THE JERUSALEM TALMUD

FOURTH ORDER: NEZIQIN

TRACTATES *BAVA QAMMA*, *BAVA MEṢI'A*, AND *BAVA BATRA*

# STUDIA JUDAICA

## FORSCHUNGEN ZUR WISSENSCHAFT DES JUDENTUMS

BEGRÜNDET VON
E. L. EHRLICH

HERAUSGEGEBEN VON
G. STEMBERGER

BAND XLV

WALTER DE GRUYTER · BERLIN · NEW YORK

# THE JERUSALEM TALMUD
## תלמוד ירושלמי

FOURTH ORDER: NEZIQIN
סדר גזיקין
TRACTATES *BAVA QAMMA*, *BAVA MEṢIʿA*,
AND *BAVA BATRA*
מסכתות בבא קמא, בבא מציעא, ובבא בתרא

EDITION, TRANSLATION, AND COMMENTARY

BY

HEINRICH W. GUGGENHEIMER

WALTER DE GRUYTER · BERLIN · NEW YORK

ISBN 978-3-11-068115-4
e-ISBN (PDF) 978-3-11-021799-5

This volume is text- and page-identical with the hardback published in 2008.

Library of Congress Control Number: 2020942697

Bibliographic information published by the Deutsche Nationalbibliothek
The Deutsche Nationalbibliothek lists this publication in the
Deutsche Nationalbibliografie;
detailed bibliographic data are available on the Internet at http://dnb.dnb.de.

© 2020 Walter de Gruyter GmbH, Berlin/Boston

Printing and binding: CPI books GmbH, Leck

www.degruyter.com

## Preface

The present volume is the eleventh in this series of the Jerusalem Talmud, the first in a three volume edition, translation, and Commentary of the Fourth Order of this Talmud. The principles of the edition regarding text, vocalization, and Commentary have been spelled out in detail in the Introduction to the first volume. The text in this volume is based on the manuscript text of the Yerushalmi edited by J. Sussman for the Academy of the Hebrew Language, Jerusalem 2001. The author has exercised his own independent judgment on what may or may not be corrupt in the text. The text essentially represents an outline, to be fleshed out by a teacher's explanation. The translation should mirror this slant; it should not endow the text with literary qualities which the original does not posses. In particular, the translation is not intended to stand separate from the Commentary.

The extensive Commentary is not based on emendations; where there is no evidence from manuscripts or early prints to correct evident scribal errors, the proposed correction is given in the Notes. As in the preceding volume, for each paragraph the folio and line numbers of the text in the Krotoschin edition are added. It should be remembered that these numbers may differ from the *editio princeps* by up to three lines. It seems to be important that a translation of the Yerushalmi be accompanied by the text, to enable the reader to compare the interpretation with other translations. The problems posed by the fragmentary nature of Tractate *Neziqin* are discussed in the Introduction.

Again I wish to thank my wife, Dr. Eva Guggenheimer, who acted as critic, style editor, proof reader, and expert on the Latin and Greek vocabulary. Her own notes on some possible Latin and Greek etymologies are identified by (E. G.). Mrs. Judith Guggenheimer helped with bibliographical matters.

Special thanks are due Mr. Marc Guenoun of Systems Support Services Ltd., who repaired the author's computer to make continued use of the old MLS wordprocessor possible.

# Contents

| | |
|---|---:|
| Introduction to Tractate Neziqin | 1 |
| Bava Qamma Chapter 1, ארבעה אבות | |
| Halakhah 1 | 11 |
| Halakhah 2 | 26 |
| Halakhah 3 | 36 |
| Halahkah 4 | 38 |
| Halakhah 5 | 40 |
| Bava Qamma Chapter 2, כיצד הרגל | |
| Halakhah 1 | 42 |
| Halakhah 2 | 48 |
| Halakhah 3 | 50 |
| Halakhah 4 | 54 |
| Halakhah 5 | 56 |
| Halakhah 6 | 59 |
| Halakhah 7 | 62 |
| Halakhah 10 | 64 |
| Bava Qamma Chapter 3, המניח את הכד | |
| Halakhah 1 | 66 |
| Halakhah 2 | 73 |
| Halakhah 3 | 76 |
| Halakhah 4 | 79 |

| | |
|---|---:|
| Halakhah 5 | 85 |
| Halakhah 6 | 89 |
| Halakhah 7 | 90 |
| Halakhah 8 | 91 |
| Halakhah 11 | 93 |
| Halakhah 12 | 97 |

## Bava Qamma Chapter 4, שור שנגח ארבעה

| | |
|---|---:|
| Halakhah 1 | 101 |
| Halakhah 2 | 107 |
| Halakhah 3 | 110 |
| Halakhah 5 | 113 |
| Halakhah 6 | 118 |
| Halakhah 7 | 124 |
| Halakhah 8 | 127 |
| Halakhah 9 | 129 |
| Halakhah 10 | 130 |

## Bava Qamma Chapter 5, שור שנגח את הפרה

| | |
|---|---:|
| Halakhah 1 | 134 |
| Halakhah 2 | 135 |
| Halakhah 3 | 137 |
| Halakhah 4 | 138 |
| Halakhah 5 | 139 |
| Halakhah 6 | 141 |
| Halakhah 7 | 145 |
| Halakhah 9 | 149 |
| Halakhah 10 | 152 |

## Bava Qamma Chapter 6, הכונס

| | |
|---|---:|
| Halakhah 1 | 155 |
| Halakhah 2 | 159 |
| Halakhah 3 | 164 |
| Halakhah 4 | 165 |

| | |
|---|---|
| Halakhah 5 | 168 |
| Halakhah 6 | 170 |
| Halakhah 7 | 171 |
| Halakhah 8 | 176 |

Bava Qamma Chapter 7, מרובה

| | |
|---|---|
| Halakhah 1 | 178 |
| Halakhah 2 | 182 |
| Halakhah 3 | 184 |
| Halakhah 4 | 186 |
| Halakhah 5 | 189 |
| Halakhah 6 | 193 |
| Halakhah 8 | 195 |
| Halakhah 10 | 196 |

Bava Qamma Chapter 8, החובל

| | |
|---|---|
| Halakhah 1 | 200 |
| Halakhah 2 | 205 |
| Halakhah 3 | 206 |
| Halakhah 4-5 | 209 |
| Halakhah 6 | 212 |
| Halakhah 7-8 | 214 |
| Halakhah 10 | 218 |
| Halakhah 11 | 220 |

Bava Qamma Chapter 9, הגוזל עצים

| | |
|---|---|
| Halakhah 1 | 223 |
| Halakhah 2 | 227 |
| Halakhah 3 | 229 |
| Halakhah 4 | 231 |
| Halakhah 5 | 232 |
| Halakhah 7 | 238 |
| Halakhah 11 | 241 |
| Halakhah 14 | 243 |

| | |
|---|---:|
| Halakhah 15 | 245 |
| Halakhah 16 | 247 |

## Bava Qamma Chapter 9, הגוזל ומאכיל

| | |
|---|---:|
| Halakhah 1 | 251 |
| Halakhah 2 | 256 |
| Halakhah 3 | 259 |
| Halakhah 4 | 260 |
| Halakhah 5 | 261 |
| Halakhah 6 | 262 |
| Halakhah 7 | 264 |
| Halakhah 9 | 266 |
| Halakhah 10 | 267 |
| Halakhah 11 | 268 |

## Bava Meṣi'a Chapter 1, שנים אוחזין

| | |
|---|---:|
| Halakhah 1 | 271 |
| Halakhah 2 | 276 |
| Halakhah 3 | 278 |
| Halakhah 4 | 279 |
| Halakhah 5 | 283 |
| Halakhah 6 | 288 |
| Halakhah 7 | 291 |
| Halakhah 8 | 294 |

## Bava Meṣi'a Chapter 2, אילו מציאות

| | |
|---|---:|
| Halakhah 1 | 298 |
| Halakhah 2 | 301 |
| Halakhah 3 | 303 |
| Halakhah 4 | 305 |
| Halakhah 5 | 308 |
| Halakhah 7 | 314 |
| Halakhah 8 | 315 |
| Halakhah 9 | 316 |

| | |
|---|---:|
| Halakhah 10 | 318 |
| Halakhah 11 | 320 |
| Halakhah 13 | 325 |

## Bava Meṣi'a Chapter 3, המפקיד

| | |
|---|---:|
| Halakhah 1 | 329 |
| Halakhah 3 | 332 |
| Halakhah 4 | 334 |
| Halakhah 7 | 337 |
| Halakhah 8 | 339 |
| Halakhah 10 | 341 |
| Halakhah 11 | 342 |
| Halakhah 12 | 344 |
| Halakhah 13 | 345 |

## Bava Meṣi'a Chapter 4, הכסף

| | |
|---|---:|
| Halakhah 1 | 348 |
| Halakhah 2 | 356 |
| Halakhah 3 | 363 |
| Halakhah 4 | 368 |
| Halakhah 5 | 369 |
| Halakhah 8 | 373 |
| Halakhah 9 | 375 |

## Bava Meṣi'a Chapter 5, איזהו נשך

| | |
|---|---:|
| Halakhah 1 | 379 |
| Halakhah 3 | 385 |
| Halakhah 5 | 389 |
| Halakhah 6 | 394 |
| Halakhah 7 | 400 |
| Halakhah 8 | 407 |
| Halakhah 10 | 414 |
| Halakhah 13 | 417 |

## Bava Meṣi'a Chapter 6, השוכר את האומנין

| | |
|---|---|
| Halakhah 1 | 420 |
| Halakhah 2 | 425 |
| Halakhah 3 | 426 |
| Halakhah 4 | 430 |
| Halakhah 7 | 434 |
| Halakhah 8 | 436 |

## Bava Meṣi'a Chapter 7, השוכר את הפועלין

| | |
|---|---|
| Halakhah 1 | 438 |
| Halakhah 2 | 441 |
| Halakhah 5 | 444 |
| Halakhah 6 | 445 |
| Halakhah 7 | 446 |
| Halakhah 8 | 447 |
| Halakhah 9 | 448 |
| Halakhah 10 | 450 |

## Bava Meṣi'a Chapter 8, השואל את הפרה

| | |
|---|---|
| Halakhah 1 | 455 |
| Halakhah 2 | 457 |
| Halakhah 3 | 458 |
| Halakhah 4 | 460 |
| Halakhah 5 | 461 |
| Halakhah 6 | 462 |
| Halakhah 8 | 464 |
| Halakhah 9 | 465 |
| Halakhah 10 | 466 |
| Halakhah 11 | 468 |

## Bava Meṣi'a Chapter 9, המקבל שדה מחבירו

| | |
|---|---|
| Halakhah 1 | 470 |
| Halakhah 2 | 472 |
| Halakhah 3 | 473 |

| | |
|---|---|
| Halakhah 4 | 474 |
| Halakhah 5 | 475 |
| Halakhah 6 | 476 |
| Halakhah 7 | 477 |
| Halakhah 8 | 479 |
| Halakhah 9 | 480 |
| Halakhah 10 | 481 |
| Halakhah 11 | 482 |
| Halakhah 13 | 484 |
| Halakhah 14 | 486 |
| Halakhah 16 | 490 |

Bava Meṣi'a Chapter 10, הבית והעליה

| | |
|---|---|
| Halakhah 1 | 493 |
| Halakhah 2 | 498 |
| Halakhah 3 | 498 |
| Halakhah 4 | 500 |
| Halakhah 7 | 502 |
| Halakhah 8 | 505 |

Bava Batra Chapter 1, השותפין

| | |
|---|---|
| Halakhah 1 | 508 |
| Halakhah 2 | 510 |
| Halakhah 4 | 512 |
| Halakhah 6 | 516 |
| Halakhah 7 | 517 |

Bava Batra Chapter 2, לא יחפור

| | |
|---|---|
| Halakhah 1 | 525 |
| Halakhah 2 | 528 |
| Halakhah 3 | 531 |
| Halakhah 4 | 535 |
| Halakhah 5 | 537 |
| Halakhah 6 | 539 |

| | |
|---|---|
| Halakhah 9 | 541 |
| Halakhah 11-13 | 543 |
| Halakhah 14 | 547 |

## Bava Batra Chapter 3, חזקת הבתים

| | |
|---|---|
| Halakhah 1 | 551 |
| Halakhah 2 | 559 |
| Halakhah 3 | 560 |
| Halakhah 4 | 566 |
| Halakhah 5 | 568 |
| Halakhah 6 | 574 |
| Halakhah 7 | 575 |
| Halakhah 8 | 577 |
| Halakhah 9 | 581 |
| Halakhah 10 | 582 |
| Halakhah 12 | 587 |

## Bava Batra Chapter 4, המוכר את הבית

| | |
|---|---|
| Halakhah 1 | 589 |
| Halakhah 2 | 591 |
| Halakhah 3 | 593 |
| Halakhah 4 | 594 |
| Halakhah 5 | 596 |
| Halakhah 6 | 598 |
| Halakhah 7 | 599 |
| Halakhah 8-11 | 601 |

## Bava Batra Chapter 5, המוכר את הספינה

| | |
|---|---|
| Halakhah 1 | 608 |
| Halakhah 5 | 617 |
| Halakhah 7 | 619 |
| Halakhah 8 | 621 |
| Halakhah 11 | 624 |
| Halakhah 14 | 628 |

Bava Batra Chapter 6, המוכר פירות

   Halakhah 1     629
   Halakhah 3     637
   Halakhah 4     639
   Halakhah 7     641

Bava Batra Chapter 7, האומר לחבירו

   Halakhah 1     644
   Halakhah 2     647
   Halakhah 3     648
   Halakhah 5     650

Bava Batra Chapter 8, יש נוחלין

   Halakhah 1     652
   Halakhah 3     659
   Halakhah 4     666
   Halakhah 5     668
   Halakhah 6     671
   Halakhah 7     678
   Halakhah 8     679
   Halakhah 9     683
   Halakhah 10     689

Bava Batra Chapter 9, מי שמת

   Halakhah 1     692
   Halakhah 3     698
   Halakhah 4     700
   Halakhah 5     703
   Halakhah 6     703
   Halakhah 7     706
   Halakhah 8     708
   Halakhah 9     713
   Halakhah 10     716
   Halakhah 12     717

| | |
|---|---|
| Bava Batra Chapter 10, גט פשוט | |
| Halakhah 1 | 720 |
| Halakhah 2 | 728 |
| Halakhah 3 | 730 |
| Halakhah 4 | 731 |
| Halakhah 5 | 732 |
| Halakhah 6 | 733 |
| Halakhah 8 | 735 |
| Halakhah 12 | 737 |
| Halakhah 13 | 738 |
| Halakhah 14 | 739 |
| Halakhah 15 | 740 |
| Halakhah 16 | 742 |
| Halakhah 17 | 745 |

## Indices

| | |
|---|---|
| Index of Biblical Quotations | 747 |
| Index of Talmudic Quotations | |
|     Babylonian Talmud | 749 |
|     Jerusalem Talmud | 752 |
|     Mishnah | 753 |
|     Tosephta | 754 |
|     Midrašim | 755 |
|     Rabbinical Literature | 756 |
| Index of Greek, Latin, and Hebrew words | 756 |
| Author Index | 757 |
| Subject Index | 758 |

# Introduction to Tractate Neziqin

The thirty Chapters of Tractate *Neziqin*, dealing with most aspects of Civil Law, are usually divided into three parts, or "gates", known as the First Gate, *Bava qamma*, the Middle Gate, *Bava meṣia'*, and the Last Gate, *Bava batra*. The nature of this Tractate poses important, probably undecidable, problems[1].

In the Babli, the three parts of the Tractate are more or less independent of each other; they form the center of all talmudic law. In the Yerushalmi, the Escurial manuscript discovered by E. S. Rosenthal, written in Galilean dialect, treats *Neziqin* as one Tractate of 30 Chapters. The Leiden manuscript text is very much babylonized and separates it into the three Babli tractates. The author already had occasion to note[2] that different tractates in the Leiden codex represent very different histories of transmission; *Neziqin* is an example of pronounced babylonization.

The first obvious difference between this and other parts of the Yerushalmi is its shortness. In the *editio princeps*, the 30 Chapters of the Tractate occupy 17 folios; the 29 Chapters of the remaining five Tractates of the same order fill 30 folio pages. By contrast, in M. Zuckermandel's edition of the Tosephta, the 33 Chapters of *Neziqin* cover 69 pages, whereas the 35 Chapters of the other Tractates of the Fourth Order (excluding *Idiut*) only cover 50 pages. A number of Chapters are very short and practically without Amoraic material, consisting only of a collection of *baraitot* relating to some of the Mishnayot. The only Chapters approximating normal length are those with relevance to ritual law, such as *Bava meṣia'* 4-5 on the prohibition of overcharging and taking interest from Jews, or of relevance for laws of personal status, as *Bava batra* 9 on inheritance. Most other Chapters give the impression that the Academy had a drawer in which materials were kept for lectures on the Mishnayot, and that the text is simply a copy of these notes, not all of them in the correct place[3]. A good first impression of the difference in length and style is given by a count of the quotes from Amoraïm in the different Chapters:

| | | | | | | | | | | | |
|---|---|---|---|---|---|---|---|---|---|---|---|
| *Baba qamma* | 42 | 35 | 44 | 57 | 27 | 30 | 21 | 20 | 41 | 33 | total 350 |
| *Baba meṣia'* | 52 | 31 | 42 | 81 | 52 | 21 | 12 | 16 | 23 | 19 | 349 |
| *Baba batra* | 22 | 49 | 97 | 26 | 29 | 32 | 16 | 67 | 69 | 69 | 476. |

In other tractates, a short Chapter typically has about 60 such references.

A second difference appears in the main personalities quoted. In other Tractates, while the basic teachings are in the names of R. Joḥanan and his aides R. Simeon ben Laqish and R. Eleazar, his successors as heads of the Academy of Tiberias, rabbis Ḥiyya bar Abba, Ze'ira, Jeremiah, and Yose, play a similarly important rôle. But in *Neziqin*, their rôle is minor. As J. Sussman[1] has noted, this is not a sign of an early redaction since also R. Yose ben Abun, the very last major figure mentioned in the Yerushalmi, appears not infrequently[4].

The only influence comparable to that of R. Joḥanan and his school is that of Rav and his school (Jeremiah and Huna) in Babylonia. By contrast, in the Babli the dominant influence is that of Samuel and his school, represented by Ravs Jehudah and Naḥman. No Babylonians younger than second generation Amoraïm are mentioned in the Tractate. Also, in many cases statements by Amoraïm are attributed to authorities in *Neziqin* other than those in other Tractates.

A few paragraphs in *Neziqin* are copied verbally from other Tractates (*Bava qamma* 3:8 copied in *Makkot* 2:4, 4:5 partially copied from *Giṭṭin* 5:4, 4:9 from *Sanhedrin* 6:2, 7:10 from *Pesaḥim* 5:3 and *Avodah zarah* 1:6; *Bava batra* 1:1 from *Nedarim* 5:1); but most parallel texts are independently formulated, rather than copied, in clear deviation from common Yerushalmi style[5].

In the early Nineteenth Century, S. I. L. Rappaport in his articles in the periodical *Kerem Ḥemed* explained the difference by postulating that rabbinic courts in Galilee did not adjudicate matters of civil law. This opinion was rejected by Zacharias Frankel[6], who pointed out that other Tractates, *Ketubot, Qiddušin, Šebuot* treat many aspects both of the material law governing money matters and of the relevant procedural law in great detail. He postulated that under the pressure of the Roman Christian authorities, the teachers of the Academy in Tiberias did not find the time to compose a full Tractate *Neziqin*. His student Israel Lewy insisted that the Tractate was edited, and wrote[7] that "these differences and the shortness characteristic of *Neziqin* may be explained most simply by assuming that it is the result of an editorial process different from that applied to the other Tractates.[8]"

In 1931, Saul Lieberman published a monograph[9] in which he argued that the Tractate is so short because it represents a first stage in its development and that the difference in attributions shows that it was not edited in Tiberias but in Caesarea (which in his opinion was Caesarea maritima). In addition, he pointed to the difference in technical language between *Neziqin* and the rest of the Yerushalmi as evidence of separate editorial activity. Lieberman's thesis was accepted by Louis Ginzberg in his "The Palestinian Talmud"[10] but rejected by J. N. Epstein in his posthumously edited "Introduction to the Literature of the Amoraïm"[11] as not sustained by the evidence. The Escurial ms. shows that the Leiden ms.'s babylonized technical language is an accident of transmission, rather than a conscious editorial practice. Lieberman answered Epstein's criticism in an appendix to his edition of *Sifry zuṭa*[12] where he points out a series of statements which are attributed to Tiberian scholars in the other parts of the Yerushalmi but in *Neziqin* to scholars connected with Caesarea[13].

Finally, in 1994, J. Neusner published a book[14] full of invective in which he tried to demolish Lieberman's thesis and establish the (false) claim that the position of *Neziqin* in the Yerushalmi be totally parallel to that of the corresponding Tractates in the Babli.

It seems to the author that the only thesis compatible with the evidence is Rappaport's. The Yerushalmi states in *Sanhedrin* 1:1 (Note 156) that during R. Simeon ben Ioḥai's lifetime, i. e., in the aftermath of the war of Bar Kokhba, civil jurisdiction was removed from rabbinic courts. There is no evidence that this jurisdiction was restored to rabbinic courts by any of the Severan emperors, nor during the military anarchy, and certainly not under the absolute monarchy. In fact, the story about R. Jonathan acting as a judge (*Baba batra* 3:14) shows that he acted as a Roman, not a rabbinic, judge.

The evidence of Egyptian papyri, and also of the remains of the Syrian-Roman law, shows that the Empire of the Principate tolerated the local laws of the subject populations of the East[15]. This toleration was slowly eroded under the absolute monarchy; Justinian's codification which established Roman law as *the* law of the Empire has to be seen as the culmination of a long process. On the other hand, since the Church after

Constantine demanded jurisdiction over personal status, parallel jurisdiction could not be withheld from rabbinic courts. This explains the detailed exposition of marriage law in all its ramifications in the Third Order of the Mishnah as well as procedural law in the Fourth Order. But since, in theory, rabbinical courts did not want to surrender their claim to universal jurisdiction, Tractate *Sanhedrin* is a somewhat incongruous compilation of rules for actual communal courts for personal status and religious affairs, actual courts of arbitration in money matters, and hypothetical courts for criminal cases and torts.

If Tractate *Neziqin* is a collection of lecture notes[16], it follows that the use of exact copies of texts in the other Tractates was a deliberate editorial decision. Similarly, the discrepancies in the names of tradents between this Tractate and others is easily explained since in both Talmudim names serve as labels to characterize coherent logical systems, i. e., opinions attributed to one and the same tradent cannot disagree with one another[17]. Since the other Tractates of the Yerushalmi are edited in the Tiberian tradition, it is understandable that many statements are labelled as belonging to logical systems developed by members of the Tiberian school. This is edition, rather than tradition.

The text of the Escurial manuscript (which covers the text from *Bava qamma* 1:1 to *Bava batra* 9:5) was edited by its discoverer, Eliezer Shimshon Rosenthal, with a critical apparatus, comparing the text to the Leiden ms. and any available Genizah fragments[18]. In the commentary, the Leiden ms. is referred to as L, the Escurial ms. as E.

It has been remarked by several authors[19] that rabbinic law, as an expression of popular tradition, is mostly influenced not by Roman, but by local law. Such influences have been duly noted in the Commentary. For most of talmudic law, the Graeco-Egyptian influences are noticeable in formal matters, while the core remains solidly based on the biblical text. Since Judaism rejects the notion of systematic theology, the theological interpretation of legal precepts remains a matter of individual interpretation. The absence of aggadic material in the Yerushalmi *Neziqin* indicates that such interpretation was not a teaching subject for the Galilean academies.

The first nine Chapters of *Bava qamma* treat torts. The first Chapter defines liabilities following the biblical treatment of torts in *Ex.* 21-22. Torts caused by human action require full restitution, but those caused by animals in certain cases only entitle the victim to partial indemnification. Damages caused by livestock are classified as being caused either by goring (where there is a difference on whether an animal gores unexpectedly or does it habitually), or by trampling or feeding. Details of the rules are treated in Chapters Two to Six, with damages caused by humans also treated in Chapters Two (end) and Three. Chapter Six, intermediate between the Chapters dealing with torts caused by animals and those caused by humans, treats the obligation of acting with reasonable care at all times.

Chapter Seven treats theft. The punishment for theft is double restitution in general, quadruple for rustling cattle and quintuple for stealing goats and sheep.

Chapter Eight treats injuries inflicted by humans, an extended commentary on *Ex.* 21:18-27.

Chapter Nine treats the civil aspects of the crime of armed robbery.

The Tenth Chapter is an Introduction to the topics covered by the first Chapters of *Bava meṣia'*. It starts with the obligations, or absence of such, of children of a robber who robbed in order to feed them. Then it treats more generally property which became ownerless because the original owners gave up hope of recovery.

The first nine Chapters of *Bava meṣia'* contain a medley of religious laws regarding money matters. The first two Chapters deal with the obligation of a finder to return his find to its owner. The first Chapter treats questions of ownership if the owner cannot be identified and the person of the finder is in question, the ways of acquisition of ownerless property, and the proper treatment of documents found. The second Chapter details the rules about which finds a finder may keep, and which ones he is required to publicly advertise for the owner. The third Chapter treats losses of items given in deposit or as loans. The fourth Chapter treats overcharging or underpaying, in concretization of *Lev.* 25:14. The fifth Chapter contains the prohibition of taking interest from fellow Jews. The sixth Chapter regulates dealings with contractors and artisans; the seventh is dedicated to the law protecting workers, i. e., day laborers. Chapter Eight treats loans and barter. Chapter Nine contains the laws for sharecroppers and agricultural contractors.

Chapter Ten treats the rules of condominium of real estate, hereby starting a main topic of *Bava batra, viz.,* real estate law. The first Chapter of *Bava batra* continues the treatment of condominium property and starts with the rules on neighborly relations; these are continued in the second Chapter. Chapter Three starts out with the acquisition of title to property in the absence of documentary proof and ends with complements to the rules of neighborly relations. Chapter Four starts the topic of standard rules of sale; applied to real estate this entails the description of what is and what is not included in a standard contract of sale of real estate. Chapter Five does the same for movables, first for means of transportation, then for agricultural produce. This topic is continued in the sixth Chapter, which also deals with implied uses of agricultural and similar real estate. Chapter Seven treats sale of agricultural property. Chapters Eight and Nine are devoted to inheritances and wills. The latter Chapter contains an interesting case in which a clause in the Babli can be understood only as a reference to the corresponding Yerushalmi (Note 112).

Chapter Ten details the rules of deeds and similar documents, in particular the Greek way of writing sealed documents, and rules applying to guarantors.

---

1   Comparatively recent texts which discuss the problems posed by the Tractate are
Gerd A. Wewers, *Probleme der Bavot Traktate. Ein redaktionskritischer und theologischer Beitrag zum Talmud Yerushalmi*, Tübingen 1984.
יעקב זוסמן. ושוב לירושלמי נזיקין. מחקרי תלמוד, קובץ מחקרים בתלמוד ובתחומים גובלים, א, ירושלם תש״ן (1990) 155 - 135 .
2   Introduction to Tractate *Gittin*, p. 4.
3   Z. Frankel (מבוא הירושלמי, p. 21b-22a) already noted that the Mishnayot preceding the Chapters of the Yerushalmi are not part of the original Yerushalmi text. This was emphasized several times by S. Lieberman and is made obvious by the Genizah texts. Defective correspondences between Halakhah and Mishnah therefore were caused by the copyist who introduced the Mishnah into the text.
4   The mention of the *chrysargyros* tax, introduced by Constantine, as a traditional tax (*Baba qamma* 3:1, Note 21) points to the middle of the Fourth Century as the *terminus post quem* of the compilation of *Neziqin*. The tax was abolished by Anastasios I (491-518), too late to give a meaningful *terminus ante quem*.
5   A somewhat intermediate role is played by Tractate *Sanhedrin* which contains both verbal copies and extensive rewritings of parallel paragraphs.
6   מבוא הירושלמי (Breslau, 1870) p. 48b (Reprint Jerusalem 1967). His opinion is accepted by J. I. Halevi in דורות הראשונים.
7   *Jahresbericht des jüdisch-theologischen Seminars Fraenckel'scher Stiftung*, Breslau 1895 (reprinted by Kedem Publishing, Jerusalem 1970) p. 21: "Diese Differenzen und die dem Traktat Nesikin eigene Kürze dürften wohl am Einfachsten sich durch die Annahme erklären lassen, dass derselbe einer anderen Redaction, als die anderen Traktate, angehört."
8   This analysis was accepted by S. Schechter in Note 20 to *The Talmud*, Studies

in Judaism, 3rd series, Philadelphia 1924, 194-237, and in the recent surveys by Gerd A. Wewers and Jacob Sussman (Note 1). Sussman's paper analyzes the deviations of *Neziqin* from general Yerushalmi style in some detail; the book by Wewers gives a very thorough and thoughtful analysis.

9   תלמודה של קיסרין, Supplement 2 of the journal תרביץ.

10   English Introduction to *A Commentary on the Palestinian Talmud*, Texts and Studies of the Jewish Theological Seminary of America, vol. X, New York 1941 (reprinted 1971); p. xxxvii. His assertion that the Tractate is intended as a lawyers' manual cannot be accepted; the material contained in the Halakhot mostly is far from practical.

11   Edited by E. Z. Melamed, Jerusalem 1958. J. Sussman correctly points out that the mention of Galilean Amoraïm of all generations and the rather frequent mention of R. Yose ben R. Bun exclude the possibility that *Neziqin* was edited much earlier than the other Tractates. Cf. also Note 4.

12   ספרי זוטא, תלמודה של קיסרין Jerusalem 1968.

13   Sussman notes that the place at which the Tractate was edited cannot be determined.

14   Why There Never Was a "Talmud of Caesarea", Saul Lieberman's Mistakes. *South Florida Studies in the History of Judaism*, No. 108. Altlanta GA 1994.

15   The papyri show no evidence that Caracalla's decree, extending citizenship to almost all inhabitants of the Empire, simultaneously abolished all non-Roman laws; *contra* Ginzberg, *loc. cit.* p. xxxi.

16   In 'תורה שבעל פה' פשוטה כמשמעה - כוחו של קוצו של יו"ד, מחקרי תלמוד ג, קובץ מחקרים בתלמוד ובתחומים גובלים מוקדש לזכרו של פרופ' אפרים א' אורבך, ירושלים תשסה (2005) 209-384, J. Sussman argues that *all* of Talmudic literature, including the very intricately structured Babylonian Talmud, has to be understood as oral literature. As Wewers formulates: Openness and incompleteness are important characteristics of the editorial work (*Offenheit und Unabgeschlossenheit sind wesentliche Merkmale der redaktionellen Arbeit*).

17   H. Guggenheimer, *Logical Problems in Jewish Tradition*, in: Confrontations with Judaism, Ph. Longworth, ed., London 1966; pp. 173, 191-192.

The Escurial text in places follows a name tradition different from that of the Leiden text; this does not imply that any of the traditions be corrupt in these places.

By a completely different chain of reasoning, G. A. Wewers also concluded that the name labels attached to traditions belong to the editing process: *Die Traditionen sind nicht im direkt positivistischen Sinn authentisch.*

18   ירושלמי נזיקין, יוצא לאור על פי כתב יד אסקוריאל בצירוף מבוא ע"י אליעזר שמשון רוזנטל. הוסיף מבוא ופירוש שאול ליברמן. The Israel Academy of Sciences, Jerusalem 1980.

19   For an in-depth study, cf. A. Gulak (*Bava batra* 4, Note 18). Cf. also L. Ginzberg (*loc. cit.*, p. xxx).

## ארבעה אבות פרק ראשון

(fol. 2a) **משנה א**: אַרְבָּעָה אָבוֹת נְזִיקִין הַשּׁוֹר וְהַבּוֹר וְהַמַּבְעֶה וְהַהֶבְעֵר. לֹא הַשּׁוֹר כַּהֲרֵי הַמַּבְעֶה וְלֹא הַמַּבְעֶה כַּהֲרֵי הַשּׁוֹר. לֹא זֶה וָזֶה שֶׁיֵּשׁ בָּהֶן רוּחַ חַיִּים כַּהֲרֵי הַבּוֹר שֶׁאֵין בָּהּ רוּחַ חַיִּים לֹא זֶה וָזֶה שֶׁדַּרְכָּן לֵילֵךְ וּלְהַזִּיק כַּהֲרֵי הָאֵשׁ שֶׁאֵין דַּרְכּוֹ לֵילֵךְ וּלְהַזִּיק. הַצַּד הַשָּׁוֶה שֶׁבָּהֶן שֶׁדַּרְכָּן לְהַזִּיק וּשְׁמִירָתָן עָלֶיךָ וּכְשֶׁהִזִּיק חָב הַמַּזִּיק לְשַׁלֵּם תַּשְׁלוּמֵי נֶזֶק בְּמֵיטַב הָאָרֶץ.

**Mishnah 1**: There are four main categories of damages[1]: The bull[2], and the pit[3], and the devourer[4], and the setting on fire[5]. The bull is not like the devourer, nor the devourer like the bull[6]; neither of them who are alive is like the pit[7] which is not alive, nor either of them which move in causing damage is like the fire[7] which does not move in causing damage. The common theme of them is that they are usually causing damage and you are obligated to watch them, and if damage was caused the person causing the damage is obligated to pay the damages in best quality land[8].

1   Most rules of payment for damages may be derived from the examples of damages treated in *Ex.* 21-22, as explained in the Halakhah.

2   An agressive bull goring with his horns; *Ex.* 21:28-32;35-36.

3   A person digging a pit in the public domain is responsible for any damage caused by his action; *Ex.* 21:33-34.

4   Damage caused by an animal other than goring: feeding ("the tooth") and trampling ("the foot"), *Ex.* 22:4. The Aramaic root בעי is found in Pseudo-Jonathan to *Num.* 22:2 as translation of Hebrew לחך "to devour". The unusual expression מַבְעֶה is used to subsume two legal terms under one.

5   *Ex.* 22:5.

6   Since goring, trampling, and devouring are all ascribed to the same animal, the question arises why the bull has to be mentioned in two different categories both in the Mishnah and in the biblical text. The details are given only in the Babli: An animal which gores is intent on causing damage; therefore the rules are different for known agressive or generally not agressive animals since these require different levels of supervision. But the rules for damage caused by feeding and trampling are the same for all animals.

7   It is obvious and confirmed by all other sources that the positions of "pit" and "fire" have to be switched.

8   If the person causing the damage cannot pay, the person collecting damages can foreclose the culprit's land with the highest value per unit of surface area. As biblical law, this applies to damages caused by unattended animals, *Ex.* 22:4.

(2a line 21) **הלכה א:** אַרְבָּעָה אָבוֹת נְזִיקִין כול'. הַשּׁוֹר זֶה הַקֶּרֶן. דִּכְתִיב כִּי יִגֹּף שׁוֹר אִישׁ אֶת שׁוֹר רֵעֵהוּ וגו'. עַד כְּדוֹן בְּתָם. בְּמוּעָד מְנַיִין. אוֹ נוֹדַע כִּי שׁוֹר נַגָּח הוּא וגו'. הַבּוֹר. כִּי יִפְתַּח אִישׁ בּוֹר וגו' בַּעַל הַבּוֹר יְשַׁלֵּם וגו'. הַמַּבְעֶה. כִּי יַבְעֶר אִישׁ שָׂדֶה אוֹ כֶרֶם וְשִׁלַּח אֶת בְּעִירֹה. זֶה הָרֶגֶל. דִּכְתִיב מְשַׁלְּחֵי רֶגֶל הַשּׁוֹר וְהַחֲמוֹר. וּכְתִיב הָסֵר מְסוּכָּתוֹ וְהָיְתָה לְבָעֵר. זֶה הַשֵּׁן. פָּרוֹץ גְּדֵירוֹ וְהָיָה לְמִרְמָס. זֶה הָרֶגֶל. וְהַהֶבְעֵר. דִּכְתִיב כִּי תֵצֵא אֵשׁ וּמָצְאָה קוֹצִים וגו'.

**Halakhah 1**: "There are four main categories of damages," etc. The bull means the horn, as is written: "If a man's bull smite another person's bull,[9]" etc. So far a harmless animal[10]. From where a notorious [dangerous] one[11]? "Or it was known that it be a goring bull,[12]" etc. The pit, "if a man open a pit," etc.; "the pit's owner has to pay,[3]" etc. The devourer: "If a person causes a field or a vineyard to be despoiled by *sending* his animals;[13]" this is the foot as it is written[14]: "Those who *send* the foot of bull and donkey." And it is written[15]: "Remove its cover and it will be despoiled," that is the tooth, "tear down its fence and it will be trampled," that is the foot. And the setting on fire, as it is written[5]: "If fire starts and finds thistles," etc.

| | |
|---|---|
| 9    *Ex.* 21:35. | in doubt because of lack of parallels. It might as well be referring to damage by excessive grazing as to destruction by trampling. |
| 10    It has no history of attacking other animals. The owner only has to pay half the damage caused. | |
| 11    For which full damages have to be paid. | 14    *Is.* 32:20. The same explanation of *Ex.* 22:4 by *Is.* 32:20 is in the Babli, 2b. |
| 12    *Ex.* 21:36. | |
| 13    *Ex.* 22:4. The meaning of יָבֻעֶר is | 15    *Is.* 5:5. |

(2a line 28) אֲנָן תַּנִּינָן. אַרְבָּעָה אָבוֹת נְזִיקִין. וְתַנֵּי רִבִּי חִייָה שְׁלֹשָׁה עָשָׂר. נֶזֶק צַעַר רִיפּוּי שֶׁבֶת וּבוֹשֶׁת שׁוֹמֵר חִנָּם וְהַשּׁוֹאֵל נוֹשֵׂא שָׂכָר וְהַשּׂוֹכֵר. אֱמוֹר מֵעַתָּה. מַה דְּתַנִּינָן אֲנָן לְהֶכְשֵׁר נְזָקִין. מַה דְּתַנֵּי רִבִּי חִייָה בֵּין לְהֶכְשֵׁר נְזָקִין בֵּין לְנִיזְקֵי גוּפוֹ. רִבִּי חַגַּיי שָׁאַל. הֵיךְ תַּנִּינָן. אַרְבָּעָה אָבוֹת נְזִיקִין. אִם הַכֹּל אָמוּר בְּשׁוֹר אֶחָד נִיתְנֵי שְׁלֹשָׁה. וְאִם הַכֹּל אָמוּר בְּשׁוֹר שְׁלֹשָׁה נִיתְנֵי חֲמִשָּׁה. אֶלָּא כְּמָה דְאִישְׁתָּעֵי קְרָיָא אִישְׁתָּעִיַת מַתְנִיתָא.

We have stated: "Four main categories of damages." But Rebbi Hiyya stated thirteen[16]: Damages, suffering, medical costs, loss of earning power, shame[17]; the unpaid trustee, and the borrower, the paid trustee, and the renter[18]. Say now, what we stated [refers to] responsibility for damages[19]. What Rebbi Hiyya stated [refers to] both responsibility for damages and bodily injury[20]. Rebbi Haggai asked: How can we state "four main categories"? If everything was said about one bull; let us state "three," if it was said about three bulls, let us state "five"[21]! But as it is presented in the verse, thus it is presented in the Mishnah[22,23].

16   Tosephta 9:1; Babli 4b in the name of R. Hoshaia. The list contains 9 items; together with the 4 mentioned in the Mishnah there are 13.

17   These five kinds of payment are due for injuries suffered at the hands of another person, Mishnah 8:1; it is based on *Ex.* 21:19. "Suffering" means [payment for]bodily pain; "shame" refers to [payment for] mental anguish caused by loss of face.

18   These four entries do not refer to kinds of payments for damages but to the obligations of persons who hold other people's property in case that property is lost, stolen, or damaged, as specified in Mishnah *Bava meṣi'a* 7:9 (based on *Ex.* 22:6-12). The unpaid trustee does not pay if he can swear that he did not use the property; the borrower pays for everything; the paid trustee and the renter have to pay for what was lost or stolen but may swear that it was not their fault if the damage was caused by an act of God or forcible robbery.

19   A literal translation would be: "Qualification for damages". The reference is to Mishnah 2: "Anything which I am obliged to guard, I qualify [myself as responsible] for damages." [Noted by S. Pinchas, *New explanations of some unclear passages in the Yerushalmi*, Sinai 133 (2004) 174-180 (Hebrew); but the relation was already noted by Eliahu Fulda.]. All damages payable for actions of one's animals are really fines for the owner's negligence in watching his animal.

20   In the Babli, 4b, this explanation is attributed to Samuel.

21   Of the categories of damages indicated in the Mishnah, three refer to actions of cattle: goring, trampling, and feeding. If one classifies the damages according to their origins, there should be three (cattle, humans, fire); if by categories there should be five.

22   Since *foot* and *tooth* are interpretations of one and the same verse, they are counted as one in the Mishnah.

23   A similar expression is used in *Berakhot* 2:4 (Note 192).

(2a line 34) תּוֹלְדוֹת הַקֶּרֶן. נְגִיחָה נְגִיפָה נְשִׁיכָה רְבִיצָה בְּעִיטָה דְחִייָה. רִבִּי יִצְחָק מַקְשֵׁי. נְגִיפָה נְגִיחָה עִיקָר הֵן וְאַתְּ עֲבִיד לוֹן תּוֹלְדוֹת. אֶלָּא מַתְחִיל בָּעִיקָר וּמְסַיֵּים בְּתוֹלְדוֹת.

The derivatives of the horn[24]: Goring[25], hitting[26], biting[27], wallowing, kicking, and pushing[28]. Rebbi Isaac asked: Hitting and goring are fundamental[29], and you call them derivative? But he starts with the fundamentals and ends with the derivatives[30].

[24] In a differently formulated version in *Šabbat* 7 (9d l. 61), "pushing" is missing. In the Babli, 2b, the list is even shorter. In *Mekhilta dR. Ismael, Mišpaṭim* 12, the formulation of the list is attributed to R. Josia. The Babli's list is also in *Mekhilta dR. Simeon ben Ioḥai, Mišpaṭim*, p. 278.

[25] The biblical expression (*Ex.* 21:28,31) used to describe the attack by an animal on a human.

[26] *Ex.* 22:35, used for attacks on other animals.

[27] Since the animal bites with the intent of causing damage, biting is put in the category of goring, "horn", rather than under feeding, "the mouth".

[28] Pushing with its body, not its horns.

[29] Anything mentioned in the biblical text is fundamental; any damage not mentioned in the biblical text is a derivative of one of the biblical causes.

[30] In the Babli, this is a declarative statement.

(2a line 37) תּוֹלְדוֹת הַבּוֹר. כָּל־פִּירְקָא תְּלִיתָיָיא דְּתַנִּינָן בִּנְזִיקִין. רִבִּי תַנֵּי. הִנִּיחַ גַּחֶלֶת בִּרְשׁוּת הָרַבִּים וּבָא אַחֵר וְנִתְקַל בָּהּ וּצְלוֹחִיתוֹ בְיָדוֹ. נִשְׂרְפוּ כֵלָיו וְנִשְׁבְּרָה צְלוֹחִיתוֹ חַיָּיב עַל הַצְּלוֹחִית מִשּׁוּם בּוֹר וְעַל הַכֵּלִים מִשּׁוּם אֵשׁ.

Derivatives of the pit: The entire third Chapter of Mishnah *Neziqin*[31]. Rebbi stated: Somebody put a glowing coal in the public domain, another person came and stumbled over it while a flask was in his hand[32]. If as a consequence that person's clothing was singed and the flask in his hand was broken, he[33] is obligated for the flask because of 'pit', and for the garments because of 'fire'.

31 *Bava qamma* Chapter 3. The "pit" is the paradigm for any obstacle put in the public domain by a private person.

32 A typical scenario discussed in Chapter 3.

33 The person who caused the accident by leaving the burning coal in the public domain.

(2a line 40) תּוֹלְדוֹת הָרֶגֶל. תַּנֵּי. בְּהֵמָה שֶׁנִּכְנְסָה לִרְשׁוּת הַיָּחִיד וְהִזִּיקָה בֵּין בְּיָדָהּ בֵּין בְּרַגְלָהּ בֵּין בְּקַרְנָהּ בֵּין בְּעוֹל שֶׁעָלֶיהָ בֵּין בְּשָׂלִיף שֶׁיֵּשׁ בָּהּ בֵּין בַּעֲגָלָה שֶׁהִיא מוֹשֶׁכֶת. מְשַׁלֵּם נֶזֶק שָׁלֵם. וְהַמַּזִּיק בַּכַּרְמְלִית מְשַׁלֵּם נֶזֶק שָׁלֵם.

Derivatives of the 'foot': It was stated[34]: For an animal which entered a private property[35] and caused damage, whether by its forefoot, or by its hindfoot, or by its horn[36], or by the yoke on it, or by a sack on it, or by the carriage it was drawing, one pays full damages. And one who causes damage in a *karmelit* pays full damages[37].

34 Tosephta 1:6; a different version in the Babli 17b.

35 Since *Ex.* 22:4 limits strict responsibility of the owner to an animal of his which causes damage "on another person's field"; full damages for *foot* and *tooth* are due only for damages caused on private property of a person other than the animal's owner.

36 Not by goring but by causing damage walking.

37 This sentence refers to the topic of Chapter Two and states that the notion of "private domain" for torts is not identical with the same notion for property rights. *Karmelit* is a part of the public domain not really accessible to the public. The two main examples are "the sides of a thoroughfare", the part of a street close to the houses if that part is not easy to use for walking because of stairs extending from houses or the fronts of the houses do not form a straight line. The other is "valley", a rural access path which is public domain, not a thoroughfare but meant only as path for use by the farmers working adjacent fields. For the rules of the Sabbath, *karmelit* is neither private nor public.

(2a line 44) תּוֹלְדוֹת הַשֵּׁן. הָווֹן בְּעָיָין מֵימַר. פָּרָה שֶׁאָכְלָה שְׂעוֹרִים וַחֲמוֹר שֶׁאָכַל כַּרְשִׁינִין וְכֶלֶב שֶׁלִּיקְלֵק אֶת הַשֶּׁמֶן וַחֲזִיר שֶׁאָכְלָה בָשָׂר כּוּלְהוֹן תּוֹלְדוֹת הַשֵּׁן אִינּוּן. אָמַר רִבִּי יִצְחָק. כּוּלְהוֹן עִיקַּר שֵׁן אִינּוּן. וְהָא תָאנֵי. תּוֹלְדוֹת הַשֵּׁן. בְּשֶׁדֶּרְסָה עַל גַּבֵּי נוֹד מָלֵא שֶׁמֶן. וּבְסִיכָה גוּפָהּ נֶהֱנָה. כְּמָה דְתֵימַר תַּמָּן הַשֵּׁן אוֹכֶלֶת וְהַגּוּף נֶהֱנֶה. אוֹף הָכָא נֶהֱנָה גוּפָהּ. רִבִּי יִרְמְיָה בָּעֵי. הָיְתָה מְהַלֶּכֶת וּפוֹלֶטֶת עֲשָׂבִים מַהוּ. אָמַר רִבִּי יוֹסֵי. מָה אִם הַמַּנִּיחַ גַּחֶלֶת לִרְשׁוּת הָרַבִּים עַד מָקוֹם שֶׁהִיא מִתְהַלֶּכֶת הִיא מַזֶּקֶת. מַאי כְדוֹן. אָמַר רִבִּי יוֹסֵי בֵּירִבִּי בּוּן. תִּיפְתָּר בְּמַנִּיחַ סַכִּין סְמוּכָה לִרְשׁוּת הָרַבִּים. כְּמָה דְתֵימַר תַּמָּן. הָאֵשׁ נוֹגֵעַ מִצַּד אֶחָד וְנִתְחַלְחֵל כּוּלּוֹ. אוֹף הָכָא. אָדָם נוֹגֵעַ מִצַּד אֶחָד וְנִתְחַלְחֵל כּוּלּוֹ. רִבִּי יוֹסֵי בֵּירִבִּי בּוּן בְּשֵׁם רִבִּי לֵוִי. בּוֹר מָלֵא מַיִם וְנָפַל שָׁמָּה גְּדִי קָטָן וְנִכְנְסוּ מַיִם דֶּרֶךְ אָזְנָיו וְנִתְחַלְחֵל כּוּלּוֹ. וָכָא נִתְחַלְחֵל כּוּלּוֹ. רִבִּי יִרְמְיָה בָּעֵי. הָיְתָה מְהַלֶּכֶת וּמְעַקֶּרֶת עֲשָׂבִים בְּגוּפָהּ וּבְקַרְנָהּ מַהוּ. שִׁינּוּי הוּא. דַּרְכָּהּ לָכֵן.

Derivatives of the tooth. They wanted to say that if a cow ate barley[38], or a donkey ate leeks, or a dog licked olive oil, or a pig[39] ate meat, all of these are derivatives of the tooth. Rebbi Isaac said, all these are of the essence of the tooth. But did we not state "derivatives of the tooth"? If it stepped on a skin full of oil[40], since its body enjoys anointing. As one says in general, the tooth eats and the body enjoys, so also here the body enjoys. Rebbi Jeremiah asked: If in walking if was disgorging grasses[41], what is the rule? Rebbi Yose said, just as one who puts a burning coal to[42] the public domain, it causes damage as far as it moves[43]. What does this mean? Rebbi Yose ben Rebbi Abun said, explain it if somebody puts a knife close to the public domain[44]. As you say there, if the fire touches one side, it trembles in its entirety, so also here, a human touches[45] on one side and trembles in his entirety. Rebbi Yose ben Rebbi Abun in the name of Rebbi Levi: If a pit is full of water and a small lamb fell in, if water enters its ears it trembles in its entirety, so here it trembles in its entirety. Rebbi Jeremiah asked: If in walking it tore out grasses with its body or its horns, what is the rule? Is this out of the ordinary? It is its common behavior[46].

38   Babli 19b. It will be established later that the owner of an animal is guilty of negligence if he does not prevent his animal from causing foreseeable damage. But if the animal shows unusual, not foreseeable, behavior, he pays only half the damage caused by it. One might assume that if an animal eats anything that does not belong to its regular feed the owner should pay only half of the damages. This is rejected; all edibles are potential feed for all animals.

39   Rashba reads: "A cat ate a large piece of meat".

40   The animal steps on a container of olive oil, breaks it, and by this has its foot drenched in oil. One has to judge this under the rules of damage by "tooth", not "foot".

41   Usually ruminants lie down while ruminating. Kosher animals are all ruminants. If an animal was ruminating while walking, losing some of its cud in walking and thereby causing damage: is this foreseeable or not foreseeable damage?

42   The expression מניח ל is very unusual. One would have expected either מניח ב or an additional word like מַנִּיחַ סָמוּךְ לִרְשׁוּת הָרַבִּים "puts close to the public domain". This may be intended here, viz., that the hot coal was put on the border but not strictly inside the public domain.

43   The animal is expected to cause damage anywhere it moves; the damage is foreseeable.

44   And somebody in the public domain is hurt by it. He shows that this damage has to be judged under the rules of damage by fire.

45   The knife.

46   The animal's owner is responsible for the entire damage.

(2b line 11) רִבִּי בּוּן בַּר חִיָּיה בְּשֵׁם רִבִּי שְׁמוּאֵל בַּר רַב יִצְחָק. אִם לֹא נֶאֱמַר שׁוֹר הָיִיתִי לָמֵד שׁוֹר מִן הַבּוֹר. מָה אִם הַבּוֹר שֶׁאֵין דַּרְכּוֹ לֵילֵךְ וּלְהַזִּיק חַיָּב

לְשַׁלֵּם. שׁוֹר שֶׁדַּרְכּוּ לֵילֵךְ וּלְהַזִּיק לֹא כָּל־שֶׁכֵּן. אוֹ מָה הַבּוֹר מְשַׁלֵּם נֶזֶק שָׁלֵם אַף הַשּׁוֹר מְשַׁלֵּם נֶזֶק שָׁלֵם. אוֹ מָה הַשּׁוֹר מְשַׁלֵּם חֲצִי נֶזֶק אַף הַבּוֹר מְשַׁלֵּם חֲצִי נֶזֶק. אִילּוּ לֹא נֶאֱמַר שׁוֹר הָיִיתִי לָמֵד שׁוֹר מִן הַבּוֹר. אוֹ אִילּוּ לֹא נֶאֱמַר בּוֹר הָיִיתִי לָמֵד בּוֹר מִן הַשּׁוֹר. וְלָמָּה תְנִינָתָהּ הָכָא. דְּאִית לֵיהּ מִילִּין סַגִּין. כֵּן. לֹא הֲרֵי מוֹשָׁב כַּהֲרֵי מִשְׁכָּב וְלֹא הֲרֵי מִשְׁכָּב כַּהֲרֵי מוֹשָׁב. נִיחָא לֹא הֲרֵי מוֹשָׁב כַּהֲרֵי מִשְׁכָּב. אִם מוֹשָׁב בְּטֶפַח יִטְמָא מִשְׁכָּב בְּאַרְבָּעָה טְפָחִים. מִפְּנֵי שֶׁטִּימֵּא מִשְׁכָּב בְּאַרְבָּעָה טְפָחִים יִטְמָא מוֹשָׁב בְּטֶפַח. אִילּוּ לֹא נֶאֱמַר מִשְׁכָּב הָיִיתִי לָמֵד מִשְׁכָּב מִן הַמּוֹשָׁב. אִילּוּ לֹא נֶאֱמַר מוֹשָׁב הָיִיתִי לָמֵד מוֹשָׁב מִן הַמִּשְׁכָּב. וְלָמָּה תְנִינָתָהּ הָכָא. דְּאִית לִתְנוּיֵיהּ סַגִּין מִילִּין. כֵּן. לֹא פָרָשַׁת נֵירוֹת כַּהֲרֵי פָרָשַׁת שִׁילּוּחַ טְמֵאִין וְלֹא פָרָשַׁת שִׁילּוּחַ טְמֵאִין כַּהֲרֵי פָרָשַׁת נֵירוֹת. אִילּוּ לֹא נֶאֱמַר פָּרָשַׁת שִׁילּוּחַ טְמֵאִין הָיִיתִי לָמֵד פָּרָשַׁת שִׁילּוּחַ טְמֵאִין מִפָּרָשַׁת נֵירוֹת. וְלָמָּה תְנִינָתָהּ הָכָא. דְּאִית לִתְנוּיֵיהּ סַגִּין מִילִּין. כֵּן. הַצַּד הַשָּׁוֶה שֶׁבָּהֶן שֶׁהֵן בְּצַו מִיַּד וּלְדוֹרוֹת. אַף כָּל־שֶׁהוּא בְּצַו מִיַּד וּלְדוֹרוֹת. אָמַר רַבִּי לָא. צָרִיךְ הוּא שֶׁיֵּאָמֵר לְכָל אֶחָד וְאֶחָד. וְהַשּׁוֹר מְלַמֵּד שֶׁהַבְּעָלִים מִיטַפְּלִין בַּנְּבֵילָה. דִּכְתִיב וְהַמֵּת וְהָיָה לוֹ וּכְתִיב בַּבּוֹר וְהַמֵּת יִהְיֶה לוֹ. תַּנֵּי רַבִּי יִשְׁמָעֵאל. יָצְאוּ קַרְקָעוֹת שֶׁאֵינָן מִיטַּלְטְלִין. יָצָא אָדָם שֶׁאֵין לוֹ הֲנָיָה בְּמוֹתוֹ. וְהָאֵשׁ מְלַמֶּדֶת עַל כּוּלְּהֶן שֶׁהוּא חַיָּב עַל הָאוֹנְסִין.

Rebbi Abun bar Ḥiyya in the name of Rebbi Samuel bar Rav Isaac: If "the bull" had not been written, I would have inferred the bull from the pit[47]. Since for the pit, which is not usually moving, one has to pay full damages, not so much more for the bull which usually is moving[48]? Either since for the pit one pays full damages, also the bull pays full damages, or since the bull pays half damages, also for the pit one should have to pay half damages[49]. If "the bull" had not been written, I would have inferred the bull from the pit; if "the pit" had not been written, I would have inferred the bull from the pit. Why was it stated here?

Because there are many things⁵⁰. Similarly, the seat is not like the bed and the bed is not like the seat⁵¹. One understands that the seat is not like the bed. The seat a square *ṭephaḥ* large can become impure; the bed four *ṭephaḥim* large can become impure⁵². Because He declared a bed four *ṭephaḥim* large as impure, would a seat a square *ṭephaḥ* large become impure⁵³? If the seat had not been written, I would have inferred seat from bed. Why was it stated here? Because there are many things to be stated. Similarly, the paragraph on lighting the candles is not like the paragraph about exiling the impure and the paragraph on exiling the impure is not like the paragraph about lighting the candles⁵⁴. If the paragraph about exiling the impure had not been written, I would have inferred the rules of the paragraph on exiling the impure from the paragraph on lighting the candles. Why was it stated here? Because there are many things to be stated⁵⁵. So what is equal about them is that they are "command" here and in future generations, so everything by "command" is for here and for future generations⁵⁶. Rebbi La said, it is necessary that all⁵⁷ be written; and the bull teaches that the owners have to deal with the cadaver⁵⁸. But it is written, "and the cadaver shall be his", and it is written for the pit, "and the cadaver shall be his"⁵⁹! Rebbi Ismael said, this excludes real estate which cannot be moved⁶⁰; it excludes a human because there can be no usufruct from him in death⁶¹. But the fire teaches for all of them that one is responsible for accidents⁶².

47   He wants to prove that the different categories mentioned in the biblical text are necessary; one cannot be subsumed under the other.

48   But for damages inflicted through goring by an animal which has no history of doing so the owner pays only half, *Ex.* 21:35.

49   This is the preceding argument in a different formulation. Since the

rules of payment are different for bull and pit, they cannot be subsumed under one rule.

50 The later text shows that one should read here: "Because there are many things to be stated;" the differences between the rules for bull and pit are many.

51 In the rules of impurity of the sufferer from gonorrhea, *Lev.* 15:4-5 proclaims the impurity of his bed and v. 6 that of his seat. Why do seat and bed have to be mentioned separately? In the *baraita* of R. Ismael (*Sifra*, Introduction 5) the rules common to seat and bed are declared valid for any implement used for human rest, as illustration of the third hermeneutical rule "a principle derived from one paragraph".

52 Babli *Me'ilah* 18a. While textiles in general can become impure, small snippets cannot. Cloth being woven cannot become impure unless it has a size which makes it usable. This depends on the intended use. Cloth intended as cover of a seat becomes impure once it contains a square of side length of one handbreadth (probably 9.1 cm); for the cover of a bed one requires a square of four handbreadths.

53 There is no logical necessity here. The rules for the impurity of beds are detailed in *Sifra Meṣora'*, *Pereq Zabim, Pereq 2, Parašah 2;* those for seats are in *Pereq* 3:1-4.

54 *Baraita* of R. Ismael (*Sifra*, Introduction 6) as illustration of the second part of the third hermeneutical rule "a principle derived from two paragraphs"; the main argument is in *Sifry Num.* 1. In *Num.* 5:1-4, Moses is instructed to *command* the Children of Israel to remove lepers, sufferers from gonorrhea, and those impure from the impurity of the dead from the camp. It is noted that the command was executed immediately. In *Num.* 8:3 it is stated that Aaron lit the lights in the Sanctuary exactly as the Eternal had *commanded* Moses. R. Ismael infers that everywhere in the Pentateuch, a *command* is to be executed immediately (and permanently).

55 As Ravad notes in his Commentary to *Sifra*, these differences are nowhere noted.

56 Quoted in *Sifra Ṣaw* 1:1, *Emor Parašah* 13:1;

57 The four categories mentioned in the Mishnah.

58 *Ex.* 21:36, speaking of the bull with a history of goring, requires the owner of the goring bull to pay full damages and concludes "the cadaver

shall be his." This "his" (and the parallel in v. 34) is interpreted as "the claimant's" in Babli 10b,53b; *Mekhilta dR. Ismael, Mišpaṭim* 11,12; *Mekhilta dR. Simeon b. Ioḥai* p. 186. The argument is that since full damages are due, one could assume that the payor had acquired the carcass and no mention of it would be necessary.

59   This seems to disprove R. La's statement. If the same rule is explicit for the agressive goring bull and the pit, one would have to assume that it does not hold for any other kinds of damages.

60   This is difficult to understand since real estate cannot fall into a pit. In Tosephta 6:14, one excludes payment for broken vessels if there is no residual value in the pieces.

61   Similarly in Tosephta 6:14; Babli 53b.

62   This is another commentary on R. La's statement. Also damages for losses by fire teach another principle. Since *Ex.* 22:5 reads "If fire gets out of control . . . the person who started the fire has to pay," even if he started the fire perfectly legally on his own property. This establishes general liability for damages caused by accident. A similar text is in *Mekhilta dR. Ismael Mišpaṭim* 14. The Babli, 26b, derives a similar principle from *Ex.* 21:24-25.

(2b line 34) אָמַר רִבִּי יוֹסֵי. הָדָא אָמְרָה. אָדָם שֶׁחָבַל בַּחֲבֵירוֹ תְּחִילָּה אַף עַל פִּי שֶׁחָזַר וְנַעֲשָׂה נִזָּק חַיָּיב. דִּכְתִיב וּמַכֵּה בְהֵמָה יְשַׁלְמֶנָּה. יְשַׁלֵּם פְּחָתָהּ.

Rebbi Yose said: This means that a person who injured another first has to pay even if he later becomes injured, as is written: "He who injures an animal has to pay for it," he has to pay the diminution in value[63].

63   The statement of R. Yose belongs to the discussion of the last part of the Mishnah, that if damage was caused the person responsible is obligated to pay for the damages. The sentence starting with "as is written" does not belong to R. Yose's text.

(2b line 36) **פִּיסְקָא.** וּכְשֶׁהִזִּיק חָב הַמַּזִּיק כּוּל׳. אָמַר רִבִּי חֲנִינָה. מַכֶּה בְהֵמָה יְשַׁלְּמֶנָּה. יְשַׁלֵּם פְּחָתָהּ. בַּר פְּדָיָיה אָמַר. אִם טָרֹף יִטָּרֵף יְבִיאֵהוּ עֵד מְקוֹם הַטְּרֵיפָה לֹא יְשַׁלֵּם. אָמַר רִבִּי נָסָא. צוֹרְכָה לְהָדָא דְּרִבִּי חֲנִינָה וְצוֹרְכָה לְהָדָא דְּבַר פְּדָיָיה. אִילּוּ אִתְאָמַרַת דְּרִבִּי חֲנִינָה וְלֹא אִתְאָמַרַת דְּבַר פְּדָיָיה. הָיִיתִי אוֹמֵר. לְהֶכְשֵׁר נִיזְקֵיה לֹא יְשַׁלֵּם כְּלוּם. לְנִזְקֵי גּוּפָהּ יְשַׁלֵּם פְּחָתָהּ. הֲוֵי. צוֹרֶךְ הוּא שֶׁיֵּאָמֵר דְּבַר פְּדָיָיה. אוֹ אִילּוּ אִתְאָמַרַת דְּבַר פְּדָיָה וְלֹא אִתְאָמַרַת דְּרִבִּי חֲנִינָה. הָיִיתִי אוֹמֵר. לְהֶכְשֵׁר נִזְקֵיה יְשַׁלֵּם פְּחָתָהּ. לְנִזְקֵי גּוּפָה יְשַׁלֵּם אֶת הַכֹּל. הֲוֵי. צוֹרֶךְ שֶׁיֵּאָמֵר דְּרִבִּי חֲנִינָה וְצוֹרֶךְ שֶׁיֵּאָמֵר דְּרִ׳ פְּדָיָיה.

New Paragraph. "If damage was caused the person responsible is obligated to pay for the damages," etc. Rebbi Hanina said, "he who injures an animal has to pay for it[64]," he has to pay the diminution in value. Bar Pedaiah said, "if it was torn, he shall bring it up to the place of the carcass, for which he does not have to pay.[65]" Rebbi Nasa said, the quote of Rebbi Hanina is needed and the quote of Bar Pedaiah is needed. If only the quote of Rebbi Hanina was given but not that of Bar Pedaiah, I would have said that if he made the damage possible he should not have to pay anything but for bodily damage he has to pay the diminution in value[66]. Therefore, Bar Pedaiah's quote is necessary. But if only the quote of Bar Pedaiah was given but not that of Rebbi Hanina, I would have said that if he made the damage possible[67] he has to pay the diminution in value, but for bodily damage he has to pay the whole[68]. Therefore, the quote of Rebbi Hanina is needed and the quote of Bar Pedaiah is needed.

64 *Lev.* 24:18, incorrect quote. In the Babli, 10b, R. Ammi (Immi) explains יְשַׁלְּמֶנָּה "pay for it" by יַשְׁלִימֶנָּה "shall supplement it," i. e., pay the difference between the value of the living animal and the carcass. This argument has to be read into the quote here.

65 *Ex.* 22:12. The sentence has become unintelligible because it mixes

quote and two distinct interpretations. Verses 9-12 refer to the person who undertook to watch over another's property and is paid for his services. If there was a loss because of theft, the watchman has to pay because he failed to prevent the theft (v. 11). If livestock was lost to predatory animals, the watchman "has to bring it עַד". The masoretic vocalization עֵד means (*Mekhilta dR. Ismael, Mišpaṭim* 15 in the name of R. Joshia; Babli 11a) that witnesses who testify that the loss was caused by a lion or similar large animal against which the watchman was powerless, will free the watchman from his obligation to pay. He will have to pay for losses caused by smaller animals which attack by stealth. The other interpretations read עד, either עַד I "until", or עַד III "torn, robbed by the enemy". In the Babli, 11a, and *Mekhilta dR. Simeon ben Ioḥai* 22:12, Abba Shaul reads "he shall bring the torn," meaning that he does not have to pay for the residual value of the carcass. In *Mekhilta dR. Ismael, Mišpaṭim* 15, R. Jonathan reads "he has to bring the owners to the place [of the attack]" to support his claim that the attack was by a large animal against whom he was powerless. The insertion of "up to the place" into Bar Pedaiah's quote follows R. Jonathan, but his interpretation is that of Abba Shaul.

66    Since the verse in *Lev.* only requires payment by a person who attacks an animal, not if the damage was caused by negligence.

67    By his negligence.

68    As one would understand from *Lev.* 24:18 without R. Immi's interpretation.

(2b line 45) רַב יְהוּדָה בְּשֵׁם שְׁמוּאֵל. אֵין שָׁמִין לֹא לַגַּנָּב וְלֹא לַגַּזְלָן וְלֹא לַשּׁוֹאֵל אֶלָּא לִנְזָקִין. וַאֲנִי אוֹמֵר. אַף לַשּׁוֹאֵל אֵין שָׁמִין. וְאַבָּא מוֹדֶה לִי. וּמָאן הוּא אַבָּא. רִבִּי אוֹ רַבָּה בַּר אֲבוּהַּ. אָמַר רַב חִסְדָּא. נַעֲשָׂה עִיקָר טְפֵילָה. אֲתָא רַב יְהוּדָה בְּשֵׁם שְׁמוּאֵל. אֵין שָׁמִין לֹא לַגַּנָּב וְלֹא לַגַּזְלָן וְלֹא לַשּׁוֹאֵל אֶלָּא לִנְזָקִין. וְהַשּׁוֹמְרִין כִּנְזָקִין הֵן.

⁶⁹Rav Jehudah in the name of Samuel: One estimates⁷⁰ neither for the thief nor for the robber nor for the borrower but only for damages, and I⁷¹ am saying that even for the borrower one does not estimate, and Abba agrees with me. Who is Abba? Rebbi⁷² or Rabba bar Abuha⁷³. Rav Ḥisda said, this treats the main event as an accessory⁷⁴. There came⁷⁵ Rav Jehudah in the name of Samuel: One estimates neither for the thief nor for the robber nor for the borrower⁷⁶ but only for damages, and watchmen fall under the rules of damages⁷⁷.

69   A consistent text is in the Babli, 11a.

70   Thiefs, robber, and borrowers who broke what they borrowed have to pay the entire damage which they caused, without deduction for the residual value of what they might return of the things they took.

71   This is Samuel speaking. After he reported the traditional opinion, he adds his own extension of the rule.

72   This certainly should read: "Rav", who in the Babli is recorded as having ruled in an actual case that the borrower has to pay in full.

73   Rav Abba, a slightly younger contemporary of Samuel and, like Samuel, teacher of R. Naḥman bar Jacob.

74   Since the borrower has to pay for accidental damage, *Ex.* 22:13, it should be obvious that he has to pay in full by biblical standards. One cannot understand why Samuel would treat the case of the borrower as an appendix to the laws of torts.

75   Here the name of a Galilean Amora who adopted the positions of Rav Jehudah and Samuel is missing.

76   The Babli, 11a and *Bava meṣi'a* 97a, comes to the opposite conclusion.

77   As explained in the preceding paragraph.

(2c line 2) רַב יְהוּדָה שָׁלַח שָׁאַל לְרִבִּי לְעָזָר. הָאַנָּס וְהַגַּנָּב וְהַגּוֹזְלָן מָהוּ לָשׁוּם לָהֶן. אָמַר לֵיהּ. אֵין שָׁמִין לֹא לַגַּנָּב וְלֹא לַגּוֹזְלָן. וּמְנַיִין שֶׁאֵין שָׁמִין לָהֶן. אָמַר רַבָּה בַּר מָמָל. חַיִּים שְׁנַיִם מְשַׁלֵּם. חַיִּים וְלֹא מֵתִים. גְּזֵילָה מְנַיִין. אָמַר רִבִּי אָבִין. וְהֵשִׁיב אֶת הַגְּזֵילָה כַּאֲשֶׁר גָּזַל.

[78]Rav Jehudah sent and asked Rebbi Eleazar: Does one estimate for the extortionist, the thief, and the robber? He answered him: one estimates neither for the thief nor for the robber. From where that one does not estimate for them? Rebbi Abba bar Mamal said, "alive, he shall pay double[79];" alive, not dead. That refers to theft; from where for robbery? Rebbi Abin said, "he shall return the robbed object in the state in which he robbed it.[80]"

78  There exists a parallel text, from a different redaction, in *Qiddušin* 1:4, Notes 466-468.

79  Ex. 22:3; the thief has to pay in full if he cannot return the stolen animal in the shape in which he stole it.

80  Lev. 5:23. The explanation adds one letter to the biblical text, changing the somewhat redundant description וְהֵשִׁיב אֶת־הַגְּזֵלָה אֲשֶׁר גָּזַל "let him return the robbed object which he robbed" into וְהֵשִׁיב אֶת־הַגְּזֵלָה כַּאֲשֶׁר גָּזַל "let him return the robbed object *in the state in which he robbed it*."

(fol. 2a) **משנה ב:** כָּל־שֶׁחַבְתִּי בִּשְׁמִירָתוֹ הִכְשַׁרְתִּי אֶת נִזְקוֹ. הִכְשַׁרְתִּי בְּמִקְצָת נִזְקוֹ חַבְתִּי בְּתַשְׁלוּמֵי נִזְקוֹ כְּהֶכְשֵׁר כָּל־נִזְקוֹ. נְכָסִים שֶׁל בְּנֵי בְרִית וּנְכָסִים הַמְיוּחָדִים חוּץ מֵרְשׁוּת הַמְיוּחֶדֶת לַמַּזִּיק וּרְשׁוּת הַנִּיזָּק וְהַמַּזִּיק בְּתַשְׁלוּמִים.

**Mishnah 2:** [81]Anything I am obligated to watch[82] I did set up for damage claims. If I partially set up for damage claims I am liable for claims as if I had set up for any claims[83]. [84]Properties of people of the covenant[85] and private property, except for property belonging solely to the person responsible for the damage[86]; but property common to the person suffering the damage and the person responsible for the damage[87] falls under the rules of restitution.

| | |
|---|---|
| 81 Compared to the Mishnah in the Babli and in the independent Mishnah mss., this Mishnah is very much abridged. The Halakhah in parts refers to the longer version.<br><br>The Mishnah is explained in detail in the Tosephta 1:1.<br><br>82 E. g., cattle or a pit in the ground.<br><br>83 If there was a shallow pit in the ground and a person came and deepened it to become a real danger, | that person becomes liable for any damages caused by the pit.<br><br>84 Missing here: "Properties not subject to the laws of misappropriation of *sancta*," i. e., the laws of restitution only apply to profane objects.<br><br>85 Damages to Gentile property cannot be prosecuted in rabbinic court.<br><br>86 Where usually the property owner cannot be sued.<br><br>87 Who might have to share the cost of damages. |

(2c line 7) **הלכה ב:** כָּל־שֶׁחַבְתִּי בִשְׁמִירָתוֹ כול׳. תַּנֵּי רִבִּי חִיָּיה. זֶה הַשּׁוֹר וְהַבּוֹר. וְהָאֵשׁ לֹא תָנָה. אָמַר רִבִּי יִרְמִיָה. הָאֵשׁ לְהֶכְשֵׁר נְזָקָיו. אָמַר רִבִּי יוֹסֵי. וְאִין כֵּינִי הָאֵשׁ לְהֶכְשֵׁר נְזָקָיו מְקַבֵּל עָלָיו הַהַתְרָיָיה בְּדַעַת זוֹ וְלוֹקֶה. מַאי כְדוֹן. הָאֵשׁ לְהֶכְשֵׁר נְזָקָיו מְקַבֵּל עָלָיו נֶזֶק צַעַר רִיפּוּי שֶׁבֶת וּבוֹשֶׁת.

**Halakhah 2:** "Anything I am obligated to watch I did set up for damage claims," etc. Rebbi Hiyya stated[88]: This refers to cattle and pit. But he did not state "fire"[89]. Rebbi Jeremiah said, the fire set up for damage claims[90]? Rebbi Yose said, if the fire were [more than] damage claims, should he not accept warning according to this opinion and be whipped[91]? How is this? The fire in setting up for damage claims he accepts [responsibility] for damages, suffering, medical costs, loss of earning power, shame[17,92].

| | |
|---|---|
| 88 Tosephta 1:1.<br>89 The same question in the Babli, 9b.<br>90 If a person is injured by fire, | even if the fire was started completely legally, he is treated as being injured by the direct action of the person starting the fire. This responsibility |

exceeds by far the responsibility of a rancher to watch his herd or of the person digging a pit in the public domain.

91 Injuring another person is a criminal act subject to prosecution. We do not find that a person making a legal fire might be criminally prosecuted.

92 This is the excess liability which puts fire in a category different from cattle and pit.

(2c line 11) הִכְשַׁרְתִּי בְּמִקְצָת נִזְקוֹ כְּהֶכְשֵׁר כָּל־נִזְקוֹ. זֶה הַבּוֹר. דְּתַנֵּי. חָפַר בּוֹר עֲשָׂרָה טְפָחִים וּבָא אַחֵר וְעָמַק בּוֹ טֶפַח הָאַחֲרוֹן חַיָּיב. רִבִּי אוֹמֵר. אַחַר הָאַחֲרוֹן לְמִיתָה וְאַחַר הָרִאשׁוֹן לִנְזָקִין. אָמַר רִבִּי יִצְחָק. כֵּינִי מַתְנִיתָא. אַחַר אַחֲרוֹן לְמִיתָה וְאַחַר שְׁנֵיהֶן לִנְזָקִין. חָפַר בּוֹ עֲשָׂרָה טְפָחִים וּבָא אַחֵר וְסִיְּידוֹ וְכִיְּירוֹ שְׁנֵיהֶן חַיָּיבִין. מִפְּנֵי שֶׁסִּיְּירוֹ וְכִיְּירוֹ יְהֵא חַיָּיב. בְּשֶׁאָמַר לוֹ. סוּד אֶת הַ(בַּיִת) [בּוֹר] הַזֶּה וּקְנֵה אוֹתוֹ. דָּמַר רִבִּי אִמִּי בְּשֵׁם רִבִּי לָעֶזָר. שְׁמִירַת נְזָקִין כִּשְׁמִירַת קִנְיָין. אָמַר רִבִּי סִימוֹן. תִּיפְתָּר בְּחוֹפֵר בַּחוֹלוֹת. דְּתַנֵּי. חָפַר זֶה עֲשָׂרָה וְזֶה עֲשָׂרָה זֶה עֶשְׂרִים וְזֶה עֶשְׂרִים זֶה מֵאָה וְזֶה מֵאָה כּוּלְּהוֹן חַיָּיבִין. כַּמָּה שִׁיעוּרָן לְהָמִית. עֲשָׂרָה טְפָחִים. וּלְהַזִּיק. כָּל־שֶׁהוּא. סוּמְכוּס אוֹמֵר. לְעוֹמְקוֹ שְׁלֹשָׁה וְרָחְבּוֹ אַרְבָּעָה. רִבִּי לָעֶזָר הַקַּפָּר אוֹמֵר. כִּמְלוֹאוֹ שֶׁלַּנּוֹפֵל. וּמַהוּ מְלוֹאוֹ שֶׁלַּנּוֹפֵל. אֲפִילוּ תַרְנְגוֹל וַאֲפִילוּ גָמָל.

"If I partially set up for damage claims" "as if I had set up for any claims." This is the pit[88], as it was stated[93]: If somebody dug a pit ten handbreadths deep[94] and another came and deepened it another handbreadth, the latter is responsible. Rebbi[95] says, one goes after the latter in case of death and after the former for damages. Rebbi Isaac says: So is the *baraita*: After the latter in case of death and after both of them for damages[96]. If he dug [a pit] ten handbreadths deep and another person came, whitewashed and lined it, both of them are liable[97]. Is he liable because he whitewashed and lined it[98]? When he told him, whitewash this (house) [pit][99] and acquire it[100], for Rebbi Immi said in the name of Rebbi

Eleazar, the prevention of damages follows the rules of guarding an acquisition[101]. Rebbi Simon said, explain it when he was digging in the dunes[102]. And it was stated: If each of them dug ten, or each one twenty, or each one a hundred, they are all liable[93,103]. How deep does it have to be[104]? To be deadly, ten handbreadths[105]. To do damage, anything. Symmachos says[106], three in depth and four in width. Rebbi Eleazar the caper grower says, the length of the animal which falls in. What means the length of the animal which falls in? Whether chicken or camel.

93 Tosephta 6:8; Babli 10a (missing in Munich ms.), 51a.

94 Since it is stated later in the Halakhah that an animal might be killed if it falls into a pit ten handbreadths deep, it is clear that here it must be assumed that the first digger stopped short of a full ten handbreadths. The second digger then turned an obstacle which might cause damage into an obstacle which endangered the life of animals. In Tosephta and Babli one reads "nine handbreadths".

95 This also is the reading of the Babli and one Tosephta ms. In the Vienna ms. of the Tosephta and the *editio princeps*: R. Jehudah.

96 This is the Babli's version of Rebbi's statement. For material damage, anybody who digs in the public domain and does not securely cover the pit is liable for damages.

97 Tosephta 6:9, Babli 51a.

98 In *Mekhilta dR. Ismael Mišpaṭim* 11, and Babli the second one is liable not because he improved the pit but because he did not cover it correctly when he had finished his work, as *Ex.* 21:33 states: "If somebody would open a pit or dig a pit without covering it." Therefore, the last one to work on the pit is liable if he failed to cover it.

99 The text in brackets is that of the original scribe (correct); that in parentheses is the corrector's, copied in *editio princeps* (incorrect).

100 By ḥazaqah, cf. *Ketubot* 5:5, Note 100.

101 Any transfer of property is at the same time transfer of liability for that property.

102 Where a simple pit would have disappeared in a short time. The second person by installing permanent walls only created the danger.

103 In the Babylonian sources, one person digs ten, the next enlarges it two twenty, the third digs down to 100.

104 To require a cover to protect the digger from damage suits; Tosephta 6:12.

105 This is undisputed in both Talmudim. If an animal is killed falling into a pit less than ten handbreadths deep, it is purely a matter of material damage.

106 He disagrees only with the statement that any pothole in the public domain is cause for a damage suit; he requires a minimal size.

(2c line 22) פִּיסְקָא. נְכָסִים שֶׁאֵין בָּהֶן מְעִילָה. דְּתַנֵּי. הַנְּכָסִין הַלָּלוּ נִיקְנִין עִם נְכָסִין שֶׁיֵּשׁ בָּהֶן מְעִילָה. רַב יְהוּדָה בְשֵׁם שְׁמוּאֵל. דְּרִבִּי יוֹסֵי הַגָּלִילִי הִיא. דְּתַנֵּי. וּמָעֲלָה מַעַל בַּיי. רִבִּי יוֹסֵי הַגָּלִילִי אוֹמֵר. לְהָבִיא קָדָשִׁים קַלִּין. בֶּן עַזַּאי אוֹמֵר. לְהָבִיא אֶת הַשְּׁלָמִים. אַבָּא יוֹסֵי בֶּן דּוֹסַאי אוֹמֵר. לֹא הָיָה בֶן עַזַּאי אוֹמֵר אֶלָּא עַל הַבְּכוֹר בִּלְבָד. וּמַה בֵינֵיהוֹן. מָאן דָּמַר שְׁלָמִים כָּל־שֶׁכֵּן מַעֲשֵׂר. וּמָאן דָּמַר מַעֲשֵׂר הָא בְכוֹר לֹא. רִבִּי שִׁמְעוֹן אוֹמֵר. אֶחָד קָדְשֵׁי קָדָשִׁים וְאֶחָד קָדָשִׁים קַלִּין. קָדָשִׁים שֶׁחַיָּיב בְּאַחֲרָיוּתָן קוֹרֵא אֲנִי בָהֶן בַּעֲמִיתוֹ וְכִיחֵשׁ. וְשֶׁאֵינוֹ חַיָּיב בְּאַחֲרָיוּתָן קוֹרֵא אֲנִי בָהֶן בַּיי וְכִיחֵשׁ. רַב הוּנָא אָמַר. אֶחָד קָדָשִׁים כְּשֵׁירִין וְאֶחָד קָדָשִׁים פְּסוּלִין. קָדָשִׁים שֶׁחַיָּיב בְּאַחֲרָיוּתָן אֲפִילוּ הֵן לַיי קוֹרֵא אֲנִי בָהֶן בַּעֲמִיתוֹ וְכִיחֵשׁ וְשֶׁאֵינוֹ חַיָּיב בְּאַחֲרָיוּתָן קוֹרֵא אֲנִי בָהֶן בַּיי וְכִיחֵשׁ וְלֹא בַּעֲמִיתוֹ וְכִיחֵשׁ.

New paragraph. "Properties not subject to the laws of misappropriation of *sancta*.[84,107]" As it was stated: "These properties[108] are acquired together with properties subject to the laws of misappropriation of *sancta*[109]." Rav Jehudah in the name of Samuel: This[110] follows Rebbi Yose the Galilean, as it was stated[111]: "'He commits larceny before the Eternal[112],' Rebbi Yose the Galilean says, this includes simple *sancta*[113].

Ben Azzai says, this includes well-being sacrifices[114]. Abba Yose ben Dosai[125] says, Ben Azzai said this only for the firstling[116]." What is between them? He who says well-being sacrifices certainly include tithes[117]. But he who says tithes[117] excludes the firstling[117]. "Rebbi Simeon says, both most holy and simple *sancta*; about any *sancta* for which he is responsible if alienated[118], I am reading 'against his neighbor and he lied[112]'; but about any *sancta* for which he is not responsible if alienated, I am reading 'against the Eternal and he lied'"[119]. Rav Huna said, both qualified and disqualified *sancta*[120], if he is responsible if alienated, even if they are for the Eternal[121], I am reading "against his fellow and he denied", but if he is not responsible if alienated[122], I am reading "against the Eternal and he lied" but not "against his fellow and he lied".

107 The laws of torts are "between a man and his neighbor," which exludes all Temple property and those sacrifices which do not remain the owner's property.

108 Since this *baraita* is not quoted elsewhere, it is not known what "these properties" are. Some commentators want to read הַנְּכָסִים שֶׁחִלְּלוֹ "properties which he redeemed" (from the Temple administrator). This is very far-fetched.

109 Since the Temple acquires and sells property by monetary transaction without any other act of acquisition (*Qiddušin* 1:6), other property can be acquired together with Temple property under the same rules. For example, if the Temple treasurer sold some Temple property together with his own, the entire transaction is legal if done under Temple rules. Similarly, if a person acquires two animals, one dedicated as "Heaven's property" (elevation, purification, or reparation offering) subject to the laws of misappropriation of *sancta*, the other as "simple sacrifice" (well-being sacrifice) which remains private property, the holier sacrifice determines the rules.

110 He disagrees with the interpretation given and holds that the

Mishnah means what it says; only sacrificial animals not under the laws of misappropriation of sancta are subject to the laws of torts.

111  *Sifra Wayyiqra Dibbura Deḥoba Pereq* 22(3); Babli *Bava qama* 12b-13a, *Temurah* 8a; a related text in Tosephta 7:21. Partial quotes in *Bava batra* 123b, *Qiddušin* 52b, *Sanhedrin* 112a, *Zebaḥim* 114a, *Bekhorot* 53b.

112  Lev. 5:21.

113  In the Babli: "Simple sancta which are his property." The question raised is the status of firstlings and animal tithe, which are Heaven's property in the hands of the rancher. Since *Lev.* 5:21 reads: "If a person sins, commits fraud against the Eternal, and lies against his fellow . . ." it perfectly describes wrongdoing involving simple sancta which in one action represents wrong both against the Eternal and one's fellow man.

114  And all sacrifices following rules of well-being sacrifices, firstlings, and animal tithe. The firstling has to be given to a Cohen, the animal tithe is eaten by the rancher and his family in Jerusalem; in both cases the altar only receives the blood but no part of the meat.

115  In *Sifra*: דוסתי (Dositheos).

116  Animal tithes.

117  It seems that in the entire argument one should read "tithes" instead of "firstling" and vice versa. While the unblemished firstling at some time has to be handed over to a Cohen, as long as it is in the rancher's hand it is his property and can be sold; but the unblemished animal tithe by its count becomes Heaven's property and cannot be sold. The blemished firstling may be sold as food.

118  If a person vows "an animal" as sacrifice and anything happens to the animal designated as sacrifice, he is obligated to provide a replacement; he is responsible for its alienation. But if he vows "this animal" and anything happens to it, he is not obligated to provide a replacement; he is not responsible for its alienation. In *Lev.*, the first kind of vow is called נֶדֶר "vow", the second kind is נְדָבָה "free offering".

119  An anonymous *baraita* in the Babli, *Bava meṣi'a* 58a/b. Debts towards Heaven have to be discharged at the rate of 125%; those towards one's fellow man by the rate of 100%.

120  Which for some reason are not accepted by the altar.

121  Most holy sacrifices which either are holocausts on the altar or whose meat is eaten by male Cohanim

within the Temple precinct.

122 Even for well-being sacrifices, most of which is eaten by the donor's family.

(2c line 34) **פִּיסְקָא.** נְכָסִים שֶׁהֵן שֶׁלִּבְנֵי בְרִית. פְּרָט לְשׁוֹר שֶׁלְיִשְׂרָאֵל שֶׁנָּגַח לְשׁוֹר שֶׁלְנָכְרִי. מְנָכְסִין הַמְיוּחָדִין. וְלֹא מִנִּכְסֵי הֶפְקֵר. חוּץ מֵרְשׁוּת הַמְיוּחֶדֶת לַמַּזִּיק שֶׁהוּא פָטוּר. נוֹהֲגִין הֵן בִּרְשׁוּת הַנִּיזָּק וְהַמַּזִּיק. אָמַר רְבִּי יִרְמְיָה. אִילּוּ תַּנָא. חוּץ מֵרְשׁוּת הַמְיוּחֶדֶת לַמַּזִּיק וְשָׁתַק. הָיִיתִי אוֹמֵר. אֶחָד חָצֵר שֶׁלְשׁוּתָּפִין וְאֶחָד חָצֵר שֶׁאֵינָהּ לִשְׁנֵיהֶן חַיֶּיבֶת. וְלָמָּה תַנָא. נוֹהֲגִין הֵן בִּרְשׁוּת הַנִּיזָּק וְהַמַּזִּיק. אֶלָּא זֶה שׁוֹמֵר חִנָּם וְהַשׁוֹאֵל נוֹשֵׂא שָׂכָר וְהַשׂוֹכֵר. אָמַר רְבִּי יוֹסֵי. מִכֵּיוָן דְתַנָא. חוּץ מֵרְשׁוּת הַמְיוּחֶדֶת לַמַּזִּיק. אֵין אָנוּ יוֹדְעִין שֶׁהֵן נוֹהֲגִין בִּרְשׁוּת הַנִּיזָּק וְהַמַּזִּיק. וְלָמָּה תַנָא. נוֹהֲגִין הֵן בִּרְשׁוּת הַנִּיזָּק וְהַמַּזִּיק. אֶלָּא לְהוֹצִיא חָצֵר שֶׁאֵינָהּ שֶׁלִּשְׁנֵיהֶן. אִית תַּנָּיֵי תַּנֵּי. חָצֵר שֶׁלְשׁוּתָּפִין חַיֶּיבֶת וְחָצֵר שֶׁאֵינָהּ לִשְׁנֵיהֶן פְּטוּרָה. אִית תַּנָּיֵי תַּנֵּי. אֲפִילוּ חָצֵר שֶׁאֵינָהּ לִשְׁנֵיהֶם חַיֶּיבֶת. מָאן דָּמַר. חָצֵר שֶׁלְשׁוּתָּפִין חַיֶּיבֶת וְחָצֵר שֶׁאֵינָהּ לִשְׁנֵיהֶן פְּטוּרָה. דִכְתִיב מֵיטַב שָׂדֵהוּ. וּמָאן דָּמַר. אֲפִילוּ חָצֵר שֶׁאֵינָהּ לִשְׁנֵיהֶן חַיֶּיבֶת. דִכְתִיב וּבִיעֵר בִּשְׂדֵה אַחֵר. מִכָּל מָקוֹם.

New paragraph. "Properties of people of the Covenant," excluding cattle of a Jew which gored cattle of a Gentile[123]. "Private property," excluding ownerless property. "Except for property belonging solely to the person responsible for the damage" who cannot be sued[124]. "But [the rules] apply to property common to the person suffering the damage and the person responsible for the damage."

Rebbi Jeremiah said, if it were stated "except for property belonging solely to the person responsible for the damage" and had stopped, I would have said that [responsibility applies] both to a common courtyard and to a courtyard belonging to neither party. Why did it state: "[the rules] apply to property common to the person suffering the damage and the person responsible for the damage"[125]? [To indicate] that it applies to the unpaid trustee, the borrower, the paid trustee, and the renter[18,126].

Rebbi Yose said, since it stated "except for property belonging solely to the person responsible for the damage", would we not know that "[the rules] apply to property common to the person suffering the damage and the person responsible for the damage"? Why was it stated that "[the rules] apply to property common to the person suffering the damage and the person responsible for the damage"? To exclude a courtyard belonging to neither of them[127].

Some Tannaïm state: A condominium courtyard is obligated, a courtyard belonging to neither of them is free. Some Tannaïm state: Even a courtyard belonging to neither of them is obligated. He who says, a condominium courtyard is obligated, a courtyard belonging to neither of them is free, for it is written: "the best of his fields.[128]" But he who says, even a courtyard belonging to neither of them is obligated, for it is written: "It ravages another person's field.[128]"

123 The Gentile cannot claim damages in a Jewish court. In particular, claims for half damages are only possible between Jewish parties; for all others it is all or nothing.

124 Since any animal not belonging to the owner of the property is trespassing; the rancher does not have to interfere if his animals defend their territory.

125 Since this statement is already implied by the preceding one.

126 If somebody received an animal under the terms of one of the four kinds of trusteeship and that animal did damage, the owner is responsible.

127 The formulation "courtyard" instead of "property" indicates that in this case both animals are illegally in the place where the damage occurred.

128 *Ex.* 22:4, speaking of damage inflicted by animals grazing (tooth) and trampling (foot). This paragraph only deals with damage caused by foot and tooth.

## HALAKHAH 2

(2c line 49) רִבִּי יָסָא בְּשֵׁם רִבִּי יוֹחָנָן. חָצֵר הַשּׁוּתָּפִין חַיֶּיבֶת. אָמַר רִבִּי יָסָא. וַאֲנָא דְאַייתִיתָהּ מֵהָדָא דְתַנֵּי רִבִּי הוֹשַׁעְיָא. אַרְבָּעָה כְּלָלוֹת הָיָה רִבִּי שִׁמְעוֹן בֶּן אֶלְעָזָר אוֹמֵר מִשּׁוּם רִבִּי מֵאִיר בִּנְזָקִין. כָּל־מָקוֹם שֶׁיֵּשׁ רְשׁוּת לְנִיזָּק וּלְמַזִּיק כְּגוֹן פּוּנְדְּקִי וַחֲצַר הַשּׁוּתָּפִין וְכַיּוֹצֵא בָהֶן. עַל הַשֵּׁן וְעַל הָרֶגֶל פָּטוּר. עַל הַנְּגִיחָה וְהַנְּגִיפָה וְהַנְּשִׁיכָה וְהָרְבִיצָה וְעַל הַבְּעִיטָה וְהַדְּחִייָה אִם תָּם מְשַׁלֵּם חֲצִי נֶזֶק וּמוּעָד מְשַׁלֵּם נֶזֶק שָׁלֵם מִן הָעֲלִייָה. לַנִּיזָּק וְלֹא לַמַּזִּיק חַייָב בַּכֹּל. לַמַּזִּיק וְלֹא לַנִּיזָּק פָּטוּר מִן הַכֹּל. וְהַכֹּל מוֹדִין בְּשֶׁאֵין רְשׁוּת לֹא לָזֶה וְלֹא לָזֶה כְּגוֹן בִּקְעָה וּרְשׁוּת הָרַבִּים וְכַיּוֹצֵא בָהּ. עַל הַשֵּׁן וְעַל הָרֶגֶל פָּטוּר. עַל הַנְּגִיחָה וְעַל הַנְּגִיפָה וְהַנְּשִׁיכָה וְהָרְבִיצָה וְהַבְּעִיטָה וְהַדְּחִייָה תָּם מְשַׁלֵּם חֲצִי נֶזֶק וּמוּעָד מְשַׁלֵּם נֶזֶק שָׁלֵם מִן הָעֲלִייָה.

Rebbi Yasa in the name of Rebbi Johanan: A condominium courtyard is obligated[129]. Rebbi Yasa said: and I deduced that from what Rebbi Hoshaia stated[130]: Four principles about damages Rebbi Simeon ben Eleazar enunciated in Rebbi Meïr's name: Any place which is permitted to both the person who sustained the damage and the person who caused it, such as a hostelry or a condominium courtyard and similar situations, he is not liable for tooth and foot; for goring, and hitting, and biting, and wallowing, and kicking, and pushing by a tame animal he pays half the damages, for a notorious one he pays full damages from [real estate] of the best quality. [Permitted] to the person who sustained the damage but not the person who caused it, he pays everyting. [Permitted] to the person who caused the damage but not the person who sustained it, he is free from everything. And everybody agrees that if neither of them had access, as a valley[131] or public property[132] and similar situations, he is not liable[133] for tooth and foot; for goring, and hitting, and biting, and wallowing, and kicking, and pushing from a tame animal he pays half the damages[10], for a notorious one he pays full damages from his storage room[11].

129 Based on the preceding paragraph and the following Tosephta, one would have expected "free", not "obligated". I. Lewy emends the text in this sense, but R. Eliahu Fulda notes: "I do not feel empowered to emend."

130 Tosephta 1:9, Babli 14a.

131 בקעה "valley" is agricultural land accessible only by footpaths, without roadway. During the growing season it is clear that the only animals allowed there are the owners' beasts used for agricultural work; one has to assume that the Tosephta refers to the time between harvest and new ploughing. In both Babylonian texts, the "valley" is classified as permitted to both parties.

132 It is difficult to understand what is meant; in both Babylonian texts, "public domain" is classified as permitted to both parties. One has to assume that what is meant is neither a public road nor commons, but public property barred to private animals, such as a park. In the Babylonian texts, the sentence refers to a courtyard owned by a third party.

133 In both Babylonian texts: "is liable".

משנה ג: שׁוּם כֶּסֶף שָׁוֶה כֶסֶף בִּפְנֵי בֵית דִּין וְעַל פִּי עֵדִים בְּנֵי חוֹרִין בְּנֵי בְרִית. וְהַנָּשִׁים בִּכְלָל הַנֶּזֶק וְהַנִּזָּק וְהַמַּזִּיק בְּתַשְׁלוּמִין. (fol. 2a)

**Mishnah 3**: Estimation[134] and determination[135] of money's worth is by a court based on testimony of free persons of the Covenant. Women are under the rule of torts[136] and sometimes both the person who causes and the one who suffers the damage pay[137].

134 The estimation of the damage sustained.

135 The determination of the value of land which the person liable for the damage has to pay.

136 In contrast to minors and slaves

who cannot be sued.

137 In cases of damage through goring by a tame animal, when the owner of the animal only pays for half the damage. This is considered a fine; a restitution would be payment of full damages; the rules of fines do not apply to Gentiles.

(2c line 59) **הלכה ג:** שׁוּם כֶּסֶף שָׁוֶה כֶסֶף כול׳. אֵין אוֹמְרִים תֵּצֵא פָרָה בְטַלִּית. אֶלָּא שָׁמִין אֶת הַנְּכָסִין בְּבֵית דִּין. שָׁוֶה כֶסֶף. מְלַמֵּד שֶׁאֵין בֵּית דִּין שָׁמִין אֶלָּא נְכָסִים שֶׁיֵּשׁ לָהֶן אַחֲרָיוּת. וְאִם תָּפַשׂ הַנִּיזָּק בְּמִטַּלְטְלִין שָׁמִין לוֹ מֵהֶן. בִּפְנֵי בֵית דִּין. מְלַמֵּד שֶׁאֵין שָׁמִין לוֹ אֶלָּא בִּפְנֵי בֵית דִּין. עַל פִּי עֵדִים. שֶׁאֵין שָׁמִין אֶלָּא עַל פִּי עֵדִים. בְּנֵי חוֹרִין וּבְנֵי בְרִית. יָצְאוּ גּוֹיִים וַעֲבָדִים וּפְסוּלֵי עֵדוּת. וְנָשִׁים בִּכְלַל הַנֶּזֶק. לְפִי שֶׁלֹּא תָפַשׂ הַכָּתוּב אֶלָּא אֶת הָאִישׁ צָרִיךְ לְרַבּוֹת אֶת הָאִשָּׁה. תַּנֵּי רִבִּי יִשְׁמָעֵאל. וְאֵלֶּה הַמִּשְׁפָּטִים אֲשֶׁר תָּשִׂים לִפְנֵיהֶם. וְהַנִּיזָק וְהַמַּזִּיק בְּתַשְׁלוּמִין. מְשַׁלְּמִין חֲצִי נֶזֶק. מִכַּן שֶׁמְּחַצִּין אֶת הַנֶּזֶק. מִכָּן שֶׁזֶּה מַפְסִיד חֲצִי נֶזֶק וְזֶה מַפְסִיד חֲצִי נֶזֶק.

**Halakhah 3**: "Estimation and determination of money's worth," etc. [138]One does not say that a cow be compensated for by a stole[139], but one appraises all property in court. "Money's worth," this teaches that the court only appraises mortgageable property[140]. But if the person suffering damage appropriated movables, one appraises those[141]. "By a court", this teaches that one only appraises in court[142]. "Based on testimony", for one only appraises by testimony[143]. "Of free persons of the Covenant", this excludes Gentiles, and slaves, and persons disqualified for testimony[144]. "Women are under the rule of torts"; since the verse[145] speaks only of men, it is necessary to include women: Rebbi Ismael stated, "these are the laws which you shall put before them[146]" "And sometimes[10] both the person who causes and the one who suffers the damage pay"; they pay half the damage. From here, that one splits the damage; each one loses half the value of the damage.

138 The Halakhah is a parallel, shorter version of Tosephta 1:2,3 and parallel *beraitot* in the Babli, 14b, 15a.

139 In Tosephta and Babli (and a Genizah fragment of the Yerushalmi): "a cow is compensated for by a stole and a stole by a cow", explained in the Babli that the stole injured the cow and the cow tore the stole. This sentence is only an amplification of the expression "estimation of money's worth".

140 The Babli, 14b, after a lengthy discussion comes to the conclusion that "money's worth" in contrast to "money" means real estate whose value can only be established by appraisal, not by barter.

141 The two Babylonian sources point out that in case the person liable for damages had died, the injured party is absolutely barred from appropriating movables from the estate.

142 The two Babylonian sources insist that the only court competent in the matter is the permanent court of the community. This interpretation also has to be accepted in the Yerushalmi since imposing fines is restricted to judges qualified to sit in criminal cases.

143 Since payment of half the damages has the status of a fine, not of restitution, the court cannot recognize an admission of liability by either of the parties since "nobody can be sentenced to a fine based on his confession" (Babli 14b).

144 While the same statement is also found in the Tosephta, it is clear that people disqualified for testimony, such as professional gamblers, are excluded by the requirement of testimony in court.

145 *Ex.* 21-22.

146 The introductory sentence, *Ex.* 21:1, is formulated gender neutral. In the Babli, 15b, this argument is attributed to R. Eleazar.

(fol. 2a) **משנה ד:** חֲמִשָּׁה תַמִּין וַחֲמִשָּׁה מוּעָדִין הַבְּהֵמָה אֵינָהּ מוּעֶדֶת לֹא לִיגַּח וְלֹא לִיגּוֹף וְלֹא לִישׁוֹךְ וְלֹא לִרְבּוֹץ וְלֹא לִבְעוֹט. הַשֵּׁן מוּעֶדֶת לוֹכַל אֶת הָרָאוּי לָהּ. שׁוֹר הַמּוּעָד וְשׁוֹר הַמַּזִּיק בִּרְשׁוּת הַנִּיזּוֹק וְהָאָדָם.

**Mishnah 4**: Five harmless[147] and five notorious animals. An animal is not known to gore, nor to hit, nor to bite, nor to lie down, nor to kick.

The tooth is known to eat what is appropriate for it[148]. A notorious bull, a bull of the person who causes the damage on the property of the person who suffered the damage, and the human[149].

147 Domesticated animals (cattle, sheep, or goats) are not supposed to be agressive unless known to be so. The shephard is not required to watch the animals as if they were ready to be agressive. Even if it is known that an animal is prone to bite, one need not assume that it also will gore, hit with its body, kick with its feet, or lie down on other animals or vessels in order to cause damage. For each one of these categories, the danger from the animal has to be established separately; otherwise the owner only pays half of the damage caused.

148 If a shepherd leads his flock through a market place, he must assume that his animals will eat any fruit or vegetables near them when they pass by, and he has to take appropriate precautions or pay full damages. But he does not have to assume that his animals will start to eat clay vessels or other inedible matter.

A sentence is missing here, found in E, the Mishnah in the Babli, and the independent Mishnah: "The foot is notorious to break anything in its way." As the Mishnah stands here, there are only four categories of notorious sources of damage.

149 These three categories pay full damages under any circumstances.

**הלכה ד:** חֲמִשָּׁה תַמִּין וַחֲמִשָּׁה מוּעָדִין כּוֹל'. אָמַר רִבִּי יוֹחָנָן. דְּרִבִּי טַרְפוֹן הִיא. בִּרְשׁוּת הַנִּיזָּק. רִבִּי טַרְפוֹן אוֹמֵר. נֶזֶק שָׁלֵם. וַחֲכָמִים אוֹמְרִים. חֲצִי נֶזֶק. (2c line 69)

**Halakhah 4**: "Five harmless and five notorious animals," etc. Rebbi Joḥanan said, this[150] follows Rebbi Ṭarphon: "In the domain of the person sustaining the damage, Rebbi Ṭarphon said, full damages; but the Sages say, half damages."

150 That any damage caused in another person's domain has always to be paid in full. The quote is from Mishnah 2:7. In the Babli, 15b, the statement is attributed to Samuel who takes pains to make clear that the first half of the Mishnah not be in dispute.

**משנה ה:** הַזְּאֵב וְהָאֲרִי הַדּוֹב וְהַנָּמֵר וְהַבַּרְדְּלִיס וְהַנָּחָשׁ הֲרֵי אִילּוּ מוּעָדִין. רִבִּי אֱלִיעֶזֶר אוֹמֵר. בִּזְמַן שֶׁהֵן בְּנֵי תַרְבּוּת אֵינָן מוּעָדִין. וְהַנָּחָשׁ מוּעָד לְעוֹלָם. מַה בֵּין תָּם לְמוּעָד. אֶלָּא שֶׁהַתָּם מְשַׁלֵּם חֲצִי נֶזֶק מִגּוּפוֹ וְהַמּוּעָד מְשַׁלֵּם נֶזֶק שָׁלֵם מִן הָעֲלִיָּיה. (fol. 2a)

**Mishnah 5**: The wolf and the lion, the bear, and the tiger[151], and the panther[152], and the snake, are notorious[153]. Rebbi Eliezer says, when they are trained[154] they are not notorious; except for the snake which always is notorious[155]. What is the difference between tame and notorious? The tame pays half the damages from its body[156] and the notorious pays full damages from the storage room[157].

151 As in Arabic, the word denotes leopard, panther, or tiger, i. e., a predator with a striped or dotted fur.

152 Most moderns identify the word as Greek πάρδαλις "panther", Arabic ابرد . Rashi everywhere translates *putois* "pole cat". In the Babli, 16a, Rav Jehudah translates ברדלס by נפריזא which the later Rav Joseph explains as אפא, ὕαινα ὄφις "hyena-snake". The latter explanation is excluded here by the Halakhah.

153 The owner of dangerous pets is always 100% responsible.

154 Trained circus performers.

155 The snake charmer does not control his snakes the way a trainer controls his performing animals.

156 *Ex.* 21:35: "They shall sell the bovine and split the money."

157 I. e., from the owner's valuables if he does not have enough cash.

**הלכה ה:** הַזְּאֵב וְהָאֲרִי וְהַדּוֹב כול׳. תַּנֵּי. רְבִּי מֵאִיר אוֹמֵר. אַף(2c line 72) הַצָּבוּעַ. אָמַר רִבִּי יוֹסֵי בֵּירִיבִּי אָבִין. לֹא אָמַר רבי מֵאִיר אֶלָּא בַּצָּבוּעַ זָכָר שֶׁיֵּשׁ לוֹ שָׁעָה שֶׁהוּא קָשֶׁה כָאֲרִי.

**Halakhah 5**: "The wolf, and the lion, and the bear," etc. It was stated[158]: Rebbi Meïr says, also the hyena. Rebbi Yose ben Rebbi Abin said, Rebbi Meïr only said this for a male hyena which at times is as dangerous as a lion.

158   Tosephta 1:4; Babli 16a.

## כיצד הרגל פרק שני

(fol. 2d) **משנה א**: כֵּיצַד הָרֶגֶל מוּעֶדֶת לְשַׁבֵּר בְּדֶרֶךְ הִילּוּכָהּ. הַבְּהֵמָה מוּעֶדֶת לְהַלֵּךְ כְּדַרְכָּהּ וּלְשַׁבֵּר. הָיְתָה מְבַעֶטֶת אוֹ שֶׁהָיוּ צְרוֹרוֹת מְנַתְּזִין מִתַּחַת רַגְלֶיהָ וְשִׁיבְּרָה אֶת הַכֵּלִים מְשַׁלֵּם חֲצִי נֶזֶק. דָּרְסָה עַל הַכְּלִי וּשְׁבָרַתּוּ וְנָפַל עַל כְּלִי אַחֵר וּשְׁבָרוֹ עַל הָרִאשׁוֹן מְשַׁלֵּם נֶזֶק שָׁלֵם וְעַל הָאַחֲרוֹן מְשַׁלֵּם חֲצִי נֶזֶק.

**Mishnah 1**: How is the foot notorious to break anything in its way[1]? An animal is notorious to break anything in its way. If it was kicking[2] or if pebbles were ricocheting from under its feet and breaking vessels, he pays half of the damage[3]. If it stepped on a vessel and broke it[4] when [the pieces] fell on another vessel and broke that, for the first he pays full damages[5] and half damages for the last[6].

1   This refers to Mishnah 1:4; cf. Chapter 1, Note 158.
2   When it was not known to do that habitually.
3   Since this is unforseeable damage.
4   When the shepherd should have taken care not to lead his animals to a place where a vessel could legitimately stand in his animal's way.
5   He violated his duty of due diligence.
6   The second vessel was broken by the shards of the first; that is an unforeseeable circumstance.

(2d line 39) **הלכה א**: כֵּיצַד הָרֶגֶל מוּעֶדֶת כוֹל׳. וְאֵין דַּרְכָּהּ לְהַתִּיז צְרוֹרוֹת. אָמַר רִבִּי אִמִּי. בְּשֶׁהָיָה כְּלִי נָתוּן בִּידֵי אָדָם. אֲבָל אִם הָיָה מוּנָח בִּרְשׁוּת הָרַבִּים הוֹאִיל וְזֶה מוּנָח בִּרְשׁוּת וְזוֹ מְהַלֶּכֶת בִּרְשׁוּת פָּטוּר. רַבָּה בַּר מָמָל אָמַר.

בָּהּ שְׁתֵּי דְרָכִים. אַחַת יֵשׁ בָּהּ עֲשָׂבִים וּצְרוֹרוֹת וְאַחַת אֵין בָּהּ עֲשָׂבִים וּצְרוֹרוֹת. הִנִּיחָה אֶת שֶׁאֵין בָּהּ עֲשָׂבִים וּצְרוֹרוֹת וְהִילְּכָה בְזוֹ שֶׁיֵּשׁ בָּהּ עֲשָׂבִים וּצְרוֹרוֹת אַף עַל פִּי שֶׁהוּא מוּנָח בִּרְשׁוּת הָרַבִּים פָּטוּר. רִבִּי לְעָזָר אוֹמֵר. כָּל־דָּבָר שֶׁהוּא מִחוּץ לְגוּפָהּ לֹא חִלְּקוּ בוֹ חֲכָמִים בֵּין בִּרְשׁוּת הַיָּחִיד בֵּין בִּרְשׁוּת הָרַבִּים לַחֲצִי כוֹפֶר.

**Halakhah 1**: "How is the foot notorious," etc. Does not an animal usually make pebbles ricochet[7]? Rebbi Immi said, if the vessel was held by a human[8]. But if it was lying in the public domain[9], since it was rightfully lying there and [the animal] was rightfully walking there, he is free[10].

Rebbi Abba bar Mamal said, if there were two roads. On one there are grasses and pebbles[11], on the other there are no grasses or pebbles[12]. It[13] disregarded the one with no grasses or pebbles and went on that with grasses and pebbles; even though it was in the public domain he is free[14].

Rebbi Eleazar[15] said, in anything not concerning its body[16], the Sages made no difference between private and public domain in the matter of half damages[17].

7 Then an animal should be watched lest it cause stones to ricochet with all damages paid in full.

8 It was not lying in the street. Then it is an uncommon outcome; the shepherd is not obligated to watch for it; one pays half damages.

9 A thoroughfare.

10 Since a shepherd has the right to lead his flock on a public road, anybody who puts a vessel into the public domain, even if it creates no nuisance, must assume that it will be broken. Therefore, nothing is due.

11 A badly maintained road which becomes overgrown and its surface loosened.

12 A well-maintained street; one may assume that all passers-by are going to use it.

13 The animal, which has no need to be anywhere at a fixed time, went

after the grasses growing on the decaying street.

14   The expression אע״פ (אַף עַל פִּי) "even though" is difficult to understand. Since even a badly maintained road is a road and built for use, animals, not only humans, are allowed to use it and, therefore, to trample on anything lying on the road. It seems that one should rather read מִפְּנֵי "because of", meaning that there are no squatters' rights on an unused part of a public road.

R. Abba bar Mamal does not comment on the Mishnah but on R. Immi's explanation with which he disagrees; he holds that an animal on a public road never causes claimable damage by simply walking there.

15   In the Babli, 19b: R. Johanan.

16   ′ Not by any of the actions specified in Mishnah 1:4.

17   Clearly nobody can claim damages if he put vessels in a roadway and they are broken, but he can claim damages if vessels on his own property are broken by pebbles ricocheting from the public road. Therefore, he also can claim damages if his vessels were on the unpaved side of the public domain. This supports R. Immi.

(2d line 47) מַהוּ שֶׁתִּתְקַבֵּל הָעֲדָאָה בְּדָבָר שֶׁהוּא חוּץ לְגוּפָהּ. רִבִּי זְעִירָא אָמַר. מְקַבֶּלֶת. רִבִּי אִילָא אָמַר. אֵינָהּ מְקַבֶּלֶת. אָמַר רִבִּי זְעִירָא. מַתְנִיתָה פְלִיגָא עֲלוֹי. שׁוֹר שֶׁמִּתְחַכֵּךְ בַּכּוֹתֶל וְנָפַל עַל הָאָדָם וַהֲרָגוֹ חַיָּיב בַּכּוֹפֶר וּפָטוּר מִמִּיתָה. וְכִי יֵשׁ כּוֹפֶר בְּתָם. וַאֲפִילוּ כְרִבִּי אִילָא לֵית הִיא פְלִיגָא. וְלָמָּה פָטוּר מִמִּיתָה. בְּשֶׁהוּעֲדָה לִהְיוֹת מַפֶּלֶת אֶת הַכְּתָלִים. כְּשֶׁהִפִּילָה אֶת הַכּוֹתֶל לֹא הָיָה אָדָם שָׁם.

Is it subject to a declaration of notoriety in a matter extraneous to its body[18]? Rebbi Ze'ira said, one accepts. Rebbi Illa said, one does not accept. Rebbi Ze'ira said, a *baraita* disagrees with him: An ox which rubs itself against a wall[19] which fell on a human and killed him is obligated for weregilt but free from death[20]. Does there exist weregilt for a harmless animal[21]? But it does not disagree with Rebbi Illa[22]. Why is it free from death if it was notorious to destroy walls? When it destroyed it, no human was there[23].

18   The verse makes a clear distinction between "harmless" cattle, which are not known to gore humans, and "notorious" cattle which have a history of such attacks. If a "harmless" animal kills a human, it must be killed (*Ex.* 21:28). If a "notorious" animal kills, it must be stoned and the owners have to pay weregilt (*Ex.* 21:29-30). Since there is a difference in legal status, the notoriety of an animal must be based on a judicial finding. Now these rules apply to all attacks which are classified as "horn", i. e., those enumerated in Mishnah 1:4. The question is whether the rules extend to damages caused by "tooth" and "foot"; e. g., whether an animal can be declared dangerous because it has a way to send pebbles flying wherever it walks, which would make its owner liable for full damages in all cases.

19   If the animal pushed against the wall the way it would push an unfriendly other animal, that clearly would be a "hit" as defined by Mishnah 1:4 and be classified as "horn", or, in the language of the *baraita*, "by its body". But here it is assumed that the animal rubs to free itself from fleas or otherwise for its comfort, not in any agressive way. Cf. Mishnah 4:7 (Tosephta 4:5); Babli 44a.

20   This does not agree with any case of "horn"; cf. Note 18.

21   Since weregilt is only required for killings by notorious animals, the *baraita* accepts that declarations of notoriety are possible for behavior not classified as "horn".

22   Since an animal causing death of a human has to be killed, whether harmless or notorious, it is clear that the statement of the *baraita* cannot be derived from the rules of "horn". But then the previous argument about weregilt does not apply.

23   Even if the animal attacked the wall as if it were a hostile animal, and the incident has to be classified as "horn", it cannot be killed if its attack only weakened the wall which collapsed at some later time, when the attacking animal already had stopped pushing.

Also in the Babli, 18b, the question is decided in R. Illa's sense.

(2d line 53) אָמַר רִבִּי לֶעֱזָר. הִטִּילָה גְלָלִים מְשַׁלֵּם נֶזֶק שָׁלֵם. דְּלֹ כֵן מָה אֲנָן אָמְרִין. צָרִיךְ שֶׁיְּהֵא הַמִּקְלוֹט בְּיָדוֹ. הָדָא דְּתֵימָא. בְּשֶׁאֵין דַּרְכָּהּ לְכֵן. אֲבָל

בִּשְׁדַּרְכָּהּ לְכֵן צָרִיךְ שֶׁיְּהֵא הַמְּקַלּוֹט בְּיָדוֹ.

Rebbi Eleazar said: If it produced dung, one pays full damages. For if it were not so, what would we say? He has to have a receptacle handy? That is to say, if it does not do so habitually. But if it does so habitually, he has to have a receptacle handy[24].

24 As often in *Neziqin*, the text seems to be a note jotted down in preparation of a lecture, not fully developed. In the Babli, 18a, one reads: "If [an animal] laid dung into dough, R. Jehudah says, [the owner] pays full damages, but R. Eleazar says, half damages." If this is a parallel, then R. Eleazar mentioned here is the Tanna, ben Shamua, not the Amora, bar Pada.

Now it is clear that cattle will always produce dung. Therefore, cow dung in a place open to cattle, such as a grazing area or a public road, cannnot be a cause for damage claims. This is the statement missing in the text, to which the note "for if it were not so" refers. The question remains whether in using a road, e. g., passing through a market place, the herder has to make sure that his animals are safely away from any merchandise. If there is an animal whose preferred place for defecating is near edibles, its owner is required to follow it, bucket in hand, to avoid having to pay full damages.

(2d line 56) רִבִּי הוֹשַׁעְיָה רַבָּה וְרִבִּי יוּדָן נְשִׂיָּיא הֲווֹן יָתְבִין. אָעַל רִבִּי בָּא בַּר מָמָל וְשָׁאַל. כִּישְׁכְּשָׁה בִּזְנָבָהּ. כְּגוֹן אִילֵּין פִּירְדָתָא. מָהוּ. וְלָא אֲמָרִין לֵיהּ כְּלוּם. בָּתַר כֵּן אָמַר לֵיהּ רִבִּי הוֹשַׁעְיָה רַבָּה. דְּלָא כֵּן מָה נָן אֲמָרִין. צָרִיךְ שֶׁיְּהֵא תוֹפֵשׂ בִּזְנָבָהּ. הֲדָא דְּתֵימַר. בְּשֶׁאֵין דַּרְכָּהּ לְכֵן. אֲבָל בִּשְׁדַּרְכָּהּ לְכֵן צָרִיךְ שֶׁיְּהֵא תוֹפֵשׂ בִּזְנָבָהּ. וּמַה פְּשִׁיטָא לוֹן. בְּנֶזֶק שָׁלֵם. וּמַה צְרִיכָה לוֹן. בַּחֲצִי נֶזֶק.

Rebbi Hoshaia the Elder and Rebbi Jehudah Neśia were sitting. Rebbi Abba bar Mamal came to them and asked: If it wagged its tail[25] as those mules do, what are the rules? They did not tell him. Later, Rebbi Hoshaia the Elder told him, for if it were not so, what would we say? Does he have to grab its tail? That is, if it does not usually do it. But if it usually does it, he has to grab its tail[26]. What is obvious to us? The problem of full damages[27]. What is problematic for us? Half damages[28].

| | |
|---|---|
| 25  It wagged its tail excessively and caused damage close to a place where it legally can pass; the situation is parallel to that discussed in the preceding paragraph. | 26  To avoid damage; cf. Note 24, end.<br>27  That no full damages are due.<br>28  And it remains undecided in the Babli, 19b. |

פִּיסְקָא. דָּרְסָה עַל הַכְּלִי וּשְׁבָרַתּוּ. רִבִּי יִרְמְיָה בָּעֵי. דָּרְסָה עַל נוֹד מָלֵא שֶׁמֶן. עַל הַנּוֹד מְשַׁלֵּם נֶזֶק שָׁלֵם וְעַל הַשֶּׁמֶן מְשַׁלֵּם חֲצִי נֶזֶק. הָיְתָה טַבְלָה מוּנַחַת וּזְכוּכִית עָלֶיהָ. דָּרְסָה עַל גַּבֵּי הַטַּבְלָה וְנִשְׁתַּבְּרוּ הַזְּכוּכִית. עַל הַטַּבְלָה מְשַׁלֵּם נֶזֶק שָׁלֵם וְעַל הַזְּכוּכִית מְשַׁלֵּם חֲצִי נֶזֶק. הָיוּ שְׁתֵּי טַבְלָיוֹת זוֹ עַל גַּבֵּי זוֹ. דָּרְסָה עַל הָעֶלְיוֹנָה וְנִשְׁתַּבְּרָה הַשְּׁנִיָּה. עַל הָעֶלְיוֹנָה מְשַׁלֵּם נֶזֶק שָׁלֵם וְעַל הַתַּחְתּוֹנָה חֲצִי נֶזֶק. הָיְתָה טַבְלָה מוּנַחַת בִּרְשׁוּת הָרַבִּים דָּרְסָה עָלֶיהָ וְהִתִּיזָה וְהָלְכָה וְנִשְׁתַּבְּרָה בִּרְשׁוּת הַיָּחִיד. אַחַר מִי אַתְּ מְהַלֵּךְ אַחַר דְּרִיסָתָהּ אוֹ אַחַר שְׁבִירָתָהּ. אִין תֵּימַר. אַדְּרִיסָתָהּ פָּטוּר. אַשְּׁבִירָתָהּ חַיָּב.

New Paragraph. "If it stepped on a vessel and broke it." Rebbi Jeremiah asked: If it stepped on a skin full of oil[29], he pays full damages for the skin[30] and half damages for the oil[31]. If there was a table lying there and glass on top of it. If it stepped on the table[29] and by that the glass broke[30]. He pays full damages fort the table and half damages for the glass. If there were two tables on top of one another[29]. If it stepped on the upper one and the lower one was broken[30]. He pays full damages fort the upper table and half damages for the lower. If the table was lying in the public domain[32], [the animal] stepped on it and it ricocheted, went and broke into a private domain[33]. What do you follow, the stepping or its breaking? If you say, after stepping³⁴, he is free [from paying] for its stepping on it; if you say, after its breaking, then he is guilty for the breaking³⁵.

29  Not in the public domain nor in its owner's.

30  Damages by "foot" not in an authorized domain.

31  For indirectly caused damages even in the domain of a person sustaining the damage one only pays half damages. The Babli agrees, 19a.

32  Where one has the right to lead one's animals and payment for damages by "foot" are excluded.

33  Where full payment is due for damages.

34  Substitution of עַל by prothetic אַ is Babylonian usage.

35  The Babli, 17b/18a, after a lengthy discussion decides that in case of damage caused by a chain of events, the location of the trigger event determines liabilities. It also notes that rules of payment of less than full damages for events not classified as "horn" are traditional, rather than biblical.

(fol. 2d) **משנה ב:** הַתַּרְנוֹגְלִין מוּעָדִין לְהַלֵּךְ כְּדַרְכָּן וּלְשַׁבֵּר. הָיָה דְלִיל קָשׁוּר בְּרַגְלוֹ אוֹ שֶׁהָיָה מְהַדֵּס וְשִׁיבֵּר אֶת הַכֵּלִים מְשַׁלֵּם חֲצִי נֶזֶק.

**Mishnah 2**: Chickens³⁶ are notorious³⁷ for breaking things in their usual walk. If a thread³⁸ was bound to its foot or it was scraping³⁹ and broke vessels, he pays half damages.

36  The usual Babylonian Amoraic and modern term for "chicken", based on Aramaic/Syriac, is תַּרְנְגוֹל. But almost all Mishnah mss. and also the early Babli prints in this Mishnah have תרנוגל, mirroring the original Sumerian *turlugallu*.

37  Its owner has to pay full damages.

38  Something thin, root דל.

39  Arukh reads חדס, from Arabic خدش "to tear with one's nails; to scrape".

(2d line 71) **הלכה ב:** הַתַּרְנוֹגָלִין מוּעָדִין כול'. רַב הוּנָא אָמַר. בְּשֶׁנִּקְשַׁר מֵאֵילָיו. אֲבָל אִם קְשָׁרוֹ הוּא מְשַׁלֵּם נֶזֶק שָׁלֵם. תַּנֵּי. תַּרְנוֹגָלִין שֶׁהִידְּסוּ אֶת הָעִיסָה וְאֶת הַפֵּירוֹת אוֹ שֶׁנִּיקְרוּ מְשַׁלֵּם נֶזֶק שָׁלֵם. הִידְסוּ עָפָר עַל גַּבֵּי עִיסָה אוֹ עַל גַּבֵּי פֵּירוֹת מְשַׁלְּמִין חֲצִי נֶזֶק. הָיוּ מְחַטְטִין בַּחֶבֶל וְנִפְסַק הַדְּלִי אוֹ שֶׁנִּשְׁבַּר מְשַׁלֵּם נֶזֶק שָׁלֵם. נָפַל עַל חֲבֵירוֹ. עַל הָעֶלְיוֹן מְשַׁלֵּם נֶזֶק שָׁלֵם וְאַתַּחְתּוֹן חֲצִי נֶזֶק. וְאֵינוֹ כְעוֹשֶׂה בּוֹר בְּמָקוֹם אֶחָד וּמַזִּיק בְּמָקוֹם אַחֵר. אָמַר רַבִּי יוֹסֵי בֵּירַבִּי בּוּן. מִכֵּיוָן שֶׁאֵין דַּרְכּוֹ לִיפּוֹל אֶלָּא בְּאוֹתוֹ הַבּוֹר כְּמִי שֶׁהוּא בוֹרוֹ. תַּנֵּי. תַּרְנוֹגָלִין שֶׁנָּפְלוּ לְגִינָה וְשִׁיבְּרוּ אֶת הַיָּרָק וְקִירְטְמוּ הַחִילְפִין מְשַׁלֵּם נֶזֶק שָׁלֵם. סוּמְכוֹס אָמַר. עַל הַקִּירְטוּם מְשַׁלֵּם נֶזֶק שָׁלֵם וְעַל הַשִּׁיבּוּר מְשַׁלֵּם חֲצִי נֶזֶק. תַּרְנְגוֹל הַפּוֹרֵחַ מִמָּקוֹם לְמָקוֹם וְהִזִּיק בְּגוּפוֹ מְשַׁלֵּם נֶזֶק שָׁלֵם. בָּרוּחַ שֶׁבֵּין כְּנָפָיו מְשַׁלֵּם חֲצִי נֶזֶק. סוּמְכוֹס אוֹמֵר. נֶזֶק שָׁלֵם. נָפַח בַּכֵּלִים וּשְׁבָרָן מְשַׁלֵּם נֶזֶק שָׁלֵם.

**Halakhah 2**: "Chickens are notorious," etc. Rav Huna said[39], if it[40] became tied by itself. But if he tied it[41], he pays full damages. It was stated[42]: "If chickens scraped dough or fruit, or they pecked, he pays full damages[43]. If they scraped dust on dough or on fruit, one pays half of the damages[44]. If they were picking at a rope[45] and the pail was separated[46] or broke, he pays full damages. If one[47] fell on another; for the uppermost he pays full damages; for the lower one half damages; it is not comparable to a pit at one place which causes damage at another place[48]." Rebbi Yose ben Rebbi Abun said, since it usually falls only into this cistern, it is as if it were his pit. It was stated[42]: "If chickens fell in a garden, broke vegetables, and cut rosemary[49], he pays full damages. Symmachos said, for cutting he pays full damages, for breaking he pays half damages. If a chicken flew from one place to another and did damage with its body, he pays full damages. By the wind between its wings, he pays half damages; Symmachos says, full damages. If it blew at vessels and broke them, he pays full damages[50].

39   Babli 19b.

40   The thread on the chicken's foot. The chicken's owner can be faulted for insufficient watchfulness.

41   If the owner tied the thread himself, perhaps to identify the chicken, and the thread caused damage, this is no longer a case only of insufficient watchfulness. The owner has to pay full damages under the heading of "pit".

42   Tosephta 2:1; Babli 17b.

43   This is damage of "foot", for which they are notorious.

44   This is uncommon damage.

45   The Tosephta adds correctly: connected to a pail of a cistern.

46   It fell into the cistern and cannot be recovered.

47   One pail on another; cf. Notes 30 ff.

48   And therefore it cannot be characterized as "pit" which pays full damages in all cases.

49   This translation is tentative; it follows Rashi, *Giṭṭin* 68b. In *Berakhot* 53b, Rashi explains: spikenard. Loew, *Flora* I, p. 10 wants to explain: stems (based on the Tosephta which switches the verbs referring to *ḥilfin* and vegetables.) At other places (Mishnah *Kelim* 17:17), the Gaonic commentary identifies חלף with Arabic خلاف "willow"; sometimes it means حلفة "Alfalfa grass".

50   For indirect damage, caused by the turbulence generated by the chicken's wings, he pays half damages. But damage caused by the bird directly blowing at something is like damage caused by touch of its body.

(fol. 2d) **משנה ג:** כֵּיצַד הַשֵּׁן מוּעֶדֶת לוֹכַל אֶת הָרָאוּי לוֹ. הַבְּהֵמָה מוּעֶדֶת לוֹכַל פֵּירוֹת אוֹ יְרָקוֹת. אָכְלָה כְסוּת אוֹ כֵלִים מְשַׁלֵּם חֲצִי נָזֶק. בַּמֶּה דְבָרִים אֲמוּרִים. בִּרְשׁוּת הַנִּיזָּק אֲבָל בִּרְשׁוּת הָרַבִּים פָּטוּר. וְאִם נֶהֱנִית מְשַׁלֵּם מַה שֶּׁנֶּהֱנִית.

**Mishnah 3**: How is the tooth notorious to eat what is fitting for it? A domesticated animal[51] is notorious for eating fruits and vegetables. If it ate a garment or vessels, he pays half damages[52]. When has this been said? In the domain of the person sustaining the damage. But on public property[10] he is free; but if it benefited, he pays what it benefited[53].

51  Cattle, sheep, or goats.
52  This leaves open the question of the owner's responsibility if a plant-eating animal eats meat.
53  This is a general principle, applicable to all kinds of damages.

(3a line 8) **הלכה ג**: כֵּיצַד הַשֵּׁן מוּעֶדֶת כול׳. רֵישׁ לָקִישׁ אָמַר. עַל הָרִאשׁוֹנָה הוּשְׁבָה. רִבִּי יוֹחָנָן אָמַר. עַל כּוּלָּהּ הוּשְׁבָה. מִחְלָפָה שִׁיטָתֵיהּ דְּרֵישׁ לָקִישׁ. תַּמָּן אָמַר רֵישׁ לָקִישׁ בְּשֵׁם רִבִּי הוֹשַׁעְיָה. עָמְדָה וְאָכְלָה מִפֵּירוֹת הַצִּבּוּרִין חַיָּיבֶת. וְכָא הוּא אָמַר אָכֵין. אָמְרֵי. תַּמָּן בְּשֵׁם רִבִּי הוֹשַׁעְיָה. בְּרַם הָכָא בְּשֵׁם גַּרְמֵיהּ. מִילְּתֵיהּ דְּרֵישׁ לָקִישׁ אָמְרָה בָעֲטָה מְהַלֶּכֶת בָּרְבוּצָה פָּטוּר. מִילְּתֵיהּ דְּרִבִּי יוֹחָנָן אָמְרָה בָעֲטָה מְהַלֶּכֶת בָּרְבוּצָה חַייָב. לֹא סוֹף דָּבָר בָּעֲטָה מְהַלֶּכֶת בָּרְבוּצָה אוֹ רְבוּצָה בַּמְהַלֶּכֶת. בָּעֲטָה מְהַלֶּכֶת בַּמְהַלֶּכֶת. אָמַר רִבִּי אִמִּי. לֹא אָמַר רֵישׁ לָקִישׁ אֶלָּא בָעֲטָה מְהַלֶּכֶת בָּרְבוּצָה פְּטוּרָה. אֲבָל רְבוּצָה בַּמְהַלֶּכֶת אוֹ מְהַלֶּכֶת בַּמְהַלֶּכֶת חַייָבֶת. תַּנֵּי רִבִּי הוֹשַׁעְיָה. כּוּלָּהּ פָּטוּר. טַעֲמָא דְּרִבִּי הוֹשַׁעְיָה. אֵין קֶרֶן בִּרְשׁוּת הָרַבִּים. רַב אָמַר. עָמְדָה וְאָכְלָה מִפֵּירוֹת הַצִּבּוּרִין [חַייֶבֶת]. מַה הֵקִילוּ בַשֵּׁן שֶׁאָכְלָה מְהַלֶּכֶת בֵּין הָעוֹמֶדֶת. חוֹמֶר בַּקֶּרֶן שֶׁבָּעֲטָה מְהַלֶּכֶת אֶת הָעוֹמֶדֶת. אִילְפַּי אָמַר. עָמְדָה וְאָכְלָה מִפֵּירוֹת הַצִּבּוּרִין חַייָבֶת. מַה הֵקִילוּ בַשֵּׁן שֶׁאָכְלָה מְהַלֶּכֶת {בֵּין הָעוֹמֶדֶת} [מִן הַמְהַלֶּכֶת]. חוֹמֶר בַּקֶּרֶן שֶׁבָּעֲטָה מְהַלֶּכֶת אֶת הַמְהַלֶּכֶת.

**Halakhah 3**: "How is the tooth notorious," etc. Rebbi Simeon ben Laqish[54] said, it[55] refers to the first part. Rebbi Johanan said, it refers to all[56]. The argument of Rebbi Simeon ben Laqish seems inverted. There, Rebbi Simeon ben Laqish said in the name of Rebbi Hoshaia: If it stood still and ate from heaped produce, it[57] is responsible[58]. And here, he says so? They said, there in the name of Rebbi Hoshaia; but here, in his own name. Rebbi Simeon ben Laqish's word implies that if a walking [animal] kicks one which is lying down[59], is it[57] free [from payment]. Rebbi Johanan's word implies that if a walking [animal] kicks one which is lying down, it[57] is obligated[60]. Not only if the walking [animal] kicks one which is lying down or one which is lying down kicks the walking one. If a walking [animal] kicks a walking one? Rebbi Immi said, Rebbi Simeon ben Laqish said, only if a walking [animal] kicks one which is lying down, it[57] is free [from payment]. But in the case of one lying down against one walking or one who was walking against one walking, it[57] is obligated[59]. Rebbi Hoshaia stated: It[57] always is free. What is Rebbi Hoshaia's reason; is there no "horn" in the public domain[60]? Rav said, if it stood still and ate from heaped produce, [it is obligated][61]. Since the leniency for "tooth" is in case it ate walking from the standing[62]; the restriction for "horn" is in case the walking animal kicked the one standing still[63]. Ilfai said: If it stood still and ate from heaped produce, it[57] is obligated. Since the leniency for "tooth" is that it ate walking {from the standing}[64] [from the walking]; the restriction for "horn" is in case the walking animal kicked the walking one[65].

54 The abbreviation Resh Laqish for Rebbi Simeon ben Laqish is Babylonian; in the Yerushalmi it is a sign of an intrusion of Babylonian spelling.

55 The animal's owner does not have to pay if his animal ate food in the public domain. If it ate vessels or garments, the damage is classified as "horn" and the owner has to pay half damages unless the animal has been certified as a notorious eater of vessels or garments, when full damages are due. In the Babli, 20a, this opinion is

attributed to Samuel and R. Joḥanan. Since in money matters the Babli recognizes Samuel and R. Joḥanan as authorities, the Babli endorses this opinion.

56  Even for vessels and garments no payment is due if they were left exposed on a public thoroughfare. In the Babli, this is the opinion of Rav and R. Simeon ben Laqish. Since the Yerushalmi recognizes R. Joḥanan over R. Simeon ben Laqish, it endorses this opinion.

57  In reality not the animal is responsible but its owner.

58  R. Simeon ben Laqish should have qualified his statement; even animals feeding in the public domain will cost their owners if their behavior deviates from the norm.

59  Babli 20a; for an animal to lie down and ruminate on a thoroughfare is deviant behavior.

60  He rejects the notion that deviant behavior of one party justifies the other. In the Babli, R. Joḥanan is presumed to agree with R. Simeon ben Laqish in this case.

60  Certainly the main place where one could expect damage by "horn" is the public domain. Rebbi Hoshaia's statement must have been corrupted in transmission.

61  The addition is the reading common to E and the Rome fragment edited by A. H. Freimann (*Tarbiz* 6, 56-63). Rav (and Ilfai, quoted later in the paragraph) hold that the exemption for "tooth" granted in the public domain only holds if the road is used as road, not as place for grazing. If the shepherd allows the animals of his herd to stand for grazing, he is responsible for any damage done. "Heaped produce" is grain arranged in an orderly heap, a sign of illegal use of the public domain for private use.

62  If cattle, sheep, or goats are driven as a herd, they may eat from what was stored in the public domain.

63  Even though the herder of the animal standing still should have driven it away.

64  E and Vatican mss. read: מְהַלֶּכֶת מִן הַמְהַלֶּכֶת "the walking animal ate from another walking animal". This refers to Ilfai's statement in the Babli, 20a: "An animal in the public domain which stretched out its neck and ate from upon another animal is obligated;" a statement explained away in the Babli. The change has to be rejected as an attempt to harmonize the Yerushalmi with the Babli.

65  While Ilfai agrees with Rav on the rules of "tooth", he disagrees with

him on "horn" and holds that for "horn" injuries the owner of the agressive animal always has to pay.

**משנה ד:** כֵּיצַד מְשַׁלֵּם מַה שֶׁנֶּהֱנֵית אָכְלָה מִתּוֹךְ הָרְחָבָה מְשַׁלֵּם מַה שֶׁנֶּהֱנֵית. מִצִּדֵּי הָרְחָבָה מְשַׁלֵּם מַה שֶׁהִזִּיקָה. מִפֶּתַח הַחֲנוּת מְשַׁלֵּם מַה שֶׁנֶּהֱנֵית מִתּוֹךְ הַחֲנוּת מְשַׁלֵּם מַה שֶׁהִזִּיקָה. (fol. 2d)

**Mishnah 4:** How does he pay for what it benefited from? If it ate on the public square, he pays for what it benefited from[66]. On the borders of the public square[67], he pays for what it damaged. From the door of a store[68], he pays for what it benefited from; inside the store he pays for what it damaged.

[66] At a place open for public use, the animal's owner pays only the price of animal feed even if it ate human food.

[67] The space is not for use; its status is of domain open neither for the person responsible for causing the damage nor the person suffering it.

[68] If the owner of the store encroached on the public domain to exhibit his wares.

**הלכה ד:** כֵּיצַד מְשַׁלֵּם מַה שֶׁנֶּהֱנֵית כול'. רַב אָמַר. עָקְמָה צַוָּארָהּ וְאָכְלָה מְשַׁלֵּם מַה שֶׁהִזִּיקָה. וְהָא תַנִּינָן. מִפֶּתַח הַחֲנוּת מְשַׁלֵּם מַה שֶׁנֶּהֱנֵית מִתּוֹךְ הַחֲנוּת מְשַׁלֵּם מַה שֶׁהִזִּיקָה. מַאי כְדוֹן. אָמַר רִבִּי יוֹסֵי בֵּירִבִּי בּוּן. תִּיפְתָּר בְּשֶׁהָיָה חֲמוֹר טָעוּן גְּדָיִים וּבִשְׁעַת עֲבָרָתוֹ פָּשְׁטוּ צַוָּארֵיהֶן וְאָכְלוּ מִפֶּתַח הַחֲנוּת מְשַׁלֵּם מַה שֶׁנֶּהֱנֵית מִתּוֹךְ הַחֲנוּת מְשַׁלֵּם מַה שֶׁהִזִּיקָה. רַב אָמַר. אָכְלָה שְׂעוֹרִים מְשַׁלֵּם תֶּבֶן. וְהָתַנֵּי רִבִּי חִייָה וּפְלִיג. לְפִיכָךְ אִם אָכְלָה חִיטִּין שֶׁהֵן רְעוּת לָהּ הֲרֵי זוּ פְטוּרָה. שִׁינַּת וְאָכְלָה מְשַׁלֵּם נֶזֶק שָׁלֵם. מַהוּ שִׁינַּת וְאָכְלָה מְשַׁלֵּם נֶזֶק שָׁלֵם. הָיְתָה קוּפָּתוֹ מוּשְׁפֶּלֶת לַאֲחוֹרָיו בִּרְשׁוּת הָרַבִּים וּפָשְׁטָה פָרָה

אֶת פִּיהָ וְאָכְלָה מִמֶּנָּה מְשַׁלֵּם נֶזֶק שָׁלֵם.  סוּג שֶׁנָּתוּן בְּפֶתַח הֶחָנוּת חֶצְיוֹ מִבִּפְנִים וְחֶצְיוֹ מִבַּחוּץ וּפָשְׁטָה פָרָה אֶת פִּיהָ וְאָכְלָה מִמֶּנָּה מְשַׁלֵּם נֶזֶק שָׁלֵם.

**Halakhah 4**: "How does he pay for what it benefited from," etc. Rav said, if it bent its neck and ate, he pays for what it damaged[69]. But did we not state: "From the door of a store, he pays what it benefited from; inside the store he pays for what it damaged"? How is that? Rebbi Yose ben Rebbi Abun said, explain it that a donkey carried lambs and when it passed by, they bent their necks and ate; from the door of a store, he pays what they benefited from; inside the store he pays for what they damaged.

Rav said, if it ate barley, he pays for straw[70]. But did not Rebbi Hiyya state and disagree? [71]"Therefore, if it ate wheat which is bad for it, it is free. If it changed and ate, he pays full damages. What means 'if it changed and ate, he pays full damages'? If somebody had his chest hanging on his back and a cow stretched out its neck and ate from it, [its owner] pays full damages[72]. If a large container was at the entrance to a store, partially outside and partially inside; if a cow stretched its neck and ate from it, he pays full damages[72]."

69 This is a direct continuation of the argument of Halakhah 3. The exemption of "tooth" only applies to an animal grazing in walking; not to one turning out of its way to feed. The same opinion is held by Rav in the Babli, 21a; there, the authoritative opinion is that of Samuel who exempts all feeding in the public domain.

70 Probably, not straw without grain is meant but עָמִיר, entire stalks with the kernels, as formulated in the Babli, 20a.

71 Tosephta 1:7; partially quoted in the Babli, 20a.

72 Since the remaining grain is no longer fit for human consumption.

**משנה ה:** הַכֶּלֶב וְהַגְּדִי שֶׁקָּפְצוּ מֵרֹאשׁ הַגַּג וְשִׁיבְּרוּ אֶת הַכֵּלִים מְשַׁלְּמִין (fol. 2d) נֶזֶק שָׁלֵם מִפְּנֵי שֶׁהֵן מוּעָדִין. כֶּלֶב שֶׁנָּטַל אֶת הַחֲרָרָה וְהָלַךְ לוֹ לְגָדִישׁ אָכַל אֶת הַחֲרָרָה וְהִדְלִיק אֶת הַגָּדִישׁ עַל הַחֲרָרָה מְשַׁלֵּם נֶזֶק שָׁלֵם וְעַל הַגָּדִישׁ מְשַׁלֵּם חֲצִי נֶזֶק.

**Mishnah 5:** For a dog or a kid goat which jumped from a roof and broke vessels one pays full damages[73] because they are notorious. If a dog stole a hot pitta[74] and went to a stack of sheaves; while it was eating the hot pitta it ignited the stack. For the pitta [its owner] pays full damages, for the stack[75] he pays half damages.

73  Even if the vessels were in the public domain.

74  חררה is a piece of dough being baked over an open fire.

75  Which is lost by indirect action of his property.

**הלכה ה:** הַכֶּלֶב וְהַגְּדִי שֶׁקָּפְצוּ מֵרֹאשׁ הַגַּג כול׳. אִית תַּנָּיֵי תַנֵּי. (3a line 35) שֶׁקָּפְצוּ. אִית תַּנָּיֵי תַנֵּי. שֶׁנָּפְלוּ. אָמַר רִבִּי יוֹחָנָן. כֵּינִי מַתְנִיתָא. שֶׁקָּפְצוּ. נָפְלוּ לֹא בְדָא.

**Halakhah 5:** "For a dog or a kid goat which jumped from a roof," etc. There are Tannaïm who state: "jumped". There are Tannaïm who state: "fell". Rebbi Johanan said, so is the Mishnah: "jumped". But "fell" does not apply[76].

76  One cannot say that dogs or kid goats are notoriously apt to fall from roofs; therefore, their owners either are free or at most pay half damages. The Babli disagrees, 21b.

כֶּלֶב שֶׁנָּטַל אֶת הַחֲרָרָה. רֵישׁ לָקִישׁ אָמַר. בְּמַצִּית אֶת הָאוּר עַל (3a line 36) כָּל־שִׁיבּוֹלֶת וְשִׁיבּוֹלֶת. רִבִּי יוֹחָנָן אָמַר. נַעֲשָׂה כְּזוֹרֵק אֶה הַחֵץ מִמָּקוֹם לְמָקוֹם. אָמַר רִבִּי יִצְחָק בַּר טַבְלַיי. מַתְנִיתָא מְסַייְעָא לְרֵישׁ לָקִישׁ. הָיָה גְדִי כָּפוּת לוֹ

וְעֶבֶד סָמוּךְ לוֹ וְנִשְׂרַף עִמּוֹ חַיָּיב. עֶבֶד כָּפוּת לוֹ וּגְדִי סָמוּךְ לוֹ פָּטוּר. אִם אוֹמֵר אַתְּ שֶׁאֵין כְּזוֹרֵק אֶה הַחֵץ מִמָּקוֹם לְמָקוֹם. עַל שִׁיבּוֹלֶת הָרִאשׁוֹנָה נִתְחַיֵּיב מִיתָה. מִיכָּן וְהֵילָךְ תַּשְׁלוּמִין. אָמַר רִבִּי יוֹסֵי. וְאַתְּ שְׁמַע מִינָהּ. שׁוֹרוֹ שֶׁהִדְלִיק אֶת הַגָּדִישׁ בַּשַּׁבָּת חַיָּיב. וְהוּא שֶׁהִדְלִיק אֶת הַגָּדִישׁ בַּשַּׁבָּת פָּטוּר. אִם אוֹמֵר אַתְּ שֶׁאֵינוֹ כְּזוֹרֵק אֶה הַחֵץ מִמָּקוֹם לְמָקוֹם. וְיֵיעָשֶׂה כְּמִי שֶׁחָלוּ עָלָיו תַּשְׁלוּמִין. מִיכָּן וְהֵילָךְ יְהֵא חַיָּיב בְּתַשְׁלוּמִין. חַד בַּר נַשׁ אַפִּיק פְּלַטִּירָה בְּפוֹרָה. עָבַר חַמְרָא וְתַבְרֵיהּ. אָתָא עוֹבְדָא קוֹמֵי רִבִּי יִצְחָק בַּר טָבְלַיי. אָמַר לֵיהּ. לֹא חַיָּיב לָךְ כְּלוּם. וְלֹא עוֹד אֶלָּא שֶׁאִם נִיזוֹק חַיָּיב בְּנִזְקוֹ.

"A dog stole a hot pitta." Rebbi Simeon ben Laqish said, only if he lit every single ear of grain[77]. Rebbi Johanan said, he is like a person who shoots an arrow from one place to another[78]. Rebbi Isaac bar Tevelai said, a Mishnah supports Rebbi Simeon ben Laqish: "If a kid goat was bound to it and a slave was close by and was burned, he is obligated. If the slave was bound and the kid goat close by, he is free.[79]" But[80] if you say that he is not like a person who shoots an arrow from one place to another, then for the first ear he is guilty of a capital crime; for the remainder he should be liable for repayment. Rebbi Yose said, you also understand that from: "If his cattle set fire to a stack of sheaves on the Sabbath, he is obligated. But if he set fire to a stack of sheaves on the Sabbath, he is free.[81]" But if you say that he is not like a person who shoots an arrow from one place to another, then should he not become obligated since for the remainder he should be liable for repayment[80]. A person did put out a hot water bottle[82] outside[83]. A donkey passed by and broke it. The case came before Rebbi Isaac bar Tevelai, who said to him: He does not owe you anything. Not only that but if [the donkey] suffered damage, [you] would be obligated for its damages[84].

77 The Babli, 22a, explains that R. Simeon ben Laqish holds that damage by fire is like any other damage caused by a person's property. Therefore, the fire not directly caused by the dog should not lead to liability of the dog's owner.

The Vatican fragment reads נעשה במצית את האור. This is a conflation of the Leiden text with a reading נַעֲשֶׂה כְּמָצִית אֶת הָאוּר "he is considered *as if* he had lit every stalk separately", that every stalk creates a new obligation.

78 This is action from a distance; the owner is liable even if his property only shot the arrow or started the fire.

79 Mishnah 6:7. If a person set fire to a haystack, he has to pay for the hay and everything inside. If an animal was bound in the haystack, a slave was close to it, and both were burned, the arsonist has to pay for the animal; he is not responsible for the slave, who was not bound and could have saved himself. But if the slave was bound and the animal free, then the arsonist is a murderer. Nobody is both executed and pays for the same crime; even if he cannot be convicted for lack of eye-witnesses to the crime he cannot be made to pay (*Terumot* 7:1, *Ketubot* 3:1). Therefore, he cannot be made to pay for the animal.

80 The argument advanced by R. Isaac bar Tevelai is not spelled out. The counter argument is presented: If the arsonist were personally liable only for the first stalk which he lit then by the time the fire reached the bound slave it no longer was his fire and there is no reason why he should not be made to pay for the animal. Only R. Johanan's position is consistent with the Mishnah.

81 Mishnah 3:12; cf. *Terumot* 7:1, Note 44.

82 Since making fire on the Sabbath is a capital crime, he cannot be sued for civil damages. But if his animals start a fire, no crime is involved, and the owner is fully responsible in a civil suit.

82 Explanation of E. S. Rosenthal, from Greek πυριατήρ "hot water bottle". Another possibility would be to read with S. Krauss (τὰ) πρατήρια "merchandise".

83 Latin *foris*, "outside, in the open". The Escurial text and the Vatican fragment offer a second reading פירון (cf. Latin *forum* "outside place, public place; market"), and a parallel text חד בר נש אמלי אסרטא "a person filled the thoroughfare".

84 Your merchandise has the status of "pit in the public domain".

## HALAKHAH 6

**משנה ו**: אֵי זֶהוּ תָם וְאֵי זֶהוּ מוּעָד. מוּעָד שֶׁהֵעִידוּ בּוֹ שְׁלֹשָׁה יָמִים. תָּם שֶׁיַּחֲזוֹר בּוֹ שְׁלֹשָׁה דִּבְרֵי רִבִּי יְהוּדָה. רִבִּי מֵאִיר אוֹמֵר מוּעָד שֶׁהֵעִידוּ בּוֹ שְׁלֹשָׁה פְעָמִים. וְתָם שֶׁהַתִּינוֹקוֹת מְמַשְׁמְשִׁין בּוֹ. (fol. 2d)

**Mishnah 6**: Which one is tame and which one is notorious? Notorious if there was testimony against it for three days. Tame if it behaved during three [days], the words of Rebbi Jehudah[85]. Rebbi Meïr says, notorious if there was testimony against it three times[86]; tame if children touched it.

85  In his opinion, a vicious animal can regain the status of tame.

86  In the Babli, this is read as including testimony about three different incidents in one day, or on three widely spaced occasions. The notorious animal regains a status of tame only if it regularly can be touched by children. In *Mekhilta dR. Ismael* (*Neziqin* 10), this interpretation is attributed to R. Yose.

**הלכה ו**: אֵי זֶהוּ תָם וְאֵי זֶהוּ מוּעָד כול׳. מַה טַעֲמָא דְרִבִּי יוּדָן. מִתְּמוֹל שְׁלְשׁוֹם. מַה מְקַיֵּים רִבִּי מֵאִיר מִתְּמוֹל שִׁלְשׁוֹם. פָּתַר לָהּ בְּהַפְלֵג נְגִיחוֹת. שֶׁאִם יָצָא בַיּוֹם רִאשׁוֹן וְנָגַח. בַּשֵּׁנִי וְלֹא נָגַח. בַּשְּׁלִישִׁי נָגַח. אֵין נַעֲשֶׂה שׁוֹר מוּעָד עַד שֶׁיִּגַּח שְׁלֹשָׁה יָמִים זֶה אַחַר זֶה. יָצָא בַיּוֹם רִאשׁוֹן וְנָגַח שְׁוָורִין. בַּשֵּׁנִי וְנָגַח כְּלָבִים. בַּשְּׁלִישִׁי וְנָגַח חֲזִירִים. עַל יְדֵי שְׁלֹשָׁה מִינִין לִשְׁלֹשָׁה יָמִים מַהוּ שֶׁיֵּעָשֶׂה שׁוֹר מוּעָד. יָצָא בַיּוֹם רִאשׁוֹן וְנָגַח. בַּשֵּׁנִי לֹא יָצָא. בַּשְּׁלִישִׁי יָצָא וְנָגַח. יָבָא כְתַפְלוּגְתָּא דְרַב אָדָא בַּר אַחֲוָא וּדְרַב הוּנָא. דְּאִיתְפַּלְגוּן. נִידָּה שֶׁבָּדְקָה עַצְמָהּ בַּיּוֹם רִאשׁוֹן וּמְצָאַתָהּ טָמֵא. בַּשֵּׁנִי לֹא בָדְקָה. בַּשְּׁלִישִׁי בָדְקָה וּמְצָאַתָהּ טָמֵא. רַב אָדָא בַּר אַחֲוָא בְּשֵׁם רַב. נִידָה וַדַּאי. רַב הוּנָא בְּשֵׁם רַב אָמַר. נִדָּה סָפֵק. אָמַר רַב הוּנָא. תַּמָּן הֲוִינָא בְרֹאשָׁהּ וְתַמָּן הֲוִינָא בְסֵיפָהּ וְתַמָּן הֲוִינָא בְּאֶמְצָעִיתָהּ. אִישְׁתְּאַלַת לְרַב וְאָמַר. סָפֵק. אִישְׁתְּאַלַת לְרַב וַאֲמַר. וַדַּאי. וְחָזַר וַאֲמַר. סָפֵק. רַב אָדָא בַּר אַחֲוָא לֹא הֲוָה תַּמָּן אֶלָּא כַּךְ מַר. וַדַּאי.

"Which one is tame and which one is notorious," etc. What is Rebbi Jehudah's reason? "From yesterday and the day before.[87]" How does Rebbi Meïr confirm "from yesterday and the day before"? He explains it by separate gorings[88], that if it was let out the first day and gored, the second day and it did not gore, the third day it gored, it is not declared a notorious bull unless it gored on three consecutive days[89]. If it was let out the first day and gored bulls, the second it gored dogs, the third it gored pigs: would it be declared a notorious bull for three different kinds on three days[90]? If it was let out the first day and gored, the second day it was not let out, the third day it was let out and gored, we come to the disagreement between Rav Ada bar Aḥawa and Rav Huna, who disagreed[91]: A menstruating woman[92] checked herself the first day and found herself impure. The second day she did not check. On the third day she checked and found herself impure. Rav Ada bar Aḥawa said in the name of Rav: she certainly is *niddah*[93]. Rav Huna said in the name of Rav: it is doubtful whether she is *niddah*[93,94]. Rav Huna said, I was there at the beginning, I was there at the end, and I was there in the middle when Rav was asked, and he said, it is doubtful. Rav was asked and he said, it is certain; then he reversed himself and said, it is doubtful. Rav Ada bar Aḥawa was only there when he said, it is certain.

---

87 *Ex.* 21:36; a notorious bull is one who was known to gore "yesterday and the day before." Babli 23b.

88 In the Rome fragment: כהפליג גגיחות, "if it spread out its gorings".

89 In the Babli, 24a, R. Meïr is credited with the argument that if three different gorings on three different days make a bull notorious then three gorings on the same day certainly will have the same effect. The plural "bulls" in the next sentence negates this interpretation in the Yerushalmi which might follow the

*Mekhilta* and attributes that argument to R. Yose (Note 86).

The Babli, 37a, notes that a bull can be declared notorious on alternate days if it was observed to gore on days 1,3,5 and was tame on days 2,4.

90 The question is not answered, probably because it never arose in practice.

91 In the Babli, *Niddah* 68a, the opinion attributed here to R. Ada is Rav's and that of Rav Huna is Levi's. Since the Babli follows Rav but the opinion of Rav Ada is discredited in the Yerushalmi, the Talmudim come to opposite conclusions.

92 The text here is incomprehensible; one has to insert two words from the parallel Babli text. *Lev.* 15:19 decrees that a menstruating woman is impure for seven days; then she may immerse herself in a *miqweh* and is pure. But if she has a disccharge "many days outside her period", she is declared זָבָה "suffering from flux", and *Lev.* 15:25-30 decrees that after she is healed she has to undergo a period of purification and a Temple ceremony to regain purity. Since "days" mean a minimum of two, "many days" mean a minimum of three (cf. H. Guggenheimer, *Logical problems in Jewish tradition*, in: Ph. Longworth, ed., *Confrontations with Judaism*, London 1966, pp. 171-196.) Therefore it is clear that one deals here with a menstruating woman who checks herself *on the seventh day* and finds herself impure. She therefore cannot become pure at the end of the seventh day but falls under the severe rules of the sufferer from flux only if she has a discharge during three consecutive days.

93 Instead of *niddah*, "the menstruating woman", this has to be read *zavah*, "the woman suffering from flux" instead; cf. the preceding Note.

94 She has to follow the rules of *zavah* but, if the Temple will be miraculously rebuilt overnight, she would not bring a sacrifice.

רַב יִרְמְיָה בְּשֵׁם רַב. הֲלָכָה כְּרִבִּי מֵאִיר בְּתַמָּה. וּכְרִבִּי יוּדָה (3a line 63) בְּהַעֲדָאָה. דְּתַנֵּי. שׁוֹר שֶׁנָּגַח שְׁלֹשָׁה פְּעָמִים בְּיוֹם אֶחָד אֵינוֹ מוּעָד. וּמַה תַּלְמוּד לוֹמַר מִתְּמוֹל שִׁלְשׁוֹם. אֶלָּא שֶׁאִם חָזַר בּוֹ שְׁלֹשָׁה יָמִים זֶה אַחַר זֶה אֵינוֹ נִידוֹן אֶלָּא כְתָם. הֲוֵינָן סָבְרִין מֵימַר. הֲלָכָה כְּרַב הוּנָא דּוּ אָמַר. מֵעֵין וּשְׁנֵיהֶם.[95] אָתָא רַב יִרְמְיָה בְּשֵׁם רַב. הֲלָכָה כְּרִבִּי מֵאִיר בְּתַמָּה וּכְרִבִּי יְהוּדָה בְּהַוְדָעָה.

Rav Jeremiah in the name of Rav: Practice follows Rebbi Meïr for the tame animal and Rebbi Jehudah for testimony[96], as we have stated[97]: "A bull which gored three times on the same day is not notorious. Why does the verse say 'from yesterday and the day before'? For if it mended its ways for three days one after the other it is judged to be tame." We were thinking to say that practice follows Rav Huna who said following both of them[98]. This is confirmed by Rav Jeremiah in the name of Rav: Practice follows Rebbi Meïr for the tame [bull] and Rebbi Jehudah for testimony.

95   Reading שניהם with the Rome ms. and E.

96   Testimony before the court which declares a bull notorious. The Babli, 24a, agrees and declares this to be the opinion of the Tanna R. Yose.

97   Similar texts are in the mss. of *Mekhilta dR. Ismael* (*Neziqin* 10), ed. Horovitz-Rabin p. 284.

98   Practice partially follows both RR. Jehudah and Meïr.


**משנה ז:** שׁוֹר הַמַּזִּיק בִּרְשׁוּת הַנִּיָּזק כֵּיצַד נָגַח נָגַף נָשַׁךְ רָבַץ בָּעַט בִּרְשׁוּת הָרַבִּים מְשַׁלֵּם חֲצִי נֶזֶק. בִּרְשׁוּת הַנִּיָּזק רִבִּי טַרְפוֹן אוֹמֵר נֶזֶק שָׁלֵם וַחֲכָמִים אוֹמְרִים חֲצִי נֶזֶק. (fol. 2d)

**Mishnah 7**: How does one treat the bull of the person causing the damage in the domain of the person sustaining the damage? If it gored, hit, bit, wallowed, or kicked, in the public domain he pays half of the damages. In the domain of the person sustaining the damage, Rebbi Tarphon said, full damages; but the Sages say, half damages[99].

**משנה ח**: אָמַר לָהֶן רִבִּי טַרְפוֹן. מַה בִּמְקוֹם שֶׁהֵיקֵל עַל הַשֵּׁן וְעַל הָרֶגֶל בִּרְשׁוּת הָרַבִּים שֶׁהוּא פָטוּר הֶחֱמִיר עֲלֵיהֶן בִּרְשׁוּת הַנִּיָּזק לְשַׁלֵּם נֶזֶק שָׁלֵם. מְקוֹם שֶׁהֶחֱמִיר עַל הַקֶּרֶן בִּרְשׁוּת הָרַבִּים לְשַׁלֵּם חֲצִי נֶזֶק אֵינוֹ דִין שֶׁנַּחֲמִיר

עֲלֵיהֶן בִּרְשׁוּת הַנִּיזָק לְשַׁלֵּם נֶזֶק שָׁלֵם. אָמְרוּ לוֹ דַּיּוֹ לַבָּא מִן הַדִּין לִהְיוֹת כַּנִּדּוֹן. מַה בִּרְשׁוּת הָרַבִּים חֲצִי נֶזֶק אַף בִּרְשׁוּת הַנִּיזָק חֲצִי נֶזֶק.

**Mishnah 8**: Rebbi Tarphon said to them: Since in a case where He was lenient with [damage by] tooth or foot in the public domain, where one is free, He was restrictive for them in the domain of the person sustaining the damage, when full damages must be paid, and He was restrictive regarding damage by the horn in the public domain, where one has to pay half damages; is it not logical that we should be restrictive in this case in the domain of the person sustaining the damage, that full damages must be paid? They said to him, it is sufficient for the result of an argument *de minore ad majus* that it should be like the premiss[100]. Since in the public domain [one pays] half damages, also in the domain of the person sustaining the damage half damages.

**משנה ט**: אָמַר לָהֶן. אֲנִי לֹא אָדִין קֶרֶן מִקֶּרֶן אֲנִי אָדִין קֶרֶן מֵרֶגֶל. וּמַה אִם בִּמְקוֹם שֶׁהֵיקֵל עַל הַשֵּׁן וְעַל הָרֶגֶל בִּרְשׁוּת הָרַבִּים הֶחֱמִיר בַּקֶּרֶן. מְקוֹם שֶׁהֶחֱמִיר עֲלֵיהֶן בִּרְשׁוּת הַנִּיזָק אֵינוֹ דִין שֶׁנַּחְמִיר בַּקֶּרֶן. אָמְרוּ לוֹ דַּיּוֹ מִן הַדִּין לִהְיוֹת כַּנִּדּוֹן. מַה בִּרְשׁוּת הָרַבִּים חֲצִי נֶזֶק אַף בִּרְשׁוּת הַנִּיזָק חֲצִי נֶזֶק.

**Mishnah 9**: He said to them, I do not argue horn from horn, I argue horn from foot! Since in a case where He was lenient with [damage by] tooth or foot in the public domain, He was restrictive for damage by the horn, when He was restrictive with [damage by] tooth or foot in the domain of the person sustaining the damage; is it not logical that we should be restrictive [in case of damage] by the horn? They said to him, it is sufficient for the result of an argument *de minore ad majus* that it should be like the premiss. Since in the public domain [one pays] half damages, also in the domain of the person sustaining the damage half damages.

99   Cf. Halakhak 1:4, Note 160.
100   This is an intrinsic limitation of arguments *de minore ad majus*, derived from *Num.* 12:14 (*Sifry Num.* 106; Babli 25a), discussed by the author (*loc. cit.* Note 92, p. 183).

**הלכה ז**: שׁוֹר הַמַּזִּיק בִּרְשׁוּת הַנִּיזָּק כּוֹל' עַד סוֹף. אָמַר רִבִּי יוֹחָנָן. דְּרִבִּי טַרְפוֹן הִיא. בִּרְשׁוּת הַנִּיזָּק. רִבִּי טַרְפוֹן אוֹמֵר. נֶזֶק שָׁלֵם. וַחֲכָמִים אוֹמְרִים. חֲצִי נֶזֶק. (3a line 68)

**Halakhah 7**: "The bull of the person causing the damage in the domain of the person sustaining the damage," etc. to the end. [101]Rebbi Johanan said, this follows Rebbi Tarphon: "In the domain of the person sustaining the damage, Rebbi Tarphon said, full damages; but the Sages say, half damages."

101   This is Halakhah 1:4.

**משנה י**: אָדָם מוּעָד לְעוֹלָם בֵּין שׁוֹגֵג בֵּין מֵזִיד בֵּין עֵר בֵּין יָשֵׁן. סִימָּא אֶת עֵין חֲבֵירוֹ וְשִׁבַּר אֶת הַכֵּלִים מְשַׁלֵּם נֶזֶק שָׁלֵם. (fol. 2d)

**Mishnah 10**: A human is always notorious: Whether in error, or intentionally, whether awake, or sleeping, if he blinded another person or broke vessels, he pays full damages[102].

102   Irrespective of the circumstances, he pays full restitution for all possible kinds of damages.

**הלכה י**: אָדָם מוּעָד לְעוֹלָם כּוֹל'. אָמַר רִבִּי יִצְחָק. מַתְנִיתָא בְּשֶׁהָיוּ שְׁנֵיהֶם יְשֵׁינִין. אֲבָל אִם הָיָה אֶחָד מֵהֶן יָשֵׁן וּבָא חֲבֵירוֹ לִישָׁן אֶצְלוֹ זֶה שֶׁבָּא לִישָׁן אֶצְלוֹ הוּא הַמּוּעָד. (3a line 70)

**Halakhah 10:** "A human is always notorious," etc. Rebbi Isaac said: The Mishnah if both of them were sleeping[103]. But if one was sleeping and another one came to sleep near him, the one who came to sleep near him is notorious[104].

103   In the Rome fragment: "So is the Mishnah: if both of them were sleeping."

104   Tosaphot (4a, *s.v.* כיון) quotes an expanded version: In the Yerushalmi it is noted that a person sleeping is liable only if he went to sleep near vessels, but if he was sleeping when vessels were deposited near him and he broke them, he does not have to pay because others caused the damage; similarly, if one was sleeping, another person went to sleep near him, and they injured one another, the first is free and the later one has to pay.

Since none of the ms. sources has this extended text, it may be an example of the Ashkenazic "book Yerushalmi".

# המניח את הכד פרק שלישי

(fol. 3b) **משנה א**: הַמַּנִּיחַ אֶת הַכַּד בִּרְשׁוּת הָרַבִּים וּבָא אַחֵר וְנִתְקַל בָּהּ וּשְׁבָרָהּ פָּטוּר. וְאִם הוּזַּק בָּהּ בַּעַל הֶחָבִית חַיָּיב בִּנְזָקָיו.

**Mishnah 1**: If somebody puts his jar down in the public domain and another person stumbled over it and broke it, [the second person] does not have to pay[1]; if he was hurt, the owner of the amphora[2] has to pay his damages[3].

1  Even though a human is always notorious, there are cases where he does not have to pay.

2  The Mishnah uses interchangeably all words which denote clay vessels used for storage, whether jar or amphora.

3  Creating an obstacle in the public domain is damage by "pit".

(3b line 62) **הלכה א**: הַמַּנִּיחַ אֶת הַכַּד בִּרְשׁוּת הָרַבִּים כול'. וְאֵין דֶּרֶךְ אָדָם לַהֲנִיחָן בִּרְשׁוּת הָרַבִּים. רַב אָמַר. בִּמְמַלֵּא אֶת כָּל־רְשׁוּת הָרַבִּים. אֲבָל אִם אֵינָהּ מְמַלֵּא אֶת כָּל־רְשׁוּת הָרַבִּים אֵין דֶּרֶךְ אָדָם לִהְיוֹת מַנִּיחָם בִּרְשׁוּת הָרַבִּים. שְׁמוּאֵל אָמַר. אוֹ בִּמְמַלֵּא אֶת כָּל־רְשׁוּת הָרַבִּים אוֹ עַד שֶׁתְּהֵא נְתוּנָה עַל קֶרֶן זָוִית. אָמַר רַבִּי לְעָזָר. וַאֲפִילוּ אֵינָהּ מְמַלֵּא כָּל־רְשׁוּת הָרַבִּים אִם יְטִילֶנָּה מִיכָּאן וְיִתְּנֶנָּה כָּאן הֲרֵי זֶה בוֹר וַאֲפִילוּ אֵינָהּ נְתוּנָה עַל קֶרֶן זָוִית אֵין דֶּרֶךְ אָדָם לִהְיוֹת מַנִּיחָן בִּרְשׁוּת הָרַבִּים.

**Halakhah 1**: "If somebody puts his jar down in the public domain," etc. Is it not usual for a person to put things[4] in the public domain? Rav said, if it was filling[5] the entire public domain[6]. But if it does not fill the entire public domain, is it not usual to put things in the public domain? Samuel said, either if it was filling the entire public domain or if it is at a corner[7]. Rebbi Eleazar[8] said, even if it does not fill the entire public domain (if he took it from here and put it down there he would create a "pit")[9] and even if it was at a corner; it is not usual for a person to put things[4] in the public domain[10].

4   Both in the Rome (R) and E mss. instead of להניחן one reads להיות מבחין (E), להיות מבחן (R): "do not people usually look where they are going in the public domain?" A person walking in the street should be obligated to observe a minimum of precaution. Then why does the Mishnah give a blanket exemption to the person who breaks another person's vessel in the publich domain? The same readings are found at the end of the paragraph as declarative statements.

5   This should be read as feminine, מְלֵאָה [cf. J. N. Epstein, Tarbiz 6 fasc. 1 (1934), p. 64-65.]

6   Babli 27b. If one does not stop traffic, one is permitted to put down his load in the public domain.

7   The person who turns around the corner could not see the obstacle in front of him. In the Babli, this is attributed to R. Joḥanan; Samuel applies the Mishnah to accidents in the dark. (In R, the statements of Rav and Samuel are conflated to one short text.)

8   In the Babli, his is confirmed as the Galilean point of view.

9   This has to be eliminated as dittography from the following paragraph; it is not in the parallel mss.

10  Anything left lying in the public domain creates a "pit".

(3b line 69) הָיְתָה מְמַלֵּא כָּל־רְשׁוּת הָרַבִּים אִם יְטִילֶנָּה מִיכָּן וְיִתְּנֶנָּה כָּאן נַעֲשָׂה בוֹר.   אֶלָּא יְטוֹל הַמַּקֵּל וִישַׁבְּרֶנָּה אוֹ יַעֲבוֹר עָלֶיהָ וְאִם נִשְׁבְּרָה נִשְׁבְּרָה. נִישְׁמְעִינָהּ מִן הָדָא. שׁוֹר שֶׁעָלָה עַל חֲבֵירוֹ וּבָא בַּעַל הַשּׁוֹר לִשְׁמוֹט אֶת שֶׁלּוֹ אוֹ הוּא שֶׁשִּׁימֵּט אֶת עַצְמוֹ וְנָפַל וָמֵת פָּטוּר. אִם דְּחָייוֹ וְנָפַל וָמֵת חַיָּיב. וְלָא יְכִיל מֵימַר לֵיהּ. אִילּוּ שְׁבַקְתָּהּ הֲוִינָא יָהִיב לָךְ נִזְקָהּ.   עוֹד הוּא דּוּ יְכִיל מֵימַר לֵיהּ.

אִילּוּ שְׁבַקְתָּהּ הֲוִיתָהּ יְהִיב לִי חֲצִי נֶזֶק. הַגַּע עַצְמָךְ שֶׁהָיָה מוּעָד. לֹא כָּל־מִמָּךְ שֶׁאֱהֵא מְחַזֵּר עִמָּךְ עַל בָּתֵּי דִינִין.

If it was filling the entire public domain, if he took it from here and put it down there he would create a "pit"[11]. But could he take a stick and break it or step over it and if it broke, it broke[12]? Let us hear from the following: If a bull mounted another[13] and the [latter's] owner came to draw away his own, or [the bull] slipped away, and [the attacker] fell down and died, he is free from payment. If he pushed [the attacker] which then fell down and died, he must pay[14]. Could he[15] not tell him, if you had not interferred, I would have paid your damages? But he could have answered, If I had not interferred, you would have paid me half the damage[16]! Think of it, if it was notorious? It is not in your power to drag me through the courts[17].

11  If the jars block the entire path, a passer-by cannot remove one of them and put it down again in the public domain since then he would create the obstacle and would be liable for any damages his "pit" would cause in the future. The Babli agrees, 31b, that any obstacle created in the public domain is under the rules of "pit".

12  Since the passer-by has the right of way, can he forcibly make himself a path without penalty, or does he normally walk and is free from paying only for incidental damage.

13  In the Babli, 28a: "If a bull mounted another *to kill him*".

14  Therefore, the passer-by is not allowed to break the jars to clear the way for himself.

15  Could the owner of the attacking bull sue the owner of the defending animal for the value of the dead bull, claiming that even if his bull had killed the other's animal he could have paid the damages.

16  The attacking bull is under the rules of "horn"; the owner of the defending animal never could have hoped to recover his entire loss.

17  Since damages caused by a notorious animal can only be collected by a suit, the owner of the defending

animal is justified in his action; the owner of the attacking bull has no claim against him.

(3b line 72) הִנִּיחַ חָבִית בִּרְשׁוּת הָרַבִּים וּבָא אַחֵר וְהִנִּיחַ אַחֶרֶת סְמוּכָה לָהּ וּבָא הָרִאשׁוֹן לִיטוֹל שֶׁלּוֹ אִם יְטִילֶנָּה מִיכָּן וְיִתְּנֶינָה כָּאן נַעֲשָׂה בוֹר. אֶלָּא יְטוֹל אֶת הַמַּקֵּל וִישַׁבְּרֶנָּה אוֹ יַעֲבוֹר עָלֶיהָ וְאִם נִשְׁבְּרָה נִשְׁבְּרָה. נִישְׁמְעִינָהּ מִן הָדָא. שׁוֹר שֶׁעָלָה בַּחֲבֵירוֹ וּבָא בַּעַל הַשׁוֹר וּשְׁמָטוֹ מִתַּחְתָּיו אִם עַד שֶׁלֹּא עָלָה שְׁמָטוֹ וְנָפַל וָמֵת פָּטוּר. וְאִם דָּחֵהוּ וְנָפַל וָמֵת חַיָּיב. אָמַר רִבִּי יוֹסֵי. וְתִישְׁמַע מִינָהּ. רָאָה אַמַּת הַמַּיִם שׁוֹטֶפֶת וּבָאָה לְתוֹךְ שָׂדֵהוּ עַד שֶׁלֹּא נִכְנְסוּ הַמַּיִם לְתוֹךְ שָׂדֵהוּ רַשַּׁאי לְפַנּוֹתָם לְמָקוֹם אַחֵר. מִשֶּׁנִּכְנְסוּ אֵין רַשַּׁאי לְפַנּוֹתָם לְמָקוֹם אַחֵר. אֲהֵן כְּרִיסוֹ אַרְגִּירָא עַד דְּלָא יֵיתֵי אֲהֵן כְּרִיסוֹ אַרְגִּירָא שָׁרֵי מֵימַר. פְּלָן עֲבִיד עֲבִידְתִּי פְּלָן עֲבִיד עֲבִידְתִּי. מִן דְּיֵיתֵי אֲהֵן כְּרִיסוֹ אַרְגִּירָא אָסוּר. הָדֵן אִכְסְנַיי פָּרְכָּא עַד דְּלָא יֵיתוֹן רוֹמָאִי שָׁרֵי (מיחשדוניה) [מְשַׁחְדִינֵיהּ].[18] מִן דְּיֵיתוֹן רוֹמָאִי אֲסִיר.

Somebody put down an amphora in the public domain and then another person came and put another one close to the first. If the first person comes to take his own and would move [the second] and put it down at another place, he would create a "pit"[11]. But could he take a stick and break it or step over it and if it broke, it broke[12]? Let us hear from the following: If a bull came to mount another[13] and the [latter's] owner came to draw away his own, if he drew him away before it could mount, and [the attacker] fell down and died, he is free from payment. If he pushed [the attacker] which then fell down and died, he must pay[14]. Rebbi Yose said, we can hear from this that if one saw a flood threatening in his irrigation canal, before the flood reached his field he is permitted to divert the water to another place[19]; after the flood reached his field he is not permitted to divert it to another place[20]. If the *chrysargyros*[21] was imposed, before [the collector of] *chrysargyros* arrived, one is permitted to say, X is following my profession, Y is following my professon. Once the [the collector of] *chrysarguros* arrived, it is forbidden. It is permitted to bribe the quartermaster[22] before the Roman [soldiers] arrive[23]; after the Roman [soldiers] arrive it is forbidden.

18   Reading of R and E "to bribe"; for the reading of L "to suspect", which does not fit the context.

19   Which would damage the property of other farmers whose fields are irrigated by the same canal.

20   This is like pushing the agressive bull off its victim, which makes the victim's owner liable for damage to the agressive bull.

21   Χρυσάργυρος, "alloy of gold and silver; tribute of gold and silver", a Roman tax imposed by Constantine I, repealed by Anastasios I. The tax was imposed on professions and forced artisans into guilds. A certain sum was collected from each profession in a taxing district [cf. A. Dessau, *Finanzen des alten Rom*, Handwörterbuch der Staatswissenschaften, Jena 1900, vol. 3, pp. 949-955]. Before the repartition of the tax, the taxpayer might indicate that certain people exercised the same profession as himself without being registered as members of the guild. By this act, he increased the pool of taxpayers and reduced his own share of the tax load. But after repartition of the tax, such a denunciation would lead to the others having to pay tax without his own obligation being reduced; that is forbidden.

22   אכסניי פרכא, from Greek ξενία "hospitality, lodging"; πάροχος, Latin *parochus* (pure Latin term *copiarius*) "purveyor; furnisher of conveniences to travelling magistrates and officers in Roman provinces". If the expression is taken as one word, cf. ξενοπάροχος, Latin *xenoparochus*, "one who provides for strangers" (E. G.).

23   The bribe is given to spare one's house from receiving soldiers to put up. The entire paragraph is quoted *in extenso* and commented on in the *Responsa* of Simeon b. Ṣemaḥ Duran, vol. 3, # 46.

(3c line 12) הִנִּיחַ אַבְנוֹ בִּרְשׁוּת הָרַבִּים וּבָא אַחֵר וְהִנִּיחַ אַחֶרֶת סְמוּכָה לָהּ וּבָא אַחֵר וְנִתְקַל בְּזוֹ וְנֶחְבַּט בְּזוֹ. מִי חַיָּב בְּנִזְקוֹ. הָרִאשׁוֹן אוֹ הַשֵּׁינִי. נִשְׁמְעִינַהּ מִן

הֲדָא. שׁוֹר שֶׁדָּחַף לַחֲבֵירוֹ וְנָפַל לַבּוֹר. בַּעַל הַשּׁוֹר חַיָּיב וּבַעַל הַבּוֹר פָּטוּר. רַבִּי נָתָן אוֹמֵר. בְּמוּעָד זֶה נוֹתֵן מֶחֱצָה וְזֶה נוֹתֵן מֶחֱצָה וּבְתָם בַּעַל הַשּׁוֹר נוֹתֵן שְׁנֵי חֲלָקִים וּבַעַל הַבּוֹר רְבִיעַ. אָמַר רִבִּי חֲנִינָה. כֵּינִי מַתְנִיתָא. בַּעַל הַשּׁוֹר נוֹתֵן שְׁלֹשָׁה חֲלָקִים וּבַעַל הַבּוֹר נוֹתֵן רְבִיעַ. (הִנִּיחַ אַבְנוֹ בִּרְשׁוּת הָרַבִּים וּבָא אַחֵר וְהִנִּיחַ אַחֶרֶת סְמוּכָה לָהּ וּבָא אַחֵר וְנִתְקַל בְּזוֹ וְנֶחְבַּט בְּזוֹ. מִי חַיָּיב בְּנִזְקוֹ. הָרִאשׁוֹן אוֹ הַשֵּׁנִי.)

הִנִּיחַ אַבְנוֹ בִּרְשׁוּת הָרַבִּים וּבָאת הָרוּחַ וְהִפְרִיחָתָהּ לִרְשׁוּת הַיָּחִיד וּבָא אַחֵר וְנִתְקַל בָּהּ. מַהוּ שֶׁיְּהֵא חַיָּיב בְּנִזְקוֹ.

הִנִּיחַ אַבְנוֹ בִּרְשׁוּת הָרַבִּים וּבָא אַחֵר וְנִתְקַל בָּהּ וְהִיתִּיזָהּ לִרְשׁוּת הַיָּחִיד וּבָא אַחֵר וְנִתְקַל בָּהּ. מַהוּ שֶׁיְּהֵא חַיָּיב בְּנִזְקוֹ.

אָמַר רִבִּי יוֹחָנָן. הִנִּיחַ אַבְנוֹ וּמַשָּׂאוֹ בִּרְשׁוּת הָרַבִּים וּבָא אַחֵר וְנִתְקַל בָּהֶן וּצְלוֹחִיתוֹ בְּיָדוֹ. בֵּין שֶׁנִּתְקַל בָּאֶבֶן וְנֶחְבַּט בַּקַּרְקַע בֵּין שֶׁנֶּחְבַּט בָּאֶבֶן וְנִתְקַל בַּקַּרְקַע חַיָּיב עַל נִיזְקֵי אָדָם וּפָטוּר עַל נִיזְקֵי צְלוֹחִיתוֹ. מִילְתֵיהּ דְּרִבִּי יוֹחָנָן אָמְרָה. בּוֹר שֶׁלַּנְּזָקִין פָּטוּר עַל הַכֵּלִים. וְאִם בְּדֶרֶךְ הַטָּחָה הִטִּיחַ אֲפִילוּ עַל נִיזְקֵי צְלוֹחִית חַיָּיב.

A person put down a stone in the public domain, another person put down another stone next to the first, a third person stumbled over the first and struck the other[24]. Who has to pay damages, the first or the second person? Let us hear from the following[25]: "A bull pushed another ox which then fell into a pit. The owner of the bull has to pay[26]; the 'owner'[27] of the pit is free. Rebbi Nathan says, if the attacker was notorious, each of them pays one half[28]; if it was tame, the owner of the bull[29] pays two thirds[30] and the 'owner' of the pit[29] a quarter." Rebbi Hanania said, so is the *baraita*: The owner of the bull[29] pays three quarters and the 'owner' of the pit[29] a quarter[31]. (A person put down a stone in the public domain, another person put down another stone next to the first, a third person stumbled over the first and struck the other. Who has to pay damages, the first or the second person?)[32]

A person put down a stone in the public domain, the wind blew it onto a private domain, another person stumbled over it. Is [the first] responsible for damages[33]?

A person put down a stone in the public domain, another person stumbled over it and made it roll into a private domain where a third person stumbled over it. Is [the first] responsible for damages[33]?

Rebbi Joḥanan said: A person put down a stone and his load in the public domain, a second person stumbled over it while he held a flask in his hand. Whether he stumbled over the stone and hit the ground or hit the stone and stumbled over the ground, [the first] has to pay damages to the person but is free from damages to the flask[34]. The statement of Rebbi Joḥanan implies that for "pit" damages one is free from damages to vessels. But if he hit it in walking[35], he[36] has to pay even for the flask.

24  He is injured by the second stone but would not have been injured had he not stumbled over the first.

25  Tosephta 6:1; quoted also in the Babli, 53a.

26  Under the rules of "horn", full damages if the ox was notorious, half damages if it was tame (Tosaphot 53a, s.v. בעל).

27  The pit or any obstacle classified as "pit" is in the public domain; it is not property of the person who created the obstacle. But the verse, *Ex.* 21:34, calls him "owner of the pit". In the language of the Babli (29b, *Pesaḥim* 6b) "it is not a person's property but the verse treats it as if it were his property." The biblical expression is used as a technical term to denote liability.

28  As explained in the Babli, R. Nathan holds that the 'owner' of the pit, the place where the attacked animal died, is the primary payor and, under the rules of "pit", has to pay 100% of the damages. Then he has

regress on the owner of the attacking bull for half of his cost.

29   Even though the reading of the text is confirmed by the Rome and Escurial mss., it seems that one has to read "pit" for "bull" and vice versa in all occurrences.

30   In all of Talmudic literature, the expression "*n* parts" means "*n* parts of *n*+1", following Egyptian arithmetic practice. In the statement here, all commentators, from Eliahu Fulda to S. Lieberman, claim that "two parts" means "two parts out of four", i. e., one half. This contradicts Talmudic practice. One has to accept the statement of R. Ḥanina (in the Rome ms.: R. Isaac) that the text is corrupt and has to be corrected. Only the corrected text is mentioned in Babli and Tosephta.

31   As explained in the Babli, the 'owner' of the pit has regress on the owner of the tame bull only for half the damages. Since the owner of a notorious bull has to pay $1/2$, the owner of a tame bull pays $1/4$ of the damages to the 'owner' of the pit who had paid all damages to the owner of the animal which was killed.

32   Dittography of the corrector for the printed edition, faithfully reproduced in the Venice print.

33   The question is not answered; it is decided in the negative since a claimant could not prove the law to be on his side.

34   Since *Ex.* 21:34 limits damages under the category of "pit" to humans and livestock, excluding its load (Mishnah 5:9; Tosephta 6:14; Babli 28b; *Mekhilta dR. Ismael, Neziqin* 11).

35   If the person was not injured by the obstacle classified as "pit", the 'owner' of the pit is liable for damages. Babli 28b.

36   The 'owner' of the "pit".

**משנה ב:** נִשְׁבְּרָה כַדּוֹ בִּרְשׁוּת הָרַבִּים וְהוּחְלַק אֶחָד בַּמַּיִם אוֹ שֶׁלָּקָה (fol. 3b) בַּחֲרָסֶיהָ חַיָּב. רִבִּי יְהוּדָה אוֹמֵר בְּמִתְכַּוֵּן חַיָּב בְּשֶׁאֵינוֹ מִתְכַּוֵּן פָּטוּר.

**Mishnah 2**: If his jar was broken in the public domain and another person slipped on the water or was hurt by one of its shards, he must pay.

Rebbi Jehudah said, if intentionally, he has to pay; if unintentionally, he is free.

(3c line 28) **הלכה ב:** נִשְׁבְּרָה כַדּוֹ בִּרְשׁוּת הָרַבִּים כול'. רִבִּי לָעְזָר אָמַר. בְּשָׁעַת נְפִילָה נֶחְלְקוּ. אֲבָל לְאַחַר נְפִילָה כָּל־עַמָּא מוֹדֵיי שֶׁחַיָּיב. אָמַר רִבִּי יוֹחָנָן. בֵּין בְּשָׁעַת נְפִילָה בֵּין לְאַחַר נְפִילָה הִיא הַמַּחֲלוֹקֶת. מְתִיב רִבִּי יוֹחָנָן לְרִבִּי לָעְזָר. אִם בְּשָׁעַת נְפִילָה פָּטוּר. אֵינוֹ קַל וָחוֹמֶר לְאַחַר נְפִילָה. וְלָמָּה פָּטוּר בְּשָׁעַת נְפִילָה. שֶׁכֵּן אָדָם מַבְקִיר נְזָקָיו בִּרְשׁוּת הָרַבִּים. אִית מַתְנִיתָא מְסַייְעָא לְדֵין וְאִית מַתְנִיתָא מְסַייְעָא לְדֵין. דְּתַנֵּי. מוֹדִין חֲכָמִים לְרִבִּי יוּדָן בְּמַנִּיחַ אַבְנוֹ וּמַשּׂאוֹ בִּרְשׁוּת הָרַבִּים וּבָא אַחֵר וְנִתְקַל בָּהֶן פָּטוּר. שֶׁעַל מְנָת כֵּן הִנְחִיל יְהוֹשֻׁעַ לְיִשְׂרָאֵל אֶת הָאָרֶץ. הָא אִם לֹא הִנְחִיל יְהוֹשֻׁעַ לְיִשְׂרָאֵל אֶת הָאָרֶץ עַל מְנָת כֵּן חַיָּיב. עַל דַּעְתֵּיהּ דְּרִבִּי יוֹחָנָן. בְּמִתְכַּוֵּין לַחֲרָסִין. עַל דַּעְתֵּיהּ דְּרִבִּי לָעְזָר. בְּמִתְכַּוֵּין לְהַזִּיק. רִבִּי זֵירָא וְרִבִּי לָא תְּרֵיהוֹן אֱמָרִין. מוֹדֶה רִבִּי יוּדָה לַחֲכָמִים בְּמַבְקִיר שׁוֹר שֶׁנָּגַח בִּרְשׁוּת הָרַבִּים שֶׁחַיָּיב. לֹא דוֹמֶה נֶזֶק עוֹמֵד לְנֶזֶק מְהַלֵּךְ.

**Halakhah 2:** "If his jar was broken in the public domain," etc. Rebbi Eleazar said, they disagree at the moment of the accident. But after the accident everybody agrees that he must pay[37]. Rebbi Joḥanan said, the disagreement is both at the moment of the accident and afterwards[38]. Rebbi Joḥanan objected to Rebbi Eleazar: If he does not have to pay at the moment of the accident, is it not an inference *de minore ad majus* afterwards[39]? Why should he be free at the moment of the accident? For a person declares his damaged property in the public domain as ownerless[40]. A *baraita* supports both of them, as it was stated: "The Sages agree with Rebbi Jehudah that somebody who puts down his stone or his load in the public domain does not have to pay if another person stumbled over it, for on this condition did Joshua distribute the Land[41]." Therefore, if Joshua had not distributed the Land on this condition, he would have to pay. In the opinion of Rebbi Joḥanan, if he intended use of the potsherds[42]. In the opinion of Rebbi Eleazar, if he intended to cause damage[43]. Rebbi Ze'ira and Rebbi La both say that Rebbi Jehudah agrees with the Sages that one has to pay if he declares his bull who gored in the public domain ownerless. Stationary damage cannot be compared to walking damage.

37 As explained at length in the Babli, 29a/b, Rebbi Jehudah holds that in using the public domain one has to be mindful of others who use the same space. Therefore a person who runs into the scene of an accident is negligent and has no claim for damages. The majority hold that follow-up accidents are the responsibility of the person who caused the first accident. R. Jehudah will agree that if he did not remove the obstacle which the accident created, he becomes 'owner' of his 'pit' by biblical decree.

38 Since the public domain is strewn with shards and other debris, these are ownerless and no responsibility can be pinned on anybody.

The position of R. Joḥanan is not clear in any of the Talmudim. The Rome text presents two opinions attributed to R. Johanan, the one quoted here and "they disagree at the moment of the accident, but after the accident everybody agrees that he is free."

39 That he should be freed from liability as explained in the preceding Note. Rome text: "is it not an inference *de minore ad majus* that afterwards he has to pay?" In S. Lieberman's opinion (in his notes to A. H. Freimann's edition of the Rome text), the Rome ms. represents an amalgamation of two different sources.

40 Accepted in the Babli, 29a/b.

41 Everybody has the right to fair use of public property. It is perfectly normal that one should be able to put down one's load for a time before continuing on his journey, and other people have to be aware of this and be considerate. Private property on public grounds becomes 'pit' only at the

moment it is left there unsupervised.

In general, "conditions on which Joshua did distribute the Land" refer to public uses of private property; cf. *Ketubot* 13:7 Note 107, *Nazir* 7:1 Note 40. This condition is not mentioned in any other source.

42    Here starts the discussion of what R. Jehudah calls "intentional accident" which makes the owner of the jar liable. If the owner of the jar intends to use the shards (e. g., as writing material), he does not declare them ownerless and the reason given for freeing him from payment does not apply.

43    If he does not clean up after the accident, he shows that he does not care about what happens to others; this explains R. Eleazar's opinion that after the accident even R. Jehudah requires payment.

(fol. 3b) **משנה ג**: הַשּׁוֹפֵךְ מַיִם בִּרְשׁוּת הָרַבִּים וְהֻזַּק בָּהֶן אַחֵר חַיָּב בְּנִזְקוֹ. הַמַּצְנִיעַ אֶת הַקּוֹץ וְאֶת הַזְּכוּכִית וְהַגּוֹדֵר אֶת גְּדֵרוֹ בְּקוֹצִים וְגָדֵר שֶׁנָּפַל לִרְשׁוּת הָרַבִּים וְהֻזְּקוּ בָהֶן אֲחֵרִים חַיָּב בְּנִזְקוֹ.

**Mishnah 3**: He who pours out water in the public domain[44] is liable for the damage if another person is hurt because of this. He who puts away a thorn, or glass, or who fences his fence with thorns, or [owns] a fence which collapsed into the public domain, is liable for the damage if other persons are hurt because of this[45].

44    Illicit use of public domain.

45    This sentence is somewhat too compressed. If somebody puts away dangerous things (a thorn, broken glass) in the public domain he is liable for any ensuing damage. The same holds if he fences in his orchard by a thorny hedge and the thorns grow into the public domain; he is liable for hurt caused within the public domain. If any of his property, fence, or wall collapses into the public domain, he is liable for any damages caused.

(3c line 40) **הלכה ג:** הַשּׁוֹפֵךְ אֶת הַמַּיִם בִּרְשׁוּת הָרַבִּים כול׳. רַב הוּנָא אָמַר. בְּשֶׁנֶּחְבַּט בְּקַרְקָעוֹ. אֲבָל אִם נִתְלַכְלְכוּ כֵלָיו חַיָּיב. רַב אָמַר. אֲפִילוּ נִתְלַכְלְכוּ כֵלָיו פָּטוּר. מִילְתֵיהּ דְּרַב אָמְרָה. בּוֹר שֶׁלַּנְּזָקִין פָּטוּר עַל הַכֵּלִים.

**Halakhah 3:** "He who pours out water in the public domain," etc. Rav Huna said, when he was falling to the ground. But if his garments were dirtied, one is liable. Rav said, even if his garments were dirtied, he is not liable[46]. The word of Rav implies one is not liable for 'pit' damages of vessels.

46  Since the text is confirmed by the parallel mss., it cannot be amended. In the Babli, 30a, Rav holds that the person pouring out the water is liable only for clothing, not for injury to the person slipping in the water; Rav Huna objects. Since pouring out water is intentional, even R. Jehudah (Mishnah 2) will agree that 'pit' was created at the moment of the pouring; in this case there is no difference in liability during or after the pouring. One has to conclude that the Yerushalmi reports a Babylonian tradition diametrically opposed to that reported in the Babli: Everybody agrees that for personal injury the person who is to blame has to pay; for vessels it is a dispute (cf. Note 34).

(3c line 43) הַמַּצְנִיעַ אֶת הַקּוֹץ וְאֶת הַזְּכוּכִית לְתוֹךְ כּוֹתְלוֹ שֶׁלַּחֲבֵירוֹ וּבָא בַּעַל הַכּוֹתֶל וּסְתָרוֹ וְהוּזַּק בָּהֶן אַחֵר חַיָּיב. חֲסִידִים הָרִאשׁוֹנִים הָיוּ מוֹצִיאִין אוֹתָן לְתוֹךְ שָׂדֶה עַצְמוֹ וּמַעֲמִיקִין לָהֶן ג׳ טְפָקִים כְּדֵי שֶׁלֹּא תַעֲלֵם הַמַּחֲרֵישָׁה.

"If somebody hides a thorn or [a piece of] glass in another person's wall; if the owner of the wall then tears it down and a third person is hurt, he is liable. The pious people of earlier times used to take them out[47] into their fields, lower than three handbreadths so that the plough would not lift them[48]."

47 This is the text of the mss. and the Tosephta; it was changed by the corrector of the Venice edition to מצניעין "they buried them".

48 Tosephta 2:6; Babli 30a. It is unclear who has to pay; probably it is the person who put the glass into the hole in the wall. In the interpretation of the Babli, he only has to pay if the wall was already weakened and one could foresee that it had to be taken down; this certainly is not the position of the Yerushalmi.

(3c line 46) פִּיסְקָא. הַגּוֹדֵר גְּדֵירוֹ בַּקּוֹצִים. אָמַר רִבִּי יוֹחָנָן. תִּיפְתָּר דִּבְרֵי הַכֹּל בְּמַפְרִיחַ. רִבִּי בּוּן בַּר חִיָּיה בְּעָא קוֹמֵי רִבִּי זְעִירָא. וְלָמָּה לִי נָן פְּתִרִין לָהּ כְּרִבִּי יוֹסֵי בֵּירְבִּי יוּדָה דְּאָמַר. שְׁלֹשָׁה שֶׁהֵן סְמוּכִין לִרְשׁוּת כִּרְשׁוּת. אָמַר לֵיהּ. וּמַה בִּישׁ לָךְ דְּאִיכָּא רִבִּי יוֹחָנָן מֵימַר לָךְ. תִּיפְתָּר דִּבְרֵי הַכֹּל בְּמַפְרִיחַ.

New Paragraph. "He fences his fence with thorns." Rebbi Joḥanan said, explain it according to everybody if it grew outwardly[49]. Rebbi Abun bar Ḥiyya asked before Rebbi Ze'ira: Why do we not explain it following Rebbi Yose ben Rebbi Jehudah who said, three [handbreadths] close to a domain are counted with the domain[50]? He answered, why are you not satisfied with what Rebbi Joḥanan said; explain it according to everybody if it grew outwardly.

49 If the thorns grow into the public domain, the owner of the hedge is responsible. If the hedge is cut exactly at the border of the private domain, most authorities in the Babli, 30a, hold that people do not walk too close to a wall or a hedge and, therefore, the owner of the hedge is not liable for injuries occurring on his property line.

50 In Babylonian sources, Babli 50a, Tosephta 6:4, he is quoted as requiring any potential danger in a private domain to be at least *four* handbreadths away from the boundary. The Yerushalmi version is repeated in Halakhah 5:7 Note 62.

(3c line 50) וְגָדֵר שֶׁנָּפַל לִרְשׁוּת הָרַבִּים. רִבִּי אַבָּהוּ בְּשֵׁם רֵישׁ לָקִישׁ אָמַר. דְּרִבִּי מֵאִיר הִיא. דְּרִבִּי מֵאִיר אָמַר. כָּל־הַמַּזִּיק שֶׁלֹּא עַל יְדֵי מַעֲשֶׂה חַיָּב. וְהָדָא אֲמָרָה דָא. נָתְנוּ לוֹ זְמַן לָקוֹץ אֶת הָאִילָן וְלִסְתּוֹר אֶת הַכּוֹתֶל וְנָפְלוּ לְתוֹךְ הַזְּמַן פָּטוּר. לְאַחַר הַזְּמַן חַיָּב. וְכַמָּה הוּא הַזְּמָן. תַּנֵּי רִבִּי הוֹשַׁעְיָה. ל יוֹם.

"A fence which collapsed into the public domain." Rebbi Abbahu in the name of Rebbi Simeon ben Laqish: This is Rebbi Meïr's, since Rebbi Meïr said, one is liable for damage caused by inaction. This is the following[51]: "If he was given a deadline by which to cut the tree or demolish the wall and they collapsed, if it happened within the term, he is not liable; after the term, he is liable." How much is a term? Rebbi Hoshaia stated: 30 days[52].

51 Mishnah *Bava meṣi'a* 10:4, dealing with a wall or a tree close to the public domain which may constitute a danger of imminent collapse; a court order is issued to the owner to eliminate the danger.

52 Also in *Bava meṣi'a* 10:4; in the Babli, *Bava meṣi'a* 118a as statement of R. Joḥanan. In the Tosephta (*Bava qama* 2:5, *Bava meṣi'a* 11:7): At least thirty days.

(fol. 3b) **משנה ד:** הַמּוֹצִיא אֶת תִּבְנוֹ וְאֶת גַּפְתּוֹ לִרְשׁוּת הָרַבִּים לְזָבָלִים וְהוּזַּק בָּהֶן אַחֵר חַיָּב בְּנִזְקוֹ. וְכָל־הַקּוֹדֵם בָּהֶן זָכָה. הַחוֹפֵךְ אֶת הַגָּלָל בִּרְשׁוּת הָרַבִּים וְהוּזַּק בָּהֶן אַחֵר חַיָּב בְּנִזְקוֹ.

**Mishnah 4**: If somebody take out his straw and his pressed olives[53] into the public domain to compost, he is liable for any damages another person might incur because of this. Anybody may take it and acquire it[54]. If somebody turns over cow droppings in the public domain[55], he is liable for any damages another person might incur because of this.

53 After they have been pressed for the production of olive oil and are squeezed dry. This is an illegal use of the public domain.

54 By rabbinic convention, anything deposited illegally in the public domain becomes ownerless; it becomes the property of the first person to take it up and remove it from the public domain. The Mishnah in the Babli and most independent Mishnah mss. have this principle spelled out by Rabban Simeon ben Gamliel.

55 This is an act of acquisition; he may collect the droppings but at the same time he becomes the owner of the corresponding 'pit'.

(3c line 55) **הלכה ד:** הַמּוֹצִיא אֶת תִּבְנוֹ וְאֶת גִּפְתוֹ כול׳. בַּמֶּה זָכָן. דְּבֵית יַנַּאי אָמְרֵי. בְּשָׁבְחָן. שְׁמוּאֵל אָמַר. בְּגוּפָן.

חִזְקִיָּה אָמַר. וְהוּא שֶׁהָפְכָהּ עַל פָּנֶיהָ לִזְכּוֹת בָּהּ. מִילְתֵיהּ דְּחִזְקִיָּה אָמְרָה. הַמִּטַּלְטְלִין נִקְנִין בַּהֲפִיכָה. אֶלָּא הַמִּטַּלְטְלִין מַהוּ שֶׁיִּקְנוּ בִגְרִירָה. אָמַר רִבִּי בּוּן בַּר חִיָּיה. נִרְאִין דְּבָרִים בָּעַמּוּדִין וּבְעוֹרוֹת קָשִׁין. אֲבָל בְּעוֹרוֹת רַכִּין לֹא קָנָה עַד שֶׁיַּגְבִּיהַּ.

**Halakhah 4:** "If somebody take out his straw and his pressed olives," etc. What did he acquire? The House of Yannai said, the increase in value. Samuel said, the substance[56].

Hizqiah said, only if he turned it over to acquire[57]. The word of Hizqiah implies that movables can be acquired by turning them over[58]. [59]But could they be acquired by dragging? Rebbi Abun bar Hiyya said, this is reasonable for pillars and hard hides[60]. But soft hides one does not acquire unless one lifts them up.

56 The person who picks up the composted material from the public domain gets it all without paying according to Samuel; the House of Yannai would require him to pay the price of the original material to the previous owner. Babli 30b, in the names of Rav and Ze'iri.

57 This now refers to cow dung. The parallel mss. and Medieval quotes

all have an additional sentence: If he did not turn it over with the intention of acquiring, it was not acquired.

58  This is rather obvious since by Mishnah *Qiddušin* 1:5 all movables can be acquired by lifting; turning over seems to be impossible without lifting.

59  From here to the end of the Halakhah there is a parallel in *Qiddušin* 1:5, Notes 514 ff., in a different formulation with mostly different speakers.

60  Which cannot be lifted by a single person; *Qiddušin* 1:5, Note 514.

(3c line 60) אָמַר רִבִּי אָחָא. לֵיי דָא פָּשְׁטָה עַל שִׁיטָתְהוֹן דְּרַבָּנָן. בֶּן סוֹרֵר וּמוֹרֶה מָהוּ שֶׁיְּהֵא חַיָּיב בְּתַשְׁלוּמֵי כֶפֶל בִּגְנֵיבָה הָרִאשׁוֹנָה. אוֹ מֵאַחַר שֶׁהוּא בְהַתְרָיַית מִיתָה יְהֵא פָטוּר. נִשְׁמְעִינָהּ מִן הָדָא. הַגּוֹנֵב כִּיס חֲבֵירוֹ וְהוֹצִיאוֹ בַּשַּׁבָּת חַיָּיב. שֶׁכְּבָר נִתְחַיֵּיב בִּגְנֵיבַת כִּיס עַד שֶׁלֹּא קָדְשָׁה עָלָיו הַשַּׁבָּת. וְלֹא בְהַתְרָיַית מִיתָה הוּא וְתֵימַר חַיָּיב. וָכָא אַף עַל פִּי שֶׁהוּא בְהַתְרָיַית מִיתָה יְהֵא חַיָּיב. אָמַר רִבִּי יַנַּאי בַּר יִשְׁמָעֵאל. רִבִּי הוֹשַׁעְיָה תַנִּיתָהּ כְּדַעְתֵּיהּ. דְּתַנֵּי. הַמּוֹצִיא אַף עַל פִּי שֶׁלֹּא הִנִּיחַ חַיָּיב. וְדִכְוָותָהּ. הַמּוֹצִיא אַף עַל פִּי שֶׁלֹּא נָטַל לְהוֹצִיא חַיָּיב. שֶׁאֵין הַתְרָיָיתוֹ אֶלָּא בִּשְׁעַת הוֹצָאָתוֹ. תַּנֵּי. אִם הָיָה גוֹרֵר בּוֹ וְיוֹצֵא פָטוּר. שֶׁחָלוּ עָלָיו מִיתָה וְתַשְׁלוּמִין כְּאַחַת. הָא אִם לֹא חָלוּ עָלָיו שְׁנֵיהֶן כְּאַחַת חַיָּיב בַּתַּשְׁלוּמִין. אָמַר רִבִּי יוֹסֵי בְּירִבִּי בּוּן. תִּיפְתָּר דַּהֲוּוֹן אִילֵּין כִּיסַיָּיא רַבְרְבִין. שֶׁדַּרְכָּן לִיקָנוֹת בִּגְרִירָה. וְלֵית שְׁמַע מִן הָדָא כְּלוּם.

Rebbi Aḥa said, would that not[61] be obvious from the reasoning of the rabbis?[62] [63]Is the rebellious son liable for double restitution for his first theft?[64] Or since he is warned of a capital offense should he be freed? Let us hear from the following: If somebody steals another's wallet[65] and removes it on the Sabbath he is liable since he already is liable for the theft of the wallet before he comes in conflict with the holiness of the Sabbath. Is he not forewarned of a capital offense and you say, he is liable! Here[66] also, even though he is forewarned of a capital offense, you say that he has to be liable. Rebbi Yannai bar Ismael said, Rebbi Hoshaia follows his own opinion, as we have stated: He who takes out is guilty even if he did not put down[67]. Similarly, he who takes out is guilty even if he did not take up with the intent to take out[68], for warning is possible only at the moment of his taking out. It was stated: If he was dragging it until he left[68], he is free since the obligations of capital crime and restitution falls on him simultaneously. Therefore, if both obligations do not fall on him simultaneously, he is liable. Rebbi Yose ben Rebbi Abun said, explain it with large pouches which usually are dragged[60]; one cannot infer anything from this[69].

61  Reading with the Rome fragment ליה for ליי in the text. With this paragraph, the fragment ends.

62  The negative answer is only given at the end of the paragraph.

63  The principle that monetary fines are barred in cases of criminal punishment is detailed in *Terumot* 7:1 Notes 51-71, *Ketubot* 3:1 Note 30, *Qiddušin* 1:5 Notes 515-519. Except for the example of the rebellious son, the passage in *Qiddušin* is a differently formulated close parallel to the text here.

64  The rebellious son (*Deut.* 21:18-21) is stoned if convicted of financing an extravagant lifestyle by repeated theft from his parents. For a first theft he cannot be prosecuted as rebellious son; one would expect that all the rules of theft apply to him. But he cannot be prosecuted as rebellious son if he never was convicted of the first theft. Of the 200% of the stolen amount which the law on theft requires him to pay, the first 100% are restitution. But the second 100% are a fine. Can the fine be collected if in some indeterminate future the conviction might be an integral part of a capital case?

65  The theft occurs in the victim's home. The thief is guilty of theft at the moment he lifts the wallet; he is guilty of desecrating the Sabbath only when he removes it from the house into the public domain.

66  The case of the rebellious son.

67  For the rabbis, the Sabbath is desecrated only by a complete prohibited action. Transport has three parts: Lifting an article, transporting it (which under certain circumstances is

prohibited on the Sabbath) and putting the article down. For the rabbis, a person cannot be prosecuted for desecration of the Sabbath if he takes an object in a private domain, takes it out to the public domain and never stops moving until the end of the Sabbath (R. Joḥanan in *Šabbat* 1:1 2b l. 40, Babli *Ketubot* 31a). R. Hoshaia disagrees. However, the reason might be that he follows Ben Azai (*Šabbat* 1:1, 2c l. 41; Babli *Ketubot* 31b) who holds that walking is like standing still. Everybody agrees that standing still while carrying something is equivalent to putting it down.

68  This Tanna holds that an article cannot be acquired by dragging it on the floor, but only by lifting; cf. Babli *Šabbat* 91b, *Bava batra* 86a.

69  There is no indication that smaller articles can be acquired by dragging.

(3c line 72) מְתִיבִין הָא מַתְנִיתָא. זִימְנִין דְּמוֹתְבִין לָהּ וּמְסַיְּיעִין לְרִבִּי יוֹחָנָן. זִימְנִין דְּמוֹתְבִין לָהּ וּמְסַיְּיעִין לְרִישׁ לָקִישׁ. יֵשׁ אוֹכֵל אֲכִילָה אַחַת וְחַיָּיב עָלֶיהָ אַרְבַּע חַטָּאוֹת וְאָשָׁם אֶחָד. טָמֵא שֶׁאָכַל חֵלֶב וְהוּא נוֹתָר מִן הַמּוּקְדָּשִׁין בְּיוֹם הַכִּיפּוּרִים. רִבִּי מֵאִיר אוֹמֵר. אִם הָיְתָה שַׁבָּת וְהוֹצִיאוֹ בַשַּׁבָּת. אָמְרוּ לוֹ. אֵינוֹ הַשֵּׁם. אֵימַת דְּמְתִיבִין וּמְסַיְּיעִין לְרִבִּי יוֹחָנָן. הוֹצִיאוֹ בַשַּׁבָּת אֵין כָּאן הֲנָחָה. וְלָמָּה אָמְרוּ. אֵינוֹ הַשֵּׁם. אֵימַת דְּמְתִיבִין וּמְסַיְּיעִין לְרִישׁ לָקִישׁ. הוֹצִיאוֹ בְיוֹם הַכִּיפּוּרִים יְהֵא פָטוּר. אָמַר רִבִּי יוֹסֵי בֵּירִבִּי בּוּן. אַתְיָיא דְרִבִּי מֵאִיר כְּרִבִּי עֲקִיבָה. דְּתַנֵּי. מִנַּיִין לְיוֹם הַכִּיפּוּרִים שֶׁחָל לִהְיוֹת בַּשַּׁבָּת וְשָׁגַג וְעָשָׂה מְלָאכָה מִנַּיִין שֶׁחַיָּיב עַל זֶה בִּפְנֵי עַצְמוֹ וְעַל זֶה בִּפְנֵי עַצְמוֹ. תַּלְמוּד לוֹמַר. שַׁבָּת הִיא. יוֹם הַכִּיפּוּרִים הוּא. דִּבְרֵי רִבִּי עֲקִיבָה. רִבִּי יִשְׁמָעֵאל אוֹמֵר. אֵין חַיָּיב אֶלָּא אַחַת.

One objects from the Mishnah; sometimes one objects in support of Rebbi Joḥanan[70], sometimes one objects in support of Rebbi Simeon ben Laqish[71]. [72]"A person may eat once and be liable for four purification and one reparation sacrifices: An impure person who ate suet which was leftover sacrifice on the Day of Atonement[73]. Rebbi Meïr said, if it was a

Sabbath and he took it out[74] on the Sabbath. They told him, it is not from that category[75]." When they objected in support of Rebbi Johanan: If he took it out on the Sabbath, there is no putting down[76]. Why did they say, it is not from that category[77]? When they objected in support of Rebbi Simeon ben Laqish: Why is he not liable if he took it out on the Day of Atonement[78]? Rebbi Yose ben Rebbi Abun said, Rebbi Meïr follows Rebbi Aqiba, as it was stated[79]: From where that if one unintentionally worked on a Day of Atonement which fell on the Sabbath, he is liable for each one separately? The verse says, "it is Sabbath[80]," "it is the Day of Atonement.[81]" Rebbi Ismael said, he is liable only once[82].

70   In his dispute with R. Hoshaia; Note 67.

71   It is not known to which statement or disagreement this refers. It seems that one refers to the question whether carrying from one domain to another is forbidden on the Day of Atonement since it is forbidden on the Sabbath (even though this opinion is characterized in the Babli, *Keritut* 14a, as "stupidity").

72   Mishnah *Keritut* 3:4; quoted partially *Šabbat* 1:1, 2c l. 43.

73   Three purification offerings are due for the inadvertent eating of sacrificial meat by an impure person (*Lev.* 7:20), suet (v. 23), and leftover sacrificial meat (v. 18), a fourth for eating on the Day of Atonement (*Lev.* 23:29). A reparation sacrifice is due for the unauthorized use of *sancta* (*Lev.* 5:15).

74   He put the meat in his mouth in one domain, went out and ate it in another domain.

75   This sin is committed by carrying, not eating.

76   If the person ate in walking, the piece of meat disappears without coming to rest.

77   According to R. Johanan, eating the piece *is* putting it down. Since for him transporting on the Sabbath is not punishable without bringing the object being transported to rest, the liability is triggered not by carrying outside but by eating. This would be in the same category as the other transgressions.

78   Why could R. Meïr not mention transporting on the Day of Atonement?

The E text has here an addition:

הוֹצִיאוֹ] בַּשַּׁבָּת וְהִנִּיחוֹ. וְלָמָּה אָמְרוּ אֵינוֹ הַשֵּׁם. אֵימַר תִּיפְתָּר בְּשֶׁאֲכָלָהּ. וַאֲכִילָה הֲנָחָה הִיא. לֹא מִסְתַּבְּרָה דְלֹא הוֹצִיאוֹ בַּשַּׁבָּת חַיָּיב. הֲרֵי שֶׁהוֹצִיאוֹ [בַּיּוֹם הַכִּפּוּרִים יְהֵא פָטוּר.

If he took it out] on the Sabbath and put it down. Why did they say: "it is not from that category"? I would say in explanation that he ate it. Is eating not putting it down? Therefore, it is only reasonable that if he took it out on the Sabbath, he be liable. Then if he took it out [on the Day of Atonement why should he not be liable?

The additional text is between the brackets, ] [. It seems that the scribe of L lost the text between הוציאו and שהוציאו. But since the text does not add anything to the discussion, the addition might be a gloss that entered the text.

79   *Sifra Emor Parašah* 9(8); Babli *Ḥulin* 101a (with R. Yose the Galilean instead of R. Ismael); Tosephta *Keritut* 2:17 (attributions switched).

80   *Lev.* 23:3.

81   *Lev.* 23:28. In this opinion, R. Meïr details obligation of 6 purification offerings.

82   Since there is only one punishment in case of willful transgression, there can be only one sacrifice in case of inadvertent sin.

**משנה ה:** שְׁנֵי קַדָּרִין שֶׁהָיוּ מְהַלְּכִין זֶה אַחַר זֶה וְנִתְקַל הָרִאשׁוֹן וְנָפַל וְנִתְקַל הַשֵּׁנִי בָּרִאשׁוֹן הָרִאשׁוֹן חַיָּיב בְּנִזְקֵי הַשֵּׁנִי. זֶה בָּא בְּחָבִיתוֹ וְזֶה בָּא בְקוֹרָתוֹ נִשְׁבְּרָה כַדּוֹ שֶׁל זֶה בְקוֹרָתוֹ שֶׁל זֶה פָּטוּר שֶׁלָּזֶה רְשׁוּת לְהַלֵּךְ וְלָזֶה רְשׁוּת לְהַלֵּךְ. (fol. 3b)

**Mishnah 5**: Two potters were walking one behind the other. The first stumbled and the second stumbled over the first; the first is liable for the damage done to the second. One came with an amphora, the other came with a beam. If the jug of the one was broken by the other's beam he is not liable since each of them had the right to walk there[83].

83 The owner of the jug had the duty to keep his distance from any obstacle which endangered his vessel.

(3d line 7) **הלכה ה:** שְׁנֵי קַדָּרִין שֶׁהָיוּ מְהַלְּכִין כול'. רִבִּי יוֹחָנָן בָּעָא. מַהוּ שֶׁיִּתֵּן לָרִאשׁוֹן שָׁהוּת כְּדֵי עֲמִידָה. אָמַר רִבִּי יוֹסֵי. פְּשִׁיטָא לְרִבִּי יוֹחָנָן לִיתֵּן לָרִאשׁוֹן שָׁהוּת כְּדֵי עֲמִידָה. וְלֹא מִסְתַּבְּרָה דְלָא מִן הַשֵּׁינִי וְהֶלְךְ מַהוּ לַשֵּׁינִי לִיתֵּן שָׁהוּת כְּדֵי עֲמִידָה. נִישְׁמְעִינָה מִן הָדָא. הַקַּדָּרִים הַמְהַלְּכִין זֶה אַחַר זֶה. נִתְקַל הָרִאשׁוֹן וְנָפַל וּבָא חֲבֵירוֹ וְנָפַל וּבָא חֲבֵירוֹ וְנִתְקַל בּוֹ וְנָפַל. הָרִאשׁוֹן מְשַׁלֵּם לַשֵּׁינִי וְהַשֵּׁינִי לַשְּׁלִישִׁי. וְאִם מַחֲמַת הָרִאשׁוֹן נָפְלוּ כוּלָּן הוּא מְשַׁלֵּם עַל יְדֵי כוּלָּן. וְחַיָּיבִין עַל נִיזְקֵי אָדָם וּפְטוּרִין עַל נִיזְקֵי כֵלִים. וְאִם הִזִּיקוּ זֶה אֶת זֶה כוּלָּן פְּטוּרִין. חַמָּרִים שֶׁהָיוּ מְהַלְּכִין זֶה אַחַר זֶה. וְנִתְקַל הָרִאשׁוֹן וְנָפַל וּבָא חֲבֵירוֹ וְנָפַל וּבָא חֲבֵירוֹ וְנִתְקַל בּוֹ וְנָפַל. הָרִאשׁוֹן מְשַׁלֵּם לַשֵּׁינִי וְהַשֵּׁינִי לַשְּׁלִישִׁי. וְאִם מַחֲמַת הָרִאשׁוֹן נָפְלוּ כוּלָּן הוּא מְשַׁלֵּם עַל יְדֵי כוּלָּן. חֲמוֹרִים שֶׁהָיוּ מְהַלְּכִין זֶה אַחַר זֶה. נִתְקַל הָרִאשׁוֹן וְנָפַל וּבָא חֲבֵירוֹ וְנִתְקַל בּוֹ וְנָפַל אֲפִילוּ מֵאָה כוּלָּן חַיָּיבִין. אִית תַּנָּיֵי תַנֵּי. כוּלָּן פְּטוּרִין. אָמַר רִבִּי לָא. מָאן דָּמַר. חַיָּיבִין. בְּשֶׁהִרְבִּיצוּם בַּעֲלֵיהֶן. נָפְלוּ אֵין אוֹנְסִין לַבְּהֵמָה. חֲמוֹרִים שֶׁהָיוּ רַגְלֵי אֶחָד מֵהֶן רָעוֹת אֵין רַשָּׁאִין לַעֲבוֹר עָלָיו. מַהוּ רַשָּׁאִין לַעֲבוֹר עָלָיו. דֶּרְסִין עֲלוֹי וְעָבְרִין. הָיָה אֶחָד רֵיקָן וְאֶחָד טָעוּן מַעֲבִירִין אֶת הָרֵיקָן מִפְּנֵי הַטָּעוּן. אֶחָד פָּרוּק וְאֶחָד טָעוּן מַעֲבִירִין אֶת הַפָּרוּק מִפְּנֵי הַטָּעוּן. הָיוּ שְׁנֵיהֶן טְעוּנִין שְׁנֵיהֶן פְּרוּקִין יַעֲשׂוּ פְשָׁרָה בֵּינֵיהֶן. שְׁתֵּי עֲגָלוֹת שְׁתֵּי סְפִינוֹת אַחַת טְעוּנָה וְאַחַת רֵיקָנִית מַעֲבִירִין פְּרוּקָה מִפְּנֵי הַטְּעוּנָה. שְׁתֵּיהֶן פְּרוּקוֹת אוֹ טְעוּנוֹת יַעֲשׂוּ פְשָׁרָה בֵּינֵיהֶן. הַנִּכְנָס לַמֶּרְחָץ נוֹתֵן כָּבוֹד לַיּוֹצֵא. וְהַיּוֹצֵא מִבֵּית הַכִּסֵּא נוֹתֵן כָּבוֹד לַנִּכְנָס.

**Halakhah 5**: "Two potters were walking one behind the other," etc. Rebbi Johanan asked: Does one give time to the first to get up[84]? Rebbi Yose said, it is obvious for Rebbi Johanan to give time to the first to stand up. But it is reasonable otherwise from the second one onwards[85], does one give time to the second to stand up? Let us hear from the following: [86]"Potters were walking one behind the other. The first stumbled and fell, the next one stumbled and fell, the next one stumbled and fell. The first one pays to the second, and the second to the third. But if all fell because of the first, he pays for all of them. They are liable for damage to humans but not liable for damage to vessels[87]. But if they (damaged) [warned][88] one another, none are liable. Donkey drivers were walking one behind the other. The first stumbled and fell, the next one stumbled and fell, the next one stumbled and fell. The first one pays to the second, and the second to the third. But if all fell because of the first, he pays for all of them. Donkeys were walking one behind the other. The first stumbled and fell, the next one stumbled and fell: even 100, all are liable." Some Tannaïm state, none are liable. Rebbi La said, he who says 'liable', if their owner let them lie down. He who says 'not liable', if they fell, since animals are not responsible for accidents[89]. "If the feet of a donkey were bad, one is not allowed to step over him. [ ][90]" What does it mean, 'to step over him?' They step on his body and pass by[91]. "If one was free, the other loaded, the loaded one has the right of way before the free one. One unloaded[92], the other one loaded, the loaded one has the right of way before the unloaded one. If both were loaded or both unloaded, let them agree between themselves[93]. Two carriages or two ships, one empty, the other loaded, the loaded one has the right of way before the unloaded one. If both were unloaded or loaded, let them agree between themselves." [94]"The person entering the bath house gives precedence to[95] the person leaving; the person leaving the toilet gives precedence to the person entering."

84 Is stumbling alone an indication of insufficient attention which makes the stumbled person liable to damages? Or is the person who notices that he is falling down required to alert the persons following him to be careful? Or is stumbling an accident for which he is not responsible; his liability then would start only if he does not expeditously clear the way for others. Also in the Babli, 31a, R. Joḥanan is reported to accept the third alternative.

85 If somebody sees an accident in the road in front of him, does he have to stop faster to avoid a multiple collision?

86 The following text to the end of the paragraph, except for some interspersed editorial comments, is closely related to Tosephta 2:8-10 (partially quoted in the Babli 31a); these texts are used to correct a scribal error and fill a lacuna in the text.

87 By the rules of 'pit'. The Babli, 31b, denies the definition of 'pit' to the first person who caused the mass collision.

88 Reading of Tosephta and Babli.

89 The owner of an animal is not responsible for accidents caused by it. The sentence about donkey drivers was inserted only to show the difference between the drivers and their animals.

90 With the parallels, one has to insert: "If it fell, they are permitted to step over it."

91 If the path is narrow and does not allow for a bypass.

92 It carries empty packaging.

93 In the Babli, *Sanhedrin* 32b, the one who gives up his right of way can demand payment from the other party.

94 *Derekh Ereṣ Rabba*, Chapter 10; *Derekh Ereṣ (Maḥzor Vitry)* Chapter 8, end.

95 Yields the right of way.

(3d line 30) זֶה בָּא בְּחָבִיתוֹ וְזֶה בָּא בְּקוֹרָתוֹ. רַבִּי זֵירָא בָּעֵי. שְׁנוּ וְהִזִּיקוּ מַהוּ. נִשְׁמְעִינָהּ מִן הָדָא. חֲמִשָּׁה שֶׁיָּשְׁבוּ עַל סַפְסָל אֶחָד וּבָא אַחֵר וְיָשַׁב בּוֹ וְנִשְׁבַּר. הוּא מְשַׁלֵּם עַל יְדֵי כּוּלָּן. וְאִם מֵחֲמַת כּוּלָּן נִשְׁבַּר כּוּלָּן חַיָּיבִין.

"One came with an amphora, another came with a beam." Rebbi Ze'ira asked: If they changed[96] and caused damage, what is the rule? Let us hear from the following: [97]"Five people sat on a couch; another came, sat on it, and it broke. He pays for all of them. But if it broke because of all of them[98], they are all liable."

96   One of the people suddenly changed his speed so that the other crashed into him. One might read this paragraph in connection with the next Mishnah.

97   Tosephta 2:9; partially in Babli 10b.

98   They invited the sixth; this caused the overload.

**משנה ו:** הָיָה בַּעַל קוֹרָה רִאשׁוֹן וּבַעַל הֶחָבִית אַחֲרוֹן נִשְׁבְּרָה הֶחָבִית בַּקוֹרָה פָּטוּר. וְאִם עָמַד בַּעַל הַקוֹרָה חַיָּב. וְאִם אָמַר לוֹ לְבַעַל הֶחָבִית עֲמוֹד פָּטוּר. הָיָה בַּעַל הֶחָבִית רִאשׁוֹן וּבַעַל הַקוֹרָה אַחֲרוֹן. נִשְׁבְּרָה הֶחָבִית בַּקוֹרָה חַיָּב. וְאִם עָמַד בַּעַל הֶחָבִית פָּטוּר. וְאִם אָמַר לוֹ לְבַעַל הַקוֹרָה עֲמוֹד חַיָּב. וְכֵן זֶה בָּא בְנֵירוֹ וְזֶה בָּא בְפִשְׁתָּנוֹ. (fol. 3b)

**Mishnah 6**: If the carrier of the beam was first and the carrier of the amphora last. If the jar broke on the beam, he[99] is not liable[100]; but if the carrier of the beam stopped walking, he is liable, except that he is not liable if he said to the carrier of the amphora: stop! If the carrier of the amphora was first and the carrier of the beam last. If the jar broke on the beam, he[99] is liable, but if the carrier of the amphora stopped walking, he is not liable, except that he[99] is liable if he[101] said to the carrier of the beam: stop! The same applies if one carries fire and the other flax[102].

99   The carrier of the beam.
100  Nobody using the public domain is required to have eyes in the back of his head.
101  The carrier of the amphora.
102  And the flax was burned.

(3d line 33) **הלכה ו:** הָיָה בַּעַל הַקּוֹרָה[103] כול'. לֹא כֵן אָמַר רַב. בִּמְמַלֵּא כָּל־רְשׁוּת הָרַבִּים. וְזוֹ מְמַלָּא כָּל־רְשׁוּת הָרַבִּים. אָמַר. כֵּיוָן שֶׁעָמַד נַעֲשָׂה כְקֶרֶן זָוִית.

**Halakhah 6**: "If the carrier of the beam," etc. Did not Rav say: If he filled the entire public domain[6,104]? (And this filled the entire public domain.)[105] One said, since he stopped, he is like a street corner[7].

103  Spelling of the Babli and the independent Mishnah mss.

104  The Mishnah only applies to a narrow path; on a wide road the second person is required not to walk directly behind the one carrying a dangerous load.

105  A corrector's addition; probably taken unthinkingly from the first paragraph of the Chapter.

(fol. 3b) **משנה ז:** שְׁנַיִם שֶׁהָיוּ מְהַלְּכִין בִּרְשׁוּת הָרַבִּים אֶחָד רָץ וְאֶחָד מְהַלֵּךְ אוֹ שֶׁהָיוּ שְׁנֵיהֶן רָצִין וְהִזִּיקוּ זֶה אֶת זֶה שְׁנֵיהֶן פְּטוּרִין.

**Mishnah 7**: Two were walking in the public domain, or one was running and one was walking, or both were running. If they caused damage one to the other, neither of them is liable[105].

105  Since both acted within their rights.

(3d line 35) **הלכה ז:** שְׁנַיִם שֶׁהָיוּ מְהַלְּכִין כול'. יוֹסֵי הַבַּבְלִי אוֹמֵר. הָיָה רָץ בִּרְשׁוּת הָרַבִּים וְהִזִּיק חַיָּיב. שְׁשִׁינָה הַמִּנְהָג. הָיָה עֶרֶב שַׁבָּת בֵּין הַשְּׁמָשׁוֹת פָּטוּר. אָמְרֵי. הוּא יוֹסֵי הַבַּבְלִי הוּא יוֹסֵי בֶּן יְהוּדָה הוּא יוֹסֵי קָטֹנְתָה. וְלָמָּה נִקְרָא שְׁמוֹ קָטֹנְתָה. שֶׁהָיָה קָטֹן חֲסִידִים.

**Halakhah 7**: "Two were walking" etc. [106]"Yose the Babylonian said: If one ran in the public domain and caused damage, he is liable. Late Friday evening he is not liable[107]." They said, Yose the Babylonian is

Yose ben Jehudah, is Yose the small one[108]. Why is he called Yose the small one? Because he was the last of the pious[109].

106 Tosephta 2:11; Babli 32a in the language of the Tosephta.

107 Anybody exceeding the speed limit is liable for any damage. But late Friday night everybody is running.

108 A longer list is in the Babli, *Pesaḥim* 113b, bottom.

109 A different version in *Soṭah*: Yerushalmi 9:17, Note 275; Babli 49b; Tosephta 15:5; *Yoma* 52b.

(fol. 3b) **משנה ח:** הַמְבַקֵּעַ בִּרְשׁוּת הַיָּחִיד וְהִזִּיק בִּרְשׁוּת הָרַבִּים בִּרְשׁוּת הָרַבִּים וְהִזִּיק בִּרְשׁוּת הַיָּחִיד בִּרְשׁוּת הַיָּחִיד וְהִזִּיק בִּרְשׁוּת הַיָּחִיד אַחֵר חַיָּב.

**Mishnah 8**: If somebody split [wood] in a private domain[110] and caused damage in the public domain, in the public domain[111] and caused damage in a private domain, in a private domain and caused damage in another private domain, he is liable.

110 A legitimate act which requires precautions to be taken because it is intrinsically dangerous.

111 An illegitimate act.

(3d line 39) **הלכה ח:** הַמְבַקֵּעַ בִּרְשׁוּת הַיָּחִיד כול׳. אָמַר רִבִּי יוֹסֵי בֶּן חֲנִינָה. הָיָה עוֹמֵד וּמְבַקֵּעַ עֵצִים בַּחֲצֵירוֹ וְנִכְנַס פּוֹעֵל לִתְבּוֹעַ שְׂכָרוֹ וְנִתְּזָה הַבְּקַעַת וְהִזִּיקַתּוּ חַיָּב. וְאִם מֵת אֵינוֹ גּוֹלֶה. וְהָתַנֵּי רִבִּי חִייָה. פָּטוּר. לֹא פְלִיגֵי. מַה דָּמַר רִבִּי יוֹסֵי. בְּשֶׁרָאָהוּ. וּמַה דָּמַר רִבִּי חִייָה. בְּשֶׁלֹּא רָאָהוּ. אִם בְּשֶׁלֹּא רָאָהוּ כֵּיוָן שֶׁאָמַר לוֹ הִיכָּנֵס חַיָּב. וְהָתַנֵּי רִבִּי חִייָה. פָּטוּר. כֵּיוָן שֶׁאָמַר לוֹ הִיכָּנֵס צָרִיךְ לִשְׁמוֹר עַצְמוֹ. וְאִית דְּבָעֵי מֵימַר. כֵּיוָן שֶׁאָמַר לוֹ הִכָּנֵס נַעֲשֵׂית כְּחָצֵר הַשּׁוּתָּפִין. דָּמַר רִבִּי יוֹחָנָן בְּשֵׁם רִבִּי יַנַּאי. הַשּׁוּתָּפִין קוֹנִין זֶה מִזֶּה בְּחָצֵר וְחַיָּיבִין זֶה בִּנְזָקֵי זֶה וְזֶה בִּנְזָקֵי זֶה. לֹא כֵן אָמַר רַב. בִּמְמַלֵּא כָּל־רְשׁוּת

הָרַבִּים. וְזוֹ מְמַלְּאָ כָּל־רְשׁוּת הָרַבִּים. אָמְרֵי. מִכֵּיוָן שֶׁדַּרְכּוֹ לְהַלֵּךְ בְּחָצֵר כְּמִי שֶׁהוּא מְמַלֵּא כָּל־הֶחָצֵר.

**Halakhah 8**: "If somebody split [wood] in a private domain," etc. [112]Rebbi Yose ben Ḥanina said, if he was splitting wood in his courtyard when a worker entered to claim[113] his wages, and a splinter ricocheted and damaged him, he is liable. If he died he does not go into exile[114]. But did not Rebbi Ḥiyya state, "he is not liable"? They do not disagree. What Rebbi Yose said, if he had seen him, but what Rebbi Ḥiyya said, if he had not seen him. If he had not seen him, once he said to him: enter, {should he not be liable? But did not Rebbi Ḥiyya state, "he is not liable"? Since he told him: enter, he has to take precautions[115]. Some want to say, since he told him to enter} it becomes like the courtyard of partners, about which Rebbi Joḥanan said in the name of Rebbi Yannai[116]: Partners acquire from one another in a courtyard and are mutually liable for damages. But did not Rav say: If he filled the entire public domain[6,104]? And did this fill the entire public domain? They said, since he[117] walks in the entire courtyard, it is as if he had filled the entire courtyard.

112 The entire paragraph is copied in *Makkot* 2:4. The text bracketed here is an addition by the corrector, probably from *Makkot*, recognizable by his standard Babli spelling. The same topic is discussed in the Babli, 32b/33a.

113 In *Makkot*: "To collect". In any case, the person entering did not trespass.

114 The responsibility of the person splitting wood in his own backyard is in civil, not in criminal law. The text in *Makkot* adds: "Because it is not as in a forest," referring to *Deut.* 19:5 which describes the circumstances under which the homicide has to dwell in a city of refuge. The Babli, 33a, quotes the end of the same verse, describing how the blade of an ax "finds his neighbor and he dies", to exclude one who walks into the path of danger (cf. *Sifry Deut.* 183).

115  In Tosephta 6:27 it is stated explicitly that the worker, who has the right to go and collect his wages, enters on his own responsibility unless invited in, at which moment the responsibility shifts to his employer.

116  *Nedarim* 5:1, Notes 22-23

117  The worker, looking for his employer to collect his wages.

(fol. 3b) **משנה ט:** שְׁנֵי שְׁוָורִים תַּמִּים שֶׁחָבְלוּ זֶה אֶת זֶה מְשַׁלְּמִים בַּמוֹתָר חֲצִי נֶזֶק. שְׁנֵיהֶן מוּעָדִין מְשַׁלְּמִין בַּמוֹתָר נֶזֶק שָׁלֵם. אֶחָד תָּם וְאֶחָד מוּעָד. מוּעָד בְּתָם מְשַׁלֵּם בַּמּוֹתָר נֶזֶק שָׁלֵם. תָּם בְּמוּעָד מְשַׁלֵּם בַּמּוֹתָר חֲצִי נֶזֶק.

**Mishnah 9**: Two tame bulls which injured one another; one pays half for the excess damage[118]. If both are notorious, one pays in full for the excess damage. One tame and one notorious; the notorious over the tame pays in full for the excess damage; the tame over the notorious pays half for the excess damage.

**משנה י:** וְכֵן שְׁנֵי אֲנָשִׁים שֶׁחָבְלוּ זֶה אֶת זֶה מְשַׁלְּמִים בַּמוֹתָר נֶזֶק שָׁלֵם. אָדָם בְּמוּעָד וּמוּעָד בְּאָדָם מְשַׁלְּמִים בַּמּוֹתָר נֶזֶק שָׁלֵם. אָדָם בְּתָם וְתָם בְּאָדָם אָדָם בְּתָם מְשַׁלֵּם בַּמּוֹתָר נֶזֶק שָׁלֵם. תָּם בְּאָדָם מְשַׁלֵּם בַּמּוֹתָר חֲצִי נֶזֶק. רִבִּי עֲקִיבָה אוֹמֵר. אַף תָּם שֶׁחָבַל בְּאָדָם מְשַׁלֵּם בַּמּוֹתָר נֶזֶק שָׁלֵם.

**Mishnah 10**: Similarly, two people who injured one another pay in full for the excess damage[119]. A human and a notorious animal, or a notorious animal and a human, one pays in full for the excess damage. A human and a tame animal; the human over the tame pays in full for the excess damage; the tame over the human pays half for the excess damage. Rebbi Akiba says, also a tame animal which injured a human pays the excess damage in full[120].

**משנה יא:** שׁוֹר שָׁוֶה מָנֶה שֶׁנָּגַח לְשׁוֹר שָׁוֶה מָאתַיִם וְאֵין הַנְּבֵילָה יָפָה כְּלוּם נוֹטֵל אֶת הַשׁוֹר. שׁוֹר שָׁוֶה מָאתַיִם שֶׁנָּגַח לְשׁוֹר שָׁוֶה מָאתַיִם וְאֵין הַנְּבֵילָה יָפָה כְּלוּם אָמַר רַבִּי מֵאִיר עַל זֶה נֶאֱמַר וּמָכְרוּ אֶת הַשׁוֹר הַחַי וְחָצוּ אֶת כַּסְפּוֹ. אָמַר לוֹ רַבִּי יְהוּדָה וְכֵן הֲלָכָה קִיַּמְתָּה וּמָכְרוּ אֶת הַשׁוֹר הַחַי וְחָצוּ אֶת כַּסְפּוֹ וְלֹא קִיַּמְתָּה וְגַם אֶת הַמֵּת יֶחֱצוּן. וְאֵי זֶה זֶה. זֶה שׁוֹר שָׁוֶה מָאתַיִם שֶׁנָּגַח לְשׁוֹר שָׁוֶה מָאתַיִם וְהַנְּבֵילָה יָפָה חֲמִשִּׁים זוּז שֶׁזֶּה נוֹטֵל חֲצִי הַחַי וַחֲצִי הַמֵּת וְזֶה נוֹטֵל חֲצִי הַחַי וַחֲצִי הַמֵּת.

**Mishnah 11:** A bull worth a mina[121] which gored a bull worth 200 and the cadaver is not worth anything; he[122] takes the bull. A bull worth 200 which gored a bull worth 200 and the cadaver is not worth anything; Rebbi Meïr said, about this case it was said[123]: "They shall sell the living bull and split the proceeds." Rebbi Jehudah said to him, you upheld "they shall sell the living bull and split the proceeds," but you did not uphold [123]"and also the cadaver they shall split." What is this? That is a bull worth 200 which gored a bull worth 200 and the cadaver is worth 50 zuz[124], in which case each owner takes half of the living bull and half from the cadaver[125].

118  Since each owner has to pay damages to the other, in effect only the owner of the bull causing the greater damage has to pay for the excess damage his animal did cause, by the statutory rate of 50% for the tame, 100% for the notorious.

119  Since a human always is notorious (2:10).

120  He holds that the rules of *Ex.* 21 do not apply to damages caused to humans.

121  100 denars.

122  The owner of the dead bull. It is presumed that the aggressor was tame and the damage be paid from its body (Mishnah 1:5).

123  *Ex.* 21:35.

124  The Babylonian half-šeqel, *zūz*, is identified with the Roman denar.

125  Tosephta 3:3; *Mekhilta dR. Ismael, Neziqin* 12.

**הלכה יא:** (3d line 53) שׁוֹר שָׁוֶה מָנָא כול'. שׁוֹר שָׁוֶה מָנָא שֶׁנָּגַח לְשׁוֹר שָׁוֶה מָנָא הִכְחִישׁוֹ חֲמִשִׁים זוּז. נוֹטֵל אֶת הַשּׁוֹר. שֶׁאֵין לוֹ אֶלָּא חֲצִי חֲבָלוֹ. לְפִיכָךְ אִם מֵת הַשּׁוֹר אוֹ שֶׁהִכְחִישׁ אֵין לוֹ אֶלָּא אוֹתוֹ הַשּׁוֹר בִּלְבַד. שׁוֹר שָׁוֶה מָנָא שֶׁנָּגַח לְשׁוֹר שָׁוֶה מָאתַיִם הִכְחִישׁוֹ חֲמִשִׁים זוּז. חָזַר הָאַחֲרוֹן וְחָבַל בּוֹ שְׁלֹשָׁה שֶׁלְּזָהָב. הָרִאשׁוֹן מְשַׁלֵּם לַשֵּׁינִי חֲצִי דִינָר זָהָב. שׁוֹר שָׁוֶה מָאתַיִם שֶׁנָּגַח שׁוֹר שָׁוֶה מָאתַיִם. הִשְׁבִּיחַ וַהֲרֵי הוּא יָפֶה אַרְבַּע מֵאוֹת. שֶׁאִילּוּ לֹא נְגָחוֹ הָיָה יָפֶה שְׁמוֹנֶה מֵאוֹת זוּז. אִם עַד שֶׁלֹּא עָמַד בַּדִּין הִשְׁבִּיחַ אֵין לוֹ אֶלָּא כִּשְׁעַת נִזְקוֹ. הִכְחִישׁ אֵין לוֹ אֶלָּא כִּשְׁעַת עֲמִידָתוֹ בְּבֵית דִּין בִּלְבַד. אָמַר רִבִּי לָא. כֵּינִי מַתְנִיתָא. הִשְׁבִּיחַ הַמַּזִּיק. אִם עַד שֶׁלֹּא עָמַד בַּדִּין הִשְׁבִּיחַ אֵין לוֹ אֶלָּא כִּשְׁעַת נִזְקוֹ. הִכְחִישׁ אֵין לוֹ אֶלָּא כִּשְׁעַת עֲמִידָתוֹ בְּבֵית דִּין.

**Halakhah 11**: "A bull worth a mina" etc. [126]"A bull worth a mina which gored a bull worth a mina; weakened (it) in the amount of 50 *zuz*; he takes the bull, for he gets only half the amount of the injury and therefore, if the bull died or was weakened, he only has that bull[127].

A bull worth a mina which gored a bull worth 200 and weakened it in the amount of 50 *zuz*; then the second [bull] couter-attacked and injured it to the amount of three gold [denars]. The first pays half a gold denar to the second[128].

A bull worth 200 which gored a bull worth 200. It increased in value and now is worth 400; but if it had not gored it, it would now be worth 800 *zuz*. If it improved before the trial it is judged as at the time of the damage[129]. If it was weakened, it is judged as at the time of the trial." Rebbi La said, so is the *baraita*: The agressor improved; if it improved before the trial it is judged as at the time of the damage; if it weakened, it is judged as at the time of the trial[130].

126 The text of this *baraita* is similar to Tosephta 2:5, but the latter is not an edition of the text underlying the Yerushalmi.

127 This sentence assumes that the first bull be tame. The first bull kills the second; the first is weakened by the fight and now is worth only half the value of the bull it killed. The owner of the dead bull takes the living one as exact payment.

128 One must read with the Tosephta: "The *second* pays half a gold denar to the *first*." The first bull damaged the second in the amount of 50 silver denar. The second damaged the first for 3 gold denar = 75 silver denar. The excess loss to be compensated for is 25 silver denar = 1 gold denar. If the bulls were tame, half a gold denar would be due.

129 The owner of the second bull can only claim the diminution of value immediately after the attack, which certainly is less than the 200 denar value of the bull at that moment, not the 400 denar of future loss.

130 When expert testimony may be taken.

(3d line 63) מָאי טַעֲמָא דְּרִבִּי מֵאִיר. אָמַר קְרָא וּמָכְרוּ אֶת הַשּׁוֹר הַחַי וְחָצוּ אֶת כַּסְפּוֹ. וּמָה מְקַיֵּים רִבִּי יְהוּדָה וְגַם אֶת הַמֵּת יֶחֱצוּן. מִיכָּן שֶׁזֶּה מַפְסִיד חֲצִי נֶזֶק וְזֶה מַפְסִיד חֲצִי נֶזֶק.

What is Rebbi Meïr's reason? The verse says, [123]"they shall sell the living bull and split its proceeds." How does Rebbi Jehudah support [123]"and also the cadaver they shall split"? From here that each one loses half the damages[131].

131 Babli 34a; Tosephta 3:3; *Mekhilta dR. Ismael Neziqin* 12; cf. Halakhah 1:3, end. The verse proves that half damages for 'horn' are paid exclusively from the proceeds of the sale of the attacking animal.

(fol. 3b) **משנה יב:** יֵשׁ חַיָּיב עַל מַעֲשֵׂה שׁוֹרוֹ וּפָטוּר עַל מַעֲשֵׂה עַצְמוֹ. פָּטוּר עַל מַעֲשֵׂה שׁוֹרוֹ וְחַיָּיב עַל מַעֲשֵׂה עַצְמוֹ. שׁוֹרוֹ שֶׁבִּייֵּשׁ פָּטוּר וְהוּא שֶׁבִּייֵּשׁ חַיָּיב. שׁוֹרוֹ שֶׁסִּימָה אֶת עֵין עַבְדּוֹ וְהִפִּיל אֶת שִׁנּוֹ פָּטוּר וְהוּא שֶׁסִּימָא אֶת עֵין עַבְדּוֹ וְהִפִּיל אֶת שִׁנּוֹ חַיָּיב. שׁוֹרוֹ שֶׁחָבַל בְּאָבִיו וּבְאִמּוֹ חַיָּיב וְהוּא שֶׁחָבַל בְּאָבִיו וּבְאִמּוֹ פָּטוּר. שׁוֹרוֹ שֶׁהִדְלִיק אֶת הַגָּדִישׁ בַּשַּׁבָּת חַיָּיב וְהוּא שֶׁהִדְלִיק אֶת הַגָּדִישׁ בַּשַּׁבָּת פָּטוּר מִפְּנֵי שֶׁנִּידּוֹן בְּנַפְשׁוֹ.

**Mishnah 12**: A person may be liable for the action of his bull but not liable for his own action, not liable for the action of his bull but liable for his own action: If his bull puts to shame, he is not liable;[132] but if he put to shame, he is liable. If his bull blinded the eye of his slave or knocked out his tooth, he is not liable; but if he himself blinded the eye of his slave or knocked out his tooth, he is liable[133]. If his bull injured his father or his mother, he is liable[134]; but if he himself injured his father or his mother, he is not liable[135]. If his bull set fire to a stack of sheaves on the Sabbath; he is liable, but if he set fire to a stack of sheaves on the Sabbath, he is not liable since he will be tried for a capital crime[135].

**משנה יג:** שׁוֹר שֶׁהָיָה רוֹדֵף אַחַר שׁוֹר אַחֵר וְהוּזַק. זֶה אוֹמֵר שׁוֹרְךָ הִזִּיק וְזֶה אוֹמֵר לֹא כִּי אֶלָּא בַּסֶּלַע לָקָה הַמּוֹצִיא מֵחֲבֵירוֹ עָלָיו הָרְאָיָה.

**Mishnah 13**: If a bull was pursuing another bull which was damaged. This one says, your bull did the damage, but the other one says, it was hurt by a rock; the burden of proof is on the claimant[136].

**משנה יד:** הָיוּ שְׁנַיִם רוֹדְפִים אַחַר אֶחָד זֶה אוֹמֵר שׁוֹרְךָ הִזִּיק וְזֶה אוֹמֵר שׁוֹרְךָ הִזִּיק שְׁנֵיהֶן פְּטוּרִין. וְאִם הָיוּ שְׁנֵיהֶן שֶׁל אִישׁ אֶחָד שְׁנֵיהֶן חַיָּיבִין.

**Mishnah 14**: If two [bulls] were pursuing another [bull]; each of them says: your bull did the damage; neither of them is liable. But if they belonged to one owner, he is liable for both of them.

**משנה טו**: הָיָה אֶחָד גָּדוֹל וְאֶחָד קָטוֹן הַנִּיזָּק אוֹמֵר הַגָּדוֹל הִזִּיק וְהַמַּזִּיק אוֹמֵר לֹא כִּי אֶלָּא הַקָּטָן הִזִּיק. אֶחָד תָּם וְאֶחָד מוּעָד הַנִּיזָּק אוֹמֵר מוּעָד הִזִּיק וְהַמַּזִּיק אוֹמֵר לֹא כִּי אֶלָּא תָם הִזִּיק. הַמּוֹצִיא מֵחֲבֵירוֹ עָלָיו הָרְאָיָה.

**Mishnah 15**: If one was large, the other small. The person sustaining the damage says that the large one did the damage[137] but the person causing the damage says that the small one did the damage, the burden of proof is on the claimant.

**משנה יו**: הָיוּ הַנִּיזָּקִין שְׁנַיִם אֶחָד גָּדוֹל וְאֶחָד קָטָן וְהַמַּזִּיקִים שְׁנַיִם אֶחָד גָּדוֹל וְאֶחָד קָטָן. הַנִּיזָּק אוֹמֵר הַגָּדוֹל הִזִּיק אֶת הַגָּדוֹל וְקָטָן אֶת הַקָּטָן וְהַמַּזִּיק אוֹמֵר לֹא כִּי אֶלָּא קָטוֹן אֶת הַגָּדוֹל וְגָדוֹל אֶת הַקָּטָן. אֶחָד תָּם וְאֶחָד מוּעָד הַנִּיזָּק אוֹמֵר מוּעָד הִזִּיק אֶת הַגָּדוֹל וְתָם אֶת הַקָּטָן וְהַמַּזִּיק אוֹמֵר לֹא כִּי אֶלָּא תָם אֶת הַגָּדוֹל וּמוּעָד אֶת הַקָּטָן. הַמּוֹצִיא מֵחֲבֵירוֹ עָלָיו הָרְאָיָה.

**Mishnah 16**: If two were damaged, one large and one small, and the [bulls] doing the damage were two, one large and one small. The person sustaining the damage says that the large one damaged the large one[137] and the small one the small; but the person causing the damage says that the small one did damage the large one and the large one the small. [Or] one tame and one notorious, the person sustaining the damage says that the notorious one damaged the large one[138] and the tame one the small; but the person causing the damage says that the tame one did damage the large one and the notorious one the small. The burden of proof is on the claimant.

132  An animal cannot insult a human; cf. Chapter 1, Note 17.

133  The rules of *Ex.* 21:26-27 decree only that a slave gain his freedom if he is mistreated by his owner personally.

134  As for injury to any third person.

135  Since he committed a capital crime (*Ex.* 21:15) and nobody has to pay if he is tried for his life (*Terumot*

7:1, Notes 3-73; *Ketubot* 3:1).

136   Without proof that stands up in court he cannot collect any damages.

137   Since for claims of damages caused by a 'tame' animal the amount which can be recovered is limited by the value of the attacking animal (Note 131, Mishnah 1:5), the person suffering the loss is interested in raising that limit.

138   In order to recover his entire loss without limitation.

**הלכה ט:** שְׁנֵי שְׁוָורִין תַּמִּים כול'. בֶּן פְּדָיָיא אָמַר. כָּל־הַמְקַלְקְלִין פְּטוּרִין חוּץ מִן הַמַּבְעִיר וְהָעוֹשֶׂה חַבּוּרָה. אָמַר רִבִּי יוֹחָנָן. בְּמַעֲבִיר אֵינוֹ חַיָּיב עַד שֶׁיְּהֵא צָרִיךְ לָאֵפֶר. וְהָעוֹשֶׂה חַבּוּרָה עַד שֶׁיְּהֵא צָרִיךְ לַדָּם. וְהָתַנִּינָן. שׁוֹרוֹ. שׁוֹרוֹ צָרִיךְ אֶת הָאֵפֶר. (3d line 49)

**Halakhah 9**[139]: "Two tame bulls," etc. [140]Ben Pedaia said: Spoilers are not liable[141] except for one making a fire and one causing a wound. Rebbi Joḥanan said, one making a fire only if he needs the ashes; one causing a wound only if he needs the blood[142]. But did we not state: "His bull"[143]? His bull needs ashes[144].

139   The ms. has the text placed correctly after Halakhah 11 but with a wrong header, "Halakhah 9". In the *editio princeps*, the paragraph was then wrongly inserted after Halakhah 8; it refers to Mishnah 12.

140   The parallels are *Šabbat* 2:2 (5a l. 31), *Erubin* 10:12 (26c l. 47), *Pesaḥim* 6:1 (33b l. 34); Babli *Bava qamma* 34b, *Šabbat* 106a, *Beṣah* 12b, *Yebamot* 16b, *Sanhedrin* 62b.

141   "Liable" and "not liable" here mean "guilty" and "not guilty" under the laws of the Sabbath. In the first introductory paragraph to the laws of the Sabbath (*Ex.* 16:29) only leaving the camp was forbidden. In the Ten Commandments (*Ex.* 20:10), "all work" is forbidden without a definition of what constitutes "work". The missing definition is deduced from *Ex.* 35. That Chapter starts with a repetition of the Sabbath prohibitions and then proceeds with the instructions for the building of the Tabernacle. One concludes that the work necessary for building the Tabernacle is the work forbidden on the Sabbath (*Mekhilta dR.*

*Ismael, Wayyaqhel*). Then in v. 33 the work of Beṣalel and Aholiab, the builders of the Tabernacle, is defined as מְלֶאכֶת מַחֲשֶׁבֶת "thinking work". The only work which constitutes a punishable desecration of the Sabbath is intentional constructive work. Therefore, any purely destructive work is not punishable.

142  Without exception, destructive work without positive effects is not punishable.

143  In the Mishnah here.

144  As the Babli explains, 35a, an intelligent bull which has a wound on its back sets a fire because it needs the ashes to wallow in them to ease its pain.

(3d line 66) **הלכה יב:** יֵשׁ חַיָּיב עַל מַעֲשֵׂה שׁוֹרוֹ כול'. רִבִּי יוּדָן בָּעֵי. הָדֵין עֲמָדַת בֵּית דִּין מַהוּ. נִשְׁמְעִינָהּ מֵהָדָא. שְׁנַיִם שֶׁזָּרְקוּ שְׁתֵּי צְרוֹרוֹת וְשִׁיבְּרוּ שְׁתֵּי כַדִּים אַחַת שְׁלֵייָן וְאַחַת שֶׁלְּשֶׁמֶן. זֶה אוֹמֵר. שֶׁלְּיַיִן שָׁבַרְתִּי. וְזֶה אוֹמֵר. שֶׁלְּיַיִן שָׁבַרְתִּי. שְׁנֵיהֶן מְשַׁלְּמִין שֶׁלְּיַיִן. אַחַת רֵיקָנִית וְאַחַת מְלֵיאָה. זֶה אוֹמֵר. רֵיקָנִית שָׁבַרְתִּי. וְזֶה אוֹמֵר. רֵיקָנִית שָׁבַרְתִּי. שְׁנֵיהֶן מְשַׁלְּמִין אֶת הָרֵיקָנִית. שִׁיבְּרוּ חָבִית אַחַת. זֶה אוֹמֵר. אַתָּה שְׁבַרְתָּהּ. וְזֶה אוֹמֵר. אַתָּה שְׁבַרְתָּהּ. שְׁנֵיהֶן פְּטוּרִין.

**Halakhah 12:** "A person may be liable for the action of his bull," etc. Rebbi Yudan asked: How is the court trial[145]? Let us hear from the following: "Two persons threw two pebbles and broke two jugs, one full of wine and one full of oil. Each of them said, I broke the one full of wine. Both of them pay for the wine. One empty and one full; each of them said, I broke the empty one. Both of them pay for the empty one. If they broke one amphora. Each of them said, you broke it. Neither of them is liable.

145  This really is a continuation of examples to Mishnaiot 13-16 applying the principle that "the burden of proof is on the claimant", even if the resulting judgment be logically inconsistent.

## שור שנגח ארבעה וחמשה פרק רביעי

(fol. 4a) **משנה א:** שׁוֹר שֶׁנָּגַח אַרְבָּעָה וַחֲמִשָּׁה שְׁוָרִין זֶה אַחַר זֶה יְשַׁלֵּם לָאַחֲרוֹן שֶׁבָּהֶן. אִם יֵשׁ בּוֹ מוֹתָר יַחֲזִיר לְשֶׁלְּפָנָיו וְאִם יֵשׁ בּוֹ מוֹתָר יַחֲזִיר לְשֶׁלִּפְנֵי פָנָיו הָאַחֲרוֹן אַחֲרוֹן נִשְׂכָּר דִּבְרֵי רבי מֵאִיר. רַבִּי שִׁמְעוֹן אוֹמֵר שׁוֹר שָׁוֶה מָאתַיִם שֶׁנָּגַח שׁוֹר שָׁוֶה מָאתַיִם וְאֵין הַנְּבֵילָה שָׁוָה כְלוּם זֶה נוֹטֵל מָנֶה וְזֶה נוֹטֵל מָנֶה. חָזַר וְנָגַח לְשׁוֹר אַחֵר שָׁוֶה מָאתַיִם הָאַחֲרוֹן נוֹטֵל מָנֶה וְשֶׁלְּפָנָיו זֶה נוֹטֵל חֲמִשִּׁים וְזֶה נוֹטֵל חֲמִשִּׁים. חָזַר וְנָגַח שׁוֹר שָׁוֶה מָאתַיִם הָאַחֲרוֹן נוֹטֵל מָנָא וְשֶׁלְּפָנָיו חֲמִשִּׁים זוּז וּשְׁנַיִם הָרִאשׁוֹנִים דִּינְרֵי זָהָב.

**Mishnah 1**: A bull which gored four or five bulls, one after the other[1], should pay for the last of them[2]. If there is anything left, it should revert to the penultimate. If then there is anything left, it should revert to the one before the penultimate. The later one is always advantaged, the words of Rebbi Meïr. Rebbi Simeon[3] says, if a bull worth 200 gored a bull worth 200 and the carcass is not worth anything, each one takes a mina. If then it gored another bull worth 200, the last one takes 100 and the preceding each take 50. If then it gored another bull worth 200, the last one takes 100, the preceding one takes 50 zuz[4], and the two first ones each a gold denar[5].

1  A tame bull went on a goring spree before it could be declared notorious in court. The damage which it caused has to be liquidated by the rules of the tame bull; i. e., the bull has to be sold and from the proceeds half the damages have to be paid.

2  According to R. Meïr, a bull

which gored becomes the property of its victim's owner. The original owner has a claim to the excess of the sale price over the claim for restitution.

Assuming that the bull was worth $a$; it gored $n$ bulls, worth $a_1, a_2, \ldots, a_n$. The owner of the last bull claims $a_n/2$ from the owner of the bull gored as the penultimate. If $a - a_n/2 > 0$, the owner of that bull satisfies himself up to the amount $a_{n-1}/2$. If $a - a_n/2 - a_{n-1}/2 > 0$, the preceding owner can satisfy himself up to $a_{n-2}/2$, and so on until all of the proceeds $a$ are used up. In practically all cases, the owner of the attacking bull ends up with nothing.

3  He holds that the original owner

and the owner of the victim become co-owners of the attacking bull. The last owner takes $a/2$; the owner of the penultimate victim then is a 50% owner of the remaining $a/2$, and so on. In this way, the owner of the $j$-th bull gored gets $a/2^{n-j+1}$; the owner of the attacking bull is left with the same amount as the one given to the owner of the first victim, $a/2^n$.

If the values of the bulls are distinct, the last owner takes $a_n/2$, the one before him

$$\min(a_{n-1}/2,\ a/2 - a_n/4)$$

and so on.

4  Silver denars.

5  25 silver denars.

(4a line 45) **הלכה א:** שׁוֹר שֶׁנָּגַח אַרְבָּעָה וַחֲמִשָּׁה שְׁוָרִין כול׳. אָמַר רִבִּי יַנַּאי. בָּא עָלָיו רִבִּי מֵאִיר מִשְּׁנֵי צְדָדִין. מַה נַּפְשָׁךְ. שֶׁלָּךְ הוּא תְּנֵיהוּ לוֹ. אֵינוֹ שֶׁלָּךְ תְּנֵיהוּ לִי שֶׁאֶגָּבֵנּוּ. וְלֹא כֵן אָמַר רִבִּי לֶעְזָר. שְׁמִירַת נְזָקָיו כִּשְׁמִירַת קִנְיָינוֹ. אָמַר לוֹ רִבִּי יוּדָן. וּמְסָרוֹ לוֹ לִנְזָקִין וְאֵינוֹ אֶלָּא מַשְׁכּוֹן בְּיָדוֹ.

**Halakhah 1:** "A bull which gored four or five bulls," etc. [6]Rebbi Yannai said, Rebbi Meïr attacks him[7] from two sides: As you take it, if it is yours[8], give it to me. If it is not yours[9], hand it over to me that I may satisfy my claim. But did not Rebbi Eleazar say, the guarding of damages parallels the guarding of acquisitions[10]? [11]Rebbi Jehudah told him, it was delivered to him for his damages but it remains a pledge[12].

6  The basic explanation of this paragraph is given by Nachmanides,

*Milḥamot Hashem*, to Mishnah 4:1.

7  The arguments given to the

owner of the bull gored last against the owner of the bull gored as the penultimate.

8   As explained in Note 2.

9   But you are part owner as claimed by R. Simeon.

10   The property rights given by the Torah to the owner of the dead bull is one of ownership, not possession (cf. *Qiddušin* 1, Note 352). Therefore, the potential owner of the bull cannot be liable for the damages done by an animal not in his actual possession.

11   In the Babli, 26b, this is labelled as R. Aqiba's opinion.

12   Since he becomes owner for monetary gain, he is obligated for damages as if he were a paid trustee. The second argument attributed to R. Meïr really is valid only if the penultimate owner actually took possession of the offending bull.

(4a line 49) וּמַה בֵּינֵיהוֹן. רִבִּי יוֹחָנָן אָמַר. הֶקְדֵּשׁ בֵּינֵיהוֹן. עַל דַּעְתֵּיהּ דְּרִבִּי יוּדָה. מַקְדִּישׁ הָרִאשׁוֹן. עַל דַּעְתֵּיהּ דְּרִבִּי מֵאִיר. שְׁנֵיהֶן מַקְדִּישִׁין אוֹתוֹ. הוֹקִיר. עַל דַּעְתֵּיהּ דְּרִבִּי יוּדָה. הוֹקְרָה לָרִאשׁוֹן. עַל דַּעְתֵּיהּ דְּרִבִּי מֵאִיר. הוֹקְרָה לַשֵּׁינִי. עָשָׂה שָׂכָר. עַל דַּעְתֵּיהּ דְּרִבִּי יְהוּדָה. הַשָּׂכָר לָרִאשׁוֹן. עַל דַּעְתֵּיהּ דְּרִבִּי מֵאִיר. הַשָּׂכָר לִשְׁנֵיהֶן. הִשְׁבִּיחַ. עַל דַּעְתֵּיהּ דְּרִבִּי יוּדָן. הִשְׁבִּיחַ לָרִאשׁוֹן. עַל דַּעְתֵּיהּ דְּרִבִּי מֵאִיר. הִשְׁבִּיחַ לִשְׁנֵיהֶן.

What is between them? Rebbi Johanan said, dedication is between them. In Rebbi Jehudah's opinion, the first [owner][13] may dedicate[14]. In Rebbi Meïr's opinion, [only] both together may dedicate it[15]. If it went up in price. In Rebbi Jehudah's opinion, it increased for the first. In Rebbi Meïr's opinion, it increased for the second. If it was rented out, in Rebbi Jehudah's opinion, the rent belongs to the first. In Rebbi Meïr's opinion, [the rent] belongs to both of them. If it improved[16], in Rebbi Jehudah's opinion, the improvement belongs to the first. In Rebbi Meïr's opinion, the improvement belongs to both of them.

13  In this paragraph, one assumes that the bull gored only once. The first owner is the original one; the second is the the owner of the dead bull.

14  The second owner is co-owner, but as long as he did not actually take possession of the bull, the first can pay him off as mortgage-holder and be both owner and in possession. Therefore, only he may dedicate since nobody can dedicate what is not in his possession (cf. *Ketubot* 5:5, Notes 105-106; Tosephta 5:1; Babli 33b).

15  While the bull is still in the possession of the first, ownership belongs to the second. They can only act together. The same reasoning applies to the following examples.

16  Cf. Chapter 3, Note 130.

(4a line 53) אָמַר רִבִּי יוֹחָנָן. רִבִּי יוּדָה וְרִבִּי שִׁמְעוֹן שְׁנֵיהֶן אָמְרוּ דָבָר אֶחָד. כְּמָה דְרִבִּי יוּדָה אָמַר. קָנָה. כֵּן רִבִּי שִׁמְעוֹן אָמַר. קָנָה. אֶלָּא שֶׁרִבִּי יוּדָן אוֹמֵר. קָנָה לַחַי קָנָה לַמֵּת. וְרִבִּי שִׁמְעוֹן אוֹמֵר. לֹא קָנָה אֶלָּא לַמֵּת בִּלְבָד.

Rebbi Joḥanan said, Rebbi Jehudah and Rebbi Simeon stated the same. Just as Rebbi Jehudah said, he acquired, so Rebbi Simeon said, he acquired[17], only that Rebbi Jehudah says, he acquired the living and the dead[18]; but Rebbi Simeon says he only acquired the (dead)[19].

17  The owner of the injured animal becomes part owner with the owner of the attacker.

18  Chapter 3, Note 135; Tosephta 3:3. The owner of the attacker also becomes part owner of the carcass.

19  This certainly should read: the living. R. Simeon only discusses the case that the carcass be without value; this skirts the issue of ownership of an injured animal.

(4a line 55) תַּמָּן תַּנִּינָן. וְכֵן שְׁלֹשָׁה שֶׁהִטִּילוּ לַכִּיס. הוֹתִירוּ אוֹ פָּחֲתוּ כָּךְ הֵן חוֹלְקִין. אָמַר רִבִּי בּוּן. נִרְאִין דְּבָרִים בְּשֶׁנְּטָלוּ מַרְגָּלִית. דִּיכוֹל מֵימַר לֵיהּ אִילּוּלֵי עֲשַׂרְתֵּי דִינָרַיי לֹא הֲוִיתָהּ מְזַבִּין כְּלוּן. אֲבָל דָּבָר שֶׁדַּרְכּוֹ לְחַלֵּק מְבִיאִין לָאֶמְצַע וְחוֹלְקִין. אָמַר רִבִּי לְעָזָר וַאֲפִילוּ דָּבָר שֶׁדַּרְכּוֹ לְחַלֵּק. דִּיכִיל מֵימַר לֵיהּ.

אַתְּ פְּרַגְמַטְיָא דִידָךְ סַגִּין וְאַתְּ מַנְעָא מַזְבְּנְתָּא. אֲנָא פְּרַגְמַטְיָא דִידִי קָלִיל וַאֲנָא הָפַךְ וּמִתְהַפֵּךְ בְּדִידִי וּמָטֵי בָךְ. עַד כְּדוֹן בְּשֶׁהָיְיתָה פְּרַגְמַטַיִיו נְתוּנָה כָאן. הָיְתָה פְּרַגְמַטַיִיו נְתוּנָה בְּרוֹמֵי. דִיכִיל מֵימַר לֵיהּ. עַד דְּאַתְּ סָלִיק לְרוֹמֵי אֲנָא הָפַךְ וּמִתְהַפֵּךְ בְּדִידִי הָכָא וּמָטֵי בָךְ.

[20]There, we have stated: "Similarly, if three who invested together lost or gained they would split in this manner." Rebbi Abun said, the statement looks reasonable if they bought a precious stone because he can say to him, without my ten denars you could not have bought anything. But anything that usually is split {smaller units that can be bought with less capital} one adds together and splits {proportionally to the capital invested}. Rebbi Eleazar says, even things that usually are split [are divided evenly], because he can say to him, you have a lot of merchandise and you have difficulty selling it. I have little merchandise and turn it over rapidly and make as much as you do. So far if his merchandise was here. What if his merchandise was in Rome? He can say to him, by the time you went to Rome, I turn mine over rapidly here and make as much as you do.

20    Mishnah *Ketubot* 10:4. The text and its relation to the corresponding one in *Ketubot* 10:4 is explained there in Notes 73-75.

(4a line 66) תַּנֵּי. שְׁלֹשָׁה שֶׁהֵטִילוּ לַכִּיס וְנִגְנְבוּ כָּךְ הֵן חוֹלְקִין. וְהָתַנֵּי. בְּאִילוּ אֲבָנִים וְנִגְנְבוּ מֶחֱצָה לָזֶה וּמֶחֱצָה לָזֶה. אָמַר רִבִּי שַׁמַּי. סְלָעִים גַּסּוֹת הֵן וְאֶיפְשָׁר לִבְלוֹל לָצֵאת יְדֵי כוּלָּן. אֲבָל אֲבָנִים דַּקּוֹת הֵן וְלֵית יְדַע אִי מִן הָדֵין נְסַב אִי מִן הָדֵין נְסָב. מְסֻפָּק כָּל־אֶחָד נוֹטֵל לְפִי כִיסוֹ. מַה חָמִית בִּגְנֵיבָה מֵימַר אֲנָן קַיָּימִין אוֹ אֵינָן קַיָּימִין אֶלָּא בִּמְשֻׁתָּיֵיר. אָמַר רִבִּי יוֹסֵי בֵּירִבִּי בּוּן. וַאֲפִילוּ תֵימַר. בִּגְנֵיבָה אֲנָן קַיָּימִין. נִמְצֵאת מִידַּת הַדִּין לוֹקָה. הַגַּע עַצְמָךְ.

דַּהֲוָה לְדֵין חַמְשִׁין וּלְדֵין מֵאָה וְחַמְשִׁין. נִגְנְבוּ חַמְשִׁין אִישְׁתַּכַּח דְּהָדֵין דַּחֲמִשִׁיתָא דְּלָא מַפְסִיד כְּלוּם.

It was stated: [21]Three who invested together and suffered theft, absorb [the loss] in the same way[22]. But was it not stated: If those [precious] stones were stolen, half for each one[23]. Rebbi Shammai said, tetradrachmas are large[24] and it is possible to subdivide exactly but stones are easy[24] and it is impossible to know which part in it belongs to whom. Because of the doubt, each one takes proportional to his investment. What did you see to say that we deal with theft, maybe one deals only with what is left[25]? Rebbi Yose ben Rebbi Abun said, even if you say that we deal with theft, would not equity be hurt? Think of it, if one invested 50 and the other 150. If 50 was stolen, would not the one with 50 not lose anything[26]?

21  Tosephta *Ketubot* 10:4.

22  The distribution algorithm described in *Ketubot* 10:4 (Note 62).

23  Each of the investors absorbs the same amount of loss.

24  Probably one should interchange the positions of "large" and "easy". Money can be divided easily and exactly; precious stones are a one or nothing affair as noted in the preceding paragraph.

25  Which is money and therefore easily distributed.

26  This is difficult to understand. There are 150 left and the sum total of the claims is 200. By the method of Mishnah *Ketubot* 10:4, the first 50 are claimed by both investors, the remaining 100 only by the second. Therefore, the first gets 25, the second 125; each one loses 25. If the loss were distributed proportional to the investment, the first investor would take 37.5, the second 113.5. It is a matter of opinion which method be more equitable.

(4a line 75) תַּמָּן תַּנִּינָן. הָאַחֲרוֹן נוֹטֵל מָנֶה וְשֶׁלְּפָנָיו חֲמִשִּׁים זוּז. וּשְׁנַיִם הָרִאשׁוֹנִים דֵּינָרֵי זָהָב. רִבִּי שְׁמוּאֵל בְּשֵׁם רִבִּי זְעִירָא. וְכֵן לְשָׂכָר. אָמַר רִבִּי יוֹסֵי. הָדָא דְּרִבִּי זֵירָא פְּלִיגָא עַל דְּרִבִּי לְעָזָר. אָמַר רִבִּי מָנִי. קַשְׁיָיתָהּ קוֹמֵי רִבִּי יוּדָן. אָמַר לִי. לֹא מוֹדֶה רִבִּי לְעָזָר שֶׁאִם הִתְנוּ בֵּינֵיהֶן שֶׁזֶּה נוֹטֵל לְפִי כִיסוֹ וְזֶה נוֹטֵל לְפִי כִיסוֹ. שְׁוָורִים כְּמוּתָנִין הֵן. חָזַר וְאָמְרָהּ קוֹמֵי רִבִּי יוֹסֵי. אָמַר לֵיהּ. בְּפֵירוּשׁ פְּלִיגֵי. רִבִּי לְעָזָר אָמַר. סְתַמָּן חוֹלְקִין בְּשָׁוֶה. רִבִּי זְעִירָא אָמַר. סְתַמָּן זֶה נוֹטֵל לְפִי כִיסוֹ וְזֶה נוֹטֵל לְפִי כִיסוֹ.

[27]There, we have stated: "If [the ox] gored an ox worth 200, the last one takes 100, the one before him 50, and the two first ones each a gold denar." Rebbi Samuel in the name of Rebbi Ze'ira: The same holds for earnings. Rebbi Yose said, the statement of Rebbi Ze'ira disagrees with Rebbi Eleazar. Rebbi Mani said, I asked this before Rebbi Yudan. He said to me: does Rebbi Eleazar not agree if they contracted between themselves that each can take according to his contribution? Oxen are as if contracted. He turned around and said this before Rebbi Yose, who answered him, they disagree explicitly: Rebbi Eleazar said, if nothing was said, they split evenly; Rebbi Ze'ira said, if nothing was said, each takes according to his contribution.

27    Cf. *Ketubot* 10:4, Notes 76-79.

(fol. 4a) **מִשְׁנָה ב:** שׁוֹר שֶׁהוּא מוּעָד לְמִינוֹ וְאֵינוֹ מוּעָד לְשֶׁאֵינוֹ מִינוֹ. מוּעָד לָאָדָם וְאֵינוֹ מוּעָד לַבְּהֵמָה. מוּעָד לַקְּטַנִּים וְאֵינוֹ מוּעָד לַגְּדוֹלִים. אֶת שֶׁהוּא מוּעָד לוֹ מְשַׁלֵּם נֶזֶק שָׁלֵם וְאֶת שֶׁאֵינוֹ מוּעָד לוֹ מְשַׁלֵּם חֲצִי נֶזֶק. אָמְרוּ לִפְנֵי רִבִּי יְהוּדָה הֲרֵי שֶׁהָיָה מוּעָד בַּשַּׁבָּתוֹת וְאֵין מוּעָד בִּימוֹת הַחוֹל. אָמַר לָהֶם בַּשַּׁבָּתוֹת

מְשַׁלֵּם נֶזֶק שָׁלֵם וּבִימוֹת הַחוֹל מְשַׁלֵּם חֲצִי נֶזֶק. אֵימָתַי הוּא תָם מִשֶּׁיַּחֲזוֹר בּוֹ שְׁלֹשֶׁת יְמֵי שַׁבָּתוֹת.

**Mishnah 2**: A bull which is notorious for its kind but not notorious for other species, notorious for humans but not notorious for animals, notorious for small ones but not notorious for large ones, pays full damages for what it is notorious for, but half damages for what it is not notorious for. They asked before Rebbi Jehudah: If it was notorious on the Sabbath but not on weekdays? He answered, it pays full damages on Sabbaths but half damages on weekdays. When does it revert to be tame? If it changed its ways for three Sabbath days[28].

28  Following R. Jehuda's opinion in Mishnah 2:6.

(4b line 6) **הלכה ב**: שׁוֹר שֶׁהוּא מוּעָד לְמִינוֹ כול'. מִכֵּיוָן שֶׁהָרַג אָדָם אֶחָד אֵינוֹ מוּעָד. רַב אָמַר. בְּשֶׁהָרַג שְׁלֹשָׁה גּוֹיִם. רִבִּי יוֹסֵי בֶּן חֲנִינָה אָמַר. בְּשֶׁרָדַף שְׁלֹשָׁה רְדִיפוֹת וְהֵן מְשַׁעֲרִין שֶׁיֵּשׁ בִּרְדִיפָתוֹ נְגִיחָה.

**Halakhah 2** "A bull which is notorious for its kind," etc. After it killed one human, is it not notorious[29]? Rav said, if it killed three Gentiles[30]. Rebbi Yose ben Ḥanina said, if it pursued three times and it was estimated that every pursuit was for goring[31].

29  Any animal which killed "a man or a woman" has to be killed (*Ex.* 21:28). How can such an animal ever become notorious after three times if it is killed after the first time?

30  Who are not subsumed under the appellation "man or woman". Babli 41a, in the name of Rav Sheshet.

31  For endangering humans, an animal may become notorious for trying three times.

(4a line 9) שֶׁאִים יָצָא בַּיּוֹם רִאשׁוֹן וְנָגַח שְׁוָורִים. בַּשֵּׁינִי וְנָגַח כְּלָבִים. בַּשְּׁלִישִׁי וְנָגַח חֲזִירִים. עַל יְדֵי ג׳ מִינִין לְג׳ יָמִים מַהוּ שֶׁיֵּעָשֶׂה שׁוֹר מוּעָד. יָצָא בַּיּוֹם רִאשׁוֹן וְנָגַח. בַּשֵּׁינִי לֹא יָצָא. בַּשְּׁלִישִׁי יָצָא וְנָגַח וכו׳. יָבֹא כִפְלוּגְתָּא דְּרַב אָדָא בַּר אַחְוָוא וּדְרַב הוּנָא. דְּאִיתְפַּלְגוּן. נִידָה שֶׁבֶּדְקָה עַצְמָהּ. בַּיּוֹם רִאשׁוֹן בֶּדְקָה וּמְצָתָהּ טָמֵא. בַּשֵּׁינִי לֹא בֶדְקָה. בַּשְּׁלִישִׁי בֶּדְקָה וּמְצָתָהּ טָמֵא. רַב אָדָא בַּר אַחְוָוא בְּשֵׁם רַב. נִידָה וַדַּאי. רַב הוּנָא בְּשֵׁם רַב אָמַר. נִדָּה סָפֵק. אָמַר רַב הוּנָא. תַּמָּן הֲוִינָא בְּרֵישָׁא וּבְסֵיפָהּ וּבְאֶמְצָעִיתָהּ. אִישְׁתָּאַלַת לְרַב וְאָמַר. סָפֵק. אִישְׁתָּאַלַת לְרַב וְאָמַר. וַדַּאי. חָזַר וְאָמַר. סָפֵק. וְרַב אָדָא בַּר אַחְוָוא לֹא הֲוָה תַּמָּן אֶלָּא כַּד מַר. וַדַּאי.

[32]If it was let out the first day and gored bulls, the second it gored dogs, the third it gored pigs: would it be declared a notorious bull for three different kinds on three days? If it was let out the first day and gored, the second day it was not let out, the third day it was let out and gored, we come to the disagreement between Rav Ada bar Ahawa and Rav Huna, who disagreed: A menstruating woman checked herself the first day and found herself impure. The second day she did not check. On the third day she checked and found herself impure. Rav Ada bar Ahawa said in the name of Rav: she certainly is *niddah*. Rav Huna said in the name of Rav: it is doubtful whether she is *niddah*. Rav Huna said, I was there at the beginning, I was there at the end, and I was there in the middle when Rav was asked, and he said, it is doubtful. Rav was asked and he said, it is certain; then he reversed himself and said, it is doubtful. Rav Ada bar Ahawa was only there when he said, it is certain.

רַב יִרְמְיָה בְּשֵׁם רַב אָמַר. הֲלָכָה כְּרִבִּי מֵאִיר בְּתַמָּה וּכְרִבִּי יוּדָה בְּהַוְּעָדָאָה.

Rav Jeremiah said in the name of Rav: Practice follows Rebbi Meïr for the tame animal and Rebbi Jehudah for testimony.

32 Halakhah 2:6, Notes 90-96.

(4b line 20) הָוֵינָן סָבְרִין מֵימַר. מַאי טַעֲמָא דְרִבִּי יוּדָה. מִכֵּיוָן דּוּ חֲמִי לוֹן לְבִישִׁין נְקִיִּין עוֹד הוּא מְשַׁנֶּה דַעְתֵּיהּ.

We wanted to ask: what is the reason of Rebbi Jehudah[33]? Because it sees us dressed[34] cleanly, it changes its behavior.

33 He accepts that a bull may be notorious only for the Sabbath. Is it reasonable to expect animals to change their behavior according to a human calendar?

34 E reads מניין נקיין, a misspelling for מָנִין נְקִיִּין "clean garments". Quoted in Hebrew translation by Tosaphot 37a s.v. הרי; explaining that the bull does not recognize its master and attendants wearing Sabbath clothing.

(fol. 4a) **משנה ג**: שׁוֹר שֶׁל יִשְׂרָאֵל שֶׁנָּגַח שׁוֹר שֶׁל הֶקְדֵּשׁ וְשֶׁל הֶקְדֵּשׁ שֶׁנָּגַח לְשׁוֹר שֶׁלְּיִשְׂרָאֵל פָּטוּר שֶׁנֶּאֱמַר שׁוֹר רֵעֵהוּ וְלֹא שׁוֹר הֶקְדֵּשׁ.

Mishnah 3: The bull of an Israel which gored a bull of Temple property or the bull of Temple property which gored a bull of an Israel are not liable since it was said "his neighbor's bull"[35], not a bull of Temple property.

**משנה ד**: שׁוֹר שֶׁל יִשְׂרָאֵל שֶׁנָּגַח לְשׁוֹר שֶׁל נָכְרִי פָּטוּר וְשֶׁלַּנָּכְרִי נָכְרִי שֶׁנָּגַח לְשׁוֹר שֶׁל יִשְׂרָאֵל בֵּין תָּם בֵּין מוּעָד מְשַׁלֵּם נֶזֶק שָׁלֵם.

Mishnah 4: The bull of an Israel which gored a bull of a non-Jew is not liable; the bull of a non-Jew which gored a bull of an Israel pays full damages, whether tame or notorious.

35 *Ex.* 21:35.

**הלכה ד:** (4b line 22) שׁוֹר שֶׁלַּיִשְׂרָאֵל שֶׁנָּגַח לְשׁוֹר שֶׁלַּנָכְרִי כוּל'. רַב אָמַר. רָאָה וַיַּתֵּר גּוֹיִם. הִתִּיר מָמוֹנָם שֶׁלַּגּוֹיִם. חִזְקִיָּה אָמַר. הוֹפִיעַ מֵהַר פָּרָן. וְהוֹפִיעַ פָּנִים כְּנֶגֶד אוּמוֹת הָעוֹלָם. רִבִּי יוֹסֵי בֶּן חֲנִינָה אָמַר. הוֹרִידָן מִנִּכְסֵיהֶן. רִבִּי אַבָּהוּ בְּשֵׁם רִבִּי יוֹחָנָן אָמַר. כְּדִינֵיהֶן. אָמַר רִבִּי לָא. לֹא עַל הָדָא אִיתְאֲמָרַת אֶלָּא בְּהָדָא דְּתַנֵּי רִבִּי חִייָה. שׁוֹר שֶׁלַּגּוֹי שֶׁנָּגַח שׁוֹר שֶׁלַּגּוֹי אַחֵר חֲבֵירוֹ. אַף עַל פִּי שֶׁקִּיבֵּל עָלָיו לָדוּן כְּדִינֵי יִשְׂרָאֵל בֵּין תָּם בֵּין מוּעָד מְשַׁלֵּם נֶזֶק שָׁלֵם. עַל הָדָא אִיתְאֲמָרַת. רִבִּי אַבָּהוּ בְּשֵׁם רִבִּי יוֹחָנָן אָמַר. כְּדִינֵיהֶן.

**Halakhah 4**: "The bull of an Israel which gored a bull of a non-Jew," etc. Rav said, "He saw and permitted Gentiles[36]," He permitted the Gentiles' money[37]. Ḥizqiah said, "He appeared from Mont Paran[38]," He appeared in front of the Gentiles; Rebbi Yose ben Ḥanina said, He made them poor[39]. Rebbi Abbahu in the name of Rebbi Joḥanan said, following their laws[40]. Rebbi La said, this was not said referring to this topic, but to what Rebbi Ḥiyya stated[41]: If a Gentile's bull gored another Gentile's bull, even though they accepted to be judged by the laws of Israel, he is liable for full damages whether tame or notorious. On that it was said that Rebbi Abbahu said in the name of Rebbi Joḥanan, following their laws.

---

36   Hab. 3:6. The usual translation is: "He saw and made peoples jump" (by an earthquake).

37   In the Babli, 38a, a statement of R. Abbahu, applies to those Gentiles who violate the Noahide commandments. Cf. *Lev. rabba* 13(2); *Tanḥuma Buber Šemini* 10; *Deut. rabba Eqeb* 1 (some mss.).

38   *Deut.* 33.2. The list of peoples living around Sinai is traditionally interpreted as a list of those to whom the Torah was offered first but who declined, and only Israel did accept (Babli *Avodah zarah* 2b; *Sifry Deut.* 343; *Pesiqta dR. Cahana Berakhah*, ed. Buber 199b; *Tanḥuma Berakhah* 4 (Buber 3); *Pseudo-Jonathan Deut.* 32:2); *Midrash Tannaïm Deut.* 32:2.

39   This statement possibly is fragmentary; cf. the formulations in the sources indicated in the preceding two

Notes.

40  It is stressed in *Ex.* 21:1 that the laws of that Chapter is *before them*; it applies only to intra-Israelite lawsuits. An application to suits involving Gentiles is illegitimate (*Sifry Deut.* 16; *Mekhilta dR. Ismael Neziqin* 1). Gentile law does not recognize payment for half the damages.

41  Tosephta 4:2.

(4b line 29) מַעֲשֶׂה שֶׁשִּׁילַּח הַמַּלְכוּת שְׁנֵי אִיסְרַטְיוֹטוֹת לִלְמוֹד תּוֹרָה מֵרַבָּן גַּמְלִיאֵל. וְלָמְדוּ מִמֶּנּוּ מִקְרָא מִשְׁנָה תַּלְמוּד הֲלָכוֹת וַאֲגָדוֹת. וּבְסוֹף אָמְרוּ לוֹ. כָּל־תּוֹרַתְכֶם נָאָה וּמְשׁוּבַּחַת חוּץ מִשְּׁנֵי דְבָרִים הַלָּלוּ שֶׁאַתֶּם אוֹמְרִים. בַּת יִשְׂרָאֵל לֹא תְיַיֵּלֵד לַנָּכְרִית אֲבָל נָכְרִית מְיַילֶּדֶת לְבַת יִשְׂרָאֵל. בַּת יִשְׂרָאֵל לֹא תָנִיק בְּנָהּ שֶׁלַּנָּכְרִית אֲבָל נָכְרִית מֵנִיקָה לְבַת יִשְׂרָאֵל בִּרְשׁוּתָהּ. גְּזֵילוֹ שֶׁלְּיִשְׂרָאֵל אָסוּר וְשֶׁלַּנָּכְרִי מוּתָּר. בְּאוֹתָהּ שָׁעָה גָּזַר רַבָּן גַּמְלִיאֵל עַל גְּזֵילוֹת נָכְרִי שֶׁיְּהֵא אָסוּר מִפְּנֵי חִילּוּל הַשֵּׁם. שׁוֹר שֶׁלְּיִשְׂרָאֵל שֶׁנָּגַח לְשׁוֹר שֶׁלַּנָּכְרִי פָּטוּר כול'. בַּדָּבָר הַזֶּה אֵין אָנוּ מוֹדִעִין לַמַּלְכוּת. אֲפִילוּ כֵן לָא מָטוֹן לְסוּלָמֵיהּ דְּצוֹר עַד דְּשָׁכְחוּן כּוּלוֹ.

[42]It happened that the [Roman] government sent two officials to study Torah with Rabban Gamliel. They learned from him Bible, Mishnah, Talmud, practice, and homilies. At the end, they told him: All of your teachings are beautiful and commendable except two things which you say: "A Jewish woman shall not act as midwife to a Gentile, but a Gentile woman may act as midwife for a Jewish woman; a Jewish woman shall not nurse the child of a Gentile, but a Gentile woman may nurse for a Jewish woman with her consent; what was robbed from a Jew is forbidden but from a Gentile it is permitted[43]." At that moment did Rabban Gamliel decide that what was robbed from a Gentile be forbidden because of desecration of the Name. "The bull of an Israel which gored a bull of a non-Jew is not liable," etc. But we shall not inform the government of this. Nevertheless, by the time they reached the Tyrian ladder they had forgotten everything.

42 Babli 38a; *Sifry Deut.* 344; *Midrash Tannaïm* (*Midrash Haggadol Deut.* 32:2).

43 In this version, a Jew could be a fence for goods stolen from a Gentile. In *Midrash Haggadol*: "what was robbed from a Jew is forbidden but *what was lost by* a Gentile is permitted." The entire sentence is missing in the Babli.

(fol. 4a) **משנה ה:** שׁוֹר שֶׁל פִּיקֵחַ שֶׁנִּגַּח שׁוֹר שֶׁל חֵרֵשׁ שׁוֹטֶה וְקָטָן חַיָּיב. שׁוֹר שֶׁל חֵרֵשׁ שׁוֹטֶה וְקָטָן שֶׁנָּגַח לְשׁוֹר שֶׁל פִּיקֵחַ פָּטוּר. שׁוֹר שֶׁל חֵרֵשׁ שׁוֹטֶה וְקָטָן שֶׁנָּגְחוּ מַעֲמִידִין לָהֶן אֶפִּיטְרוֹפוֹס וּמְעִידִין בָּהֶן בִּפְנֵי אֶפִּיטְרוֹפוֹס. נִתְפַּקַּח הַחֵרֵשׁ נִשְׁתַּפָּה הַשּׁוֹטֶה וְהִגְדִּיל הַקָּטָן חָזַר לְתַמּוּתוֹ דִּבְרֵי רִבִּי מֵאִיר. רִבִּי יוֹסֵי אוֹמֵר הֲרֵי הוּא בְחֶזְקָתוֹ. שׁוֹר הָאָצְטַדִין אֵינוֹ חַיָּיב מִיתָה שֶׁנֶּאֱמַר כִּי יִגַּח וְלֹא שֶׁיַּגִּיחוּהוּ אֲחֵרִים.

**Mishnah 5**: If a bull of a sane person gored the bull of a deaf-mute, insane, or underaged person, he is liable. If a bull of a deaf-mute, insane, or underaged person gored the bull of a sane person, he is not liable[44]. If a bull of a deaf-mute, insane, or underaged person gored, one[45] appoints a guardian for them and receives testimony about them[46] in the presence of the guardian[47]. If the deaf-mute became hearing, the insane normal, the underaged of age, it returns to be tame, the words of Rebbi Meïr[48]; Rebbi Yose said, it remains in its prior state. A bull of the stadion[49] is not to be killed since it is said: "if it gores," not that others train it to gore.

44 Since these persons cannot appear in court, they cannot be sued.

45 In the Mishnah in the Babli: "The court".

46 About the animal, to have it declared notorious. Once the animal is declared notorious, the guardian will have to pay damages from the estate of his wards.

47 Since testimony in general may

not be taken in the absence of the parties. In the case of the goring bull, it is stated in *Ex.* 21:29 that testimony must be "in presence of the owner' (Midrash Haggadol *ad loc.*).

48 He holds that "tame" or "noto-rious" is not a property of the animal but a qualification of the legal status of its owner. If the owner became a person in law, his status would have to be determined anew.

49 Trained for bullfights.

(4b line 39) **הלכה ה:** שׁוֹר שֶׁלְּפִיקֵחַ כול'. כֵּינֵי מַתְנִיתָא. שׁוֹר שֶׁלְּחֵרֵשׁ שׁוֹר שֶׁלְּשׁוֹטֶה שׁוֹר שֶׁלְּקָטָן.

**Halakhah 5**: "If a bull of a sane person," etc. So is the Mishnah[50]: The bull of a deaf-mute, the bull of an insane, the bull of an underaged.

50 The Mishnah should not be read as freeing only the underaged deaf-dumb insane person from liability.

(4b line 40) וְהָא תַנִּינָן. שׁוֹר חֵרֵשׁ שׁוֹטָה וְקָטָן שֶׁנָּגְחוּ מַעֲמִידִין לָהֶן אֶפִּיטְרוֹפוֹס וּמְעִידִין לָהֶן בִּפְנֵי אֶפִּיטְרוֹפִין. עַד כְּדוֹן בְּשֶׁהוּעֲדוּ לִפְנֵי הַבְּעָלִים וּמְסָרוּם לָאֶפִּיטְרוֹפִין. הוּעֲדוּ לִפְנֵי אֶפִּיטְרוֹפִין וּמְסָרוּם לַבְּעָלִים מָהוּ. נִישְׁמְעִינָהּ מִן הָדָא. שְׁאָלוֹ בְּחֶזְקַת שֶׁהוּא תָם וְנִמְצָא מוּעָד הַבְּעָלִים מְשַׁלְּמִין חֲצִי נֶזֶק וְהַשּׁוֹאֵל חֲצִי נֶזֶק. אָמַר רִבִּי אֶלְעָזָר. דְּרִבִּי יוֹסֵי הִיא. דְּרִבִּי יוֹסֵי אָמַר. הֲרֵי הוּא בְחֶזְקָתוֹ. וְאֵין כְּרִבִּי יוֹסֵי יְשַׁלֵּם אֶת הַכֹּל. בְּשֶׁשְּׁאָלוֹ בְּחֶזְקַת שֶׁהוּא תָם. וְאֵין בִּשֶּׁשְּׁאָלוֹ בְּחֶזְקַת שֶׁהוּא תָם לֹא יְשַׁלֵּם כְּלוּם. בְּיוֹדֵעַ בּוֹ שֶׁהוּא נַגְחָן. הֵמִית בִּפְנֵי הַשּׁוֹאֵל וּמְסָרוֹ לַבְּעָלִים עַד שֶׁלֹּא נִגְמַר דִּינוֹ פָּטוּר. מִשֶּׁנִּגְמַר דִּינוֹ חַיָּיב. רִבִּי יַעֲקֹב אָמַר. אַף מִשֶּׁנִּגְמַר דִּינוֹ עַד שֶׁלֹּא נִסְקַל פָּטוּר.

Did we not state: "If a bull of a deaf-mute, insane, or underaged person gored, one appoints a guardian for them and receives testimony about them in the presence of the guardian"[51]? So far if testimony was taken in the presence of the owner and he delivered to the guardian. If testimony was taken in the presence of the guardian and he delivered to the owner[52]? Let us hear from the following: [53]"If somebody borrowed it with the understanding that it was tame but it turned out to be notorious, the owner pays half of the damages and the borrower pays half of the damages[54]." Rebbi Eleazar said, this is Rebbi Yose's, since Rebbi Yose said, it remains in its prior state. But if this is Rebbi Yose's, he[55] should pay in full. If he borrowed it with the understanding that it was tame[56]. But if he borrowed it with the understanding that it was tame, he should not have to pay anything. If he knew that it was apt to gore[57].

It was stated[58]: "If it killed while at the borrower's, who handed it back to the owners, before judgment was rendered he is not liable[59], after judgment was rendered[60] he is liable. Rebbi Jacob said, even after judgment was rendered but before it was stoned, he is not liable[61]."

51    The Mishnah seems self-contradictory. Either incompetent persons are not liable or they have to be represented by guardians whose duty it will be to indemnify the victims of the animals of the incompetent. The question is also asked in the Babli, 39a. It is answered there but here left unanswered. One may not assume that the treatment of the Babli is valid for the Yerushalmi. It is more likely that the question is not answered because the Mishnah has a straightforward interpretation: The incompetent are not liable, but it is the duty of the court to intervene and appoint guardians responsible for future control of the dangerous animals (*Midrash Haggadol Ex.* 21:36).

52    This text seems to be devoid of sense. One may adopt the emendation of *Pene Moshe* and switch the objects: "So far if testimony was taken in the presence of the *guardian* and he delivered to the *owner*. If testimony was taken in the presence of the *owner* and he delivered to the *guardian*?" This text refers to the disagreement between R. Meïr and R. Yose. For the latter, a notorious beast always remains notorious. For R. Meïr the designation of "notorious" lapses if the animal is handed over to the grown-up owner by the guardian. What would be his

opinion if an owner of a notorious beast developed a mental illness and his estate were handed to a guardian by the court? Does he also hold that the designation of "notorious" lapses in this case?

53   Babli 40a, Tosephta 5:4.

54   The owner has to pay full damages for the notorious animal. Since he failed to inform the borrower, he has regress on him only for half the damages since the borrower is responsible to watch the animal to make sure it causes no damage as "tame". (For the different versions of the Tosephta, cf. S. Lieberman in *Tosefta kiFshutah*.)

55   Since for R. Yose the status of the animal does not change with a change of control, the borrower should be liable for the entire damage.

56   Same explanation given in the Babli, 40a.

57   But the borrower was not informed that the animal had been declared notorious by action of the court.

58   Tosephta 5:4; cf. Babli 44b/45a, 98b.

59   Since he handed back a bull, he does not have to replace it even though after judgment the bull will not be worth anything.

60   That the bull has to be killed and its carcass forbidden for usufruct (*Ex.* 21:28).

61   Since he returned the bull; its changed legal status is not apparent.

(4b line 50) אָמַר רִבִּי יוֹחָנָן. בַּתְּחִילָה אֵין מְמַנִּין אַפִּיטְרוֹפִין עַל מְנָת לַחוֹב לָהֶן אֶלָּא לִזְכוּת לָהֶן. וְאִם חָבוּ חָבוּ. רִבִּי יוֹסֵי בֶּן חֲנִינָה אָמַר. בֵּין בַּתְּחִילָה בֵּין בַּסּוֹף אֵין מְמַנִּין אַפִּיטְרוֹפִין עַל הַיְתוֹמִין לֹא לִזְכוּת וְלֹא לְחוֹבָה. מַתְנִיתָא פְלִיגָא עַל רִבִּי יוֹסֵי בֶּן חֲנִינָה. מַעֲמִידִין לָהֶן אַפִּיטְרוֹפִין וּמְעִידִין לָהֶן בִּפְנֵי אַפִּיטְרוֹפִין. אָמַר לֵיהּ. שַׁנְיָיא הִיא בְּשׁוֹר שֶׁלֹּא יֵצֵא וְיַזִּיק.

[62]Rebbi Joḥanan said, as a matter of principle one[63] does not appoint guardians for orphans to their detriment, but only to their profit; but if they are detrimental, they are detrimental. Rebbi Yose bar Ḥanina said, neither as a matter of principle nor as a reaction, neither for profit nor for detriment. A Mishnah disagrees with Rebbi Yose bar Ḥanina: "One

appears a guardian for them" There is a difference about an ox, lest it continue to cause damage.

62 This paragraph has an exact correspondence in *Giṭṭin* 5:4 (47a l. 15), Notes 111-115. The next paragraph is a reformulation of the topic discussed there, Notes 100-101, 116-122.

63 The court, if the father had failed to appoint a guardian before his death.

(4b line 55) שׁוֹרוֹ שֶׁלְּתוֹמִין וְשֶׁלְּאֶפִּיטְרוֹפִּין שֶׁיָּצָא וְהִזִּיק מָהוּ. רִבִּי יוֹחָנָן אָמַר. מִשֶּׁלִּיתוֹמִין. שֶׁאִים אַתָּה אוֹמֵר. מִשֶּׁלְּאֶפִּיטְרוֹפִּין. לֹא נַעֲשָׂה אָדָם מֵעוֹלָם אֶפִּיטְרוֹפּוֹס. רִבִּי יוֹסֵי בֶּן חֲנִינָה אָמַר. מִשֶּׁלְּאֶפִּיטְרוֹפִּין. וַתְיָיא דְרִבִּי יוֹסֵי בֶּן חֲנִינָה כְּאַבָּא שָׁאוּל וּדְרִבִּי יוֹחָנָן כְּרַבָּנִין. דְּתַנִּינָן תַּמָּן. אֶפִּיטְרוֹפּוֹס שֶׁמִּינָהוּ אֲבִי הַיְתוֹמִים יִשָּׁבַע. מִינָּהוּ בֵּית דִּין לֹא יִשָּׁבַע. שֶׁבֵּית דִּין מַבְחִינִין אוֹתוֹ. אַבָּא שָׁאוּל אוֹמֵר חִילוּף הַדְּבָרִים. אֶפִּיטְרוֹפּוֹס שֶׁמִּינָהוּ אֲבִי הַיְתוֹמִים לֹא יִשָּׁבַע. דְּבָעֵי מְמַשְׁכְּנָה לֵיהּ. מִינָּהוּ בֵּית דִּין יִשָּׁבַע. אִית בַּר נָשׁ בָּעֵי מִיתַּן כַּמָּה וּמִיתְקְרֵי הֵימָן.

If a bull of orphans and guardians went out and did damage, what is the rule? Rebbi Joḥanan said, [the damage is paid] from the orphan's property. For if you say from the guardians', nobody ever will agree to become a guardian. Rebbi Yose ben Ḥanina said, from the guardians'. Rebbi Yose ben Ḥanina follows Abba Shaul and Rebbi Joḥanan the rabbis, as it was stated there: "A guardian appointed by the orphans' father shall be made to swear; if he was appointed by the court he shall not be made to swear," for the court will check him out. "Abba Shaul says, it is the other way around," a guardian appointed by the orphans' father shall not be made to swear; it would be as if he would take a pledge from him. If he was appointed by the court he shall be made to swear, since a person will do much to be called trustworthy.

(4b line 63) אָמַר אַבָּא בַּר רַב הוּנָא. הָדָא אֲמָרָה. הַמַּכִּישׁ בְּהֶמַת חֲבֵירוֹ וְהָלְכָה וְהִזִּיקָה חַיָּיב בִּנְזָקֶיהָ.

Abba bar Rab Huna said: This[64] implies that somebody who hit another person's animal which as a consequence went and did damage is responsible for the damage caused[65].

64  The statement which excepts the bull trained to fight from retribution; the Mishnah puts all the blame on its trainers.

65  Even though in general one does not allow suits for indirectly caused damages.

( fol. 4a ) **משנה ו:** שׁוֹר שֶׁנָּגַח אֶת הָאָדָם וָמֵת מוּעָד מְשַׁלֵּם אֶת הַכּוֹפֶר וְתָם פָּטוּר מִן הַכּוֹפֶר וְזֶה וָזֶה חַיָּיבִין מִיתָה וְכֵן בַּבֵּן וְכֵן בַּבַּת.  נָגַח עֶבֶד אוֹ אָמָה נוֹתֵן שְׁלֹשִׁים סְלָעִים בֵּין שֶׁהוּא יָפֶה מָנֶא וּבֵין שֶׁאֵינוֹ יָפֶה אֶלָּא דִינַר זָהָב.

**Mishnah 6**: A bull which gored a human who then died, if it is notorious [the owner] pays weregilt[66], if tame he is not liable for weregilt; in both cases they have to be killed[67]. The same holds for a son or a daughter[68]. It it gored a male or female slave, [the owner] pays 30 tetradrachmas[69], whether he was worth a mina or was worth only a gold[70] denar.

66  *Ex.* 21:30.

67  *Ex.* 21:28,29.

68  There is no difference whether the victim was adult or underage. The statement is only necessary since the verse, *Ex.* 21:31, stresses that the same rules apply to underage as to adult victims.

69  *Ex.* 21:32.

70  This reading is also found in some Babli mss., Alfasi, and the Naples print of the Mishnah. In other texts: "one (silver) denar".

(4b line 64) **הלכה ו:** שׁוֹר שֶׁנָּגַח אֶת הָאָדָם כול'. תַּנֵּי. וּבַעַל הַשּׁוֹר נָקִי. נָקִי מֵחֲצִי כוֹפֶר. דִּבְרֵי רִבִּי אֱלִיעֶזֶר. אָמַר לוֹ רִבִּי עֲקִיבָה. רִבִּי. וַהֲלֹא מוּקְדָּם הוּא לְבֵית הַסְּקִילָה חֲמוּרָה. אָמַר לוֹ. לֹא אָמַרְתִּי אֶלָּא בְנִתְכַּווֵן לַהֲרוֹג אֶת הַבְּהֵמָה וְהָרַג אֶת הָאָדָם כול'. עַד דּוּ מַקְשֵׁי לָהּ עַל דְּרִבִּי לְעֶזֶר יַקְשִׁינָהּ עַל דִּידֵיהּ. אָמַר רִבִּי מְיָישָׁא. תִּיפְתָּר בְּשֶׁעָבַר וּשְׁחָטוֹ. וְאִית דְּבָעֵי מֵימַר. מָאן דְּיַלְפָהּ מִן דְּרִבִּי לִעֶזֶר עוֹד הוּא אָמַר כֵּן. לֹא אָמַרְתִּי אֶלָּא בְשֶׁנִּתְכַּווֵן לַהֲרוֹג אֶת הַבְּהֵמָה וְהָרַג אֶת הָאָדָם. לְנָכְרִי וְהָרַג יִשְׂרָאֵל. לִנְפָלִים וְהָרַג שֶׁלְּקַיָּימָה. פָּטוּר. מַה מְקַיֵּים רִבִּי עֲקִיבָה וּבַעַל הַשּׁוֹר נָקִי. נָקִי מִדְּמֵי עָבֶד. וְלֵית לֵיהּ לְרִבִּי לְעֶזֶר נָקִי מִדְּמֵי עָבֶד. אִם כּוֹפֶר יוּשַׁת עָלָיו. בְּמוֹעֵד הַכָּתוּב מְדַבֵּר. וְלֵית לֵיהּ לְרִבִּי עֲקִיבָה נָקִי מֵחֲצִי כוֹפֶר. נֶאֱמַר כָּאן הַשּׁוֹר יִסָּקֵל וְנֶאֱמַר לְהַלָּן הַשּׁוֹר יִסָּקֵל. מַה שּׁוֹר שֶׁנֶּאֱמַר לְהַלָּן בְּמוֹעֵד הַכָּתוּב מְדַבֵּר אַף הַשּׁוֹר יִסָּקֵל שֶׁנֶּאֱמַר כָּאן בְּמוֹעֵד הַכָּתוּב מְדַבֵּר. וְלֵית כְּתִיב סָקוֹל יִסָּקֵל הַשּׁוֹר. אָמַר. מוּטָב יְלַמֵּד הַשּׁוֹר יִסָּקֵל מִשּׁוֹר יִסָּקֵל וְאַל יְלַמֵּד הַשּׁוֹר יִסָּקֵל מִסָּקוֹל יִסָּקֵל הַשּׁוֹר.

**Halakhah 6**: "A bull which gored a human," etc. It was stated[71]: "But the owner of the bull is free[72]," free from half the weregilt, the words of Rebbi Eliezer. Rebbi Aqiba said to him, Rabbi, is he not destined for the severity of the stoning place[73]? He answered him, I said this only for one which intended to kill an animal but killed a human[74], etc.[75] Before he objects to Rebbi Eliezer, should he not object to himself[76]? Rebbi Miasha said, explain it if he transgressed and slaughtered it[77]. But some want to say, from what[78] we learn from Rebbi Eliezer who said, I said this only for one which intended to kill an animal but killed a human, a Gentile but killed an Israel[40], still birth but killed a viable [child][79], he is not liable. How does Rebbi Aqiba explain "the owner of the bull is free"[72,76]? Free from paying for a slave. Does not Rebbi Eliezer agree that he is free from paying for a slave? "If weregilt is imposed on him,[80]" the verse speaks of the notorious⁸¹. Does not Rebbi Aqiba agree that he is free from half the weregilt? It is said here, "the bull shall be stoned⁸²," and it says there, "the bull shall be stoned.⁸³" Since about "the bull" mentioned there, the verse speaks of the notorious, so also about "the bull shall be stoned" mentioned here, the verse speaks of the notorious⁸⁴. But is it not written: "The bull by stoning shall be stoned⁷²"? It is better that "the bull shall be stoned" shall be interpreted following "the bull shall be stoned" rather than that "the bull shall be stoned" should be interpreted following "the bull by stoning shall be stoned"⁸⁴.

71  Babli 41b; cf. *Mekhilta dR. Ismael Neziqin* 10 (Horovitz-Rabin p. 283); *Mekhilta dR. Simeon ben Iohai* 21:28, *Midrash Tannaïm* (*Midrash Haggadol Ex.* 21:28, ed. Margaliut p. 484.)

72  *Ex.* 21:28.

73  As the formulation of the Babli makes explicit, since any damages caused by a tame animal are paid from its body and a bull which killed a human is stoned and its carcass forbidden for usufruct, there is nothing from which either damages or fine might be paid.

74  The bull was attacking another animal when a human intervened and was killed. In that case, the bull is not condemned to be stoned and is not forbidden for usufruct.

75  A list of similar situations as given later in the paragraph.

76  Below, R. Aqiba is quoted as holding that the verse frees the owner of a tame bull from paying for the death of a slave. He should have told himself that his interpretation is impossible.

77  As stated in Mishnah 9, the bull's meat becomes forbidden only when it is stoned. If the owners slaughter it immediately after the attack, before the court had time to intervene, the meat is valuable and its proceeds are available to cover damages.

78  Reading מִן "from" instead of מאן "who" (I. Lewy).

79  Killing a fetus or a newborn which is not viable is forbidden but not prosecutable as murder; the same holds for killing a *terepha*, a terminally ill

person.
80  Ex. 21:30.
81  Therefore, the notion of weregilt is not applicable to the tame bull; the exemption needs no verse.
82  Ex. 21:29. This verse imposes weregilt for the killing of a free person by a notorious bull.
83  Ex. 21:32. This verse imposes a fine for the killing of a slave.
84  Therefore, no fine is imposed for the killing of a slave by a tame bull.

(4c line 3) אָמַר רִבִּי יָסָא. מִילָה שְׁמָעִית מִן דְּרִבִּי שְׁמוּאֵל בַּר רַב יִצְחָק הָכָא וְלֵית אֲנָא יְדַע מַה הִיא. אָמַר לֵיהּ רִבִּי זְעִירָא. דִּילְמָא דָא הִיא. בַּתְּחִילָה אֵינוֹ מְדַבֵּר אֶלָּא בְּתָם. הֶחֱזִיר אֶת הַמּוּעָד לַכּוֹפֶר. הֶחֱזִיר אֶת שְׁנֵיהֶן לִנְזָקִין. יָכוֹל כְּשֵׁם שֶׁהֶחֱזִירוֹ לִנְזָקִין כָּךְ הֶחֱזִירוֹ לִדְמֵי עֶבֶד. תַּלְמוּד לוֹמַר וּבַעַל הַשּׁוֹר נָקִי. נָקִי מִדְּמֵי עֶבֶד. אָמַר רִבִּי לָא. בְּכָל־אָתָר אַתְּ מַחְמִיר בְּעֶבֶד יוֹתֵר מִן הַכֹּל. שֶׁאֲפִילוּ מוּכֵּה שְׁחִין נוֹתֵן שְׁלֹשִׁים סֶלַע. חָיֵיתִי אוֹמֵר. אַף בְּאָבִיו וּבְאִמּוֹ כֵּן. תַּלְמוּד לוֹמַר וּבַעַל הַשּׁוֹר נָקִי. נָקִי מִדְּמֵי וְלָדוֹת. בְּכָל־אָתָר אַתְּ מַחְמִיר בְּמוּעָד יוֹתֵר מִתָּם וְהָכָא אַתְּ מַחְמִיר בְּתָם יוֹתֵר מִבְּמוּעָד. אֶלָּא כֵּינִי. אֲנָשִׁים מִתְכַּוְּונִין חַיָּיבִין. שְׁוָורִין שֶׁאֵינָן מִתְכַּוְּונִין פְּטוּרִין. הָא אִם הָיוּ מִתְכַּוְּונִין יְהוּ חַיָּיבִין. תַּלְמוּד לוֹמַר וּבַעַל הַשּׁוֹר נָקִי. נָקִי מִדְּמֵי וְלָדוֹת. תַּנֵּי חוֹרָן תַּנֵּי. וּבַעַל הַשּׁוֹר נָקִי. נָקִי מִדְּמֵי עֶבֶד. וְלֵית כְּתִיב וְכִי יִנָּצוּ אֲנָשִׁים. אֲנָשִׁים וְלֹא שְׁוָורִים. אָמַר רִבִּי חַגַּיי. כֵּינִי מַתְנִיתָא. אֲנָשִׁים שֶׁאֵין מִתְכַּוְּונִין חַיָּיבִין. שְׁוָורִים שֶׁאֵין מִתְכַּוְּונִין פְּטוּרִין. הָא אִם הָיוּ מִתְכַּוְּונִין יְהוּ חַיָּיבִין. תַּלְמוּד לוֹמַר וּבַעַל הַשּׁוֹר נָקִי. נָקִי מִדְּמֵי עֶבֶד. וְלֵית כְּתִיב כִּי יִנָּצוּ כִּי יְרִיבוּן. וַהֲלֹא הִיא מַצּוּת הִיא מְרִיבָה. אִי מַה לְהַלָּן בְּמִתְכַּוֵּון אַף כָּאן בְּמִתְכַּוֵּון. מַה כָּאן בְּשֶׁאֵינוֹ מִתְכַּוֵּון אַף לְהַלָּן בְּשֶׁאֵינוֹ מִתְכַּוֵּון. מַאי כְדוֹן. כֵּיי דָּמַר רִבִּי שְׁמוּאֵל בַּר רַב יִצְחָק. בַּתְּחִילָה אֵינוֹ מְדַבֵּר אֶלָּא בְּתָם כוֹל׳.

Rebbi Yasa said, I heard something[85] from Rebbi Samuel ben Rav Isaac in this matter, but I do not remember what it was. Rebbi Ze'ira told him, maybe it was the following: At the start the discussion refers to the tame animal. It added weregilt for the notorious. Then it added damages for both of them[86]. I could think that as it added damages, it added the payment for the slave[87]; the verse says "but the owner of the bull is free[72];" free from paying for a slave. Rebbi La said[88], everywhere you are more restrictive for a slave than anything else since even if he is scabbed one pays thirty tetradrachmas; I would have said also (for his father and his mother)[89] the same; the verse says "but the owner of the bull is free[72];" free from paying for fetuses[90]. Everywhere you are more restrictive for a notorious than for a tame one, would you be more restrictive here for a tame one than for a notorious[91]? But it must be so: Men who act unintentionally are liable; bulls who act unintentionally are not liable. Does this mean that if they acted intentionally, they were liable? The verse says, "but the owner of the bull is free[72];" free from paying for a slave[92]. Another Tanna stated: "But the owner of the bull is free[72];" free from paying for a slave[92]. But is it not written: "If people quarrel[93]", people but not bulls. Rebbi Haggai said, so is the *baraita*: Men who act unintentionally are liable; bulls who act unintentionally are not liable. Does this mean that if they acted intentionally, they were liable? The verse says, "but the owner of the bull is free[72];" free from paying for a slave[92]. But is it not written: "When they quarrel[93]," "when they brawl[94]". Is not quarrel the same as brawl[95]? Since there the act was intentional, so here the act was intentional; or since here the act was unintentional, so here the act was unintentional. What about this[96]? As Rebbi Samuel ben Rav Isaac said, at the start it treats the tame animal, etc.

85  A *baraita*.
86  Ex. 21:28 discusses the tame bull which kills a human. Verses 29-32 deal with the notorious bull which is killing.

Verses 35-36 then deal with both kinds of bulls as damaging goods.

87 Since the payment for killed slaves is not treated as weregilt but as payment of damages to the owner for the loss of his slave, might it not be treated as part of the rules for payment of damages?

88 A different but parallel argument is in the Babli, 42b.

89 It seems that one has ro read: "a male or female slave".

90 There is an obvious lacuna here which is filled by E: "But the owner of the bull is free;" *free from paying for a slave. It was stated in the name of Rebbi Eleazar ben Azariah: "but the owner of the bull is free,"* free from paying for fetuses.

The scribe's error was induced by the repetition of the same text. For the statement of R. Eleazar ben Azariah, cf. Note 71.

The payment for fetuses refers to *Ex.* 21:22: If quarrelling people unintentionally hit a pregnant woman who then has a miscarriage, they have to indemnify her husband. The argument in the text presupposes the statement later in the text: "'people' but not bulls." (cf. *Midrash Haggadol* to *Ex.* 21:22) This exempts the owner of a notorious bull from payment if it causes a miscarriage. Therefore, there is no reason to think that the owner of a tame bull should pay. Why should R. Eleazar b. Azariah have to mention it?

92 It seems that one has to read here: "for fetuses".

93 *Ex.* 21:22.

94 *Ex.* 21:18, specifying the payments due for intentionally inflicted injuries.

95 There is missing the corresponding rhetorical question "and fight the same as quarrel"? It is in E. The arguments are used to impose the payments mentioned in *Ex.* 21:18 for intentional injuries on the unintentional injuries mentioned in 21:22, and vice-versa (*Nazir* 9:5, Notes 183-184; *Sanhedrin* 9:3, 27a l. 58; *Midrash Haggadol* 21:22).

96 Which of the two contradictory arguments is to be accepted? Neither.

(4c line 22) וּמִנַּיִין לְנִזְקֵי הָעֶבֶד. תַּלְמוּד לוֹמַר אוֹ בֵן יִגָּח אוֹ בַת יִגָּח. וְאִם עֶבֶד וגו'. רִבִּי חִייָה בַּר וָא וְרִבִּי שְׁמוּאֵל בַּר רַב יִצְחָק. חַד אָמַר. לֹא תְהֵא תוֹסֶפֶת יְתֵירָה עַל הָעִיקָר. וְחָרָנָה אָמַר. מְשַׁלֵּם לוֹ כָּל-נִזְקוֹ.

From where damages for a slave[97]? The verse says, "or it gores a son, or it gores a daughter, . . . , and if a slave[98], etc." Rebbi Hiyya bar Abba and Rebbi Samuel bar Isaac. One said, the addition may not be more than the main thing[99]. But the other said, he has to pay the entire damages.[100]

97 If a slave was injured by an animal but was not killed. May his owner sue the animal's owner for damages.

98 Verses *Ex.* 21:31,32 treat attacks on minors and on slaves in parallel. It is implied that any payments due for an injured child are due for a slave.

99 Since for a slave killed the payment is 30 tetradrachmas, payments for an injured slave can be at most 30 tetradrachmas. This opinion is not found in the Babli.

100 All payments due for a free person (medical costs, lost wages, payment for pain and suffering) are due for a slave without limitation. The Babli, 43b, attributes this opinion to R. Samuel b. R. Isaac.

**משנה ז:** שׁוֹר שֶׁהָיָה מִתְחַכֵּךְ בַּכּוֹתֶל וְנָפַל עַל הָאָדָם נִתְכַּווֵן לַהֲרוֹג אֶת הַבְּהֵמָה וְהָרַג אֶת הָאָדָם לַנָּכְרִי וְהָרַג בֶּן יִשְׂרָאֵל לַנְּפָלִים וְהָרַג בֶּן קַיָּימָא פָּטוּר. (fol. 4a)

**Mishnah 7:** A bull which was rubbing itself against a wall which then fell on a human, [or which] intended to kill an animal but killed a human[74], a Gentile but killed a Jew[40], stillbirth but killed a viable child[79], is free from prosecution.

**הלכה ז:** שׁוֹר שֶׁהָיָה מִתְחַכֵּךְ בַּכּוֹתֶל כול׳. וְאִישׁ כִּי יַכֶּה כָּל־נֶפֶשׁ (4c line 26) אָדָם. לְהָבִיא אֶת הַמַּכֶּה וְיֵשׁ בּוֹ לְהָמִית. אִית תַּנָּיֵי תַנֵּי. אֵין בּוֹ כְּדֵי לְהָמִית. אָמַר רִבִּי לָא. וַאֲפִילוּ יֵשׁ בּוֹ לְהָמִית וּבָא אַחֵר וְהֵמִית הַמֵּמִית חַיָּיב. וְהֵמִית

אִישׁ אוֹ אִשָּׁה. מַה הָאִישׁ מוֹרִישׁ נִזְקָיו לְבָנָיו אַף אִשָּׁה מוֹרִישָׁה נְזָקֶיהָ לְבָנֶיהָ. וְאֵין הַבַּעַל יוֹרֵשׁ אֶת אִשְׁתּוֹ. אָמַר רֵישׁ לָקִישׁ. כָּךְ פֵּירְשָׁהּ רִבִּי הוֹשַׁעְיָה אֲבִי הַמִּשְׁנָה. בַּכּוֹפֶר שֶׁלְּאַחַר מִיתָה שָׁנוּ.

**Halakhah 7**: "A bull which was rubbing itself against a wall," etc. "A man who kills any human soul,[101]" to include a hit which is potentially deadly. Some Tannaïm state, even if it is not deadly[102]. Rebbi La said, even if it is deadly but a third person came and killed, the killer is guilty[103]. "And it killed a man or a woman[104]," just as a man lets his sons inherit his injury claims, so a woman lets her sons inherit her injury claims. But does not a man inherit from his wife[105]? Rebbi Simeon ben Laqish said, so did Rebbi Hoshaiah, the father of the Mishnah, explain: One teaches here about weregilt which is due after death[106].

101  Lev. 21:17.

102  The Babli, *Sanhedrin* 78a, explains that the verse can be read either as "a man who kills a human totally" or as "a man who kills anything of a man." In the first version, if one attacker wounds a person and a second one finishes him off, the second attacker is the murderer even if the wounds inflicted by the first are potentially lethal. In the second version, the heirs of a person killed by a gang have indemnity claims against all gang members taking part in the attack even if none of them can be prosecuted for first degree murder.

103  A tannaïtic statement in *Sifra Emor Pereq* 20(1).

104  Ex. 21:29.

105  How can her children (or in the absence of children, her paternal relatives) inherit anything from her if she is survived by her husband?

106  (*Mekhilta dR. Simeon b. Iohai* 21:29, p. 181). The biblical right of inheritance by the husband, based on *Num.* 27:11, excludes future claims (Babli 42b; *Bava batra* 8:6 Note 129). Since there is no weregilt for a living person, the husband cannot inherit.

(4c line 32) תַּנֵי. הַמּוֹכֵר שׁוֹר לַחֲבֵירוֹ וְנִמְצָא נַגְחָן. רַב אָמַר. מִקַּח טָעוּת הוּא. וּשְׁמוּאֵל אָמַר. יָכִיל הוּא מֵימַר לֵיהּ. לִשְׁחִיטָה מְכַרְתִּיו לָךְ. וְנָתַן פִּדְיוֹן נַפְשׁוֹ. אִית תַּנָּיֵי תַנֵי. נֶפֶשׁ מַזִּיק. אִית תַּנָּיֵי תַנֵי. נֶפֶשׁ נִיזָּק. מָאן דְּאָמַר. נֶפֶשׁ נִיזָּק. הִכָּהוּ הָרִאשׁוֹן הַכָּיַית מִיתָה וּבָא הַשֵּׁינִי וּבִילְבְּלוֹ. אִין תֵּימַר. יֵשׁ נְזָקִים בְּכוּלּוֹ. הָרִאשׁוֹן נוֹתֵן נֶזֶק וְהַשֵּׁינִי נוֹתֵן כּוּפְרוֹ. אִין תֵּימַר. אֵין נְזָקִין בְּכוּלּוֹ. הָרִאשׁוֹן נוֹתֵן כּוּפְרוֹ וְהַשֵּׁינִי פָטוּר. כְּמָאן דְּאָמַר. פִּדְיוֹן נַפְשׁוֹ שֶׁלְּמַזִּיק. אִין תֵּימַר. יֵשׁ נְזָקִין בְּכוּלּוֹ. הָרִאשׁוֹן נוֹתֵן כּוּפְרוֹ וְהַשֵּׁינִי פָטוּר. אִין תֵּימַר. אֵין נְזָקִין בְּכוּלּוֹ. שְׁנֵיהֶן פְּטוּרִין.

If somebody sells a bull to another person and it turns out to be goring. Rav said, it is an acquisition in error, but Samuel says, he can tell him: I sold it to you to be slaughtered[107].

"He shall give weregilt for his person.[108]" Some Tannaïm state: The attacker's person. Some Tannaïm state: The person suffering the damage. Following him who said, the person suffering the damage, [assume] the first one injured him fatally and then the second came and kept him in confusion[109]. If you say that damages are fully required[110], the first one pays damages and the second pays the weregilt. If you say that damages are not fully required[111], the first one pays weregilt but the second is not liable. Following him who said, the attacker's person, if you say that damages are fully required, the first one pays weregilt and the second is not liable[112]. If you say that damages are not fully required, neither one is liable[113].

107 According to Rav, the buyer can force the annulment of the sale and receive his money back. According to Samuel, since a bull can be sold either for meat or for work, it is up to the buyer to specify for which use he is buying since for livestock there do not exist generally valid criteria of quality. (Ševi'it 5:8, Notes 70,71; Babli 46a, *Bava batra* 92a).

| | |
|---|---|
| 108 *Ex.* 21:30. It is not clear to whom the verse refers in mentioning "his", cf. *Ketubot* 3:10, Note 151 and all sources quoted there, in particular Babli 40a. | 110 Damages are due even though weregilt was paid. |
| | 111 There is no claim for damages if there is one for weregilt. |
| 108 The bull of owner A injured a person who was prevented by the bull of owner B to seek immediate medical attention; the person then died. | 112 Since the action of B's bull was strictly defensive, he is not an attacker. |
| | 113 If neither of them can be held criminally liable, neither of them can be held financially liable. |

(fol. 4a) **משנה ח:** שׁוֹר הָאִשָּׁה שׁוֹר הַיְתוֹמִין שׁוֹר אֶפִּיטְרוֹפּוֹס שׁוֹר הַמִּדְבָּר שׁוֹר הַהֶקְדֵּשׁ שׁוֹר הַגֵּר שֶׁמֵת וְאֵין לוֹ יוֹרְשִׁין הֲרֵי אֵלּוּ חַיָּיבִין מִיתָה. רִבִּי יְהוּדָה אוֹמֵר שׁוֹר הַמִּדְבָּר שׁוֹר הַהֶקְדֵּשׁ שׁוֹר הַגֵּר שֶׁמֵת וְאֵין לוֹ יוֹרְשִׁין פְּטוּרִין מִן הַמִּיתָה מִפְּנֵי שֶׁאֵין לָהֶן בְּעָלִים.

**Mishnah 8**: A bull belonging to a woman, a bull belonging to orphans[114], a bull under a guardian[115], a wild bull, a bull of Temple property, a bull belonging to a proselyte who died without heirs, these are subject to the death penalty[116]. Rebbi Jehudah says that a wild bull, a bull of Temple property, a bull belonging to a proselyte who died without heirs[117], are not subject to the death penalty since they have no owners.

| | |
|---|---|
| 114 Minors for whom no guardian was appointed. | 116 If they killed a person. |
| 115 Property of orphans. | 117 Whose estate is ownerless; cf. *Qiddushin* 1:1, Note 30. |

(4c line 40) **הלכה ח:** שׁוֹר הָאִשָּׁה שׁוֹר הַיְתוֹמִין כול'. מַאי טַעֲמָא דְּרִבִּי יוּדָן. וְהוּעַד בִּבְעָלָיו וְלֹא יִשְׁמְרֶנּוּ. אֵין בְּעָלִים לָאֵילוּ לְעִנְיַין נְזָקִין. תַּנֵּי רִבִּי הוֹשַׁעְיָה לְעִנְיַין נְזָקִין רִבִּי מֵאִיר מְחַיֵּיב וְרִבִּי יוּדָן פּוֹטֵר. לַכּוֹפֶר מָה. רִבִּי פְּדָת בְּשֵׁם רִבִּי

הוֹשַׁעְיָה. הַכֹּל מוֹדִין בַּכּוֹפֶר שֶׁהוּא חַיָּיב. וְאִין דְּאָמְרִין. רִבִּי יוֹחָנָן בְּשֵׁם רִבִּי יַנַּאי. כְּשֵׁם שֶׁחוֹלְקִין בִּנְזָקִין כָּךְ הֵן חוֹלְקִין בַּכּוֹפֶר. רִבִּי יִרְמְיָה בָּעֵי קוֹמֵי רִבִּי זְעִירָא. הֵיךְ עָבְדִין עוֹבְדָא. אָמַר לֵיהּ. כְּרִבִּי הוֹשַׁעְיָה. לְעִנְיַין נְזָקִין רִבִּי מֵאִיר מְחַיֵּיב וְרִבִּי יוּדָן פּוֹטֵר. הָא לַכּוֹפֶר דִּבְרֵי הַכֹּל חַיָּיב.

**Halakhah 8**: "A bull belonging to a woman, a bull belonging to orphans," etc. What is Rebbi Jehudah's reason? "It was testified to before its owners and they did not watch it;[118]" those have no owners who could be responsible for damages. Rebbi Hoshaia stated: In matters of damages[119], Rebbi Meïr declares liable but Rebbi Jehudah declares not liable. What about weregilt? Rebbi Pedat in the name of Rebbi Hoshaia: Everybody agrees that he is liable for weregilt. But some say, Rebbi Johanan in the name of Rebbi Yannai: Just as they disagree for damages so they disagree for weregilt[120]. Rebbi Jeremiah asked before Rebbi Ze'ira: How does one actually act? He said to him, following Rebbi Hoshaia that in matters of damages, Rebbi Meïr declares liable but Rebbi Jehudah declares not liable; therefore, in matters of weregilt everybody agrees that he is liable.

118  *Ex.* 21:29. Tosephta 4:6. The verse speaks of the notorious bull; one seems to understand that no ownerless bull can be brought to court.

119  Damage claims are possible only against humans. One must refer to a bull who did damage before its owner dedicated it to the Temple, or was property of a proselyte while the latter was still living.

120  The language of the Tosephta seems to support R. Johanan. The formulation of the Babli, 44b (in the name of Rav Huna and a *baraita*) is inconclusive. (The Babli, 44a, reports a similar disagreement, between Rav and Samuel, referring to Mishnah 7.)

( fol. 4a ) **משנה ט:** שׁוֹר שֶׁהוּא יוֹצֵא לִיסָּקֵל וְהִקְדִּישׁוֹ בְּעָלָיו אֵינוֹ מוּקְדָּשׁ וְאִם שְׁחָטוֹ בְּשָׂרוֹ אָסוּר. אִם עַד שֶׁלֹּא נִגְמַר דִּינוֹ הִקְדִּישׁוֹ בְּעָלָיו מוּקְדָּשׁ וְאִם שְׁחָטוֹ בְּשָׂרוֹ מוּתָּר.

**Mishnah 9**: If one dedicates a bull which is led out to be stoned, it is not dedicated, and if it was slaughtered, its meat is forbidden[121]. If its owner dedicated it before sentence was pronounced, it is dedicated, and if it was slaughtered, its meat is permitted.

121  Ex. 21:28 reads in part: "The bull shall be stoned; its meat shall not be eaten." If the bull is killed by stoning, it is not ritually slaughtered and automatically its meat is forbidden as carcass meat. The specific mention of the prohibition of the meat is interpreted to mean that it becomes forbidden the moment sentence is pronounced. If the owner wants to save something of the value of the bull, he has to slaughter it immediately after it killed [*Mekhilta dR. Ismael, Neziqin* 10; *dR. Simeon ben Iohai* 21:28, p. 178; Yerushalmi *Pesaḥim* 2:1 (28c l. 34), '*Orlah* 3:1 Note 26; Babli *Pesaḥim* 22b].

(4c line 40) **הלכה ט:** שׁוֹר שֶׁהוּא יוֹצֵא לִיסָּקֵל כול'. תַּנֵּי. שׁוֹר שֶׁהָיָה יוֹצֵא לִיסָּקֵל וְנִמְצְאוּ עֵידָיו זוֹמְמִין. רִבִּי יוֹחָנָן אָמַר. כָּל־הַקּוֹדֵם בּוֹ זָכָה. רֵישׁ לָקִישׁ אָמַר. יֵיאוּשׁ טָעוּת הוּא. וְכֵן עֶבֶד הַיּוֹצֵא לֵיהָרֵג וְנִמְצְאוּ עֵידָיו זוֹמְמִין. רִבִּי יוֹחָנָן אָמַר. זָכָה לְעַצְמוֹ. רֵישׁ לָקִישׁ אָמַר. יֵיאוּשׁ טָעוּת הוּא.

**Halakhah 9**: "A bull which is led out to be stoned," etc. It was stated[122]: If a bull was led out to be stoned when its witnesses were found to be false, Rebbi Joḥanan said, the first to come acquires it[123]; Rebbi Simeon ben Laqish said, it was false despair[124]. Similarly, if a slave was led out to be killed when his witnesses were found to be false, Rebbi Joḥanan said, he acquired himself[125]; Rebbi Simeon ben Laqish said, it was false despair.

122 *Sanhedrin* 6:2(23b l.25) an exact copy, 10:8(29d l.14) a reformulation.

123 Since the court declares the bull to be forbidden for usufruct, it cannot remain the property of its owner. When the prohibition of usufruct is lifted because the sentence was declared false, the bull is ownerless. If a third party grabs the bull before the owner can take it back, that third party now is the legal owner. The Babli, *Keritut* 24a, holds that R. Johanan will agree that the bull never was ownerless if the judgment was overturned on the initiative or appeal by the owner.

124 He holds that ownership never was annulled, only that the owner gave up hope of ever having use of the bull again. The bull remains the property of its owner who may use it once the prohibition of usufruct is lifted.

125 He is free and needs no bill of manumission.

( fol. 4a ) **משנה י:** מְסָרוֹ לְשׁוֹמֵר חִנָּם וְלַשּׁוֹאֵל וְלַנּוֹשֵׂא שָׂכָר וְהַשּׂוֹכֵר נִכְנְסוּ תַּחַת הַבְּעָלִים. מוּעָד מְשַׁלֵּם נֶזֶק שָׁלֵם וְתָם מְשַׁלֵּם חֲצִי נֶזֶק. קְשָׁרוֹ בְּעָלָיו בְּמוֹסֵירָה וְנָעַל בְּפָנָיו כָּרָאוּי וְיָצָא וְהִזִּיק אֶחָד תָּם וְאֶחָד מוּעָד חַיָּיב. רִבִּי יְהוּדָה אוֹמֵר תָּם חַיָּיב וּמוּעָד פָּטוּר שֶׁנֶּאֱמַר וְלֹא יִשְׁמְרֶנּוּ בְּעָלָיו וְשָׁמוּר הוּא זֶה. רִבִּי אֱלִיעֶזֶר אוֹמֵר אֵין לוֹ שְׁמִירָה אֶלָּא סַכִּין.

**Mishnah 10**: If it was handed over to an unpaid trustee, or a borrower, or a paid trustee, or a lessee, they entered instead of the owner[126]; a notorious animal pays full damages, a tame one half damages. If he tied it down with a rope and locked it in as he should, if then it broke out and caused damage he is liable whether tame or notorious[127]. Rebbi Jehudah says, for the tame he is liable, for the notorious he is not liable since it was said: "if its owner would not guard it[128]," but it was guarded. Rebbi Eliezer says, this one can be guarded only by the knife[129].

126 The four cases of temporary guardians of other people's property are defined in Mishnah *Bava meṣi'a* 6:8. For damages caused while the animal was in the temporary control of another person, the person in control may be responsible in place of the owner. This limited liability is detailed in the second part of the Mishnah.

127 In the Halakhah, the Babli, *Mekhilta dR. Simeon b. Ioḥai,* and most independent Mishnah texts, this is identified as R. Meïr's opinion. In Tosephta 5:7 and *Mekhilta dR. Ismael, Neziqin* 10, R. Meïr declares the owner of the tame bull not liable in this case, only the owner of a notorious bull. In all of these sources there is a third opinion, by R. Eliezer ben Jacob, that neither is liable.

128 *Ex..* 21:36. There is no corresponding verse regarding a tame bull.

129 Once a bull has been declared notorious, it has to be slaughtered immediately.

(4c line 46) **הלכה י:** מְסָרוֹ לְשׁוֹמֵר חִנָּם כול׳. אָמַר רִבִּי לְעָזָר. דִּבְרֵי רִבִּי מֵאִיר. שְׁמִירַת נְזָקִין כִּשְׁמִירַת שׁוֹמֵר חִנָּם. דִּבְרֵי רִבִּי יוּדָן. שְׁמִירַת נְזָקִין כְּשׁוֹמֵר שָׂכָר. אָמַר רִבִּי לְעָזָר. דִּבְרֵי רִבִּי מֵאִיר. מָסַר שׁוֹר לְשׁוֹמֵר חִנָּם. יָצָא וְהִזִּיק פָּטוּר. יָצָא וְנִטְרַף פָּטוּר. לְשׁוֹמֵר שָׂכָר. יָצָא וְהִזִּיק חַייָב. יָצָא וְנִטְרַף פָּטוּר. אָמַר רִבִּי לְעָזָר. דִּבְרֵי רִבִּי יוּדָן. מָסַר שׁוֹר מוּעָד לְשׁוֹמֵר חִנָּם. יָצָא וְהִזִּיק חַייָב. יָצָא וְנִטְרַף פָּטוּר. לְשׁוֹמֵר שָׂכָר. יָצָא וְהִזִּיק חַייָב. נִטְרַף חַייָב. אָמַר רִבִּי לְעָזָר. וַהֲלֹא שָׁמוּר הוּא וְהַתּוֹרָה מְחַייְבַתּוּ. אָמַר רִבִּי לְעָזָר. כָּל־שְׁמִירָה שֶׁאָמְרָה תּוֹרָה אֲפִילוּ הִקִּיפוּ חוֹמַת בַּרְזֶל אֵין מְשַׁעֲרִין אוֹתוֹ אֶלָּא בְגוּפוֹ. לְפִיכָךְ רוֹאִין אוֹתוֹ אִם רָאוּי לִשְׁמִירָה פָּטוּר וְאִם לָאו חַייָב.

**Halakhah 10**: "If it was handed over to an unpaid trustee," etc. Rebbi Eleazar said, the words of Rebbi Meïr that watching for damages is on the level of an unpaid trustee[130]; Rebbi Jehuda said that watching for damages is on the level of a paid trustee[131].

Rebbi Eleazar said, the words of Rebbi Meïr: If one handed over a bull[132] to an unpaid trustee, if it went off and did damage, he is not liable[130]; if it went out and became torn[133], he is not liable[134]. To a paid trustee, if it went off and did damage, he is liable; if it went out and became torn, he is not liable[135].

Rebbi Eleazar said, the words of Rebbi Jehudah: If one handed over a notorious bull to an unpaid trustee, if it went off and did damage, he is liable; if it went out and became torn, he is not liable[136]. To a paid trustee, if it went off and did damage, he is liable; if it went out and became torn, he is liable[137]. Rebbi Eleazar said, was it not watched? But the Torah declared him liable.

Rebbi Eleazar said, for every guarding required by the Torah, even if it was done by enclosing in an iron wall, one only qualifies by personal presence[138]. Therefore one determines whether he is qualified for watching; then he is not liable, otherwise he is liable.

130 The unpaid trustee has to pay only if anything happens because of his negligence. Therefore, it seems that R. Eleazar refers to R. Meïr's position as articulated in Tosephta and *Mekhilta dR. Ismael*, Note 127.

131 The paid trustee has to pay for any damage which it was in his power to prevent. R. Jehudah frees the person guarding a notorious bull from being liable only because of an exemption granted by the verse.

132 In E and Rashba: "a tame bull". This seems to be required by the next paragraph.

133 The bull is attacked and severely damaged by another.

134 In E and Rashba: "is liable". In Rashba's explanation, the person who accepts the duty to watch over an animal becomes liable if the animal is damaged.

The text of L seems to be preferable since the unpaid trustee is freed from liability if he can swear that the damage was not caused by his negligence.

135 It seems that one has to read: "is liable". The clause is missing in Rashba's quote.

136 Since even the paid shepherd does not have to pay for the torn, by

*Ex.* 22:12.

137 Even though *Ex.* 22:12 frees the paid trustee from paying for a torn animal, here he should have prevented the bull from getting out in the first place.

138 Mechanical devices cannot replace personal supervision. Even the unpaid trustee will be liable if he relies on a mechanical device instead of his personal supervision.

## שור שנגח את הפרה פרק חמישי

(fol. 4c) **משנה א:** שׁוֹר שֶׁנָּגַח אֶת הַפָּרָה וְנִמְצָא עוּבָרָהּ בְּצִידָהּ וְאֵין יָדוּעַ אִם עַד שֶׁלֹּא נְגָחָהּ יָלְדָה אִם מִשֶּׁנְּגָחָהּ יָלְדָה מְשַׁלֵּם חֲצִי נֶזֶק לַפָּרָה וּרְבִיעַ לַוָּלָד.

**Mishnah 1**: A bull gored a cow and her fetus[1] was found beside her. If it is not known whether she gave birth before she was gored[2] or gave birth after she was gored, he pays half the damages for the cow[3] and a quarter for the fetus[4].

1 A dead fetus after a miscarriage.
2 In that case, the owner of the bull would not have to pay for the miscarriage.
3 The normal amount for damage caused by a tame bull.
4 Since the owner of the cow cannot prove that the bull caused the miscarriage but neither can the owner of the bull prove that his animal did not cause it, and the bull's attack on the cow is proved by two witnesses, the claim of damages for the fetus is "money in doubt" which is split evenly, cf. *Ketubot* 2:1, Note 9.

(4d line 40) **הלכה א:** שׁוֹר שֶׁנָּגַח אֶת הַפָּרָה כול׳. וְכִי כָּל־הַפָּרוֹת מַפִּילוֹת. נְהַלֵּךְ בָּהֶן אַחַר הָרוֹב וְאָמוֹר. מֵחֲמַת נְגִיחָה הִפִּילָה. זֹאת אוֹמֶרֶת שֶׁלֹּא הִילְכוּ בְּמִידַת הַדִּין בְּמָמוֹן אַחַר הָרוֹב אֶלָּא בְּמִיעוּט. אָמַר רִבִּי יוֹסֵי. בְּמָקוֹם אַחַר הִילְכוּ בְּמִידַת הַדִּין בְּמָמוֹן אַחַר הָרוֹב. כְּהָדָא דְתַנֵּי רִבִּי אָחָא. גָּמָל הָאוֹחֵר בֵּין הַגְּמַלִּים וְנִמְצָא שָׁם אֶחָד מֵת חַיָּיב. אֲנִי אוֹמֵר. בְּיָדוּעַ שֶׁזֶּה הֲרָגוֹ.

**Halakhah 1**: "A bull gored a cow", etc. [5]Do all cows have miscarriages? Should we follow the majority of cases? This implies that in criminal cases and in money matters one does not apply a majority argument. Rebbi Yose said, in another case they applied a majority argument in criminal cases and in money matters, as Rebbi Aḥa stated: [6]"If a camel was in heat among camels and one finds one of them dead, I am saying that certainly the one in heat killed it."

5   This is a slight reformulation of a passage in *Ketubot* 2:1, Notes 9-11.

6   Tosephta 3:6.

(fol. 4c) **משנה ב:** וְכֵן פָּרָה שֶׁנָּגְחָה אֶת הַשּׁוֹר וְנִמְצָא וַלְדָהּ בְּצִידָהּ וְאֵין יָדוּעַ אִם עַד שֶׁלֹּא נָגְחָה יָלְדָה אִם מִשֶּׁנָּגְחָה יָלְדָה מְשַׁלֵּם חֲצִי נֶזֶק מִן הַפָּרָה וּרְבִיעַ מִן הַוָּלָד.

**Mishnah 2**: And similarly, if a cow gored an ox and her calf is found next to her, but it is not known whether she gave birth before or after she gored[7], he pays half the damage from the cow and a quarter from the calf.

7   If at the moment of her goring the calf was part of her body, it is available to be sold to cover the damages. But if it was born before the goring, it is not available to the owner of the bull. Therefore, the claim of the bull's owner on the calf cannot exceed a quarter of its value.

(4d line 45) וְאָמַר רִבִּי יַנַּאי. כֵּינִי מַתְנִיתָא. מְשַׁלֵּם חֲצִי נֶזֶק מִן הַפָּרָה וּבַעַל הַוְּלָדוֹת עוֹלֶה לְבַעַל הַפָּרָה רְבִיעַ. אָמַר רִבִּי יוֹסֵי. זֶה נוֹתֵן מֶחֱצָה וְזֶה נוֹתֵן מֶחֱצָה. מַה מַפְקָה מִבֵּינֵיהוֹן. מֵתוּ הַוְּלָדוֹת. מָאן דָּמַר. מְשַׁלֵּם חֲצִי נֶזֶק לַפָּרָה וּרְבִיעַ נֶזֶק לַוָּלָד. אָהֵן יְהִיב נִיזְקֵיהּ וְאָהֵן יְהִיב נִיזְקֵיהּ. מָאן דָּמַר. מְשַׁלֵּם חֲצִי נֶזֶק מִן הַפָּרָה וּבַעַל הַוְּלָדוֹת עוֹלֶה לְבַעַל הַפָּרָה רְבִיעַ. אָהֵן יְהִיב נִיזְקֵיהּ. וְאָהֵן אָמַר. לֹא לְדֵין בָּעִית אַיְיִדֵי לִיקוּמֵיךְ.

**8**And Rebbi Yannai said, so is the Mishnah: He pays half of the damage from the cow and the owner of the calves returns a quarter to the owner of the cow[9]. Rebbi Yose said, each of them gives half[10]. What is the difference between them? If the calves died. According to him who said, he pays half of the damage from the cow and a quarter of the damage from the calf, each one pays his part of the damage. According to him who said, he pays half of the damage from the cow and the owner of the calves returns a quarter to the owner of the cow, one pays the damage, but the other one says, I did not want these, here they are before you[11].

8   In mss. and *editio princeps*, this paragraph is part of Halakhah 1. But it clearly refers to Mishnah 2.

9   He refers the Mishnah to the case where the rancher sold the expected calf of his pregnant cow to a third party. The owner of the bull has to be indemnified by the cow's owner alone, but the latter has regress on the calf's owner up to a quarter of its value.

The Babli, 46b, has another approach: If the cow is available, he collects half his damages from the cow. If the cow is not available, he collects a quarter of his damages from the calf.

10   He holds that the owner of the bull has to collect separately, first half of his claim of half the the damages up to a quarter of the calf's value and then the remainder from the cow's owner.

11   Even if the carcass of the calf is not worthless, he may return the dead bodies and claim his money back.

(4c line 50) **הלכה ב:** וְכֵן פָּרָה שֶׁנֶּגְחָה אֶת הַשּׁוֹר כול'. רִבִּי בּוּן בַּר כַּהֲנָא בְּעָא קוֹמֵי רִבִּי אִימִּי. מִפְּנֵי שֶׁהוּא סָפֵק. הָא אִילּוּ וַדָּאי זֶה נוֹתֵן מֶחֱצָה וְזֶה נוֹתֵן מֶחֱצָה. כָּךְ אֲנִי אוֹמֵר. רַגְלָהּ שֶׁלְּאָדָם אֶחָד כּוּלָּהּ שֶׁלְּאָדָם אֶחָד. זֶה נוֹתֵן מֶחֱצָה וְזֶה נוֹתֵן מֶחֱצָה. אָמַר לֵיהּ. בְּמוֹעֵד הִיא מַתְנִיתָא. רַגְלָהּ מְכוּרָה לָךְ. מָכַר חֶצְיָיהּ. רַגְלָהּ שְׁנִייָה מְכוּרָה לָךְ. מָכַר חֲצִי חֶצְיָיהּ. אָמַר רֵישׁ לָקִישׁ. כָּל־אִילֵּין שְׁמוּעָתָא דְּלֵוִי אִינּוּן.

**Halakhah 2**: "And similarly, if a cow gored an ox," etc. Rebbi Abun bar Cahana asked before Rebbi Immi: Because it is in doubt; therefore if it were certain, each one would give half[12]? Would I say that a foot of a person is the entire person? Each one would give half? He said to him, the Mishnah deals with a notorious animal[13]. [14]"Its foot is sold to you," he sold half[15]. "Its second foot is sold to you," he sold half of the [remaining] half[16]. Rebbi Simeon ben Laqish said, all these traditions are Levi's[17].

12  Why is the calf treated on an equal footing with the cow? Is not the calf here only an appendix to the cow?

13  It is difficult to accept this reading since the Mishnah clearly speaks of half damages, but it is confirmed by all quotes of this paragraph in Medieval sources.

14  A similar text is in Tosephta 'Arakhin 3:9,10.

15  The side to which the foot belongs.

16  Since he did not say that he was selling the other half, something is not sold. Therefore, sale of the unborn calf can be treated as sale of a quarter interest in the cow. If the cow were notorious, the owner of the calf would be liable as holder of a quarter interest in the cow.

17  As the Babli points out, 46a, both Mishnaiot have to be rejected. Instead of an appeal to Symmachos's principle that "one splits money in doubt", one rules that "the burden of proof is on the claimant" and in the absence of witnesses the owner of the injured animal has no chance to prove any claim he might have on the calf. R. Simeon ben Laqish seems to attribute to Levi the acceptance of Symmachos's rule in these cases.

(fol. 4c) **משנה ג**: הַקַּדָּר שֶׁהִכְנִיס קְדֵירוֹתָיו לַחֲצַר בַּעַל הַבַּיִת שֶׁלֹּא בִּרְשׁוּת וְשִׁבְּרָתָן בְּהֶמְתּוֹ שֶׁל בַּעַל הַבַּיִת פָּטוּר וְאִם הוּזְּקָה בָּהֶן בַּעַל הַקְּדֵירוֹת חַיָּיב וְאִם הִכְנִיס בִּרְשׁוּת בַּעַל הֶחָצֵר חַיָּיב.

**Mishnah 3**: If a potter put his pots in a private courtyard without permission and an animal of the owner broke them, [the owner] is not liable; if [the animal] was hurt, the owner of the pots is liable. But if he puts them there with permission, the owner of the courtyard is liable.

(4c line 56) **הלכה ג**: הַקַּדָּר שֶׁהִנִּיחַ קְדֵירוֹתָיו כול׳. הִכְנִיס קְדֵירוֹתָיו לַחֲצַר בַּעַל בַּיִת שֶׁלֹּא בִּרְשׁוּת וּבָא שׁוֹר מִמָּקוֹם אַחֵר וְשִׁבְּרָן פָּטוּר. הוּזַּק בָּהֶן פָּטוּר. הָדָא אָמְרָה. הַקֶּרֶן פְּטוּרָה בֶּחָצֵר שֶׁאֵינָהּ שֶׁלִּשְׁנֵיהֶן.

**Halakhah 3**: "If a potter put his pots," etc. If he put his pots in a private courtyard without permission and a bull came from another place and broke them, he[18] is not liable. If it was hurt by them, he is not liable[19]. This implies that 'horn'[20] is not liable in a courtyard which belongs to neither party[21].

| | | | |
|---|---|---|---|
| 18 | The bull's owner. | 20 | Probably one should read: 'foot'. |
| 19 | The potter. | 21 | Chapter 1, Halakhah 2. |

(fol. 4c) **משנה ד**: הִכְנִיס פֵּירוֹתָיו לַחֲצַר בַּעַל הַבַּיִת שֶׁלֹּא בִּרְשׁוּת וַאֲכָלָתַן בְּהֶמְתּוֹ שֶׁל בַּעַל הַבַּיִת פָּטוּר וְאִם הוּזְקָה בָּהֶן בַּעַל הַפֵּירוֹת חַיָּיב וְאִם הִכְנִיס בִּרְשׁוּת בַּעַל הֶחָצֵר חַיָּיב.

**Mishnah 4**: If somebody put his produce in a private courtyard without permission and an animal of the owner ate them, [the owner] is not liable; if [the animal] was hurt, the owner of the produce is liable. But if he puts them there with permission, the owner of the courtyard is liable.

(4c line 56) **הלכה ד:** הִכְנִיס פֵּירוֹתָיו לַחֲצַר בַּעַל הַבַּיִת כול'. הִכְנִיס פֵּירוֹתָיו לַחֲצַר בַּעַל הַבַּיִת שֶׁלֹּא בִּרְשׁוּת וּבָא שׁוֹר מִמָּקוֹם אַחֵר וַאֲכָלָן פָּטוּר. הוּזַק בָּהֶן פָּטוּר. הָדָא אֲמְרָה. שֶׁהַשֵּׁן פְּטוּרָה בֶחָצֵר שֶׁאֵינָהּ שֶׁלִּשְׁנֵיהֶן.

**Halakhah 4**: "If somebody put his produce in a private courtyard," etc. If he put his produce in a private courtyard without permission and a bull came from another place and ate them, he is not liable. If it was hurt by them, he is not liable. This implies that the 'tooth' is not liable in a courtyard which belongs to neither party.

(fol. 4d) **משנה ה:** הִכְנִיס שׁוֹרוֹ לַחֲצַר בַּעַל הַבַּיִת שֶׁלֹּא בִּרְשׁוּת וּנְגָחוֹ שׁוֹרוֹ שֶׁל בַּעַל הַבַּיִת אוֹ שֶׁנְּשָׁכוֹ כַּלְבּוֹ שֶׁל בַּעַל הַבַּיִת פָּטוּר. נָגַח הוּא שׁוֹרוֹ שֶׁל בַּעַל הַבַּיִת חַיָּיב. נָפַל לְבוֹרוֹ וְהִבְאִישׁ מֵימָיו חַיָּיב. הָיָה אָבִיו אוֹ בְנוֹ לְתוֹכוֹ מְשַׁלֵּם אֶת הַכּוֹפֶר וְאִם הִכְנִיס בִּרְשׁוּת בַּעַל הֶחָצֵר חַיָּיב. רִבִּי אוֹמֵר בְּכוּלָּן עַד שֶׁיְּקַבֵּל עָלָיו לִשְׁמוֹר.

**Mishnah 5**: If somebody put his bull in a private courtyard without permission and the owner's bull gored it or his dog bit it, [the owner] is not liable; if it gored the owner's bull, he[18] is liable. If it fell into his[22] cistern and caused it to stink, he is liable. If his[22] father or son were inside[23], he pays weregilt. But if he put it in by permission, the owner of the courtyard is liable; Rebbi says, in all these cases[24], only if he[21] agreed to watch.

| | | | |
|---|---|---|---|
| 21 | The courtyard's owner. | | bull. |
| 23 | And were killed by the falling | 24 | Mishnaiot 3-5. |

(4c line 62) **הלכה ה:** הִכְנִיס שׁוֹר לַחֲצַר בַּעַל הַבַּיִת כול'. הִכְנִיס שׁוֹר לַחֲצַר בַּעַל הַבַּיִת שֶׁלֹּא בִּרְשׁוּת וּבָא שׁוֹר מִמָּקוֹם אַחֵר. נָגַח נָגַף רָבַץ בָּעַט נָשַׁךְ מְשַׁלֵּם נֶזֶק שָׁלֵם. דִּבְרֵי רִבִּי מֵאִיר. וַחֲכָמִים אוֹמְרִים. עַל הַשֵּׁן וְעַל הָרֶגֶל חַיָּיב. עַל הַנְּגִיחָה וְעַל הַנְּגִיפָה וְעַל הַנְּשִׁיכָה וְעַל הָרְבִיצָה וְעַל הַבְּעִיטָה וְעַל הַדְּחִייָה תָּם מְשַׁלֵּם חֲצִי נֶזֶק. מוּעָד מְשַׁלֵּם נֶזֶק שָׁלֵם מִן הָעֲלִייָה.

**Halakhah 5:** "If somebody put a bull in a private courtyard," etc. [25]"If somebody put a bull in a private courtyard without permission, and a bull came from another place. If it gored, hit, bit, walloped, or kicked, he pays full damages, the words of Rebbi Meïr[26]. But the Sages say, for 'tooth' and 'foot' he is liable[27]; for goring, or hitting, or biting, or walloping, or kicking, or pushing, a tame [bull] pays half the damages, a notorious full damages from storage."

25 Tosephta 5:10,9. A very incomplete quote in the Babli, 48a.

26 For him, half damages for 'horn'

only applies in the public domain.

27 Cf. Halakhah 1:2.

(4c line 62) רַב יְהוּדָה בְּשֵׁם שְׁמוּאֵל. הֲלָכָה כְרִבִּי. רַב זְעִירָא אָמַר. הֲלָכָה כְרִבִּי. אָמַר רִבִּי יִרְמְיָה. הַכֹּל מוֹדִין בַּבַּיִת שֶׁהוּא אוֹמֵר לוֹ. הַכָּנֵס וַאֲנִי מְשַׁמְּרוֹ. הַכֹּל מוֹדִין בַּשָּׂדֶה שֶׁאוֹמֵר לוֹ. הַכְנִיסֵהוּ וְשׁוֹמְרֵהוּ. מַה פְלִיגִין. בֶּחָצֵר. רִבִּי אוֹמֵר. חָצֵר כְּשָׂדֶה. וַחֲכָמִים אוֹמְרִים. חָצֵר כַּבַּיִת. תַּמָּן תַּנִּינָן. הַמַּגְדִּישׁ בְּתוֹךְ שְׂדֵה חֲבֵירוֹ שֶׁלֹּא בִּרְשׁוּת. גְּדִישִׁים בַּשָּׂדֶה כְּכֵלִים בַּבַּיִת. אָמַר רִבִּי יוֹסֵי בֵּי רִבִּי בּוּן. תִּיפָּתֵר בָּהִיא דְאִית לָהּ מִסְגָּר.

Rav Jehudah in the name of Samuel: Practice follows Rebbi[28]. Rav Ze'ira said, practice follows Rebbi. Rebbi Jeremiah said, everybody agrees that in a house, if he tells him, "put it in," [he implies] "and I shall watch it." Everybody agrees that on a field, if he tells him, "put it in," [he implies] "and you watch it." Where do they disagree? In a courtyard. Rebbi says, a courtyard is like a field, but the Sages say, a courtyard is like a house. There, we have stated[29]: If somebody assembles sheaves in another person's field without permission." [R. Isaac said,][30] sheaves on a field are like vessels in a house[31]? Rebbi Yose ben Rebbi Abun said, explain it by one which has a lock[32].

28  Babli 48b.
29  Mishnah 6:3. There, it is stated that if the owner gave permission, he is liable for damages; this seems to contradict R. Jeremiah's explanation.
30  Reading of E and Halakhah 6:3.
31  Because of their value, they always are guarded.
32  The field is fenced and locked in.

(fol. 4d) **משנה ו:** שׁוֹר שֶׁהָיָה מִתְכַּוֵּן לַחֲבֵירוֹ וְהִכָּה אֶת הָאִשָּׁה וְיָצְאוּ יְלָדֶיהָ פָּטוּר מִדְּמֵי וְלָדוֹת. וְאָדָם שֶׁהָיָה מִתְכַּוֵּן לַחֲבֵירוֹ וְהִכָּה אֶת הָאִשָּׁה וְיָצְאוּ יְלָדֶיהָ מְשַׁלֵּם דְּמֵי וְלָדוֹת. כֵּיצַד מְשַׁלֵּם דְּמֵי וְלָדוֹת. שָׁמִין אֶת הָאִשָּׁה כַּמָּה הִיא יָפָה עַד שֶׁלֹּא יָלְדָה וְכַמָּה הִיא יָפָה מִשֶּׁיָּלְדָה. אָמַר רַבָּן שִׁמְעוֹן בֶּן גַּמְלִיאֵל אִם כֵּן מִשֶּׁהָאִשָּׁה יוֹלֶדֶת מַשְׁבַּחַת. אֶלָּא שָׁמִין אֶת הַוְולָדוֹת כַּמָּה הֵן יָפִין וְנוֹתְנִים לַבַּעַל. וְאִם אֵין לָהּ בַּעַל נוֹתְנִים לְיוֹרְשָׁיו. הָיְתָה שִׁפְחָה וְנִשְׁתַּחְרְרָה אוֹ גִּיּוֹרֶת פָּטוּר.

**Mishnah 6**: If a bull intended [to hurt] another bull but hit a woman who then had a miscarriage, he is not liable. But if a man intended [to hurt] a neighbor but hit a woman who then had a miscarriage, he pays for the children[33]. How does he pay for the children? One estimates the worth of the woman before and after she gave birth[34]. Rabban Simeon ben Gamliel said, but the value of a woman increses after giving birth![35] But one estimates how much the children would have been worth and gives [the value] to the husband; if she does not have a husband, to the latter's heirs. If she was a freedwoman or a proselyte[36], he is not liable.

33 *Ex.* 21:22 speaks only about quarrelling men hitting a woman, not animals attacking.

34 How much she would be worth on the slave market.

35 Before she gave birth, a potential buyer would discount the price to account for the risk of death in childbirth.

36 If she was pregnant when she was manumitted or converted, she has no legal father of the children. Also if a woman was married to a freedman or a proselyte who died childless, the attacker does not have to pay since the husband has no heir (but cf. Babli 49a/b, *Mekhilta dR. Simeon b. Ioḥai* 21:22).

(4c line 75) **הלכה ו:** שׁוֹר שֶׁהָיָה מִתְכַּוֵּן כול'. שׁוֹר שֶׁהָיָה מִתְכַּוֵּן לַחֲבֵירוֹ. הָא אִם הָיָה מִתְכַּוֵּין לָאִשָּׁה חַיָּיב. וְלֹא שַׁנְיָיא הִיא בֵּין שֶׁהוּא מִתְכַּוֵּין לְהַכּוֹת אֶת הָאִשָּׁה בֵּין שֶׁנִּתְכַּוֵּון לְהַכּוֹת חֲבֵירוֹ. וְלָמָּה תַנִּינָה הָכָא. אָמַר אַבָּא בַּר רַב חָנָה. בְּגִין מַתְנֵי הָא דְּבַתְרָהּ. אָדָם שֶׁהָיָה מִתְכַּוֵּן לַחֲבֵירוֹ וְהִכָּה אֶת הָאִשָּׁה וְיָצְאוּ יְלָדֶיהָ מְשַׁלֵּם דְּמֵי וְלָדוֹת.

**Halakhah 6:** "If a bull intended," etc. A bull which intended [to attack] another; therefore, if it intended to hit the woman is he liable? Does it make a difference whether it intended to hit the woman or intended to hit another [bull][37]? Then why was it stated here? Abba bar Rav Ḥana[38] said, because he had to state the next clause: "But if a human intended [to hurt] another human but hit a woman who then had a miscarriage, he pays for the children."

37 Since *Ex.* 21:22 speaks only of men; animals are excluded irrespective of their actions. The same argument is in the Babli, 49a, in the name of Rav Ada bar Aḥawa.

38 One might wonder whether to read "Abba bar bar Ḥana".

(5a line 3) תַּנֵּי. הָאוֹמֵר לַחֲבֵירוֹ. שִׁפְחָה וֻלְדָּנִית אֲנִי מוֹכֵר לָךְ בָּנֶיהָ מַשְׁבִּיחִין אוֹתָהּ. רַבָּן שִׁמְעוֹן בֶּן גַּמְלִיאֵל אוֹמֵר. קוֹטִיסְמֵי הִיא זוֹ. כְּתִיב כִּי יִנָּצוּ אֲנָשִׁים וְנָגְפוּ אִשָּׁה הָרָה וְיָצְאוּ יְלָדֶיהָ. אַבָּא יוֹסֵי בֶּן חָנָן אוֹמֵר. מִמַּשְׁמָע שֶׁנֶּאֱמַר וְיָצְאוּ יְלָדֶיהָ אֵינִי יוֹדֵעַ שֶׁהִיא הָרָה. מַה תַּלְמוּד לוֹמַר הָרָה. מַגִּיד שֶׁאֵין מִתְחַיֵּיב עַד שֶׁיַּכֶּה בִּמְקוֹם עוּבְּרָהּ. הָא אִם הִכָּה עַל כַּף יָדָהּ אוֹ עַל כַּף רַגְלָהּ פָּטוּר. כַּאֲשֶׁר יוֹשֵׁת³⁹ עָלָיו בַּעַל הָאִשָּׁה. שׁוֹמְעֵנִי אַף עַל פִּי שֶׁאֵין הֵהֵרְיוֹן שֶׁלּוֹ. תַּלְמוּד לוֹמַר הָרָה. מַגִּיד שֶׁאֵינוֹ מְשַׁלֵּם אֶלָּא לְבַעַל הֵהֵרְיוֹן. רִבִּי עוּקְבָּא שָׁאַל. בָּא עַל אִמּוֹ בָּא עַל אֲחוֹתוֹ אַף הוּא בַּעַל הֵרָיוֹן הוּא. תַּלְמוּד לוֹמַר בַּעַל. אֶת שֶׁרָאוּי לִיקָרוֹת בַּעַל. יָצְאוּ אֵילוּ שֶׁאֵינָן רְאוּיִין לִהְיוֹת בַּעַל.

It was stated: "I am selling you a fertile slave girl, her children increase her value. Rabban Simeon ben Gamliel says, this is buttocks[40]."

It is written[41]: "If quarrelling men hit a pregnant woman and she loses her children." [42]Abba Yose ben Ḥanan said, from the meaning of "and she loses her children" would I not know that she was pregnant? Then why does the verse say "pregnant"? It tells you that he is not liable unless he hits her at the place of her pregnancy. Therefore, if he hit her on the palm of her hand or the sole of her foot, he is not liable[43]. "As the woman's husband will put on him". Do I understand, even if the pregnancy is not his[44]? The verse says, "pregnant". It tells that he pays only to the master of the pregnancy. Rebbi Uqba[45] asked, if somebody sleeps with his mother or his sister, is that one not also the master of the pregnancy? The verse says "husband", somebody who may be called "husband". This excludes those who cannot be called[45a] "husband"[46].

39   In the biblical text יָשִׁית.
40   Greek κάθισμα "buttocks, behind; seat; sinking". It may be that the word is used here in a slightly pornographic meaning.
41   Ex. 21:22.

42  *Mekhilta dR. Ismael Neziqin* 8; partially quoted in the Babli, 49a.

43  In E and *Or Zarua'* (vol. 3, #236), one reads: "If he hit her on the palm of her hand or the sole of her foot, *on her head or any of her limbs, would we understand that he be liable? The verse says, "pregnant"* (it tells you that he is not liable . . .).

44  If he married a pregnant girl.

45  In the Medieval parallel sources [*Tosaphot* 43a, *Or zarua', Yalqut Šim'oni Qonṭeros Aḥaron* (Ashkenazi), *Rashba ad* 43a (Sephardi)], "R. Aqiba", an unlikely text.

45a  The translation follows the reading להיקרות of E, not the bland "to be" of L.

46  Since an incestual marriage is no marriage at all (*Qiddušin* 3:12), *Or zarua'* (*loc. cit.*) deduces from here that the adulterous father of a bastard fetus has a claim on the money since he could have married the woman had she not been otherwise married. The Babli, 43a, explicitly gives the claim to the money to the boyfriend of an unmarried pregnant woman.

(5a line 13) רִבִּי יָסָא בְּשֵׁם רִבִּי יוֹחָנָן. עוֹבָרִין אֵין יוֹצְאִין בְּשֵׁן וָעַיִן. נִיחָא בְּשֵׁר. וָעַיִן. אָמַר רִבִּי יֵסֵא בִּירְבִּי בּוּן. כֵּינִי מַתְנִיתָא. עוֹבָרִין אֵין יוֹצְאִין בְּשֵׁן וָעַיִן שֶׁל אִמָּן.

Rebbi Yasa in the name of Rebbi Joḥanan: Fetuses do not gain freedom by 'tooth and eye.'[47] One understands "eye". Tooth?[48] Rebbi Yose ben Rebbi Abun said, so is the *baraita*: Fetuses do not gain freedom by their mother's 'tooth and eye.'[49]

47  A slave gains his freedom if his master severely injures one of his limbs, exemplified by "tooth and eye"; *Ex.* 21:26-27, *Qiddušin* 1:3, Note 380.

48  The translation follows E. In L, the terms are exchanged, following the biblical mention of "tooth" before "eye". But a fetus has no tooth, only eyes. The Babli, *Qiddušin* 24b, understands the statement as meaning that the child of a slave mother is born free if he was injured in the womb by his master.

49  This contradicts the Yerushalmi's doctrine (*Qiddušin* 1:3, Notes 403-407) that a slave woman and her fetus cannot have different status;

it follows the minority opinion of R. Johanan (*Qiddušin* 1:3, Notes 408) that there can be no partial manumission except in the case of a slave belonging to two joint owners.

(fol. 4d) **משנה ז:** הַחוֹפֵר בּוֹר בִּרְשׁוּת הָרַבִּים וְנָפַל לְתוֹכוֹ שׁוֹר אוֹ חֲמוֹר וָמֵת חַיָּב. אֶחָד הַחוֹפֵר בּוֹר שִׁיחַ וּמְעָרָה חֲרִיצִים וּנְעִיצִים חַיָּב. אִם כֵּן לָמָּה נֶאֱמַר בּוֹר. מַה הַבּוֹר שֶׁהוּא כְדֵי לְהָמִית עַד עֲשָׂרָה טְפָחִים אַף כָּל־דָּבָר שֶׁיֶּשׁ בּוֹ כְדֵי לְהָמִית עַד עֲשָׂרָה טְפָחִים. הָיוּ פְחוּתִין מֵעֲשָׂרָה טְפָחִים וְנָפַל לְתוֹכוֹ שׁוֹר אוֹ חֲמוֹר וָמֵת פָּטוּר וְאִם הוּזַּק בּוֹ חַיָּב.

**Mishnah 7:**[50] One who digs a pit in the public domain is liable if an ox or a donkey fell in and died. Anyone who digs a pit, a ditch, a cave, rectangular excavations, or bases for poles, is liable. Then why is it said "a pit"? Just as a pit to be life-threatening must be ten handbreadths[51] deep, so everything to be life-threatening must be ten handbreadths deep. If it was less than ten handbreadths deep when an ox or a donkey fell in and died, he is not liable[52], but if they were damaged, he is liable[53].

**משנה ח:** הַחוֹפֵר בּוֹר בִּרְשׁוּת הַיָּחִיד וּפְתָחוֹ לִרְשׁוּת הָרַבִּים אוֹ בִּרְשׁוּת הָרַבִּים וּפְתָחוֹ לִרְשׁוּת הַיָּחִיד בִּרְשׁוּת הַיָּחִיד וּפְתָחוֹ לִרְשׁוּת הַיָּחִיד אַחֵר חַיָּב.

**Mishnah 8:** One who digs a pit in a private domain and opens it to the public domain[54], in the public domain and opens it to a private domain, in a private domain and opens it to another private domain, is liable[55].

50  In the Babli and most independent Mishnah mss., Mishnah 7 is Mishnah 8 and vice versa.

51  About 1 yard.

52  Since *Ex.* 21:33-34 is not applicable.

53  For any obstacle put into the public domain, the person responsible is liable for full damages (Chapter 1, Note 3).

54    If the pit is so close to the public domain that an unsuspecting passer-by might be tripped by it, it is counted as obstacle in the public domain. If the private domain is separated from the public domain or another private domain by a fence at least 10 handbreadths high, the owner can do what he pleases on his property (Babli 50a).

55    Again, if the pit is too close to the other property, it is putting an unauthorized obstacle on somebody else's property.

**הלכה ז:** הַחוֹפֵר בּוֹר בִּרְשׁוּת הָרַבִּים כול'. כְּתִיב כִּי יִפְתַּח אִישׁ בּוֹר וְכִי יִכְרֶה אִישׁ בּוֹר. אֶחָד בּוֹר לִנְזָקִין וְאֶחָד בּוֹר לְמִיתָה. אָמַר רִבִּי יִצְחָק. אֶחָד בּוֹר שֶׁלְּמִיתָה וְאֶחָד בּוֹר לִנְזָקִין שְׁנֵיהֶן מִמִּקְרָא אֶחָד נִתְרַבּוּ. וּכְשֶׁהוּא בָא לְבוֹר שֶׁלְּמִיתָה אַתְּ מַר. פָּטוּר עַל הַכֵּלִים. וּכְשֶׁהוּא בָא לְבוֹר שֶׁלִּנְזָקִין אַתְּ מַר. חַייָב עַל הַכֵּלִים. אֵין לִי אֶלָּא בְּשֶׁחָפַר. לָקַח יָרַשׁ נִיתַּן לוֹ בְמַתָּנָה מְנַיִין. שֶׁנֶּאֱמַר אוֹ כִי יִכְרֶה אִישׁ בּוֹר. וְכִי יֵשׁ לוֹ רְשׁוּת לְהַבְקִיר נְזָקָיו בִּרְשׁוּת הָרַבִּים. אָמַר רִבִּי יוֹסֵי בֵּירִבִּי בּוּן. תִּיפְתָּר כְּרִבִּי יוֹסֵי בֵּירִבִּי יְהוּדָה דְּאָמַר. שְׁלֹשָׁה (דְּבָרִים) שֶׁהֵן סְמוּכִין לִרְשׁוּת כִּרְשׁוּת.

**Halakhah 7:** "One who digs a pit in the public domain," etc. It is written[56]: "If a man open a pit" and "if a man dig a pit." One pit for damages, the other pit for death[57]. Rebbi Isaac said, both the pit of death and the pit of damages were added from the same verse, but when it comes to the pit of death you say he is not liable for vessels, but when it comes to the pit of damages you say he is liable for vessels[58]! This is not only if he dug, from where if he bought, inherited, or it was given to him as a gift? The verse says, "if a man acquire a pit.[59]" Has one the right to abandon his damages in the public domain[60]? Rebbi Yose ben Rebbi Abun said, explain it following Rebbi Yose ben Rebbi Jehudah who said, three [handbreadths][61] close to a domain are like that domain[62].

56   *Ex.* 21:33.

57   The verse mentions "opening" for a pit which is not deep enough to kill an animal, and "digging" for a pit

deep enough to kill.

58   In the next Halakhah one deduces "an ox but not an ox with his vessels" from the language of the verse. Why does this not apply to damages in case the animal survives the fall? No answer is given; it must be that the award of damages in this case is a matter of common, not biblical law.

59   Understanding יכרה as not derived from I כרה "to dig" but from II כרה "to buy" (*Deut* 2:6, *Hos.* 3:2); in the Babli (*Soṭah* 13a, *Roš Haššanah* 26a) this is charaterized as Phoenician.

60   Since 'pit' is an obstacle in the public domain, how is it possible to acquire if from another person?

61   Reading טפחים for דברים "things" in the text.

62   This defines what means "close to another domain" in Mishnah 8 (Note 54). In the Babli, 50a, he requires a distance of at least 4 handbreadths. A private domain can be bought or inherited with all its liabilities.

(5a line 23) רִבִּי מָנָא בָּעֵי.  מָהוּ שֶׁיֵּעָשֶׂה אֶת הָעוֹמֶק כְּגוּבָהּ.  וְהֵיכִי דָמֵי.  אִין בְּהַהוּא דָאָתֵי מִן עֵיל חָמֵי לֵיהּ.  אֶלָּא בְּהַהוּא דַאֲתֵי מִן לְרַע.

Rebbi Mana asked: Can the depth be considered like the height? How is that[63]? If about him who comes from up high, he sees it. But for him who comes from below[64].

63   As I. Lewy correctly notes, היכי דמי is pure Babli language.

64   In the absence of parallel texts, any interpretation of this paragraph is speculative. The explanation of Eliahu Fulda seems the most natural: The pit is dug on an incline; it does not go deeper than the surrounding valley. For an ox coming down from the hill, the pit is simply a slightly steeper declivity, but for one climbing up from the valley it is a real obstacle.

**משנה ט:** בּוֹר שֶׁל שְׁנֵי שׁוּתָּפִין עָבַר עָלָיו הָרִאשׁוֹן וְלֹא כִיסָּהוּ וְהַשֵּׁינִי וְלֹא כִיסָּהוּ הַשֵּׁינִי חַיָּיב.  כִּיסָּהוּ הָרִאשׁוֹן וּבָא הַשֵּׁינִי וְגִילֵּהוּ הַשֵּׁינִי חַיָּיב.  כִּיסָּהוּ הָרִאשׁוֹן וּבָא הַשֵּׁינִי וּמְצָאוֹ מְגוּלֶּה וְלֹא כִיסָּהוּ הַשֵּׁינִי חַיָּיב.  כִּיסָּהוּ כָּרָאוּי וְנָפַל לְתוֹכוֹ שׁוֹר אוֹ חֲמוֹר וָמֵת פָּטוּר.  לֹא כִיסָּהוּ כָּרָאוּי וְנָפַל לְתוֹכוֹ (fol. 4d)

שׁוֹר אוֹ חֲמוֹר וָמֵת חַיָּב. נָפַל לְפָנָיו מִקּוֹל הַכְּרִיָּיה חַיָּב לְאַחֲרָיו מִקּוֹל הַכְּרִיָּיה פָּטוּר. נָפַל לְתוֹכוֹ שׁוֹר וְכֵלָיו וְנִשְׁתַּבְּרוּ חֲמוֹר וְכֵלָיו וְנִתְקָרְאוּ חַיָּב עַל הַבְּהֵמָה וּפָטוּר עַל הַכֵּלִים. נָפַל לְתוֹכוֹ שׁוֹר חֵרֵשׁ שׁוֹטֶה וְקָטָן חַיָּב. בֵּן אוֹ בַת עֶבֶד אוֹ אָמָא פָּטוּר.

**Mishnah 9**: A pit dug by two partners; if the first went by and did not cover it, the second and did not cover it, the second is liable. If the first covered it, the second came and uncovered it, the second is liable. If the first covered it, the second came, found it uncovered but did not cover it, the second is liable. If he covered it appropriately[65] but an ox or a donkey fell in and died, he is not liable[66]. If he did not cover it appropriately and an ox or a donkey fell in and died, he is liable. If it fell forward because of the noise of the excavation, he is liable, backward because of the noise of the excavation, he is not liable[67]. If an ox and its equipment[68] fell in and broke, a donkey and its equipment[69] was torn, he is liable for the animal but not liable for the equipment. If the ox falling in was deaf-mute, insane, or young, he is liable[70]; a son or daughter, a slave or slave-girl, he is not liable[71].

[65] This will be defined in the Halakhah.

[66] *Ex.* 21:33 explicitly absolves him if the pit is covered.

[67] An animal falling backward is an unusual occurrence that cannot be foreseen; also in this case the animal fell on the ground and not into the pit.

[68] Harness and plough.

[69] Cover and saddle.

[70] These categories do not apply to animals.

[71] Humans are supposed to watch where they are going.

**הלכה ט**: בּוֹר שֶׁלִּשְׁנֵי שׁוּתָּפִין כול'. (5a line 25) הֵיךְ אֵיפְשַׁר לְבוֹר שֶׁלִּשְׁנֵי שׁוּתָּפִים. אָמַר רִבִּי יַנַּאי. תִּיפָּתֵר שֶׁנְּתָנוּ אֶבֶן שְׁנֵיהֶן אֶבֶן הָאַחֲרוֹנָה. וְלָמָּה לֹא פָתַר

לָהּ בְּחָפַר זֶה עֲשָׂרָה וְזֶה עֲשָׂרָה. דּוּ בָעֵי מִיפְתְּרִינֵיהּ בְּבוֹר שֶׁלַּעֲשָׂרָה טְפָחִים שֶׁלִּשְׁנֵי שׁוּתָפִין.

**Halakhah 9**: "A pit dug by two partners," etc. How is a pit of two partners possible[72]? Rebbi Yannai said, explain it if they both together put in the last stone[73]. And why did they not explain that each of them dug ten handbreadths[74]? Because he wants to explain it for a pit ten handbreadths deep[75] of two partners.

72  Since the pit is dug in the public domain, it is the sole responsibility of the digger; there can be no joint ownership.

73  They together secured the rim lest the pit collapse. In the Babli, 51a, this explanation is ascribed to R. Johanan, R. Yannai's student.

74  Halakhah 1:2, Note 107.

75  The mininum depth for which the digger is responsible if an animal is killed. The Mishnah is always formulated to apply to the borderline case.

(5a line 28) עָבַר עָלָיו הָרִאשׁוֹן וְלֹא כִיסָּהוּ וְהַשֵּׁינִי וְלֹא כִיסָּהוּ הַשֵּׁינִי חַיָּיב. רִבִּי בָּא בַּר בִּיזְנָא רִבִּי יָסָא בְשֵׁם רִבִּי יוֹחָנָן. נוֹתְנִין לוֹ שָׁהוּת לִכְרוֹת אֲרָזִים מִן הַלְּבָנוֹן. אִית בָּהּ לְחוּמְרָא וְאִית בָּהּ לְקוּלָּא. פְּעָמִים שֶׁסְּמוּכִין לַלְּבָנוֹן. פְּעָמִים שֶׁרְחוֹקִין לַלְּבָנוֹן.

"If the first went by and did not cover it, the second and did not cover it, the second is liable." Rebbi Abba bar Bizna[76], Rebbi Yasa in the name of Rebbi Johanan: One gives him time to cut cedars from Lebanon[77]. That can be a stringency and it can be a leniency[78]. Sometimes he is close to the Lebanon, sometimes he is far from the Lebanon.

76  An Amora of this name is not otherwise known. With all quotes in Medieval authors one should read "bar Bina (Abbina)".

77  In the interpretation of the Babli (52a): The first partner is freed

from liability if the second had time to bring wood from Lebanon after being informed that the pit was not covered.

78   It is missing the main point of a legal rule, to be equally applicable to everybody. In the Babli, Samuel therefore states that the first is freed from liability the moment the second becomes aware of the situation.

(5a line 32) כִּסָּהוּ כָּרָאוּי. עַד הֵיכָן כִּסָּהוּ. יָבֹא כַּיי דְּתַנִּינָן תַּמָּן. כְּדֵי שֶׁתְּהֵא עֲגָלָה מְהַלֶּכֶת טְעוּנָה אֲבָנִים.

"If he covered it appropriately." How much does it have to be covered? It shall be as we have stated there: "That [it can withstand] a truck full of stones driving over it.[79]"

אָמַר רבִּי יַנַּאי. לְתוֹכוֹ בֵּין שֶׁלְּפָנָיו בֵּין שֶׁלְּאַחֲרָיו פָּטוּר. חוּצָה לוֹ לְפָנָיו פָּטוּר לְאַחֲרָיו חַיָּיב.

Rebbi Yannai said, in front of him, whether forward ot behind he is (not) liable. Outside, forward he is (not) liable, behind he is [not] liable[80].

79   Mishnah *Bava batra* 3:12; cf. *Bikkurim* 1:1, Notes 19-20.

80   This refers to the case that the animal was frightened by the noise of the excavation. It is clear that in the entire statement, "not liable" has to be replaced by "liable", and vice versa. This is confirmed by Tosephta 6:13 which frees from liability only if the animal falls backward outside the pit; *Mekhilta dR. Ismael Neziqin* 11 (ed. Horovitz-Rabin p. 289), *Mekhilta dR. Simeon b. Iohai* 21:33 (ed. Epstein-Melamed p. 185 l. 13).

(5a line 35) נָפַל לְתוֹכוֹ שׁוֹר וְכֵילָיו וְנִשְׁתַּבְּרוּ חֲמוֹר וְכֵילָיו וְנִתְקָרְאוּ חַיָּיב עַל הַבְּהֵמָה וּפָטוּר עַל הַכֵּלִים. שְׁמוּאֵל אָמַר. בְּשֶׁהִתְרִיפוּ מַחֲמַת אֲוֵירוֹ. אֲבָל אִם נֶחְבַּט בַּקַּרְקַע חַיָּיב. רִבִּי יוֹחָנָן וְרֵישׁ לָקִישׁ תְּרֵיהוֹן אָמְרִין. אֲפִילוּ נֶחְבַּט בַּקַּרְקַע פָּטוּר. דֶּרֶךְ נְפִילָה פָּטְרָה תּוֹרָה. וְנָפַל שָׁמָּה שׁוֹר אוֹ חֲמוֹר. שׁוֹר וְלֹא שׁוֹר בְּכֵלָיו. חֲמוֹר וְלֹא חֲמוֹר בְּכֵלָיו. שֶׁהָיָה בְדִין. מָה אִם בּוֹר נְזָקִין שֶׁפָּטוּר מִן

הַמִּיתָה חַיָּיב עַל הַכֵּלִים. בּוֹר שֶׁלַּעֲשָׂרָה טְפָחִים שֶׁחַיָּיב עַל הַמִּיתָה אֵינוֹ דִין שֶׁיְּהֵא חַיָּיב עַל הַכֵּלִים. תַּלְמוּד לוֹמַר וְנָפַל שָׁמָּה שׁוֹר אוֹ חֲמוֹר. שׁוֹר וְלֹא שׁוֹר בְּכֵלָיו. חֲמוֹר וְלֹא חֲמוֹר בְּכֵלָיו.

"If an ox and its equipment[68] fell in and broke, a donkey and its equipment[69] and was torn, he is liable for the animal but not liable for the equipment." Samuel said, when it became disoriented because of the air[81], but if it hit the ground he is liable. Rebbi Joḥanan and Rebbi Simeon ben Laqish both say, even if it hit the ground, he is not liable[82]: The Torah absolved from liability when it fell down. "An ox or a donkey fell in there;[56]" "an ox" and not an ox and its equipment; "a donkey" and not a donkey and its equipment[83]. Since it looked logical: If a pit of damages[58], where one is not liable for death, one is liable for vessels; would it not be logical that for a pit ten handbreadths deep, for which one is liable for death, should one not be liable for vessels?[84] The verse says, "an ox or a donkey fell in there;" "an ox" and not an ox and its equipment; "a donkey" and not a donkey and its equipment.

81 The bad air exuding from the pit.

82 In the Babli, 53a, Samuel's statement is attributed to Rav, R. Joḥanan and Resh Laqish's to Samuel. Since in the Babli practice follows Samuel and in the Yerushalmi R. Joḥanan, both Talmudim decide in the same way.

83 Cf. Halakhah 3:1, Note 34, and the references given there.

84 *Mekhilta dR. Ismael Neziqin* 11 p. 288 l. 16.

(5a line 44) נָפַל לְתוֹכוֹ שׁוֹר חֵרֵשׁ שׁוֹטֶה וְקָטָן חַיָּיב. אָמַר רִבִּי לְעָזָר. כֵּינֵי מַתְנִיתָא. שׁוֹור וְהוּא חֵרֵשׁ שׁוֹר וְהוּא שׁוֹטֶה [שׁוֹר וְהוּא קָטָן]. בֶּן אוֹ בַת עֶבֶד אוֹ אָמָה פָּטוּר.

"If the ox falling in was deaf-mute, insane, or young, he is liable". Rebbi Eleazar said, so is the Mishnah: an ox which is deaf-mute, an insane ox[85], [an underage ox][86]; "a son or daughter, a slave or slave-girl, he is not liable".

85 One should not read the Mishnah as: "An ox, a deaf-mute, an insane, or a minor," the last three items referring to humans.

86 Addition from E and a Genizah fragment; also required by general Talmudic style.

(fol. 4d) **משנה י:** אֶחָד הַשּׁוֹר וְאֶחָד כָּל־הַבְּהֵמָה לִנְפִילַת הַבּוֹר לְהַפְרָשַׁת הַר סִינַי וּלְתַשְׁלוּמֵי כֶפֶל וּלְהָשִׁיב אֲבֵידָה לִפְרִיקָה לַחֲסִימָה לַכִּלְאַיִם וְלַשַּׁבָּת. וְכֵן חַיָּה וָעוֹף כַּיּוֹצֵא בָהֶן. אִם כֵּן לָמָּה נֶאֱמַר שׁוֹר אוֹ חֲמוֹר. אֶלָּא שֶׁדִּיבֶּר הַכָּתוּב בַּהוֹוֶה.

**Mishnah 10**: The ox and any domestic animal equally are under the rules of falling into a pit, separating from Mount Sinai[88], paying double restitution, returning lost property, unloading, muzzling, interbreeding, and the Sabbath. Wild animals and birds follow the same rules. Then why was it said "ox or donkey"? But the verse speaks of the actuality[87].

87 At the time of the promulgation of the Law, these were the most frequent cases.

88 *Ex.* 19:13.

(5a line 46) **הלכה י:** אֶחָד הַשּׁוֹר וְאֶחָד כָּל־הַבְּהֵמָה לִנְפִילַת הַבּוֹר כול'. לִנְפִילַת הַבּוֹר וְנָפַל שָׁמָּה שׁוֹר אוֹ חֲמוֹר. לְהַפְרָשַׁת הַר סִינַי אִם בְּהֵמָה אִם אִישׁ לֹא יִחְיֶה. לְתַשְׁלוּמֵי כֶפֶל כָּפֶל מִשּׁוֹר עַד חֲמוֹר. לְהָשִׁיב אֲבֵידָה הָשֵׁב תְּשִׁיבֵם. לִפְרִיקָה

## HALAKHAH 10

עָזוֹב תַּעֲזוֹב. לַחֲסִימָה לֹא תַחְסוֹם שׁוֹר בְּדִישׁוֹ. לַכִּלְאַיִם בְּהֶמְתְּךָ לֹא תַרְבִּיעַ כִּלְאַיִם. לַשַּׁבָּת לְמַעַן יָנוּחַ שׁוֹרְךָ וַחֲמוֹרֶךָ.

**Halakhah 10:** "The ox and any domestic animal equally are under the rules of falling into a pit," etc. Falling into a pit, "and an ox or a donkey fell in there.[56]" Separating from Mount Sinai, "neither animal nor man shall live.[88]" Paying double restitution, "from ox to donkey[89]". To return lost property, "you shall certainly return them[90]." Unloading, "do remove[91]." Muzzling, "do not muzzle an ox while threshing[92]." Interbreeding, "your animal you shall not breed *kilaim*[93]." The Sabbath, "that your ox and your donkey may rest[94]."

| | | | |
|---|---|---|---|
| 89 | *Ex.* 22:3, the penalty for the thief found with livestock. | 92 | *Deut.* 25:4. |
| 90 | *Deut.* 22:1. | 93 | *Lev.* 19:19. |
| 91 | *Ex..* 23:5. | 94 | *Ex.* 23:12. |

(5a line 51) וְכֵן חַיָּה וָעוֹף כַּיּוֹצֵא בָהֶן. שְׁמוּאֵל אָמַר. אַוָּז יָם עִם אַוָּז יִשּׁוּב כִּלְאַיִם זֶה בָּזֶה. אָמַר רִבִּי יוֹסֵי. מַתְנִיתָא לֹא אָמְרָה כֵן. אֶלָּא שׁוֹר עִם בַּר חֲמוֹר עִם חֲמוֹר בַּר כִּלְאַיִם זֶה בָּזֶה. רֵישׁ לָקִישׁ אָמַר. מִשְׁנָה שְׁלֵימָה שָׁנָה רִבִּי. וְכֵן חַיָּה וָעוֹף כַּיּוֹצֵא בָהֶן. אָמַר רִבִּי יוֹחָנָן. וַאֲנָא דְּאַיְיתִיתֵיהּ מִן דְּבֵית לֵוִי. תַּרְנְגוֹל עִם פָּיסִיוֹנִי תַּרְנְגוֹל עִם הַתַּוָּסֶת אַף עַל פִּי שֶׁדּוֹמִין זֶה לָזֶה כִּלְאַיִם זֶה בָּזֶה.

"Wild animals and birds follow the same rules." [95]Samuel said, the sea goose is *kilaim* with domesticated goose. Rebbi Yose said, the Mishnah does not say so, but an ox and a bison are *kilaim* with one another; a donkey and a wild donkey are *kilaim* with one another[96]. Rebbi Simeon ben Laqish said, Rebbi stated a complete Mishnah: "Wild animals and birds follow the same rules.[97]" Rebbi Johanan said, and I brought this from the House of Levi[98]: A rooster with a pheasant[99], a rooster with a peacock-hen[100] are *kilaim* even though they are similar one to the other.

95   In *Kilaim* 8:6: R. Samuel, but in the Babli, 55a, in the name of Samuel.

96   Contradicting the rabbis in *Kilaim* 8:6, Notes 97-98. The Genizah fragment here has an addition: "A pig and a wild boar are *kilaim;*" this is from Tosephta *Kilaim* 1:8.

97   If two related kinds of land animals are *kilaim*, then certainly land and water fowl are *kilaim* and one does not need a specific statement for this.

98   Babli 55a, in the name of R. Simeon ben Laqish.

99   Greek φασιανός.

100   טָוָס, Greek ταώς "Peacock".

הכונס פרק ששי

(fol. 5a) **משנה א**: הַכּוֹנֵס צֹאן לַדִּיר וְנָעַל בְּפָנֶיהָ כָּרָאוּי וְיָצְתָה וְהִזִּיקָה חַיָּב. נִפְרְצָה בַלַּיְלָה אוֹ שֶׁפְּרָצוּהָ לִסְטִים וְיָצְתָה וְהִזִּיקָה פָּטוּר. הוֹצִיאוּהָ לִסְטִין הַלִּסְטִין חַיָּבִין.

**Mishnah 1**: [1]He who brings a flock[2] into a corral and locks them in as he should[3], but they managed to get out and caused damage, is liable. If they broke out in the night[4] or robbers broke in and they managed to get out and caused damage, he is not liable. If robbers let them out[5], the robbers are liable.

1   In the Babli and the independent Mishnah mss., the text reads:

He who brings a flock into a corral and locks it as he should, but they managed to get out and caused damage, is *not liable*. *If he did not lock them in as he should, they managed to get out and caused damage*, he is liable.

It seems that this text also underlies the Yerushalmi Halakhah; the shortened version may be a scribal error.

2   Sheep and goats are notorious for eating everything edible in their way; in this respect they can be compared to a bull known to be goring.

3   The Babli, 55b, defines "locking in as one should" as a minimal standard: fencing, including the doors, which can withstand a normal wind but not necessarily a storm. There is no reason to assume that the same minimal standard is accepted in the Yerushalmi.

4   When it could not have been noticed by the rancher.

5   As the Halakhah explains, the robbers are liable only if they led the flock out for their own purpose. The case that they broke into the corral and the flock left through the breach is covered by the preceding sentence.

(5b line 29) **הלכה א**: הַכּוֹנֵס צֹאן לַדִּיר כול'. רִבִּי לָא בְּשֵׁם רִבִּי יַנַּאי. בְּמַחֲלוֹקֶת. רִבִּי לָעְזָר אָמַר. דִּבְרֵי הַכֹּל הוּא. אָמַר רִבִּי לָא. מִסְתַּבְּרָא הָדָא דְרִבִּי לָעְזָר. שֶׁהֲרֵי אֵין כְּתִיב שְׁמִירָה בְּגוּפוֹ אֶלָּא בְקֶרֶן. מַאי כְדוֹן. רִישׁ לָקִישׁ אָמַר. בְּמַחֲלוֹקֶת. רִבִּי לָעְזָר אוֹמֵר. דִּבְרֵי הַכֹּל הִיא. וְאִית דְּאָמְרִין. דְּרִבִּי לִיעֶזֶר בֶּן יַעֲקֹב הִיא. דְּאָמַר. בֵּין כָּךְ וּבֵין כָּךְ פָּטוּר.

**Halakhah 1:** "He who brings a flock into a corral," etc. Rebbi La in the name of Rebbi Yannai: In disagreement[6]. Rebbi Eleazar said, it[7] is everybody's opinion. Rebbi La said, Rebbi Eleazar's statement is convincing since watching the animal itself is written only for "horn"[8]. What about it? Rebbi Simeon ben Laqish said, in disagreement. Rebbi Eleazar said, it is everybody's opinion. Some say, it follows Rebbi Eliezer ben Jacob who said[9], in no case is he liable[10].

6  The Babli refers the Mishnah to a disagreement in Mishnah 4:10 about a bull which was tied down with a rope and locked in, where R. Meïr does not absolve the owner from liability but R. Jehudah does. It is asserted that the Mishnah in the version of the Babli and the independent Mishnah mss. is R. Jehudah's, but the Mishnah in the version of the Yerushalmi is R. Meïr's.

7  The long version of the Mishnah.

8  Only for a notoriously goring bull does *Ex.* 21:36 require that the animal be under the control of a human 24 hours a day; Babli 55b. It follows that for damages classified as "tooth" or "foot", even R. Meïr may agree to the long version of the Mishnah.

9  In the case of Mishnah 4:10; the text is Tosephta 5:7; cf. Chapter 4 Note 127.

10  R. Jehudah would agree with the short version of the Mishnah.

(5b line 33) עַד כְּדוֹן בְּשֶׁהָיְתָה גְדוּרָה מִד' רוּחוֹת. הָיְתָה גְדוּרָה מִשָּׁלֹשׁ רוּחוֹתָיו וּפְרוּצָה מֵרוּחַ אַחַת וְיָצְאת מִמְּקוֹם הַפִּרְצָה מָהוּ. נִישְׁמְעִינָהּ מִן הָדָא. נָפַל כּוֹתְלוֹ מִקּוֹל הַזּוּעוֹת מִקּוֹל הָרְעָמִים. אִם עָמַד וּבְנָאוֹ כְּצוּרְכּוֹ פָּטוּר. וְאִם לָאו חַיָּיב. כְּלוּם צְרִיכָה לֹא בְּשֶׁנָּפְלוּ שָׁם שְׁלֹשָׁה כְּתָלִים בְּרִיאִים מִמֶּנָּה.

[11] So far if [the corral] was fenced in on four sides. If it was fenced in on three sides and breached on one side[12], and [an animal] left through the breach, what is the rule? Let us hear from the following[13]: "If his wall fell in from the noise of earthquakes[14] or thunder and he rebuilt it as required, he is not liable[15], otherwise he is liable.[16]" The only problem is if three better built walls fell together with it[17].

11  In case the animals escaped in the night.

12  As the text stands, it seems to make no sense. Nobody can claim that animals are "locked in as they should be" if they are brought to an area open on one side. E reads "[the robbers] breached"; it has to be rejected since the Genizah text supports L. One has to explain that the corral is fenced in on all four sides but while three sides are strong enough to withstand a concerted push by the flock, the fourth side is not. In that case, was the escape of the flock to be foreseen and should the rancher be liable?

13  Tosephta *Bava Mesi'a* 11:7.

14  In the Genizah text and the Tosephta: "because of an earthquake".

15  If he followed the local building code, but the wall collapsed again and somebody was hurt in the collapse, the builder is not liable.

16  Therefore, the rancher is liable for damages by animals escaping through a substandard fence.

17  The question remains whether a builder is responsible for damages from the collapse of a substandard wall (or fence) when the same incident also destroyed walls built to local standards.

(5b line 38) תַּנֵּי. רְבִּי יְהוֹשֻׁעַ אוֹמֵר. אַרְבָּעָה אֵין חַייָבִין לְשַׁלֵּם מִן הַדִּין וְאֵין הַשָּׁמַיִם מוֹחֲלִין לָהֶן עַד שֶׁיְשַׁלְּמוּ. הַיּוֹדֵעַ עֵדוּת לַחֲבֵירוֹ וְאֵינוֹ מְעִידוֹ אֵין חַייָב לְשַׁלֵּם מִן הַדִּין וְאֵין הַשָּׁמַיִם מוֹחֲלִין לוֹ עַד שֶׁיְשַׁלֵּם. הַשּׂוֹכֵר עֵידֵי שֶׁקֶר וְגָבָה אֵין חַייָב לְשַׁלֵּם מִן הַדִּין וְאֵין הַשָּׁמַיִם מוֹחֲלִין לוֹ עַד שֶׁיְשַׁלֵּם. הַכּוֹבֵשׁ קָמָה לִפְנֵי הָאוֹר וְהַפּוֹרֵץ גָּדֵר לִפְנֵי בְהֵמָה אֵין חַייָב לְשַׁלֵּם מִן הַדִּין וְאֵין הַשָּׁמַיִם מוֹחֲלִין לוֹ עַד שֶׁיְשַׁלֵּם.

It was stated[18]: Rebbi Joshua said, four persons are not required to pay[19] but Heaven will not forgive them until they pay up: A person who knows testimony beneficial to another but does not testify[19a] is not required to pay but Heaven will not forgive him until he pays up. A person who hires false witnesses[20] against another and collects is not required to pay but Heaven will not forgive him until he pays up. A person who bends standing grain towards a fire[21] or who makes a breach in a fence for animals[22] is not required to pay but Heaven will not forgive him until he pays up.

18  Tosephta *Šebuot* 3:1-3, Babli 55b.

19  He holds that damages caused indirectly cannot be recovered in court.

19a  He refuses to appear as a witness in another person's civil case who as a consequence loses his suit. The person refusing to be a witness has the moral obligation to idemnify the other.

20  In money matters. This is indirect causation since "there is no agency in criminal matters"; the responsibility of a person knowingly committing a criminal act is not diminished by his performing the act for the benefit of another person.

21  He causes a wildfire to burn agricultural produce which but for his intervention might have been spared.

22  He lets the animals find the breach later on their own. This case explains why robbers who break into a corral and thereby create a possibility for the animals in the corral to escape cannot be sued for the damage caused later by the animals.

(5b line 44) הוֹצִיאוּהָ לִיסְטִין הַלִסְטִין חַיָּבִין. אָמַר רַב הוֹשַׁעְיָה. בְּשֶׁהוֹצִיאוּהָ לְגוֹזְלָהּ. אֲבָל אִם הוֹצִיאוּהָ לְאַבְּדָהּ הַלִּיסְטִין פְּטוּרִין.

"If robbers let it out, the robbers are liable." Rav Hoshaia said, if they let it out as part of their robbery[23]. But if they let it out to get lost, the robbers are not liable[22].

23 Since they took the animals as their property, they take the liability with them.

(fol. 5a) **משנה ב:** הִנִּיחָהּ בַּחַמָּה אוֹ שֶׁמְּסָרָהּ בְּיַד חֵרֵשׁ שׁוֹטֶה וְקָטָן וְיָצְתָה וְהִזִּיקָה חַיָּב. מְסָרָהּ לָרוֹעֶה נִכְנַס הָרוֹעֶה תַּחְתָּיו. נָפְלָה לַגִּנָּה וְהִזִּיקָה מְשַׁלֶּמֶת מַה שֶׁנֶּהֱנֵית. יָרְדָה כְדַרְכָּהּ וְהִזִּיקָה מְשַׁלֶּמֶת מַה שֶׁהִזִּיקָה. כֵּיצַד מְשַׁלֶּמֶת מַה שֶׁהִזִּיקָה. שָׁמִין בֵּית סְאָה בְּאוֹתָהּ שָׂדֶה כַּמָּה הָיְתָה יָפָה וְכַמָּה הִיא יָפָה. רַבִּי שִׁמְעוֹן אוֹמֵר אָכְלָה פֵּירוֹת גְּמוּרִין מְשַׁלֶּמֶת פֵּירוֹת גְּמוּרִין אִם סְאָה סְאָה אִם סָאתַיִם סָאתַיִם.

**Mishnah 2**: If he left it[24] in the sun[25] or handed it over to a deaf-and-dumb, an insane, or an underage person[26], he is liable. If he handed it over to a shepherd, the shepherd takes his place. If it fell[27] into a garden and caused damage[28], it[29] pays for what it profited[30]. If it entered in due course[31], it pays for what it damaged. How does it pay for what it damaged? One estimates a *bet se'ah*[32] of the field; how much was it worth and how much is it worth[33]. Rebbi Simeon says, if it ate ripe produce it pays for ripe produce[34], whether one or two *se'ah*.

24 Even though Mishnah 1 is formulated for a flock, Mishnah two always refers to a single animal.

25 If the corral has no shade, the animal can be expected to try to break out to find shade somewhere. Since the owner causes the break, he is liable for all consequences.

26 These three categories are the paradigm of irresponsible persons. Appointing these as shepherds is the equivalent of letting the animals roam freely without supervision.

27 By accident.

28 In most Babli and Mishnah mss., "and profited", by eating the produce around it. A "garden" is an irrigated plot.

29 In the Halakhah and some Mishnah and Alfassi mss., in the entire Mishnah one reads מְשַׁלֵּם "he (the owner) pays", instead of מְשַׁלֶּמֶת "it (the

animal) pays".

30 The animal's owner does not have to pay the high-priced vegetables which his animal ate but only the value of animal feed of corresponding nutritional content.

31 Under the control of the owner, not by accident.

32 2'500 square cubits, the standard size of a field; cf. *Peah* 2:1, Note 31.

33 The animal's owner only pays the diminution in value of the crop as if the damaged parcel had been part of a standard field whose yield is sold wholesale.

34 The exact retail value of what it destroyed.

(5b line 46) **הלכה ב:** הִנִּיחָתּ בַּחַמָּה כול׳. תַּנֵּי. רוֹעֶה שֶׁמָּסַר צֹאנוֹ לָרוֹעֶה. הָרִאשׁוֹן חַיָּיב וְהַשֵּׁנִי פָּטוּר. רַב וְרֵישׁ לָקִישׁ תְּרֵיהוֹן אָמְרִין. מִכֵּיוָן שֶׁמְּסָרָהּ לְבֶן דַּעַת פָּטוּר.

**Halakhah 2**: It was stated[35]: "If a shepherd handed his flock over to another shepherd, the first is liable, the second is not liable.[36]" Rav and Rebbi Simeon ben Laqish both said, since he handed it over to a responsible person, he is not liable[37].

35 Tosephta 6:20.

36 If the owner did not give prior authorization for the change of control; cf. *Qiddušin* 1:4, Note 449; *Ketubot* 9:5, Notes 127-146. The first shepherd remains liable to the owner; he might sue the second shepherd once he paid the owner. The Babli, 56b, makes an exception if the second shepherd is employed by the first as his helper since then one may assume an implied consent for the transfer of control.

37 Since the Mishnah insists that the owner remain liable if he hands over control to an irresponsible person, one may infer that any change of control between responsible persons implies a change of liability.

(5b line 48) מְסָרָהּ לָרוֹעֶה נִכְנַס הָרוֹאֶה תַחְתָּיו. וְנָפְלָה לַגִּינָּה וְהִזִּיקָה מְשַׁלֵּם מַה שֶּׁנֶּהֱנֵית. רַב הוּנָא אָמַר. כְּשֶׁנֶּחְבְּטָה עַל גַּבֵּי עֲשָׂבִים. אֲבָל עָמְדָה וְרָעֲתָה מְשַׁלֵּם מַה שֶּׁהִזִּיקָה.

"If he handed it over to a shepherd, the shepherd takes his place. If it fell into a garden and caused damage, he[29] pays for what it profited." Rav Huna[38] said, if it fell on vegetables[39]. But if it stood up and grazed, he pays for what it damaged[40].

38  In the Babli, 57b/58a, "Rav".

39  "Paying for the benefit" may be more than "paying for the damage". If the animal would have had broken bones if the fall had not been cushioned by the vegetation, the benefit to the owner is quite large.

40  If the shepherd does not immediately remove the animal from the field, the subsequent damage is not considered caused by the accident but under the shepherd's control.

(5b line 50) יָרְדָה כְדַרְכָּהּ וְהִזִּיקָה מְשַׁלֵּם מַה שֶּׁהִזִּיקָה. רִבִּי יוֹסֵי בְּרִבִּי חֲנִינָה אָמַר. אוֹתָהּ הַשָּׂדֶה פְטוּרָה וְשָׂדֶה אַחֶרֶת חַייֶבֶת. רִבִּי יוֹחָנָן וְרִישׁ לָקִישׁ תְּרֵיהוֹן אָמְרִין. אֲפִילוּ רָעֲת כָּל־הַשָּׂדֶה פְטוּרָה. לְעוֹלָם אֵינָהּ חַייֶבֶת עַד שֶׁתֵּצֵא מִתּוֹכָהּ לִרְשׁוּת הָרַבִּים וְתִיכָּנֵס מֵרְשׁוּת הָרַבִּים לְשָׂדֶה אַחֶרֶת. אֶלָּא נָפְלָה לְגִנָּה וְיָרְדָה לְתוֹךְ גִּנָּה אַחֶרֶת מָהוּ. עַל דַּעְתֵּיהּ דְּרִבִּי יוֹסֵי בֶּן חֲנִינָה דְּאָמַר. אוֹתָהּ הַשָּׂדֶה פְּטוּרָה. וְכָא חַייֶבֶת. עַל דַּעְתִּין דְּרִבִּי יוֹחָנָן וְרִישׁ לָקִישׁ דִּינּוּן אָמְרִין. אֲפִילוּ רָעֲת כָּל־הַשָּׂדֶה פְטוּרָה. לְעוֹלָם אֵינָהּ חַייֶבֶת עַד שֶׁתֵּצֵא מִתּוֹכָהּ לִרְשׁוּת הָרַבִּים וּמֵרְשׁוּת הָרַבִּים לְשָׂדֶה אַחֶרֶת. אֶלָּא נָפְלָה לְמָקוֹם שֶׁרְאוּיָה לֵירֵד. יָרְדָה לְמָקוֹם שֶׁרְאוּיָה לִיפּוֹל. אָמַר רִבִּי יוֹסֵי בַּר חֲנִינָה. הִיא מַתְנִיתָהּ. אֶלָּא נָפְלָה לְמָקוֹם שֶׁרְאוּיָה לִיפּוֹל. נָפְלָה לְמָקוֹם שֶׁרְאוּיָה לֵירֵד. דָּא צְרִיכָא לְדָא וְדָא צְרִיכָא לְדָא. דָּא צְרִיכָא לְדָא. שֶׁמְּשַׁלֵּם מַה שֶׁנֶּהֱנֵית. וְדָא צְרִיכָא לְדָא. שֶׁמְּשַׁלֵּם מַה שֶׁהִזִּיקָה.

"If it entered in due course, he[29] pays for what it damaged."[40] Rebbi Yose ben Rebbi Ḥanina said, on that field itself he is not liable, but for another field he is liable[41]. Rebbi Joḥanan and Rebbi Simeon ben Laqish both said, even if it grazed on that entire field he is not liable; he only is liable if it left the field for the public domain and from the public domain entered another field[42]. But what is the rule if it fell into a garden and then entered another garden? In the opinion of Rebbi Yose ben Rebbi Ḥanina who said, on that field itself he is not liable, here he will be liable[43]. In the opinion of Rebbi Joḥanan and Rebbi Simeon ben Laqish who both said, even if it grazed on that entire field he is not liable; he only is liable if it left the field for the public domain and from the public domain entered another field. But if it fell into a place which it could have entered, or it entered a place into which it could have fallen?[44] Rebbi Yose bar Ḥanina said, that is the Mishnah; it fell into a place into which it only could have fallen[45]. But if it fell into a place which it could have entered? Each case is problematic for one of them[46]. One needs the first case, that he pays what it profited[45]; the other[47] needs the other case, that he pays what it damaged.

40  This quote from the Mishnah is out of place since the following discussion still refers to the case that the animal accidentally fell into an area used for growing produce.

41  He disagrees with Rav Huna and holds that for *all* damages caused by an animal falling into a growing area by accident, only the corresponding value of animal feed is due. In the Babli, 58a, this position is attributed to Rav Cahana.

In the entire paragraph, "liable" means "liable for the full value of the destroyed produce".

42  In the Babli, 58a, R. Joḥanan holds that a change in the status of liability occurs as soon as the person responsible realizes that the animal left the field into which it had fallen.

43  Since he imposes full liability as soon as the animal leaves the field of the accident.

44  In a case which could be classified in two different ways, which section of the Mishnah is applicable?

45  A genuine accident. The leniency of the Mishnah only applies to a case in which the animal fell into a plot not accessible to it by walking.

46  R. Yose ben Ḥanina and R. Joḥanan.

47  Even R. Joḥanan will agree that an animal falling into a field accessible to it by walking is judged by the rules of entering, not falling.

(5b line 63) תַּנֵּי. אֵין שָׁמִין בֵּית כּוֹר מִפְּנֵי שֶׁהוּא פּוֹגֵם. וְלֹא בֵית קַב מִפְּנֵי שֶׁמַּשְׁבִּיחַ. אֶלָּא שָׁמִין בֵּית סְאָה בְּאוֹתָהּ שָׂדֶה כַּמָּה הָיְתָה יָפָה וְכַמָּה הִיא יָפָה. אָמַר רִבִּי יוּדָה. אֵימָתַי. בִּזְמַן שֶׁאָכְלָה יִיחוּרֵי תְאֵנִים וְקִירְטְמָה לוּלְבֵי גְפָנִים. אֲבָל אִם אָכְלָה בוֹסֶר אוֹ פַגִּין שָׁמִין לוֹ פֵּירוֹת גְּמוּרִין. אָמַר רִבִּי יוּדָן מִשּׁוּם רִבִּי עֲקִיבָה. אָכְלָה פֵּירוֹת גְּמוּרִין מְשַׁלֵּם פֵּירוֹת גְּמוּרִין נְטִיעוֹת שָׁמִין לוֹ נְטִיעוֹת. נְטִיעוֹת שָׁמִין לוֹ בֵּית סְאָה. רִבִּי שִׁמְעוֹן בֶּן יְהוּדָה אוֹמֵר מִשּׁוּם רִבִּי עֲקִיבָה. תְּבוּאָה שֶׁלֹּא הֵבִיאָה שְׁלִישׁ נִידּוֹנֶת כִּנְטִיעוֹת. דְּבֵי רִבִּי יַנַּאי אָמְרֵי. שָׁמִין תַּרְקַב בְּשִׁשִּׁים תַּרְקַבִּים. רִבִּי יוֹסֵי בֵּירִבִּי חֲנִינָה אוֹמֵר. שָׁמִין קֶלַח בְּס' קְלָחִים.

It was stated[48]: "One does not estimate a *bet kor*[49] because it would diminish, nor a *bet qab*[50] because it would inflate. But one estimates a *bet se'ah*[32] of the field in question, how much it was worth and how much is it worth now. Rebbi Jehudah said, when? If it ate shoots of the fig tree or plucked shoots of vines. But if it ate unripe grapes or unripe figs, one estimates them as fully grown fruits. Rebbi Jehudah said in the name of Rebbi Aqiba: If it ate fully grown produce, he pays for fully grown produce, [fruits of][51] trees, one estimates trees for him. Trees one estimates by the *bet se'ah*[52]. Rebbi Simeon ben Jehudah said in the name of Rebbi Aqiba: Produce not yet one-third ripe is estimated under the rules of trees.[53]" In the House of Rebbi Yannai they said, one estimates a three-*qab* in sixty three-*qabs*[54]. Rebbi Yose ben Rebbi Hanina said, one estimates a stalk in sixty stalks[55].

48  Tosephta 6:21 (partially with different tradents); *Mekhilta dR. Simeon ben Iohai* p. 195. Parts are quoted in the Babli, 58b/59a, as Amoraic statements.

49  30 *bet se'ah* = 75'000 square cubits. At this wholesale level, the damage done by the animal would be considered minimal and the farmer deprived of just compensation.

50  One sixth of a *bet se'ah*. In a plot of this size the damage would be

complete and the farmer overpaid.

51 Reading of the Genizah text.

52 In a minimal orchard, ten trees grow on a *bet se'ah* (cf. *Ševi'it* 1:2, Note 18). One has to estimate the diminution of value in the wholesale price of the yield of ten trees.

53 To be estimated on a field the size of a *bet se'ah*.

54 A damaged plot the size of half a *bet se'ah* is estimated in 30 *bet se'ah*, not 60.

55 A similar statement is in the Babli, 58b.

(5b line 72) חַד בַּר נַשׁ גָּנַב חָדָא כְּפוּנִי. אָתָא עוֹבְדָא קוֹמֵי שְׁמוּאֵל. אָמַר לֵיהּ. זִיל שַׁיְימָא לֵיהּ בְּרֵישׁ דְּקָלָא. אָמַר רִבִּי יוֹסֵי בֵּירְבִּי בּוּן. כְּבָשָׂהּ דַּאֲחִינִי הֲוָה.

A person stole a hard date[56]. The case came before Samuel who said to him[57], go and estimate for him at the top of the date palm[58]. Rebbi Yose ben Rebbi Abun said, it was a preserve of unripe dates[59].

56 Which is barely edible.

57 Probably to his student and aide, Rav Jehudah, to determine the amount of restitution due.

58 The place most exposed to the sun, which produces the sweetest and most expensive dates.

59 The treatment turned an almost wooden fruit into a delicacy for which a comparison with the sweetest kind of fresh date might be appropriate.

(fol. 5a) **משנה ג:** הַמַּגְדִּישׁ לְתוֹךְ שָׂדֵה חֲבֵירוֹ שֶׁלֹּא בִרְשׁוּת וַאֲכָלָתַן בְּהֶמְתּוֹ שֶׁל בַּעַל הַשָּׂדֶה פָּטוּר. וְאִם הִזִּיקָה בָהֶן בַּעַל הַמַּגְדִּישׁ חַיָּב. וְאִם הִגְדִּישׁ בִּרְשׁוּת בַּעַל הַשָּׂדֶה חַיָּב.

**Mishnah 3:** If somebody stacks his sheaves on another person's field without permission and the field's owner's animals ate them, he[60] is not liable. If it was damaged by it[61], the owner of the stack is liable. But if he stacked his sheaves with permission, the field's owner is liable.

| 60 The field's owner; cf. Mishnah 5:4. | 61 If the produce stacked there was inappropriate as animal feed. |
|---|---|

**הלכה ג:** הַמַּגְדִּישׁ לְתוֹךְ שְׂדֵה חֲבֵירוֹ כול'. אָמַר רִבִּי יִצְחָק. גְּדִישִׁים בַּשָּׂדֶה כְּכֵלִים בַּבַּיִת. אָמַר רִבִּי יוֹסֵי בֵּי רִבִּי בּוּן. תִּיפָּתָר בְּהַהִיא דְּאִית לֵיהּ מִסְגָּר. (5b line 75)

[62]If somebody stacks his sheaves on another person's field without permission." R. Isaac said, are sheaves on a field like vessels in a house? Rebbi Yose ben Rebbi Abun said, explain it by one which has a lock.

62    Halakhah 5:5, Notes 29-32.

**משנה ד:** הַשּׁוֹלֵחַ אֶת הַבְּעֵירָה בְּיַד חֵרֵשׁ שׁוֹטֶה וְקָטָן פָּטוּר בְּדִינֵי אָדָם וְחַיָּיב בְּדִינֵי שָׁמַיִם. שִׁילְּחָהּ בְּיַד פִּיקֵּחַ הַפִּיקֵּחַ חַיָּיב. אֶחָד הֵבִיא אֶת הָאֵשׁ וְאֶחָד הֵבִיא אֶת הָעֵצִים הַמֵּבִיא אֶת הָעֵצִים חַיָּיב. אֶחָד הֵבִיא אֶת הָעֵצִים וְאֶחָד הֵבִיא אֶת הָאוּר הַמֵּבִיא אֶת הָאוּר חַיָּיב. בָּא אַחֵר וְלִיבָּה הַמְלַבֶּה חַיָּיב. לִיבָּהוּ הָרוּחַ הֲרֵי כוּלָּן פְּטוּרִין. (fol. 5a)

**Mishnah 4**: He who causes a fire through the hand of a deaf-mute, an insane, or an underage person[63] is not liable in human law[64] but liable in Heaven's law[65]. If he causes it through a hearing person, the hearing person is liable[66]. If one person brings the fire and another one the wood, the one bringing the wood is liable. If one brings the wood and another one the fire, the one bringing the fire is liable[67]. If another person came and fanned the flames, the one who fanned is liable. If the wind fanned it[68], none of them is liable[69].

| 63 These are irresponsible; no liability can be imposed on them. | The expression "to send a fire" is a pun on the expression "sending בעירה" |
|---|---|

(*Ex.* 22:4), his animal, and paying for בערה "arson" in v. 5; cf. Ibn Ezra *ad loc.*

64   Damages by indirect arson cannot be recovered.

65   He cannot hope for divine forgiveness unless he pays the damages.

66   Since "there is no agency in criminal matters", cf. Note 20.

67   If several ingredients are necessary, the person contributing the last ingredient makes the act possible and, therefore, bears full liability.

68   And without wind the fire would not have caused damage.

69   Since they did not directly cause the damages.

(5c line 1) **הלכה ד:** הַשּׁוֹלֵחַ אֶת הַבְּעִירָה כול'. חִזְקִיָּה אָמַר. בְּשֶׁמָּסַר לוֹ נַחֶלֶת. אֲבָל מָסַר לוֹ שַׁלְהֶבֶת חַיָּיב. אָמַר רִבִּי יוֹחָנָן. הִיא נַחֶלֶת הִיא שַׁלְהֶבֶת. וְקַשְׁיָא עַל דַּעְתֵּיהּ דְּחִזְקִיָּה. אִילּוּ מִי שֶׁרָאָה נַחַלְתּוֹ שֶׁלַּחֲבֵירוֹ מְגוּלְגֶּלֶת וְהוֹלֶכֶת וְאֵין כוֹלֶה אוֹתָהּ. שֶׁמָּא אֵינוֹ פָטוּר. אָמְרֵי. תִּיפְתָּר בְּשֶׁמָּסַר לוֹ נַחֶלֶת הֶפְקֵר. אִינַמֵי שַׁלְהֶבֶת הֶפְקֵר. וְלֵית שְׁמַע מִינָהּ כְּלוּם.

**Halakhah 4**: "He who sets a fire," etc. [70]Hizqiah said, if he handed him[71] a glowing coal. But if he handed him an open flame he is liable[72]. Rebbi Johanan said, coal and flame are the same[73]. It is difficult according to Hizqiah, for if somebody saw another person's glowing coal rolling by and did not extinguish it, is he not free from liability[74]? They said, explain it if he handed him an ownerless glowing coal, or also an ownerless flame, and one cannot infer anything[75].

70   A similar discussion is in the Babli, 59b-60a; but the underlying argument there seems to be different.

71   The irresponsible person.

72   In that case, he is directly responsible for the fire; it is not indirect causation.

73   Since after handing the fire to the deaf-and-dumb, insane, or underaged, he cannot know what they are going to do with it; the causation of the damage is still indirect. R. Johanan will agree that if somebody hands a fire to an irresponsible person and then guides that person until the fire is set, he is the arsonist and liable for all damages.

74   The passive bystander who fails to prevent a fire cannot be sued for damages. Then what is the difference

between an irresponsible and a responsible person in this matter?

75 The responsible person will acquire the coal or burning object by picking it up and becomes liable in all respects; an irresponsible person cannot acquire.

E has a different version of the last sentence, which avoids the Babylonian expression אינמי:

תִּיפְתָּר שֶׁמָּסַר לוֹ שַׁלְהֶבֶת שֶׁל הֶקְדֵּשׁ וְלֵית שֵׁ״מ כְּלוּם.

"Explain it if he handed him a flame belonging to the Sanctuary, and one cannot infer anything."

Taking the Sanctuary's property is sinful; only the adult can sin.

(5c line 6) אִית תַּנָּיֵי תַנֵּי. וְלִיבָּה. אִית תַּנָּיֵי תַנֵּי. וְנִיבָה. מָאן דָּמַר. וְלִיבָּה. דִּכְתִיב בְּלַבַּת אֵשׁ. מָאן דָּמַר. וְנִיבָה. וְהָיָה בְלִבִּי כְּאֵשׁ בּוֹעֶרֶת.

Some Tannaïm state: וְלִיבָּה. Some Tannaïm state: וְנִיבָה. He who says וְלִיבָּה. As it is written, "in the flaming fire"[76]. He who says וְנִיבָה, "it was in my heart like burning fire.[77]"

76 *Ex.* 3:2.
77 *Jer.* 20:9. A similar argument is in the Babli, 60a.

It seems that the difference between the versions is simply a dialectal switch between the liquids *l* and *n*; but a biblical source is sought. In the Babli, the reference is to *Is.* 57:19, where the "fruit of the lips" is interpreted as "speech". The verse from *Jer.* quoted here then points out that speech can be fiery, i. e., with one's mouth one can fan a fire.

(5c line 8) תַּמָּן אָמְרִין. בְּרוּחַ שֶׁלְּאוֹנְסִין הִיא מַתְנִיתָא. אֲבָל בְּרוּחַ שֶׁהָעוֹלָם מִתְנַהֵג בּוֹ חַיָּיב. רִבִּי יוֹחָנָן וְרֵישׁ לָקִישׁ תְּרֵיהוֹן אָמְרִין. אֲפִילוּ רוּחַ שֶׁהָעוֹלָם מִתְנַהֵג בּוֹ פָּטוּר. שֶׁפְּעָמִים בָּא פְּעָמִים לֹא בָא.

There[78], they say, the Mishnah speaks of a catastrophic wind, but in case of normal wind he is liable. Rebbi Joḥanan and Rebbi Simeon ben Laqish both say, even in case of normal wind he is not liable; for sometimes it blows, sometimes it does not blow[79].

78 Babli 60a, in the name of Rava, the representative of Galilean Halakhah.
79 Wind is unpredictable; wind which is fanning a fire cannot be planned. If without the wind the fire would not have spread, the person starting the fire is not liable.

**משנה ה:** הַשּׁוֹלֵחַ אֶת הַבְּעֵירָה וְאָכְלָה עֵצִים אוֹ אֲבָנִים אוֹ עָפָר חַיָּיב (fol. 5b) שֶׁנֶּאֱמַר כִּי תֵצֵא אֵשׁ וּמָצְאָה קוֹצִים וגו'. עָבְרָה גָּדֵר שֶׁהוּא גָּבוֹהַּ אַרְבַּע אַמּוֹת אוֹ דֶרֶךְ הָרַבִּים אוֹ נָהָר פָּטוּר.

**Mishnah 5**: He who sets a fire which consumes wood, or stones, or dust, is liable since it is said: "If fire gets out of control and finds thorns, etc."[80] If it crossed a wall four cubits high[81], or a public road[82], or a brook[83], he is not liable.

80 *Ex.* 22:5. The Halakhah will explain the proof from the verse.
81 A stone or brick wall which will not burn.
82 At least 16 cubits wide (Halakhah 6, Mishnah *Bava batra* 6:7).
83 At least 8 cubits wide (Halakhah 6).

**הלכה ה:** הַשּׁוֹלֵחַ אֶת הַבְּעֵירָה וְאָכְלָה עֵצִים כול'. מַה קוֹצִים (5c line 11) מְיוּחָדִין שֶׁדַּרְכָּן לִידָּלֵק אַף אֵין לִי אֶלָּא דְבָרִים שֶׁדַּרְכָּן לִידָּלֵק. תַּלְמוּד לוֹמַר גָּדִישׁ. אוֹ מַה גָּדִישׁ מְיוּחָד שֶׁתָּלוּשׁ מִן הַקַּרְקַע אַף אֵין לִי אֶלָּא דָבָר הַתָּלוּשׁ מִן הַקַּרְקַע. תַּלְמוּד לוֹמַר קָמָה. אוֹ מַה אִילוּ וְאִילוּ מְיוּחָדִין שֶׁדַּרְכָּן לִידָּלֵק אַף אֵין לִי אֶלָּא דָבָר שֶׁדַּרְכּוֹ לִידָּלֵק. לִיחֲכָה נִירוֹ סִיפְסְפָה אֲבָנָיו מְנַיִין. תַּלְמוּד לוֹמַר אוֹ הַשָּׂדֶה. וְיֹאמַר קוֹצִים קָמָה גָדִישׁ וְאַל יֹאמַר שָׂדֶה. עַל דַּעֲתֵּיהּ דְּרִבִּי יוּדָן נִיחָא. דְּאָמַר מְשַׁלֵּם כָּל־מַה שֶׁבְּתוֹכוֹ. וְעַל דַּעֲתִּין דְּרַבָּנִין דְּאָמְרֵי. אֵינוֹ מְשַׁלֵּם אֶלָּא גָדִישׁ חִטִּים וְגָדִישׁ שְׂעוֹרִים. לְאֵי זֶה דָבָר נֶאֱמַר שָׂדֶה וּלְאֵי זֶה דָּבָר נֶאֱמַר גָּדִישׁ.

"He who sets a fire which consumes wood,[84]" etc. Since thorns are flammable, do I only include flammable material? The verse says, "a stack". Since a stack of sheaves is particular in that it was harvested, do I only include harvested material? The verse says, "standing grain." Since all of these are particular in that they are flammable, do I only include flammable material? If it swept his furrow or damaged his stone, from where? The verse says, "or the field.[85]" Should it only have mentioned thorns, standing grain, and stack, but not mentioned field? In the opinion of Rebbi Jehudah[86] this is acceptable since he says, he pays for everything inside. But according to the rabbis, who say that he only pays for a stack of wheat or barley sheaves, why did it mention "field"[87], why did it mention "stack"[88]?

84 The full verse reads: "If fire gets out of control and finds thorns, or consumes a stack of sheaves, or standing grain, or the field, the person who set the blaze shall certainly pay." Similar discussions on what the different examples mentioned in the verse imply are in the Babli 60a, *Mekhilta dR. Ismael, Neziqin* 14 (ed. Horovitz-Rabin p. 297), *Mekhilta dR. Simeon ben Iohai* p. 196.

85 The earth constituting the field.

86 Mishnah 7. Since R. Jehudah requires the arsonist to pay for everything of value stored inside the stack, nothing of value would have been excluded if "field" had not been mentioned.

87 To include stones and require the arsonist also to pay for the work needed to plough the field anew.

88 To include everything stacked, even limestone assembled to be burned into lime (*Mekhilta dR. Ismael*).

(5c line 20) עָבְרָה גָדֵר שֶׁגְּבוֹהָה אַרְבַּע אַמּוֹת אוֹ דֶרֶךְ הָרַבִּים אוֹ נָהָר פָּטוּר. אָמַר רַבָּה. בְּקוֹדַחַת הִיא מַתְנִיתָא. אֲבָל בִּמְקַקְטֶפֶת דִּבְרֵי הַכֹּל חַיָּיב. רִבִּי יוֹחָנָן אָמַר. בִּמְקַקְטֶפֶת הִיא מַתְנִיתָא. אֲבָל בְּקוֹדַחַת פָּטוּר.

"If it crossed a wall four cubits high, or a public road, or a brook, he is not liable." Rebbi Abba said, the Mishnah speaks of burning fire[89]. But if it is wind-whipped everybody agrees that he is liable[90]. Rebbi Joḥanan said, the Mishnah speaks of wind-whipped fire, but if it is burning he is not liable[90].

89  A fire which spreads by burning the flammable material next to it, to be distinguished from wind-whipped fire which jumps over fire clearings and waterways.

90  Since it can be expected to cross a fire clearing of 16 cubits and more.

91  If the fire unexpectedly crosses a fire wall.

(fol. 5b) **משנה ו:** הַמַּדְלִיק בְּתוֹךְ שֶׁלּוֹ עַד כַּמָּה תַּעֲבוֹר הַדְּלֵיקָה. רִבִּי אֶלְעָזָר בֶּן עֲזַרְיָה אוֹמֵר רוֹאִין אוֹתָהּ כְּאִילּוּ הִיא בְּאֶמְצַע בֵּית כּוֹר. רִבִּי לִיעֶזֶר אוֹמֵר שֵׁשׁ עֶשְׂרֵה אַמּוֹת כְּדֶרֶךְ רְשׁוּת הָרַבִּים וְרִבִּי עֲקִיבָה אוֹמֵר חֲמִשִּׁים אַמָּה וְרִבִּי שִׁמְעוֹן אוֹמֵר שַׁלֵּם יְשַׁלֵּם הַמַּבְעִיר אֶת הַבְּעֵירָה הַכֹּל לְפִי הַדְּלֵיקָה.

**Mishnah 6**: If somebody starts a fire inside his property, how far does it have to spread[92]? Rebbi Eleazar ben Azariah says, one looks at it as if he started it at the center of a *bet kor*[93]. Rebbi Eliezer says, sixteen cubits like a public road; and Rebbi Aqiba says, 50 cubits; and Rebbi Simeon says "the person setting the fire shall certainly pay,[94]" everything depends on the setting of the fire.

92  That the spreading of the fire was not foreseeable and the person starting the fire would no longer be liable.

93  Which is 75'000 square cubits (Note 49). The edge length of a *bet kor* therefore is 273.86 cubits and the distance of the center from the side is 136.93 cubits. For him, the liability stops if a strip 137 cubits wide around the fire is protected against the spread of the fire.

94  *Ex.* 22:5.

(5c line 24) **הלכה ו:** הַמַּדְלִיק בְּתוֹךְ שֶׁלּוֹ כול'. תַּנֵּי. מַעֲשֶׂה שֶׁעָבְרָה דְלִיקָה אֶת הַיַּרְדֵּן. שֶׁהָיְתָה קָשָׁה. עַד כַּמָּה תַעֲבֹר הַדְּלִיקָה. רִבִּי לִיעֶזֶר אוֹמֵר שֵׁשׁ עֶשְׂרֵה אַמּוֹת כְּדֶרֶךְ הָרַבִּים. בִּשְׁעַת הָרוּחַ שְׁלֹשִׁים אַמָּה. רִבִּי יְהוּדָה אוֹמֵר. שְׁלֹשִׁים אַמָּה. בִּשְׁעַת הָרוּחַ חֲמִשִּׁים אַמָּה. רִבִּי עֲקִיבָה אוֹמֵר. חֲמִשִּׁים אַמָּה. בִּשְׁעַת הָרוּחַ מֵאָה אַמָּה. מַעֲשֶׂה בָּעֲרָב שֶׁקָּפַץ הָאוּר יוֹתֵר מִשְּׁלֹשׁ מֵאוֹת אָמָּה. אֵימָתַי. בִּזְמַן שֶׁקָּפַץ. אֲבָל אִם הָיוּ עֵצִים מְצוּיִין לְפָנָיו אוֹ שֶׁהָיָה מְסַפְסֵף וְהוֹלֵךְ אֲפִילוּ עַד מִיל חַיָּיב. עָבְרָה נָהָר אוֹ שְׁלוּלִית רְחָבִין שְׁמוֹנֶה אַמּוֹת פָּטוּר.

**Halakhah 6**: "If somebody starts a fire inside his property," etc. [95]"It happened that a fire crossed the Jordan, because it was a firestorm[96]. How far may a fire spread[97]? Rebbi Eliezer says sixteen cubits like a public road, if there is wind thirty cubits. Rebbi Jehudah says thirty cubits, if there is wind fifty cubits. Rebbi Aqiba says 50 cubits, if there is wind a hundred cubits. It happened in Arabia that a fire jumped more than three hundred cubits. When is this? If it jumps. But if there is wood or it burns continuously[98], he is liable even up to a *mil*[99]. If it crossed a river or a pond eight cubits wide, he is not liable."

95 Tosephta 6:22-23; cf. *Mekhilta dR. Ismael, Neziqin* 14 (ed. Horovitz-Rabin p. 297), Babli 61a.

96 A large fire can create its own storm which carries the flames beyond the expected limits.

97 How wide a strip has to be cleared of flammable material to protect the person who set the fire from damage claims?

98 If the safety strip is not cleared of all flammable material.

99 2'000 cubits.

(fol. 5b) **משנה ז:** הַמַּדְלִיק אֶת הַגָּדִישׁ וְהָיוּ בוֹ כֵלִים רִבִּי יְהוּדָה אוֹמֵר יְשַׁלֵּם כָּל־מַה שֶּׁבְּתוֹכוֹ וַחֲכָמִים אוֹמְרִים אֵינוֹ מְשַׁלֵּם אֶלָּא גָדִישׁ שֶׁל חִטִּין אוֹ גָדִישׁ שֶׁל שְׂעוֹרִין. הָיָה גְּדִי כָפוּת לוֹ וְעֶבֶד סָמוּךְ לוֹ וְנִשְׂרַף עִמּוֹ חַיָּיב. עֶבֶד כָּפוּת לוֹ וּגְדִי

סָמוּךְ לוֹ וְנִשְׂרַף עִמּוֹ פָּטוּר. וּמוֹדִין חֲכָמִים לְרַבִּי יְהוּדָה בַּמַּדְלִיק אֶת הַבִּירָה שֶׁהוּא מְשַׁלֵּם כָּל־מַה שֶׁבְּתוֹכָהּ שֶׁכֵּן דֶּרֶךְ בְּנֵי אָדָם לְהַנִּיחַ בַּבָּתִּים.

**Mishnah 7**: He who sets fire to a stack of sheaves which contains implements, Rebbi Jehudah says, he has to pay everything contained in it but the Sages say, he pays only for a stack of wheat sheaves or a stack of barley sheaves[100]. If a goat was tied to it, and a slave was nearby[101], and they were burned, he is liable. If a slave was tied to it, and a goat was nearby, and they were burned, he is not liable[102]. But the Sages agree with Rebbi Jehudah that one who sets fire to a building has to pay everything contained in it since people regularly store things in houses.

100 He has to pay only for what was visible from the outside.

101 Since the slave was not bound, he could have escaped. The arsonist is not guilty of murder; he is liable for all material damage which he may cause.

102 Since the slave could not have escaped, the arsonist is a murderer. Even if he cannot be criminally prosecuted for lack of eye witnesses or for other reasons, he cannot be sued for monetary damages (*Ketubot* 3:1, Notes 29ff., *Terumot* 7:1, Notes 3-73, and sources given there.)

**הלכה ז:** הַמַּדְלִיק אֶת הַגָּדִישׁ כול׳. (5c line 31) רַבִּי אַבָּהוּ בְּשֵׁם רַבִּי יוֹחָנָן. מוֹדִין חֲכָמִים לְרַבִּי יוּדָן בִּכְלֵי גוֹרֶן שֶׁדַּרְכָּן לְהַטְמִין. מַחְלְפָה שִׁיטַת רַבִּי יוּדָן. תַּמָּן הוּא אוֹמֵר. פְּרָט לְטָמוּן. וְהָכָא הוּא אָמַר. לְרַבּוֹת הַטָּמוּן. וְלֵית רַבִּי יוּדָן דְּרִישׁ הָכָא אֶלָּא גָדִישׁ. לְאֵי זֶה דָבָר נֶאֱמַר גָּדִישׁ. שֶׁמְּשַׁלֵּם כָּל־מַה שֶׁבְּתוֹכוֹ. מַחְלְפָה שִׁיטַת רַבָּנִין. תַּמָּן אָמְרִין. לְרַבּוֹת טָמוּן. וְכָא אָמְרִין. פְּרָט לְטָמוּן. וְלֹא כֵן אָמַר רַבִּי אַבָּהוּ בְּשֵׁם רַבִּי יוֹחָנָן. מוֹדִין חֲכָמִים לְרַבִּי יוּדָן בִּכְלֵי גוֹרֶן שֶׁדַּרְכָּן לִיטָמֵן. אָמַר רַבִּי הוֹשַׁעְיָה. בְּשֶׁאֵין עֵדִים. אֲבָל אִם יֵשׁ עֵדִים כָּל־עַמָּא מוֹדוּ עַל הָדָא דְרִבִּי (יוסי) דְּתַנֵּי כֵן. הָיָה גָּדִישׁ חִטִּים מְחוּפֶּה שְׂעוֹרִין. אוֹ גָדִישׁ שְׂעוֹרִין מְחוּפֶּה בְחִטִּין. נוֹתֵן לוֹ גָּדִישׁ שְׂעוֹרִים. כְּהָדָא חַד בַּר נַשׁ אַפְקַד גַּבֵּי חַבְרֵיהּ חַד שַׂק צְרִיר וְאִירְעוֹ אוֹנֶס. אָהֵן אָמַר. סִיגִין הֲוָה מָלֵא. וְאָהֵן הֲוָא אָמַר. מְטַקְסִין הֲוָה מָלֵא. הֲרֵי זֶה נִשְׁבָּע וְנוֹטֵל.

**Halakhah 7**: "He who sets fire to a stack of sheaves," etc. Rebbi Abbahu in the name of Rebbi Johanan: The Sages agree with Rebbi Jehudah about threshing tools which usually are hidden there[103]. The argument of Rebbi Jehudah seems inverted. There[104] he says except what is hidden, but here he says including what is hidden? But does not Rebbi Jehudah simply explain "stack"? Why was "stack" written? That he has to pay for all that is in it[105]. The argument of the rabbis seems inverted. There they say, including what is hidden; but here they say, except what is hidden? But did not Rebbi Abbahu say in the name of Rebbi Johanan: The Sages agree with Rebbi Johanan about threshing tools which usually are hidden there?[106] Rebbi Hoshaia said, if there are no witnesses. But if there are witnesses, everybody agrees with Rebbi (Yose)[107] as it was stated: [108]"If it was a stack of wheat sheaves covered with barley or a stack of barley sheaves covered with wheat, he pays for a stack of barley." As the following: A person deposited a tied sack with another person, when something happened. This one said, it was full of dross, but the other said, it was full of raw silk. [ ][109] He swears and collects[110].

103 The Babli (61b) agrees in the name of Rava, the proponent of Galilean Halakhah.

104 Mishnah *Peah* 6:9. The parallel treatment there in Halakhah 6:9 (Notes 151-154) is more explicit.

105 The difference has nothing to do with positions of R. Jehudah, but with his interpretation of *Ex.* 22:5. The verse states that the arsonist has to pay for "thorns, or a stack, or standing grain, or a field." Since even without mention of "stack" the arsonist would have to pay for the grain, the inclusion of "stack" can only mean "everything in a stack, whether recognizable from the outside or not."

106 They do not disagree with R. Jehudah. Their difference is about the standards of proof required from the victims of a fire. R. Jehudah holds that the arsonist would have to disprove any claim while the rabbis hold that the claimant still has the burden of proof

unless he is supported by current agricultural practice.

107  One has to read: Jehudah, with Rosh (Chapter 6, #16).

108  Tosephta 6:24, Babli 62a.

109  Add with Rosh and Alfasi (#125): "Rav said."

110  The text is elliptic; it is best explained following Nahmanides (and all Spanish commentators of the Babli.) The first problem is what is the connection between the story and the question at hand; the second is why the claimant may swear and collect. Nahmanides (as quoted by Rashba *ad 62a* and others) thinks that the sack was lost in a fire; the owner of the sack claims payment from the person responsible for the fire. Now Mishnah *Šebuot* 7:1 states that in general one only accepts an oath of a person who can absolve himself of payment by the oath. To collect money based on an oath is possible only in very few cases, one of them being the victim of a robbery. In the Babli, 62a, it is stated that R. Jehudah equates loss by fire to loss by robbery. Since the Yerushalmi holds that the Sages mostly agree with R. Jehudah, everybody must hold that the victim of a fire may swear and collect. In the case described, since the sack was deposited tightly tied, the argument of the person with whom the sack was deposited (who may have set the fire himself), that the sack might have contained scrap metal, is not more than a conjecture and may be disregarded.

By the biblical law of deposits (*Ex.* 22:6-8), the person holding the deposit has to swear that he did nothing to impair the deposit; then he is not liable. If he set the fire, he cannot swear and, therefore, should be required to pay without the other side being forced to swear. However, this only applies if the nature of the deposit was known. If the contents of the sack were not ascertained by the trustee when he accepted the sack, the rule that the person who cannot swear must pay is irrelevant.

(5c line 44) רִבִּי יוֹחָנָן בָּעֵי. מַהוּ שֶׁיִּטְעֲנוּ לוֹ דָּבָר שֶׁאֵין רְאוּיִין לוֹ. נִשְׁמְעִינָהּ מִן הָדָא. דַּאֲרִיסֵיהּ דְּבַר זִיזָא אַפְקַד גַּבֵּי חַד בַּר נַשׁ לִיטְרָא דְהַב. מִית בַּר זִיזָא וּמִית אֲרִיסֵיהּ דְּבַר זִיזָא. אָתָא עוֹבְדָא קוֹמֵי רִבִּי יִשְׁמָעֵאל בֵּירִבִּי יוֹסֵי. אָמַר. מָאן הוּא דְלָא יָדַע דְּכָל־מַאי דְאִית לַאֲרִיסֵיהּ דְּבַר זִיזָא לְבַר זִיזָא אִינּוּן. יִתְיְיהֲבוּן לִבְנוֹי דְּבַר זִיזָא. הֲוֹון לְבַר זִיזָא בְּנִין וַרְבְרְבִין וּבְנִין דְּקִיקִין. אָמַר.

## HALAKHAH 7

יִסְבּוֹן רַבְרְבִין פַּלְגָּא. וְכַד רְבוּ דְקִיקַיָּא יִסְבּוֹן פַּלְגָּא. דְּמָךְ רִבִּי יִשְׁמָעֵאל בֵּירִבִּי יוֹסֵי. אֲתַא עוֹבְדָא קוֹמֵי רִבִּי חִייָה. אָמַר. אִין מִן הָדָא לֵית שְׁמַע מִינָּהּ כְּלוּם. [ ]. יִתְיִיהֲבוֹן לִבְנוֹי דַּאֲרִיסָה. אָמַר לֵיהּ מָרֵיהּ דְּפִיקְדוֹנָא. כְּבָר יְהָבִית פַּלְגָּא. אָמַר לֵיהּ. מַה שֶׁנָּתַתָּה עַל פִּי בֵית דִּין נָתַתָּה. וּמַה שֶׁאַתָּה נוֹתֵין עַל פִּי בֵית דִּין אַתָּה נוֹתֵן. מָהוּ דְיֵימְרוֹן בְּנוֹי דַּאֲרִיסֵיהּ דְּבַר זִיזָא לִבְנוֹי דְּבַר זִיזָא. יָבוֹן לוֹן מַה דְּנַסְתּוּן. יָכְלִין מֵימַר לוֹן. מַה שֶׁנַּעֲשָׂה עַל פִּי בֵית דִּין נַעֲשָׂה. מָהוּ דְיֵימְרוֹן דְּקוּקַיָּיא לְרַבְרְבַיָּיא. נִיפְלוֹג עִמְּכוֹן. יָכְלִין מֵימַר לוֹן. מְצִיאָה מָצָאנוּ. אָמַר רִבִּי יִצְחָק. לֵית בֵּין רַבְרְבַיָּיא לִדְקוּקַיָּיא אֶלָּא כְּמִי שֶׁנִּיתַּן לָהֶן מַתָּנָה.

Rebbi Johanan asked: Can one argue for him an argument which does not apply to him[111]? Let us hear from the following: Bar Ziza's sharecropper deposited a pound[112] of gold with somebody. Bar Ziza and Bar Ziza's sharecropper died; the case came before Rebbi Ismael ben Rebbi Yose. He said, does not everybody know that all Bar Ziza's sharecrooper had was Bar Ziza's property? It should be given to Bar Ziza's sons. Bar Ziza had adult and underage sons. He said, the adult one should take half and when the underage ones grow up, they should receive half. Rebbi Ismael ben Rebbi Yose died; the case came before Rebbi Hiyya who said, that argument[113] means nothing [since there are people who do not flout their wealth][114]; it should be given to the sharecropper's sons. The trustee told him, I already disbursed half of it. He told him, what you gave, you gave by court order and what you will give, you will give by court order. May the sharecropper's sons say to Bar Ziza's sons, give us what you took? They can tell them, what was done was done by court order. May the underage ones say to the adult, let us share with you? May they tell them, we found a find? Rebbi Isaac said, the case between the adult and underaged ones is compared to one who gave a gift[115].

111  The entire paragraph is in a slightly different formulation in *Šebuot* 7:2, 37d.

Since the Sages agree with R. Jehudah that for matters within general practice one believes the claimant of fire damages without proof, must the "general practice" be interpreted narrowly or may one admit, e. g., practices of rich people for a poor claimant?

112  A Roman pound, 345 g, an enormous value in the early 3rd Century.

113  R. Ismael ben R. Yose's.

114  Missing here, added from the text of Alfasi (#125) and the parallel in *Šebuot*. In the latter text, the position of R. Ḥiyya is explicitly endorsed by R. Joḥanan who quotes *Prov.* 13:7: "There are those who pose as rich and have nothing, pose as poor and have great wealth".

115  Since R. Ismael ben R. Yose said that "it should be given to Bar Ziza's sons," all have to share equally.

(fol. 5b) **משנה ח**: גֵּץ שֶׁיָּצָא מִתַּחַת הַפַּטִּישׁ וְהִזִּיק חַיָּיב. גָּמָל שֶׁהָיָה טָעוּן פִּשְׁתָּן וְעוֹבֵר בִּרְשׁוּת הָרַבִּים נִכְנְסָה פִשְׁתָּנוֹ לְתוֹךְ הַחֲנוּת וְדָלְקָה בְּנֵרוֹ שֶׁל חֶנְוָנִי וְהִדְלִיק אֶת הַבִּירָה בַּעַל הַגָּמָל חַיָּיב. הִנִּיחַ הַחֶנְוָנִי נֵרוֹ מִבַּחוּץ הַחֶנְוָנִי חַיָּיב. רִבִּי יְהוּדָה אוֹמֵר בְּנֵר חֲנוּכָּה פָּטוּר.

**Mishnah 8**: If a spark came from under a hammer and caused damage, he[116] is liable. If a camel was loaded with flax and while it walked in the public domain the flax entered a store, was lit by the storekeeper's light, and set the building on fire, the camel's owner is liable. If the store owner put his light outside[117], the store owner is liable. Rebbi Jehudah says, in case of a Ḥanukkah light he is not liable[118].

116  The person working the hammer.

117  An illicit use of the public domain.

118  Where an outside display is required.

**הלכה ח:** גֵּץ הַיּוֹצֵא מִתַּחַת הַפַּטִּישׁ כול'. תַּנֵּי רִבִּי יוּדָן. בְּנֵר חֲנוּכָּה (5c line 59) פָּטוּר מִפְּנֵי שֶׁהוּא רְשׁוּת. וַחֲכָמִים אוֹמְרִין. בֵּין כָּךְ וּבֵין כָּךְ חַיָּיב. כְּגוֹן אֵילוּ שֶׁהֵן עוֹשִׂין סוּכּוֹת בְּפִתְחֵי חֲנוּיוֹתֵיהֶם בֶּחָג מִפְּנֵי שֶׁהוּא רְשׁוּת וּבָא אַחֵר וְהוּזַּק בָּהֶן חַיָּיב.

**Halakhah 8**: "If a spark is coming from under a hammer," etc. [119]"Rebbi Jehudah stated: In case of a Hanukkah light he is not liable because he acted with permission[118]. But the Sages say, in any case he is liable, as, e. g., those who build huts in front of their stores on Tabernacles because it is permitted[120]; but if somebody else is hurt by them, he is liable."

---

119 Tosephta 6:28.
120 Because of the religious requirement, the use of public space for a hut is permitted under the jurisdiction of the Jewish court but it cannot supersede the right of others to unhindered access to the public domain.

## מרוכה פרק שביעי

(fol. 5c) **משנה א:** מְרוּבָה מִידַּת תַּשְׁלוּמֵי כֶפֶל מִמִּידַּת תַּשְׁלוּמֵי אַרְבָּעָה וַחֲמִשָּׁה שֶׁמִּידַּת תַּשְׁלוּמֵי כֶפֶל נוֹהֶגֶת בֵּין בְּדָבָר שֶׁיֵּשׁ בּוֹ רוּחַ חַיִּים וּבְדָבָר שֶׁאֵין בּוֹ רוּחַ חַיִּים. וּמִידַּת תַּשְׁלוּמֵי אַרְבָּעָה וַחֲמִשָּׁה אֵינָהּ נוֹהֶגֶת אֶלָּא בְשׁוֹר וָשֶׂה בִּלְבַד שֶׁנֶּאֱמַר כִּי יִגְנֹב אִישׁ שׁוֹר אוֹ שֶׂה וגו'. אֵין הַגּוֹנֵב אַחַר הַגַּבָּב מְשַׁלֵּם תַּשְׁלוּמֵי כֶפֶל וְלֹא הַטּוֹבֵחַ וְלֹא הַמּוֹכֵר אַחַר הַגַּבָּב מְשַׁלֵּם תַּשְׁלוּמֵי אַרְבָּעָה וַחֲמִשָּׁה.

**Mishnah 1**: The obligation to make double restitution[1] is more frequent than that of paying quadruple or quintuple restitution since the obligation to make double restitution applies both to living things and to inanimate objects; but the obligation of paying quadruple or quintuple restitution only applies to oxen and sheep, as it is said: "If a man steal an ox or a sheep,[2]" etc. He who steals from a thief does not pay double restitution, nor does the one who slaughters or sells after a thief pay quadruple or quintuple restitution.

1 The general punishment of a thief, *Ex.* 22:3,8.

2 *Ex.* 21:37 decrees quintuple payment for stolen cattle sold or slaughtered by the thief and quadruple payment for stolen sheep or goats.

(5d line 33) **הלכה א:** מְרוּבָה מִידַּת תַּשְׁלוּמֵי כֶפֶל כול'. מְנָן תֵּיתֵי לֵיהּ. מֵאִם הִמָּצֵא תִמָּצֵא וגו'. אֵין לִי אֶלָּא שׁוֹר וַחֲמוֹר וָשֶׂה. כְּשֶׁהוּא אוֹמֵר חַיִּים. לְרַבּוֹת כָּל־בַּעֲלֵי חַיִּים. הַגְּנֵיבָה. לְרַבּוֹת אֶת הַמִּיטַּלְטְלִין. וְלָמָּה שׁוֹר וַחֲמוֹר וָשֶׂה. אִם דָּבָר שֶׁיֵּשׁ בּוֹ הֲנָיָיה לַמִּזְבֵּחַ נִיתְנֵי שׁוֹר וָשֶׂה. [ ]6 תַּנֵּי רִבִּי יִשְׁמָעֵאל. יָצְאוּ

קַרְקָעוֹת שֶׁאֵין מִיטַּלְטְלִין. יָצְאוּ עֲבָדִים שֶׁאֵין לְךָ בָּהֶן אֶלָּא תַשְׁמִישׁ. יָצְאוּ שְׁטָרוֹת שֶׁאֵין לְךָ בָּהֶן אֶלָּא רְאָיָיה.

**Halakhah 1**: "The obligation to make double restitution is more frequent," etc. From where does he get this? From "if being found it is found[3]". This includes not only ox, or donkey, or sheep: Since He says "alive", it includes all living beings[4]. "The stolen goods", to include movables. Why "ox, or donkey, or sheep"? If it were restricted to anything useful for the altar, one should have stated "ox and sheep"[5]. [If it were restricted to anything useful for the priests, one should have stated "ox and donkey."][6] Rebbi Ismael stated: It excludes real estate which is not movable; it excludes slaves from whom you only have service; it excludes documents which only are for proof[7].

3 *Ex.* 22:3: "If the stolen goods being found are found alive in his hand, be it ox, or donkey, or sheep, doubly shall he pay." Since in 21:37 quadruple or quintuple restitution was ordered for selling or slaughtering stolen cattle or sheep, the mention of "donkey" extends the set of objects subject to double restitution beyond that subject to multiple restitution.

4 Babli 83b, *Mekhilta dR. Ismael Neziqin* 13, *Mekhilta dR. Simeon ben Iohai* p. 194.

5 Since a donkey is an impure animal excluded from the altar, its mention declares the law to be a strictly profane matter.

6 Addition of E, confirmed by a Genizah fragment. At first look, the argument seems to prove that double restitution be required only for animals whose firstborn are either given to the Cohen (cattle and sheep, *Ex.* 34:19), or for which a substitute is given to the Cohen (donkeys, *Ex.* 34:20,13:13). The extended arguments in the Babli, 64a, and even more so in *Mekhilta dR. Simeon ben Iohai*, p. 194, note that the explicit mention of "stolen goods" shows that the list is incomplete and, therefore, no restriction is intended..

7 Babli 64b; for these only simple restitution is required. Documents which prove a claim do not in themselves represent money's worth.

(5d line 44) רִבִּי אַבָּהוּ שָׁאַל. לָמָּה לֹא שָׁנִינוּ שְׁמִידַת תַּשְׁלוּמֵי כֶפֶל נוֹהֶגֶת בְּטוֹעֵן טַעֲנַת גַּנָּב בְּשׁוּתָּפִין. מַה שֶׁאֵין כֵּן בְּתַשְׁלוּמֵי אַרְבָּעָה וַחֲמִשָּׁה.

Rebbi Abbahu asked: Why did we not state that double restitution is due if a claim of theft is made in a partnership[8], where quadruple or quintuple restitution does not apply[9]?

8   In any trust relation, the person making a false claim that something was stolen which he himself took has to make double restitution, *Ex.* 22:8.

9   The Babli quotes R. Ḥiyya bar Abba in the name of R. Joḥanan that quadruple or quintuple restitution applies in case of a fraudulent claim of theft, 62b.

(5d line 46) תַּנֵּי. וְגוּנַּב מִבֵּית הָאִישׁ. וְלֹא מִבֵּית הָאִשָּׁה. כָּל־עַצְמוֹ אֵין כְּתִיב רֵעֵהוּ אֶלָּא בְשׁוֹאֵל. וְתֵימַר הָכֵין. אֵין הַגּוֹנֵב אַחַר הַגַּנָּב מְשַׁלֵּם תַּשְׁלוּמֵי [כֶפֶל וְלֹא הַטּוֹבֵחַ וְלֹא הַמּוֹכֵר אַחַר הַגַּנָּב מְשַׁלֵּם תַּשְׁלוּמֵי] אַרְבָּעָה וַחֲמִשָּׁה. גָּנַב וְנִגְנְבָה מִמֶּנּוּ [וְאַחַר כָּךְ נִמְצֵאת הַגְּנֵיבָה לְמִי הוּא מְשַׁלֵּם. לָרִאשׁוֹן לַשֵּׁנִי לִשְׁנֵיהֶם. גָּנַב וְנִגְנְבָה מִמֶּנּוּ] וְתָפְשׂוּ הַבְּעָלִים אֶת הַשֵּׁנִי וְנִשְׁבַּע לָהֶן. אִין תֵּימַר. מוֹצִיאִין מִן הַשֵּׁנִי. מֵבִיא קָרְבָּן עַל הַשְּׁבוּעָה. אִין תֵּימַר. אֵין מוֹצִיאִין מִן הַשֵּׁנִי. אֵינוֹ מֵבִיא קָרְבָּן שְׁבוּעָה. גָּנַב וְנִגְנְבָה מִמֶּנּוּ וְנִמְלַךְ הַשֵּׁנִי לְהַחֲזִיר. אִין תֵּימַר. יַחֲזִיר לַבְּעָלִים. פְּעָמִים שֶׁאֵין מוֹדִיעִין לַגַּנָּב. אִין תֵּימַר. יַחֲזִיר לַגַּנָּב. פְּעָמִים שֶׁאֵין מוֹדִיעִין לַבְּעָלִים. כֵּיצַד יַעֲשֶׂה. יַחֲזִיר לַבְּעָלִים בִּפְנֵי גַנָּב.

It was stated: "It was stolen from the man's house"[10], but not from the woman's house[11]? Is not "his neighbor" only written in respect of the borrower[12]? But one has to say that "he who steals from a thief does not pay [double restitution, nor does the one who slaughters or sells after a thief pay][13] quadruple or quintuple restitution. If something was stolen which then was stolen from him; [14][when in the end the stolen object was found, to whom does he pay? To the first owner, to the second[15], to both of them[16]? If something was stolen which then was stolen from him[15]]; the owners apprehended the second thief who swore to them[17]. If you say that one takes it away from the second, he has to bring a sacrifice for the oath. If you say that one does not take it away from the second, he does not have to bring a sacrifice for his oath. If something was stolen which then was stolen from him[15] and the second thief decides to return it[18], if you say that he has to return it to the owners, they might not inform the first thief[19]. If you say that he has to return it to the first thief, that one might not inform the owners[20]. What does he have to do? He returns it to the owners in the presence of the thief.

10  Ex. 22:6, speaking of the responsibilities of the unpaid trustee. (Different *baraitot* explaining the verse are in *Šebuot* 8:1, fol. 38b). The verse ends: If the thief is found he has to make double restitution.

11  Since this interpretation does not make sense, it is natural to read the verse meaning that the thief stealing from the trustee has to pay double but the thief stealing from the thief does not. In the Babli, *Bekhorot* 11a, the expression is read to exclude stealing from public property from double restitution.

12  Ex. 22:13. In fact, "his neighbor" is also written for the paid trustee, Ex. 22:9. In all these cases, it is emphasized that one only deals with the principal, not that anything was stolen from a thief. E reads: "Only the borrower is called neighbor."

13  This is a quote from the Mishnah, complete only in E. In the Genizah fragment, after the first few words the rest is indicated by "etc." In the Leiden ms. it is missing; the scribe skipped from תשלומי to תשלומי.

14  Addtion from E supported by the Genizah fragment. It is again missing in L because the scribe omitted the text between two identical expressions.

15  The thief.

16  The answer is given at the end of the paragraph.

17  He swore falsely that he did not steal the object from them. If the owners can recover the object from the second thief, he swore falsely and has to bring a reparation sacrifice as described in *Lev.* 5:1-13. But if the owners can only demand payment of the object's worth, he did not swear falsely since he did not steal from them.

18 Who also will confess from whom he took the object.
19 That he has to pay simple restitution since the object already was returned.
20 That he owes them double restitution.

**משנה ב:** גָּנַב עַל פִּי שְׁנַיִם וְטָבַח וּמָכַר עַל פִּיהֶם אוֹ עַל פִּי שְׁנַיִם אֲחֵרִים מְשַׁלֵּם תַּשְׁלוּמֵי אַרְבָּעָה וַחֲמִשָּׁה. גָּנַב וּמָכַר בַּשַּׁבָּת גָּנַב וּמָכַר לַעֲבוֹדָה זָרָה גָּנַב וְטָבַח בְּיוֹם הַכִּפּוּרִים גָּנַב מִשֶּׁל אָבִיו וְטָבַח וּמָכַר וְאַחַר כָּךְ מֵת אָבִיו גָּנַב וְטָבַח וְאַחַר כָּךְ הִקְדִּישׁ מְשַׁלֵּם תַּשְׁלוּמֵי אַרְבָּעָה וַחֲמִשָּׁה. גָּנַב וְטָבַח לִרְפוּאָה אוֹ לַכְּלָבִים הַשּׁוֹחֵט וְנִמְצָא טְרֵפָה הַשּׁוֹחֵט חוּלִין בָּעֲזָרָה מְשַׁלֵּם תַּשְׁלוּמֵי אַרְבָּעָה וַחֲמִשָּׁה. רַבִּי שִׁמְעוֹן פּוֹטֵר בִּשְׁנֵי אֵילוּ. (fol. 5c)

**Mishnah 2:** He who stole according to the testimony of two people[21] and slaughtered or sold according to their testimony or the testimony of two others, has to pay quadruple or quintuple restitution. He who stole and sold on the Sabbath[22], stole and sold to pagan worship[23], stole and slaughtered on the Day of Atonement[24], stole from his father, slaughtered, or sold, and then his father died,[25] stole, slaughtered, and then dedicated it to the Temple[26], has to pay quadruple or quintuple restitution. He who stole and slaughtered for medical purposes or for the dogs, he who slaughtered and it turned out torn[27], he who slaughtered a profane animal in the Temple courtyard[28], has to pay quadruple or quintuple restitution. Rebbi Simeon frees from liability in these two cases[29].

21 To recover stolen property is a civil matter and is judged according to civil law. But for the owners to collect double, quadruple, or quintuple restitution requires a criminal conviction of the thief which can be based only on the testimony of at least two eye witnesses to the act.

22 This is forbidden but in itself is not a capital crime which would

preempt the imposition of a fine. But if he slaughtered on the Sabbath he committed a capital crime and could not be sentenced to a fine; cf. Chapter 6, Note 102.

23  As long as he does not himself participate in pagan worship, no capital crime has been committed.

24  The punishment for this deadly sin is left to Heaven, not the human court.

25  Even though he is an heir, he has to pay to his co-heirs their share in the fine payable to the estate.

26  Since he already was subject to the fine when he dedicated, the dedication cannot erase the liability.

27  On inspection the animal was found to be sick and the meat unfit for human consumption.

28  The slaughtered animal is forbidden for any use.

29  He holds that slaughter which does not prepare meat for human consumption technically is called "killing" rather than "slaughter" and is not covered by the rule of *Ex.* 21:37.

**הלכה ב:** וְלֹא כֵן אָמַר רִבִּי אַבָּהוּ בְּשֵׁם רִבִּי יוֹחָנָן הֵזִיד בְּחֵלֶב וְשָׁגַג (5d line 53) בְּקָרְבָּן מַתְרִין בּוֹ וְלוֹקֶה וּמֵבִיא קָרְבָּן. רִבִּי בּוּן בַּר חִיָּיה בְּשֵׁם רִבִּי שְׁמוּאֵל בַּר רַב יִצְחָק כְּדֵי רִשְׁעָתוֹ. שְׁנֵי דְּבָרִים מְסוּרִין לְבֵית דִּין הַתּוֹפֵס אֶחָד מֵהֶן. יָצָא דָבָר שֶׁמָּסוּר לַשָּׁמַיִם.

[29]Did not Rabbi Abbahu say in the name of Rebbi Johanan: If he is intentional about fat but in error about a sacrifice, he can be warned, is whipped, and brings a sacrifice. [30]Rebbi Abun bar Ḥiyya in the name of Rebbi Samuel bar Rav Isaac: (*Deut.* 25:2) "Because of his guilt." If two alternatives are presented to the court, one chooses one of them. This excludes matters in the power of Heaven.

29  This is the beginning of the discussion about when a fine can or cannot be imposed. The correct text is in *Terumot* 6:1, Notes 5,6. There is no sacrifice which might atone for an intentional sin.

30  *Terumot* 7:1, Notes 2,14.

(fol. 5d) **משנה ג:** גָּנַב עַל פִּי שְׁנַיִם וְטָבַח וּמָכַר עַל פִּיהֶן וְנִמְצְאוּ זוֹמְמִין מְשַׁלְּמִין לוֹ אֶת הַכֹּל. גָּנַב עַל פִּי שְׁנַיִם וְטָבַח וּמָכַר עַל פִּי שְׁנַיִם אֲחֵרִים אֵילוּ וָאֵילוּ נִמְצְאוּ זוֹמְמִין הָרִאשׁוֹנִים מְשַׁלְּמִים כֶּפֶל וְהָאַחֲרוֹנִים מְשַׁלְּמִים תַּשְׁלוּמֵי שְׁלֹשָׁה. נִמְצְאוּ הָאַחֲרוֹנִים זוֹמְמִין הוּא מְשַׁלֵּם תַּשְׁלוּמֵי כֶפֶל וְהֵם מְשַׁלְּמִים תַּשְׁלוּמֵי שְׁלֹשָׁה. אֶחָד מִן הָאַחֲרוֹנִים זוֹמֵם בָּטְלָה עֵדוּת שְׁנִיָּה. אֶחָד מִן הָרִאשׁוֹנִים זוֹמֵם בָּטְלָה כָּל־הָעֵדוּת שֶׁאִם אֵין גְּנֵיבָה אֵין טְבִיחָה וְאֵין מְכִירָה.

**Mishnah 3**: One was convicted of theft on the testimony of two witnesses and of slaughtering or selling on their testimony; if they are found perjured they pay everything[31] to him. If he was convicted of theft on the testimony of two witnesses and of slaughtering or selling on the testimony of two others who all were found perjured, the first group pays double restitution and the second group triple[32]. If the second group were found perjured, he pays double restitution[33] while they pay triple[34]. If one of the second group was found perjured, the second testimony is invalidated[35]. If one of the first group is found perjured, the entire testimony is invalidated since if there is no theft there is no slaughter or sale[36].

31  *Deut.* 19:19 requires that the punishment of a perjured witness be the statutory punishment which would have been imposed on the accused. Testimony can be shown to be perjured only by other testimony which establishes that the witness was not in a position to see the act which he testifies about; cf. *Ketubot* 2:11, Note 199.

32  As pointed out at the end of the Mishnah, everybody is permitted to sell or slaughter his livestock. The act becomes criminal only if the animal was stolen. Therefore the testimony of the second group is predicated on that of the first group; they only have to pay the difference their testimony would make in the sentence imposed on the defendant had their testimony been true. For the imputed sale of a stolen sheep they pay double, for that of a stolen ox triple damages.

33  For the valid conviction of theft.

34  Or double, as the case may be.

35  A single witness in a criminal proceeding is disregarded, *Deut.* 19:15.

36  No possibility to prosecute for sale or slaughter.

**הלכה ג:** גָּנַב עַל פִּי שְׁנַיִם כול'. (5d line 57) עַד כְּדוֹן בְּשֶׁבָּאוּ עֵידֵי גְנֵיבָה וְעֵדֵי טְבִיחָה כְּאַחַת. בָּאוּ עֵידֵי גְנֵיבָה וְלֹא קִיבְּלוּם וְאַחַר כָּךְ בָּעוּ עֵידֵי טְבִיחָה. אָמְרִין לָהֶן. הֱווּ יוֹדְעִין שֶׁכְּבָר בָּאוּ עֵידֵי גְנֵיבָה וְלֹא קִיבַּלְנוּם וְעַל יְדֵיכֶם אָנוּ מְקַבְּלִין אוֹתָן. נִמְצְאוּ עֵידֵי טְבִיחָה זוֹמְמִין מְשַׁלְּמִין עַל יְדֵי עֵידֵי גְנֵיבָה. רַבִּי חִזְקִיָּה לֹא מַר כֵּן אֶלָּא. עַד כְּדוֹן בְּשֶׁבָּאוּ עֵידֵי גְנֵיבָה וְעֵידֵי טְבִיחָה כְּאַחַת. בָּאוּ עֵידֵי טְבִיחָה וְלֹא קִיבְּלוּ אוֹתָן וְאַחַר כָּךְ בָּעוּ עֵידֵי גְנֵיבָה. אוֹמְרִין לוֹהֶן. הֱווּ יוֹדְעִין שֶׁכְּבָר בָּאוּ עֵידֵי טְבִיחָה וְלֹא קִיבַּלְנוּם וְעַל יְדֵיכֶם אָנוּ מְקַבְּלִין אוֹתָן. וְנִמְצְאוּ זוֹמְמִין עֵידֵי גְנֵיבָה. מְשַׁלְּמִין עַל יְדֵי עֵידֵי טְבִיחָה.

[37]**Halakhah 3**: "One was convicted of theft on the testimony of two witnesses," etc. So far if the witnesses for theft and those for slaughter came together[38]. If witnesses for theft appeared but were not accepted[39] and after that came witnesses for slaughter. One tells them "witnesses for theft already had appeared but were not accepted, but on the strength of your testimony[40] we shall accept them." If the witnesses for slaughter turn out to be perjured, they pay because of the witnesses for theft[41]. Rebbi Hizqiah does not say so but: So far if the witnesses for theft and those for slaughter came together. If witnesses for slaughter appeared but were not accepted[42] and after that came witnesses for theft. One tells them "witnesses for slaughter already had appeared but were not accepted, but on the strength of your testimony we shall accept them." If the witnesses for theft turn out to be perjured[43], they pay because of the witnesses for slaughter.

37  In L, Halakhah 3 comes after Halakhah 4, but in the Genizah and E texts, and *editio princeps*, the order is as given here.

38  Since slaughter or sale are not criminal unless the animal was stolen, it

is clear that the Mishnah refers to a case in which both theft and slaughter are dealt with in the same court procedure.

39   Their testimony did not stand up under preliminary cross-examination. Failing there is not proof of perjury.

40   Which supports the testimony of the witnesses to the theft.

41   Since without proof of theft, testimony of slaughter cannot be accepted in court; the witnesses to the slaughter have to pay double or triple restitution only because they caused the testimony to the theft to be accepted.

42   They cannot be heard as long as there were no witnesses to the theft.

43   In that case the testimony about slaughter is "testimony of the wicked" which has to be thrown out of court (*Ex.* 23:1). But since the witnesses to the theft caused the testimony about slaughter to be accepted, they have to pay the entire quadruple or quintuple restitution.

(fol. 5d) **משנה ד**: גָּנַב עַל פִּי שְׁנַיִם וְטָבַח וּמָכַר עַל פִּי עֵד אֶחָד אוֹ עַל פִּי עַצְמוֹ מְשַׁלֵּם תַּשְׁלוּמֵי כֶפֶל וְאֵינוֹ מְשַׁלֵּם תַּשְׁלוּמֵי אַרְבָּעָה וַחֲמִשָּׁה.

**Mishnah 4**: A person convicted of theft on the testimony of two witnesses, who slaughtered or sold by the testimony of a single witness or his own confession, pays double restitution but does not have to pay quadruple or quintuple[44].

44   Since the testimony of a single witness is not admissible in a criminal procedure, he cannot be convicted of slaughtering or selling and does not have to pay the fine. Similarly, since a person is always related to himself and relatives are barred from being witnesses in criminal proceedings, his confession is inadmissible and he never pays a fine on his own admission. In civil procedure one has to pay on the basis of his admission.

(5d line 65) **הלכה ד**: גָּנַב עַל פִּי שְׁנַיִם כול׳. אָמַר רִבִּי זְעִירָא. הָדָא אָמְרָה. עַד זוֹמֵם אֵין נִפְסָל בְּבֵית דִּין אֶלָּא מֵעַצְמוֹ הוּא נִפְסָל. פָּתַר לָהּ בְּהַתְרָיָיה. וְתַנֵּי כֵן.

אָמַר רִבִּי יוֹסֵי. בַּמֶּה דְבָרִים אֲמוּרִים. בִּשְׁתֵּי עֵדִיוֹת וּבִשְׁתֵּי הַתְרָיוֹת. אֲבָל בְּעֵדוּת אַחַת וּבְהַתְרָייָה אַחַת כָּל־עֵדוּת שֶׁבְּטֵלָה מִקְצָתָהּ בָּטְלָה כּוּלָּהּ. מַהוּ שֶׁבָּטְלָה מִקְצָתָהּ בָּטְלָה כּוּלָּהּ. הָיוּ עוֹמְדִין וּמְעִידִין עָלָיו בָּעֲשָׂרָה בְנִיסָן שֶׁגָּנַב שׁוֹר בְּאֶחָד בְּנִיסָן. טָבַח וּמָכַר בָּעֲשָׂרָה בְנִיסָן. הוּזַמּוּ בַחֲמִשָּׁה עָשָׂר בְּנִיסָן. כָּל־עֵדוּת שֶׁהֵעִידוּ מֵעֲשָׂרָה בְנִיסָן עַד חֲמִשָּׁה עָשָׂר בְּנִיסָן לְמַפְרֵיעַ הֲרֵי אִילּוּ פְסוּלוֹת. אָמַר רִבִּי בָּא בַּר מָמָל. תִּיפְתָּר בִּמְעִידִין עָלָיו בְּכֶרֶךְ אֶחָד. וְלֵית שְׁמַע מִינָהּ כְּלוּם. וְתַנֵּי כֵן. הֵן הָיוּ הָרִאשׁוֹנִים וְהֵן הָיוּ הָאַחֲרוֹנִים. הוּזַמּוּ בָרִאשׁוֹנָה אֵין כְּךָ כְּלוּם. בַּשְּׁנִיָּיה הֲרֵי אִילּוּ עֵדוּת אֶחָד. שְׁלִישִׁית הֲרֵי אִילּוּ שְׁתֵּי עֵדִיּוֹת. וְהֵיכִי דָמֵי. אִם בִּמְעִידִין עָלָיו בְּכֶרֶךְ אֶחָד. לֵית שְׁמַע מִינָהּ כְּלוּם. לָא אַתְייָא דָא אֶלָּא עַל יְדֵי עֵדוּת סַגִּיאָ.

**Halakhah 4**: "A person convicted of theft on the testimony of two witnesses," etc. [45]Rebbi Ze'ira said, this implies that a perjured witness is not disqualified by the court but is disqualified by himself[46]. Explain it by warning[47], as it was stated: "Rebbi Yose said, when has this been said? For two testimonies with two warnings. But for one testimony and one warning any testimony which is partially disqualified is totally disqualified[48]." What does it mean that if it is partially disqualified it is totally disqualified? If they were standing and testifying against him on then tenth of Nisan that he had stolen an ox on the first of Nisan. He slaughtered or sold on the tenth of Nisan. They were shown to be perjured on the fifteenth of Nisan. Any testimony which they delivered between the tenth and the fifteenth of Nisan is retroactively disqualified. Rebbi Abba bar Mamal said, explain it if they deliver their testimony in one group and you cannot infer anything, as we have stated: [49]"They were the first and they were the later [witnesses]. If they were shown to be perjured at first, there is nothing. At the second time, there is one testimony. At the third time, there are two testimonies." And how is[50] that if they give testimony in one group, you cannot infer anything? It comes only based on multiple testimony[51].

on multiple testimony[51].

45   A differently edited text is in *Makkot* 1:8; the subject of this paragraph is hinted at in *Bava batra* 3:6. The paragraph refers to Mishnah 3, not Mishnah 4.

46   In the Babli 72b, *Sanhedrin* 27a, as opinion of Abbai. The testimony of a proven criminal is invalid since by accepting such testimony the court would become the accomplice of an evildoer, which is forbidden in *Ex.* 23:1. The question is whether testimony becomes invalid only after the witness has been convicted of a felony or by his felonious act. While in general testimony of a criminal becomes unacceptable only after conviction, perjury carries its own conviction and all testimony rendered after one which was determined to be perjured automatically becomes void.

The argument presented by R. Ze'ira is based on the end of Mishnah 3: If the first testimony was perjured, the second testimony becomes void. But at the time that the second group of witnesses testified it was not known that the first testimony was perjured. This proves that a later discovery of perjury invalidates testimony retroactively.

47   Criminal intent can be proven only if the person was duly warned that his intended action was criminal (cf. *Kilaim* 8:1 Note 9, *Sotah* 7:1 Note 26, *Nazir* 8:1 Note 46). The court before accepting testimony has to warn the witnesses of the consequences of perjury. If both groups of witnesses were warned simultaneously, there is only one testimony and R. Ze'ira's argument does not prove anything.

48   Babli 73a; Tosephta 6:23.

49   Tosephta *Bava batra* 2:9. A person claims ownership of real estate currently in the possession of another person. Neither party has documentary proof. The claimant can show that he was a prior owner or is the heir of a prior owner. The person in possession claims to have bought or otherwise legally acquired the property. If the person can show by testimony that the claimant had failed to protest during three years in which he had undisturbed and continuous possession, the court will declare him the legal owner. (This is one of the many meanings of ḥazaqah, cf. *Ketubot* 5:5 Note 100). If the same group testifies three times on the possessor's behalf, covering three years, and one of their testimonies later was found to be perjured, that and all subsequent testimonies are thrown out by the court.

50   היכי דמי is an expression otherwise known only from the Babli. E and the

parallel in *Makkot* have היכי אמר, idiomatic Galilean Aramaic.

51  R. Abba bar Mamal's argument is rejected. Since possession is established by separate testimonies regarding three successive years, it is impossible to explain the Tosephta as referring to a single testimony. R. Zeʿira's inference is confirmed.

**משנה ה:** גָּנַב וְטָבַח בַּשַּׁבָּת. גָּנַב וְטָבַח לַעֲבוֹדָה זָרָה. גָּנַב מִשֶּׁלְאָבִיו וּמֵת אָבִיו וְאַחַר כָּךְ טָבַח וּמָכַר. גָּנַב וְהִקְדִּישׁ וְאַחַר טָבַח וּמָכַר מְשַׁלֵּם תַּשְׁלוּמֵי כֶפֶל וְאֵינוֹ מְשַׁלֵּם תַּשְׁלוּמֵי אַרְבָּעָה וַחֲמִשָּׁה. רִבִּי שִׁמְעוֹן אוֹמֵר קֳדָשִׁים שֶׁהוּא חַיָּיב בְּאַחֲרָיוּתָן מְשַׁלֵּם תַּשְׁלוּמֵי אַרְבָּעָה וַחֲמִשָּׁה וְשֶׁאֵינוֹ חַיָּיב בְּאַחֲרָיוּתָן פָּטוּר. (fol. 5d)

**Mishnah 5**: One who stole and slaughtered on the Sabbath[52], or stole and slaughtered for idolatry[53], or stole from his father and after his father's death slaughtered or sold[54], or stole, dedicated it[55], and afterwards slaughtered or sold, pays double restitution but not quadruple or quintuple. Rebbi Simeon says, for *sancta* for which he is liable by a warranty[56] he has to pay quadruple or quintuple, but if there is no warranty, he is not liable.

52  Stealing animals on the Sabbath is forbidden as on weekdays and incurs the same penalty. But slaughtering on the Sabbath is a capital crime which cannot be punished by an additional fine (cf. Note 22 and *Ketubot* 3:1, *Terumot* 7:1).

53  Pagan worship is a capital crime; a fine can be imposed for the theft but not for the slaughter.

54  Since he is a co-heir, he slaughtered or sold what is partially his own and cannot be sanctioned for the act.

55  As a sacrifice in the Temple. Temple property is not under the rules of civil law; illicit use is subject to the rules of *Lev.* 5:14-16, imposing a payment of 125% of the value taken.

56  If the thief made a vow in which he obligated himself for a certain sacrifice and then dedicated the stolen animal for that sacrifice, the animal still was in his possession since if it died or was lost he would be required to provide a replacement. But if he simply

dedicated the stolen animal as a sacrifice, implying that he would not be obligated to provide a replacement if it were lost or died, the animal would become Heaven's possession and its slaughter or sale would not trigger the obligation of quadruple or quintuple restitution.

(6a line 2) **הלכה ה:** גָּנַב וְטָבַח בַּשַּׁבָּת כול׳. וְלֹא כֵן אָמַר רִבִּי אַבָּהוּ בְּשֵׁם רִבִּי יוֹחָנָן מֵזִיד בְּחֵלֶב שׁוֹגֵג בְּקָרְבָּן מַתְרִין בּוֹ וְלוֹקֶה וּמֵבִיא קָרְבָּן. מָאן תַּנִּיתָהּ. [וְרִבִּי שִׁמְעוֹן. דְּתַנִּינָן.] רִבִּי שִׁמְעוֹן אוֹמֵר קֳדָשִׁים שֶׁחַייָב בְּאַחֲרָיוּתָן מְשַׁלֵּם תַּשְׁלוּמֵי אַרְבָּעָה וַחֲמִשָּׁה וְשֶׁאֵין חַייָב בְּאַחֲרָיוּתָן פָּטוּר.

"One who stole and slaughtered on the Sabbath," etc. [29]Did not Rabbi Abbahu say in the name of Rebbi Joḥanan: If he is intentional error about fat but in error about a sacrifice, he can be warned, is whipped, and brings a sacrifice. Who stated it[57]? [Rebbi Simeon, as we have stated][58]: "Rebbi Simeon says, for *sancta* for which he is liable by a warranty he has to pay quadruple or quintuple[59], but if there is no warranty, he is not liable."[60]

57 The statement in the Mishnah that the thief does not pay multiple restitution for slaughter or sale after dedication.

58 Added from E supported by a Genizah fragment.

59 Since these are not Heaven's property.

60 The argument is rejected in the Babli which holds that R. Simeon does not at all address the problem of the Mishnah (76a-78a).

(6a line 6) רִבִּי יוֹסְטָא בֵּירִבִּי מָתוּן שָׁאַל. הַפּוֹדֶה כַלְכָּלָה מִיַּד הַגּוּזְבָּר מָהוּ שֶׁיִּבָּטֵל[61] לְמַעְשְׂרוֹת. מָתִיב רֵישׁ לָקִישׁ. וְהָתַנִּינָן. גָּנַב וְהִקְדִּישׁ וְאַחַר טָבַח וּמָכַר. כְּמָה דְאַתְּ אָמַר תַּמָּן. הַמַּקְדִּישׁ אֵינוֹ כְמוֹכֵר. וְדִכְוָתָהּ הַפּוֹדֶה אֵינוֹ כְלוֹקֵחַ. מִילְּתֵיהּ דְּרֵישׁ לָקִישׁ אֲמָרָהּ. מְכִירָה כְפִדְיוֹן. אֲמְרֵי. רָאוּי הוּא לִפְדוֹתוֹ וּלְאוֹכְלוֹ.

Rebbi Justus ben Rebbi Matton asked: If somebody redeems a string of dry figs from the Temple treasurer, does it become *tevel* for tithes[62]? Rebbi Simeon ben Laqish asked: Did we not state[63] about him who "stole, dedicated it, and afterwards slaughtered or sold"? As you say there, the one who dedicates is not like a seller[64], so one who redeems is not like a buyer. The word of Rebbi Simeon ben Laqish implies that selling is like redeeming. They said, he has the choice of redeeming and eating it[65].

61 Read with E and Genizah texts: שֶׁיִּטָּבֵל. This word has been translated.

62 Produce becomes obligated for tithes only at the very end of harvest. A profane sale triggers the obligation of tithes for previously exempt produce (*Ma'serot* 4:1, Note 7.)

63 In the Mishnah.

64 If dedication were the equivalent of a sale, the thief who dedicated the stolen animal should immediately be obligated for quadruple or quintuple restitution by the act of dedication alone. Since dedication is not a sale, redemption cannot be a buy.

65 R. Simeon ben Laqish's argument is rejected: Dedication is not a sale because the person dedicating retains the right of first refusal (*Ma'serot* 1:1 Note 23). R. Justus's problem is not resolved.

(6a line 11) אָמַר רִבִּי לְעָזָר. רָאוּ אוֹתוֹ שׁוֹחֵט שׁוֹר שָׁחוֹר בַּיַּעַר חֲזָקָה גָּנוּב הוּא. חָשׁ לוֹמַר. שֶׁמָּא הָיָה רָבוּץ. תִּיפְתָּר בְּשֶׁרָאוּהוּ מוֹשֵׁךְ.

Rebbi Eleazar said: If they saw him slaughtering a black ox in a forest, it is *prima facie* evidence that it was stolen[66]. Could you not assume that it was lying down[67]? Explain it if they saw him dragging it[68].

66 The animal was slaughtered at a place where it was not easily seen and where usually cattle are not found and slaughter does not happen. Then the court can accept testimony about the slaughter to be used later if the police can find witnesses to the theft.

67 Since cattle periodically lie down to ruminate, could the ox not have chosen a shady place for his convenience?

68 Viz., the animal into the forest.

The Babli, 69b, points out that it is necessary for the thief to be seen dragging the animal to establish the theft. A person who slaughters a ruminating ox without moving the animal first did not steal before slaughtering and can be sued only for simple restitution.

(6a line 12) יֵשׁ בְּטוֹבֵחַ מַה שֶׁאֵין בְּמוֹכֵר וְיֵשׁ בְּמוֹכֵר שֶׁאֵין בְּטוֹבֵחַ. שֶׁהַטּוֹבֵחַ בַּשַּׁבָּת חַיָּיב וְהַמּוֹכֵר בַּשַּׁבָּת פָּטוּר. אָמַר רִבִּי יַנַּאי בֵּירִבִּי יִשְׁמָעֵאל. מָצִינוּ שֶׁהַמְּכִירָה חַיָּיבִין עָלֶיהָ בַּשַּׁבָּת. הַגַּע עַצְמָךְ. בָּאוֹמֵר לַחֲבֵירוֹ. תְּלוֹשׁ מִן הַקַּרְקַע הַזֶּה וּקְנֵה אוֹתוֹ. לֹא קְנָיָיו. אָמַר רִבִּי יוֹסֵי בֵּירִבִּי בּוּן. תְּלִישָׁה הִיא שֶׁמְּחַיֶּיבֶת אוֹתוֹ וְלֹא מְכִירָה.

There is a rule about the slaughterer which does not apply to the seller and to the seller which does not apply to the slaughterer, for he who slaughters on the Sabbath is criminally liable but he who sells on the Sabbath cannot be prosecuted[69]. Rebbi Yannai ben Rebbi Ismael said, we find a case of sale for which one is criminally liable on the Sabbath. Think of it, if somebody said to another: tear something off from this ground[70] to acquire, did he not acquire? Rebbi Yose ben Rebbi Abun said, the tearing makes him liable, not the sale[71].

69 The seller violates the positive commandment to rest on the Sabbath, but he did not violate any prohibition. Criminal prosecution is possible only for violation of a prohibition. The Mishnah is correct in only mentioning slaughter but not sale in connection with the Sabbath.

70 Which is an act of harvesting, forbidden in *Ex.* 34:21.

71 The Babli disagrees, 70b, and holds that no quadruple or quintuple restitution is due if the sale is simultaneous with and conditioned on a prohibited action.

**משנה ו:** מְכָרוֹ חוּץ מֵאֶחָד מִמֵּאָה שֶׁבּוֹ אוֹ שֶׁהָיְתָה לוֹ בּוֹ שׁוּתָפוּת. הַשּׁוֹחֵט וְנִתְנַבְּלָה בְיָדוֹ הַנּוֹחֵר וְהַמְעַקֵּר מְשַׁלֵּם תַּשְׁלוּמֵי כֶפֶל וְאֵינוֹ מְשַׁלֵּם תַּשְׁלוּמֵי אַרְבָּעָה וַחֲמִשָּׁה.

**Mishnah 6**: One who sold it except for a one percent interest in it[72], or had a partnership interest in it[73], one who slaughtered and it became a carcass in his hand[74], or one who stabs or tears out[75], pays double restitution but not quadruple or quintuple.

**משנה ז:** גָּנַב בִּרְשׁוּת הַבְּעָלִים טָבַח וּמָכַר חוּץ מֵרְשׁוּתָן. אוֹ שֶׁגָּנַב חוּץ מֵרְשׁוּתָן וְטָבַח וּמָכַר בִּרְשׁוּתָן. אוֹ שֶׁגָּנַב וְטָבַח וּמָכַר חוּץ מֵרְשׁוּתָן מְשַׁלֵּם תַּשְׁלוּמֵי אַרְבָּעָה וַחֲמִשָּׁה. אֲבָל אִם גָּנַב וְטָבַח וּמָכַר בִּרְשׁוּתָם פָּטוּר.

**Mishnah 7**: He who stole on the owner's property but slaughtered or sold off their property[76], or stole off their property and slaughtered or sold on their property, or stole and slaughtered or sold off their property has to pay quadruple or quintuple restitution. But if he stole and slaughtered or sold on their property[77], he is not liable.

72   If he did not sell the animal outright, *Ex.* 21:37 is not applicable. As *Mekhilta dR. Simeon ben Iohai* (p. 191) explains, slaughter and sale are treated on an equal footing in the verse. Since slaughter is all or nothing, a sale must be all or nothing.

73   It was not completely stolen; cf. Note 54.

74   If the carcass is unfit for Jewish consumption, he killed the animal but did not slaughter it; *Ex.* 21:37 is not applicable.

75   He kills the animal by tearing out some vital organ; the carcass is not fit for Jewish consumption.

76   By moving the animal off the property he took possession. This makes him a thief and subject to the law of quadruple or quintuple restitution.

77   If he never took possession, he cannot be called a thief and cannot be prosecuted under the terms of *Ex.* 21:37.

**הלכה ו-ז:** (6a line 18) מְכָרוֹ חוּץ מֵאֶחָד מִמֵּאָה שֶׁבּוֹ כול'. גָּנַב בִּרְשׁוּת הַבְּעָלִים כול'. רִבִּי זְעִירָא בָּעֵי. מְכָרָהּ חֶצְיָין מָהוּ. מָכַר חֶצְיָיהּ לָזֶה וְחֶצְיָיהּ לָזֶה מָהוּ. נִישְׁמְעִינָהּ מִן הָדָא. מְכָרָהּ חוּץ מִיָּדָהּ חוּץ מֵרַגְלָהּ הוּץ מִקַּרְנָהּ חוּץ מִגִּיזָתָהּ מְשַׁלֵּם תַּשְׁלוּמֵי אַרְבָּעָה וַחֲמִשָּׁה. רִבִּי לֶעְזָר בֵּירִבִּי שִׁמְעוֹן אוֹמֵר. חוּץ מִקַּרְנָהּ מְשַׁלֵּם תַּשְׁלוּמֵי כֶפֶל. חוּץ מִגִּיזּוֹתֶיהָ מְשַׁלֵּם תַּשְׁלוּמֵי אַרְבָּעָה וַחֲמִשָּׁה. רִבִּי אוֹמֵר. חוּץ מִדָּבָר שֶׁהַנְּשָׁמָה תְלוּיָה בָהּ מְשַׁלֵּם תַּשְׁלוּמֵי אַרְבָּעָה וַחֲמִשָּׁה. חוּץ מִדָּבָר שֶׁאֵין הַנְּשָׁמָה תְלוּיָה בָהּ פָּטוּר.

**Halakhah 6-7:** "One who sold it except for a one percent interest in it," etc. "He who stole on the owner's property," etc. Rebbi Ze'ira asked: If he sold it in halves, what is the rule[78]? If he sold half of it to one person and the other half to another, what is the rule? Let us hear from the following[79]: "If he sold it except for its forefoot, except for its hindfoot, except for its horn, except for its shearings[80], he pays quadruple or quintuple restitution. Rebbi Eleazar ben Rebbi Simeon[81] says, except for its horn he pays double restitution, except for its shearings he pays quadruple or quintuple restitution[82]. Rebbi says, except for a vital organ he pays quadruple or quintuple restitution; except for a non-vital organ he is not liable."

78  He sold the entire animal to one person but in two transactions.

79  Tosephta 7:18; essentially the same text is in the Babli, 78b, only except that the Babli in the statements of the anonymous Tanna and of Rebbi for "he pays" has "he does not pay" and vice-versa (similarly in *Mekhilta dR. Simeon ben Iohai* p. 191). The Babli text conforms to the Mishnah; the Yerushalmi-Tosephta text contradicts the Mishnah and defies rational explanation. Since the text is confirmed by all three Yerushalmi and both Tosephta mss., it cannot be emended, as noted by Rashba, *Novellae ad* 78b.

80  Since the sheep could be sold except for its wool and then the seller could shear it before delivery, the sheep was essentially sold completely in two transactions. Therefore, the answer to R. Ze'ira's question depends entirely on

whether in this case one reads "he pays" or "he does not pay".

81   In all other sources: R. Simeon ben Eleazar.

82   He agrees with the Mishnah but holds that the wool is external to the sheep, not part of its intrinsic body.

**משנה ח:** הָיָה מוֹשְׁכוֹ וְיוֹצֵא וּמֵת בִּרְשׁוּת הַבְּעָלִים פָּטוּר.  הִגְבִּיהוֹ אוֹ שֶׁהוֹצִיאוֹ חוּץ מֵרְשׁוּת הַבְּעָלִים וָמֵת חַיָּב. (fol. 5d)

**Mishnah 8**: If he was drawing it to lead it out but it died on the owner's property, he is not liable[83]. If he lifted it[84] or had led it outside the owner's property when it died, he is liable.

**משנה ט:** נְתָנוֹ לִבְכוֹרוֹת בְּנוֹ לְבַעַל חוֹבוֹ לְשׁוֹמֵר חִנָּם וְלַשׁוֹאֵל לְנוֹשֵׂא שָׂכָר וְלַשׂוֹכֵר וְהָיָה מוֹשְׁכוֹ וּמֵת בִּרְשׁוּת הַבְּעָלִים פָּטוּר.  הִגְבִּיהוֹ אוֹ שֶׁהוֹצִיאוֹ חוּץ מֵרְשׁוּת הַבְּעָלִים וָמֵת חַיָּב.

**Mishnah 9**: If he gave it for his first-born son[85], to his creditor, to an unpaid guardian or a borrower, to a paid guardian or a renter, and that person was drawing it to lead it out but it died on the owner's property, he is not liable[86]. If he[87] lifted it or had led it outside the owner's property when it died, he[88] is liable.

83   Drawing an animal by its halter or leading it on the owner's property is not an act of acquisition. If the animal died before it left the owner's property it was not stolen and no restitution is due.

84   If the thief lifts the animal (e. g., a sheep or a goat) on the owner's property with the intent of stealing it, he acquired it and as a thief becomes liable for double restitution.

85   In lieu of paying 5 šeqalim to a Cohen as redemption money, he tells the Cohen to take a sheep from such and such a flock, implying that the flock was his. If the Cohen takes the animal in good faith, the person who tricked him into taking it becomes the thief. The same holds for the other cases mentioned in the Mishnah.

86   Since there was no theft even if

87  The intended recipient.      88  The instigator.

**הלכה ח-ט:** הָיָה מוֹשְׁכוֹ וְיוֹצֵא וּמֵת כול'. נְתָנוֹ לִבְכוֹרוֹת בְּנוֹ כול'. (6a line 25)
אָמַר רִבִּי מָנָא. מָאן דָּמַר לִי הָדָא מִילְתָא אֲנָא נָסִיב בְרנייתיה. מָהוּ פָטוּר.
נִפְטַר מֵחוֹבוֹ אוֹ נִפְטַר מִגְּנֵיבָה.

**Halakhah 8-9**: "If he was drawing it to lead it out but it died," etc.; "If he gave it for his first-born son," etc. Rebbi Mana said, if somebody would explain to me the following, I would carry his ברנייה[89] : What means "is not liable"? Is he not liable for his obligation or not liable for theft[90]?

89  The word and its meaning are unclear. In E, the reading is בנרייחיה, the Genizah text reads either בנליתא or ברלייתה or בולנייתה. None of these words has a parallel in Talmudic literature.

90  In Mishnah 9, what means "is not liable"? If the Cohen or the creditor accepted the assignment but then the animal died in the assignee's hand before a theft happened, are they barred from asking the person who tricked them for payment or is the explanation as given in Note 85, that no theft did occur? The Babli, 80a, only considers the second alternative.

**משנה י:** אֵין מְגַדְּלִין בְּהֵמָה דַקָּה בְּאֶרֶץ יִשְׂרָאֵל אֲבָל מְגַדְּלִין בְּסוּרְיָיא (fol. 5d)
וּבַמִּדְבָּרוֹת שֶׁבְּאֶרֶץ יִשְׂרָאֵל. אֵין מְגַדְּלִין תַּרְנְגוֹלִין בִּירוּשָׁלַיִם מִפְּנֵי הַקֳּדָשִׁים
וְלֹא כֹהֲנִים בְּאֶרֶץ יִשְׂרָאֵל מִפְּנֵי הַטְּהָרוֹת. וְלֹא יְגַדֵּל יִשְׂרָאֵל חֲזִירִין בְּכָל־מָקוֹם
וְלֹא יְגַדֵּל אָדָם אֶת הַכֶּלֶב אֶלָּא אִם כֵּן הָיָה קָשׁוּר בַּשַּׁלְשֶׁלֶת. אֵין פּוֹרְסִין נְשָׁבִין
לַיּוֹנִים אֶלָּא אִם כֵּן הָיָה רָחוֹק מִן הַיִּישּׁוּב שְׁלֹשִׁים רִיס.

**Mishnah 10**: One does not raise sheep and goats in the Land of Israel[91] but one raises them in Syria[92] and in the non-arable tracts[93] in the Land of Israel. One does not raise chickens in Jerusalem because of the sacrifices[94], nor may Cohanim in the Land of Israel do so because of purities[95]. A Jew may not raise pigs, and a person should not raise a dog unless it is tied by a chain. One does not set traps for pigeons unless thirty stadia[96] distant from any settlement.

91  Since they eat anything they see, if raised near agricultural land they would eat any crop and any sapling and their owner would by necessity become a robber, robbing farmers of their crops.

92  Which has plenty of empty spaces.

93  מִדְבָּר, from Aramaic דבר "to lead", is a place where sheep are lead to graze because it is not agricultural land. For such a "desert" in a non-desert region cf. Gen. 37:22; the word is also used for the grasses which sheep find in the prairie, Targum Onqelos to Ex. 3:1.

94  Chickens were always kept in the open. They dig up all kinds of things; in Jerusalem they might dig up the remains of a human bone. This is incompatible with the duty to eat "simple sancta" all over the walled city of Jerusalem.

95  They have to be pure in order to eat heave; chickens would present too great a risk.

96  A parasang (5523m). Since a parasang in the Talmudim is usually identified with 4 mil, this would make the mil 1281m and the underlying cubit 64cm. It is assumed that at this distance no pigeons which are private property can be found.

(6a line 28) **הלכה י:** אֵין מְגַדְּלִין בְּהֵמָה דַקָּה כול׳. אָמַר רִבִּי בָּא. כְּגוֹן מָהִיר שֶׁהִיא שִׁשָּׁה עָשָׂר מִיל עַל שִׁשָּׁה עָשָׂר מִיל.

**Halakhah 10**: "One does not raise sheep and goats in the Land of Israel," etc. Rebbi Abba said, for example Mahir which is sixteen by sixteen mil[97].

97  Pesahim 5:3, 'Avodah zarah 1:6; Eccl. rabba 1(34), v. 1:13. The place has not been identified; in Eccl. r. it seems to indicate a place in Transjordan of 16 square parasangs without agriculture.

(6a line 29) תַּנֵּי. אֵין מְגַדְּלִין תַּרְנְגוֹלִין בִּירוּשָׁלַיִם מִפְּנֵי הַקֳּדָשִׁים וְלֹא כֹהֲנִים בְּאֶרֶץ יִשְׂרָאֵל מִפְּנֵי הַטָּהֳרוֹת. יָכוֹל אַף בִּירוּשָׁלַיִם כֵּן. אוֹ יָבֹא כַיֵי דָּמַר רִבִּי

יְהוֹשֻׁעַ בֶּן לֵוִי. יְרוּשָׁלַ͏ִם הַבְּנוּיָה וגו'. עִיר שֶׁמְחַבֶּרֶת יִשְׂרָאֵל זֶה לָזֶה.

It was stated: "One does not raise chickens in Jerusalem because of the sacrifices, nor may Cohanim in the Land of Israel because of purities." I could think also in Jerusalem in this way[98], but it might follow what Rebbi Joshua ben Levi said, "Jerusalem the built-up[99]" etc., the city which joins Israel one to the other.

98  That people eating sacrifices may not raise chickens but all others may.

99  *Ps.* 122:3. The argument is about the second half of the verse which is not quoted: "A city joined together." All its inhabitants are joined in its holiness.

In *Ḥagigah* 3:6, The same remark by R. Joshua ben Levi's is given quite a different interpretation.

(6a line 33) כְּתִיב טְמֵאִים הֵם לָכֶם. מַה תַּלְמוּד לוֹמַר וּטְמֵאִים יִהְיוּ לָכֶם. אֶלָּא אֶחָד אִיסּוּר אֲכִילָה וְאֶחָד אִיסּוּר הֲנָייָה. כָּל־דָּבָר שֶׁאִיסּוּרוֹ [דְּבַר תּוֹרָה אָסוּר לַעֲשׂוֹת בּוֹ סְחוֹרָה. וְכָל־דָּבָר שֶׁאִיסּוּרוֹ] מִדִּבְרֵיהֶן מוּתָּר לַעֲשׂוֹת בּוֹ סְחוֹרָה. וַהֲרֵי חֲמוֹר. לִמְלַאכְתּוֹ הוּא גָדֵל. וַהֲרֵי גָּמָל. לִמְלַאכְתּוֹ הוּא גָדֵל.

[100]It is written[101]: "They are impure for you". Why does it say[102] "they shall be impure for you"? One is for the prohibition of eating, the other for the prohibition of usufruct. Anything forbidden [by the Torah is forbidden for trade, but everything whose prohibition][103] is rabbinical is permitted for trade. But is there not the donkey? It is raised for work. Is there not the camel? It is raised for work.

100  This is from *Ševi'it* 7:4, Notes 75-76 (*'Orlah* 3:1, *Pesaḥim* 2:1).

101  *Lev.* 11:28.

102  *Lev.* 11:35.

103 Text missing in the Leiden ms. (the scribe skipped from איסורו to איסורו), taken from E, supported by the Genizah text and the parallels.

(6a line 36) לֹא יְגַדֵּל אָדָם אֶת הַכֶּלֶב אֶלָּא אִם כֵּן קָשׁוּר בְּשַׁלְשֶׁלֶת. אָמַר רִבִּי יוֹסֵי בֵּירִבִּי חֲנִינָה. כָּל־הַמְגַדֵּל כֶּלֶב רַע בְּתוֹךְ שֶׁלּוֹ עָלָיו הַכָּתוּב אוֹמֵר לַמָּס מֵרֵעֵהוּ חָסֶד וגו'.

"A person should not raise a dog unless it is tied by a chain." Rebbi Yose ben Rebbi Ḥanina said: About anybody who raises a biting dog the verse says: "He who refuses kindness to his neighbor,[104]" etc.

104 *Job* 6:14; Babli *Šabbat* 63a/b. As Eliahu Fulda explains, a biting dog will frighten away the poor who cannot come and ask for alms.

(6a line 39) אֵין פּוֹרְסִין נְשָׁבִין לַיּוֹנִים אֶלָּא אִם כֵּן הָיָה רָחוֹק מִן הַיִּישּׁוּב שְׁלֹשִׁים רִיס. [הָכָא אַתְּ אָמַר. שְׁלֹשִׁים רִיס.] וּלְהַלָּן אַתְּ אָמַר. נ אַמָּה. אָמַר רִבִּי יוֹסֵי בֵּרִבִּי בּוּן. לִרְעוֹת מְרִיעָה נ' אַמָּה. לִפְרוֹחַ פּוֹרַחַת אֲפִילוּ אַרְבָּעַת מִילִין.

"One does not set traps for pigeons unless distant thirty stadia from any settlement." [Here, you say thirty stadia.][105] But there[106], you say 50 cubits. Rebbi Yose ben Rebbi Abun said, they feed within fifty cubits[107]; they fly even four *mil*[96].

105 Text missing in the Leiden ms.; added from E supported by the Genizah text.

106 Mishnah *Bava batra* 2:5: One may not have a dove-cot within 50 cubits of agricultural land, to prevent the pigeons from eating the farmer's seeds.

107 Babli 83a (in the name of Abbai).

# החובל פרק שמיני

(fol. 6a) **משנה א:** הַחוֹבֵל בַּחֲבֵירוֹ חַיָּיב עָלָיו מִשּׁוּם חֲמִשָּׁה דְבָרִים בְּנֶזֶק בְּצַעַר בְּרִיפּוּי בְּשֶׁבֶת וּבְבוֹשֶׁת. בְּנֶזֶק כֵּיצַד סִימָּא אֶת עֵינוֹ קָטַע אֶת יָדוֹ שָׁבַר אֶת רַגְלוֹ רוֹאִין אוֹתוֹ כְּאִילוּ הוּא עֶבֶד נִמְכַּר כַּמָּה הָיָה יָפֶה וְכַמָּה הוּא יָפֶה. צַעַר כְּנָיוֹ בַּשְׁפוּד אוֹ בַּמַּסְמֵר וַאֲפִילוּ עַל צִיפָּרְנוֹ מְקוֹם שֶׁאֵינוֹ עוֹשֶׂה חַבּוּרָה אוֹמְדִין כַּמָּה אָדָם כַּיּוֹצֵא בָזֶה רוֹצֶה לִיטּוֹל לִהְיוֹת מִצְטַעֵר כָּךְ.

**Mishnah 1**: One who injures another person owes him under five categories: Damages, suffering, medical costs, loss of earnings[1], and embarrassment. How are damages determined? If he blinded his eye, or cut off his hand, or broke his leg, one considers it as if he were sold as a slave; how much was he worth and how much is he worth now[2]. Suffering: If he burned him with a spit, or with a nail, even on his fingernails where it does not cause a wound[3], one estimates how much a person in his state would ask to be paid in order to be willing to suffer such pain.

1  Payment of medical costs and replacement of lost earnings are biblical obligations, *Ex.* 21:19.

2  Since slaves are bought for their working power (Halakhah 7:1), what has to be estimated is the loss of earning power.

3  If no open wound is caused, no damages are due. The payment for pain is independent of the payment for damages.

(6b line 20) **הלכה א:** הַחוֹבֵל בַּחֲבֵירוֹ כול'. תַּנֵּי. הַחוֹבֵל בַּחֲבֵירוֹ חֲמִשָּׁה נוֹתֵן לוֹ חֲמִשָּׁה. אַרְבָּעָה נוֹתֵן לוֹ אַרְבָּעָה. שְׁלֹשָׁה נוֹתֵן לוֹ שְׁלֹשָׁה. שְׁנַיִם נוֹתֵן לוֹ שְׁנַיִם.

אֶחָד נוֹתֵן לוֹ אֶחָד. וְהֵיכִי. הִכָּהוּ עַל יָדוֹ וְקִטְעָהּ נוֹתֵן לוֹ חֲמִשָּׁה. נֶזֶק צַעַר רִיפּוּי שֶׁבֶת וּבוֹשֶׁת. הִכָּהוּ עַל יָדוֹ וְצָבַת נוֹתֵן לוֹ ד'. צַעַר רִיפּוּי שֶׁבֶת וּבוֹשֶׁת. הִכָּהוּ עַל רֹאשׁוֹ וְצָבַת נוֹתֵן לוֹ ג'. צַעַר רִיפּוּי שֶׁבֶת. בְּמָקוֹם שֶׁאֵינוֹ נִרְאָה נוֹתֵן לוֹ ב'. צַעַר רִיפּוּי. בְּטוֹמוֹס שֶׁבְּיָדוֹ נוֹתֵן לוֹ א'. בּוֹשֶׁת.

**Halakhah 1:** "One who injures another person," etc. It was stated[4]: "One who injures another person in five [respects] pays him for five categories, in four he pays him four, in three he pays him three, in two he pays him two, in one he pays him one." How? If he hit him on his hand and severed it, he pays him five times: Damages, suffering, medical costs, loss of earnings, and embarassment. If he hit him on his hand and it became swollen[5], he pays four times: Suffering, medical costs, loss of earnings, and embarassment. If he hit him on his head which became swollen, he pays three times, suffering, medical costs, loss of earnings[6]. At a place where it is not visible he pays twice, suffering and medical costs[7]. With a tome[8] in his hand he pays only once, for embarrassment.

4 Tosephta 9:1.

5 Since the damage is not permanent, no damages are due.

6 Maimonides (*Hilkhot Hovel umazziq* 2:2) and Rosh (Chapter 8, §1) read: embarrassment. This is reasonable since a person with a swollen head is embarrassed but not disabled. But the Genizah text supports the Leiden reading; the error, if it is one, must be a very old one. E hs a lacuna at this place.

7 This supports the reading of Maimonides and Rosh.

8 Latin *tomus* "cut", Greek τόμος "piece, slice". There is no injury or hurt; therefore payment is only due for embarrassment. E reads בניומוס, a scribal error. A differently formulated parallel in *Sifra Emor Pereq* 20(4) reads "בְּלוּחַ וּבְפִינַקָּס וּבְטוֹמוֹס נְיָירוֹת" "with a plank, or a wooden writing tablet (πίναξ), or a bundle of papers."

(6b line 26) רִבִּי יִרְמְיָה בָּעֵי. קָטַע יָדוֹ וְחָזַר וְקָטַע יָדוֹ מִלְּמַעֲלָן מַהוּ שֶׁיִּתֶּן לוֹ צַעַר שֶׁל שָׁעָה רִאשׁוֹנָה.

Rebbi Jeremiah asked: If he severed his hand and returned and severed the arm, does he have to pay additionally for the pain inflicted the first time[9]?

9  If the case came to court only after the second attack. In the Babli, 85b, it is considered obvious that suffering and embarrassment must be treated separately for each attack whereas the other payments can be combined.

(6b line 28) כְּתִיב עַיִן תַּחַת עַיִן שֵׁן תַּחַת שֵׁן. וּבְמָקוֹם אַחֵר הוּא אוֹמֵר לֹא תָחוֹס עֵינֶיךָ. אֶחָד שׁוֹגֵג וְאֶחָד מֵזִיד. יֹאמַר שׁוֹגֵג וְאַל יֹאמַר מֵזִיד. שֶׁאִילּוּ נֶאֱמַר שׁוֹגֵג וְלֹא נֶאֱמַר מֵזִיד הָיִיתִי אוֹמֵר. שׁוֹגֵג יְשַׁלֵּם מָמוֹן מֵזִיד [וְיִקְטַע אֶת יָדוֹ. הֲוֵי צוֹרֶךְ הוּא שֶׁיֹּאמַר מֵזִיד. אוֹ אִילּוּ נֶאֱמַר מֵזִיד וְלֹא נֶאֱמַר שׁוֹגֵג הָיִיתִי אוֹמֵר. מֵזִיד יְשַׁלֵּם מָמוֹן שׁוֹגֵג] לֹא יְשַׁלֵּם כְּלוּם. הֲוֵי צוֹרֶךְ לוֹמַר שׁוֹגֵג וְצוֹרֶךְ לוֹמַר מֵזִיד. שֶׁאִם הָיָה סוּמָא וְסִימָּא אֶת עֵינוֹ קִיטֵּעַ וְקִיטֵּעַ אֶת יָדוֹ הֵיאַךְ זֶה מִתְקַיְּים וַעֲשִׂיתֶם לוֹ כַּאֲשֶׁר זָמַם לַעֲשׂוֹת לְאָחִיו. מַגִּיד שֶׁאֵינוֹ מְשַׁלֵּם אֶלָּא מָמוֹן.

It is written: "An eye for an eye, a tooth for a tooth[10]." At another place, He says: "Do not be softhearted.[11]" One refers to inadvertent acts, the other to intentional ones[12]. He could mention the inadvertent but not mention the intentional. But if the inadvertent had been mentioned but not the intentional, I would have said that for the inadvertent act he shall pay money, for the intentional [have his hand cut off. Therefore it was necessary to mention the intentional. Or if the intentional had been mentioned but not the inadvertent, I would have said that for the intentional act he shall pay money, for the inadvertent][13] he should not pay at all. Therefore it was necessary to mention both inadvertent and intentional. And if he blinded a blind man or cut off the arm of an amputee, how could one fulfill: "Do to him as he intended to do to his brother"[14]? This indicates that he only pays money.

10  Lev. 24:20, speaking of payment for either animal or man.
11  Deut. 19:21, 25:12.
12  Cf. *Sifry Deut.* 293. The quote *Deut.* 19:21 refers to the punishment of the perjured witnesses. Since in injury cases the false accuser wanted to extort money and therefore would have to pay money, it is concluded that *Deut.* 25:12 which prescribes punishment for intentional injury also must mean payment of money. Therefore *Lev.* 24:20 refers to payment for unintentional injury.

13  Text missing in the Leiden ms., supplied from E and supported by the Genizah text.
14  *Deut.* 19:19, referring to the punishment of perjured witnesses. The quote is confirmed by all three ms. sources but probably the reference should be to *Lev.* 23:19: "As a person injures another, so should be done to him". The Babli, 84a, in quoting a similar *baraita* refers to *Lev.* 24:22: "A uniform law shall it be for you"; cf. also *Sifra Emor Pereq* 20(7).

צַעַר. (6b line 34) כְּוִיָּיו בַּשְׁפּוּד אוֹ בַּמַּסְמֵר וַאֲפִילוּ עַל צִיפּוֹרְנוֹ מָקוֹם שֶׁאֵינוֹ עוֹשֶׂה חַבּוּרָה. כְּתִיב כְּוִיָּיה תַּחַת כְּוִיָּיה וגו'. הֵיכִי דָמֵי. אִם בְּשֶׁפְּצָעוֹ וְהוֹצִיא דָמוֹ כְּבָר כְּתִיב פֶּצַע תַּחַת פָּצַע. מַה תַּלְמוּד לוֹמַר חַבּוּרָה. אֶלָּא שֶׁאִם כְּוִיָּיו בַּשְׁפּוּד עַל כַּף יָדוֹ וְצָבַת עַל כַּף רַגְלוֹ וְצָבַת. אוֹ שֶׁהִטִּיל עָלָיו שֶׁלֶג אוֹ צִינִּים בְּמָקוֹם שֶׁאֵינוֹ נִרְאֶה חַיָּיב לְרַפּוֹתוֹ.

"Suffering: If he burned him with a spit, or with a nail, even on his fingernails where it does not cause a wound." How is this[15]? If he wounded him so that he lost blood, it already is written: "A wound for a wound[16]." Why does the verse say "a contusion"? To tell you that if he burned him with a spit on the palm of his hand and it swelled, on the sole of his foot and it swelled, or he put snow or ice on him at a place which is not visible, he has to pay his medical expenses.[17]

15  The Genizah and E texts do not have דמי; cf. Chapter 7, Note 50.
16  *Ex.* 21:25. Of the three expressions mentioned there, the third one, חַבּוּרָה, "contusion", already seems to be subsumed under the first, כְּוִיָּה, "burn", or the second, פֶּצַע, "open wound". A similar discussion is in the

Babli, 84b.

17  A somewhat different text is in *Mekhilta dR. Ismael Neziqin* 8: "If he wounded him so that he lost blood, it already is written: 'A wound for a wound'; if he caused a contusion, is there not written 'a contusion for a contusion'? Why is written 'a burn for a burn'? To tell you that if he burned him with a spit on the palm of his hand or on the sole of his foot and *it was not noticeable*, or he put snow on his head and gave him a cold, he has to pay for his *suffering*."

(6b line 39) אוֹמְדִין כַּמָּה אָדָם כַּיּוֹצֵא בָזֶה רוֹצֶה לִיטוֹל לִהְיוֹת מִצְטַעֵר בְּכָךְ. אָמַר רִבִּי זְעִירָה. חֲמֵיי בַּר נַשׁ וְאָמְרִין לֵיהּ. כַּמָּה אַתְּ בָּעֵי לְמִיתַּן וְלָא יֵיאַבֵךְ אָהֵן צַעֲרָא. וּמַה דְּהוּא אָמַר יָהֵבִין לֵיהּ. אָמַר מַר עוּקְבָה. כַּמָּה אָדָם רוֹצֶה לִיטוֹל הִיא מַתְנִיתָא. וְתֵימַר אָכֵן. אֶלָּא חֲמֵיי בַּר נַשׁ וְאָמְרִין לֵיהּ. כַּמָּה אַתְּ בָּעֵי מֵיסַב וְיֵאַבֵךְ אָהֵן צַעֲרָא. וּמַה דּוּ אָמַר יָהֵבִין לֵיהּ. תַּנֵּי. בֶּן עַזַּאי אוֹמֵר. נוֹתְנִין נִכְאֵי מָזוֹן. מָהוּ נִכְאֵי מָזוֹן. בְּקַדְמִיתָא הֲוִינָא אָכִיל טְלוֹפְחִין וְיָרָק. וּכְדוֹן לֵית בִּי מֵיכַל אֶלָּא בֵּיעִין וְתַרְנוּגַלִּין. וּמַה דּוּ אָמַר יָהֵבִין לֵיהּ. אָמַר רִבִּי יוֹסֵי בַּר יַעֲקֹב. אָהֵן רוֹמַיי כַּד מִבְאַשׁ לֹא נָפִיק לִקְרָבָא עַד דְּיֵיכוֹל מַה דְחָסֵר יוֹמִין בְּיוֹמִין.

"One estimates how much a person in his state would ask to be paid in order to be willing to suffer such pain." Rebbi Ze'ira said, one sees a person and asks him, how much would you give that such pain would not be inflicted on you? And what he says, he has to give[18]. Mar Uqba said, the Mishnah is "how much a person would ask to be paid," and you say so? But one sees a person and asks him, how much would you ask that such pain not be inflicted on you? And what he says, he has to give[19]. Ben Azai said, one gives food invalidity[20]. What is food invalidity? Before that, I was eating lentils and vegetables but now I can only eat eggs and chicken. What he asks one[21] gives him. Rebbi Yose ben Jacob said, a Roman who was sick would not go into battle until he could eat all he had been missing those days.

18  The court determines the payment for suffering by asking a randomly chosen member of the public. The amount indicated by that person is imposed on the attacker.

19  *Mekhilta dR. Ismael Neziqin* 8 explains this as the meaning of payment "burn for burn".

20  Tosephta 9:3. The Erfurt text reads "the cost of food", for the additional cost of a sick person's diet.

21  The court imposes the additional costs on the attacker.

(fol. 6a) **משנה ב:** רִיפּוּי הִכָּהוּ חַיָּב לְרַפֹּאתוֹ. עָלוּ בוֹ צְמָחִים אִם מֵחֲמַת הַמַּכָּה חַיָּב שֶׁלֹּא מֵחֲמַת הַמַּכָּה פָּטוּר. חָיְיתָה וְנִסְתְּרָה חָיְיתָה וְנִסְתְּרָה חַיָּב לְרַפֹּאתוֹ. חָיְיתָה כָּל־צָרְכָּהּ אֵינוֹ חַיָּב לְרַפֹּאתוֹ.

**Mishnah 2**: Medical costs. If he hit a person, he has to pay that person's medical costs. In case a growth on that person's body developed, if it was a consequence of the injury, he has to pay medical costs. If it started to heal but regressed several times, he has to pay medical costs. After it was healed completely he no longer has to pay medical costs.

(6b line 49) **הלכה ב:** רִיפּוּי הִכָּהוּ חַיָּב לְרַפֹּאתוֹ כול׳. רִבִּי יִרְמְיָה בָּעֵי. עָלוּ בּוֹ צְמָחִין סְבִיבוֹת הַמַּכָּה וְנִסְתְּרָה מֵחֲמַת הַמַּכָּה מָהוּ. מִן מַה דִכְתִיב וְרַפֹּא יְרַפֵּא. שֶׁאִם עָבַר עַל דְּבַר רוֹפֵא [פָּטוּר].²² תַּנֵּי חוֹרִין וְרַפֹּא יְרַפֵּא. שֶׁאִם עָלַת גַּרְגּוּתְנִי חַיָּב לְרַפֹּאתוֹ. תַּנֵּי. רִבִּי יוֹסֵי בֵּירִבִּי יוּדָן אוֹמֵר. עָלוּ בוֹ צְמָחִים סְבִיבוֹת הַמַּכָּה אַף עַל פִּי שֶׁנִּסְתְּרָה [מֵחֲמַת]²³ הַמַּכָּה חַיָּב לְרַפֹּאתוֹ וְאֵין חַיָּב לִיתֵּן לוֹ דְּמֵי שָׁבְתּוֹ. רִבִּי שִׁמְעוֹן אוֹמֵר. חִידּוּשׁ חִידֵּשׁ הַכָּתוּב בַּפָּרָשָׁה הַזֹּאת שֶׁיִּתֵּן לוֹ שֶׁבֶת וְרִפּוּי. רַק שִׁבְתּוֹ יִתֵּן וְרַפֹּא יְרַפֵּא.

**Halakhah 2**: "Medical costs. If he hit a person, he has to pay that person's medical costs," etc. Rebbi Jeremiah asked: If there was a growth around the wound and complications ensued because of the wound, what is the rule²⁴?

Since it is written[1]: "And healing he shall heal," if [the patient] did not follow the doctor's instructions, he is [not liable][25]. It was stated in another *baraita*: If [the wound] was covered with scab, he must pay for medical treatment. It was stated[25]: "Rebbi Yose ben Rebbi Jehudah[26] says, if there was a growth around the wound, even if complications ensued because of the wound, he must pay for medical treatment but he is not liable to pay for his loss of earnings. Rebbi Simeon[27] says, in this paragraph[1] Scripture introduced a novelty stating that he has to pay for loss of earnings together with medical treatment: 'Only his loss of earnings he shall compensate and healing he shall heal.'"

22  Added from the Genizah text.
23  Added from E and Genizah texts.
24  Is the attacker liable for delayed consequences of his attack?
25  For continued medical care. Babli 85a, Tosephta 9:4.
26  In the parallel texts, this is R. Jehudah's own opinion.
27  In the Babli, this is quoted as "the Sages'" opinion. Whenever one is obligated to pay for medical treatment, he automatically is obligated to pay for lost earnings. This answers R. Jeremiah's question in full.

(fol. 6a) **משנה ג:** שָׁבֶת. רוֹאִין אוֹתוֹ כְּאִילוּ הוּא שׁוֹמֵר קִישּׁוּאַיִן שֶׁכְּבָר נָתַן לוֹ דְּמֵי יָדוֹ וּדְמֵי רַגְלוֹ. בּוֹשֶׁת. הַכֹּל לְפִי הַמְבַיֵּישׁ וְהַמִּתְבַּיֵּישׁ. הַמְבַיֵּישׁ אֶת הֶעָרוֹם הַמְבַיֵּישׁ אֶת הַסּוֹמָא וְהַמְבַיֵּישׁ אֶת הַיָּשֵׁן וְיָשֵׁן שֶׁבִּיֵּישׁ פָּטוּר. נָפַל מִן הַגַּג וְהִזִּיק וּבִיֵּישׁ חַיָּיב עַל הַנֶּזֶק וּפָטוּר עַל הַבּוֹשֶׁת שֶׁנֶּאֱמַר וְשָׁלְחָה יָדָהּ וְהֶחֱזִיקָה בִּמְבוּשָׁיו אֵינוֹ חַיָּיב עַל הַבּוֹשֶׁת עַד שֶׁיְּהֵא מִתְכַּוֵּין.

**Mishnah 3**: Loss of earnings. One considers him as if he were a watchman of pumpkins since he already compensated him for the loss of his hand or loss of his foot[28].

Embarrassment. Everything depends on the person embarrassing and the one embarrassed[29]. One who embarrassed a naked person[30], or embarrassed a blind person[31], or embarrassed a sleeping person[32] is liable, but the sleeper who embarrassed is not liable. If a person fell from a roof and caused damage and embarrassed, he is liable for the damage but not liable for the embarrassment since is was said[33]: "She reached out with her hand and grabbed him at his private parts;" one is not liable for embarrassment unless if was intended.

28 Once long-term disability has been compensated for, short term inability to work has to be compensated on the level of his remaining long term earning power.

29 The lower the social standing of the agressor, the more weighty is his insult. The higher the social standing of the victim, the more damaging is the insult.

30 Who is in an embarrassing situation.

31 Who cannot see the reaction of others to his embarrassment.

32 Who does not notice his embarrassment.

33 Deut. 25:11.

(6b line 56) **הלכה ג:** שֶׁבֶת. רוֹאִין אוֹתוֹ כול׳. הָכָא אַתְּ מַר. רוֹאִין אוֹתוֹ כִּילוּ שׁוֹמֵר קִישּׁוּאִין. וְהָכָא אַתְּ מַר. הָיָה עוֹשֶׂה מָנָה בַּיּוֹם נוֹתֵן לוֹ מָנָה. סֶלַע נוֹתֵן לוֹ סֶלַע. אָמַר רִבִּי יִצְחָק. תְּרֵין שְׁבָתִּין אִינּוּן. הִכָּהוּ עַל יָדוֹ וְקִטְעָהּ אֵין רוֹאִין אוֹתוֹ כִּילוּ עוֹשֶׂה מָנָה בַּיּוֹם אֶלָּא רוֹאִין אוֹתוֹ כִּילוּ חִיגֵּר יוֹשֵׁב וְשׁוֹמֵר קִישּׁוּאִין. שֶׁכְּבָר נָתַן לוֹ דְמֵי יָדוֹ וּדְמֵי רַגְלוֹ. שֶׁאִם כְּוָיוֹ עַל כַּף יָדוֹ וְצָבַת עַל כַּף רֹאשׁוֹ וְצָבָה. אוֹ שֶׁהִטִּיל עָלָיו שֶׁלֶג אוֹ צוֹנֵן בְּמָקוֹם שֶׁאֵינוֹ נִרְאֶה. חַייָב לְרַפּוֹתוֹ.

**Halakhah 3**: "Loss of earnings. One considers him," etc. Here you say, "one considers him as if he were a watchman of pumpkins." But there, you say[33], "if he was earning a mina per day, he pays him a mina; a tetradrachma, he gives him a tetradrachma." Rebbi Isaac said, there are two kinds of inability to work. If he hit him on his hand and cut it off, one does not consider him as if he earned a mina a day but one considers him as if he were a lame person watching pumpkins, because he already compensated him for the loss of his hand or loss of his foot. But if he burned him on the palm of his hand and it swelled, on the flat of his head and it swelled, or he put on him snow or cold water at a place which is not visible, then he has to pay his medical expenses[34].

33  Tosephta 3:3. The entire argument of this paragraph is formulated in the Tosephta in a way which is both more concise and more clear; it is obvious that the Tosephta was not known to the compilers of the Yerushalmi.

The principle involved is very clear. If damages for long-term inability were paid, short term inability is compensated for at the reduced rate applicable to the future. But if the impairment is temporary and no damages are due, the full normal earning power has to be compensated for.

34  The last sentence is a quote from Halakhah 1 (Note 17). According to the preceding Halakhah, the obligation of paying for medical care implies the obligation to pay for loss of temporary earnings.

(6b line 63) תַּנֵּי. וְשָׁלְחָה יָדָהּ. וְלֹא אֵשֶׁת שָׁלִיחַ בֵּית דִּין. תַּנֵּיֵי חוֹרָן תַּנֵּי. וְשָׁלְחָה יָדָהּ. לְרַבּוֹת אֵשֶׁת שָׁלִיחַ בֵּית דִּין. מָאן דָּמַר. וְשָׁלְחָה יָדָהּ. וְלֹא אֵשֶׁת שָׁלִיחַ בֵּית דִּין. בְּשֶׁהִכָּהוּ בִּרְשׁוּת. מָאן דָּמַר. לְרַבּוֹת אֵשֶׁת שָׁלִיחַ בֵּית דִּין. בְּשֶׁהִכָּהוּ שֶׁלֹּא בִרְשׁוּת. תַּנֵּי. לֹא אֵשֶׁת שְׁנַיִם.

[35]It was stated: "She reached out with her hand," but not the court marshal's wife. Another Tanna stated, "she reached out with her hand," including the court marshal's wife. He who said, "she reached out with her hand," but not the court marshal's wife, if he whipped with permission. He who said, "she reached out with her hand," including the court marshal's wife, if he whipped without permission. It was stated: Not the wife of two men[36].

35 This paragraph is alluded to in the Babli, 28a, and *Sifry Deut.* #292. The verse *Deut.* 25:11 reads: "If men quarreled, a person with his brother, and the wife of one of them intervened to save her husband from the hand of one who hit him when she reached out with her hand and grabbed him at his private parts." Grabbing a person's private parts is given as an example of an action intended to embarrass. It is clear in the paragraph that "wife of x" stands for "x" himself. The court marshall meting out punishment is protected from a damage suit by the person suffering the punishment as long as he strictly follows the court's instructions. He is not protected for actions taken on his own initiative.

36 Since a woman cannot have two husbands, one derives from the expression "the wife of one of them" that two people trading mutual insults have no case in court.

(fol. 6a) **משנה ד**: זֶה חוֹמֶר בָּאָדָם מִבַּשׁוֹר שֶׁהָאָדָם מְשַׁלֵּם אֶת הַנֶּזֶק וּמְשַׁלֵּם דְּמֵי וְלָדוֹת וְשׁוֹר אֵינוֹ מְשַׁלֵּם אֶלָּא נֶזֶק וְאֵינוֹ מְשַׁלֵּם דְּמֵי וְלָדוֹת.

**Mishnah 4**: This is more severe regarding a human than an ox since a human pays damages[37] and pays for unborn children[38], but the ox pays only damages and does not pay for unborn children.

**משנה ה**: הַמַּכֶּה אָבִיו וְאִמּוֹ וְלֹא עָשָׂה בָּהֶם חַבּוּרָה הַחוֹבֵל בְּיוֹם הַכִּיפּוּרִים חַיָּיב בְּכוּלָּן. הַחוֹבֵל בְּעֶבֶד עִבְרִי חַיָּיב בְּכוּלָּן חוּץ מִן הַשֶּׁבֶת בִּזְמַן שֶׁהוּא שֶׁלּוֹ. הַחוֹבֵל בְּעֶבֶד כְּנַעֲנִי שֶׁלַּאֲחֵרִים חַיָּיב בְּכוּלָּן. רִבִּי יְהוּדָה אוֹמֵר אֵין לַעֲבָדִים בּוֹשֶׁת.

**Mishnah 5**: A person who hits his father or mother without causing a concussion[39] or who causes injury on the Day of Atonement[40] is liable for everything. He who injures a Hebrew slave[41] is liable for everything except for lost earnings if he is his own. He who injures another person's Canaanite slave[42] is liable for everything. Rebbi Jehudah says, slaves have no claim for embarrassment.

37 And the other four categories of payments mentioned in Mishnah 1. These are enumerated by the Mishnah in the Babli and most independent Mishnah mss.

38 *Ex.* 21:22 prescribes that an attack on a woman which leads to a miscarriage but does not endanger the woman's life entitles the woman's husband to go to court and exact payment for the loss of prospective children.

39 *Ex.* 21:15 declares hitting father or mother to be a capital crime. Hitting one of the parents without causing visible damage is a sin but not a crime. Therefore there is no obstacle to pressing monetary claims. Cf. Mishnah 7.

40 Desecrating the Day of Atonement is a deadly sin but not a prosecutable crime; it is outside the purview of the human court. Injuring somebody on the Sabbath is a capital crime. Cf. Mishnah 7.

41 Hebrew slavery was an institution permanently abolished, never resurrected in the Second Commonwealt; cf. *Qiddušin* 1:2, Note 150. The argument is purely theoretical.

42 Any Gentile slave becoming potentially Jewish by circumcision and immersion in a *miqweh*; cf. *Qiddušin* 1:3, Note 328. A person severely injuring his own slave has to set him free (*Ex.* 21:26-27).

(6b line 56) **הלכה ד-ה:** זֶה חוֹמֶר בָּאָדָם מִבַּשּׁוֹר כול׳. הַמַּכֶּה אָבִיו וְאִמּוֹ כול׳. תַּנֵּי. וְהָעֵדִים שֶׁאָמְרוּ מְעִידִין אָנוּ עַל פְּלוֹנִי שֶׁסִּימָּא שְׁתֵּי עֵינָיו כְּאַחַת. שֶׁהִפִּיל שְׁתֵּי שִׁינָיו כְּאַחַת. אֵינוֹ נוֹתֵן לוֹ כְּלוּם. זוֹ אַחַר זוֹ יוֹצֵא לַחֵירוּת בָּרִאשׁוֹנָה וְנוֹתֵן לוֹ דְמֵי שְׁנִיָּיה. רִבִּי אַבָּהוּ בְשֵׁם רִבִּי יוֹחָנָן. זֹאת אוֹמֶרֶת שָׁמִין לַעֲבָדִים בּוֹשֶׁת. רִבִּי לָא בְשֵׁם רִבִּי יוֹחָנָן. הַמַּקְדִּישׁ מַעֲשֵׂה יְדֵי עַצְמוֹ כּוּפָּן קִידֵּשׁ. חָזַר וְתַנָּא. הַמַּקְדִּישׁ מַעֲשֵׂה יְדֵי עַבְדּוֹ יוֹצִיא לוֹ מֵהֶן פַּרְנָסָתוֹ וְהַשְּׁאָר הֶקְדֵּשׁ. הָכָא אַתְּ אָמַר. הַשְּׁאָר הֶקְדֵּשׁ. וְהָכָא אַתְּ מַר. כּוּלוֹ קוֹדֶשׁ. אָמַר רִבִּי אָחָא. מְצֻוִּוים יִשְׂרָאֵל לְפַרְנֵס בְּנֵי חוֹרִין יוֹתֵר מֵעֲבָדִים. לֹא כֵן אָמַר רִבִּי יוֹחָנָן. הַקּוֹטֵעַ יְדֵי עֶבֶד חֲבֵירוֹ רַבּוֹ נוֹטֵל נִזְקוֹ צַעֲרוֹ רִיפּוּי שִׁבְתּוֹ בּוֹשְׁתּוֹ. וַהֲלָא יִתְפַּרְנֵס מִן הַצְּדָקָה. אָמַר רִבִּי אָחָא. מְצֻוִּוים יִשְׂרָאֵל לְפַרְנֵס עֲבָדִים קִיטְעִין יוֹתֵר מִן הַשְּׁלֵימִין. וְהָא רִבִּי יוֹחָנָן אֲכִיל קוֹפָד וְיָהִיב לְעַבְדֵּיהּ. שָׁתֵי חֲמַר וְיָהִיב לְעַבְדֵּיהּ.

וְקָרֵי אֲנַפְשֵׁיי הֲלֹא בְבֶטֶן עוֹשֵׂינִי עָשֵׂהוּ. אֲמְרֵי. תַּמָּן בִּמְידַת הַדִּין. בְּרַם הָכָא בְּמִידַת הָרַחֲמִים.

**Halakhah 4-5**: "This is more severe regarding a human than an ox," etc. "A person who hits his father or mother," etc. It was stated[43]: If the witnesses said, we testify that X blinded both of his eyes simultanously, or that he knocked out two of his teeth simultaneously, he does not have to pay anything. One after the other, he gains his freedom by the first and he pays him damages for the second[44]. Rebbi Abbahu in the name of Rebbi Joḥanan: This implies that one estimates embarrassment for slaves[45]. [46]Rebbi La in the name of Rebbi Joḥanan: If a person dedicates his earnings, he dedicates everything[47]. If he dedicates the earnings of his slave, he[48] can take from there his upkeep and the remainder is dedicated. Here you say, the remainder is dedicated, but there you say, everything is holy. Rebbi Aḥa said, Jews are more obligated to support free people than slaves[49]. But did not Rebbi Joḥanan say: If somebody cuts off the hands of somebody else's slave, his master collects damages, suffering, medical costs, loss of earnings, and embarrassment, and that one should be supported by welfare[50]. Rebbi Aḥa said, Jews are more obligated to support amputated slaves than unimpaired ones. But did not Rebbi Joḥanan also give to his slave when he ate meat? Give also to his slave when he drank wine? And recited for himself the verse[51]: "Did not His maker make me in the womb"? They said, there a rule of law, here a rule of mercy.

43   A similar statement is in *Mekhilta dR. Ismael, Neziqin* 9.

44   Ex. 21:26-27 states that a slave gains his freedom if his master blinds him or knocks out one of his teeth. If the master injures the slave repeatedly, the slave gains his freedom by the first injury and, therefore, can claim full payment for the second as a free Jew (Babli *Giṭṭin* 42b). But if a double

injury was inflicted in one blow, the slave was not free and has no claim beyond his automatic freedom.

45  Since there is no exception made for shame in the previous statement.

The statement is difficult to understand since at the moment of the second injury the slave already is a free Jew rather than a slave. As R. Eliahu Fulda points out, it also is superfluous since R. Johanan always follows the anonymous Mishnah as practice. Since the Yerushalmi is so elliptic, it may not be excluded that it follows the Babli (*Giṭṭin* 42b) in holding that the slave is automatically free only for eye and tooth which are mentioned in the verse, but for other injuries for which the court will force the slave's freedom a bill of manumission would be required. Then R. Abbahu's statement becomes relevant for the case of a slave in his period between servitude and freedom.

46  A text similar to the remainder of this paragraph is in *Ketubot* 5:5, Notes 120-130.

47  Everything he earns automatically is Temple property; he cannot take anything to feed himself but has to beg his sustenance from others. Tosephta *'Arakhin* 3:8 does not support this statement.

48  The slave can support himself from his own earnings; only the excess becomes Temple property; Tosephta *'Arakhin* 3:8, Babli *Giṭṭin* 12a.

49  Slaves would not be able to feed themselves from alms.

50  Babli *Giṭṭin* 12b.

51  *Job* 31:15.

(fol. 6a) **משנה ו:** חֵרֵשׁ שׁוֹטֶה וְקָטָן פְּגִיעָתָן רָעָה הַחוֹבֵל בָּהֶן חַיָּיב וְהֵם שֶׁחָבְלוּ בַּאֲחֵרִים פְּטוּרִין. הָעֶבֶד וְהָאִשָּׁה פְּגִיעָתָן רָעָה הַחוֹבֵל בָּהֶן חַיָּיב וְהֵם שֶׁחָבְלוּ בַּאֲחֵרִים פְּטוּרִין אֲבָל מְשַׁלְּמִין לְאַחַר זְמַן. נִתְגָּרְשָׁה הָאִשָּׁה וְנִשְׁתַּחְרֵר הָעֶבֶד חַיָּיבִין לְשַׁלֵּם.

**Mishnah 6**: It is bad to meet a deaf-mute, an insane, or an underage person[52]: Anybody who injures them is liable but they who cause injury are not liable. It is bad to meet a woman[53] or a slave[54]: Anybody who injures them is liable but they who cause injury are not liable, but they might have to pay later. If the woman was divorced or the slave manumitted, they have to pay.

52 These are not prosecutable and cannot be sued. Even if they were healed or grew up they cannot be sued for what they did when they were not responsible.

53 A married woman, any of whose private property is administered by her husband who has the usufruct and therefore can block any payment which would diminish his income. A married woman whose husband had waved his right of administration and usufruct before marriage is counted as a male for the rules of this Mishnah.

54 Any whose property is his master's. This rule was contested by the Sadducees, Mishnah *Yadayim* 4:7.

(6c line 5) **הלכה ו:** חֵרֵשׁ שׁוֹטֶה וְקָטָן פְּגִיעָתָן רָעָה כול'. תַּנֵּי. וְהָעֵדִים שֶׁאָמְרוּ מְעִידִים אָנוּ עַל פְּלוֹנִי שֶׁסִּימָּא עֵין עַבְדּוֹ וְהִפִּיל שִׁינוֹ שֶׁכֵּן הָרַב אוֹמֵר. וְנִמְצְאוּ זוֹמְמִין. מְשַׁלְּמִין לָעֶבֶד. וְכוּלֵּיהּ מִן אָהֵן עוֹבְדָא מֵימַר כֵּן. אָמַר רִבִּי נָסָה. וִינוּן דַּמְרוֹן כֵּן. מְעִידִין אָנוּ עַל פְּלוֹנִי שֶׁנִּכְנַס תַּחַת יָדוֹ שָׁלֵם וְיָצָא חָבוּל בִּשְׁתַּיִם. יוֹצֵא לַחֵירוּת בָּרִאשׁוֹנָה וְנוֹתֵן לוֹ דְּמֵי שְׁנִיָּיה.

"It is bad to meet a deaf-mute, an insane, or an underage person," etc. It was stated[55]: If the witnesses said, we testify that X blinded the eye of his slave and broke his tooth, for that is what the master said, and they are found to be perjured, they pay to the slave[56]. How can they say this about the case[57]? Rebbi Nasa said, those might say the following: We testify about X that [the slave] came to his hand unimpaired and left with two injuries[58]. Then he gains his freedom with the first and he has to pay him for the second[59].

55 Tosephta *Makkot* 1:4.

56 The master in fact blinded the slave and broke his tooth. Since the payment for the loss of an eye is much larger than that for the loss of a tooth, it is to the advantage of the master to free his slave for the eye and to pay only for the tooth. If the witnesses are

found to be perjured, they have to pay the difference of the payments for eye and tooth to the slave, irrespective of what happened in reality.

57  How can such a case really occur? The same question can be asked about the case treated in the preceding Halakhah since even if it looked as if both eyes were blinded simultaneously, it might have been that one was injured a fraction of a second before the other.

58  This is unproblematic testimony.

59  Since the burden of proof is on the claimant, the slave becomes free on the injury to the eye and receives payment for the injury to the tooth unless he can prove by witnesses that his tooth was knocked out first.

(fol. 6a) **משנה ז**: הַמַּכֶּה אָבִיו וְאִמּוֹ וְעָשָׂה בָהֶם חַבּוּרָה וְהַחוֹבֵל בַּחֲבֵירוֹ בַּשַּׁבָּת פָּטוּר מִכּוּלָּן מִפְּנֵי שֶׁהוּא נִידּוֹן בְּנַפְשׁוֹ. וְהַחוֹבֵל בְּעֶבֶד כְּנַעֲנִי שֶׁלּוֹ פָּטוּר מִכּוּלָּן.

**Mishnah 7**: A person who hits his father or mother causing a concussion[39] or who causes injury to a fellow man on the Sabbath[40] is not liable for anything since he is tried for his life[60]. One who injures his own Canaanite slave is not liable for anything.

**משנה ח**: הַתּוֹקֵעַ לַחֲבֵירוֹ נוֹתֵן לוֹ סֶלַע. רִבִּי יְהוּדָה אוֹמֵר מִשּׁוּם רִבִּי יוֹסֵי הַגְּלִילִי מָנֶה. סְטָרוֹ נוֹתֵן לוֹ מָאתַיִם זוּז לְאַחַר יָדוֹ נוֹתֵן לוֹ אַרְבַּע מֵאוֹת זוּז. צָרַם בְּאָזְנוֹ תָּלַשׁ בִּשְׂעָרוֹ רָקַק וְהִגִּיעַ בּוֹ הָרוֹק הֶעֱבִיר טַלִּיתוֹ מִמֶּנּוּ פָּרַע רֹאשָׁהּ שֶׁל אִשָּׁה נוֹתֵן אַרְבַּע מֵאוֹת זוּז וְהַכֹּל לְפִי כְבוֹדוֹ.

**Mishnah 8**: He who hits another[61] pays him a tetradrachma[62]; Rebbi Jehudah says in the name of Rebbi Yose the Galilean, a *mina*[63]. If he slapped him, he pays 200 *zuz*[64], with the back of his hand he gives him 400 *zuz*. If he hurt him on his earlobe, tore out some of his hair, spat on him and the spit touched him, removed his stole, uncovered a woman's hair[65], he pays 400 zuz; everything corresponding to his honor[66].

**משנה ט**: אָמַר רִבִּי עֲקִיבָה אֲפִילוּ עֲנִי שֶׁבְּיִשְׂרָאֵל רוֹאִין אוֹתָן כְּאִילוּ הֵן בְּנֵי חוֹרִין שֶׁיָּרְדוּ מִנִּכְסֵיהֶן שֶׁהֵן בְּנֵי אַבְרָהָם יִצְחָק וְיַעֲקֹב. מַעֲשֶׂה בְּאֶחָד שֶׁפָּרַע רֹאשָׁהּ שֶׁל אִשָּׁה וּבָאת לִפְנֵי רִבִּי עֲקִיבָה וְחִייְבוֹ לִיתֵּן לָהּ אַרְבַּע מֵאוֹת זוּז. אָמַר לוֹ רִבִּי תֵּן לִי זְמָן וְנָתַן לוֹ. שִׁימְּרָהּ עוֹמֶדֶת עַל פֶּתַח חֲצֵירָהּ וְשִׁיבֵּר אֶת הַפַּךְ בְּפָנֶיהָ וּבוֹ כְּאִיסָּר שֶׁמֶן גִּילַּת אֶת רֹאשָׁהּ וְהָיְתָה מְטַפַּחַת וּמַנַּחַת עַל רֹאשָׁהּ וְהֶעֱמִיד לָהּ עֵדִים וּבָא לִפְנֵי רִבִּי עֲקִיבָה אָמַר לוֹ לָזֶה אֲנִי נוֹתֵן אַרְבַּע מֵאוֹת זוּז. אָמַר לוֹ לֹא אָמַרְתָּ כְּלוּם שֶׁהַחוֹבֵל בְּעַצְמוֹ אַף עַל פִּי שֶׁאֵינוֹ רַשַּׁאי פָּטוּר וַאֲחֵרִים שֶׁחָבְלוּ בוֹ חַיָּיבִים. הַקּוֹצֵץ אֶת נְטִיעוֹתָיו עַל פִּי שֶׁאֵינוֹ רַשַּׁאי פָּטוּר וַאֲחֵרִים שֶׁקִּצְצוּ אֶת נְטִיעוֹתָיו חַיָּיבִים.

**Mishnah 9**: Rebbi Aqiba said, even the poorest in Israel are treated as aristocrats who lost their property[67], for they are descendents of Abraham, Isaac, and Jacob. In a case where somebody uncovered a woman's hair, she came before Rebbi Aqiba who obligated him to pay her 400 *zuz*. He said to him, Rabbi, give me some time, which he did. He watched her at the entrance of her courtyard and broke a flask before her which contained an *as* worth of oil[68]. She uncovered her hair, splashed her hand with the oil and worked it onto her head. He had her observed by witnesses and came before Rebbi Aqiba, telling him, to such a one[69] I have to give 400 *zuz*? He told him, you did not say anything since a person who injures himself, while he is not allowed to do that[70], is not liable, but others who injure him are liable; a person who cuts down his fruit trees, while he is not allowed to do that[71], is not liable, but others who cut down his fruit trees are.

60  Even if he cannot be tried because of lack of eyewitnesses or other reasons; cf. *Terumot* 7:1, Note 16.

61  The meaning of this sentence is not clear. '*Arukh*: He blows his horn into the victim's ear. Rashi quotes the *Arukh* and adds his teacher's explanation: He hit him on his ear. Maimonides in his Mishnah Commentary: He hit him with his fist.

In his Code (חובל ומזיק 9:3): He hit him with his flat hand.

62  The word סלע used in both Talmudim for tetradrachma is not the Hebrew "rock" but the Sumerian *silà* used in Accadic as the unit of volume ($^1/_{300}$ of a *gur*, בור).

63  100 *denarii*.

64  Accadic *zūzum*, from זוז "to split", the half-šeqel piece, identified with the Roman *denarius*. The possession of 200 *zuz* disqualifies its holder from receiving public assistance (Mishnah *Peah* 8:8); it is a considerable sum.

65  A married woman will indicate her status by having her hair covered in public. In the Babli and some Mishnah mss. it is stated explicitly "uncovered a woman's hair in public".

66  The sums stated in the Mishnah are maxima, applicable to the highest levels of society; the court may lower them in appropriate cases.

67  He disagrees with the last statement of the preceding Mishnah; the sums mentioned are mandatory in all cases.

68  A very small amount.

69  Who uncovers herself for a very small gain.

70  *Gen.* 9:5, *Deut.* 4:15.

71  *Deut.* 20:19; *Ševi'it* 4:10, Notes 109-110.

(6c line 10) **הלכה ז-ח**: הַתּוֹקֵעַ לַחֲבֵירוֹ נוֹתֵן לוֹ סֶלַע. אָמַר רִבִּי עֲקִיבָה אֲפִילוּ עָנִי שֶׁבְּיִשְׂרָאֵל כוּל׳. תַּנֵּי רַב קַרְנִי. לַבְּעִיטָה אַחַת. לָרְכוּבָה שָׁלֹשׁ. לַסְקְלוֹנְקִית חָמֵשׁ עֶשְׂרֵה. חַד אָמַר בְּשֵׁם רֵישׁ לָקִישׁ. הַמְבַיֵּישׁ אֶת הַזָּקֵן נוֹתֵן לוֹ דְּמֵי בוֹשְׁתּוֹ מְשֻׁלָּם. חַד בַּר נָשׁ אִיקְפַּד לְרִבִּי יוּדָה בַּר חֲנִינָה. אָתָא עוֹבְדָא קוֹמֵי רֵישׁ לָקִישׁ וּקְנָסֵיהּ לִטְרָא דְּדָהָב.

**Halakhah 7-8**: "He who hits another pays him a tetradrachma." "Rebbi Aqiba said, even the poorest in Israel," etc. Rav Qarni stated: For a kick, one. For an elbow, three. For *sqlvnqyt* fifteen[72]. Somebody said in the name of Rebbi Simeon ben Laqish: He who puts an Elder to shame has fully to pay for his shame. A person insulted Rebbi Jehudah ben Ḥanina[73]. The case came before Rebbi Simeon ben Laqish who fined him a pound of gold.

| | |
|---|---|
| 72   In the parallel in Babli, 27b, the quote appears in Rav Ḥisda's name. There, pushing with the elbow cost 3 tetradrachmas, a kick with the foot 5, and סנוקרת 13. The unexplained סנוקרת (which also is the reading of E here) according to R. Ḥananel (i. e., Gaonic tradition) means a hook with the fist under the chin; according to Rashi hitting somebody with a donkey saddle. | The Genizah text reads יסקינוקינית, the *Metivot* fragment סקלוקינת. J. N. Epstein (תרביץ 2/1 ללקסיקון התלמודי p. 123-127) proposes Accadic *sunkirtu* (*su-un-kir-tum*) "camel's hump" as origin. {Cf. Latin *sculpturigo* "scratching", *sculptorium* "back scratcher" (E. G.).}<br><br>73   The case is mentioned in *Ketubot* 4:8, Note 202. |

(6c line 16) רָקַק וְהִגִּיעַ בּוֹ הָרוֹק. עַד הֵיכָן הִגִּיעַ בּוֹ הָרוֹק. עַד גּוּפוֹ עַד כֵּלָיו. אֶלָּא רָקַק וְלֹא הִגִּיעַ בּוֹ הָרוֹק מָהוּ. אָמַר רִבִּי יוֹסֵי. הָדָא אָמְרָה. הַמְבַיֵּישׁ אֶת חֲבֵירוֹ בִּדְבָרִים פָּטוּר.

"If one spat on him and the spit touched him." How far does the spit have to reach? On his body, on his garments?[74] But what is the rule if he spat and the spittle did not reach him? Rebbi Yose said, this implies that somebody who insults another person verbally is not liable[75].

| | |
|---|---|
| 74   The question is not answered. One may conclude that there is no difference. The Babli, 91a, comes to the opposite conclusion, *viz.*, that spitting on somebody's garments is not punishable.<br><br>75   Since certainly spitting is not | punishable if the spit falls to the ground before it reaches the intended victim, verbal spit which never touches cannot be punishable (in contrast to contemporary Roman or Egyptian laws.) |

(6c line 18) תַּנֵּי רִבִּי אַבָּהוּ קוֹמֵי רִבִּי יוֹחָנָן. הוֹרַגְתָּהּ קוֹצְצָתָהּ נְטִיעוֹתָיי. וַהֲלָה אוֹמֵר. אֵינִי יוֹדֵעַ. חַייָב. אָמַר לוֹ. הֵן תַּנִּיתָהּ אִילֵין לְמַקְרִילוֹת לְמַקְבִּילוֹת. אָמַר לֵיהּ. אֲנָא הוּא דְטָעִית וְאִינּוּן דַּמְרִין כֵּן. מְעִידִין אָנוּ אִישׁ פְּלוֹנִי שֶׁהָרַג שׁוֹר פְּלוֹנִי. וַהֲלָה אוֹמֵר אֵינִי יוֹדֵעַ. חַייָב. [אָמַר. הָא אֲמִירָה.]

Rebbi Abbahu stated before Rebbi Johanan: "You killed my ox, you cut down my fruit trees," and the other says, I do not know, he is liable. He said to him, certainly you state that to the rabble[76]. He answered, it is my fault, they said the following: "We testify against X that he killed ox Y" and the other says, I do not know, he is liable. [He said, that was stated.][77]

76 As J. Levy notes, the unexplained words מקרילות (Genizah מקליקות ,מקבילות) are onomatopoetic and intended as an insult. The Babli in such a situation uses חִילֵק וּבִילֵק "split and desolation" to designate the totally unworthy. R. Abbahu's statement is not worth to be heard since nobody can be responsible for an undocumented claim about which he notes his own ignorance.

77 Not in the Leiden ms., added from the E and Genizah texts. R. Johanan notes that the statement in its present form is obviously true, hence unnecessary.

The Genizah text has a better version in R. Abbahu's statement: "We testify against X that he killed Y's ox or cut down his fruit trees."

**משנה י**: אַף עַל פִּי שֶׁהוּא נוֹתֵן לוֹ אֵינוֹ נִמְחָל לוֹ עַד שֶׁיְבַקֵּשׁ מִמֶּנּוּ (fol. 6a) שֶׁנֶּאֱמַר וְעַתָּה הָשֵׁב אֵשֶׁת הָאִישׁ כִּי נָבִיא הוּא. וּמְנַיִין שֶׁלֹּא יְהֵא הַמּוֹחֵל אַכְזָרִי שֶׁנֶּאֱמַר וַיִּתְפַּלֵּל אַבְרָהָם אֶל הָאֱלֹהִים וגו'.

**Mishnah 10**: Even though he did pay, he will not be forgiven[78] unless he asks for forgiveness, as it is said: "Now return the man's wife since he is a prophet[79]." From where that the person asked to forgive shall not be cruel? It is said[80]: "Abraham prayed to the Omnipotent, etc."

78 The person who injures another cannot obtain mercy in Heaven unless he first has asked forgiveness on earth.

79 Gen. 20:7. The reference as usual is to the part of the verse which is not quoted: "Let him pray for you that you will live." This implies that Abraham first had to forgive

Avimelekh before the latter obtained    80    Gen. 20:17.
Heavenly mercy.

(6c line 22) **הלכה י**: אַף עַל פִּי שֶׁהוּא נוֹתֵן לוֹ כול'. [וְכֵן אַתָּה מוֹצֵא בְּרֵיעֵי אִיוֹב וְעַתָּה קְחוּ לָכֶם שִׁבְעָה פָרִים וְשִׁבְעָה אֵלִים וגו' וַיֵּלְכוּ אֱלִיפַז הַתֵּימָנִי וּבִלְדַּד הַשּׁוּחִי וְצוֹפַר הַנַּעֲמָתִי וַיַּעֲשׂוּ וגו' וּבְסוֹף הָעִנְיָין מַהוּא אוֹמֵר וַי'י שָׁב אֶת שְׁבוּת אִיּוֹב אֵימָתַי בְּהִתְפַּלְּלוֹ בְּעַד רֵעֵהוּ וגו' וַיּוֹסֶף י'י אֶת כָּל־אֲשֶׁר לְאִיּוֹב לְמִשְׁנֶה.]

**Halakhah 10**: "Even though he did pay," etc. [81][And so you find with Job's friends. [82]"Now yourselves take seven bulls and seven rams, etc." "Eliphas the Temanite, Bildad the Shuhite, and Ṣophar the Naamite went and did, etc." What does it say at the end? "The Eternal changed Job's fortunes." When? "When he was praying for his neighbor, etc." "The Eternal doubled everything that Job had had."]

81    Paragraph missing in the Leiden ms., added from the Genizah text. E's text is somewhat longer.

82    *Job* 42:8-10. Tosephta 9:29.

(6c line 22) תַּנֵּי. רִבִּי יוּדָה אוֹמֵר מִשּׁוּם רַבָּן גַּמְלִיאֵל. הֲרֵי הוּא אוֹמֵר וְנָתַן לְךָ רַחֲמִים וגו'. סִימָן זֶה יְהֵא בְּיָדְךָ. כָּל־זְמַן שֶׁאַתְּ רַחֲמָן הַמָּקוֹם מְרַחֵם עָלֶיךָ. אֵינְךָ מְרַחֵם אֵין הַמָּקוֹם מְרַחֵם לָךְ. רַב אָמַר. אָדָם שֶׁשָּׂרַח לַחֲבֵירוֹ וּבִיקֵּשׁ מִמֶּנּוּ וְלֹא קִיבְּלוֹ יַעֲשֶׂה שׁוּרַת בְּנֵי אָדָם וִיפַיְּיסֶנּוּ. דִּכְתִיב יָשׁוֹר עַל אֲנָשִׁים וגו'. וְאִם עָשָׂה כֵן מַה כָּתוּב תַּמָּן. פָּדָה מִשְׁאוֹל נַפְשׁוֹ מֵעֲבוֹר בַּשַּׁחַת וגו'. אָמַר רִבִּי יוֹסֵי. הָדָא דְתֵימַר שֶׁלֹּא הוֹצִיא לוֹ שֵׁם רָע. אֲבָל הוֹצִיא לוֹ שֵׁם רַע אֵין לוֹ מְחִילָה עוֹלָמִית.

It was stated[83]: Rebbi Jehudah says in the name of Rabban Gamliel. Since it says that[84] "He will give you mercy etc.", let the following be a sign in your hand: Whenever that you show mercy, the Omnipresent will have mercy on you. If you do not show mercy, the Omnipresent will not have mercy on you. [85]Rav said: If a person misbehaved towards another and asked for pardon but the other did not respond, let him assemble a row of people and ask for pardon, as it is written[86]: "Form a row of men, etc.[87]" If he does so, what is written there? [88]"He redeemed his soul from the pit, not to go to destruction etc." Rebbi Yose said, that is if he did not defame, but the defamer is never pardoned.

83 Tosephta 9:30; Babli *Šabbat* 151b.
84 *Deut.* 13:18.
85 *Yoma* 8:9 (45c), Babli 87b.
86 *Job* 33:27.
87 "Let him say, I sinned, I did evil without caring."
88 *Job* 33:28.

(fol. 6a) **משנה יא**: הָאוֹמֵר סַמֵּא אֶת עֵינִי קְטַע אֶת יָדִי שַׁבֵּר אֶת רַגְלִי חַיָּיב עַל מְנָת לִפְטוֹר חַיָּיב. קָרַע אֶת כְּסוּתִי שַׁבֵּר אֶת כַּדִּי חַיָּיב. עַל מְנָת לִפְטוֹר פָּטוּר. עָשֵׂה כֵן לְאִישׁ פְּלוֹנִי עַל מְנָת לִפְטוֹר חַיָּיב בֵּין בְּגוּפוֹ בֵּין בְּמָמוֹנוֹ.

**Mishnah 11**: If one says: Blind my eye, cut off my hand, break my leg, he is liable[89]. On condition not to be liable[90], he is liable. Tear my garment, break my pitcher, he is liable. On condition not to be liable, he is not liable[91]. Do that to another person, on condition not to be liable, he is liable whether about his person or his money[89].

89 It is forbidden to injure another person (except for medical treatment). Since "there is no agency for committing crimes", a person committing a crime on the instigation of another is not absolved from liability.
90 Even if the instigator/victim agrees beforehand that no liability would be involved.
91 Since this is purely a money matter.

(6c line 31) **הלכה יא:** הָאוֹמֵר סַמֵּא אֶת עֵינִי קְטַע אֶת יָדִי כול'. הָאוֹמֵר. סַמֵּא עֵינִי שֶׁמַּזִּיקַתְנִי. קְטַע יָדִי שֶׁמַּזִּיקַתְנִי. חַייָב. עַל מְנָת לִפְטוֹר. חַייָב. אָמַר רִבִּי לְעָזָר. בָּהֵן שֶׁהוּא כְלָאו מַתְנִיתָא. אֲבָל בָּהֵן שֶׁהוּא כְהֵן פָּטוּר. מִילְתֵיהּ דְּרִבִּי לְעָזֶר מִשּׁוּם פְּגַם מִשְׁפָּחָה. רֵישׁ לָקִישׁ אָמַר. בָּהֵן שֶׁהוּא כְהֵן הִיא מַתְנִיתָא. אֲבָל בָּהֵן שֶׁהוּא כְלָאו חַייָב. מִילְתֵיהּ דְּרֵישׁ לָקִישׁ אָמְרָה שֶׁשָּׁמִין לַקְרוֹבִין בּוֹשֶׁת. תַּנֵּי. יִשְׂרָאֵל שֶׁאֲנָסוּהוּ גוֹיִם וְנָטְלוּ מִמֶּנּוּ מָמוֹן חֲבֵירוֹ בְּפָנָיו פָּטוּר. נָטַל וְנָתַן בְּיַד חַייָב. אָמַר רִבִּי יוֹסֵי. הָדָא דְתֵימַר בְּשֶׁאָמְרוּ לוֹ מָמוֹן סְתָם. אֲבָל מָמוֹן פְּלוֹנִי אֲפִילוּ נָטַל וְנָתַן בְּיַד פָּטוּר.

**Halakhah 11**: "If one say: Blind my eye, cut off my hand," etc. "If he says, blind my eye because it damages me, cut off my hand because it damages me, he is liable. On condition not to be liable, he is liable."[92] Rebbi Eleazar said, the Mishnah deals with a "yes" which really means "no". But for a "yes" which does mean "yes" he is not liable[93]. The statement of Rebbi Eleazar is about the family's loss of standing. Rebbi Simeon ben Laqish said, the Mishnah deals with a "yes" which means "yes". But for a "yes" which means "no", he is liable[94]. The statement of Rebbi Simeon ben Laqish imples that one estimates the relatives' loss of standing[95].

It was stated[96]: "If Gentiles forced a Jew and took from him another person's money in his presence, he is not liable. If he handed it over, he is liable." Rebbi Yose said, that means if they simply demanded "money"[97]. But "X's money", he is not liable even if he handed it over[98].

---

92  Tosephta 9:32: "If one says: blind my eye because it damages me, cut off my hand because it damages me, he is not liable." This may be a Babylonian version.

93  If a person asks to be mutilated, it is obvious that this person cannot sue for damages. Then the question arises, what does the Mishnah mean by holding the person who does the mutilation liable? The relatives can sue because they have to bear the

shame of having a mutilated member in their family. If the person doing the mutilation can show that the immunity granted him by the victim was honest, they cannot sue.

94   Even for the willful destruction of property.

95   He gives the relatives the right to sue in any case. In the Babli, 93a, R. Simeon ben Laqish's position is attributed to his teacher R. Hoshaia, R. Eleazar's position to his teacher R. Johanan. Since R. Simeon ben Laqish is a higher authority than R. Eleazar but R. Johanan is higher than R. Hoshaia, implicitly the two Talmudim decide in opposite ways.

96   Tosephta 9:33; quoted in Babli 117a.

97   One may use another person's money to save his own life but he has to pay for it.

98   Cf. *Terumot* 8:10, Note 248.

## הגוזל עצים פרק תשיעי

(fol. 6c) **משנה א**: הַגּוֹזֵל עֵצִים וַעֲשָׂאָן כֵּלִים צֶמֶר וַעֲשָׂאוֹ בְגָדִים מְשַׁלֵּם כְּשָׁעַת הַגְּזֵילָה. גָּזַל פָּרָה מְעוּבֶּרֶת וְיָלְדָה רָחֵל טְעוּנָה וּגְזָזָהּ מְשַׁלֵּם דְּמֵי פָרָה מְעוּבֶּרֶת לֵילֵד דְּמֵי רָחֵל טְעוּנָה לִיגָּזֵז. גָּזַל פָּרָה וְעִיבְּרָה אֶצְלוֹ וְיָלְדָה רָחֵל וְנִטְעֲנָה עִמּוֹ וּגְזָזָהּ מְשַׁלֵּם כְּשָׁעַת הַגְּזֵילָה. זֶה הַכְּלָל כָּל־הַגַּזְלָנִין מְשַׁלְּמִין כְּשָׁעַת הַגְּזֵילָה.

**Mishnah 1**: One who robbed[1] wood and turned it into utensils, wool and turned it into garments[2], pays their value at the time of the robbery. If he robbed a pregnant cow and it calved, a sheep in its wool and he shore it[3], he pays the price of a pregnant cow ready to calve, or a sheep in its wool ready to be shorn. If he robbed a cow which became pregnant in his possession and it calved, or a sheep which grew wool with him and he shore it, he pays their value at the time of the robbery. This is the principle: All robbers pay for value at the time of the robbery.

1 The robber, who takes things openly and by force, has to make restitution with possibly a 25% fine, *Lev.* 5:21-24. The thief who takes things by stealth has to pay double.

2 Once the nature of the robbed item was changed, the robber became its owner and only owes the monetary value to the original owner.

3 And now it is not in the state in which it was robbed.

(6d line 22) **הלכה א**: הַגּוֹזֵל עֵצִים וַעֲשָׂאָן כֵּלִים כול'. הָכָא אַתְּ מַר. לִיבּוּן כְּשִׁינּוּי. וְהָכָא אַתְּ מַר. אֵין לִיבּוּן כְּשִׁינּוּי. הֵן דְּתֵימַר. לִיבּוּן כְּשִׁינּוּי. בְּשֶׁעֲשָׂאוֹ צוֹפִים. וְהֵן דְּתֵימַר. אֵין לִיבּוּן כְּשִׁינּוּי. בְּשֶׁהִנִּיחוֹ כְּמוֹת שֶׁהוּא. מָצִינוּ לִיבּוּן בְּלֹא צוֹפִים. שֶׁמָּא יֵשׁ צוֹפִים בְּלֹא לִיבּוּן. אָמַר רִבִּי יוּדָן. קַל הוּא שֶׁהִיקְלִי

בְּנִזְלָן שֶׁיְּשַׁלֵּם כְּשָׁעַת הַגְּזִילָה. גָּזַל שָׁלַח וְלִיבְּנוּ. אִית לָךְ מֵימַר בְּשֶׁעֲשָׂאוֹ צוּפִים.
עוֹד קַל הוּא שֶׁהִיקֵלִי בְּנִזְלָן שֶׁיְּהֵא מְשַׁלֵּם כְּשָׁעַת הַגְּזִילָה.

**Halakhah 1**: "One who robbed wood and turned it into utensils," etc. Here[4], you say that bleaching is a change, and there[5] you say that bleaching is not a change. If you say that bleaching is a change, if he made it into wool flakes[6]. If you say that bleaching is not a change, if he left it unchanged. We find bleaching without flakes. Are there flakes without bleaching[7]? Rebbi Yudan said, it is a leniency instituted for the robber that he pay their value at the time of the robbery[8]. If somebody robbed raw hide and cleaned it, can you say that he turned it into flakes[9]? Again it is a leniency instituted for the robber that he pay the value at the time of the robbery.

4   Tosephta 10:2 states that raw wool that was bleached does not have to be returned; only its value as raw wool has to be paid. Babli 93b.

5   The Mishnah, which says that only turning wool into a garment is a change by which the robber becomes the owner; this implies that cleaning, spinning, and dying the wool prior to weaving is not a change which absolves the robber from returning the wool as is.

6   Arabic صوف, Samaritan Aramaic צוף. The wool flakes can be used to stuff pillows; they cannot be spun into thread. The robber changed raw material into a finished product.

7   At least the raw wool has to be washed before being turned into flakes.

8   Since robbers, in contrast to thieves, are known, it should be made easy for them to return the robbed goods and avoid prosecution. This is the position of the House of Hillel as explained in the next paragraph. The Mishnah represents the teaching of the House of Hillel.

9   Nonetheless, he only owes the value of the hide and cannot be forced to return it as is.

(6d line 28) גָּזַל מָרִישׁ וּבְנָאוֹ בַּבִּירָה. בֵּית שַׁמַּאי אוֹמְרִים. יְקַעְקֵעַ כָּל־הַבִּירָה כּוּלָּהּ וְיִתְּנֶנּוּ לוֹ. וּבֵית הִלֵּל אוֹמְרִים. יִתֵּן לוֹ דָּמָיו מִפְּנֵי תַקָּנַת שָׁבִים. יָרַד

לְחָרְבָּה וּבְנָיָיהּ שֶׁלֹּא בִרְשׁוּת שָׁמִין לוֹ וְיָדוֹ עַל הַתַּחְתּוֹנָה. בְּנָיָיהּ בִּרְשׁוּת שָׁמִין לוֹ וְיָדוֹ עַל הָעֶלְיוֹנָה. בִּיקֵּשׁ לִיטוֹל אֲבָנָיו וְעֵצָיו אֵין שׁוֹמְעִין לוֹ. רִבִּי יַעֲקֹב בַּר אָחָא בְּשֵׁם רִבִּי יְהוֹשֻׁעַ בֶּן לֵוִי. מִשּׁוּם יִישׁוּב אֶרֶץ יִשְׂרָאֵל. רַב נַחְמָן בַּר יִצְחָק שָׁאַל. אִילוּ מִי שֶׁנִּכְנַס לְחוֹרְבָתוֹ שֶׁלַּחֲבֵירוֹ וּפֵירֵק חֲבִילָתוֹ לְשָׁעָה וּבִיקֵּשׁ לִיטְלוֹ שֶׁמָּא אֵין שׁוֹמְעִין לוֹ. כֵּיוָן דְּשָׁמַע דָּמַר רִבִּי יַעֲקֹב בַּר אָחָא. מִשּׁוּם יִישׁוּב אֶרֶץ יִשְׂרָאֵל. אָמַר. הָאֲמִירָה. אֶלָּא בָּנָה בְּמָקוֹם שֶׁאֵין רָאוּי לִבְנוֹת וְנָטַע בְּמָקוֹם שֶׁאֵין רָאוּי לִיטַע. רַב אָמַר. שָׁמִין לוֹ אֶלָּא שֶׁמַּעֲרִימִין עָלָיו לִיכָּנֵס לְשָׁם בִּימוֹת הַחַמָּה וּבִימוֹת הַגְּשָׁמִים. אָמַר לוֹ. הָא תַנִּיתָהּ. שָׁמִין לוֹ וְיָדוֹ עַל הַתַּחְתּוֹנָה.

[10]"One who robbed a beam and built it into a large building. The House of Shammai say, he has to tear down the entire building and return it. But the House of Hillel say, he has to pay its worth to support the penitents. If he went into another person's ruined building and rebuilt it without permission, one estimates for him and his hand is disadvantaged[11]. If he rebuilt it with permission, one estimates for him and his hand is advantaged[12]. If he wanted to take his wood and stones, one does not listen to him." Rebbi Jacob bar Aḥa in the name of Rebbi Joshua ben Levi: Because of the settlement in the Land of Israel[13]. Rav Naḥman bar Isaac[14] asked: If somebody temporarily entered another person's ruin to put down his bundle, when he wanted to take it up again does one not listen to him[15]? When he heard what Rebbi Jacob bar Aḥa had said, because of the settlement in the Land of Israel, he said: That is a statement[16]. But if he built[17] at a place unfit for building, or planted trees at a place unfit for planting, Rav said one estimates[18] for him[11] but one tricks him to permit entry both in summer and in winter[19]. One said to him: Was that not already stated: "One estimates for him and his hand is disadvantaged?"

10  Tosephta 10:5-7; Babli *Giṭṭin* 55a. A different version of the entire paragraph is in *Giṭṭin* 5:5 (Notes 158-168).

11  He only can expect the lesser of his expenses or the value created.

12  The Tosephta explains that he is entitled to the larger of his expenses or the value created.

13  In this version, the rule only applies to the Land of Israel. In the version in *Giṭṭin* the reason is "because of civilization", that one does not wilfully destroy houses, applicable worldwide.

14  In E, the Genizah fragment, and in *Giṭṭin*: Naḥman bar Jacob. This reading is also confirmed by the Babli, *Bava meṣi'a* 101a. Since otherwise only Babylonian authorities of the first two generations are mentioned in *Neziqin*, L's reading is a scribal error.

15  Then why can the illegal builder not take his logs with him? In the Babli, *Bava meṣi'a* 101a, Rav Naḥman is quoted as letting the illegal builder take his materials instead of accepting the estimated value.

16  A valid statement.

17  Without permission.

18  In E: "One listens".

19  "Him" refers to the legal owner of the land. It is explained in the Babli, *Bava meṣi'a* 101a, that the person who planted is advantaged (Note 12) if the owner restricts entrance to the newly planted area.

(6d line 40) אָמַר רִבִּי זֵירָה. הָדָא אָמְרָה. גָּזַל שְׁמֵינָה וְהִכְחִישָׁה מַחֲזִיר לוֹ אֶת הַשּׁוּמָן. אָמַר רַב חִסְדָּא. הָדָא אָמְרָה. גָּזַל כְּחוּשָׁה וְהִשְׁמִינָה מַחֲזִירָהּ בְּעֵינָהּ.

Rebbi Ze'ira said, this implies that if he robbed a fattened animal and it became thin[20], he has to replace the fat. Rav Ḥisda said, this implies that if he robbed a thin animal and fattened it, he has to return it as is[21].

20  This is a natural change; it is not enough to make the robber an owner. But since the Mishnah states that he has to give back the value at the time of robbery, he has to make up for value lost. Cf. Babli 65a for the case of a thief.

21  Since the robber never became the owner (cf. Note 2).

(6d line 42) מִפְּנֵי שֶׁעִיבְּרָה אֶצְלוֹ וְיָלְדָה. מְשַׁלֵּם כְּשָׁעַת הַגְּזֵילָה. מָאן תַּנִּיתָהּ. רִבִּי יַעֲקֹב. דְּתַנֵּי. זֶה הַכְּלָל. שֶׁהָיָה רִבִּי יַעֲקֹב אוֹמֵר. כָּל־גְּזֵילָה שֶׁהִיא קַיֶּימֶת בְּעֵינֶיהָ וְלֹא נִשְׁתַּנֵּית מִבְּרִייָתָהּ אוֹמֵר לוֹ. הֲרֵי שֶׁלְּךָ לְפָנֶיךָ. וְהַגַּנָּב לְעוֹלָם מְשַׁלֵּם כְּשָׁעַת הַגְּנֵיבָה.

Because it became pregnant at his place and calved he pays its value at the time of the robbery[22]. Who stated this? Rebbi Jacob, as it was stated[23]: "This is the principle about which Rebbi Jacob said: About any robbed object which exists as before and was not changed from the state in which it was created[24], he tells him: Here is your property before you. And the thief always pays the value at the time of theft."

22  E has an addition: "Therefore, if it did not become pregnant at his place and calved he pays . . ." This addition is out of place.

23  An anonymous statement in Tosephta 10:3.

24  Even if now it is worthless, as, e. g., leavened matter after Passover which was robbed before Passover. Since the deficiency is not visible, the robber can return the leavened matter to discharge his obligation while a thief has to pay double the value it had at the time of the theft.

(fol. 6c) **משנה ב:** גָּזַל בְּהֵמָה וְהִזְקִינָה עֲבָדִים וְהִזְקִינוּ מְשַׁלֵּם כְּשָׁעַת הַגְּזֵילָה. רִבִּי מֵאִיר אוֹמֵר יֹאמַר לוֹ בָּעֲבָדִים הֲרֵי שֶׁלְּךָ לְפָנֶיךָ.

**Mishnah 2**: If he robbed an animal and it aged, slaves and they aged[25], he has to pay their value at the time of the robbery. Rebbi Meïr says, he may say about slaves: Here is your property before you[26].

25  They do not look the same as at the time of the robbery and are not worth the same; the robber cannot return them but has to pay up.

26  Since slaves are treated according to the law of real estate (Mishnah *Bava batra* 3:1, *Qiddušin* 1:2 Notes 347 ff.) and real estate can never

be acquired by a robber, for him a slave can never be acquired by a robber and ages as the original owner's property.

(6d line 46) **הלכה ב:** גָּזַל בְּהֵמָה וְהִזְקִינָה כול'. רַב הוּנָא אָמַר. בְּשֶׁגָּזַל עֵגֶל וְנַעֲשָׂה שׁוֹר. אֲבָל גָּזַל שׁוֹר וְהִזְקִין אוֹמֵר לוֹ. הֲרֵי שֶׁלָּךְ לְפָנֶיךָ. שְׁמוּאֵל אָמַר. אֲפִילוּ גָּזַל עֵגֶל וְנַעֲשָׂה שׁוֹר אוֹמֵר לוֹ. הֲרֵי שֶׁלָּךְ לְפָנֶיךָ. תַּנֵּי רַב קַרְנָא. וַאֲפִילוּ גָּזַל עֵגֶל וְנַעֲשָׂה שׁוֹר וְטָבַח וּמָכַר מְשַׁלֵּם תַּשְׁלוּמֵי ד' וְה' עֵגֶל. אָמַר אָבוֹי דִשְׁמוּאֵל בַּר אִמִּי בְּשֵׁם רַב יְהוּדָה. הֲלָכָה כְּרִבִּי מֵאִיר.

**Halakhah 2**: "If he robbed an animal and it aged," etc. Rav Huna said, if he robbed a calf and it became a bull[27]; but if he robbed a bull and it aged, he tells him: Here is your property before you[28]. Samuel said, even if he robbed a calf and it became a bull, he tells him[29]: Here is your property before you. Rav Qarna stated: Even if he robbed[30] a calf and it became a bull before he slaughtered or sold it, he pays quadruple or quintuple the value of a calf[31]. The father of Samuel bar Immi said in the name of Rav Jehudah[32]: Practice follows Rebbi Meïr.

27 This is a change in the nature of the animal; he cannot return it but must pay.

28 In the Babli, 96b, Rav Pappa disagrees and holds that the weakened animal cannot be returned.

29 He holds that it still is called cattle, not changed from the date of its birth.

30 One has to read "stole" since robbers are not under the law of quadruple or quintuple restitution.

31 He follows Samuel that the bull is still the same animal as the calf. In the Babli, 65b, R. Ilai (La) is quoted as following the Mishnah and Rav Huna that the change of the calf into a bull is an essential change which lets the thief become the owner, not only the possessor, of the animal. If he slaughtered or sold the animal after it reached sexual maturity, he slaughtered or sold his own property and only pays double restitution for the theft.

32 The student of Samuel. In the Babli, 96b, the statement is in the name of Rav.

משנה ג: (fol. 6c) גָּזַל מַטְבֵּעַ וְנִסְדַּק וְנִרְקְבוּ פֵּירוֹת וְהִרְכִּיבוּ יַיִן וְהֶחֱמִיץ מְשַׁלֵּם כְּשָׁעַת הַגְּזֵילָה. מַטְבֵּעַ וְנִפְסַל תְּרוּמָה וְנִטְמֵאת חָמֵץ וְעָבַר עָלָיו הַפֶּסַח בְּהֵמָה וְנֶעֶבְדָה בָהּ עֲבֵירָה אוֹ שֶׁנִּפְסְלָה מֵעַל גַּבֵּי הַמִּזְבֵּחַ אוֹ שֶׁהָיְתָה יוֹצֵאת לִיסָקֵל אוֹמֵר לוֹ הֲרֵי שֶׁלָּךְ לְפָנֶיךָ.

**Mishnah 3**: If he robbed a coin and it was split, fruits and they rotted, wine and it spoiled, he pays their value at the time of the robbery[33]. A coin and it was declared invalid, heave and it became impure[34], leavened matter and Passover passed[35], an animal which was used for sin[36], or which became disqualified from the altar[37], or which was taken out to be stoned[38], he tells him: Here is your property before you[39].

33  In all these cases, the thing robbed was changed materially; it cannot be returned.

34  It lost its value as food and only can be used as fuel.

35  It is rabbinically forbidden for all usufruct.

36  Either it was used for idolatry which makes it forbidden as sacrifice, or was used for bestiality which makes it subject to a death sentence.

37  The living animal no longer can be offered as a sacrifice.

38  After it killed a human.

39  Since these defects are not visible, following R. Jacob the robbed objects can be returned as they are (Babli 98b).

(6d line 51) הלכה ג: גָּזַל מַטְבֵּעַ וְנִסְדַּק כול'. רַב הוּנָא אָמַר. בְּשֶׁפְּסָלַתּוּ מַלְכוּת. שְׁמוּאֵל אָמַר בְּשֶׁנִּסְדַּק וַדַּאי. רִבִּי יוּדָה בֶּן פָּזִי בְּשֵׁם רִבִּי יוֹסֵי בַּר חֲנִינָה. וְהֵן שֶׁהִרְכִּיבוּ מִן הַכְּנִימָה. אֲבָל אִם הִרְכִּיבוּ מִתּוֹלַעַת כִּבְרִיאָין הֵן. רַב הוּנָא אָמַר. בְּשֶׁפְּסָלַתּוּ מַלְכוּת. אֲבָל פְּסָלַתּוּ מְדִינָה אוֹמֵר לוֹ הֲרֵי שֶׁלָּךְ לְפָנֶיךָ. שְׁמוּאֵל אָמַר. אֲפִילוּ פְּסָלַתּוּ מַלְכוּת אוֹמֵר לוֹ. הֲרֵי שֶׁלָּךְ לְפָנֶיךָ.

**Halakhah 3**: "If he robbed a coin and it was split," etc. Rav Huna said, if the government invalidated it. Samuel said, if really it was split[40]. Rebbi Jehudah ben Pazi in the name of Rebbi Yose ben Ḥanina: Only if they rotted because of maggots but if they rotted because of worms they are like healthy ones⁴¹. Rav Huna said, if the government invalidated it, but if the country invalidated it⁴², he may say to him: Here is your property before you. Samuel said, even if the government invalidated it, he may say to him: Here is your property before you.

40   Rav Huna considers a coin invalidated by the government as a piece of metal, not a coin. Therefore its nature was changed and it is as if it was split. Samuel considers an invalidated coin still as a coin. In the Babli, 97a, Rav Huna is quoted with the opinion here ascribed to Samuel, and Rav Jehudah, Samuel's student, with that ascribed to Rav Huna.

41   This refers to the rotten fruits mentioned in the Mishnah. If the fruits were damaged by larvae but now are free of insects they are usable, not lost or changed. Before the days of pesticides almost no fruits were completely free of any insect damage.

42   As in the military anarchy of the Roman empire when the silver-washed copper coins given out as silver were no longer used by the public which switched to the gold standard (cf. E. and H. Guggenheimer, *Notes on the Talmudic Vocabulary* 8, Lešonēnū 37(1973) 105-112.)

(6d line 56) רִבִּי יוּדָן לָא נְחִית לְבֵית וַעֲדָא. קָם עִם רִבִּי מָנָא. אָמַר לֵיהּ. מַה חִידוּת הֲוָה לְכוֹן בְּבֵי מִדְרָשָׁא יוֹמָא דֵין. אָמַר לֵיהּ. מִילָּה פָלָן. אָמַר לֵיהּ. וְלֹא מַתְנִיתָא הִיא. תְּרוּמָה וְנִטְמֵאת. אָמַר לֵיהּ. תִּיפְתָּר בְּשֶׁנִּטְמֵאת מֵאֵילֶיהָ וְלֵית שְׁמַע מִינָהּ כְּלוּם.

Rebbi Yudan did not go to the house of assembly. He met Rebbi Mana and asked him, what was new for you in the house of study today? He told him, such and such a subject. He replied, is that not a Mishnah, "heave and it became impure"? He replied, explain it if it became impure by itself⁴⁴ and you cannot infer anything.

43   Seemingly on the subject of an induced invisible change in value, whether it constitutes acquisition or not.

44   For example, if a dead reptile was found in the utensil containing the

heave. Then it implies nothing about the status of the object if the robber caused the change.

(6d line 60) חִילְפַּיי אָמַר. נִשְׁבַּע לוֹ קוֹדֶם הַפֶּסַח. אַחַר הַפֶּסַח מְשַׁלֵּם לוֹ חָמֵץ יָפֶה. אָמַר רִבִּי מָנָא. אֲזָלִית לְקַיְסָרִין וְאַשְׁכְּחִית לְרִבִּי חִזְקִיָּה דְּדָרִישׁ לָהּ מִשּׁוּם דְּרִבִּי יַעֲקֹב בַּר אָחָא. אִין אִית בַּר נָשׁ פְּלִיג עַל חִילְפַּיי שֶׁאֵין מְשַׁלֵּם חָמֵץ יָפֶה. הַכֹּל מוֹדִין בְּחָמֵץ שֶׁמְּשַׁלֵּם חָמֵץ יָפֶה.

Hilfai said, if he[45] swore to him before Passover, then after Passover he pays him for fully useable leavened matter. Rebbi Mana said, I went to Caesarea and asked Rebbi Ḥizqiah, who quoted this in the name of Rebbi Jacob bar Aḥa, is there anybody who disagrees with Hilfai so that he would not have to pay for fully useable leavened matter? Everybody agrees about leavened matter that he has to pay for fully useable leavened matter.

45   The robber was challenged by its owner to return to him his leavened matter before Passover and swore that he did not have it. Because of the oath he now is obligated for valuable leavened matter; he is barred from returning after Passover the leavened matter which now is worthless.

(fol. 6c) **מִשְׁנָה ד:** נָתַן לְאוּמָּנִין לְתַקֵּן וְקִילְקְלוּ חַיָּיבִין לְשַׁלֵּם. נָתַן לְחָרָשׁ שִׁידָּה תֵּיבָה וּמִגְדָּל לְתַקֵּן וְקִילְקֵל חַיָּיב לְשַׁלֵּם. וְהַבַּנַּאי שֶׁקִּיבֵּל עָלָיו אֶת הַכּוֹתֶל לְסוֹתְרוֹ וְשִׁיבַּר אֶת הָאֲבָנִים אוֹ שֶׁהִזִּיק חַיָּיב לְשַׁלֵּם. הָיָה סוֹתֵר מִצַּד זֶה וְנָפַל מִצַּד אַחֵר פָּטוּר וְאִם מֵחֲמַת הַמַּכָּה חַיָּיב.

**Mishnah 4**: If one gave something to artisans to repair and they broke it, they are liable. If one gave a chest, a box, or a cupboard to a woodworker to repair and he broke it, he is liable. And the builder who contracted to take down a wall is liable to pay if he ruined the stones or caused damage. If he was taking it down on one side when if collapsed on the other side he is not liable, but when it happened because of the pounding he is liable.

**הלכה ד:** נָתַן לְאוּמָּנִין לְתַקֵּן וְקִילְקְלוּ כול'. רַב הוּנָא אָמַר. וְהוּא שֶׁקָּבַע בּוֹ מַסְמֵר הָאַחֲרוֹן כְּדֵי לִזְכּוֹת לְכֵלָיו. (6d line 64)

**Halakhah 4:** "If one gave something to artisans to repair and they broke it," etc. Rav Huna said, only if he put in the last nail to acquire the rights to his utensils[46].

46 The Babli, 98a, infers from the second sentence of the Mishnah, which clearly refers to existing containers given to be fixed, that the "something" given in the first sentence is raw material, given to be turned into a utensil. The question then arises whether the artisan who ruins the utensil has to pay only for the material or for the finished utensil (since the client has to find another artisan and pay the latter.) About this question, Rav Huna (in the Babli, Rav Assi) notes that the artisan is liable only for the raw material as long as he did not put in the last nail. Once the object is finished, the artisan has the right to retain it until his bill be paid. Therefore, he then holds the object under the rules of the paid trustee and is liable for damage to it (Tosephta 10:8).

**משנה ה:** נָתַן צֶמֶר לַצַּבָּע וְהִקְדִּיחָהּ הַיּוֹרָה נוֹתֵן לוֹ דְּמֵי צַמְרוֹ. צְבָעוֹ כָאוּר אִם הַשֶּׁבַח יָתֵר עַל הַהוֹצָאָה נוֹתֵן לוֹ אֶת הַיְצִיאָה וְאִם הַיְצִיאָה יְתֵירָה עַל הַשֶּׁבַח נוֹתֵן לוֹ אֶת הַשֶּׁבַח. (fol. 6c)

**Mishnah 5:** If one gave wool to the dyer and the vat burned it, he gives him the value of his wool[47,48]. If he dyed it poorly, if the increased value is more than the expenses[49], he gives him his expenses; if the expenses are more than the increased value he gives him the increased value.

**משנה ו**: לִצְבּוֹעַ לוֹ אָדוֹם וּצְבָאוֹ שָׁחוֹר שָׁחוֹר וּצְבָאוֹ אָדוֹם רִבִּי מֵאִיר אוֹמֵר נוֹתֵן לוֹ דְּמֵי צַמְרוֹ. רִבִּי יְהוּדָה אוֹמֵר אִם הַשֶּׁבַח יֶתֶר עַל הַיְצִיאָה נוֹתֵן לוֹ אֶת הַיְצִיאָה וְאִם הַיְצִיאָה יְתִירָה עַל הַשֶּׁבַח נוֹתֵן לוֹ אֶת הַשֶּׁבַח.

**Mishnah 6**: To dye it red and he dyed it black, black and he dyed it red, Rebbi Meïr says, he gives him the value of his wool[47]. Rebbi Jehudah says, if the increased value is more than the expenses, he gives him his expenses; if the expenses are more than the increased value he gives him the increased value.

47  By his unprofessional work he changed the material from his prior state and acquired it as his property for which he has to pay.

48  In this case, the material is lost; it is impossible to refer to improved value.

49  The dyer's cash expenses for dye and fuel.

(6d line 66) **הלכה ה:** נָתַן צֶמֶר לַצַּבָּע כול'. רַב הוּנָא אָמַר. שֶׁהִקְדִּיחוֹ סַמְמָנִין. אֲבָל הִקְדִּיחָתָה יוֹרָה אוֹמֵר לוֹ. הֲרֵי שֶׁלָּךְ לְפָנֶיךָ. שְׁמוּאֵל אָמַר. אֲפִילוּ הִקְדִּיחוֹ סַמְמָנִין אוֹמֵר לוֹ. הֲרֵי שֶׁלָּךְ לְפָנֶיךָ.

**Halakhah 5**: "If one gave wool to the dyer," etc. Rav Huna said, if chemicals burned it[50], but if the vat burned it[51], he may say to him: Here is your property before you. Samuel said, even[52] if chemicals burned it, he may say to him: Here is your property before you.

50  The dye ruined the wool.

51  By overheating with too little fluid in the vat before dye was added. Then the wool was not changed from its original state. Rav Huna has to emend the text of the Mishnah.

52  This means: Only if chemicals burned it; otherwise one follows the text of the Mishnah.

(6d line 68) מָהוּ אִם הַשֶּׁבַח יֶתֶר עַל הַהוֹצָאָה נוֹתֵן לוֹ אֶת הַהוֹצָאָה. בַּר נַשׁ דִּיהַב לְחַבְרֵיהּ חֲמִשָּׁה מִינֵי עֲמַר וַחֲמִשָּׁה מִינֵי סַמְמָנִין וְעַשְׂרָה מָנוֹי אַגְרֵיהּ.

אָמַר לֵיהּ. צִיבְעֵיהּ סוֹמָק וְצִבְעֵי אוּכָם. אָמַר לֵיהּ. אִילּוּ צְבַעְתֵּיהּ סוֹמָק הֲוָה טָב עֶשְׂרִים וַחֲמִשָּׁה מָנוֹי וּכְדוֹ דְצַבַעְתֵּיהּ אוּכָם לֵית הוּא טָב אֶלָּא עֶשְׂרִים מָנוֹי. אַתְּ אוֹבָדְתְּ דִּידָךְ. אֲנָא לָא אוֹבֵד דִּידִי. אָמַר רִבִּי יוֹנָה. וְתִשְׁמַע מִינֵּיהּ. בַּר נָשׁ דִּיהַב לְחַבְרֵיהּ חֹ דֵּינָרִין דְּזָבִין לֵיהּ חִיטִין מִטִּיבֶּרְיָא וּזְבַן לֵיהּ מִצִּיפּוֹרִי. אָמַר לֵיהּ. אִילּוּ זְבַנְתְּ לִי מִטִּיבֶּרְיָא הֲווֹן עֶשְׂרִין וַחֲמִשָּׁה מוֹדְיָי. כְּדוֹן דְּזַבְנַתְּ מִצִּיפּוֹרִי לֵיתִנּוּן אֶלָּא עֶשְׂרִין מוֹדְיָי. אַתְּ אוֹבָדְתְּ דִּידָךְ. אֲנָא לָא אוֹבֵד דִּידִי.

What means "if the increased value is more than the expenses, he gives him his expenses"? A person gave to another five lots[53] of wool, five portions of dye, and ten minas for his wages. He told him, dye it red, but the other dyed it black. He told him, if you had dyed it red, it would have been worth 25 minas, now that you dyed it black it is worth only 20 minas. You lost yours, I did not lose mine[54]. Rebbi Jonah[55] said, you can understand from here that if a person gave to another eight denars to buy for him wheat in Tiberias but he bought for him in Sepphoris, he may say to him, if you had bought for me in Tiberias there would have been 25 *modii*[56]; now that you bought in Sepphoris there are only 20 *modii*. You lost yours, I did not lose mine[57].

53 The translation follows the reading of E and Tosaphot 100b, s.v. אם, which read מנוי "portions" rather than מיני "kinds". The same reading is found in שיטה מקובצת ad 100b. E starts the sentence by: אית בר נש "there is a man".

54 He deducts 5 minas from the dyer's wages. This argument is about value, not cost.

55 E and שיטה מקובצת read: R. Yose.

56 *Modius*, a Roman measure of volume, 64 *quartarii*, about 8.5 l, $2/3$ of a *se'ah*.

57 He deducts the price of 5 *modii* from the broker's fee.

תַּנֵּי. הַנּוֹתֵן מָעוֹת לַחֲבֵירוֹ לִיקַּח לוֹ חִיטִים וְלָקַח לוֹ שְׂעוֹרִים. אִם (7a line 1) פָּחֲתוּ פָּחֲתוּ לוֹ וְאִם הוֹתִירוּ הוֹתִירוּ לוֹ. וְתַנֵּי חוֹרָן. אִם פָּחֲתוּ פָּחֲתוּ לוֹ וְאִם הוֹתִירוּ לִשְׁנֵיהֶן. [מָן דְּאָמַר אִם פָּחֲתוּ פָּחֲתוּ לוֹ וְאִם הוֹתִירוּ הוֹתִירוּ לוֹ רִבִּי

## HALAKHAH 5

מֵאִיר. מַה טַעֲמָא דְּרַבִּי מֵאִיר. שֶׁלֹּא נִתְכַּוֵּון הַמּוֹכֵר לְזַכּוֹת אֶלָּא לַלּוֹקֵחַ. וּמָן דְּמַר אִם פָּחֲתוּ פָּחֲתוּ לוֹ וְאִם הוֹתִירוּ לִשְׁנֵיהֶן רַבִּי יְהוּדָה.] מַאי טַעֲמָא דְּרַבִּי יוּדָן. שֶׁלֹּא נִתְכַּוֵּון הַמּוֹכֵר לְזַכּוֹת אֶלָּא לְבַעַל הַמָּעוֹת. וְלָמָּה אֵין חוֹלֵק עִמּוֹ. שֶׁאָסוּר לֵיהָנוֹת מֵחֲבֵירוֹ. מֵעַתָּה אֲפִילוּ אָמַר לוֹ לִיקַח לוֹ חִטִּים וְלָקַח לוֹ חִטִּים. [אָמַר רַבִּי יוֹחָנָן. בְּשָׁעָה שֶׁאָמַר לוֹ לִיקַח לוֹ בָּהֶן חִטִּין וְלָקַח לוֹ חִטִּין] לֹא נִתְכַּוֵּון הַמּוֹכֵר לְזַכּוֹת אֶלָּא לְבַעַל הַמָּעוֹת. וּבְשָׁעָה שֶׁאָמַר לוֹ לִיקַח לוֹ חִטִּים וְלָקַח לוֹ שְׂעוֹרִים לֹא נִתְכַּוֵּון מוֹכֵר לְזַכּוֹת אֶלָּא לַלּוֹקֵחַ וְקִיֵּים מַה בְּיָדֵיהּ. אָמַר רַבִּי נָסָא. בְּשָׁעָה שֶׁקִּיֵּים שְׁלִיחוּתוֹ לֹא נִתְכַּוֵּון הַמּוֹכֵר לְזַכּוֹת לְבַעַל הַמָּעוֹת. לֹא קִיֵּים שְׁלִיחוּתוֹ נִתְכַּוֵּון לְזַכּוֹת לַלּוֹקֵחַ. וְלָמָּה חוֹלֵק עִמּוֹ. אָמַר. הוֹאִיל וּבָאת לוֹ הֲנָייָה מִתַּחַת יָדוֹ אַף הוּא חוֹלֵק עִמּוֹ.

It was stated: One gives money to another to buy wheat for him, but the man bought barley. If it went down in price, it went down in price for him; if it rose in price, it rose for him[58]. We stated otherwise[59]: "If it went down in price, it went down in price for him; if it rose in price, it rose for both of them.[60]" [61][He who said if it went down in price, it went down in price for him; if it rose in price, it rose for him, is Rebbi Meïr. What is Rebbi Meïr's reason? Because the seller intended to transfer ownership only to the buyer[62]. But he who said, if it went down in price, it went down in price for him; if it rose in price, it rose for both of them, is Rebbi Jehudah.] What is Rebbi Jehudah's reason? Because the seller intended to transfer ownership only to the owner of the money[63]. Why does he (not)[64] split with him? Because it is forbidden to take advantage of another person[65]. Then even if one gave him money to buy wheat and he bought wheat?[66] [67][Rebbi Joḥanan said, if he had given money to buy wheat and he bought wheat,] the seller intended to transfer ownership only to the owner of the money. If he had given money to buy wheat and he bought barley, the seller intended to transfer ownership only to the buyer, who is stuck with what he has on his hands. Rebbi Nasa said, if he was true to his agency, did the seller not intend to transfer ownership to the owner of the money? If he was not true to his agency, he intended to transfer ownership to the buyer[68]. Then why does he split with him? He said, because he realizes a profit by means of the other man's money, he splits with him[65].

58  Since the agent did not fulfill the conditions of his agency, he acquired the barley for himself and has to carry the entire financial risk in selling the barley and buying wheat instead. Since the risk is entirely the agent's, the eventual gain also is his.

59  Tosephta *Bava meṣi'a* 4:20.

60  The unfaithful agent is disadvantaged. Nevertheless, one has to find a reason for the unequal treatment of loss and gain.

61  Added from E; there is no Genizah text for the remainder of the Tractate. The addition seems necessary and the oversight of the Leiden scribe is easily explained. In the Babli, 102b, the identification of the Tannaïm is ascribed to R. Joḥanan who, however, is quoted there to the effect that R. Jehudah does not accept that unfaithful execution of an agency makes the agent the owner of the object acquired.

62  In *Demay* 6:12 (Notes 194-196), this opinion is attributed to R. Jehudah. Since ownership is transferred when the seller hands over the goods, it matters to whom the seller intended to transfer title. Usually the seller does not know whether the buyer is acting on his own account or as an agent; the law will have to tell the seller what to intend.

63  In *Demay* 6:12 (Notes 194-196), this opinion is attributed to R. Yose. R. Meïr is not mentioned there.

64  It seems that this word should be deleted; it is missing in the quote given by *Bet Yosef, Ḥošen Mišpaṭ* §123.

65  One should not trade with another person's money. In the Babli, *Bava meṣi'a* 117b, this is a statement of R. Joḥanan.

66  According to R. Jehudah, anything bought through an agent should need another transfer of ownership from agent to principal. This clearly is not practice.

67  Added from E, not in L.

68  R. Nasa agrees with R. Joḥanan in practice but formulates it in a way applicable to any situation.

(7a line 12) הָתִיב רִבִּי שְׁמוּאֵל בַּר בָּא קוֹמֵי רִבִּי יוֹחָנָן. וְהָתַנִּינָן. אֶחָד הַמַּקְדִּישׁ נְכָסָיו וְאֶחָד הַמַּעֲרִיךְ עַצְמוֹ אֵין לוֹ בִּכְסוּת אִשְׁתּוֹ וּבָנָיו. אָמַר. לֹא עָלַת עַל דַעְתּוֹ לוֹמַר בִּכְסוּת אִשְׁתּוֹ וּבָנָיו. וְהָתַנִּינָן. עֶרְכִּי עָלַי. כֵּיוָן שֶׁאָמַר עֶרְכִּי עָלַי לֹא קָבַע לְעַצְמוֹ אֶלָּא נ סֶלַע. הָאוֹמֵר. עֶרְכִּי עָלַי עַל מְנָת שֶׁלֹא לְסַדֵּר מַה שֶׁעַל אִשְׁתִּי וּבָנָי. רִבִּי נָסָא בְשֵׁם רִבִּי בּוּן בַּר חִייָה. הָאוֹמֵר. עֶרְכִּי עָלַי עַל מְנָת שֶׁלֹּא לְסַדֵּר מֵחֵפֶץ פְּלוֹנִי. אֵין מְסַדְּרִין לוֹ מֵאוֹתוֹ חֵפֶץ. רַב הוֹשַׁעְיָה בְשֵׁם שְׁמוּאֵל בַּר אַבָּא. זֹאת אוֹמֶרֶת שֶׁאֵין שָׁמִין עֲרָכִין מִן הַמִּטַּלְטְלִין דְּבַר תּוֹרָה אֶלָּא מִדִּבְרֵיהֶן.

Rebbi Samuel bar Abba objected before Rebbi Joḥanan. Did we not state[69]: "Both the person who dedicates[70] and the one who vows his own valuation[71] exclude their wives' and children's clothing.[72]" He answered, nobody thought to include their wives' and children's clothing[73]. But did we not state: "My valuation on myself"; at the moment when he said, my valuation on myself, he only obligated himself for fifty tetradrachmas[71]. If he says, my valuation on myself on condition not to pledge what is worn by my wife and children? Rebbi Nasa in the name of Samuel bar Abba: One who says, my valuation on myself on condition not to pledge a particular thing, one cannot use that particular thing as a pledge[74]. Rav Hoshaia in the name of Samuel bar Abba: This implies that one does not foreclose valuations from movables by biblical decree[75] but only from the rabbis.

69 Mishnah 'Arakhin 6:5.
70 He dedicates his entire property to the Temple. The administrators of the Temple have to foreclose all of his properties.
71 He vows the amount specified in Lev. 27:1-8 as valuation, which for an adult male is fixed in v. 3 as 50 holy sheqel, interpreted as 50 tetradrachmas (Qiddushin 1:1, Note 339).
72 The Mishnah there also excludes "dye which was dyed for them (the wife and children)." If R. Joḥanan is correct and by law the seller intends

to benefit the owner of the money by which he is paid, who told the dyer or the clothier to transfer his intent from the husband, the giver of the money, to the wife and children, the beneficiaries?

73 The problem in *Arakhin* has nothing to do with our problem here since a vow is always subject to the exclusions stipulated by the person making the vow.

74 Again, this is a reformulation of the previous statement in a form universally applicable.

75 If the administrators of the Temple operated according to a biblical decree, all stipulations would be invalid (cf. *Ketubot* 9:1, Note 5). If stipulations are respected, the process of foreclosure of movables cannot be biblical.

(fol. 6c) **משנה ז:** הַגּוֹזֵל אֶת חֲבֵירוֹ שָׁוֶה פְרוּטָה וְנִשְׁבַּע לוֹ יוֹלִיכֶנּוּ אַחֲרָיו אֲפִילוּ לְמָדַי. לֹא יִתֵּן לֹא לִבְנוֹ וְלֹא לִשְׁלוּחוֹ אֲבָל נוֹתֵן לִשְׁלִיחַ בֵּית דִּין. וְאִם מֵת יַחֲזִיר לְיוֹרְשָׁיו.

**Mishnah 7**: He who robbed at least a *peruṭa*'s worth from a fellow man and swore to him[76] should deliver it to him even in Media[77]. He should deliver neither to [the victim's] son nor to his agent[78], but he may deliver to an agent of the court[79], and if [the victim] had died, he has to make restitution to his heirs.

**משנה ח:** נָתַן לוֹ אֶת הַקֶּרֶן וְלֹא נָתַן לוֹ אֶת הַחוֹמֶשׁ מָחַל לוֹ עַל הַקֶּרֶן וְלֹא מָחַל לוֹ עַל הַחוֹמֶשׁ מָחַל לוֹ עַל זֶה וְעַל זֶה חוּץ מִפָּחוֹת מִשְׁוֵה פְרוּטָה בַּקֶּרֶן אֵינוֹ צָרִיךְ לֵילֵךְ אַחֲרָיו.

**Mishnah 8**: If he had returned the capital[80] but not the fifth[1,81], or [the victim] had forgiven him the capital but not the fifth or had forgiven him both except for less than a *peruṭa*'s worth of the capital[82], he need not follow him.

**משנה ט**: נָתַן לוֹ אֶת הַחוֹמֶשׁ וְלֹא נָתַן לוֹ אֶת הַקֶּרֶן מָחַל לוֹ עַל הַחוֹמֶשׁ וְלֹא מָחַל לוֹ עַל הַקֶּרֶן מָחַל לוֹ עַל זֶה וְעַל זֶה חוּץ מִשָּׁוֶה פְרוּטָה בַּקֶּרֶן צָרִיךְ לֵילֵךְ אַחֲרָיו.

**Mishnah 9**: If he had returned the fifth but not the capital, or [the victim] had forgiven him the fifth but not the capital or had forgiven him both except for a *peruṭa*'s worth of the capital, he has to follow him.

**משנה י**: נָתַן לוֹ אֶת הַקֶּרֶן וְנִשְׁבַּע לוֹ עַל הַחוֹמֶשׁ הֲרֵי זֶה מְשַׁלֵּם חוֹמֶשׁ עַל חוֹמֶשׁ עַד שֶׁיִּתְמָעֵט הַקֶּרֶן פָּחוֹת מִשָּׁוֶה פְרוּטָה. וְכֵן בְּפִקָּדוֹן אוֹ בִתְשׂוּמֶת יָד אוֹ בְגָזֵל אוֹ עָשַׁק אֶת עֲמִיתוֹ אוֹ מָצָא אֲבֵדָה וְכִחֵשׁ בָּהּ וְנִשְׁבַּע עַל שָׁקֶר הֲרֵי זֶה מְשַׁלֵּם קֶרֶן וְחוֹמֶשׁ וְאָשָׁם.

**Mishnah 10**: If he paid the capital but swore on the fifth, he pays a fifth for the fifth until the capital[83] becomes less than a *peruṭa*'s worth. And so "for a deposit, or a partnership, or robbery, or if he oppressed his neighbor, or found lost property and denied it, and swore falsely,[84]" has to pay the capital, and a fifth, and a reparation sacrifice.

76  The victim had asked him to return the robbed item when he swore that he had not robbed him. When later he admits to the robbery, *Lev.* 5:23-25 makes it clear that after a false oath there can be no atonement nor any divine forgiveness until the falsely denied debt was paid in full. The "fifth" is computed from above, a fifth of the entire payment which is a fourth of the amount of the robbery.

77  Meaning any far-away place which is difficult to reach.

78  While one can liquidate a debt through the creditor's agent, one cannot fulfill the religious duty of restitution by proxy.

79  Duly appointed in a public act at the request of the victim (cf. *Bava meṣi'a* 3:6).

80  The value of the robbed item.

81  The verse requires personal restitution. The additional 25% constitute a fine; it is additional money, not restitution, and can be liquidated by agent or by mail.

82  Less than a *peruṭa*'s worth is not money; cf. *Qiddušin* 1:1, Note 7.

83  As is explained in the Halakhah, the "capital" is the object of the false

oath. For the embezzlement or robbery, the "fifth" is 25% of the original amount. For a false oath about these 25%, the additional fine is 6.25% of the original amount. In the next step, 1.5625% would have to be added and so on. But once the amount in dispute becomes less than a *peruṭa*'s worth, the process stops since that amount no longer represents money.

84  Lev. 5:21.

(7a line 20) **הלכה ז:** הַגּוֹזֵל אֶת חֲבֵירוֹ שָׁוֶה פְרוּטָה כול'. כֵּינִי מַתְנִיתָא. עַד שֶׁיִּתְמָעֵט חוֹמֶשׁ הָאַחֲרוֹן פָּחוֹת מִשָּׁוֶה פְרוּטָה. אָמַר רִבִּי יוֹנָתָן. בִּנְתִינַת חוֹמֶשׁ נַעֲשָׂה חוֹמֶשׁ קֶרֶן. לֹא אַתְיָא אֶלָּא בְשָׁעַת עֵדִים וּבְשָׁעַת קָרְבָּן.

**Halakhah 7:** "He who robbed at least a *peruṭa*'s worth from a fellow man," etc. So is the Mishnah: Until the last fifth becomes less than a *peruṭa*'s worth[85]. Rebbi Jonathan said: By handing over the fifth, the fifth becomes capital[86]. This only applies with witnesses[87] and at the time of sacrifices[88].

85  This refers to Mishnah 10, cf. Note 83.

86  If the robber starts paying the fifth, it becomes capital in the terminology of the Mishnah.

87  For if the robber confessed in presence of the victim and the latter agreed to be paid later, the sum becomes a loan and has to be paid under the law of loans rather than that of restitution; it can be repaid to the creditor's agent. The Babli, 108a, disagrees and holds that the fifth be due only on the confession by the robber but not on the testimony of witnesses. The explanations of Ibn Ezra (*Num.* 5:7) and Ḥizquni (*Lev.* 5:24) who require a simple fifth on the confession and two fifths on testimony of witnesses are based on the Yerushalmi.

88  Since payment of the fifth is stated as a precondition to atonement by sacrifice, the payment of the fifth cannot be enforced in the absence of a Temple; cf. Rashi 63b, *s.v.* הודה מעצמו.

(fol. 6c) **משנה יא:** אֵיכָן פִּקְדּוֹנִי. אָמַר לוֹ אָבַד מַשְׁבִּיעֲךָ אֲנִי וְאָמַר אָמֵן וְהָעֵדִים מְעִידִין אוֹתוֹ שֶׁאֲכָלוֹ מְשַׁלֵּם אֶת הַקֶּרֶן. הוֹדָה מֵעַצְמוֹ מְשַׁלֵּם קֶרֶן וְחוֹמֶשׁ וְאָשָׁם.

**Mishnah 11:** Where is my deposit? He told him 'it was lost[89]'. 'I will make you swear' and he said 'amen'[90]. If witnesses testify against him that he ate it, he pays the capital[91]. If he confessed on his own, he has to pay the capital, and a fifth, and a reparation sacrifice.

**משנה יב:** אֵיכָן פִּקְדּוֹנִי. אָמַר לוֹ נִגְנַב מַשְׁבִּיעֲךָ אֲנִי וְאָמַר אָמֵן וְהָעֵדִים מְעִידִין אוֹתוֹ שֶׁגְּנָבוֹ מְשַׁלֵּם תַּשְׁלוּמֵי כָּפֶל. הוֹדָה מֵעַצְמוֹ מְשַׁלֵּם קֶרֶן וְחוֹמֶשׁ וְאָשָׁם.

**Mishnah 12:** Where is my deposit? He told him 'it was stolen'. 'I will make you swear' and he said 'amen'. If witnesses testify against him that he stole it, he pays double restitution[92]. If he confessed on his own, he has to pay the capital, and a fifth, and a reparation sacrifice[93].

89   As an unpaid trustee he does not have to pay if it was lost and the trustee never had used it for himself.
90   This is the oath.
91   As a robber; cf. Note 87.
92   For the unpaid trustee who claimed falsely that the deposit was stolen, double restitution is required by Ex. 22:8.
93   Nobody pays multiple restitution on his own confession since a confession is not acceptable in a criminal trial. He pays a fifth and brings the sacrifice for the false oath, Lev. 5:23-25.

(7a line 23) **הלכה יא:** אֵיכָן פִּקְדּוֹנִי. וְאָמַר לוֹ אָבַד כוֹל'. תַּנֵּי. אֵין מְקַבְּלִין פִּיקָּדוֹן מִנָּשִׁים וַעֲבָדִים וּקְטַנִּים. קִיבֵּל מֵאִשָּׁה יַחֲזִיר לָהּ. מֵתָה יַחֲזִיר לְבַעֲלָהּ. מֵעֶבֶד יַחֲזִיר לוֹ. וְאִם מֵת יַחֲזִיר לְרַבּוֹ. מִקָּטָן יַחֲזִיר לוֹ. מֵת יַחֲזִיר לְאָבִיו. וְעוֹשֶׂה בָהֶן סְגוּלָּה. וְכוּלָּן שֶׁאָמְרוּ בִּשְׁעַת מוֹתָן יִינָּתְנוּ לִפְלוֹנִי שֶׁהֵן שֶׁלּוֹ. יַעֲשֶׂה פֵּירוּשׁ לְפֵירוּשׁוֹ. רִבִּי זְבִידָא בְּשֵׁם רִבִּי בָּא בַּר מָמָל. וּבִלְבַד בְּעֵדִים. כְּהָדָא אִיתָת דְּרִבִּי בָּא בַּר חָנָה מִי דָּמְכָא אָמְרָה. אָהֵן קִידּוּשָׁא דִבְרַתִּי. וְהוּא אָמַר.

לֵית הוּא אֶלָּא דִידִי. אָתָא עוֹבְדָא קוֹמֵי רַב אָמַר. אֵין אָדָם מָצוּי לְשַׁקֵּר בִּשְׁעַת מִיתָה.

**Halakhah 11**: "Where is my deposit? He told him 'it was lost'," etc. It was stated[94]: "One does not accept deposits from women, or slaves, or underage children[95]. If one accepted from a woman, he should return it to her; if she died, he should return it to her husband[96]. If one accepted from a slave, he should return it to him; if he died, he should return it to his master. From an underage child, he should return it to him, if he died he should return it to his father, and make it a safe investment[97]. If any of these said at the moment of their death, it should be given to X because it is his property, one should follow his interpretation[98]." Rebbi Zebida in the name of Rebbi Abba bar Mamal: Only before witnesses[99]. As the following[100]: When Rebbi Abba bar Hana's wife was dying, she said, these rings belong to my daughter. But he said no, they are mine. The case came before Rav who said, people are not given to lying at the time of their death[101].

94  Tosephta 11:1; Babli *Bava batra* 51b.

95  Since usually they have no independent property, one has to suspect that the deposit might be stolen property.

96  Who is her heir.

97  It seems that this sentence should be rearranged as in the Tosephta: "From an underage child, he should make it a safe investment, return it to him (once he reaches the age in which he legally can do business); if he died he should return it to his father."

98  The translation follows the extensive discussion of the expression פירוש לפירושו by S. Lieberman in *Tosefta kiFshutah Neziqin*, p. 134.

99  Dispositions of a last will which do not follow the general rule should be executed only in the presence of witnesses, to protect the trustee against claims of the legal heirs.

100  Another version of the same story is told in the Babli, *Bava batra* 52a. There, the husband is Abba bar bar Hana. This is the correct attribution

since Abba bar Ḥana, the elder R. Ḥiyya's brother, died before the birth of his son, therefore also before his wife. In Halakhah 10:1, "R. Abba bar Ḥana" speaks of "my oncle R. Ḥiyya". This proves that the person called Abba bar Ḥana in the Yerushalmi is called Abba bar bar Ḥana in the Babli.

101 A statement of Rava in the Babli, *Bava batra* 175a.

**משנה יג**: הַגּוֹזֵל אֶת אָבִיו וְנִשְׁבַּע לוֹ וָמֵת הֲרֵי זֶה מְשַׁלֵּם קֶרֶן וְחוֹמֶשׁ לְבָנָיו אוֹ לְאֶחָיו וְאִם אֵינוֹ רוֹצֶה אוֹ שֶׁאֵין לוֹ לֹוֶה וּבַעֲלֵי הַחוֹב בָּאִין וְנִפְרָעִין. (fol. 6d)

**Mishnah 13**: He who robbed from his father and swore to him when he[102] died has to pay capital and fifth to his sons or brothers[103]. But if he refuses[104], or does not have the money, he takes a loan and the creditors come and make themselves paid[105].

**משנה יד**: הָאוֹמֵר לִבְנוֹ קוֹנָם שֶׁאַתָּה נֶהֱנֶה לִי אִם מֵת יוֹרִישֶׁנּוּ. בְּחַיַּי וּבְמוֹתִי אִם מֵת לֹא יוֹרִישֶׁנּוּ וְיִתֵּן לְבָנָיו אוֹ לְאֶחָיו וְאִם אֵין לוֹ לֹוֶה וּבַעֲלֵי הַחוֹב בָּאִין וְנִפְרָעִין.

**Mishnah 14**: If somebody says to his son: A *qônām*[106] that you cannot enjoy anything from me, when he dies he can inherit from him[107]. During my lifetime and after my death, when he dies he cannot inherit from him but should give it[108] to his sons or his brothers, and if he has nothing[109] he may take a loan; the creditors come and make themselves paid[105].

102 The father.
103 Since the Yerushalmi does not discuss this Mishnah, we do not know whether the intention is that the robber has to pay to the father's brothers or other sons ot to his own sons or brothers. In any case he cannot obtain atonement as long as a *peruta* from the robbery remains in his hand.
104 He does not want to pay anything to his family.
105 He takes a loan, pays his obligations, and when the loan comes due directs the creditor to the

recipients of his payments. Then he has fulfilled his obligation without losing any of his money.

106 An expression of making a vow; Mishnah *Nedarim* 1:1.

107 Since a deceased person has no property, the estate is no longer the father's money.

108 The inheritance.

109 To eat.

(7a line 31) **הלכה יד:** הָאוֹמֵר לִבְנוֹ קוֹנָם שֶׁאַתְּ נֶהֱנֶה לִי כול'. אָמַר רִבִּי יִרְמְיָה. חֲמֵי אֵיךְ תַּנִּינָן הָכָא. הָאוֹמֵר לִבְנוֹ. קוֹנָם שֶׁאַתְּ נֶהֱנֶה לִי. אִם מֵת יוֹרִשֵׁנּוּ. בְּחַיַּי וּבְמוֹתִי. אִם מֵת לֹא יוֹרִישֶׁנּוּ. וְהָתַנֵּי. בְּחַיַּי. אִם מֵת יִירָשֶׁנּוּ. בְּמוֹתִי. אִם מֵת יִירָשֶׁנּוּ. בְּחַיַּי וּבְמוֹתִי. אִם מֵת לֹא יוֹרִישֶׁנּוּ. מַה בֵּין אָהֵן דָּמַר חָדָא חָדָא לָהֶן דָּמַר תַּרְתֵּי תַּרְתֵּי. רַב יִרְמִיָה וְרִבִּי יוֹסֵי בֶּן חֲנִינָה תְּרֵיהוֹן אָמְרִין. קוֹנָם לְבַיִת זֶה שֶׁאֵינִי נִכְנָס בְּחַיַּי וּבְמוֹתִי. לְבַיִת זֶה. אֲסָרוֹ עָלָיו בֵּין בַּחַיִּים בֵּין לְאַחַר מִיתָה. אָמַר רִבִּי יוֹסֵי. תַּנִּינָן בִּנְזִיקִין מַה דְּלֹא תַנִּינָן בִּנְדָרִים. קוֹנָם הֲנָייַת נְכָסַיי אִילוּ עָלַי בְּחַיַּי וּבְמוֹתִי. כֵּיוָן שֶׁאָמַר. אִילוּ. אֲסָרָן עָלָיו בֵּין בַּחַיִּים בֵּין לְאַחַר מִיתָה.

**Halakhah 14:** "If somebody says to his son: A *qônām* that you cannot enjoy anything from me," etc. [110]Rebbi Jeremiah said, look what we did state here: "If somebody says to his son, 'a *qônām* that you can not enjoy anything from me,' if he dies, the son inherits; 'during my lifetime and after my death,' if he dies, he cannot inherit." Did we not state, 'during my lifetime', he inherits; 'after my death', he inherits, 'during my lifetime and after my death', he cannot inherit? What is the difference between the one who says it one by one and the one who says it by twos? Rav Jeremiah and Rebbi Yose ben Ḥanina both say, 'a *qônām* that I shall not enter this house during my lifetime and after my death', since he said "this house", he forbade it on himself during lifetime and after death. Rebbi Yose said, we have stated in *Neziqin* what we did not state in *Nedarim*: 'A *qônām* that I cannot enjoy these my properties during my lifetime and after my death,' from the moment he said "these" he forbade them to himself during his lifetime and after his death.

110  This text is a reformulation of a text in *Nedarim* 5:2, explained there in Notes 35-43.

**משנה טו:** (fol. 6d) הַגּוֹזֵל אֶת הַגֵּר וְנִשְׁבַּע לוֹ וָמֵת הֲרֵי זֶה מְשַׁלֵּם קֶרֶן וְחוֹמֶשׁ לַכֹּהֲנִים וְאָשָׁם לַמִּזְבֵּחַ שֶׁנֶּאֱמַר וְאִם אֵין לָאִישׁ גּוֹאֵל לְהָשִׁיב הָאָשָׁם אֵלָיו הָאָשָׁם וגו׳. הָיָה מַעֲלֶה אֶת הַכֶּסֶף וְאֶת הָאָשָׁם וָמֵת הַכֶּסֶף יִנָּתֵן לְבָנָיו וְהָאָשָׁם יִרְעֶה עַד שֶׁיִּסְתָּאֵב וְיִמָּכֵר וְיִפְּלוּ דָמָיו לִנְדָבָה. נָתַן אֶת הַכֶּסֶף לְאַנְשֵׁי מִשְׁמָר וָמֵת אֵין הַיּוֹרְשִׁין יְכוֹלִין לְהוֹצִיא מִיָּדָם שֶׁנֶּאֱמַר אִישׁ אֲשֶׁר יִתֵּן לַכֹּהֵן לוֹ יִהְיֶה.

**Mishnah 15**: One who robbed from a proselyte[111], swore to him, and [the proselyte] died, has to pay the capital and the fifth to the priests and the reparation offering to the altar as it is said[112]: "If the man has no heirs to give the reparation to, the reparation etc." If he was bringing the money and the reparation offering when he[113] died, the money should be given to his sons[114] and the reparation offering[115] shall graze until it becomes disqualified[116], then be sold, and the amount be given for voluntary offerings[117]. If he had given the money to the men of the watch[118] when he died, the heirs cannot ask it back from them since it is said[119]: "What a man give to a Cohen shall be the latter's."

111  Who failed to start a Jewish family. By becoming a Jew, he became a new person, no longer related to his previous Gentile family.

112  *Num.* 5:8: "If the man has no heirs to give the reparation to, the reparation shall be returned to the Eternal, to the priests, except for the atonement ram by which he can reach atonement." While the sacrificial meat of the ram is eaten by the priests in the Temple courtyard, they eat from the Eternal's table and it never becomes their property.

113  The robber.

114  His death was atonement. Since he does not need atonement after death, the money does not need to be given to the priests; it becomes part of the estate.

115 If it was dedicated as such by its owner, the dedication cannot be undone.

116 As a sacrifice, either by developing a defect or outliving its third birthday (Mishnah *Parah* 1:3).

117 The account from which elevation offerings were paid if otherwise the altar would have been empty.

118 The priests were organized into 24 watches; each watch served from one Sabbath morning to the next. The watch on duty had the exclusive rights to all emoluments accruing to priests during their term of office.

119 *Num.* 5:10.

(7a line 40) **הלכה טו:** הַגּוֹזֵל אֶת הַגֵּר כול׳. חִילְפָּיי וְרִבִּי יוֹסֵי בַּר חֲנִינָה אָמְרֵי. דְּרִבִּי יוֹסֵי הַגְּלִילִי הִיא. דְּדָרַשׁ רִבִּי יוֹסֵי הַגְּלִילִי. בַּמֶּה הַכָּתוּב מְדַבֵּר. בְּגוֹזֵל אֶת הַגֵּר וְנִשְׁבַּע לוֹ וָמֵת שֶׁמְּשַׁלֵּם קֶרֶן וָחוֹמֶשׁ לַכֹּהֲנִים וְאָשָׁם לַמִּזְבֵּחַ. וְאִם אֵין לָאִישׁ גּוֹאֵל. הַטָּעוּן כַּפָּרָה חַיָּיב. יָצָא זֶה שֶׁאֵין טָעוּן כַּפָּרָה. דָּרַשׁ רִבִּי עֲקִיבָה כְּשֶׁבָּא מֵזוּפְרִין. בַּמֶּה הַכָּתוּב מְדַבֵּר. בְּגוֹזֵל אֶת הַגֵּר וְנִשְׁבַּע לוֹ וָמֵת שֶׁמְּשַׁלֵּם קֶרֶן וָחוֹמֶשׁ לַכֹּהֲנִים וְאָשָׁם לַמִּזְבֵּחַ. שֶׁנֶּאֱמַר וְאִם אֵין לָאִישׁ גּוֹאֵל וגו׳. אֵין לָךְ אָדָם בְּיִשְׂרָאֵל שֶׁאֵין לוֹ גּוֹאֵל אֶלָּא זֶה הַגֵּר. רַב וְרֵישׁ לָקִישׁ אָמְרֵי. רִבִּי עֲקִיבָה הִיא. דְּאָמַר תּוּשָׁב אַשְׁמָה בְּכָל־מָקוֹם.

**Halakhah 15**: "One who robbed from a proselyte," etc. Hilfai and Rebbi Yose bar Hanina said, this is Rebbi Yose the Galilean's, as Rebbi Yose the Galiean explained: Of what does the verse speak? About one who robbed from a proselyte, swore to him, who then died, that he would pay the capital and the fifth to the priests and the reparation offering to the altar. "If the man have no relative," he who needs atonement is obligated; this excludes the one who does not need atonement. Rebbi Aqiba explained when he came from Zephyrium[120]: About one who robbed from a proselyte, swore to him, who then died, that he would pay the capital and the fifth to the priests and the reparation offering to the altar, as it is said: "If the man have no relative," etc. The only person in Israel who has no relative is the proselyte. Rav and Rebbi Simeon ben

Laqish said, it is Rebbi Aqiba's who said that the wrongly acquired property has to be returned in any case[121].

120 Possibly the town in Cyprus (Cape Paphos).

121 The paragraph is elliptic; its meaning can be ascertained from the parallels in the Babli 109a, Tosephta 10:16,17, *Sifry Num.* #4 (*Num. rabba* 8(7), *Yalquṭ* #701). Both R. Yose the Galilean and R. Aqiba agree that "the man without relative" must be a proselyte who failed to start a Jewish family. (In *Sifry*, this statement is attributed to R. Ismael.) The rules of inheritance imply that the property of the deceased proselyte becomes ownerless; therefore anything held by another person at the proselyte's death becomes property of the holder. If the robber confessed his guilt after the proselyte's death, the money becomes the Eternal's property Who gives it to the priests. If the robber confessed his guilt to the proselyte, even if the proselyte agrees to payment at a later date, turning the debt into a loan, when he dies the robber does not acquire the money since he cannot atone for his guilt as long as the money is in his hand. If the robber dies before he returned the money, for R. Yose the Galilean the money becomes part of the robber's estate since the dead "do not need atonement." R. Aqiba holds that the money does not become part of the estate since "wrongly acquired property has to be returned in any case," and the heirs have to turn the money over to the priests. *Sifry* notes that R. Aqiba agreed with R. Yose the Galilean before he went to Zephyrium but there changed his opinion. (The Tosephta attributes R. Yose the Galilean's argument to R. Aqiba).

**משנה יו:** נָתַן הַכֶּסֶף לִיהוֹיָרִיב וְאָשָׁם לִידַעְיָה יָצָא. אָשָׁם לִיהוֹיָרִיב וְכֶסֶף לִידַעְיָה אִם קַיָּים הָאָשָׁם יַקְרִיבוּהוּ בְּנֵי יְדַעְיָה וְאִם לָאו יַחֲזוֹר וְיָבִיא אָשָׁם אַחֵר שֶׁהַמֵּבִיא גְזֵילוֹ עַד שֶׁלֹּא הֵבִיא אֲשָׁמוֹ יָצָא. אֲשָׁמוֹ עַד שֶׁלֹּא הֵבִיא גְזֵילוֹ לֹא יָצָא. נָתַן אֶת הַקֶּרֶן וְלֹא נָתַן אֶת הַחוֹמֶשׁ אֵין חוֹמֶשׁ מְעַכֵּב. (fol. 6d)

**Mishnah 16**: If he gave the money to Yehoiarib and the reparation offering to Yedaiah[122], he has fulfilled his obligation. The reparation offering to Yehoiarib and the money to Yedaiah, if the offering still is alive it should be brought by Yedaiah[123]; otherwise he was to come back and bring another reparation offering; for he who brings the robbed item before he brings the reparation offering has fulfilled his obligation, but he who brings the reparation offering before he brings the robbed item has not fulfilled his obligation. If he paid the capital but not the fifth, the fifth is no obstacle[124].

122 In the list of watches, *1Chr.* 24:7-18, Yehoiarib is the first and Yedaiah the second watch. The restitution may precede the offering but cannot follow it. As explained at the end of the Mishnah, the reparation offering (whether for swearing falsely to a native born Jew or to a proselyte) cannot be accepted by the Temple if it was not ascertained that restitution was made since both in *Lev.* 5:25 as in *Num.* 5:8 the sacrifice is clearly demanded *after* restitution had been made. There can be no ritual cleansing if the human aspect was not attended to.

123 Since the priests of Yehoiarib have no right to officiate in Yedaiah's week; this is the "right sold by the forefathers" (*Deut.* 18:8).

124 Non-payment of the fifth does not invalidate the sacrifice but the sacrifice does not absolve from paying the fifth at a later date.

(7a line 48) **הלכה יו:** נָתַן אֶת הַכֶּסֶף לִיהוֹיָרִיב כול'. רִבִּי חִזְקִיָּה אָמַר. בִּשְׁתֵּי שַׁבָּתוֹת פְּלִיגִין. רִבִּי יוֹסֵי אוֹמֵר. בְּשַׁבָּת אַחַת. מָאן דָּמַר. בִּשְׁתֵּי שַׁבָּתוֹת. נָתַן אֶת הַכֶּסֶף לִיהוֹיָרִיב בְּמִשְׁמָר יְדַעְיָה וְאָשָׁם לִידַעְיָה בְּמִשְׁמָר יְהוֹיָרִיב יָצָא. רִבִּי אוֹמֵר. אִם כְּדִבְרֵי רִבִּי יוּדָן אִם הִקְרִיבוּ בְּנֵי יְהוֹיָרִיב אֶת הָאָשָׁם לֹא נִתְכַּפֵּר לָהֶן אֶלָּא יוֹלִיךְ אֶת הַכֶּסֶף מִבְּנֵי יְדַעְיָה אֶל בְּנֵי יְהוֹיָרִיב. וְיַקְרִיבוּ בְּנֵי יְהוֹיָרִיב אֶת הָאָשָׁם וְיִתְכַּפֵּר לָהֶן. זֹאת אוֹמֶרֶת. אַנְשֵׁי מִשְׁמָר שֶׁזָּכוּ מִשְׁמָר שֶׁלֹּא בְשַׁבָּתָן אֵין מוֹצִיאִין אוֹתוֹ מִיָּדָן. מָאן דָּמַר. בְּשַׁבָּת אַחַת פְּלִיגִין. נָתַן אֶת הַכֶּסֶף לִיהוֹיָרִיב בְּמִשְׁמָר יְדַעְיָה אָשָׁם לִידַעְיָה בְּמִשְׁמָר יְהוֹיָרִיב לֹא יָצָא כוּל'. זֹאת אוֹמֶרֶת. אַנְשֵׁי מִשְׁמָר שֶׁזָּכוּ בְקָרְבָּן בְּשַׁבָּתָן אֵין מוֹצִיאִין אוֹתָן מִיָּדָן. וְאִם עִיבֵּר מִשְׁמָר בְּנֵי יְהוֹיָרִיב. כֵּינִי מַתְנִיתָא. וְאִם הָיָה שֶׁעִיבֵּר לְאַחַר יָמִים זָכוּ בְּנֵי

יְהוֹיָרִיב אֶת הָאָשָׁם לֹא נִתְכַּפֵּר לָהֶן. אֶלָּא יוֹלִיךְ אֶת הַכֶּסֶף מִבְּנֵי יְדַעְיָה אֵצֶל בְּנֵי יְהוֹיָרִיב וְיַקְרִיבוּ בְנֵי יְדַעְיָה אֶת הָאָשָׁם וְיִתְכַּפֵּר לָהֶנם. זֹאת אוֹמֶרֶת. אַנְשֵׁי מִשְׁמָר שֶׁזָּכוּ בְקָרְבָּן בְּשַׁבָּתָן. נִתְעַצְּלוּ וְלֹא הִקְרִיבוּהוּ מוֹצִיאִין אוֹתָן מִיָּדוֹ.

**Halakhah 16**: "If he gave the money to Yehoiarib," etc. Rebbi Hizqiah said, they disagree[125] about two weeks, Rebbi Yose said about one week. He who said about two weeks, "if he gave the money to Yehoiarib on Yedaiah's watch and the reparation offering to Yedaiah on Yehoiarib's watch, he has fulfilled his obligation.[126] Rebbi said, following Rebbi Jehudah's words if the men from Yehoiarib offered the reparation offering there was no atonement; but the money should be transferred from the men of Yedaiah to the men of Yehoiarib; the men from Yehoiarib then shall offer the reparation offering for atonement." This implies that one removes the money given to men of a watch not during their week. He who said that they disagree about one week, if he gave the money to Yehoiarib on Yedaiah's watch and the reparation offering to Yedaiah on Yehoiarib's watch[127], means that he did not fulfill his obligation, etc. This implies that one does not remove a sacrifice which men of a watch received during their week. But if the watch of the men of Yehoiarib dragged their feet, then the *baraita* implies that they dragged their feet after the men of Yehoiarib received the reparation offering after days[128], and there is no atonement. But one has to transfer the money from the men of Yedaiah to the men of Yehoiarib, the men of Yedaiah[129] shall offer the reparation offering, and there will be atonement. This implies that if men of a watch received a sacrifice during their week but were lazy and did not offer it, one removes it from their hand.

125   There is no disagreement in the Mishnah. The entire Halakhah is based on the *baraita* quoted in the following; paralleled in Tosephta 10:18 (Babli 111a), except that in the text here the disagreement is missing.

126   What is missing here is the statement of the diagreement: "If the offering was given to Yehoiarib and the money to Yedaiah, R. Jehudah requires the money to be transferred to the offerers of the sacrifice, the Sages that the sacrifice be transferred to the recipients of the money."

Both watches acted incorrectly by not checking whether the money had been delivered before the sacrifice. If each watch received their part during their week then clearly the situation is that of the Mishnah where a new offering is needed if the first one is not available to the second watch. But if the second watch received the money at the same time the first received the sacrifice, then R. Jehudah and the Sages disagree about who has to give up his part.

127   The sacrifice one week before the delivery of the money.

128   The watch cannot keep the animal for 24 weeks until their turn comes again.

129   In E: "Yehoiarib". This clearly is a corruption. But the text common to both mss. is also incorrect. Since the hypothesis was that the money had been given to Yehoiarib, it is clear that one has to read: "One has to transfer the money from the men of *Yehoiarib* to the men of *Yedaiah*."

## הגוזל ומאכיל פרק עשירי

(fol. 7a) **משנה א**: הַגּוֹזֵל וּמַאֲכִיל אֶת בָּנָיו וּמַנִּיחַ לִפְנֵיהֶן פְּטוּרִין מִלְשַׁלֵּם. אִם הָיָה דָבָר שֶׁיֵּשׁ בּוֹ אַחֲרָיוּת נְכָסִים חַיָּיבִין לְשַׁלֵּם. אֵין פּוֹרְטִין לֹא מִתֵּיבַת הַמּוֹכְסִין וְלֹא מִכִּיס שֶׁל גַּבָּאִין וְאֵין נוֹטְלִין מֵהֶם צְדָקָה אֲבָל נוֹטֵל הוּא מִתּוֹךְ בֵּיתוֹ אוֹ מִן הַשּׁוּק.

**Mishnah 1**: If somebody robbed to feed his children and they inherited from him, they are not liable to pay[1]; if it was mortgageable property they have to pay[2]. One changes money[3] neither from the chest of the publican[4] nor the wallet of the tax collector and one does not accept charity from these, but one accepts from their house[5] or from the market place[5].

1   Even if they were the ones benefiting from the robbery.

2   A different formulation is in the Halakhah: "they have to return it"; cf. Note 14.

3   To exchange small coins for large or vice-versa. But one may take from them coins as change from a large coin used to pay the tolls even though the coins probably were taken by extortion.

4   The Mishnah presupposes the system of toll and tax farming where the contractor paid the government the expected amount of taxes in advance and then had to collect more than that amount to pay his employees and to make a profit. Since therefore he had to instruct his employees to collect more than was due by the government's computation, there is no toll or tax collector's box which does not contain money tainted by extortion.

5   Charity given by the publican or tax collector from his private money is not tainted; only that money collected in the course of his duty necessarily contains extortion money.

6   Where the publican or tax collector went in private affairs and pays from his own wallet.

(7b line 37) **הלכה א:** הַגּוֹזֵל וּמַאֲכִיל אֶת בָּנָיו כול'. תַּנֵּי. יִשְׂרָאֵל שֶׁלּוֶוה בְּרִיבִּית וְעָשָׂה תְשׁוּבָה חַייָב לְהַחֲזִיר. מֵת וְהִנִּיחַ לִפְנֵי בָנָיו עָלָיו הַכָּתוּב אוֹמֵר יָכִין וְצַדִּיק יִלְבָּשׁ. הִנִּיחַ לִפְנֵיהֶן פָּרָה אוֹ טַלִּית חַייָבִין לְהַחֲזִיר. אֲזַל תְּנַייָהּ לְגַזְלַייָא.

**Halakhah 1**: "If somebody robbed to feed his children," etc. It was stated[7]: "A Jew who is engaged in lending with interest and repented, has to return it[8]. If he died and left it to his children, about him the verse says 'he prepares but the just will wear it.[9]' If he left them a cow or a stole, they have to return it." He went and stated that for robberies[10].

7 Tosephta *Bava meṣi'a* 5:25-26; in a different version Babli 94b.

8 The ill-gotten gains.

9 *Job* 27:17. As usual, the reference is to the part of the verse not quoted: "he (the sinner) distributes clean money."

10 Even though the statement starts with illegal interest income, it is not usual to obtain a cow or a stole as interest. The last sentence, therefore, has to refer to robbed goods.

(7b line 40) אִם הָיָה דָבָר שֶׁיֵּשׁ לוֹ אַחֲרָיוּת נְכָסִים חַייָבִין לְהַחֲזִיר. אֵי זֶהוּ דָבָר שֶׁיֵּשׁ לוֹ אַחֲרָיוּת. רִבִּי יוֹנָתָן אוֹמֵר. בְּשֶׁהִנִּיחַ לִפְנֵיהֶן קַרְקַע. רֵישׁ לָקִישׁ אָמַר. בְּשֶׁהִנִּיחַ לִפְנֵיהֶן גּוּף הַגְּזִילָה. רַב אָמַר. יוֹרֵשׁ כִּמְשׁוּעְבָּד. כְּשֵׁם שֶׁאֵין מִלְוָה בְּעֵדִים גּוֹבָה מִמְּשׁוּעְבָּדִים כָּךְ אֵינָהּ גּוֹבָה מִיּוֹרְשִׁין. שְׁמוּאֵל אָמַר. דְּאִיקְנֵי אֵינוֹ גּוֹבָה מִמְּשׁוּעְבָּדִים. הָא מִבְּנֵי חָרֵי גּוֹבָה. וְלֵית הִיא פְּלִיגָא עַל רַב. דְּרַב אָמַר. יוֹרֵשׁ כִּמְשׁוּעְבָּד. כְּשֵׁם שֶׁאֵין מִלְוָה בְּעֵדִים גּוֹבָה מִמְּשׁוּעְבָּדִים כָּךְ אֵינָהּ גּוֹבָה מִיּוֹרְשִׁין. פָּתַר לָהּ בְּשֶׁהִנִּיחַ לִפְנֵיהֶן קַרְקַע. וַאֲפִילוּ כִשְׁמוּאֵל לֵית הִיא פְּלִיגָא. לֹא כֵן אָמַר שְׁמוּאֵל. דְּאִיקְנֵי אֵינוֹ גּוֹבָה מִמְּשׁוּעְבָּדִים. פָּתַר לָהּ בְּשֶׁהִנִּיחַ לִפְנֵיהֶן גּוּף הַגְּזִילָה.

"If it was mortgageable property they have to return it." What is mortgageable property? Rebbi Jonathan says, if they inherited real estate. Rebbi Simeon ben Laqish said, if they inherited robbed items[11]. Rav said, an heir is like the holder of encumbered property. Just as a loan executed before witnesses cannot be collected from encumbered property, so it cannot be collected from heirs[12]. Samuel said, what was received cannot be foreclosed on mortgaged property, but on free property it can be foreclosed[13]. But does [the Mishnah] not disagree with Rav? Since Rav said, an heir is like a holder of encumbered property; just as a loan executed before witnesses cannot be collected from encumbered property, so it cannot be foreclosed from heirs[14]. Explain it if he left them real estate[15]. But might it[16] not disagree with Samuel? Did not Samuel say, what was received cannot be foreclosed on mortgaged property? Explain it if they inherited robbed items[17].

11 The Babli, 113a, quotes this in the name of Rebbi; E reads "Johanan" instead of Jonathan.

12 *Giṭṭin* 3:8 (Note 146), 8:7 (Note 104), *Bava meṣi'a* 1:6; Babli 111b (in the name of Rami bar Ḥama). A loan executed without a public document is not subject to a title search; the loan cannot be collected either from mortgaged property or from the innocent buyer of property pledged for the oral loan.

13 Babli 111b, in the name of Rava. Since the loan made before witnesses can be collected from unencumbered property, it can be collected from unencumbered property of the estate.

In the Babli, *Bava batra* 175b, Samuel agrees with Rav that an undocumented loan cannot be collected from the heirs; the opinion expressed here, that it can be enforced against the heirs but not against buyers of the property, is attributed there (176a) to Rav Pappa and declared judicial practice.

14 But the Mishnah requires robbed real estate to be paid for. The question makes sense only in the formulation of the Mishnah, not the quote at the beginning of the present paragraph since both R. Jonathan and R. Simeon ben Laqish agree that originally robbed real estate available after the robber's death must be returned to its original owners.

15 There is no question of "paying for it", only of "returning it."

16 The Mishnah.

17 Which has to be returned according to everybody, for reasons other than the rules of foreclosure.

(7b line 50) גָּזַל טַלִּית וּנְתָנָהּ לְאַחֵר. רַבִּי לָעְזָר בְּשֵׁם רִבִּי חִיָּיה אָמַר. מוֹצִיאִין מֵרִאשׁוֹן וְלֹא מִשֵּׁינִי. רִבִּי יוֹחָנָן אָמַר בְּשֵׁם רִבִּי יַנַּאי. מוֹצִיאִין אַף מִן הַשֵּׁינִי. רִבִּי בָּא בַּר מָמָל אָמַר. אַף רִבִּי חִיָּיה כְּדַעְתֵּיהּ. דְּרִבִּי חִיָּיה אָמַר. מוֹצִיאִין אַף מִשֵּׁינִי.

[18]If he robbed a stole and gave it to another person. Rebbi Eleazar said in the name of Rebbi Ḥiyya, one takes away from the first one but not from the second[19]. Rebbi Joḥanan in the name of Rebbi Yannai said, one takes away even from the second. Rebbi Abba bar Mamal said, even Rebbi Ḥiyya will agree with this since Rebbi Ḥiyya said, one takes away even from the second[20].

18 This is a reformulation of the discussion in *Terumot* 7:5, Notes 92-95. The Babli, 115a, deals with the case that the robber sold the garment.

19 Tosephta 10:20.

20 In this version, R. Abba bar Mamal contradicts R. Eleazar. In the version of *Terumot,* one only states that R. Ḥiyya agrees that the robber cannot be sued if the recipient voluntarily gives the item back to its original owner.

(7b line 53) נִתְחַלְּפוּ כֵלָיו בְּבֵית הָאוּמָן יִשְׁתַּמֵּשׁ בָּהֶן וְיֵצֵא וִיבַקֵּשׁ אֶת שֶׁלּוֹ. בְּבֵית הָאָבֵל אוֹ בְּבֵית הַמִּשְׁתֶּה אַל יִשְׁתַּמֵּשׁ בָּהֶן אֶלָּא יֵצֵא וִיבַקֵּשׁ אֶת שֶׁלּוֹ. אָמַר רִבִּי בָּא בַּר חָנָה. לֹא הֲוָה רִבִּי חִיָּיה חֲבִיבִי פָּתַר לָהּ אֶלָּא כְּגוֹן הָדֵין בַּר קוֹרָא. שֶׁכָּל־הַנּוֹטֵל מֵאֶצְלוֹ נוֹטֵל בִּרְשׁוּת וְכָל־הַמֵּנִיחַ אֶצְלוֹ מֵנִיחַ בִּרְשׁוּת.

If his vessels were switched at the artisan's he may use them while he goes out and searches for his own. At a mourner's house or at a wedding, he may not use them while he goes out and searches for his own[21]. Rebbi Abba bar Ḥanan said, my uncle Rebbi Ḥiyya explained this[22] only as in the case of one Bar Qora where everybody who takes from him takes by permission and everybody who puts something up there does so with permission.

| | |
|---|---|
| 21 Babli *Bava batra* 46a, where the difference between both rules is explained it is stated that the artisan may sometimes sell vessels on the order | of their owner whereas a switch at a social function always is in error.<br>22 The permission to use the artisan's vessels. |

(7b line 57) הַגַּנָּבִים שֶׁבָּאוּ בַּמַּחְתֶּרֶת וְעָשׂוּ תְשׁוּבָה חַיָּיבִין לְהַחֲזִיר. עָשָׂה אֶחָד מֵהֶן תְּשׁוּבָה חַיָּיב לְהַחֲזִיר אֶת שֶׁלּוֹ. וְאִם הָיָה מוֹצִיא וְנוֹתֵן לָהֶן הוּא מְשַׁלֵּם עַל יְדֵי כּוּלָן.

[23]"If thieves who stole by stealth repented, they have to make restitution[24]. If one of a gang repented, he has to make restitution for himself. But if he traded for them[25], he has to make restitution for all of them."

| | |
|---|---|
| 23 Tosephta 10:39.<br>24 To clear their consciences. There is no question of double restitution which is possible only by judgment. | 25 If he traded the loot to fences and distributed the money among the gang, he is responsible for the fact that the victims of the theft cannot recover their property. |

(7b line 60) תַּנֵּי. הַגּוֹזֵל וּמַאֲכִיל בָּנָיו בֵּין גְּדוֹלִים בֵּין קְטַנִּים פְּטוּרִין מִלְּשַׁלֵּם. הִנִּיחַ לִפְנֵיהֶן בֵּין גְּדוֹלִים בֵּין קְטַנִּים חַיָּיבִין לְשַׁלֵּם. סוּמְכוּס אוֹמֵר. גְּדוֹלִים חַיָּיבִין קְטַנִּים פְּטוּרִין. אִם אָמְרוּ. אֵין אָנוּ יוֹדְעִין אִם עָשָׂה אָבִינוּ חֶשְׁבּוֹן בָּאַחֲרוֹנָה הֲרֵי אֵילוּ פְּטוּרִין. הָתִיב רִבִּי בָּא בַּר מָמָל. הַגַּע עַצְמָךְ בְּשֶׁהִנִּיחַ לִפְנֵיהֶן קַרְקַע. לֹא הַכֹּל מֵהֶן לוֹמַר. אֵין אָנוּ יוֹדְעִין מַה חֶשְׁבּוֹן עָשָׂה אָבִינוּ בָּאַחֲרוֹנָה. הָתִיב רַב הַמְנוּנָא. הַגַּע עַצְמָךְ שֶׁהָיְתָה גְזֵילָה מְפוּרְסֶמֶת. לֹא הַכֹּל מֵהֶן לוֹמַר. אֵין אָנוּ יוֹדְעִין מַה עָשָׂה אָבִינוּ חֶשְׁבּוֹן בָּאַחֲרוֹנָה. הָתִיב רַב שֵׁשֶׁת. אֲפִילוּ קְטַנִּים נִטְעֲנִין לָהֶן בְּבֵית דִּין. מָה אִית לָךְ לְמֵימַר. אָמַר רִבִּי מָנָא. תִּיפְתָּר בְּשֶׁטְּעָנוּ הֵן. אֵין אָנוּ יוֹדְעִין כּוּל'. יַדְעִין אֲנָן דַּעֲסַק אֲבוּנָן עִמָּךְ עַל הָדֵין חוּשְׁבְּנָא. וְלֵית נָן יַדְעִין מַה נְפַק מִדִּינָא.

It was stated[26]: "If somebody robbed to feed his children, whether adult or underage, they are not liable to pay. If they inherited from him, both adult and underage are liable to pay. Symmachos says, the adults are liable, the underaged are not liable[27]. If they said, we do not know whether our father accounted for it at the end, they are not liable." Rebbi Abba bar Mamal objected: Think of it, if they inherited real estate, they are not able to say, we do not know whether our father accounted for it at the end[28]. Rav Hamnuna objected: Think of it, if it was a notorious robbery; they are not able to say, we do not know whether our father accounted for it at the end. Rav Sheshet objected: For the underaged the court will argue[29]. What can you say? Rebbi Mana said, explain it if they argue, we do not know, etc., we know that our father was in dispute with you on this account, but we do not know how it was resolved[30].

26 Tosephta 10:21; Babli 112a.

27 The underaged cannot be sued since they have no standing in court and no witnesses in civil suits are admitted without both parties being present. Underaged heirs can be sued in court only in foreclosure proceedings based on documents, in which case the court will appoint a guardian who can examine the validity of the document for them.

28 The Mishnah states unconditionally that robbed real estate has to be returned.

29 The court-appointed attorney will argue for the underaged that they cannot know whether their father arranged himself with his victim.

30 This is a credible defense; the claimant either has to prove that there were no contacts or provide documentary proof that the claim was not settled.

**משנה ב:** נָטְלוּ מוֹכְסִין אֶת חֲמוֹרוֹ וְנָתְנוּ לוֹ חֲמוֹר אַחֵר גָּזְלוּ הַלִּיסְטִין (fol. 7a) כְּסוּתוֹ וְנָתְנוּ לוֹ כְּסוּת אַחֶרֶת הֲרֵי אִילּוּ שֶׁלּוֹ מִפְּנֵי שֶׁהַבְּעָלִין מִתְיָיאֲשִׁין מֵהֶן.

הַמַּצִּיל מִיַּד הַנָּהָר מִיַּד הַלִיסְטִין אִם נִתְיָיאֲשׁוּ הַבְּעָלִין הֲרֵי אֵילוּ שָׁלּוּ. וְכֵן נְחִיל שֶׁל דְּבוֹרִים אִם נִתְיָיאֲשׁוּ הַבְּעָלִין הֲרֵי אֵילוּ שָׁלּוּ. אָמַר רִבִּי יוֹחָנָן בֶּן בְּרוֹקָה נֶאֱמֶנֶת אִשָּׁה אוֹ קָטָן לוֹמַר מִכָּאן יָצָא נְחִיל זֶה וּמְהַלֵּךְ בְּתוֹךְ שָׂדֵהוּ וְנוֹטֵל אֶת נְחִילוֹ וְאִם הִזִּיק מְשַׁלֵּם מַה שֶׁהִזִּיק. אֲבָל לֹא יָקוֹץ אֶת הַסּוֹכָה עַל מְנָת לִתֵּן דָּמִים. רִבִּי יִשְׁמָעֵאל בְּנוֹ שֶׁל רִבִּי יוֹחָנָן בֶּן בְּרוֹקָה אוֹמֵר אַף קוֹצֵץ וְנוֹתֵן דָּמִים.

**Mishnah 2**: If the publicans took his donkey and gave him another donkey, or armed robbers[31] took his garment and gave him another garment, they are his since the owners had given up hope of recovery[32]. Things saved from a flood or from armed robbers are his if the owners had given up hope of recovery. Similarly, a swarm of bees is his if the owners had given up hope of recovery. Rebbi Johanan ben Beroqa said, a woman or a child are trusted if they say: "This swarm of bees came from here."[33] [The beekeeper] may enter another's field to take his swarm; if he caused damage he has to pay what he damaged, but he cannot cut off a branch[34] intending to pay for it. Rebbi Ismael, Rebbi Johanan ben Beroqa's son, said: he may even cut a branch and pay for it.

31   In contrast to a גַּזְלָן, a לִיסְטִיס (λῃστής) always is an *armed* robber.
32   Any lost article for which the owners had given up hope of recovery is ownerless property and becomes the property of the finder. (This is the principle underlying the first two Chapters of *Bava meṣi'a*.) It does not matter that the owners lost hope because of unlawful acts by others.
33   By this they determine the ownership of the swarm of bees, allow the bee-keeper to try to capture the swarm and prohibit anybody else from taking it. While women are barred from formal testimony, they are admitted to indicate facts. Children are never believed about what they remember, but here they indicate a fact immediately after it happened; their indication can be taken as unbiased truth.

Swarming bees are lost if not captured immediately. Therefore the rules about swarms of bees belong to the rules of things that cannot be recovered later.
34   On which the bees have settled.

(7b line 70) **הלכה ב:** נְטָלוּ מוֹכְסִין כול׳. תַּנֵּי. הַמַּצִּיל מִן הַגַּיִיס מִן הַדְּלֵיקָה מִשְׁנוּנִית הַיָּם מִשְׁלוּלִית הַנָּהָר הֲרֵי אִילּוּ שֶׁלּוֹ.

**Halakhah 2:** "If the publicans took," etc. It was stated: "Things saved from an army, or a fire, from a whirlpool in the sea, a whirlpool of a river, are his.[35]"

35 A similar statement in Tosephta *Bava meṣi'a* 2:2 adds: "because the owners gave up hope of recovery."

(7b line 72) וְכֵן נְחִיל שֶׁל דְּבוֹרִים אִם נִתְיָיאֲשׁוּ בְעָלָיו הֲרֵי אִילּוּ שֶׁלּוֹ. רִבִּי חִינְנָא בַר פַּפָּא בְשֵׁם רִבִּי יוֹחָנָן. מַתְנִיתָא בְּנָחִיל שֶׁגְּזָלוֹ מִן הַהֲלִיכָה וּבְפוֹרֵחַ. וּבִלְבַד עַל אָתָר. אֲבָל אִם יָצָא וְחָזַר אֲנִי אוֹמֵר. מִפְּנֵי יִרְאָה וּפִיתּוּי אֲמָרוּ. תַּנֵּי. רִבִּי יִשְׁמָעֵאל בֶּן רִבִּי יוֹחָנָן בֶּן בְּרוֹקָה אוֹמֵר. תְּנַאי בֵּית דִּין הוּא לָקוּץ זֶה סוֹכָה וְנוֹתֵן דָּמִים. שֶׁעַל מְנָת כֵּן הִנְחִיל יְהוֹשֻׁעַ לְיִשְׂרָאֵל אֶת הָאָרֶץ.

[36]"Similarly, a swarm of bees is his if the owners had given up hope of recovery." Rebbi Ḥinena bar Pappos in the name of Rebbi Joḥanan: The Mishnah is about a swarm taken in flight and from a schoolboy[37], and only immediately[38]. But if one left and returned, I am saying that he[39] said it because of fear, or being seduced. It was stated[40]: Rebbi Joḥanan ben Beroqa says, it is a stipulation by the court that this one may cut a branch and pay for it since on this condition did Joshua distribute the Land to Israel[41].

36 Another formulation of the same topic is in *Ketubot* 2:11, Notes 203-209.

37 But not a younger child (Rashba, *Novellae ad* 114b.)

38 "Immediately" refers to the testimony of women and children, who can determine ownership, even in their own behalf, on the pursuit ot the swarm.

39 The underage witness.

40 Babli 82b,114b.

41 The last remark is not in the Babli. For the list of stipulations about land use ascribed to Joshua, cf. *Nazir* 7:1, Note 40.

## HALAKHAH 3

(fol. 7b) **משנה ג:** הַמַּכִּיר כֵּלָיו אוֹ סְפָרָיו בְּיַד אַחֵר אִם יָצָא לוֹ שֵׁם גְּנֵיבָה בָּעִיר יִשָּׁבַע כַּמָּה הוֹצִיא וְיִטּוֹל. וְאִם לָאו לֹא הֵימֶנּוּ שֶׁאֲנִי אוֹמֵר מְכָרָן לְאַחֵר וּלְקָחָן זֶה מִמֶּנּוּ.

**Mishnah 3**: If one recognizes his own vessels or books in the hand of another[42], if the theft was a known fact in town, [the other] shall swear to him how much he paid and take this amount[43]. Otherwise[44] he[45] cannot be believed, for I am saying that he had sold the items to a third party and the other had bought them from there.

42   And he can prove that they were his.
43   The owner can force the present owner to sell him his heirlooms for the price which he had paid to thief or fence.
44   If the police had not been notified of the theft.
45   The person who claims that his property was in the hand of another.

(7c line 1) **הלכה ג:** הַמַּכִּיר כֵּלָיו אוֹ סְפָרָיו כול׳. אָמַר רִבִּי בָּא בַּר מָמָל. בְּדִין הוּא שֶׁלֹּא יִשָּׁבַע. וְלָמָּה אָמְרוּ. יִשָּׁבַע. שֶׁלֹּא יְהוּ בַעֲלֵי בָתִּים נִטְפָּלִין לַגַּנָּבִים. רִבִּי יְהוֹשֻׁעַ בֶּן לֵוִי אָמַר. וְהוּא שֶׁיָּצָא לוֹ שֵׁם שֶׁנִּגְנְבוּ סְפָרָיו. רַב אָמַר. צָרִיךְ לְהָבִיא רְאָייָה שֶׁלָּן עִמּוֹ בְּאוֹתוֹ הַלַּיְלָה. אַסִּי אָמַר. אִם טָעַן לוֹמַר. מִפְּלוֹנִי לְקַחְתִּים. נֶאֱמָן. אָתָא עוֹבְדָא קוֹמֵי רִבִּי נָסָא וְלֹא קִיבֵּל. מַה פְּלִיג. אָמְרֵי. בַּר נַשׁ דְּעֵקִין הֲוָה. בְּגִין כֵּן לֹא קָבִיל.

"If one recognizes his own vessels or books," etc. Rebbi Abba bar Mamal said, it would have been correct that they should not have to swear[46]. Why did they say they have to swear? That homeowners should not be fences[47]. Rebbi Joshua ben Levi said, only if it was a known fact that his books had been stolen[48]. Rav said, he has to bring proof that he stayed there[49] the night in question. Assi said, if he claims: "I bought them from X," he is to be believed[49]. A case came before Rebbi Nasa and he did not accept it. Does he disagree? They said, he was a known troublemaker[50]; therefore he did not accept the case[51].

46 There certainly is no biblical reason why the case should be treated differently from any other claim about money.

47 If thieves find no buyers they will stop stealing.

48 The claimant can only force an oath on the owner of his books if the theft of specific books was made public.

49 If the prior owner was not at his place at the time of the theft, one might suspect that the theft occurred with the owner's connivance. This does not mean that he has no chance of getting back his books through a regular suit, but the rules of the Mishnah cannot be applied.

49 If X is not available at the time to testify. The claimant would have to disprove the defendant's assertion.

50 Explaining the *hapax* דעקין from Arabic زعق "to produce fear by shouting", cf. Hebrew צעק.

51 Since the Mishnah puts it into the hands of the judge to decide when a theft "is publicly known", it can be read as allowing judicial discretion in deciding whether a case look legitimate or not.

(fol. 7b) **משנה ד:** זֶה בָּא בְּחָבִיתוֹ שֶׁל יַיִן וְזֶה בָּא בְּכַדּוֹ שֶׁל דְּבַשׁ. נִסְדְּקָה חָבִית שֶׁל דְּבַשׁ וְשָׁפַךְ זֶה אֶת יֵינוֹ וְהִצִּיל אֶת הַדְּבַשׁ לְתוֹכָהּ אֵין לוֹ אֶלָּא שְׂכָרוֹ. אִם אָמַר אַצִּיל אֶת שֶׁלָּךְ וְאַתָּה נוֹתֵן לִי דְמֵי שֶׁלִּי חַיָּיב לִיתֵּן לוֹ.

**Mishnah 4**: One comes with his amphora of wine, the other comes with his jug of honey. If the amphora[52] of honey sprang a leak, if the other one poured out his wine and saved the honey into it, he only has his wages[53]. But if he said, I shall save yours if you pay me the value of mine, he[54] is liable to pay him.

52 Cf. Chapter 3, Note 2.

53 For the work, not for the lost wine.

54 If the owner of the more valuable merchandise agreed, he has to keep the terms of this oral contract.

**הלכה ד:** זֶה בָּא בְחָבִיתוֹ שֶׁלְּיַיִן כול׳. תַּנֵּי. שְׁנַיִם בַּמִּדְבָּר בְּיַד זֶה (7c line 7) חָבִית מַיִם וּבְיַד זֶה חָבִית דְּבַשׁ. נִסְדַּק חָבִית מַיִם. תְּנַיי בֵּית דִּין הוּא שֶׁיִּשְׁפּוֹךְ זֶה דְּבָשׁוֹ וְיַצִּיל אֶת מֵימָיו. שֶׁהַמַּיִם מְחַיֶּיה בַּמִּדְבָּר וְלֹא הַדְּבַשׁ. תַּנֵּי. פּוֹעֵל וְעָנִי שֶׁעָלוּ לְרֹאשׁ אִילָן וְשִׁיבְּרוּ סוֹכָה. בִּזְמַן שֶׁדֶּרֶךְ פּוֹעֲלִין לַעֲלוֹת בָּאִילָן פְּטוּרִין. וְאִם לָאו חַיָּיבִין.

**Halakhah 4**: "One comes with his amphora of wine," etc. It was stated[55]: "Two people are in the desert; in the hand of one is an amphora of water, in the other's hand an amphora of honey. If the water amphora springs a leak it is a stipulation of the court that the other pour out his honey in order to save the water since water sustains life in the desert but not honey." It was stated[56]: "If a worker and a poor man climbed on a tree and broke a branch; if workers are supposed to climb the tree they are not liable, otherwise they are liable."

55 Tosephta 10:28. The Tosephta adds: "When they come to an inhabited area, [the owner of the water] has to pay the value of the honey." There is not much reason to believe that this or a similar text is understood in the Yerushalmi's *baraita*; cf. *Tosefta kiFshutah Neziqin* p. 56.

56 Tosephta 10:29. About the dangers and rules of the poor climbing trees to claim their *peah*, cf. *Peah* 4:1.

**משנה ה:** שָׁטַף נָהָר חֲמוֹרוֹ וַחֲמוֹר חֲבֵירוֹ שֶׁלּוֹ יָפֶה מָנֶה וְשֶׁל חֲבֵירוֹ (fol. 7b) מָאתַיִם הִנִּיחַ אֶת שֶׁלּוֹ וְהִצִּיל אֶת שֶׁל חֲבֵירוֹ אֵין לוֹ אֶלָּא שְׂכָרוֹ. אִם אָמַר אַצִּיל אֶת שֶׁלָּךְ וְאַתָּה נוֹתֵן לִי דְּמֵי שֶׁלִּי חַיָּיב לִיתֵּן לוֹ.

**Mishnah 5**: If a river washed away his donkey and another's donkey; his was worth a mina, the other's 200. If he abandoned his own and saved the other's, he only has his wages[53]. But if he said, I shall save yours if you pay me the value of mine, he[54] is liable to pay him.

(7c line 12) **הלכה ה:** שָׁטַף נָהָר אֶת חֲמוֹרוֹ כול'. תַּנֵּי. הִנִּיחַ שֶׁלּוֹ לְהַצִּיל שֶׁלַּחֲבֵירוֹ וְעָלָה שֶׁלַּחֲבֵירוֹ מֵאֵילָיו אֵין נִזְקָק לוֹ כְּלוּם. אֶלָּא הִנִּיחַ שֶׁלּוֹ לְהַצִּיל שֶׁלַּחֲבֵירוֹ וְעָלָה שֶׁלּוֹ מֵאֵילָיו. מָהוּ דְיֵימַר לוֹ. נִתְיָיאַשְׁתִּי. נִשְׁמְעִינָהּ מִן הָדָא. שָׁטַף נָהָר חֲמוֹרוֹ וְהָיָה צָוַח וְאוֹמֵר. לֹא נִתְיָיאַשְׁתִּי. רֵישׁ לָקִישׁ אָמַר. כָּל־זְמַן שֶׁצָּוַח לֹא נִתְיָיאַשׁ. רַבִּי יוֹחָנָן אָמַר. חֲזָקָה מְיָיאֵשׁ הוּא.

**Halakhah 5:** "If a river washed away his donkey," etc. It was stated: If he abandoned his to save the other's, but the other's climbed out by himself, he does not owe him anything[57]. But if he abandoned his to save the other's, and his own climbed out by himself, may he say, "I did not abandon hope of recovery"[58]? Let us hear from the following: If a river washed away his donkey and he was crying: "I did not abandon hope of recovery!" Rebbi Simeon ben Laqish said, as long as he is crying he did not abandon hope of recovery. Rebbi Joḥanan said, there is a presumption[59] that he had abandoned hope.

57 In the Babli, 116a, it is stated that he is due payment for his work.

58 Does the fact that he did not try to save his own donkey imply that he has given up hope of recovering it? If so, the donkey is ownerless and it becomes the property of anybody taking it. If he has not given up hope of recovering it, everybody taking hold of the donkey is required to return it to its owner.

59 For the meaning of חֲזָקָה, cf. *Ketubot* 5:5, Note 100.

(fol. 7b) **משנה ו:** הַגּוֹזֵל שָׂדֶה וּנְטָלוּהָ מַסִּיקִין אִם מַכַּת מְדִינָה הִיא אוֹמֵר לוֹ הֲרֵי שֶׁלָּךְ לְפָנֶיךָ וְאִם מַחֲמַת הַגַּזְלָן חַיָּיב לְהַעֲמִיד לוֹ שָׂדֶה. שְׁטָפָהּ נָהָר אוֹמֵר לוֹ הֲרֵי שֶׁלָּךְ לְפָנֶיךָ.

**Mishnah 6:** Somebody had robbed a field which subsequently was taken by discharged veterans[60]. If it is a provincial plague, he may tell him: Here is your property before you[61]. But if it was because of the robber[62], he has to give him a field. If a river had washed it away, he may say to him: Here is your property before you[63].

60 "Retired Roman veterans who received a provincial's property", from Latin *missicius, missitius*, adj., "discharged from military service" (M. Gil).

In a Genizah ms. of the Mishnah: "If armed robbers took it." Parallel sources leave no doubt that the Leiden ms. text is the correct one.

61 If the properties of many provincials had been taken, the robber can tell the original owner that it is up to him to try to get indemnification.

62 If the veterans were directed to take the land because it had come to the attention of the authorities that it was in the wrong hands, the robber has to indemnify the original owner with another field of equal value.

63 Since it also would have been damaged in the original owner's hand.

(7c line 18) **הלכה ו:** הַגּוֹזֵל שָׂדֶה מֵחֲבֵירוֹ כול'. אָמַר רִבִּי יוֹחָנָן. וַהֲלֹא אָמְרוּ. אֵין הַקַּרְקַע נִגְזֶלֶת. וְלָמָּה אָמְרוּ חַיָּיב לְהַעֲמִיד לוֹ שָׂדֶה. קְנָס קְנָסוּהוּ. נְטָלוּהוּ מֵסִיקִין מִן הַגַּזְלָן מַחֲמַת הַנִּגְזָל. מָהוּ דוּ יְכִיל מֵימַר לֵיהּ. מִכָּל־מָקוֹם הַב לִי דִידִי וּמָאן דְּבָעֵי יֵיתֵי וְיִסַּב מִינִּי. רִבִּי יְהוֹשֻׁעַ בֶּן לֵוִי אָמַר. אֵין אָדָם נִתְפָּס עַל חֲבֵירוֹ וְחַיָּיב לִיתֵּן לוֹ. אֶלָּא בְאַרְנוֹן וּבְגוּלְגּוֹלֶת. רַב אָמַר. יְכִיל מֵימַר לֵיהּ. אַתְּ שְׁרֵי עֲבִיטָיךְ מִינִּי.

**Halakhah 6**: "Somebody had robbed a field from another person[64]," etc. [65]Rebbi Joḥanan said, but did they not say that "real estate cannot be robbed"[66]? Why did they say, "he has to give him a field"[67]? It is a fine by which they fined him. If the discharged veterans took it from the robber because of the robbed[68], could he tell him, in any case give me what is mine and let any claimant come and deal with me? Rebbi Johua ben Levi said, nobody is held responsible for his neighbor and the latter has to repay him except *annona* and head-tax. Rav said, he can tell him, you redeemed your pledge with my money[69].

64  The longer text is that of the Babli and most independent Mishnah mss. (but not the Genizah text of this Mishnah).

65  In another formulation, this paragraph appears in *Nedarim* 4:2 (Notes 27-33) and *Ketubot* 13:2 (35d l. 39).

66  Nothing the robber does can give him title to the real estate.

67  Even if the field was taken from the robber, in law it was taken from the robbed.

68  Because he was in arrears with payments to the government, the veterans were directed to his property.

69  If the government required A to pay for B's obligation, B always has to indemnify A. It has to be noted that Rav lived under Parthian and Persian rule, R. Joshua ben Levi in the Roman Empire.


(fol. 7b) **משנה ז**: הַגּוֹזֵל אֶת חֲבֵירוֹ אוֹ שֶׁלָּוָה מִמֶּנּוּ אוֹ שֶׁהִפְקִיד לוֹ בַּיִּשּׁוּב לֹא יַחֲזִיר לוֹ בַּמִּדְבָּר. עַל מְנָת לָצֵאת בַּמִּדְבָּר יַחֲזִיר לוֹ בַּמִּדְבָּר.

**Mishnah 7**: He who robbed from another, or took a loan from him, or accepted a deposit in a built-up area cannot give it back to him in the desert. [If it was given] with the intent to depart for the desert, he can give it back to him in the desert.

**משנה ח**: הָאוֹמֵר לַחֲבֵירוֹ גְּזַלְתִּיךָ וְהִלְוִיתַנִי הִפְקַדְתָּ אֶצְלִי וְאֵינוֹ יוֹדֵעַ אִם הֶחֱזַרְתִּי לָךְ וְאִם לֹא הֶחֱזַרְתִּי לָךְ חַיָּיב לְשַׁלֵּם. אֲבָל אָמַר לוֹ אֵינִי יוֹדֵעַ אִם גְּזַלְתִּיךָ אִם הִלְוִיתַנִי אִם הִפְקַדְתָּהּ אֶצְלִי אִם לֹא הִפְקַדְתָּ פָּטוּר מִלְּשַׁלֵּם.

**Mishnah 8**: He who says to another: I robbed you, or I took a loan from you, you deposited with me, but I do not known whether I returned it to you or did not return it, is liable to pay. But if he said to him: I do not know whether I robbed you, or I took a loan from you, or you deposited with me or did not deposit, he is not liable to pay.

(7c line 23) **הלכה ח:** הָאוֹמֵר לַחֲבֵירוֹ גְּזַלְתִּיךָ כול'. רִבִּי יוֹחָנָן אָמַר. בָּבָא לָצֵאת יְדֵי שָׁמַיִם. גְּזַלְתִּיךָ וְהִלְוִיתַנִי הִפְקַדְתָּ אֶצְלִי וְהֶחֱזַרְתִּי לָךְ. וַהֲלָה אוֹמֵר. אֵינִי יוֹדֵעַ. רִבִּי יִרְמְיָה סָבַר מֵימַר. חַייָב לְהַעֲמִיד לוֹ מִן הַדִּין. רִבִּי יוֹסֵי סָבַר מֵימַר. עוֹד הִיא לָצֵאת יְדֵי שָׁמַיִם. הוֹצֵאתִי מִן הַכִּיס וְנָתַתִּי לָךְ. וְהוּא אוֹמֵר. אֵינִי יוֹדֵעַ. רַב הוּנָא אָמַר. אוֹמְרִין לוֹ. אַתְּ לֵית יָדַע אָהֵן יָדַע.

**Halakhah 8**: "He who says to another: I robbed you," etc. Rebbi Johanan said, if he wants to clear himself before Heaven[70]. I robbed you, or I took a loan from you, you deposited with me; did I return it to you? The other party says, I do not know[71]. Rebbi Jeremiah wanted to say, he is required to make good as a matter of law. Rebbi Yose wanted to say, still it is to become clear before Heaven. I took from the wallet and gave to you, and the other party says, I do not know. Rav Huna said, one tells him: You do not know but the other party knows[72].

70   Without a definitive claim from the other party, there is no case for the courts. "Liable" and "not liable" in this Mishnah refer to moral, not legal, obligations. Babli 118a.

71   This seems to be a reformulation of the Mishnah; in that case R. Jeremiah would disagree with R. Johanan. Sabbatai Cohen (*Šakh*, *Ḥošen Mišpaṭ* §95 Note 67) reads "*You* robbed me, etc. I did return it to you, but the other party says, I do not know."

72   Cf. *Šebuot* 6, end (37b l. 64). There are two possible interpretations.

*Šakh*: They both agree that something was paid but neither party checked whether the exact amount was given. There is no claim, neither legal nor moral.

*Pene Moshe*: One party asserts that the debt was liquidated; the other party is not sure. Neither one has proof. Rav Huna asserts in the Babli 118a (also *Ketubot* 12b) that "between 'certain' and 'possible' claims, the 'certain' claim is preferred [by the courts]".

(fol. 7b) **משנה ט:** הַגּוֹנֵב טָלֶה מִן הָעֵדֶר וְהֶחֱזִירוֹ וָמֵת אוֹ נִגְנַב חַיָּיב בְּאַחֲרָיוּתוֹ. לֹא יָדְעוּ הַבְּעָלִים לֹא בִגְנֵיבָתוֹ וְלֹא בַחֲזִירָתוֹ וּמָנוּ אֶת הַצֹּאן וּשְׁלֵימָה הִיא פָּטוּר מִלְּשַׁלֵּם.

**Mishnah 9**: If one stole a lamb from the flock[73] and returned it[74], if it died or was stolen he is liable. If the owners were unaware both of the theft and the return, he is no longer liable after they counted the flock and found it complete[75].

73  And the owners noticed the theft.

74  Silently, without notifying the owners. Then the lamb still remains his responsibility.

75  Since the owners did not notice the theft, they do not have to be informed of the return.

(7c line 29) **הלכה ט:** הַגּוֹנֵב טָלֶה מִן הָעֵדֶר כול'. אָמַר רִבִּי יוֹחָנָן. אִם יָדְעוּ הַבְּעָלִים בַּגְּנֵיבָה צְרִיכִין לֵידַע בַּחֲזִירָה. לֹא יָדְעוּ בַּגְּנֵיבָה אֵין צְרִיכִין לֵידַע בַּחֲזִירָה. רֵישׁ לָקִישׁ אָמַר. אַף עַל פִּי שֶׁלֹּא יָדְעוּ בַּגְּנֵיבָה צְרִיכִין לֵידַע בַּחֲזִירָה. אָמַר רִבִּי לֶעְזָר. אִין הֲוָה כְגוֹן הָהֵין בְּרָחָא אֵין צְרִיכִין לֵידַע בַּחֲזִירָה. מַהוּ כְגוֹן הָהֵין בְּרָחָא. אִית דְּמָרִין. חוּטְרָא. אִית דְּמָרִין. פַּנְדּוּרָה. אִית דְּמָרִין. תַּיְישָׁא רַבָּא.

**Halakhah 9**: "If one stole a lamb from the flock," etc. Rebbi Johanan said, if the owners knew of the theft, they have to be notified of the return. If they did not know of the theft, they do not have to be notified of the return. Rebbi Simeon ben Laqish said, even if they did not know of the theft, they have to be notified of the return[76]. Rebbi Eleazar said, if it was similar to the case of a ram[77], they do not have to be notified of the return. What means "similar to the case of a ram"? Some say, the shepherd's staff. Some say, a *pandura*[78]. Some say, the bell-wether.

76  He reads the first sentence of the Mishnah to apply to all cases, whether the owner knew or did not know. If they did not know, only a count of the flock frees the thief from responsibility.

77  In case it is obvious that the theft was returned, even without counting.

78  Greek πανδοῦρα, a kind of guitar.

**משנה י:** אֵין לוֹקְחִין מִן הָרוֹעִים צֶמֶר וְחָלָב וּגְדָיִים וְלֹא מִשׁוֹמְרֵי פֵירוֹת עֵצִים וּפֵירוֹת אֲבָל לוֹקְחִין כְּלֵי פִשְׁתָּן מִן הַנָּשִׁים בַּגָּלִיל וַעֲגָלִים בַּשָּׁרוֹן. וְכוּלָן שֶׁאָמְרוּ לְהַטְמִין אָסוּר. וְלוֹקְחִין בֵּיצִים וְתַרְנוֹגָלִין מִכָּל־מָקוֹם. (fol. 7b)

**Mishnah 10:** One does not buy wool, or milk, or lambs from shepherds[79], nor wood or fruits from orchard watchmen; but one may buy linen garments from women in Galilee, and calves in the Sharon[80]. In all cases it is forbidden if they[81] told to hide. One buys eggs and chickens everywhere.

79  Since shepherds usually are not the owners of their flock, one has to assume that they sell stolen goods.

80  In both cases, the trade was in the hand of women who ran the business for their husbands.

81  If the seller tells the buyer to hide the merchandise, the buyer has to know that he is buying stolen goods. He is forbidden to buy.

**הלכה י:** אֵין לוֹקְחִין מִן הָרוֹעִים כול'. תַּנֵּי. אֵין מְקַבְּלִין פִּקְדוֹנוֹת לֹא מִנָּשִׁים וְלֹא מֵעֲבָדִים וְלֹא מִקְּטַנִּים. קִיבֵּל מִן הָאִשָּׁה יַחֲזִיר לָהּ. מֵתָה יַחֲזִיר לְבַעֲלָהּ. (7c line 34)

**Halakhah 10:** "One does not buy from shepherds," etc. It was stated[82]: "One does not accept deposits from women, or slaves, or underage children. If one accepted from a woman, he should return it to her; if she died, he should return it to her husband."

82   Cf. Halakhah 9:11, Note 94 ff.

(fol. 7b) **משנה יא:** מוֹכִין שֶׁהַכּוֹבֵס מוֹצִיא הֲרֵי אִילוּ שֶׁלּוֹ וְשֶׁהַסּוֹרֵק מוֹצִיא הֲרֵי אִילוּ שֶׁל בַּעַל הַבַּיִת. הַכּוֹבֵס נוֹטֵל שְׁלֹשָׁה חוּטִין וְהֵן שֶׁלּוֹ יוֹתֵר מִיכֵּן שֶׁל בַּעַל הַבַּיִת. אִם הָיָה שָׁחוֹר עַל גַּבֵּי לָבָן נוֹטֵל אֶת הַכֹּל וְהֵן שֶׁלּוֹ.

**Mishnah 11**: Fibers which remain at the washer's are his[83], but what the carder produces[84] are the consignor's. The washer takes three threads and they are his, more than that belong to the consignor. If it was black on a white background he takes all of them and they are his[85].

83   They are a negligible amount.
84   It is his job to produce fibers which can be used to manufacture felt.
85   Threads of another kind added by weavers to the end of a cloth, to be removed when the garment is washed before being worn for the first time.

(7c line 37) **הלכה יא:** מוֹכִין שֶׁהַכּוֹבֵס מוֹצִיא כול׳. אַבָּא הוֹשַׁעְיָה אִישׁ טְרִייָא הֲוָה קַצָּר וַהֲוָה עָבַד לֵיהּ חָדָא אִסְטְדָכִין מִן חַד עֲמָר. דְּלָא יְהוֹוֹן בְּרִייָתָא אָמְרִין. מִדִּידָן לְבַשׁ.

**Halakhah 11**: "Fibers which remain at the washer's," etc. Abba Hoshaia from Tireh[86] was a washer. He made himself a tunic[87] of a single kind of wool lest people say: He wears our property[88].

86   A frequent place name.
87   In the word, ד is not a safe reading. The Venice printer read איסטרכין. Brill reads איסטכרין, Greek στιχάριον, "variegated tunic".
88   In the Tosephta, 11:14, it is noted that even he took black and white fibers following the Mishnah. This Abba Hoshaia cannot be the fourth generation Amora mentioned in *Eccl. rabba* 1:5.

(fol. 7b) **משנה יב:** הַחַיָּט שֶׁשִּׁיֵּיר מִן הַחוּט כְּדֵי לִתְפוֹר בּוֹ וּמַטְלִית שֶׁהִיא שָׁלֹשׁ עַל שָׁלֹשׁ חַיָּיב לְהַחֲזִיר לַבְּעָלִין. מַה שֶׁהֶחָרָשׁ מוֹצִיא בַּמַּעֲצָד הֲרֵי אִילּוּ שֶׁלּוֹ וּבַכַּשִּׁיל שֶׁל בַּעַל הַבַּיִת. וְאִם הָיָה עוֹשֶׂה אֵצֶל בַּעַל הַבַּיִת אַף הַנְּסוֹרֶת שֶׁל בַּעַל הַבַּיִת.

**Mishnah 12**: The tailor[89] who had enough thread left to sew with it, and cloth three by three finger breadths[90], has to return if to its owners. What the woodworker[89] takes off with a small plane is his, with a large one belongs to the consignor; if he works at the latter's place even the chips are the consignor's.

89  He receives all materials from the consignor.

90  Which can be used as a handkerchief.

(7c line 39) **הלכה יא:** הַחַיָּט שֶׁשִּׁיֵּיר מִן הַחוּט כול׳. תַּנֵּי רִבִּי חִייָה. מְלֹא מַחַט. דְּבֵי רִבִּי חִייָה פָּתְרִין לָהּ. כְּפָלַיִם כִּמְלֹא מַחַט. תַּנֵּי בַּר קַפָּרָא. מְלֹא מְשִׁיכַת הַמַּחַט. דְּבֵי רבי יַנַּאי פָּתְרִין לָהּ. כְּפָלַיִם בִּמְשִׁיכַת מַחַט. מַה וּפְלִיג. מַה דְּתַנֵּי רִבִּי חִייָה. מְלֹא מַחַט. דְּבֵי רִבִּי יַנַּאי פָּתְרִין לָהּ. כְּפָלַיִם בִּמְלֹא מַחַט. מַה דְּתַנֵּי בַּר קַפָּרָא. מְלֹא מְשִׁיכַת הַמַּחַט. דְּבֵי רִבִּי יַנַּאי פָּתְרִין לָהּ. כְּפָלַיִם בִּמְשִׁיכַת הַמַּחַט.

**Halakhah 12**: "The tailor who had enough thread left," etc. Rebbi Ḥiyya stated: A needle full[91]. The House of Rebbi Ḥiyya explained: Twice a needle full[92]. Bar Qappara stated: The stitching with a needle[93]. The House of Rebbi Yannai explained: twice the stitching of a needle. Do they disagree? What Rebbi Ḥiyya stated, a needle full, the House of Rebbi Ḥiyya explained: Twice a needle full. What Bar Qappara stated: the stitching with a needle, the House of Rebbi Yannai explained: twice the stitching of a needle.

91 Enough thread to start working.

92 In the Babli, 119b (in the name of Rav Assi): Twice the length of the needle.

93 Enough thread to sew a few permanent stitches of a garment.

## שנים אוחזין פרק ראשון

**משנה א:** (fol. 7c) שְׁנַיִם אוֹחֲזִין בְּטַלִּית זֶה אוֹמֵר אֲנִי מְצָאתִיהָ וְזֶה אוֹמֵר אֲנִי מְצָאתִיהָ זֶה אוֹמֵר כּוּלָהּ שֶׁלִּי וְזֶה אוֹמֵר כּוּלָהּ שֶׁלִּי. זֶה יִשָּׁבַע שֶׁאֵין לוֹ בָהּ פָּחוּת מֵחֶצְיָהּ וְזֶה יִשָּׁבַע שֶׁאֵין לוֹ בָהּ פָּחוּת מֵחֶצְיָהּ וְיַחֲלוֹקוּ. זֶה אוֹמֵר כּוּלָהּ שֶׁלִּי וְזֶה אוֹמֵר חֶצְיָהּ שֶׁלִּי. הָאוֹמֵר כּוּלָהּ שֶׁלִּי יִשָּׁבַע שֶׁאֵין לוֹ בָהּ פָּחוּת מִשְּׁלֹשָׁה חֲלָקִים וְהָאוֹמֵר חֶצְיָהּ שֶׁלִּי יִשָּׁבַע שֶׁאֵין לוֹ בָהּ פָּחוּת מֵרְבִיעַ. זֶה נוֹטֵל שְׁלֹשָׁה חֲלָקִים וְזֶה נוֹטֵל רְבִיעַ.

**Mishnah 1:** [1]If two persons hold on to one toga and each of them says "I found it" [or] "it wholly belongs to me"[2], each of them has to swear that he owns no less than half of it and they shall divide it evenly[3]. If one says "it wholly belongs to me" and one says "half of it belongs to me", the one who says "it wholly belongs to me" shall swear that he owns no less than three parts[4] and the one who says "half of it belongs to me" shall swear that he owns no less than a quarter[5]. The first one takes three parts, the second takes a fourth.

1  The main application of the Mishnah is to bankruptcy problems where the amount available for distribution is not sufficient to cover all claims. The principle underlying the distribution has been explained at length in *Ketubot* 10:4, Note 62.

2  Each of them has to grab a similar length of cloth, to establish equality of claims.

3  There are no witnesses nor other kinds of proof; the case has to be settled by judicial oath. It is obvious that if the two claimants do not agree to possess the object in common it has to be split evenly. If both of them are

ready to swear that the object entirely belongs to him, at least one of them is swearing falsely. Since the formulation of the oath is in the hand of the judges, they must be careful not to teach the parties to swear to a falsehood; they cannot let them swear about full ownership, for the court is warned (*Ex.* 23:1) "not to lend a hand to a wicked person to be an extortionary witness", i. e., it is forbidden to administer an oath to a known felon (Mishnah *Šebuot* 7:4). But if each party only swear to the amount it actually will receive, it is possible that both swear to the truth. The formulation "no less than" implies that the oath is true even if one of them is the full owner; the language of the oaths does not contradict the claims brought before the court.

4  $3/4$. The language of "parts" follows the Egyptian (and Roman) pattern; $n$ *parts* always means $n/_{n+1}$.

5  As explained in *Ketubot*, the underlying principle is: "Amounts in doubt are split evenly". If neither party has proof by document or witnesses and A claims 100% of an amount available but B only claims 50%, 50% are assigned to A as undisputed amount. The remaining 50% are in dispute and have to be split evenly; each of the the parties receives 25%.

(7d line 26) **הלכה א:** שְׁנַיִם אוֹחֲזִין בַּטַּלִּית כוּל׳. תַּנֵּי. אָדָם שֶׁאָמַר לַחֲבֵירוֹ. תֵּן לִי מָנֶה שֶׁאַתָּה חַיָּיב לִי. אָמַר לוֹ. לֹא הָיוּ דְבָרִים מֵעוֹלָם. הָלַךְ וְהֵבִיא עֵדִים שֶׁחַיָּיב לוֹ נ זוּז. רִבִּי חִייָה רֹבָה אָמַר. הוֹדָיַית עֵדִים כְּהוֹדָיַית פִּיו וְיִשָּׁבַע עַל הַשְּׁאָר. רִבִּי יוֹחָנָן אָמַר. אֵין הוֹדָיַית עֵדִים כְּהוֹדָיַית פִּיו שֶׁיִּשָּׁבַע עַל הַשְּׁאָר. אָמַר רִבִּי לָא. מִשְׁנַיִם אוֹחֲזִין בַּטַּלִּית דְּרִבִּי חִייָה רוֹבָה. מִכֵּיוָן שֶׁתָּפוּשׂ בְּחֶצְיָיהּ. (א)לֹא⁶ כְּמִי שֶׁהֵבִיא עֵדִים שֶׁחֶצְיָיהּ שֶׁלּוֹ. וְתֵימַר. נִשְׁבָּע וְנוֹטֵל. אוּף הָדָא דַמְיָא לָהּ.

**Halakhah 1:** "If two people hold on to one stole," etc. [7]It was stated: One person said to another, give me the mina[8] which you owe me. He answered, it never happened. He went and brought witnesses that the other owed him 50 *zuz*. The elder Rebbi Ḥiyya said, the confession of the witnesses is the same as his own confession; he has to swear about the remainder⁹. Rebbi Johanan said, the confession of the witnesses is not the same as his own confession that he should have to swear¹⁰. Rebbi La said, Rebbi Hiyya the elder's statement is implied by "if two people hold on to one stole". Since he holds on to half of it, is it not as if he brought witnesses that one half belongs to him? Could one not say that he swears and collects¹¹? Is this a similar case¹²?

6   The Leiden scribe wrote אלא "but"; the E text has לא "not". The latter is chosen as the correct text.

7   A parallel but different text is in *Ketubot* 2:1, Notes 12-15.

8   The Greek *mina* of 100 drachmas (denars). *Zuz*, "half sheqel" is the talmudic name of the denar.

9   A similar text, formulated as R. Hiyya's statement, is quoted in the Babli, 3a. The oath required here is the biblical "oath imposed by the judges", Mishnah *Ševu'ot* 6:1 based on *Ex.* 22:8. The rabbinic interpretation of the biblical expression אֲשֶׁר יֹאמַר כִּי הוּא זֶה is "if he [the defendant] agrees that there be a case." If the defendant in a civil suit, in which there are no witnesses or documents, denies the entire claim, he does not have to swear a biblical oath (he may have to swear a rabbinical oath). But if he agrees to part of the claim, he has to swear a biblical oath to free himself from the remainder. Only if the claim is advanced as tentative, then any admission by the defendant is a gift to the claimant and by rabbinic rule no oath of any kind is due. (Cf. *Gittin* 5:3, Note 84).

10   Since *Ex.* 22:8 insists on the defendant's agreeing to part of the claim, witnesses can never force a judicial oath. This opinion is not mentioned in the Babli. In *Ketubot* (*loc. cit.* Note 7), R. Johanan denies that the oath is biblical; its rules cannot be determined by biblical arguments.

11   The argument is refuted. Since each party claims the entire stole, each one is disputing half of a claim. There is no claimant nor defendant; even R. Hiyya must agree that the oath imposed by the Mishnah is not biblical.

12   For R. Hiyya, the case of the *baraita* is biblical; R. La's argument is impossible. (In *Ketubot*, R. La quotes R. Johanan's statement in the next paragraph.)

(7d line 33) רַבָּה בַּר מָמָל וְרַב עַמְרָם סְלִיקוּ הֵן דְּרַב בֵּינַיֵּי אֲמַר לֵיהּ. אֵין מוֹסְרִין שְׁבוּעָה לְחָשׁוּד. אֲמַר לֵיהּ. אֲפִילוּ לְשׁוֹן שְׁבוּעָה אֵין מוֹסְרִין לוֹ. כֵּיצַד נִשְׁבַּע. רַב הוּנָא אָמַר. שְׁבוּעָה שֶׁיֵּשׁ לִי בָהּ וְאֵין לִי בָהּ פָּחוֹת (מִשְׁוֶה פְרוּטָה) [מֶחֱצָיָהּ]. אָמַר רִבִּי יוֹחָנָן. אִם מִזּוֹ שְׁבוּעַת תַּקָּנָה הִיא.

This topic[13] came up between Rebbi Abba bar Mamal and Rav Amram. One said, one does not entrust an oath to a suspect person[14]. The other said, one does not even formulate an oath for such a one[15]. Rav Huna said: "An oath that I have property rights to it to the amount of no less than (the value of a *peruṭah*)[16] [half of its value][17]. Rebbi Joḥanan said, if it is about this, it is an institutional oath[18].

13   The oath prescribed in the Mishnah.
14   How is this oath possible? Cf. Note 3.
15   The formulation of the oath in the Mishnah still leaves the court open to a charge of administering an oath which helps a person to be dishonest since one could read the text as: "An oath that I have no claim to it, less than half." Therefore, a positive statement of claim has to be inserted into the formula. The same formula is attributed to Rav Huna in the Babli, 5b.
16   Reading of the Leiden ms., a scribal error.
17   Text of E, confirmed by the Babli.
18   He disagrees with R. Ḥiyya and holds that the oath is purely an *ad hoc* instituted rabbinical ordinance. In the words of the Babli (3a), "lest it be easy to assert unfounded claims on another person's property."

(7d line 37) תַּנֵּי. שְׁנַיִם שֶׁהָיוּ תוֹפְסִין בִּשְׁטָר. זֶה אוֹמֵר. שֶׁלִּי וְאָבַד מִמֶּנִּי. וְזֶה אוֹמֵר. שֶׁלִּי הוּא שֶׁפְּרַעְתִּיו לָךְ. יִתְקַיֵּים הַשְּׁטָר בְּחוֹתְמָיו. דִּבְרֵי רִבִּי. רַבָּן [שִׁמְעוֹן בֶּן][18a] גַּמְלִיאֵל אוֹמֵר. יַחֲלוֹקוּ. אָמַר רִבִּי לְעָזָר. הַכֹּל הוֹלֵךְ אַחַר הַתָּפוּס בָּעֵדִים. אָמַר רַב חִסְדָּא. אֵין שְׁמַעְתּוּנֵיהּ אָתְיָיא כְּרַבָּן שִׁמְעוֹן.

It was stated[19]: "If two persons were holding a document[20] and one said, it is mine but I had lost it; the other said, it is mine since I paid you. The document should be validated by its signatories, the words of Rebbi[21]. Rabban Simeon ben Gamliel said, they should split[21]." Rabbi Eleazar said, it all depends on who is holding the signatures[22]. Rav Ḥisda said, if this[23] is true information, it follows Rabban Simeon[24].

18a  Text of E, missing in L.
19  Tosephta 1:15; *Giṭṭin* 1:1, Notes 68-71; Babli *Bava meṣi'a* 7a, *Bava batra* 170a.
20  An IOU; the persons involved are the creditor and the debtor.
21  He holds that a paid IOU either should be torn up or the receipt should be written on the document or be attached to it.
22  Since only the signatures validate the document. He follows the reformulation of the Mishnah in the Tosephta (1:1): "If two people hold on to one toga, each one takes what he holds in his hand." Presumably they split the remainder.
23  The opinion reported in the name of R. Eleazar the Amora.
24  Since for Rebbi an IOU without a receipt is valid, irrespective of who holds it.

(7d line 41) זֶה אוֹמֵר חֶצְיָהּ שֶׁלִּי. וְזֶה אוֹמֵר. שְׁלִישָׁהּ שֶׁלִּי. הָאוֹמֵר חֶצְיָהּ שֶׁלִּי יִשָּׁבַע שֶׁאֵין לוֹ בָהּ פָּחוֹת מֵרְבִיעַ. וְהָאוֹמֵר שְׁלִישָׁהּ שֶׁלִּי יִשָּׁבַע שֶׁאֵין לוֹ בָהּ פָּחוֹת מִשְּׁתוּת. כְּלָלוֹ שֶׁלְּדָבָר. אֵינוֹ נִשְׁבָּע אֶלָּא עַל חֲצִי שֶׁהוֹדָה.

One says, half is mine; the other says, a third is mine. The one who says that half is his shall swear that no less than a quarter be his; the one who says that a third is his shall swear that no less than a sixth be his. The principle involved: One only swears on half of what he agreed to[25].

25  On the face of it, the paragraph is unintelligible. R. E. Fulda comments: "I do not feel empowered to emend." The corresponding Tosephta (1:2) is clear:
"One says, *all* is mine; the other says,

a third is mine. The one who says that all is his shall swear that no less than five parts ($5/6$) are his; the one who says that a third is his shall swear that no less than a sixth is his. The principle involved: One only swears on half of what he agreed to."

In the case of the Tosephta, the second claimant surrenders $2/3$ to the first. Only $1/3$ is in dispute; it is split evenly. The first one receives $2/3 + 1/6 = 5/6$; the second receives $1/6$. Rabbinic practice decrees that one only swears on half of the amount which is in dispute; in this case each would swear that he owns no less that one sixth in addition to what he has by consensus [Maimonides, *To'en wenit'an* 9:8 (*Maggid Mišneh* ad 9:9), *Šulḥan 'Arukh Ḥošen Mišpaṭ* 138:2 (Note)].

In the Yerushalmi the total of the claims only adds up to $5/6$; they can be satisfied in full. There is no reason why anybody should swear. One has to explain the *baraita* as dealing with a case of bankruptcy in which the claims themselves are not sufficiently documented and can each be considered only by an affirmatory oath.

(fol. 7c) **משנה ב:** הָיוּ שְׁנַיִם רוֹכְבִין עַל גַּבֵּי בְהֵמָה אוֹ שֶׁהָיָה אֶחָד רוֹכֵב וְאֶחָד מְהַלֵּךְ. זֶה אוֹמֵר כּוּלָהּ שֶׁלִּי וְזֶה אוֹמֵר כּוּלָהּ שֶׁלִּי. זֶה יִשָּׁבַע שֶׁאֵין לוֹ בָהּ פָּחוּת מֶחֱצְיָיהּ וְזֶה יִשָּׁבַע שֶׁאֵין לוֹ בָהּ פָּחוּת מֶחֱצְיָיהּ וְיַחֲלוֹקוּ. בִּזְמַן שֶׁהֵן מוֹדִין אוֹ שֶׁיֵּשׁ לָהֶן עֵדִים חוֹלְקִין בְּלֹא שְׁבוּעָה.

**Mishnah 2**: If two persons were riding on an animal or one was riding and one was walking, each of them says "it wholly belongs to me"[26], each of them has to swear that he owns no less than half of it and they shall divide it evenly. If they agree[27] or if they have witnesses, they divide without an oath.

26   It will be explained in Mishnah 3 that the finder is not the person who first saw the abandoned property but the one who lifted it to acquire. It would be reasonable to expect that if a walker and a rider simultaneously

came upon some lost property the walker had a better chance to grab the object first. But in the absence of proof these arguments are irrelevant to the court; both parties must be given equal standing.

27 Even after the court gave its verdict, the parties are free to come to an amicable settlement.

(7d line 46) **הלכה ב**: הָיוּ שְׁנַיִם רוֹכְבִין עַל גַּבֵּי בְהֵמָה כול׳. אָמַר רִבִּי חוּנָא. תַּנֵּי תַמָּן. אִשָּׁה שֶׁהָיְתָה רְכוּבָה עַל גַּבֵּי בְהֵמָה וּשְׁנַיִם מַנְהִיגִין אוֹתָהּ. וְאוֹמֶרֶת. אִילוּ עֲבָדַיי וְהַחֲמוֹר וְהַמַּשָּׂאוּי שֶׁלִּי. וְזֶה אוֹמֵר. זוֹ אִשְׁתִּי וְזֶה עַבְדִּי וְהַחֲמוֹר וְהַמַּשָּׂאוּי שֶׁלִּי. וְזֶה אוֹמֵר. זוֹ אִשְׁתִּי וְזֶה עַבְדִּי וְהַחֲמוֹר וְהַמַּשָּׂאוּי שֶׁלִּי. צְרִיכָה גֵט מִשְּׁנֵיהֶן. וּצְרִיכָה לְשַׁחְרֵר אֶת שְׁנֵיהֶן. וּשְׁנֵיהֶן מְשַׁחְרְרִין זֶה אֶת זֶה. וּבַחֲמוֹר וּבַמַּשָּׂאוּי שֶׁלָּשְׁתָּן שָׁוִין.

**Halakhah 2**: "If two persons were riding on an animal," etc. Rebbi Huna said: It was stated there[28]: "A woman comes[29] riding on an animal and two men lead her. She says: these are my slaves; the donkey and the load are mine. Each of them says: this is my wife, the other is my slave, and the donkey and the load are mine[30]. She needs a bill of divorce from both of them[31] and has to manumit both of them. They have to manumit one another. In the donkey and the load they are equal co-owners.

28 A different, incompatible version is in the Babli, *Qiddušin* 65b, in the name of Rav Aḥdevoi bar Ammi who lived a generation before R. Huna and was known for his construction of impossible situations.

29 From overseas, without identification papers.

30 Since the rules of court proceedings state that "once somebody testified (under cross-examination), he cannot testify a second time", they cannot come back to court and change their statements (cf. *Ševi'it* 10:5 Note 96, *Bikkurim* 3:4 Note 72, *Ketubot* 3:3 Note 56; Babli *Ketubot* 18b). In line with the principles of Mishnah 1, the court has to impose a solution compatible with all statements.

31 Since the woman denies being

married and there are no witnesses, she certainly has no claim to *ketubah* from either of the men. From Mishnah *Qiddušin* 3:11 it would seem that therefore she can marry another person without a bill of divorce, as stated explicitly in the Babli; but the formulation in the Yerushalmi does not seem to support this statement.

(fol. 7c) **משנה ג**: הָיָה רוֹכֵב עַל הַבְּהֵמָה וְרָאָה אֶת הַמְּצִיאָה וְאָמַר לַחֲבֵירוֹ תְּנֶיהָ לִי וּנְטָלָהּ אָמַר אֲנִי זָכִיתִי בָהּ זָכָה בָהּ. אִם מִשֶּׁנְּתָנָהּ לוֹ אָמַר אֲנִי זָכִיתִי בָהּ תְּחִילָּה לֹא אָמַר כְּלוּם.

**Mishnah 3**: Somebody was riding on an animal when he saw a find and said to another person: "give it to me". If [that one] took it and said: "I acquired it", he acquired it[32]. If after he had handed it over, he said: "I acquired it first," he did not say anything[33].

32 Since ownerless property only can be acquired by action, never by intent or declaration (cf. *Ketubot* 5:5, Note 100.

33 The rider acquired the object by grabbing it in his hand; he is the presumed owner. The walker is now a claimant and "the burden of proof is on the claimant". If he did not articulate his claim before handing over the object there can be no witnesses and no proof.

(7d line 51) **הלכה ג**: הָיָה רָכוּב עַל הַבְּהֵמָה כול'. אָמַר רִבִּי יִצְחָק. הָדָא הִילְכְתָא לֵית שְׁמַע מִינָהּ כְּלוּם לֹא מֵרֹאשָׁהּ וְלֹא מְסוֹפָהּ. הָיָה רָכוּב עַל גַּבֵּי בְהֵמָה וְרָאָה אֶת הַמְּצִיאָה וְאָמַר לַחֲבֵירוֹ. תְּנֶיהָ לִי. נְטָלָהּ וְאָמַר. אֲנִי זָכִיתִי בָהּ. זָכָה בָהּ. אִילּוּ אָמַר. זְכֵה לִי. זָכָה. הֲוֵי לֵית שְׁמַע מִינָהּ כְּלוּם לֹא מֵרֵישָׁא וְלֹא מְסֵיפָא.

**Mishnah 3**: "Somebody was riding on an animal," etc. Rebbi Isaac says, from this rule one cannot infer anything, not from its beginning nor from its end. "Somebody was riding on an animal when he saw a find and said to another person: 'give it to me'. If [that one] took it and said: 'I acquired it', he acquired it". If he had said, "acquire it for me", he would have acquired it. That means, from this rule one cannot infer anything, not from its beginning nor from its end[34].

34   As *Pene Moshe* points out, this refers to the disagreement between R. Johanan and R. Simeon ben Laqish (*Peah* 4:6, Note 112), on whether a person can acquire a find for another person by lifting it. The Mishnah does not help in solving the dispute. The first sentence does not help since it does not exclude that had the rider said, "acquire it for me" instead of "give it to me", the walker would have acquired it for the rider by lifting and would not have been able to claim that he acquired it. The second sentence does not have to be quoted since it obviously is irrelevant for the disagreement between R. Johanan and R. Simeon ben Laqish.

(fol. 7d) **משנה ד:** רָאָה אֶה הַמְצִיאָה וְנָפַל עָלֶיהָ וּבָא אַחֵר וְהֶחֱזִיק בָּהּ זֶה שֶׁהֶחֱזִיק בָּהּ זָכָה בָהּ. רָאָה אוֹתָן רָצִין אַחַר מְצִיאָה אַחַר צְבִי שָׁבוּר אַחַר גּוֹזָלוֹת שֶׁלֹּא פֵּירֵיחוּ וְאָמַר זָכַת לִי שָׂדִי זָכַת לוֹ. הָיָה צְבִי רָץ כְּדַרְכּוֹ אוֹ שֶׁהָיוּ גּוֹזָלוֹת מִפְרִיחִין וְאָמַר סָכַת לִי שָׂדִי לֹא אָמַר כְּלוּם.

**Mishnah 4**: If somebody saw a find and fell upon it[35] when another person grabbed it, the one who grabbed it acquired it. If one saw people running after a find[36], after an injured deer, after young pigeons unable to fly, and he said: "my field shall acquire it for me", it acquired it for him[37]. If the deer was running normally, or the pigeons were flying, and he said: "my field shall acquire it for me", he did not say anything[38].

35 Without moving the find, it is not acquired. The second person in grabbing the find must have moved it a little; therefore, he acquired it.

36 Lying on an open field after it was harvested, before the field was ploughed.

37 A person's real estate acquires for its owner any property lying there of which he is cognizant; cf. *Gittin* 6:2, Note 71.

38 Animals and birds on a field are not lying there; real estate cannot acquire moving objects.

(7d line 56) **הלכה ד**: רָאָה אֶה הַמְּצִיאָה כול'. רֵישׁ לָקִישׁ אָמַר אַבָּא כֹּהֵן בַּר דְּלָיָה. אָדָם זָכָה בַּמְצִיאָה בְּתוֹךְ ד' אמות שֶׁלּוֹ. רִבִּי יוֹחָנָן אָמַר. וְהוּא שֶׁתִּפּוֹל לְתוֹךְ יָדוֹ. מַתְנִיתָהּ פְּלִיגָא עַל רֵישׁ לָקִישׁ. נָטַל מִקְצָת הַפֵּיאָה וְזָרַק עַל הַשְּׁאָר אֵין לוֹ בָּהּ כְּלוּם. אָמַר. תִּיפְתָּר בְּשֶׁלֹּא אָמַר. יִזְכּוּ לִי בְד' אַמּוֹת שֶׁלִּי. וְאָמוֹר דְּבַתְרָהּ. נָפַל עָלֶיהָ וּפָרַס טַלִּיתוֹ עָלֶיהָ מַעֲבִירִין אוֹתוֹ מִמֶּנָּה. עוֹד הִיא בְּשֶׁלֹּא אָמַר. יִזְכּוּ לִי בְד' אַמּוֹת שֶׁלִּי. וְהַתַנֵּי רִבִּי חִיָּיה. שְׁנַיִם שֶׁהָיוּ מִתְכַּתְּשִׁין בָּעוֹמֶר וּבָא עָנִי וַחֲטָפוֹ מִלִּפְנֵיהֶן זָכָה בוֹ. עוֹד הִיא בְּשֶׁלֹּא אָמַר. יִזְכּוּ לִי בְד' אַמּוֹת שֶׁלִּי. וְהָתַנִּינָן. רָאָה אֶה הַמְּצִיאָה וְנָפַל עָלֶיהָ וּבָא אַחֵר וְהֶחֱזִיק בָּהּ. זֶה שֶׁהֶחֱזִיק בָּהּ זָכָה בָהּ. עוֹד הִיא בְּשֶׁלֹּא אָמַר. יִזְכּוּ לִי בְד' אַמּוֹת שֶׁלִּי. וְהָתַנִּינָן. קָרוֹב לָהּ מְגוֹרֶשֶׁת. קָרוֹב לוֹ אֵינָהּ מְגוֹרֶשֶׁת. מֶחֱצָה לְמֶחֱצָה מְגוֹרֶשֶׁת וְאֵינָהּ מְגוֹרֶשֶׁת. חִזְקִיָּה אָמַר. בִּשְׂכַר הַלִּיבְּלָר הִיא מַתְנִיתָא. הֲתִיבוֹן. וְהָכְתִיב וַאֲנִי בְעוֹנְיִי הֲכִינוֹתִי וגו'. וְהֵיכִי. אִם בִּנְתוּנִין בְּתוֹךְ יָדוֹ עָשִׁיר הוּא. אִי בְּשֶׁאֵינָן נְתוּנִין לְתוֹךְ יָדוֹ יֵשׁ אָדָם מַקְדִּישׁ דָּבָר שֶׁאֵינוֹ שֶׁלּוֹ. הֲוֵי אוֹמֵר. בִּנְתוּנִין בְּתוֹךְ ד' אַמּוֹת שֶׁלּוֹ. אָמַר רִבִּי אָבִין. מַהוּ בְעוֹנְיִי. שֶׁאֵין עֲשִׁירוּת לִפְנֵי מִי שֶׁאָמַר וְהָיָה הָעוֹלָם. דָּבָר אַחֵר. שֶׁהָיָה מִתְעַנֶּה וּמַקְדִּישׁ סְעוּדָתוֹ לַשָּׁמַיִם.

**Halakhah 4**: "If somebody saw a find" etc. Rabbi Simeon ben Laqish said [in the name of] Abba Cohen bar Delaiah[39]: A person acquires a find within four cubits from himself[40]. Rebbi Johanan said, only if it fell into his hand[41]. A Mishnah disagrees with Rebbi Simeon ben Laqish: [42]"If he took some of the *peah* and threw it on the rest, he has nothing of it."[43]

He[44] answered: Explain it if the did not say that his four cubits should acquire it for him. But does it not say afterwards: "If he fell on it or spread his talith on it, one removes him from it?" That is the same, if he did not say that his four cubits should acquire it for him. But did not Rebbi Hiyya state[45]: "If two were pushing one another because of a sheaf and another poor person came and grabbed it from before them, he is entitled to it[35]." It is the same; he did not say that his four cubits should acquire it for him.

But did we not state: "If somebody saw a find and fell upon it when another person grabbed it, the one who grabbed it acquired it." It is the same, he did not say that his four cubits should acquire it for him.

But did we not state[46]: "If it landed close to her it is a bill of divorce, close to him it is no bill of divorce, half and half she is divorced and not divorced." Hizqiah said, the Mishnah speaks of the scribe's fee[47].

[48]They objected: Is it not written: "I in my poverty did prepare[49]"? How is that? If it was in his possession, he was rich. If it was not in his possession, how can a person dedicate what is not his? It must be that it was within four cubits from him[50]. Rebbi Abin said, what means "in my poverty?" That there is no wealth before Him Who commanded and the world came into existence! Another explanation: he fasted[51] and donated the price of his meal to Heaven.

39 "Resh Laqish" for "R. Simeon ben Laqish" and the omission of "in the name of" are typically Babylonian style.

40 *Peah* 4:2, Note 31; *Gittin* 8:3. If a person stands in the public domain, an ownerless object is within four cubits of him but of no other person, then he has the right to acquire the object and no other person has the right to enter the circle of four cubits around him to take the object. It is clear that taking possession requires

intent by the acquirer (cf. Babli *Bava meṣi'a* 10a/b).

41   No acquisition in the public domain can be effected by thought.

42   The remainder of this paragraph essentially is from *Peah* 4:2, Notes 40-46; *Giṭṭin* 8:3 (49c line 10).

43   Taking *Peah*, the uncut grain at the end of a field, is done from a private domain. But since the Torah grants the poor the right to enter a field after the end of the harvest to collect *peah* and forgotten stalks and sheaves, the harvested field has the status of public domain for the poor. A poor person acquires *peah* by taking it. He cannot then take his property and spread it over the remainder of standing produce to claim ownership, neither can he lie down on it for the same purpose. As with any acquisition, an action seems to be needed.

44   R. Simeon ben Laqish, defending his position.

45   Tosephta *Peah* 2:2.

46   Mishnah *Giṭṭin* 8:2.

47   In *Giṭṭin* 8:3, Note 47, the expression is: "The scribe of the second bill of divorce earns money." Since divorce is a unilateral act by the husband, he has to pay the scribe. But if the wife is "divorced and not divorced", a second bill of divorce is in the interest of both parties. The husband needs it in order to free himself from the duty to pay for his divorced wife's upkeep (*Giṭṭin* 8:2, Note 36), while the ex-wife needs it in order to be able to remarry. Therefore, they share the cost of the second bill.

48   The text is a reformulation of *Peah* 4:2, Notes 29-39; *Giṭṭin* 8:3 (49c l. 8).

49   *1Chr.* 22:14. David in his poverty prepared 100'000 talents of gold and 1'000'000 talents of silver for the future Temple. How can a super-rich person be called poor?

50   *Peah* 4:2, Note 50.

51   Reading עני as "to be deprived".

(7d line 74) תַּנֵּי. הָאוֹמֵר. יִזְכֶּה לִי בֵיתִי בִּמְצִיאָה שֶׁנָּפְלָה לְתוֹכָהּ. לֹא אָמַר כְּלוּם. יָצָא שֵׁם לִמְצִיאָתוֹ דְּבָרָיו קַיָּימִין. כְּהָדָא אֲרִיסֵיהּ דְּרִבִּי בָּא בַּר מִינָא סָלִיק לְדִיקְלָא אַשְׁכַּח גּוֹזָלִין וְנַסְתּוֹן. אֲזַל שְׁאַל לְרַב. לֹא אָמַר לֵיהּ כְּלוּם. אֲזַל חֲזַר. אָמַר רִבִּי בָּא בַּר מִינָא. קַשְׁיָיא לוֹן חֲזָרוּתֵי יֹתֵר מִמְּצִיאָתוֹ.

It was stated: "One who says, my house[51] shall acquire for me any find that fell into it, did not say anything. If the find was known, his words stand[52]." As in the case of Rebbi Abba bar Mina's[53] sharecropper who climbed a date palm[54], found pigeon chicks there, and took them. He went to ask the master, who said nothing to him[55]. He went and returned them. Rebbi Abba bar Mina said, his returning is more difficult for us[56] than his finding.

51  Any of his real estate.

52  Tosephta 1:4. There, the text reads: "One who says, my house shall acquire for me any find that *will fall* into it, did not say anything." This text is intelligible. Real estate acquires for its proprietor by the owner's will, as expressed in the second sentence. A future find is not foreseeable and cannot be the object of today's will. In the Halakhah, the past has to be read as future.

53  It is not impossible that he be R. Abba bar Zamina as conjectured by R. Eliahu Fulda.

54  On R. Abba's property.

55  He was not quite sure whether the chicks belonged to himself, as property owner, or to his sharecropper, the finder.

56  Since he treated them as ownerless property that nevertheless had an owner, even if it was not clear who the owner was.

**משנה ה:** מְצִיאַת בְּנוֹ וּבִתּוֹ הַקְּטַנִּים וְעַבְדּוֹ וְשִׁפְחָתוֹ הַכְּנַעֲנִים מְצִיאַת אִשְׁתּוֹ הֲרֵי אֵילוּ שֶׁלּוֹ. מְצִיאַת בְּנוֹ וּבִתּוֹ הַגְּדוֹלִים וְעַבְדּוֹ וְשִׁפְחָתוֹ הָעִבְרִים מְצִיאַת אִשְׁתּוֹ שֶׁגֵּרְשָׁהּ אַף עַל פִּי שֶׁלֹּא נָתַן לָהּ אֶת כְּתוּבָּתָהּ הֲרֵי אֵילוּ שֶׁלָּהֶן. (fol. 7d)

**Mishnah 5:** The find of his small son or daughter[57], or of his Canaanite[58] male or female slave, his wife's find[59], these are his. The find of his adult son or daughter, or of his Hebrew male or female slave[60], his wife's find after he divorced her even though he did not yet pay her *ketubah*[61], these are their own.

57 Even though in general קטן has to be translated as "underage", the Mishnah might refer to children who do not earn their upkeep, irrespective of age.

58 Of non-Jewish origin, whose person is his master's property. Cf. Mishnah *Qiddušin* 1:3.

59 It is part of the *Ketubah* contract that the wife's earnings, including her finds, are the husband's, since the latter is responsible for his wife's expenses. This clause can be modified by contract if the wife earns her own money and renounces her claim to her upkeep by the husband (*Ketubot* 7:1, Note 9).

60 A purely theoretical statement, Hebrew slavery having disappeared with the Babylonian exile; Cf. Mishnah *Qiddušin* 1:2.

61 Then he still is obligated to pay for her upkeep but has no claim to her earnings.

(8a line 3) **הלכה ה**: מְצִיאַת בְּנוֹ וּבִתּוֹ הַקְּטַנִּים כול׳. אָמַר רִבִּי יוֹחָנָן. בְּשֶׁאֵינָן טְפוּלִין לְאָבִיהֶן. אֲבָל אִם הָיוּ טְפוּלִין לְאָבִיהֶן מְצִיאָתָן שֶׁלּוֹ. רֵישׁ לָקִישׁ אָמַר. אֵין אָדָם זוֹכֶה לַחֲבֵירוֹ בִמְצִיאָה. אָמַר רִבִּי [הִילָא]. לֹא דְאָמַר רִבִּי שִׁמְעוֹן אֲכֵן אֶלָּא דְקָשֵׁי לֵיהּ עַל הָדָא דְתַנֵּי רִבִּי הוֹשַׁעְיָה. הַשּׂוֹכֵר אֶת הַפּוֹעֵל לַעֲשׂוֹת בְּכָל־מְלָאכָה מְצִיאָתוֹ לַבַעַל הַבַּיִת. אָמַר רֵישׁ לָקִישׁ. אָדָם שֶׁיֵּשׁ בּוֹ רְשׁוּת לַחֲזוֹר בּוֹ תְּהֵא מְצִיאָתוֹ לְרַבּוֹ.

**Halakhah 5**: "The find of his small son or daughter," etc. Rebbi Johanan said, only if they are not dependent on their father. But if they are dependent on their father, their finds belong to the latter[62]. Rebbi Simeon ben Laqish says, a person cannot acquire a find for another[63]. Rebbi [Hila][64] said: Not that Rebbi Simeon had formulated thus, but he had a problem with what Rebbi Hoshaiah stated: If a person hires a worker for *any* work, the latter's finds belong to the employer. Rebbi

Simeon ben Laqish said, should the finds of a person who can resign at any moment belong to his employer[65]?

62   This is the only opinion registered in the Babli, 12b, and in *Ketubot* 6:1, Note 21.

63   Therefore, קטן in the Mishnah means "underage"; the finds of aduult children, 12.5 years for girls and 13 years for boys, belong to them even though they still live in their father's house.

64   Word missing in L and *editio princeps*; added from E..

65   The last two sentences are formulated similarly in *Peah* 4:6, Notes 108-110. The statement naturally is not applicable to a worker hired to scout for finds (Babli 12b).

(8a line 8) מַה בֵּין עֲבָדוֹ וְשִׁפְחָתוֹ הָעְבְרִים לְעַבְדוֹ וְשִׁפְחָתוֹ הַכְּנַעֲנִים. אָמַר רִבִּי יוֹחָנָן. עַבְדוֹ וְשִׁפְחָתוֹ הָעְבְרִים הוֹאִיל וְאֵינוֹ רַשַּׁאי לְשַׁנּוֹתוֹ מִמְּלַכְתּוֹ מְצִיאָתוֹ לְעַצְמוֹ. עַבְדוֹ וְשִׁפְחָתוֹ הַכְּנַעֲנִים הוֹאִיל וְרַשַּׁאי לְשַׁנּוֹתָן מִמְּלַאכְתָּן מְצִיאָתָן לְרַבָּן. הֲתִיבוֹן. הֲרֵי אִשְׁתּוֹ שֶׁאֵינוֹ רַשַּׁאי לְשַׁנּוֹת מִמְּלַכְתָּהּ וּמְצִיאָתָהּ שֶׁלּוֹ. דְּתַנִּינָן תַּמָּן. כּוֹפָהּ לַעֲשׂוֹת בַּצֶּמֶר. וְאֵינוֹ כּוֹפָהּ לַעֲשׂוֹת בְּדָבָר אַחֵר. אָמַר רִבִּי בָּא בַּר מִינָא וְרִבִּי יָסָא בְּשֵׁם רִבִּי יוֹחָנָן. טַעַם אַחֵר בָּאִשָּׁה. מַה טַּעַם אַחֵר בָּאִשָּׁה. רִבִּי חַגַּי אָמַר. מִפְּנֵי הַקְּטָטָה. רִבִּי יוֹסֵה אוֹמֵר. שֶׁלֹּא תְהֵא מַבְרַחַת נִכְסֵי בַעֲלָהּ וְאוֹמֶרֶת. מְצִיאָה הִיא. הֲתִיבוֹן בַּעֲדִים לֹא אָסְרוּ זֶה אֶלָּא מִפְּנֵי זֶה.

What is the difference between his Hebrew male and female slaves and his Canaanite male and female slaves? Rebbi Joḥanan said, since he is not empowered to change the employment of his male[66] or female[67] Hebrew slave, that one's find belongs to himself. Since he is empowered to change the employment of his male or female Canaanite slave, their find belongs to their master. They objected: He is not empowered to change the employment of his wife, but her find belongs to him. As we have stated there: "He forces her to work with wool,[68]" he cannot force her to work any other material[69]. [70]Rebbi Abba bar Mina and Rebbi Yasa in the name of Rebbi Joḥanan: there is another reason in the case of the wife. What is another reason in the case of the wife? Rebbi Ḥaggai said, because of quarrel[71]. Rebbi Yose said, lest she smuggle away her husband's property and say: it is a find. They objected: before witnesses[72,73]? They forbade[74] one because of the other[74].

66  Lev. 26:39 prohibits to let the male Hebrew slave "work slave's work". This is interpreted in *Mekhilta dR. Ismael Neziqin* 1, *Mekhilta dR. Simeon ben Ioḥai* p. 160, *Sifra Behar Pereq* 7(3) that the slave must be employed in the trade he exercised before being sold.

67  Since she is underage, it is a question whether her find belongs to her father or her master. She probably should not have been mentioned in this connection; the use of the singular in the remainder of the sentence is correct, as compared to the plural used in the next sentence.

68  Mishnah *Ketubot* 5:6

69  Cf. *Ketubot* 5:6, Note 163.

70  An expanded version of this discussion is in *Ketubot* 6:1, Notes 17-21.

71  This is the only reason mentioned in the Babli, 12b, *Ketubot* 40b. The husband should not be angry that he has to pay for all of his wife's needs but cannot get his hands on her find.

72  If she finds an object before witnesses, there is no reason for R. Yose's rule. In *Ketubot*, several similar instances are invoked.

73  E has a longer text, but shorter than the analogous one in *Ketubot*, to explain the question:

מַה מַפְקָה בֵּינֵיהוֹן. מָצְאת בְּעֵדִים. מָאן דָּמַר מִפְּנֵי הַקְּטָטָה. אֵין כָּאן קְטָטָה. וּמָאן דָּמַר שֶׁלֹּא תְהֵא מַבְרַחַת נְכָסִים מִשֶּׁל בַּעֲלָהּ וְאוֹמֶרֶת מְצִיאָה מָצָאתִי. הָא בְּעֵדִים לֹא אֲסָרוּ זֶה אֶלָּא מִפְּנֵי זֶה.

What is the difference between them? If she found it in the presence of witnesses. For him who says, because of quarrel, would there not be quarrel? For him who says, lest she smuggle away her husband's property and say: I found a find, it follows that before witnesses they forbade one because of the other.

74 The wife's find is handed over to the husband even in cases where it was not necessary.

The use of "forbade" seems inadequate here; one would expect "decreed" or "instituted" the rule. In *Ketubot*, no verb is mentioned in this sentence. R. Yose holds that the worst case has to be presumed in all situations since detailed investigation probably is impossible.

(8a line 17) מְצִיאַת אִשְׁתּוֹ שֶׁגֵּירְשָׁהּ. רִבִּי יוֹסָנָא בְּשֵׁם רִבִּי אָחָא. אָדָם שֶׁגֵּירַשׁ אִשְׁתּוֹ וְלֹא נָתַן לָהּ כְּתוּבָּתָהּ חַיָּיב בִּמְזוֹנוֹתֶיהָ עַד שֶׁיִּתֵּן לָהּ פְּרוּטָה אַחֲרוֹנָה. אָמַר רִבִּי יוֹסֵי. מַתְנִיתָא אָמְרָה כֵן. מְצִיאַת אִשְׁתּוֹ שֶׁגֵּירְשָׁהּ. אָמַר רִבִּי הוֹשַׁעְיָה. שֶׁלֹּא תֹאמַר. הוֹאִיל וְחַיָּיב בִּמְזוֹנוֹתֶיהָ עַד שֶׁיִּתֵּן לָהּ פְּרוּטָה הָאַחֲרוֹנָה תְּהֵא מְצִיאָתָהּ שֶׁלּוֹ. לְפוּם כָּךְ צָרַךְ מִתְנִיתָא.

"His wife's find after he divorced her." Rebbi Yosana in the name of Rebbi Aḥa: A man who divorced his wife without paying her *ketubah* is liable for her upkeep until he gave her the last penny[75]. Rebbi Yose said, the Mishnah says this, "his wife's find after he divorced her.[76]" Rebbi Hoshaiah said, the Mishnah is needed lest you say that because he is liable for her upkeep until he gave her the last penny, her find should be his.

75 A similar rule, in the name of R. Isaac, is in *Ketubot* 6:2 (30c line 57) Note 22. Alfasi (*Ketubot* Chapter 13, # 390) proves that the Babli disagrees and limits the husband's liability to the amount of the *ketubah*.

76 If the husband had no financial responsibility for his ex-wife there would be no reason for him to claim her find.

(fol. 7d) **משנה ו:** מָצָא שְׁטָרֵי חוֹב אִם יֵשׁ בָּהֶם אַחֲרָיוּת נְכָסִים לֹא יַחֲזִיר שֶׁבֵּית דִּין נִפְרָעִין מֵהֶן. אֵין בָּהֶם אַחֲרָיוּת נְכָסִים יַחֲזִיר שֶׁאֵין בֵּית דִּין נִפְרָעִין מֵהֶן דִּבְרֵי רִבִּי מֵאִיר. וַחֲכָמִים אוֹמְרִים בֵּין כָּךְ וּבֵין כָּךְ לֹא יַחֲזִיר שֶׁבֵּית דִּין נִפְרָעִין מֵהֶן.

**Mishnah 6**: One who found documents of indebtedness containing an alienation clause should not return them since the court will foreclose on their basis[77]. If they do not contain an alienation clause, he should return them since the court will not foreclose on their basis[78], the words of Rebbi Meïr. But the Sages say, in no case should he return them since the court will foreclose on their basis[79].

[77] The standard document of indebtedness was written as a mortgage covering all the real estate in the debtor's possession at the moment of the execution of the deed. In contrast to general Egyptian and Roman practice the debtor was allowed to sell his real estate. but the alienation clause stated that the sale did not break the mortgage lien. If the debtor was unable to pay, the creditor could have regress on the buyer, who then would have to sue the debtor for his loss. The finder might not return the deed which he found since the mortgage might have been paid but the receipt somehow became separated from the document. If the deed was returned to the creditor, the latter might use it against an innocent buyer who would not know that it had been liquidated. This standard mortgage might have its root in the Ptolemaic and later Roman-Egyptian *obligatio omnium bonorum*, but probably it came with its Accadic name *šatārum* "written document" from Babylonian practice.

[78] Since the deed cannot be used against a third party, one assumes that the debtor has the means to prove that the debt was paid. In the Tosephta, 1:5, the formulation is: should return it if the debtor agrees.

[79] They rule that an alienation clause is always implied in a written bill of indebtedness; its absence only shows the incompetence of the scribe formulating the contract.

**הלכה ו**: (8a line 23) מָצָא שְׁטָרֵי חוֹב כול'. תַּנֵּי בְשֵׁם רְבִּי מֵאִיר. בֵּין שְׁטָר שֶׁיֵּשׁ בּוֹ אַחֲרָיוּת נְכָסִין וּבֵין שְׁטָר שֶׁאֵין בּוֹ אַחֲרָיוּת נְכָסִין גּוֹבָה מִנְּכָסִין בְּנֵי חוֹרִין. עַל דַּעְתֵּיהּ דְּרִבִּי מֵאִיר לְאֵי זֶה דָבָר הוּא מַחֲזִיר. לָצוּר עַל פִּי צְלוֹחִיתוֹ. רַב אָמַר. יוֹרֵשׁ כִּמְשׁוּעְבָּד. כְּשֵׁם שֶׁמִּלְוָה בְעֵדִים אֵינָהּ נִגְבֵּית מִמְּשׁוּעְבָּדִים כָּךְ אֵינָהּ נִגְבֵּית מִן הַיּוֹרְשִׁין. שְׁמוּאֵל אָמַר. דְּאִיקְנֵי אֵינוֹ גוֹבֶה מִמְּשׁוּעְבָּדִים. הָא מִבְּנֵי חוֹרֵי גָבֵי. הָכָא אָתְּ מַר. גּוֹבָה. וְהָכָא אָתְּ מַר. אֵינוֹ גוֹבָה. לֹא דָמֵי מִי שֶׁשִּׁיעְבֵּד מִקְצָת לְמִי שֶׁלֹּא שִׁיעְבֵּד כָּל־עִיקָר.

**Halakhah 6**: "One who found documents of indebtedness," etc. It was stated in the name of Rebbi Meïr: Both based on a document containing an alienation clause or a document containing no alienation clause, he collects from unincumbered property[80]. Following this opinion of Rebbi Meïr, to what purpose does he return it? To cover the mouth of his pitcher[81]. [82]Rav said, an heir is like the holder of encumbered property. Just as a loan executed before witnesses cannot be collected from encumbered property, so it cannot be collected from heirs. Samuel said, what was received cannot be foreclosed on mortgaged property, but on free property it can be foreclosed. Here you say, it can be collected, but there you say, it cannot be collected[83]. There is no comparison between one who agreed to a small lien and one who never agreed to a lien.

---

80  Property which is in the debtor's possession without being subject to any third party lien. In this version of R. Meïr's position, a creditor who wants to be secure has to write a contract which forbids the debtor to either sell his property or to mortgage it to another person.

81  In this context, the remark is a non sequitur. It seems to refer to another tradition of R. Meïr's, quoted in the Babli, 13a, by Samuel: A contract containing no alienation clause cannot be used to foreclose. This means that such a contract is hardly worth the paper it is written on.

E has a different text with an additional sentence:

תַּנֵּי בְשֵׁם רִבִּי מֵאִיר. בֵּין שְׁטָר שֶׁיֵּשׁ בּוֹ אַחֲרָיוּת נְכָסִין וּבֵין שְׁטָר שֶׁאֵין בּוֹ אַחֲרָיוּת נְכָסִין גּוֹבָה מִנְּכָסִין מְשׁוּעֲבָּדִים. וַחֲכָמִים אוֹמ' שְׁטָר שֶׁיֵּשׁ בּוֹ אַחֲרָיוּת נְכָסִין גּוֹבָה מִנְּכָסִין מְשׁוּעֲבָּדִים וְשֶׁאֵין בּוֹ אַחֲרָיוּת נְכָסִין אֵינוּ גוֹבָה מִנְּכָסִין מְשׁוּעֲבָּדִים.

It was stated in the name of Rebbi Meïr: Both based on a document containing an alienation clause or a document containing no alienation clause, he collects from incumbered property. But the Sages say, he collects from incumbered property based on a document containing an alienation clause, but based on a document containing no alienation clause, he cannot collect from incumbered property.

S. Lieberman suggests to read תַּמָּן אוֹמְרִים "there (in Babylonia), they say" instead of "but the Sages say." This then properly refers the entire discussion to positions of R. Meïr quoted in the Halakhah. One could also suggest to read אֲחֵרִים אוֹמְרִים "others say," and refer to the opinion stated as R. Meïr's in *Ketubot* 4:9, Note 217, which is identical with that quoted here in the name of the "Sages".

82   The following two sentences are from *Bava Qamma* 10:1, Notes 12-13. Rav's statement is a reformulation, Samuel's a copy.

83   Unencumbered property can be foreclosed on basis of an IOU missing an alienation clause. The property of the recipient of a gift cannot be foreclosed.

(8a line 31) אָמַר רִבִּי לְעָזָר. שֶׁאֲנִי אוֹמֵר. כָּתַב לִלְווֹת וְלֹא לָוָה. אָמַר רִבִּי לְעָזָר. אִם הָיָה הַלּוֹוֶה מוֹדֶה הֲרֵי זֶה יַחֲזִיר. אָמַר רִבִּי לְעָזָר. אִם הוּחְזַק הַשְּׁטָר בְּיַד הַמַּלְוֶה הֲרֵי זֶה יַחֲזִיר. וּתְלִיתָהוֹן מְתַבְּרִין. וַחֲכָמִים אוֹמְרִים בֵּין כָּךְ וּבֵין כָּךְ לֹא יַחֲזִיר. רִבִּי אַבָּהוּ בְּשֵׁם רִבִּי יוֹחָנָן. מִפְּנֵי קֵינוֹנִיָּיא. רִבִּי יָסָא בְּשֵׁם רִבִּי יוֹחָנָן. אִם הָיָה זְמַנּוּ יוֹצֵא לְבוֹ בַּיּוֹם יַחֲזִיר.

Rebbi Eleazar said, for I am saying that he wanted to take a loan but did not[84]. Rebbi Eleazar said, if the debtor agreed, he should return it. Rebbi Eleazar said, if the document was generally known to be in the creditor's hand, he should return it. But all three are broken[85], "the Sages say, in no case should he return them." Rebbi Abbahu in the name of Rebbi Joḥanan: Because of conspiracy[86]. Rebbi Yasa in the name of Rebbi Joḥanan: If its date was that very day, he should return it[87,88].

84   He explains the reason of the Sages. Mishnah *Bava Batra* 10:5 permits to write a mortgage document for the debtor and have it signed even though the creditor not be present at that moment. As the Babli, 12b, explains, the problem with this is that the mortgage might have been executed in April but the loan was given only in October. If the debtor sold real estate in the meantime, the buyer in effect bought unencumbered property while the mortgage document falsely classified it as encumbered. Therefore, the Babli restricts the permission to mortgage deeds with which the title to the land is immediately deposited with the creditor, the Egyptian ὑπάλλαγμα (cf. R. Taubenschlag, *The Law of Graeco-Roman Egypt in the Light of the Papyri*, pp. 208 ff.) The Yerushalmi (*loc. cit.* Halakhah 10:5) gives standing in court only to unilateral promises of payment for future services.

85   All three statements of R. Eleazar are rejected in practice.

86   Greek κοινωνία, cf. *Yebamot* 3:9, Note 133. Lender and borrower might conspire to defraud the innocent buyer; see Note 84.

87   The document was dated the day it was found; the witnesses are still available who can testify to its genuineness.

88   E here has an addition which is irrelevant:

וַאֲפִילוּ אֵין זְמַנּוֹ יוֹצֵא לָבוֹא בַּיוֹם יַחֲזִיר. מָהוּ פְלִיג. וּמַד רִבִּי אַבָּהוּ בְּשֵׁם רִבִּי יוֹחָנָן. מִפְּנֵי קֵינוֹנְיָיה. וּמַד רִבִּי יוֹחָנָן. אִם הָיָה זְמַנּוֹ יוֹצֵא לָבוֹא בַּיוֹם יַחֲזִיר.

But could he not return it if the date was not of the same day? Do they disagree? But Rebbi Abbahu said\* in the name of Rebbi Joḥanan: Because of conspiracy. Rebbi Joḥanan said\*: If its date was that very day, he should return it.

\*   Reading ומד for ומר

**משנה ז:** מָצָא גִיטֵּי נָשִׁים וְשִׁיחֲרוּרֵי עֲבָדִים דְּיַיתֵיקֵי מַתָּנָה וְשׁוֹבְרִין (fol. 7d) הֲרֵי זֶה לֹא יַחֲזִיר שֶׁאֲנִי אוֹמֵר כְּתוּבִין הָיוּ וְנִמְלַךְ עֲלֵיהֶם שֶׁלֹּא לִתְּנָן.

**Mishnah 7**: One who found women's bills of divorce[89] or slaves' bills of manumission, dispositions[90] of gift or receipts[91] should not return them since I say that they were written but he changed his mind not to deliver them.

[89] The divorcee would need the bill to collect her *ketubah*. If the *ketubah* was paid, the bill should be torn up. Therefore, one could assume that the woman would take care to watch over the document and, in case it was lost, to publicly announce its loss and ask the public to return it to her. In the absence of such a public announcement, the finder has to assume that the bill was not delivered. Similar arguments apply to the other documents enumerated in the Mishnah.

[90] Greek διαθήκη, usually referring to testamentary gifts.

[91] Documents which prove the liquidation of a mortgage.

(8a line 36) **הלכה ז**: מָצָא גִיטֵי נָשִׁים כול'. תַּנֵי. מָצָא גִיטִין וּכְתוּבוֹת הֲרֵי זֶה יַחֲזִיר. וּכְתוּבָּה לֹא הִיא חֲזָקָה.

**Halakhah 7**: "One who found women's bills of divorce," etc. It was stated: One whou found women's bills of divorce with *ketubot*[92] should return them." Is the *ketubah* not *prime facie* evidence?

[92] He found a bill of divorce and attached to it a *ketubah* which either had a receipt written on it or was torn where the witnesses had signed as proof of liquidation of the debt. Then the bill certainly had been delivered to the woman, the *ketubah* had been paid, and no monetary consequences would follow the return of the bill to the woman. The *baraita* does not contradict the Mishnah.

E has a different formulation of the last sentence:

וּכְתוּבָּה לֹא הוּחְזְקָה בְּיַד הָאִשָּׁה.

Was the *ketubah* not *prima facie* evidence in the woman's hand?

(8a line 37) שְׁטָר שֶׁלָּוָה בּוֹ וּפְרָעוֹ לֹא יַחֲזוֹר וְיִגְבֶּה בּוֹ מִפְּנֵי מֵירַע כּוֹחָן שֶׁל לְקוּחוֹת. רִבִּי יָסָא בְּשֵׁם רִבִּי יוֹחָנָן. וַאֲפִילוּ לְבוֹ בַיּוֹם. רִבִּי זֵירָא בְּעָא קוֹמֵי רִבִּי יָסָא. הָכָא אַתְּ מַר. אֲפִילוּ לְבוֹ בַיּוֹם. וְהָכָא אַתְּ מַר. אִם זְמַנּוֹ יוֹצֵא לְבוֹ בַיּוֹם יַחֲזִיר. אָמַר לֵיהּ. אָדָם מָצוּי לִלְווֹת וְלִפְרוֹעַ לְבוֹ בַיּוֹם. וְאֵין אָדָם עָשׂוּי לִפְרוֹעַ וְלִלְווֹת לְבוֹ בַיּוֹם. רִבִּי חַגַּיי בְּעָא קוֹמֵי רִבִּי יָסָא. הוּא הַזְּמָן וְהֵן הָעֵדִים וְהוּא הַמִּלְוָה מָהוּ מִפְּנֵי מֵירַע כּוֹחָן שֶׁל לְקוּחוֹת. אָמַר לֵיהּ. בְּשֶׁלֹּא נִשְׁתַּעְבְּדוּ נְכָסִים. וְיֵשׁ אוֹמְרִים. בְּשֶׁלֹּא חָתְמוּ הָעֵדִים עַל אוֹתָהּ הַמִּלְוָה.

If a person took a documented loan and paid it back, he cannot use the document to take a second loan because it diminishes the power of the buyers. Rebbi Yasa in the name of Rebbi Johanan: Even on the same day[93].

Rebbi Ze'ira asked before Rebbi Yasa: Here you say, even on the same day. But there[94], you say, if its date was that very day, he should return it! He answered, a person is apt to take a loan and repay it the same day, but a person is not apt to repay a loan and take it the same day[95,93].

Rebbi Haggai asked before Rebbi Yasa: It is the same day, the same witnesses, and the same amount. What is the meaning of "it diminishes the power of the buyers"[96]? He answered, if the property had not been mortgaged[97]. But some say, if the witnesses did not sign for *this* loan[98,93].

93 The same statement is in the Babli, 17a.
94 In the preceding Halakhah.
95 It is a matter of *prima facie* evidence, as in the cases of the Mishnah.
96 The formulation implies that the creditor can unlawfully foreclose property from the innocent buyer in case of nonpayment of the debt.
97 If the first loan was not given as a mortgage.
98 All the statements of R. Haggai are true; nevertheless the document is invalid since the witnesses did not certify the loan actually given but a predecessor loan.

(fol. 7d) **משנה ח:** מָצָא אִגְּרוֹת שׁוּם וְאִגְּרוֹת מָזוֹן וּשְׁטָרֵי חֲלִיצָה וּמֵאוּנִין וּשְׁטָרֵי בֵירוּרִין וְכָל־מַעֲשֵׂה בֵית דִין הֲרֵי זֶה יַחֲזִיר. מָצָא בַחֲפִיסָה אוֹ בִגְלוֹסְקָמָא תַּכְרִיךְ שֶׁל שְׁטָרוֹת אוֹ אֲגוּדָה שֶׁל שְׁטָרוֹת הֲרֵי זֶה יַחֲזִיר. וְכַמָּה הִיא אֲגוּדָה שֶׁל שְׁטָרוֹת שְׁלֹשָׁה קְשׁוּרִין זֶה בָזֶה. רַבָּן שִׁמְעוֹן בֶּן גַּמְלִיאֵל אוֹמֵר אֶחָד הַלּוֹוֶה מִשְּׁלֹשָׁה יַחֲזִיר לַלּוֹוֶה שְׁלֹשָׁה הַלּוֹוִים מֵאֶחָד יַחֲזִיר לַמַּלְוֶה. מָצָא שְׁטָר בֵּין שְׁטָרוֹתָיו וְאֵין יָדוּעַ מַה טִיבוֹ יְהֵא מוּנָח עַד שֶׁיָּבוֹא אֵלִיָּהוּ. אִם יֵשׁ עִמָּהֶן סִמְפּוֹן יַעֲשֶׂה מַה שֶׁבְּסִימְפּוֹן.

**Mishnah 8:** One who found letters of appraisal[99], letters of sustenance[100], or documents of *ḥaliṣah*[101] or repudiation[102], or documents of arbitration[103], or any other court document, should return them. If he found in a basket[104] or in a box[105] a bundle[106] or joined documents he should return them. How many are joined documents? Three documents connected one to the other. Rabban Simeon ben Gamliel says, if one persons borrows from three, he should return it to the borrower; if three persons borrow from one, he should return it to the lender. If he found a document among his documents whose nature was unknown to him[107], it should lie there until Elijah comes[108]. If it has an agreement[109] attached to it, he should follow the agreement.

[99] Court documents in which the value of property in execution is appraised for the creditor.

[100] Court documents empowering a widow to sell from her late husband's property for her sustenance.

[101] Court documents authorizing a childless widow to remarry outside her late husband's family.

[102] Court documents confirming that an underage, fatherless girl walked out on a marriage arranged by her mother or her brothers.

[103] Court documents in which the parties to a civil suit appoint a panel of arbitration judges and promise to abide by their judgment.

[104] Arabic حنف "basket, bag".

[105] Greek γλωσσοκομεῖον "chest, box".

106 Documents rolled and tied together. In joined documents one is joined to the next.
107 According to Rashi, a third party document; according to Maimonides and Ravia, a valid IOU in a bundle of receipted documents.
108 The announcer of the Messiah is reputed to know all the answers.
109 Greek σύμφωνον "contract", an expression used in Byzantine era papyri for special stipulations within a written contract (cf. Taubenschlag, Note 84, p. 224). The commentators of the Babli and Alfasi follow the Geonim and Rashi in explaining *symphon* as a receipt; R. Hananel explains "receipt or codicill".

(8a line 45) **הלכה ח**: מָצָא אִגְרוֹת שׁוּם כול׳. רַב יִרְמְיָה בְּשֵׁם רַב. אִם הָיָה אִישֵׁר הַדַּיָּינִין הֲרֵי זֶה יַחֲזִיר. רִבִּי חָמָא אָבוֹי דְרִבִּי הוֹשַׁעְיָה אָמַר. אַשְׁלֵי דַיָּינִין שֶׁבַּגָּלוּיוֹת גּוֹזְלֵי דַיָּינִין שֶׁבְּאֶרֶץ יִשְׂרָאֵל.

**Halakhah 8**: "One who found letters of appraisal," etc. Rav Jeremiah in the name of Rav: If it contained a certification by the court, it should be returned[110]. Rebbi Ḥama the father of Rebbi Hoshaia said, the tamarisks among the judges of the diaspora are like chicks among the judges of the Land of Israel[111].

110 Even a private document.
111 The statement of Rav, the mightiest of the Babylonian authorities, is in error. As the Galilean authorities explain in the Babli, 16b, the only case in which a court certified mortgage document can be returned, is an instruction by the court that ownership of a well-defined property of the debtor is transferred to the creditor in liquidation of the mortgage. In this case, no third party buyer is endangered. But a document certified for unspecified foreclosure cannot be returned since an innocent third party might be damaged.

(8a line 48) רַב הַמְנוּנָא אָמַר. נִכְתְּבָה אוֹנוֹ בְּאֶחָד בְּנִיסָן נִיתַּן הַכֶּסֶף בַּעֲשָׂרָה בְּנִיסָן צְרִיכִין לִכְתּוֹב. אַף עַל פִּי שֶׁכָּתַבְנוּ כָּתַב בְּאֶחָד בְּנִיסָן כֵּן נִגְמַר שֶׁיִּתֵּן

הַכֶּסֶף בַּעֲשָׂרָה בְּנִיסָן.

Rav Hamnuna said, if the sale contract was written on the first of Nisan but payment was only on the tenth of Nisan[112], they have to write: Even though we wrote the document on the first of Nisan it was agreed that payment be made on the tenth of Nisan.

112 Then ownership will only be transferred on the 10th; the piece of property will be at the disposal of the creditors of the seller, not of the buyer, between the 1st and the 10th. In the interpretation of *Sefer Ha'ittur* I 30a, the Babli disputes the validity of any sale document predating the transfer of ownership.

(8a line 50) רַב יִרְמְיָה בְּשֵׁם רַב. סִימְפּוֹן שֶׁיּוֹצֵא מִתַּחַת יְדֵי הַמַּלְוֶה בִּכְתַב יְדֵי מַלְוֶה פָּסוּל. אֲנִי אוֹמֵר. מִתְעַסֵּק הָיָה בִּשְׁטָרוֹתָיו. הָא מִתַּחַת יְדֵי אַחֵר כָּשֵׁר. רִבִּי יִצְחָק בַּר נַחְמָן בְּשֵׁם שְׁמוּאֵל. לְעוֹלָם אֵין סִימְפּוֹן כָּשֵׁר עַד שֶׁיֵּצֵא מִתַּחַת יְדֵי הַמַּלְוֶה בִּכְתַב יְדֵי הַלֹּוֶה. וְהָא תַנִּינָן. שֶׁלֹּא פִיקַּדְנוּ אַבָּא וְשֶׁלֹּא אָמַר לָנוּ אַבָּא וְשֶׁלֹּא מָצִינוּ שְׁטָר בֵּין שְׁטָרוֹתָיו שֶׁשְּׁטָר זֶה פָרוּעַ. הָא אִם נִמְצָא פָרוּעַ. מַאי כְדוֹן. אָמַר רִבִּי יוֹסֵי בֵּירִבִּי בּוּן. תִּיפְתַּר כְּגוֹן הָדָא דִיַתֵיקֵי. שֶׁאֵין אָדָם מָצוּי לִפְגֹם דִּייַתֵיקִין שֶׁלּוֹ.

Rav Jeremiah in the name of Rav: A stipulation produced by the creditor in the creditor's handwrtiting is invalid[113], for I am saying that he has trained in writing documents. This implies that in the hand of another it would be valid. Rebbi Isaac bar Naḥman in the name of Samuel: A stipulation is only valid if it is in the possession of the creditor but written by the debtor. But did we not state[114]: "That our father did not charge us, that our father did not tell us, that we did not find a document among our father's documents that this note was paid." Therefore, it might be found paid. What about this? Rebbi Yose ben Rebbi Abun said, explain it that it was a testamentary gift., since people are not likely to impair their testamentary gifts[115].

113 The same statement is in the Babli, 20b. *Sefer Ha'iṭṭur* I 41a (Notes מט to גא) gives two slightly different versions of parts of this paragraph.

114 Mishnah *Šebuot* 7:9, quoted *Ketubot* 9:7 (Note 177), *Sanhedrin* 8:6 (20b l. 62), Babli 20b, *Šebuot* 45. This is the oath required from heirs if they sue for payment of IOU's they inherited. It is clear that the creditor's heirs are not the creditor himself.

115 Attachments to documents of testamentary gifts written by the donor are to be accepted at face value. The same statement is repeated in *Šebuot* 7:9, 38a l. 48.

## אילו מציאות פרק שני

**משנה א:** (fol. 8a) אֵילוּ מְצִיאוֹת שֶׁלּוֹ וְאֵילוּ חַיָּיב לְהַכְרִיז. אֵילוּ מְצִיאוֹת שֶׁלּוֹ מָצָא פֵירוֹת מְפוּזָּרִין מָעוֹת מְפוּזָּרוֹת כְּרִיכוֹת בִּרְשׁוּת הָרַבִּים וְעִיגוּלֵי דְבֵילָה כִּכָּרוֹת שֶׁל נַחְתּוֹם מַחֲרוֹזוֹת שֶׁל דָּגִים וַחֲתִיכוֹת שֶׁל בָּשָׂר וְגִיזֵּי צֶמֶר הַבָּאוֹת מִמְּדִינָתָן וַאֲנִיצֵי פִשְׁתָּן וּלְשׁוֹנוֹת שֶׁל אַרְגָּמָן הֲרֵי אֵילוּ שֶׁלּוֹ.

**Mishnah 1:** Which finds are his and which ones does he have to make public[1]? The following finds are his: If he found scattered produce, scattered coins[2], bundles of grain in the public domain[3], or fig cakes, baker's loaves, strings of fish, cuts of meat, local fleece-wool, bundles of flax, or strips of purple wool[4]; these are his[5].

1   As explained in Mishnah 6, there is a biblical requirement that the finder not return a found object unless the person claiming to be the owner clearly identifies the object by some marks or properties not generally known. Therefore, objects without identifying properties cannot be returned and become the finder's immediately since it may be assumed that the owner immediately gave up hope of recovery, so that an ownerless object was picked up.

2   If these are common produce or common coins, they have no identifying marks nor can they be identified by the place where they were lost.

3   Small bundles which are blown away by the wind or moved by passing animals or people; they cannot be expected to be found at the place where they were lost. Since most farmers make such bundles, their shape is no identifying mark.

4   All these are local products, made uniformly by several producers and, therefore, without individual identifying marks.

5   In the Babli and most independent Mishnah mss.: "The words of R. Meïr." Since an anonymous Mishnah is supposed to be R. Meïr's,

the addition is unnecessary. The individual opinions expressed in the next Mishnah are clarifications, not dissenting opinions.

(8b line 50) **הלכה א:** אֵילוּ מְצִיאוֹת שֶׁלּוֹ כול'. מְנַיִין לְיִיאוּשׁ בְּעָלִין מִן הַתּוֹרָה. רִבִּי יוֹחָנָן בְּשֵׁם רִבִּי שִׁמְעוֹן בֶּן יְהוֹצָדָק. כֵּן תַּעֲשֶׂה לַחֲמוֹרוֹ וגו'. אֶת שֶׁאָבוּד לוֹ וּמָצוּי לָךְ אַתְּ חַיָּיב לְהַכְרִיז. וְאֶת שֶׁאֵינוֹ אָבוּד לוֹ וּמָצוּי לָךְ אֵין אַתְּ חַיָּיב לְהַכְרִיז. יָצָא יֵיאוּשׁ בְּעָלִין שֶׁאָבוּד מִמֶּנּוּ וּמִכָּל־אָדָם.

**Halakhah 1**: "Which finds are his," etc. From where may an owner's hopelessness[6] be deduced from the Torah? Rebbi Joḥanan said in the name of Rebbi Simeon ben Yehoṣadaq: "So you shall proceed with his donkey,[7]" etc. What is lost by him but may be found by anybody you have to make public. But what is not lost by him but may be found by anybody you do not have to make public. This excludes the owner's hopelessness about that which was lost by him or anybody.

6  That a lost article becomes ownerless the moment the owner realizes his loss since he has no hope of recovery. Then appropriating a find which has no distinguishing marks is not theft. This leaves open the question, discussed at length in the Babli, why keeping a find without marks is not theft even before the original owner became conscious of his loss.

7  *Deut.* 22:3: "So you shall proceed with his donkey, so you shall proceed with his garment, so you shall proceed with anything *lost by your neighbor and which you found*; you cannot avoid taking notice." As usual, the argument is about a part of the verse which is not quoted. The clause in Italics seems to be superfluous; if he did not lose and you did not find, there would be no case. It must be that you found something which can be traced back to your neighbor.

(8b line 54) תַּנֵּי. מָצָא כְּרִיכוֹת בִּרְשׁוּת הָרַבִּים אֵינוֹ חַיָּיב לְהַכְרִיז. בִּרְשׁוּת הַיָּחִיד חַיָּיב לְהַכְרִיז. אֲלוּמוֹת בֵּין בִּרְשׁוּת הָרַבִּים בֵּין בִּרְשׁוּת הַיָּחִיד חַיָּיב לְהַכְרִיז.

It was stated⁸: "One who found bundles of grain in the public domain⁹ does not have to make it public; in a private domain¹⁰ he has to make it public¹¹. Sheaves¹² he has to make public, whether in the public or the private domain."

8   Tosephta 2:5; Babli 22b.
9   Small bundles of standard size on the road leading from the fields to town.
10  On a field or a narrow path, not accessible to persons not engaged in agriculture at that place.
11  In this situation, the bundle might not have been moved from the place and the place might count as identifying mark.
12  Large sheaves for which size, kind, and place might count as identifying marks.

(8b line 56) עִיגוּלֵי דְבֵילָה. הָדָא דְתֵימַר בְּאִילֵּין עִיגוּלַיָּיא רַבְרְבַיָּא. בְּרַם בְּאִילֵּין זְעִירַיָּיא דְאָתְיָין מִבְּצְרָה חַיָּיב לְהַכְרִיז מִשּׁוּם סִימָנֵי מָקוֹם. חֲתִיכוֹת שֶׁלְבָשָׂר וּבְתוֹכָן כִּכָּר אַחַת אוֹ כּוּלְיָה אַחַת חַיָּיב לְהַכְרִיז. מַחֲרוֹזוֹת שֶׁלְדָגִים וּבְתוֹכָן יָרָק אֶחָד אוֹ לָכִיס אֶחָד חַיָּיב לְהַכְרִיז.

"Fig cakes." That is, large cakes. But small cakes which come from Bostra¹³ he has to make public since they are typical for that place. Cuts of meat and among them a loaf¹⁴ or a kidney he has to make public. Strings of fish¹⁵ strung together with a vegetable or a whitefish¹⁵ he has to make public.

13  They are not locally made and may exhibit characteristics which distinguish them from other imported produce.
14  E reads כָּבֵד אֶחָד "a liver". This seems to be a more reasonable text. Meat which is not a standard cut produced by every butcher has to be announced.
15  Routinely made by every fisherman when he brings his catch to market.
15  Cf. *Kilaim* 1:6, Note 117.

(fol. 8a) **משנה ב:** רבִּי יְהוּדָה אוֹמֵר. כָּל־דָּבָר שֶׁיֵּשׁ בּוֹ שִׁנּוּי חַיָּיב לְהַכְרִיז. כֵּיצַד מָצָא עִיגּוּל וּבְתוֹכוֹ חֶרֶס כְּכָר וּבְתוֹכוֹ מָעוֹת. רבִּי שִׁמְעוֹן בֶּן אֶלְעָזָר אוֹמֵר כָּל־כְּלֵי אֶנְפּוֹרְיָא אֵינוֹ חַיָּיב לְהַכְרִיז.

**Mishnah 2**: Rebbi Jehudah says, anything out of the ordinary[16] one has to make public. How is this? If he found a fig cake containing a potsherd, or a loaf containing coins. Rebbi Simeon ben Eleazar said, merchandise of any kind[17] one does not have to make public.

16 The deviation from the norm serves as identifying mark.

17 S. Lieberman, following B. Mussaphia, identifies as Greek ἐμπορία. If a new vessel is offered for trade and looks like any other new vessel of the same manufacture, no identification is possible. In the Tosephta, 2:1, R. Simeon ben Eleazar explicitly states that vessels which show signs of use must be advertised.

(8b line 60) **הלכה ב:** רבִּי יְהוּדָה אוֹמֵר. כָּל־דָּבָר שֶׁיֵּשׁ בּוֹ שִׁינּוּי כול'. תַּנֵּי. בִּמְשׁוּקָע בּוֹ. הָכָא אַתְּ מַר. בִּמְשׁוּקָע בּוֹ. וְכָא אַתְּ מַר. בִּנְתוּן בּוֹ דֶּרֶךְ הִינּוּחַ. הֵן דְּתֵימַר בִּמְשׁוּקָע בּוֹ. בִּרְשׁוּת הָרַבִּים. וְהֵן דְּתֵימַר בִּנְתוּן בּוֹ דֶּרֶךְ הִינּוּחַ. בִּרְשׁוּת הַיָּחִיד. וַאֲפִילוּ בִּרְשׁוּת הָרַבִּים בִּנְתוּן בּוֹ דֶּרֶךְ הִינוּחַ אֲנִי אוֹמֵר. דֶּרֶךְ נְפִילָה נָפְלָה עָלָיו.

**Halakhah 2**: "Rebbi Jehudah says, anything out of the ordinary," etc. It was stated: If it is embedded in it[18]. Here you say, if it is embedded in it. But there[19] you say, if it lies on top of it. When you say, if it is embedded in it, in the public domain[20]. When you say, if it lies on top of it, in a private domain. Maybe even in the public domain? If it lies on top of it, I am saying that if fell there.

18 Kneaded into the fig cake or baked into the loaf.

19 Tosefta 2:8: One who found a container and produce in front of it, a wallet and coins in front of it, must make it public.

20 Where the place is not a distinguishing mark.

(8b line 65) רִבִּי שִׁמְעוֹן בֶּן אֶלְעָזָר אוֹמֵר. כְּלֵי אֶנְפּוֹרְיָא אֵינוֹ חַיָּיב לְהַכְרִיז. אָמְרָהּ רִבִּי יוֹחָנָן וְתַנֵּי לָהּ. וְאֵילוּ הֵן. כְּגוֹן בַּדֵּי מְחָטִין וְצִינּוֹרִיּוֹת וּמַחֲרוֹזוֹת שֶׁלְּקַרְדּוּמוֹת. אֲמוֹרֵיהּ דְּרִבִּי יִצְחָק בַּר טַבְלַיי אַשְׁכָּח עֲזִיל כְּרִיךְ בְּמִקְטוֹרָה. אֲתָא גַּבֵּי רִבִּי יִצְחָק וְאוֹרֵי לֵיהּ כְּהָדָא דְרִבִּי שִׁמְעוֹן בֶּן אֶלְעָזָר דְּמַתְנִיתָן. אֲמוֹרֵיהּ דְּרִבִּי יוֹחָנָן אַשְׁכָּח עֲזִיל כְּרִיךְ בְּמִקְטוֹרָא. אֲתָא לְגַבֵּי רִבִּי יוֹחָנָן. אָמַר לֵיהּ. הֵן אַשְׁכַּחְתִּינֵיהּ. בְּסִימְטָא. בְּפַלָטְיָא. דּוּ בָעֵי מִיפְטְרִינָהּ כְּהָדָא דְרִבִּי שִׁמְעוֹן בֶּן אֶלְעָזָר דְּמַתְנִיתָן.

"Rebbi Simeon ben Eleazar said, merchandise of any kind[17] one does not have to make public." Rebbi Johanan made this public and stated about it[21]: "The following are these. For example needle strips[22], fire tongs[23], and strips of axes[24]. The Amora of Rebbi Isaac bar Tevlai found a web rolled in a scarf[25]. He came before Rebbi Isaac bar Tevlai who instructed him following Rebbi Simeon ben Eleazar. The Amora of Rebbi Johanan found a web rolled in a scarf. He came before Rebbi Johanan who asked him, where did you find it? In an alley[26], in a public square[27]? For he wanted to free him following Rebbi Simeon ben Eleazar.

21 Tosephta 2:1; Babli 24a.
22 Intact books of needles; an unused mass-produced article without individual marks.
23 Where it is easy to see that they were never used.
24 Since one only uses one axe at a time, these were never used.
25 Latin *amictorium* "loose garment, throw, scarf, etc.". *Arukh* explains as "burnoose". In Ashkenazic rabbinic Hebrew used for "coat".
26 Latin *semita*. A semi-private place, whose location might be a distinguishing mark and would have to be advertised.
27 Latin *platea*, Greek πλατεῖα. Here R. Simeon ben Eleazar's rule applies.

(fol. 8a) **משנה ג:** וְאֵילוּ חַיָּב לְהַכְרִיז. מָצָא פֵירוֹת בִּכְלִי אוֹ כְלִי כְּמוֹת שֶׁהוּא. מָעוֹת בְּכִיס אוֹ כִיס כְּמוֹת שֶׁהוּא. צִיבּוּרֵי פֵירוֹת צִיבּוּרֵי מָעוֹת שְׁלֹשָׁה מַטְבֵּיעוֹת זֶה עַל גַּב זֶה. כְּרִיכוֹת בִּרְשׁוּת הַיָּחִיד וְכִיכָּרוֹת שֶׁל בַּעַל הַבַּיִת וְגִיזֵּי צֶמֶר הַלְּקוּחוֹת מִבֵּית הָאוּמָּן. כַּדֵּי יַיִן וְכַדֵּי שֶׁמֶן חַיָּב לְהַכְרִיז.

**Mishnah 3**: But the following must be made public[28]: If one found produce in a container or simply a container, coins in a wallet or simply a wallet, heaps of produce, heaps of coins[29], three coins one on top of the other[30], bundles of grain in a private domain[3], home-baked loaves[31], fleece wool taken from an artisan's house[32]. Pitchers of wine and pitchers of oil he has to make public.

28  Because there are distinguishing marks which the legitimate owner can identify if only the bare fact that such-and-such an item was found was made public.

29  The amount and kind of the coins can be indicated.

30  The particular way in which the coins were arranged is a distinguishing mark.

31  They have peculiar shapes which distinguish them from professionally produced loaves.

32  Showing signs of processing.

(8b line 72) **הלכה ג:** וְאֵילוּ חַיָּב לְהַכְרִיז כול'. רַב יְהוּדָה אָמַר. ג מַטְבֵּיעוֹת שֶׁלְּג מְלָכִים. אָמַר רִבִּי אֶלְעָזָר. וַאֲפִילוּ שֶׁלְּשָׁתָּן שֶׁלְּמֶלֶךְ אֶחָד וַעֲשׂוּיִין גּוֹדָלִין. שֶׁלְּג מְלָכִים וַעֲשׂוּיִין ג גּוֹדָלִין. אוֹ אֲפִילוּ שֶׁלְּשָׁתָּן שֶׁלְּמֶלֶךְ אֶחָד וַעֲשׂוּיִין גּוֹדָלִין.

**Halakhah 3**: "But the following must be made public," etc. Rav Jehudah says three coins of three kings[33]. Rebbi Eleazar said, or even three from one king if they form a tower[34]? Of three kings and they are in three towers? Or even three of one king as a tower[35].

33  Three coins from three mints are certainly an identifying mark. In the Babli, 25a, this is a statement by the Galilean R. Ḥanina.

34  If the loser can indicate both the kind of coin and the way they were arranged, he is identified as the owner. In the Babli, 25a, the only arrangement

counted as identifying mark is that of a tower, the coins one on top of the other.

35   This is the final answer. The claimant must identify either three different mintings or one kind of coin and the way they were arranged. Then it would be improbable that the arrangement was accidental.

(8b line 75) כַּדֵּי יַיִן וְכַדֵּי שֶׁמֶן חַיָּיב לְהַכְרִיז. אָמַר רִבִּי יוֹחָנָן. אִין הֲוָה כְגוֹן אָהֵן מַצּוּבָה אֵין חַיָּיב לְהַכְרִיז. מַהוּ כְגוֹן אָהֵן מַצּוּבָה. כְּגוֹן אָהֵן קַרְפֵּיפָה שֶׁלִּשְׁלֹשָׁה בְנֵי אָדָם. מִכֵּיוָן דְּלָא יָדַע לְמָאן מְחַזְרָה אֵין חַיָּיב לְהַכְרִיז. אָמַר רִבִּי יוֹסֵי. אַתְּ שְׁמַע מִינָּהּ. בַּר נַשׁ הֲוָה מְהַלֵּךְ חוֹרֵי רִבִּי חֲלַפְתָּא נְפַל מִינַּייהוּ חַד דֵּינָר. מִכֵּיוָן דְּלָא יָדַע לְמָאן מְחַזְרָה אֵין חַיָּיב לְהַכְרִיז. שִׁמְעוֹן בַּר וָה הֲוָה מְהַלֵּךְ חוֹרֵי רִבִּי לְעָזָר. נְפַל מִינֵּיהּ דֵּינָר. אוֹשְׁטֵיהּ לֵיהּ שִׁמְעוֹן בַּר וָה. אָמַר לֵיהּ. כְּבַר נִתְיָיאַשְׁתִּי מִינֵּיהּ. אָמְרֵי. לֹא אִיתְכַּוֵּון רִבִּי לֶעְזָר אֶלָּא לְזַכְּיֵיהּ לְרִבִּי שִׁמְעוֹן בַּר וָא בְּגִין דַּהֲוָה אִינַשׁ מִסְכֵּן.

"Pitchers of wine and pitchers of oil he has to make public."[36] Rebbi Joḥanan said, if it was like a tripod[37] one does not have to make it public. What means, like a tripod? For example, a corral belonging to three people. Since one does not know to whom to return it, he does not have to make it public. Rebbi Yose[38] said, one understands from here that if a person went behind Rebbi Ḥalafta and a denar fell down from them, since one does not know to whom to return it, he does not have to make it public[39]. Simeon bar Abba was walking behind Rebbi Eleazar; a denar fell down from him. Simeon bar Abba presented it to him. He answered, I already had given up hope about this. They said, Rebbi Eleazar only intended it for Rebbi Simeon bar Abba because he was poor[40].

36   This quote from the Mishnah is out of place since one continues the discussion of single coins found.

37   Three coins forming a regular triangle. This arrangement does not count as identifying mark.

A corral is an enclosed space where nobody dwells permanently. If there are three tool sheds or three cow sheds in the corral, it may well be triangular.

38   This clearly refers to R. Yose the Amora, not the Tanna ben Ḥalafta. The meaning of the mention of "R. Ḥalafta" in his statement is not clear.

39   If there are no identifying marks and there is a doubt even between only two people, the find does not have to be returned.

40   Since he refused to accept alms, R. Eleazar found a way to give him money in a way understood only by scholars

**משנה ד**: מָצָא אַחַר הַגָּפָה אוֹ אַחַר הַגָּדֵר גּוֹזָלוֹת מְקוּשָׁרִין אוֹ בִשְׁבִילִין שֶׁבַּשָּׂדוֹת הֲרֵי זֶה לֹא יִגַּע בָּהֶן. מָצָא כְּלִי בָּאֲשָׁפוֹת אִם מְכוּסֶּה לֹא יִגַּע בּוֹ וְאִם מְגוּלֶה נוֹטֵל וּמַכְרִיז. מָצָא בַּגַּל וּבְכוֹתֶל יָשָׁן הֲרֵי אֵילוּ שֶׁלּוֹ. מָצָא בְּכוֹתֶל חָדָשׁ מֶחֱצָיוֹ וְלַחוּץ שֶׁלּוֹ מֶחֱצָיוֹ וְלִפְנִים שֶׁל בַּעַל הַבַּיִת. אִם הָיָה מַשְׂכִּירוֹ לַאֲחֵרִים אֲפִילוּ בְּתוֹךְ הַבַּיִת הֲרֵי אֵילוּ שֶׁלּוֹ. (fol. 8a)

**Mishnah 4**: If one found pigeon chicks bound together behind a temporary or permanent fence or on paths between fields[41], he should not touch them[42]. If one found a vessel on garbage heaps, if it was covered he should not touch it[42], if in the open he should take it and make it public[43]. What one found in a heap or an old wall[44] belongs to him. At a new wall[45], from the middle to the outside belongs to him, from the middle to the inside belongs to its owner. If he was renting out to others, even what is inside the house belongs to him[46].

41   Not easily accessible to the public.

42   One may not touch other people's property which possibly was deposited somewhere, neither lost nor abandoned, since, as Maimonides writes (*Gezelah wa'abedah* 15:1), in the worst case the owner would lose his property and in the best he would be obligated to provide a distinguishing mark to regain his property.

43   An intact vessel usually is not abandoned.

44   A wall is old if it no longer

shields anything.

45   A stone wall built with niches.

46   Anything left in a rental apartment after the renter moved out belongs to the landlord.

(8c line 8) **הלכה ד:** מָצָא אַחַר הַגַּפָּה כול׳. רַב יְהוּדָה אָמַר. וּבִלְבַד גּוֹזָלוֹת מְקוּשָּׁרִין בְּכַנְפֵיהֶן. רִבִּי בָּא בַּר זַבְדָּא אַשְׁכַּח חֲמָר מִכְסֵי בַּחֲפִיסָה וְנָסְתֵּיהּ. אֲזַל שְׁאַל לְרַב. אֲמַר לֵיהּ. לָא עֲבַדְתְּ טָבוֹת. אֲמַר לֵיהּ. חַזְרִיהּ. אֲמַר לֵיהּ. לָא. דְּנֵימַר אֲתָא מָרֵיהּ בְּעֵי לֵיהּ וְלָא אַשְׁכְּחֵיהּ וְאִיתְאַיֵּישׁ מִינֵּיהּ.

**Halakhah 4:** "If one found behind a temporary fence", etc. Rav Jehudah said: Only pigeon chicks tied together at their wings[47]. Rebbi Abba bar Zavda found a ring covered in a box[48] and took it. He came and asked Rav, who told him, you did not act correctly. He said, shall I return it? He answered, no, for we might say that his owner came, looked for it, did not find it and gave up hope for it[49].

47   As the Babli explains, 25b, it was general usage to tie pigeon chicks together at their wings for transport, sale, etc. If these chicks were taken, no distinguishing marks otherwise were available and the owner could never get them back even if the find was advertised.

48   E reads בחספה "with a potsherd". L is confirmed by Tosaphot (25b *s.v.* ואם).

49   The Babli, 25b, does not tell the story but quotes its result: R. Abba bar Zavda says in the name of Rav that "if possibly it was deposited, one should not take it, but if he took it, he should not return it." In Rashi's interpretation, one has to advertise the find. Following Maimonides (*l. c.* Note 42), the finder keeps it. Ravad disagrees and holds that since the finder took it illegally, he cannot acquire but the object must lie untouched until the prophet Elijah comes and determines the owner. The last two opinions can be read into the Yerushalmi text which notes that the owner probably gave up hope of recovery and, therefore, could not regain the object even when the find was advertised.

(8c line 11) תַּנֵי. מָצָא בָּאַשְׁפָּה חַיָּיב לְהַכְרִיז. שֶׁדֶּרֶךְ הָאַשְׁפָּה לְהִיטַּלְטֵל. מָצָא בַּגַּל וּבְכוֹתֶל יָשָׁן הֲרֵי אֵילּוּ שֶׁלּוֹ. שֶׁאֲנִי אוֹמֵר. שֶׁלֶּאֱמוֹרִיִּים הָיוּ. תַּנֵי. מָצָא בֵין פַּסִּים לַפַּסִּים. מִן הָאֶגֶף וְלִפְנִים כְּלִפְנִים. מִן הָאֶגֶף וּלְחוּץ כְּלַחוּץ. אִם הָיָה מְפוּלָּשׁ לִפְנִים אֲפִילּוּ מֵחֶצְיוֹ וְלַחוּץ הֲרֵי אֵילּוּ שֶׁלְּבַעַל הַבַּיִת. אִם הָיָה מְפוּלָּשׁ לַחוּץ אֲפִילּוּ מֵחֶצְיוֹ וְלִפְנִים הֲרֵי אֵילּוּ שֶׁלְּמוֹצְאֵיהֶן.

It was stated: What one found on a garbage heap he has to make public, for garbage is moved[50]. What one found in a heap or an old wall[44] belongs to him, for I am saying that it belonged to the Emorites[51]. It was stated[52]: If one found between planks[53], from the door and inside is like inside, from the door and outside is like outside. If it was opening to the inside, even from from the middle to the outside belongs to the owner of the property; if it was opening to the outside, even from the middle to the inside belongs to the finders.

50  Also quoted in the Babli, 25b; Tosephta 2:11. S. Lieberman explains that, in contrast to the garbage heap in the public domain mentioned in the Mishnah, one speaks here of a private garbage heap which periodically is emptied into a landfill. Therefore, everything lying there is either abandoned or lost and must be taken and advertised.

51  Tosephta 2:12. Archeological finds are ownerless and can be taken by the finder.

52  A similar, but not necessarily compatible, text is in Tosephta 2:13.

53  A temporary fence made of wooden planks. The planks do not touch but are placed close enough to one another that no goat can pass between them. The problem is the status of the empty spaces between the planks.

(8c line 16) הָיָה מַשְׂכִּירָן לַאֲחֵרִים אֲפִילּוּ מָצָא בְתוֹךְ הַבַּיִת הֲרֵי אֵילּוּ שֶׁלּוֹ. אָמַר רִבִּי יִרְמְיָה. בְּפוּנְדָּק אִתְפַּלְּגוּן. אֲבָל בֶּחָצֵר כָּל־עַמָּא מוֹדוּ שֶׁחַיָּיב לְהַכְרִיז. אָמַר רִבִּי יוֹסֵי. בֶּחָצֵר אִתְפַּלְּגוּן. אֲבָל בְּפוּנְדָּק כָּל־עַמָּא מוֹדוּ שֶׁהוּא שֶׁלְּמוֹצְאוֹ.

"If he was renting out to others, even what is inside the house belongs to him."⁵⁴ Rebbi Jeremiah says, they disagree about a hostelry⁵⁵, but in a courtyard everybody agrees that he is required to make it public. Rebbi Yose said, they disagree about a courtyard, but in a hostelry everybody agrees that it belongs to its finder.

54    This quote is not really connected with the following, which refers to Tosephta 2:2, in which R. Simeon ben Eleazar states that "what is saved from the mouth of a lion or a wolf, from the surge of the ocean or a river, or found on a public thoroughfare, belongs to the finder since the owners had given up hope." Since this is stated as an individual opinion, it follows that the anonymous majority require publication in all cases.

55    Greek πανδοκεῖον, τό.

(fol. 8b) **משנה ה:** מָצָא בַחֲנוּת הֲרֵי אֵילוּ שֶׁלּוֹ. בֵּין הַתֵּיבָה וְלַחֶנְוָנִי הֲרֵי הוּא שֶׁל חֶנְוָנִי. לִפְנֵי הַשּׁוּלְחָנִי הֲרֵי אֵילוּ שֶׁלּוֹ. בֵּין הַכִּסֵּא וְלַשּׁוּלְחָנִי הֲרֵי הוּא שֶׁל שׁוּלְחָנִי. הַלּוֹקֵחַ פֵּירוֹת מֵחֲבֵירוֹ אוֹ שֶׁשִּׁילַח לוֹ חֲבֵירוֹ פֵּירוֹת וּמָצָא בְתוֹכוֹ מָעוֹת הֲרֵי אֵילוּ שֶׁלּוֹ. וְאִם הָיוּ צְרוּרִין נוֹטֵל וּמַכְרִיז.

**Mishnah 5**: What one found in a store is his⁵⁶. Between the counter and the storekeeper it is the storekeeper's. Before the moneychanger it is his⁵⁶. Between the chair⁵⁷ and the moneychanger it is the moneychanger's. If one bought produce from another person or another person sent him produce and he found coins in it, they are his⁵⁸. But if they were bundled⁵⁹, he takes them and makes it public.

**משנה ו:** אַף הַשִּׂמְלָה הָיְתָה בִּכְלָל כָּל־אֵילוּ וְלָמָּה יָצָאת. לְהַקִּישׁ אֵלֶיהָ לוֹמַר לָךְ מַה שִׂמְלָה מְיוּחֶדֶת שֶׁיֵּשׁ בָּהּ סִימָנִין וְיֵשׁ לָהּ תּוֹבְעִין אַף כָּל־דָּבָר שֶׁיֵּשׁ בָּהּ סִימָנִין וְיֵשׁ לָהּ תּוֹבְעִין חַיָּיב לְהַכְרִיז.

**Mishnah 6** The garment[60] was subsumed under "anything"; why was it mentioned separately? To bracket with it and tell you, just as a garment is special in that it has distinguishing marks and claimants, so about everything which has distinguishing marks and claimants you have to give public notice[61].

56  Because most probably one of the previous customers lost the money which by its nature has no distinguishing marks.

57  Where the customer sits who has his money exchanged.

58  The coins probably were lost by a person engaged in harvest or transport, not the seller of the produce.

59  Where the number of coins, their value, and the way they were tied together are distinguishing marks.

60  *Deut.* 22:3: "So you shall treat his donkey, so you shall treat *his garment*, so you shall treat *anything* lost by your fellow man, which is lost by him but you found it; you are not allowed to disregard it."

61  *Sifry Deut.* 224. This justifies the arguments in Halakhah 4 that even if there are distinguishing marks, one does not have to advertise if there are no claimants.

(8c line 20) **הלכה ח:** מָצָא בַחֲנוּת הֲרֵי אֵילוּ שֶׁלּוֹ כול'. אָמַר רִבִּי לֶעָזָר. כֵּינִי מַתְנִיתָא. עַל גַּבֵּי כִסֵא שֶׁלּוֹ עַל גַּבֵּי תֵיבָה שֶׁלּוֹ.

**Halakhah 5:** "What one found in a store is his," etc. Rebbi Eleazar said, so is the Mishnah: On his chair, on his counter[62].

62  The Babli, 26b, in the name of R. Eleazar infers from the Mishnah that forgotten coins on the counter of store or bank are the finder's. The language of the Yerushalmi rather points to the opposite conclusion, *viz.*, that they are the storekeeper's or the banker's.

(8c line 21) שִׁמְעוֹן בֶּן שָׁטַח הֲוָה עֲסִיק בְּהָדָא כִיתָּנָא. אָמְרִין לֵיהּ תַּלְמִידוֹי. רִבִּי. אַרְפֵּי מִינָךְ וַאֲנָן זְבָנִין לָךְ חֲדָא חֲמָר וְלֵית אַתְּ לָעֵי סוּגִין. אַזְלוֹן זְבָנוֹן לֵיהּ חֲדָא חֲמָר מֵחַד סִירְקָאי וּתְלֵי בֵיהּ חֲדָא מַרְגְּלִי. אָתוֹן לְגַבֵּיהּ אָמְרִין לֵיהּ.

מִן כְּדוֹן לֵית אַתְּ צְרִיךְ לָעֵי תּוּבָן. אֲמַר לוֹן. אָמְרִין לֵיהּ. לָמָה. אָמְרִין לֵיהּ. זְבִינָן לָךְ חַד חֲמָר מֵחַד סִירְקָיֵי וּתְלִי בֵּיהּ חָדָא מַרְגְּלִי. אֲמַר לוֹן. וְיָדַע בָּהּ מָרָהּ. אָמְרִין לֵיהּ. לָא. אֲמַר לוֹן. אִיזֵל חֲזַר. לֹא כֵן אָמַר רַב הוּנָא בֵּיבַי בַּר גּוֹזְלוֹן בְּשֵׁם רַב. הָתִיבוֹן קוֹמֵי רִבִּי. אֲפִילוּ כְּמָאן דָּמַר. גְּזֵילוֹ שֶׁלְּגוֹי אֲסוּרָה. כָּל־עַמּוֹ מוֹדֵיי שֶׁאֲבֵידָתוֹ מוּתֶּרֶת. מַה אַתּוּן סָבְרִין שִׁמְעוֹן בֶּן שָׁטַח בַּרְבְּרוֹן הֲוָה. בְּעֵי שִׁמְעוֹן בֶּן שָׁטַח מַשְׁמַע בְּרִיךְ אֱלָהֲהוֹן דִּיהוּדָאֵי מֵאַגַּר כָּל־הָדֵין עָלְמָא.

[63]Simeon ben Shetaḥ[64] was working with linen. His students said to him, Rabbi, in order to make it easier for you we want to buy a donkey, then you will not have to work so hard. They went and bought a donkey from a Saracen; a pearl was hanging on its neck. They came to him saying, because of this you will not have to work anymore. He said to them, why? They told him, we bought for you a donkey from a Saracen and a pearl is hanging on its neck. He asked them, does its owner know about this? They answered, no. He told them, go and return it.

But did not Rav Huna, Bevay bar Gozlan, in the name of Rav say, they objected before Rebbi: Even according to him who says that an object robbed from a Gentile is forbidden, everybody agrees that what he lost is permitted[65].

Do you think that Simeon ben Shetaḥ was a barbarian[66]? Simeon ben Shetaḥ wanted to hear: Praised be the God of the Jews, more than any gain in this world.

63  An abbreviated Hebrew version of this story is in *Deut. rabba* 3(5).
64  The head of the Synhedrion in Alexander Yannai's time.
65  *Bava qama* 113b.
66  Greek βάρβαρος, "barbarous, foreign".

## HALAKHAH 5    311

(8c line 31) וְיַיְדָא אֶמְרָה דָא.   רִבִּי חֲנִינָה מִשְׁתָּעֵי הָדֵין עוֹבְדָא.   רַבָּנִין סַבַּיָּיא זְבָנִין חַד כְּרִי דְחִיטִּין מֵאִילֵין דְּאִיסְרָטוֹס[67] וְאַשְׁכְּחוֹן בֵּיהּ בֵּיהּ חָדָא צְרָרָא דְדֵינָרֵי וַחֲזָרוּנֵיהּ לְהוֹן.   אָמְרִין.   בְּרִיךְ אֱלָהֲהוֹן דִּיהוּדָאֵי.

The following implies the same. Rebbi Ḥanina reports the following case: The elder rabbis bought a heap of wheat from the household of the general and found in it a bundle of denars. They returned it to them. They said, praised be the God of the Jews.

67    E: דאסטרטוס. Greek στρατιώτης "soldier, miliary man".

(8c line 34) אַבָּא אוֹשַׁעְיָה אִישׁ טוּרְיָיא [הֲוָה קַצָּר.   עָלַת מַלְכְּתָא מַסְחֵי גוֹ מְגִירָה דְמַיָּא וְאוֹבְדַת בִּינְדִילוֹנִין דִּילָהּ וְאַשְׁכְּחָהּ.   מִי נָפְקָא אוֹשְׁטֵיהּ לָהּ.   אָמְרָה.   אֲהֵין לָךְ.   לִי אֲהֵן מַהוּ חָשׁוּב עֲלַי אִית לִי טָבִין מִנֵּיהּ אִית לִי סוּגִין מִנֵּיהּ.   אָמַר לֵיהּ.   אוֹרָיְתָא גָזְרַת דְּנַחְזוֹר.   אָמְרָה.   בְּרִיךְ אֱלָהֲהוֹן דִּיהוּדָאֵי.

Abba Oshaia from Tireh [was a washer. The queen came to bathe in a water pond. She lost her בינדילונין[68]; he found it. When she left, he handed it to her.][69] She said, this is for you; it is not important for me and I have more of this. He told her, the Torah decided that we have to return it. She said, praised be the God of the Jews.

68   Lieberman suggests Greek δεράνιον, Byzantine δεράιον "necklace". *princeps*, but already noted in the 17th Cent. by R. Menaḥem di Lonzano in his textual notes on the Yerushalmi.

69   From E, missing in L and *editio*

(8c line 36) רִבִּי שְׁמוּאֵל בַּר סוֹסַרְטַיי סָלַק לְרוֹמֵי.   אוֹבְדַת מַלְכְּתָא דִילֵנִיהּ דִּידָהּ וְאַשְׁכְּחֵיהּ.   אַפְקַת כְּרוּז בַּמְּדִינְתָּא.   מָאן דְּמַחֲזַר לָהּ בְּגוֹ ל יוֹמִין יָסַב אָכֵן וְאָכֵן.   בָּתַר ל יוֹמִין אִיתְרִים רֵישֵׁיהּ.   לָא חֲזָרֵיהּ גוֹ ל יוֹמִין.   בָּתַר ל יוֹמִין חֲזָרֵיהּ.   אָמְרָה לֵיהּ.   לָא הֲוֵית בִּמְדִינְתָּא.   אֲמַר לָהּ.   אִין.   אָמְרָה לֵיהּ.   וְלָא שְׁמַעַת קָלָא דִכְרוּזָא.   אֲמַר לָהּ.   אִין.   אָמְרָה לֵיהּ.   וּמָה מַר.   אֲמַר לָהּ.   מָאן

דְּמַחֲזַר לָהּ בְּגוֹ ל יוֹמִין יְסַב אָכֵן וְאָכֵן. בָּתַר ל יוֹמִין יִתָּרִים רֵישֵׁיהּ. אָמְרָה
לֵיהּ. וְלָמָּה לָא חֲזַרְתִּינֵיהּ גּוֹ ל יוֹמִין. אֲמַר לָהּ. דְּלָא תֵימְרוּן בְּגִין דַּחַלְתֵּיךְ
עֲבָדִית אֶלָּא בְּגִין דַּחַלְתֵּיהּ דְּרַחֲמָנָא. אָמְרָה לֵיהּ. בְּרִיךְ אֱלָהֲהוֹן דִּיהוּדָאֵי.

Rebbi Samuel bar Sosarṭai went to Rome. The queen had lost her דיליניה but he found it. A herold went through the city: One who will return it within 30 days will receive such and such; after 30 days his head will be lifted from him. He did not return it within 30 days. After 30 days he returned it. She asked him, had you not been in the city? He answered, yes. She asked him, had you not heard the voice of the herold? He answered, yes. She asked him, what did he say? He answered, one who will return it within 30 days will receive such and such; after 30 days his head will be lifted from him. She asked him, why did you not return it within 30 days? He answered, one should not say that I acted out of fear of you, but out of fear of the Merciful. She said to him, praised be the God of the Jews.

(8c line 46) אֲלֶכְּסַנְדְּרוֹס מְקֶדוֹן סְלִיק גַּבֵּי מַלְכָּא קַצְיָיא. חָמָא לֵיהּ דְּהַב סַגִּין
כְּסַף סַגִּין. אֲמַר לֵיהּ. לָא דְהַבָךְ וְלָא כַסְפָּךְ אֲנָא צָרִיךְ. לָא אֲתִית אֶלָּא מֵיחְמֵי
פְּרוֹכְסִין דִּידְכוֹן הֵיךְ אַתּוּן יָהֲבִין הֵיךְ אַתּוּן דַּיְינִין. עַד דּוּ עָסוֹק עִמֵּיהּ אֲתָא
בַּר נָשׁ חַד דְּאָיֵין עִם חַבְרֵיהּ דִּזְבַן חָדָא (חֶלְקָה וַחֲסִפְתָהּ) [קִיקְלָא וַחֲפַרוֹנָהּ]
וְאַשְׁכְּחוֹן בָּהּ סִימָא דְדִינָרֵי. אֲהֵן דִּזְבַן הֲוָא מַר. קִיקִילְתָּא זְבָנִית סִימָא לָא
זְבָנִית. אֲהֵן דְּזַבִּין הֲוָא מַר. קִיקִילְתָּא וְכָל דְּאִית בָּהּ זַבִּינִית. עַד דְּעִינוּן
עֲסִיקִין דֵּין עִם דֵּין אֲמַר מַלְכָּא לְחַד מִינַּייְהוּ. אִית לָךְ בַּר זָכַר. אֲמַר לֵיהּ. אִין.
אֲמַר לְחַבְרֵיהּ. אִית לָךְ בְּרַת נוּקְבָה. אֲמַר לֵיהּ. אִין. אֲמַר לוֹן. אַסְבּוּן דֵּין
לְדֵין וְסִימָא יְהֵי לִתְרַוַּיְיהוֹן. שָׁרֵי גְּחִיךְ. אֲמַר לֵיהּ. לָמָּה אַתְּ גְּחִיךְ. לָא דָּנִית
טָבָאוּת. אֲמַר לֵיהּ. אִילּוּ הֲוָה הָדֵין דִּינָא גַּבְּכוֹן הֵיךְ הֲוֵיתוֹן דָּנִין. אֲמַר לֵיהּ.
קָטְלִין דֵּין וְדֵין וְסִימָא עֲלַת לְמַלְכָּא. אֲמַר לֵיהּ. כָּל־הָכִי אַתּוּן רָחֲמִין דְּהַב
סוֹגִי. עֲבַד לֵיהּ אֲרִיסְטוֹן. אַפִּיק קוֹמֵי קוֹפָד דִּדְהַב תַּרְנוֹגַלִּין דִּדְהַב. אֲמַר לֵיהּ.

דְּהַב אֲנָא אָכֵל. אֲמַר לֵיהּ. תִּיפַּח רוּחֵיהּ דְּהַהוּא גַבְרָא. דְּהַב לֵית אַתּוּן אָכְלִין וְלָמָה אַתּוּן רָחֲמִין דְּהַב סוּגִין. אֲמַר לֵיהּ. דַּנְחָא עֲלֵיכוֹן שִׁמְשָׁא. אֲמַר לֵיהּ. אִין. נְחִית עֲלֵיכוֹן מִיטְרָא. אֲמַר לֵיהּ. אִין. אֲמַר לֵיהּ. דִּילְמָא אִית גַּבֵּיכוֹן בְּעִיר דָּקִיק. אֲמַר לֵיהּ. אִין. תִּיפַּח רוּחֵיהּ דְּהַהוּא גַבְרָא. לֵית אַתּוּן חַיִּין אֶלָּא בִּזְכוּת בְּעִירָא דָּקִיקָא. דִּכְתִיב אָדָם וּבְהֵמָה תּוֹשִׁיעַ יי.

[70]Alexander the Macedonian went to the king of Cassia[71]. He saw that he had much gold, much silver. He told him, I do not need your gold nor your silver; I came only so see your practice[72], how you are dealing, how you are judging. While he was still discussing with him, there came a man having a dispute with another, for he bought (a plot, entered it) [a garbage heap, dug in it][73] and found a treasure trove of denars. The buyer said, I bought a garbage heap, I did not buy a treasure. The seller said, I sold a garbage heap and all it contains. While they still were arguing with one another, the king asked one of them, do you have a male son? He answered, yes. He asked the other one, do you have a female daughter? He answered, yes. He told them, marry them to each other and the treasure should belong to both. He[74] started to laugh. He[75] asked him, why are you laughing? Did I not judge correctly? He asked him, if the case came before you, how would you have judged? He[74] told him, one kills both of them and the treasure falls to the king. He[75] told him, do you love gold so much? He[75] made him a meal and brought before him golden meat, golden chicken. He[74] asked him, can I eat gold? He[75] told him, the spirit of this person should be wiped out. You cannot eat gold, why do you love gold so much? He[75] asked him, does the sun shine upon you? He[74] answered, yes. Does rain fall on you? He[74] answered, yes. He[75] asked him, do you have small animals? He[74] answered, yes. The spirit of this person should be wiped out; you live only by the merit of the small animals, as it is written[76]: "Man and animal You are saving, o Eternal!"

| | |
|---|---|
| 70 Parallel versions of this story are in *Gen. rabba* 33(1), *Lev. rabba* 27(1). | text, the one in brackets is the text of E and the Midrashim. The sequel shows that the latter text is original. |
| 71 In the Midrashim: Behind the Mountains of Darkness. | 74 Alexander. |
| 72 Greek πρᾶξις. | 75 The savage king. |
| 73 The text in parentheses is the L | 76 *Ps.* 36:7. |

(fol. 8b) **משנה ז**: וְעַד אֵימָתַי חַיָּיב לְהַכְרִיז. עַד כְּדֵי שֶׁיֵּדְעוּ שְׁכֵינָיו דִּבְרֵי רַבִּי מֵאִיר. רַבִּי יְהוּדָה אוֹמֵר שְׁלֹשָׁה רְגָלִים וְאַחַר הָרֶגֶל הָאַחֲרוֹן שִׁבְעַת יָמִים כְּדֵי שֶׁיֵּלֵךְ לְבֵיתוֹ שְׁלֹשָׁה וְיַחֲזוֹר שְׁלֹשָׁה וְיַכְרִיז יוֹם אֶחָד.

**Mishnah 7**: How long does one have to make it public[77]. Until his neighbors know, the words of Rebbi Meïr. Rebbi Jehudah says, three holidays, and after the last holiday seven days so that one goes home during three days, comes back during three days, and makes it public for one day[78].

| | |
|---|---|
| 77 To actively seek out the owner. | everybody hear all declarations and can inform his neighbors about the objects found. The person who lost an advertised object then can go to Jerusalem. |
| 78 Presuming that every person who made the pilgrimage to Jerusalem publicly declare there his finds (at the "stone of claimants", Babli 28b) so that | |

(8c line 63) **הלכה ז**: עַד מָתַי חַיָּיב לְהַכְרִיז כּוּל׳. תַּנֵּי. בָּרִאשׁוֹנָה הָיוּ מַכְרִיזִין שְׁלֹשָׁה רְגָלִים וְאַחַר רֶגֶל הָאַחֲרוֹן שִׁבְעַת יָמִים כְּדֵי שֶׁיֵּלֵךְ שְׁלֹשָׁה וְיַחֲזוֹר שְׁלֹשָׁה וְיַכְרִיז יוֹם אֶחָד. מִשֶּׁחָרַב בֵּית הַמִּקְדָּשׁ הִתְקִינוּ שֶׁיְּהוּ מַכְרִיזִין שְׁלֹשָׁה יָמִים. מִן הַסַּכָּנָה וְאֵילָךְ הִתְקִינוּ שֶׁיְּהֵא מוֹדִיעַ לִקְרוֹבָיו וְלִשְׁכֵינָיו וְדַיּוֹ.

**Halakhah 7**: "How long does one have to make it public," etc. It was stated[79]: In earlier times one made it public during three holidays, and after the last holiday seven days so that one goes home during three days, comes back during three days, and makes it public during one day. After the destruction of the Temple they instituted that one has to make it public during three days[80]. Starting from the danger[81] they instituted that one has to inform his relatives and neighbors[82]; this is sufficient.

79  Tosephta 2:17; a different version in the Babli 28b.
80  In the Tosephta, 30 days. In the Babli, "one has to give notice in the synagogues and houses of study", no time limit given. In one Babli ms: "One *only* has to give notice in the synagogue." A similar notice is implied by Halakhah 8.
81  Hadrian's persecutions when all synagogues were closed and religious assemblies were forbidden (S. Lieberman).
82  In the Tosephta and some Babli texts, "his relatives, neighbors, and acquaintances."

משנה ח: אָמַר אֶת הָאֲבֵידָה וְלֹא אָמַר אֶת סִימָנֶיהָ הֲרֵי זֶה לֹא יִתֵּן. (fol. 8b)
וְהָרַמַּאי אַף עַל פִּי שֶׁאָמַר סִימָנֶיהָ הֲרֵי זֶה לֹא יִתֵּן לוֹ שֶׁנֶּאֱמַר עַד דְּרוֹשׁ אָחִיךָ אוֹתוֹ. עַד שֶׁתִּדְרוֹשׁ אֶת אָחִיךָ אִם רַמַּאי הוּא אִם אֵינוֹ רַמַּאי.

**Mishnah 8**: If one described the lost object but not its identifying marks, he[83] should not deliver. To the swindler one should not deliver even if he describes its identifying marks, since it is said: "Until investigating your brother about it,[84]" until you investigate your brother whether he be a swindler or no swindler.

83  The finder may deliver only after satisfying himself that the claimant is the legal owner.
84  *Deut.* 22:2; *Sifry Deut.* 223.

הלכה ח: אָמַר אֶת הָאֲבֵידָה כול'. אֵי זֶהוּ רַמַּאי. עֲבַד גַּרְמֵיהּ (8c line 67)
מְחַזֵּר מְצִיאָן. וַעֲבַד חָדָא רַבָּה וְטָבָה. הֵיךְ הוּא עָבִיד רַבָּה וְטָבָה. חֲמֵי לֵיהּ

בִּירִיָּיתָא מְחַזֵּר מְצִיאָן וּמַפְקִידִין גַּבֵּיהּ וְהוּא נָסִיב כּוּלָּהּ וַאֲזִיל לֵיהּ. וְאִית דְּאָמְרִין. אֲזִיל לִכְנִישְׁתָּא וּשְׁמַע סִימָנִין וַאֲזַל לִכְנִישְׁתָּא חוֹרֵי וַאֲמַר סִימָנָא וּנְסַב לֵיהּ.

**Halakhah 8**: "If one described the lost object," etc. What is a swindler? He shows himself as one who returns finds and uses this for a big coup. How does he make a big coup? He shows himself to people as one who returns finds so they will give him valuables in trust. He takes all of them and disappears. But some say, he goes to one synagogue and hears about distinguishing marks; then he goes to another synagogue, describes the indentifying marks and takes [the finds] away.

(fol. 8b) **משנה ט**: כָּל־דָּבָר שֶׁעוֹשֶׂה וְאוֹכֵל יַעֲשֶׂה וְיֹאכַל. וְדָבָר שֶׁאֵינוֹ עוֹשֶׂה וְאוֹכֵל יִמָּכֵר שֶׁנֶּאֱמַר וַהֲשֵׁבוֹתוֹ לוֹ. רְאֵה הֵיאַךְ תְּשִׁיבֶנּוּ לוֹ. מַה יְּהֵא בַדָּמִים. רִבִּי טַרְפוֹן אוֹמֵר יִשְׁתַּמֵּשׁ בָּהֶן לְפִיכָךְ אִם אָבְדוּ חַיָּיב בְּאַחֲרָיוּתָן. רִבִּי עֲקִיבָה אוֹמֵר לֹא יִשְׁתַּמֵּשׁ בָּהֶן לְפִיכָךְ אִם אָבְדוּ אֵינוֹ חַיָּיב בְּאַחֲרָיוּתָן.

**Mishnah 9**: Anything which works and eats[85] shall work and eat[86]. What does not work but eats[87] should be sold because it is said[84], "and return it to him," plan to return it to him[88]. What happens with the money? Rebbi Tarphon says, he may use it; therefore if it is lost he is liable for its alienation. Rebbi Aqiba says, he may not use it; therefore if it is lost he is not liable for its alienation.

85  E. g., cattle or donkeys.
86  While the finder waits for the owner to claim his animal.
87  Any other kind of animal.
88  The find has to be kept in such a way that it can be returned without presenting to its owner a bill for expenses during the waiting period.

(8c line 67) **הלכה ט:** כָּל־דָּבָר שֶׁעוֹשֶׂה וְאוֹכֵל כּוֹל'. תַּנֵּי. שֶׁלֹּא יֹאכַל עֵגֶל לַעֲגָלִים סַיָּיח לַסַּיָּיחִין וְתַרְנְגוֹל לְתַרְנְגוֹלִין. עוֹבְדָא הֲוָה בְּחַד בַּר נַשׁ דְּאַשְׁכַּח חֲמִשָּׁה עֲגָלִין וַהֲוָה מַזְבִּין וּמוֹכְלִינוֹן עַד דְּקָמוֹן עַל חַד. רַב יְהוּדָה בְּשֵׁם רַב. הֲלָכָה כְּרִבִּי טַרְפוֹן בְּדָבָר שֶׁיֵּשׁ בּוֹ סִימָן. רִבִּי בָּא וְרַב יְהוּדָה בְּשֵׁם רַב. מַעֲשֶׂה הָיָה וְהוֹרֵי רִבִּי כְּרִבִּי טַרְפוֹן בְּדָבָר שֶׁיֵּשׁ בּוֹ סִימָן. רַב יְהוּדָה אָמַר. תַּלְמִיד חָכָם אֵין צָרִיךְ לִיתֵּן סִימָן. אָמַר רַב הוּנָא. הַכֹּל מוֹדִין שֶׁאִם הָיָה צְרוֹר מָעוֹת לֹא יִגַּע בָּהֶן.

**Halakhah 9**: "Anything which works and eats," etc. It was stated: There should not be given food in the value of a calf to calves, a foal to foals, or a chicken to chickens[89]. It happened that a man found five calves; he was selling and feeding until only one was left.

Rav Jehudah in the name of Rav: Practice follows Rebbi Tarphon[90] about objects with distinguishing marks[91]. Rebbi Abba and Rav Jehudah in the name of Rav: It happened that Rebbi instructed following Rebbi Tarphon in a case about objects with distinguishing marks. Rav Jehudah said, a scholar does not have to indicate a distinguishing mark. Rav Huna said, everybody[92] agrees that if it was a bundle of coins he may not touch them[93].

89 The Yerushalmi sets no time limit on how long the finder has to care for animals he found. Tosefta (2:20) and Babli (28b) give different limits. The statement here in contrast notes that by the time the bill for the food of an animal in a herd approaches the cost of one animal, the finder should sell the herd (under the supervision of the court, in order to escape financial responsibilities.)

90 In the Babli, 29b, Rav Jehudah in the name of Samuel.

91 Objects without distinguishing marks immediately become the finder's property.

92 Even R. Aqiba.

93 Babli 29b.

(8d line 3) יְהוּדָה בְּרִיבִּי עָאַל לִכְנִישְׁתָּא. שְׁבַק סַנְדָּלוֹי וְאָזְלִין. אָמַר. אִילּוּ לָא אֲזָלִית לִכְנִישְׁתָּא לָא אָזְלוֹן סַנְדָּלַיי. רִבִּי יוֹסֵי הֲוָה יָתִיב וּמַתְנֵי וְעַל מִיתָא. מָן דְּקָם לָא אָמַר לֵיהּ כְּלוּם. וּמָן דְּיָתִיב לֵיהּ לֹא אָמַר לֵיהּ כְּלוּם.

The great Jehudah went to the synagogue. He took off his sandals and they disappeared. He said, if I had not gone to the synagogue, my sandals would not have disappeard[94].

Rebbi Yose was sitting and teaching when a dead body was brought in. He did not say anything either to those who got up or to those who remained sitting[95].

94  He followed the oriental usage not to enter a synagogue with his shoes on his feet. The story belongs to Halakhah 8; it shows that swindlers (or in this case, thieves) are found even in a synagogue or among scholars.

95  A reformulation of a text in *Berakhot* 3:1; *Nazir* 7:1 Note 34. It has no relevance for the topics discussed here.

(fol. 8b) **משנה י:** מָצָא סְפָרִים קוֹרֵא בָּהֶן אַחַת לִשְׁלֹשִׁים יוֹם וְאִם אֵינוֹ יוֹדֵעַ לִקְרוֹת גּוֹלְלָן. אֲבָל לֹא יִלְמוֹד בָּהֶן בַּתְּחִילָּה וְלֹא יִקְרָא אַחֵר עִמּוֹ. מָצָא כְּסוּת מְנַעֲרָהּ אַחַת לִשְׁלֹשִׁים יוֹם וְשׁוֹטְחָהּ לְצָרְכָּהּ אֲבָל לֹא לִכְבוֹדוֹ. כְּלֵי כֶסֶף וּכְלֵי נְחוֹשֶׁת מִשְׁתַּמֵּשׁ בָּהֶן לְצָרְכָן אֲבָל לֹא לְשָׁחֳקָן. כְּלֵי זָהָב וּכְלֵי זְכוּכִית לֹא יִגַּע בָּהֶן עַד שֶׁיָּבוֹא אֵלִיָּהוּ. מָצָא שַׂק אוֹ קוּפָּה וְכָל־דָּבָר שֶׁאֵין דַּרְכּוֹ לִיטּוֹל הֲרֵי זֶה לֹא יִטּוֹל.

**Mishnah 10**: One who found book-scrolls reads in them once every thirty days; if he is illiterate, he rolls them up[96]. But he should not study a new subject in them, nor should a second person read with him[97]. One who found a garment shakes it out every thirty days; he spreads it out for its conservation, but not to show off[98]. Silver and brass vessels he uses for their preservation, but not to rub off[99]. Gold and glass vessels he should not touch until the prophet Elijah comes[100]. If one found a sack or a chest or anything which he does not take up, he need not take it[101].

96  The rules of the Mishnah are based on the finder's biblical obligation to keep the find in as good condition as possible (cf. Note 88). Leather or parchment scrolls deteriorate if they are not rolled up for a long time.

97  Intensive use is apt to damage the scroll.

98  Displaying a garment which is too expensive for his means in order to enhance one's credit standing is illegitimate use of another person's property.

99  These vessels get tarnished if they are not used. But they cannot be used in a way which would require heavy rubbing for cleansing since this would diminish their weight.

100  Cf. Note 49.

101  If his social standing would be impaired if he was seen carrying something that in normal circumstances is carried only by servants, he may disregard the biblical commandment to take up the find.

(8d line 6) **הלכה י:** מָצָא סְפָרִים קוֹרֵא בָהֶן אַחַת לְל יוֹם. תַּנֵּי. מָצָא סְפָרִים כול׳. אִם אֵינוֹ יוֹדֵעַ לִקְרוֹת גּוֹלְלָן. לֹא יִקְרָא פָּרָשָׁה וְיִשְׁנֶה. וְלֹא יִקְרָא פָּרָשָׁה וִיתַרְגְּמֶם. וְלֹא יִפְתַּח בָּהּ יוֹתֵר מִג׳ דַּפִּין. וְלֹא יִקְרוּ בוֹ ג׳ בְּכֶרֶךְ אֶחָד. בַּמֶּה דְבָרִים אֲמוּרִים. בַּחֲדָשִׁים. אֲבָל בִּישִׁינִים שְׁנֵים עָשָׂר חוֹדֶשׁ. כְּלֵי כֶסֶף מִשְׁתַּמֵּשׁ בָּהֶן בְּצוֹנִין אֲבָל לֹא בְחַמִּין מִפְּנֵי שֶׁמַּשְׁחִירָן. כְּלֵי נְחוֹשֶׁת מִשְׁתַּמֵּשׁ בָּהֶן בַּחַמִּין אֲבָל לֹא עַל יְדֵי הָאוֹר מִפְּנֵי שֶׁמַּפְחִיתָן. מַגְרֵיפוֹת וְקַרְדּוּמוֹת מִשְׁתַּמֵּשׁ בָּהֶן בְּרַךְ אֲבָל לֹא בְקָשָׁה. מַגְרֵיפָה מְקַבֵּל בָּהּ אֶת הַטִּיט וּמְדִיחָהּ וּמַנִּיחָהּ בִּמְקוֹמָהּ. קוֹרְדּוֹם מְבַקֵּעַ בּוֹ עֵצִים אֲבָל לֹא צִינִּים וַעֲצֵי זַיִת. כְּשֵׁם שֶׁאַתְּ אוֹמֵר בְּמוֹצֵא כָּךְ אַתָּה אוֹמֵר בְּמַפְקִיד. הַמַּפְקִיד כְּסוּת אֵצֶל חֲבֵירוֹ מְנַעֲרָהּ אַחַת לְל יוֹם. וְאִם הָיְתָה מְרוּבָּה גּוֹבָהּ שְׂכָרוֹ מִמֶּנָּה.

**Halakhah 10:** "One who found book-scrolls," etc. It was stated[102]: "One who found book-scrolls reads in them once every thirty days; if he is illiterate he rolls them up. He should not read a paragraph and repeat it, nor should he read a paragraph and translate it[103], nor should he open more than three pages[104], nor should three persons read from the same tome. When has this been said? For new ones[105]. But for old ones twelve months.

Silver vessels he may use cold but not hot because it blackens them[106]. Brass vessels he may use hot but not on the fire because it diminishes them. Rakes and axes he may use on soft material but not on hard. With a rake he may receive mortar, wash it, and put it back in its place. With an ax he may split wood[107], but not stone-palm or olive wood.

What has been said about a find is valid equally for deposits. If one deposits a garment with another person, he has to shake it out once every thirty days. If it is much work, he can collect his expenses[108] from it.

102  Tosephta 2:21-22; in the Babli 29b-30a a series of *baraitot*; partial parallel in *Sifry Deut.* 224.

103  If it is a Torah scroll, it may not be used to prepare either for the reading or the Aramaic translation in the synagogue.

104  To avoid tearing the scroll inadvertently.

105  Whose leather or parchment is stiff and there is a danger lest it break if not moved from time to time.

106  They become tarnished.

107  Soft wood, not hardwood.

108  Such as hiring help to take care of the garment.

**משנה יא:** אֵי זוֹ הִיא אֲבֵידָה. מָצָא חֲמוֹר אוֹ פָרָה רוֹעִין בַּדֶּרֶךְ אֵין זוֹ אֲבֵידָה. חֲמוֹר וְכֵלָיו הֲפוּכִין וּפָרָה רָצָה בֵּין הַכְּרָמִים הֲרֵי זוֹ עֲבֵידָה. הֶחֱזִירָהּ (fol. 8b) וּבָרְחָה הֶחֱזִירָהּ וּבָרְחָה אֲפִילוּ אַרְבָּעָה וַחֲמִשָּׁה פְּעָמִים חַיָּיב לְהַחֲזִירָהּ שֶׁנֶּאֱמַר הָשֵׁב תְּשִׁיבֵם. הָיָה בָּטֵל מִסֶּלַע לֹא יֹאמַר לוֹ תֵּן לִי סֶלַע אֶלָּא נוֹתֵן לוֹ שְׂכָרוֹ כְּפוֹעֵל בָּטֵל. אִם יֵשׁ בֵּית דִּין מַתְנֶה עִמּוֹ בִּפְנֵי בֵּית דִּין. אִם אֵין שָׁם בֵּית דִּין בִּפְנֵי מִי מַתְנֶה. שֶׁלּוֹ קוֹדֵם.

**Mishnah 11**: What is a lost animal[109]? If he found a donkey or a cow grazing on the road[110], this is no lost animal. A donkey whose gear is upside-down or a cow running in a vineyard are lost animals. If he returned it but it ran away, returned it but it ran away even four or five times, he is obligated to return it since it is said[111]: "Return it returning." If he was losing time worth a tetradrachma[112], he cannot say, give me a tetradrachma but [the owner] may pay him at the rate of an unemployed worker. If there is a court[113], he can stipulate with him[114] before the court. If there is no court, before whom could he stipulate? His own comes first[115].

משנה יב: מְצָאָהּ בְּרֶפֶת אֵינוֹ חַיָּב בָּהּ. בִּרְשׁוּת הָרַבִּים חַיָּב בָּהּ. הָיְתָה בֵּין הַקְּבָרוֹת אַל יִטַּמֵּא לוֹ. אִם אָמַר לוֹ אָבִיו הִיטַּמֵּא אוֹ שֶׁאָמַר לוֹ אַל תַּחֲזִיר לֹא יִשְׁמַע לוֹ. פֵּירֵק וְטָעַן פֵּירֵק וְטָעַן אֲפִילוּ אַרְבָּעָה וַחֲמִשָּׁה פְּעָמִים חַיָּב שֶׁנֶּאֱמַר עָזוֹב תַּעֲזֹב. הָלַךְ וְיָשַׁב לוֹ וְאָמַר הוֹאִיל וְעָלֶיךָ מִצְוָה אִם רְצִיתָה לִפְרוֹק פְּרוֹק פָּטוּר שֶׁנֶּאֱמַר עִמּוֹ. הָיָה חוֹלֶה אוֹ זָקֵן חַיָּב. מִצְוָה מִן הַתּוֹרָה לִפְרוֹק אֲבָל לֹא לִטְעוֹן. רִבִּי שִׁמְעוֹן אוֹמֵר אַף לִטְעוֹן. רִבִּי יוֹסֵי הַגְּלִילִי אוֹמֵר אִם הָיָה עָלָיו יוֹתֵר מִמַּשּׂאוֹ אֵינוֹ זָקוּק לוֹ שֶׁנֶּאֱמַר תַּחַת מַשָּׂאוֹ מַשּׂאוֹי שֶׁהוּא יָכוֹל לַעֲמוֹד בּוֹ.

**Mishnah 12**: [116]If one found it in the cow-shed, he has no obligation; in the public domain he is obligated. But if it was between graves, he[117] may not defile himself. If his father told him to defile himself, or told him not to return it, he should not listen to him[118]. [119]If he unloaded and loaded, unloaded and loaded even four or five times, he is obligated since it is said: "restoring restore"[120]. If he[121] sat down and said, since it is your[122] religious obligation, if you want to unload, unload, he[122] is free since it is said: "with him". It is a religious obligation to unload, but not to load; Rebbi Simeon says, also to load[123]. Rebbi Yose the Galilean said, if the load was more than the ordinary, he need not do anything since it is said: "under *its* load," a load which it can carry[124].

109  The Mishnah refers to *Deut.* 22:1 and *Ex.* 23:4 which state the duty to return straying animals to their owners.

110  Even if no person was near watching the animal.

111  *Deut.* 22:1. The infinitive construction is regularly interpreted as implying repetition; cf. *Sifry Deut.* 222.

112  If the person finding the animal is highly paid and his time is worth much more than that of an agricultural hired hand, the question arises whether he can be forced to miss his lucrative trade in order to return a stray animal.

113  According to Rashi, this may be an *ad hoc* court composed of three of the finder's acquaintances who can empower him to charge full compensation for his time. Since the Yerushalmi does not discuss the Mishnah, its position cannot be ascertained.

114  This word is also in Alfasi's text but only in one ms. of the Babli. R. Yosef Ḥabiba (*Nimmuqe Yosef*) in his commentary to Alfasi points out that the word makes no sense since the finder's obligation already has terminated if the animal's owner is around.

115  There is no obligation to incur monetary loss in following *Deut.* 22:1.

116  This is a continuation of Mishnah 11. On the owner's property, no animal is staying.

117  If the possible helper was a Cohen.

118  Since both son and father are required to follow God's commandments, if the father commands not to obey God, he must be disobeyed (*Mekhilta dR. Ismael, Neziqin* Chapter 20; ed. Horovitz-Rabin p. 325.)

119  Here begins the rabbinic interpretation of *Ex.* 23:5.

120  *Ex.* 23:5; in rabbinic interpretation, the root here is עזב II. Ibn Ezra in both his commentaries *ad loc.* calls this "far fetched". Onqelos, Pseudo-Jonathan, and Saadia translate as if it were written twice, first עזב I "abandon", then עזב II "put in good order." This may be a pun intended in the biblical text.

121  The owner of a animal which stumbled.

122  The person who comes to help. *Mekhilta dR. Simeon ben Iohai*, p. 215.

123  Implied by the parallel *Deut.* 22:4: "uplifting you shall uplift with him." *Mekhilta dR. Ismael, Neziqin* 20 (p. 326); *Sifry Deut.* 225.

124  *Mekhilta dR. Ismael, Neziqin* 20 (p. 325).

(8d line 18) **הלכה יא:** אֵי זוֹ הִיא אֲבֵידָה כול'. מָצָא בְרָפֶת אֵין חַיָּיב בָּהּ. בִּרְשׁוּת הָרַבִּים חַיָּיב. בֵּין הַקְּבָרוֹת אַל יִטַּמֵּא. אָמַר לוֹ אָבִיו. הִיטַּמֵּא. אוֹ

שֶׁאָמַר לוֹ אָבִיו. אַל תַּחֲזִיר. אַל יִשְׁמַע לוֹ. בְּכָל אָתָר אַתְּ מַר. מִצְוַת עֲשֵׂה קוֹדֶמֶת לְמִצְוַת לֹא תַעֲשֶׂה. וָכָא אַתְּ מַר. אֵין מִצְוַת עֲשֵׂה קוֹדֶמֶת לְמִצְוַת לֹא תַעֲשֶׂה. שַׁנְיָיא הִיא שֶׁהוּא וְאָבִיו חַיָּיבִין בִּכְבוֹד הַמָּקוֹם.

**Halakhah 11**: "What is a lost animal," etc. "If one found it in the cowshed, he has no obligation; in the public domain he is obligated. Between graves, he may not defile himself. If his father told him to defile himself, or told him not to return it, he should not listen to him." Everywhere you say that a positive commandment has precedence over a prohibition, but here, you say that a positive commandment does not have precedence over a prohibition[125]? There is a difference since both he and his father are required to honor the Omnipresent[118, 126].

125 The positive commandment is to honor father and mother, to fear mother and father. The obligation to help with a fallen animal is formulated as a prohibition: one is forbidden to be oblivious of the animal's pain; the Cohen is forbidden to enter a cemetary. Therefore, why should the father's command not be obeyed in preference to obeying biblical prohibitions.

126 In the Babli, 32a, this is explained as direct obligation formulated in *Lev.* 19:3.

(8d line 23) תַּנֵּי. רוֹבֵץ וְלֹא רָבְצָן. וְחָזַר תַּנֵּי. פּוֹרֵק עִמּוֹ אֲפִילוּ מֵאָה פְּעָמִים בַּיּוֹם. הֵן דְּתֵימַר. רוֹבֵץ וְלֹא רָבְצָן. בְּהַהוּא דְּמַפִּיל גַּרְמֵיהּ. וְהֵן דְּתֵימַר. פּוֹרֵק עִמּוֹ אֲפִילוּ מֵאָה פְּעָמִים. בְּהַהוּא דְּאָנִיס.

It was stated: "Lying down" but not one which habitually lies down[127]. But then it was stated: "He unloads with him even a hundred times[127*] in a day." When you said, "lying down" rather than one which habitually lies down, about one which lies down by himself. When you said, "he unloads with him even a hundred times," in an accident.

127 *Mekhilta dR. Ismael, Neziqin* 20 (p. 325); Babli 33a.

It has been noted by modern Bible commentators that רבץ (Accadic *rabaṣu*, Arabic ربض) describes an animal resting comfortably on its knees and that, therefore, *Ex.* 23:5 is an exhortation not to be a busybody offering help when it is not needed, whereas *Deut.* 22:4 is the obligation to help where it is needed. The problem with this interpretation is that it does not fit the general context of the Chapter in *Ex.* Therefore, the rabbinic interpretation is preferable which essentially treats all words in *Ex.* 23:5 as ambiguous.

127* Tosephta 2:24.

(8d line 26) כִּי תִפְגַּע. יָכוֹל פְּגִיעָה מַמָּשׁ. תַּלְמוּד לוֹמַר. כִּי תִרְאֶה. אִי כִּי תִרְאֶה יָכוֹל אֲפִילוּ רָחוֹק מֵאָה מִיל. תַּלְמוּד לוֹמַר. כִּי תִפְגַּע. הָא כֵיצַד. שִׁיעֲרוּ חֲכָמִים אֶחָד מִשִּׁבְעָה וּמֶחֱצָה בְּמִיל. וְזֶהוּ רִיס. עָזוֹב תַּעֲזוֹב זוֹ פְּרִיקָה. הָקֵם תָּקִים זוֹ טְעִינָה. רַבִּי שִׁמְעוֹן בֶּן לָקִישׁ אוֹמֵר. כְּשֵׁם שֶׁפּוֹרְקוֹ מִן הַתּוֹרָה כָּךְ טוֹעֲנוֹ מִן הַתּוֹרָה. חֲמוֹר יִשְׂרָאֵל וּמַשָּׂאוֹי שֶׁלְּגוֹי דִּבְרֵי הַכֹּל פּוֹרֵק וְטוֹעֵן. חֲמוֹר גּוֹי וּמַשָּׂאוֹי שֶׁל יִשְׂרָאֵל. כְּדִבְרֵי חֲכָמִים לֹא פוֹרֵק וְלֹא טוֹעֵן. כְּדִבְרֵי רַבִּי שִׁמְעוֹן פּוֹרֵק וְלֹא טוֹעֵן.

[128]"If you hit upon.[129]" I could think, really if you hit upon him; the verse says, "if you see.[130]" Concerning "if you see," I could think even at a distance of a hundred[131] *mil*? The verse says, "if you hit upon." How is this? The Sages estimated one in $7^1/_2$ of a *mil*, i. e., a *stadion*[131].

[128]Putting in order you shall put in order,[129]" this is unloading. "Uplifting you shall uplift,[130]" this is loading. Rebbi Simeon ben Ioḥai says, just as his unloading is [an obligation] from the Torah, so his loading is from the Torah[133]. [134]If the donkey was a Jew's but the load a Gentile's, everybody says that he unloads and loads. If the donkey was a Gentile's but the load a Jew's, according to the Sages one neither unloads nor loads. According to Rebbi Simeon one unloads but does not load.

128 Babli 32a; *Mekhilta dR. Ismael Neziqin* 20 p. 323, *dR. Simeon bar Iohai* p. 215, *Sifry Deut.* 222, *Midrash Tannaïm* (*Midrash Haggadol*) 22:4.
129 *Ex.* 23:5.
130 *Deut.* 22:4.
131 E has מלוא מיל "a full *mil*", which for practical purposes is as impossible as 100 *mil*.
132 An *itinerant stadion* of about 148 m or 266 $2/3$ cubits.
133 Whereas for the Sages he may ask to be paid for helping in loading; cf. Note 134.
134 Babli 32b; other sources cf. Note 128.

**משנה יג**: (fol. 8b) אֲבֵידָתוֹ וַאֲבֵידַת אָבִיו שֶׁלּוֹ קוֹדֶמֶת. אֲבֵידָתוֹ וַאֲבֵידַת רַבּוֹ שֶׁלּוֹ קוֹדֶמֶת. אֲבֵידַת אָבִיו וַאֲבֵידַת רַבּוֹ שֶׁל רַבּוֹ קוֹדֶמֶת לְשֶׁל אָבִיו שֶׁאָבִיו הֱבִיאוֹ לְחַיֵּי הָעוֹלָם הַזֶּה. וְרַבּוֹ שֶׁלִּימְּדוֹ חָכְמָה הֱבִיאוֹ לְחַיֵּי הָעוֹלָם הַבָּא. וְאִם אָבִיו שָׁקוּל כְּנֶגֶד רַבּוֹ אֲבֵידַת אָבִיו קוֹדֶמֶת. הָיָה אָבִיו וְרַבּוֹ נוֹשְׂאִין מַשָּׂאוּי מַנִּיחַ אֶת שֶׁל רַבּוֹ וְאַחַר כָּךְ מַנִּיחַ אֶת שֶׁל אָבִיו. הָיָה אָבִיו וְרַבּוֹ בְּבֵית הַשְּׁבִי פּוֹדֶה אֶת רַבּוֹ וְאַחַר כָּךְ פּוֹדֶה אֶת אָבִיו. אֲבָל אִם הָיָה אָבִיו תַּלְמִיד חָכָם פּוֹדֶה אֶת אָבִיו וְאַחַר כָּךְ פּוֹדֶה אֶת רַבּוֹ.

[135]**Mishnah 13**: Between his lost property and his father's lost property, his own has precedence. Between his lost property and his teacher's lost property, his own has precedence. Between his father's lost property and his teacher's lost property, his teacher's lost property has precedence, for his father brought him to the life of this world, but his teacher who taught him wisdom brought him to the life of the future world. But if his father was his teacher's equal, his father's lost property has precedence. If his father and his teacher were carrying loads, he unloads his teacher's and after that his father's. If his father and his teacher were jailed, he redeems his teacher and after that redeems his father; but if his father was learned he redeems his father and after that redeems his teacher.

135 Mishnah and Halakhah are treated more thoroughly in *Horaiot* 3:7, 48b (cf. also end of Mishnah *Keritut* 6:9, Tosephta *Horaiot* 2:5,6).

(8d line 34) **הלכה יג:** אֲבֵידָתוֹ וַאֲבֵידַת אָבִיו כול'. תַּנֵּי. אֵי זֶהוּ רַבּוֹ שֶׁלִּימְּדוֹ חָכְמָה. כָּל־שֶׁפָּתַח לוֹ תְּחִילָּה. דִּבְרֵי רִבִּי מֵאִיר. רִבִּי יוּדָן אוֹמֵר. כָּל־שָׁרוֹב תַּלְמוּדוֹ מִמֶּנּוּ. רִבִּי יוֹסֵי אוֹמֵר. כָּל־שֶׁהֵאִיר עֵינָיו בְּמִשְׁנָתוֹ. רַב כְּרִבִּי מֵאִיר. וְרִבִּי יוֹחָנָן כְּרִבִּי יוּדָה. שְׁמוּאֵל כְּרִבִּי יוֹסֵי.

רַב כְּרִבִּי מֵאִיר. חַד בַּר נָשׁ פָּתַח פּוּמֵיהּ דְּרַב. וּשְׁמַע דִּדְמָךְ וּבְזַע עֲלוֹי.

רִבִּי יוֹחָנָן כְּרִבִּי יוּדָה. רִבִּי יוֹחָנָן הֲוָה סָלִיק מְטִיבֶּרְיָה לְצִיפּוֹרִי. חָמָא חַד בַּר נָשׁ נָחַת מִן תַּמָּן. אֲמַר לֵיהּ. מַה קָלָא בִמְדִינְתָּא. אֲמַר לֵיהּ. חַד רַבָּן דְּמַךְ וְכָל־עַמָּא פָּרְיָין מִיטַּפְּלָא בֵיהּ. יָדַע רִבִּי יוֹחָנָן דְּהוּא רִבִּי חֲנִינָה. שְׁלַח וְאַיְיתֵי מָאנִין טָבִין דְּשׁוּבְתָא וּבְזָעוֹן. וְלֹא כֵן תַּנֵּי. כָּל־קֶרַע שֶׁאֵינוֹ שֶׁל בֶּהָלָה אֵינוֹ קֶרַע. רִבִּי יוֹחָנָן בָּעָא מֵיעֲבַד דְּרַבָּה וּמוֹקִרִיתֵיהּ. וְלָא יָדְעִין אִין מִשּׁוּם דַּהֲוָה רַבֵּיהּ אִין מִשּׁוּם שְׁמוּעוֹת הָרָעוֹת. מִילְּתֵיהּ דְּרִבִּי חִיָּיה בַּר וָא בְצִיפּוֹרִי. חָמָא כּוּלֵּי עָלְמָא פָּרְיֵי. אֲמַר לֵיהּ. לָמָּה כּוּלֵּי עָלְמָא פָּרְיֵי. אָמְרִין לֵיהּ. רִבִּי יוֹחָנָן יָתִיב דְּרִישׁ בְּבֵי מִדְרָשָׁא דְּרִבִּי בְּנָיָיה וְעַל עַמָּא פָּרְיֵי מִישְׁמְעִינֵיהּ. אָמַר. בְּרִיךְ רַחֲמָנָא דַחֲמֵי לִי פּוֹרִין עַד דַּאֲנָא בַחַיִּים. וּבַאֲגַדְתָּא פָּשְׁטִית לֵיהּ חוּץ מִמִּשְׁלֵי וְקֹהֶלֶת. הָדָא אֲמָרָה. כָּל־תַּלְמִיד וְתַלְמִיד.

שְׁמוּאֵל כְּרִבִּי יוֹסֵי אָמַר. חַד בַּר נָשׁ אַסְבַּר לִשְׁמוּאֵל בִּשְׁנֵי מַפְתֵּיחוֹת אֶחָד יוֹרֵד לְאַמַּת בֵּית הַשִּׁיחִי וְאֶחָד פּוֹתֵחַ כִּיוָן. שֶׁהָיָה מוֹרִיד יָדוֹ עַד שִׁיחָיו הָיָה פּוֹתֵחַ כִּיוָן. וּשְׁמַע דִּדְמָךְ וּבְזַע עֲלוֹי.

**Halakhah 13**: "Between his lost property and his father's lost property," etc. It was stated[136]: "Who is his teacher who taught him wisdom? The one who taught him first[137], the words of Rebbi Meïr. Rebbi Jehudah says, the one from whom he received most of his instruction. Rebbi Yose said, anyone who explained a Mishnah to him." Rav followed Rebbi Meïr, Rebbi Johanan Rebbi Jehudah, and Samuel Rebbi Yose.

Rav followed Rebbi Meïr. A person was Rav's first teacher. He heard that he had died and tore his garment for him.

Rebbi Joḥanan followed Rebbi Jehudah. Rebbi Joḥanan was climbing from Tiberias to Sepphoris when he saw a man descending from there. He asked him, what is new in the big city? He told him, one of the great rabbis died and everbody was running to occupy themselves with him[138]. Rebbi Joḥanan understood that it was Rebbi Ḥanina. He sent and brought his good Sabbath clothes and tore them[139]. But did we not state: Any tear which is not in panic is not a tear[140]? Rebbi Joḥanan wanted to do more and show his appreciation. But we do not know whether it was because he was his teacher or because of bad news. There is the case of Rebbi Ḥiyya bar Abba in Sepphoris[141]. He saw that everybody was running. He asked, why is everybody running? They told him, Rebbi Joḥanan is preaching in Rebbi Banaia's study house and everybody is running to hear him. He said, praised be the Merciful Who showed me people running while I am alive. In *Agadah* I explained him everything except Proverbs and Ecclesiastes[142]. This means every single student[143].

Samuel followed Rebbi Yose. A person explained to Samuel: "Two keys, for one he has to go down to his arm-pit and one opens straight;[144]" that he lowered his hand under his arm-pit until he could insert the key straight. He heard that this one had died and tore his garment for him[145].

---

136 A different version in the Babli 33a, Tosephta 2:30, *Horaiot* 2:5. (The latter text is not in the Yerushalmi appended to the *editio princeps* of the Babli.)

137 The elementary school teacher who taught him reading and writing.

138 For the burial.

139 In the Babli, *Mo'ed Qaṭan* 25a, "13 silk stolas."

140 Since really it is forbidden to destroy usable things, tearing one's clothes in mourning is acceptable only as an expression of acute pain. How

could R. Johanan make an elaborate ceremony out of it? In the Babli, *Mo'ed Qaṭan* 25a, the statement is amoraic, attributed to Samuel.

141 This sentence seems to be incomplete. In the *Horaiot* text: "R. Hananiah (read: R. Hanina) was leaning on R. Hiyya bar Abba in Sepphoris."

142 This proves that R. Hanina was a teacher of R. Johanan, even though in legal matters R. Johanan was the student of R. Hoshaia.

143 Even if he is a student only in homiletics.

144 Mishnah *Tamid* 3:6. The doors of the Temple hall could be opened only from the inside. When the door was locked, a Cohen entered from a small side door which led to a guard room. The lock of this side door was hidden; the Cohen had to take the key, reach with his entire arm, up to his arm-pit, behind the partition wall and then insert the key. The second door, from the guard room into the Temple hall, could then be opened by a regular key inserted straight into the keyhole.

145 In *Horaiot*: He removed his phylacteries as s sign of mourning.

## המפקיד פרק שלישי

**משנה א:** (fol. 8d) הַמַּפְקִיד אֵצֶל חֲבֵירוֹ בְּהֵמָה אוֹ כֵלִים וְנִגְנְבוּ אוֹ שֶׁאָבְדוּ שִׁילֵּם וְלָא רָצָה לִישָּׁבַע שֶׁהֲרֵי אָמְרוּ שׁוֹמֵר חִנָּם נִשְׁבָּע וְיוֹצֵא. נִמְצָא הַגַּנָּב מְשַׁלֵּם תַּשְׁלוּמֵי כֶפֶל טָבַח וּמָכַר מְשַׁלֵּם תַּשְׁלוּמֵי אַרְבָּעָה וַחֲמִשָּׁה. לְמִי מְשַׁלֵּם לְמִי שֶׁהַפִּיקָדוֹן אֶצְלוֹ.

**Mishnah 1**: If one deposited an animal or vessels with another[1] and they were stolen or lost: If the other paid and did not want to swear[2] although they said that the unpaid trustee swears and is absolved[3], in case the thief was found, he pays double restitution[4]; if he slaughtered or sold it, he pays quadruple or quintuple restitution[5]. To whom does he pay? To the person with whom it was deposited[6].

**משנה ב:** נִשְׁבַּע וְלָא רָצָה לְשַׁלֵּם נִמְצָא הַגַּנָּב מְשַׁלֵּם תַּשְׁלוּמֵי כֶפֶל טָבַח וּמָכַר מְשַׁלֵּם תַּשְׁלוּמֵי אַרְבָּעָה וַחֲמִשָּׁה. לְמִי מְשַׁלֵּם לְבַעַל הַפִּיקָדוֹן.

**Mishnah 2**: If the other had sworn and did not pay, in case the thief was found, he pays double restitution; if he slaughtered or sold it, he pays quadruple or quintuple restitution. To whom does he pay? To the owner of the deposit.

1   Without paying for the service. The paid trustee has to pay except for an act of God or armed robbery.

2   Since he avoids all oaths because of religious scruples.

3   Mishnah 7:8, based on *Ex.* 22:6-8. He has to swear (1) that the object deposited is not in his possession and (2) that he was not negligent.

4   *Ex.* 22:6.

5   *Ex.* 21:37.

6   Who had acquired the right to the deposited object by paying for it.

(9a line 35) **הלכה א:** הַמַּפְקִיד אֵצֶל חֲבֵירוֹ כול'. מֶנָן תֵּיתֵי לֵיהּ. אִם הִמָּצֵא תִמָּצֵא בְיָדוֹ הַגְּנֵיבָה. וְכִי אֵין אָנוּ יוֹדְעִין שֶׁאִם יִמָּצֵא הַגַּנָּב יְשַׁלֵּם שְׁנָיִם. וּמַה תַּלְמוּד לוֹמַר שְׁנַיִם יְשַׁלֵּם. אִם אֵינוֹ עִנְיָין לוֹ תְּנֵיהוּ עִנְיָין לְשֶׁלְּפָנָיו. רִבִּי [ ] עָאַל לְפִירְקָא דְרִבִּי יוּדָן. אָמַר קוֹמֵיהּ הָדָא. אָמַר לֵיהּ. אֱמוֹר דְּבַתְרָהּ. נִשְׁבַּע וְלֹא רָצָה לְשַׁלֵּם נִמְצָא הַגַּנָּב מְשַׁלֵּם תַּשְׁלוּמֵי כָפֶל. טָבַח וּמָכַר מְשַׁלֵּם תַּשְׁלוּמֵי אַרְבָּעָה וַחֲמִשָּׁה. לְמִי מְשַׁלֵּם. לְבַעַל הַפִּיקָדוֹן. וִישַׁלֵּם לְמִי שֶׁהַפִּיקָדוֹן אֶצְלוֹ. רִבִּי נָסָה בְשֵׁם רִבִּי יוֹנָה. חַיִּים שְׁנַיִם יְשַׁלֵּם. לְמָקוֹם שֶׁהַקֶּרֶן מְהַלֵּךְ שָׁם הַכֶּפֶל מְהַלֵּךְ. רִבִּי יוֹחָנָן וְרִבִּי לָעְזָר. רִבִּי נָסָה מוֹסִיף בְשֵׁם רִבִּי יוֹסֵי בֶּן חֲנִינָה. לֹא סוֹף דָּבָר שִׁילֵּם אֶלָּא מִיכֵּיוָן שֶׁקִּיבֵּל עָלָיו לְשַׁלֵּם כְּמִי שֶׁשִּׁילֵּם.

**Halakhah 1**: "If one deposited an animal or vessels with another," etc. From where does he bring this[7]? "If the stolen object be found in his hand[8]." Do we not know that if the thief is found that he has to pay double[9]? Why does the verse say, "double he shall pay"? If the verse is not needed for the case[10], use it for the following subject[11]. Rebbi [ ][12] went to the "term"[12*] of Rebbi Yudan and asked this question before him. He answered, refer to what is stated afterwards: "If the other had sworn and did not pay, in case the thief was found, he pays double restitution; if he had slaughtered or sold it, he pays quadruple or quintuple restitution. To whom does he pay? To the owner of the deposit." Should he not pay to the person with whom it was deposited[13]? Rebbi Nasa in the name of Rebbi Jonah: "Alive, double he shall pay[14]." To the place where the capital goes, there the double fine goes[15]. Rebbi Johanan and Rebbi Eleazar; Rebbi Nasa adds in the name of Rebbi Yose ben Hanina: Not only when he paid, but even when he stated his willingness to pay it is as if he had paid[16].

7  That the fine has to be paid to the trustee if the latter had refused to swear.

8  *Ex.* 22:3: "If the stolen object be

found in his hand ... double he shall pay."

9   Since this is explicit in *Ex.* 22:6 (for money or vessels), why does it have to be stated in v. 3 for livestock?

10   If the objects were stolen from their owner; *Ex.* 21:37-22:3.

11   If they were stolen from the unpaid trustee, *Ex.* 22:6-8.

12   The name of an Amora is missing here. The discussion cannot be between Rebbi and the Tanna R. Jehudah (bar Ilai) since Rebbi was a student of R. Jehudah's son and never used Aramaic in learned discussions. E reads "Rav Naḥman". S. Lieberman suggests that he might be R. Naḥman from Jaffa [*Gen. r.* 53(4)], one of the rabbis of Caesarea.

12*   The "term" is the twice-yearly period of public lectures.

13   Since one has to assume that the thief has to pay to the person from whom he stole. Then the trustee would have to pay the restitution to the object's owner but could retain the fine for himself.

14   *Ex.* 22:3.

15   Since it says "double", not "he has to pay the value of the theft and then a fine in an equal amount", it follows that double restitution is one payment to one recipient.

16   Babli 34a,37a. Since by necessity the transaction between owner and trustee happened before the thief was apprehended, when neither one of the two were in possession, the right to ownership is transferred by agreement, rather than by actual payment.

(9a line 44) אָמַר. מְשַׁלֵּם אֲנִי. חוֹשְׁשִׁין שֶׁמָּא שָׁלַח בּוֹ יָד. אָמַר. נִשְׁבָּע אֲנִי. וְרָאָה אוֹתָן שֶׁמְּנַלְגְּלִין עָלָיו שְׁבוּעוֹת אֲחֵרוֹת וְאָמַר. מְשַׁלֵּם אֲנִי. חוֹשְׁשִׁין. אָמַר רִבִּי יוֹסֵי. לֹא חִיְּיבָה אוֹתוֹ הַתּוֹרָה שְׁבוּעָה לְהַחֲמִיר עָלָיו אֶלָּא לְהָקֵל. שֶׁאִם רָצָה לְשַׁלֵּם יְשַׁלֵּם וְאִם רָצָה לִישָּׁבַע יִשָּׁבַע. הָיוּ לוֹ עֵדִים שֶׁנִּגְנְבָה בְאוֹנֶס הָדָא הִיא דָּמַר רִבִּי לְעָזָר. הַמּוֹכֵר קְנָסָיו לְאַחֵר לֹא עָשָׂה כְלוּם. הָיוּ לוֹ עֵדִים שֶׁנִּגְנְבָה בִּפְשִׁיעָה הֲרֵי הוּא בִּכְלָל יְשַׁלֵּם. וְאַחַר כָּךְ נִמְצֵאת הַגְּנֵיבָה לְמִי מְשַׁלֵּם. לָרִאשׁוֹן אוֹ לַשֵּׁינִי אוֹ לִשְׁנֵיהֶן.

If he said, I am paying, one may suspect that possibly he took it for himself[17]. If he said, I am swearing, but then he saw that other oaths were added[18] and he said, I am paying, one is suspicious[19]. Rebbi Yose said, the

Torah did not impose an oath on him to restrict him but to ease for him; for if he wants to pay, he shall pay, and if he wants to swear, he shall swear[20]. If he had witnesses that it was forcibly stolen[21], to that case refers what Rebbi Eleazar said: If somebody sells his claims of fines to someone else, he did not do anything[22]. If he had witnesses that it was stolen because of negligence, he comes under the category of "he shall pay"[23]. If afterwards the stolen object was found, to whom does [the thief] pay? To the first, or to the second, or to both of them?

17   One forces him to swear a rabbinic oath that the article is not in his possession.

18   Since once a person is required to swear by biblical standards, the opposing party can make him swear on any other claims even if those claims alone would not be sufficient to force an oath: *Soṭah* 2:6, Notes 166-169.

19   The oath required from every non-payor. For rabbinic oaths one cannot force additions; cf. *Rosh Šebuot* 7, end of Section 18 (Alfasi *Šebuot* 7, # 1186.)

20   *Ex.* 22:7-8. R. Yose denies the possibility of the imposition of a rabbinic oath if there is no case for a biblical oath.

21   Then he does not pay without swearing an oath.

22   If the trustee pays even though he is not required to swear in order to be freed from payment, he did not acquire the right to claim double restitution from the thief. If the thief is caught, he has to pay double to the owner of the object who then will return to the trustee what the latter had paid and retain the amount of the fine for himself.

23   *Ex.* 22:8 explicitly obligates the trustee for damages caused by his negligence. In this case, the Mishnah does not apply and there is no statement that the claims were transmitted to the trustee.

(fol. 8d) **משנה ג:** הַשּׂוֹכֵר פָּרָה מֵחֲבֵירוֹ וְהִשְׁאִילָהּ לְאַחֵר וּמֵתָה כְדַרְכָּהּ יִשָּׁבַע הַשּׂוֹכֵר שֶׁמֵּתָה כְדַרְכָּהּ וְהַשּׁוֹאֵל יְשַׁלֵּם לַשּׂוֹכֵר. אָמַר רִבִּי יוֹסֵי כֵּיצַד הַלָּה עוֹשֶׂה

סְחוֹרָה בְּפָרָתוֹ שֶׁלַּחֲבֵירוֹ. אֶלָּא תַּחֲזוֹר הַפָּרָה לַבְּעָלִים.

**Mishnah 3**: If somebody lease[24] a cow from another person and then lends[25] it out to a third person. If it died a natural death, the lessee shall swear that it died a natural death and the borrower has to pay the lessee. Rebbi Yose said, how can this one treat another person's cow as his merchandise[26]? But [the value of] the cow shall be returned to its owner.

24 Mishnah 7:8 states that the lessee pays for what is lost or stolen but not for what is robbed, or by natural causes is broken or dies.
25 The borrower pays for anything that happens to the object he rented (Mishnah 7:8).
26 Why should the lessee get the value of the cow and its owner get nothing?

**הלכה ג:** הַשּׂוֹכֵר פָּרָה מֵחֲבֵירוֹ כול׳. וְיֵשׁ לוֹ רְשׁוּת לְהַשְׁאִיל. וְלֹא (9a line 51) כֵן תַּנֵּי רִבִּי חִייָה. אֵין הַשּׁוֹאֵל רַשַּׁאי לְהַשְׁאִיל וְלֹא הַשּׂוֹכֵר רַשַּׁאי לְהַשְׂכִּיר וְלֹא הַשּׁוֹאֵל רַשַּׁאי לְהַשְׂכִּיר וְלֹא הַשּׂוֹכֵר רַשַּׁאי לְהַשְׁאִיל אֶלָּא אִם כֵּן נָטַל רְשׁוּת מִן הַבְּעָלִים. רִבִּי לָא בְשֵׁם רִבִּי יַנַּאי. וְהוּא שֶׁנְּתָנוֹ לוֹ לְהַשְׂכִּיר. וָכָא. וְהוּא שֶׁנְּתָנוֹ לָהּ רְשׁוּת לַעֲשׂוֹת בָּהּ אֶפִּיטְרוֹפָּא. רִבִּי אַבָּהוּ שָׁאַל. שְׁאָלוּהָ בְּעָלִים מְשׁוּכֵּר וָמֵתָה כְדַרְכָּהּ יִשָּׁבַע הַשּׂוֹכֵר שֶׁמֵּתָה כְדַרְכָּהּ וְהַשּׁוֹאֵל מְשַׁלֵּם לַשּׂוֹכֵר. וְאִין כֵּינִי אֲפִילוּ אֲכָלוּהָ. אָמַר רִבִּי אַבִינָא. אֲכָלוּ שֶׁלָּהֶן אָכְלוּ. אָמַר רִבִּי יוֹסֵי. הֵיאךְ הַלָּה עוֹשֶׂה סְחוֹרָה בְּפָרָתוֹ שֶׁלָּזֶה. אֶלָּא תַּחֲזוֹר פָּרָה לַבְּעָלִים.

**Halakhah 3**: "If somebody lease a cow from another person," etc. [27]But does he have permission to lend it? Did not Rebbi Hiyya state: "The borrower cannot lend, nor the lessee lease, nor the borrower lease, nor the lessee lend, unless he received permission from the owners." Rebbi La said in the name of Rebbi Yannai: Only if he gave permission to lease. And here, only if he gave permission to let him be a steward[28]. Rebbi Abbahu asked: If the owners borrowed it and it died of natural causes, should the lessee swear that it died a natural death and the borrower pay the renter[29]? Rebbi Abinna said, if they ate it, they ate their own property. "Rebbi Yose said, how can this one treat another person's cow as his merchandise? But [the value of] the cow shall be returned to its owner[30]."

27  This paragraph is a fragment from a lengthy discussion in *Ketubot* 9:5, Notes 128-145; *Qiddušin* 1:4, Note 451.

28  This sentence does not belong here; it refers to the question in *Ketubot* whether a wife who has been entrusted by her husband with the care of his properties may delegate her duties to her sons.

29  If the owner is the borrower, the rule of the anonymous majority leads to a paradoxical result.

30  Therefore, practice has to follow R. Yose.

(fol. 8d) **משנה ד:** אָמַר לִשְׁנַיִם גָּזַלְתִּי אֶת אֶחָד מִכֶּם מָנֶה וְאֵינִי יוֹדֵעַ אֵי זֶה מִכֶּם. אוֹ אָבִיו שֶׁל אֶחָד מִכֶּם הִפְקִיד אֶצְלִי מָנֶה וְאֵינִי יוֹדֵעַ אֵי זֶה הוּא. נוֹתֵן לָזֶה מָנֶה וְלָזֶה מָנֶה שֶׁהוֹדָה מִפִּי עַצְמוֹ.

**Mishnah 4**: If one says to two people, I robbed a *mina* from one of you but I do not know who it was or, the father of one of you deposited a *mina* with me but I do not know who it is, has to pay a *mina* to each of them since he himself confessed.

**משנה ה:** שְׁנַיִם שֶׁהִפְקִידוּ אֵצֶל אֶחָד זֶה מָנֶה וְזֶה מָאתַיִם. זֶה אוֹמֵר שֶׁלִּי מָאתַיִם וְזֶה אוֹמֵר שֶׁלִּי מָאתַיִם נוֹתֵן לָזֶה מָנֶה וְלָזֶה מָנֶה וְהַשְּׁאָר יְהֵא מוּנָּח עַד שֶׁיָּבוֹא אֵלִיָּהוּ.

**Mishnah 5**: If two people deposited with a third party, one a *mina* and one 200 [*zuz*]. Each of them says, the 200 are mine. He shall give each of them a *mina* and the remainder shall be deposited until Elijah comes[31].

**משנה ו:** וְכֵן שְׁנֵי כֵלִים אֶחָד יָפֶה מָנֶה וְאֶחָד יָפֶה אֶלֶף זוּז זֶה אוֹמֵר יָפֶה שֶׁלִּי וְזֶה אוֹמֵר יָפֶה שֶׁלִּי נוֹתֵן אֶת הַקָּטָן לְאֶחָד מֵהֶן וּמִתּוֹךְ הַגָּדוֹל נוֹתֵן דְּמֵי הַקָּטָן לַשֵּׁנִי וְהַשְּׁאָר יְהֵא מוּנָח עַד שֶׁיָּבוֹא אֵלִיָּהוּ. אָמַר רִבִּי יוֹסֵי אִם כֵּן מַה הִפְסִיד הָרַמַּאי. אֶלָּא הַכֹּל יְהֵא מוּנָח עַד שֶׁיָּבֹא אֵלִיָּהוּ.

**Mishnah 6**: Similarly two vessels, one worth a *mina*, the other worth 1'000 *zuz*. Each of them says, the valuable one is mine. He shall give the small vessel to one of them, from the value of the large one he shall give the value of the small one to the other and the remainder shall be deposited until Elijah comes. Rebbi Yose said, if that be so, what did the trickster lose? But everything shall be deposited until Elijah comes[32].

31  In the Babli and all independent Mishnah mss., R. Yose's objection (Mishnah 6) is also quoted here.

The prophet Elijah, precursor of the Messiah, is supposed to know the answer to all unsolved questions.

32  Since Mishnaiot 5 and 6 are not discussed in the Yerushalmi, it is impossible to know its position relative to all modifications made by the Babli in their interpretation.

(9a line 60) **הלכה ד:** אָמַר לִשְׁנַיִם גָּזַלְתִּי כוּל'. רִבִּי אַבָּהוּ בְּשֵׁם רִבִּי יוֹחָנָן. כָּאן בְּעוֹרְרִין כָּאן בְּשׁוּתְּקִין. רִבִּי יָסָא בְּשֵׁם רִבִּי יוֹחָנָן. כָּאן בְּשֶׁיֵּשׁ עֵדִים יוֹדְעִין וְכָאן בְּשֶׁאֵין עֵדִים יוֹדְעִין. רַב יִרְמְיָה בְּשֵׁם רַב. כָּאן בְּנִשְׁבָּע כָּאן בְּשֶׁלֹּא נִשְׁבָּע. תַּמָּן אָמְרִין בְּשֵׁם רַב. שָׁם בְּנִשְׁבָּע כָּאן בְּשֶׁלֹּא נִשְׁבָּע. רִבִּי יִרְמְיָה בְּעֵי. אִם בְּשֶׁנִּשְׁבָּע הָיָה לוֹ לִשְׁתּוֹק. רִבִּי יִרְמְיָה סָבַר מֵימַר. הָיָה לוֹ לִשְׁתּוֹק וְלֹא לְהוֹדוֹת. רִבִּי יָסָא סָבַר מֵימַר. הָיָה לוֹ לִשְׁתּוֹק וְלֹא לִישָּׁבַע. רִבִּי יוֹחָנָן אָמַר. אִם בְּשֶׁנִּשְׁבָּע הָיָה לוֹ לַעֲשׂוֹת שְׁלוּחַ בֵּית דִּין. רִבִּי יוֹחָנָן סָבַר מֵימַר. שְׁלוּחַ בֵּית דִּין שֶׁעָשָׂה גוֹזֵל. תַּנָּיֵי חוֹרָן תַּנֵּי. שְׁלִיחַ בֵּית דִּין שֶׁעָשָׂה נִגְזָל. [וְכֵן תַּנֵּי. רִבִּי שִׁמְעוֹן בֶּן לְעָזָר אוֹמֵר. שְׁלִיחַ בֵּית דִּין שֶׁעָשָׂה הַנִּגְזָל] וְלֹא שְׁלִיחַ בֵּית דִּין שֶׁעָשָׂה גוֹזֵל. אָמַר רִבִּי אִילָא. אוֹף אֲנָן תַּנִּינָא וְאָמְרִינָן. הִיא גְזֵילָה הִיא בְעֵילָה הִיא מִלְוָה. הַכֹּל מוֹדִין בְּפִיקָדוֹן דְּמַתְנִיתָא מֵהָדָא אָמַר לִשְׁנַיִם. גָּזַלְתִּי מִכֶּם מָנֶה וְאֵינִי יוֹדֵעַ אֵי זֶה הוּא.

**Halakhah 4**: "If one says to two people, I robbed," etc. [33]Rebbi Abbahu in the name of Rebbi Joḥanan: Here if they complain, there if they are silent. Rebbi Yasa in the name of Rebbi Joḥanan: Here, if witnesses know; there, if no witnesses know. Rav Jeremiah in the name of Rav: Here if he swore; there if he did not swear. There, they say in the name of Rav: Here if he swore; there if he did not swear[34]. Rebbi Jeremiah wanted to say, he should have kept silent and not confessed. Rebbi Yasa wanted to say, he should have kept silent and not have sworn. Rebbi Joḥanan said, if he swore, he should have appointed an officer of the court. Rebbi Joḥanan seems to say, an officer of the court determined that one was a robber, not a court which determined that one was robbed. Other Tannaïm stated, a court which determined that one was robbed, [as it was stated, Rebbi Simeon ben Eleazar said, a court which determined that one was robbed,][35] not a court which determined that one was a robber. Rebbi Ila said, we also have stated that the rules are identical for robbery, intercourse[36], and loan[37]. Everbody agrees about the deposit mentioned in the Mishnah, from the following: "If he said to two people, I robbed a mina from one of you but I do not know which one of you it was."

33  This Halakhah is a sketch, or a first draft, of the discussion in *Yebamot* 15:10, Notes 153-178. The problem discussed is the discrepancy between Mishnah 4 and Mishnah *Yebamot* 15:10 which states that if somebody repents after having robbed one of a group of five people but does not know who it was, and each of them claims to be the victim, R. Tarphon says that he puts the amount of the robbery before them and lets them fight about the distribution. R. Aqiba agrees that this is the legal situation but holds that the robber is not free in the eyes of Heaven unless he pay the amount of the robbery to each of them. Mishnah 4 contains no hint of this controversy; we have to assume that it represents the opinions of both R. Tarphon and R. Aqiba. The

question is what is the difference between the two situations? The discussion is explained there in detail.

34   Cf. *Yebamot* 15:10, Note 157.

35   Addition of E; justified by its parallel in *Yebamot*.

36   Cf. *Yebamot* 15:9, Note 152. A man became betrothed by intercourse (violating a rabbinic prohibition) to one of two women. He does not remember who it was; they both claim to be his wife. Following R. Aqiba, he has to pay two *ketubot*.

37   In the unlikely case that somebody took a loan from one of two people who both claim to be his creditors and he does not remember whose debtor he is.

(fol. 8d) **משנה ז**: הַמַּפְקִיד פֵּירוֹת אֵצֶל חֲבֵירוֹ אֲפִילוּ הֵן אוֹבְדִין לֹא יִגַּע בָּהֶן. רַבָּן שִׁמְעוֹן בֶּן גַּמְלִיאֵל אוֹמֵר מוֹכְרָן בִּפְנֵי בֵית דִּין מִפְּנֵי הָשֵׁב אֲבֵידָה לַבְּעָלִין.

**Mishnah 7**: If somebody deposits produce with another person, even if it is becoming unusable[38] he should not touch it[39]. Rabban Simeon ben Gamliel said, he shall sell it under the supervision of the court[40] as returning lost property to its owner.

38   Either being spoiled, or being eaten by animals, or becoming ritually prohibited.

39   The Babli explains that this only refers to produce of the depositor's own farm; for trade produce the anonymous Tanna will agree with Rabban Simeon.

40   To insure himself against future claims by the depositor.

(9a line 71) **הלכה ז**: הַמַּפְקִיד פֵּירוֹת אֵצֶל חֲבֵירוֹ כול׳. אָמַר רִבִּי אַבָּהוּ אִם אוֹמֵר אַתְּ אֲבוּדִין הֵן אַל יִגַּע בָּהֶן. אַף הוּא מַמְצִיא לָהֶן. רִבִּי אַבָּא בַּר יַעֲקֹב בְּשֵׁם רִבִּי יוֹחָנָן רִבִּי אַבָּהוּ בְּשֵׁם רִבִּי יוֹחָנָן. הֲלָכָה כְּרַבָּן שִׁמְעוֹן בֶּן גַּמְלִיאֵל. כְּהָדָא רִבִּי יוֹחָנָן חֲקוֹקָה אַפְקַד גַּבֵּי רִבִּי חִייָה רוֹבָה חַד דִּיסִיקְיָה מַלְיָיא חָמֵץ. אָתָא שָׁאַל לְרִבִּי. אָמַר. יִמָּכֵר עַל פִּי בֵית דִּין בִּשְׁעַת הַבִּיעוּר. חַד בַּר נָשׁ אַפְקִיד גַּבֵּי רִבִּי חִייָה בַּר אַשִׁי חַד גְּרָב דְּכוּתָח. אָתָא שָׁאַל לְרַב. אָמַר. יִמָּכֵר עַל פִּי בֵית דִּין בִּשְׁעַת הַבִּיעוּר.

**Halakhah 7:** "If somebody deposits produce with another person," etc. Rebbi Abbahu said, if you would say that he should not touch them even if they are going to spoil, he will invent situations[41]. Rebbi Abba bar Jacob in the name of Rebbi Joḥanan, Rebbi Abbahu in the name of Rebbi Joḥanan: Practice follows Rabban Simeon ben Gamliel[42]. For example, Rebbi Joḥanan from Ḥaqoq deposited with the Elder Rebbi Ḥiyya[43] a saddle bag[44] full of leavened material. He came to ask Rebbi, who said it should be sold under the surpervision of the court when it would have to be destroyed[45]. A person deposited with Rabbi Ḥiyya bar Ashi an amphora full of *kutaḥ*[46]. He came to ask Rav, who said it should be sold under the surpervision of the court when otherwise it would have to be destroyed.

41 He explains R. Simeon ben Gamliel's ruling. If the trustee is prohibited from doing anything, he might invent a story that the produce did spoil when in reality he took it. But a sale under the supervision of the court avoids this.

42 Babli 38b, rejected there by the Babylonian authorities.

43 In the Babli, *Pesaḥim* 13a, a person deposited with R. Joḥanan from Ḥaqoq. Cf. *Pesaḥim* 1:6 (27c l. 74).

44 Greek διράκκιον, cf. *Berakhot* 3:5, Note 239.

45 Leavened material in possession of a Jew becomes permanently prohibited for usufruct at noon of the 14th of Nisan. Such material held in deposit should not be touched until 11 o'clock on that day, for the owner might come and dispose of it himself. But at 11 o'clock it should be sold to a Gentile lest it become worthless.

46 A Babylonian kind of soft cheese curdled by mold growing on old bread. This cheese is considered leavened material. [(N. B.) Might the acoustic similarity of the name of *cottage* cheese (*Ricotta*), soft cheese comparable to *kutaḥ*, be more than a coincidence? (E.G.)]

**משנה ח**: (fol. 8d) הַמַּפְקִיד פֵּירוֹת אֵצֶל חֲבֵירוֹ הֲרֵי זֶה יוֹצִיא לוֹ חֶסְרוֹנוֹת. לַחִטִּין וְלָאוֹרֶז תִּשְׁעַת חֲצָאֵי קַבִּין לַכּוֹר. לַשְּׂעוֹרִין וְלַדּוֹחַן תִּשְׁעָה קַבִּין לַכּוֹר. לַכּוּסְמִין וּלְזֶרַע פִּשְׁתָּן שָׁלֹשׁ סְאִין לַכּוֹר הַכֹּל לְפִי הַמִּידָה הַכֹּל לְפִי הַזְּמָן. אָמַר רִבִּי יוֹחָנָן בֶּן נוּרִי וְכִי מָה אִיכְפַּת לָהֶן לָעַכְבָּרִין וַהֲלֹא אוֹכְלוֹת בֵּין מֵהַרְבָּה וּבֵין מִקִּמְעָא. אֶלָּא אֵינוֹ מוֹצִיא לוֹ אֶלָּא כּוֹר אֶחָד בִּלְבָד. רִבִּי יְהוּדָה אוֹמֵר אִם הָיְתָה מִדָּה מְרוּבָּה אֵינוֹ מוֹצִיא לוֹ חֶסְרוֹנוֹת מִפְּנֵי שֶׁהֵן מוֹתִירוֹת.

**Mishnah 8**: If somebody deposits produce with another person[47], the latter returns it deducting losses[48], for wheat and rice $9/2$ *qab* per *kor*[49], for barley and millet nine *qab* per *kor*[50], for spelt and linseed three *se'ah* per *kor*[51]; everything proportional to quantity and time elapsed[52]. Rebbi Johanan ben Nuri said, do the rats care, do they not eat from much as from little[53]? But he only deducts what corresponds to one *kor*[54]. Rebbi Jehudah says, if it was a large quantity, he does not deduct because of the surplus[55].

**משנה ט**: (fol. 9a) יוֹצִיא לוֹ שְׁתוּת לַיַּיִן. רִבִּי יְהוּדָה אוֹמֵר חוֹמֶשׁ. יוֹצִיא לוֹ שְׁלֹשֶׁת לוּגִּין שֶׁמֶן לְמֵאָה לוֹג וּמֶחֱצָה שְׁמָרִים לוֹג וּמֶחֱצָה בֶּלַע. אִם הָיָה שֶׁמֶן מְזוּקָּק אֵינוֹ מוֹצִיא לוֹ שְׁמָרִים. אִם הָיוּ קַנְקַנִּים יְשָׁנוֹת אֵינוֹ מוֹצִיא לוֹ בֶּלַע. רִבִּי יְהוּדָה אוֹמֵר אַף הַמּוֹכֵר שֶׁמֶן מְזוּקָּק לַחֲבֵירוֹ כָּל־יְמוֹת הַשָּׁנָה הֲרֵי זֶה מְקַבֵּל עָלָיו לוֹג וּמֶחֱצָה שְׁמָרִים לְמֵאָה.

**Mishnah 9**: He deducts one sixth of wine; Rebbi Jehudah says a fifth. He deducts three *log* of oil per hundred, a *log* and a half lees[56], a *log* and a half absorption[57]. If it was refined oil, he does not deduct lees; if the vessels were old, he does not deduct absorption. Rebbi Jehudah says, also if somebody sells refined oil during the entire year, [the buyer] accepts a *log* and a half lees per hundred[58].

47 It is understood that the recipient stores the depositor's produce with his own. He has to return a given quantity, not exactly the produce given to him. If it is understood that he has to keep the other farmer's produce

separate, he simply returns the original produce in the original vessels without calculation.

48   Grain eaten by mice and other pests.

49   One *kor* is 30 *se'ah*; 1 *se'ah* is 24 *log*. The loss ratio is $9/1440 = 1/16$ or .625%.

50   1.25%.

51   10%.

52   The ratios indicated are per year.

53   This is incorrect; they breed quickly if there is an abundance of food.

54   He accepts proportionality in time but not in quantity. For him the amounts stated in the Mishnah are upper limits of what may be deducted in one year.

55   In his place, quantities over 1 *kor*, 0.384 m$^3$, are measured with an ample supplement which should take care of the losses.

56   Fragments of olives swimming in the oil, to be filtered out.

57   Oil absorbed by the walls of the porous clay vessels in which the oil is stored.

58   If the oil is sold at the going rate for unrefined oil, the seller may deliver refined oil, delivering only 98.5% of the quantity contracted for.

(9b line 2) הלכה ח: הַמַּפְקִיד פֵּירוֹת אֵצֶל חֲבֵירוֹ כול'. אָמַר רִבִּי אִמִּי. בְּשָׁעַת הַגּוֹרֶן שָׁנוּ. תַּמָּן אָמְרִין. אִילֵּין עַכְבָּרַיָּיא רְשִׁיעַיָּה כַּד חַמְיָין פֵּירֵי סַגִּין קַרְיָין לַחֲבֵירֵיהוֹן וְאָכְלִין עִמְּהוֹן. אָמַר רִבִּי יוֹחָנָן. אוֹבָדוֹת הֵן מִתְפַּזְּרוֹת הֵן.

**Halakhah 8**: "If somebody deposits produce with another person," etc. Rebbi Immi said, they stated this at harvest time[59]. There, they say that these evil rats, if they see plenty of produce, call their friends and eat with them; Rebbi Joḥanan said, they waste, they squander[60].

59   The percentages are computed for a full year, from one harvest to the next; Babli 40a.

60   All give reasons why practice cannot follow R. Joḥanan ben Nuri.

(9b line 5) יוֹצִיא לוֹ שְׁתוּת לַיַּיִן. רִבִּי יְהוּדָה אוֹמֵר חוֹמֶשׁ. אָמַר רַב אוֹשַׁעְיָה. בְּשֶׁלֹּא אָמַר לוֹ. שֶׁמֶן מְזוּקָּק אֲנִי מַעֲמִיד לָךְ כָּל־הַשָּׁנָה. אֲבָל אִם אָמַר לוֹ כֵּן

חַיָּיב לְהַעֲמִיד לוֹ שֶׁמֶן מְזוּקָק.

"He deducts one sixth of wine; Rebbi Jehudah says a fifth." Rav Oshaia said, if he did not tell him; "I am providing you with refined oil the entire year." But if he said so, he has to provide him with refined oil[61].

61  If he simply sold "oil" at the going rate, he can deliver a slightly smaller quantity of refined oil. But if he advertised "refined oil", he has to deliver the full measure of refined oil, irrespective of price.

(fol. 9a) **מִשְׁנָה י:** הַמַּפְקִיד חָבִית אֵצֶל חֲבֵירוֹ וְלֹא יִחֲדוּ לוֹ הַבְּעָלִים מָקוֹם וְטִילְטְלָהּ וְנִשְׁבְּרָה אִם מִתּוֹךְ יָדוֹ נִשְׁבְּרָה לְצוֹרְכוֹ חַיָּיב לְצוֹרְכָהּ פָּטוּר. אִם מִשֶּׁהִנִּיחָהּ נִשְׁבְּרָה בֵּין לְצוֹרְכוֹ בֵּין לְצוֹרְכָהּ פָּטוּר. יִיחֲדוּ לוֹ הַבְּעָלִים מָקוֹם וְטִילְטְלָהּ וְנִשְׁבְּרָה בֵּין מִתּוֹךְ יָדוֹ בֵּין מִשֶּׁהִנִּיחָהּ לְצוֹרְכוֹ חַיָּיב לְצוֹרְכָהּ פָּטוּר.

**Mishnah 10**: If somebody deposits an amphora with another person without insisting on a separate place[62], when it was moved and broke in his hand, if [the moving] was for his needs, he is liable; for its needs he is not liable. If it broke after it was put down, whether it was for his or its needs, he is not liable[63]. If its owner insisted on a separate place[64] but it was moved and broke, whether in his hand or after it was put down, for his needs he is liable, for its needs he is not liable.

62  Then the trustee may move the amphora using regular care.
63  Unless the trustee was negligent in moving.
64  Then the trustee is not authorized to move the amphora except in an emergency.

(9b line 8) **הֲלָכָה י:** הַמַּפְקִיד חָבִית אֵצֶל חֲבֵירוֹ כול׳. לֹא כֵן אָמַר רִבִּי לְעָזָר. לְמָה הַדָּבָר דּוֹמֶה. לְגוֹנֵב חָבִית מִמַּרְתֵּף חֲבֵירוֹ. אַף עַל פִּי שֶׁלֹּא יָדְעוּ הַבְּעָלִים בִּגְנֵיבָהּ צְרִיכִין לֵידַע בַּחֲזָרָה. אָמַר. שַׁנְיָיה הִיא שֶׁיֵּשׁ רְשׁוּת [לְשׁוֹמֵר] עָלֶיהָ.

אָמַר רִבִּי לָעְזָר. אִית אָמַר. שֶׁיֵּשׁ רְשׁוּת לְשׁוֹמֵר עָלֶיהָ. מָהוּ לְצָרְכָּהּ. בְּשֶׁיִּיחֲדוּ לָהּ הַבְּעָלִים בְּאוֹתוֹ מָקוֹם. אֲבָל בְּמָקוֹם אַחֵר בֵּין לְצוֹרְכוֹ בֵּין לְצוֹרְכָהּ פָּטוּר. אִית אִנּוּן אֱמְרִין. שֶׁאֵין רְשׁוּת לְשׁוֹמֵר עָלֶיהָ לֹא שַׁנְיָיא בֵּין בְּאוֹתוֹ מָקוֹם בֵּין בְּמָקוֹם אַחֵר לְצוֹרְכוֹ חַיָּיב לְצוֹרְכָהּ פָּטוּר.

**Halakhah 10**: "If somebody deposits an amphora with another person," etc. Did not Rebbi Eleazar say, to what can the situation be compared? One who steals an amphora from another person's wine cellar. Even if the owner does not realize the theft, it is necessary that he know of its return[65]. He said, there is a difference because [the trustee][66] has authority over it[67]. Rebbi Eleazar said, some say because the trustee has authority over it. What means "for its needs"? If the owner insisted on a specified place, at another place, whether it is for his needs or its needs, he is (not)[68] liable. There are those who say that the trustee is not authorized; there is no difference whether at this place or at another place; for his needs he is liable, for its needs he is not liable.

65   Tosephta *Bava qamma* 10:33. Applied to the case in which the trustee has agreed to keep the amphora at a designated place, if later he moves the amphora from that place (except in case of emergency to save it from destruction), he is a thief and even if he returns the amphora to its place he remains fully liable for anything that happens to the amphora until he informs its owner that he did move it and returned it.

66   Addition of E. Even without the addition it is clear that the trustee is referred to.

67   Since the trustee has emergency powers over the amphora, if he moves it he is not a thief.

68   Both mss. offer the same scribal error, "not liable" in place of "liable".

**מ﬩נה יא:** הַמַּפְקִיד מָעוֹת אֵצֶל חֲבֵירוֹ צְרָרָן וְהִפְשִׁילָן לַאֲחוֹרָיו אוֹ (fol. 9a) שֶׁמְּסָרָן לִבְנוֹ אוֹ לְבִתּוֹ הַקְּטַנִּים וְנָעַל בִּפְנֵיהֶן שֶׁלֹּא כָרָאוּי חַיָּיב שֶׁלֹּא שָׁמַר

כְּדֶרֶךְ הַשּׁוֹמְרִין וְאִם שָׁמַר כְּדֶרֶךְ הַשּׁוֹמְרִים פָּטוּר.

**Mishnah 11**: If somebody deposits coins with another person who binds them together and carries them on his back[69] or gives them to his underage son or daughter, or locks them insufficiently, he is liable because he did not take care the way people take care. But if he took care the way people take care, he is not liable[70].

69 Where they are easily stolen.
70 Taking care of money is no different from taking care of any other object. If his care would have been enough for a vessel, it is enough for coins.

(9b line 15) **הלכה יא**: הַמַּפְקִיד מָעוֹת אֵצֶל חֲבֵירוֹ כול'. אָמַר רִבִּי יוֹסֵי. וְתִשְׁמַע מִינָהּ. בַּר נַשׁ דִּיהַב לְחַבְרֵיהּ פליטורין בַּשּׁוּקָא. מְסָרָן לִבְנוֹ וּבִתּוֹ הַקְּטַנִּים נִגְנְבוּ אוֹ אָבְדוּ פָּטוּר מִלְּשַׁלֵּם. שֶׁאֲנִי אוֹמֵר. לֹא עַל דַּעַת פליטורין בַּשּׁוּק.

**Halkhah 11**: "If somebody deposits coins with another person," etc. Rebbi Yose said: One understands from this that in case a man gave *plyṭvryn*[71] to another in the market place and that one handed it over to his underage son or daughter, if they were stolen or lost he is not liable since I say that nobody is in the market place because of *plyṭvryn*[72].

71 E reads first פליסורין, then כליסורין. The first reading is supported by the text quoted by Menaḥem di Lonzano. S. Lieberman reads this as Greek κλυστήριον, "a clyster", which fits the context. The explanations proposed by earlier commentators are not reasonable.
72 If private matters are handed over by the depositor in an inappropriate manner, the trustee is not required to behave appropriately.

(9b line 18) מָתַי אָמְרוּ. שׁוֹמֵר חִנָּם נִשְׁבַּע וְיוֹצֵא. בִּזְמַן שֶׁשִּׁימֵּר כְּדֶרֶךְ הַשּׁוֹמְרִין. נָעַל כָּרָאוּי קָשַׁר כָּרָאוּי נְתָנָן בָּאֲפוּנְדָּתוֹ צְרָרָן בְּסַדִּינוֹ וְהִשְׁלִיכָן לְפָנָיו. נְתָנָן בְּשִׁידָה וּבְתֵיבָה וּבְמִגְדָּל. נִגְנְבוּ אוֹ אָבְדוּ חַיָּיב בִּשְׁבוּעָה וּפָטוּר מִלְּשַׁלֵּם. וְאִם

יֵשׁ עֵדִים שֶׁעָשָׂה כֵן אַף מִשְּׁבוּעָה פָּטוּר. נָעַל שֶׁלֹא כָרָאוּי קָשַׁר שֶׁלֹא כָרָאוּי הִפְשִׁילָן לַאֲחוֹרָיו נְתָנָן בְּרֹאשׁ גַּגּוֹ וְנִגְנְבוּ חַיָּיב לְשַׁלֵּם. נְתָנָן בְּמָקוֹם שֶׁנּוֹהֵג לִיתֵּן שֶׁלּוֹ אִם הָיָה רָאוּי לִשְׁמִירָה פָּטוּר וְאִי לֹא חַיָּיב.

When did they say that the unpaid trustee swears and is absolved? If he took care of it the way caretakers do: He locked as he should, tied as he should, put it into his money-belt[73], tied it into his poncho and kept it in front of him, put it into a cupboard, a chest, or a safety box; if they were stolen or lost he is required to swear but not liable to pay[73a]. If there are witnesses that he did so, he even is freed from the oath. He locked carelessly, tied carelessly, put it on his back[74], left it on his roof; if it was stolen he is liable for payment. If he put it at a place where he usually keeps his own things, if it was kept safe as it should have been he is not liable, otherwise he is liable[75].

73 E reads instead of באפונדתו (from the Latin *funda* "money belt") באפר אפורין which S. Lieberman reads as Greek παράφορον "loose belt".

73a The unpaid trustee does not swear automatically if the object entrusted to him is lost; the judges have to find that he is entitled to swear.

74 E has an addition: "He hung it outside his money-belt, tied it into his scarf and put it on his back."

75 A person careless with his own belongings is not absolved from liability if he proves that he treated others' property no worse than his own.

(fol. 9a) **משנה יב:** הַמַּפְקִיד מָעוֹת אֵצֶל הַשֻּׁלְחָנִי אִם צְרוּרִין לֹא יִשְׁתַּמֵּשׁ בָּהֶן וְאִם מוּתָּרִין יִשְׁתַּמֵּשׁ בָּהֶן. אֵצֶל בַּעַל הַבַּיִת בֵּין צְרוּרִין בֵּין מוּתָּרִין לֹא יִשְׁתַּמֵּשׁ בָּהֶן. הַחֶנְוָונִי כְּבַעַל הַבַּיִת דִּבְרֵי רִבִּי מֵאִיר. רִבִּי יְהוּדָה אוֹמֵר כְּשֻׁלְחָנִי.

**Mishnah 12:** "If somebody deposits coins with a money changer, if they are tied together, he may not use them, if loose, he may use them.

With a householder, whether tied together or loose he may not use them[76]. The storekeeper is like a householder, the words of Rebbi Meïr; Rebbi Jehudah says, like a money changer.

76  The Mishnah in the Babli and the independent Mishnah mss. adds: Anybody permitted to use the money is liable if it is lost; anybody not permitted to use it is not liable (beyond the usual liability of the unpaid trustee) for coins.

(9b line 25) **הלכה יב:** הַמַּפְקִיד מָעוֹת אֵצֶל הַשּׁוּלְחָנִי כול׳. רַב הוּנָא אָמַר רִבִּי יִרְמְיָה בְּעֵי. מַה. צְרוּרִין בְּחוֹתָם אוֹ צְרוּרִין בְּלֹא חוֹתָם. אִין תֵּימַר בְּחוֹתָם שֶׁלֹּא בְחוֹתָם מוּתָּר. אִין תֵּימַר שֶׁלֹּא בְחוֹתָם. כָּל־שֶׁכֵּן בְּחוֹתָם.

**Halakhah 12**: "If somebody deposits coins with a money changer," etc. Rav Huna said that Rebbi Jeremiah[77] asked how[78]? Tied under seal or tied together without seal. If you say under seal, without seal he may. If you say without seal, so much more under seal.

77  The Babylonian, known as Rav Jeremiah in the Babli.
78  What is the meaning of "tied together" which prohibits the money changer from using the coins. In the Babli, 43a, a statement attributed by different mss. to different authors states that only money deposited under seal cannot be used.

(fol. 9a) **משנה יג:** הַשּׁוֹלֵחַ יַד בַּפִּיקָּדוֹן בֵּית שַׁמַּאי אוֹמְרִים יִלְקֶה בְחָסֵר וְיָתֵר. וּבֵית הִלֵּל אוֹמְרִים כְּשָׁעַת הוֹצָאָה רִבִּי עֲקִיבָה אוֹמֵר כְּשָׁעַת הַתְּבִיעָה. הַחוֹשֵׁב לִשְׁלוֹחַ יַד בַּפִּיקָּדוֹן בֵּית שַׁמַּאי מְחַיְּיבִין וּבֵית הִלֵּל אוֹמְרִים אֵינוֹ חַייָב עַד שָׁעָה שֶׁיִּשְׁלַח יָד. כֵּיצַד. הִיטָּא אֶת הֶחָבִית וְנָטַל מִמֶּנָּה רְבִיעִית וְנִשְׁבְּרָה אֵינוֹ מְשַׁלֵּם אֶלָּא רְבִיעִית. הִגְבִּיהָהּ וְנָטַל מִמֶּנָּה רְבִיעִית וְנִשְׁבְּרָה מְשַׁלֵּם אֶת הַכֹּל.

**Mishnah 13**: If a person appropriates a deposit[79], the House of Shammai say, he shall be hit by less or more[80], but the House of Hillel say, [at the price] at the time of delivery; Rebbi Aqiba says, at the time of claim. If somebody intends to take the deposit, the House of Shammai hold him liable but the House of Hillel say, he is liable only from the moment he takes it[81]. How is this? If he tilted the amphora[82] and took a *quartarius*, and then it broke, he pays only for a *quartarius*[83]. If he lifted it[84] and took a *quartarius*, and then it broke, he pays for all.

79    Illegally.
80    He pays the larger of its values at the time of deposit and at the time it should have been delivered to the depositor.
81    The Mishnah in the *editio princeps* of the Babli adds: "For it is written (*Ex.* 22:7): If he did not stretch out his hand to his neighbor's possession." It is not in the mss. of the Babli or the Mishnah. The verse implies that theft occurs only by a thief's act of acquisition, such as moving the object.
82    But the amphora never lost contact with the floor on which it was standing and no part in contact with the floor changed position.
83    Because the trustee-thief acquired only the *quartarius* of wine.
84    Thereby acquiring the [responsability for the] amphora.

(9b line 27) **הלכה יג**: הַשּׁוֹלֵחַ יַד בְּפִיקָדוֹן. כֵּינִי מַתְנִיתָא. כְּשָׁעַת תְּבִיעָתוֹ בַּבֵּית דִּין. רַב יִרְמְיָה בְשֵׁם רַב. הֲלָכָה כְּרִבִּי עֲקִיבָה. אֲפִילוּ בֵית הִלֵּל חֲלוּקִין עָלָיו. רִבִּי בּוּן בַּר חִייָה. מַעֲשֶׂה הֲוָה וְהוֹרָה רִבִּי כְּרִבִּי עֲקִיבָה. אָמַר רַב הוֹשַׁעְיָה. בְּשֶׁאֵין עֵדִים. אֲבָל אִם יֵשׁ עֵדִים כָּל־עַמָּא מוֹדְוֵיי עַל הָדָא דְּרִבִּי עֲקִיבָה. אָתָא עוֹבְדָא קוֹמֵי רִבִּי נָסָא וְהוֹרִי כְּרִבִּי עֲקִיבָה.

**Halakhah 13**: "If a person appropriates a deposit," etc. So is the Mishnah: At the time of claim in court[85]. Rav Jeremiah in the name of Rav: Practice follows Rebbi Aqiba[86]. Even though the House of Hillel disagree with him? Rebbi Abun bar Ḥiyya: It happened that there was a case and Rebbi instructed following Rebbi Aqiba. Rav Hoshaia said, if there are no witnesses. But if there are witnesses, everybody agrees with Rebbi Aqiba's position[87]. There came a case before Rebbi Nasa and he instructed following Rebbi Aqiba.

85 The "time of claim" mentioned in the Mishnah is not the time of the claim of the owner on the trustee for return of his property but the moment the case is brought to court. Since the court is supposed to hear each case on the day it was brought, the value of the object can be determined by asking local dealers.

86 The Babli agrees in the name of Samuel, 43b.

87 In the Babli, 43b, even R. Aqiba agrees that if there are witnesses to the theft, the moment of the theft determines the value.

(9b line 33) וּמַה טַעֲמוֹן דְּבֵית שַׁמַּי. עַל־כָּל דְּבַר פֶּשַׁע. מַה מְקַיְּימִין בֵּית הִלֵּל. עַל־כָּל דְּבַר פֶּשַׁע. יָכוֹל אֵין לִי אֶלָּא הוּא. כול׳.

And what is the reason of the House of Shammai? "Any talk of criminality.[88]" How do the House of Hillel explain "any talk of criminality"? I could think only if he acts alone[89], etc.

88 *Ex.* 22:8. The same argument is in the Babli 44a, *Qiddušin* 42b; *Mekhilta dR. Simeon ben Iohai* p. 202.

89 The trustee is guilty in civil law even if the taking of the depositor's property was done by the trustee's agent; *Mekhilta dR. Simeon ben Iohai* p. 202.

This is explained at the start of a lengthy text in *Šebuot* 8:1 (38c l. 37 - 38d l. 1) which really is a commentary on Mishnah *Bava meṣi'a* 3:13. E copies this text here; R. H. Y. D. Azulai (פתח עינים) published a slightly shorter text from a ms. of R. Menaḥem Lonzano who copied it from a ms. of Yerushalmi *Bava meṣia'*. E's text is an exact copy of *Šebuot*, and Azulai's text is identical with these two except for some omissions of repetitions. It seems that these texts are later additions, not original to the text of *Neziqin* nor in its spirit. The present edition therefore will treat these texts as copies from *Šebuot*.

## הכסף פרק רביעי

(fol. 9b) **משנה א:** הַכֶּסֶף קוֹנֶה אֶת הַזָּהָב וְהַזָּהָב אֵינוֹ קוֹנֶה אֶת הַכֶּסֶף. הַנְּחוֹשֶׁת קוֹנָה אֶת הַכֶּסֶף וְהַכֶּסֶף אֵינוֹ קוֹנֶה אֶת הַנְּחוֹשֶׁת. מָעוֹת הָרָעוֹת קוֹנוֹת אֶת הַיָּפוֹת וְהַיָּפוֹת אֵינָן קוֹנוֹת אֶת הָרָעוֹת. אֲסִימוֹן קוֹנֶה אֶת הַמַּטְבֵּעַ וְהַמַּטְבֵּעַ אֵינוֹ קוֹנֶה אֶת אֲסִימוֹן. הַמִּיטַלְטְלִין קוֹנִין אֶת הַמַּטְבֵּעַ וְהַמַּטְבֵּעַ אֵינוֹ קוֹנֶה אֶת הַמִּיטַלְטְלִין. זֶה הַכְּלָל. כָּל־הַמִּיטַלְטְלִין קוֹנִין זֶה אֶת זֶה.

**Mishnah 1:** [1]Silver acquires gold but gold does not acquire silver[2]. Brass acquires silver but silver does not acquire brass[3]. Bad coins[4] acquire good ones but good ones do not acquire bad ones. A blank[5] acquires a coin but a coin does not acquire a blank. Movables acquire coins but coins do not acquire movables[2]. This is the rule: all movables acquire one another[6].

1  A general reference to this Mishnah and the first paragraph of the Halakhah is in D. Sperber, *Roman Palestine 200-400, Money and Prices*, Ramat Gan 1974; Chapters XI, XIV.

2  It is accepted in rabbinic law (in the name of R. Yannai in Halakhah 4:2, in the Babli 46b in the name of R. Johanan) that in Biblical law money acquires both ownership and possession though this is denied in the other Yerushalmi Tractates in the name of R. Johanan, (*Ševi'it* 8:1 Note 15, *Erubin* 7:11 24d l. 3). But it is universally accepted that in rabbinic practice payment only establishes a *claim* to ownership and possession, not a *fact*. This is to avoid fraudulent transactions in which the seller sells non-existent goods and then claims that they were lost, e. g., by fire, between sale and delivery when they already were owned by the buyer but not yet in his possession. On the other hand, in a barter transaction taking possession by one party automatically transfers both

ownership and possession to the other party (*Qiddušin* 1:6). If a person loses because the other party who took money in a commercial transaction then refuses to go through with the sale and offers to refund the money, he can ask the court to publicly curse the defaulting party but he has no legal way to force completion of the sale (Mishnah 2). But if the buyer took possession of the merchandise, then the sale is completed; the seller can force payment in court and is not required to take the article back. This means that transactions involving money are considered a kind of barter in which coins always are passive but never active objects of barter.

There is no doubt that gold or silver bars are merchandise, objects of trade and barter. The question is about coins. If gold coins are exchanged for silver coins and vice-versa, the question is which of the species are considered as merchandise and which as coins in the transaction. The Babli and all sources depending on it (Mishnah and Tosephta mss.) state that "Gold acquires silver but silver does not acquire gold," the opposite of the Yerushalmi. The Halakhah states that originally, the Yerushalmi Mishnah was identical with the Babli; the change can be dated to the early Third Century.

D. Sperber has argued convincingly that this is not a question of gold or silver standard since both the Roman and the Parthian, later Persian, empires actually were on a gold-and-silver standard. But the Persian empire never experienced the disastrous manipulation of silver coinage which started with Caracalla and ended with the hyper-inflation of the military anarchy, only to be brought under control by Diocletian's currency reform. By contrast, even the worst Roman emperors did not adulterate gold coinage (if they minted gold at all.) Therefore, in Babylonia silver coin was the common vehicle of trade while gold coin was used only in very large transactions or as a vehicle for hoarding. This means that silver coin was "money" but gold coin was "merchandise" even when gold coin did not trade at an agio over the official ratio. But in the Roman empire in the period of formulation of the Mishnah (roughly 190-230) silver coins changed from dependable vehicle of commerce to objects to be disposed of as quickly as possible; silver became a merchandise relative to gold coin.

3  In good times, brass coins are local currency only which cannot be used at far-away places; they are tokens rather than coins. When tokens

are exchanged for coins, the tokens are the merchandise. In bad times, when "silver" coins were brass coins slightly washed in a silver solution, brass coins did not exist.

4   Coins taken out of circulation; they are not money in the legal sense.

5   Metal disks ready to be stamped in the mint. They are not money until stamped.

6   Mishnah *Qiddušin* 1:6.

(9c line 26) **הלכה א:** הַכֶּסֶף קוֹנֶה אֶת הַזָּהָב כול׳. זֶהוּ כְּלָלוֹ שֶׁלְּדָבָר. כָּל־הַיָּרוּד מֵחֲבֵירוֹ קוֹנֶה אֶת חֲבֵירוֹ. אָמַר רִבִּי חִייָה בַּר אֲשִׁי. מָאן תַּנִּיתָהּ. רִבִּי שִׁמְעוֹן בֵּרִבִּי. אָמַר לֵיהּ אָבוֹי. חֲזוֹר בָּךְ וְתַנִּי כְהָדָא. הַזָּהָב קוֹנֶה אֶת הַכֶּסֶף. אָמַר לֵיהּ. לֵינָא חָזַר בִּי. דְּעַד דַּהֲוָה חֵילָךְ עֲלָךְ אַתְּנִיתָנִי. הַכֶּסֶף קוֹנֶה אֶת הַזָּהָב. מִילְתֵיהּ דְּרִבִּי אָמְרָה. זָהָב כְּפֵירוֹת. מַתְנִיתָא אָמְרָה. כֶּסֶף כְּפֵירוֹת. [מַתְנִיתָא דְּרִבִּי חִייָה אָמְרָה. זָהָב כְּפֵירוֹת. מִילְתֵיהּ אָמְרָה. כְּסֵדֶף כְּפֵירוֹת. כְּהָדָא] בְּרַת רִבִּי חִייָה רוּבָּה אוֹזְפַת לְרַב דֵּינָרִין. אָתַת שְׁאֲלַת לָאֲבוּהּ. אָמַר לָהּ. שְׁקִילִי מִינֵּיהּ דֵּינָרִין טָבִין וּתְקִילִין. מֵבְרַת רִבִּי חִייָה יָלְפִין. אָמַר רִבִּי אִידִי. אוֹף אַבָּה אֲבוֹי דִּשְׁמוּאֵל בְּעָא קוֹמֵי רִבִּי. מַהוּ לִלְווֹת דֵּינָרִין בְּדֵינָרִין. אָמַר לֵיהּ. מוּתָּר. אָמַר רִבִּי יַעֲקֹב בַּר אָחָא. אוֹף רִבִּי יוֹחָנָן וְרֵישׁ לָקִישׁ תְּרֵיהוֹן מָרִין. מוּתָּר לִלְווֹת דֵּינָרִין בְּדֵינָרִין. קָרַט בְּקָרַט מוּתָּר. לְקָן בְּלֵקָן אָסוּר.

**Halakhah 1**: "Silver acquires gold," etc. This is a summary of the matter: Anything worth less that the other acquires the other. Rebbi Ḥiyya bar Ashi said, who stated this? Rebbi Simeon ben Rebbi[7]. His father told him, change your opinion and state the following: "Gold acquires silver.[8]" He told him, I do not change my opinion since when your faculties were unimpaired, you instructed me to state: "Silver acquires gold." The word of Rebbi implies that gold is like produce[9]. The Mishnah implies that silver is like produce[9]. [Rebbi Ḥiyya's *baraita* implies that gold is like produce[10], but his word implies that silver is like produce, as in the following:][11] The elder Rebbi Ḥiyya's daughter lent denars[12] to Rav. She came and asked her father, who told her: Take from him good and full weight denars[13]. Do we learn from Rebbi Hiyya's daughter[14]? Rebbi Idi said, also Abba, Samuel's father, asked before Rebbi: May one lend denars against denars[12]? He answered him, it is permitted[15]. Rebbi Jacob bar Aha said, also Rebbi Johanan and Rebbi Simeon ben Laqish both instruct: It is permitted to lend denars against denars. *Qerat* against *qerat* is permitted, *lekan* against *lekan* is forbidden[16].

7   Babli 44a.

8   The version accepted in Babylonia sees the world as it should be; not the temporary state at the beginning military anarchy in the Roman empire when the currency was manipulated.

9   It has the power of merchandise to transfer possession and finalize a deal.

10   Tosephta 3:13.

11   Addition of E. The characterization of the Tosephta as Galilean might raise doubts as to the genuineness of the addition.

12   Gold denars.

13   Babli 44b. The problem here is the prohibition of taking interest, which is defined as "payment for waiting" (Babli 65a). Therefore, it is forbidden to lend merchandise on condition to receive the same amount of merchandise in return at a specified future time since in the meantime the value of the merchandise might have increased and the lender would be repaid more in monetary value than what he lent out. It is required to determine the monetary value of the articles to be lent before they are transferred. The only exceptions are (a) short term loans and (b) bridge loans where the borrower already owns the borrowed items while they are stored at another locality. If R. Hiyya holds that silver is merchandise, how can he allow his daughter to lend gold coin against gold coin? The Babli explicitly states that during the term of the loan, gold rose in price against silver.

14   The story is irrelevant for the problem of this Halakhah since Rav states in Halakhah 5:7 (Note 135) that between close relatives the taking of interest is permitted. Rav was the student of his uncle R. Hiyya until he returned to Babylonia in 218; he was R. Hiyya's daughter's cousin. All we can

learn is that Rav's statement is really R. Ḥiyya's. [S. Abramson in *Sinai* 89 (1981) pp. 217-218.] It is not stated whether the lender was Pazi or Martha.

15 The answer of a young R. Jehudah ben Rabban Simeon.

16 Sperber's analysis (*l. c.* pp. 92-93) makes it probable that the last sentence is not R. Joḥanan's and R. Simeon ben Laqish's, but is the editor's deduction from the preceding statement. He notes that *qeraṭ* can either be the Greek κεράτιον, a gold weight, $1/1728$ *libra aurei*, in Dioclation's system equal in value with the silver *siliqua*, $1/24$ *solidus*, or Syriac קרטא, *quarta* (*pars sicli*), one denar.

Since we are dealing with coins, the preferred meaning is that of *siliqua*, an honest silver coin which did not exist during R. Joḥanan's lifetime. *Lekan* was proposed in *Ma'aśer Šeni* 4:1, Note 22, as "small measure or weight", i. e. local small change which in the Mishnah had been defined as merchandise when compared with silver. {The computation of R. Eliahu Fulda in *Ma'aśer Šeni* 4:1, who wanted to prove that the *lekan* was $1/62.5$ of a *solidus*, was already shown to be in error by H. Y. Sheftel [Encyclopedia of biblical and rabbinic coins, measures, weights, areas, and time, Berdiczew 1907 (Hebrew)]}.

(9c line 36) תַּמָּן תַּנִּינָן. כָּל־הַנַּעֲשָׂה דָמִים בְּאַחֵר כֵּיוָן שֶׁזָּכָה זֶה נִתְחַיֵּיב זֶה בַּחֲלִיפָיו. אָמַר רִבִּי יוֹחָנָן לֹא שָׁנוּ אֶלָּא שׁוֹר בְּפָרָה אוֹ חֲמוֹר בְּשׁוֹר. הָא צִיבּוּר בְּצִיבּוּר לֹא קָנָה. רַב יִרְמְיָה בְּשֵׁם רַב. אֲפִילוּ צִבּוּר בְּצִיבּוּר קָנָה. רִבִּי אַבָּא בַּר מִינָה בְּשֵׁם רַב. הַמַּחֲלִיף אברוקלון בְּאמבורוקלון קָנָה.

There, we have stated: If anything is given instead of money, if one entered in possession, the other is obligated for its exchange[17]. Rebbi Joḥanan said, they stated this only about an ox for a cow, or a donkey for an ox; but heap against heap one did not acquire. Rav Jeremiah in the name of Rav: Even heaps among heaps he did acquire[18]. Rebbi Abba bar Mina in the name of Rav: One who exchanged אברוקלון against אמבורוקלון did acquire[19].

17 Cf. Note 2, *Qiddušin* 1:6, Note 521.

18 *Qiddušin* 1:6, Note 525. If one of the parties took possession, the other

19 The reading of R. Ḥananel and 'Arukh is: One who exchanged אמבורקלין against אמבורקלין did acquire. Arukh explains as "bundles of sheets" which in Italian (dialect of Rome) would be called ברוקלי (variants, ברוקלון, ברוקלו) or טרצילו. תרצילו, טורצלי, תרוצולו, תורצלו). The second word is identified by Krauss in Additamenta ad librum Aruch Completum as turzello. M. Sachs (J. Levy, S. Krauss) identifies אמבורוקלון as Latin involucrum "wrapper; covering; envelope", from involvo "to wrap up, roll up.". Turzello, from Latin tortus "a twisting, winding", from torqueo "to twist, to turn" is an acceptable translation of involucrum. In this interpretation, the statement implies that the laws of barter also apply if something is exchanged against an object of the same kind. It is difficult to understand why this should not be so.

H. Y. D. Azulay, in his פתח עיניים, quotes from the ms. of R. Menaḥem di Lonzano בדיקלין באמה בדיקלין. E: אמלוקנין באמבוליקין.

However, Maimonides connects the statement with the later Mishnaiot whose subject is the cancellation of a sale because of overcharging by the seller or underpaying by the buyer. He reads the statement as meaning that a barter is concluded the moment one of the parties takes possession of the object coming to him, and no legal recourse exists for the party realizing that he made a bad bargain. He must hold that אמבורוקלון and אברוקלון are two different objects. It is possible that he reads the two words as "needle" and "silk cloth" since he writes (Mekhirah 13:1): "One who barters vessels agains vessels or animals against animals, even a needle for silk cloth or a kid goat for a horse, has no claim of overcharging since he might prefer a needle to silk cloth." The horse is specifically exempt from the rules of overcharging in Halakhah 4, Note 132. (Ravad objects and thinks that Maimonides misunderstood the Yerushalmi.) The commentary Migdal 'Oz (R. Šem-Ṭob Gabbai) reads אמטרקלין, אמבורקלין but gives no explanation of the words beyond noting that these clearly denote different objects.

(9c line 40) רִבִּי זֵירָא רַב יְהוּדָה בְשֵׁם שְׁמוּאֵל. לָזֶה פָּרָה וְלָזֶה חֲמוֹר וְהֶחֱלִיפוּ זֶה בָּזֶה. וּמָשַׁךְ בַּעַל הַחֲמוֹר אֶת הַפָּרָה וּבָא בַּעַל הַפָּרָה לִמְשׁוֹךְ הַחֲמוֹר וּמְצָאָהּ שְׁבוּרָה. בַּעַל הַחֲמוֹר עָלָיו לְהָבִיא רְאָיָיה שֶׁהָיָה חֲמוֹרוֹ שָׁלֵם בְּשָׁעָה שֶׁמָּשַׁךְ.

מָאן דְּלָא סָבַר הָא מִילְתָא לָא סָבַר בְּנִזְקִין כְּלוּם. אָמַר רִבִּי זֵירָא. לֵינָה סָבַר הָדָא מִילְתָא וְלֵינָה סָבַר בְּנִזְקִין כְּלוּם. תַּמָּן תַּנִּינָן. הָיוּ בָהּ מוּמִין וְעוֹדָהּ בְּבֵית אָבִיהָ כול'. רִבִּי חוּנָה רִבִּי פִּינְחָס רִבִּי חִזְקִיָּה סָלְקוּן גַּבֵּי רִבִּי יוֹסֵי לְנַדְּפָה. אָמְרִין קוֹמוֹי הָדָא וְאָמַר לוֹן. אֱמוֹר דְּבָתְרָהּ. נִכְנְסָה לִרְשׁוּת הַבַּעַל צָרִיךְ לְהָבִיא רְאָיָה. וְלֹא הָאָב שֶׁהוּא צָרִיךְ לְהָבִיא רְאָיָה. וְתֵימַר הַבַּעַל צָרִיךְ לְהָבִיא רְאָיָה. אוֹף הָכָא הַבַּעַל צָרִיךְ לְהָבִיא רְאָיָה.

[20]Rebbi Ze'ira[21], Rav Jehudah in the name of Samuel: One had a cow and one a donkey. They exchanged one for the other. The donkey's owner took the cow. When the cow's owner came to take the donkey and found that it had a fracture, the donkey's owner had to bring proof that his donkey was well at the moment he took the cow. Anybody who does not agree to this does not know anything about civil law. Rebbi Ze'ira said, I do not agree, I do not know anything about civil law. There, we have stated[22]: "If she had bodily defects, as long as she was in her father's house," etc. Rebbi Huna, Rebbi Phineas, and Rebbi Hizqiah went to visit Rebbi Yose to sharpen wits. They quoted the statement[22] and he told them, look at the next statement: "Once she entered the husband's domain, the husband has to prove." Would not the father have to prove? But you are saying that the husband has to prove; here also, the owner has to prove.

20 This text is an outline of the detailed argument in *Qiddušin* 1:6, Notes 532-542.

21 In *Qiddušin*, R. Abba. Since R. Ze'ira objects to the statement in both texts, and the *Qiddušin* text is reproduced in the next paragraph, the attribution here is incorrect.

22 Mishnah *Ketubot* 7:9. After the definitive wedding, the husband discovers that his bride has a bodily defect and divorces her for that. He does not want to pay her *ketubah*. A *prima facie* argument is that the defect happened where it was discovered. Therefore, if the bride was still in her father's house, the father has to prove that at the time of the preliminary

wedding his daughter was without blemish. If the bride now is in her husband's house, the husband has to prove that she was already blemished at the preliminary wedding when he agreed to be financially responsible for her. Similarly, the rule is that if the donkey was in his first owner's stable when the buyer found it with a broken leg that the stable's owner has to prove that it was healthy at the time he took possession of the cow.

(9c line 50) רִבִּי בָּא רַב יְהוּדָה בְשֵׁם שְׁמוּאֵל. לָזֶה פָרָה וְלָזֶה חֲמוֹר וְהֶחֱלִיפוּ. מָשַׁךְ בַּעַל הַחֲמוֹר אֶת הַפָּרָה לֹא קְנָאָהּ. חֲמוֹר מָהוּ שֶׁתִּקָּנֶה. רִבִּי בָּא אָמַר. קָנָה. רִבִּי יָסָא אָמַר. לֹא קָנָה. אָמַר רִבִּי מָנָא. אִית הָכָא מִילֵּי דְיוֹדֵי בָהּ רִבִּי יוֹסֵי. אָדָם שֶׁאָמַר לַחֲבֵירוֹ. פָּרָתִי אֲנִי מְבַקֵּשׁ לִמְכּוֹר. אָמַר לֵיהּ. בְּכַמָּה. אָמַר לֵיהּ. בְּחֹ דֵּנָרִין. אֲזַל סָמְכֵיהּ גַּבֵּי טַרְפּוֹנִיטִיָּא. בְּצַפְרָא עֲבַר וְאַשְׁכְּחֵיהּ תַּמָּן קָאִים. אָמַר לֵיהּ. מָה אַתְּ עָבִיד הָכָא. אָמַר לֵיהּ. אֲנָא בָּעֵי מֵיסַב דֵּינָרִין דְּאַסְמִיכְתָּנִי. אָמַר לֵיהּ. מָה אַתְּ בָּעֵי מִיזְבּוֹן לָךְ בְּהוֹן. אָמַר לֵיהּ. חֲמוֹר. אָמַר לֵיהּ. חֲמוֹרָךְ אֶצְלִי. מָשַׁךְ זֶה לֹא קָנָה זֶה מָשַׁךְ זֶה לֹא קָנָה זֶה. אֶלָּא כָּל־אֶחָד נִקְנֶה בְגוּפוֹ.

[23](Rebbi Abba, Rav Jehudah in the name of Samuel: One had a cow and one a donkey. They exchanged them.) The donkey's owner took the cow; he did not acquire it[24]. Would the donkey be acquired? Rebbi Abba said, he acquired. Rebby Yasa said, he did not acquire. Rebbi Mana said, there is a situation in which Rebbi Yose would agree: A man said to another, I want to sell my cow. He asked him, for how much? He answered, for eight denars. He went and gave him a draft on his banker[25]. In the morning he went and found him open for business. He asked him, what are you doing here? He answered, I want to collect the denars in the draft I have on you. He asked him, what do you want to buy with them? He answered, a donkey. He told him, your donkey is with me. If either of them took possession, the other did not acquire but each animal separately has to be taken in possession[26].

23 This paragraph is similar to one in *Qidduš in* 1:6, Notes 543-549. The initial sentence is out of place in this paragraph; it should be the start of the preceding one, cf. Note 21. The missing starting sentence would indicate that the parties to a trade determined the monetary value of the animals traded. No money actually changed hands because they agreed that the prices of the items exchanged were equal. The question now arises whether the transaction has to be classified as sell-and-buy, in which case each party has to take possession by an act of acquisition, or as barter, when the taking of possession of one party automatically transfers possession also to the other party.

24 Obviously, this statement does not fit the preceding sentence; it refers to the statement of R. Abba, Rav Hamnuna, Rav Ada bar Ahawa in the name of Rav (*Qidduš in* 1:6, 60d l. 75, Note 543): A cow was originally sold for a fixed sum. Then the buyer had second thoughts and offered the seller a donkey instead of money. If now they exchange the animals, it is not barter. Since the first to take the other's animal takes something for which he did not pay, and the sale was not a credit sale, he cannot have acquired the animal until the other party also takes his. The only problem left open is whether the second party also has to execute a conscious act of acquisition; this is required by R. Yose but waved by R. Abba.

25 For the unexplained word טרפוניטיה, *Migdal Oz* (*loc. cit.* Note 19) reads טרפיזטא א τραπεζίτης "banker", the Greek equivalent of Mishnaic שׁוּלְחָנִי. In *Qidduš in* it simply says, "he gave him a draft for money, פריטייא"; the last term might refer to Greek πρατήριον, τό "place for selling, market" (E. G.)

26 Since three people are involved, the seller of the cow, the buyer of the cow, and the banker as seller of the donkey, this is a sale and a separate buy, not a barter. Two separate acts of acquisition are unquestionably required.

(fol. 9b) **משנה ב:** כֵּיצַד מָשַׁךְ מִמֶּנּוּ פֵּירוֹת וְלֹא נָתַן לוֹ מָעוֹת אֵינוֹ יָכוֹל לַחֲזוֹר נָתַן לוֹ מָעוֹת וְלֹא מָשַׁךְ לוֹ פֵּירוֹת יָכוֹל לַחֲזוֹר בּוֹ. אֲבָל אָמְרוּ מִי שֶׁפָּרַע מֵאַנְשֵׁי דוֹר הַמַּבּוּל עָתִיד לְהִיפָּרַע מִמִּי שֶׁאֵינוֹ עוֹמֵד בְּדִבּוּרוֹ. רַבִּי שִׁמְעוֹן אוֹמֵר כָּל־שֶׁהַכֶּסֶף בְּיָדוֹ יָדוֹ עַל הָעֶלְיוֹנָה.

**Mishnah 2**: How is this? If he collected from him the produce but did not give him the money[27], he cannot retract. If he gave the money but did not collect the produce, he can retract[28], but they said: He Who exacted retribution from the people of the Flood will in future collect from him who does not keep his word[29]. Rebbi Simeon said, the one who holds the money is advantaged[30].

27 He is in possession even though he is not yet the owner. The transaction was concluded. If the buyer does not pay, the seller has a valid case in court for collection of a debt.

28 Since Mishnah 1 implies that handing over money is not an act of taking possession, both parties can still annul the contract. The seller can return the money and the buyer has no case for breach of contract; the buyer can ask for the money back and refuse to take delivery.

29 The injured party can go to court and ask for official moral condemnation of the party who reneged on the contract at the last minute.

30 The moment the buyer paid, he lost his right to renege on the contract. Only the seller retains the option of returning the money and not delivering the goods if the contract is still open.

(9c line 58) **הלכה ב:** כֵּיצַד מָשַׁךְ הֵימֶנּוּ פֵּירוֹת כול'. אָמַר רִבִּי אָחָא. כְּתִיב כִּי מָלְאָה הָאָרֶץ חָמָס מִפְּנֵיהֶם. וּמָה הָיָה חֲמָסָן. הֲוָה בַּר נַשׁ נְפִיק טְעִין קוּפָּה מְלֵיאָה תּוּרְמוֹסִין וְהָיוּ מִתְכַּוְּונִין וְנוֹטְלִין פָּחוֹת מִשְׁוֶה פְרוּטָה דָּבָר שֶׁאֵינוֹ יוֹצֵא בַדַּיָּינִין. אָמַר רִבִּי חִייָה בַּר וָוה. רַבָּה רַבָּה. כְּמַעֲשֵׂי אִילוּ כֵּן מַעֲשֵׂי אִילוּ.

**Halakhah 2**: "How is this? If he collected the produce from him," etc. Rebbi Aḥa said, it is written: "For the earth was filled with oppression because of them.[31]" What was their oppression? If a person came carrying a box full of lupines they all asembled and each one was taking less than the worth of a *peruṭah*, a case which cannot be brought before the judges[32]. Rebbi Ḥiyya bar Abba said, "much, much"[33]. The acts of these were identical to the acts of those.

358  NEZIQIN BAVA MEṢIʿA CHAPTER FOUR

31   *Gen.* 6:13. *Gen. rabba* 31(5), in the name of R. Ḥanina.

32   The farmer in the end was left with nothing but so many thieves took only a minute amount that he did not have a case against anybody.

33   *Gen.* 6:5 about the generation of the flood; *Gen.* 18:20 about Sodom and Gomorrha, identical expressions. *Gen. rabba* 28(3); R. Berekhiah in the name of R. Joḥanan.

(9c line 63) אָמַר רִבִּי חֲנִינָה. הֲלָכָה כְרִבִּי שִׁמְעוֹן. וְלָא אֲמִרִין לָהּ לְכָל־אַפִּין. רַב יִרְמְיָה בְשֵׁם רַב. מַעֲשֶׂה הָיָה וְהוֹרָה רִבִּי כְרִבִּי שִׁמְעוֹן. רִבִּי חִייָה בַּר יוֹסֵף יְהַב דִּינָר לִמְלִחְתָא. חֲזַר בֵּיהּ הַהוּא. אֲמַר. לָא יָדַע דִּכְבָר יְהָבוֹן מַגְלָא גוֹ שְׁקֵיהּ דְּהַהוּא גַבְרָא. מִי שֶׁפָּרַע מֵאַנְשֵׁי דוֹר הַמַּבּוּל עָתִיד לִיפָּרַע מִמִּי שֶׁאֵינוֹ עוֹמֵד בְּדִיבּוּרוֹ. חֲזַר בֵּיהּ. חַד בַּר נַשׁ יְהַב דִּינָרִין לַמְטַכְסָא. חֲזַר בֵּיהּ. אֲתָא עוֹבְדָא קוֹמֵי רִבִּי חִייָה בַּר יוֹסֵף וְרִבִּי יוֹחָנָן. רִבִּי חִייָה בַּר יוֹסֵף אֲמַר. אוֹ יִתֵּן לוֹ כְּדֵי עֵירְבוֹנוֹ אוֹ יִמְסוֹר אוֹתוֹ לְמִי שֶׁפָּרַע. וְרִבִּי יוֹחָנָן אֲמַר. אוֹ יִתֵּן לוֹ כָל־מִקָּחוֹ אוֹ יִמְסוֹר אוֹתוֹ לְמִי שֶׁפָּרַע. רִבִּי לָא אֲמַר. רִבִּי זֵירָה אֲמַר. מִקְצַת דָּמִים נָתַן לוֹ. מוֹדֶה רִבִּי חִייָה בַּר יוֹסֵף לְרִבִּי יוֹחָנָן בְּמֶקַח שֶׁאֵין דַּרְכּוֹ לִיקָנוֹת חֲצָיִין כְּגוֹן פָּרָה וְטַלִּית.

Rebbi Ḥanina said, practice follows Rebbi Simeon[34], but we do not say this in all cases[35]. Rav Jeremiah in the name of Rav: A case came before Rebbi and he instructed following Rebbi Simeon. [36]Rebbi Ḥiyya bar Joseph gave a *denar* for salt. That one reneged[37]. He said, does he[38] not know that already a sickle is put on the thigh of that man, "He Who exacted retribution from the people of the Flood will in the future collect from him who does not keep his word"? [39]A person paid for raw silk[40]. He reneged[37]. The case came before Rebbi Ḥiyya bar Joseph and Rebbi Joḥanan. Rebbi Ḥiyya bar Joseph said, either he delivers for the amount of the pledge[41] or one may turn him over to "Him Who exacted retribution.". Rebbi Joḥanan said, either he delivers the entire contract or one may turn him over to "Him Who exacted retribution.[42]" Rebbi La said, it was a case of a pledge; Rebbi Ze'ira said, he had given him partial payment[43]. Rebbi Ḥiyya bar Joseph agrees with Rebbi Joḥanan in a sale which is not usually split, such as of a cow or a stole.

34  In the Babli, R. Joḥanan rules following R. Simeon (48b) but Rav Ḥisda explicitly disagrees (49b).

35  As explained later in this paragraph, the ruling does not apply to partial payments in all its forms.

36  A completely different version of this story is in the Babli, 48b; it is a contamination of this story with the next one.

37  The seller refused to fill the contract and gave the money back to him.

38  R. Ḥiyya bar Joseph told the seller to exert moral pressure on him even if he could not bring the case to court because of R. Ḥanina's ruling.

39  A different version of this story is in *Qiddušin* 2:1, Notes 101-107.

40  Greek μέταξα.

41  Since the money was given as surety, not as payment, R. Simeon's rule cannot be applied to the contract. But he holds that a contract can be enforced in parts. In the Babli, 49a, this is Rav's position.

42  A partial payment validates the entire deal; cf. *Qiddušin* 2:1, Note 106.

43  There is no difference between the two situations as regards R. Simeon's rule.

(9c line 73) רִבִּי יַעֲקֹב בַּר אִידִי רִבִּי אַבָּהוּ בְּשֵׁם רִבִּי יוֹחָנָן. טַבַּעַת אֵין בָּהּ מִשּׁוּם עֵירָבוֹן. כָּל־הַנּוֹשֵׂא וְנוֹתֵן בִּדְבָרִים אֵין מוֹסְרִין אוֹתוֹ לְמִי שֶׁפָּרַע. רִבִּי יַעֲקֹב בַּר זַבְדִּי רִבִּי אַבָּהוּ בְּשֵׁם רִבִּי יוֹחָנָן. אָמַר לִיתֵּן מַתָּנָה לַחֲבֵירוֹ וּבִיקֵשׁ לַחֲזוֹר בּוֹ חוֹזֵר. [רִבִּי יַעֲקֹב בַּר זַבְדִּי בְּעָא קוֹמֵי רִבִּי אַבָּהוּ. וְאָהֵין הוּא לָיו צֶדֶק הִין צֶדֶק.] אָמַר. בְּשָׁעָה שֶׁאָמַר צָרִיךְ לוֹמַר בְּדַעַת גְּמוּרָה. מִבָּתָר כֵּן אִין חָזַר בֵּיהּ לֹא חָזַר בֵּיהּ. הָדָא דְּתֵימַר בְּעָנִי. אֲבָל בְּעָשִׁיר נַעֲשָׂה נֶדֶר. רַב מִפְקֵד לַשַּׁמָּשֵׁיהּ. אֵימַת דְּנֵימַר לָךְ. תִּתֵּן מַתָּנָה לְבַר נַשׁ. אִין הֲוָה מִסְכֵּן הַב לֵיהּ מִיָּד. וְאִין עָתִיר אִימְלִיךְ בִּי תִּנְיָינוּת.

Rebbi Jacob bar Idi, Rebbi Abbahu in the name of Rebbi Joḥanan: A ring does not have the status of a pledge[44]. Nobody dealing in words only may one deliver to "Him Who exacted retribution"[45]. Rebbi Jacob bar Zavdi, Rebbi Abbahu in the name of Rebbi Joḥanan: If one promised a gift to another and wanted to renege on it, he may renege.[46] [Rebbi Jacob bar Zavdi asked before Rebbi Abbahu: Is that "true no, true yes[47]"?][48] He said, at the moment when he said it, he had to speak with full deliberation[49]. After that, if he changes his mind, he cannot change it, that is, if [the recipient] is poor[50]. But for a rich person, is that a vow? Rav commanded his servant: If I tell you to give a gift to a person, if he is poor, give it to him immediately. But if he is rich, take counsel with me a second time[51].

44 Since it has to be returned as is, it is only a reminder without legal consequences. Cf. *Ševi'it* 10:9, Note 131; Babli 48b.

45 *Ševi'it* 10:9, Notes 129-130; Babli 49a, Tosephta 3:14. As long as there was no action of acquisition, the person who goes back on his word can be considered untrustworthy but is not subject to judicial censure.

46 *Ševi'it* 10:9, Notes 133-142; *Ma'aśer Šeni* 4:7 Note 129 Babli 49a.

47 Lev. 19:36.

48 Text added from E. Since the answer is given in L, the question must have been in the original text. For the duty to be honest in monetary matters as a biblical command, cf. *Ševi'it* 10:9, Note 134; *Giṭṭin* 6:1, Note 39.

49 The obligation to be honest does not imply a prohibition to change one's mind. In the *Giṭṭin* text, it is R. Jacob bar Zavdi who gives the answer to R. Yose [Babli 49a, *Bekhorot* 13b; *Sifra Bekhorot Pereq* 8(7)].

50 Giving alms is not a gift to the poor but a gift to God and as such is final upon being promised (Mishnah *Qiddušin* 1:6.

*Kaftor waPeraḥ* Chapter 44 reads: "If somebody promised to give a gift and wants to change his mind, he may change his mind. But if he said, I am speaking with full deliberation, he cannot change his mind. That is, for a rich recipient. But for a poor recipient it becomes a vow." This seems to be more of a paraphrase than an exact quote.

51 This contradicts the statement in *Ševi'it* 10:9 that Rav never changed his mind once he had promised a gift.

(9d line 4) רִבִּי יוֹחָנָן יְהַב דֵּינָרִין לִקְרִיבוֹי עַל מְשַׁח. יְקַר מְשַׁח. אָתָא שָׁאַל לְרִבִּי יַנַּאי. אָמַר לֵיהּ. מִדְּבַר תּוֹרָה מָעוֹת קוֹנִין. וְלָמָּה אָמְרוּ אֵין קוֹנִין. שֶׁלֹּא יֹאמַר לוֹ. נִשְׂרְפוּ חִטֶּיךָ בָּעֲלִיָּיה. רִבִּי שְׁמוּאֵל בַּר סוֹסַרְטַאי בְּשֵׁם רִבִּי אַבָּהוּ. אִם אָמַר לוֹ. נִשְׂרְפוּ חִטֶּיךָ בָּעֲלִיָּיה. נֶאֱמָן. רִבִּי יִצְחָק מַקְשֵׁי. מַה נָן קַייָמִין. אִם בְּשָׁקָנוּ לוֹ מָעוֹתָיו שֶׁלּוֹ נִשְׂרְפוּ. וְאִי לֹא קָנוּ לוֹ מָעוֹתָיו שֶׁלָּזֶה נִשְׂרְפוּ.

Rebbi Joḥanan gave denars to a relative of his for oil. The oil rose in price[52]. He went and asked Rebbi Yannai who told him, by Torah standards money acquires, but why did they say it does not acquire? Lest [the seller] tell him, your wheat was burned in the storage room[53]. Rebbi Samuel ben Sosartai in the name of Rebbi Abbahu: If [the seller] told him, your wheat was burned in the storage room, he is trustworthy[54]. Rebbi Isaac objected: Where do we hold? If his money had acquired for him, his property would have been burned[55]. But if his money had not acquired for him, the other's property was burned.

52 And the relative wanted to annul the contract.
53 Really ""the upper storey", usually used as storage area in farm-houses. Cf. Babli 46b, 47a, 47b, *Erubin* 81b, 7:1 (24d l. 3); *Ḥulin* 83a; *Qiddušin* 26a,28b; *Ševi'it* 8:1 (38a l. 2) Note 15. The opinion attributed here to R. Yannai is that of R. Joḥanan in the Babli, of R. Simeon ben Laqish in the Yerushalmi *Erubin* and *Ševi'it*.
54 The testimony must be accepted by the court unless shown to be perjured by two independent witnesses.
55 Then the statement of R. Samuel ben Sosartai would have made sense. But since rabbinically money cannot acquire, if the seller claims that the wheat was burned after he had received payment, his claim is irrelevant since the wheat was not yet delievered. The seller has to provide the buyer with other grain irrespective of what happened.

(9d line 10) רִבִּי סִימוֹן בְּשֵׁם רִבִּי יְהוֹשֻׁעַ בֶּן לֵוִי. בַּר נַשׁ דִּיהַב לְחַבְרֵיהּ י׳ דֵּינָרִין. אָמַר לֵיהּ. אִית לִי גַּבָּךְ ק׳ (דֵּינָרִין) [גַּרְבִּין] מֵהֲדֵין בֵּיתָא. שָׁרֵי. מֵהֲדֵין כַּרְמָא. אָסוּר. מַה בֵּין כֶּרֶם לַבַּיִת. בַּיִת אֵינוֹ מָצוּי לִיפּוֹל. כֶּרֶם מָצוּי לִיפּוֹל. אָמַר רִבִּי

יוֹסֵי. אַתְּ שְׁמַע מִינָהּ. בַּר נָשׁ דִּיהַב לְחַבְרֵיהּ יּ דֵּינָרִין. אָמַר לֵיהּ. בִּמְנָת
דְּתֵיקוּם לִי בְהוֹן קׄ גַּרְבִּין. מִכֵּיוָן שֶׁשָּׁלַח יָדוֹ בָּהֶן צָרִיךְ לְהַעֲמִיד לוֹ מִקְחוֹ.

Rebbi Simon in the name of Rebbi Joshua ben Levi: A person who gave ten denars to another and told him, I have to get from you 100 (denars)[56] [barrels] from that house, is permitted; from that vineyard, is prohibited[57]. What is the difference between house and vineyard? A house is not expected to collapse, a vineyard occasionally collapses[58]. Rebbi Yose said, you understand from this that if a person gave ten denars to another and told him, I have to get 100 barrels from you, once he[59] used them he is required to deliver the merchandise.

56 *Denars* is the reading of the Leiden ms. and the *editio princeps*; but it is impossible. *Barrels* is the reading of E, supported by the quote in *Sefer Ha'ittur* I, p. 22 (Note 92): גרבין חמרא *Wine barrels*, copied in *Mordekhai Bava meṣi'a* #449 as גריוי 10 gold denars would be an appropriate price for 100 clay barrels of wine.

57 The "house" is the wine cellar. Since the object of sale already exists in the possession of the seller, the transaction is not a forbidden trade to circumvent the prohibition of interest. But a trade on futures of wine from yet ungrown grapes is impossible, cf. *Ketubot* 5:5, Note 113.

58 Occasionally there is no harvest.

59 In the interpretation of *Sefer Ha'ittur* (accepted by *Mordekhai, loc. cit.*), R. Yose states that for wine, already stored in barrels, the argument of R. Yannai does not apply and the sale was concluded by the seller accepting the money. This argument is justly rejected by R. Joseph Caro (*Bet Yosef Ḥošen Mišpaṭ* 199,2) as against talmudic principles. In addition, while wine in clay barrels stored in a stone cellar is not likely to be burned, it easily may be lost by breakage of the barrels. Therefore, it seems that this paragraph is a direct continuation of the previous one and R. Ḥanina's ruling that practice follows R. Simeon is qualified further in that the seller has lost his right of refusal once he used the money in his business.

The biblical expression שָׁלַח יָד בְּ (*Ex.* 22:7) means "illegally to take" (for one's own use).

(9d line 15) רְבִּי שִׁמְעוֹן בֶּן לָקִישׁ אָמַר. אוֹ קָנֹה מִיַּד עֲמִיתֶךָ. מִיַּד עֲמִיתֶךָ אַתְּ צָרִיךְ מְשִׁיכָה. אֵין אַתְּ צָרִיךְ מְשִׁיכָה מִיָּד הַגּוֹי. עַל דַּעְתֵּיהּ דְּרִבִּי שִׁמְעוֹן בֶּן לָקִישׁ. לְאֵי זֶה דָבָר מוֹסְרִין אוֹתוֹ לְמִי שֶׁפָּרַע. אָמַר רִבִּי יוֹסֵי בֵּירִבִּי בּוּן. וַתְיָיא כְּהָדֵין תַּנָּאָה דְתַגֵּי. הַנּוֹשֵׂא וְנוֹתֵן בִּדְבָרִים אֵין מוֹסְרִין אוֹתוֹ לְמִי שֶׁפָּרַע.

Rebbi Simeon ben Laqish said, "or buying from your neighbor's hand"[60], from you neighbor's hand you need an act of acquisition; you do not need an act of acquisition from the Gentile's hand[61]. In Rebbi Simeon ben Laqish's opinion, why does one deliver a person to "Him Who exacted retribution"[62]? Rebbi Yose ben Rebbi Abun said, it follows the Tanna who stated: "Nobody dealing in words only may one deliver to "Him Who exacted retribution"[45,63].

60 *Lev.* 25:14, containing the prohibition of overcharging or underpaying in commercial transactions.

61 The principle that in biblical law payment transfers not only ownership but also possession is restricted to transactions involving Gentiles; for transactions between Jews the transfer needs an actual "taking" from the prior owner's hand; Babli 47b.

62 Since a deal between Jews is not valid in biblical law without actual transfer, why should the court be involved in a dispute regarding such a deal? E reads here: why does one *not* deliver a person to "Him Who ... "?

63 This Tanna holds that taking the money is a "transfer from hand to hand", which gives the transaction biblical status. The only case which the court will refuse to hear is one where no concrete action has yet taken place.

(fol. 9b) **מִשְׁנָה ג:** הַהוֹנָאָה אַרְבָּעָה כֶּסֶף מֵעֶשְׂרִים וְאַרְבָּעָה כֶּסֶף לַסֶּלַע שְׁתוּת לַמֶּקַח. עַד אֵימָתַי מוּתָּר לְהַחֲזִיר עַד כְּדֵי שֶׁיַּרְאֶה לַתַּגָּר אוֹ לִקְרוֹבוֹ. הוֹרָה רִבִּי טַרְפוֹן בְּלוֹד הַהוֹנָיָיה שְׁמוֹנָה כֶּסֶף לַסֶּלַע שְׁלִישׁ לַמֶּקַח וְשָׂמְחוּ תַגְּרֵי לוֹד. אָמַר לָהֶן כָּל־הַיּוֹם מוּתָּר לְהַחֲזִיר. אָמְרוּ לוֹ יַנִּיחַ לָנוּ רִבִּי טַרְפוֹן אֶת מְקוֹמֵינוּ וְחָזְרוּ

לְדִבְרֵי חֲכָמִים. אֶחָד הַלּוֹקֵחַ וְאֶחָד הַמּוֹכֵר יֵשׁ לָהֶם הוֹנָיָיה. כְּשֵׁם שֶׁהוֹנָיָיה לַהֶדְיוֹט כָּךְ הוֹנָיָיה לַתַּגָּר. רִבִּי יְהוּדָה אוֹמֵר אֵין לַתַּגָּר הוֹנָיָיה. מִי שֶׁהוּטַּל עָלָיו יָדוֹ עַל הָעֶלְיוֹנָה שֶׁהוּא אוֹמֵר לוֹ תֶּן לִי אֶת מְעוֹתַי אוֹ תֶּן לִי מַה שֶׁהוֹנִיתָנִי.

**Mishnah 3**: Cheating[64] is four obols per tetradrachma of 24 obols[65], one sixth of the sale price. Until when may one return [the merchandise]? Until one can show it to a trader[66] or a relative. Rebbi Tarphon instructed in Lydda that cheating is eight obols per tetradrachma, a third of the sale price, and the traders of Lydda were rejoicing. He told them, one may return [the merchandise] the entire day; they said, let Rebbi Tarphon keep our place quiet; they returned to the words of the Sages. Just as a private person can be cheated, so a trader can be cheated. Rebbi Jehudah says, a trader has no claim of being cheated[67]. The person overcharged has the advantage; if he so desires, he says, give me my money back[68], or give me back by what you overcharged me[69].

64 Overcharging (or underpaying) the current rate, forbidden in *Lev.* 25:14. Overcharges of less than $16^2/_3\%$ are not recoverable in court.

65 A drachma (in the Roman Empire identified with the denar) is 6 obols.

66 A market maker in that commodity.

67 Since he has to know what the going rate is for what he sells. This implies that for R. Jehudah a trader is permitted to have a sale with reductions of at least $16^2/_3\%$ of the going rate; the Sages would only permit a sale with reductions $<16^2/_3\%$.

68 The buyer returns the article and gets his money back.

69 He keeps the article.

(9d line 20) **הלכה ג**: הָאוֹנָאָה אַרְבָּעָה כֶּסֶף כול'. רַב אָמַר שִׁיעוּר הוּא. רִבִּי יוֹחָנָן אָמַר. לֵית הוּא שִׁיעוּרָא. רַב אָמַר. כָּל־הַנּוֹשֵׂא וְנוֹתֵן בְּמִנַת שֶׁאֵין לוֹ אוֹנָאָה יֵשׁ לוֹ אוֹנָאָה. תַּנֵּי רִבִּי לֵוִי. הָאוֹנָאָה פְּרוּטָה וְהַהוֹנָאָה פְּרוּטָה. אֶלָּא הוֹנָאָה עַצְמָהּ מַהוּ. תַּנֵּי. נִקְנָה הַמֶּקַח חוֹזֵר לוֹ הוֹנָיָיתוֹ. דִּבְרֵי רִבִּי יְהוּדָה הַנָּשִׂיא. רִבִּי יוֹחָנָן אָמַר. בָּטֵל מְקָחוֹ.

**Halakhah 3**: "Cheating is four obols," etc. Rav said, this is the rate[70]; Rebbi Joḥanan said, it is not the rate[71]. Rav said, if somebody trades on condition that the rules of cheating not apply to him, the rules of cheating do apply to him[72]. Rebbi Levi[73] stated: Cheating applies to a *peruṭah*, cheating can be by a *peruṭah*[74]. But what is the status of cheating[75]? It was stated: The item was acquired, he returns the overcharge, the words of Rebbi Jehudah the Prince[76]; Rebbi Joḥanan said, the sale is annulled.

70 Since the Mishnah ties the definition of overcharging to the money changing hands: the sixth has to be computed as one sixth of the sale price both for overcharging or for underpaying. If an article worth 6 was sold for 7 the overcharge was $1/7$. If it was sold for 5, the undercharge was 20% and the sale can be annulled on the demand of the seller. In the Babli, 49b, this opinion is attributed to Samuel; Rav holds that the basis of computation always is the current market price.

71 The larger of sale or market price is the base of computation.

72 Biblical prohibitions cannot be abolished by private conventions; Mishnah *Ketubot* 9:1.

73 R. Levi was the preacher in R. Joḥanan's academy. His statement is attributed in the Babli 55a to Levi (bar Sisi), the student of Rebbi. Since here R. Levi is mentioned together with his contemporary R. Joḥanan, and in the Babli Levi bar Sisi together with his contemporary Rav Cahana, there is a genuine discrepancy in the traditions of both Talmudim.

74 The rules of cheating apply even to transactions whose total value does not add up to the smallest silver coin, the obol. (In Hasmonean times, when the obol really was a silver coin, it was 24 *peruṭot*.) In the Babli, Rav Cahana denies the applicability. E reads וההודאה שוה פרוטה "the confession of a *peruṭah*'s worth" instead of וההונאה פרוטה. This is an echo of Mishnah 6 and *Šebuot* 6:1 and is out of place here.

75 If the overcharge was less than $16 2/3\%$, the buyer has no recourse. If it is more than $16 2/3\%$, he can annul the sale. What if it is exactly $16 2/3\%$? The Mishnah gives the injured party the choice of either receiving the amount of the overcharge or returning the object.

76 Rebbi's grandson, contemporary of R. Joḥanan.

(9d line 24) כַּהֲנָא בְּעָא קוֹמֵי רַב. בְּשָׁעָה שֶׁהַמּוֹכֵר מִתְאוּנֶה מִתְאוּנֶה עַד חוֹמֶשׁ. בְּשָׁעָה שֶׁהַלּוֹקֵחַ מִתְאוּנֶה מִתְאוּנֶה עַד שְׁתוּת. אָמַר לֵיהּ. הִיא הוֹנָיָיתוֹ וּמִצְטָרְפִין עַד שְׁתוּת. מָכַר לוֹ שָׁוֶה ה' בְּו' יְכִיל מֵימַר לֵיהּ. חַד דֵּינָר אִיגְרַבְתְּ. סַב דֵּינָרָךְ. אָמַר רִבִּי זֵירָא. יְכִיל מֵימַר לֵיהּ. לֵית אִיקְרֵי דִיהֲוֹן בְּרִיָּיתָא אָמְרִין. פְּלוֹנִי אִיגִחָךְ. וְאִית דְּבָעֵי מֵימַר. יְכִיל מֵימַר לֵיהּ. לֵית הוּא יְקָרִי מַלְבּוּשׁ בָּהּ דֵּינָרִין. רִבִּי יוֹחָנָן רִבִּי אֶלְעָזָר וְרִבִּי הוֹשַׁעְיָה אָמְרֵי. מָה טַעֲמָא דְאָהֵן תַּנָּיָיא. יָדַע אֲנָא דְּלָא הֲוַת מִיקָמְתִי טָבָא אֶלָּא ה' דֵּינָרִין. עַל דַּהֲוַת דְּחִיק לֵיהּ יְהַב עַל אַשְׁתָּהּ דֵּינָרִין. סַב דִּידָךְ וְהַב דִּידִי.

Cahana asked before Rav: If the seller is being cheated, he is cheated up to a fifth; if the buyer is being cheated, he is cheated up to a sixth[77]! He answered him, it and the amount of cheating add up to a sixth[78]. If he sold him what was worth five for six, can [the seller] not say, you were taken in for a denar, take your denar![79] Rebbi Ze'ira said, the other can say to him, it is not to my honor that people say, this one was made a laughing stock. Some say, he can say to him, it is not to my honor to wear a garment of five denars. Rebbi Johanan, Rebbi Eleazar and Rebbi Hoshaia say, what is that Tanna's reason[80]? "I know that my merchandise was worth only five denars, but because he needed it, I gave it to him for six. Take yours and return mine."

77 According to Rav, if an article worth 6 is sold for 7, the buyer can invoke the statute against cheating because he was overcharged $16^2/_3$%. But the seller can claim an additional payment if he was only paid 5, when he really was underpaid 20%, which should lead to an outright cancellation of the transaction.

78 The objection really is well taken; for the buyer the percentage is computed from below, for the seller from above.

79 Since the customer was overcharged by 20%, he can automatically annul the sale. Why can the seller not pay him the amount overcharged and force the customer to keep the merchandise?

80 The one who says that the higher of market or sale price is the basis of computation.

(9d line 28) מָכַר לוֹ שָׁוֶה ה' בְּו'. לֹא הִסְפִּיק לִישָּׂא וְלִיתֵּן עַד שֶׁהוֹקִיר מְשֻׁבָּע. רִבִּי יַעֲקֹב בַּר אִידִי רִבִּי אַבָּהוּ בְּשֵׁם רִבִּי יוֹחָנָן. כְּשֵׁם שֶׁבָּטֵל מֶקַח מֵאֵצֶל זֶה כָּךְ בָּטֵל מִזֶּה. תַּמָּן תַּנִּינָן. אַרְבַּע מִידוֹת בַּמּוֹכְרִין. מָכַר לוֹ חִטִּים יָפוֹת וְנִמְצְאוּ רָעוֹת לוֹקֵחַ יָכוֹל לַחֲזוֹר בּוֹ. רָעוֹת וְנִמְצְאוּ יָפוֹת מוֹכֵר יָכוֹל לַחֲזוֹר בּוֹ. [הָא הַלּוֹקֵחַ אֵינוֹ יָכוֹל לַחֲזוֹר בּוֹ.] אָמַר רִבִּי יוֹסֵי בֵּירִבִּי בּוּן. וַתְיָיא כְּהָדֵין תַּנָּא. הַנּוֹשֵׂא וְנוֹתֵן בִּדְבָרִים אֵין מוֹסְרִין אוֹתוֹ לְמִי שֶׁפָּרַע.

If he sold him what was worth five for six; [the buyer] did not have time to ask around until it appreciated to be worth seven. Rebbi Jacob bar Idi, Rebbi Abbahu in the name of Rebbi Johanan: Since the sale is annulled for one[81], it also is annulled for the other[82]. There, we have stated[83]: "Four situations in sales. If he sold him high quality wheat and it turned out to be low quality, the buyer can annul the transaction. Low quality and it turned out to be high quality, the seller can annul the transaction." [Therefore, the buyer cannot annul the transaction.][84] Rebbi Yose ben Rebbi Abun said, it follows this Tanna: "Nobody dealing in words only may one deliver to "Him Who exacted retribution"[45,85].

81   The buyer originally was overcharged by 20%, which gives him the right to annul the transaction, even though at the moment he could realize a $16^2/_3\%$ gain.

82   The seller can take back the merchandise and sell it again at a higher price.

83   Mishnah *Bava batra* 5:8.

84   Text of E, missing in L; but it is clearly understood that the Mishnah *Bava batra* was quoted to contradict R. Johanan's statement that the seller can annul the sale because the buyer could.

85   Even according to R. Johanan, the seller can retract his committment to a sale only as long as no money has changed hands; otherwise the buyer could haul him into court publicly to be cursed. The Babli, *Bava batra* 83b/84a flatly rejects the possibility that a dishonest trader enjoy a privilege from which the honest trader was barred.

(fol. 9b) **משנה ד:** וְכַמָּה תְּהֵא הַסֶּלַע חֲסֵירָה וְלֹא יְהֵא בָּהּ הוֹנָיָיה. רִבִּי מֵאִיר אוֹמֵר אַרְבָּעָה אִיסוֹרוֹת מֵאִיסָּר לַדֵּינָר. רִבִּי יְהוּדָה אוֹמֵר אַרְבָּעָה פּוּנְדְּיוֹנוֹת מִפּוּנְדְּיוֹן לַדֵּינָר. רִבִּי שִׁמְעוֹן אוֹמֵר שְׁמוֹנָה פּוּנְדְיוֹנוֹת מִשְּׁנֵי פּוּנְדְּיוֹנוֹת לַדֵּינָר.

**Mishnah 4**: By how much could a tertradrachma be deficient without it being cheating? Rebbi Meïr says four *assarii*, one *assarius* per denar. Rebbi Jehudah says four *dupondii*, a *dupondius* per denar. Rebbi Simeon says eight *dupondii*, two *dupondii* per denar[86].

86  1 *denarius argenteus* = 12 *dupondii* = 24 *assarii*. R. Simeon holds that the standards for coins are the universal standards for everything else. R. Jehudah admits a tolerance of 8.33%, R. Meïr only 4.166%.

(9d line 39) **הלכה ד:** וְכַמָּה תְּהֵא הַסֶּלַע חֲסֵירָה כול׳. תַּנֵּי. יוֹתֵר מִכֵּן מוֹצִיאָהּ בְּשָׁוָה. סֶלַע עַד שֶׁקֶל דֵּינָר עַד רוֹבַע. פָּחוֹת מִכֵּן אֲפִילוּ הוּא כְּאִיסָּר אֵין יָכוֹל לְהוֹצִיאָהּ. הָיְתָה יוֹצֵא עַל אֲסִימוֹן בְּסֶלַע וְעַל הַמַּטְבֵּעַ בְּשֶׁקֶל. עַל אֲסִימוֹן בְּשֶׁקֶל וְעַל הַמַּטְבֵּעַ בְּסֶלַע. אֵין לוֹ אֶלָּא צוּרַת הַמַּטְבֵּעַ. לֹא יִתְּנֶנָּה לֹא לְחָרָם וְלֹא לְהָרָג מִפְּנֵי שֶׁמְּרַמִּין בּוֹ אֶת אֲחֵרִים. אֶלָּא נוֹקְבָהּ וְתוֹלָהּ בְּצַוְּואר בְּנוֹ. בַּמֶּה דְּבָרִים אֲמוּרִים. בְּדֵינָרִין וּבְסְלָעִין. אֲבָל בְּדֵינָר זָהָב וּבְמַטְבְּעוֹת כֶּסֶף מוֹצִיאִין בְּשָׁוְיֵיהֶן. כְּשֵׁם שֶׁמּוֹצִיאִין לְחוּלִּין כָּךְ מוֹצִיאִין לְמַעֲשֵׂר שֵׁינִי. וּבִלְבַד שֶׁלֹּא יִתְכַּוֵּין לְהוֹצִיאָן.

**Halakhah 4**: "By how much could a tertradrachma be deficient," etc. It was stated: [87]"More than that[88] he spends it for its worth, a tetradrachma up to a *šeqel*[89], a denar up to a quarter [*šeqel*]. If it is less than this even by an *assarius*, he may not spend it. If it was circulating as a blank for a tetradrachma or as a *šeqel* coin, as a blank for a *šeqel* or as a tetradrachma coin, he only has the shape of the coin[90]. He should give it neither to a person who condemns property[91] nor to a tax assessor[91] since they defraud people, but he drills a hole into it and hangs it on his son's neck. When has this been said? About tetradrachmas and denars.

But gold denars and silver coins[92] one may spend according to their value[93]. Just as one spends it for profane things one may spend it for Second Tithe provided one does not plan it[94]."

87 Similar texts in Tosephta 3:17-19, Babli 52a.

88 If the coin is below the tolerances indicated in the Mishnah.

89 A Mishnaic *šeqel* is two denars, half a tetradrachma (a Tyrian *šeqel*). The quarter *šeqel* then is half a denar.

90 Whether it can be used or not depends on the shape of the coin which it pretends to be.

91 חרם is the receiver of the inheritance tax, חרג (הרג) the receiver of property tax; cf. *Nedarim* 3:4-5, Note 97.

92 Honest silver coin which can be traded for its silver content.

93 These coins have to be weighed before being used as currency.

94 In Temple times, Second Tithe produce was redeemed for coin which was spent on food in Jerusalem, to be eaten there in purity. Since the redemption is a transaction between a person and himself, occasionally deficient coins may be used since he knows the deficiency. But one may not collect deficient coins during the year and then use the collected coins for redemption (*Ma'aśer Šeni* 2:7, Note 96).

(fol. 9b) **משנה ה:** עַד אֵימָתַי מוּתָּר לְהַחֲזִיר. בַּכְּרַכִּין עַד כְּדֵי שֶׁיַּרְאֶה לַשּׁוּלְחָנִי וּבַכְּפָרִין עַד עַרְבֵי שַׁבָּתוֹת. אִם הָיָה מַכִּירָהּ אֲפִילוּ לְאַחַר שְׁנֵים עָשָׂר חֹדֶשׁ מְקַבְּלָהּ מִמֶּנּוּ וְאֵין לוֹ עָלָיו אֶלָּא תַּרְעוֹמֶת. וְנוֹתְנָהּ לְמַעֲשֵׂר שֵׁנִי וְאֵינוֹ חוֹשֵׁשׁ שֶׁאֵינָהּ אֶלָּא נֶפֶשׁ רָעָה.

**Mishnah 5**: How much time does one have to return it[95]? In walled cities[96] until one can show it to a banker, in villages until Sabbath eve. If he recognizes it, he should take it back even after twelve months, but he has only a complaint against him[97]. He may use it for Second Tithe without hesitation since it is only miserly[94,98].

**משנה ו**: הָאוֹנָיָיה אַרְבָּעָה כֶסֶף. וְהַטַּעֲנָה שְׁתֵּי כָסֶף. וְהַהוֹדָיָיה שָׁוֶה פְרוּטָה. חָמֵשׁ פְּרוּטוֹת הֵן הַהוֹדָיָיה שָׁוֶה פְרוּטָה וְהָאִשָּׁה מִתְקַדֶּשֶׁת בְּשָׁוֶה פְרוּטָה. הַנֶּהֱנֶה שָׁוֶה פְרוּטָה מִן הַהֶקְדֵּשׁ מָעַל. הַמוֹצֵא שָׁוֶה פְרוּטָה הַיָּב לְהַכְרִיז. הַגּוֹזֵל אֶת חֲבֵירוֹ שָׁוֶה פְרוּטָה וְנִשְׁבַּע לוֹ יוֹלִיכֶנּוּ אַחֲרָיו אֲפִילוּ לְמָדַי.

**Mishnah 6**: Cheating is by four oboli[99], claim is about two oboli, confession is about one *peruṭah*[100]. There are five *peruṭot*[101]: Confession is about one *peruṭah*[100]; a woman is preliminarily married by one *peruṭah*'s worth[102]; one who used one *peruṭah*'s worth of Temple property committed larceny[103]; one who finds one *peruṭah*'s worth has to make it public; one who robbed another of one *peruṭah*'s worth and swore about it, has to return it to him even in Media[104].

**משנה ז**: חֲמִשָּׁה חוּמְשִׁין הֵן. הָאוֹכֵל תְּרוּמָה וּתְרוּמַת מַעֲשֵׂר וּתְרוּמַת מַעֲשֵׂר שֶׁל דְּמַאי וְהַחַלָּה וְהַבִּיכּוּרִים מוֹסִיף חוֹמֶשׁ. הַפּוֹדֶה נֶטַע רְבָעִי וּמַעֲשֵׂר שֵׁנִי שֶׁלּוֹ מוֹסִיף חוֹמֶשׁ. הַפּוֹדֶה אֶת הֶקְדֵּישׁוֹ מוֹסִיף חוֹמֶשׁ. הַנֶּהֱנֶה שָׁוֶה פְרוּטָה מִן הַהֶקְדֵּשׁ מוֹסִיף חוֹמֶשׁ. הַגּוֹזֵל אֶת חֲבֵירוֹ שָׁוֶה פְרוּטָה וְנִשְׁבַּע לוֹ מוֹסִיף חוֹמֶשׁ.

**Mishnah 7**: There are five fifths[105]: He who eats heave, or heave of the tithe[106], or heave of the tithe of *demay*[107], or *ḥallah*[108], or first fruits[109], adds a fifth[110]. He who redeems his vineyard in the fourth year[111] or his Second Tithe[112], adds a fifth. He who redeems his own gifts to the Temple, adds a fifth[113]. He who used one *peruṭah*'s worth of Temple property, adds a fifth[103]. He who robbed another of one *peruṭah*'s worth and swore about it, adds a fifth[114].

---

95   The defective coin which fails the standards of Mishnah 4.

96   Greek χάραξ, χάρακος "palisade".

97   If the person who handed out the defective coin recognizes that it is the coin given out illegally, he has a moral duty to take it back even when the legal period in which he can be forced to take it back has expired. If he refuses, the injured party has the right to complain (i. e., tell about the

case to other people) but has no recourse in court.

98  After the destruction of the Temple and the disappearence of the ashes of the red cow (cf. *Berakhot* 1:1, Note 3) when food can no longer be eaten in purity, the coin has to be destroyed. For that purpose it even is preferable to use defective coins.

99  Mishnah 3.

100  The court will not impose a judicial oath unless it be a case in which the claim is at least 2 oboli and the defendant admits to owing at least 1 *peruṭah*; Mishnah *Šebuot* 6:1.

101  The *peruṭah* appears as minimal standard in five legal categories.

102  Mishnah *Qiddušin* 1:1.

103  He has to pay a 25% fine and bring a sacrifice, *Lev.* 5:15-16.

104  Mishnah *Bava qamma* 9:7.

105  Five cases in which a payment of 125% of the amount is due.

106  If he eats in error, Mishnah *Terumot* 6:1; *Lev.* 22:14, *Num.* 18:26.

107  This only applies to *demay* (produce of which it is not known whether it was tithed), but not to the heave of its tithe; Mishnah *Demay* 1:2, Note 67.

108  *Num.* 15:20.

109  Mishnah *Bikkurim* 2:1.

110  All these cases are considered identical since each of them is called "heave" in a verse.

111  *Lev.* 19:24, 27:31.

112  Mishnah *Ma'aśer Šeni* 5:5; *Deut.* 14:25.

113  *Lev.* 27:19.

114  *Lev.* 5:24.

(9d line 48) **הלכה ה:** עַד אֵימָתַי מוּתָּר לְהַחֲזִיר כול׳. חִזְקִיָּה אָמַר. לְצוֹרְפָהּ בִּירוּשָׁלֵם מְצָרְפָהּ כְּיָפָה. בָּא לְחַלְּלָהּ בִּגְבוּלִין מְחַלְּלָהּ בְּרָעָה. וְהָתַנִּינָן. בּוֹרֵר הַיָּפָה שֶׁבָּהֶן וּמְחַלְּלָן עָלֶיהָ. וְיָבוֹר הָרָעָה וְיַעֲשֶׂה אוֹתָהּ [כְּיָפָה]. אָמַר. שַׁנְיָיא הִיא הָכָא שֶׁכְּבָר הוּכַח בּוֹ מַעֲשֵׂר שֵׁינִי.

**Halakhah 5:** "How much time does one have to return it," etc. [115]Hizqiah said, to add it for Jerusalem, he adds it as good coin. If he uses it to redeem in the countryside, he redeems with the underweight coin. But did we not state: "He chooses the better one of the two and exchanges it for them"? Why can he not take the worse [coin] and treat it [as a good one][115a]. He[116] said, there is a difference here because it already was shown to be Second Tithe[117].

115  Cf. Babli 52b. The paragraph is the parallel to *Ma'aśer Šeni* 2:7, Notes 96-98. It is clear that an underweight coin in Jerusalem in Temple times, when silver coinage was honest silver, could be spent according to its true value by weight. The Mishnah permits to redeem Second Tithe by an underweight coin as if it were full weight. The question asked is why Mishnah *Ma'aśer Šeni* 2:6 requires one to choose the better one for Second Tithe if two similar coins, one of Second Tithe and one profane, were commingled and it is not known which one is the sanctified one. Since one may use an underweight coin for redemption, why does one have to choose the fuller weight coin in case of doubt?

115a  Addition of E.

116  In *Ma'aśer Šeni*: R. Jonah.

117  One may use a profane underweight coin for redemption; once it is sanctified it has to be treated with respect.

(9d line 51) נוֹתְנָהּ לְמַעֲשֵׂר שֵׁנִי וְאֵינוֹ חוֹשֵׁשׁ שֶׁאֵינָהּ אֶלָּא נֶפֶשׁ רָעָה. יַעֲקֹב בַּר זַבְדִּי רִבִּי יוֹחָנָן בְּשֵׁם רִבִּי סִימוֹן. כָּל־מַעֲשֵׂר שֵׁינִי שֶׁאֵין בְּקַרְנוֹ שָׁוֶה פְרוּטָה אֵין מוֹסִיף חוֹמֶשׁ. רִבִּי יוֹחָנָן בְּשֵׁם רִבִּי יַנַּאי. כָּל־מַעֲשֵׂר שֵׁינִי שֶׁאֵין בְּחוּמְשׁוֹ שָׁוֶה פְרוּטָה אֵין מוֹסִיף חוֹמֶשׁ. אִית מַתְנִיתָא מְסַייְעָא לְדֵין וְאִית מַתְנִיתָא מְסַייְעָא לְדֵין. דְּתַנֵּי. מִמַּעְשְׂרוֹ. פְּרָט לְפָחוֹת מִשָּׁוֶה פְרוּטָה. הָדָא אָמְרָה. עַד שְׁיְּהֵא בְקַרְנוֹ שָׁוֶה פְרוּטָה. תַּנֵּיי חוֹרָן תַּנֵּי. מִמַּעְשְׂרוֹ חֲמִשִׁיתָיו. פְּרָט לְפָחוֹת מִשָּׁוֶה פְרוּטָה. הָדָא אָמְרָה. עַד שְׁיְּהֵא בְחוּמְשׁוֹ שָׁוֶה פְרוּטָה. אָמַר רָבִין בַּר מָמָל. מַתְנִיתָא לָא כְהָדֵין וְלָא כְהָדֵין. דְּתַנִּינָן. ה' פְרוּטוֹת הֵן. וְלֹא תַנִּינָן עַד שְׁיְּהֵא בְקַרְנוֹ שָׁוֶה פְרוּטָה. וְתַנִּינָן ה' חוֹמְשִׁין הֵן. וְלֹא וְלֹא תַנִּינָן עַד שְׁיְּהֵא בְחוּמְשׁוֹ שָׁוֶה פְרוּטָה.

"He may use it for Second Tithe without hesitation since it is only miserly." [118]Jacob bar Zavdi, Rebbi Joḥanan in the name of Rebbi Simon[119]: One does not add a fifth for any Second Tithe which in itself is not worth a *peruṭah*. Rebbi Joḥanan in the name of Rebbi Yannai: One does not add a fifth for any Second Tithe for which the fifth is not worth a *peruṭah*[120]. A *baraita* supports the one, a *baraita* supports the other.

As it was stated: "From its tithe,[121]" except what is worth less than a *peruṭah*.[122] This means, not unless itself is worth a *peruṭah*. Another Tanna states: "From its tithe[121], its fifths[123]" except if it is worth less than a *peruṭah*. This means, not unless the fifth is worth a *peruṭah*. Rebbi Abin bar Mamal[124] said, our Mishnah follows neither one since we have stated "there are five *peruṭot*", but we did not state "not unless itself is worth a *peruṭah*"; we have stated "there are five fifths", but we did not state "not unless the fifth is worth a *peruṭah*".

118  Cf. Babli 53b. A parallel, different treatment is in *Ma'aśer Šeni* 4:3, Notes 57-63.

118  For obvious chronological reasons this must read: R. Simon (in *Ma'aśer Šeni*: R. Yose ben R. Simon) in the name of R. Joḥanan.

120  The Babli presents this as R. Simeon ben Laqish's opinion. The Yerushalmi *Ma'aśer Šeni* quotes only the second opinion.

121  Lev. 27:31.

122  As always in rabbinic interpretation, the prefix מ is partitive: Not for all tithe has a fifth to be given in redemption. *Sifra Beḥuqqotai Pereq* 12(10); Babli 53b.

123  Lev. 5:23. The plural "fifths" is interpreted to mean that if somebody is obligated to pay a fifth and then reneges and swears falsely that he does not owe it, the first fifth becomes principal on which another fifth is due. This may continue until the fifth becomes less that a *peruṭah*. *Sifra Wayyiqra Parašah* 13(12); Babli 53b.

124  Everywhere else, including *Ma'aśer Šeni*, he is called Abba bar Mamal. There, it is shown that quite a number of "*peruṭot*" are missing from the Mishnah.

(fol. 9b) **משנה ח:** וְאֵילוּ דְבָרִים שֶׁאֵין לָהֶן הוֹנָיָיה. הָעֲבָדִים וְהַשְּׁטָרוֹת וְהַקַּרְקָעוֹת וְהַהֶקְדֵּישׁוֹת. אֵין בָּהֶן לֹא תַשְׁלוּמֵי כֶפֶל וְלֹא תַשְׁלוּמֵי אַרְבָּעָה וַחֲמִשָּׁה. שׁוֹמֵר חִנָּם אֵינוֹ נִשְׁבָּע וְנוֹשֵׂא שָׂכָר אֵינוֹ מְשַׁלֵּם. רִבִּי שִׁמְעוֹן אוֹמֵר קֳדָשִׁים שֶׁהוּא חַייָב בְּאַחֲרָיוּתָן יֵשׁ לָהֶן הוֹנָיָיה וְשֶׁאֵינוֹ חַייָב בְּאַחֲרָיוּתָן אֵין לָהֶן

הוֹנָיָיה. רִבִּי יְהוּדָה אוֹמֵר אַף הַמּוֹכֵר סֵפֶר תּוֹרָה בְּהֵמָה וּמַרְגָּלִית אֵין לָהֶן הוֹנָיָיה. אָמְרוּ לוֹ לֹא אָמְרוּ אֶלָּא אֶת אֵילוּ.

**Mishnah 8**: The following are not under the rules of cheating[125]: Slaves[126], securities[127], real estate[128], and Temple property[129]; they are not under the rules of double or quadruple or quintuple restitution[130]. An unpaid trustee does not have to swear, a paid trustee does not pay. Rebbi Simeon says, sacrifices which he is obligated to warrant[131] are under the rules of cheating; those for which he is not obligated to warrant are not under the rules of cheating. Rebbi Jehudah says, also he who sells a Torah scroll, an animal, or a pearl is not under the rules of cheating. They told him, they said only these.

125  There is no recourse in court for overpaying or underpaying.

126  In *Lev.* 25:45, Gentile slaves are put under the rules of real estate.

127  Documents of indebtedness. What one buys is not the paper on which the IOU is written but the future claim. What one buys "from the hand of your neighbor" (*Lev.* 25:14) is the paper; therefore the IOU is not under the rules of that verse.

128  *Lev.* 25:14 only refers to movables.

129  *Lev.* 25:14 only refers to "your neighbor," not to public property.

130  If slaves, securities, or Temple property was stolen (e. g., Temple animals).

131  If one vows to bring "a sacrifice", he has not fulfilled his obligation until the animal was sacrificed. Before that moment, it remains the personal property of the offerer and is covered by *Lev.* 25:14. But if he vows to offer "this animal", he has fulfilled his duty at the moment the animal was delivered to the Temple. After that it is Temple property; cf. Mishnah *Bava qamma* 7:5.

(9d line 61) **הלכה ח**: וְאֵילוּ דְבָרִים שֶׁאֵין לָהֶן הוֹנָיָיה כול׳. תַּנֵּי. רִבִּי יוּדָה אוֹמֵר. אַף סֵפֶר תּוֹרָה בְּהֵמָה וּמַרְגָּלִית אֵין לָהֶן הוֹנָאָה. סֵפֶר תּוֹרָה אֵין קֵץ לְדָמָיו. בְּהֵמָה וּמַרְגָּלִית צְרִיכִין לְזַוְוגָם. אָמְרוּ לוֹ. וַהֲלֹא הַכֹּל אָדָם רוֹצֶה

לָזוּג. תַּנֵּי. רִבִּי יוּדָה בֶּן בְּתֵירָה אוֹמֵר. טַיָּיף וְסוּס וּתְרִיס בַּמִּלְחָמָה אֵין לָהֶן הוֹנָיָיה.

**Halakhah 8**: "The following are not under the rules of cheating," etc. It was stated[132]: "Rebbi Jehudah says, also a Torah scroll, an animal, and a pearl are not under the rules of cheating. A Torah scroll, for its value is infinite. An animal and a pearl need to be paired. They said to him, does not a person want to pair everything?" It was stated: "Rebbi Jehudah ben Bathyra says, a sword, a horse, and a shield are not under the rules of cheating at wartime."

132 Babli 58b, Tosephta 3:24.

(fol. 9c) **משנה ט:** כְּשֵׁם שֶׁהוֹנָיָיה בְּמֶקַח וּבְמִמְכָּר כָּךְ הוֹנָיָיה בִּדְבָרִים. לֹא יֹאמַר לוֹ בְּכַמָּה חֵפֶץ זֶה וְהוּא אֵינוֹ רוֹצֶה לִיקַּח. אִם הָיָה בַּעַל תְּשׁוּבָה לֹא יֹאמַר לוֹ זְכוֹר מַעֲשֶׂיךָ הָרִאשׁוֹנִים. אִם הוּא בֶן גֵּרִים לֹא יֹאמַר לוֹ זְכוֹר מַה הָיוּ מַעֲשֵׂה אֲבוֹתֶיךָ שֶׁנֶּאֱמַר וְגֵר לֹא תוֹנֶה וְלֹא תִלְחָצֶנּוּ כִּי גֵרִים הֱיִיתֶם בְּאֶרֶץ מִצְרָיִם..

**Mishnah 9**: Just as there is cheating in trade so there is cheating by words. One should not say to another: how much for this object, if he is not interested in buying. If somebody was a repentant sinner, one should not say to him: remember your earlier deeds. If somebody was the son of a proselyte, one may not say to him: remember the deeds of your forefathers, for it is written[133]: "A sojourner you may neither cheat nor oppress, for you were sojourners in the Land of Egypt."

**משנה י:** אֵין מְעָרְבִין פֵּירוֹת בְּפֵירוֹת אֲפִילוּ חֲדָשִׁים בַּחֲדָשִׁים וְאֵין צָרִיךְ לוֹמַר חֲדָשִׁים בִּישָׁנִים. בֶּאֱמֶת בַּיַּיִן הִתִּירוּ לְעָרֵב קָשֶׁה בְּרַךְ מִפְּנֵי שֶׁהוּא מַשְׁבִּיחוֹ. אֵין מְעָרְבִין שִׁמְרֵי יַיִן בְּיַיִן אֲבָל נוֹתֵן לוֹ אֶת שְׁמָרָיו. מִי שֶׁנִּתְעָרֵב

מַיִם בְּיֵינוֹ לֹא יִמְכְּרֶנּוּ בַּחֲנוּת אֶלָּא אִם כֵּן הוֹדִיעוֹ וְלֹא לַתַּגָּר אַף עַל פִּי שֶׁהוֹדִיעוֹ שֶׁאֵינוֹ אֶלָּא לְרַמּוֹת בּוֹ.  מָקוֹם שֶׁנָּהֲגוּ לְהַטִּיל מַיִם יִטִּילוּ.

**Mishnah 10**: One[134] does not mix produce, not even new with new; no need to say new with old. In truth[135] they permitted to mix strong wine with weak since it improves it. One[136] does not mix wine lees with wine, but one delivers the lees with the wine. If water became mixed with somebody's wine, he should not sell it in the store unless he declares it, and not to a trader for that one would only use it to trick people; at a place where they usually put water into the wine they may do so.

**משנה יא**: הַתַּגָּר נוֹטֵל מֵחָמֵשׁ גְּרָנוֹת וְנוֹתֵן לְתוֹךְ מְגוּרָה אַחַת מֵחָמֵשׁ גִּתּוֹת וְנוֹתֵן לְתוֹךְ פִּיטָם אֶחָד וּבִלְבַד שֶׁלֹּא יִתְכַּוֵּן לְעָרֵב.  רַבִּי יְהוּדָה אוֹמֵר לֹא יְחַלֵּק הַחֶנְוָנִי קְלָיוֹת וֶאֱגוֹזִין לַתִּינוֹקוֹת מִפְּנֵי שֶׁהוּא מַרְגִּילָן לָבֹא אֶצְלוֹ וַחֲכָמִים מַתִּירִין.  וְלֹא יִפְחוֹת אֶת הַשַּׁעַר וַחֲכָמִים אוֹמְרִים זָכוּר לַטּוֹב.  לֹא יָבוֹר אֶת הַגְּרִיסִין כְּדִבְרֵי אַבָּא שָׁאוּל וַחֲכָמִים מַתִּירִין.  וּמוֹדִין שֶׁלֹּא יָבוֹר מֵעַל פִּי הַמְּגוּרָה שֶׁאֵינוֹ אֶלָּא גוֹנֵב אֶת הָעָיִן.  אֵין מְפַרְקְסִין לֹא אֶת הָאָדָם וְלֹא אֶת הַבְּהֵמָה וְלֹא אֶת הַכֵּלִים.

**Mishnah 11**: The trader may buy from five threshing floors and put into one chest, wine from five wine presses and put into one barrel[137], on condition that he not intend to mix[138]. Rebbi Jehudah says, a store owner should not distribute roasted kernels and nuts to children because he induces them to come to him, but the Sages permit. He should not reduce the price, but the Sages say, may he be remembered as a benefactor[139]. He should not clean the groats following Abba Shaul, but the Sages permit it. However, they agree that he may not clean the upper layer of the chest[140] since that gives a dishonest impression. One may not put make-up on humans[141], animals, or vessels.

133   Ex. 22:20; *Mekhilta dR. Ismael Neziqin* 18, *Mekhilta dR. Simeon ben Iohai* p. 210.
134   The farmer.
135   "In truth" characterizes undisputed practice.
136   The winery.
137   Greek πίθος.
138   He may only pour wines of the same kind into one barrel.
139   The Sages oppose restrictions which hinder competition.
140   A store may not dress up the upper layer of merchandise, which is seen by the buyer, and then sell lesser quality from below. This is cheating.
141   Slaves one offers for sale.

(9d line 66) **הלכה ט:** כְּשֵׁם שֶׁהָאוֹנָאָה בְּמֶקַח וּבְמִמְכָּר כול'. אֵין מְפַרְקְסִין. רְבִּי אַבְדּוֹמָא מַלָּחָא הֲוָה מְפַטֵּר סְרָדְוָתֵיהּ. אָמַר לֵיהּ יַעֲקֹב בַּר אָחָא. וְהָתַנִּינָן. אֵין מְפַרְקְסִין. מִילְתֵיהּ אֲמָרָה שֶׁיֵּשׁ פִּירְקוּס בָּאוֹכְלַין. רְבִּי זֵירָא הֲוָה עָסַק בְּהָדָא כִּיתָנָא. אָתָא גַבֵּיהּ רְבִּי אַבָּהוּ. אָמַר לֵיהּ. מָה אֲנָא מְשַׁפְּרָא עִיבִידִיתֵיהּ. אָמַר לֵיהּ. אֵיזִיל עֲבִיד מַה דְאַתְּ יָדַע. רְבִּי אַבָּהוּ הֲוָה עָסִיק בְּאִילֵּין לְסוּטַיָּא. אָתָא שְׁאַל לְרְבִּי יוֹסֵי בֶּן חֲנִינָה. אָמַר לֵיהּ. מְנָן בְּאִילֵּין לְסוּטַיָּא. אָמַר לֵיהּ. אֵיזִיל עֲבִיד מַה דְאַתְּ יָדַע. רַבָּה שֶׁקֶר טָהֵר. תַּנֵּה רְבִּי יַעֲקֹב עֲמַסּוֹנַיָּיא. מַהוּ אֵין מְפַרְקְסִין. דְּלָא יֵימָא לֵיהּ. צוּר גַּרְמָךְ.

**Halakhak 9**: "Just as there is cheating in trade," etc. "One may not put on make-up." Rebbi Eudaimon the salt dealer was mollifying his spread[142]. Jacob bar Aḥa said to him, did we not state: "one may not put on make up"? His word implies that there is make-up on food. Rebbi Ze'ira was working with flax. He went to Rebbi Abbahu and asked him, may I make my work look good? He told him, go and apply all you know. Rebbi Abbahu was working on those shawls[143]. He came to ask Rebbi Yose ben Ḥanina, how am I with those shawls? He told him, go and apply all you know. Rebbi Abba painted a bathtub. Rebbi Jacob from Emmaus stated: What means: "one may not put on make up"? One may not say to him[141], paint yourself.

142 The translation of this sentence is tentative and is based on the meaning of the corresponding words فتر, سرد in Arabic. R. Eliahu Fulda (followed by Levy and Kohut) explains that he washed his sieve in soap to produce better looking salt grains. R. M. Margalit explains without any lexical justification that he washed pieces of meat to make them look better. Jastrow translated: R. Eudaimon the sailor mollified his sails. But sails are not edible and they are not made from loose tissue with lots of holes, سر.

143 Yerushalmi *Šabbat* 4, 8b l. 69 translates רדדים (*Is.* 3:23) by לסוטות.

## איזהו נשך פרק חמישי

(fol. 10a) **משנה א:** אֵי זֶהוּ נֶשֶׁךְ וְאֵי זֶהוּ תַרְבִּית. אֵי זֶהוּ נֶשֶׁךְ הַמַּלְוֶה סֶלַע בַּחֲמִשָּׁה דֵינָרִין וְסָאתַיִם חִטִּים בְּשָׁלֹשׁ מִפְּנֵי שֶׁהוּא נוֹשֵׁךְ. וְאֵי זֶהוּ תַרְבִּית הַמַּרְבֶּה בַּפֵּירוֹת. כֵּיצַד לָקַח הֵימֶנּוּ חִטִּים בְּדִינָר זָהָב הַכּוֹר. וְכֵן הַשַּׁעַר. עָמְדוּ חִטִּים בִּשְׁלֹשִׁים דֵּינָרִין אָמַר לוֹ תֶּן לִי חִטַּי שֶׁאֲנִי מוֹכְרָן וְלוֹקֵחַ אֲנִי בָּהֶן יַיִן אָמַר לוֹ הֲרֵי חִטִּין עֲשׂוּיוֹת עָלַי בִּשְׁלֹשִׁים דֵּינָרִין וַהֲרֵי לָךְ אֶצְלִי יַיִן וְיַיִן אֵין לוֹ.

**Mishnah 1**: What is biting[1] and what is increase[2]? What is biting, lending a tetradrachma for five denars, two *se'ah* of wheat for three; because this bites. What is increase? Paying more for produce. How is this? One bought from another wheat for a gold denar the *kor* at the going rate[3]. Wheat appreciated to thirty denars. He told him, deliver my wheat, for I want to sell it and buy wine with the proceeds. The other said, let your wheat be given to me for thirty denars[4] and you have wine with me[5], but he has no wine[6].

**משנה ב:** הַמַּלְוֶה אֶת חֲבֵירוֹ לֹא יָדוּר בַּחֲצֵירוֹ חִנָּם וְלֹא יִשְׂכּוֹר מִמֶּנּוּ בְּפָחוֹת מִפְּנֵי שֶׁהוּא רִבִּית.

**Mishnah 2**: A creditor may not dwell on the debtor's premises for free or rent it below the going rate, for this would be interest[7].

---

1 Interest which is prohibited by biblical law (*Lev.* 25:36) must be *biting*, i. e. cost the debtor money, and *increase*, result in monetary gain for the lender.

2 תַּרְבִּית "increase", refers to rabbinic interest prohibitions in which the *biting* feature is missing. Transactions which are perfectly legitimate in general can become forbidden as rabbinic interest if enacted between borrower and lender. There are

different shades of rabbinically prohibited interest. Transactions which result in gain for the lender for deferral of repayment of a debt are plain interest payments. Services the debtor renders to the creditor which carry no monetary value are אֲבַק רִבִּית "dust of interest".

3 For later delivery.

4 So far, the transaction is perfectly legal.

5 They fixed the amount of wine which was the monetary equivalent of a *kor* of wheat at the time of the second transaction.

6 Since at the time of delivery the seller might have to buy wine at a higher price, the quantity of wine delivered would contain a "premium paid to the buyer for waiting to receive delivery". The latter is the definition of rabbinically forbidden interest. This prohibits all trades in futures (even to a farmer, who might have a bad harvest and be forced to buy grain in the open market to cover the quantities he contracted for at the start of the growing season.)

7 רִבִּית is the common rabbinic expression for "interest".

(10a line 58) **הלכה א:** אֵי זֶהוּ נֶשֶׁךְ כּוֹל׳. אָמַר רִבִּי יַנַּאי. זֶהוּ רִבִּית שֶׁהוּא יוֹצֵא בַדַּיָּינִין. בָּעוּ קוֹמֵי רִבִּי יוֹחָנָן. רִבִּית מָהוּ שֶׁיֵּצֵא בַדַּיָּינִין. אָמַר לוֹ. אִם מִזּוּ אֵין אָנוּ מְנִיחִין לִגְדוֹלֵי אֶרֶץ יִשְׂרָאֵל כְּלוּם. מוֹדֵי רִבִּי יוֹחָנָן שֶׁאֵין שְׁטָר זוֹקֵק לַחֲבֵירוֹ. מוֹדֶה רִבִּי יוֹחָנָן שֶׁאִם הָיָה הַשְּׁטָר קַיָּים דִּמְנַכִּין לֵיהּ.

**Halakhah 1:** "What is biting," etc. Rebbi Yannai said, this[8] is interest which is taken away by the judges. They asked before Rebbi Johanan, can interest be taken away by the judges? He said, if it were so, nothing would be left for the great people of the Land of Israel[9]. Rebbi Johanan agrees that no document obligates another[10]. Rebbi Johanan agrees that if the document exists one subtracts [the interest][11].

8 The interest described as "biting" in the Mishnah, where the rate of interest is spelled out beforehand. In the Babli, 61b, this is the opinion of R. Eleazar. Everybody agrees that rabbinic interest, where the effective rate depends on market forces, is not recoverable in court.

9 To return interest taken is a moral but not a legal duty; Babli 61b.

10  While a court will not force a creditor to return the interest he already received, it cannot accept documents subjecting the debtor to a fixed rate of interest. If several documents are submitted to the court in a dispute between two parties, and one claim, containing a stated interest rate, was already paid off, the interest paid thereon cannot be deducted from the capital in dispute in the document which was not yet liquidated.

11  If a document subjecting the debtor to a fixed rate of interest comes before the court, they have to delete the interest clause.

(10a line 61) אֵי זֶהוּ תַרְבִּית. תַּנֵּי. יִשְׂרָאֵל שֶׁהִלְוָה בְּרִיבִּית לְיִשְׂרָאֵל אֵינוֹ גּוֹבֶה לֹא אֶת הַקֶּרֶן וְלֹא אֶת הָרִיבִּית. דִּבְרֵי רַבִּי מֵאִיר. וַחֲכָמִים אוֹמְרִים. גּוֹבֶה אֶת הַקֶּרֶן וְלֹא אֶת הָרִיבִּית. כְּתִיב אֶת כַּסְפְּךָ לֹא תִתֵּן לוֹ בְּנֶשֶׁךְ. אֵין לִי אֶלָּא נֶשֶׁךְ בְּכֶסֶף וְרִיבִּית בְּאוֹכֶל. נֶשֶׁךְ בְּאוֹכֶל וְרִיבִּית בְּכֶסֶף מְנַיִין. תַּלְמוּד לוֹמַר אַל תִּקַּח מֵאִתּוֹ נֶשֶׁךְ וְתַרְבִּית. הִקִּישׁ נֶשֶׁךְ לְתַרְבִּית וְתַרְבִּית לְנֶשֶׁךְ. מַה נֶּשֶׁךְ כֶּסֶף אַף תַּרְבִּית כֶּסֶף. מַה תַּרְבִּית אוֹכֶל אַף נֶשֶׁךְ אוֹכֶל.

"What is increase?" It was stated[12]: A Jew who lent to another Jew with interest can collect neither principal[13] nor interest, the words of Rebbi Meïr. But the Sages say, he may collect the capital but not the interest. [14]It is written: "Your money you shall not give him by biting[15]." Not only money by biting and food by increase. From where increase in money and biting in food? The verse says, "do not take from him biting and increase,[16]" it brackets biting with increase and increase with biting. Since biting refers to money, increase also refers to money; since increase refers to food, biting also refers to food[17].

12  Babli 72a, *Bava qamma* 30b, *Bava batra* 94b; Yerushalmi *Giṭṭin* 4:4 (Notes 129,130), *Pesaḥim* 2:2 (29a l. 38).

13  Not as a matter of biblical law but as a fine. For him, the court will refuse to look at a document containing a stated rate of interest which therefore becomes barred from any action needing the sanction of a court.

14  Babli 60b.

15  The reference includes the second half of *Lev.* 25:36, "and against

increase do not give your food."

16   Lev. 25:35, "and fear your God, I am the Eternal." This establishes the prohibition of stated interest as a moral imperative, subject to the jurisdiction of Heaven, not the human court. The argument identifies תַּרְבִּית in v. 35 and מַרְבִּית in v. 36.

17   In each case every instance of taking stated interest is two sins by one action.

(10a line 68) לָקַח מִמֶּנּוּ חִיטִים. אָמַר רִבִּי בָּא בַּר כָּהֲנָא. הַשַּׁעַר שֶׁהוּא יָפֶה לָעוֹלָם. פָּחוּת מִיכֵּן וַוי לְזָבוּנָא. יוֹתֵר מִכֵּן וַוי לִמְזַבְּנָה.

"One bought wheat from another." Rebbi Abba bar Cahana said, the rate which is valid for everybody[18]. Less than that, woe to the seller; more than that, woe to the buyer!

18   The going rate mentioned in the Mishnah is the rate at which the seller is ready to sell to any buyer. It is presumed that market forces are effective at all times.

(10a line 70) אָמַר לוֹ. תֶּן לִי חִיטַּיי שֶׁאֲנִי מוֹכְרָן. בְּמַה קָנָה. רַב נַחְמָן בַּר יַעֲקֹב סָבַר מֵימַר. חַייָב לְהַעֲמִיד (לַחֲבֵירוֹ) [לוֹ מִן הַדִּין]. רִבִּי אַבָּהוּ בְּשֵׁם רִבִּי יוֹחָנָן. קָנוּ לוֹ מָעוֹתָיו דְּבַר תּוֹרָה.

"He told him, deliver my wheat, for I want to sell it." How did he acquire[19]? Rav Naḥman bar Jacob was of the opinion that he had to deliver (to the other person)[20] [by law. Rebbi Abbahu in the name of Rebbi Joḥanan: His money acquired for him by biblical law.][21]

19   Since the Mishnah forbids taking money for merchandise which is not yet in the seller's hand, it must assume that the contract is binding; otherwise it could not be forbidden. E has here an extended quote from the Mishnah.

20   Reading of the Leiden ms. and *editio princeps*. As stated in the previous note, this is a trivial inference.

21   Reading of E. The Mishnah here follows R. Yannai and R. Joḥanan (Chapter 4, Note 2) that by biblical standards paying money transfers both

ownership and possession. The seller obligates himself by taking money or money's worth. In *Qiddušin* 2:6, Note 138, R. Ḥiyya bar Abba, successor of R. Joḥanan in Tiberias, disagrees in the name of R. Joḥanan.

(10a line 71) הַמַּלְוֶה אֶת חֲבֵירוֹ. חַד בַּר נָשׁ אַשְׁאַל לְחַבְרֵיהּ דֵּינָרִין אַשְׁרוּנֵיהּ גּוֹ בֵּיתֵיהּ. אֲמַר לֵיהּ. הַב לִי אֲגַר בֵּיתִי. אֲמַר לֵיהּ. הַב לִי דֵּינָרַיי. אֲתָא עוֹבְדָא קוֹמֵי רִבִּי בָּא בַּר מִינָא. אֲמַר לֵיהּ. וְקַיֵּים לֵיהּ מַה דַּהֲוָה חֲמֵי לְמֵישְׁרֵי.

"A creditor." A person lent money to another, who let him live in his house, then said, give me the rent for my house. The first one said, give me my money[22]. The case came before Rebbi Abba bar Mina[23], who told him to give what was a reasonable rent.

22  The text is quoted by Ran *Ketubot* 13 (on Alfasi # 391; 63a in the Wilna edition of Alfasi). There, the creditor first asked for his money; the debtor responded by asking for rent.

23  In Ran: Abba bar Zamina.

(10a line 74) תַּנֵּי. יֵשׁ דְּבָרִים שֶׁהֵן רִבִּית וּמוּתָּרִין. כֵּיצַד. לוֹקֵחַ אָדָם שְׁטָרוֹת חֲבֵירוֹ בְּפָחוֹת וּמִלְוֹנוֹתוֹ שֶׁלַּחֲבֵירוֹ בְּפָחוֹת וְאֵינוֹ חוֹשֵׁשׁ מִשּׁוּם רִבִּית. וְיֵשׁ דְּבָרִים שֶׁאֵינָן רִבִּית וַאֲסוּרִין מִשּׁוּם הַעֲרָמַת רִבִּית. כֵּיצַד. קִיבֵּל הֵימֶנּוּ שָׂדֶה בְּי' כּוֹר חִיטִין. אָמַר לוֹ. תֶּן לִי סֶלַע אֶחָד. אָמַר לוֹ אֵין לִי אֶלָּא כּוֹר אֶחָד חִיטִין. טוֹל לָךְ. וְחָזַר וְלָקַח מִמֶּנּוּ בְּכֹד. אֵין זֶה רִבִּית אֲבָל אָסוּר מִשּׁוּם הַעֲרָמַת רִבִּית. אֲמַר לֵיהּ. לֵית אַתְּ צְרִיךְ וְהַב אֲגַר כֵּלִים אוֹ אֲגַר הַכַּתָּפִין אֲקוֹלִי וְסַב דֵּינָרְךָ.

It was stated[24]: "There are things which are interest but are permitted. How is that? A person may buy another's promissory notes at a discount, or bills of debt at a discount, and need have no compunctions because of interest[25]. Other things are not interest but are forbidden because of circumventing interest. How is that? One received from another a field for ten *kor* of wheat[26]. . . . A person said to another, lend me a tetradrachma[27]. He answered, I only have a *kor* of wheat, take it. If he then turned around and bought it back for 24 it is not interest but forbidden because of circumventing interest.²⁸" He might have said to him, you do not have to do this and take your denar but then you have to pay for vessels and porters of the containers²⁹.

24  Tosephta 5:3, Babli 62b.

25  As a matter of principle, while interest, a "premium for waiting to receive money due", is forbidden, discount, a premium for paying early, is unquestionably permitted. The securities are due sometime in the future; the lender needs money now. He sells his securities at a discount.

26  This statement is both corrupt and incomplete (in both mss.). Most likely it refers to Mishnah 3: A farmer rents a field and is given the choice of either paying 10 in advance for the year or each month 1 (of whichever unit it may be.) Since in talmudic tradition rental fees are payable at the end of the rental period, the difference of 2 for the year is discount rather than interest; it is unquestionably permitted.

27  The continuation shows that one must read "mina", 100 denars, for "tetradrachma".

28  Since a *mina* equals 25 tetradrachmas, the lender makes 1 tetradrachma on the deal. The question arises, why is this not true interest?

29  Since the borrower would have had expenses of a tetradrachma if he actually had sold the wheat on the market, the lender can save him the expense by taking the wheat back while deducting the putative costs. But since for the lender it actually is a "premium for waiting," it is prohibited as "circumventing interest".

(10b line 5) רִבִּי לָא אָמַר בְּנוֹתֵן לוֹ שְׂכַר רַגְלוֹ. רִבִּי זֵירָא אָמַר. נַעֲשָׂה כְּמַשְׂכִּיר לוֹ דִּירָה בְּיוֹקֶר.

Rebbi La said, he pays him the wages of his foot; Rebbi Ze'ira said, he rents him the dwelling at an inflated price³⁰.

30  It seems that these statements refer to the following Mishnah 3, that it is permitted to rent a dwelling at a discount if the rental fee is paid for a year in advance. R. La holds that the discount is not a simple finance operation but represents real savings for the landlord who does not have to go every month to collect his rent. R. Ze'ira holds that rental fees are not

really determined by the market; every landlord has the choice for how much he wants to rent out his real estate. If there exists no market price, one cannot talk about over- or under-charging.

(fol. 10a) **משנה ג:** מַרְבִּין עַל הַשָּׂכָר וְאֵין מַרְבִּין עַל הַמֶּכֶר. כֵּיצַד הִשְׂכִּיר לוֹ אֶת הֶחָצֵר וְאָמַר לוֹ אִם מֵעַכְשָׁיו אַתָּה נוֹתֵן לִי הֲרֵי הוּא לָךְ בְּעֶשֶׂר סְלָעִים לַשָּׁנָה וְאִם שֶׁלְחֹדֶשׁ בְּחֹדֶשׁ בְּסֶלַע לַחֹדֶשׁ מוּתָּר. מָכַר לוֹ אֶת שָׂדֵהוּ וְאָמַר לוֹ אִם מֵעַכְשָׁיו אַתָּה נוֹתֵן לִי הֲרֵי הִיא לָךְ בְּאֶלֶף זוּז וְאִם לַגּוֹרֶן בִּשְׁנֵים עָשָׂר מָנֶה אָסוּר.

**Mishnah 3**: One may increase rental fees but not sale price. How is this? He leased a courtyard saying to him[31], if [you pay] now it is yours for ten tetradrachmas a year but if paid monthly it is a tetradrachma per month; this is permitted[32]. He sold his field and said to him[33], if [you pay] now it is yours for 1'000 *zuz*, but if after the threshing floor[34] it is twelve *mina*; this is forbidden.

**משנה ד:** מָכַר לוֹ אֶת שָׂדֵהוּ וְנָתַן לוֹ מִקְצָת דָּמִים וְאָמַר לוֹ אֵימָתַי שֶׁתִּרְצֶה הָבֵא מָעוֹת וְטוֹל אֶת שֶׁלָּךְ אָסוּר. הִלְוָוהוּ עַל שָׂדֵהוּ וְאָמַר לוֹ אִם אֵי אַתָּה נוֹתֵן לִי מִכָּאן וְעַד שָׁלֹשׁ שָׁנִים הֲרֵי הִיא שֶׁלִּי הֲרֵי הִיא שֶׁלּוֹ. וְכָךְ הָיָה בַּיְיתוֹס בֶּן זוֹנִין עוֹשֶׂה עַל פִּי חֲכָמִים.

**Mishnah 4**: If one sold his field, [the buyer] made a partial payment and [the seller] said, anytime you wish bring the remainder and take yours; this is forbidden[35]. If one lent money on a field and said, if you do not repay me in three years from now, it will be mine, it is his[36]; Boethos ben Zenon[37] acted thus following the Sages.

| | | | |
|---|---|---|---|
| 31 | The landlord to the renter. | 34 | When the farmer sells his crop; this is the only time of the year when he has ample cash. |
| 32 | As explained in Note 26. | | |
| 33 | The seller to the buyer. | | |

35 If the field is sold now but the yield remains the seller's until it is fully paid for, the yield collected by the seller is a "premium for waiting."

36 A mortgage with a forfeiture clause.

37 In the Babli, 63a, 'Arakhin 31a; Tosephta 4:2: On the instruction of R. Eleazar ben Azariah.

(10b line 7) **הלכה ג:** מַרְבִּין עַל הַשָּׂכָר כול׳. תַּנֵּי. הַמּוֹכֵר שָׂדֶה לַחֲבֵירוֹ וְאָמַר לוֹ. עַל מְנָת שֶׁאֱהֵא בָהּ אָרִיס. עַל מְנָת שֶׁאֱהֵא בָהּ שׁוּתָף. עַל מְנָת שֶׁהַמַּעְשְׂרוֹת שֶׁלִּי. עַל מְנָת שֶׁכְּשֶׁתִּמְכְּרֶנָּה לֹא תִמְכְּרֶנָּה אֶלָּא לִי. שֶׁכָּל־זְמַן שֶׁאֲנִי רוֹצֶה נוֹתֵן דָּמֶיהָ וְנוֹטְלָהּ. מוּתָּר. הָיָה חַיָּיב לוֹ מָעוֹת וְכָתַב לוֹ שָׂדֵהוּ בְמֶכֶר. כָּל־זְמַן שֶׁהַמּוֹכֵר אוֹכֵל פֵּירוֹת מוּתָּר. כָּל־זְמַן שֶׁהַלּוֹקֵחַ אוֹכֵל פֵּירוֹת אָסוּר. רִבִּי יוּדָה אוֹמֵר. בֵּין כָּךְ וּבֵין כָּךְ מוּתָּר. אָמַר רִבִּי יוּדָה. כָּךְ הָיָה בָּיֵיתוֹס בֶּן זוֹנִין עוֹשֶׂה עַל פִּי חֲכָמִים. אָמְרוּ לוֹ. מִשָּׁם רְאָייָה. מוֹכֵר אוֹכֵל פֵּירוֹת הָיָה. רִבִּי יוֹחָנָן וְרִבִּי לָעְזָר וְרִבִּי הוֹשַׁעְיָה אָמְרֵי. מִבָּתֵּי עָרֵי חוֹמָה לָמַד רִבִּי יְהוּדָה. דְּתַנֵּי. שָׁנָה הָאֲמוּרָה בַתּוֹרָה עָרֵי חוֹמָה הֲרֵי הֵן כְּמִין רִבִּית וְאֵינָהּ רִבִּית. תַּנַּיי חוֹרָן תַּנֵּי. הֲרֵי זוֹ רִיבִּית אֶלָּא שֶׁהִיתִּירָהּ הַתּוֹרָה. מָאן דָּמַר. הֲרֵי זוֹ כְּמִין רִבִּית וְאֵינָהּ רִבִּית. רִבִּי מֵאִיר. מָאן דָּמַר. הֲרֵי זוֹ רִיבִּית אֶלָּא שֶׁהַתּוֹרָה הִיתִּירָהּ. רִבִּי יוּדָה. אָמַר רִבִּי אִידִי. כַּד סָלְקִית מִגְלוּתָא אַשְׁכְּחִית עוֹבְדָא קוֹמֵי רִבִּי אַמִּי. הֲרֵי זוֹ כְּמִין רִבִּית וְאֵינָהּ רִבִּית. אָמַר רִבִּי חִזְקִיָּה. לֹא אָמְרוּ אֶלָּא זוֹ רִבִּית שֶׁהִיתִּירָהּ הַתּוֹרָה. כָּאן הַתּוֹרָה הִתִּירָהּ. הָא בְמָקוֹם אַחֵר לֹא. אֲפִילוּ כֵן לֹא אַשְׁגַּח רִבִּי אַמִּי. אָמַר. בַּייתָא עִם דַּייָרָא דָּאִיר.

**Halakhah 3:** "One may increase rental fees," etc. It was stated[38]: "If somebody sells a field to another and stipulates, on condition that I shall work it as a sharecropper, on condition that I shall be part owner, on condition that the tithes shall be mine[39], on condition that if you sell it, you will sell it only to me, that anytime I want I may pay you back and take it; this is permitted." [40]"If he owed him money and wrote his field over to him as a sale, any time the seller[41] eats the yield it is permitted; any time the buyer[42] eats the yield, it is forbidden. Rebbi Jehudah says, in any case it is permitted. Rebbi Jehudah said, that is what Boethos ben Zenon did following the Sages[37]. They said to him, is that a proof? The seller was eating the yield." Rebbi Johanan, Rebbi Eleazar, and Rebbi Hoshaia said, Rebbi Jehudah learned from the houses of walled cities[43]. As it was stated: The year mentioned in the Torah regarding walled cities is like interest but it is not interest[44]. Another Tanna stated: This is interest but the Torah permitted it[45]. He who said, it is like interest but it is not interest, Rebbi Meïr[46]. He who said, this is interest but the Torah permitted it, Rebbi Jehudah[46],[47] Rebbi Idi said, when I came from the Diaspora, I found that a case[48] was before Rebbi Immi of "it is like interest but it is not interest.[49]" Rebbi Hizqiah said, they only said that "this is interest but the Torah permitted it." There[50], the Torah permitted it, therefore not in any other case. Nevertheless, Rebbi Immi did not consider it[51], for he said: a house dwells with its inhabitants[52].

38  Tosephta 4:4.

39  *Demay* 6:3 (Notes 77,84); Babli *Bava batra* 63a. In this case, the seller must be a Cohen or Levite; he reserves for himself the place at which the grain used as tithe grows. The condition is impossible for an Israel since for him it would be a trade in futures which is null and void.

40  Babli 63a; *Megillah* 27b, *Arakhin* 31a.

41  The debtor.

42  The creditor who in the end will return the field to its owner and in the meantime receives the field's yield as "premium for waiting."

43  *Lev.* 25:29-30. The sale of a house in a walled city implies an automatic right for the seller to buy back his house at the exact sale price during one full year. During that year, the buyer has the house as owner for his unrestricted use.

44  Since no interest rate was spelled out, no biblical prohibition was violated.

45  He holds that rabbinic interest prohibitions are basically biblical as long as they involve a clear "premium for waiting." The only rabbinic interest prohibitions which are purely a "fence around the law" are those which only

involve a possible, but not a certain, premium (such as "increase" defined in Mishnah 1.)

46   It seems that one has to switch the positions of R. Meïr (i. e., "the rabbis") and R. Jehudah; cf. Babli 'Arakhin 31a. E here has a lacuna.

47   E here has an addition: "What is R. Jehudah's reason? Any interest which involves one permitted aspect is permitted." The permitted aspect in this case is that the debtor decides not to repay his debt. Since the loan was structured as a conditional sale, the buyer retroactively is justified in harvesting the yield from the date of sale. This is Abbaye's reading of R. Jehudah's position in the Babli (63a); the addition seems to be a gloss by a student of the Babli.

48   E has an addition: הַדָּר בַּחֲצַר חֲבֵירוֹ שֶׁלֹּא מִדַּעְתּוֹ "about one who dwelt on another's property without the latter's knowledge." If this addition be relevant, it must have been the creditor who lived on property which belonged to the debtor but was held by the latter neither for rental nor fot his own use, cf. ברכיהו ליפשיץ *מחזי כמטון* מחקרי תלמוד ג (2005) p. 438-460.

49   It is more likely that the problem was a sale which in the end was rescinded but in the meantime the buyer lived in the house.

50   A house in a walled city, and the case before R. Immi was not in this category.

51   He ruled according to R. Jehudah.

52   When the sale was rescinded, the full price was to be returned without any deductions for rental during the period in which the buyer used it. R. Immi did not necessarily follow R. Jehudah's argument as presented in the Halakhah; he holds that an uninhabited house deteriorates much more than an inhabited one and, therefore, the buyer is due some consideration for the upkeep of the house. Then this consideration might as well be the entire rent.

E's text contradicts the interpretation of J. N. Epstein in *Tarbiz* 8 (1937) 395-397 who considers the case before R. Immi as antichretic lease (cf. 6:7, Notes 77-78 and *Giṭṭin* 4:6, Note 168.) But antichretic loans are endorsed in Mishnah 6:7 in certain cases.

**משנה ה:** (fol. 10a) אֵין מוֹשִׁיבִין חֶנְוָנִי לְמַחֲצִית שָׂכָר לֹא יִתֵּן לוֹ מָעוֹת לִיקַּח בָּהֶן פֵּירוֹת לְמַחֲצִית שָׂכָר אֶלָּא אִם כֵּן נוֹתֵן לוֹ שְׂכָרוֹ כְּפוֹעֵל בָּטֵל. אֵין מוֹשִׁיבִין תַּרְנוּגָלִין לְמֶחֱצָה וְאֵין שָׁמִין עֲגָלִים וּסְיָיחִים לְמֶחֱצָה אֶלָּא אִם כֵּן נוֹתֵן לוֹ שְׂכַר עֲמָלוֹ וּמְזוֹנוֹת. אֲבָל מְקַבְּלִין עֲגָלִים וּסְיָיחִים לְמֶחֱצָה וּמְגַדְּלִין אוֹתָן עַד שֶׁיְּהוּ שְׁלָשִׁין וַחֲמוֹר עַד שֶׁתְּהֵא טוֹעֶנֶת.

**Mishnah 5:** One does not hire a shop clerk for half the gain[53]; one does not give him money to buy produce for half the gain unless one pays him wages as an unemployed[54] worker. One does not give chickens to breed[55] for half, nor does one hand over calves and foals for care for half the risk unless one pays for his work and food[56]. But one takes in[57] calves and foals for half and grows them until they are one-third grown[58], and a donkey[59] until it becomes a beast of burden.

53 I. e., half the gain or loss, because then the material or the money provided to the trader is a loan and the 50% gain, the profit from the loan, is a "premium for waiting". But if the trader receives a basic wage, he is an employee rather than an independent agent receiving a loan.

54 This word appears in the Tosephta but is missing in the Babli.

55 To split the difference in price between chicks and eggs.

56 Again if the rancher not only will get 50% of the gain but also will be responsible for 50% of any loss. Then the investment is a loan, and the rules of the prohibition of interest are applicable. Cf. Note 84.

59 When all the risk is borne by the investor. This is a monetary equivalent of the investor paying the rancher for his work.

58 It is possible to read this as "three years old".

59 Used in rabbinic Hebrew both for he- and she-asses.

**הלכה ה:** (10b line 23) אֵין מוֹשִׁיבִין חֶנְוָנִי כול׳. חַד בַּר נַשׁ אַשְׁאַל לְחַבְרֵיהּ דֵּינָרִין. אֲמַר לֵיהּ. סַב בּ דֵּינָרִין אַגְרָךְ וּמַה דִּינוּן עָבְדִין דִּילִי וְלָךְ.

**Halakhah 5:** "One does not hire a shop clerk," etc.[54] A person lent another one denars. He said to him, take two denars[55] as your wages and what they will bring shall be mine and yours.

54 E has here an addition: וּבְמָקוֹם "שֶׁנָּהֲגוּ לַעֲלוֹת שָׂכָר כַּתָּף לְמָעוֹת מַעֲלִין. At a place where one is used to pay carrier's wages as money, one pays." This refers to the Mishnah, that one must pay the clerk a minimum wage. It is stated that the minimum cannot be less than what is customary locally. This seems to contradict the next sentence.

According to S. Lieberman (*Tosefta kiFshutah Bava Meṣi'a* p. 211) כתף "porter" means "work, exertion"; cf. Halakhah 6, Tosephta 5:6.

55 The wages required by the Mishnah can be a token sum. In practice, the Babli agrees in the name of Samuel (69a).

(10b line 25) תַּנֵּי. הַנּוֹתֵן מָעוֹת לַחֲבֵירוֹ לִיקַח בָּהֶן פֵּירוֹת לְמַחֲצִית וְאָמַר. לֹא לָקַחְתִּי. אֵין לוֹ עָלָיו אֶלָּא תִּרְעוֹמֶת. וְאִם יָדוּעַ שֶׁלָּקַח הֲרֵי זֶה מוֹצִיא מִמֶּנּוּ עַל כּוֹרְחוֹ.

It was stated[56]: "If somebody gives money to another to buy produce with it for half [the gain]; if that one says, I did not buy[57], he only has a complaint on him[58]. But if it was known[59] that he bought, the other forcibly extracts from him."

הַנּוֹתֵן מָעוֹת לַחֲבֵירוֹ לִיקַח בָּהֶן פֵּירוֹת לְמַחֲצִית שָׂכָר. רָצָה אֶחָד מֵהֶן לְיַישְׁנָן חֲבֵירוֹ מְעַכֵּב עַל יָדוֹ. אִם הָיָה עֶרֶב שְׁבִיעִית אֵין חֲבֵירוֹ מְעַכֵּב עַל יָדוֹ שֶׁשְּׁנֵיהֶן עַל מְנָת כֵּן לְקָחוּם.

[60]"If somebody gives money to another to buy produce with it for half the gain and one of them wants to age it, the other may hinder him[61]. But if it was the eve of a Sabbatical year, the other may not hinder him because it was understood that it was bought for that purpose[62]."

הַנּוֹתֵן מָעוֹת לַחֲבֵירוֹ לִיקַח בָּהֶן פֵּירוֹת לְמַחֲצִית שָׂכָר. אִם אָמַר. הֵא לָךְ מָנֶה שֶׁאֵינוֹ יָכוֹל לַעֲמוֹד בִּפְרוֹטְרוֹט. הֲרֵי זֶה אָסוּר. רָאָה פֵירוֹת מוֹקִירִין הֲרֵי זֶה מוּתָּר.

[63]"If somebody gives money to another to buy produce with it for half the gain and one says, here you have a *mina* for I cannot be bothered with the details, that is forbidden. But if he saw that grain was going up in price, it is permitted[64].

הַנּוֹתֵן מָעוֹת לַחֲבֵירוֹ לִיקַח בָּהֶן פֵּירוֹת לְמַחֲצִית שָׂכָר רַשַּׁאי הַלּוֹקֵחַ לִיקַח מֵאוֹתוֹ הַמִּין. כְּשֶׁמּוֹכֵר לֹא יִמְכּוֹר שְׁנַיִם כְּאַחַת אֶלָּא מוֹכֵר זֶה רִאשׁוֹן וְזֶה אַחֲרוֹן.

If somebody gives money to another to buy produce with it for half the gain, the trader is permitted to buy of the same kind. When he sells, he may not sell everything together but sells this first and that later[65].

הַנּוֹתֵן מָעוֹת לַחֲבֵירוֹ לִיקַח בָּהֶן פֵּירוֹת לְמַחֲצִית שָׂכָר רַשַּׁאי לִיקַח מִכָּל־מִין שֶׁיִּרְצֶה. לֹא יִקַּח לוֹ בָּהֶן כְּסוּת וְעֵצִים. אָמַר רִבִּי יִצְחָק. הָדָא אָמְרָה. הַמְבַטֵּל כִּיס חֲבֵירוֹ אֵין לוֹ עָלָיו אֶלָּא תִּרְעוֹמֶת. הַמְבַטֵּל שְׂדֵה חֲבֵירוֹ חַיָּיב לִשְׁפּוֹת לוֹ. הַמְבַטֵּל סְפִינַת חֲבֵירוֹ וַחֲנוּת חֲבֵירוֹ מָהוּ.

[66]"If somebody gives money to another to buy produce with[67] for half the gain, the trader is permitted to buy any kind he wants, but he should not buy a garment or wood[68]." [69]Rebbi Isaac said, this implies that if one who leaves another's capital unemployed, he only has a complaint on him[58]. If he leaves another's field unused, he is obligated to serve him[70]. If he leaves another's ship or store unused[71], what [is the rule][72]?

הַמּוֹלִיךְ פֵּירוֹת מִמָּקוֹם הַזּוֹל לִמְקוֹם הַיּוֹקֶר. אָמַר לַחֲבֵירוֹ. תְּנֵם לִי וַאֲנִי נוֹתֵן לָךְ כְּדֶרֶךְ שֶׁאַתָּה נוֹתְנָן לְמָקוֹם פְּלוֹנִי. אִם בְּאַחֲרָיוּת הַנּוֹתֵן אָסוּר וְהַלּוֹקֵחַ מוּתָּר. הַמּוֹלִיךְ חֲבִילָה מִמָּקוֹם לְמָקוֹם. אָמַר לוֹ. תְּנֶיהָ לִי וַאֲנִי נוֹתֵן לָךְ כְּדֶרֶךְ שֶׁאַתְּ נוֹתֵן בְּמָקוֹם פְּלוֹנִי. אִם בְּאַחֲרָיוּת הַנּוֹתֵן אָסוּר וְהַלּוֹקֵחַ מוּתָּר. אֲבָל חֲמָרִים הַמַּקְבְּלִין מִבַּעֲלֵי בָתִּים מַעֲמִידִין לָהֶן פֵּירוֹת בִּמְקוֹם הַיּוֹקֶר כְּשַׁעַר הַזּוֹל. רִבִּי יוּדָה בַּר פָּזִי. עַד מָקוֹם שֶׁדַּרְכּוֹ לֵילֵךְ וְלָבוֹא בּוֹ בַיּוֹם. רַב הוּנָא אָמַר. נַעֲשָׂה שְׁלוּחוֹ. וְהָא מְתִיבִין [לְרַב] הוּנָא. שָׁלִיחַ שֶׁנֶּאֱנַס חַיָּיב עַל הָאוּנָסִין.

שֶׁנֶּאֱנָס פָּטוּר עַל הָאוֹנָסִין. לֹא פְעָמִים מַתָּנֶה שׁוֹמֵר חִנָּם לִהְיוֹת כְּשׁוֹאֵל. וְהָתַנֵּי רִבִּי הוֹשַׁעְיָה. כְּשֵׁם שֶׁחַיָּיב בְּכוּלָּהּ כָּךְ חַיָּיב בְּמִקְצָתָהּ. מַאי כְדוֹן מַיְיתֵה. תַּמָּן מְשַׁלֵּם כְּשַׁעַר הַיּוֹקֶר. בְּרַם הָכָא מְשַׁלֵּם כְּשַׁעַר הַזּוֹל.

[73]"A person was transporting from a lowprice place to a highprice one. Another said to him, give it to me, I shall pay you what you would charge at place X. If the responsibility is the giver's, it is forbidden, but the buyer's is permitted[74]. A person was transporting a package from place to place. Another said to him, give it to me, I shall pay you what you would charge at place X. If the responsibility is the giver's, it is forbidden, but the buyer's is permitted. But donkey drivers who receive from householders[75] obtain produce for a highprice place at lowprice rates[76]." Rebbi Jehudah bar Pazi: At a place where usually they can go and return the same day[77]. Rav Huna said, he becomes his agent[78]. But did one not object to [Rav][79] Huna: If an agent fell victim to an accident, is he liable[80]? If he was the victim of an accident, he is not liable. Does it not happen that an unpaid trustee accepts to be like a borrower[81]? But did not Rebbi Hoshaia state: Just as he is liable for the entirety, so he is liable for a part[82]! Why does one quote this? There, he would pay a high price, but here he pays at the low rate[83].

56    Tosephta 4:22.
57    After some time he returns the money and claims that he did not trade.
58    The injured party has the right to complain (i. e., tell about the case to other people) but has no recourse in court for the gain lost by leaving his money inactive for some time.
59    If the other's commercial activity can be proven by any means, the injured party can sue in court.
60    Tosephta 4:18. There, the second sentence appears in the name of R. Jehudah.
61    In the absence of a prior agreement, if they bought grain at harvest time and one of the parties wants to defer selling until close to the

next harvest when prices will be appreciably higher, the other partner can object and prefer a quick penny to a slow dollar.

62   Since there is no harvest in the Sabbatical year, the price of grain is certain to rise. In this case, the presumption is that the parties bought the grain for storage and later sale.

63   Tosephta 4:17.

64   The person who did the trading wants to pay the person who gave the money a lump sum and not be bothered with providing a detailed accounting. In general, this is (rabbinically) forbidden even though the trader would do it for his own convenience. But if it is obvious that the other's share in the gain would be more than a *mina*, only that the other party is ready to take less but receive his money immediately, it would be a permitted discount.

65   The trader is permitted to invest of his own money in the same commodity which he buys together with another in order to get a better price for the larger order. But when he sells, he has to sell the quantiity for which he is trustee first and only then may he sell for his own account, when it is to be expected that the large quantity will have lowered the price somewhat.

66   Tosephta 4:21.

67   Without specific instructions.

68   This would be illicit use of another person's money.

69   This remark does not belong here; it is repeated as Halakhah 9:3. It is a commentary on Tosephta 4:22, Notes 56-58. *Or zarua'* (vol. 2. p. 93, #339) quotes it as the Yerushalmi's commentary to that Tosephta.

70   A sharecropper is not permitted to leave a field fallow (unless it is good agricultural practice in crop rotation and done with the landlord's knowledge). He cannot say that he is required only to deliver 50% of the gain, which means 0 if there is no gain. שפה means "to serve food".

71   When given to him for 50% of the net gain.

72   *Or zarua'* (Note 69) quotes the Yerushalmi 9:3 as leaving the question unanswered, but adds that in Chapter 4 the answer is: He is not liable.

73   Tosephta 4:8 (*Tosefta ki-Fshutah Bava Meṣ'ia* p. 198), Babli 72b/73a.

74   The other person takes the merchandise, brings it to the high-priced place, sells it there, and pays the owner on his return. In the meantime he has the use of the money he received for the sale. If this second person is responsible for any accidents, the original owner gets a "premium for

waiting" in that he does not have to spend time and money for the trip and does not need insurance; this is rabbinically forbidden. But if the risk remains the original owner's, it is a legitimate business deal and permitted.

75 They collect produce from farmers at a stated low rate, transport it to a highprice city, sell it there and buy supplies cheaper in the city than in the countryside, sell in the countryside and pay the farmers at the end. They do business without investing their own money.

76 In Tosephta and Babli: "They do not have to worry about interest prohibitions." This has to be understood here also.

77 Then no interest would be due and interest restrictions do not apply.

78 The donkey driver is the farmer's agent for selling the latter's produce. Interest rules do not apply to agency.

79 From E, missing in L by scribal error.

80 Since the donkey driver has to pay the farmer for his grain, irrespective of what happened on the road, he cannot be an agent.

81 An agent is not liable for accidents only if he strictly acts in the principal's interest. If he is permitted to use the other's money for his own trades, be becomes liable as a borrower while remaining an agent (Babli 94a).

82 This really is the same question again. An agent cannot be responsible for part of the merchandise if he is not responsible for the entirety. How can the donkey-driver be an agent if he collects produce from many farmers? S. Lieberman follows R. Eliahu Fulda in assigning these last sentences to Halakhah 5:7.

83 Usually an agent is told what he is expected to do. If he is a buying agent, he is expected to pay the price which the principal agreed to. But here, he is only required to pay the farmer at the agreed local rate; he can reasonably be expected to be liable for accidents even if he acts as an agent.

(fol. 10a) **משנה ו:** שָׁמִין פָּרָה וַחֲמוֹר וְכָל־דָּבָר שֶׁדַּרְכּוֹ לַעֲשׂוֹת וְלֶאֱכוֹל. מָקוֹם שֶׁנָּהֲגוּ לַחֲלוֹק אֶת הַוְּלָדוֹת מִיַּד חוֹלְקִין מָקוֹם שֶׁנָּהֲגוּ לְנַדֵּל יְנַדְּלוּ. רַבָּן שִׁמְעוֹן בֶּן גַּמְלִיאֵל אוֹמֵר שָׁמִין עֵגֶל עַל אִמּוֹ וְסַיָּיח עִם אִמּוֹ וּמַפְרִין עַל שָׂדֵהוּ וְאֵינוֹ חוֹשֵׁשׁ מִשּׁוּם רִיבִּית.

**Mishnah 6**: One hands a cow or a donkey over for care as well as anything which works and eats[84]. At a place where one usually divides the young immediately, one divides; at a place where one usually raises them, they should be raised. Rabban Simeon ben Gamliel says, one hands over a calf with its mother, a foal with its mother[85], and one invests in improving a field and does not worry about interest[86].

84 This is the text also of most Mishnah and Babli mss.; only the *editio princeps* of the Babli follows Rashi in reading: "One estimates the value of a cow and a donkey and anything which works and eats *for the middle*," i. e., the owner of the animal and the person who cares for it and is the beneficiary of its work split any increase or loss arising from the animal 50-50. Maimonides, whose Mishnah text is identical with the Yerushalmi and the mss., does not comment on it, but in his Code (*Šutafim* 8:3) formulates that the owner and the tenant farmer share profits on a 50-50 basis; he does not mention that the farmer has to carry 50% of the risk and even 100% of the risk if the animal dies through of his fault (Note 102). In modern terms the Mishnah states that an investment is not a loan, and that the worker and the capitalist who provides the means of production are free to conclude any contractual arrangement.

While the dictionaries and the commentators identify this שם with Aramaic שם "to estimate, determine its value", for the translation it is identified with Arabic سام،سوم "to impose a task" ("to let graze freely" in the *af'ala* stem). In the Halakhah, both meanings are used.

85 Even though the calf is not productive, the tenant farmer is obligated to provide food and care for his share in its future value.

86 It is legal for the tenant farmer to ask the landlord to invest money in his field, to be repaid by future increases in yield. That is yield of investment, rather than interest.

(10b line 49) **הלכה ו**: שָׁמִין פָּרָה וַחֲמוֹר כול'. תַּנֵּי. שָׁם הוּא אָדָם מֵחֲבֵירוֹ בְּהֵמָה בִּמְנָת לַעֲלוֹת לוֹ וְלָד אֶחָד וְגִיזָה אַחַת לַשָּׁנָה. תַּרְנְגוֹלֶת בִּי בֵּצִים לַחוֹדֶשׁ. הַשָּׁמָה תַּרְנְגוֹלֶת מְחַבֵּירָתָהּ מִיטַפֶּלֶת בְּאֶפְרוֹחִין כָּל־זְמַן שֶׁצְּרִיכִין לְאִימָן.

מִיטַפֵּל בִּבְהֵמָה דַקָּה ל יוֹם וּבְגַסָּה נ יוֹם. רבי יוֹסֵי אוֹמֵר. (בְּגַסָּה) [בַּדַּקָּה] ג
חֳדָשִׁים מִפְּנֵי שֶׁטִּיפוּלָה מְרוּבָּה. יוֹתֵר מִיכֵּן חֶלְקוֹ שֶׁלְּבַעַל הַבַּיִת וְהִשְׁוָה עָלָיו.
הַכֹּל כְּמִנְהַג הַמְּדִינָה. מַהוּ חֶלְקוֹ שֶׁלְּבַעַל הַבַּיִת וְהִשְׁוָה עָלָיו. בַּר נָשׁ דִּיהַב
לְחַבְרֵיהּ ק דִּינָרִין ק דִּינָרִין עַבְדוֹן כ דִּינָרִין. אָהֵן נָסַב פַּלְגָּא וְאָהֵן פַּלְגָּא שֶׁלְּבַעַל הַבַּיִת
אִיתְעַבְדוּן עֲלוֹי קֶרֶן. בְּנֵי אֵינָשׁ עַבְדִין כֵּן. אֶלָּא נָסְבִין וְיָהֲבִין וּבְסֵיפָה פַּלְגִין.
הַשָּׁם בְּהֵמָה לַחֲבֵירוֹ חַיָּיב בָּאַחֲרָיוּתוֹ. בִּבְהֵמָה טְמֵיאָה יִ"ב חֹדֶשׁ. בָּאָדָם כ"ד
חֹדֶשׁ. מָקוֹם שֶׁנָּהֲגוּ לַעֲלוֹת שָׂכָר כַּתָּף לְמָעוֹת מַעֲלִין. וּוְלָדוֹת לַבְּהֵמָה מַעֲלִין.
הַכֹּל כְּמִנְהַג הַמְּדִינָה.

**Halakhah 6**: "One hands a cow or a donkey over for care," etc. It was stated: "A person may receive from another an animal on condition to deliver to him one lamb and one shearing per year, a chicken for ten eggs a month. [87]The woman receiving a chicken has to care for the chicks as long as those depend on their mother. [88]One cares for small animals 30 days and for large animals 50 days. Rebbi Yose says, for (large) [small][89] animals three months because they need special care. After that, he gives the owner his part equally, everything according to local practice." What means "he gives the owner his part equally"? A person gave to another 100 denars; they produced 20 denars. Each takes half of it; the half of the owner remains with him as capital[90]. Do people do that[91]? But they trade, and at the end they divide it up. [92]"A person receiving an animal for care is responsible for it, for an unclean animal[93] twelve months, for a human 24 months[94]. At a place where work[95] is compensated separately, one pays; for offspring of animals, one pays[96], everything following local custom."

---

87  Tosephta 5:5. For the entire Halakhah, the basic commentary is S. Lieberman, *Tosefta ki-Fshutah Bava Meṣi'a* pp. 211-216.

88  Tosephta 5:7, Babli 69a.

89  "Large" is L's, "small" the E text. The latter is supported by Tosephta, Babli, Mishnah *Bekhorot* 4:1.

90  The contract is amended automatically to increase the owner's share in the herd.
91  In E: People do not do that.
92  Tosephta 5:5, Babli 69a.
93  A horse or a donkey, which are not kosher. This is the minimum duration of a contract for care of such animals; the contract period can be shorter for edible animals raised for their meat.
94  The contract period for a wet-nurse.
95  Work exceeding the daily routine.
96  The terms described at the start of the paragraph are not prescriptive; without special written stipulation local custom prevails.

(10b line 61) רַבָּן שִׁמְעוֹן בֶּן גַּמְלִיאֵל אוֹמֵר שָׁמִין כּוֹל'. אֲפִילוּ בְּמָקוֹם שֶׁמַּעֲלִין שְׂכַר כַּתָּף לְמָעוֹת. וְאֵינוּ חוֹשֵׁשׁ מִשּׁוּם רִבִּית.

הַשָּׂם בְּהֵמָה מֵחֲבֵירוֹ עַד כַּמָּה חַיָּיב בְּאַחֲרָיוּתָהּ. סוּמְכוֹס אוֹמֵר. הַגּוֹדָרוֹת יב חֹדֶשׁ. בְּאַתוֹנוֹת כ"ד חֹדֶשׁ. עָמַד עָלָיו בְּתוֹךְ הַזְּמַן שָׁמִין לוֹ. אַחַר הַזְּמַן אֵין שָׁמִין לוֹ. לֹא דוֹמֶה טִיפּוּל שָׁנָה אַחַת לִשְׁתֵּי שָׁנִים.

הַשָּׂם בְּהֵמָה לַחֲבֵירוֹ אֵין פָּחוֹת מִי"ב חֹדֶשׁ. מֵתָה בַּבּוֹסְיָא יָהַב כּוּלֵּיהּ. דְּלָא בְּבוֹסְיָא יָהַב פַּלְגָּא. כֵּיצַד. שָׁמָהּ בְּמָנֶה וְהִשְׁבִּיחָהּ וְשָׁוָה מָאתַיִם. מֵתָה בַּבּוֹסְיָא יָהַב שִׁשָּׁה שֶׁלְּזָהָב. דְּלָא בְּבוֹסְיָא יָהַב חֲמִשִּׁים זוּז. הִכְחִישָׁה וְיָפָה חֲמִשִּׁים זוּז. מֵתָה בַּבּוֹסְיָא יָהַב ג' שֶׁלְּזָהָב. דְּלָא בְּבוֹסְיָא יָהַב חֲמִשִּׁים זוּז.

הַשָּׂם בְּהֵמָה מֵחֲבֵירוֹ אֵין פָּחוֹת מִי"ב חֹדֶשׁ. עָשָׂה בָהּ כָּל־יְמוֹת הַחַמָּה וְאָמַר לְמָכְרָהּ בִּימוֹת הַגְּשָׁמִים כּוֹפִין אוֹתוֹ שֶׁיֹּאכִילָהּ כָּל־יְמוֹת הַגְּשָׁמִים. הֶאֱכִיל כָּל־יְמוֹת הַגְּשָׁמִים וְאָמַר לְמָכְרָהּ בִּימוֹת הַחַמָּה כּוֹפִין אוֹתוֹ שֶׁיַּעֲשֶׂה בָהּ כָּל־יְמוֹת הַחַמָּה.

[97]"Rabban Simeon ben Gamliel says, one hands over, etc., even at a place where one pays additional money for exertion, and one is not worried because of interest.[85]"

[98]"If one accepts an animal for care from another person, how long does he have to care for it? Symmachos says, small asses twelve months, adult donkeys 24 months[99]. If he terminates the care in the middle of the

term, one estimates for him; after the term one does not estimate for him, but care for one year is not comparable to two years[100]."

[101]"If it dies because of gross negligence, he gives everything; not because of gross negligence, he gives half[102]. How is this? It was estimated as one *mina*[103] and improved and now is worth 200. If it dies because of gross negligence, he gives six gold denars[104]; if not because of gross negligence, he gives 50 *zuz*.[105]"

[106]"If one accepts an animal for care from another person, it is for no less than twelve months. If he occupied himself with it all through the summer and he says to sell it, one forces him to feed it all through the winter. If he fed it all through the winter and he wants to sell it in the summer, one forces him to occupy himself with it all through the summer.[107]"

97   Tosephta 5:5.
98   Tosephta 5:8; Babli 69a.
99   In E and both other sources, the minimum time is 18 months for adult she-asses, 24 months for the young. This seems reasonable.

In E, the name Symmachos is correctly spelled סימכוס.

The translation follows S. Lieberman (*l. c.* Note 87 p. 213-4) in identifying גודרות (in E: העדרות) as γαϊδάρια, plural of γαϊδάριον, "small donkey", a word frequently found in Egyptian papyri (it seems originally Persian *gaudar*, "calf"). He also notes that since in all of Talmudic literature חֲמוֹר denotes both male and female donkeys, one may assume that the word אָתוֹן, "she-ass" in Biblical texts, also denotes both male and female donkeys.

100   If one of the parties wants to terminate the contract (for cause, as shown later in the Halakhah), the determination of the difference in value of the animals at the start and at the end of the time of care is a matter for the courts. Otherwise, this is not the case since the sale price will determine the final value. It is noted that the increase in value of calves is not constant in time; the increase in the first year of a two-year contract is less than half of the final value.

101   Tosephta 5:11-12.

102 Since the tenant farmer is given a 50% interest in the gain, he also must bear a 50% risk of loss. The element of risk is what distinguishes investment from loan and exempts the transaction from the laws of interest. If the death is due to gross negligence of the caregiver, the owner may sue him for his loss.

103 At the start of the contract period.

104 150 silver denars. He pays 100 for the animal and 50 for the owner's part in the improvement which was lost through the caregiver's fault.

105 Half the original value.

106 Tosephta 5:9.

107 If either of the parties wants to terminate the contract before its expiration date, the other party can go to court and force the continuation until the end of the contract period.

(10b line 74) תַּנֵי. רַבָּן שִׁמְעוֹן בֶּן גַּמְלִיאֵל אוֹמֵר מַפְרִין עַל שָׂדֵהוּ וְאֵין חוֹשֵׁשׁ מִשּׁוּם רִבִּית. כֵּיצַד. קִיבֵּל הֵימֶינוּ בְּי׳ כּוֹרִין חִטִּין. אָמַר לוֹ. תֶּן לִי סֶלַע אֶחָד וַאֲנִי נוֹתֵן לָךְ י״ב כּוֹרִין לַגּוֹרֶן מוּתָּר. רִבִּי יוֹחָנָן אָמַר. מִפְּנֵי שֶׁהַשָּׂדֶה מְצוּיָה לְהִתְבָּרֵךְ. רֵישׁ לָקִישׁ אָמַר. נַעֲשָׂה כְּמַשְׂכִּיר לוֹ שָׂדֶה בְּיוֹקֶר. מַה בֵּינֵיהוֹן. חֲנוּת וּסְפִינָה. מָאן דָּמַר. מִפְּנֵי שֶׁהַשָּׂדֶה מְצוּיָה לְהִתְבָּרֵךְ. מַפְרִין עַל חֲנוּת וּסְפִינָה. מָאן דָּמַר. נַעֲשָׂה כְּמַשְׂכִּיר לוֹ שָׂדֶה בְּיוֹקֶר. חֲנוּת וּסְפִינָה אֵין מַפְרִין. אָמַר רִבִּי יַעֲקֹב בַּר אָחָא. בְּפֵירוּשׁ פְּלִיגֵי. רִבִּי יוֹחָנָן אָמַר. מַפְרִין עַל חֲנוּת וּסְפִינָה. רֵישׁ לָקִישׁ אָמַר. אֵין מַפְרִין. מַתְנִיתָא מְסַייְעָא לְרֵישׁ לָקִישׁ. אֵין מַפְרִין עַל חֲנוּת וּסְפִינָה וְעַל דָּבָר שֶׁאֵינוֹ עוֹשֶׂה בְגוּפוֹ.

[108]It was stated: "Rabban Simeon ben Gamliel said, one invests in improving a field and does not worry about interest. How is this? One leased a field for ten *kor* of wheat and said to him, give me a tetradrachma[109] and I shall give you twelve *kor* at threshing time, it is permitted." Rebbi Johanan said, because the field may bring an extraordinary yield[110]. Rebbi Simeon ben Laqish said, it is as if he increased the rent for the field. What is the difference between them? A store or a ship[111]. According to him who said, because the field may bring an extraordinary yield, one invests in a store or a ship[112]. According

to him who said, it is as if he increased the rent for the field, one may not invest in a store or a ship[113]. Rebbi Jacob bar Aḥa said, they disagree explicitly: Rebbi Joḥanan said, one invests in a store or a ship. Rebbi Simeon ben Laqish said, one may not invest in a store or a ship, nor in anything which is not invested in the object itself[114].

108 Tosephta 5:13, Babli 69b.

109 In the parallel sources: 200 denars, 2 *minas*. This seems to be the correct text since it is unlikely that much improvement can be bought for 4 silver denars, and it is incomprehensible that the rent should increase by 50 silver denars a year for a loan of 4. But in E the text is: תֶּן לִי סֶלַע אַחַת וַאֲנִי נוֹתֵן לָךְ כּוֹר אֶחָד. "Give me one tetradrachma and I shall give you one *kor*."

110 The improvement of the object justifies the increase in rent.

111 As will be noted at the end, this refers to an additional investment by the owner in merchandise to be sold in the store or transported on the ship.

112 A larger inventory may yield larger earnings.

113 A perpetual rent for an investment in merchandise would be interest.

114 R. Simeon ben Laqish agrees that an investment in a renovation of the store, or to provide the ship with better sails or steering gear, is legitimate (opinion of Rav Naḥman in the Babli).

(fol. 10a) **משנה ז:** אֵין מְקַבְּלִין צֹאן בַּרְזֶל מִיִּשְׂרָאֵל מִפְּנֵי שֶׁהוּא רִיבִּית. אֲבָל מְקַבְּלִין צֹאן בַּרְזֶל מֵהַגּוֹיִם וְלוֹוִין מֵהֶן וּמַלְוִין אוֹתָן בְּרִיבִּית וְכֵן בְּגֵר תּוֹשָׁב. מַלְוֶה הוּא יִשְׂרָאֵל מָעוֹתָיו שֶׁל נָכְרִי מִדַּעַת הַנָּכְרִי אֲבָל לֹא מִדַּעַת יִשְׂרָאֵל.

**Mishnah 7:** One may not receive mortmain property[115] from a Jew because that is interest. But one may receive mortmain property from Gentiles, one may borrow from them and lend them on interest, and similarly from a sojourner[116]. A Jew can lend a Gentile's money on interest by the Gentile's instruction but not by a Jew's[117].

115  Property given in perpetuity, for which rental is due in perpetuity irrespective of whether the original objects are still in existence. Risk-free income is interest; this also is the definition of interest in modern Mathematics of Finance.

116  A Gentile who follows the seven Noaḥide commandments, in particular the prohibition of idolatry.

117  In particular, not his own initiative.

(10c line 8) **הלכה ז:** אֵין מְקַבְּלִין צֹאן בַּרְזֶל מִיִשְׂרָאֵל כול׳. אֵי זֶהוּ צֹאן בַּרְזֶל. הָיוּ לְפָנָיו מֵאָה צֹאן. אָמַר לוֹ. הֲרֵי הֵן עֲשׂוּיוֹת עָלָיו בְּק שֶׁלְּזָהָב וְלָדָן וַחֲלָבָן וְגִיזָּתָן שֶׁלָּךְ וְאִם מֵתוּ אַתְּ חַיָּיב בְּאַחֲרָיוּתֵיהֶן וְאַתְּ מַעֲלֶה לִי סֶלַע שֶׁלְּכָל־אַחַת וְאַחַת מִשֶּׁלָּךְ בָּאַחֲרוֹנָה. אָסוּר.

**Halakhah 7**: "One may not receive mortmain property from a Jew," etc. [118]"What is mortmain property? He had 100 sheep and told another: They are valued for you at 100 gold [denars]; their young, their milk, and their shearings are yours, but if they die you are liable for them and you pay me a tetradrachma for every one of them at the end of the year[119]. This is forbidden[119a]."

118  Tosephta 5:13.

119  This example has an interest rate of 16%.

119a  In the Tosephta: permitted.

(10c line 12) רְבִּי יִרְמְיָה בָּעֵי. תַּמָּן אַתְּ מַר. נוֹשֵׂא שָׂכָר חַיָּיב עַל הָאוֹנָסִין אָסוּר. וָכָא אַתְּ מַר. נוֹשֵׂא שָׂכָר חַיָּיב עַל הָאוֹנָסִין מוּתָּר. לֹא פְעָמִים שֶׁמַּתְּנָה שׁוֹמֵר חִנָּם לִהְיוֹת כְּשׁוֹאֵל. רְבִּי יִרְמְיָה בָּעֵי. תַּמָּן אַתְּ מַר. צֹאן בַּרְזֶל לָרִאשׁוֹן. וָכָא אַתְּ מַר. לַשֵּׁינִי. אָמַר רְבִּי יוֹסֵי. תַּמָּן שֶׁעִיקָּרָן לָרִאשׁוֹן וְלָדָן לָרִאשׁוֹן. בְּרַם הָכָא עִיקָּרָן לַשֵּׁינִי וְלָדָן לַשֵּׁינִי.

Rebbi Jeremiah asked: There[120] you say that a paid trustee who would be responsible for accidents is forbidden. But here[121] you say that a paid trustee who is responsible for accidents is permitted. Does it not happen that an unpaid trustee agrees to be like a borrower[81,122]?

Rebbi Jeremiah asked: There¹²³ you say that mortmain belongs to the first, but here you say to the second¹²⁴. Rebbi Yose said, there since the essence belongs to the first, the offspring are counted for the first¹²⁵. But here the essence belongs to the second since the offspring belong to the second¹²⁶.

120   Mishnah 5, which forbids handing over calves to be raised unless the rancher is paid for his work.

121   Mishnah 6, which allows such contracts for adult animals without restrictions.

122   The quote from Halakhah 5 is slightly out of place here. Since the rancher is supposed to use the animal for his purposes, he cannot be under the rules of the unpaid trustee; he is a paid trustee. But this is really irrelevant for the question; the main point is that the transaction involves an element of risk which shields it from the laws of interest, Note 115.

123   Mishnah *Bekhorot* 2:4, quoted in the Babli 70b. The offspring of a Gentile's mortmain animals in the hands of a Jewish tenant farmer are not subject to the laws of the firstling since the mothers are considered the Gentile's property.

124   In the Halakhah here, the offspring is defined as the tenant's property.

125   Since the owner can repossess the mother if the tenant is in arrears with his payment, the Gentile retains a monetary interest in the mother. This is enough to free the offspring from the rules of firstlings.

126   As explained in the Halakhah. For the majority opinion in Mishnah *Bekhorot* 2:4, the offspring's offspring is subject to the rules of firstlings for the same reason.

(10c line 16) וְלֹוִין מֵהֶן וּמַלְוִין אוֹתָן בְּרִבִּית כול׳. רִבִּי אוֹמֵר. תּוֹשָׁב הָאָמוּר בְּעֶבֶד עִבְרִי אֵינִי יוֹדֵעַ מַה טִיבוֹ. גֵּר צֶדֶק הָאָמוּר בְּרִבִּית אֵינִי יוֹדֵעַ מַה טִיבוֹ.

"One may borrow from them and lend them on interest, and similarly from a sojourner." Rebbi said, I do not know the definition of "sojourner" quoted in reference to the Hebrew slave. I do not know the definition of "proselyte" quoted in reference to interest¹²⁷.

127  In the Babli, 91a, "sojourner" is quoted in connection with interest, "proselyte" in connection with the Hebrew slave. There is no need to adapt the Babli's reading.

The first reference is to *Lev.* 25:47: "If the hand of a stranger *and* sojourner with you be opulent but your brother wax poor next to him and be sold to the stranger sojourner with you or to the essence of the stranger's family." Rebbi notes that the verse implies that "stranger *and* sojourner" is the same as "stranger sojourner". Therefore, he objects to the usual explanation (*Qiddušin* 20b; *Sifra* ad 25:47):

"Stranger" is the proselyte; "sojourner" is the Noaḥide stranger, "stranger's family" is the idolater, "essence" is an idolatrous temple. But he has no better interpretation to offer.

The second question is about *Lev.* 25:35,36: "If your brother wax poor and his hand totter with you; you have to support him, stranger *and* sojourner and living with you. Do not take from him interest and increase, . . ." Here again, *Sifra* explains that "stranger" is the proselyte; "sojourner" is the Noaḥide stranger, but the second statement contradicts our Mishnah.

(10c line 18) מַלְוֶה יִשְׂרָאֵל מָעוֹת שֶׁל נָכְרִי מִדַּעַת נָכְרִי אֲבָל לֹא מִדַּעַת יִשְׂרָאֵל. יִשְׂרָאֵל שֶׁלָּוָה מִגּוֹי וּבִיקֵּשׁ לְהַחֲזִירָם לוֹ. אָמַר לוֹ יִשְׂרָאֵל אַחֵר. תְּנֵם לִי וַאֲנִי נוֹתֵן כְּדֶרֶךְ שֶׁאַתְּ נוֹתֵן לוֹ. אָסוּר. וְאִם הֶעֱמִידוֹ עִם הַגּוֹי מוּתָּר. [אָמַר רבִּי יוֹסֵי. וְהוּא שֶׁהֶעֱמִידוֹ עִם הַגּוֹי.]

גּוֹי שֶׁלָּוָה מִיִּשְׂרָאֵל וּבִיקֵּשׁ לְהַחֲזִירָם לוֹ. אָמַר לוֹ יִשְׂרָאֵל אַחֵר. תְּנֵם לִי וַאֲנִי מַעֲלֶה לוֹ רִיבִּית. מוּתָּר. וְאִם הֶעֱמִידוֹ אֵצֶל יִשְׂרָאֵל אָסוּר. אָמַר רבִּי יוֹסֵי. וְהוּא שֶׁהֶעֱמִידוֹ אֵצֶל יִשְׂרָאֵל.

יִשְׂרָאֵל שֶׁלָּוָה וְגוֹי מִיִּשְׂרָאֵל וְנִתְגַּיֵּיר. בֵּין שֶׁזְּקָפָן עַד שֶׁלֹּא נִתְגַּיֵּיר בֵּין מִשֶּׁנִּתְגַּיֵּיר גּוֹבֶה הַקֶּרֶן וְלֹא הָרִיבִּית  אֲבָל גּוֹי שֶׁלָּוָה מִיִּשְׂרָאֵל וְנִתְגַּיֵּיר. אִם עַד שֶׁלֹּא נִתְגַּיֵּיר זְקָפָן עָלָיו בְּמִלְוָה גּוֹבֶה הַקֶּרֶן וְהָרִיבִּית. מִשֶּׁנִּתְגַּיֵּיר גּוֹבֶה הַקֶּרֶן וְלֹא הָרִיבִּית. בַּר קַפָּרָא אוֹמֵר. גּוֹבֶה הַקֶּרֶן וְאֶת הָרִיבִּית. אָמַר רבִּי יַעֲקֹב בַּר אֲחָא. טַעֲמָא דְּבַר קַפָּרָא. מִכֵּיוָן שֶׁאַתְּ מַבְרִיחוֹ מִן הָרִיבִּית אַף הוּא נַעֲשָׂה גֵּר שֶׁקֶר.

"A Jew can lend a Gentile's money on interest by the Gentile's instruction but not by a Jew's." [128]"A Jew had loaned money from a Gentile and wanted to return it when another Jew said to him, give it to me and I shall pay him the same rate as you are paying; this is forbidden[129]. But if he introduced him to the Gentile, it is permitted." [Rebbi Yose said, only if he let him stand with the Gentile.][130]

[131]"A Gentile had borrowed money from a Jew and wanted to return it when another Jew said to him, give it to me and I shall pay him the same rate as you are paying; this is permitted. But if he introduced him to the Gentile, it is forbidden." Rebbi Yose said, only if he let him stand with the Gentile.

[132]"A Jew had borrowed money from a Gentile or a Gentile from a Jew when he converted. Whether the loan was finalized before or after his conversion, he can collect the principal but not the interest.[133] But if a Gentile had borrowed money from a Jew and converted, if the loan was finalized before he converted, he can collect principal and interest; after he converted, he can collect principal but not interest. Bar Qappara said, he can collect both principal and interest." Rebbi Jacob bar Aḥa said, Bar Qappara's reason is that if you exempt him from interest he is turned into an insincere proselyte[134].

128 Tosephta 5:16; Babli 71b. For the remainder of the Halakhah, cf. *Tosefta kiFshutah Bava Meṣi'a* pp. 220-229.

129 If the Jew receives the money from the Jew not on the Gentile's command; this is forbidden by the Mishnah.

130 Added from E supported by Nachmanides's quote from the Yerushalmi in his *Novellae ad* 71b.

The question is, what is the role of the Gentile in this matter. Even though R. Yasa holds in *Demay* 6:1 (Note 10) and *Terumot* 1:1 (Note 76) that a Gentile can appoint a Jew as his agent, and the Tosephta can be interpreted in this sense that the borrower has to get the lender's agreement to transfer the loan to another borrower, R. Yose denies this and requires that the loan actually be transferred by the Gentile. The Amora R. Yose was the student of R. Jeremiah, student of R. Ze'ira, student of R. Yasa.

131   Tosephta 5:17; Babli 71b. As long as the money is given by the Gentile, it is permitted. R. Yose holds that the Gentile cannot be the Jew's agent; therefore, the transaction is prohibited only if the Jew is an agent, not if the Jew agrees to the Gentile's action.

132   Tosephta 5:21, Babli 72a.

133   E has a longer text:

יִשְׂרָאֵל שֶׁלָּוָה מִגּוֹי וְגוֹי מִישְׂרָאֵל וְנִתְגַּיֵּיר.  בֵּין שֶׁזְּקָפָן עַד שֶׁלֹּא נִתְגַּיֵּיר בֵּין מִשֶּׁנִּתְגַּיֵּיר גּוֹבֶה הַקֶּרֶן וְלֹא הָרִיבִּית [דִּבְרֵי רִבִּי מֵאִיר.  רִבִּי יוֹסֵה אוֹמֵר.  יִשְׂרָאֵל שֶׁלָּוָה מִגּוֹי וְנִתְגַּיֵּיר.  בֵּין שֶׁזְּקָפָן עַד שֶׁלֹּא נִתְגַּיֵּיר בֵּין שֶׁזְּקָפָן עָלָיו מִשֶּׁנִּתְגַּיֵּיר גּוֹבֶה הַקֶּרֶן וְאֶת הָרִיבִּית.]

A Jew had borrowed money from a Gentile or a Gentile from a Jew when he converted. Whether the loan was finalized before or after his conversion, he can collect the principal but not the interest [the words of Rebbi Meïr. Rebbi Yose says, if the Jew had borrowed money from a Gentile, whether the loan was finalized before or after his conversion, he can collect both principal and interest.]

The text attributed to R. Meïr is the same in Tosephta and Babli. The text attributed to R. Yose is the same in the Babli; it is the same as attributed to Bar Qappara in the Halakhah. In the Tosephta, R. Yose (the Tanna) holds that the Gentile debtor cannot pay interest after conversion but a Jewish debtor of a loan executed before the Gentile's conversion has to pay interest (since the obligation he entered into was legitimate at the time it was assumed.) The E text as it stands is either superfluous or defective; the L text certainly is defective since the third sentence of the paragraph contradicts the second. The two sentences most likely belong to two different authors, as attested by the Tosephta.

134   Who therefore might have difficulty in finding a Jewish mate; his rule is to the ex-Gentile's benefit.

(10c line 30) לוֶוה אָדָם מִבָּנָיו וּבְנוֹתָיו בְּרִיבִּית אֶלָּא שֶׁמְּחַנְּחָן בְּרִיבִּית.  אָמַר רַב.  כְּגוֹן אֲנָא לְרַבָּה בַּר בַּר חָנָה וְרַבָּה בַּר בַּר חָנָה לִי.  לֹא יְהֵא אָדָם לוֶוה בְּשֶׁקֶל וּמַלְוֶה בְּסֶלַע.  אֲבָל גּוֹי לוֶוה בְּשֶׁקֶל וּמַלְוֶה בְּסֶלַע.

יִשְׂרָאֵל לֹוֶה מִגּוֹי וְגוֹי מִיִשְׂרָאֵל וְיִשְׂרָאֵל נַעֲשֶׂה לוֹ עָרֵב וְאֵינוֹ חוֹשֵׁשׁ מִשּׁוּם רִבִּית. יִשְׂרָאֵל שֶׁמִּינָה גוֹי אֶפִּיטְרוֹפָּא אוֹ סַנְטָר מוּתָּר לִלְווֹת מִמֶּנּוּ בְּרִיבִּית. וְגוֹי שֶׁמִּינָה יִשְׂרָאֵל אֶפִּיטְרוֹפָּא אוֹ סַנְטָר אָסוּר לִלְווֹת מִמֶּנּוּ בְּרִיבִּית. מָעוֹת גוֹי שֶׁהָיוּ מוּפְקָדִין אֵצֶל יִשְׂרָאֵל אָסוּר לִלְווֹת בְּרִיבִּית. מָעוֹת יִשְׂרָאֵל שֶׁהָיוּ מוּפְקָדִין אֵצֶל גוֹי מוּתָּר לִלְווֹת מִמֶּנּוּ בְּרִיבִּית. זֶה הַכְּלָל. כָּל־שֶׁהוּא בָּאַחֲרָיוּת יִשְׂרָאֵל אָסוּר. בָּאַחֲרָיוּת גוֹי מוּתָּר.

[135]"A person may borrow from his sons or daughters on interest, but he educates them for interest." Rav said, e. g., I from Rabba bar bar Ḥana or Rabba bar bar Ḥana from me. "A person may not borrow for a *šeqel* and lend out for a tetradrachma; but a Gentile may borrow for a *šeqel* and lend out for a tetradrachma.[136]"

[137]A Jew may borrow from a Gentile, and a Gentile from a Jew, and a Jew can become his guarantor without any worries about interest. If a Jew appointed a Gentile as guardian or steward[138], it is permitted to borrow from him on interest. But if a Gentile appointed a Jew as guardian or steward, it is prohibited to borrow from him on interest.

[139]It is forbidden to borrow on interest a Gentile's money deposited with a Jew; it is permitted to borrow on interest a Jew's money deposited with a Gentile. This is the principle: Anything which the Jew has to warrant[140] is forbidden, what the Gentile has to warrant is permitted.

135  Tosephta 5:15; Babli 75a. The Babli version, "to lend his children and family" is presupposed here; otherwise Rav could not point to deals between him and his cousin's son Rabba bar bar Ḥana. The Babli prohibits this practice; it only permits deals between scholars who know that interest is forbidden and give the money as a gift.

136  A Jew cannot be a banker, taking deposits from Jews at 2% interest (one *šeqel* per *mina*) in order to lend to Gentiles at 4%. But a Gentile banker can take deposits from Jews or Gentiles to lend to other Jews at a higher rate.

137  Tosephta 5:20; quoted in Tosaphot 71b, *s. v.* בגון.

| | |
|---|---|
| 138 The word was identified by S. Lieberman as Latin *saltuarius*, administrator of an agricultural domain. Since the Gentile gives the loan, interest is permitted even if the capital is a Jew's. | 139 Tosephta 5:19.<br>140 Since the banker is obligated to pay his depositors even if a borrower defaults, the deposits are treated as the banker's property. |

(fol. 10a) **משנה ח:** אֵין פּוֹסְקִין עַל הַפֵּירוֹת עַד שֶׁיֵּצֵא הַשַּׁעַר. הָיָה הוּא תְּחִלָּה לַקּוֹצְרִים פּוֹסֵק עִמּוֹ עַל הַגָּדִישׁ וְעַל הֶעָבִיט שֶׁל עֲנָבִים וְעַל הַמַּטְעָן שֶׁל זֵיתִים וְעַל הַבֵּיצִין שֶׁל יוֹצֵר וְעַל הַסִּיד מִשְּׁיִּשְׁקַע כִּבְשָׁנוֹ. פּוֹסֵק עִמּוֹ עַל הַזֶּבֶל כָּל־יְמוֹת הַשָּׁנָה. רִבִּי יוֹסֵי אוֹמֵר אֵין פּוֹסֵק עַל הַזֶּבֶל עַד שֶׁיְּהֵא לוֹ זֶבֶל בָּאַשְׁפּוֹת. וַחֲכָמִים מַתִּירִין. פּוֹסֵק עִמּוֹ כְּשַׁעַר הַגָּבוֹהַּ. רִבִּי יְהוּדָה אוֹמֵר אַף עַל פִּי שֶׁלֹּא פָסַק עִמּוֹ כְּשַׁעַר הַגָּבוֹהַּ יָכוֹל הוּא לוֹמַר תֶּן לִי כָזֶה אוֹ תֶּן לִי אֶת מְעוֹתָיי.

**Mishnah 8**: One does not contract for produce until a rate was established[141]. If he was the first to harvest, he may contract[142] for the stack of sheaves, or the vat of grapes, or the barrel of olives, or for potter's clay and lime when it was loaded in his oven. One may contract for manure the entire year; Rebbi Yose says, one may not contract for manure unless he has manure on his dungheap, but the Sages permit it[143]. One contracts for wholesale price[144]; Rebbi Jehudah says, even if one did not contract for wholesale price he may say to him, give me some like that or return my money[145].

**משנה ט:** מַלְוֶה אָדָם אֶת אֲרִיסָיו חִיטִּין בְּחִיטִּין לְזֶרַע אֲבָל לֹא לֶאֱכֹל שֶׁהָיָה רַבָּן גַּמְלִיאֵל מַלְוֶה אֶת אֲרִיסָיו חִיטִּין בְּיוֹקֶר וְהוּזְלוּ אוֹ בְזוֹל וְהוֹקִירוּ וְנוֹטֵל מֵהֶן כְּשַׁעַר הַזּוֹל. לֹא שֶׁהֲלָכָה כֵן אֶלָּא שֶׁרָצָה לְהַחֲמִיר עַל עַצְמוֹ.

**Mishnah 9**: A person may lend to his sharecroppers wheat for wheat[146] as seed grain but not as food; but Rebban Gamliel lent his sharecroppers wheat grain; if at high price and the rate went down or at low price and the rate went up, he took from them at the low rate[147], not because this is practice but because he wanted to be strict with himself.

[141] In the absence of a functioning commodities exchange, a trader may not conclude a contract for future delivery of a commodity for a fixed price if he receives the money immediately. For he might have to buy the commodity later at a higher price and then the material delivered would convey a "premium for waiting". Once the rate is established and the seller can immediately hedge his trade by another contract, the transaction is legitimate even if the seller does not have any of the commodity which he sells and for which he is paid.

[142] Before a rate was established, the farmer can sell at any price level he sees fit if the basic produce is in his hand. He can sell grain on the basis of the harvested sheaves, wine on the basis of the harvested grapes, olive oil on the basis of the harvested olives. The potter can sell finished pottery once he has the raw material in storage.

[143] Since on a farm manure is continually produced.

[144] It is possible to write a contract that the money be paid now for a later delivery at the then going wholesale rate.

[145] Since money does not acquire (Chapter 4, Note 2), the buyer can require delivery at the going rate, if it is less than the one stipulated earlier, or annul the contract without being subject to judicial censure since he only paid for future delivery.

[146] He gives them a certain amount as seed grain and receives the same amount back at harvest time. As a commercial transaction this is forbidden since in case the rate at the new harvest was higher than at sowing time there would be an element of interest (cf. Note 180). But seed grain for the landlord's own domain is an investment, not a loan.

[147] The statement of the Mishnah would have been unnecessary since it already was stated that investments do not fall under the rules of loans, were it not that Rabban Gamliel (in the low-inflation environment of Nerva's and Trajan's times) used to provide his sharecroppers with seed grain for which he determined the price and then at the next harvest took it back at the lower of last year's and this year's prices, to avoid even the semblance of taking interest.

(10c line 39) **הלכה ח:** אֵין פּוֹסְקִין עַל הַפֵּירוֹת כול׳. מָהוּ לִפְסוֹק בְּשַׁעַר שֶׁלַּסִּירְקִי. רִבִּי יוֹחָנָן אָמַר. פּוֹסְקִין. רֵישׁ לָקִישׁ אָמַר. אֵין פּוֹסְקִין. רִבִּי בּוּן בַּר חִיָּיה בְּעָא קוֹמֵי רִבִּי זֵירָא. לֹא מִסְתַּבְּרָה דְּיוֹדֵי רֵישׁ לָקִישׁ לְרִבִּי יוֹחָנָן בְּשַׁעַר סִירְקִי שֶׁלְּצִיפּוֹרִין שֶׁאֵינָהּ פּוֹסֶקֶת. אָמַר רִבִּי בּוּן בַּר כַּהֲנָא. וְתָמָּה אֲנָא אֵיךְ רַבָּנָן פְּלִיגֵי. בֵּין פּוֹסֵק לַפֵּירוֹת בֵּין פּוֹסֵק לַמָּעוֹת בֵּין מִלְוָה לַפֵּירוֹת. אָמַר רִבִּי יִרְמְיָה. בְּמִלְוָה אִיתְפְּלִיגוּ. אֲבָל (בְּפוּנְדָּק) [בְּפִיסוֹק] כָּל־עַמָּא מוֹדוּ שֶׁאָסוּר. אָמַר רִבִּי יוֹסֵה. בְּפִיסוּק אִיתְפַּלְּגוּן. אֲבָל בְּמִלְוָה כָּל־עַמָּא מוֹדוּ שֶׁמּוּתָּר. דְּבֵי רִבִּי יַנַּאי אֲמְרֵי. פּוֹסְקִין עַל הַשַּׁחַת. רִבִּי יוֹסֵי בֶּן חֲנִינָה אוֹמֵר. אַף עַל חַלּוֹת דְּבָשׁ. רִבִּי יוֹחָנָן אוֹמֵר. כָּל־הָעֲיָירוֹת הַסְּמוּכוֹת לִטִיבֶּרְיָא כֵּיוָן שֶׁיָּצָא שַׁעַר שֶׁלְּטִיבֶּרְיָא פּוֹסְקִין.

**Halakhah 8**: "One does not contract for produce," etc. May one contract based on Saracens' rates[148]? Rebbi Joḥanan says, one may contract; Rebbi Simeon ben Laqish said, one may not contract[149]. Rebbi Abun bar Ḥiyya asked before Rebbi Ze'ira: Would it not be reasonable that Rebbi Simeon ben Laqish agree with Rebbi Joḥanan about rates of Saracens of Sepphoris, since that is uninterrupted[150]? Rebbi Abun bar Cahana said, I am wondering about what the rabbis disagree? Whether contracting for produce[151], or contracting for money[152], or a loan on produce[153]? Rebbi Jeremiah said, they disagree about a loan, but about (a hostelry) [a contract][154] everybody agrees that it is forbidden[155]. Rebbi Yose said, they disagree about a contract, but about a loan everybody agrees that it is permitted. In the House of Rebbi Yannai they said, one contracts for cattle feed[156]. Rebbi Yose ben Ḥanina said, also on honeycombs. Rebbi Joḥanan said, in all villages near Tiberias one contracts once the rate was established at Tiberias.

148 The rate quoted by Arab traders who in most cases are itinerant and might not be around at the time of delivery.

149  In the Babli, 72b, this is attributed to R. Johanan and accepted as practice.

150  While it is the going rate on a Saracens' market, it is not called "Saracens' rate".

151  Contracting for a fixed amount of produce.

152  Fixing the unit price.

153  Taking a loan of produce now to be repaid at the next harvest. If at that time the rate is expected to be higher, this certainly is forbidden (Note 6). But if 6 months before the next harvest the prices probably are higher, this might be permitted.

154  The text in parentheses is L's, a scribal error. The text in brackets is E's.

155  Since the seller cannot be sure to find the merchandise at a reasonable price if the exchange does not exist permanently.

156  Mostly taken year round from the spontaneous growth of fallow fields.

(10c line 48) הָיָה הוּא תְּחִילָּה לַקּוֹצְרִין פּוֹסֵק עִמּוֹ עַל הַגָּדִישׁ כול'. רַב אָמַר. מְחוּסָּר מַעֲשֵׂה אֶחָד פּוֹסֵק. מְחוּסָּר כַּמָּה מַעֲשִׂים אֵינוֹ פוֹסֵק. רִבִּי יוֹחָנָן וְרֵישׁ לָקִישׁ תְּרֵיהוֹן אָמְרִין. אֲפִילוּ מְחוּסָּר כַּמָּה מַעֲשִׂים פּוֹסֵק. וְהָא מַתְנִיתָא פְּלִיגָא עַל רַב. הָיָה הוּא תְּחִילָּה לַקּוֹצְרִין כול'.

"If he was the first to harvest, he may contract for the stack of sheaves," etc. Rav said, if one processing stage was missing, one may contract; if several processing stages were missing, one may not contract[157]. Rebbi Johanan and Rebbi Simeon ben Laqish both say, even if several processing stages were missing, one may contract. But the Mishnah disagrees with Rav: "If he was the first to harvest,[158]" etc.

157  The farmer may contract to sell his produce if no more than one operation is needed to prepare the produce as it is customarily delivered.

158  Since the vintner may contract to sell wine once he harvested his grapes, which have to be transported to the wine press, be pressed, the juice fermented, filtered, and cured, it is obvious that Rav is in error. In the Babli 74a, Rav is quoted as permitting two processing stages but not three; Samuel represents the opinion here attributed to the Galilean Sages.

## HALAKHAH 8

(10c line 52) אַבָּא בַּר זְמִינָא יְהַב חַד דֵּינָר לַקַּפֵּילָא וּנְסַב מִינֵּיהּ בְּשָׁעָה זְלִילָה דְכָל־שַׁתָּא. וְלֹא מוֹדֵי רַב. רִבִּי חִיָּיה רוֹבָה הֲוָה לֵיהּ כִּיתָּן. אָתוּ חֲמָרַיָּא מִיזְבְּנָא מִינֵּיהּ. אָמַר לוֹן. לֵית בְּדַעְתִּי מְזַבְּנָתָהּ כְּדוֹן אֶלָּא בְפוּרְיָא. אָמְרוּ לֵיהּ. זַבְּנָהּ לָן כְּדוֹן מַה דְּאַתְּ עָתִיד מִיזַבְּנָתָהּ בְּפוּרְיָא. אֲתָא שְׁאַל לְרִבִּי. אֲמַר לֵיהּ. אָסוּר. נְפַק קְבָעָהּ בְּמַתְנִיתָא וְתַנֵּי כֵן. הָיָה חַיָּיב לוֹ מָעוֹת וּבָא לִיטּוֹל מִמֶּנּוּ בַּגּוֹרֶן וְאָמַר לוֹ. עֲשֵׂם עָלַי כְּשַׁעַר שֶׁבַּשּׁוּק וַאֲנִי אַעֲלֶה לָךְ כָּל־יֹ"ב חֹדֶשׁ. אָסוּר. דְלֹא כְאִיסָּרוֹ הַבָּא בְיָדוֹ. אָמַר רַב. מוֹדֵי רִבִּי חִיָּיה חֲבִיבִי דִּי לָן יָהֲבִין לֵיהּ וְקָנָה מִכְּבָר שָׁרֵי. אַגְרָא מִן כְּבָר וְקָנָה בָּתַר כֵּן שָׁרֵי. קָנָה מִן כְּבָר וְאַגְרָא בָּתַר כֵּן אָסוּר.

Abba bar Zamina gave a denar to the food merchant and took from him at the cheapest rate of the entire year. Rav[159] did not agree. Rebbi Hiyya the Elder had flax. The donkey drivers wanted to buy from him. He told them, it is not my intention to sell this before Purim[160]. They said to him, sell it to us now at the price which you would sell it for at Purim[161]. He went to ask Rebbi, who told him, it is forbidden. He went out, formulated this in a *baraita*, and stated the following: [162]"If one was owing money and the other wanted to take from him on the threshing floor, when he told him, credit it to my account by the market rate[163] and I shall provide you all twelve months[164]; this is forbidden for it is not as if the *assarion* came to his hand[165]." Rav said, my uncle Rebbi Hiyya will agree that if they paid him and he immediately acquired, then it is permitted. If he paid beforehand and acquired afterwards, it is permitted[166]; if he acquired earlier and paid afterwards, it is forbidden[161].

159 A name must be missing here since the first generation Amora Rav could not express an opinion about dealings three generations later.

160 When one would expect the price to be the highest of the year.

161 They intended to transport the flax to a region where flax was more expensive, and pay him on their return. The flax then is a loan and the higher

payment later is a "premium for waiting."
162  Tosephta 4:23; a different version in the Babli, 62b.
163  The wholesale rate at harvest time, which is the lowest of the entire year.
164  Paying his debt by delivery of produce in installments at a reduced rate implies hidden interest payments.
165  In contrast to the Mishnah, where money changes hands at the time the contract is signed.
166  This is the case of the Mishnah.

(10c line 61) רִבִּי לָעָזָר יְהַב דֵּינָר לְחַד בַּר נַשׁ. אָמַר לֵיהּ. מַה דְּהֵינוּן עָבְדִין מִיכָּן וְעַד חֲנוּכָּה דִידִי [וְדִידָךְ]. מִתַּמָּן וּלְהַלָּן לֵית לִי עִמָּךְ עֲסוֹק אִין פָּחֲתִין וְאִין יְתִירִין דִּידָךְ. בָּעָה מִיתֵּן לֵיהּ בָּתַר חֲנוּכָּה וְלָא קַבִּיל. רִבִּי לָעָזָר חָשַׁשׁ עַל קָרוֹב לְשָׂכָר וְרָחוֹק לְהֶפְסֵד. וְתַנֵּי כֵן. קִירוּב שָׂכָר וְרִיחוּק הֶפְסֵד זוֹ מִידַּת רְשָׁעִים. קִירוּב הֶפְסֵד וְרִיחוּק שָׂכָר זוֹ מִידַּת צַדִּיקִים. קָרוֹב לָזֶה וְלָזֶה רָחוֹק לָזֶה וְלָזֶה זוֹ מִידַּת כָּל־אָדָם. רִבִּי יִצְחָק יְהַב דֵּינָרִין לְבַר נַשׁ. בָּעָא מֵיעֲבַד לֵיהּ כְּהָדָא דְרִבִּי לָעָזָר וְלָא קַבִּיל עִילָוֵוי. כַּהֲנָא יְהַב מ׳ דֵּינָרִין לְבַר נַשׁ מִיזְבָּן לֵיהּ כִּיתָּנָא. יָקְרָא כִיתָּן. אֲתָא שְׁאַל לְרַב. אֲמַר לֵיהּ. אֵיזִיל סָב מִינֵּיהּ מ׳ כּוֹרִין רַבְרְבִין.

Rebbi Eleazar invested a denar with a person and told him, what it earns between now and Hanukkah is mine [and yours]¹⁶⁷, afterwards I do not have any part with you, whether they earn or lose it is yours¹⁶⁸. He wanted to give to him after Hanukkah but he did not accept¹⁶⁹. Rebbi Eleazar had misgivings because of "close to gain and far from loss," as it was stated¹⁷⁰: "Close to gain and far from loss is the way of the wicked¹⁷¹. Close to loss and far from gain is the way of the just. Close and far equally to both is the way of everybody¹⁷²." Rebbi Isaac invested denars with a person. He wanted to stipulate as did Rebbi Eleazar but the other did not accept¹⁷³. Cahana invested 40 denars with a person to buy flax for him. Flax went up in price¹⁷⁴. He went to ask Rav, who told him to go and collect 40 large *kor*¹⁷⁵.

167  Reading of E, split 50-50. In the light of the following comments, this seems to be the correct reading.

168  The trader did not have to return the investment immediately.

169  Since the trader bore the entire risk, R. Eleazar did not accept riskless income which is interest.

170  Tosephta 4:16, Babli 70a.

171  As the Tosephta states, the yield of an investment in which the investor is partially shielded from risk is partially interest and therefore forbidden.

172  As long as risk is evenly distributed among all investors, the question of interest does not arise.

173  He did not want to appear as wicked to let R. Isaac feel just.

174  When they sold the flax and made money.

175  Money made on investments is not interest. (A gold denar is given as the normal price for a *kor* of grain, Note 3. The excess of a large over a regular *kor* represents Cahana's gain.) In the Babli, *Bava qamma* 103a, Rav similarly holds that if from the start the money was given as investment, Cahana was entitled to the gain, but not if it was given as a loan.

(10c line 70) בִּיקֵּשׁ רבִּי לְהַתִּיר קְלִיטוֹ שֶׁלָּיָם וְלֹא הִנִּיחוֹ רבִּי יִשְׁמָעֵאל בֵּירבִּי יוֹסֵי. וְאִית דָּמְרִין. רבִּי יִשְׁמָעֵאל בֵּירבִּי יוֹסֵי בִּיקֵּשׁ לְהַתִּיר וְלֹא הִנִּיחוֹ רבִּי. מַאי קְלִיטוֹ שֶׁלָּיָם. בַּר נָשׁ דִּיהַב לְחַבְרֵיהּ קׄ דֵּינָרִין. [אָמַר לֵיהּ. יְבָלִי עֶשְׂרִין דֵּינָרִין. אִין פּוֹחֲתִין דִּידָךְ וְאִין אוֹתְרוֹן דִּידָךְ. אָבְדוּ מִשֶּׁל שְׁנֵיהֶם. אָמַר רבִּי חוּנָה.] כְּגוֹן אִילֵּין דִּיהֲבִין עִיבִידְתָּא לְאִילֵּין דְּמַפְרְשִׁין לָרִיסִים מְתַּרְתֵּין קְסוֹסְטְבָן אוֹ מִגׄ קְסוֹסְטְבָן. אֵין זוֹ רִבִּית אֶלָּא הַטְרָשָׁא.

Rebbi wanted to permit the ocean's absorption but Rebbi Ismael ben Rebbi Yose did not admit it; some say that Rebbi Ismael ben Rebbi Yose wanted to permit but Rebbi did not admit it. What is the ocean's absorption? A person gave 100 denars to another. [He tells him, my yield is 20 denars. If it is less, it is on your account, if it is more, it is for your account. If it is lost, it is of both[175]. Rebbi Huna said,][176] for instance those who give merchandise to those who depart overseas to the stadia[177] for two or three *xestes*[178]. That is not interest but property.

175  He gives money for overseas trade. If everything goes well, his rate of return in 20%; the fixed rate would characterize this as interest. But if the ship sinks, "the ocean absorbs it," he bears half the loss. The 50 denars at risk make this an investment. The problem is whether the transaction as a whole be classified as a loan or an investment.

176  Addition from E.

177  Probably Greece or Southern Italy. The text of E is לכיסין; Lieberman reads לְנִיסִין, Greek νῆσοι "islands".

178  A ξέστης is the equivalent of a Roman *sextarius*, as a measure about .53 l. Maybe the idea is that the gain from a successful voyage overseas brings in enough money to be measured by volume (cf. *Yebamot* 6:4, Note 75).

(10c line 75) רִבִּי יוֹסֵה וְרִבִּי לֶעְזָר בֶּן עֲזַרְיָה אָמְרוּ דָבָר אֶחָד. דְּתַנִּינָן תַּמָּן. הָיָה לוֹ דָּבָר מוּעָט מוֹסִיף עָלָיו וְהוֹלֵךְ. וְרִבִּי אֶלְעָזָר בֶּן עֲזַרְיָה אוֹסֵר עַד שֶׁיַּעֲמִיק שְׁלֹשָׁה [אוֹ עַד שֶׁיַּגְבִּיהַּ שְׁלֹשָׁה] אוֹ עַד שֶׁיִּתֵּן עַל הַסֶּלַע.

Rebbi Yose and Rebbi Eleazar ben Azariah[179] said the same thing, as we have stated there: "If he had little, he may continuously add to it, but Rebbi Eleazar ben Azariah says only if he raises or lowers it by three [hand-breadths] or puts it on a rock."

179  R. Yose in the Mishnah denying an exception to the rules of interest for manure; R. Eleazar ben Azariah in Mishnah *Ševi'it* 3:2 (Notes 18-22) denying an exception to the rules of the Sabbatical year for accumulation of manure.

(fol. 10a) **משנה י:** לֹא יֹאמַר אָדָם לַחֲבֵירוֹ הַלְוֵינִי כּוֹר חִיטִּין וַאֲנִי אֶתֵּן לָךְ מִן הַגּוֹרֶן. אֲבָל אוֹמֵר לוֹ הַלְוֵינִי עַד שֶׁיָּבֹא בְּנִי אוֹ עַד שֶׁאֶמְצָא הַמַּפְתֵּחַ. וְהִלֵּל אוֹסֵר. וְכָךְ הָיָה הִלֵּל אוֹמֵר לֹא תַלְוֶה אִשָּׁה כִּכָּר לַחֲבֵירָתָהּ עַד שֶׁתַּעֲשֶׂנּוּ בְדָמִים שֶׁמָּא יוֹקִירוּ הַחִטִּים וְנִמְצָא בָאוֹת לִידֵי רִבִּית.

**Mishnah 10**: A person may not say to another, lend me a *kor* of wheat and I shall return it to you from the threshing-floor[180], but he may tell him, lend me until my son comes or until I find the key[181], but Hillel forbids. Similarly, Hillel[182] said that a woman may not lend a loaf to another unless she fixed its price, for possibly wheat may rise in price and they would be entangled in problems of interest.

משנה יא: אוֹמֵר אָדָם לַחֲבֵירוֹ נַכֵּשׁ עִמִּי וַאֲנַכֵּשׁ עִמָּךְ עֲדוֹר עִמִּי וְאֶעְדוֹר עִמָּךְ. וְלֹא יֹאמַר לוֹ נַכֵּשׁ עִמִּי וְאֶעְדוֹר עִמָּךְ עֲדוֹר עִמִּי וַאֲנַכֵּשׁ עִמָּךְ. כָּל־יְמֵי גָּרִיד אֶחָד כָּל־יְמֵי רְבִיעָה אַחַת. לֹא יֹאמַר לוֹ חֲרוֹשׁ עִמִּי בַגָּרִיד וַאֲנִי עִמָּךְ בָּרְבִיעָה.

**Mishnah 11**: A man may say to another, weed with me and I shall be weeding with you, hoe with me and I shall be hoeing with you, but he shall not tell him, weed with me and I shall be hoeing with you, hoe with me and I shall be weeding with you. All the dry season is one, all the wet season is not; one may not say to him, plough with me in the dry season and I shall be ploughing with you in the wet season[183].

משנה יב: רַבָּן גַּמְלִיאֵל אוֹמֵר יֵשׁ רִיבִּית מוּקְדֶּמֶת וְיֵשׁ רִבִּית מְאוּחֶרֶת. כֵּיצַד נָתַן אֶת עֵינָיו לִלְווֹת מִמֶּנּוּ הָיָה מְשַׁלֵּחַ לוֹ וְאוֹמֵר בִּשְׁבִיל שֶׁיַּלְוֵינִי זוֹ הִיא רִיבִּית מוּקְדֶּמֶת. לָוָה מִמֶּנּוּ וְהֶחֱזִיר לוֹ אֶת מָעוֹתָיו הָיָה מְשַׁלֵּחַ לוֹ וְאָמַר בִּשְׁבִיל מְעוֹתֶיךָ שֶׁהָיוּ בְטֵילוֹת אֶצְלִי זוֹ הִיא רִבִּית מְאוּחֶרֶת. רִבִּי שִׁמְעוֹן אוֹמֵר יֵשׁ רִבִּית דְּבָרִים. לֹא יֹאמַר לוֹ דַּע אִם בָּא אִישׁ פְּלוֹנִי מִמָּקוֹם פְּלוֹנִי.

**Mishnah 12**: Rabban Gamliel says, there exists predated and postdated interest. How is this? If one indended to borrow from him and sent him [a gift] saying, so you should lend me; that is predated interest. If one had borrowed and returned the money when he sent him [a gift] saying, that is for your money which was not earning for you while it was with me; that is postdated interest. Rebbi Simeon says, there exists verbal interest.

One should not say to him, you should know that **X** came from place **Y**[184].

180 This is the general prohibition of lending commodities against the same amount of commodities since lending and repayment might represent very different values on the spot market.

181 Short term loans for which no big change in commodity prices is to be expected.

182 While the records of Hillel's time, the reigns of Caesar and Augustus, do not indicate inflationary pressures, it is possible that in Egypt and the neighboring countries the price of wheat was very sensitive to the requisitions for the provision of Rome and therefore unpredictable.

183 One may not offer to exchange agricultural work against agricultural work if these would represent vastly different expenditures if they needed hired hands.

184 To let the debtor take care of the guest for the creditor.

**הלכה י:** לֹא יֹאמַר אָדָם לַחֲבֵירוֹ כוּל׳. תַּנֵּי. לֹא יֹאמַר אָדָם לַחֲבֵירוֹ. הַלְוֵינִי כּוֹר חִיטִּים וַאֲנִי אֶתֵּן לָךְ לַגּוֹרֶן. הָא עַד שְׁתַּיִם שָׁלֹשׁ שַׁבָּתוֹת מוּתָּר. וְהִלֵּל אוֹסֵר. שְׁמוּאֵל אָמַר. הֲלָכָה כְּהִלֵּל. (10d line 1)

**Halakhah 10**: "A person may not say to another," etc. It was stated: "A person may not say to another, lend me a *kor* of wheat and I shall return it to you from the threshing-floor," therefore for two or three weeks it is permitted; "but Hillel forbids.[185]" Samuel said, practice follows Hillel[186].

185 E adds: "But he may tell him, lend me until my son comes or until I find the key, but Hillel forbids;" therefore two or three weeks is forbidden. The formulation of L shows that his short text is original; the implication of both texts is the same.

186 Babli 75a; the editors of the Babli reject Samuel's statement.

**משנה יג:** אֵילוּ עוֹבְרִין בְּלֹא תַעֲשֶׂה הַמַּלְוֶה וְהַלֹּוֶה וְהֶעָרֵב וְהָעֵדִים (fol. 10a) וַחֲכָמִים אוֹמְרִים אַף הַסּוֹפֵר. עוֹבְרִים עַל בַּל תִּתֵּן וּמִשּׁוּם וְעַל בַּל תִּקַּח מִמֶּנּוּ וְעַל לֹא תִהְיֶה לוֹ כְּנוֹשֶׁה וְעַל לֹא תְשִׂימוּן עָלָיו נֶשֶׁךְ וְלִפְנֵי עִוֵּר לֹא תִתֵּן מִכְשׁוֹל וְיָרֵאתָ מֵאֱלֹהֶיךָ אֲנִי ל'.

**Mishnah 13**: The following transgress prohibitions: The creditor, and the debtor, and the guarantor, and the witnesses; the Sages say, also the scribe. They transgress "do not give,[187]" and "do not take from him,[188]" and "do not be a creditor,[189]" and "do not burden him with interest,[189]" and "before a blind man do not put an obstacle; and fear your God, I am the Eternal.[190]"

187 *Lev.* 25:37.
188 *Lev.* 25:36.
189 *Ex.* 22:24.
190 *Lev.* 19:14. While the preceding verses spell out the guilt of the parties, this verse explains the guilt of the scribe, who is supposedly learned in the law and has to know that he participates in an illegal activity. The extended interpretation of *Lev.* 19:14 is one of the signs of pharisaic doctrine; it is intimated that the Sadducees, the opponents of the Sages, would absolve the scribe from guilt.

**הלכה יג:** וְאֵילוּ עוֹבְרִין בְּלֹא תַעֲשֶׂה כול'. אָמַר רִבִּי יָסָא. בּוֹא (10d line 5) וּרְאֵה כַּמָּה סְמִיּוֹת עֵינֵי מַלְוֵי רִבִּית. אָדָם קוֹרֵא לַחֲבֵירוֹ עוֹבֵד עֲבוֹדָה זָרָה וּמְגַלֶּה עֲרָיוֹת וְשׁוֹפֵךְ דָּמִים וּמְבַקֵּשׁ לֵירֵד עִמּוֹ לְחַיָּיו. וַהֲלָא שׂוֹכֵר הָעֵדִים וְהַלִּבְלָר וְאוֹמֵר לָהֶן. בּוֹאוּ וְהָעִידוּ שֶׁכָּפַר בַּמָּקוֹם. לְמַדְךָ שֶׁכָּל־הַמַּלְוֶה בְרִיבִּית כּוֹפֵר בָּעִיקָּר. רִבִּי שִׁמְעוֹן בֶּן אֶלְעָזָר אוֹמֵר. יוֹתֵר מִמַּה שֶּׁכּוֹפְרִין בָּעִיקָּר כּוֹפְרִין שֶׁעוֹשִׂין הַתּוֹרָה פְּלַסְטְרוֹן וְאֶת מֹשֶׁה טִיפֵּשׁ וְאוֹמְרִים. אִילּוּ הָיָה מֹשֶׁה יוֹדֵעַ שֶׁכָּךְ הָיִינוּ מַרְוִיחִין לֹא הָיָה כוֹתְבוֹ. רִבִּי עֲקִיבָה אוֹמֵר. קָשָׁה הָרִיבִּית שֶׁאַף הַטּוֹבָה רִבִּית. הֲרֵי שֶׁאָמַר לִיקַּח לוֹ יָרָק מִן הַשּׁוּק אַף עַל [וִ שֶׁנָּתַן לוֹ מְעוֹתָיו הֲרֵי זֶה רִבִּית. רִבִּי שִׁמְעוֹן אוֹמֵר. קָשָׁה הָרִיבִּית שֶׁאַף שְׁאֵילַת שָׁלוֹם רִבִּית. לֹא שָׁאַל לוֹ שָׁלוֹם מִיָּמָיו וְעַל שֶׁלָּוָה מִמֶּנּוּ הִקְדִּים לוֹ שָׁלוֹם הֲרֵי זֶה רִבִּית. וְכֵן הָיָה רִבִּי שִׁמְעוֹן בֶּן אֶלְעָזָר אוֹמֵר. כָּל־מִי שֶׁיֵּשׁ לוֹ מָעוֹת וְאֵינוֹ מַלְוָן בְּרִיבִּית עָלָיו הַכָּתוּב

אוֹמֵר כַּסְפּוֹ לֹא נָתַן בְּנֶשֶׁךְ וגו'. אָמַר רִבִּי שְׁמוּאֵל בַּר אִימִּי. הַמִּיטְמוּט הַזֶּה לֹא הָיִינוּ יוֹדְעִין מָהוּ. וּבָא שְׁלֹמֹה וּפֵירַשׁ הַצֵּל לְקוּחִים לַמָּוֶת וגו'.

**Halakhah 13**: "The following transgress prohibitions," etc. [191]"Rebbi Yose[192] said, come and see how blind are the eyes of people who lend on interest. If a person calls another one idolator, or adulterer, or murderer, the other will want to destroy him. But this one pays witnesses and a scribe and tells them, come and testify that I negated the roots [of Judaism]. Rebbi Simeon ben Eleazar said, they negate much more than the roots, for they declare the Torah false[193] and Moses an idiot and say, if Moses had known how much we are earning, he would not have written it. Rebbi Aqiba says, interest is difficult since even a favor can be interest. If one[194] told him to buy vegetables on the market for him, even though he gave him the money, this is interest. Rebbi Simeon said, interest is difficult since even greeting can be interest. If he never greeted him but because he took a loan from him he is quick to greet him, this is interest[195]. [196]In this sense, Rebbi Simeon ben Eleazar used to say, about a person who has money and does not lend it on interest the verse says[197]: 'his money he did not lend on interest,' etc. Rebbi Samuel bar Immi[198] said, we would not know what this tottering was if Salomon had not come and explained: 'to save those taken to death.'[199]"

191  Tosephta 6:17-18; a short quote also in the Babli, 75b.

192  One has to read R. Yose, the Tanna, instead of R. Yasa, the Amora.

193  Greek πλαστός, ή, όν, "fabricated".

184  If the creditor uses the debtor to run errands for him without paying for the latter's time, it is interest.

195  In the Tosephta, this is R. Aqiba's statement.

196  Babli 71a.

197  *Ps.* 15:6. "One who does this will never totter."

198  In the Tosephta, R. Simeon or R. Shemaia. R. Simeon bar Immi was a third generation Amora. In *Midrash Ps.* 15(6), R. Samuel (ed. S. Buber, Note

31).

199 *Prov.* 24:11: "To save those taken to death, and tottering to be killed, if you refrain." The root used in *Prov.* 24:11 is the same as that in *Ps.* 15:6; it is presumed to have the same meaning. As usual, the argument is about those parts of the verses which are not quoted.

## השוכר את האומנין פרק ששי

(fol. 10d) **משנה א**: הַשּׂוֹכֵר אֶת הָאוּמָּנִין וְהִטְעוּ זֶה אֶת זֶה אֵין לָהֶם זֶה עַל זֶה אֶלָּא תַרְעוֹמֶת. שָׂכַר אֶת הַחֲמָר וְאֶת הַקַּדָּר פֶּרֵייָא פֶּרֵין וַחֲלִילִין לַכַּלָּה אוֹ לַמֵּת פּוֹעֲלִין לְהַעֲלוֹת פִּשְׁתָּנוֹ מִן הַמִּשְׁרָה וְכָל־דָּבָר שֶׁהוּא אָבֵד וְחָזְרוּ בָהֶן מָקוֹם שֶׁאֵין אָדָם שׂוֹכֵר עֲלֵיהֶן אוֹ מַטְעָן.

**Mishnah 1**: If somebody hired tradesmen[1] and they tricked one another[2], they only have mutual complaints on one another[3]. If somebody hired a donkey driver, or a teamster[4], carriage carriers[5], or flute players for a bride or a burial, workers to bring his flax from the soaking pond, or anything in danger of being lost, if they reneged at a place where nobody is available[6], he hires at their expense or tricks them.

1    Independent contractors.

2    This Chapter is the continuation of Chapter Four. While in trade there is a notion of fair price, and overcharge or underpayment are reasons to annul the contract, there is no mechanism to establish fair rates for services (or labor wages, Chapter 7); the notions of overcharge or underpayment do not apply. In addition, a contract for services becomes final only with the start of work; before that time each party is in principle free to annul the contract at any moment. While this right is unalienable for workers (Halakhah 2), for contractors it is restricted to cases where no irreparable loss would be caused to the other party.

3    The injured party in general has no recourse in court. But if the injured party tells others about the bad treatment he received, it is no slander.

4    Reading קרר "teamster" instead of קדר "potter".

5    Reading with D. Hoffmann πορεῖο φόροι. [Cf. Greek πόρευμα "means of transportation or φέρετρον "bier, litter, frame" (E.G.)] [Musaphia reads περιφέραια "circumference,

circle" and interprets as "curved trumpets". *Arukh* explains "a kind of litter" without indicating an etymology Rashi: prepared wood to construct a litter, φορεῖον.}

6    If the contractor had agreed to a certain price but then, when the employer was in a situation in which it was impossible for him to quickly find a replacement that would save him from a big loss, reneged on the contract and demanded a much higher price, he can either try to get a replacement at a much higher rate and then sue the original contractor for the difference, or he can agree to the exorbitant amount and then pay only the original rate with the blessing of the court.

(10d line 56) **הלכה א:** הַשּׂוֹכֵר אֶת הָאוּמָּנִין כול'. הִטְעוּ זֶה אֶת זֶה מָהוּ. אִיתֵּיי אַתּוּן עָבְדִין עִמִּי הֵיךְ אַתּוּן עָבְדִין מִן חָמֵשׁ רָבָּן. וְאַשְׁכְּחוֹן עָבְדִין מִן עֲשַׂר רָבָּן לִמְלָאכָה. אַתּוּן עָבְדִין עִמִּי הֵיךְ אַתּוּן עָבְדִין מִן עֲשָׂרָה יוֹמִין. וְאַשְׁכְּחוֹן עָבְדִין מִן חֲמִשָּׁה יוֹמִין. (הִטְעָן) [הִטְעוּ] בַּעַל הַבַּיִת מָהוּ. אִיתֵּיי אַתּוּן עָבְדִין עִם חֲבֵירֵיכוֹן הֵיךְ הִנּוּן עָבְדִין [מִי רָבָּן. וְאַשְׁכְּחוֹן עָבְדִין מֵהּ רָבָּן לִמְלָאכָה. אִיתֵּיי אַתּוּן עָבְדִין עִם חֲבֵירֵיכוֹן הֵיךְ הִנּוּן עָבְדִין] מָה יָמִין. וְאַשְׁכְּחוֹן עָבְדִין מִי יָמִין. בַּמֶּה דְּבָרִים אֲמוּרִים. שֶׁלֹּא הָלְכוּ הַחַמָּרִים. אֲבָל הָלְכוּ וְלֹא מָצְאוּ תְּבוּאָה. פּוֹעֲלִין לְנַכֵּשׁ וּמָצְאוּ שָׂדֵהוּ זְלֵחָה. נוֹתֵן לָהֶן שְׂכַר הֲלִיכָה וַחֲזִירָה. וְלֹא דוֹמֶה הַבָּא טָעוּן לַבָּא רֵיקָן. עוֹשֶׂה מְלָאכָה לְיוֹשֵׁב וּבָטֵל. הַיּוֹשֵׁב בַּצֵּל לַיּוֹשֵׁב בַּחַמָּה. רִבִּי חִייָה רוֹבָה אֲגַר חַמָּרִין לְמֵיתָא לֵיהּ כִּיתָּן. הָלְכוּ וּמְצָאוּהָ לַחָה. אָמַר לוֹן רַב. פּוּק וְהַב לוֹן אַגְרוֹן מוּשְׁלָם. וַאֲמַר לְהוֹן. לָא דַּאֲנָא חַייָב מִיתֵּן לְכוֹן אַגְרֵיכוֹן אֶלָּא אֲנָא חִייָה מָסְרִית לְכוֹן.

**Halakhah 1**: "If somebody hired tradesmen," etc. [7]What means, they tricked one another? Come, work for me for five large [coins]. It turned out it was work for ten large [coins][8]. You work for me a job which needs ten days. It turned out it was work for five days[9]. What means, [they][10] tricked the householder? Come, work for me with your colleagues {for ten large [coins]. It turned out it was work for five large [coins][9]. You work for me a job which needs five days.}[10] It turned out it was work for ten days[8]. [11]"When was this said; if the donkey drivers did not start yet. But if they went and did not find grain, or workers to weed and found the field flooded, he has to pay them for going and coming[12]. But one cannot compare coming loaded with coming empty, or working with being idle, sitting in the shadow with sitting in the sun.[13]" Rebbi Hiyya the Elder hired donkey drivers to bring his flax. They went and found it wet[13]. (Rav)[14] said to him, go and pay them their full fee. He said to them, not that I would be obligated to pay you your fee but I, Hiyya, am handing it over to you[15].

7  The Babli has a completely different interpretation.

8  The employer tricked the contractor.

9  The contractor tricked the employer.

10  Reading of E, supported by Ran (Commentary to the Mishnah). L reads: The employer tricks them. Both statements apply.

11  Tosephta 7:1; Babli 76b.

12  In the Babli and in 2 out of 3 Tosephta sources: "their fee completely."

13  When it would spoil in transport.

14  The Tosephta and the Babli allow the employer to pay only for the actual work done, not the contract sum.

14  One has to read "Rebbi", since Rav was in no position to tell his uncle and teacher what to do, and in the Babli, 76b, he is quoted as accepting his uncle's original opinion.

15  As a voluntary gift; by this declaration he barred himself from appealing to the court to get his money back and established practice to pay the full fee due.

(10d line 69) בַּמֶּה דְבָרִים אֲמוּרִים. שֶׁלֹּא הִתְחִילוּ. אֲבָל אִם קִבֵּל מִמֶּנּוּ שָׂדֶה לִקְצוֹר בְּבֹ סְלָעִים קָצַר חֶצְיָיהּ וְהִנִּיחַ חֶצְיָיהּ. בֶּגֶד לֶאֱרוֹג בְּבֹ סְלָעִים אָרַג חֶצְיוֹ וְהִנִּיחַ חֶצְיוֹ שָׁמִין לוֹ. כֵּיצַד שָׁמִין לוֹ מַה שֶּׁעָשָׂה. אִם הָיָה מַה שֶּׁעָשָׂה יָפֶה וֹ דֵינָרִין נוֹתֵן לוֹ סֶלַע אוֹ יִגְמוֹר מְלַאכְתּוֹ. וְאִם סֶלַע נוֹתֵן לוֹ סֶלַע. רִבִּי דוֹסָא אוֹמֵר. שָׁמִין מַה שֶּׁעָתִיד לֵיעָשׂוֹת. אִם הָיָה מַה שֶּׁעָתִיד לַעֲשׂוֹת יָפָה ג דֵינָרִין נוֹתֵן לוֹ שֶׁקֶל אוֹ יִגְמוֹר מְלַאכְתּוֹ. וְאִם שֶׁקֶל נוֹתֵן לוֹ שֶׁקֶל. רִבִּי זֵירָא בְּשֵׁם רַב הוּנָא רִבִּי בִּינָה רִבִּי יִרְמְיָה בְּשֵׁם רַב. הֲלָכָה כְּרִבִּי דוֹסָא.

בַּמֶּה דְבָרִים אֲמוּרִים. בְּדָבָר שֶׁאֵינוֹ אָבֵד. אֲבָל בְּדָבָר הָאָבֵד שׂוֹכֵר עָלָיו מִמָּקוֹם אַחֵר וּמַטְעוֹ וְאוֹמֵר לוֹ. סֶלַע פָּסַקְתִּי לָךְ בּ אֲנִי נוֹתֵן לָךְ. נוֹטֵל מִזֶּה וְנוֹתֵן לָזֶה. אָמַר רִבִּי אִילָא. וּבִלְבַד עַד כְּדֵי שְׂכָרוֹ. עַד כְּדוֹן וּבִלְבַד עַד כְּדֵי שְׂכַר אוֹתוֹ הַיּוֹם. וּבִלְבַד עַד כְּדֵי שְׂכָרוֹ לַשָּׁעָה. בַּמֶּה דְבָרִים אֲמוּרִים. בְּמָקוֹם שֶׁאֵינוֹ מוֹצֵא לִשְׂכּוֹר פּוֹעֲלִים. אֲבָל אִם רָאָה חַמָּרִין שֶׁמְמַשְׁמְשִׁין וּבָאִין אוֹ שֶׁפָּרַק סְפִינָתוֹ בְּלִמֵן. אָמַר לוֹ. צֵא וּשְׂכוֹר לָךְ אַחַת מִכָּל־אֵילוּ. אֵין לוֹ עָלָיו אֶלָּא תַרְעוֹמֶת.

[11]"When was this said? Before they started. But if he accepted to harvest a field for two tetradrachmas, harvested half and left half uncut, a garment to weave for two tetradrachmas, wove half and left half unwoven, one estimates for him. How does one estimate what he did? If what he did was worth six denar, he gives him a *sela'* or he has to finish his work[16]. If it was worth a tetradrachma he gives him a tetradrachma; Rebbi Dosa says, one estimates what remains to be done[17]. If what remains to be done was worth three denar, he gives him a *šeqel* or he has to finish his work[18]. If it was a *šeqel*, he gives him a *šeqel*[19]." Rebbi Ze'ira in the name of Rav Huna, Rebbi Bina, Rebbi Jeremiah[20] in the name of Rav: practice follows Rebbi Dosa.

[11]"When was this said? If nothing is in danger to be lost. But if it is in danger to be lost, he hires others on his account[21] or tricks him and tells him, I contracted with you for one tetradrachma, I shall give you two. He takes from one and gives to the other." Rebbi Ila said, only up to his wages[22]. So far, only up to his wages for that day, or only up to his wages for that hour? [11]"When was this said? At a place where no workers are ready to be hired. But if one saw that donkey drivers approached, or that he was unloading his ship in a port[23], he[24] may tell him, go and hire yourself one of these; he only has a complaint on him."

16  According to Rashi, the anonymous Tanna holds that a contractor, like a hired worker, has an unlimited right to stop his work. Therefore, the contractor is always paid what is due him; for half the contract work done he must be paid half the contract sum. Even if the replacement contractor will charge 6 denars for work specified in the original contract for a *sela'* or 4 denars, the additional costs are to be borne by the employer.

17  The Babli, 67a, explains that R. Dosa follows Mishnah 2 and restricts the unlimited right to leave work without notice to workers only. The contractor can only claim the difference between the contract sum and what was paid to his replacement.

18  This is difficult to understand. Instead of "3 denars", in the Tosephta, the reading is "5 denars", in the Babli "6 denars". The Babli is clear: The contract sum was 8 denars. If the substitute contractor gets 6, the original one gets 2 denars, or one *šeqel*. S. Lieberman conjectures that in L the numeral was spelled out, as it is in E, and that שלשה was a copyist's error for ששה, the Babli's reading.

19  This reading is confirmed by the Tosephta; the Babli reads as in the preceding sentence, "if a tetradrachma, he gives a tetradrachma." M. Margalit in *Pene Moshe* (supported by D. Pardo, *Ḥasde David*) writes that in case the first contractor finished exactly half the job, he is paid the smaller of half the contract sum or the amount another contractor takes to finish the job. If that would be one *šeqel*, the original contractor also gets only one *šeqel*; since he broke the contract, the earlier obligation of his employer was abrogated.

20  The Babylonian. The statement is not mentioned in the Babli but is accepted by Maimonides.

21  In this case, the anonymous Tanna agrees with R. Dosa that the original contractor cannot claim more than the difference between the original contract sum and the amount paid to the second contractor.

22  If the substitute contractor charges more than the original amount, the defaulting contractor cannot be sued for the difference. (Babli 78a).

23  Greek λιμήν.

24  The first contractor can get out of the contract without penalty. "He" is the contractor," "him" the employer.

**משנה ב:** הַשּׂוֹכֵר אֶת הָאוּמָּנִין וְחָזְרוּ בָּהֶן יָדָן לַתַּחְתּוֹנָה. אִם בַּעַל הַבַּיִת חוֹזֵר בּוֹ יָדוֹ לַתַּחְתּוֹנָה. כָּל־הַמְשַׁנֶּה יָדוֹ לַתַּחְתּוֹנָה וְכָל־הַחוֹזֵר בּוֹ יָדוֹ לַהַתַּחְתּוֹנָה. (fol. 10d)

**Mishnah 2:** If somebody hired tradesmen[1] and they backed out they are disadvantaged[25]; if the householder backs out, he is disadvantaged[26]. Anyone changing the terms of a contract is disadvantaged[27]; anyone backing out of a contract is disadvantaged.

25  The contractor can only claim the difference between the contract sum and what was paid to his substitute..

26  He has to pay the contractor's claims in full.

27  Mishnah *Bava Qamma* 9:5.

**הלכה ב:** הַשּׂוֹכֵר אֶת הָאוּמָּנִין כול׳. רַב אָמַר. כִּי לִי בְנֵי יִשְׂרָאֵל עֲבָדִים. אֵין יִשְׂרָאֵל קוֹנִין זֶה אֶת זֶה. אָמַר רִבִּי יוֹחָנָן. עֶבֶד עִבְרִי הִיא מַתְנִיתָא. עַל דַּעְתֵּיהּ דְּרַב. בֵּין פּוֹעֵל בֵּין בַּעַל הַבַּיִת יָכוֹל לַחֲזוֹר בּוֹ. עַל דַּעְתֵּיהּ דְּרִבִּי יוֹחָנָן. פּוֹעֵל יָכוֹל לַחֲזוֹר בּוֹ וְלֹא בַעַל הַבַּיִת. (11a line 7)

**Halakhah 2:** "If somebody hired tradesmen," etc. Rav said, "because the Children of Israel are My servants[28]," Jews cannot buy one another. Rebbi Joḥanan said, this was stated about a Hebrew slave[29]. In Rav's opinion, both a worker and an employer can back out; in Rebbi Joḥanan's opinion the worker can back out but not the employer[30].

28  *Lev.* 25:55.

29  The verse is in the paragraph about a Hebrew slave of a Gentile, who has to be freed in the Jubilee year.

30  It seems that the attributions have to be switched. Rav, who quotes the verse, holds that a contract which bars a worker from quitting his job is invalid as "stipulating against the words of the Torah", must hold that any employment contract which specifies a fixed term of employment can be enforced only against the employer, not the employee. In the Babli 10a this is universally accepted. This does not exclude that the worker who quits his

job in the middle of work be financially disadvantaged (Babli 77a). R. Joḥanan, who holds that the verse is irrelevant in the context, must read the Mishnaiot as applying both to contractors and workers; both can renege on their obligations if they accept the penalties spelled out there.

(fol. 10d) **משנה ג:** הַשׂוֹכֵר אֶת הַחֲמוֹר לְהוֹלִיכָהּ בָּהָר וְהוֹלִיכָהּ בַּבִּקְעָה. בַּבִּקְעָה וְהוֹלִיכָהּ בָּהָר אֲפִילוּ זוֹ עֲשָׂרָה מִילִין וְזוֹ עֲשָׂרָה מִילִין וָמֵתָה חַיָּיב לְשַׁלֵּם. שָׂכַר אֶת הַחֲמוֹר וְהִבְרִיקָה אוֹ שֶׁנִּשְׂאֵת בָּאַנְגָּרִייָא אוֹמֵר לוֹ הֲרֵי שֶׁלָּךְ לְפָנֶיךָ. מֵתָה אוֹ נִשְׁבְּרָה חַיָּיב לְהַעֲמִיד לוֹ חֲמוֹר.

**Mishnah 3**: Somebody who rented a donkey to lead it on the mountain but led it in the valley, in the valley but led it on the mountain, even if both ways were ten *mil*, if it died he has to pay[31]. If he rented a donkey and it developed eye trouble[32] or it was taken to government service[32a], he tells him[33], here is your property before you. If it died or broke a limb, he has to provide him[34] with another donkey.

31 Even though a renter does not have to pay if the rented animal dies (Mishnah 7:9), since he "changed the terms of a contract, he is disadvantaged."

32 Cf. Arabic بَرِقَ "to have trouble seeing".

32a Greek ἀγγαρεία.

33 The owner tells the renter that this is a common risk which anybody working with animals has to live with; he does not have to provide him with another animal.

34 The owner has to provide the renter with a new animal.

(11a line 11) **הלכה ג:** הַשּׂוֹכֵר אֶת הַחֲמוֹר כול׳. נִיחָא בָּהָר וְהוֹלִיכָהּ בַּבִּקְעָה. בַּבִּקְעָה וְהוֹלִיכָהּ בָּהָר. רִבִּי שִׁמְעוֹן בֶּן יָקִים אָמַר. בְּשֶׁמֵּתָה מֵחֲמַת אֲוִיר. רִבִּי דּוֹסְתַּי בֶּן יַנַּאי אָמַר שֶׁהִכִּישָׁהּ נָחָשׁ. רִבִּי יוֹחָנָן אָמַר. רִבִּי מֵאִיר הִיא דְּאָמַר. כָּל־הַמְשַׁנֶּה עַל דַּעַת בַּעַל הַבַּיִת נִקְרָא גַזְלָן.

**Halakhah 3**: "Somebody who rented a donkey," etc. One understands on the mountain, but he led it in the valley. In the valley, but he led it on the mountain? Rebbi Simeon ben Yaqim said, if it died because of the air[35]. Rebbi Dositheos ben Yannai said, if it was bitten by a snake[36]. Rebbi Joḥanan said, it is Rebbi Meïr's who said, anybody who deviates from the owner's instructions is called a robber[37].

35 Even though mountain air is healthier, some animals cannot stand the change in climate. In the Babli, 78a, the argument is inverted.

36 Which are infrequent in agricultural areas.

37 *Qiddušin* 2:1, Note 70.

(11a line 14) שָׂכַר הַחֲמוֹר וְהִבְרִיקָה. דְּבָזָק. אוֹ שֶׁנַּעֲשֵׂית אַנְגֶּרְיָא. אִית תַּנָּיֵי תַּנֵּי. אַנְגֶּרְיָא כְּמִיתָה. וְאִית תַּנָּיֵי תַנֵּי. אוֹמֵר לוֹ. הֲרֵי שֶׁלָּךְ לְפָנֶיךָ. מָאן דְּתַנֵּי. אַנְגֶּרְיָא כְּמִיתָה. בְּאוֹתוֹ שֶׁיָּכוֹל לְפַשֵּׂר. מָאן דָּמַר. אוֹמֵר לוֹ. הֲרֵי שֶׁלָּךְ לְפָנֶיךָ. בְּאוֹתוֹ שֶׁאֵין יָכוֹל לְפַשֵּׂר

תַּנֵּי. רְבִּי שִׁמְעוֹן בֶּן אֶלְעָזָר אוֹמֵר. כְּדֶרֶךְ הֲלִיכָתָהּ אֵין חַיָּיב לְהַעֲמִיד לוֹ חֲמוֹר אַחֵר. שֶׁלֹּא כְדֶרֶךְ הֲלִיכָתָהּ חַיָּיב לְהַעֲמִיד לוֹ חֲמוֹר אַחֵר. אָמַר רְבִּי אַבָּהוּ בְּשֵׁם רְבִּי יוֹסֵי בֶּן חֲנִינָה. בְּקַפְּנְדָּרְיָא אֵין חַיָּיב לְהַעֲמִיד לוֹ חֲמוֹר אַחֵר. בַּסִּילִיקֵי חַיָּיב לְהַעֲמִיד לוֹ חֲמוֹר אַחֵר. רְבִּי אַבָּהוּ בְּשֵׁם רְבִּי יוֹסֵי בֶּן חֲנִינָה. אֲגָרָהּ מִיכָּא לְלוֹד וְאִינְסִיבַת אַנְגֶּרְיָא לְלוֹד. אֵין חַיָּיב לְהַעֲמִיד לוֹ חֲמוֹר אַחֵר. מִיכָּא לְלוֹד וְאִינְסִיבַת אַנְגֶּרְיָא לְצוֹר. חַיָּיב לְהַעֲמִיד לוֹ חֲמוֹר אַחֵר.

"If he rented a donkey and it developed eye trouble," it was stumbling[38]. "Or it was taken to government service." There are Tannaïm who state, government service is like death[39]; but there are Tannaïm who state, he tells him, here is your property before you. He who stated, government service is like death, if he[40] can find an accomodation; he who says, he tells him, here is your property before you, if he cannot find an accomodation.

⁴¹"It was stated, Rebbi Simeon ben Eleazar says, if it happened on the road, he does not have to provide him with another donkey; if it did not happen on the road, he has to provide him with another donkey.⁴²" Rebbi Abbahu said in the name of Rebbi Yose ben Ḥanina: At a short-cut⁴³ he does not have to provide him with another donkey; on the king's highway⁴⁴ he has to provide him with another donkey. Rebbi Abbahu in the name of Rebbi Yose ben Ḥanina: If he hired it from here to Lydda and it was taken into government service from here to Lydda, he does not have to provide him with another donkey⁴⁵; from here to Lydda and it was taken into government service from here to Tyre⁴⁶, he has to provide him with another donkey.

38  This is Rava's explanation in the Babli, 78b.

39  Tosephta 7:7; in the Babli 78b this is a statement of Rav.

40  The donkey's owner with the government official who wants to take the donkey, to make sure the animal is returned to him after a short period.

41  Tosephta 7:7; Babli 78b. For the entire paragraph cf. *Tosefta kiFshutah Bava Meṣia'* pp. 251-252.

42  If the donkey was taken by the government while it was on the road, the owner may say to the lessee that it was his bad luck to be in the wrong place at the wrong time. But if the officials went to look in all the barns, it could not have been the lessee's bad luck and the owner has to provide a replacement. (Explanation of R. Hananel, quoted in Tosaphot 78b. s. v. אם.)

43  Latin *compendiarium* [*iter*]; cf. *Berakhot* 1:1, Note 36. Since the government officials found him alone on a narrow path, it is his fault that the animal was taken.

44  Greek (ὁδός) βασιλική. Since everybody walks there, the lessee is not to blame. This argument is roughly equivalent to that of Note 42.

45  This is a temporary inconvenience; the donkey will be available to the lessee after a short interval.

46  It is up to the owner, not the lessee, to go to Tyre and to reclaim his animal. The lessee cannot be left without a beast of burden for a very long time.

(11a line 25) מֵתָה אוֹ נִשְׁבְּרָה חַיָּיב לְהַעֲמִיד לוֹ חֲמוֹר. רִבִּי יוֹחָנָן אָמַר. בְּשֶׁאָמַר לוֹ חֲמוֹר סְתָם. אֲבָל אִם אָמַר לוֹ חֲמוֹר זֶה יָכִיל מֵימַר לֵיהּ. לְדֵין בְּעִית אַייתִי לִי קוֹמִין. רַב הוּנָא אָמַר. חַיָּיב לְטַפֵּל בּוֹ בְּאוֹתוֹ מָקוֹם. אָמַר רִבִּי זֵירָא. אִם יֵשׁ בִּטְפֵילָה כְּדֵי לִשְׂכּוֹר לוֹ גַּייְדּוֹר קָטָן אֵינוֹ חַיָּיב לְהַעֲמִיד לוֹ חֲמוֹר אַחֵר. וְאִם לָאו חַיָּיב לְהַעֲמִיד לוֹ חֲמוֹר אַחֵר. אָמַר רִבִּי הוּנָא. אִם יֵשׁ בִּנְבֵילָה כְּדֵי לִיקַח גַּייְדּוֹר קָטָן אֵינוֹ חַיָּיב לְהַעֲמִיד לוֹ חֲמוֹר אַחֵר. וְאִם לָאו חַיָּיב לְהַעֲמִיד לוֹ חֲמוֹר אַחֵר.

"If it died or broke a limb, he has to provide him with a donkey." Rebbi Johanan said, if [the lessee] requested "a donkey" without specifications. But if he requested "this donkey", [the lessor] may tell him, you wanted this one, bring it before us. Rav Huna said, he[47] has to deal with it on place. Rebbi Ze'ira said, if he can get enough from his effort to lease a small donkey, he does not need to provide him with another donkey. Otherwise, he has to provide him with another donkey. Rebbi Huna[47a] said, if the cadaver is worth enough to buy a small donkey, he does not need to provide him with another donkey. Otherwise, he has to provide him with another donkey[48].

47  The lessee, not the lessor is obligated to sell the carcass or the injured animal.

47a  In E: Rebbi Ila.

48  The dispute between R. Ze'ira and R. Huna is quoted in the Babli, 79a, as a dispute between Samuel and Rav. Samuel and R. Ze'ira hold that the lessee is empowered to use the proceeds for his needs within the terms of the lease; only an eventual residual would go to the lessor. Rav and R. Huna hold that the receipts for the carcass or the injured animal represent capital which, therefore, has to be delivered to the lessor who for his part is required to provide a substitute animal to the lessee.

(fol. 10d) **משנה ד:** הַשּׂוֹכֵר אֶת הַחֲמוֹר לְהוֹלִיכָהּ בָּהָר וְהוֹלִיכָהּ בַּבִּקְעָה אִם הֶחֱלִיקָה פָּטוּר וְאִם הוּחַמָּה חַיָּב. לְהוֹלִיכָהּ בַּבִּקְעָה וְהוֹלִיכָהּ בָּהָר אִם הֶחֱלִיקָה חַיָּב וְאִם הוּחַמָּה פָּטוּר וְאִם מֵחֲמַת הַמַּעֲלָה חַיָּב.

**Mishnah 4**: Somebody rented a donkey to lead it on the mountain but led it in the valley; if it slipped, he is not liable[49]; if it suffered a heat stroke, he is liable. In the valley, but he led it on the mountain; if it slipped, he is liable; if it suffered a heat stroke, he is not liable but if it happened because of the ascent[50], he is liable.

**משנה ה:** הַשּׂוֹכֵר אֶת הַפָּרָה לַחֲרוֹשׁ בָּהָר וְחָרַשׁ בַּבִּקְעָה אִם נִשְׁבַּר הַקַּנְקָן פָּטוּר. בַּבִּקְעָה וְחָרַשׁ בָּהָר אִם נִשְׁבַּר הַקַּנְקָן חַיָּב. לָדוּשׁ בַּקִּטְנִית וְדָשׁ בַּתְּבוּאָה פָּטוּר. בַּתְּבוּאָה וְדָשׁ בַּקִּטְנִית חַיָּב מִפְּנֵי שֶׁהַקִּטְנִית מְחַלֶּקֶת.

**Mishnah 5**: Somebody rented a cow to plough[51] on the mountain but ploughed in the valley, if the plough's peg[52] broke, he is not liable. In the valley but he ploughed on the mountain, if the plough's peg broke, he is liable[53]. To thresh legumes[54] but he threshed grain, he is not liable; to thresh grain but he threshed legumes, he is liable, for legumes make [the floor] slippery.

**משנה ו:** הַשּׂוֹכֵר אֶת הַחֲמוֹר לְהָבִיא עָלֶיהָ חִטִּין וְהֵבִיא עָלֶיהָ שְׂעוֹרִין תְּבוּאָה וְהֵבִיא עָלֶיהָ תֶּבֶן חַיָּב. וְכַמָּה יוֹסִיף עַל מַשָּׂאוֹ וִיהֵא חַיָּב. סוֹמְכוֹס אוֹמֵר מִשּׁוּם רִבִּי מֵאִיר סְאָה לַגָּמָל שְׁלשָׁה קַבִּין לַחֲמוֹר.

**Mishnah 6**: Somebody who rented a donkey to use it to transport wheat but transported barley, grain but transported straw, is liable[55]. How much did one add to the load that he became liable? Symmachos said in the name of Rebbi Meïr: one *se'ah* for a camel, three *qab*[56] for a donkey[57].

49   A mountain donkey can be presumed to be sure-footed. If it slipped it is not the lessee's fault; the lessor cannot sue the lessee even

though the lessee violated the conditions of the lease.

50  If the donkey died of heat stroke while climbing in the mountains, the lessor can sue the lessee for the value of the donkey since the lessee violated the conditions of the lease.

51  He rented the plough with the cow.

52  The central peg with which the plough is steered; the most delicate part of the plough; cf. *Berakhot* 2:4, Note 206.

53  For the uneven terrain puts more stress on the steering mechanism.

54  Beans or peas.

55  The Mishnah in the Babli and the independent Mishnah mss. add: Because volume is difficult to carry (Maimonides's text: because volume is as difficult as weight.) The specific weight of barley is less than that of wheat; the same specified weight will mean a larger load for barley than for wheat. The Mishnah also adds that the standard volume to be carried by a donkey is a *letekh*, 15 *se'ah,* about 190 liter.

56  Half a *se'ah*, about 6.4 l.

57  A contract to carry a certain volume allows an excess volume of $1/_{30}$ of the stipulated amount. This makes the standard load carried by a camel 1 *kor*, 30 *se'ah.*

(11a line 32) **הלכה ד:** הַשּׂוֹכֵר אֶת הַחֲמוֹר כול׳. תַּנֵּי כַּמָּה יוֹסִיף עַל מַשָּׂאוֹ וִיהֵא חַיָּיב. סוּמְכוּס אוֹמֵר מִשּׁוּם רִבִּי מֵאִיר. סְאָה לַגָּמָל וְגֹ קַבִּין לַחֲמוֹר. קַב לַכַּתָּף וְגֹ סָאִין לַעֲגָלָה. וּסְפִינָה לְפִי מַה שֶׁהִיא.

**Halakhah 4**: "Somebody who rented a donkey," etc. "How much did one add to the load that he became liable? Symmachos said in the name of Rebbi Meïr: one *se'ah* for a camel, three *qab* for a donkey, one *qab* for a porter, and three *se'ah* for a cart. But a ship according to its size"[58].

58  Tosephta 7:10, Babli 80b.

(11a line 35) שִׁיָּירָה שֶׁנָּפַל עָלֶיהָ גַּיִיס מְחַשְּׁבִין לְפִי מָמוֹן וְלֹא לְפִי נְפָשׁוֹת. שָׁלְחוּ לִפְנֵיהֶן תַּיָּיר מְחַשְּׁבִין לְפִי נְפָשׁוֹת. אֵין מְשַׁנִּין עַל הַמִּנְהָג שֶׁלַּשַּׁיָּירָה. סְפִינָה שֶׁעָמַד עָלֶיהָ נַחְשׁוֹל וְהֵיקֵל מִמַּשּׂוֹאָהּ מְחַשְּׁבִין לְפִי מַשָּׂאוֹי וּלְפִי מָמוֹן וְלֹא לְפִי נְפָשׁוֹת. אֲבָל הַשּׂוֹכֵר מְחַבֵּירוֹ קָרוֹן אוֹ סְפִינָה מְחַשְּׁבִין לְפִי מַשָּׂאוֹי

וּלְפִי נְפָשׁוֹת וְלֹא לְפִי מָמוֹן.

שַׁיָּרָה שֶׁנָּפַל עָלֶיהָ גַיִיס וְעָמַד אֶחָד מֵהֶן וְהִצִּיל מִיָּדָן הִצִּיל לָאֶמְצַע. וְאִם נָתְנוּ לוֹ רְשׁוּת הִצִּיל לְעַצְמוֹ. חַמָּרִין שֶׁנָּפְלוּ עֲלֵיהֶן לִיסְטִין וְעָמַד אֶחָד מֵהֶן וְהִצִּיל הִצִּיל לָאֶמְצַע. וְאִם הִתְנָה עִמָּם בְּבֵית דִּין הִצִּיל לְעַצְמוֹ. הַשּׁוּתָּפִין שֶׁמָּחֲלוּ לָהֶן מוּכְסִין מָחֲלוּ לָאֶמְצַע. וְאִם אָמְרוּ. לְשֵׁם פְּלוֹנִי מָחַלְנוּ. מַה שֶּׁמָּחֲלוּ מָחֲלוּ לוֹ.

הַגַּבָּאִין וְהַמּוּכְסִין תְּשׁוּבָתָן קָשָׁה. הֲרֵי אֵילּוּ מַחֲזִירִין לְמִי שֶׁמַּכִּירִין. וּלְמִי שֶׁאֵין מַכִּירִין יַעֲשׂוּ מֵהֶן צוֹרְכֵי צִיבּוּר.

[59]"If a caravan was attacked by soldiers[60] one computes according to value but not according to persons. If they sent a scout ahead of them, one computes[61] according to persons. One does not deviate from the usage of caravans[62]."

[63]"If a ship encounters a calamity[64] and one lightens its load, one computes according to weight and value but not according to persons. But one who rents a carriage or a ship from another person computes according to load and persons but not according to value[65]."

[66]"If a caravan was attacked by soldiers[60] and one of its members managed to save something from their hand, he saved equally [for all]; but if they gave him permission[67], he saved for himself. If donkey-drivers were attacked by robbers and one of theirs managed to save something from their hand, he saved equally [for all]; but if he stipulated with them in court, he saved for himself. If toll collectors forgave to partners, they forgave equally [for all]; but if they indicated, we forgave to Mr. X, what they forgave, they forgave him."

[68]"The repentance of publicans and toll collectors is difficult[69]. They should return to those whom they know; [moneys taken] from people they do not know they should use for the public good."

59 Tosephta 7:13; Babli *Bava qamma* 116b.

60 The meaning of גייס is as variable as the corresponding Arabic جيش "troup; army; soldiers". In this context it is presumed that they came to plunder, not to kill. Therefore, what is left after they are gone is divided proportionally to the value of the original cargoes.

61 Payment for the scout's salary. In Tosephta and Babli: "One computes *also* according to the number of persons."

62 Local rules always supersede general rules.

63 Tosephta 7:14; Babli *Bava qamma* 116b.

64 It is not clear from the frequent mention of נַחְשׁוֹל שֶׁבַּיָּם whether the reference be to a storm or to a single giant wave. The translation compares the word to Arabic نحس "unlucky, ominous, calamitous, disastrous".

65 For the transporter, the value of the merchandise carried should not make any difference.

66 Tosephta 8:25; Babli *Bava qamma* 116b.

67 In the interpretation of the Babli this refers to the case of a prior agreement that in case of an attack, everyone will keep what he can save. This agrees with the explicit rule for donkey caravans which prescribes a prior arrangement by a court document.

68 Tosephta 8:25; Babli *Bava qamma* 94b.

69 Their problem is the generally accepted doctrine (Mishnah *Yoma* 8:9) that sins between man and fellow man are not forgiven by Heaven unless the sinner asks forgiveness from his fellow man. Since under the antique system of tax farming, neither the tax- nor the toll-collector could make a living if they only exacted the legal amounts, they will have sinned against a great number of people whom they do not know by name.

(fol. 10d) **משנה ז:** כָּל־הָאוּמָּנִין שׁוֹמְרֵי שָׂכָר וְכוּלָּן שֶׁאָמְרוּ טוֹל אֶת שֶׁלָּךְ וְהָבֵא מָעוֹת שׁוֹמֵר חִנָּם. שְׁמוֹר לִי וְאֶשְׁמוֹר לָךְ שׁוֹמֵר שָׂכָר. שְׁמוֹר לִי וְאָמַר לוֹ הַנַּח לְפָנֶיךָ שׁוֹמֵר חִנָּם. הַמַּלְוָה עַל הַמַּשְׁכּוֹן שׁוֹמֵר שָׂכָר. רִבִּי יוּדָה אוֹמֵר הִלְוָהוּ מָעוֹת שׁוֹמֵר חִנָּם הִלְוָהוּ פֵּירוֹת שׁוֹמֵר שָׂכָר. אַבָּא שָׁאוּל אוֹמֵר מוּתָּר אָדָם לְהַשְׂכִּיר מַשְׁכּוֹנוֹ שֶׁל עָנִי לִהְיוֹת פּוֹסֵק עָלָיו וְהוֹלֵךְ מִפְּנֵי שֶׁהוּא כְּמֵשִׁיב אֲבֵידָה.

**Mishnah 7**: All artisans are paid trustees[70], but in any case where he said, take what is yours and bring money, he becomes an unpaid trustee[71]. Watch over what is mine and I shall watch over what is yours, paid trustee[72]. Watch over what is mine, and he said, put it down before you, an unpaid trustee[73]. He who gives a loan on a pledge is a paid trustee[74]; Rebbi Jehudah said, if he lent money, he is an unpaid trustee[75], if produce, a paid trustee[76]. Abba Shaul said, a person is authorized to rent out a poor person's pledge to continuously slice off [from the loan] because he is like a person who returns lost property[77].

70 As such, he is liable if the article was stolen or lost, in contrast to the unpaid trustee who swears but does not pay (Mishnah 7:9). Since the artisan earns his money by creating or repairing other people's possessions, he is rewarded for having them.

71 From the moment the client is informed that his order is ready, the artisan no longer has a monetary interest in keeping the object.

72 The mutual services are worth money.

73 As the Halakhah points out, the Mishnah really should read: "put it down before *me*", as in the Babli and the Mishnah manuscript corrected by Maimonides in his autograph Commentary.

74 The pledge will save the creditor an application to the court for forclosure in case the loan was not repaid. This convenience is worth money in the opinion of this Tanna.

75 In his opinion, the possibility of a future advantage is not money's worth today.

76 Giving a loan in produce against a pledge transfers the risk of spoilage to the borrower. This is an immediate advantage to the creditor which makes him a paid trustee.

77 The creditor of a loan on a pledge by a poor person has automatic permission to transform the loan into an antichretic loan in which the yield of the pledge is used to amortize ("slice off") the loan. Once the loan is repaid, the pledge is returned to the borrower who otherwise probably would have no possibility of redeeming his pledge. Cf. *Giṭṭin* 4:6, Note 168.

## HALAKHAH 7

(11a line 46) **הלכה ז:** כָּל־הָאוּמָּנִין שׁוֹמְרֵי שָׂכָר כּוּל׳. הָדָא אַנְטִיכְרֵיסִיס רִבִּית הוּא.

**Halakhah 7:** "All artisans are paid trustees," etc. This ἀντίχρησις[78] is interest.

78 In E correctly: אנטיכריסיס "Substitution of usufruct for interest." The antichretic loan described by Abba Shaul is unquestionably permitted since it is easily verifiable that all earnings of the pledge be used to reduce the amount of the loan. What is questionable is a loan in which the creditor himself uses the pledge and credits the borrower's account with a specified amount per accounting period. It is held that such a set-up automatically contains a certain amount of interest and is permissible only between Jews and Gentiles.

(11a line 47) שְׁמוּאֵל אָמַר. כְּשֶׁאָמַר לוֹ. הַנַּח לְפָנַיי. אֲבָל אָמַר לוֹ. הַנַּח לְפָנֶיךָ. אֵינוֹ לֹא שׁוֹמֵר חִנָּם וְלֹא שׁוֹמֵר שָׂכָר.

Samuel[79] said, if he said, put it down before me. But if he said, put it down before yourself, he is neither an unpaid nor a paid trustee[80].

79 Reading of E and *editio princeps*. L has ששאל "that he asked", a scribal error. In the Babli, 81b, the statement is attributed to Rav's student Rav Huna.

80 The Yerushalmi version really is a rejection of any responsibility by the person asked to act as trustee.

(11a line 49) אָמַר רִבִּי יוֹחָנָן. רוֹצֶה אָדָם לִיתֵּן כַּמָּה וְלִמְכּוֹר פֵּירוֹתָיו עַל יְדֵי מַשְׁכּוֹן. רִבִּי אַבָּהוּ בְּשֵׁם רִבִּי יוֹסֵי בֶן חֲנִינָה. רוֹצֶה אָדָם לִיתֵּן כַּמָּה וְלִמְכּוֹר פֵּירוֹתָיו לְמִי שֶׁיְּפַייְּסֶנּוּ עַל יְדֵי מַשְׁכּוֹן.

Rebbi Johanan said, a person is ready to give something so that he can sell his produce based on a pledge[81]. Rebbi Abbahu in the name of Rebbi Yose ben Hanina said, a person is ready to give something so that he can sell his produce to somebody who will appease him by a pledge[82].

81  He gives a reason for R. Jehudah to declare the lender of produce to be a paid trustee. The creditor not only transfers the risk of spoilage to the borrower but also has his claim covered by a pledge.

82  He differs with R. Johanan in extending the status of paid trustee not only to the person who lends against a pledge but also to the lender without pledge who only receives a pledge later against extension of the loan for an additional period.

(fol. 10d) **משנה ח:** הַמַּעֲבִיר חָבִית מִמָּקוֹם לְמָקוֹם וְנִשְׁבְּרָה בֵּין שׁוֹמֵר חִנָּם בֵּין שׁוֹמֵר שָׂכָר יִשָּׁבֵע. רִבִּי אֱלִיעֶזֶר אוֹמֵר זֶה וְזֶה יִשָּׁבַע וְתָמֵיהַּ אֲנִי אִם יְכוֹלִין זֶה וְזֶה לְהִישָׁבַע.

**Mishnah 8**: One who transports an amphora from place to place and it breaks shall swear[83], whether unpaid or paid trustee. Rebbi Eliezer said, both shall swear[84], but I am wondering whether any of them be able to swear[85].

83  That it did not happen because of his negligence.

84  This is the rule he was taught by his teachers.

85  Since the paid trustee is liable whether it was his fault or not, why and about what should he swear? The unpaid trustee is not liable if he swears, but how can he be sure that nothing he did contributed to the accident?

(11a line 52) **הלכה ח:** הַמַּעֲבִיר חָבִית מִמָּקוֹם לְמָקוֹם כול'. תַּנֵּי רִבִּי נְחֶמְיָה קַדָּר מָסַר קַדְרוֹי לְבַר נַשׁ תְּבָרִין. אָרִים גּוּלְתֵיהּ. אֲתָא גַבֵּי רִבִּי יוֹסֵי בֶּן חֲנִינָה אֲמַר לֵיהּ. אֵיזִיל אֲמַר לֵיהּ. לְמַעַן תֵּלֵךְ בְּדֶרֶךְ טוֹבִים. אֲזַל וַאֲמַר לֵיהּ וִיהַב גּוּלְתֵיהּ. אֲמַר לֵיהּ. יְהַב לָךְ אַגְרָךְ. אֲמַר לֵיהּ. לָא. אֲמַר לֵיהּ. זִיל וֶאֱמוֹר לֵיהּ וְאָרְחוֹת צַדִּיקִים תִּשְׁמוֹר. אֲזַל וַאֲמַר לֵיהּ וִיהַב לֵיהּ אַגְרֵיהּ.

**Halakhah 8**: "One who transports an amphora from place to place," etc. It was stated[86]: [87]Rebbi Nehemiah the potter gave his pots to a person who broke them. He[88] confiscated his[89] coat. He[89] went to Rebbi Yose ben Ḥanina, who told him, go and tell him: [90]"That you should go in the ways of good prople." He[89] went and told him[88] who then returned his coat. He[91] asked him, did he[88] pay your wages? He[89] said, no. He[91] told him, go and tell him: "And to the paths of the just you shall keep." He[89] went and told him[88] who then paid his wages.

86 Since R. Yose ben Ḥanina was a second generation Amora, this expression is inappropriate.

87 In the Babli, 83a, the story is told about Rabba bar bar Ḥana and Rav. Its upshoot is that while the teamster who breaks something in transport is liable, if he is poor one should not insist on the letter of the law.

88 R. Nehemiah the potter. The reading is confirmed by *Kaftor wa-Peraḥ* 44 (ed. Luncz, Jerusalem 1899, p. 615) against the opinion of S. Lieberman who here suspects a lacuna.

89 The transporter.

90 *Prov.* 2:20.

91 R. Yose ben Ḥanina.

## השוכר את הפועלין פרק שביעי

(fol. 11a) **משנה א:** הַשּׂוֹכֵר אֶת הַפּוֹעֲלִין וְאָמַר לָהֶן לְהַשְׁכִּים וּלְהַעֲרִיב מְקוֹם שֶׁנָּהֲגוּ שֶׁלֹּא לְהַשְׁכִּים וּלְהַעֲרִיב אֵינוֹ יָכוֹל לְכוֹפָן. מְקוֹם שֶׁנָּהֲגוּ לָזוּן יָזוּן לְסַפֵּק מְתִיקָה יְסַפֵּק הַכֹּל כְּמִנְהַג הַמְּדִינָה. מַעֲשֶׂה בְּרַבִּי יוֹחָנָן בֶּן מַתְיָא שֶׁאָמַר לִבְנוֹ צֵא שְׂכוֹר לָנוּ פּוֹעֲלִין וּפָסַק לָהֶן מְזוֹנוֹת. וּכְשֶׁבָּא אֵצֶל אָבִיו אָמַר לוֹ אֲפִילוּ אַתָּה עוֹשֶׂה לָהֶן כִּסְעוּדַת שְׁלֹמֹה בִּשְׁעָתוֹ לֹא יָצָאתָ יְדֵי חוֹבָתָךְ עִמָּהֶן שֶׁהֵן בְּנֵי אַבְרָהָם יִצְחָק וְיַעֲקֹב אֶלָּא עַד שֶׁלֹּא יַתְחִילוּ בַּמְּלָאכָה צֵא וֶאֱמוֹר לָהֶן עַל מְנָת שֶׁאֵין לָכֶם אֶלָּא פַת וְקִטְנִית בִּלְבַד. רַבָּן שִׁמְעוֹן בֶּן גַּמְלִיאֵל אוֹמֵר לֹא הָיָה צָרִיךְ הַכֹּל כְּמִנְהַג הַמְּדִינָה.

**Mishnah 1**: One who hires workers[1] and tells them to start early and work late[2], at a place where it is not customary to start early or work late cannot force them to do so. At a place where it is customary to feed them, he has to feed them; to supply a snack, he has to supply it, always following local custom. It happened that Rebbi Joḥanan ben Matthew said to his son, go and hire workers for us. He awarded them food, but when he returned to his father, the latter told him, even if you serve them Solomon's meal in his time[3] you did not fulfill your pledge since they are descendants of Abraham, Isaac, and Jacob. But before they start work go and tell them: On condition that your only claim be for bread and legumes. Rabban Simeon ben Gamliel said, that was unnecessary; one always follows local custom.

| 1 | On daily wages. |
| 2 | It is universally accepted that a working day is from sunrise to sundown. An early riser starts work at |

dawn and a late worker works until dusk.

3   30 *kor* fine flour, 60 *kor* coarse flour, 10 feed-lot cattle, 20 grass fed cattle, 100 sheep, also fallow-buck, gazelle, roe-buck, and fattened geese (*1K.* 5:3).

(11b line 40) **הלכה א:** הַשּׂוֹכֵר אֶת הַפּוֹעֲלִין כול׳. אָמַר רַב הוֹשַׁעְיָה. זֹאת אוֹמֶרֶת. הַמִּנְהָג מְבַטֵּל אֶת הַהֲלָכָה. אָמַר רִבִּי אִימִּי. כָּל־הַמּוֹצִיא מֵחֲבֵירוֹ עָלָיו לְהָבִיא רְאָיָיה חוּץ מִזוֹ.

**Halakhah 1**: "One who hires workers," etc. Rav Hoshaia said, this means that usage supersedes practice[4]. Rebbi Immi said, everywhere the burden of proof is on the claimant except here[5].

4   At least in civil law. As a statement of Rav this also is in *Yebamot* 12:1, Note 21. The rule is never stated explicitly in the Babli but has generated a very great number of responsa in all periods of rabbinic literature.

5   In employment law, the party accused of not following local custom has to prove that in fact he is following it.

(11b line 42) בְּנֵי טִיבֶּרְיָא לֹא מַשְׁכִּימִין וְלֹא מַעֲרִיבִין. בְּנֵי בֵית מָעוֹן מַשְׁכִּימִין וּמַעֲרִיבִין. בְּנֵי טִיבֶּרְיָא שֶׁעָלוּ לִשְׂכַּר בֵּית מָעוֹן נִשְׂכָּרִין כִּבְנֵי מָעוֹן. בְּנֵי בֵית מָעוֹן שֶׁיָּרְדוּ לִשְׂכַּר טִיבֶּרְיָא נִשְׂכָּרִין כְּטִיבֶּרְיָא. אֲבָל שְׁעוּלָה מִטִּיבֶּרְיָא לִשְׂכּוֹר פּוֹעֲלִין מִבֵּית מָעוֹן יְכִילוּ מֵימַר לוֹן. כֵּן סַלְקַת בְּמַחְשַׁבְתְּכוֹן דְּלָא הֲוִינָא מַשְׁכַּח מֵינַר פּוֹעֲלִין מִטִּיבֶּרְיָא. אֶלָּא בְּגִין דְּשַׁמְעִית עֲלֵיכוֹן דְּאַתּוּן מַשְׁכִּימִין וּמַעֲרִיבִין בְּגִין כָּךְ סַלְקִית הָכָא. מָקוֹם שֶׁאֵין מִנְהָג. יְהוּדָה בֶּן בּוּנִי רִבִּי אִמִּי רַב יְהוּדָה. תָּנֵיי בֵּית דִּין הוּא שֶׁתְּהֵא הַשְׁכָּמָה שֶׁלְּפוֹעֲלִין וְהָעֲרָבָה שֶׁלְּבַעַל הַבַּיִת. וּמַה טַעֲמָא. תָּשֶׁת חוֹשֶׁךְ וִיהִי לָיְלָה. הַכְּפִירִים שׁוֹאֲגִים לַטָּרֶף. תִּתֵּן לָהֶם יִלְקוֹטוּן. תִּזְרַח הַשֶּׁמֶשׁ יֵאָסֵפוּן. יֵצֵא אָדָם לְפָעֳלוֹ. (עַרְבִית) [עַרְבֵי שַׁבָּתוֹת] בֵּין הַשְׁכָּמָה בֵּין הָעֲרָבָה מִשֶּׁלְּבַעַל הַבַּיִת. עַד אֵיכָן. עַד כְּדֵי לְמַלְּאוֹת לוֹ חָבִית מַיִם וְלִצְלוֹת לוֹ דָּגָה וּלְהַדְלִיק לוֹ נֵר.

In Tiberias one does not work early or late[2]. In Bet Ma'on[6] one works early and late. People from Tiberias who climb up to be hired in Bet Ma'on are hired on the terms of Bet Maon. People from Bet Ma'on who descend to Tiberias are hired on the terms of Tiberias. But an employer from Tiberias who climbs up to hire workers in Bet Maon can tell them, you should not think that I could not find workers to hire in Tiberias but came up because I heard that you start early and work late[7]. At a place where there is no common usage, Jehudah ben Buni, Rebbi Immi, Rav Jehudah: It is a stipulation of the court that the early part of morning belong to the workers and the late part of evening to the employer[8]. What is the reason? "You make darkness, there is night; the young lions roar for prey; You give to them, they are collecting; the sun shines, they return; man leaves for his work[9]." (In the evening)[10] [Fridays][11] both early rising and late going is at the employer's expense[12]. How much? That he may fill an amphora of water, fry himself a fish[13], and light the candle.

6 A place on the slope of the mountain overlooking Tiberias (*Soṭah* 1:8, Note 280). According to Josephus, *Vita* 12, it is situated 4 stadia from Tiberias, less than 600 m.

7 The hiring contract always follows the local custom of the place of contracting, not the place of work.

8 A workday for a journeyman starts at sunrise and ends at nightfall.

9 *Ps.* 104:19-23,28. The only relevant verses are v. 22-23: "The sun shines ... man goes out to work, his labors until evening." This implies that a workday does not start before sunrise but continues after sunset until nightfall. The same argument in the Babli, in the name of R. Simeon ben Laqish (83a/b).

10 Reading of L, rejected by all commentators.

11 Reading of E.

12 On Friday a full working day does not start before sunrise but only continues until the later afternoon, leaving enough time for the worker to return home and prepare for the Sabbath before sundown.

13 The quickest way to prepare cooked food.

(11b line 54) עַל דַּעְתֵּיהּ דְּרִבִּי יוֹחָנָן בֶּן מִתְיָה. אָדָם שֶׁהָלַךְ לְקַדֵּשׁ אִשָּׁה מִמָּקוֹם אַחֵר צָרִיךְ לְהַתְנוֹת עִמָּהּ וְלוֹמַר לָהּ. עַל מְנָת דְּתַעַבְדִי כֵּן וְכֵן וְתֵאכְלִי כֵּן וְכֵן.

In the opinion of Rebbi Joḥanan ben Matthew[14], a man who goes to another place to preliminarily marry a woman has to stipulate with her and tell her, on condition that you work so and so much and eat for such and such costs.

14 Who relies neither on local usage nor on the stipulations of the Mishnah.

(fol. 11a) **משנה ב**: אֵילוּ אוֹכְלִין מִן הַתּוֹרָה. הָעוֹשֶׂה בִמְחוּבָּר לַקַּרְקַע בְּשָׁעַת גְּמַר מְלָאכָה וּבְתָלוּשׁ מִן הַקַּרְקַע עַד שֶׁלֹּא נִגְמְרָה מְלַאכְתָּן וּבְדָבָר שֶׁגִּידּוּלָיו מִן הָאָרֶץ.

**Mishnah 2**: The following eat by Torah law[15]: He who works on produce connected to the ground at the completion of work[16], or separated from the ground before the completion of work[17], only things grown from the earth[18].

**משנה ג**: וְאֵילוּ שֶׁאֵינָן אוֹכְלִין. הָעוֹשֶׂה בִמְחוּבָּר לַקַּרְקַע בְּשָׁעָה שֶׁאֵינָהּ גְּמַר מְלָאכָה וּבְתָלוּשׁ מִן הַקַּרְקַע מֵאַחַר שֶׁנִּגְמְרָה מְלַאכְתָּן וּבְדָבָר שֶׁאֵין גִּידּוּלָיו מִן הָאָרֶץ.

**Mishnah 2**: But the following may not eat: He who works on produce connected to the ground before the completion of work[19], or separated from the ground after the completion of work[20], or things not grown from the earth[18].

**משנה ד**: הָיָה עוֹשֶׂה בְיָדוֹ אֲבָל לֹא בְרַגְלָיו בְּרַגְלָיו אֲבָל לֹא בְיָדָיו אֲפִילוּ בִּכְתֵיפוֹ הֲרֵי זֶה אוֹכֵל. רִבִּי יוֹסֵי בֵּי רִבִּי יְהוּדָה אוֹמֵר עַד שֶׁיַּעֲשֶׂה בְיָדָיו וּבְרַגְלָיו.

**Mishnah 4**: If he was working with his hand but not with his feet, with his feet but not with his hands, even with his shoulder, he may eat. Rebbi Yose ben Rebbi Jehudah says, only if he works with hands and feet[21].

15 The agricultural worker empowered by *Deut.* 23:25-26 to eat from grain and grapes.

16 The only time he may eat from standing produce is at harvest time if he is occupied in harvesting.

17 As long as the produce is not subject to the laws of tithing, i. e., ready to be stored.

18 The worker at a hydroponic farm has no right to eat from the produce, nor may the worker in a dairy drink from the milk.

19 The agricultural worker during the growing season.

20 The worker on food after it became subject to the laws of tithing.

21 Like the harvester of grain or grapes mentioned in the verse.

(11b line 56) **הלכה ב:** אֵילוּ אוֹכְלִין מִן הַתּוֹרָה כּוּל'. אָמַר רִבִּי לָא. כִּי תָבוֹא בְּכֶרֶם רֵעֶךָ. וְכִי עָלַת עַל דַּעַת שֶׁיֹּאכַל עֵצִים וַאֲבָנִים. מַה תַּלְמוּד לוֹמַר עֲנָבִים. שֶׁלֹּא יְקַלֵּף בַּתְּאֵינִים וִימַצְמֵץ בָּעֲנָבִים.

**Halakhah 2**: "The following eat by Torah law," etc. Rebbi La said, "if you come into your neighbor's vineyard.[22]" Could anybody think that he would eat wood or stones? Why does the verse say "grapes"? That he may not skin figs or suck grapes[23].

22 *Deut.* 23:25: "If you come into your neighbor's vineyard, you may eat grapes to satisfy yourself." What else is there to eat in a vineyard?

23 Different, tannaïtic, arguments are in the Babli 87b; *Ma'serot* 2:7 (Notes 142-149); *Sifry Deut.* 266.

(11b line 56) הָיָה עוֹשֶׂה בְיָדָיו אֲבָל לֹא בְרַגְלָיו. אָמַר רִבִּי לָא. כְּתִיב כִּי תָבֹא בְקָמַת רֵעֶךָ וְגוֹ'. בְּיָדָיו אוֹ אוֹגֵד בְּרַגְלָיו מְקַמֵּץ אֲפִילוּ עַל כְּתֵיפוֹ טוֹעֵן. רִבִּי יוֹסֵי בֵּי רִבִּי יְהוּדָה אוֹמֵר עַד שֶׁיַּעֲשֶׂה בְיָדָיו וְרַגְלָיו וְגוּפוֹ. יָצָא עוֹשֶׂה בְיָדָיו אֲבָל לֹא בְרַגְלָיו. בְּרַגְלָיו אֲבָל לֹא בְגוּפוֹ.

רִבִּי יוֹסֵי בֵּירִבִּי יוּדָן אוֹמֵר דַּיִישׁ. מַה דַּיִישׁ מְיוּחָד דָּבָר שֶׁגִּידוּלוֹ מִן הַקַּרְקַע. יָצָא הַחוֹלֵב הַמְגַבֵּן הַמְחַבֵּץ שֶׁאֵין גִּידוּלֵי קַרְקַע. מַה דַּיִישׁ מְיוּחָד דָּבָר שֶׁלֹּא נִגְמְרָה מְלַאכְתּוֹ. יָצָא הַיַּיִן מִשֶּׁיִּקְפֶּה [וְהַשֶּׁמֶן] מִשֶּׁיָּרַד לָעוּקָה הַבּוֹדֵל בַּתְּמָרִים וְהַמְפָרֵד בַּגְּרוֹגְרוֹת דָּבָר שֶׁנִּגְמְרָה מְלַאכְתּוֹ. מַה דַּיִישׁ שֶׁלֹּא בָא לְזִיקַת הַמַּעְשְׂרוֹת. יָצָא הַלָּשׁ וְהַמְקַטֵּף וְהָאוֹפֶה שֶׁבָּא לְזִיקַת מַעְשְׂרוֹת.

" If he was working with his hand but not with his feet." Rebbi La said, it is written: "If you come into your neighbor's standing grain," etc.[24] With his hands, binding. With his feet, he compresses. Even with his shoulder, he carries.

[25]"Rebbi Yose ben Rebbi Jehudah says, only if he works with hands and feet; this excludes him who works with his hands but not with his feet, with his feet but not with his hands."

[26]"Rebbi Yose ben Rebbi Jehudah says, threshing. Since threshing is special in that it refers to something grown from the earth, this excludes the one who milks, makes cheese with rennet or with mold, which is not something grown from the earth. Since threshing is special in that it refers to something not completely processed; this excludes wine after it was fermented, [olive oil][27] after it descended into the vat, one who isolates dates or separates dried figs, done after complete processing. Since threshing comes before the obligation of tithes, this excludes him who kneads dough, separates into cakes, or bakes, which comes after it became obligated for tithes."

24 *Deut.* 23:26. This quote is not followed up here; it refers to the discussion in *Ma'serot* 2:6, Notes 122-123.

25 Tosephta 8:7; Babli 91b; *Ma'serot* 2:6, Note 117.

26 Tosephta 8:7; Babli 89a; *Ma'serot* 2:6, Notes 118-121. The argument refers to *Deut.* 25:4, the prohibition to muzzle the ox while he is threshing. It is declared that the rights of the laborer are no less than

the rights of the ox. The other sources have an additional set of inferences which is quoted in E as:

דְּיֵישׁ מַה דַּיִישׁ מְיוּחָד שֶׁהוּא תָּלוּשׁ מִן הַקַּרְקַע. יָצָא הַמְעַדֵּר בִּגְפָנִים הַמְנַכֵּשׁ בְּשׁוּם וּבִבְצָלִים וּבִקְפְלוֹטִין דָּבָר שֶׁהוּא מְחוּבָּר לַקַּרְקַע.

Threshing, just as threshing is particular in that it applies to plucked [grain]. This excludes him who weeds among vines, weeds among garlic, and onions, and leeks, which are connected to the ground.

Since this text parallels a statement of the Tosephta and the Yerushalmi *Ma'serot* but is formulated in the Yerushalmi *Neziqin* style, it has to be accepted as original; missing in L.

27 From E, missing in L.

**משנה ה:** (fol. 11b) הָיָה עוֹשֶׂה בַתְּאֵנִים לֹא יֹאכַל בָּעֲנָבִים בָּעֲנָבִים לֹא יֹאכַל בַּתְּאֵנִים אֲבָל מוֹנֵעַ הוּא אֶת עַצְמוֹ עַד שֶׁמַּגִּיעַ לִמְקוֹם הַיָּפוֹת וְאוֹכֵל. וְכוּלָּן לֹא אָמְרוּ אֶלָּא בִּשְׁעַת גְּמַר מְלָאכָה אֲבָל מִשּׁוּם הָשֵׁב אֲבֵידָה לַבְּעָלִים אָמְרוּ הַפּוֹעֲלִין אוֹכְלִין בַּהֲלִיכָתָן מֵאֻמָּן לְאֻמָּן וּבַחֲזִירָתָן מִן הַגַּת וַחֲמוֹר שֶׁתְּהֵא פּוֹרֶקֶת.

**Mishnah 5**: If one was working on figs he may not eat grapes, on grapes he may not eat figs; but he may restrain himself until he reaches the place of the good ones and eat there[28]. In all cases they only referred to the time of finishing[29] work, but because of returning lost property to its owner[30] they said that workers may eat when they go from row to row, and when they return from the wine press, and a donkey while offloading.

28 The farmer cannot hinder his agricultural worker from eating of his best produce.

29 This is also the reading of Alfasi and Maimonides; the latter infers from here (*Śekhirut* 12:2-3) that at harvest time the worker may eat only during breaks in harvesting, not while he is actually working; he may not harvest with his right hand and eat

with his left. The word "finishing" is not in any Ashkenazic text, nor in the *editio princeps* of the Babli. The Provençal *Meïri* writes the word in his Mishnah text but not in the quotes from the Mishnah in his commentary.

30   In order to minimize the time for which the employer pays but which the worker uses to eat during working hours, traditional rules encourage him to eat only while going from one job to another or waiting for others to finish a task from where he can start his work. A worker who does not follow this rule is within his rights but cannot be expected to be rehired.

(11b line 68) **הלכה ה:** הָיָה עוֹשֶׂה בַּתְּאֵנִים כול'. אָמַר רִבִּי לָא. כְּתִיב כִּי תָבוֹא בְכֶרֶם רֵעֶיךָ וְאָכַלְתָּ עֲנָבִים כְּנַפְשְׁךָ שָׂבְעֶךָ. וְכִי מַה יֵשׁ בַּכֶּרֶם לוֹכַל אֶלָּא עֲנָבִים. לְלַמְּדָךְ הָיָה עוֹשֶׂה בָּעֲנָבִים לֹא יֹאכַל בַּתְּאֵינִים.

**Halakhah 5**: "If one was working on figs," etc. Rebbi La said, it is written: "If you come into your neighbor's vineyard, you may eat grapes to satisfy yourself." What else is there in the vineyard to eat but grapes? To teach you that if he was working on grapes he may not eat figs[31].

31  *Deut.* 23:25. E quotes the entire first part of the Mishnah which is from the text of *Sifry Deut.* 266 on this verse. It seems therefore that the text of L is original.

(fol. 11b) **משנה ו:** אוֹכֵל פּוֹעֵל קִישׁוּת אֲפִילוּ בְדֵינָר וְכוֹתֶבֶת אֲפִילוּ בְדֵינָר. רִבִּי אֶלְעָזָר חִסְמָא אוֹמֵר לֹא יֹאכַל פּוֹעֵל יוֹתֵר עַל שְׂכָרוֹ. וַחֲכָמִים מַתִּירִין אֲבָל מְלַמְּדִין אֶת הָאָדָם שֶׁלֹּא יְהֵא רַעַבְתָן וְהֵא סוֹתֵם הַפֶּתַח מִלְּפָנָיו.

**Mishnah 6**: A worker may eat zucchini even for a denar's worth, or dates even for a denar's worth. Rebbi Eleazar Ḥasma said, a worker may not eat more than his wages[32] and the Sages permit it[33], but one instructs a man not to be voracious lest he close the door before him[34].

32 His wages for the day's work. The Halakhah shows that this was less that a silver *denar*. In Mishnah *Ševi'it* 8:4 it is intimated that the daily wages might be as low as one *assarius* or a quarter denar. (In *Matth.* 20:2 one denar; but this is an aggadic text.)

33 In *Sifry Deut.* 266, both parties learn from *Deut.* 23:25: "you may eat grapes to *satisfy yourself.*" For R. Eleazar Ḥasma the criterion is *yourself*, for the Sages *to satisfy*.

34 Nobody will hire him in the future if he is known to abuse his rights.

(11b line 71) **הלכה ו:** אוֹכֵל פּוֹעֵל קִישׁוּת אֲפִילוּ בְדֵינָר. רִבִּי לְעָזָר בֶּן אַנְטִיגְנָס אוֹמֵר בְּשֵׁם רִבִּי רִבִּי לְעָזָר בֵּירִבִּי יַנַּאי. זֹאת אוֹמֶרֶת. אוֹכֵל פּוֹעֵל יוֹתֵר עַל שְׂכָרוֹ. וְאִית דְּאָמְרִין רִבִּי יוֹחָנָן בְּשֵׁם רִבִּי יַנַּאי. זֹאת אוֹמֶרֶת שֶׁיֹּאכַל פּוֹעֵל אֶשְׁכּוֹל רִאשׁוֹן וְאֶשְׁכּוֹל אַחֲרוֹן.

**Halakhah 6:** "A worker may eat zucchini even for a denar's worth," etc. Rebbi Eleazar ben Antigonos says in the name of Rebbi Eleazar ben Rebbi Yannai, this means that a worker may eat more than his [daily] wages[32]. But some say, Rebbi Joḥanan in the name of Rebbi Yannai: This means that a worker may eat the first or the last bunch of grapes[35].

35 Both the first and the last bunches of grapes would fetch a premium on the market of fresh fruits; nevertheless the farmer may not prohibit his hired hand from eating them. In the Babli, 93a, this is formulated as: Even if the entire yield is only one bunch, the worker may eat it.

(fol. 11b) **משנה ז:** קוֹצֵץ אָדָם עַל יְדֵי עַצְמוֹ עַל יְדֵי בְנוֹ וּבִתּוֹ הַגְּדוֹלִים עַל יְדֵי עַבְדוֹ וְשִׁפְחָתוֹ הַגְּדוֹלִים עַל יְדֵי אִשְׁתּוֹ מִפְּנֵי שֶׁיֵּשׁ בָּהֶן דַּעַת. אֲבָל לֹא עַל יְדֵי בְנוֹ וּבִתּוֹ הַקְּטַנִּים וְלֹא עַל יְדֵי עַבְדּוֹ וְשִׁפְחָתוֹ הַקְּטַנִּים וְלֹא עַל יְדֵי בְהֶמְתּוֹ מִפְּנֵי שֶׁאֵין בָּהֶן דַּעַת.

**Mishnah 7**: A person may contract for himself, for his adult son or daughter, for his adult male and female slaves, for his wife, because they have understanding. But he may not contract for his underage son or daughter, nor for his underage male and female slaves, nor for his animal, because they have no understanding[36].

[36] This Mishnah is explained only in a short section of the Babli, 92b/93a, which is summarized by Maimonides (*Śekhirut* 12:14): "A worker who worked together with his wife, children, and slaves for one employer may contract with the employer that none of them will eat from what they are working on. That is, if they are adults, because they have understanding and therefore can give up their rights. But for those underage he cannot contract, since they eat not from their father's, nor from their employer's, but from Heaven's." Cf. also *Ma'serot* 2:6, Note 129.

(fol. 11b) **משנה ח:** הַשּׂוֹכֵר אֶת הַפּוֹעֲלִין לַעֲשׂוֹת עִמּוֹ בְּנֶטַע רְבָעִי שֶׁלּוֹ הֲרֵי אֵילוּ לֹא יֹאכְלוּ. אִם לֹא הוֹדִיעָן פּוֹדֶה וּמַאֲכִילָן. נִתְפָּרְסוּ עִגּוּלָיו נִתְפַּתְּחוּ חָבִיּוֹתָיו הֲרֵי אֵילוּ לֹא יֹאכְלוּ. אִם לֹא הוֹדִיעָן מְעַשֵּׂר וּמַאֲכִילָן.

**Mishnah 8**: If somebody hires workers to work with him in his fourth-year plantation, they may not eat. If he did not inform them, he has to redeem it and feed them[37]. If his fig cakes were dislodged or his amphoras opened, they may not eat. If he did not inform them, he has to tithe and feed them[38].

[37] Newly planted fruit trees in their first three years have to be stripped of their fruits as forbidden *'orlah*. In the fourth year the yield may be redeemed and then eaten in place, or brought to the Temple and eaten there in purity (*Lev.* 19:23-24; Tractate *'Orlah*). Since eating from the fruit is a recognized privilege of agricultural workers, if they are not informed that they are to work on forbidden fruit they could not ask for higher wages to

compensate for the fruit.

38   It was stated in Mishnah 3 that workers on food processed to the stage of tithes have no privilege of eating from it. It is forbidden to eat titheable but untithed food   If the workers were hired under the impression that they had the privilege, the employer has to provide them with permitted food.

(11b line 75) **הלכה ח:** הַשּׂוֹכֵר אֶת הַפּוֹעֲלִין כול'. כָּל־שֶׁכְּיוֹצֵא בּוֹ בָא לְזִיקַת מַעְשְׂרוֹת וְאִיסּוּר אַחֵר גָּרַם לוֹ. שְׂכָרוֹ סְתָם פּוֹדֶה וּמַאֲכִיל מְעַשֵּׂר וּמַאֲכִיל. קָצַץ עִמּוֹ הֲרֵי זֶה אוֹכֵל. וְכָל־שֶׁאֵין כְּיוֹצֵא בּוֹ בָא לְזִיקַת הַמַּעְשְׂרוֹת וְאִיסּוּר אַחֵר גָּרַם לוֹ. שְׂכָרוֹ סְתָם אֵינוֹ אוֹכֵל. קָצַץ עִמּוֹ הֲרֵי זֶה אוֹכֵל.

**Halakhah 8:** "If somebody hires workers to work," etc. Anything which is of a kind apt to be under the rules of tithing but another prohibition caused it [to be forbidden to eat], if one hired [a worker] without mentioning it, he has to redeem and feed, tithe and feed[39]. If [the worker] contracted for it, he eats[40]. But if it is of a kind exempt from the rules of tithing[41] but another prohibition caused it [to be forbidden to eat], if one hired [a worker] without mentioning it, that one cannot eat[42]; if he contracted for it, he eats.

39   This is the case of the Mishnah; the "other prohibition" is the fourth-year status of the orchard.

40   This is obvious; any worker may contract to receive part or all of his wages as food. It is only needed here as a parallel to the next statement.

41   For example, any unripe fruit as mentioned in *Ma'serot* 1:2.

42   If this is from a fourth-year orchard, the worker has no claim to the fruit even if he was not informed beforehand.

(fol. 11b) **משנה ט:** שׁוֹמְרֵי פֵירוֹת אוֹכְלִין מֵהִילְכוֹת מְדִינָה אֲבָל לֹא מִן הַתּוֹרָה. אַרְבָּעָה שׁוֹמְרִין הֵן שׁוֹמֵר חִנָּם וְהַשּׁוֹאֵל נוֹשֵׂא שָׂכָר וְהַשּׂוֹכֵר. שׁוֹמֵר חִנָּם נִשְׁבַּע

עַל הַכֹּל וְהַשּׁוֹאֵל מְשַׁלֵּם אֶת הַכֹּל וְנוֹשֵׂא שָׂכָר וְהַשּׂוֹכֵר נִשְׁבָּעִין עַל הַשְּׁבוּרָה וְעַל הַשְּׁבוּיָה וְעַל הַמֵּתָה וּמְשַׁלְּמִין אֶת הָאֲבֵידָה וְאֶת הַגְּנֵיבָה.

**Mishnah 9**: Watchmen of produce[43] eat because of local practice but not from the Torah. There are four kinds of keepers: The unpaid trustee and the borrower, the paid keeper and the renter. The unpaid trustee swears about everything[44], the borrower pays for everything. The paid keeper and the renter swear about the broken, the kidnapped, and the dead[45] but pay for the lost and the stolen.

43 They do not actually work and are not covered by Mishnah 3.
44 If anything happens to the goods entrusted to him he does not pay if he is able to swear that he did not take anything and that it was not his fault; *Ex.* 22:6-8.
45 They do not pay for what happened beyond their control; *Ex.* 22:11-12.

**הלכה ט**: (11c line 4) שׁוֹמְרֵי פֵּירוֹת אוֹכְלִים מֵהִילְכוֹת מְדִינָה כול׳. רַב הוּנָא אָמַר. בְּשׁוֹמְרֵי פֵּירוֹת הִיא מַתְנִיתָא. אֲבָל בְּשׁוֹמְרֵי גִינּוֹת וּפַרְדֵּיסִין אוֹכְלִין מִן הַתּוֹרָה. שְׁמוּאֵל אָמַר. בְּשׁוֹמְרֵי גִינּוֹת וּפַרְדֵּיסִין הִיא מַתְנִיתָא. אֲבָל בְּשׁוֹמְרֵי פֵּירוֹת אֵין אוֹכְלִין לֹא מִתּוֹרָה וְלֹא מֵהִילְכוֹת מְדִינָה. תַּנֵּי רִבִּי חִייָה וּמְסַייֵעַ עַל רַב הוּנָא. וְטָמֵא הַכֹּהֵן עַד הָעָרֶב. לְרַבּוֹת אֶת הַשּׁוֹמְרִין שֶׁיְּהוּא מְטַמְּאִין בְּגָדָיו.

**Halakhah 9**: "Watchmen of produce eat because of local practice," etc. Rav Huna[46] said, the Mishnah refers to watchmen of produce[47]. But watchmen of vegetable gardens and orchards eat by Torah law. Samuel said, the Mishnah refers to watchmen of vegetable gardens and orchards[43]. But watchmen of produce eat neither by Torah law nor by local practice[48]. Rebbi Hiyya stated in support of[49] Rav Huna: "The Cohen shall be impure until evening," to include watchmen, that they make their garments impure[50].

46 In the Babli, 93a, the opinion of Rav Huna is quoted as that of his teacher Rav; Samuel's opinion is reproduced there.

47 After the harvest.

48 If the produce is ready to be sold, it only has to be watched to prevent loss.

49 This use of עַל when one would expect לְ may be the root of German-Jewish כָּשֵׁר עַל פֶּסַח "usable for Passover" instead of כָּשֵׁר לְפֶסַח used by all other Jewish groups.

50 This refers to the law of the Red Cow, *Num.* 19, in particular 19:7. The priest who supervises the burning of the cadaver of the red cow becomes impure simply by watching the procedure even if he touches nothing and does nothing himself. This proves that watching alone is counted as an activity in Torah law, as asserted by Rav Huna.

(fol. 11b) **משנה י:** זְאֵב אֶחָד אֵינוֹ אוֹנֶס וּשְׁנֵי זְאֵיבִין אוֹנֶס. רִבִּי יְהוּדָה אוֹמֵר בְּשָׁעַת מִשְׁלַחַת זְאֵבִים אַף זְאֵב אֶחָד אוֹנֶס.

**Mishnah 10:** 51One wolf is not an unavoidable accident, two wolves are. Rebbi Jehudah says, in times when wolves appear in packs, even a single wolf is an unavoidable accident.

**משנה יא:** שְׁנֵי כְלָבִים אֵינָן אוֹנֶס. יַדּוּעַ הַבַּבְלִי אוֹמֵר מִשּׁוּם רִבִּי מֵאִיר. מֵרוּחַ אַחַת אֵינוֹ אוֹנֶס מִשְׁתֵּי רוּחוֹת אוֹנֶס.

**Mishnah 11:** Two dogs are not an unavoidable accident. Yaddua the Babylonian says in the name of Rebbi Meïr: From the same direction it is not an unavoidable accident; from two different directions it is an unavoidable accident

**משנה יב:** הַלִּיסְטִין הֲרֵי הֵן אוֹנֶס. הָאֲרִי וְהַדּוֹב וְהַנָּמֵר וְהַבַּרְדְּלִיס וְהַנָּחָשׁ הֲרֵי אֵילוּ אוֹנְסִין. אֵימָתַי בִּזְמַן שֶׁבָּאוּ מֵאֲלֵיהֶן אֲבָל אִם הוֹלִיכָן לִמְקוֹם גְּדוּדֵי חַיָּה וְלִיסְטִין אֵין אֵילוּ אוֹנְסִין.

**Mishnah 12**: Robbers are an unavoidable accident. A lion, and a bear, and a leopard, and a panther[52], and a snake are unavoidable accidents. When? If they came by themselves. But if he led [the flock] to a place of troops of wild animals or robbers, these are not unavoidable accidents.

משנה יג: מֵתָה כְדַרְכָּהּ הֲרֵי זֶה אוֹנֶס. סִכְפָּהּ וָמֵתָה אֵינוֹ אוֹנֶס. עָלַת לְרָאשֵׁי צוּקִין וְנָפְלָה הֲרֵי זֶה אוֹנֶס. הֶעֱלָה לְרָאשֵׁי צוּקִין וְנָפְלָה אֵינוֹ אוֹנֶס. מַתְנֶה שׁוֹמֵר חִנָּם לִהְיוֹת פָּטוּר מִשְּׁבוּעָה וְהַשּׁוֹאֵל לִהְיוֹת פָּטוּר מִלְּשַׁלֵּם נוֹשֵׂא שָׂכָר וְהַשּׂוֹכֵר לִהְיוֹת פְּטוּרִין מִשְּׁבוּעָה וּמִלְּשַׁלֵּם.

**Mishnah 13**: If [an animal] dies a natural death it is an unavoidable accident. If he tortured it and it died, it is not an unavoidable accident. If it climbed to the top of a cliff and fell, it is an unavoidable accident. If he led it onto the top of a cliff and it fell, it is not an unavoidable accident. The unpaid keeper may stipulate that he be free from swearing, the borrower that he not be liable to pay, the paid keeper and the renter that they not be liable to swear or to pay[53].

משנה יד: כָּל־הַמַּתְנֶה עַל מַה שֶׁכָּתוּב בַּתּוֹרָה תְּנָיָיו בָּטֵל. וְכָל־תְּנַאי שֶׁהוּא מַעֲשֶׂה בִתְחִילָּתוֹ תְּנָיָיו בָּטֵל. וְכָל־שֶׁאֶיפְשָׁר לוֹ לְקַיְּמוֹ בְסוֹפוֹ וְהִתְנָה עָלָיו מִתְּחִילָּתוֹ תְּנָיָיו קַיָּים.

**Mishnah 14**: The stipulation of anybody who stipulates against what is written in the Torah is invalid. Any stipulation which follows a prior action is invalid[54]. But any stipulation which it is possible to fulfill at the end and he stipulated it at the start is valid[54].

51  The next four Mishnaiot deal with the responsibilities of the paid keeper and the renter, who may free themselves from paying for an unavoidable accident by swearing but have to pay for avoidable accidents. The prime example of the paid keeper is the shepherd, for whom these rules are formulated.

52  Greek πάρδαλις, Latin *pardalis*.

53  In money matters there is freedom in contracting. Even though

the rules of responsibility of keepers are biblical (Notes 44,45), they are default rules to be used in the absence of contrary stipulations. It follows that Mishnah 14 deals only with stipulations other than money matters.

54   An action cannot be invalidated retroactively. If a man preliminarily marries a woman and after that tries to impose conditions on the act, he remains unconditionally married.

55   But any condition which was intended to be impossible to keep is void. If a man divorces his wife saying, this is your letter of divorce on condition that you cross the ocean on your feet, or that you fly in the air like a bird, she is unconditionally divorced (Tosephta *Giṭṭin* 5:12).

(11c line 9) **הלכה י:** זְאֵב אֶחָד אֵינוֹ אוֹנֶס כול׳. כָּל־הַמַּתְנֶה עַל מַה שֶׁכָּתוּב בַּתּוֹרָה כול׳. תַּנֵּי. כָּל־הַמַּתְנֶה עַל מַה שֶׁכָּתוּב בַּתּוֹרָה. תְּנַאי מָמוֹן תְּנָאוֹ קַייָם. תְּנַאי שֶׁאֵינוֹ שֶׁלְּמָמוֹן תְּנָאוֹ בָטֵל. כֵּיצַד. אָמַר לְאִשָּׁה. הֲרֵי אַתְּ מְקוּדֶּשֶׁת לִי עַל מְנָת שֶׁאֵין לִיךְ עָלַי שְׁאֵר כְּסוּת וְעוֹנָה. הֲרֵי זוֹ מְקוּדֶּשֶׁת [וּתְנָייוֹ קַייָם. עַל מְנָת] שֶׁאִם מֵתִי לֹא תְהֵא זְקוּקָה לְייבּוּם. הֲרֵי זוֹ מְקוּדֶּשֶׁת וּתְנָאוֹ בָטֵל.

**Halakhah 10**: "One wolf is not an unavoidable accident," etc. "The stipulation of anybody who stipulates against what is written in the Torah," etc. It was stated: [56]"The stipulation of anybody who stipulates against what is written in the Torah, monetary stipulations are valid, non-monetary stipulations are invalid." How is this? If one said to a woman: be preliminarily married to me on condition that you have no claim on me for sustenance, clothing, and marital relations, she is preliminarily married [and his stipulation is valid. "On condition][57] that it I die you shall not be obligated for levirate marriage, she is preliminarily married but his stipulation is invalid."

56   Tosephta *Qiddušin* 3:8; cf. *Qiddušin* 1:2, Notes 262-271 (Babli *Qiddušin* 19b).

57   Addition from E, missing in L.

The addition is unquestionably correct even though it is pointed out in *Qiddušin* 1:2 (Note 268) that only the first two conditions are of monetary character. There, the problem is explained away by restricting the possibility of such a condition to preliminary marriage with a very young girl who is not available for sexual relations. But from the story of R. Tarphon who in times of famine preliminarily married 300 women to give them access to heave (*Yebamot* 4:12 Note 197; Tosephta *Ketubot* 5:1) and certainly did not offer them sustenance and clothing from his own means, it seems that if some of the conditions are of monetary character and the nonmonetary stipulation is not operative at the moment (since marital relations are obligatory and permitted only after definitive marriage), the stipulation is valid and if it is valid at the moment it is made it remains valid even after the nonmonetary stipulation becomes operative.

(11c line 9) זֶה הַכְּלָל שֶׁהָיָה רִבִּי יְהוּדָה בֶן תֵּימָא אוֹמֵר. כָּל־דָּבָר שֶׁאֵיפְשָׁר לְהִתְקַיֵּים וְהִתְנָה עִמָּהּ לֹא נִתְכַּוֵּון אֶלָּא לְהַפְלִיגָהּ. בֵּין שֶׁאָמַר בִּכְתָב בֵּין שֶׁאָמַר בְּפֶה. כָּל־הַמִּתְקַיְּיִין בְּפֶה מִתְקַיְּיִים בִּכְתָב. וּכְפַר עוֹתְנַי כִּגְלִיל וְאַנְטִיפַּטְרִס כִּיהוּדָה. אֶת שֶׁבֵּינְתַיִים מַטִּילִין אוֹתוֹ לְחוּמְרוֹ.

[58]"This is the principle enunciated by Rebbi Jehudah ben Tema: Anything which is impossible to keep but he stipulated for her only to put her off[55,59]. Whether we put it in writing or said it orally, everything valid orally is valid when written[60]". [61]"And Kefar Othnay belongs to Galilee, Antipatris to Judea; the places in between are interpreted stringently[62]."

58    Tosephta *Gittin* 5:12; Babli 94a, *Gittin* 84a; cf. *Tosefta kiFshutah Gittin* pp. 886-887.

59    The majority opinion in the Tosephta and the Babli holds that a bill of divorce given with an impossible stipulation is invalid.

60    In general, conditions written into a bill of divorce invalidate the entire bill. Cf. *Gittin* 3:1, Notes 40-56.

61    Tosephta *Gittin* 5:7; Babli *Gittin* 76a. This refers to a man who before departing gave his wife a bill of divorce and stated that she should be divorced if he left Judea, or if he reached Galilee, etc. On the *via maris* Antipatris (near Petah Tiqwah) was the border station in Judea and Kefar

Othnay (Kafr Uthnay near Megiddo) the border station in Galilee; Mishnah *Gittin* 7:8.

62 Since the position of the stretch of the *via maris* passing through Samaria is indeterminate in *halakhah*, if the husband, e. g., left Judea but did not reach Galilee the wife is "divorced and not divorced."

## השואל את הפרה פרק שמיני

(fol. 11c) **משנה א:** הַשּׁוֹאֵל אֶת הַפָּרָה וְשָׁאַל בְּעָלֶיהָ עִמָּהּ. שָׁאַל אֶת הַפָּרָה וְשָׂכַר בְּעָלֶיהָ עִמָּהּ. שָׁאַל אֶת הַבְּעָלִים אוֹ שְׂכָרָן וּלְאַחַר כָּךְ שָׁאַל אֶת הַפָּרָה וָמֵתָה פָּטוּר שֶׁנֶּאֱמַר אִם בְּעָלָיו עִמּוֹ לֹא יְשַׁלֵּם.

**Mishnah 1**: If somebody borrowed a cow and asked its owner [to work with him], or borrowed a cow and paid its owner [to work with him], or asked or paid its owner [to work with him] and then borrowed the cow: if it died he is not liable since it was said: "if its owner was with it he does not pay[1]."

**משנה ב:** אֲבָל שָׁאַל אֶת הַפָּרָה וְאַחַר כָּךְ שָׁאַל אֶת הַבְּעָלִים אוֹ שְׂכָרָן וָמֵתָה חַיָּיב שֶׁנֶּאֱמַר אִם בְּעָלָיו אֵין עִמּוֹ שַׁלֵּם יְשַׁלֵּם.

**Mishnah 2**: But if he borrowed the cow and afterwards asked or paid its owner [to work with him] and it died he is liable since it was said: "if its owner was not with it, certainly he shall pay.[2]"

1 Ex. 22:14. The verse is read to mean that the borrower is not liable to pay for an animal which dies while working for him if its owner also was working for him all the time the animal was working. The owner need not be near the animal at the moment of its death.

2 Ex. 22:15.

(11c line 70) **הלכה א:** הַשּׁוֹאֵל אֶת הַפָּרָה כול׳. אָמַר רִבִּי אִילָא. מִמַּשְׁמַע שֶׁנֶּאֱמַר שַׁלֵּם יְשַׁלֵּם אֵין אָנוּ יוֹדְעִין אִם בְּעָלָיו עִמּוֹ לֹא יְשַׁלֵּם. מַה תַּלְמוּד לוֹמַר בְּעָלָיו אֵין עִמּוֹ שַׁלֵּם יְשַׁלֵּם. אֶלָּא מִכֵּיוָן שֶׁשָּׁאַל אֶת הַפָּרָה וְלֹא שָׁאַל בְּעָלָהּ עִמָּהּ אַף עַל פִּי שֶׁהַבְּעָלִים חוֹרְשִׁין עַל גַּבָּהּ וָמֵתָה חַיָּיב.

אֲבָל שָׁאַל אֶת הַפָּרָה וְאַחַר כָּךְ שָׁאַל בְּעָלָהּ אוֹ שְׂכָרָן וָמֵתָה חַיָּיב. אָמַר רִבִּי לָא. מִמַּשְׁמָע שֶׁנֶּאֱמַר אִם בְּעָלָיו עִמּוֹ לֹא יְשַׁלֵּם אֵינִי יוֹדֵעַ שֶׁאִם אֵין בְּעָלָיו עִמּוֹ שַׁלֵּם יְשַׁלֵּם. וּמַה תַלְמוּד לוֹמַר בְּעָלָיו עִמּוֹ לֹא יְשַׁלֵּם. אֶלָּא מִכֵּיוָן שֶׁשָּׁאַל אֶת הַפָּרָה וְשָׂכַר בְּעָלָהּ עִמָּהּ אַף עַל פִּי שֶׁהַבְּעָלִים חוֹרְשִׁין בְּמָקוֹם אַחֵר וָמֵתָה פָּטוּר.

**Halakhah 1**: "If somebody borrowed a cow," etc. Rebbi Ila said, from the meaning of what is said, "certainly he shall pay"; would we not have known that if its owner was with it he does not pay? Why does the verse say, "if its owner was not with it, certainly he shall pay"? But since he borrowed the cow and did not ask its owner at the same time, even if the latter was ploughing with it when it died, he is liable.

"But if he borrowed the cow and afterwards asked or paid its owner [to work with him] and it died he is liable." Rebbi La said, from the meaning of what is said, "if its owner was not with it, certainly he shall pay," would I not have known that if its owner was not with it, certainly he shall pay? Why does the verse say, "if its owner was with it he does not pay"? But since he borrowed the cow and did ask its owner at the same time, even if the latter was ploughing at another place when it died, he is not liable[3].

3   A similar, tannaïtic, text is in the Babli, 95b, and *Mekhilta dR. Simeon bar Iohai* 22:14 (p. 206-207). In the language of *Mekhilta dR. Ismael* (*Neziqin* 16, p. 306): The borrower has to pay if the cow was out of its owner's control even for one moment.

(fol. 11c) **משנה ג:** הַשּׁוֹאֵל אֶת הַפָּרָה שְׁאָלָהּ חֲצִי יוֹם וּשְׂכָרָהּ חֲצִי יוֹם שְׁאָלָהּ הַיּוֹם וּשְׂכָרָהּ לְמָחָר שָׁכַר אַחַת וְשָׁאַל אַחַת הַמַּשְׁאִיל אוֹמֵר שְׁאוּלָה מֵתָה בְּיוֹם שֶׁהָיְתָה שְׁאוּלָה מֵתָה בְּשָׁעָה שֶׁהָיְתָה שְׁאוּלָה מֵתָה וְהַלָּה אוֹמֵר אֵינִי יוֹדֵעַ חַיָּיב. הַשּׂוֹכֵר אוֹמֵר שְׂכוּרָה מֵתָה בַּיּוֹם שֶׁהָיְתָה שְׂכוּרָה מֵתָה בְּשָׁעָה שֶׁהָיְתָה שְׂכוּרָה

מֵתָה וְהַלָּה אוֹמֵר אֵינִי יוֹדֵעַ פָּטוּר. זֶה אוֹמֵר שְׁאוּלָה וְזֶה אוֹמֵר שְׂכוּרָה יִשָּׁבַע הַשּׂוֹכֵר שֶׁהַשְּׂכוּרָה מֵתָה. זֶה אוֹמֵר אֵינִי יוֹדֵעַ וְזֶה אוֹמֵר אֵינִי יוֹדֵעַ יַחֲלוֹקוּ.

**Mishnah 3**: Somebody borrowed a cow; he borrowed it for half a day and leased[4] it for half a day, or borrowed it for one day and leased it for the next, or borrowed for one and leased for one. The lessee says, the borrowed one died, or it died on the day it was borrowed, or it died during the time it was borrowed, and the other one says "I do not know", he is liable[5]. The lessor says, the leased one died, or it died on the day it was leased, or it died during the time it was leased, and the other one says "I do not know", he is not liable[5]. One says the borrowed and the other one says the leased; let the lessee swear that the leased one died[6]. If both say "I do not know" they shall split[7].

4 The lessor does not have to pay if the cow died; that risk was covered by the rental fee (*Ex.* 22:14).

5 Since one party claims certainty and the other ignorance, judgment has to be given to the party claiming certainty.

5 Both claim certainty but neither has proof. The claimant has to swear in order to collect.

7 The value of the cow is "money in doubt" which has to be split evenly (Chapter 1, Note 5). The lessee /borrower has to pay half the value of the cow which died.

(11d line 6) **הלכה ב**: הַשּׁוֹאֵל אֶת הַפָּרָה כול׳. לַיְלָה שֶׁבֵּינְתַיִים מָהוּ. אִית מָרִין. דֶּרֶךְ הַפָּרוֹת לָלוּן עַל בְּעָלֵיהֶן וְזוֹ עַל יְדֵי שֶׁשּׂוֹכְרָהּ אֶצְלוֹ לֹא לָנָה כִּשְׁאוּלָה הִיא אֶצְלָהּ וְהוּא חַיָּיב. וְאִית מָרִין. אֵין דֶּרֶךְ הַפָּרוֹת לָלוּן עַל בְּעָלֵיהֶן וְזוֹ כִּשְׂכוּרָה אֶצְלוֹ וּפָטוּר.

**Halakhah 2**: "Somebody borrowed a cow," etc. What is the status of the night in between[8]? Some say, usually cows rest at their owners', and this one, because it is leased to him, stays overnight and is as if loaned to him; he is liable. But some say, usually cows do not rest at their owners',

**8** He borrowed for one day and leased for the next; the cow dies during the night.

(11d line 10) **הלכה ג:** הַשּׁוֹאֵל אֶת הַפָּרָה כול'.

### E

תַּנֵּי. הַשְׁאִילֵינִי פָּרָתָךְ עֲשָׂרָה יָמִים וְהִשְׁאֵל לִי בָהֶן חֲמִשָּׁה יָמִים. מֵתָה. מִשִּׁעְבּוּד הָרִאשׁוֹנִים. מִשִּׁעְבּוּד הָאַחֲרוֹנִים מֵתָה.

הַשְׁאִילֵינִי פָּרָתָךְ עֲשָׂרָה יָמִים וְהִשְׁאֵל לִי בָהֶם רִאשׁוֹנִים. וּמֵתָה בתוֹךְ הָאַחֲרוֹנִים. מִשִּׁעְבּוּד הָרִאשׁוֹנִים מֵתָה. מִשִּׁעְבּוּד הָאַחֲרוֹנִים מֵתָה.

הַשְׁאִילֵינִי פָּרָתָךְ לְאַחַר עֲשָׂרָה יָמִים. אָמַר לֵיהּ. סַבָּהּ מִן כְּבָר. מֵתָה. מִשִּׁעְבּוּד הָרִאשׁוֹנִים מֵתָה. מִשִּׁעְבּוּד הָאַחֲרוֹנִים מֵתָה.

### L

תַּנֵּי. הַשְׁאִילֵינִי פָּרָתָךְ י׳ יָמִים וְהַשְׁאֵל לִי בָהֶן ה׳ יָמִים רִאשׁוֹנִים. מֵתָה בתוֹךְ הָאַחֲרוֹנִים מִשִּׁעְבּוּד הָרִאשׁוֹנִים מֵתָה.

הַשְׁאִילֵינִי פָּרָתָךְ לְאַחַר עֲשֶׂר יָמִים. אָמַר לֵיהּ. סַבָּהּ מִן כְּבָר. מֵתָה. מִשִּׁעְבּוּד הָאַחֲרוֹנִים מֵתָה.

### E

It was stated: 'Lend me your cow for ten days and you shall be lent to me[9] the first five days.' If it died, was it subject to the first days' servitude? It died subject to the later days' servitude[10].

'Lend me your cow for ten days and you shall be lent to me the first of these.' If it died during the

### L

It was stated: 'Lend me your cow for ten days and you shall be lent to me[9] the first five days.' If it died during the last days, it died subject to the first days' servitude[10].

'Lend me your cow after ten days.' The other one said, 'take it now.' If it died, it died subject to the later days' servitude[12].

later days, was it subject to the first days' servitude? it died subject to the later days' servitude[11].

'Lend me your cow after ten days.' The other one said, 'take it now.' If it died, was it subject to the first days' servitude[13]? It died subject to the later days' servitude.

9  I. e., work with me during five days.
10  The text of L contradicts the principle established in Note 3. Therefore the text of E has to be accepted; the borrower has to pay for the dead cow.
11  This second paragraph is an almost verbatim copy of the preceding; it should be deleted.
12  In all cases, it already was established in Note three that the borrower is liable if the animal was not under its owner's control for even one minute.
13  The rhetorical question should be read in all three paragraphs.

(11d line 14) הַשְׁאִילֵינִי פָרָתָךְ וַאֲנִי נִשְׁאַל לָךְ. הַשְׁאִילֵינִי פָרָתָךְ וּבוֹא וַעֲשֵׂה עִמִּי. הַשְׁאִילֵינִי קַרְדּוֹמָךְ וּבוֹא וְנַכֵּשׁ עִמִּי. הַשְׁאִילֵינִי תַמְחוּיָיךְ וּבוֹא וֶאֱכוֹל עִמִּי. שְׁאָלָהּ מִן הַבַּיָּיר אוֹ מִן הַסַּנְטָר אוֹ מִן הָאִיקוֹמְנוֹס וָמֵתָה כְּמִי שֶׁהַבְּעָלִים עִמּוֹ.

Lend me your cow and I shall respond to your request[14]; lend me your cow and come work with me; lend me your axe and come weed with me; lend me your plate and come eat with me. If he borrowed it from the superintendent of cisterns, the steward[15], or the administrator and it died, it is as if the owners were with it[16].

14  It is not clear what this means. In the other three cases the borrower asks the owner to be with the animal, tool, or vessel; the biblical rule of the borrower applies. Therefore, one has to assume that in the first case also the borrower asks for animal and owner and is ready to reciprocate with his animal and time.

15  Chapter 5, Note 138. The steward is the organizer of the work on the estate; the administrator (οἰκονόμος) is the paymaster and the accountant. On large estates, both could be slaves, cf. *Bava batra* 4:7.

16  On an estate of absentee owners, the employees authorized to dispose of certain items do represent the owners. If the employee worked with the borrower, it is as if the owner worked with him.

(fol. 11c) **משנה ד:** הַשׁוֹאֵל אֶת הַפָּרָה וְשִׁילַּח לוֹ בְיַד בְּנוֹ וּבְיַד עַבְדּוֹ וּבְיַד שְׁלוּחוֹ אוֹ בְיַד בְּנוֹ בְיַד עַבְדּוֹ בְיַד שְׁלוּחוֹ שֶׁלַּשּׁוֹאֵל וָמֵתָה פָּטוּר. אָמַר לוֹ הַשּׁוֹאֵל שַׁלְּחָהּ לִי בְּיַד בְּנִי וּבְיַד עַבְדִּי וּבְיַד שְׁלוּחִי אוֹ בְיַד בִּנְךָ אוֹ בְיַד עַבְדְּךָ אוֹ בְיַד שְׁלוּחֶךָ אוֹ שֶׁאָמַר לוֹ הַמַּשְׁאִיל הֲרֵינִי מְשַׁלְּחָהּ לָךְ בְּיַד בְּנִי בְּיַד עַבְדִּי בְּיַד שְׁלוּחִי אוֹ בְיַד בִּנְךָ אוֹ בְיַד עַבְדְּךָ אוֹ בְיַד שְׁלוּחֶךָ וְאָמַר לוֹ הַשּׁוֹאֵל שַׁלַּח וְשִׁילְּחָהּ וָמֵתָה חַיָּיב. וְכֵן בְּשָׁעָה שֶׁמַּחֲזִירָהּ.

**Mishnah 4**: If somebody borrowed a cow and [the lender] sent it through his son, or his slave, or his agent, or through the borrower's son, or slave, or agent, and it died, he is not liable[17]. If the borrower said, send it to me through my son, or slave, or agent, or through your son, or slave, or agent, or if the lender said, I am going to send it to you through my son, or slave, or agent, or through your son, or slave, or agent, and the borrower said: send! If it died, he is liable[18]. The same holds when he returns it[19].

17  If everything is done on the lender's initiative, the cow is not delivered until it reaches its destination; it still is under its owner's

control.

18 If the delivery is on the borrower's initiative or explicit agreement, the cow is under the borrower's control during delivery. If anything happened, he is liable.

19 The person on whose orders the delivery takes place carries the financial responsibility.

(11d line 17) **הלכה ד**: אָמַר לוֹ הִשְׁאִילָה לִי כול׳.

**Halakhah 4**: "If he said to him, lend me," etc.

(fol. 11c) **משנה ה**: הַמַּחֲלִיף פָּרָה בַחֲמוֹר וְיָלְדָה וְכֵן הַמּוֹכֵר שִׁפְחָתוֹ וְיָלְדָה זֶה אוֹמֵר עַד שֶׁלֹּא מָכַרְתִּי וְזֶה אוֹמֵר מִשֶּׁלְּקַחְתִּי יַחֲלוֹקוּ. הָיוּ לוֹ שְׁנֵי עֲבָדִים אֶחָד גָּדוֹל וְאֶחָד קָטָן וְכֵן שְׁתֵּי שָׂדוֹת אַחַת גְּדוֹלָה וְאַחַת קְטַנָּה. הַלּוֹקֵחַ אוֹמֵר הַגָּדוֹל לָקַחְתִּי וְהַמּוֹכֵר אוֹמֵר אֵינִי יוֹדֵעַ זָכָה בַּגָּדוֹל. הַמּוֹכֵר אוֹמֵר הַקָּטוֹן מָכַרְתִּי וְהַלָּה אוֹמֵר אֵינִי יוֹדֵעַ אֵין לוֹ אֶלָּא קָטָן. זֶה אוֹמֵר גָּדוֹל וְזֶה אוֹמֵר קָטָן יִשָּׁבַע הַמּוֹכֵר שֶׁהַקָּטָן מָכַר. זֶה אוֹמֵר אֵינִי יוֹדֵעַ וְזֶה אוֹמֵר אֵינִי יוֹדֵעַ יַחֲלוֹקוּ.

**Mishnah 5**: Somebody exchanged a cow for a donkey and it gave birth, or he sold his slave girl and she gave birth. If one said, [it happened] before I sold, the other said, after I bought, they shall split[20]. If he had two slaves, one adult and one young, or two fields, one large and one small. The buyer says, I bought the large one, and the seller says, I do not know: he acquired the large one[21]. The seller says, I sold the small and the other party says, I do not know: he has only the small one[21]. If one says the large one and the other says the small, let the seller swear that he sold the small one[22]. If both say, I do not know, they shall split[23].

20 If neither of them has proof.
21 Even if neither of them has proof, judgment has to be given to the one who claims certainty against one who asserts uncertainty.
22 Both assert their claim with

(11d line 18) **הלכה ה:** הַמַּחֲלִיף פָּרָה כול'. אָמַר רִבִּי יוֹחָנָן. זוֹ לְהוֹצִיא מִידֵי סוּמָכוֹס שָׁאוֹמֵר. כָּל־הַסְפֵיקוֹת יַחֲלוֹקוּ. אָמַר רִבִּי לָא. תִּיפְתָּר בְּשֶׁזֶּה אוֹמֵר. בָּרִיא לִי. וְזֶה אוֹמֵר. בָּרִיא לִי. רִבִּי יוֹסֵי בָּעֵי. אִם בְּשֶׁזֶּה אוֹמֵר. בָּרִיא לִי. וְזֶה אוֹמֵר. בָּרִיא לִי. עַל דָּא אָמַר רִבִּי יוֹחָנָן לְהוֹצִיא מִדִּבְרֵי סוּמָכוֹס.

**Halakhah 5**: "Somebody exchanged a cow," etc. Rebbi Joḥanan said, this[24] contradicts Symmachos who says that in *all* cases of doubt one splits evenly[25]. Rebbi La said, explain it if both of them say, I am certain[26]. Rebbi Yose explained, if both of them say, I am certain, that is what Rebbi Joḥanan refered to when he said, this contradicts Symmachos's words.

24  If both parties submit their claim as certain as in the case of Note 22.

25  But in cases where both claims are tentative, the rule is universally accepted and we do not need Symmachos's statement. Cf. Babli 100a.

26  He holds that Symmachos gave his rule only in cases where nobody submits a certain claim.

(fol. 11c) **משנה ו:** הַמּוֹכֵר זֵיתָיו לָעֵצִים וְעָשׂוּ פָּחוֹת מֵרְבִיעִית לַסְּאָה הֲרֵי אֵילוּ לְבַעַל הַזֵּיתִים. עָשׂוּ רְבִיעִית לַסְּאָה זֶה אוֹמֵר זֵיתַיי גִּידֵּילוּ וְזֶה אוֹמֵר אַרְצִי גִידְּלָהּ יַחֲלוֹקוּ.

**Mishnah 6**: Somebody sold his olive trees for their wood[27]. If they produced less than a *quartarius* [of oil] per *se'ah*[28], it belongs to the owner of the olive trees. A *quartarius* [of oil] per *se'ah*, one says, my olive trees grew [the olives], the other says, my land grew them: they shall split evenly[29].

**משנה ז:** שָׁטַף הַנָּהָר זֵיתָיו וּנְתָנָם לְתוֹךְ שְׂדֵה חֲבֵירוֹ זֶה אוֹמֵר זֵיתַיי גִידֵּילוּ וְזֶה אוֹמֵר אַרְצִי גִידְּלָה יַחֲלוֹקוּ.

**Mishnah 7**: If a river flooded his olive trees and carried them to another's field[30]; one says, my olive trees grew them, the other says, my land grew them: they shall split evenly.

27   It is forbidden to cut down fruit bearing trees (*Ševi'it* 4:9, Notes 109-113). But one is permitted to cut down a fruit tree which does no longer yield a commercially useful crop, or if its wood is more valuable than its crop.

28   If the yield in oil is $< 1/96$ of the volume of olives harvested. This is such a minute quantity that nobody is supposed to quarrel about it.

29   The buyer, instead of cutting down the tree for its wood, left it standing on the seller's ground until the next harvest. Then the seller may claim part of the yield.

30   The Mishnah presupposes not that the trees were torn away by the flood but that the flood eroded the earth around the trees which then were carried away with their roots still embedded in the original owner's earth. Then the owner of the parcel on which they were deposited can dig a hole in which to set the tree with its original earth and hope for a normal harvest.

When the flood swept land away, it becomes ownerless since the owner is presumed to have abandoned hope of recovery (Halakhah 2:1); it does not have to be returned (Tosephta 2:2; *Šeqalim* 7:3).

(11d line 22) **הלכה ו:** הַמּוֹכֵר זֵיתָיו לָעֵצִים כול׳. רִבִּי יוֹחָנָן בָּעֵי. הִרְטִיבוּ מַה הֵן.

רַב הוּנָא אָמַר. בְּשֶׁשְּׁטָפָן בְּגוּשֵׁיהֶן. רִבִּי יוֹסֵי בֶּן חֲנִינָה אָמַר. שְׁנֵי עָרְלָה בֵּינֵיהֶן.

**Halakhah 6**: "Somebody sold his olive trees for their wood," etc. Rebbi Johanan asked, what is their status if they become moist[31]?

[32]Rav Huna said, if it swept them away in their earth. Rebbi Yose ben Hanina said, the years of *'orlah* are their dispute[33].

31 If the olives only contain 1% of recoverable oil, they probably are not edible. What is the status of the crop if somehow they become edible? The question is not answered.

32 This refers to Mishnah 7.

33 In the Babli, 101a, the entire discussion is in the name of R. Simeon ben Laqish.

If the trees are swept away with their roots exposed, the farmer who replants them on his property must observe the first three years as *'orlah* (Mishnah *'Orlah* 1:3). There is no yield to quarrel about. Therefore, the Mishnah presupposes that the earth in which the tree was planted was eroded and the tree was swept away with it, as explained in the Mishnah. R. Yose b. Hanina notes that the original owner has a claim only for the three years in which the new owner would not have had any yield, were it not for the original owner's earth in which the roots were embedded. After three years the entire harvest is the second owner's.

(fol. 11c) **משנה ח:** הַמַּשְׂכִּיר בַּיִת לַחֲבֵירוֹ בִּימוֹת הַגְּשָׁמִים אֵינוֹ יָכוֹל לְהוֹצִיאוֹ מִן הֶחָג עַד הַפֶּסַח. וּבִימוֹת הַחַמָּה שְׁלֹשִׁים יוֹם וּבַכְּרַכִּין אֶחָד יְמוֹת הַחַמָּה וְאֶחָד יְמוֹת הַגְּשָׁמִים שְׁנֵים עָשָׂר חֹדֶשׁ. וּבַחֲנוּיוֹת אֶחָד כָּרַכִּין וְאֶחָד עֲיָירוֹת שְׁנֵים עָשָׂר חֹדֶשׁ. רַבָּן שִׁמְעוֹן בֶּן גַּמְלִיאֵל אוֹמֵר חֲנוּת שֶׁל נַחְתּוֹמִין וְשֶׁל צַבָּעִין שָׁלֹשׁ שָׁנִים.

**Mishnah 8**: He who rents a dwelling to another person cannot remove him from there during the rainy season, from Tabernacles to Passover, but in the dry season on thirty days' notice. But in walled cities,[33] whether in the dry or the rainy season, on twelve months' notice. For a store[34], whether in a walled city or in a village, twelve months. Rabban Simeon ben Gamliel said, a baker's or dyer's store[35], three years.

33 Where there is a permanent shortage of apartments and it is unlikely that a replacement dwelling can be found within one month.

34 The store owner frequently sells on credit and needs time to collect

(11d line 24) **הלכה ו:** הַמַּשְׂכִּיר בַּיִת לַחֲבֵירוֹ כול׳. תַּנֵּי. כָּל־אֵילוּ שֶׁאָמְרוּ ל יוֹם וְי'ב חוֹדֶשׁ לֹא שֶׁיִּדּוֹר בְּתוֹכָן ל יוֹם וְי'ב חוֹדֶשׁ אֶלָּא שֶׁיּוֹדִיעוֹ קוֹדֶם ל יוֹם וְקוֹדֶם י'ב חוֹדֶשׁ. בֵּית הַבַּד כָּל שָׁעַת בֵּית הַבַּד. בֵּית הַגַּת כָּל שָׁעַת הַגַּת. בֵּית הַיּוֹצְרָה אֵין פָּחוֹת מִשְּׁנֵים עָשָׂר חוֹדֶשׁ. אָמַר רִבִּי יוֹסֵי. בַּמֶּה דְבָרִים אֲמוּרִים. בְּאֵילֵין שֶׁהֵן עוֹשִׂין בֶּעָפָר שָׁחוֹר. אֲבָל בְּאֵילֵין שֶׁעוֹשִׂין בֶּעָפָר לָבָן כּוֹנֵס גּוֹרְנוֹ וּמִסְתַּלֵּק.

**Halakhah 8**: "He who leases a dwelling to another person," etc. It was stated: [36]"Anywhere they mention 30 days or twelve months it does not mean that one has to dwell there 30 days or twelve months but notice must be given before 30 days or twelve months[37]. An oil press, the entire period it is in use. A wine press, the entire period it is in use. A potter's atelier no less than twelve months. Rebbi Yose[38] said, when has this been said? For those who work with black earth. But one who works with white earth collects his stock and leaves."

36   Tosephta 8:27; the first sentence also in the Babli 101b.
37   Tosephta and Babli add: The tenant is held to the same deadlines if he wants to terminate the lease. But for the duration of a contract of lease there are no general rules.
38   In the Tosephta: R. Nehemiah.

(fol. 11c) **משנה ט:** הַמַּשְׂכִּיר בַּיִת לַחֲבֵירוֹ הַמַּשְׂכִּיר חַיָּיב בַּדֶּלֶת בַּנֶּגֶר וּבַמַּנְעוּל וּבְכָל־דָּבָר שֶׁהוּא מַעֲשֵׂה אוּמָּן. אֲבָל דָּבָר שֶׁאֵינוֹ מַעֲשֵׂה אוּמָּן הַשּׂוֹכֵר עוֹשֵׂהוּ. הַזֶּבֶל שֶׁל בַּעַל הַבַּיִת. אֵין לַשּׂוֹכֵר אֶלָּא הַיּוֹצֵא מִן הַתַּנּוּר וּמִן הַכִּירַיִם בִּלְבַד.

**Mishnah 9**: He who leases a dwelling to another person: the lessee must provide the door, the key-bolt and the door handle and everything that requires expert installation. But anything that does not require experts, the lessor does it. Manure[39] belongs to the lessee; the lessor only has what comes from the oven and the cooking stove[40].

39 Which accumulates in the courtyard and is sold as fertilizer.

lord's courtyard; the tenant may sell the ashes as fertilizer.

40 Even if they are in the land-

(11d line 30) **הלכה ט**: הַמַּשְׂכִּיר בַּיִת לַחֲבֵירוֹ כול'. הוֹרֵי רבִּי יִצְחָק בַּר חֲקוּלָה מְזוּזָה מַעֲשֵׂה אוּמָּן.

**Halakhah 9**: "He who leases a dwelling to another person," etc. Rebbi Isaac ben Ḥaqula instructed that a *mezuzah* requires expert installation[41].

41 If a Jewish landlord leases a dwelling to a Jew, it must come with the required box of scriptural verses on

the doorpost (*Deut.* 6:9, 11:20). The Babli disagrees, 102a.

(fol. 11c) **משנה י**: הַמַּשְׂכִּיר בַּיִת לַחֲבֵירוֹ לַשָּׁנָה נִתְעַבְּרָה הַשָּׁנָה נִתְעַבְּרָה לַשּׂוֹכֵר. הִשְׂכִּיר לוֹ לֶחֳדָשִׁים נִתְעַבְּרָה הַשָּׁנָה נִתְעַבְּרָה לַמַּשְׂכִּיר. מַעֲשֵׂה בְצִיפּוֹרִין שֶׁשָּׂכַר מֶרְחָץ מֵחֲבֵירוֹ בִּשְׁנֵים עָשָׂר זָהָב לַשָּׁנָה מִדֵּינָר זָהָב לַחֹדֶשׁ וּבָא מַעֲשֵׂה לִפְנֵי רַבָּן שִׁמְעוֹן בֶּן גַּמְלִיאֵל וְלִפְנֵי רבִּי יוֹסֵי וְאָמְרוּ יַחֲלוֹקוּ אֶת חֹדֶשׁ הָעִיבּוּר.

**Mishnah 10**: He who leases a dwelling to another person by the year, if the year was intercalated[42], it was intercalated for the lessor. If he leased by the month, if the year was intercalated it was intercalated for the lessee. It happened in Sepphoris that a person leased a bathhouse from another for twelve gold denars per year, one gold denar per month[43]. The case came before Rabban Simeon ben Gamliel and Rebbi Yose who said, they should split the intercalated month.

42 Before the publication of calendar computations in the Fourth Century, the uninitiated could not know which lunar year would be decreed to have a thirteenth month added to it.

43 The contract was written so that the lease was both per year and per month. The rent for the thirteenth month was "money in doubt."

**הלכה י** (11d line 31): הַמַּשְׂכִּיר בַּיִת לַחֲבֵירוֹ כול'. וְהֵיכִי. אִם בְּשָׁבָא עָלָיו בְּסוֹף הַחוֹדֶשׁ גְּבֵיי לֵיהּ כּוּלָהּ. וְאִם בְּשָׁבָא עָלָיו בְּרֹאשׁ חוֹדֶשׁ אָמַר לֵיהּ. פּוּק לָךְ. שְׁמוּאֵל אָמַר. כֵּינֵי מַתְנִיתָא. בְּשָׁבָא עָלָיו בְּאֶמְצַע הַחוֹדֶשׁ. רַב אָמַר. דִּינָא דְנַר. אָמַר רִבִּי לָא. לֵית דָּא פְּשְׁטָא עַל שִׁיטַת בֶּן נַנָּס דּוּ אָמַר. בִּיטֵּל לָשׁוֹן אַחֲרוֹן אֶת הָרִאשׁוֹן.

**Halakhah 10**: "He who leases a dwelling to another person," etc. Why? If he came to claim at the end of the month, can he collect everything[44]? And if he came to him at the beginning of the month, he can tell him, get out[45]. Samuel says, the Mishnah is so: If he came to claim in the middle of the month[46]. Rav said, a rule to collect[47]. Rebbi La said, this clearly does not follow the rule of Ben Nannas who said, the later language supersedes the earlier one[48].

44 Since the tenant is already living in the house, the landlord is the claimant and on him is the burden of proof that the contract was written as a monthly lease.

45 The tenant claims that he has the right to live there rent free; the burden of proof is on him. The restrictions on evictions spelled out in Mishnah 8 only apply to tenants who are not in arrears with their payments.

46 This is a case of "money in doubt"; Babli 102b.

47 He disagrees with the Mishnah and would have ruled for the landlord; Babli 102b. דָּנַר is short for דְּאָגַר; E reads here: דִּינָא דְגָרְדֵּיי דָּנוּ "they gave a judgment of weavers". The text of L seems preferable.

48 In Mishnah *Bava batra* 7:4. Since months are mentioned last, the lease is per month only and every month is payable. This is Rav's reason in the Babli.

(fol. 11c) **משנה יא:** הַמַּשְׂכִּיר בַּיִת לַחֲבֵירוֹ וְנָפַל חַיָּיב לְהַעֲמִיד לוֹ בַּיִת. הָיָה קָטָן לֹא יַעֲשֶׂנּוּ גָדוֹל. גָּדוֹל לֹא יַעֲשֶׂנּוּ קָטָן. אֶחָד לֹא יַעֲשֶׂנּוּ שְׁנַיִם. שְׁנַיִם לֹא יַעֲשֶׂנּוּ אֶחָד. לֹא יִפְחוֹת מִן הַחַלּוֹנוֹת וְלֹא יוֹסִיף עֲלֵיהֶן אֶלָּא מִדַּעַת שְׁנֵיהֶן.

**Mishnah 11**: He who leases a dwelling to another person and it collapsed has to provide him with a dwelling. If it was small he may not make it large, large he may not make it small. One room he shall not make into two, two he may not make into one. He may not reduce the number of windows nor add to them except with the agreement of both parties.

(11d line 36) **הלכה יא:** הַמַּשְׂכִּיר בַּיִת לַחֲבֵירוֹ כול׳. רֵישׁ לָקִישׁ אָמַר. בְּמַעֲמִידוֹ עַל גַּבָּיו. רִבִּי יוֹחָנָן אָמַר. בְּאוֹמֵר לוֹ. בַּיִת כָּזֶה אֲנִי מַשְׂכִּיר לָךְ. אֶלָּא הַמַּשְׂכִּיר בַּיִת לַחֲבֵירוֹ וּבִיקֵּשׁ לְמוֹכְרוֹ. אָמַר רִבִּי אִמִּי. לֹא [עֲלְתָה][49] עַל דַּעַת שֶׁזֶּה יָמוּת בָּרָעָב. רִבִּי זֵירָא וְרִבִּי הִילָא תְּרֵיהוֹן מָרִין. מִכֹּל קָנוּי לוֹ. אֶלָּא דוּ אָמַר לֵיהּ. שִׁיבְקֵיהּ. דְּשָׁרֵי עַד יְמַלֵּא אֲנַקְלְווֹסִיס דִּידֵיהּ. אֲתָא עוֹבְדָא קוֹמֵי רִבִּי נִיסִי וְלָא קַבִּיל. מַה פְּלִיג. אָמְרֵי. בְּרַתֵּיהּ הֲוַות מְמַשְׁכְּנָה גַּבֵּי חַד רוֹמַי. [וְלָא הֲוָה לֵיהּ לְמִפְרְקָהּ. וְהוֹרָה רִבִּי אַסִּי שֶׁיִּמְכּוֹר.][49] בְּגִין כֵּן הוֹרֵי כְרִבִּי אִימִי.

**Halakhah 11**: "He who leases a dwelling to another person," etc. Rebbi Simeon ben Laqish said, if he puts him into it[50]. Rebbi Johanan said, if he told him, a dwelling like this I shall lease to you[51]. But if a person leasing a house wants to sell it? Rebbi Immi said, nobody thinks that this one should die of hunger[52]. Rebbi Ze'ira and Rebbi Hila both say, while certainly it is acquired by him, he has to tell him, let him dwell there until the time of his recall[53,54]. There came a case before Rebbi Nisi[55] and he did not accept this. Does he disagree? They said, his daughter was given as a pledge to a Roman [and he did not have the wherewithal to redeem her and Rebbi Assi instructed to sell;] therefore he instructed following Rebbi Immi[56].

49  From E, confirmed by *'Or zarua'* §328; *Rosh* Chapter 8 # 25.

50  The strict requirements of the Mishnah only apply if the lessor makes a sales pitch about the qualities of the particular dwelling.

51  Even if only the kind of dwelling is mentioned.

52  For him, a sale breaks a lease.

53  Greek ἀνάκλησις "recall, restoration". *'Or zarua'* reads עַד מִישְׁלָם זִמְנֵיהּ "until his time is up."

54  While a sale during a lease is certainly valid, there is an obligation of the seller to include a paragraph in the sales document which protects the tenant for the remainder of his lease.

55  This probably should read: Assi, with *'Or zarua'*, *Rosh*, and the later text.

56  In an emergency one follows R. Immi. The rule of RR. Ze'ira and Ila is a recommendation, not the law. This is implied in R. Immi's formulation.

## המקבל שדה מחבירו פרק תשיעי

(fol. 11d) **משנה א:** הַמְקַבֵּל שָׂדֶה מֵחֲבֵירוֹ מְקוֹם שֶׁנָּהֲגוּ לִקְצוֹר יִקְצוֹר לַעֲדוֹר יַעֲדוֹר לַחֲרוֹשׁ אַחֲרָיו יַחֲרוֹשׁ הַכֹּל כְּמִנְהַג הַמְּדִינָה. כְּשֵׁם שֶׁחוֹלְקִין בַּתְּבוּאָה כָּךְ חוֹלְקִין בַּתֶּבֶן וּבַקַּשׁ. כְּשֵׁם שֶׁחוֹלְקִין בַּיַּיִן כָּךְ חוֹלְקִין בַּזְּמוֹרוֹת וּבַקָּנִים וּשְׁנֵיהֶן מְסַפְּקִין אֶת הַקָּנִים.

**Mishnah 1**: One who contracts with another for a field[1], at a place where one usually cuts, he has to cut[2], to uproot, he has to uproot[3], to plough after harvest, he has to plough, everything according to local usage. Just as they divide the grain, so they divide straw and chaff. Just as they divide the wine, so they divide the vine tendrils[4] and the props[5]; they both provide the props together.

1   Either as a sharecropper or as a tenant for a fixed amount per year. The percentage given to the owner of the land has to be specified in each case; all other conditions follow the rules of the Mishnah unless they are contracted otherwise.

2   At harvest time, one cuts the grain with sickle or scythe.

3   One tears out the entire plant with its roots.

4   Cut during the pruning of the vines.

5   To which the vines are tied. Since they are bought in common, they are disposed of in common.

(12a line 28) **הלכה א:** הַמְקַבֵּל שָׂדֶה מֵחֲבֵירוֹ כול'. מְקוֹם שֶׁנָּהֲגוּ לִקְצוֹר וְתָלַשׁ. אָמַר לֵיהּ. אַתְּ בְּעִיתָהּ. לִתְלוֹשׁ וְקָצַר. אָמְרִין לוֹ. פּוּק דְּרִיתָהּ.

**Halakhah 1**: "One who contracts with another for a field" etc. If he uprooted at a place where one usually cuts, he[6] may tell him: "you make it sterile." Where one uproots and he cuts, one tells him, go out and make it clean.

6    This gives the reasons why the landlord can force the contractor to follow customary rules. The same arguments are in the Babli, 103b.

(12a line 29) תַּנֵּי. הַמְקַבֵּל שָׂדֶה מֵחֲבֵירוֹ הֲרֵי זֶה קוֹצֵר וּמְעַמֵּר וְדָשׁ וְזוֹרֶה וּבוֹרֵר. הַחוֹפֵר וְהַכַּיָּיל וְהַסַּנְטָר שׁוֹמְרֵי הָעִיר וְהָאִיקוֹנוֹמוֹס נוֹטְלִין שְׂכָרָן מִן הָאֶמְצַע. הַכַּיָּיר וְהַבַּלָּן וְהַסֵּפָר בִּזְמַן שֶׁבָּאִין מִכֹּחַ הָאָרִיס נוֹטְלִין מִכֹּחַ הָאָרִיס. מִכֹּחַ בַּעַל הַבַּיִת נוֹטְלִין מִכֹּחַ בַּעַל הַבַּיִת. אֵין מְשַׁנִּין עַל מִנְהַג הַמְּדִינָה.

It was stated[7]: "One who contracts with another for a field has to harvest, bind into sheaves, thresh, winnow, and grade[8]. The digger[9], the measurer[10], the steward[11], the town watchmen, and the administrator[11] take their wages from the community[12]. The builder of furnaces[13], the maker of seals, and the scribe[14], if hired by the tenant they take[15] from the tenant; if hired by the landlord they take from the landlord. [16]One does not change local usage."

7    Tosephta 9:14.

8    Separate the grain into the different commercially recognized grades. All this work done far away from the field is included in the lease of the field.

9    He digs cisterns and is responsible for the cleaning and upkeep of the water system. This is a permanent job.

10   He measures the volumes of grain (cf. Arabic كيال) and other produce. The correct determination by *Arukh* (6 כל) was misunderstood by later commentators and lexicographers as "geometer", whose services outside of Egypt were almost never needed. This led S. Lieberman to note (*Tosefta kiFshutah Bava meṣia'* p. 285) that he does not know the definition of כייר and that the explanations of commentaries and dictionaries are unconvincing. The seal of the grain measurer was needed for bulk sale of produce.

11   Cf. 8:3, Note 15.

12   They are paid from town taxes. This presupposes that the entire town is the private property of a large landowner.

13   כּוּר is an industrial furnace. But since building furnaces is not continuous work and כּוֹר is a measure of volume (30 *se'ah*), perhaps the כייר is

identical with the כייל (E. G.).

14 Usually one reads הַבַּלָּן וְהַסַפָּר "the bath attendant and the barber" but these providers of personal services cannot be understood here. A בּוּל "seal" in Hebrew and Syriac, Latin *bulla*, is needed for commercial and financial transactions.

15 Their fees or wages.

16 E adds: אָמַר ר' לָא. הַפּוֹעֲלִים בִּזְמַן שֶׁבָּאִין מִכֹּחַ הָאָרִיס נוֹטְלִין מִכֹּחַ הָאָרִיס. מִכֹּחַ בַּעַל הַבַּיִת נוֹטְלִין מִכֹּחַ בַּעַל הַבַּיִת.
R. La said: Workers if hired by the tenant receive from the tenant; if hired by the landlord they receive from the landlord.

(fol. 11d) **משנה ב:** הַמְקַבֵּל שָׂדֶה מֵחֲבֵירוֹ וְהִיא בֵּית שְׁלָחִין אוֹ בֵית הָאִילָן. יָבַשׁ הַמַּעֲיָין וְנִקְצַץ הָאִילָן אֵינוֹ מְנַכֶּה לוֹ מֵחֲכִירוֹ. אִם אָמַר לוֹ הַשְׂכֵּר לִי שְׂדֵי בֵית שְׁלָחִין זוֹ אוֹ בֵית הָאִילָן זוֹ יָבַשׁ הַמַּעֲיָין וְנִקְצַץ הָאִילָן מְנַכֶּה לוֹ מֵחֲכִירוֹ.

**Mishnah 2:** One who contracts with another for a field[17], if it is an irrigated field or an orchard and the source dried up or the orchard was cut down, he[18] may not deduct from his leasing fee. If he said, this irrigated field or this orchard shall be leased to me[19] and the source dried up or the orchard was cut down, he may deduct from his leasing fee.

17 The nature of the field was not specified in the lease.

18 The tenant. This Mishnah does not apply to sharecroppers.

19 The nature of the field was specified in the lease.

(12a line 34) **הלכה ב:** הַמְקַבֵּל שָׂדֶה מֵחֲבֵירוֹ כול'. אָמַר רִבִּי יִצְחָק. בְּשֶׁיָּבַשׁ כָּל־הַמַּעֲיָין. בְּרַם אִין הֲוָה עָמִיק תַּרְתֵּין קוֹמִין וְאַתְּ עָבִיד ג קוֹמִין עָמִיק יָכְלִין מֵימַר לֵיהּ. לַעֲיֵ בֵיהּ וְהוּא סַגִּי.

נִקְצַץ הָאִילָן. אָמַר רִבִּי יִצְחָק. בְּשֶׁנִּקְצַץ כָּל־הָאִילָן. אֲבָל אִם נִשְׁתַּיֵּיר בּוֹ מַטָּע עֲשָׂרָה לְבֵית סְאָה יָכִיל מֵימַר לֵיהּ. בְּקַדְמִיתָא הֲווֹ דְחָשִׁין וְלָא הֲווֹ עָבְדִין סַגִּין. בְּרַם כְּדוֹן הִינּוּן דְּלִילִין וְעָבְדִין סַגִּין.

**Halakhah 2**: "One who contracts with another for a field," etc. Rebbi Isaac said, if the well dried up completely[20]. But if it was two storeys deep and now it is three storeys deep, one may tell him: exert yourself and it will be sufficient.

"The orchard was cut down." Rebbi Isaac said, if the entire orchard was cut down. But if there remained ten trees standing per *bet se'ah*[21] he may tell him: At the beginning they were sickly and were not bearing much. But now they are sparse and will be productive.

20   This refers to the second case of the Mishnah, where the nature of the area to be leased was specified in the contract. The Babli (103b) points out that the drying up of the water source must be a local phenomenon; for if it were due to a countrywide drought the tenant could reduce his rent payments according to Mishnah 9:6.

21   Ten fruit trees per *bet se'ah* constitute a minimal orchard (*Ševi'it* 1:2, Note 18), one tree per 250 square cubits. If the trees are more widely spaced, the area legally is no longer an orchard. The statement that "the entire orchard was cut down" has to be qualified to mean that "the trees were cut down to the extent that the orchard no longer exists."

משנה ג: הַמְקַבֵּל שָׂדֶה מֵחֲבֵירוֹ אִם מְשָׁזְכָה בָּהּ הוֹבִירָהּ שָׁמִין אוֹתָהּ (fol. 11d) כַּמָּה רְאוּיָה לַעֲשׂוֹת וְנוֹתְנִין לוֹ שֶׁכָּךְ כּוֹתֵב לוֹ אִם אוֹבִיר וְלֹא אַעֲבִיד אִישַׁלַּם בְּמֵיטָבָא.

**Mishnah 3**: One contracts with another for a field; if after he received[22] it he lets it lie fallow[23] one estimates how much it could yield and gives to him, for so he writes to him: If I let it lie fallow or do not work it, I shall pay as if well-worked[24].

22 The share cropper.
23 Without the landlord's agreement or against the local rules of crop rotation.
24 Since the sharecropper is presumed to be uneducated, any condition binding on him has to be formulated in Aramaic.

(12a line 39) **הלכה ג:** הַמְקַבֵּל שָׂדֶה מֵחֲבֵירוֹ כול׳. אָמַר רִבִּי יִצְחָק. הָדָא אָמְרָה. הַמְבַטֵּל כִּיס חֲבֵירוֹ אֵין לוֹ עָלָיו אֶלָא תַּרְעוֹמֶת. הַמְבַטֵּל שְׂדֵה חֲבֵירוֹ חַיָּיב לְשַׁפּוֹת לוֹ. הַמְבַטֵּל סְפִינוֹתוֹ וַחֲנוּתוֹ מָהוּ.

**Halakhah 3**: "One who contracts with another for a field," etc. Rebbi Isaac said, this[25] implies that if one lets another's money lie idle, the other only has a complaint against him. If one lets another's field lie idly, he has to compensate him adequately[26]. If one lets another's ship or store lie idly, what is the rule?

25 Not this Mishnah, but Tosephta 4:22 quoted in Halakhah 5:5, Note 56. For the definition of "complaint", see there, Note 58.
26 This is the Mishnah here.

(fol. 11d) **משנה ד:** הַמְקַבֵּל שָׂדֶה מֵחֲבֵירוֹ וְלֹא רָצָה לְנַכֵּשׁ וְאָמַר לוֹ מָה אִיכְפַּת לָךְ הוֹאִיל וַאֲנִי נוֹתֵן לָךְ חֲכוֹרָךְ אֵין שׁוֹמְעִין לוֹ מִפְּנֵי שֶׁיָּכוֹל לוֹמַר לוֹ לְמָחָר אַתְּ יוֹצֵא מִמֶּנָּה וְהִיא מַעֲלָה לְפָנַיי עֲשָׂבִים.

**Mishnah 4**: One[27] who contracts with another for a field, did not want to weed[28], and told him, what do you care since I am paying you rent? One does not listen to him[29] since he[30] may tell him, tomorrow you leave it and I'll have it overgrown with grasses.

27 The tenant farmer, not the share cropper.
28 Or flagrantly neglected any other common agricultural practice.
29 The court.
30 The landlord.

(12a line 42) **הלכה ד:** הַמְקַבֵּל שָׂדֶה מֵחֲבֵירוֹ כול'.

**Halakhah 4**: "One who contracts with another for a field," etc.

(fol. 11d) **משנה ה:** הַמְקַבֵּל שָׂדֶה מֵחֲבֵירוֹ וְלֹא עָשָׂת. אִם יֵשׁ בָּהּ כְּדֵי לְהַעֲמִיד כְּרִי חַיָּיב לְטַפֵּל בָּהּ. אָמַר רִבִּי יְהוּדָה מַה קִיצְבָהּ בַּכְּרִי. אֶלָּא אִם יֵשׁ בָּהּ כְּדֵי נְפִילָה.

**Mishnah 5**: One who contracts with another for a field and it did not produce[31]. If it is enough to make a pile, he has to work on it. Rebbi Jehudah said, what is the definition of a pile? But if it is enough for spreading.

(12a line 42) **הלכה ה:** הַמְקַבֵּל שָׂדֶה מֵחֲבֵירוֹ כול'. כַּמָּה כְּדֵי לְהַעֲמִיד בָּהּ כְּרִי. רִבִּי יַעֲקֹב בַּר אִידִי בְשֵׁם רִבִּי יְהוֹשֻׁעַ בֶּן לֵוִי. וּבִלְבַד שֶׁיַּעֲמִיד הָרַחַת. רִבִּי אַבָּהוּ בְשֵׁם רִבִּי יוֹסֵי בֶּן חֲנִינָה. וְהוּא שֶׁיְּהֵא בֵית מִכְנָס שֶׁלָּהּ לְמַעֲלָה. רִבִּי יְהוֹשֻׁעַ בֶּן לֵוִי אָמַר. חוּץ מִיצִיאוֹתָיו שֶׁלָּזֶה. רִבִּי יוֹסֵי בֶּן חֲנִינָה אָמַר. חוּץ מִיצִיאוֹתָיו שֶׁלָּזֶה וְשֶׁלָּזֶה. אָמַר רִבִּי אַבָּהוּ כְּדֵי נְפִילָה. כְּדֵי הַזֶּרַע הַנּוֹפֵל בָּהּ.

**Halakhah 5**: "One who contracts with another for a field," etc. How much is "enough to make a pile"? Rebbi Jacob bar Idi in the name of Rebbi Joshua ben Levi: that the winnowing shovel can stand upright in it[32]. Rebbi Abbahu in the name of Rebbi Yose ben Ḥanina: only that its handle be on top[33]. Rebbi Joshua ben Levi said: in addition to his expenses[34]. Rebbi Yose ben Ḥanina said: in addition to the expenses of both of them. Rebbi Abbahu said: "for spreading", to recover the seed grain which was spread on it[35].

31 And the share cropper does not work for a minimal yield.

32 It is enough if the shovel can be held standing by the grain around it

33 The shovel's blade must be completely covered by grain, only the handle be visible on top (Babli 105a).

34 There must be enough grain so it may be sold to cover the share cropper's expenses and the remainder form a pile in which a shovel can be kept standing. In the Babli (105a), R. Simeon ben Laqish says, the expenses and two *se'ah* of grain (about 25 liter).

35 This is explained in *Peah* 5:1, Notes 28-30.

(fol. 11d) **משנה ו:** הַמְקַבֵּל שָׂדֶה מֵחֲבֵירוֹ וַאֲכָלָהּ חָגָב אוֹ נִשְׁדְּפָה. אִם מַכַּת מְדִינָה הִיא מְנַכֶּה לוֹ מֵחֲכִירוֹ אִם אֵינָהּ מַכַּת מְדִינָה אֵינוֹ מְנַכֶּה לוֹ מֵחֲכִירוֹ. רַבִּי יְהוּדָה אוֹמֵר אִם קִיבְּלָהּ מִמֶּנּוּ בְּמָעוֹת בֵּין כָּךְ וּבֵין כָּךְ אֵינוֹ מְנַכֶּה לוֹ מֵחֲכִירוֹ.

**Mishnah 6**: One[27] who contracts with another for a field, but it was eaten by locusts or scorched. If it was a countrywide calamity, he reduces his leasing fee; if it was not a countrywide calamity[36], he does not reduce his leasing fee. Rebbi Jehudah says, if he contracted for a sum of money[37] in no case does he deduct from the leasing fee.

36 But only individual fields were damaged.

37 The lease has to be paid in coin, not in produce. Yerushalmi *Demay* 6:1 (Tosephta *Demay* 6:2) notes that the tenant paying in kind is called חוֹכֵר "lessee", the one paying in money is called שׂוֹכֵר "he who rents".

(12a line 48) **הלכה ו:** הַמְקַבֵּל שָׂדֶה מֵחֲבֵירוֹ כול׳. רַב הוּנָא אָמַר. בְּשֶׁנִּשְׁדְּפָה כָּל־אוֹתָהּ הָרוּחַ. שִׁמְעוֹן בָּר וָא בְּשֵׁם רִבִּי יוֹחָנָן. וְהוּא שֶׁאִוְרָעָה. [אֲבָל אִם לֹא זַרְעָהּ] דּוּ יָכִיל מֵימַר לֵיהּ. אִילּוּ הֲוַת זַרְעִתָּהּ הֲוָת עָבְדָה סַגִּין. הַגַּע עַצְמָךְ שֶׁהָיוּ שָׂדוֹת אֲחֵרוֹת וְלֹא [לָקוּ]. יָכִיל מֵימַר לֵיהּ. קוּדְשָׁא בְּרִיךְ הוּא מְגַלְגֵּל עִם רְשִׁיעַיָּיא. הָיוּ שָׁם שָׂדוֹת אֲחֵרוֹת וְלָקוּ. יָכִיל מֵימַר לֵיהּ. עַד כָּא הֲוֵינָא חַיָּיב בָּהּ. מִיכָּא וּלְהַלָּן לִינָה חַיָּיב בָּהּ.

**Halakhah 6**: "One[27] who contracts with another for a field," etc. Rav Huna said, if the entire area in that direction was scorched[38]. Simeon bar Abba in the name of Rebbi Johanan. But only if it was sown. [But if he did not sow][39], the other can tell him, if you had sown it would have produced a lot[40]. Think of it, if there were other fields [which were not hit][41,42]? He may tell him, the Holy One, praise to Him, is forbearing with the evildoers. If there were other fields which were damaged[43]? He[44] may tell him, so far I was liable in the case; from now on I am no longer liable.

38  In the Babli, 105b, all opinions agree that there is a countrywide calamity only if fields in all directions from the village were scorched.

39  Reading E, missing in L and *editio princeps*, but implied by the text.

40  There might have been so great a yield that even after the field was scorched, a reasonable harvest would have been left.

41  Reading of E and R. Eliahu Fulda; missing in L. R. Eliahu usually is careful to note his emendations. The absence of a note indicates that he had some basis for his reading. The *editio princeps* moves the period: הַגַּע עַצְמָךְ שֶׁהָיוּ שָׂדוֹת אֲחֵרוֹת. וְלֹא יָכִיל מֵימַר לֵיהּ.

"Think of it, if there were other fields. May he not tell him . . .?" The meaning is unchanged.

42  If only most but not all fields were scorched. The Babli, 105b/106a from the start only speaks of "most of the *pagus* (the agricultural area)".

43  This is the opposite case, if not all but only most of the fields were damaged; a situation which the Babli still would classify as a countrywide calamity but the Yerushalmi considers as the farmer's personal bad luck.

44  The landlord may refuse to reduce the rental fee, saying that he would be forced to agree only if all fields had been damaged.

**משנה ז**: הַמְקַבֵּל שָׂדֶה מֵחֲבֵירוֹ בַּעֲשֶׂרֶת כּוֹר חִיטִּים לַשָּׁנָה. לָקָת נוֹתֵן לוֹ מִתּוֹכָהּ. הָיוּ חִיטֶּיהָ יָפוֹת לֹא יֹאמַר לוֹ הֲרֵינִי לוֹקֵחַ מִן הַשּׁוּק אֶלָּא נוֹתֵן לוֹ (fol. 11d)

מְתוּכָהּ.

**Mishnah 7**: One[27] who contracts with another for a field, for ten *kor* of wheat per year. If it was damaged, he delivers from it[45]. If the wheat turned out to be of high quality, he may not tell him: I am buying wheat in the market, but he delivers from the yield[46].

45 If the rental fee is payable in kind, one may assume that the yield of the field given in lease is meant. If the grain produced was of inferior quality, the landlord is obliged to accept this low quality grain as payment.

46 The tenant cannot sell the high quality grain on the market, buy medium quality for his rental fee, and pocket the difference.

(12a line 55) **הלכה ז:** הַמְקַבֵּל שָׂדֶה מֵחֲבֵירוֹ כול׳. תַּנֵּי. הַמְקַבֵּל שָׂדֶה מִיִּשְׂרָאֵל מְעַשֵּׂר וְנוֹתֵן לוֹ. דִּבְרֵי רִבִּי מֵאִיר. וַחֲכָמִים אוֹמְרִים. בֵּין מֵאוֹתוֹ הַמִּין בֵּין מֵאוֹתוֹ שָׂדֶה תּוֹרֵם וְנוֹתֵן לוֹ. אֲבָל מִשָּׂדֶה אַחֶרֶת אוֹ מִמִּין אַחֵר מְעַשֵּׂר וְנוֹתֵן לוֹ. רִבִּי מֵאִיר אוֹמֵר. אַף מֵאוֹתָהּ שָׂדֶה מֵאוֹתוֹ הַמִּין תּוֹרֵם וְנוֹתֵן לוֹ. אֲבָל מִשָּׂדֶה אַחֵר אוֹ מִמִּין אַחֵר אֵין מְעַשֵּׂר וְנוֹתֵן לוֹ.

**Halakhah 7**: "One who contracts with another for a field," etc. It was stated: [47]"One who contracts[48] with another for a field tithes and delivers to him, the words of Rebbi Meïr[49]. But the Sages say, both for the same kind and for the same field[50] he lifts heave[51] and delivers to him. But from another field or another kind he tithes and delivers to him[52]. [53]Rebbi Meïr says, only for the same kind and for the same field he lifts heave and delivers to him. But from another field or another kind he does (not)[54] tithe and deliver to him."

47 Cf. Tosephta *Demay* 6:4; *Demay* 6:1 Notes 12-25.

48 As a lessee (Note 37).

49 Since the produce is delivered to the landlord as payment, in his opinion it must be fully profane in that first heave (for the Cohen) and tithe (for the Levite) be taken and charged

to the lessee's account. This means that the cost to the lessee in the Land of Israel really is 11.8% higher than the amount stipulated in the lease.

50  In case the lessee pays with the produce of the field, he may tell the landlord to give tithes himself. This applies also if the contract calls for delivery of certain produce but the tenant farmer grows other kinds besides the specified produce.

51  In earlier times, when Cohanim were able to be ritually pure and eat heave in purity, recommended 2% of the produce. In times when ashes of the red cow are no longer available, a nominal amount.

52  This is the procedure frowned upon in the Mishnah: The lessee sells his crop and pays his rent with cheaper produce bought on the market. Since then he incurs a 10% surcharge for the tithe, he will not pay with bought produce unless he is able to get an extraordinarily high price for his produce.

53  The Tosephta shows that this sentence should be attributed to R. Jehudah, not R. Meïr who always requires delivery of tithed produce. He permits delivery after lifting token heave only for agricultural property whose rent comprises all kinds of produce grown there.

54  "Not" seems to be a scribal error.

(fol. 11d) **משנה ח:** הַמְקַבֵּל שָׂדֶה מֵחֲבֵירוֹ לְזוֹרְעָהּ שְׂעוֹרִין לֹא יִזְרָעֶנָּה חִיטִּין. חִיטִּין יִזְרָעֶנָּה שְׂעוֹרִין. רַבָּן שִׁמְעוֹן בֶּן גַּמְלִיאֵל אוֹסֵר. קִטְנִית לֹא יִזְרָעֶנָּה תְּבוּאָה. תְּבוּאָה יִזְרָעֶנָּה קִטְנִית. רַבָּן שִׁמְעוֹן בֶּן גַּמְלִיאֵל אוֹסֵר.

**Mishnah 8**: One who contracts with another for a field to sow barley shall not sow wheat; for wheat he may sow barley. Rabban Simeon ben Gamliel prohibits[55]. For legumes[56] he may not sow grain; for grain he may sow legumes. Rabban Simeon ben Gamliel prohibits.

55  He holds that the tenant is always required to obey exactly the terms of his lease. The anonymous Tanna holds that barley may be substituted for wheat in crop rotation but not vice-versa.

56  Beans and similar vegetables whose roots enrich the soil with

nitrogen. The Babli contends (107a) that in Iraq grain is more beneficial to the soil than legumes.

(12a line 59) **הלכה ח:** הַמְקַבֵּל שָׂדֶה מֵחֲבֵירוֹ כול'. נִיחָא שְׂעוֹרִין לֹא יִזְרָעֶנָּה חִיטִּים. חִיטִּין לֹא יִזְרָעֶנָּה שְׂעוֹרִין. וַתְיָיא כְרִבִּי לָא אוֹ כְדִבְרֵי הַכֹּל בְּמָקוֹם שֶׁאֵין שְׂעוֹרִין כִּפְלַיִים בְּחִיטִּין. אֲבָל בְּמָקוֹם שֶׁמַּעֲלִין שְׂעוֹרִין כִּפְלַיִים בְּחִיטִּין זוֹרְעָהּ שְׂעוֹרִים.

**Halakhah 8:** "One who contracts with another for a field," etc. One understands that for barley he may not sow wheat[57]; for wheat, may he not sow barley? It follows Rebbi La[58] or is the opinion of everybody at a place where the yield of barley is not twice that of wheat. But at a place where barley produces twice as much as wheat he may sow barley[59].

57  Since wheat takes more out of the ground than does barley.
58  In the next Halakhah, following the reading of E.
59  Even if this interferes with crop rotation.

(fol. 11d) **משנה ט:** הַמְקַבֵּל שָׂדֶה מֵחֲבֵירוֹ לְשָׁנִים מוּעָטוֹת לֹא יִזְרָעֶנָּה פִּשְׁתָּן וְאֵין לוֹ קוֹרַת שִׁקְמָה. קִיבְּלָהּ מִמֶּנּוּ לְשֶׁבַע שָׁנִים. שָׁנָה רִאשׁוֹנָה זָרְעָהּ פִּשְׁתָּן וְיֵשׁ לוֹ קוֹרַת שִׁקְמָה.

**Mishnah 9:** One who contracts with another for a field for a few years may not sow flax[60] and does not have sycamore logs[61]. If he contracted for seven years[62], he may sow flax and does have sycamore logs.

60  Which exhausts the soil which then takes a number of years to recover.
61  Sycamores are planted for their wood, not their fruit. If cut down, the stump (סַדַּן הַשִּׁקְמָה "anvil of the sycamore") grows a new tree which will need at least seven years to grow to usable size. Cf. *Kilaim* 1:8 Note 150; *Ševi'it* 4:5 Note 71.
62  For a minimum of 7 years.

(12a line 62) **הלכה ט:** הַמְקַבֵּל שָׂדֶה מֵחֲבֵירוֹ כול׳. נִיחָא חִטִּין לֹא יִזְרָעֶנָּה פִּשְׁתָּן. פִּשְׁתָּן לֹא יִזְרָעֶנָּה חִיטִּין. פִּשְׁתָּן לוֹקֶה הָאָרֶץ ג שָׁנִים וְתֵימַר כֵּן. פֵּירֵשׁ רִבִּי מְנַחֵם אֲחִי רִבִּי גּוֹרְיוֹן קוֹמֵי רִבִּי לָא. מוּטָב לְזוֹרְעָהּ פִּשְׁתָּן אַחַר פִּשְׁתָּן וְלֹא שְׂעוֹרִין אַחַר שְׂעוֹרִין.

**Halakhah 9**: "One who contracts with another for a field," etc. One understands that for wheat he may not sow flax. For flax may he not sow wheat? Flax damages the soil for three years and you say so[63]? Rebbi Menaḥem, the brother of Rebbi Gorion, explained before Rebbi La: It is better to sow flax after flax but not barley after barley[64].

63   That one may not substitute wheat for flax.

64   E reads: "wheat after wheat". It seems that this reading is required by the preceding Halakhah, Note 58. The Tosephta, 9:32, allows any sequence of crops on condition that no crop be planted for two consecutive years.

(fol. 11d) **משנה י:** הַמְקַבֵּל שָׂדֶה מֵחֲבֵירוֹ לְשָׁבוּעַ אֶחָד בִּשְׁבַע מֵאוֹת זוּז הַשְּׁבִיעִית מִן הַמִּנְיָין. קִיבְּלָהּ מִמֶּנּוּ שֶׁבַע שָׁנִים בִּשְׁבַע מֵאוֹת זוּז אֵין הַשְּׁבִיעִית מִן הַמִּנְיָין.

**Mishnah 10**: If one who contracts with another for a field for a Sabbatical cycle at 700 denars, the Sabbatical year is included[65]. If he contracted for seven years at 700 denars, the Sabbatical is not included[66].

65   He has the use of the field for 7 consecutive years, which gives him the possibility of 6 harvests.

66   He contracted for 7 agricultural years or 7 harvests. He has the use of the field for 7 non-consecutive years because in the Sabbatical year the field reverts to the disposition of its owner.

(12a line 66) **הלכה י:** הַמְקַבֵּל שָׂדֶה מֵחֲבֵירוֹ כול׳. תַּנֵּי. הַמְקַבֵּל שָׂדֶה מֵחֲבֵירוֹ. זְרָעָהּ שָׁנָה אַחַת וְלֹא צִימְחָה כּוֹפִין אוֹתוֹ לְזוֹרְעָהּ שְׁנִייָה. שְׁנִייָה וְלֹא צִימְחָה

אֵין כּוֹפִין אוֹתוֹ לְזוֹרְעָהּ שְׁלִישִׁית. אָמַר רֵישׁ לָקִישׁ. הָדָא דְתֵימַר בְּשָׂדֶה שֶׁאֵינָהּ בְּדוּקָה. אֲבָל בְּשָׂדֶה שֶׁהִיא בְּדוּקָה כּוֹפִין אוֹתוֹ וְזוֹרְעָהּ שְׁלִישִׁית.

**Halakhah 10**: "If one contracts with another for a field," etc. It was stated: [67]"One contracts with another for a field; he sowed it a first year and it did not grow; one forces him to sow a second year. If the second time it did not grow, one cannot force him to sow a third year." Rebbi Simeon ben Laqish said, that is, a field which had not been checked out[68]. But if it had been checked out, one can force him to sow a third year.

---

67  Tosephta 9:16; Babli 106b.

68  It is not clear what a "checked-out field" would be. In the Babli, 106b, R. Simeon ben Laqish holds that even the second time the contractor cannot be forced to sow if the first time the plants sprouted but the crop was then destroyed by a natural disaster.

---

**משנה יא:** שְׂכִיר יוֹם גּוֹבֶה כָּל־הַלַּיְלָה וּשְׂכִיר לַיְלָה גּוֹבֶה כָּל־הַיּוֹם וּשְׂכִיר שָׁעוֹת גּוֹבֶה כָּל־הַיּוֹם וְכָל־הַלַּיְלָה. (fol. 12a)

**Mishnah 11**: A person hired for the day collects the entire night[69]; a person hired for the night collects the entire day[70]. A person hired for hours collects the entire day and the entire night[71].

**משנה יב:** שְׂכִיר שַׁבָּת שְׂכִיר חוֹדֶשׁ שְׂכִיר שָׁנָה שְׂכִיר שָׁבוּעַ יָצָא בַיּוֹם גּוֹבֶה כָּל־הַיּוֹם יָצָא בַלַּיְלָה גּוֹבֶה כָּל־הַלַּיְלָה וְכָל־הַיּוֹם.

**Mishnah 12**: A person hired for a week, a month, a year, or a Sabbatical period, if he finishes during daytime, he collects the entire day; if he finishes at nighttime, he collects the entire night and the following day.

---

69  Since he works until sundown, he cannot be paid during the day. If he was not paid by daybreak the next morning, his employer has sinned

against the rule that "one may not withhold a hireling's wages until the morning" (*Lev.* 19:13).

70   If he is not paid promptly, the employer sins against "you must pay his wages on his day" (*Deut.* 24:15).

71   This is explained in the Halakhah.

(12a line 71) **הלכה יא:** שְׂכִיר יוֹם גּוֹבֶה כָּל־הַלַּיְלָה כול'. שְׁמוּאֵל אָמַר. לְמָחָר עוֹבֵר עָלָיו מִשּׁוּם בְּיוֹמוֹ תִּתֵּן שְׂכָרוֹ. רִבִּי דוֹסָא אוֹמֵר. יוֹם אֶחָד הוּא דְּתֵימַר. עוֹבֵר עָלָיו כָּל־שִׁימוֹת הַלָּלוּ. אִין בִּגְלַל מְקַיְימָא קְרָאֵי תִּיפְתָּר בִּשְׂכִיר שָׁעוֹת יוֹם וָלַיְלָה. שֶׁיָּכוֹל לִגְבּוֹת כָּל־הַיּוֹם וְכָל־הַלַּיְלָה. וְתַנֵּי כֵן. שְׂכִיר שָׁעוֹת בַּיּוֹם גּוֹבֶה כָּל־הַיּוֹם. בַּלַּיְלָה גּוֹבֶה כָּל־הַלַּיְלָה. שְׂכִיר שָׁעוֹת בַּיּוֹם וּבַלַּיְלָה גּוֹבֶה כָּל־הַלַּיְלָה וְכָל־הַיּוֹם.

**Halakhah 11:** "A person hired for the day collects the entire night," etc. Samuel said, the next morning he is in violation on his behalf because of ""you must pay his wages on his day"[70]. Rebbi Dosa said, is there one day when you can say that he transgresses on all these counts[72]? If it is to refer to the verses, explain it about a person hired by the hour during day and night who can collect the entire day and the entire night. And it was stated thus: [73]"A person hired by the hour during the day collects the entire day; in the night he collects the entire night. A person hired by the hour during day and night collects the entire night and the entire day."

72   He refers to Tosephta 10:3 or *Sifry Deut* 278: One who retains a hireling's wages transgresses five prohibitions: "Do not oppress" (*Lev.* 19:13; *Deut.* 24:14), "do not rob" (*Lev.* 19:13), "do not withhold overnight" (*Lev.* 19:13), "the sun shall not set for him" (*Deut.* 24:15). Since *Lev.* 19:13 refers to paying in the night and *Deut.* 24:14 to paying by day, how could one person transgress all five commandments simultaneously? The Babli (111a) even has a list of 6 verses; they also combine *Lev.* 19:13 and *Deut.* 24:15.

73   Tosephta 10:2; Babli 111a; *Sifra Qedošim Parašah* 2(12).

(fol. 12a) **משנה יג:** אֶחָד שְׂכַר הָאָדָם וְאֶחָד שְׂכַר הַבְּהֵמָה וְאֶחָד שְׂכַר הַכֵּלִים יֵשׁ בּוֹ מִשּׁוּם בְּיוֹמוֹ תִּתֵּן שְׂכָרוֹ וְיֵשׁ בּוֹ מִשּׁוּם לֹא תָלִין פְּעוּלַת שָׂכִיר עַד בּוֹקֶר. אֵימָתַי בִּזְמַן שֶׁתְּבָעוֹ. לֹא תְבָעוֹ אֵינוֹ עוֹבֵר עָלָיו. הִמְחָהוּ אֵצֶל חֶנְוָנִי אוֹ אֵצֶל שׁוּלְחָנִי אֵינוֹ עוֹבֵר עָלָיו. הַשָּׂכִיר נִשְׁבָּע בִּזְמַנּוֹ וְנוֹטֵל עָבַר זְמַנּוֹ אֵינוֹ נִשְׁבָּע וְנוֹטֵל. וְאִם יֵשׁ עֵדִים שֶׁתְּבָעוֹ הֲרֵי זֶה נִשְׁבָּע וְנוֹטֵל.

**Mishnah 13:** Wages of a human, as well as wages for an animal, as well as wages for implements are subsumed under "you must pay his wages on his day"[70] and "one may not withhold a hireling's wages until the morning"[69]. When? If he claimed it. If he did not claim it, one does not transgress. If one gave him a draft on a storekeeper or a banker, he does not transgress. In his time[74] the hireling swears and takes[75]; after his time he does not swear and take[76]. But if there are witnesses that he did claim, he swears and takes[77].

74  The time when he has to be paid according to Mishnah 11.

75  The hireling claims that he was not paid; the employer claims that he did pay; neither of them has witnesses. Then the hireling is privileged; the court will allow him to swear that he was not paid and then order his employer to pay.

76  The ordinary rules of procedure apply: in the absence of proof the defendant may swear to absolve himself.

77  Even after the 12 hour period when he should have been paid. The unpaid hireling has to protect his claim by asking for his money in front of witnesses.

(12b line 1) **הלכה יג:** אֶחָד שְׂכַר הָאָדָם כול׳. כְּתִיב לֹא תַעֲשׁוֹק עָנִי וְאֶבְיוֹן מֵאַחֶיךָ. אִילּוּ יִשְׂרָאֵל. מִגֵּרְךָ. זֶה גֵּר צֶדֶק. בְּאַרְצְךָ. לְרַבּוֹת הַבְּהֵמָה וְהָעֲבָדִים. בִּשְׁעָרֶיךָ. לְרַבּוֹת הַמִּטַּלְטְלִין.

**Halakhah 13:** "Wages of a human," etc. [78]It is written[79]: "Do not oppress the poor and needy of your brothers," this refers to Israel. "Your proselytes," this refers to the just proselytes[80]. "In your land," to add animals and slaves. "In your gates," to add movables[81].

78  *Sifry Deut.* 279.

79  *Deut.* 24:14. The verse reads: Do not oppress the poor and needy hireling ...

80  He is a full Jew in contrast to the גֵּר תּוֹשָׁב "resident proselyte" who only keeps the Noahide commandments.

81  A different argument for the same implication, based on *Lev.* 19:13, is in *Sifra Qedošim Parašah* 2(9).

(12b line 3) תַּנֵּי. יָכוֹל הַמְחָהוּ אֵצֶל חֶנְוָנִי אוֹ אֵצֶל שׁוּלְחָנִי יְהֵא עוֹבֵר עָלָיו. אֵינוֹ עוֹבֵר עָלָיו אֲבָל עוֹבְרִין הֵן עָלָיו. אֵימָתַי. בִּזְמַן שֶׁתְּבָעוֹ. לֹא תְבָעוֹ אֵינוֹ עוֹבֵר עָלָיו.

It was stated[82]: I could think that if one gave him a draft on a storekeeper or a banker, he would transgress about him. He does not transgress about him but they transgress about him. When? If he claimed it. If he did not claim it, one does not transgress.

82  Tosephta 10:5; *Sifra Qedošim Parašah* 2(11).

(12b line 6) הַשָּׂכִיר בִּזְמַנּוֹ נִשְׁבַּע וְנוֹטֵל. רֵישׁ לָקִישׁ אָמַר. בְּשֶׁאָמַר לוֹ. נָתַתִּי. אֲבָל אִם אָמַר לוֹ. אֶתֵּן לְמָחָר. אִם אָמַר לוֹ. נָתַתִּי. אֵינוֹ נֶאֱמָן. רַבִּי יוֹסֵי בֶּן חֲנִינָה אָמַר. וַאֲפִילוּ לְמָחָר אִם אָמַר לוֹ. נָתַתִּי. נֶאֱמָן.

"In his time the hireling swears and takes." Rebbi Simeon ben Laqish said, if he said: I paid[83]. But if he said, I shall pay tomorrow: if then he said, I paid, he cannot be believed. Rebbi Yose ben Ḥanina said, even the next day, if he said, I paid, he is believed[84].

83  This refers to the case that the hireling did not claim his wages immediately, but comes later to claim his wages. The employer may swear that he paid only if he asserts that he paid immediately. But if he admits that he transgressed the commandment to pay immediately, the hireling retains his right to swear in order to get a court order forcing the employer to pay.

84  In any case where the hireling

did not claim his wages immediately before witnesses and the claim is presented after the time due, the employer retains the right to swear that he paid.

(fol. 12a) **משנה יד:** גֵּר תּוֹשָׁב יֵשׁ בּוֹ מִשּׁוּם בְּיוֹמוֹ תִּתֵּן שְׂכָרוֹ וְאֵין בּוֹ מִפְּנֵי לֹא תָלִין פְּעוּלַת שָׂכִיר אִתְּךָ עַד בּוֹקֶר.

**Mishnah 14**: The resident proselyte[80] is protected by "you must pay his wages on his day" but not by "one may not withhold a hireling's wages until the morning"[85].

**משנה טו:** הַמַּלְוֶה אֶת חֲבֵירוֹ לֹא יְמַשְׁכְּנֶנּוּ אֶלָּא בְּבֵית דִּין וְלֹא יִכָּנֵס לְבֵיתוֹ לִיטוֹל מַשְׁכּוֹנוֹ שֶׁנֶּאֱמַר בַּחוּץ תַּעֲמוֹד. הָיוּ לוֹ שְׁנֵי כֵלִים נוֹטֵל אֶחָד וּמַחֲזִיר אֶחָד. מַחֲזִיר אֶת הַכַּר בַּלַּיְלָה וְאֶת הַמַּחֲרֵישָׁה בַּיּוֹם. וְאִם מֵת אֵינוֹ מַחֲזִיר לְיוֹרְשָׁיו. רַבָּן שִׁמְעוֹן בֶּן גַּמְלִיאֵל אוֹמֵר אַף לְעַצְמוֹ אֵינֶנּוּ מַחֲזִיר אֶלָּא עַד שְׁלֹשִׁים יוֹם וּמִשְּׁלֹשִׁים יוֹם וּלְהַלָּן מוֹכְרָן בְּבֵית דִּין.

A person who lends to another may take a pledge from him only in court[86]. He may not enter his house to take his pledge, as it is said: "You have to stand outside.[87]" If he had two vessels[88], he takes one and returns one. He returns the pillow for the night[89] and the plough for the day. If he[90] dies, he[91] does not return it to his[90] heirs. Rabban Simeon ben Gamliel says, even to himself[90] he[91] returns it only up to 30 days; after thirty days[92] he[91] sells it in court[86]

85  The verse *Deut.* 24:14 speaks of "your proselyte... in your gates." The same expression is used in *Deut.* 14:20 to permit the sale of carcass meat to the resident proselyte. By the doctrine of invariable lexemes in the Torah, the expression in *Deut.* 24:14 refers to the resident proselyte. But *Lev.* 19:13 speaks of "your neighbor"; only the just proselyte is covered by that expression. (Halakhah 14; Babli 111b).

86  Under the supervision of the

court.
87  Deut. 24:11.
88  This expression, כֵּלִים, covers both implements and textiles.
89  Deut. 24:13.
90  The debtor.
91  The creditor.
92  The religious obligation to return the pledge is formulated in Deut. 24:13 as an obligation to return it to the debtor in person. If the debtor died, the pledge may be sold and the proceeds deducted from the amount of the debt.
92  30 days after the creditor had sued the debtor for repayment. In civil matters, a summons to court always stipulates a response within 30 days.

(12b line 8) **הלכה יד:** גֵּר תּוֹשָׁב יֵשׁ בּוֹ מִשּׁוּם בְּיוֹמוֹ תִּתֵּן שְׂכָרוֹ כּוֹל'. כְּתִיב לֹא תַעֲשׁוֹק אֶת רֵעֶךָ. פְּרָט לְגֵר תּוֹשָׁב.

**Halakhah 14**: "The resident proselyte is protected by 'you must pay his wages on his day'", etc. It is written: "Do not oppress your neighbor," excluding the resident proselyte[85].

כְּתִיב בִּנְזָקִין שֶׁיְּהֵא גוֹבֶה בָּעִידִּית. שֶׁנֶּאֱמַר מֵיטַב שָׂדֵהוּ וגו'. וּכְתִיב בְּמִלְוָה שֶׁיְּהֵא גוֹבֶה בְּבֵינוֹנִית. שֶׁנֶּאֱמַר וְהָאִישׁ אֲשֶׁר אַתָּה נוֹשֶׁה בוֹ וגו'. לָמְדוּ קַרְקָעוֹת מִן הַמַּשְׁכּוֹנוֹת. וְדִכְוָותָהּ יָלְמְדוּ מַשְׁכּוֹנוֹת מִקַּרְקָעוֹת. פֵּירַשׁ רִבִּי סִימַאי. דְּבַר תּוֹרָה שֶׁיְּהֵא שָׁלִיחַ בֵּית דִּין נִכְנָס וְגוֹבֶה בְּבֵינוֹנִית. שֶׁאִם יִכָּנֵס הַמַּלְוֶה הֲרֵי הוּא מוֹצִיא הַיָּפָה. וְאִם יִכָּנֵס הַלּוֹוֶה מוֹצִיא הָרָע. אֶלָּא שָׁלוּחַ בֵּית דִּין נִכְנָס וְגוֹבֶה בְּבֵינוֹנִית. תַּנֵּי רִבִּי יִשְׁמָעֵאל. דְּבַר תּוֹרָה שֶׁיְּהֵא הַלּוֹוֶה נִכְנָס. שֶׁנֶּאֱמַר וְהָאִישׁ אֲשֶׁר אַתָּה נוֹשֶׁה בוֹ וגו'. אָמַר רִבִּי לָא. תַּנֵּיי תַמָּן. חָבוֹל. בְּבֵית דִּין. שֶׁלֹּא בְּבֵית דִּין מְנַיִין. תַּלְמוּד לוֹמַר אִם חָבוֹל תַּחְבּוֹל. מִישְׁכְּנוֹ שֶׁלֹּא בִרְשׁוּת עוֹבֵר עַל כָּל־שֵׁם וְשֵׁם שֶׁיֵּשׁ בּוֹ. אָמַר רִבִּי לָא. הוּא גָרַם לְעַצְמוֹ [לַעֲבוֹר] עַל כָּל־שֵׁם וְשֵׁם שֶׁיֵּשׁ לוֹ.

It is written about torts that the collection be from the best quality, as it is said: "his best field, etc.[93]" And it is written about a loan that the collection be from average quality, as it is said: "and the man to whom you are creditor, etc.[87,94]" They inferred real estate from pledges[95].

Similarly, should not pledges be inferred from real estate[96]? [97]Rebbi Simai explained: It is a word of the Torah that the court's bailiff enter and collect from average quality. For if the creditor enter, he would bring out the best. And if the debtor enter, he would bring out the worst. But the court's bailiff enters and collects from average quality. Rebbi Ismael stated: It is a word of the Torah that the debtor enter, as it is said: "and the man to whom you are creditor etc.[98]"

Rebbi La said, it was stated there[99]: "to seize as pledge", by the court. Outside the court, from where[100]? The verse[101] says, "if to seize as pledge you seize as pledge." If he took the pledge without authorization, he transgresses all these verses[102]. Rebbi La said, he caused himself to transgress all these verses[103].

93   *Ex.* 22:4; Babli *Giṭṭin* 48b.

94   The inference is explained later by R. Simai.

95   Since *Deut.* 24:14 refers to a pledge of movables, it is not obvious that the same rule should be applied to the foreclosure of a mortgage.

96   If payment for torts is made by cash or movables, not in real estate, that only best quality would be acceptable. But any debt can be liquidated by money or money's worth to avoid foreclosure.

97   A parallel to the remainder of the paragraph is in *Giṭṭin* 5:1, Notes 30-32.

98   *Deut.* 24:10-11: "If you are a creditor to your neighbor for anything, do not enter his house to take his pledge. Stand outside, and the man to whom you are creditor shall bring the pledge outside to you." This clearly indicates that it is up to the debtor to determine what to give as pledge; the requirement that it be of medium quality is purely rabbinical for R. Ismael; in the words of the Babli "not to lock the door before borrowers" (Babli 113b). The obligation to stand outside extends to the bailiff (*Sifry Deut.* 276).

But R. Simai, and the Masoretes who follow him in their punctuation, read: "Stand outside, and the man, acting on behalf of the one to whom you are creditor, shall bring . . ." *The man* is the court's employee.

99   In Babylonia.

100   The court has to give author-

ization; it does not have to oversee the execution.
101 *Ex.* 22:25.
102 Tosephta 10:8: *Ex.* 22:25, *Deut.* 24:10-13, for a total of five sins committed by one action.
103 If he received the pledge through the court's bailiff and did not return it, he still would transgress *Ex.* 22:25 and *Deut.* 24:13, but not the other commandments.

(12b line 21) מִישְׁכְּנוֹ וְחָזַר וְנָתַן לוֹ.  מִידַת הַדִּין בְּיָדוֹ שֶׁיְּהֵא גוֹבֶה מִנְּכָסִין מְשׁוּעְבָּדִין.  וְאִם מַחֲזִיר לוֹ לְאֵי זֶה דָבָר שֶׁיְּמַשְׁכְּנוּ הוּא מְמַשְׁכְּנוֹ.  פֵּירַשׁ רִבִּי שֶׁמָּא תָבוֹא שְׁמִיטָה וְיַשְׁמִיט.  אוֹ שֶׁמָּא יָמוּת הַלָּה וְנִמְצְאוּ הַמִּטַּלְטְלִין בְּיַד הַיּוֹרְשִׁין.

If he took a pledge and then returned it, by law he can collect from the property mortgaged to him[104]. [105]"But if he returns it, why does he take a pledge? Rebbi explained, for maybe there will be a Sabbatical year and annul [the debt][106]. Or maybe that one[107] will die and leave the movables in the heir's hand."

104 Usually, נְכָסִין מְשׁוּעְבָּדִין denotes otherwise mortgaged real estate. But in this case it denotes the pledge, which in case of non-payment the creditor can satisfy himself from. Since by biblical law the pledge has to be returned periodically, why should the Jewish creditor of a Jew bother to take a pledge?

105 Tosephta 10:9. In the Babli, 114b-115a, in the name of R. Meïr.
106 Secured loans are not remitted in the Sabbatical year; Mishnah *Ševi'it* 10:2.
107 The borrower. If the borrower's estate contains no real estate, the creditor might be unable to force repayment of the debt.

(12b line 24) תַּנֵּי.  חוֹבֵל כְּסוּת יוֹם בַּלַּיְלָה וּכְסוּת לַיְלָה בַּיּוֹם.  מַחֲזִיר כְּסוּת יוֹם בַּיּוֹם וּכְסוּת לַיְלָה בַּלַּיְלָה.  כָּר וְסַדִּין שֶׁדַּרְכָּן לִכְסוּת בַּלַּיְלָה חוֹבְלָן בַּיּוֹם וּמַחֲזִירָן בַּלַּיְלָה.  קוּרְדּוֹם וּמַחֲרֵישָׁה שֶׁדַּרְכָּן לַעֲשׂוֹת בָּהֶן מְלָאכָה בַּיּוֹם חוֹבְלָן בַּלַּיְלָה וּמַחֲזִירָן בַּיּוֹם.  אָמַר רִבִּי לָא.  זִימְנִין דְּתִיפְתָּר הָהֵן קְרָא לֹא תָבוֹא עָלָיו

הַשֶּׁמֶשׁ. לָא תִדְנַח עֲלוֹי שִׁמְשָׁא. וְזִמְנִין דְּתִיפְתָּר לָהּ. לָא תִטְמַע עֲלוֹי שִׁמְשָׁא. דִּכְתִיב הָשֵׁב תָּשִׁיב לוֹ אֶת הָעֲבוֹט כְּבוֹא הַשֶּׁמֶשׁ. עִם מַעֲלֵי שִׁמְשָׁא. עַד בּוֹא הַשֶּׁמֶשׁ תְּשִׁיבֶנּוּ לוֹ. עַד מִטְמָעֵי שִׁמְשָׁא.

It was stated[108]: He takes a day garment as pledge during the night and a night garment during the day. He returns a day garment during the day and a night garment during the night. Pillow and bed sheet[109] which are used as cover during the night he may take as pledge during the day and return for the night. An axe and a plough which usually are used for work during the day he may take as pledge during the night and return for the day.

Rebbi La said: Sometimes one explains the verse[110] "the sun shall not come onto it," as "the sun shall not rise upon it", but sometimes one explains as "the sun shall not set upon it" since it is written "returning you shall return the pledge to him when the sun comes,[111]" at sunrise, "until the going of the sun return it to him,[101]" until sundown.

108  Cf. *Mekhilta dR. Ismael Mišpaṭim* 19 (p. 316-317); *Mekhilta dR. Simeon b. Iohai* p. 212; *Tanḥuma Mišpaṭim* 10; *Ex. rabba* 30:7; *Sifry Deut.* 277.

108  Corrected version of the scribe. First he wrote סַגוֹס σάγος "coarse coat" (expression used in *Mekhilta dR. Simeon b. Iohai, Sifry Deut.*).

110  *Deut.* 24:15 (speaking of worker's wages, not pledges).

111  *Deut.* 24:13.

**משנה יו:** (fol. 12a) אַלְמָנָה בֵּין שֶׁהִיא עֲנִיָּה בֵּין שֶׁהִיא עֲשִׁירָה אֵין מְמַשְׁכְּנִין אוֹתָהּ שֶׁנֶּאֱמַר וְלֹא תַחֲבוֹל בֶּגֶד אַלְמָנָה. הַחוֹבֵל אֶת הָרֵיחַיִם עוֹבֵר בְּלֹא תַעֲשֶׂה וְחַיָּיב מִשּׁוּם שְׁנֵי כֵלִים שֶׁנֶּאֱמַר לֹא יַחֲבוֹל רֵיחַיִם וָרָכֶב. וְלֹא רֵיחַיִם וָרֶכֶב בִּלְבַד אָמְרוּ אֶלָּא כָּל־דָּבָר שֶׁעוֹשִׂין בּוֹ אוֹכֶל נֶפֶשׁ שֶׁנֶּאֱמַר כִּי נֶפֶשׁ הוּא חוֹבֵל.

**Mishnah 16**: One may not take a pledge from a widow, whether poor or rich, since it was said[112]: "And do not take a widow's garment for a pledge." One who takes a flour mill as pledge transgresses a prohibition and is guilty for two vessels[113], as it was said: "Do not take upper and lower millstones as pledge[114]." They said, not only upper and lower millstones but everything used to make food, as it was said: "For he takes a living person for a pledge[114]."

112  *Deut.* 24:17.
113  Even though the moving millstone is useless without its stone base and vice-versa.
114  *Deut.* 24:6.

**הלכה יו:** (12b line 32) אַלְמָנָה בֵּין שֶׁהִיא עֲנִייָה בֵּין שֶׁהִיא עֲשִׁירָה אֵין מְמַשְׁכְּנִין אוֹתָהּ כול׳. תַּנֵּי. אַלְמָנָה בֵּין עֲנִייָה בֵּין עֲשִׁירָה אֵין מְמַשְׁכְּנִין אוֹתָהּ. שֶׁנֶּאֱמַר לֹא תַחֲבוֹל בֶּגֶד אַלְמָנָה. אֶחָד עֲנִייָה וְאֶחָד עֲשִׁירָה. דִּבְרֵי רִבִּי מֵאִיר. רִבִּי יְהוּדָה אוֹמֵר. עֲנִייָה אֵין מְמַשְׁכְּנִין אוֹתָהּ כָּל־עִיקָּר. עֲשִׁירָה מְמַשְׁכְּנִין אוֹתָהּ וְאֵינוֹ מַחֲזִיר. שֶׁמִּתּוֹךְ שֶׁבָּא אֶצְלָהּ מַשִּׂיאָהּ שֵׁם רַע.

**Halakhah 16**: "One may not take a pledge from a widow, whether poor or rich," etc. It was stated[115]: "One may not take a pledge from a widow, whether poor or rich, since it was said[112]: 'And do not take a widow's garment for a pledge', whether poor or rich, the words of Rebbi Meïr. Rebbi Jehudah says, from a poor one he cannot take any pledge at all, from a rich one he may take a pledge but does not return it since if he came to her he would ruin her reputation."

115  In the Babylonian tradition, Babli 115a, Tosephta 10:10, R. Meïr's opinion is attributed to R. Jehudah and R. Jehudah's to R. Simeon. In *Sifry Deut.* 281, the first statement is anonymous as in the Mishnah; R. Simeon is quoted to the effect that no woman's pledge can be returned since any woman's reputation would be ruined by frequent visits by a man not

married to her. This argument is incorporated into Pseudo-Jonathan's Targum of *Deut.* 24:17.

(12b line 37) הַחוֹבֵל זוּג שֶׁלַּסַּפָּרִין עוֹבֵר עַל זֶה בִּפְנֵי עַצְמוֹ וְעַל זֶה בִּפְנֵי עַצְמוֹ. חָבַל אֶחָד מֵהֶן אֵינוֹ עוֹבֵר [אֶלָּא] עַל אֶחָד מֵהֶן. הַמְמַשְׁכֵּן צֶמֶד פָּרוֹת עוֹבֵר עַל זֶה בִּפְנֵי עַצְמוֹ וְעַל זֶה בִּפְנֵי עַצְמוֹ. מִישְׁכֵּן אֶחָד מֵהֶן אֵינוֹ עוֹבֵר אֶלָּא עַל אֶחָד מֵהֶן בִּלְבָד.

[116]One who takes a pair of barber's scissors[117] transgresses for the two blades separately. If he took only one component, he transgresses for this one [only][118,119]. One who takes a yoke of cows[120] transgresses for each one separately. If he took only one, he transgresses for this one only.

116 For the Babylonian version, cf. Babli 116a, Tosephta 10:11.

117 Since the scissors are indispensable to the barber's livelihood, for him they are as important as is food and cannot be impounded. Even though the scissors only work as a pair (ζεῦγος), each blade separately is counted as a tool. The rules of items which cannot be taken are spelled out in Mishnah *'Arakhin* 6:3.

118 From E, missing in L, but implied by the last sentence of the paragraph.

119 Even though the part remaining in the barber's hand is almost useless, the creditor may be punished only for one misdemeanor.

120 From a farmer whose plough is drawn by a yoke of cows.

הבית והעליה פרק עשירי

(fol. 12b) **משנה א:** הַבַּיִת וְהָעֲלִיָּה שֶׁל שְׁנַיִם שֶׁנָּפְלוּ שְׁנֵיהֶן חוֹלְקִין בָּעֵצִים וּבָאֲבָנִים וּבֶעָפָר. רוֹאִין אֵילוּ אֲבָנִים הָרְאוּיוֹת לְהִשְׁתַּבֵּר. הָיָה אֶחָד מֵהֶן מַכִּיר מִקְצָת אֲבָנָיו נוֹטְלָן וְעוֹלוֹת לוֹ מִן הַחֶשְׁבּוֹן.

**Mishnah 1**: If the ground floor[1] and the upper floor belonging to two different persons collapse, they divide wood, stones, and dust between themselves[2]. One takes into consideration which stones were at risk to break[3]. If one of them recognized his stones, he takes them, and they are debited to his account.

1 בַּיִת in rabbinic Hebrew means either a one-storey (usually, one room) house or the ground floor of a multi-storey house. A building with more than two floors is called פְּלָטִין "a palace".

2 Tosephta 11:1 prescribes that in case the two apartments were of unequal size, the building material is divided proportional to the size of the apartments.

3 This is an instruction to the court if the case needs judicial intervention.

(12c line 3) **הלכה א:** הַבַּיִת וְהָעֲלִיָּה שֶׁלִּשְׁנַיִם שֶׁנָּפְלוּ כול'. תַּנֵּי. נִכְמַר כְּתַנּוּר הָעֶלְיוֹנוֹת רְאוּיוֹת לִישָׁבֵר. נָפַל לְחוּץ הַתַּחְתּוֹנוֹת רְאוּיוֹת לִישָׁבֵר.

**Halakhah 1**: "If the ground floor[1] and the upper floor belonging to two different persons collapse," etc. It was stated: If they were blackened like an oven, the upper ones were apt to break. If they fell to the outside, the lower ones were apt to break[4].

4   There are no parallels to the *baraita*, but it seems that one has to switch the statements: If the broken stones were black like the inside of an oven, they probably were foundation stones. If stones fell away from the house and are broken, they were upper floor stones (*Responsa Radbaz* vol. 5, #2112; cf. *Tosephta kiFshutah Bava mesia'* p. 304).

(12c line 5) הָיָה הָאֶחָד מַכִּיר מִקְצָת אֲבָנָיו נוֹטְלָן וְעוֹלוֹת לוֹ מִן הַחֶשְׁבּוֹן. אָמַר רִבִּי הוֹשַׁעְיָה. זאת אוֹמֶרֶת שֶׁשּׁוֹלֶטֶת הַיָד מִצַּד אֶחָד. תַּמָּן תַּנִּינָן. מֵאָה טֶבֶל מֵאָה חוּלִּין נוֹטֵל מֵאָה וְאַחַת. מֵאָה טֶבֶל וּמֵאָה מַעֲשֵׂר נוֹטֵל מֵאָה וְאַחַת. אָמַר רִבִּי יוֹסֵי. אִם אוֹמֵר אַתְּ נוֹטֵל מֵאָה אֲנִי אוֹמֵר כֹּל חוּלִּין עָלָיו בְּיָדוֹ וְנִמְצְאוּ אֵילוּ בְטִבְלָן. אֶלָּא נוֹטֵל מֵאָה וְאַחַת כְּדֵי לְהַפְרִישׁ תְּרוּמָה וּתְרוּמַת מַעֲשֵׂר מִן הַטֶּבֶל.

"If one of them recognized his stones, he takes them, and they are debited to his account." Rebbi Hoshaia said, this means that the hand rules on one side[5]. There[6], we have stated: "A hundred *tevel* in a hundred profane, he removes 101. A hundred *tevel* in a hundred tithe, he removes 101."[7] Rebbi Yose said, if you say that he takes 100, I would say that only profane came to his hand and the other remains *tevel*.[8] So he takes 101 in order to separate heave and heave of the tithe from the *tevel*.

5   It is not clear what the sentence means. It seems that R. Hoshaia's problem is that both rules given in the Mishnah, i. e., that all broken stones probably from a certain place are debited to the owner of that place, and that the person who recognizes his stones takes them for his account, disregarding a certain margin of error. If property rights ("hand") are given to one side, it rules over the entire lot in dispute. This seems to contradict common sense.

6   Mishnah *Demay* 7:9, Notes 128-129.

7   As explained there, the *tevel* in question is tithe of which heave of the tithe was not taken and which therefore is forbidden for consumption to anybody not a Cohen. The question is why 101 has to be taken as *tevel* rather than 100. The question is answered by

R. Yose.

8   While this is extremely unlikely, it is possible and the legal rule is based on this possibility. The same situation applies here. While it is unlikely that all broken stones come from one party's floor, it is possible and that is enough as a legal principle.

(12c line 10) אִילֵּין תְּקוֹעַיָּיא. רִבִּי זְעִירָא. אָמַר אַרְעַיָּא. זָקִיק אַתְּ מַטְעִינֵנִי. רִבִּי לָא. אָמַר עִילָּאֵי. בַּנַּאֵי אָמְרִין. תַּרְוֵיהוֹן אִילֵּין יְסוֹדַיָּיא. וְדָא מְסַייעָה לְמָאן דְּאָמַר בַּנַּאֵי. הָיְתָה חוּרְבָּתוֹ סְמוּכָה לְכוֹתֶל חֲצַר חֲבֵירוֹ לֹא יֹאמַר לוֹ. הֲרֵינִי מְיַיסֵּד עִמָּךְ כּוֹתֶל חֲצֵירִי וְעוֹלֶה. אֶלָּא מְיַיסֵּד עִמּוֹ מִלְּמַטָּה וְעוֹלֶה. הָיְתָה עַל גַּבֵּי שִׁיחִין אוֹ עַל גַּבֵּי מְעָרוֹת אֵינוֹ נִזְקַק לוֹ כְּלוּם. אָמַר רִבִּי יוֹסֵי בֵּירִבִּי בּוּן. תִּיפְתָּר כְּגוֹן אִילֵּין דָּרַיָּיא דְּבֵישָׁן דְּלָא יָכִיל אַרְעַיָּא בָּאנֵי עַד דְּבָנֵי עִילַּייָא.

Those bearing columns[9]. Rebbi Ze'ira: He[10] tells the bottom dweller, you are obliged to support me. Rebbi La: He[11] tells the dweller in the upper floor, the builders say that both have to build the foundations. The following supports the builders: [12]"If his ruined building was close to the wall of his neighbor's courtyard, he should not tell him: I am contributing to the foundations of your wall where it comes up, but he has to contribute to the foundations from the bottom and up[13]. If it was built on top of ditches or caves, he is not obligated for anything.[14]" Rebbi Yose ben Rebbi Abun said, explain it, for example those inhabitants of Bet Shean where the bottom dweller cannot build unless the builder of the upper floor builds[15].

9   If a condominium is rebuilt, who has to pay for those elements of the wall whose only function is to carry the weight of the upper storey and the roof?

10   The owner of the rights to the upper floor.

11   The owner of the rights to the lower floor.

12   A similar text is Tosephta 11:4.

13   His plot is situated higher than his neighbor's courtyard. Then he has

to pay not only for the part of the wall which he will use but also for the foundations on which his part of the wall will be built. Therefore, the owner of the second floor also has to pay for the additional cost incurred by the owner of the ground floor for foundations and walls built for a heavier load.

14   Since the ground floor could not be built without covering what is beneath, the costs cannot be claimed from the owner of the second floor.

15   If the house is built on a steep hillside, the excavation must be done simultaneously for both floors; otherwise debris from above would fall into the building site of the lower floor. Therefore, each one of the parties has to assume part of the cost; satisfying both Rabbis Ze'ira and La.

**משנה ב:** הַבַּיִת וְהָעֲלִיָּיה שֶׁל שְׁנַיִם נִפְחֲתָה הָעֲלִיָּיה וְאֵין בַּעַל הַבַּיִת (fol. 12b) רוֹצֶה לְתַקֵּן הֲרֵי בַּעַל הָעֲלִיָּיה יוֹרֵד וְדָר לְמַטָּה עַד שֶׁיְּתַקֵּן לוֹ אֶה הָעֲלִיָּיה. רַבִּי יוֹסֵי אוֹמֵר הַתַּחְתּוֹן נוֹתֵן אֶת הַתִּקְרָה וְהָעֶלְיוֹן אֶת הַמַּעֲזֵיבָה.

**Mishnah 2**: The ground floor and the upper floor belong to two different persons[16]; if the upper floor sprang a leak and the owner of the ground floor does not want to fix it, the owner of the upper floor descends and dwells below until he fixes the upper floor for him. Rebbi Yose says, the lower one gives the roofing[17] and the upper one the roof covering[18].

16   Following the Babli, Maimonides and Rashi explain that the house is the property of the person dwelling in the lower apartment; the dweller in the first floor rented his apartment. The landlord is required to keep the rented apartment in good repair. According to Tosaphot, the Mishnah either refers to a rental situation or to two brothers who inherited the house together. Then the expenses for necessary repairs have to be borne equally by both of them. If one of them refuses to pay his part, the other brother may use his apartment as a temporary dwelling.

17   Wooden logs or planks to make a roof.

18   Mortar and cement to make a smooth, watertight surface.

(12c line 17) **הלכה ב:** הַבַּיִת וְהָעֲלִיָּה שֶׁלִּשְׁנַיִם כול׳. תַּנֵּי. נִפְחַת מְקוֹם הַתַּנּוּר יוֹרֵד לְמַטָּה. מְקוֹם הַכִּירָה יוֹרֵד לְמַטָּה. אֶלָּא דּוּ אֲמַר לֵיהּ. עֲבִיד לָךְ סוּלָם דְּלָא תִיהֱוֵי עֲלִיל וּנְפִיק גּוֹ בֵּיתִי.

**Halakhah 2**: "The ground floor and the upper floor belong to two different persons," etc. It was stated: "If it sprang a leak above the oven, he descends. If it sprang a leak above the fireplace, he descends[19]." But he may tell him, make yourself a ladder so you do not have to ascend and descend through my dwelling[20].

19   Not to dwell there but to bake and cook in the courtyard in front of the bottom dweller's door. In the Babli, 116b, this is Rav's opinion. Samuel holds that if the top dweller has to descend for any household chores, he comes to live in the ground floor apartment.

20   In any case the second floor dweller is supposed to have his own stairs outside the first floor dweller's apartment.

(12c line 20) רִבִּי יוֹסֵי אוֹמֵר תַּחְתּוֹן נוֹתֵן אֶת הַתִּקְרָה וְעֶלְיוֹן אֶת הַמַּעֲזִיבָה. רִבִּי יוֹסְטָא בְּשֵׁם רֵישׁ לָקִישׁ. הַתַּחְתּוֹן נוֹתֵן תִּקְרָה וּלְוָחִים וְעֶלְיוֹן נוֹתֵן הַמַּעֲזִיבָה. בְּאֵי זוֹ מַעֲזִיבָה. רִבִּי יַעֲקֹב בַּר אָחָא בְּשֵׁם רִבִּי לָעְזָר. מַעֲזִיבָה עָבָה. רִבִּי אַבָּהוּ בְּשֵׁם רִבִּי לָעְזָר. מַעֲזִיבָה בֵּינוֹנִית. לֹא אֶמְרוּ אֶלָּא לְהָדִיחַ אֶת הַכּוֹסוֹת. בְּרַם אֵין הֲוָה בָּעֵי מְשַׁזְגָּא מָאנִין אוּף רִבִּי אַבָּהוּ בְּשֵׁם רִבִּי לָעְזָר מוֹדֵי בְּמַעֲזִיבָה עָבָה. הוֹרֵי רִבִּי חֲנִינָה לְאִילֵּין צִיפּוֹרָאֵי שֶׁיְּהוּא שְׁנֵיהֶן נוֹתְנִין אֶת הַתִּקְרָה וְאֶת הַלְּוָחִין. דְּאִינּוּן זְקוּקִין מֵיסַק חַמְרֵיהוֹן תַּמָּן וּמֵיסַק פֵּירֵיהוֹן תַּמָּן.

"Rebbi Yose says, the lower one contributes the roofing and the upper one the roof covering," etc. [21]Rebbi Justus in the name of Rebbi Simeon ben Laqish:: The bottom dweller contributes the logs and the planks[22]; the dweller on the upper floor contributes the roof covering[18]. Which kind of roof covering? Rebbi Jacob bar Aḥa in the name of Rebbi Eleazar: heavy roof covering. Rebbi Abbahu in the name of Rebbi Eleazar: medium roof covering, since they only spoke about rinsing cups. But if he wanted to wash clothing, also Rebbi Abbahu in the name of Rebbi Eleazar will agree that the roof covering has to be heavy[23]. Rebbi Ḥanina instructed those of Sepphoris that both of them should contribute the logs and the plates since they expect to bring up there their wine and their produce[24].

21  Babli 117a. In most mss. of the Babli the name is Justinus.
22  The logs to make a roof and the planks to create a platform on top of the roof.
23  If the flat roof is used for any activity, the roof covering must withstand prolonged use without becoming leaky.
24  If both parties intend to use the roof, both have to equally share the expenses.

(fol. 12b) **משנה ג:** הַבַּיִת וְהָעֲלִיָּה שֶׁל שְׁנַיִם שֶׁנָּפְלוּ אָמַר בַּעַל הָעֲלִיָּה לְבַעַל הַבַּיִת לִבְנוֹת וְהוּא אֵינוֹ רוֹצֶה לִבְנוֹת הֲרֵי בַּעַל הָעֲלִיָּה בּוֹנֶה אֶת הַבַּיִת וְדָר בְּתוֹכוֹ עַד שֶׁיִּתֵּן לוֹ יְצִיאוֹתָיו. רִבִּי יְהוּדָה אוֹמֵר אַף זֶה דָּר בְּתוֹךְ שֶׁל חֲבֵירוֹ צָרִיךְ לְהַעֲלוֹת לוֹ שָׂכָר אֶלָּא בַּעַל (הַבַּיִת)[25] בּוֹנֶה אֶת הַבַּיִת וְאֶת הָעֲלִיָּה וּמְקָרֶה אֶת הָעֲלִיָּה וְיוֹשֵׁב בַּבַּיִת עַד שֶׁיִּתֵּן לוֹ אֶת יְצִיאוֹתָיו.

**Mishnah 3**: If the ground floor and the upper floor belonging to two different persons collapse, and the owner of the upper floor suggests to the owner of the ground floor to rebuild but himself refuses to build, then the owner of the upper floor rebuilds the ground floor and dwells in it until he[11] pays his[10] expenses. Rebbi Jehudah says, but he who dwells in another person's [place] would have to pay him rent[26]; so the owner of the (ground)[25] floor builds ground and upper floors and makes the roof over the upper floor[27] but dwells on the ground floor until he[11] pays his[10] expenses.

25 Clearly one has to read הָעֲלִיָּה "the upper floor" with the Babli and all Mishnah mss.

26 His problem is that if the owner of the ground floor pays his share, the owner of the upper floor will have dwelt in the apartment rent free, which amounts to receiving hidden interest.

27 To make the upper floor livable, even if he does not dwell there.

(12c line 28) **הלכה ג:** הַבַּיִת וְהָעֲלִיָּה כול'. אֶלָּא בַעַל הַבַּיִת מְבַקֵּשׁ לִבְנוֹת וּבַעַל הָעֲלִיָּה אֵינוֹ רוֹצֶה. מָהוּ שֶׁיֹּאמַר לוֹ. גּוֹפְיָנוּ. נִישְׁמְעִינָהּ מֵהָדָא. הָיְתָה חוֹרְבָתוֹ סְמוּכָה לְחוֹרְבַת חֲבֵירוֹ. עָמַד הַלָּה וּבְנָאָהּ בְּלֹא רְשׁוּתוֹ הֲרֵי זֶה מְחַשֵּׁב יְצִיאוֹתָיו כְּשַׁעַר שֶׁבָּנָה וְיִתֵּן לוֹ אֶת כָּל־יְצִיאוֹתָיו. הָדָא אָמְרָה. שֶׁאֵינוֹ אוֹמֵר לוֹ. גּוֹפְיָנוּ מִן הַצַּד. כְּשֵׁם שֶׁאֵינוֹ אוֹמֵר לוֹ. גּוֹפְיָנוּ מִן הַצַּד. כָּךְ אֵין אוֹמֵר לוֹ. גּוֹפְיָנוּ מִלְמַעֲלָן.

**Halakhah 3**: "If the ground floor and the upper floor," etc. But if the owner of the ground floor wants to build and the owner of the upper floor does not, may he tell him: seal it?[28] Let us hear from the following: [29]"If his collapsed building was next to another's collapsed building[30], and he rebuilt without permission, he computes his actual expenses and he has to pay him all his expenses[31]." This implies that he cannot tell him, seal it on the side. Just as he cannot tell him, seal it on the side, so he cannot tell him, seal it on top[32].

28 Can the ground floor dweller ask the owner of the upper floor to provide a roof? If both floors were rebuilt, the roof would be a charge on the second floor's owner.

29 A related *baraita* is Tosephta 11:4.

30 And the two buiildings shared a wall.

31 If the second owner later decides to rebuild his house, he cannot use the other building's wall without paying the first builder's cost in full. But at the moment of building, he is not required to contribute.

32 The owner of the ground floor has no regress on the owner of the upper floor at the moment when he is building; he has to finish his own roof. He will be able to recoup part of his expenses only when the owner of the upper floor decides to rebuild.

(fol. 12d) **משנה ד**: וְכֵן בֵּית הַבַּד שֶׁהוּא בָנוּי בַּסֶּלַע וְגִינָּה אַחַת עַל גַּבָּיו וְנִפְחַת הֲרֵי בַּעַל הַגִּינָּה יוֹרֵד וְזוֹרֵעַ לְמַטָּה. עַד שֶׁיַּעֲשֶׂה לְבֵית בַּדּוֹ כִּיפִּין. הַכּוֹתֶל וְהָאִילָן שֶׁנָּפְלוּ לִרְשׁוּת הָרַבִּים וְהִזִּיקוּ פְּטוּרִין מִלְּשַׁלֵּם. נָתְנוּ לוֹ זְמַן לִסְתּוֹר אֶת הַכּוֹתֶל וְלָקוֹץ אֶת הָאִילָן וְנָפְלוּ בְּתוֹךְ הַזְּמַן פָּטוּר לְאַחַר הַזְּמַן חַיָּיב.

**Mishnah 4**: And so an olive press built into a rock with a vegetable garden on its top: If it caved in, the garden's owner may sow on the bottom until he build cupolas on his olive press[33]. If a wall or a tree fell into the public domain and caused damage, he is not liable to pay[34]. If he was given an order[35] to tear down the wall or cut down the tree; within the term he is not liable, after the term he is liable.

33  Olive presses (as well as wine presses) usually were built with cupolas. If the natural roof of the press hewn into the rock collapsed, the owner of the vegetable plot may use the bottom for his vegetables until the owner of the olive press rebuilds it. The owner of the vegetable garden may fill the top with soil to create a level surface.

34  Since it was an unforseeable accident.

35  By the court, on application of the building police.

(12c line 34) **הלכה ד**: וְכֵן בֵּית הַבַּד עַד הַכּוֹתֶל וְהָאִילָן כול'. אָמַר רבִּי לְעָזָר. מַעֲשֶׂה בִדְלִית אַחַת שֶׁהָיְתָה מוּדְלָה עַל פְּרְסִיקוֹ שֶׁל חֲבֵירוֹ וְנִפְשַׁח הַפְּרְסִיק. וּבָא מַעֲשֶׂה לִפְנֵי רִבִּי חִייָה הַגָּדוֹל וְאָמַר לוֹ. צֵא וְהַעֲמֵד לוֹ פְּרְסָק. אָמַר לֵיהּ רבִּי יוֹחָנָן. וְלֹא מַתְנִיתָא הִיא. וְכֵן בֵּית הַבַּד שֶׁהוּא בָנוּי בַּסֶּלַע וְגִינַּת אַחַר עַל גַּבָּיו וְנִפְחַת. שְׁמַעֲנוּ שָׁאֵין כּוֹפִין. וְהָתַנֵּי רבִּי חִייָה. כּוֹפִין. נֵימַר. וְלֹא פְלִיגֵי. מָאן דְּמַר. כּוֹפִין. שֶׁהוּא שָׁם. וּמָאן דְּמַר. אֵין כּוֹפִין. בְּשָׁאֵין עוֹמֵד שָׁם.

**Halakhah 4**: "And so an olive press," until "if a wall or a tree," etc. Rebbi Eleazar said: It happened that a vine was growing on another person's peach tree[36], and the peach tree withered[37]. The case came before the great Rebbi Ḥiyya who told him, go and provide him with a peach tree. Rebbi Joḥanan told him: Is this not a Mishnah? "And so an olive press built into a rock and another's vegetable garden is on its top"? Do we not understand that one does not force[38]? But Rebbi Ḥiyya stated that one forces[39]! We may say that they did not disagree. He who says that one forces, if he is there. But he who says that one does not force, if he is absent[40].

36 Latin *prunus persica* "Persian plum tree"

37 Killed by the vine which overgrew it.

38 The Mishnah does not require the owner of the oil press to rebuild but gives the gardener the right to use the area on top of the oil press for his purposes. The court is not empowered to force the owner of the oil press to reconstitute the vegetable garden.

39 To provide a replacement tree.

40 The Mishnah speaks of an absentee landlord. Until the absentee be notified it may take a long time; in the meantime the gardener is given the use of the area occupied by the oil press.

(12c line 40) נָתְנוּ לוֹ זְמַן לָקוּץ. כַּמָּה הוּא זְמַן. רִבִּי הוֹשַׁעְיָה אָמַר. ל יוֹם.
"If he was given an order to cut down.[41]" What is the time limit? Rebbi Hoshaia said, 30 days[42].

41 This quote shows that the Mishnah underlying the Halakhah is not the version presented in the Mishnah (and Maimonides's autograph) but the text given in the Babli and many Mishnah mss. which mention cutting down the tree before tearing down the wall.

42 In the Babli, 118a, this is attributed to R. Johanan (R. Hoshaia's student.) In the Tosephta, 11:7 and *Bava qamma* 2:5, the wording is: at least 30 days. The enforcement of a strict limit of 30 days for obeying court orders is Amoraic.

**משנה ה:** (fol. 12b) מִי שֶׁהָיָה כּוֹתְלוֹ סָמוּךְ לְגִינַת חֲבֵירוֹ וְנָפַל וְאָמַר לוֹ פַּנֵּה אֲבָנֶיךָ וְאָמַר לוֹ הִגִּיעוּךָ אֵין שׁוֹמְעִין לוֹ. מִשֶּׁקִּבֵּל עָלָיו אָמַר לוֹ הֵילָךְ אֶת יְצִיאוֹתֶיךָ וַאֲנִי נוֹטֵל אֶת שֶׁלִּי אֵין שׁוֹמְעִין לוֹ.

**Mishnah 5**: Somebody's wall bordering on another's vegetable garden collapsed. That one told him, remove your stones; if he said, they are yours[43], one[44] does not listen to him. If after the other had accepted, he told him: here are your expenses and I shall take what is mine, one does not listen to him.

**משנה ו:** הַשּׂוֹכֵר אֶת הַפּוֹעֵל לַעֲשׂוֹת עִמּוֹ בַּתֶּבֶן וּבַקַּשׁ אָמַר לוֹ תֶּן לִי אֶת שְׂכָרִי אָמַר לוֹ טוֹל מַה שֶּׁעָשִׂיתָ בִּשְׂכָרֶךָ אֵין שׁוֹמְעִין לוֹ. מִשֶּׁקִּבֵּל עָלָיו אָמַר לוֹ הֵילָךְ שְׂכָרֶךָ וַאֲנִי נוֹטֵל אֶת שֶׁלִּי אֵין שׁוֹמְעִין לוֹ.

**Mishnah 6**: Somebody hired a worker to work on straw and chaff. When he said to him, pay me my wages, he answered, take what you worked on as your wages, one does not listen to him. If after the other[45] had accepted, he told him: here are your wages and I shall take what is mine, one does not listen to him[44].

**משנה ז:** הַמּוֹצִיא זִבְלוֹ לִרְשׁוּת הָרַבִּים הַמּוֹצִיא מוֹצִיא וְהַמְזַבֵּל מְזַבֵּל. אֵין שׁוֹרִין טִיט בִּרְשׁוּת הָרַבִּים וְאֵין לוֹבְנִין לְבֵינִים אֲבָל גּוֹבְלִין טִיט בִּרְשׁוּת הָרַבִּים אֲבָל לֹא לִלְבֵינִים. הַבּוֹנֶה בִרְשׁוּת הָרַבִּים וְהַמֵּבִיא אֲבָנִים הַמֵּבִיא מֵבִיא וְהַבּוֹנֶה בּוֹנֶה. וְאִם הִזִּיק מְשַׁלֵּם מַה שֶּׁהִזִּיק. רַבָּן שִׁמְעוֹן בֶּן גַּמְלִיאֵל אוֹמֵר אַף מְתַקֵּן הוּא אֶת מְלַאכְתּוֹ לִפְנֵי שְׁלֹשִׁים יוֹם.

**Mishnah 7**: If somebody brought his manure into the public domain, he who brings, brings, and he who uses it to manure, manures[46]. One does not soak loam in the public domain[47] nor does one form bricks; one kneads loam in the public domain[48] but not bricks. If somebody builds in the public domain and somebody brings stones; he who brings, brings, and he who builds, builds[49]; but if he caused damage, he pays for what he damaged. Rabban Simeon ben Gamliel says, also he has to prepare his work 30 days in advance.[50]

43 If the neighbor pays for the removal of the building material, it is his.

44 The court will not accept the proposition; the opposing party can force a judgment for their claim.

45 The worker.

46 Temporary use of the public domain for agricultural purposes is permitted but care must be taken that the time in which the public domain is used to deposit potentially dangerous material is reduced to the absolute minimum.

47 Which takes a long time.

48 If a wall is built bordering on the public domain it is permissible to knead mortar for immediate use on the wall.

49 Again, the time in which the public domain is used to deposit potentially dangerous material must be reduced to the absolute minimum.

50 No building permit should be given without a plan to hold the use of public domain for private purposes to a minimum.

(12c line 43) **הלכה ז:** הַמּוֹצִיא זִבְלוֹ כול'. תַּנֵּי. פּוֹרֵק אָדָם זִבְלוֹ בְּפֶתַח חֲצֵירוֹ בִּרְשׁוּת הָרַבִּים לְפַנּוֹתוֹ מִיָּד. אֲבָל לַשְׁהוֹתוֹ אָסוּר. בָּא אֶחָד וְהוּזַּק הֲרֵי זֶה חַיָּיב. רִבִּי יוּדָה אוֹמֵר. בְּשָׁעַת הַזְּבָלִים פּוֹרֵק אָדָם זִבְלוֹ בְּפֶתַח חֲצֵירוֹ בִּרְשׁוּת הָרַבִּים כְּדֵי שֶׁיִּתְפָּרֵךְ בְּרַגְלֵי אָדָם וּבְהֵמָה ל יוֹם. שֶׁעַל מְנָת כֵּן הִנְחִיל יְהוֹשֻׁעַ לְיִשְׂרָאֵל אֶת הָאָרֶץ. פּוֹרֵק אָדָם עֲפָרוֹ בְּפֶתַח חֲצֵירוֹ בִּרְשׁוּת הָרַבִּים לִשְׁרוֹתוֹ וּלְהַעֲלוֹתוֹ עַל גַּבֵּי דִימוֹס מִיָּד. לַשְׁהוֹתוֹ אָסוּר. בָּא אֶחָד וְהוּזַּק בּוֹ חַיָּיב. לֹא יְהֵא גוֹבֵל בְּצַד זֶה [וּבוֹנֶה בְּצַד זֶה][51] אֶלָּא בִּמְקוֹם שֶׁבּוֹנֵהוּ. פּוֹרֵק אָדָם אֲבָנָיו בְּפֶתַח חֲצֵירוֹ בִּרְשׁוּת הָרַבִּים לְפַנּוֹתָן מִיָּד. לַשְׁהוֹתָן אָסוּר. בָּא אַחֵר וְהוּזַּק בָּהֶן חַיָּיב. מָסַר הַחוֹצֵב לַגַּמָּל הַגַּמָּל חַיָּיב. גַּמָּל לַסַּתָּת הַסַּתָּת חַיָּיב. סַתָּת לַסַּבָּל הַסַּבָּל חַיָּיב. הֶעֱלָה עַל גַּבֵּי בִימוֹס וְהָיָה מְפַקְפֵּק בָּהּ וְנָפְלָה הָאַרְדְּכַל חַיָּיב. מְסָרָהּ (הַסַּתָּת לַסַּבָּל)[52] [הַחַצָּב לַסַּתָּת][53] וְהוּזַּק בֵּין בִּסְתִיתוֹת בֵּין בָּאֶבֶן הַסַּתָּת חַיָּיב. הַסַּתָּת לַסַּבָּל וְהוּזַּק בִּסְתִיתוּת הַסַּתָּת חַיָּיב. בָּאֶבֶן הַסַּבָּל חַיָּיב. עָלְתָה וְיָשְׁבָה בְּדִימוֹס וְנָפְלָה פָּטוּר.

**Halakhah 7:** "Somebody who brought his manure," etc. It was stated: [54]"A person may unload his manure at his courtyard door in the public domain in order immediately to remove it. But it is forbidden to leave it there. If another person was injured by it, he is liable. Rebbi Jehudah says, at the time of carrying out manure[55] a person may unload his manure at his courtyard door in the public domain for it to be broken down by the feet of people and animals for 30 days, for on this condition did Joshua distribute the Land to Israel.[56]" [57]"A person may unload his dust at his courtyard door in the public domain in order immediately to mix it with water[58] and to bring it to the row of stones; it is forbidden to leave it there. If another person was injured by it, he is liable. He should not knead on one side [and build on the other][51] but on the side where he is building." [59]"A person may unload his stones at his courtyard door in the public domain in order immediately to remove them; it is forbidden to leave them there. If another person was injured by them, he is liable. If the quarryman delivered to the camel driver, the camel driver is liable. The camel driver to the stone-mason, the stone-mason is liable. The stone-mason to the porter, the porter is liable. It it was brought up to scaffolding[60], it was wobbly there and fell, the master-mason is liable. If the (stone-mason)[52] [quarryman][53] handed it to the (porter)[52] [stone mason][53] and somebody was injured either by splinters or the stone, the stone-mason is liable. The stone-mason to the porter and he[61] was injured by a splinter, the stone-mason is liable. By the stone, the porter is liable. If it was delivered, settled in the row[62], and fell, he is not liable[34]."

51  Missing in L, added from E, confirmed by the Tosephta.

52  Reading of L, erroneously copied from the next sentence.

53  Reading of E, confirmed by the Tosephta.

54  Tosephta 11:8, Babli 118b, *Bava qamma* 81b..

55  A month before ordinarily the fields have to be manured.

56  For other authorized private uses of public or other people's

| | | | |
|---|---|---|---|
| | properties, cf. *Bava batra* 5:1 Notes 16 ff. | 60 | Greek βωμός. |
| | | 61 | A third party. |
| 57 | Tosephta 11:6. | 62 | Greek δόμος "building; rows of stones or bricks in a building"; cf. *Berakhot* 2:5, Note 226. |
| 58 | To make mortar. | | |
| 59 | Tosephta 11:5; Babli 118b. | | |

(fol. 12b) **משנה ח:** שְׁתֵּי גִנּוֹת זוֹ עַל גַּב זוֹ וְהַיָּרָק בֵּינְתַיִם רִבִּי מֵאִיר אוֹמֵר שֶׁל עֶלְיוֹן. רִבִּי יְהוּדָה אוֹמֵר שֶׁל תַּחְתּוֹן. אָמַר רִבִּי מֵאִיר וּמָה אִם יִרְצֶה הָעֶלְיוֹן לִיקַּח אֶת עַפְרוֹ אֵין כָּאן יָרָק. אָמַר רִבִּי יְהוּדָה אִם יִרְצֶה הַתַּחְתּוֹן לְמַלֹּאות גִּינָתוֹ עָפָר אֵין כָּאן יָרָק. אָמַר רִבִּי מֵאִיר וְכִי מֵאַחַר שֶׁשְּׁנֵיהֶן יְכוֹלִין לִמְחוֹת זֶה עַל זֶה רוֹאִין מִנַּיִין יָרָק זֶה חָיָה. רִבִּי שִׁמְעוֹן אוֹמֵר כָּל־שֶׁהָעֶלְיוֹן יָכוֹל לִפְשׁוֹט אֶת יָדוֹ וְלִיטּוֹל הֲרֵי הוּא שֶׁלּוֹ וְהַשְּׁאָר שֶׁל תַּחְתּוֹן.

**Mishnah 8**: Two vegetable gardens, one on top of the other[63] and vegetables growing between them. Rebbi Meïr says, it is the upper's[64]. Rebbi Jehudah says, it is the lower's[65]. Said Rebbi Meïr: If the upper's owner wanted to remove his earth, there would be no vegetables. Said Rebbi Jehudah: If the lower's wanted to fill up his vegetable garden with earth, there would be no vegetables. Said Rebbi Meïr: Since both of them may object to one another one looks from where these vegetables grow[66]. Rebbi Simeon says, any which the upper's may take by stretching out his hand are his; the remainder is the lower's.

| | | | |
|---|---|---|---|
| 63 | One on the slope of a hill, the other in the valley. | 66 | The wild growing vegetable in between grows from the water with which the upper plot is irrigated. |
| 64 | The owner's of the upper plot. | | |
| 65 | The owner's of the lower plot. | | |

(12c line 57) **הלכה ח:** שְׁתֵּי גִינוֹת כול'. מַה יַעֲשׂוּ. אֶפְרַיִם בְּשֵׁם רֵישׁ לָקִישׁ אָמַר. יַחֲלוֹקוּ. דְּבֵית רִבִּי יַנַּאי אָמְרֵי. עַד י' טְפָחִים. רִבִּי יוֹחָנָן אָמַר בְּשֵׁם רִבִּי

יַנַּאי. וּבִלְבַד שֶׁלֹּא יוֹאֲנָס.

**Halakhah 8**: "Two vegetable gardens," etc. What shall one do? Ephraim[67] in the name of Rebbi Simeon ben Laqish said, they shall split[68]. In the House of Rebbi Yannai they say, up to ten handbreadths[69]. Rebbi Johanan said in the name of Rebbi Yannai: Only he shall not force himself[70].

67 In the Babli, 119a, he is called "Ephraim the scribe, R. Simeon ben Laqish's student." But there, he is quoted as deciding following R. Simeon (cf. Note 69).

68 Since it was not decided whom to follow in practice, it is "money in doubt" and must be split evenly (Chapter 1, Note 5).

69 They decide following R. Jehudah who has precedence over R. Meïr and R. Simeon (*Terumot* 3:1, Notes 25,26). The owner of private property owns the rights to its airspace without limitations (Babli *Šabbat* 7a/b), but for any domain not purely private property, the domain only extends ten handbreadths from the ground (*Kilaim* 6:2, Note 31, *Šabbat* 11:2 13a l. 32; Babli *Šabbat* 7b). Since the area between the two vegetable gardens is not the private domain of either of them, the domain of the owner of the lower plot cannot extend to more than 10 handbreadths above his ground.

70 He decides following R. Simeon, following the rule that if a dispute between two authorities in the Mishnah is not resolved, practice follows the third opinion which arbitrates between the two (Babli *Šabbat* 39b, R. Johanan in the name of R. Yannai). He qualifies the right of the owner of the upper plot in that he has a right only to those vegetables which he can reach without undue exertion. In the Babli, 119a, this opinion is quoted in the name of the House of R. Yannai.

(12c line 59) כּוֹתֶל שֶׁבֵּין שְׁתֵי מְחִיצוֹת וְנִפְרָץ. רַב וּשְׁמוּאֵל. חַד אָמַר. מְחֵצָה לָזֶה וּמְחֵצָה לָזֶה. וְחַד אָמַר. כּוּלוֹ לָזֶה וְכוּלוֹ לָזֶה. מַה מַפְקָה מִבֵּינֵיהוֹן. מָצָא מְצִיאָה. מָאן דָּמַר. מְחֵצָה לָזֶה וּמְחֵצָה לָזֶה. מֶחֱצִיוֹ וְהֵילֵךְ לָזֶה וּמֶחֱצִיוֹ וְהֵילֵךְ לָזֶה. וּמָאן דָּמַר. כּוּלוֹ לָזֶה וְכוּלוֹ לָזֶה. הַמּוֹצֵא זָכָה.

A wall between two partitions[71] which was breached. Rav and Samuel, one said, half belongs to one party, the other half to the other party. The other said, both own it entirely. What is the difference between them? If one found a find. For him who said that half belongs to one party, the other half to the other party, if it was on one side it belongs to this party, one the other side it belongs to the other party. For him who said that both own it entirely, the finder acquired it[72].

70 The scribe first wrote שתי חצירות "two courtyards" and then corrected it to שתי מחיצות "two partitions". The problem to be corrected was that a courtyard usually is a condominium of many home owners dwelling in the same compound, whereas clearly we are dealing here with only two owners.

The corrected text is confirmed by E; the scribe's original text is quoted by *Sefer ha'Ittur* (Warsaw 1883, vol. 1, part 2, p. 24b Note 14).

71 Since abandoned property on private grounds automatically belongs to the owner.

# השותפין פרק ראשון

(fol. 12d) **משנה א:** הַשּׁוּתָּפִין שֶׁרָצוּ לַעֲשׂוֹת מְחִיצָה בֶחָצֵר בּוֹנִין אֶת הַכּוֹתֶל בָּאֶמְצַע. מָקוֹם שֶׁנָּהֲגוּ לִבְנוֹת גְּוִיל גָּזִית כְּפִיסִין וּלְבֵינִים בּוֹנִים הַכֹּל כְּמִנְהַג הַמְּדִינָה. בַּגְּוִיל זֶה נוֹתֵן ג טְפָחִים וְזֶה נוֹתֵן ג טְפָחִים. בַּגָּזִית זֶה נוֹתֵן טְפָחַיִים וּמֶחֱצָה וְזֶה נוֹתֵן טְפָחַיִים וּמֶחֱצָה. בַּכְּפִיסִין זֶה נוֹתֵן טְפָחַיִים וְזֶה נוֹתֵן טְפָחַיִים. בַּלְּבֵינִים זֶה נוֹתֵן טֶפַח וּמֶחֱצָה וְזֶה נוֹתֵן טֶפַח וּמֶחֱצָה. לְפִיכָךְ אִם נָפַל הַכּוֹתֶל הַמָּקוֹם וְהָאֲבָנִים שֶׁל שְׁנֵיהֶן.

**Mishnah 1**: Condominium owners[1] who want to make a separation in the courtyard build the wall in the middle. At a place where commonly one builds with unhewn stones, or hewn stones, or half-bricks[2], or bricks, everything follows local custom[3]. For unhewn stones, each partner gives three handbreadths. For hewn stones, each gives two and one half handbreadths. For half-bricks, each gives two handbreadths. For bricks, each gives one and a half handbreadths[4]. Therefore, if the wall collapsed[5] the place and the stones belong to both of them.

1   They own separate houses built facing one courtyard; they want to build a wall so that each house opens to its own courtyard.

2   This is the definition of the Babli (3a). In *Hab.* 2:11 the word means "wood splinter".

3   If one of the parties wants to build following local custom, he can force the other party to agree with him.

4   A wall made of half-bricks is wider than one made of whole bricks since the mortar between the pieces takes up an additional half handbreadth.

5   If a wall collapsed and it is no longer known who built it, one has to assume that it was built following these rules.

(12d line 47) **הלכה א:** הַשּׁוּתָּפִין שֶׁרָצוּ לַעֲשׂוֹת מְחִיצָה כול׳. הֵיךְ תַּנִּינָן תַּמָּן. אֵין חוֹלְקִין אֶת הֶחָצֵר עַד שֶׁיְּהֵא אַרְבַּע אַמּוֹת לָזֶה וְאַרְבַּע אַמּוֹת לָזֶה. אָמְרֵי. תַּמָּן בְּשֶׁאֵין שְׁנֵיהֶן רוֹצִין. בְּרַם הָכָא בִּשְׁשְׁנֵיהֶן רוֹצִין. וַאֲפִילוּ תֵימַר הָכָא בְּשֶׁאֵין שְׁנֵיהֶן רוֹצִין. רָצָה זֶה כּוֹפִין לָזֶה. רָצָה זֶה כּוֹפִין לָזֶה. אָמַר רִבִּי יוֹחָנָן. כּוֹפִין בַּחֲצֵירוֹת וְאֵין כּוֹפִין בַּגַּגּוֹת. רִבִּי נָסָה סְבַר מֵימַר. בֶּחָצֵר שֶׁהִיא לְמַעְלָה מִן הַגַּג. אֲבָל גַּג שֶׁהוּא לְמַעְלָה מִן הֶחָצֵר כּוֹפִין. רִבִּי יוֹחָנָן סְבַר מֵימַר. בֶּחָצֵר שֶׁהִיא לְמַעְלָה מִן הַגַּג כּוֹפִין. אֲבָל גַּג שֶׁהוּא לְמַעְלָה מִן הֶחָצֵר אֵין כּוֹפִין.

**Halakhah 1:** "Condominium owners who want to make a separation," etc. As we have stated there[6]: "One does not subdivide a courtyard unless each party has four cubits." They said, there if the two parties do not agree[7]. But here if both parties agree[8]. And you may even say, here if the two parties do not agree[9]. If this one wishes, one forces the other; if the other one wishes, one forces this one. Rebbi Joḥanan said, one forces for courtyards; one does not force for roofs[10]. Rebbi Nasa wanted to say, in case of a courtyard which is higher than the roof[11]. But in case of a roof which is higher than the courtyard, one forces[12]. Rebbi Joḥanan wanted to say, in case of a courtyard which is higher than the roof one forces[13]. But in case of a roof which is higher than the courtyard, one does not force[14].

6   Mishnah 7.

7   This is spelled out in Mishnah 7: one party may force the dissolution of a condominium if each party will be left with a legal minimum of space.

8   It says explicitly that "they wish to make a separation." In that case they are not bound by minimal conditions (Babli 2b).

9   As explained in the next

sentence, "they wish" means "either of them may wish".

10  It is assumed that the parties wish to build the wall in order to insure privacy, so that one party cannot see what the other is doing in his courtyard. The courtyards were always in the back of the houses, not visible from the street. One assumes that both buildings are one-storey houses and that the wall will be built high enough that from one flat roof the neighbor's courtyard cannot be seen. There remains the question what is meant by "splitting because of the roof."

11  Two houses built on a hillside; the courtyard of the upper one is higher than the roof of the lower. According to R. Nasa, the owner of the lower house cannot go to court to force the owner of the upper house to build a wall which will guarantee the privacy of the lower house.

12  As noted before, the wall must be built high enough that from one flat roof the neighbor's courtyard cannot be seen.

13  In this case, the inhabitants cannot but see what is going on in the lower house. This violates the privacy rights of the inhabitants of the latter; the former can be forced to construct a fence which will bar them from looking down.

14  Since the use of the roof is infrequent, the damage done to the other party by an occasional glance is minor and does not warrant the construction of a fence. The Babli disagrees in the name of Samuel, 2b.

(fol. 12d) **משנה ב:** וְכֵן בַּגִּינָּה מָקוֹם שֶׁנָּהֲגוּ לִגְדּוֹר יִגְדּוֹר. אֲבָל בַּבִּקְעָה מָקוֹם שֶׁנָּהֲגוּ שֶׁלֹּא לִגְדּוֹר אֵין מְחַיְּיבִין אוֹתוֹ אֶלָּא אִם רוֹצֶה כּוֹנֵס לְתוֹךְ שֶׁלּוֹ וּבוֹנֶה וְעוֹשֶׂה חָזִית מִבַּחוּץ. לְפִיכָךְ אִם נָפַל הַכּוֹתֶל הַמָּקוֹם וְהָאֲבָנִים שֶׁלּוֹ.

**Mishnah 2:** Similarly for a vegetable garden[15]; a place which customarily is fenced in, he must fence in[16]. But in an agricultural area[17], a place which customarily is not fenced in, one does not obligate him. But if he[18] wishes, he builds inside his land and makes a façade[19] to the outside; therefore if the wall collapses both land and stones are his.

**משנה ג:** וְאִם עָשׂוּ מִדַּעַת שְׁנֵיהֶם בּוֹנִים אֶת הַכּוֹתֶל בָּאֶמְצַע וְעוֹשִׂין חָזִית מִכָּאן וּמִכָּאן. לְפִיכָךְ אִם נָפַל הַכּוֹתֶל הַמָּקוֹם וְהָאֲבָנִים לִשְׁנֵיהֶן.

**Mishnah 3**: But if they[20] did it with mutual agreement they build the wall in the middle and make façades on both sides; therefore if the wall collapses[5] both land and stones belong to both of them.

15  An irrigated area of intensive agriculture.

16  If one of the parties wishes to construct a fence the other party is forced to contribute land and money to its construction.

17  בקעה is a region of extensive agriculture.

18  One of the farmers.

19  A smooth face; the wall or fence must be covered with smooth stone plates. This characterizes the fence or wall as private property of a single owner.

20  Two property owners in the agricultural area.

**הלכה ב:** (12d line 55) וְכֵן בַּגִּינָה כול׳. תַּנֵּי. בַּגִּינָה בֵּין בְּמָקוֹם שֶׁנָּהֲגוּ לִגְדּוֹר בֵּין בְּמָקוֹם שֶׁנָּהֲגוּ שֶׁלֹּא לִגְדּוֹר כּוֹפִין. אֲבָל בַּבִּקְעָה מָקוֹם שֶׁנָּהֲגוּ לִגְדּוֹר כּוֹפִין שֶׁלֹּא לִגְדּוֹר אֵין כּוֹפִין.

**Halakhah 2**: "Similarly for a vegetable garden," etc. It was stated: For a vegetable garden, whether it be a place where it is customary to build a fence, or a place where it is not customary to build a fence, one forces[21]. But in an agricultural area, at a place where it is customary to build a fence one forces; where it is not customary to build a fence one does not force.

21  As pointed out in the Babli, 4a, Mishnah 2 is ambiguous in the case of a place where it is not customary to fence in vegetable gardens. From the first sentence, one would infer that one would not force one farmer to participate in the costs of a fence which his neighbor wants to put up, but from the second sentence it seems that only in agricultural areas he does not

have to participate. The Babli restricts the power of the court to order participation in the building of a fence to places which do not have a declared policy against erecting fences. It is possible to read this into the Yerushalmi text.

**משנה ד:** הַמַּקִּיף אֶת חֲבֵירוֹ מִשָּׁלֹשׁ רוּחוֹתָיו וְגָדַר אֶת הָרִאשׁוֹנָה וְאֶת הַשְּׁנִיָּה וְאֶת הַשְּׁלִישִׁית אֵין מְחַיְּבִין אוֹתוֹ. רַבִּי יוֹסֵי אוֹמֵר. אִם עָמַד וְגָדַר אֶת הָרְבִיעִית מְגַלְגְּלִין עָלָיו אֶת הַכֹּל. (fol. 12d)

**Mishnah 4**: Somebody's [property] surrounded another's on three sides. If he fenced in the first, and the second, and the third sides, one does not hold [the other] liable. Rebbi Yose said, if the latter then fenced in the fourth side, one rolls everything over to him[22].

**משנה ה:** כּוֹתֶל חָצֵר שֶׁנָּפַל מְחַיְּבִין אוֹתוֹ לִבְנוֹתוֹ עַד אַרְבַּע אַמּוֹת. בְּחֶזְקַת שֶׁנְּתָנָן עַד שֶׁיָּבִיא רְאָיָה שֶׁלֹּא נָתַן. מֵאַרְבַּע אַמּוֹת וּלְמַעְלָה אֵין מְחַיְּבִין אוֹתוֹ. סָמַךְ לוֹ כּוֹתֶל אַחֵר אַף עַל פִּי שֶׁלֹּא נָתַן עָלָיו אֶת הַתִּקְרָה מְגַלְגְּלִין עָלָיו אֶת הַכֹּל. בְּחֶזְקַת שֶׁלֹּא נָתַן עַד שֶׁיָּבִיא רְאָיָה שֶׁנָּתַן.

**Mishnah 5**: If the wall of a courtyard collapsed, one obligates him[23] to rebuild up to four cubits. There is a presumption that he gave, unless he brings proof that he did not give[24]. Higher than four cubits one does not obligate him, but if he built an adjacent wall, even though he did not put on roofing, one rolls everything over to him[25]. There is a presumption that he did not give, unless he brings proof that he gave[26].

22  Since he now uses the three fences put up by the other owner for his own purposes, the latter can ask for half the cost of erecting the other three fences.

23  If one of the parties wants to rebuild, the other is forced to share the costs.

24 If later the party which rebuilt the wall claims that it was not paid by the other party, he is the claimant and the burden of proof is on him.

25 If only one party is in charge of rebuilding, he cannot claim reimbursement for the costs of raising the wall higher than four cubits, even if the wall which had collapsed was higher. But if the party which is not in charge then builds a wall on his own property in the full hight of the separation wall, at a right angle to it, and now has three walls, the two newly built ones and his house, which he may use to create a new roofed space, he uses the full hight of the rebuilt wall and has to pay his share for the full hight.

26 If he did not pay his full share, putting the roofing on the other person's wall would be illegal. Therefore, the rules of torts apply rather than those of civil claims. Since it is common usage that the second party pays only for the costs of building up to four cubits, the presumption is that he did not pay for his share of the part of the wall which exceeds the customary height.

(12d line 57) **הלכה ד:** הַמַּקִּיף אֶת חֲבֵירוֹ כול׳. **הלכה ה:** כּוֹתֶל חָצֵר שֶׁנָּפַל כול׳. רַב חוּנָה אָמַר. וּבִלְבַד כְּשָׁעָה שֶׁבָּנָה עַכְשָׁיו. דְּאִין הֲוָה בָּנֵי דְּכִיפִין בָּנֵי לָהּ דְּכִיפִין. בְּרַם הָכָא הֲוָה בָּנֵי דְכִיפִין וּבְנָתֵיהּ בְּלִיבְנִין גָּבִי לֵיהּ כִּיפִין וְכָל־שָׁעָה דְנָפִיל בָּנֵי לָהּ.

**Halakha 4**: "Somebody's [property] surrounded another's," etc.
**Halakhah 5**: "If the wall of a courtyard collapsed," etc. Rav Huna said, only at the rate he is building now[27]. For if he built it arched[28], he had to build arched. But here if it was built arched and he built it with bricks, he can collect the cost of arches, and if it should collapse, he has to rebuild it[29].

27 Commentary to Mishnah 4. The farmer who only built one fence has to pay to the one who built three at most half the cost of his fences if they were built like the fourth (Babli 4b). E reads בְּשַׁעַר "at the rate" instead of L's בְּשָׁעָה "at the time"; the reading of E was translated.

28 Commentary to Mishnah 5. The wall was built in the way of Roman architecture, sturdy Roman arches with a thin filling below and a flat top. This saves material but costs more in labor.

29 The party which rebuilt the wall can require to be paid for the quality of the previous wall, but if it was executed with inferior material or workmanship he has to rebuild it at his own expense.

(12d line 60) רִבִּי יוֹסֵי אוֹמֵר. אִם עָמַד וְגָדַר אֶת הָרְבִיעִית מְגַלְגְּלִין עָלָיו אֶת הַכֹּל. רַב חוּנָא אָמַר. מְגַלְגְּלִין עָלָיו פְּשׁוּטוֹ שֶׁלַּכּוֹתֶל.

"Rebbi Yose said, if the latter then fenced in the fourth side, one rolls everything over to him.[30]" Rav Huna said, one rolls over the length of the wall to him[31].

30 While this is a quote from Mishnah 4, Rav Huna's remark refers to Mishnah 5.

31 Even if the new wall built by the other party who did not construct the original wall higher than four cubits starts in the middle of the wall of partition, he has to pay for the elevation of the wall of partition in its entire length. This also is Rav Huna's opinion in the Babli 6a, opposed by the authoritative Rav Naḥman who holds that he only has to pay for that part of the wall which he uses for his own purposes.

(12d line 64) עַד כְּדוֹן לְאָרְכּוֹ. לְרָחְבּוֹ. אָמַר רִבִּי נָסָא. כּוֹתַל חָצֵר לֹא נַעֲשָׂה אֶלָּא לְהַצִּיל לוֹ. סָבְרִין מֵימַר. שֶׁאִם רָצָה לִקְרוֹת אֵינוֹ מַקְרֶה. אָמַר רִבִּי יוֹסֵי בֵּירִבִּי בּוּן. תִּיפְתָּר עַל יְדֵי מָרִישָׁיו.

So far lengthwise. What about its width?[32] Rebbi Nasa said, the wall of the courtyard is only made to save for him[33]. They[34] intended to say that if he wanted to make a roof, he cannot make a roof[35]. Rebbi Yose ben Rebbi Abun said, explain it by his beams[36].

32 The Mishnah refers to the case that the new wall be built at a right angle to the dividing wall; the builder then intends to put on logs which form the roof parallel to the dividing wall, between his house and his new wall. He uses the dividing wall only as back wall for his new room; the dividing wall does not carry any weight. Nevertheless, it is enough to make him responsible for half the cost of the entire dividing wall. The problem now is about a wall built parallel to the dividing wall, where the house will form the back wall of the new room to be constructed. If the owner of this piece of land pays half of the cost of the dividing wall, may he put his logs on it to form a roof over his new room?

33 The purpose of the wall is to create privacy, rather than to carry any weight.

34 The members of R. Nasa's school.

35 If the wall was not built for weight-carrying from the start, no party can put any weight on it. E has an additional argument:

וְחָזַר וְתַנָּה. סָמַךְ לוֹ כּוֹתֶל אַחֵר אַף עַל פִּי שֶׁלֹא נוֹתֵן עָלָיו אֶת הַתִּקְרָה מְגַלְגְּלִין עָלָיו אֶת הַכֹּל. הָא אִם רָצָה לִקְרוֹת אֵינוֹ מְקָרֶה.

He (R. Nasa) repeated and stated: "but if he built an adjacent wall, even though he did not put on roofing, one rolls everything over to him." Therefore, even if he wanted to make a roof, he cannot make a roof.

The inference which his students wanted to draw from his statement already follows from the text of the Mishnah. The payment required is just for the wall as is, not for any additional use.

36 מְרִישׁ is a weight-carrying beam. The person building a wall parallel to the dividing wall might put up vertical beams at the two ends of the dividing wall and use them together with his newly constructed wall to make a wooden frame on which to place the roof beams. Then he gets a room of which the dividing wall simply is a wall but carries no weight. The payment of half the cost of the dividing wall is enough to make this a legitimate construction.

(fol. 12d) **משנה ו:** כּוֹפִין אוֹתוֹ לִבְנוֹת בֵּית שַׁעַר וְדֶלֶת לֶחָצֵר. רַבָּן שִׁמְעוֹן בֶּן גַּמְלִיאֵל אוֹמֵר לֹא כָל־הַחֲצֵירוֹת רְאוּיוֹת לְבֵית שַׁעַר. כּוֹפִין אוֹתוֹ לִבְנוֹת לָעִיר חוֹמָה וּדְלָתַיִם וּבְרִיחַ. רַבָּן שִׁמְעוֹן בֶּן גַּמְלִיאֵל אוֹמֵר לֹא כָל־הָעֲיָירוֹת רְאוּיוֹת לְחוֹמָה. כַּמָּה יְהֵא בָעִיר וִיהֵא כְאַנְשֵׁי הָעִיר. שְׁנֵים עָשָׂר חוֹדֶשׁ. קָנָה בָהּ בֵּית דִּירָה הֲרֵי הוּא כְאַנְשֵׁי הָעִיר מִיַּד.

**Mishnah 6**: One forces him to build a porter's lodge and a door for the courtyard[37]. Rabban Simeon ben Gamliel says, not all courtyards are appropriate for a porter's lodge. One forces[38] him to build a wall for the town with double doors and bolt. Rabban Simeon ben Gamliel says, not all towns[39] are appropriate for a wall. How long does he have to stay in a town to be like an inhabitant of the town[40]? Twelve months; if he bought an apartment he immediately is an inhabitant of the town.

37 Any owner of one of the houses opening to the courtyard can take the other owners to court and have them contribute their fair share to the building and maintenance of a secure entrance to the courtyard. According to Tosephta *Bava meṣi'a* 11:17, the condominium can force an absentee landlord to contribute to this but to nothing else.

38 The town administration can force contributions from all property owners to projects concerning their common safety.

39 Villages usually are unwalled.

40 To be a local taxpayer.

(12d line 66) **הלכה ו:** כּוֹפִין אוֹתוֹ לִבְנוֹת כול'. אָמַר רִבִּי לָא. כֵּינִי. אוֹרְחָא דְמָאן דְּמִתְפַּרְנֵס מַבְנֵי לֵיהּ שׁוּר. שֶׁנֶּאֱמַר הוֹן עָשִׁיר קִרְיַת עוּזּוֹ וגו'. תַּנֵּי. שָׁהָה שָׁם שְׁלֹשִׁים יוֹם הֲרֵי הוּא כְאַנְשֵׁי הָעִיר לְקוּפָּה. לִכְסוּת שִׁשָּׁה חֳדָשִׁים. לְפִיסִים וּלְזִימְיוֹת שְׁנֵים עָשָׂר חוֹדֶשׁ. בָּתַר כָּל־הֲלֵין מִילִּין אִיתְּמַר לְפִיסִים וּלְזִימְיוֹת יב חוֹדֶשׁ. אָמַר רִבִּי יוֹסֵי בֵּירִבִּי בּוּן. לְחִיטֵּי הַפֶּסַח בֵּין לִישָּׂא בֵּין לִיתֵּן.

**Halakhah 6**: "One forces him to build," etc. Rebbi La said: So it is; the way of a provident person is to build himself a wall, as it is said[41]: "The wealth of the rich is the fortification of his might, etc." It was stated[42]: "If he stayed there for thirty days he is like the townspeople for the charity chest, for clothing six months, for assessments[43] and penalties[44] twelve months." After all these, was twelve months said only for assessments and penalties? Rebbi Yose ben Rebbi Abun said for Passover wheat, both to take and to give[44*].

41   *Prov.* 10:15.
42   Similar, but materially different, texts are in *Peah* 8:7 (Notes 105-106), Tosephta *Peah* 4:9.
43   For imperial taxes imposed on the locality as a lump sum.
44   Greek ζημία; cf. *Peah* 1:1, Note 84. These are extraordinary taxes imposed by the imperial government.
44*  12 months are required both to be subject to the local tax to supply the needs of the local poor for Passover (Mishnah *Pesaḥim* 10:1) or to receive welfare support in this matter.

(fol. 12d) **משנה ז:** אֵין חוֹלְקִין אֶת הֶחָצֵר עַד שֶׁיְּהֵא אַרְבַּע אַמּוֹת לָזֶה וְאַרְבַּע אַמּוֹת לָזֶה וְלֹא אֶת הַשָּׂדֶה עַד שֶׁיְּהֵא בָהּ תִּשְׁעַת קַבִּין לָזֶה וְתִשְׁעַת קַבִּין לָזֶה. רִבִּי יְהוּדָה אוֹמֵר עַד שֶׁיְּהֵא בָהּ תִּשְׁעַת חֲצָאֵי קַבִּין לָזֶה וְתִשְׁעַת חֲצָאֵי קַבִּין לָזֶה. וְלֹא אֶת הַגִּנָּה עַד שֶׁיְּהֵא בָהּ חֲצִי קַב לָזֶה וַחֲצִי קַב לָזֶה. רִבִּי עֲקִיבָה אוֹמֵר בֵּית רוֹבַע. וְלֹא אֶת הַטְּרִיקְלִין וְלֹא אֶת הַמּוֹרָן וְלֹא אֶת הַשּׁוֹבָךְ וְלֹא אֶת הַטַּלִּית וְלֹא אֶת הַמֶּרְחָץ וְלֹא אֶת בֵּית הַבַּד עַד שֶׁיְּהֵא בָהֶן כְּדֵי לָזֶה וּכְדֵי לָזֶה. זֶה הַכְּלָל. כָּל־שֶׁיֵּחָלֵק וּשְׁמוֹ עָלָיו חוֹלְקִין וְאִם לָאו אֵין חוֹלְקִין. אֵימָתַי. בִּזְמַן שֶׁאֵין שְׁנֵיהֶם רוֹצִים. אֲבָל בִּזְמַן שֶׁשְּׁנֵיהֶן רוֹצִין אֲפִלּוּ בְּפָחוֹת יַחֲלוֹקוּ. וְכִתְבֵי הַקּוֹדֶשׁ אַף עַל פִּי שֶׁשְּׁנֵיהֶן רוֹצִין לֹא יַחֲלוֹקוּ.

**Mishnah 7**: One does not divide the courtyard unless there be four cubits for each one[45], nor the field unless there be nine *qab* for each one[46]; Rebbi Jehudah says, nine half *qabbim* for each one[47]. Not the vegetable garden unless there be half a *qab* for each one[48]; Rebbi Aqiba says, the area of a quarter [*qab*][49]. Not the dining hall, nor the storage room, nor the dovecote, nor the stole, nor the bathhouse, nor the olive press unless there is one for each of them. This is the principle: Anything which is divided and retains its name one divides, otherwise one does not divide. When is that? If the two of them do not agree. However, if both of them want it, they may divide even if it is less[50]. But Holy Scripture[51] they should not divide even if both of them want it.

45  In a common courtyard, the four cubits in front of the door of each house along its entire width are for the private use of its owner. Therefore, the 4 cubits mentioned here are measured starting at a distance of 4 cubits from the house along the entire width of the house, as stated by R. Joḥanan in the Halakhah and the Babli, 11a. According to the Babli, the four cubits are personal property only in front of the doors.

46  *Qab* is short for *bet qab*, the area to be sown by one *qab*, $1/6$ *se'ah*, of seed grain. The *bet se'ah* is defined as 2500 square cubits. Therefore, the *bet qab* is $416^2/_3$ square cubits. The rules will prevent the division of estates from resulting in plots too small to be worked on. For the majority, the minimal size of an inherited field is 3750 square cubits.

47  1875 square cubits.

48  $208^1/_3$ square cubits.

49  $104^1/_6$ square cubits.

50  The rules are guidelines for the courts for the resolution of disputes; they do not restrict the ability of the parties to contract following their wishes.

51  A scroll of biblical texts.

(12d line 72) **הלכה ו:** אֵין חוֹלְקִין אֶת הֶחָצֵר כול'. אָמַר רִבִּי יוֹחָנָן אַרְבַּע אַמּוֹת שֶׁאָמְרוּ חוּץ מֵאַרְבַּע אַמּוֹת שֶׁלַּפְּתָחִים. וְתַנֵּי בַּר קַפָּרָא כֵּן. אֵין חוֹלְקִין אֶת הֶחָצֵר עַד שֶׁיְּהֵא בָהּ שְׁמוֹנֶה אַמּוֹת לָזֶה וּשְׁמוֹנֶה אַמּוֹת לָזֶה. אָמַר רִבִּי יוֹחָנָן. אַרְבַּע אַמּוֹת שֶׁאָמְרוּ לֹא שֶׁהֵן לוֹ לְקִנְיָין אֶלָּא שֶׁיְּהֵא מַעֲמִיד בְּהֶמְתּוֹ לַשָּׁעָה

וּפוֹרֵק חֲבִילָתוֹ. רִבִּי יוֹנָתָן מַקְשֵׁי. כְּלוּם אָמְרוּ אַרְבַּע אַמּוֹת אֶלָּא שֶׁיְּהֵא מַעֲמִיד בְּהֶמְתּוֹ וּפוֹרֵק חֲבִילָתוֹ לַשָּׁעָה. אַשְׁכַּח תַּנֵּי. אַף חוּלְיַת הַבּוֹר יֵשׁ לָהּ אַרְבַּע אַמּוֹת. דְּבֵי רִבִּי יַנַּאי אָמְרֵי. אַף בֵּית הַתַּרְנוֹגָלִין יֵשׁ לָהֶן אַרְבַּע אַמּוֹת.

**Halakhah 7**: "One does not divide the courtyard," etc. Rebbi Joḥanan said, the four cubits which they mentioned are outside the four cubits of the doors. Bar Kappara stated thus: One does not subdivide a courtyard unless there be eight cubits for each party[45].

Rebbi Joḥanan said, the four cubits which they mentioned are not acquired by him[52] but they are for him to park his animal temporarily and unload his package[53]. Rebbi Jonathan asked: did they only say for him to park his animal temporarily and unload his package temporarily[54]? It was found stated: also the circular enclosure of a cistern has four cubits[55]. They said in the House of Rebbi Yannai: the chicken coop also has four cubits[56].

52 They remain condominium property.

53 The co-owners of the courtyard may freely pass through these four cubits but not temporarily use the space otherwise; the owner or renter of the house may use it to load and unload animals and carriages but not as permanent storage area.

54 Is it possible that these rights not be connected with property rights?

55 Tosephta *Bava meṣi'a* 11:15. The area around the common cistern has to be kept clear so that the dwellers in the courtyard have free access and are able to put their pails there. Both the cistern and the circular area surrounding it clearly are condominium property; there is no basis for R. Jonathan's question.

56 In the Babli, 11b, R. Yannai disagrees.

(13a line 7) רִבִּי יוֹחָנָן בְּשֵׁם רִבִּי בַּנָּיָיה. בַּכֹּל הַשּׁוּתָּפִין מְמַחִין זֶה עַל זֶה בֶּחָצֵר חוּץ מִן הַכְּבִיסָה מִפְּנֵי כְבוֹד בְּנוֹת יִשְׂרָאֵל. אָמַר רִבִּי מַתַּנְיָה. הָדָא דְתֵימַר.

בְּמָקוֹם שֶׁהַנָּשִׁים מְכַבְּסוֹת. אֲבָל מָקוֹם שֶׁהָאֲנָשִׁים מְכַבְּסִין לֹא בְדָא. וְדָא דְתֵימַר. חוּץ מִן הַכְּבִיסָה מִפְּנֵי כְּבוֹד בְּנוֹת יִשְׂרָאֵל. בְּרַם בַּד אַמּוֹת דְּנַפְשֵׁיהּ מַמְחֵי הוּא בְיָדֵיהּ. וְדָא דְתֵימַר. בְּכָל שׁוּתָּפִין מַמְחִין זֶה עַל זֶה בֶּחָצֵר. בְּכָל־חָצֵר. בְּרַם בַּד אַמּוֹת דְּחַבְרֵיהּ לֹא מַמְחֵי בְיָדֵיהּ. וְאִם הָיָה הַמָּקוֹם מִנְדְּרוֹן אֲפִילוּ בַּד אַמּוֹת דְּחַבְרֵיהּ מַמְחֵי בְיָדֵיהּ. דּוּ יָכִיל מֵימַר לֵיהּ. אַתְּ שָׁפִיךְ גּוּ דִידָךְ וְהוּא נְחִית גּוּ דִידִי.

[56]*Rebbi Joḥanan in the name of Rebbi Banaiah. Everything the co-owners can prevent one another from doing in the courtyard except laundering because of the honor of the daughters of Israel[57]. Rebbi Mattaniah said, this is at a place where women do the laundering, but not at a place where men do the laundering. And what was said, except laundering because of the honor of the daughters of Israel, only that in his own four cubits he may prevent it. And what was said, everything the co-owners can prevent one another from doing in the courtyard, in the entire courtyard except in the other person's own four cubits where he cannot prevent him. But if the place was at an incline, even in the other person's own four cubits he can prevent him, since he may tell him: you are pouring out in your domain but it flows down into mine.

56*   The entire paragraph is from *Nedarim* 5:1, Notes 16-20. The courtyard is there for entering and leaving the houses. Any other use is possible only if it does not disturb other inhabitants of the courtyard.

57   Babli 57b.

(13a line 16) רִבִּי יוֹחָנָן בְּשֵׁם רִבִּי לָעְזָר בְּרִבִּי שִׁמְעוֹן. מִי שֶׁאֵינוֹ רוֹצֶה לְעָרֵב נִכְנָסִין לְבֵיתוֹ וּמְעָרְבִין לוֹ בְּעַל כָּרְחוֹ. וְהָא תַנֵּי. וְהוּא אֵינוֹ רוֹצֶה לְעָרֵב. אֵינוֹ מִמְּאֵן נִכְנָסִין לְבֵיתוֹ וּמְעָרְבִין לוֹ עַל כָּרְחוֹ. מִפְּנֵי שֶׁאֵין מְמָאֵן. אֲבָל אִם הָיָה מְמָאֵן לֹא. וְתַנֵּי כֵן. כּוֹפִין הֵן בְּנֵי הַמָּבוֹי זֶה אֶת זֶה לַעֲשׂוֹת לָהֶן לֶחִי וְקוֹרָה

לַמָּבוֹי. אָמַר רִבִּי יוֹסֵי בֵּירִבִּי בּוּן. לֹא שֶׁאֵינוֹ רוֹצֶה לְעָרֵב. אֶלָּא מִנֶּפֶשׁ בִּישָׁא לָא בָּעֵי מְעָרְבָא.

[58]Rebbi Joḥanan in the name of Rebbi Eleazar ben Rebbi Simeon. If anybody does not want to participate in an *'eruv*[59] one enters his house and makes the *'eruv* against his will. But was it not stated: if he does not want to make an *'eruv*, if he does not refuse one enters his house and makes the *'eruv* against his will? Because he does not refuse. But not if he does refuse[60]. But was it not stated[61]: "The dwellers at a dead end alley may force one another to make a lath or a beam for the dead end alley.[62]" Rebbi Yose ben Rebbi Abun said, not that he refused[63] but out of ill-will he does not want to participate in an *'eruv*[64].

58 A parallel but materially different treatment of the same subject is in *'Erubin* 7:11, 24d lines 12-16.

59 A major bone of contention between Sadducees and Pharisees in Second Temple times was the interpretation of *Ex.* 19:26: "Nobody shall leave his place on the Sabbath day." It is agreed that this implies that one may carry things at will at "one's place", i. e., in one's house, and that one may not carry in the public domain. As a matter of principle, it is agreed that a condominium space, such as a courtyard, does not qualify as "one's place." In pharisaic interpretation, this is only a rabbinic interpretation; it is not biblical. As a consequence, there is a rabbinic possibility to turn the courtyard into a common space by collecting contributions to symbolically prepare food for a common meal of all dwellers around the courtyard and depositing it in one of the houses. This is called "*'eruv* (mixing) of courtyards". The whole idea of *'eruv* is rejected by Sadducees who consider reliance on it as a breach of the biblical Sabbath prohibition. It is similarly possible to turn a dead-end alley into a common courtyard of all dwellers there by affixing either a vertical lath or an horizontal beam at the entrance to the alley and then treating the alley and all courtyards which open into it as one large courtyard where then carrying is

permitted. But if even one dweller in a courtyard or a dead end alley rejects the entire idea of 'eruv, no 'eruv can be made. The presence of Gentiles is irrelevant for purposes of making an 'eruv.

60   One Sadducee living in a courtyard makes the 'eruv impossible for the entire dead end alley. No Sadducees are known from after the time of the war of Bar Kokhba except Samaritans.

61   Tosephta *Bava meṣi'a* 11:18; Babli *'Eruvin* 80a.

62   How can one force a rabbinic institution on Sadducees or Samaritans?

63   He is neither Sadducee nor Samaritan.

64   This is a particular case of the principle that "one forces people not to behave like the people of Sodom" (Babli 12b), *viz.*, to refuse anything which does not hurt himself but will benefit others.

(13a line 22) רַב חוּנָה אָמַר. חָצֵר מִתְחַלֶּקֶת לַפְּתָחִין. אָמַר רַב חִסְדָּא. לַזְּבָלִין הִיא מַתְנִיתָא. וְתַנֵּי כֵן. בְּכִירָה טֶפַח בַּזְּבָלִין לְפִי פְתָחִים. בְּאִכְסַדְרָה לְפִי אָדָם. ה' חֲצֵירוֹת שֶׁהָיוּ מִשְׁתַּמְּשׁוֹת בְּאַמָּה וְנִתְקַלְקְלָה. כּוּלָם מְתַקְּנוֹת אֶת הָעֶלְיוֹנָה. וְהָעֶלְיוֹנָה מְתַקֶּנֶת כְּנֶגְדָּהּ וְהַשְּׁאָר עִם הַשְּׁנִייָה. וְהַשְּׁנִייָה מְתַקֶּנֶת כְּנֶגְדָּהּ וְהַתַּחְתּוֹנָה מְתַקֶּנֶת עִם כּוּלָם וּמְתַקֶּנֶת כְּנֶגְדָּהּ. חֲמִשָּׁה דְיוּטוֹת שֶׁהָיוּ מִשְׁתַּמְּשׁוֹת בְּבַיִת וְנִתְקַלְקֵל. כּוּלְהָם מְתַקְּנוֹת עִם הַתַּחְתּוֹנָה. וְהַתַּחְתּוֹנָה מְתַקֶּנֶת כְּנֶגְדָּהּ וְהַשְּׁאָר עִם הַשְּׁנִייָה. וְהַשְּׁנִייָה מְתַקֶּנֶת כְּנֶגְדָּהּ. וְהָעֶלְיוֹנָה מְתַקֶּנֶת כְּנֶגְדָּהּ וּמְתַקֶּנֶת עִם כּוּלָם. הָיוּ עֲשׂוּיִן לִגְשָׁמִים יְכוֹלִין לִמְחוֹת בְּיָדָן לִכְבִיסָה. לִכְבִיסָה אֵין יְכוֹלִין לִמְחוֹת בְּיָדָן לִגְשָׁמִים.

Rav Huna said, a courtyard is divided by the number of doors[65]. Rav Ḥisda said, the *baraita* refers to manure. It was stated as follows: "For the cooking stove one handbreadth, for manure according to doors, for the covered walkway according to people.[66]"   [67]"Five courtyards which were using a water conduit and it broke. All of them repair together with the uppermost. The uppermost repairs at its place; the others with the second one. The second one repairs at its place; the lowest one repairs with all of them and at its place." [68]"Five apartments[69] are built above a house which broke. All of them repair with the lowest. The lowest repairs at its place; the others with the second one. The second one repairs at its place; the uppermost repairs with all of them and at its place. [70]If it was a storm sewer they[71] can prevent it being used for laundry. For laundry they cannot prevent it being used as storm sewer."

65 Babli 11a. According to Rashi, Rav Huna speaks about distribution of an inheritance in case the father willed a house in his compound to each child but did not specify anything about the surrounding areas. These then are distributed in proportion to the doors of the houses each child inherited.

According to Maimonides (Šekhenim 2:1) condominium ownership in the courtyard is determined by the number of doors opening into it from each house.

66 This text is thoroughly corrupt. The mention of the cooking stove may refer to the minimal distance of a cooking stove from a wall (Chapter 2, Note 22); but probably it does not correspond to anything.

The remainder of the text is a corruption of Tosephta *Bava meṣi'a* 11:12. The manure mentioned here is not animal excrement but the garbage thrown into the courtyard from the houses, which is broken by people stepping on it and in time transformed into material which can be used as fertilizer. From time to time this is swept together and then divided up among the different owners. Since one assumes that every door is used to throw garbage into the courtyard, it is reasonable to distribute the fertilizer proportional to the number of doors.

The "covered walkway", ἐξέδρα, should be read as "quartering", ξενία (אכסניא), soldiers to be given quarters by the population. They are to be given quarters proportional to the number of dwellers in each house.

67 Tosephta *Bava meṣi'a* 11:21; Babli *Bava meṣi'a* 108a. Both Babylonian sources speak of "5 vegetable gardens." If a water counduit has to be repaired, every user has to pay for the repairs up to the place where he syphons off the water.

68 Tosephta *Bava meṣi'a* 11:20.

Since a multi-storey house whose ground floor crumbles must be torn down, it is clear that one must read with the Tosephta בִּיב "pipe, sewage pipe" instead of בַּיִת "house, ground floor apartment." Every apartment which uses the sewer is required to contribute to its repair from the point of its connection to the sewage system.

69  E דייאטות; Greek δίαιτα; cf. *Yebamot* 1:6, Note 200. One should read with E בְּבִיב, מִשְׁתַּמְּשׁוֹת "they use the same *sewer*".

70  This part shows clearly that the entire *baraita* refers to a crumbling sewer system, not a crumbling house.

71  The rate payors have to pay for its upkeep.

(13a line 22) וְכִתְבֵי הַקּוֹדֶשׁ אַף עַל פִּי שֶׁשְּׁנֵיהֶן רוֹצִין לֹא יַחֲלוֹקוּ. אָמַר רִבִּי הוֹשַׁעְיָה. כְּגוֹן תִּילִים וְדִבְרֵי הַיָּמִים. אֲבָל תִּילַן בְּתִילִין חוֹלְקִין. אָמַר רִבִּי עוּקְבָא. אֲפִלּוּ תִּילָם בְּתִילִים אֵין חוֹלְקִין. שֶׁמִּתּוֹךְ שֶׁאֵין חוֹלְקִין אֵילוּ בָּאִין וְקוֹרְאִין בָּאֵילוּ וְאֵילוּ בָּאִין וְקוֹרְאִין בָּאֵילוּ

"But Holy Scripture[51] they should not divide even if both of them want it." Rebbi Hoshaia said, for example, Psalms and Chronicles. But Psalms and Psalms one may divide[72]. Rebbi Uqba said, even Psalms and Psalms one may not divide. Since one may not divide, each of them comes and reads in the other's [book][73].

72  In the Babli, 13b, Samuel explains that if the Bible is written in separate scrolls, the heirs may divide the scrolls; the collection does not have to remain intact. If Psalms are written in five different scrolls, they may be given to five different recipients.

73  In order to emphasize and remind everybody of his co-ownership. But if the heirs could split the scrolls, they would lock them away in some treasure chest and never look at them again (explanation of R. Eliahu Fulda).

## לא יחפור פרק שני

**משנה א:** (fol. 13a) לֹא יַחְפּוֹר אָדָם בּוֹר סָמוּךְ לְבוֹרוֹ שֶׁל חֲבֵירוֹ וְלֹא שִׁיחַ וְלֹא מְעָרָה וְלֹא אַמַּת הַמַּיִם וְלֹא נִבְרֶכֶת הַכּוֹבְסִין אֶלָּא אִם כֵּן הִרְחִיק מִכּוֹתֶל חֲבֵירוֹ ג׳ טְפָחִים וְסָד בְּסִיד. מַרְחִיקִין אֶת הַגֶּפֶת וְאֶת הַזֶּבֶל וְאֶת הַמֶּלַח וְאֶת הַסִּיד וְאֶת הַסְּלָעִים מִכּוֹתְלוֹ שֶׁל חֲבֵירוֹ ג׳ טְפָחִים אוֹ סָד בְּסִיד. מַרְחִיקִין אֶת הַזְּרָעִים וְאֶת הַמַּחֲרֵישָׁה וְאֶת מֵי רַגְלַיִם מִן הַכּוֹתֶל ג׳ טְפָחִים. מַרְחִיקִין אֶת הָרֵחַיִם ג׳ מִן הַשֶּׁכֶב שֶׁהֵן אַרְבָּעָה מִן הָרֶכֶב וְאֶת הַתַּנּוּר ג׳ מִן הַכִּלְיָיא שֶׁהֵן אַרְבָּעָה מִן הַשָּׂפָה.

**Mishnah 1**: A person may not dig a cistern close to his neighbor's cistern, nor a ditch, nor a cave, nor a water canal, nor a washer's pond except if he distanced himself from his neighbor's wall three handbreadths and lined with lime[1]. One removes olive peat, and manure, and salt, and lime, and rocks[2] from his neighbor's wall three handbreadths or lines with lime[3]. One distances seeds, and ploughs[4], and urine three handbreadths from the wall. One distances a grindstone[5] three from the base, which means four from the moving stone, and the oven[6] three from the base[7], which means four from its rim.

1  Any construction with water has to be at a distance of three handbreadths and must be waterproofed.

2  All except rocks are corrosive.

3  The wall must be insulated against the corrosive action of the dangerous materials.

4  One does not plough closer than three handbreadths from a wall.

5  A grain mill worked by hand, consisting of a moving grindstone and a larger stationary stone base.

6  The oven is a removable earthenware frustum of a cone sitting on a larger masonry base on which the fire burns.

7  Greek κοιλία "belly"; a stone or brick base which is concave in the middle for the fire; the frustum of the cone of the oven is placed on the rim which is higher than the place of the fire.

(13b line 23) **הלכה א:** לֹא יַחְפּוֹר אָדָם בּוֹר כבול׳. כֵּינִי מַתְנִיתָא לֹא יַחְפּוֹר אָדָם בּוֹר סָמוּךְ לְכוֹתֶל בּוֹרוֹ שֶׁל חֲבֵירוֹ. וְלֹא שִׁיחַ וְלֹא מְעָרָה וְלֹא אַמַּת הַמַּיִם וְלֹא נִבְרֶכֶת הַכּוֹבְסִין אֶלָּא אִם כֵּן הִרְחִיק מִכּוֹתֶל חֲבֵירוֹ שְׁלֹשָׁה טְפָחִים וְסָד בְּסִיד. אִם סָד בְּסִיד כָּל־שֶׁהוּא. אִם לֹא סָד בְּסִיד שְׁלֹשָׁה טְפָחִים. מֵהָדָא. מַרְחִיקִין הַגֶּפֶת וְהַזֶּבֶל וְהַמֶּלַח וְהַסִּיד וְהַסְּלָעִים מִכּוֹתֶל חֲבֵירוֹ ג׳ טְפָחִים אוֹ סָד בְּסִיד. הָכָא אַתְּ מַר. מִפְּנֵי שֶׁהַסְּלָעִים מַרְתִּיחִין. וְכָא אַתְּ מַר. אֵין מַרְתִּיחִין. אָמַר רִבִּי יוֹסֵי. כָּאן וְכָאן אֵין הַסְּלָעִים מַרְתִּיחִין. אֶלָּא מִפְּנֵי שֶׁעוֹשִׂין עָפָר תּוֹחֵחַ וּמַלְקִין אֶת אַרְצוֹת הַכּוֹתֶל.

**Halakhah 1:** "A person may not dig a cistern," etc. So is the Mishnah: "[A person may not dig a cistern close to *the wall of* his neighbor's cistern. Nor a ditch, nor a cave, nor a water canal, nor a washer's pond except if he distanced himself from his neighbor's wall three handbreadths] and lined with lime[8]. If he lined with lime, any distance. If he did not line with lime, three handbreadths. From the following: "One removes olive peat, and manure, and salt, and lime, and rocks from his neighbor's wall three handbreadths or lines with lime." Here you say, because rocks generate heat[9]. But there you say that they do not generate heat[10]. Rebbi Yose said, in no case do rocks generate heat[11]. But because they loosen the earth and damage the ground around the wall[12].

8  The text in brackets (in the Hebrew in a different type face) is from E, missing in L. According to L, one insists that in this sentence one reads וְסָד in contrast to the next, which reads אוֹ סָד. According to E, one specifies that the minimal distance is only required between the walls of the

cisterns, not the surroundings (which inside a person's domain are four cubits, cf. Chapter 1 Note 55). Then it is explained that וְסָד here and אוֹ סָד in the next sentence mean exactly the same, "or one lines."

9   Since rocks are mentioned together with olive peat and manure.

10  In Mishnah Šabbat 4:1, olive peat, manure, salt, and lime are mentioned as generating heat and therefore forbidden as material in which food can be stored for use on the Sabbath. The omission of rocks implies that they do not generate heat.

11  The Babli disagrees, 19a. Cf. Rashi, s. v. הנך משום, Tosaphot s. v. משום דמשתכי.

12  All rules of this Mishnah are derived from the principle that no activity on one person's grounds should endanger another's buildings.

(13b line 29) תַּנֵּי. בְּצוֹנָם מוּתָּר. וְהֵיךְ אֲמָרִין. רִבִּי יוֹחָנָן נְפַק מִכְּנִישְׁתָּא וְשָׁפַךְ מַיִם לוֹחֲרֵי תַרְעָא. וְלָא יָדְעִין אִי מִשּׁוּם דַּהֲוָה צוֹנָם וְאֵין מִשּׁוּם דַּהֲוָה בֵיהּ צַעַר וְלָא הֲוָה יָכִיל מְסוּבָּר.

It was stated[13]: "If it was solid rock, it is permitted[14]." As we say, Rebbi Joḥanan left the synagogue and let water behind the door. But we do not know whether it was because it was solid rock or because he suffered pain and could no bear it[15].

13  Tosephta 1:4; Babli 19b.
14  To urinate at a wall.
15  In the Babli, the statement is accepted as practice.

(13b line 31) הָדָא דְתֵימַר. בִּרְיחַיָּא דְתַמָּן. בְּרַם בְּרֵיחַיָּא דִּידָן שְׁלֹשָׁה מִן הָאִיצְטְרוֹבִיל שֶׁהֵן אַרְבָּעָה מִן הַקֶּלֶת. וְאֶת הַתַּנּוּר ג' מִן הַכְּלָיָיא שֶׁהֵן ד' מִן הַשָּׂפָה. רִבִּי יוּדָן בֶּן פָּזִי אָמַר. מִן הַשָּׂפָה הַחִיצוֹנָה וְלִפְנִים. וְרַבָּנָן אָמְרֵי. מִן הַשָּׂפָה הַפְּנִימִית וְלַחוּץ. הָיָה עָשׂוּי כְּשׁוּבָךְ מָהוּ. נִשְׁמְעִינָהּ מֵהָכָא. רִבִּי יְהוּדָה אוֹמֵר. עַד שֶׁתְּהֵא תַחְתָּיו מַעֲזִיבָה ג' טְפָחִים וּבְכִירָה טֶפַח. וְכִירָה לֹא כְּמִין שׁוֹבָךְ הִיא עֲשׂוּיָה. וְתֵימַר. בֵּין מִלְמַעֲלָן בֵּין מִלְמַטָּן טֶפַח. הָכָא בֵּין מִלְמַעֲלָן בֵּין מִלְמַטָּן ג' טְפָחִים.

This means, about grindstones there[16], but for our grindstones three from the pine cone[17] which is four from the enclosure[18]. "And the oven three from the base which are four from its rim." Rebbi Yudan bar Pazi said, from the outer rim inwards; but the rabbis say, from the inner rim outwards[19]. If if was built like a dovecote[20], what [are the rules]? Let us hear from the following[21]: "Rebbi Jehudah said, unless there be under it insulating material three handbreadths and for a stove one handbreadth." Is a stove not build like a dovecote, and you say both above and below a handbreadth? Also here, both above and below a handbreadth[22].

16  In Babylonia.

17  Greek στρόβιλος. The grindstone was shaped like a pine cone with a handle on top by which it was moved.

18  The wooden enclosure around the immovable stone basis of the grindstone.

14  The distance of four handbreadths from the oven for R. Yudan bar Pazy is measured from the outside of the wall of the oven, for the rabbis from the inside.

20  If the oven is not shaped like a cone but like a cube.

21  Tosephta 1:3; cf. Mishnah 2. The cone-shaped oven, with a fire at the bottom and a hole on top, is made to create a draft and, therefore, is much hotter than the stove which is an earthenware cube with a circular hole on top for the pot, where the fire is lit on the clay bottom.

22  If the stove is used inside the house, it needs fireproofing material on the floor, the ceiling, and the nearby wall.

(fol. 13a) **משנה ב:** לֹא יַעֲמִיד אָדָם תַּנוּר בְּתוֹךְ הַבַּיִת אֶלָּא אִם כֵּן יֵשׁ עַל גַּבָּיו גּוֹבַהּ אַרְבַּע אַמּוֹת. הָיָה מַעֲמִידוֹ בָּעֲלִיָּיה עַד שֶׁיְּהֵא תַחְתָּיו מַעֲזִיבָה ג׳ טְפָחִים וּבְכִירָה טֶפַח. וְאִם הִזִּיק מְשַׁלֵּם מַה שֶּׁהִזִּיק. רִבִּי שִׁמְעוֹן אוֹמֵר לֹא אָמְרוּ כָל־הַשִּׁיעוּרִים הָאֵילוּ אֶלָּא שֶׁאִם הִזִּיק יְהֵא פָטוּר מִלְּשַׁלֵּם.

**Mishnah 2**: A person should not put an oven in the house[23] unless there be above it a space of four cubits; or if he puts it on the upper floor unless there be under it insulating material three handbreadths and for a stove one handbreadth[22]. But if he caused damage, he must pay what he damaged[24]. Rebbi Simeon said, the reason they indicated these measures is that he not be liable to pay if he caused any damage, .

23  The ground floor which either has a dirt or a stone floor. Therefore, no fireproofing is needed below the oven. But the ceiling, which also is the floor of the second storey, is made of logs covered with plaster; it is flammable.

24  Even if he observed all rules spelled out in the Mishnah.

(fol. 13a) **משנה ג**: לֹא יִפְתַּח אָדָם חֲנוּת שֶׁל נַחְתּוֹמִין וְשֶׁל צַבָּעִין תַּחַת אוֹצְרוֹ שֶׁל חֲבֵירוֹ וְלֹא רֶפֶת בָּקָר. בֶּאֱמֶת הִתִּירוּ בַּיַּיִן אֲבָל לֹא רֶפֶת בָּקָר. חֲנוּת שֶׁבֶּחָצֵר יָכוֹל הוּא לִמְחוֹת בְּיָדוֹ וְלוֹמַר לוֹ אֵינִי יָכוֹל לִישָׁן מִקּוֹל הַנִּכְנָסִין וּמִקּוֹל הַיּוֹצְאָם. עוֹשֶׂה כֵלִים יוֹצֵא וּמוֹכֵר בְּתוֹךְ הַשּׁוּק אֲבָל אֵינוֹ יָכוֹל לִמְחוֹת בְּיָדוֹ וְלוֹמַר לוֹ אֵינִי יָכוֹל לִישָׁן מִקּוֹל הַפַּטִּישׁ וְלֹא מִקּוֹל הָרֵחַיִם וְלֹא מִקּוֹל הַתִּינוֹקוֹת.

**Mishnah 3**: A person may not open a bakery or a dye shop[25] under the storage room of another person, nor an animal barn[26]. In truth[27] they permitted for wine[28], but not an animal barn. About a store in the courtyard[29] one[30] may object and tell him, I cannot sleep because of the noise of those coming and the noise of those leaving[31]. One who manufactures vessels has to leave and sells them in the market[32]; nobody may object and tell him, I cannot sleep because of the noise of the hammer, nor because of the noise of a grindstone, nor because of the noise of children[33].

25  Both create excessive heat which might damage the goods stored there. The owner of a preexisting storage facility can go to court and request an order prohibiting the operation of a bakery or dye shop.

26  The smell would ruin most of the goods stored there.

27  A technical term indicating pre-rabbinic practice which somehow deviates from the principle just stated.

28  Which is held to age better in the heat.

29  Somebody bought a property in the courtyard to open a store where there was none before.

30  Any of the co-owners of the courtyard.

31  The customers.

32  But he can manufacture in a place which otherwise is a bedroom community as long as he does not create traffic of people who do not belong there.

33  Nobody may object to a school in his courtyard.

(13b line 39) **הלכה ב:** לֹא יַעֲמִיד אָדָם כול׳. תַּנֵּי. וְלֹא שֶׁלְּנַפָּחִין. תַּנָּה רַב קַרְנָא. אִין הֲוָה כְגוֹן קֵינִי אוֹ כְנָפַח מִתְּחִילָּה מוּתָּר. כְּנֶגֶד דִּירָתוֹ מָהוּ. אָמַר רִבִּי אָחָא. כָּל־שֶׁכֵּן כְּנֶגֶד דִּירָתוֹ. אָמַר רִבִּי יוֹנָתָן. הַמַּזִּיק אֵין לוֹ חֲזָקָה. רִבִּי יְהוֹשֻׁעַ אוֹמֵר. מַמְחֵי רַבָּנִין בְּעָשָׁן תָּדִיר. כְּהָדָא חָדָא אִיתָּא הֲוַת מַדְלְקָה חוֹלִין תְּחוֹת רִבִּי אִילְפַּיי. אִיבְעָה מַמְחַיָּיא בְיָדָהּ. אֲתָא עוּבְדָּא קוֹמֵי רִבִּי נָסָה. אָמַר. לֹא אָמְרוּ אֶלָּא בְעָשָׁן תָּדִיר.

**Halakhah 2:** "A person should not put," etc. It was stated: Nor a smithy. Rav Qarna stated: If he was like a metal worker[34], or it was built originally as a smithy[35], it is permitted. How is it in front of his dwelling[36]? Rebbi Aḥa said, certainly not in front of his dwelling[37]. Rebbi Jonathan said, a person causing damage has no claim of undisturbed posession[38]. Rebbi Joshua[39] said, the rabbis object to permanent smoke. As the following: A woman was burning sand[40] below [the apartment of] Rebbi Ilfay[41]. He wanted to object to her. The case came before Rebbi Nasa who said, they said it only about continuous smoke.

34 The biblical metal worker; *Gen.* 4:22; he only spends a small part of his time as a smith; most of his time he manufactures metal vessels.

35 A separate building. It is possible to read: If it was built as a smithy from the start, i. e., if the smithy existed before the construction of the warehouse; this is the interpretation of the Babli, 20b.

36 Out in the open.

37 This already was settled in Halakhah 1:7.

38 Babli 23a. Even if the other inhabitants of the courtyard do not object, a new owner can object if an activity is classified in law as damaging.

39 Rosh (Chapter 2, §18) reads "R. Joshua ben Levi." This reading has to be accepted.

40 Maybe to make glass. It is possible to read: She was burning the bird *Ḥol* (Phoenix, *Job* 19:18). For חולין Rosh reads קלא or קולין "roasts".

41 Rosh reads: R. Eleazar.

(13b line 44) **הלכה ג:** לֹא יִפְתַּח אָדָם כול׳. רִבִּי יַעֲקֹב בַּר אָחָא פָּנֵי חַד חֲלִיטָר מִן אִיסְטִיב לְאִיסְטִיב. רִבִּי אֶבְדּוּמִי אֲחִי רִבִּי יוֹסֵי הֲוָה חַד חֲלִיטָר שָׁרֵי תַּחְתּוֹהִי. עָבַר רִבִּי אָחָא וְלֹא מָחָה. אָמַר. רַבָּנָן עָבְרִין וְלָא מַחְוֵי. כָּעַס עֲלוֹי רִבִּי אָחָא. אִיבְאַשׁ רִבִּי אֶבְדּוּמִי אֲחִי רִבִּי יוֹסֵי אִיבְאַשׁ. סְלִיק רִבִּי יוֹסֵי מְבַקַּרְתֵּיהּ. אָמַר. אֵיזִיל וְאִיבְּעֵי מִינֵיהּ. אָזַל וָמַר בֵּי דִינָא וְרָחֵם עֲלוֹי בֵּי דִינָא וַעֲתַר לֵיהּ תַּכְרִיכִין.

**Halakhah 3**: "A person may not open," etc. Rebbi Jacob bar Aḥa moved a preparer of fried food from one stall[42] to another stall. One preparer of fried food was dwelling below [the apartment of] Rebbi Eudaimon the brother of Rebbi Yose. Rebbi Aḥa passed by and did not object[43]. He said, the rabbis are passing by and do not object. Rebbi Aḥa got angry with him. Rebbi Eudaimon the brother of Rebbi Yose became seriously ill. Rebbi Yose came to visit him. He said, I shall go and ask him[44]. He went and said, if a court had mercy on somebody would the court prepare shrouds for him?

42  Cf. Latin *stibadium* "bench", Arabic مسطبة.

43  This paragraph really should be taken together with the preceding one. It seems that the store was there before R. Eudaimon moved in. The latter therefore needed a confirmation from the head of the local court that "a person causing damage has no squatter's rights" (Note 38), which R. Aḥa refused. Since the fourth generation authority refused to enforce the pronouncement of the first generation R. Jonathan, its legal validity is in doubt.

44  He promised to pacify R. Aḥa.

(13b line 50) חַד בַּר נָשׁ זְבִין כָּל־דְּרָתֵיהּ. שִׁיֵּיר בָּהּ חַד מִסְטוּבָא וַהֲוָה עָלִיל וְיָתִיב לֵיהּ עֲלֵיהּ. אָתָא עוֹבְדָא קוֹמֵי רִבִּי יוֹנָה בִּירְבִּי יוֹסֵי. אָמְרִין. לָא כוּלָּא מִינָּךְ מֵיעַל וְיָתִיב עֲלֵיהּ וַחֲמֵי מֵיעַל וּנְפִיק גּוֹ בֵיתֵיהּ. חַד בַּר נָשׁ זְבִין פַּלְגָּא דְרָתֵיהּ שִׁיֵּיר בָּהּ חַד נַחְתּוֹמָר. אָתָא עוֹבְדָא קוֹמֵי רִבִּי יוֹנָה וְרִבִּי יוֹסֵי. אָמְרִין. אַתְּ אֲתָת עֲלוֹי הוּא לָא אֲתָא עֲלָךְ. וְתַנֵּי כֵן. אִם קָדְמָה הָרֶפֶת אוֹ חֲנוּת לָאוֹצָר אֵין יָכוֹל לִמְחוֹת.

A person sold his entire house[45]; he reserved for himself one stone bench[45a] where he went and sat. The case came before Rebbi Jonah and Rebbi Yose. They said, it is not in your power to go and sit there and observe who comes and goes in his house[46].

A person sold half his house; he reserved a bake shop for himself. The case came before Rebbi Jonah and Rebbi Yose. They said, you are coming to him; he is not coming to you, as it is stated[47]: "If the barn or the store preceded the storage room, he cannot object."

45  A private dwelling with the entire courtyard.

45a  Arabic مَنَبّ "bench, anvil".

46  Your property right does not override the buyer's right to privacy.

47  Tosephta 1:4, Babli 20b. The buyer of an apartment above a bake shop cannot complain.

(13b line 55) תַּנֵּי. בֶּאֱמֶת בְּיַיִן הִתִּירוּ אַף עַל פִּי שֶׁמְּמַעֲטוֹ. אֶלָּא שֶׁמַּשְׁבִּיחוֹ. רַב הוֹשַׁעְיָה כַּד שְׁמַע הָדֵין תַּנְיָיה יְהַב חַמְרֵיהּ גּוֹ אִגְרֵיהּ דְּבָנֵי. אַסְרְיֵהּ חַמְרֵיהּ. אָמַר. הַמִּשְׁנָה הִיטְעַתַנִי. לֹא שֶׁהִטְעָתֵי הַמִּשְׁנָה אֶלָּא דְרִיחָה דְּבָנֵי מַסְרֵי חַמְרֵיהּ.

It was stated: In truth, they permitted for wine even though it diminishes it because it improves it[48]. Rav Hoshaia when he heard this statement put his wine in the attic of the bath house. His wine became foul-smelling. He said, the Mishnah led me astray. But the Mishnah did not lead him astray; the smell of the bath house made his wine foul-smelling[49].

| | |
|---|---|
| 48 | Tosephta 1:4, Babli 20b. |
| 49 | The Babli endorses the opinion that the Mishnah be valid only for Palestinian, not Babylonian wines. |

(13b line 59) תַּנֵּי. לִשְׁכֵינוֹ יָכוֹל לַחֲזוֹר בּוֹ. מִשֶּׁקִּיבֵּל עָלָיו אֵינוֹ יָכוֹל לַחֲזוֹר בּוֹ. רַבָּן שִׁמְעוֹן בֶּן גַּמְלִיאֵל אוֹמֵר. אַף מִשֶּׁקִּיבֵּל עָלָיו יָכוֹל לַחֲזוֹר בּוֹ. דוּ יָכִיל מֵימַר לֵיהּ. אִינוּן אָזְלִין וְאַתְיָין לְהָכָא בְּעַיִין לָךְ וְלָא מַשְׁכְּחִין לָהּ וּמַרְבִּין עֲלֵינוּ הַדֶּרֶךְ. רִבִּי חֲנִינָה וְרִבִּי מָנָא. חַד אָמַר. מָהוּ לִשְׁכֵינוֹ. מַשְׁרִיתֵיהּ גּוֹ דְּרָתֵיהּ. מִשֶּׁקִּיבֵּל עָלָיו אֵין יָכוֹל לַחֲזוֹר בּוֹ. רַב הוּנָא אָמַר. מָהוּ לִשְׁכֵינוֹ. מִיפְתַּח לֵיהּ חֲנוּת. מִשֶּׁקִּיבֵּל עָלָיו אֵין יָכוֹל לַחֲזוֹר בּוֹ. אַתְיָיא דְּרַבָּן שִׁמְעוֹן בֶּן גַּמְלִיאֵל כְּרִבִּי מֵאִיר. דְּתַנִינָן תַּמָּן. וְעַל כּוּלָּן אָמַר רִבִּי מֵאִיר. אַף עַל פִּי שֶׁהִתְנָה עִמָּהּ יְכוֹלָה הִיא שֶׁתֹּאמַר. סְבוּרָה הָיִיתִי שֶׁאֲנִי יְכוֹלָה לְקַבֵּל וְעַכְשָׁיו אֵינִי יְכוֹלָה.

It was stated[50]: About his neighbor he may change his mind. Once he accepted it he can no longer change his mind[51]. Rabban Simeon ben Gamliel says, even after he accepted it, he can change his mind, for he can tell him, they come and go here, they are looking for you and do not find you, and they increase traffic here[52]. Rebbi Ḥanina and Rebbi Mana, one said, what is "his neighbor"? He let him live in his house[53]. Once he accepted it he can no longer change his mind. Rav Huna[54] said, one said, what is "his neighbor"? He opened a store for him[55]. Once he accepted it he can no longer change his mind. Rabban Simeon ben Gamliel parallels Rebbi Meïr, as we have stated there[56]: "For all of these says Rebbi Meïr that, even if he contracted with her, she can say 'I thought that I could stand it, now I cannot.'"

50  Different texts are in Tosephta 1:4, Babli 21b.

51  There are situations where one of the co-owners of the courtyard has lost his veto power even if the troublesome store was new. The question to be discussed is, what means "accepted"? If a new owner does not immediately complain, this certainly does not make him lose his right.

52  For him the veto power over a new enterprise in the courtyard remains valid if he can prove actual impairment of his quality of life by the new store.

53  Nobody can complain about his own tenant.

54  This should be: "the other", אוחרי.

55  He holds that an owner can annul a lease if the tenant causes him problems. But if he modified his building for the new tenant's business, he cannot complain.

56  Mishnah *Ketubot* 7:11, Note 163. A woman was informed of bodily defects of her prospective husband before her marriage. The majority hold that once married, she cannot ask the court to force a divorce because of the husband's defects. R. Meïr disagrees as explained in the text.

(13b line 68) אֲבָל אֵינוֹ יָכוֹל לִמְחוֹת וְלוֹמַר לוֹ. אֵינִי יָכוֹל לִישָׁן מִקּוֹל הַפַּטִּישׁ וְלֹא מִקּוֹל הָרֵחַיִם אוֹ מִקּוֹל הַתִּינוֹקוֹת. אִילֵּין דְּמַלְפִין טַלַיָּיא וְאִילֵּין דְּעָבְדִין מסוגין[א56] אִילֵּין לְאִילֵּין יָכְלִין חַבְרֵיהוֹן לְמִימְחֵי בִּידֵיהוֹן. דּוּ יָכִיל מֵימַר לֵיהּ. אִינּוּן אָזְלִין וְאָתְיָין בָּעֵי לָהּ וְלָא מַשְׁכְּחִין יָתָהּ וְהֵן מַרְבִּין עָלֵינוּ אֶת הַדֶּרֶךְ. אִילֵּין צִיפּוֹרָאֵי מַמְחִין אִילֵּין לְאִילֵּין מִסַּמְרֵיהּ דִּנְוָלַיָּה. הוֹרֵי רִבִּי אַבִּימֵי בַּר טוֹבִי מִיתֵּן חַד נְוָל בֵּין כּוֹתֶל לְכוֹתֶל. הוֹרֵי רִבִּי יִצְחָק בַּר חֲקוּלָה מְרַחֶקֶת אִילֵּין מָרוֹשְׁתִיָּהּ מִכּוֹתָלָא דְּ אַמּוֹת. אָמַר רִבִּי יוֹסֵי בֵּירִבִּי בּוּן. אִילֵּין עַמּוּדַיָּא דְרַבִּינִין מְכֹּחַ קִרְיַית אִינּוּן רַבִּינִין. שׁוּרָא דְחָמָץ מִן קָל גּוּרֵי פַרְסַיָּיא נְפַל.

"Nobody may object and tell him, I cannot sleep because of the noise of the hammer, or because of the noise of a grindstone, or because of the noise of children." Those who teach boys and those who feed one another, their fellows may object to what they are doing[57], for he can tell him, they come and go here, they are looking for you and do not find you, and they increase traffic here[58]. Those Sepphoreans can object to one another for nailing down their looms[59]. Rebbi Abime bar Tobi instructed to put one loom between two walls[60]. Rebbi Isaac bar Ḥaqula distanced a saw-horse four cubits from the wall[61]. Rebbi Yose ben Abun said, those pillars which are weakened are weakened because of the force of shouts. The wall of Ḥoms fell before the noise of the Persians' arrows[62,63].

56א Read with E and *Sefer ha'Iṭṭur* 1:2 p. 104a Note 678: מְגוּסִין. No word מסוגין is attested elsewhere.

57 The Mishnah notwithstanding there can be only one (one-room) school in a residential courtyard, and only one restaurant.

58 This text is copied from the previous paragraph; it neither fits in grammar (number) nor in argument.

59 Since the periodic concussions of the air will weaken the walls.

60 In a residential area there can be no more than one loom to a room.

61 Again to prevent the wall from being damaged by the noise caused by sawing.

62 Reading גירי "arrows" for גורי "lion whelps".

63 In Sapor I's invasion of Syria.

**משנה ד:** מִי שֶׁהָיָה כּוֹתְלוֹ סָמוּךְ לְכוֹתֶל חֲבֵירוֹ לֹא יִסְמוֹךְ לוֹ כּוֹתֶל (fol. 13a) אַחֵר אֶלָּא אִם כֵּן הִרְחִיק מִמֶּנּוּ אַרְבַּע אַמּוֹת. וּבַחֲלוֹנוֹת מִלְמַעֲלָן וּמִלְמַטָּן וּמִכְּנֶגְדָּן אַרְבַּע אַמּוֹת.

**Mishnah 4**: If somebody's wall was close to another's wall he may not build his wall close by unless he moves it four cubits away[64]. If there are windows, on top, from below, and on equal height, four cubits[65].

64 Even though his wall is mentioned twice in this sentence, there is only one wall to be built. Since the next sentence speaks of a wall, either of a house or a wall of separation, parallel to the other person's existing wall, probably the wall mentioned here is to be built at a right angle to the existing wall. In the interpretation of the Babli, 22b, there should be space between the two walls so that people may walk between them and by their walking compact the earth holding both walls.

65 If there are windows in the other house's wall, the new wall must preserve the other person's privacy. Therefore, the wall must be either 4 cubits higher or 4 cubits lower than the window. If it is of equal hight then it must be at least 4 cubits distant to allow daylight into the window.

(13b line 75) **הלכה ד:** מִי שֶׁהָיָה כּוֹתְלוֹ כול׳. דְּבֵי רִבִּי יַנַּאי אָמְרֵי. בְּבָאִין לִייַשֵּׁב עִיר בַּתְּחִילָה הִיא מַתְנִיתָא. אָמַר רִבִּי לָא. בְּכוֹתֶל אָטוּם הִיא מַתְנִיתָא. אָמַר רִבִּי יוֹסֵי. בְּכוֹתֶל סוֹדְמִין הִיא מַתְנִיתָא. אָמַר רִבִּי יוֹסֵי בֵּירִבִּי בּוּן. מַתְנִיתָא אָמְרָה כֵן. וּבַחֲלוֹנוֹת בֵּין מִלְּמַעְלָן בֵּין מִלְּמַטָּן בֵּין מִכְּנֶגְדָּן אַרְבַּע אַמּוֹת. מִלְּמַעְלָן ד׳ אַמּוֹת שֶׁלֹּא יְהֵא עוֹמֵד וְרוֹאֶה. מִלְּמַטָּן ד׳ אַמּוֹת שֶׁלֹּא יְהֵא עוֹמֵד וְרוֹאֶה. מִכְּנֶגְדָּן שֶׁלֹּא יַאֲפִיל אֶת הַצְּדָדִין. וְתַנֵּי כֵן. מַרְחִיקִין הַכּוֹתֶל מִן הַחֲלוֹן כִּמְלֹא חֲלוֹן.

**Halakhah 4**: "If somebody's wall was," etc. In the House of Rebbi Yannai they said, the Mishnah speaks of those coming first to settle in a new town[66]. Rebbi La said, The Mishnah speaks of a sealed wall[67]. Rebbi Yose said, the Mishnah speaks of a barricade[68] wall. Rebbi Yose ben Rebbi Abun said, the Mishnah says so: "If there are windows, on top, from below, and on equal height, four cubits." On top four cubits, lest he could stand and see; from below four cubits, lest he could stand and see; at equal hight lest he obscure the sides[65]. This was stated[69]: "One distances the wall from a window by the size of a window."

66  Babli 22b, in the name of R. Yose b. Ḥanina. They imply that in a settled area, a wall built at a right angle may be built adjacent to the existing wall.

67  This wall mentioned in the first sentence is solid, having no windows.

68  Arabic سدم "to close a door, to barricade"; not the wall of a house but the fence of an enclosure.

69  Tosephta 1:5, including the statement of R. Yose bar Abun.

**משנה ה:** מַרְחִיקִין אֶת הַסּוּלָם מִן הַשּׁוֹבָךְ אַרְבַּע אַמּוֹת כְּדֵי שֶׁלֹּא (fol. 13a) תִקְפּוֹץ הַנְּמִיָּה. וְאֶת הַכּוֹתֶל מִן הַמַּזְחִילָה אַרְבַּע אַמּוֹת כְּדֵי שֶׁיְּהֵא זוֹקֵף אֶת הַסּוּלָם. מַרְחִיקִין אֶת הַשּׁוֹבָךְ מִן הָעִיר חֲמִשִּׁים אַמָּה וְלֹא יַעֲשֶׂה אָדָם שׁוֹבָךְ בְּתוֹךְ שֶׁלּוֹ אֶלָּא אִם כֵּן יֵשׁ לוֹ חֲמִשִּׁים אַמָּה לְכָל רוּחַ. רִבִּי יְהוּדָה אוֹמֵר בֵּית אַרְבַּעַת כּוֹרִין מְלֹא שֶׁגֶר הַיּוֹנָה. וְאִם לְקָחוֹ אֲפִילוּ בֵית רוֹבַע הֲרֵי הוּא בְחֶזְקָתוֹ.

**Mishnah 5**: One distances the ladder[70] from a dovecote by four cubits lest a marten jump[71], and the wall four cubits from the leader[72] so it can support the ladder. One distances the dovecote from town by fifty cubits[73]. A person may not build a dovecote on his property unless he have fifty cubits in each direction[73]. Rebbi Jehudah says, the area of four *bet kor*[74], the distance one sends a pigeon. But if he bought it even with the area of a quarter [*qab*][75], it is in his power[76].

70  The permanent ladder leading to the upper floor apartment.

71  Onto the dovecote and eat the pigeons. If a builder contracts to build an access to an upper floor and disregards this rule it is malpractice and he has to rebuild the access at his own expense.

72 By which the rainwater flows from the roof to the earth. Near the leader the earth is soft and does not support anything.

73 It is axiomatic that a pigeon chick which cannot yet fly does not move farther than 50 cubits away from the dovecote. Therefore, any chick within 50 cubits belongs to the owner of the dovecote; the rule prevents property disputes about pigeon chicks.

74 The dovecote has to be the center of a square of surface area 300'000 square cubits, of side length 547.72 cubits, in its owner's possession.

75 A square of area $104^{1}/_{6}$ square cubits, of edge lengths slightly over 10 cubits; cf. Chapter 7, Note 49.

76 An existing dovecote which does not conform to the rules does not have to be removed.

(13c line 6) **הלכה ה:** מַרְחִיקִין אֶת הַסּוּלָּם כול׳ עַד בְּחֶזְקָתוֹ. אָמַר רבִּי לָעְזָר. הָדָא דְתֵימַר לְיָמִין. אֲבָל לִשְׂמֹאל זוֹקֵף מִיַּד.

**Halakhah 5:** "One distances the ladder," etc., until "in his power." Rebbi Eleazar said, that is, to the right hand side. But to the left he may put it up immediately[77].

77 If the leader is built so that the water flows to the right hand side, one may buld the ladder close to it on the other side since its stability will not be compromised.

(13c line 8) הָכָה אַתְּ מַר. נ אַמָּה וּלְהַלָּן אַתְּ מַר. ל ריס.. אָמַר רִבִּי יוֹסֵה בֵּירִבִּי בּוּן. לְעִנְיַן לִרְעוֹת רוֹעָה הִיא נ אַמָּה. לְעִנְיַן לִפְרוֹחַ פּוֹרַחַת אֲפִילוּ עַד ד׳ מִיל.

Here, you say 50 cubits. But there, you say 30 *stadia*. Rebbi Yose ben Rebbi Abun said, they feed within fifty cubits; they fly even four *mil*[78].

78 Reformulation of a paragraph in *Bava qamma* 7:10, Notes 105-107.

(fol. 13a) **משנה ו:** נִיפּוּל הַנִּמְצָא בְתוֹךְ חֲמִשִּׁים אַמָּה הֲרֵי הוּא שֶׁל בַּעַל הַשּׁוֹבָךְ חוּץ מֵחֲמִשִּׁים אַמָּה הֲרֵי הוּא שֶׁל מוֹצְאוֹ. נִמְצָא בֵּין שְׁנֵי שׁוֹבָכוֹת קָרוֹב לָזֶה שֶׁלּוֹ וְלָזֶה שֶׁלּוֹ. מֶחֱצָה עַל מֶחֱצָה שְׁנֵיהֶן יַחֲלוֹקוּ.

**Mishnah 6**: A pigeon chick which is found within 50 cubits belongs to the owner of the dovecote; farther away than 50 cubits it belongs to its finder[73]. If it was found between two dovecotes, if it is closer to one of them, it belongs to it; in the middle, both [owners] shall split evenly.

(13c line 10) **הלכה ו:** נִיפּוּל הַנִּמְצָא בְתוֹךְ חֲמִשִּׁים אַמָּה כול׳. הָדָא דְתֵימַר. בְּשֶׁאֵין דֶּרֶךְ הָרַבִּים מַפְסֶקֶת בֵּינְתַיִּים. אֲבָל בִּזְמַן שֶׁמַּפְסֶקֶת לֹא בְדָא. הָדָא יַלְפָה מֵהַהִיא וְהַהִיא יַלְפָה מֵהָדָא. הָדָא יַלְפָה מֵהַהִיא. שֶׁאִם הָיוּ שְׁנַיִם שֶׁחַיָּיב לְהַכְרִיז. וְהַהִיא יַלְפָה מֵהָדָא. שֶׁאִם הָיוּ ג׳ שֶׁהוּא שֶׁל מוֹצְאוֹ.

**Halakhah 6**: "A pigeon chick which is found within 50 cubits," etc. That is, if no public road interrupts between them[79]. But not if a public road interrupts between them[80]. This is learned from that, and that is learned from this[81]. This is learned from that: if there were two[82], he has to make it public. That is learned from this: if there were three[82], it would belong to its finder[81].

---

[79] This refers to the last case in the Mishnah, if the chick was found between two dovecotes less than 100 cubits from one another.

[80] One may assume that the chick was lost by a passer-by who gave up hope to recover it; therefore, it belongs to the finder. (Babli 23b/24a).

[81] "That" is Halakhah *Bava meṣia‘* 2:4, Notes 54-55. Something found in an apartment shared by two people has to be advertised; in a hotel frequented by 3 or more people it belongs to the finder.

[82] Dovecotes within 50 cubits of the chick.

**משנה ז**: מַרְחִיקִין אֶת הָאִילָן מִן הָעִיר עֶשְׂרִים וְחָמֵשׁ אַמָּה וְהֶחָרוּב (fol. 13a) וְהַשִּׁיקְמָה חֲמִשִּׁים אַמָּה. אַבָּא שָׁאוּל אוֹמֵר כָּל־אִילָן סְרָק חֲמִשִּׁים אַמָּה. אִם הָעִיר קָדְמָה קוֹצֵץ וְאֵינוֹ נוֹתֵן דָּמִים. וְאִם הָאִילָן קָדַם קוֹצֵץ וְנוֹתֵן דָּמִים. סָפֵק זֶה קָדַם וְזֶה קָדַם קוֹצֵץ וְאֵינוֹ נוֹתֵן דָּמִים.

**Mishnah 7**: One distances a tree from a town by 25 cubits; but carob tree or sycamore by 50 cubits; Abba Shaul says, every non-fruit tree by 50 cubits. If the town existed before the tree, one cuts it down and does not pay for it; if the tree existed before the town, one cuts it down[83] and pays for it. If there is a doubt which one existed before the other, one cuts it down but does not pay[84].

**משנה ח**: מַרְחִיקִין גּוֹרֶן קְבוּעָה מִן הָעִיר חֲמִשִּׁים אַמָּה. לֹא יַעֲשֶׂה אָדָם גּוֹרֶן קְבוּעָה בְּתוֹךְ שֶׁלּוֹ אֶלָּא אִם כֵּן יֵשׁ לוֹ חֲמִשִּׁים אַמָּה לְכָל־רוּחַ. מַרְחִיק מִנְּטִיעוֹתָיו שֶׁל חֲבֵירוֹ וּמִנִּירוֹ כְּדֵי שֶׁלֹּא יַזִּיק.

**Mishnah 8**: One distances a threshing floor 50 cubits from the town[85]. A person shall not make a threshing floor on his property unless he owns 50 cubits in each direction[86]. He distances it from another's orchards or ploughed field so that he will not cause damage[87].

83  The developer of the town has the right to cut the surrounding trees down provided that he pay for them.

84  Since the burden of proof is on the claimant.

85  Because the chaff flying from a threshing floor is unhealthy.

86  The directions are N,E,S,W. He must own a 100 by 100 square, not only a circle of 50 cubits radius.

87  In case of a dispute, the burden of proof is on him that he did not impair another person's property.

(13c line 15) **הלכה ז:** מַרְחִיקִין אֶת הָאִילָן מִן הָעִיר כול׳. מִשֵּׁם שֶׁעוֹמֵד וּמַאֲפִיל אוֹ מִשֵּׁם שֶׁנִּיאוֹ רַע. מַה מַפְקָה מִבֵּינֵיהוֹן. הָיָה עוֹמֵד בְּתוֹךְ שֶׁלּוֹ. אִין תֵּימַר מִשֵּׁם שֶׁעוֹמֵד וּמַאֲפִיל. בְּתוֹךְ שֶׁלּוֹ מוּתָּר. וְאִין תֵּימַר מִשֵּׁם שֶׁנִּיאוֹ רַע. אֲפִילוּ בְתוֹךְ שֶׁלּוֹ אָסוּר.

**Halakhah 7:** "One distances a tree from a town," etc.. Because it creates shadow where it stands or because its falling leaves[88] are dangerous? What is the difference between them? If it stands on one's own property. If you say, because it creates shadow where it stands, on his property it is permitted. But it you say, because its motion is dangerous, even on his property it is forbidden.

---

88  This translation follows the reading of E שינויי, which S. Lieberman reads as שִׁינּוּיָי, equivalent to Babli נְבְיָיחוֹ (Avodah zarah 48b).

In the parallel, Babli 24b, the word is נויי which Maimonides (Šekhenim 10:1), and Rashi by the absence of a commentary, understand as "beauty" but R. Gershom (correct text in Arukh completum s. v. ניא) explains the Babli's "because of נויי" that all places in and around the town should be freely accessible (maybe for the fire brigade.) He seems to identify the Yerushalmi's ניא with the Babli's נויי. Torczyner and Ben Jehudah, in the latter's Thesaurus, do not come to a conclusion as to meaning and etymology of the word.

---

(fol. 13a) **משנה ט:** מַרְחִיקִין אֶת הַנְּבִילוֹת וְאֶת הַקְּבָרוֹת וְאֶת הַבּוּרְסְקִי מִן הָעִיר חֲמִשִּׁים אַמָּה וְאֵין עוֹשִׂין בּוּרְסְקִי אֶלָּא לְמִזְרַח הָעִיר. רִבִּי עֲקִיבָה אוֹמֵר לְכָל־רוּחַ הוּא עוֹשֶׂה חוּץ מִמַּעֲרָבָה וּמַרְחִיק חֲמִשִּׁים אַמָּה.

**Mishnah 9:** One distances carcasses, and graves, and tanneries 50 cubits from the town, and one builds a tannery only to the East of a town[89]. Rebbi Aqiba says, one may build in any direction except to the West, and distances himself by 50 cubits.

89 Since most days of the year the wind blows from the West. The bad smell of the tannery will be downwind.

(13c line 19) **הלכה ט:** מַרְחִיקִין אֶת הַנְּבֵילוֹת כול׳. רִבִּי אַבָּהוּ בְּשֵׁם רִבִּי יוֹחָנָן. עַד מָקוֹם שֶׁעוֹשֶׂה גֶלֶד. דְּבֵית רִבִּי יַנַּאי אָמְרֵי. עַד מָקוֹם שֶׁעוֹשֶׂה וּמֵרִיחַ. וְתַנֵּי כֵן. רִבִּי עֲקִיבָה אוֹמֵר. לְכָל־רוּחַ הוּא עוֹשֶׂה וּמַרְחִיק חוּץ מִמַּעֲרָבָה מִפְּנֵי שֶׁהִיא תְדִירָה. רִבִּי מָנָא הֲוָה מְהַלֵּךְ עִם מוּכֵּי שְׁחִין. אֲמַר לֵיהּ אָבִיי. לָא תַחֲלוֹךְ מִמְּדִינְחֵיהּ אֶלָּא מִמַּעֲרָבֵיהּ.

**Halakhah 9:** "One distances carcasses," etc. Rebbi Abbahu in the name of Rebbi Johanan: To the place where one prepares the skins[90]. In the House of Rebbi Yannai they said, up to the place where one might smell what he makes[91]. It was stated so[92]: "Rebbi Aqiba says, he may build it in any direction and distances himself, except to the West because that [wind] is frequent.[89]" Rebbi Mana went to accompany a person afflicted with a skin disease. His father told him, do not walk to the East of him but rather to the West of him.

90 This explains why animal carcasses come under the same rules as tanneries: The process of making leather starts with skinning carcasses.

91 This now refers to the problem of locating a tannery. Any location is fine where the smell does not reach the town.

92 Tosephta 1:8, Babli 25a.

(fol. 13b) **משנה י:** מַרְחִיקִין אֶת הַמִּשְׁרָה מִן הַיָּרָק וְאֶת הַכְּרֵישִׁין מִן הַבְּצָלִים וְאֶת הַחַרְדָּל מִן הַדְּבוֹרִים. רִבִּי יוֹסֵי מַתִּיר בַּחַרְדָּל.

**Mishnah 10:** One distances a soaking pond[93] from vegetables, and leeks from onions[94], and mustard from bees[95]. Rebbi Yose permits

93 A person who makes a pond to soak his flax has to put it far enough from existing vegetable fields to avoid being sued for any damage to the vegetables.

94 In order to avoid cross-pollination at flowering time.

95 To avoid causing the honey to smell of mustard.

(13c line 24) **הלכה י:** מַרְחִיקִין אֶת הַמִּשְׁרָה כול'. תַּנֵּי. מַרְחִיקִין אֶת הַבְּצָלֶת מִן הַכְּרֵישִׁין. וְרִבִּי לֶעְזָר בְּרִבִּי שִׁמְעוֹן מַתִּיר. אָמַר רִבִּי יַעֲקֹב בַּר דּוֹסַאי. מִגּוֹ אִילֵּין מַתְנִיתָא. כְּשֵׁם שֶׁזֶּה מַרְחִיק זֶה מִזֶּה כָּךְ זֶה מַרְחִיק זֶה מִזֶּה. רִבִּי אַבָּהוּ בְשֵׁם רִבִּי יוֹסֵי בֶּן חֲנִינָה. מִפְּנֵי שֶׁפִּי הַדְּבוֹרִים חַד וּמַחֲרִיבוֹת הַדְּבָשׁ.

**Halakhah 10**: "One distances a soaking pond," etc. It was stated: One distances an onion bed from leeks, but Rebbi Eleazar ben Rebbi Simeon permits it. Rebbi Jacob ben Dosai said, from these teachings [it follows] that mutually they have to distance themselves one from the other[96].

Rebbi Abbahu in the name of Rebbi Yose ben Ḥanina: Because the bees' mouth becomes sharp and they destroy the honey[97].

96 The Mishnah warns a person not to plant leeks next to an existing bed of onions to avoid a damage suit; the *baraita* does the same for a person wanting to plant onions next to an existing bed of leeks. One has to conclude that in all cases the latecomer has to be careful not to hurt existing cultures and the rules of the Mishnah work both ways.

97 The person putting a bee-hive near to a bed of mustard only hurts himself, rather than the grower of mustard.

(fol. 13b) **משנה יא:** מַרְחִיקִין אֶת הָאִילָן מִן הַבּוֹר עֶשְׂרִים וְחָמֵשׁ אַמָּה וְהֶחָרוּב וְהַשִּׁיקְמָה חֲמִשִּׁים אַמָּה בֵּין מִלְּמַעְלָה בֵּין מִן הַצַּד. אִם הַבּוֹר קָדַם קוֹצֵץ וְנוֹתֵן

דָּמָיו וְאִם הָאִילָן קָדַם לֹא יָקוּץ. סָפֵק זֶה קָדַם וְסָפֵק זֶה קָדַם לֹא יָקוּץ. רִבִּי יוֹסֵי אוֹמֵר אַף עַל פִּי שֶׁהַבּוֹר קָדַם אֶת הָאִילָן לֹא יָקוּץ שֶׁזֶּה חוֹפֵר בְּתוֹךְ שֶׁלּוֹ וְזֶה נוֹטֵעַ בְּתוֹךְ שֶׁלּוֹ.

**Mishnah 11**: One distances a tree 25 cubits from a cistern, but carob tree and sycamore 50 cubits, whether on top or level[98]. If the cistern existed before, he shall cut it down and pay for it[99]; if the tree existed before, one shall not cut it down. Rebbi Yose said, even if the cistern existed before, one shall not cut it down since the one digs on his property and the other plants on his property[100].

**משנה יב**: לֹא יִטַּע אָדָם אִילָן סָמוּךְ לִשְׂדֵה חֲבֵירוֹ אֶלָּא אִם כֵּן הִרְחִיק מִמֶּנּוּ ד׳ אַמּוֹת אֶחָד גְּפָנִים וְאֶחָד כָּל־אִילָן. הָיָה גָדֵר בֵּינְתַּיִים זֶה סוֹמֵךְ לַגָּדֵר וְזֶה סוֹמֵךְ לַגָּדֵר. הָיוּ שָׁרָשָׁיו יוֹצְאִין לְתוֹךְ שְׂדֵה חֲבֵירוֹ מַעֲמִיק ג׳ טְפָחִים כְּדֵי שֶׁלֹּא יְעַכֵּב אֶת הַמַּחֲרֵישָׁה. הָיָה חוֹפֵר בּוֹר וְשִׁיחַ וּמְעָרָה קוֹצֵץ וְיוֹרֵד וְהָעֵצִים שֶׁלּוֹ.

**Mishnah 12**: A person should not plant a tree next to another's field unless he distanced himself from it by four cubits[101], whether vines or any other tree. If there was a wall between them, each one goes close to the wall[102]. If its roots extended to another's field, he lowers the roots three handbreadths in order not to hinder the plough[103]. If one was digging a cistern, or a ditch, or a cavern, he cuts and excavates and the wood is his.

**משנה יג**: אִילָן שֶׁהוּא נוֹטֶה לְתוֹךְ שְׂדֵה חֲבֵירוֹ קוֹצֵץ מְלֹא מַרְדֵּעַ עַל גַּבֵּי הַמַּחֲרֵישָׁה. הֶחָרוּב וְהַשִּׁיקְמָה כְּנֶגֶד הַמִּשְׁקוֹלֶת. בֵּית הַשְּׁלָחִין כָּל־הָאִילָן כְּנֶגֶד הַמִּשְׁקוֹלֶת. אַבָּא שָׁאוּל אוֹמֵר כָּל־אִילָן סְרָק כְּנֶגֶד הַמִּשְׁקוֹלֶת.

**Mishnah 13**: If a tree overhangs another's field, he may cut it in the height of the plough's ox-goad[104]; carob tree and sycamore along the plumb line[105]. Over an irrigated field along the plumb line[105]. Abba Shaul says, every non-fruit-bearing tree along the plumb line[105].

98  In order to avoid damage to the walls of the cistern by the roots. The required distance applies if the tree is planted on a level with the cistern or above it on a hillside. In the Babylonian sources, Babli 25b and Tosephta 1:12, it is emphasized that this also applies if the tree is planted on a hillside below the level of the cistern. In *Ševi'it* 1:2 (Notes 28-34), R. Yose ben Rebbi Abun characterizes the Babli's opinion as R. Simeon's and holds that R. Yose, who is the higher authority, allows a tree to be planted below the cistern. He will require that the cistern's bottom not be below its owner's property line on the hill. (It is not obvious that the opinions of the editors of the other parts of the Yerushalmi are accepted in *Neziqin*.)

99  He (the tree's owner) shall cut his tree down if he (the cistern's owner) pays for it.

100  Since the owner of the tree legally may plant a tree on his property, the provident owner of the neighboring plot will build his cistern at 25 cubits' distance from his property line.

101  This is good advice rather than a legal requirement. A person planting a fruit tree on his property needs a circle with a radius of 4 cubits around it for servicing the tree; he has to avoid trespassing on other people's property.

102  Since then there is no danger of trespassing. גָּדֵר, like Arabic جَدْر, is a rural stone wall made without mortar, not a fence as in modern Hebrew.

103  I. e., the field's owner is free to remove any roots in his soil down to a depth of 3 handbreadths (about 30 cm) without asking or paying anybody.

104  He may cut all overhanging branches of a fruit tree to the height of the ox-goad used with his plough.

105  The owner of the field may cut these trees vertically at his property line.

(13c line 24) **הלכה יא:** מַרְחִיקִין אֶת הָאִילָן כול'. **הלכה יב:** לֹא יִטַּע אָדָם כול'. רִבִּי יַעֲקֹב בַּר אִידִי בְּשֵׁם רִבִּי יְהוֹשֻׁעַ בֶּן לֵוִי. טַעֲמוֹן דְּרַבָּנִין. מִפְּנֵי שֶׁיִּישׁוּב הָעוֹלָם בַּבּוֹרוֹת. שִׁמְעוֹן בַּר וָוה אָמַר בְּשֵׁם רִבִּי יוֹחָנָן. כָּךְ מֵשִׁיב רִבִּי יוֹסֵי לְרַבָּנִין. כְּמָה דְאִית לְכוֹן יִישׁוּב הָעוֹלָם בַּבּוֹרוֹת אוּף אֲנָא אִית לִי יִישׁוּב הָעוֹלָם בָּאִילָנוֹת.

**Halakhah 11**: "One distances a tree," etc. **Halakhah 12**: "A person should not plant," etc. Rebbi Jacob bar Idi in the name of Rebbi Joshua ben Levi: The rabbis' reason is that civilization is based on cisterns[106]. Simeon bar Abba in the name of Rebbi Joḥanan: Rebbi Joshua answers the rabbis thus: just as you hold that civilization is based on cisterns, so I am holding that civilization is based on trees.

106 The tree's owner did not break any law in planting it, as R. Yose insists. Then why do the rabbis *force* the tree's owner to cut it down if the cistern's owner offers him money?

(13c line 32) [רִבִּי יוֹסֵה בְּשֵׁם רִבִּי יוֹחָנָן. אֵין שָׁרָשִׁים לְעִנְיַין הַבִּיכּוּרִים כְּלוּם.] אָמַר רִבִּי יוֹסֵי. וְיֵאוּת אָמַר. שֶׁאִים אוֹמֵר שָׁרָשִׁין עִיקָּר הֵן לַבִּיכּוּרִים לֹא הָיָה אָדָם יָכוֹל לְהָבִיא בִּיכּוּרִים מֵעוֹלָם. מִפְּנֵי שֶׁשָּׁרָשִׁין שֶׁלָּזֶה יוֹצְאִין לְתוֹךְ שָׁרָשָׁיו שֶׁלָּזֶה וְשֶׁלָּזֶה בְשֶׁלָּזֶה. לְפוּם כֵּן אָמַר רִבִּי יָסָא בְשֵׁם רִבִּי יוֹחָנָן. אֵין שָׁרָשִׁים לְעִנְיַין בִּיכּוּרִים כְּלוּם.

**הלכה יג**: אִילָן שֶׁהוּא נוֹטֶה לְתוֹךְ שְׂדֵה חֲבֵירוֹ כול'.

[107][Rebbi *Yasa*[108] said in the name of Rebbi Joḥanan: Roots are irrelevant for First Fruits.][109] Rebbi Yose said, he said it correctly. For if he did say that roots are important, nobody could ever bring First Fruits since the roots of one enter the other's ground and vice-versa. Therefore, Rebbi Yasa said in the name of Rebbi Joḥanan: Roots are irrelevant for First Fruits.

**Halakhah 13**: "If a tree overhangs another's field," etc.

107 Text of E, missing in L, but presupposed by R. Yose's reaction to it.
108 The correct attribution is in the quote at the end of the paragraph.

107 This refers to the discussion in *Bikkurim* 1:1 (Notes 4-20). If a vintner takes a branch of a vine, still connected to its stem, buries most of it

in the ground and only lets the end reappear on the surface (he "provines"), the end will in time develop into a new vine. First fruits have to be brought from the vintner's "own land" (*Deut.* 26:2). Therefore, if the branch was buried under a public road or another person's property, neither the grape bunches of the original vine nor those of the new one qualify for first fruits unless the branch was enclosed in a pipe which prevents it from extracting nourishment from public or otherwise owned private land. But Mishnah 12 here presupposes that roots of orchards always extend subterraneously into other domains. Why therefore should anybody be able to bring First Fruits and recite the declaration confirming that all fruits are from "his earth"? In *Bikkurim*, R. Joḥanan is quoted declaring the rules of First Fruit as "rules of robbers."

**משנה יד:** אִילָן שֶׁהוּא נוֹטֶה לִרְשׁוּת הָרַבִּים קוֹצֵץ כְּדֵי שֶׁיְּהֵא הַגָּמָל עוֹבֵר בְּרוֹכְבוֹ. רִבִּי יְהוּדָה אוֹמֵר טָעוּן פִּשְׁתָּן אוֹ חֲבִילֵי זְמוֹרוֹת. רִבִּי שִׁמְעוֹן אוֹמֵר כָּל־הָאִילָן כְּנֶגֶד הַמִּשְׁקוֹלוֹת מִפְּנֵי הַטּוּמְאָה. (fol. 13b)

**Mishnah 14**: If a tree overhangs the public domain, one has to cut it so that a camel with a rider on it may pass; Rebbi Jehudah says, loaded with flax or bundles of vine cuttings[109]. Rebbi Simeon says, any tree [must be cut] along the plumb line because of impurity[105,110].

109 They are very light and take up a large volume.

110 R. Simeon essentially rejects the rabbis' rule as following Gentile law (*Corpus iuris, Decretum de arboribus caedendis* requires that branches overhanging a public road must be cut up to a height of 15 Roman *pedes*, not quite 4.5 m.) He insists on a Jewish rationale. The impurity of the dead is transferred not only by touch but by being under one "tent" with a corpse. The crown of a tree forms such a "tent." If the tree overhangs a road but grows inside a fence or wall which obstructs the view, a person passing

under it could be inadvertently become severely impure (cf. *Nazir* 7:3, Notes 163-164). Therefore, in the Land of Israel all overhangs have to be eliminated. He has no rules for other countries.

(13c line 32) **הלכה יד:** אִילָן שֶׁהוּא נוֹטֶה לִרְשׁוּת הָרַבִּים כול׳. רִבִּי יוֹנָתָן הֲוָה דָאִין טַבָּאוּת וַהֲוָה תַּמָּן חַד רוֹמַיי וַהֲוָה מְגִירֵיהּ בְּחַקְלָא וּבְבֵיתָא. וַהֲוָה לְרִבִּי יוֹנָתָן חַד אִילָן נָטֶה גּוֹ דְּהַהוּא רוֹמַיָּה. אָתָא קוֹמֵי חַד דַּיָּין אָכֵן. אָמַר לוֹן. אֲזָלוּן וְתוֹן בְּצַפְרָא. אָמַר הַהוּא רוֹמַיָּה. בְּגִינִי לָא נְפַק דִּינָא. לְמָחָר אֲנָא מְבַטֵּל אִילוּ מִדִּידִי וַחֲמֵי הֵיאַךְ דִּינָא נָפַק. אִין הֲוָה דָאִין כָּל־עַמָּא וְלָא דָאִין נַפְשֵׁיהּ לֵית הוּא בַּר נַשׁ. בְּאַפְתֵּי רַמְשָׁא שָׁלַח רִבִּי יוֹנָתָן בָּתַר נַגָּרֵיהּ. אָמַר. פוּק קוֹץ מַה דְנָטָה גּוֹ רוֹמַיָּה. בְּצַפְרָא קָרַץ בַּעַל דִּינֵיהּ לְגַבֵּיהּ. אָמַר לֵיהּ. זִיל קוֹץ מַה דְנָטָה גּוֹ דִּידֵיהּ. אָמַר לֵיהּ רוֹמַיָּה. דִּידָךְ מַה. אָמַר לֵיהּ. פּוּק חֲמֵי יָתֵיהּ כְּמָה דִּידִי עֲבַד עֲבַד דִּידָךְ. נְפַק חֲמִיתֵיהּ. אָמַר. בָּרוּךְ אֱלָהֲהוֹן דִּיהוּדָאֵי.

**Halakhah 14**: "If a tree overhangs the public domain,," etc. [111]Rebbi Jonathan was careful in judging; there was a Roman there who was his neighbor both in the field and the house. Rebbi Jonathan had a tree overhanging the Roman's property. A similar case came before him[112]. He told them, go and return next morning[113]. This Roman said, because of me he did not decide the case. Tomorrow I will abandon my work[114] and see how the judgment goes. If he judges all people and does not judge himself, he is not human. At nightfall, Rebbi Jonathan sent for his carpenter and told him, go and cut everything that overhangs the Roman's. In the morning, the parties appeared before him. He told him, go and cut what overhangs into his property. The Roman said to him, what is with yours? He told him, go and see; what was done with mine do with yours. He went out and looked. He said, praised be the Jews' God.

111 A Hebrew version of this story is in *Tanḥuma Šofeṭim* 3 [*Ginze Schechter* I (New York 1928), p. 130]. A similar story, about R. Yannai, is in the Babli, 60a/b.

112 A case of a tree overhanging from one person's property over another's.

113 A most unusual procedure.

114 The reading of E: אוּמְנִין דִּידִי "my job" makes good sense; no conjectures are needed. The text of L must be classified as a scribal error.

(13c line 32) חָדָא אִיתָא אוֹקְרַת תְּאֵנִין לְרִבִּי יוֹנָתָן. אָמַר לָהּ. בְּבָעוּ מִינָךְ אִי אַעַלְתִּינוֹן מִינַּגְלָיָין אַפְּקִינוֹן מִינַּגְלָיָין. וְאִין אַעַלְתִּינוֹן מִיכַסְיָין אַפְּקִינוֹן מִיכַסְיָין דְּלָא יֵימְרוּן בְּרַיָּיתָא. דֵּינָרִין יְהָבַת לֵיהּ. וְאוֹקְרָא תְּאֵנִין.

רִבִּי חֲנִינָה אָעֵיל לְרִבִּי יוֹנָתָן בְּגִינִיתֵיהּ וְאַיְיכְלֵיהּ תְּאֵנִין. מִדְּנָפַק חָמָא חַד אִילָן דְּבָרַת שׁוּבְעִין חִוָּורִין. אָמַר לֵיהּ. לָמָּה לֹא אוֹכַלְתָּנִי מִן אִילֵּין. אָמַר לֵיהּ. דְּאִינּוּן לִבְרִי. רִבִּי חֲנִינָה חָשַׁשׁ מִשּׁוּם גֶּזֶל בְּנוֹ.

A woman honored Rebbi Jonathan with figs[115]. He told her, please if you brought them covered, take them away covered; but if you brought them in the open, take them away in the open, so that people should not say that she brought him denars and he honored her with figs[116].

Rebbi Ḥanina brought Rebbi Jonathan to his garden and served him figs. When he left, he saw one tree of white *benotševaʿ*[117]. He asked him, why did you not let me eat from these? He told him, they are my son's. Rebbi Ḥanina was afraid of robbing his son.

115 As a bakshish, which as a judge he could not accept.

116 But still accepts bribes.

117 Delicacy figs; cf. *Ma'serot* 2:8, Note 135.

(13c line 32) רִבִּי יָסָא בְּשֵׁם רִבִּי יוֹחָנָן. הֲלָכָה כְּרִבִּי שִׁמְעוֹן. רִבִּי חִיָּיה בְּשֵׁם רִבִּי יוֹחָנָן. כָּל־עַמָּא מוֹדוּ שֶׁהֲלָכָה כְּרִבִּי שִׁמְעוֹן.

Rebbi Yasa in the name of Rebbi Johanan: Practice follows Rebbi Simeon. Rebbi Hiyya in the name of Rebbi Johanan: Everybody agrees that practice follows Rebbi Simeon[118].

118 Since the Babli does not discuss the matter, it follows that it accepts practice following the anonymous Tanna, which is appropriate outside the Land of Israel.

## חזקת הבתים פרק שלישי

(fol. 13c) **משנה א**: חֶזְקַת הַבָּתִּים בּוֹרוֹת שִׁיחִין וּמְעָרוֹת וּמֶרְחֲצָאוֹת וְשׁוֹבָכוֹת בֵּית הַבַּדִּין בֵּית הַשְׁלָחִין וְהָעֲבָדִים וְכָל־שֶׁהוּא עוֹשֶׂה פֵּירוֹת תָּדִיר חֶזְקָתָן שָׁלֹשׁ שָׁנִים מִיּוֹם לְיוֹם. שְׂדֵה הַבַּעַל חֶזְקָתָהּ שָׁלֹשׁ שָׁנִים וְאֵינָהּ מִיּוֹם לְיוֹם.

**Mishnah 1**: Confirmation of claim of undisturbed possession[1] of houses, cisterns, ditches, and caverns, and bath houses, and dove-cotes, oil presses, irrigated land, and slaves[2], and everything which yields continuously is three years from day to day. The claim of undisturbed possession of an unirrigated field is three years, but not from day to day[3].

1  A person who claims legal acquisition of real estate but has no deed can defend himself against an accusation of being an illegal squatter and must be confirmed by the court in his rights if he can prove undisturbed possession for three consecutive years by witnesses.

There is a second meaning of חֲזָקָה "permanence of the status quo", cf. *Qiddušin* 1:1, Note 30.

2  Who in this respect follow the law of real estate; *Qiddušin* 1:3, Notes 347-355.

3  But undisturbed collection of three consecutive harvests.

(13d line 35) **הלכה א**: חֶזְקַת הַבָּתִּים בּוֹרוֹת שִׁיחִין וּמְעָרוֹת כול'. מִנַּיִן לַחֲזָקוֹת. אָמַר רִבִּי יוֹחָנָן. שָׁמַעְנוּ מֵהוֹלְכֵי אוּשָׁא מְשׁוֹר הַמּוּעָד לָמְדוּ. אָמַר רִבִּי יוֹסֵי. מָאן אִית לֵיהּ שׁוֹר הַמּוּעָד לְג' יָמִים. לֹא רִבִּי יוּדָה. דְּתַנִּינָן תַּמָּן. רִבִּי יוּדָה אוֹמֵר. לֹא אָמְרוּ ג' שָׁנִים אֶלָּא כְּדֵי שֶׁיְּהֵא בְּאִיסְפַּמְיָא וְיַחֲזִיק שָׁנָה וְיֵלְכוּ וְיוֹדִיעוּהוּ שָׁנָה וְיָבוֹא שָׁנָה.

**Halakhah 1:** "The claim of undisturbed possession of houses, cisterns, ditches, and caverns," etc. From where confirmation of claims of undisturbed possession? [4]Rebbi Joḥanan said, we heard from those who went to Usha[5] that they learned it from the notorious bull[6]. Rebbi Yose said, who holds that a bull becomes notorious after three days? Not Rebbi Jehudah? As we stated there[7]: "Rebbi Jehudah said, they said three years only for the case that if he[8] is in Spain, he[9] should be in possession for one year; they went and told him during one year, and he[8] returns within one year.[10]"

---

4   A parallel argument is in the Babli, 28a/b.

5   In the Babli identified as R. Ismael. In the aftermath of the Bar Kokhba war and its consequences, the Synhedrion was reconstituted at Usha under the leadership of R. Jehudah.

6   The rules of the notorious bull only apply to an animal which gored three times. The limit of three years is popular usage; no biblical sources are claimed.

7   Mishnah *Bava qamma* 2:6. Only R. Jehudah requires that the agressive behavior of the bull be confirmed by testimony for three consecutive days; R. Meïr holds that three incidents are sufficient, not necessarily on consecutive days. But nobody holds that legal possession can be claimed on the basis of 3 incidents of interrupted squatting.

7   Mishnah 3.

8   The original owner of the land.

9   The squatter.

10  This means that intrinsically R. Jehudah only requires one year of undisturbed possession. If the institution of חֲזָקָה is based on R. Jehudah's teaching, it is only a tenuous analogy, without any claim of Biblical origin.

(13d line 39) שִׁמְעוֹן בַּר וָא בְּשֵׁם רִבִּי יוֹחָנָן. הַמּוֹכֵר בַּיִת לַחֲבֵירוֹ כֵּיוָן שֶׁמָּסַר לוֹ מַפְתֵּחַ קָנָה. רִבִּי אִמִּי בְּשֵׁם רִבִּי יוֹחָנָן. הַמּוֹכֵר בַּיִת לַחֲבֵירוֹ כֵּיוָן שֶׁעָבַר לְתוֹכוֹ פֵּירוֹת קָנָה. אָמַר רִבִּי שְׁמוּאֵל בַּר רַב יִצְחָק. וּבִלְבַד פֵּירוֹת שֶׁרְאוּיִין לִיצָּבֵר.

## HALAKHAH 1

רִבִּי יוֹחָנָן בְּשֵׁם רִבִּי יַנַּאי. הַמּוֹכֵר בּוֹר לַחֲבֵירוֹ כֵּיוָן שֶׁמָּסַר לוֹ דְלָיָיו קָנָה. רִבִּי יְהוֹשֻׁעַ בֶּן לֵוִי בְּשֵׁם רֵישׁ לָקִישׁ. הַמּוֹכֵר צֹאן לַחֲבֵירוֹ כֵּיוָן שֶׁמָּסַר לוֹ מַשְׁכּוֹכִית קָנָה. מַאי מַשְׁכּוֹכִית. אִית דָּמְרִין. חוּטְרָא. וְאִית דָּמְרִין. פַּנְדּוּרָא. וְאִית דְּאָמְרִין. תַּיְיָשָׁא רַבָּא. רֵישׁ לָקִישׁ בְּשֵׁם בַּר קַפָּרָא. הַמּוֹכֵר קֶבֶר לַחֲבֵירוֹ כֵּיוָן שֶׁקָּבַר מֵת אֶחָד בְּכוּךְ חֲזָקָה לְכָל־הַכּוּךְ. קָבַר ג מֵתִים בִּשְׁלֹשָׁה כּוּכִין חֲזָקָה לְכָל־הַקֶּבֶר.

[11]Simeon bar Abba in the name of Rebbi Johanan: If someboldy is selling a house to another, when he delivered the key [the buyer] took possession[12]. Rebbi Immi in the name of Rebbi Johanan: If somebody is selling a house to another, when [the buyer] stored produce there, he took possession[13]. Rebbi Samuel bar Rav Isaac said, only produce usually stored. Rebbi Johanan in the name of Rebbi Yannai: If somebody is selling a cistern to another, when he handed over its pails [the buyer] took possession[14]. Rebbi Joshua ben Levi in the name of Rebbi Simeon ben Laqish[15]: If somebody sold a flock to another person, when [the seller] delivered the *maškokît*, [the buyer] took possession. What is *maškokît*? Some say, the shepherd's staff. But some say, a *pandura*[16]. And some say, the bell-wether. Rebbi Simeon ben Laqish in the name of Bar Qappara: If somebody is selling a burial chamber to another, when that one buried there one dead it is confirmation of claim for the entire chamber. When he buried three dead in three chambers, it is confirmation of claim for the entire burial cavern[16a].

11 A claim of possession must be based on a claim of ownership. But transfer of ownership is only a precondition for the transfer of possession which needs a separate action. This is detailed in *Qiddušin*, Chapter 1, from which most of this paragraph is taken.

12 Cf. *Qiddušin* 1:4, Note 435. The text here agrees with the Babli (*Bava*

*qamma* 51a/52b) against the Yerushalmi *Qiddušin*.

13   *Qiddušin* 1:4, Note 435.

14   *Qiddušin* 1:4, Note 434. There, the statement is by R. Simeon bar Abba in the name of R. Joshua ben Levi.

15   Obviously, this must read: R. Simeon ben Laqish in the name of R. Joshua ben Levi. In *Qiddušin* 1:4 (Notes 432-433), it is in the name of R. Yannai.

16   Cf. *Qiddušin* 1:4 Note 433.

16a  For the rules of burial caverns see Halakhah 6:8.

(13d line 49) וַעֲבָדִים. רִבִּי סִימוֹן אֲחוּי דְּרִבִּי יְהוּדָה בַּר זַבְדִּי בְשֵׁם רַב. תִּינוֹק כָּל־זְמַן שֶׁמּוּשְׁלָךְ בַּשּׁוּק אָבִיו אוֹ אִמּוֹ מְעִידִין עָלָיו. נֶאֱסַף מִן הַשּׁוּק צָרִיךְ שְׁנֵי עֵדִים וְאָבִיו וְאִמּוֹ נַעֲשִׂין לוֹ כִשְׁנֵי עֵדִים. אָמַר רִבִּי אַבָּהוּ. וְחָשׁוּד אָדָם לוֹמַר עַל מִי שֶׁאֵינוֹ בְנוֹ שֶׁהוּא בְנוֹ. דִּילְמָא בְּנִיכְסֵי הַגֵּר אִתְאָמְרַת. אָמְרוּ לֵיהּ. הֲרֵי כָל־רַבּוֹתֵינוּ בַגּוֹלָה מְעִידִין עָלֵינוּ שֶׁכָּךְ שָׁמַעֲנוּהּ מִפִּי רַב אָדָא בַּר אַבוּהּ. אָמַר רַב חִסְדָּא. הָדָא דְּתֵימַר בְּתִינוֹק שֶׁאֵינוֹ מַרְגִּיעַ. אֲבָל בְּתִינוֹק הַמַּרְגִּיעַ הָדָא הִיא דְּאָמַר רִבִּי יוֹחָנָן. עֲגָלִים וְסַיָּיחִים הַמְקַפְצִין מִמָּקוֹם לְמָקוֹם אֵין לָהֶן חֲזָקָה.

"And slaves." [17]Rebbi Simon the brother of Rebbi Jehudah bar Zavdi in the name of Rav: As long as a baby lies in the public domain, his father or his mother can testify about him. Once he has been collected from the public domain, one needs two witnesses and its father and mother are like two witnesses. Rebbi Abbahu said, can a person be suspected to say about one who is not his son that he is his son[18]? Maybe it was said about the property of a convert[19]? He told him, but all our teachers in the Diaspora testify that in this form we heard it from Rav Ada bar Abuh[20]. Rav Ḥisda said: That is, if the baby is not moving. But [the case of] a baby which is moving refers to what Rebbi Joḥanan said: property rights on jumping calves and lambs which move from place to place cannot be proven by possession[21].

## HALAKHAH 1    555

17 This paragraph is partially quote and partially reformulation of a paragraph in *Qiddušin* 4:2, Notes 107-111.

18 Why should not his father alone be empowered to recognize his child?

19 If he has no Jewish children, he has no heirs in Jewish law and all Jews are potentially entitled to inherit from him. If then he recognizes an otherwise unknown person as his son, he potentially damages other people's claim; the recognition needs two witnesses, *viz.*, father and mother. But once he is married in Jewish law, the Torah gives the father the sole power to recognize his child; *Deut.* 21:17.

20 In E and *Or zarua'* I §340 (end): Rabba bar Abuh. This seems to be the correct attribution.

21 Therefore, such a child is a foundling; his parents cannot act as witnesses since by their testimony they declare themselves his relatives and thus disqualify themselves. This conclusion is the opposite of the one reached in the longer text in *Qiddušin*; it parallels the conclusion reached by the Babli, 36a.

(13d line 57) רִבִּי יָסָא בְּשֵׁם רִבִּי יוֹחָנָן. שְׁתֵּי שָׂדוֹת בְּנִכְסֵי הַגֵּר הַמֵּיצַר בֵּינְתַיִים. תָּלַשׁ מֵאַחַת מֵהֶן לִקְנוֹת חֲבֵירָרְתָהּ וְלֹא לִקְנוֹת הַמֵּיצַר. הִיא נִקְנֵית וַחֲבֵירָרְתָהּ אֵינָהּ נִקְנֵית. רִבִּי זֵירָא בְעָא קוֹמֵי רִבִּי יָסָא. נִתְכַּוֵּון לִקְנוֹת [מִן] הַמֵּיצַר. וּשְׁרַע מִינָהּ. אָמַר רַב חִסְדָּא. בְּנִכְסֵי הַגֵּר תָּלַשׁ בִּצְפוֹנָהּ שֶׁלְּשָׂדֶה לִקְנוֹת דְּרוֹמָהּ וְלֹא אֶמְצָעִיתָהּ. צְפוֹנָהּ נִקְנֵית דְּרוֹמָהּ לֹא נִקְנֵית תַּמָּן תַּנִּינָן. אִם הָיָה מְחוּבָּר לַקַּרְקַע וְתָלַשׁ כָּל־שֶׁהוּא קָנָה. שְׁמוּאֵל אָמַר. לֹא קָנָה אֶלָּא מַה שֶּׁתָּלַשׁ. אָמַר רִבִּי אֲבְדּוּמָא נְחוּתָא בְּנִכְסֵי הַגֵּר אִתְּאֲמַר. רַב חִסְדָּא אָמַר רִבִּי יִצְחָק. בְּגִין דְּלָא תֵימַר קַשְׁיָא לִשְׁמוּאֵל אַתְּ מַר בְּנִכְסֵי הַגֵּר אִתְאָמְרַת

[22]Rebbi Yasa in the name of Rebbi Johanan: If two fields of a proselyte were involved[23], with a boundary strip in between. If he cut off from one of them with the intent of taking possession also of the other but not the boundary strip in between, the one was acquired by him but not the other. Rebbi Ze'ira asked before Rebbi Yasa: If he intended to

acquire starting [from]²⁴ the boundary strip and below? Rav Ḥisda said, property of a proselyte which he took possession of in the North by cutting off with the intent of also acquiring the one to the South, but did not have the intent of acquiring the strip in the middle, he acquired the one to the North but not the one to the South²⁵. There, we have stated²⁶: "If it was connected to the ground and he cut off anything, he acquired." Samuel said, he acquired only what he cut off. Rebbi Eudaimon the Emigrant said, this was said concerning the property of a proselyte²⁷. Rav Ḥisda said, Rebbi Isaac: It was reported that this was said concerning the property of a proselyte, so it should present no difficulty for Samuel²⁸.

22  This is a reformulation of a paragraph in *Qiddušin* 1:5, Notes 502-513; cf. Babli 52b/53a.

23  By becoming Jewish, the proselyte changed his ethnic status and severed his links with his biological family. If he failed to start a Jewish family, he died without heirs; the fields now are ownerless property. {It was characteristic of Egypt intercommunal law that inheritance across ethnic boundaries was impossible. So the daughter of a Roman *missicius* as Roman citizen could not inherit from her native Egyptian mother (cf. R. Taubenschlag, *loc. cit. Bava meṣia'* 1, Note 84, p. 142.)

The fields can be acquired only by performing some agricultural work, e. g., weeding. But work on a field only acquires real estate adjacent to the place on which the work was done.

24  Reading of E, missing in L, confirmed by the text in *Qiddušin*.

25  This statement is really the same as the one attributed earlier to R. Joḥanan. The genuine source is *Qiddušin* 1:5 where the two statements refer to different situations.

26  Mishnah 5:9. This refers to a standing crop on a field. After harvest, the produce is taken into possession by the buyer by moving some of the crop. The problem is, how can standing crop be acquired while the field remains the seller's property? Cf. *Qiddušin* 1:5 Note 513.

27  Since no real estate was acquired, taking some stalks can have no influence on the remainder of the

ownerless crop.

28 Since if the crop was paid for and the buyer was told by the seller to harvest it, Samuel must agree that by cutting the first stalk he takes possession of the entire crop.

(13d line 65) רַב חִסְדָּא אָמַר. מָשַׁךְ בְּהֵמָה זוֹ לִקְנוֹת קָנָה. לִקְנוֹת וּלְדוֹתֶיהָ [לֹא] קָנָה. לִקְנוֹת הִיא וּלְדוֹתֶיהָ (לֹא) קָנָה. אָמַר רִבִּי נָסָה. הָדָא דְתֵימַר. בְּשֶׁלֹּא הָיְתָה עוֹבָרָה. אֲבָל אִם הָיְתָה עוֹבָרָה עָשׂוּ אוֹתָהּ כְּאֶחָד מֵאֵיבָרֶיהָ. וְהָתַנֵּי. הַמּוֹכֵר עוּבָּרֵי בְהֶמְתּוֹ לַחֲבֵירוֹ לֹא עָשָׂה כְלוּם. וּוְלָדֵי שִׁפְחָתוֹ לַחֲבֵירוֹ לֹא עָשָׂה כְלוּם. מַעְשְׂרוֹת שָׂדֵהוּ לַחֲבֵירוֹ לֹא עָשָׂה כְלוּם. אֲוִיר חוֹרְבָתוֹ לַחֲבֵירוֹ לֹא עָשָׂה כְלוּם. אֶלָּא מוֹכֵר לוֹ בְּהֵמָה וּמְשַׁיֵּיר לוֹ עוֹבָרָהּ. מוֹכֵר לוֹ שִׁפְחָה וּמְשַׁיֵּיר לוֹ וְלָדָהּ. מוֹכֵר לוֹ שָׂדֶה וּמְשַׁיֵּיר לוֹ מַעְשְׂרוֹת. מוֹכֵר לוֹ חוֹרְבָה וּמְשַׁיֵּיר לוֹ אֲוִירָהּ.

[29]Rav Ḥisda said, "draw this animal close to you in order to take possession," he took possession[30]. "To take possession of its offspring," he did [not][31] take possession. "To take possession of it together with its offspring," he did (not)[32] take possession. Rebbi Nasa[33] said, that is, if it was not pregnant. But if it was pregnant, they treated [the fetus] as one of its limbs, as we did state[34]: He who sells the fetus of his animal to another person did not do anything; the future children of his slave girl to another person, he did not do anything; the tithes of his field to another person, he did not do anything; the airspace of his dry land to another person, he did not do anything. But he may sell him an animal and reserve her fetus for himself, sell him a slave girl and reserve her children for himself, sell him a field and reserve the tithes for himself, sell him dry land and reserve the airspace for himself.

29 This is from *Qidduŝin* 1:4, Notes 414-417.

30 Implied by Mishnah *Qidduŝin* 1:4.

31  Reading of E, missing in L, required bt the text in *Qiddušin*.
32  Reading of L, missing in E, to be deleted with the text in *Qiddušin*.
33  In *Qiddušin*: Yose.

34  This is a reformulation of an Amoraic text in *Demay* 6:3, Notes 79-83, and its slightly garbled parallel in *Qiddušin* 1:4, Notes 439-441.

(13d line 74) רִבִּי בָּא בְשֵׁם רַב חִסְדָּא. שְׁלֹשָׁה הֵן שֶׁהֵן נֶאֱמָנִין לְאַלְתָּר. הַחַיָּה וְהַשַּׁיָּירָה וְהַמְטָהֶרֶת חֲבֵרוֹתֶיהָ. הַחַיָּה בְשָׁעָה שֶׁיּוֹשֶׁבֶת עַל הַמַּשְׁבֵּר. מֵהָדָא דִכְתִיב וַתִּקַּח הַמְיַלֶּדֶת וַתִּקְשֹׁר וגו'. שַׁיָּירָא. כַּיי דָּמַר רִבִּי סִימוֹן אֲחוֵי דִיהוּדָה בַּר זַבְדִי בְשֵׁם רַב. [תִּינוֹק] כָּל־זְמַן שֶׁמּוּשְׁלָךְ לַשּׁוּק אוֹ אָבִיו אוֹ אִמּוֹ מְעִידִין עָלָיו. נֶאֱסַף צָרִיךְ שְׁנֵי עֵדִים וְאָבִיו וְאִמּוֹ נַעֲשִׂין לוֹ כִּשְׁנֵי עֵדִים. וְהַמְטָהֶרֶת חֲבֵרוֹתֶיהָ. כַּיי דְתַנִּינָן תַּמָּן. שָׁלֹשׁ נָשִׁים שֶׁהָיוּ יְשֵׁינוֹת בְּמִטָּה וְנִמְצָא דָם תַּחַת אַחַת מֵהֶן כּוּלָּן טְמֵאוֹת. בָּדְקָה אַחַת וּמָצְאתָה טָמֵא הִיא טְמֵאָה וְכוּלָּן טְהוֹרוֹת. אָמַר רִבִּי בָּא. וּבִלְבַד מֵעֵת לָעֵת.

[35]Rebbi Abba in the name of Rav Ḥisda: Three are trustworthy immediately: a midwife, a caravan, and the one who purifies her colleagues. A midwife as long as [the woman] sits on the birthing chair, from the verse: "The midwife took and wound, etc." A caravan, as Rebbi Simon, the brother of Rebbi Jehudah bar Zavdi, said in the name of Rav: As long as [a baby][36] lies in the public domain, either its father or its mother can testify about him. Once he has been collected from the public domain, one needs two witnesses; its father and mother may become its two witnesses. The one who purifies her colleagues, as we have stated there[37]: "Three women sleep on one bed. If blood was found under one of them, all three are impure. If one of them checked herself out and found herself impure, she is impure and the other two are pure." Rebbi Abba said, only within 24 hours.

35  This is a slight rewording of a paragraph in *Qiddušin* 4:2, Notes 112-117.

36  Reading of E, missing in L, required by the parallel in *Qiddušin* and the context.

37  Mishnah *Niddah* 9:4.

**משנה ב:** רִבִּי יִשְׁמָעֵאל אוֹמֵר גֹ חֳדָשִׁים בָּרִאשׁוֹנָה וּשְׁלֹשָׁה חֳדָשִׁים בָּאַחֲרוֹנָה וּשְׁנֵים עָשָׂר חֹדֶשׁ בָּאֶמְצַע הֲרֵי שְׁמוֹנָה עָשָׂר חֹדֶשׁ. רִבִּי עֲקִיבָה אוֹמֵר חֹדֶשׁ בָּרִאשׁוֹנָה וְחֹדֶשׁ בָּאַחֲרוֹנָה וּשְׁנֵים עָשָׂר חֹדֶשׁ בָּאֶמְצַע הֲרֵי אַרְבָּעָה עָשָׂר חֹדֶשׁ. אָמַר רִבִּי יִשְׁמָעֵאל בַּמֶּה דְּבָרִים אֲמוּרִים בִּשְׂדֵה הַלָּבָן אֲבָל בִּשְׂדֵה הָאִילָן כָּנַס אֶת תְּבוּאָתוֹ מָסַק אֶת זֵיתָיו כָּנַס אֶת קֵייצוֹ הֲרֵי אִילּוּ שָׁלֹשׁ שָׁנִים. (fol. 13c)

**Mishnah 2:** Rebbi Ismael says, three months in the first and three months in the last with twelve months in the middle, for a total of eighteen months[38]. Rebbi Aqiba says, one month in the first and one month in the last with twelve months in the middle, for a total of fourteen months. Rebbi Ismael said, when has this been said? A field of grain. But for an orchard, if he harvested his yield[39], lifted his olives, and collected his cut figs it counts for three years[40].

38  The three years of undisturbed possession required in Mishnah 1 are not three calendar years but three harvests with time for preparation before the harvest and processing afterwards.

39  The grape harvest, which in *Deut.* 22:9 is called "the vineyard's yield".

40  Depending on the trees in the orchard, three different undisturbed harvests establish a presumption of lawful possession.

(14a line 6) **הלכה ב:** רִבִּי יִשְׁמָעֵאל אוֹמֵר. שְׁלֹשָׁה חֳדָשִׁים הָרִאשׁוֹנִים כּוּל׳. שְׁמוּאֵל אָמַר. זוֹ דִּבְרֵי רִבִּי יִשְׁמָעֵאל וְרִבִּי עֲקִיבָה. אֲבָל חֲכָמִים אוֹמְרִים. ג

שָׁנִים קָצִיר. ג שָׁנִים בָּצִיר. ג שָׁנִים מָסִיק. רַב אָמַר. זוֹ דִבְרֵי רִבִּי יִשְׁמָעֵאל וְרִבִּי עֲקִיבָה. אֲבָל חֲכָמִים אוֹמְרִים. ג שָׁנִים מֵעֵת לָעֵת. רִבִּי שְׁמוּאֵל בַּר נַחְמָן בְּשֵׁם רִבִּי יוֹנָתָן. כְּשֵׁם שֶׁחֲלוּקִין כָּאן כָּךְ חֲלוּקִין בִּשְׁנֵי אֵלִיָּהוּ.

**Halakhah 2:** "Rebbi Ismael says, the first three months," etc. [41]Samuel said, these are the words of Rebbi Ismael and Rebbi Aqiba. But the Sages say, three years grain cutting, three years grape harvesting, three years olive harvesting. Rav said, these are the words of Rebbi Ismael and Rebbi Aqiba. But the Sages say, three years from day to day. Rebbi Samuel bar Nahman in the name of Rebbi Jonathan: Just as they disagree here, so they disgree about Elijah's years[42].

| | |
|---|---|
| 41 | Babli 36b. |
| 42 | Whether the three years' draught mentioned in *1K.* 18:1 were 14 months, 18 months, or three full years. |

(fol. 13c) **משנה ג:** שָׁלשׁ אֲרָצוֹת לַחֲזָקָה יְהוּדָה וְעֵבֶר הַיַּרְדֵּן וְהַגָּלִיל. הָיָה בִיהוּדָה וְהֶחֱזִיק בַּגָּלִיל בַּגָּלִיל וְהֶחֱזִיק בִּיהוּדָה אֵינָהּ חֲזָקָה עַד שֶׁיְּהֵא עִמּוֹ בַּמְּדִינָה. אָמַר רִבִּי יְהוּדָה לֹא אָמְרוּ שָׁלשׁ שָׁנִים אֶלָּא כְּדֵי שֶׁיְּהֵא בָאִיסְפַּמְיָא וְיַחֲזִיק שָׁנָה וְיֵלְכוּ וְיוֹדִיעוּהוּ שָׁנָה וְיָבוֹא לַשָּׁנָה הָאַחֶרֶת.

**Mishnah 1:** There are three regions for claims of undisturbed possession: Judea, Transjordan[43], and Galilee. If he was in Judea and somebody claimed undisturbed possession in Galilee, or in Galilee and somebody claimed undisturbed possession in Judea, it is not undisturbed possession unless he be in the same province[44]. Rebbi Jehudah said, they said three years only for the case that if he[8] is in Spain[45], he[9] should be in possession for one year; they went and told him during one year, and he[8] returns within one year.[10]

43 According to some interpretations, the region between the Judean foothills and the Mediterranian; cf. Ševi'it 9:2, Note 39.

44 If the original owner can prove that he was not in the province during the claimant's occupation of the land, a claim of undisturbed possession will be disallowed and the claimant evicted unless he has documentary proof of his claim.

45 Or Apamea in Phrygia; that would be presupposed in R. Ismael's and R. Aqiba's interpretations.

(14a line 12) **הלכה ג:** שָׁלֹשׁ אֲרָצוֹת לַחֲזָקָה כול׳ רַב אָמַר. בִּשְׁעַת הַחֵירוּם שָׁנוּ. אָמַר רִבִּי חֲנִינָה. שְׁנֵי עָרְלָה בֵּינֵיהוֹן.

רַב אָמַר. אֵין חֲזָקָה לַבּוֹרֵחַ וְלֹא מֵאֶרֶץ לְאֶרֶץ. שְׁמוּאֵל אָמַר. יֵשׁ חֲזָקָה לַבּוֹרֵחַ וְיֵשׁ חֲזָקָה מֵאֶרֶץ לְאֶרֶץ. אָמַר רַב נַחְמָן בַּר רַב יִצְחָק. קַרְיָיא מְסַיֵּיעַ לְמַה דָּמַר שְׁמוּאֵל. וַיִּתֵּן לָהּ הַמֶּלֶךְ סָרִיס אֶחָד וגו׳.

**Halakhah 3**: "There are three regions for claims of undisturbed possession," etc. Rav said, this was taught in emergency situations[46].

Rebbi Ḥanina said, the years of *orlah* are in dispute between them[47].

Rav said, there can be no claim of undisturbed possession from a fugitive, nor one made from one country to another. Samuel said, there can be a claim of undisturbed possession from a fugitive, and a claim of undisturbed possession made from one country to another[48]. Rav Naḥman bar Rav Isaac[48*] said, a verse supports what Samuel said: "The king gave her an adjutant,[49]" etc.

46 That a person being in a different province of the same country cannot claim undisturbed possession only applies in wartime or similar circumstances when there is no regular communication between the regions. In the Babli, 38a, this opinion is explained as following Rav's opinion that the injured party may protest anywhere, not necessarily in the presence of the

person in actual possession.

47 This refers to Mishnah and Halakhah 2. For Samuel, a new orchard which may not be harvested can never be acquired by a claim of undisturbed possession; for Rav it may be acquired after three full years. It also is possible that the statement refers to the dispute between R. Aqiba and R. Ismael. Since R. Aqiba only requires minimal preparation for a harvest, he will recognize years in which the trees cannot be harvested as included in the time required for a claim of undisturbed possession. R. Ismael, who requires extensive preparations, will not recognize those years.

48 As the Babli points out, 38b, this statement by Rav contradicts the earlier one that the rule of the Mishnah only applies to emergency situations. Samuel's position is clear; he holds that a protest can be made before any court which will sign a dated statement which may be used before the court at the place of the disputed real estate without time limit. For the position of Rav, two explanations are given there.

One is that he holds that a protest must be made in person and that his statement about the Mishnah was to explain the thinking of the Tanna, not his own. Another is that he also holds that a protest can be submitted in any court but that such an appearance in a distant court can be expected only from a fugitive because of non-payment of taxes or other debt but not from a person accused of a capital crime. Also, the choice of the word "country" instead of "province" refers to a country outside the Roman Empire, such as Persia or India, from where any communication might be difficult or impossible.

48* The identity of this Amora is not clear. The fourth generation Amora Rav Naḥman bar Isaac never is quoted as Rav Naḥman bar *Rav* Isaac.

49 *2K*. 8:6. Since the Shunamite woman needed the king's intervention after an absence of 7 years in the Land of the Philistines it follows that she could get no relief in the regular courts since a claim of undisturbed possession could be made against a proprietor living in another country.

(14a line 17) אָמַר רִבִּי לֶעְזָר. וַאֲפִילוּ שְׁתֵּי אבטיניות כְּגוֹן שלומי ונבירו וְהַיַּרְדֵּן מַפְסִיק בֵּנְתַיִים וְעוֹמֵד שָׁם וְרוֹאֶה אֶחָד הַמַּחֲזִיק בַּשָּׂדֶה וּמַחֲזִיק בְּשֶׁלּוֹ אֵינָהּ

חֲזָקָה עַד שֶׁתְּהֵא עִמּוֹ בְּאוֹתָהּ הָעִיר וּבְאוֹתָהּ הַמְּדִינָה.

Rebbi Eleazar said: Even two אבטיניות, e. g., שלומי and נבירו[50] separated by the Jordan and a person may see another taking possession of the field, his property, there is no creation of a claim of undisturbed possession unless he was in the same locality, in the same province[44].

50  In Babylonian sources (*Bekhorot* Babli 55a, Tosephta 7:3) the spelling is אבטלאות or אבטליות; with a change of liquids, also אבטיניות. In E and *Megillah* 1:1 l. 44: אבטוניות. In *Sefer haIṭṭur* 1-2, p. 88b (מודעא) אפסיטואות. *Meïri Bava batra ad* 38a (ed. A. Schreiber p. 213) אכסניות "hostelries".

'*Arukh* explains "big cities"; no acceptable etymologies are known. (If the word be Greek, the Yerushalmi transliteration would be more reliable than the Babylonian. But Jastrow's αὐτονομία is doubtful, as is Zuckermandel's ἀποτέλειοι.)

The names of the towns appear as נבירו, נמירי, נמורי; נמר or שלומי, השולמי עבר הירדן היהודי(י-) S. Klein (גבירו, נמוכי). 1925 ם determines the places as Bet Nimra in Transjordan opposite Alexandria in Cisjordan.

(14a line 20) רַב אָמַר. עִיקַּר חֲזָקָה הַכְנָסַת פֵּירוֹת. לֹא מוֹדֶה רַב בִּמְנַכֵּשׁ וּבִמְעַדֵּר. מוֹדֶה רַב בִּמְנַכֵּשׁ וּבִמְעַדֵּר. מָהוּ דְּאָמַר רַב. עִיקַּר חֲזָקָה הַכְנָסַת פֵּירוֹת. אֶלָּא שֶׁאִם רָאוּ אוֹתוֹ חוֹרֵשׁ וְקוֹצֵר וּמְעַמֵּר וְדָשׁ וּבוֹרֵר וְלֹא רָאוּהוּ מַכְנִיס פֵּירוֹת אֵינָהּ חֲזָקָה אֶלָּא הַכְנָסַת פֵּירוֹת.

[51]Rav said, the main confirmation of a claim of possession is storing the produce. Does Rav not agree about weeding and turning the soil? Rav agrees about weeding and turning the soil. What does it mean that Rav said, the main indication of a claim of possession is storing the produce? That if they saw him ploughing, and harvesting, and binding into sheaves, and threshing, and grading, but did not see him storing the produce, there is no claim of possession without storing the produce[52].

51  This is a slightly more detailed exposition of a paragraph in *Yebamot* 12:1, Note 29.

52  Since all other work could be done by a hired hand. While taking the final produce without ever having worked the land might be an indication of theft, working the land without enjoying its yield disproves ownership.

(14a line 24) רַב אָמַר. עִיקַּר חֲלִיצָה הַתָּרַת רְצוּעוֹת. לֹא כֵן אָמַר רִבִּי בָּא בְשֵׁם רַב יְהוּדָה. רִבִּי זְרִיקָן מָטֵי בָהּ בְּשֵׁם רַב. דִּבְרֵי חֲכָמִים. חָלְצָה וְלֹא רֶקְקָה רֶקְקָה וְלֹא חָלְצָה. חֲלִיצָתָהּ פְּסוּלָה עַד שֶׁתַּחֲלוֹץ וְתָרוֹק. מוֹדֶה רַב עַד שֶׁתַּחֲלוֹץ וְתָרוֹק. מֵהָדָא דְּאָמַר רַב. עִיקַּר חֲלִיצָה הַתָּרַת רְצוּעוֹת.

[53]Rav said, the essence of *ḥaliṣah*[27] is the untying of the shoelace. Did not Rebbi Abba say in the name of Rav Jehudah, Rebbi Zeriqan turns to it in the name of Rav: The words of the Sages: If she slips off but did not spit, or spat but did not take off, the *ḥaliṣah* is invalid unless she slips off and spits[28]. Rav agrees "unless she slips off and spits"; it is implied by what Rav said, the essence of slipping off is untying the shoelaces.

53  This is a reformulation of a paragraph in *Yebamot* 12:1, Notes 27-28, about the act of freeing the childless widow from levirate marriage. It is quoted here as an appendix to the previous paragraph.

(14a line 28) רִבִּי יוֹסֵי בֶּן חֲנִינָה שָׁאַל לְרִבִּי יוֹחָנָן. עֲרָר מָהוּ שֶׁצָּרִיךְ בֵּית דִּין. רִבִּי יוֹסֵה בְשֵׁם רִבִּי יוֹחָנָן. עֲרָר אֵין צָרִיךְ בֵּית דִּין. וְאִית דָּמְרִין. רִבִּי יוֹסֵי בֶּן חֲנִינָה שָׁאַל לְתַלְמִידוֹי דְּרִבִּי יוֹחָנָן. עֲרָר מָהוּ שֶׁצָּרִיךְ בֵּית דִּין. רִבִּי חִייָה בְשֵׁם רִבִּי יוֹחָנָן. עֲרָר צָרִיךְ בֵּית דִּין. שְׁמוּאֵל אָמַר. אֲפִילוּ עֲרָר עִמּוֹ בִּפְנֵי פּוֹעֲלִין עֲרָר הוּא. וְצָרִיךְ לְעוֹרֵר עַל כָּל־שָׁלֹשׁ שָׁנִים. גִּידוּל בֶּן מִינְיָימִין הֲוָה לֵיהּ עוֹבְדָא וַהֲוֵי דַיְינֵיהּ חִלְקִיָּה בַּר טוֹבִי וְרַב הוּנָא וְחִייָה בַּר רַב. אָמַר לוֹן חִייָה בַּר רַב. כֵּן אָמַר אַבָּא. מִכֵּיוָן שֶׁעֲרַר עִמּוֹ שָׁלֹשׁ שָׁנִים הָרִאשׁוֹנוֹת עוֹד אֵין צָרִיךְ לְעוֹרֵר עָלָיו. וְתַנֵּי כֵּן. הָיָה אוֹכֵל שֶׁלּוֹ שֵׁשׁ שָׁנִים. עֲרָר שָׁלֹשׁ שָׁנִים הָרִאשׁוֹנוֹת.

אָמַר לוֹ. אַתָּה מְכַרְתָּהּ לִי אַתָּה נָתַתָּהּ לִי מַתָּנָה. אֵינָהּ חֲזָקָה. מַחֲמַת טַעֲנָה הָרִאשׁוֹנָה הֲרֵי זוֹ חֲזָקָה. שֶׁכָּל־חֲזָקָה שֶׁאֵין עִמָּהּ טַעֲנָה אֵינָהּ חֲזָקָה. שְׁמוּאֵל אָמַר. אִם כֵּן אֵין אָנוּ מְנִיחִין לִגְדוֹלֵי אֶרֶץ יִשְׂרָאֵל כְּלוּם.

Rebbi Yose ben Ḥanina asked Rebbi Joḥanan: Must a protest be filed before a court? Rebbi Yose in the name of Rebbi Joḥanan: a protest does not have to be filed before a court[54]. But some say, Rebbi Yose ben Ḥanina asked Rebbi Joḥanan's student: Must a protest be filed before a court? Rebbi Ḥiyya in the name of Rebbi Joḥanan: a protest must be filed before a court[55]. Samuel said, even if he protested against him in front of workers, it is a protest[54], but he has to protest in each one of the three years. Giddul ben Minyamin had a case; his judges were Ḥilqiah bar Tobi, Rav Huna, and Ḥiyya bar Rav. Ḥiyya bar Rav told them, so said my father: Once he protested the first three years, he is not required to protest further[56]. It was stated thus[57]: "If he[58] ate it as his own for six years, he[59] protested against him the first three years; then[60] he[58] said, you sold it to me, you gave it to me as a gift, there is no claim of undisturbed possession. Because of an initial claim[60a] it would have been a claim of undisturbed possession since[61] any claim of undisturbed possession not accompanied by a claim of legal ownership is not a claim of undisturbed possession[62]." Samuel said, if it is so, nothing would be left for the great people of the Land of Israel[63].

54 A protest against unlawful occupation of land is a matter of testimony, rather than court action. It needs only two witnesses and does not have to be in writing; this is the position of the Babli (39b/40a).

55 It needs three judges and a written confirmation by the clerk of court.

In the Babli, 39a, R. Ḥiyya bar Abba is quoted as holding that a protest is a matter of witnessing, needing two witnesses but no court, and R. Abbahu that it is a matter of court record, needing three judges, both in the name of R. Joḥanan.

56 The Babli, 39b, disagrees and in addition holds that the protest has to be renewed at the end of each three-year period.

57 Tosephta 2:4.

58 The occupant.

59 The former owner.

60 In the Tosephta: "at the end", implying that the occupant was silent during the first protest.

60a An assertion of ownership at the start would be an argument accepted by the court.

61 Mishnah 3:4.

62 In the Tosephta: Any claim not asserted from the start is invalid.

63 Cf. *Bava Meṣi'a* 5:1, Note 9.


**משנה ד:** כָּל־חֲזָקָה שֶׁאֵין עִמָּהּ טַעֲנָה אֵינָהּ חֲזָקָה. כֵּיצַד אָמַר לוֹ מָה (fol. 13c) אַתָּה עוֹשֶׂה בְתוֹךְ שֶׁלִּי. שֶׁלֹּא אָמַר לִי אָדָם דָּבָר מֵעוֹלָם אֵינָהּ חֲזָקָה. אַתָּה מְכַרְתָּהּ לִי אַתָּה נְתַתָּהּ לִי מַתָּנָה הֲרֵי זוֹ חֲזָקָה. וְהַבָּא מִשּׁוּם יְרוּשָׁה אֵינוֹ צָרִיךְ טַעֲנָה.

**Mishnah 4**: Any claim of undisturbed possession not accompanied by a claim of legal ownership is not a claim of undisturbed possession. How is this? He[59] said to him, what are you doing on my property? Nobody ever said anything to me[58] is not a claim of undisturbed possession. You sold it to me, you gave it to me as a gift, is a claim of undisturbed possession. A person entering because of inheritance does not need a claim[64].

64 The heir does not have to establish his ownership by investigating how the bequeather acquired title.

(14a line 40) **הלכה ד:** כָּל־חֲזָקָה שֶׁאֵין עִמָּהּ טַעֲנָה כול׳. וְצָרִיךְ חֲזָקָה. תַּמָּן תַּנִּינָן. מוֹדֶה רִבִּי יְהוֹשֻׁעַ בְּאוֹמֵר לַחֲבֵירוֹ. שָׂדֶה זוֹ כול׳. כְּהָדָא. רְאוּבֵן אוֹכֵל שָׂדֶה בְּחֶזְקַת שֶׁהִיא שֶׁלּוֹ וְהֵבִיא שִׁמְעוֹן עֵדִים שֶׁמֵּת אָבִיו מִתּוֹכָהּ. מַפְקִין לָהּ מֵרְאוּבֵן וִיהָבִין לְשִׁמְעוֹן. אֶלָּא הָלַךְ רְאוּבֵן וְהֵבִיא עֵדִים שֶׁלֹּא מֵת אָבִיו מִתּוֹכָהּ. אָמַר רַב נַחְמָן בַּר יַעֲקֹב. אֲנָא אַפִּיקְתֵּיהּ מֵרְאוּבֵן אֲנָא מַחֲזַרְנָהּ לֵיהּ. רַב אָמַר. כְּשֶׁנְּתַתָּהּ עַל פִּי בֵית דִּין נְתַתָּהּ. מִיכָּן וְהֵילָךְ הַמּוֹצִיא מֵחֲבֵירוֹ עָלָיו הָרְאָיָיה.

**Halakhah 4**: "Any claim of undisturbed possession not accompanied by a claim of legal ownership," etc. But it needs proof of undisturbed possession[65]. There[66], we have stated: "Rebbi Joshua agrees that if somebody says to another, 'this field', etc." [67]As the following. Reuben ate from a field claiming that it was his. Simeon brought witnesses that his father died in possession. One removes [the field] from Reuben and hands it over to Simeon. Reuben went and brought witnesses that [Simeon's] father did not die in possession. Rebbi Nahman ben Jacob said, I took it from Reuben, I am returning it to him. Rav[68] said, when you gave it to him, you gave it on the basis of a court decree. From there on the burden of proof is on the claimant.

---

65  In order to be safe from actions against his title, the owner has to hold on to his deed until he has established a three years' claim of undisturbed possession.

66  Mishnah *Ketubot* 2:2. If a person informs another that property which he holds did belong to his father, he must be believed without proof that he holds legal title since "the mouth which forbade is the mouth which permitted."

67  A shortened reformulation of a paragraph in *Ketubot* 2:2, Notes 37-43.

68  Since Rav died before Rav Nahman b. Jacob became Chief Judge, one must read with the text of *Ketubot*: "The rabbis here" who disagree with the Babylonian decision and hold that a revision of a prior court decision has to be treated as a new case and must follow standard court procedure.

(14a line 46) מִי מוֹדִיעַ. אָמַר רִבִּי בָּא. עֵידֵי מִיתָה מוֹדִיעִין. הַגַּע עַצְמָךְ שָׁאֵין הָעֵדִים יוֹדְעִין. אָמַר רִבִּי יוֹסֵי. לְעוֹלָם הַשָּׂדֶה בְחֶזְקַת בְּעָלֶיהָ. מִיכָּן וְהֵילָךְ הַמּוֹצִיא מֵחֲבֵירוֹ עָלָיו הָרְאָיָיה.

Who informs[69]? Rebbi Abba said, the witnesses to the death inform. Think of it, if the witnesses did not know! Rebbi Yose said, the field always is in the possession of its owner. From there on the burden of proof is on the claimant[70].

69    This also refers to the last statement of the Mishnah, that the heir is not required to establish title.

70    An heir is always held *prima facie* as owner and possessor. The burden of proof in an attack on his title rests on the attacker.

(fol. 13d) **משנה ה:** הַשּׁוּתָּפִין וְהָאֲרִיסִין וְהָאֶפִּיטְרוֹפִין אֵין לָהֶן חֲזָקָה. אֵין לָאִישׁ חֲזָקָה בְּנִכְסֵי אִשְׁתּוֹ וְלֹא לָאִשָּׁה בְּנִכְסֵי בַעְלָהּ וְלֹא לָאָב בְּנִכְסֵי הַבֵּן וְלֹא לַבֵּן בְּנִכְסֵי הָאָב. בַּמֶּה דְבָרִים אֲמוּרִים בַּמַּחֲזִיק. אֲבָל בְּנוֹתֵן מַתָּנָה וְהָאַחִים שֶׁחָלְקוּ וְהַמַּחֲזִיק בְּנִכְסֵי הַגֵּר נָעַל גָּדַר וּפָרַץ כָּל־שֶׁהוּא הֲרֵי זוֹ חֲזָקָה.

**Mishnah 5:** Partners[71] and sharecroppers[72] have no claim of undisturbed possession. A husband has no claim of undisturbed possession in his wife's property[73], nor a wife in her husband's property[74], nor a father in his son's property[75], nor the son in his father's property[76]. When has this been said? For one who claims undisturbed possession. But if one is given a gift, or brothers distributed the estate, one takes possession of a convert's property[77], when he locked, fenced in, or made any breach that is a legal form of taking in possession[78].

71 If a property was bought by partners and one partner used the property for himself during three years, this still does not establish a claim of ownership.

72 The sharecropper is supposed to work the land. Even if he takes in the entire crop and stores it in his barn it is no proof of ownership since possibly he pays the landlord from the proceeds of the sale of some of the crop.

73 Since it is his duty to take care of her property and he is entitled to its produce, his activities cannot establish a claim of ownership.

74 Since the husband is obligated to feed his wife, it would be legal for him to give her one of his fields to work on and live off its yield; but her taking care of the property and collecting all its yield cannot establish a claim of ownership.

75 If the son inherited property from his maternal grandfather, the father is obligated to take care of it without acquiring property rights.

76 If he takes care of his aging father's property.

77 Who died without leaving a will or legal heirs.

78 This חֲזָקָה has a completely different meaning from the one presupposed in the preceding Mishnaiot. It describes the act of taking possession after acquiring ownership, as described in *Qiddušin,* Halakhah 1:5. This can be any act only the proprietor would perform, not a visitor.

(14a line 49) **הלכה ה:** הַשּׁוּתָפִין וְהָאֲרִיסִין כוּל׳. שׁוּתָף. שְׁמוּאֵל אָמַר. לֵית כָּן שׁוּתָף. שׁוּתָף אֵין לוֹ חֲזָקָה. לֹא כֵן אָמַר שְׁמוּאֵל. שׁוּתָף שֶׁיָּרַד וְנָטַע כְּנוֹטֵעַ בִּרְשׁוּת. הֵן דְּתֵימַר. שׁוּתָף שֶׁיָּרַד וְנָטַע כְּנוֹטֵעַ בִּרְשׁוּת. בְּאוֹתוֹ שֶׁעוֹמֵד שָׁם. וְהֵן דְּתֵימַר. שׁוּתָף אֵין לוֹ חֲזָקָה. בְּשֶׁאֵינוֹ עוֹמֵד שָׁם. מָהוּ מַיְיתֵי תְּחוֹתֵיהּ. הָאוּמָּנִין וְהַגּוֹזְלִין אֵין לָהֶן חֲזָקָה. רָאָה עַבְדוֹ אֵל הָאוּמָּן וְכֵילָיו אֵל הַכּוֹבֵס. אָמַר לוֹ. תֵּן לִי עַבְדִּי תֵּן לִי כֵלַיי. אָמַר לוֹ. אַתָּה נְתַתּוֹ לִי בְּמַתָּנָה אַתָּה מְכַרְתּוֹ לִי. אֵינָהּ חֲזָקָה. אַתָּה אָמַרְתָּ לִי לְמוֹכְרוֹ אַתָּה אָמַרְתָּ לִתְנוֹ לִי מַתָּנָה. הֲרֵי זוֹ חֲזָקָה.

**Halakhah 5**: "Partners and sharecroppers," etc. "A partner." Samuel said, "partner" is not mentioned here[79]. Does the partner not have a claim to undisturbed possession⁸⁰? Did not Samuel say that the partner who went and planted, planted with permission⁸¹? When you say, the partner who went and planted, planted with permission, if he⁸² was there. When you say, the partner has no claim of undisturbed possession, if he⁸³ was not there. What does he include in his stead⁸⁴? Artisans⁸⁵ and robbers⁸⁶ have no claim of undisturbed possession. ⁸⁷"If somebody saw his slave at an artisan's, or his garments at the washer's, and told him, give me my slave, give me my garments, but he answered him, you gave him to me as a gift; you sold him to me; this is no claim of undisturbed possession⁸⁸. You told me to sell him⁸⁹; you instructed⁹⁰ to give him to me as a gift, this is a claim of undisturbed possession⁹¹."

79  A different treatment of the same statement is in the Babli, 42b. Samuel deletes mention of partners from the Mishnah.

80  This is the version of L. E: שׁוּתָף יֵשׁ לוֹ חֲזָקָה. The partner has a claim to undisturbed possession.

81  If a partner took possession, worked the property and reaped all its yield, one has to assume that there was an agreement between the partners to split the property. Therefore, if another partner disputes the existence of such an agreement after three years of undisturned possession, he is a claimant and the burden of proof is on him.

82  The other partner, who can make an appearance and take part of the yield.

83  If the other partner did not live at that place, the presumption is that the partners also bought property at the other place where the other partner takes all the yield, but no presumption is created of sole proprietorship at either place. Any partner who claims dissolution of the partnership has to bring proof.

84  Since the Mishnah states "*and* sharecroppers," it is clear that some word must precede the statement.

85  This is part of the Mishnah in the Babli and the independent Mishnah mss.

86  The extortionist who claims that

the former owner handed over the property to avoid being murdered may be truthful but the argument is not heard in court. Babli 47a.

87 Tosephta 2:6, Babli 45b.

88 The artisan, while in possession, is the claimant who has to bring proof since usually he is not the owner of what he is working on. As S. Lieberman explains, if the owner decided to sell a young slave it was customary to send him to be an apprentice in order to increase his value; also vessels and garments to be sold may be given to be refurbished to increase their value.

89 The teacher who trained the slave then should find a buyer; this was customary.

90 A third person who can testify to the fact.

91 The former owner is the claimant who has to bring proof.

(14a line 57) וְהָאֲרִיסִים. רַב הוּנָא אָמַר. בָּאֲרִיס לְעוֹלָם. אֲבָל בָּאֲרִיס לְשָׁעָה יֵשׁ לוֹ חֲזָקָה. רִבִּי יוֹחָנָן וְרִישׁ לָקִישׁ תְּרֵיהוֹן מָרִין. אֲפִילוּ בָּאֲרִיס לְשָׁעָה אֵין לוֹ חֲזָקָה. וְנֵימַר. נְחַת רוּחֵיהּ מִינֵּיהּ וְשָׁבְקֵיהּ. תַּמָּן אָמְרִין. אָרִיס אֵין לוֹ חֲזָקָה. בֶּן אָרִיס יֵשׁ לוֹ חֲזָקָה. רִבִּי יוֹחָנָן וְרִישׁ לָקִישׁ אָמְרִין. אַף אָרִיס וּבֶן אָרִיס אֵין לוֹ חֲזָקָה. דְּנֵימַר. נְחַת רוּחֵיהּ מֵאָבוֹי וּשְׁבַק בְּרֵיהּ. דָּמַר רִבִּי יוֹחָנָן. אָרִיס שֶׁהוֹרִיד אָרִיס אֵין לוֹ חֲזָקָה. שֶׁדֶּרֶךְ אָרִיס לְהוֹרִיד אָרִיס.

"Sharecroppers." Rav Huna said, a permanent sharecropper[92], but a temporary sharecropper[93] has a claim of undisturbed possession. Rebbi Johanan and Rebbi Simeon ben Laqish both teach that even a temporary sharecropper has no claim of undisturbed possession, for we may say that he[94] is satisfied with him and let him[95] have it. There, they say that a sharecropper has no claim of undisturbed possession but a sharecropper's son has a claim of undisturbed possession[96]; Rebbi Johanan and Rebbi Simeon ben Laqish say, neither a sharecropper nor a sharecropper's son have a claim of undisturbed possession, for we may say that he[94] was satisfied with his father and let the son have it. As Rebbi Johanan said, a sharecropper who engaged another sharecropper has no claim of undisturbed possession since it is common for sharecroppers to engage sub-sharecroppers[97].

92  He is no sharecropper in the modern sense but rather a tenant farmer in perpetuity, usually paying his rent in kind. It was stated earlier (Note 51) that the proof of ownership of agricultural land is the storing of its yield. In this paragraph, a "claim of undisturbed possession" would be testimony that for three consecutive years the farmer collected all the harvest and stored it in his own barn without separating the landlord's portion before storage.

93  Who has a contract renewable periodically. Since in this case it is unlikely that the landlord's share should not be delivered promptly, three years on non-delivery create a presumption of ownership; Babli 47a.

94  The landlord.

95  The sharecropper's son.

96  In the interpretation of Maimonides, *Ṭo'en weniṭ'an* 14:2, this refers only to the case that the son claims to have bought the property. But if he claims that the father bought it and he inherited, the burden of proof is on him and he cannot claim undisturbed possession since the father could not have claimed it.

97  The same statement is found in the Babli, 46a.

(14a line 62) אֲבָל אָדָם שֶׁמְּפַקֵּחַ עַל נִכְסֵי אִשְׁתּוֹ יֵשׁ לוֹ חֲזָקָה. שֶׁדֶּרֶךְ הַבְּעָלִים לְפַקֵּחַ עַל נִכְסֵי נְשׁוֹתֵיהֶן. אֵין לָאִישׁ חֲזָקָה בְּנִכְסֵי אִשְׁתּוֹ. בְּחַיֵּי אִשְׁתּוֹ. אֲבָל אַחַר מִיתָתָהּ יֵשׁ לוֹ חֲזָקָה. וְלֹא לָאִשָּׁה בְּנִכְסֵי בַעְלָהּ. בְּחַיָּיו. אֲבָל לְאַחַר מִיתָתוֹ יֵשׁ לָהּ חֲזָקָה. וְלֹא לַבֵּן בְּנִכְסֵי הָאָב. בְּחַיָּיו. אֲבָל אַחַר מִיתַת הָאָב יֵשׁ לוֹ חֲזָקָה. וְלֹא לָאָב בְּנִכְסֵי הַבֵּן. בְּחַיָּיו. אֲבָל אַחַר מִיתַת הַבֵּן יֵשׁ לוֹ חֲזָקָה.

In truth, should a man supervising his wife's properties have a claim of undisturbed possession, since usually husbands supervise their wife's properties? "A husband has no claim of undisturbed possession in his wife's property" during her lifetime. But after her death he has a claim of undisturbed possession[98]. "Nor a wife in her husband's property" during his lifetime. But after his death she has a claim of undisturbed possession[99]. "Nor a son in the father's property" during his lifetime. But after the father's death he has a claim of undisturbed possession[100]. "Nor the father in his son's property" during his lifetime. But after the son's death he has a claim of undisturbed possession[101].

98    Based on his right of inheritance.
99    If she claims the property as her *ketubah*.
100   As his part of the father's estate.
101   If the son died without children and the father is his heir.

(14a line 67) רַב אָמַר.  בְּפוֹחֵת מֵעֲשָׂרָה אוֹ מוֹסִיף עַל עֲשָׂרָה.  שְׁמוּאֵל אָמַר. אֲפִילוּ פָּרַץ מְקוֹם שֶׁאֵינוֹ רָאוּי לִפְרוֹץ וְגָדַר מְקוֹם שֶׁאֵינוֹ רָאוּי לִגְדּוֹר הֲרֵי זֶה חֲזָקָה.

Rav said, if he lowered it below ten [handbreadths] or increased above ten[102]. Samuel said, even if he made a breach at a place where a breach was irrelevant or a fence where a fence was irrelevant, it is legally taking possession.

102   This refers to the last sentence of the Mishnah. A person taking possession of land he bought in the opinion of Rav must take some legally important action. A fence is legally a separation only if it is at least ten handbreadths high. Samuel holds that the kind of action is irrelevant as long as it is of the kind only a proprietor would take. In the Babli, 53a, the attributions are switched.

(fol. 13d) **משנה ו**: שְׁנַיִם מְעִידִין אוֹתוֹ שֶׁאֲכָלָהּ שָׁלֹשׁ שָׁנִים וְנִמְצְאוּ זוֹמְמִין מְשַׁלְּמִין לוֹ אֶת הַכֹּל. שָׁנִים בָּרִאשׁוֹנָה וּשְׁנַיִם בַּשְּׁנִיָּיה וּשְׁנַיִם בַּשְּׁלִישִׁית מְשַׁלְּמִין בֵּינֵיהֶם. שְׁלֹשָׁה אַחִים וְאֶחָד מִצְטָרֵף עִמָּהֶן הֲרֵי אֵילוּ שָׁלֹשׁ עֵדִיּוֹת וְהֵן עֵדוּת אַחַת.

**Mishnah 6**: Two testify for him that he ate its yield for three years; if they are found perjured they pay everything to him[102*]. Two for the first [year], two for the second, two for the third, pay together[103]. Three brothers and another joins them; these are three testimonies[104] which count as one testimony[105].

102*  Since they intended to make the owner lose his property, they have to pay the current value of the property as a fine, *Deut.* 19:19.

103   Each witness has to pay $1/6$ of the fine.

104   Two relatives cannot testify together. If each brother testifies about a different year and the outsider testifies with each of them, there is valid testimony about three years of claim of undisturbed possession.

105   Since the owner of the land can lose his property only by the total of the testimonies, for the law of perjury the three testimonies are one and each person pays $1/6$ of the fine for his testimony, which means that the single outsider pays $3/6 = 1/2$ and each brother pays $1/6$.

(14a line 70) **הלכה ו**: שְׁנַיִם מְעִידִין אוֹתוֹ כול׳. אָמַר לוֹ. מָה אַתָּה עוֹשֶׂה בְתוֹךְ שֶׁלִּי. שֶׁיֵּשׁ לִי בָהּ שְׁנֵי חֲזָקָה. וְהָלַךְ וְהֵבִיא עֵדִים שֶׁיֵּשׁ לוֹ בָהּ שְׁנֵי חֲזָקָה. וְהָלַךְ זֶה וְהוּזְמוּ עֵדָיו. הֲרֵי זֶה נוֹתֵן לוֹ הַשָּׂדֶה וְאוֹכֵל פֵּירוֹת שֶׁלְּג שָׁנִים. וְהָתַנֵּי. הַמּוֹכֵר לַחֲבֵירוֹ וְנִתְעַצֵּל לוֹקֵחַ וְלֹא הֶחֱזִיק בָּהּ וְיָרַד הַמּוֹכֵר וְהֶחֱזִיק בָּהּ. בִּיטְלָה הַחֲזָקָה אֶת הַמֶּכֶר וְאֶת הַמַּתָּנָה. אָמַר רִבִּי זֵירָא. הָדָא אֲמָרָה. עֵד זוֹמֵם אֵין נִפְסַל בְּבֵית דִּין.

**Halakhah 6**: "Two testify for him," etc. One said to another "what are you doing in my field?" "For I have the years of undisturbed possession of it." He went and brought witnesses that he had the years of undisturbed possession of it. The first one went and proved the witnesses of the second perjured. He has to give him the field and the yield of three years[105].

[106]As we have stated: If somebody sells a field to another but the buyer was lazy and did not enter into possession when the seller went and legally took possession, the taking possession invalidates the sale or the gift.

[107]Rebbi Ze'ira said, this implies that the perjurer is not disqualified by the court.

---

105  The witnesses convicted of perjury have to pay the value of the field; the person who hired them has to return the field and pay the value of the yield which he took unlawfully since he admitted taking it.

106  This refers to the last sentence of Mishnah 5 und proves that actually taking possession is necessary in addition to acquiring ownership.

107  This is explained in *Bava qamma* 7:4, Note 46. The fact of perjury, rather than conviction by the court, disqualifies the perjurer; his testimony is nonexistent even if the fact is not realized by the court at the time. Therefore, if the testimony about the first year was perjured, the true testimony about years 2 and 3 becomes void; there is no testimony about three years of undisturbed possession, and nobody has to pay.

---

**משנה ז:** אֵילוּ דְבָרִים שֶׁיֵּשׁ לָהֶם חֲזָקָה וְאֵילוּ דְבָרִים שֶׁאֵין לָהֶם (fol. 13d) חֲזָקָה. הָיָה מַעֲמִיד בְּהֵמָה בֶּחָצֵר תַּנּוּר וְכִירַיִם וְרֵיחַיִם וּמִגְדָּל תַּרְנְגוֹלִין וְנוֹתֵן זִבְלוֹ בֶּחָצֵר אֵינָהּ חֲזָקָה. אֲבָל עָשָׂה לְבֶחֶמְתּוֹ מְחִיצָה גְּבוֹהָה י' טְפָחִים וְכֵן לַתַּנּוּר וְכֵן לַכִּירַיִים וְכֵן לָרֵחַיִם. הִכְנִיס תַּרְנְגוֹלִין לְתוֹךְ הַבַּיִת וְעָשָׂה מָקוֹם לְזִבְלוֹ עָמוֹק ג' אוֹ גָבוֹהַּ ג' הֲרֵי זוֹ חֲזָקָה.

**Mishnah 7**: The following count for a claim of undisturbed possession and the following do not count for a claim of undisturbed possession[108]. If one put his animals into a courtyard, an oven, a cooking stove, or a grindstone, or raises chickens, or puts his manure in a courtyard, it does not count for a claim of undisturbed possession[109]. But if he made for his animals an enclosure ten [handbreadths] high, or did it for an oven, a cooking stove, or a grindstone, brought chickens into the house, or made a place for his manure three [handbreadths] low or three high: this counts for a claim of undisturbed possession[110].

108 For non-agricultural properties where there is no direct equivalent of storing the harvest in one's silo.

109 Since each of the co-owners of the courtyard does this, nobody can be assumed to check whether the person doing this really be entitled to it.

110 Since people will complain if he does not have property rights to do what he is doing.

(14a line 75) **הלכה ז:** אֵילוּ דְבָרִים שֶׁיֵּשׁ לָהֶם חֲזָקָה כול׳. אָמַר רִבִּי לָעֲזָר. נָהֲגוּ הַשּׁוּתָּפִין לִהְיוֹת מַתִּירִין זֶה לָזֶה בַּתַּרְנוּגָלִין. אָמַר רִבִּי יוֹסֵה. מַתְנִיתָא לֹא אָמְרָה כֵן. אֶלָּא שְׁנֵיהֶן אֲסוּרִין לְהַעֲמִיד רֵיחַיִם וְתַנּוּר וּלְגַדֵּל תַּרְנוּגָלִין. אָמַר רִבִּי לָעֲזָר. גִּידֵּל תַּרְנְגָלִין בְּחָצֵר שֶׁאֵינָהּ שֶׁלּוֹ הֲרֵי זוֹ חֲזָקָה. אָמַר רִבִּי יוֹסֵי. וְיָאוּת. מַה נַפְשָׁךְ. אִם יֵשׁ לוֹ רְשׁוּת לְנַדֵּל הֲרֵי זֶה גִּידֵּל. אִם אֵין לוֹ רְשׁוּת לְגַדֵּל הֲרֵי זוֹ חֲזָקָה.

**Halakhah 7**: "The following count for a claim of undisturbed possession," etc. Rebbi Eleazar said, co-owners usually permit chickens to one another[111]. Rebbi Yose said, a Mishnah[112] says otherwise: "Both of them are forbidden to put up there a grindstone or an oven, or to raise chickens there."

Rebbi Eleazar said, if somebody raised chickens in a courtyard which is not his, it is taking in possession[113]. Rebbi Yose said, this is correct. As you take it, if he has permission to raise chickens there, he raises them. If he does not have permission to raise, it would be legally taking in possession.

111  One does not have to ask for the other's permission to raise chickens in the common courtyard.

112  *Nedarim* 5:1 (Note 4): Co-owners who mutually made vows not to have usufruct from one another are forbidden to raise chickens in the common courtyard.

113  If the owners of the courtyard do not hinder the raising of chickens from the start, later they become claimants and bear the burden of proof to remove the chickens.

(fol. 13d) **משנה ח:** הַמַּרְזֵב אֵין לוֹ חֲזָקָה וְיֵשׁ לִמְקוֹמוֹ חֲזָקָה. הַמַּזְחִילָה יֵשׁ לָהּ חֲזָקָה. סוּלָּם הַמִּצְרִי אֵין לוֹ חֲזָקָה וְלַצּוּרִי יֵשׁ לוֹ חֲזָקָה. חַלּוֹן הַמִּצְרִית אֵין לָהּ חֲזָקָה וְלַצּוּרִית יֵשׁ לָהּ חֲזָקָה. אֵי זוֹ הִיא חַלּוֹן הַמִּצְרִית כָּל־שֶׁאֵין רֹאשׁוֹ שֶׁל אָדָם יָכוֹל לִיכָּנֵס בְּתוֹכָהּ. רִבִּי יְהוּדָה אוֹמֵר אִם יֵשׁ לָהּ מַלְבֵּן אַף עַל פִּי שֶׁאֵין רֹאשׁוֹ שֶׁל אָדָם יָכוֹל לִיכָּנֵס לְתוֹכָהּ הֲרֵי זוֹ חֲזָקָה.

**Mishnah 8**: The drain pipe does not represent a right of possession; its location represents a right of possession[114]. The leader represents a right of possession[115]. An Egyptian ladder[116] does not represent a right of possession; a Tyrian one[117] represents a right of possession. An Egyptian window does not represent a right of possession; a Tyrian one represents a right of possession[118]. What is an Egyptian window? Any where a man's head cannot enter. Rebbi Jehudah says, if it has a wooden frame it represents a right of possession even if a man's head cannot enter.

114 חֲזָקָה here has a third meaning, viz., a right possessed by one property owner which restricts the property rights of another. In all cases mentioned in the Mishnah, it is presumed that the house was built in conformity with the rules and without protest by its neighbors.

The מַזְחֵילָה "leader, drain pipe" is the fixed tube which brings the rainwater from the roof to the ground; מַרְזֵב is a small movable pipe which takes the water coming out of the leader away from the house into the courtyard. (In modern Hebrew, מַזְחֵילָה is a sled, מַרְזֵב is the leader, drain pipe.) If the leader ends on another owner's property, this owner may move the direction of the *marzeb* but may not remove it.

115 If the leader was built on the outside of a house which is in the airspace of the adjacent courtyard, it may not be removed by this courtyard's owners.

116 A small movable ladder giving access to the upper floor apartment directly from the courtyard.

117 A wide wooden ladder permanently attached to the house.

118 The owner of the adjacent lot may build a wall in front of an Egyptian window and make it useless. But he may not build within 4 cubits of a Tyrian window (Mishnah 2:4). A Tyrian window is defined in Tosephta 2:14 as being wide enough for a man's head and having a wooden frame.

(14b line 5) **הלכה ח:** הַמַּרְזֵב אֵין לוֹ חֲזָקָה. רֵישׁ לָקִישׁ אָמַר. לְהַאֲרִיךְ וּלְהַרְחִיב בּוֹ. רִבִּי יוֹחָנָן אָמַר. לְכָל־אוֹתָהּ הָרוּחַ. וְהָתַנִּינָן. הַמַּזְחֵילָה יֶשׁ לָהּ רְשׁוּת ד' אַמּוֹת. אִית לָךְ מֵימַר. כָּל־אוֹתוֹ הָרוּחַ. וְדִכְוָותָהּ הַמַּרְזֵב אֵין לוֹ חֲזָקָה לְכָל־אוֹתָהּ הָרוּחַ. וְתַנֵּי כֵן. מְקוֹם הַמַּרְזֵב בֶּחָצֵר יֵשׁ לוֹ חֲזָקָה. מְקוֹם קִילּוּחוֹ בֶּחָצֵר אֵין לוֹ חֲזָקָה.

**Halakhah 8:** "The drain pipe does not represent a right of possession." Rebbi Simeon ben Laqish said, to lengthen and to widen it[119]. Rebbi Johanan said, in all of that direction[120], as we have stated: the leader has a domain of four cubits[121]. You have to say, in all this direction[122]. Similarly, the drain tube does not represent a right of possession in all of this direction. It was stated thus[123]: "The location of the drain tube does represent a right of possession, the location of its spout does not represent a right of possession."

119  The owner of the house does not have the right to lengthen or widen his drain pipe on another's property. In the Babli, 58b, R. Ḥanina holds that the owner of the other property has the right to shorten the drain pipe but not to remove it.

120  While the owner of the other property has the right to move the drain pipe, he cannot move its spout away from before the wall to which it belongs.

121  If a drain pipe legally is built to drain a roof, the owner of the house has the right to put up a ladder in front of the pipe to clean and repair it.

122  Anywhere in front of this roof.

123  Tosephta 2:13.

(14b line 10) דְּבֵי רִבִּי יַנַּאי אָמְרֵי. עַד שְׁלֹשָׁה עֲוֹקִין בְּכִסֵּא. אָמַר רבי לָא בְשֵׁם דְּבֵי רִבִּי יַנַּאי. לְעִנְיָין טוּמְאָה אִיתְאָמְרַת. רִבִּי חִזְקִיָּה בְשֵׁם דְּבֵי רִבִּי יַנַּאי. לְעִנְיָין חֲזָקוֹת אִיתְאָמְרַת. רִבִּי יוֹסֵי בְשֵׁם דְּבֵי רִבִּי יַנַּאי. לְעִנְיָין שַׁבָּת אִיתְאָמְרַת.

[124]In the House of Rebbi Yannai they said, up to three steps it is like a chair[125]. Rebbi La said in the name of the House of Rebbi Yannai, this was said referring to impurity[126]. Rebbi Ḥizqiah said in the name of the House of Rebbi Yannai, this was said referring to rights of possession[127]. Rebbi Yose in the name of the House of Rebbi Yannai, this was said referring to the Sabbath[128].

124  A similar text, with different attributions, is in *Šabbat* 3, 6c l. 56.

125  A ladder having no more than three steps goes after the rules of chairs.

126  A chair which is made to sit on can become impure by a person whose impurity is generated by bodily excretions (such as gonorrhea or menstrual flow) who sits on it even if

he never touches it (e. g., if it is completely covered by material not subject to impurity.) A ladder can become impure only by touch or by the impurity of a corpse in a "tent".

127  A short ladder, even if built wide like a Tyrian, never can represent rights of possession.

128  In *Erubin* 7:1 it is stated that two courtyards separated by a wall higher than 10 handbreadths are two separate domains for the rules of the Sabbath. If the wall is higher, it is possible to make the two courtyards into one domain by putting up ladders, even Egyptian ones, if only the remaining height is less than 10 handbreadths. But the ladder has to have at least 4 steps.

14b line 14) אָמַר רִבִּי הוֹשַׁעְיָה. לֹא אָמְרוּ אֶלָּא בְחָצֵר. אֲבָל בְּגַגּוֹת אֲפִילוּ לְמַעֲלָה מֵד' אַמּוֹת מְעַכְּבוֹ. [רִבִּי יִצְחָק אֲמָרָהּ קוֹמֵי רִבִּי חֲנִינָא. רִבִּי חֲנִינָא אֲמָרָהּ קוֹמֵי רִבִּי פִּינְחָס בַּר חָמָא. לֹא אָמְרוּ אֶלָּא בְחָצֵר אֲבָל בְּגַגּוֹת אֲפִילוּ לְמַעֲלָה מֵאַרְבַּע אַמּוֹת מְעַכְּבוֹ.] שָׁמַע רִבִּי הוֹשַׁעְיָה וַהֲוָה בִיש לֵיהּ. אָמַר. אֲנָא אֲמָרִית שְׁמוּעָתָא וְלָא אֲמְרִית מִשְּׁמִי. לֹא אָמְרוּ אֶלָּא בְחָצֵר אֲבָל בְּגַגּוֹת אֲפִילוּ לְמַעֲלָה מֵאַרְבַּע אַמּוֹת מְעַכְּבוֹ.

Rebbi Eleazar said, they said this[129] only for a courtyard. But for roofs[130] even higher than four cubits he may prevent him. [131][Rebbi Isaac said this before Rebbi Ḥanina, Rebbi Ḥanina said this before Rebbi Phineas bar Ḥama: They said this only for a courtyard, but for roofs[130] even higher than four cubits he may prevent him.] Rebbi Hoshaia heard this and was offended. He said, I formulated this teaching but you did not say it in my name: They said this only for a courtyard, but for roofs even higher than four cubits he may prevent him.

129  It is not too clear to what this refers. The least unlikely suggestion is due to *Pene Moshe*, where it is referred to the remark in *Yebamot* 12:3 (Notes 93,94) that one may open an Egyptian window looking out on somebody else's courtyard without asking permission on condition that the opening be higher than 4 cubits above the ground. In general, the rules of privacy do not

allow the owner of a house to open windows that give him the possibility to see his neighbors' activities which before he could not see. R. Hoshaia states that the rule from *Yebamot* holds for narrow windows opening on a courtyard which cannot be used to observe the courtyard if they are high enough. But if the new window is built in the wall of an upper storey level with the roof of a house bordering on the courtyard, the argument does not apply and the owner of that house can prohibit the opening of the window by claiming "damage by looking".

The damage feared may be from the evil eye; cf. Latin *invideo* "to look in; to cast an evil eye", from which *invidia, ae* "envy, grudge" (E. G.).

130   Reading בְּגִנּוֹת for ms. בגנות "in gardens", parallel to the reading in the last sentence (which, however, is due to the second hand in L.). Since the error is found both in L and in E, it must be copied from an old source.

131   Text from the second hand in E; it or a similar text are required by the last sentence in the paragraph.

**משנה ט:** זִיז עַד טֶפַח יֵשׁ לוֹ חֲזָקָה וְיָכוֹל לִמְחוֹת. פָּחוּת מִטֶּפַח אֵין לוֹ חֲזָקָה וְאֵינוֹ יָכוֹל לִמְחוֹת. (fol. 13d)

**Mishnah 9**: A protrusion[132] down to one handbreadth establishes a right of possession but he can object; less than a handbreadth does not establish a right of possession but he cannot object.

132   An extension of the roof protruding outside the wall of the house. If it is built over a neighbor's courtyard and extends from the roof at least by one handbreadth, the neighbor may forbid it but if it was built without objection it cannot be challenged later. If it extends less, the neighbor cannot object but does not have to take it for granted; he may build a new wall incorporating the molding.

(14b line 16) **הלכה ט:** זִיז עַד טֶפַח יֵשׁ לוֹ חֲזָקָה כול'. רִבִּי לָא בְּשֵׁם רִבִּי יַנַּאי. זִיז הַיּוֹצֵא [עַד] טֶפַח מוֹצִיאוֹ אֶתְ אֲפִילוּ כַּמָּה. לְמְשׁוֹךְ כַּמָּה. נָתַן ר' הוֹשַׁעְיָה. בְּחוֹלֵק אֶת בֵּיתוֹ.

**Halakhah 9:** "A protrusion down to one handbreadth establishes a right of possession," etc. Rebbi La in the name of Rebbi Yannai: If the molding is [up to] one handbreadth wide he may extend it all the way, to draw it all the way[133]. Nathan[134], Rebbi Hoshaia: About one who divides his house[135].

133  The inserted word is from E. It seems to mean that if a house was built with a protruding mold along part of the wall with the neighbor's acquiescence, the protrusion can be extended along the entire length of the wall without requiring a new permit.

134  Correct in E: R. Nathan in the name of R. Hoshaiah.

135  It seems that this sentence belongs to the next Halakhah, where it is explained that a person may transform a one-family house into a multi-family one as long as he constructs an interior staircase and does not increase the number of doors leading from the house into the courtyard.

(fol. 13d) **משנה י:** לֹא יִפְתַּח אָדָם חֲלוֹנוֹתָיו לַחֲצַר הַשּׁוּתָּפִין. לָקַח בַּיִת בְּחָצֵר אַחֶרֶת לֹא יִפְתְּחֶנָה לַחֲצַר הַשּׁוּתָּפִין. בָּנָה עֲלִייָה עַל גַּבֵּי בֵּיתוֹ לֹא יִפְתְּחֶנָּה לַחֲצַר הַשּׁוּתָּפִין אֶלָּא אִם רָצָה בּוֹנֶה אֶת הַחֶדֶר לִפְנִים מִבֵּיתוֹ וּבוֹנֶה עֲלִייָה עַל גַּבֵּי בֵיתוֹ וּפוֹתְחָהּ לְתוֹךְ בֵּיתוֹ.

**Mishnah 10:** A person may not open windows into the common courtyard[136]. If he bought a house in another courtyard he may not open it into the common courtyard[137]. If he built a second floor on top of his house he may not open it into the common courtyard but he may build a room inside his house or a second floor on top of his house on condition that the access to it be from within his house[135].

**משנה יא**: לֹא יִפְתַּח אָדָם לַחֲצַר הַשּׁוּתָּפִין פֶּתַח כְּנֶגֶד פֶּתַח חַלּוֹן כְּנֶגֶד חַלּוֹן. הָיָה קָטָן לֹא יַעֲשֶׂנּוּ גָּדוֹל אֶחָד לֹא יַעֲשֶׂנּוּ שְׁנַיִם אֲבָל פּוֹתֵחַ הוּא לִרְשׁוּת הָרַבִּים פֶּתַח כְּנֶגֶד פֶּתַח וְחַלּוֹן כְּנֶגֶד חַלּוֹן קָטָן עוֹשֶׂה אוֹתוֹ גָּדוֹל אֶחָד עוֹשֶׂה אוֹתוֹ שְׁנַיִם.

**Mishnah 11**: In a common courtyard a person may not open a door opposite a door, a window opposite a window. If it was small, he may not enlarge it. If it was one, he may not make it double[138]. But he may open into the public domain a door opposite a door and a window opposite a window. If it was small, he may enlarge it. If it was one, he may make it double[139].

136 Once the house is built, nobody may make any changes to his house which infringes on the privacy rights of the co-owners without the explicit agreement of all co-owners. In particular one may not add windows which would enable him to see activities of his neighbors which he could not see without them.

137 If he bought a house whose back wall borders on the condominium courtyard where his other house stands, he may not open a door directly from the common courtyard into that house since the door would acquire rights to the four adjacent cubits to the detriment of the other owners and increase traffic in the courtyard. If he wants to build such a door, he must buy the building rights from his co-owners.

138 All these activities allow him to see more of his neighbors' activities.

139 Since building a door or a window open towards the public domain implies a waiver of privacy rights.

(14b line 19) **הלכה י**: לֹא יִפְתַּח אָדָם חֲלוֹנוֹתָיו כול׳. הָכָא אַתְּ מַר. פֶּתַח כְּנֶגֶד פֶּתַח מוּתָּר. וְהָכָא אַתְּ מַר. פֶּתַח כְּנֶגֶד פֶּתַח אָסוּר. הֵן דְּתֵימַר. מוּתָּר. בְּמָבוֹי. וְהֵן דְּתֵימַר. אָסוּר. בַּחֲצַר הַשּׁוּתָּפִין. וְהָתַנֵּי. כְּשֵׁם שֶׁבְּנֵי חָצֵר יְכוֹלִין לִמְחוֹת זֶה עַל יְדֵי זֶה בֶּחָצֵר כֵּן בְּנֵי מָבוֹי יְכוֹלִין לִמְחוֹת זֶה עַל יְדֵי זֶה בְּמָבוֹי. אָמַר רִבִּי

לֹא. כָּאן בְּשֶׁנָּתַן רְשׁוּת כָּאן בְּשֶׁלֹּא נָתַן רְשׁוּת. אָמַר רִבִּי יוֹחָנָן. שַׁנְיָיא הִיא בַּגַּנּוֹת שֶׁנִּיתְנוּ לַחֲפִירָה. אָמַר רִבִּי נָסָא. וְחָרָבוֹת לֹא נִיתְּנוּ לְהִיבָּנוֹת.

**Halakhah 10**: "A person may not open windows," etc. [140]Here you say, a door opposite a door is permitted, and there you say, a door opposite a door is forbidden[141]. Where you say it is permitted, in an alley[142]. And where you say it is forbidden, in a condominium courtyard. But did we not state[143]: "Just as the inhabitants of a courtyard may object to one another, so the inhabitants of an alley may object to one another"? Rebbi La said, here when permission was given, there when permission was not given[144]. Rebbi Joḥanan said, there is a difference because gardens are usually dug into[145]. Rebbi Nasa said, are ruins not to be rebuilt[146]?

140 The following explanation is based on Rashba, *Responsa* vol. 5, #106.

141 The Mishnah forbids making doors opposite doors in a courtyard but allows them on a public street. It does not say anything about an alley, a narrow dead-end street frequented only by the inhabitants of the courtyards opening into the alley and their visitors, and usually bordered by windowless walls. The status of the alley is not defined in the Mishnah. If opposite doors only be forbidden in a courtyard, they would be allowed in an alley; if they only be allowed in a thoroughfare they would be forbidden in an alley.

142 The alley is part of the public domain.

143 Tosephta 2:15.

144 In principle, R. La accepts the explanation given earlier but he holds that for opening a door directly into the alley one needs the agreement of the other inhabitants of the alley. This agreement, once given, is irrevocable. But in a courtyard any co-owner may retract his assent at any time since according to the Mishnah the door should not have been built in the first place.

145 This is the text of L. It does not refer to the question raised in the text but to a later statement in the same

Tosephta, that if a brook passes through somebody's vegetable garden, he may divert its water at will for his irrigation needs. This seems to contradict the entire tenor of the present Chapter which denies the individual the right to infringe upon pre-existing rights of others. R. Joḥanan holds that if the brook was treated as private property, in that the farmer's lot was taxed as one vegetable garden rather than two properties separated by a river, the owner must be permitted to use his property without restriction.

E reads here: שְׁנִיָּיא הִיא בַּגַגוֹת שֶׁנִּיתְּנוּ לְהַפְרִיחַ "there is a difference because *roofs* are usually *made to protrude.*" That would refer to Halakhah 9 (Note 133) but probably is a corruption.

146   Sometimes the door built later forces a door built earlier to be walled up. If an earlier house collapsed, its right to have a door into the courtyard has not disappeared; no door can be built opposite the future door of a rebuilt house.

(14b line 25) אָמַר רִבִּי יַעֲקֹב בַּר אָחָא. תַּנֵּי תַמָּן. הַפּוֹתֵחַ חַלּוֹן בְּכוֹתֶל חֲצֵירוֹ בְּמַעֲמַד חֲבֵירוֹ. (ד׳ אַמּוֹת) [רִבִּי אוֹמֵר]. פּוֹחֵת בִּשְׂמֹאל נוֹעֵל בְּיָמִין. הַגַּע עַצְמָךְ שֶׁהָיָה עוֹמֵד שָׁם. יָכִיל מֵימַר לֵיהּ. הֲוִינָא בְעִית לְעִי. הָיָה מוֹשִׁיט לוֹ צְרוֹרוֹת. יָכִיל מֵימַר לֵיהּ. מִנְחֵךְ הֲוִינָא בָּאוּ גַבְרָא.

Rebbi Jacob bar Aḥa said that there[147], one states: If somebody opens a window in the wall of somebody else's courtyard in the presence of the other (four cubits)[148], [Rebbi says][149] he takes down[149*] with his left hand and closes with his right[150]. Think of it, was he not standing there? He may tell him, I wanted to enjoy myself. If he handed him stones[151]? He may tell him, I was making fun of this[152] man.

147   In Babylonia.
148   Reading of L, a corruption.
149   Reading of E, accepted as correct.
149*   Perhaps one should read פוחת "he opens" instead of פוחח "he takes down".
150   He has to wall it up again faster than he opened it. The wall's owner

retains an unconditional right to demand the walling up of the window.

151  Helping with building material.

152  Reading בָּאוּ (vocalization of the ms.) as בְּהַהוּא (S. Lieberman, *Tarbiz* 5, 1934, pp. 100-101.)

(14b line 29) הָיוּ חֲמִשָּׁה פְּתָחִים זֶה לִפְנִים מִזֶּה שִׁיעוּר כּוּלָּן כִּמְלוֹא מַקְדֵּחַ. וְדָא מְסַיְּיעָא לְמָאן דְּמָרִין בַּנָּאֵי. חַלּוֹן שֶׁהִיא פְתוּחָה לְאִיסְטִיב לֹא נַעֲשֵׂית אֶלָּא לְהַכְנִיס אֶת הָאוֹרָה. מִכֵּיוָן שֶׁאֵין לָהּ חֲזָקָה אֵינָהּ מְבִיאָה אֶת הַטּוּמְאָה.

If there were five openings one inside another, the measure of all of them is a drill hole. This supports what the builders say, *viz.*, that a window open above a stone bench[153] is made only to let light in. Since it cannot represent a right of possession, it cannot bring impurity[154].

153  Which is inconvenient to reach.

154  This is rather elliptic; it refers to the rules of impurity of the dead, the most important rule of which is that any person or vessels under one "tent" with a corpse becomes impure. If the corpse is in a stoa of which a wall belongs to a house, any window in that wall brings the impurity into the entire house. Mishnah *Ahilut* 13:1 states that if the window was made for light only, the minimal size which makes it a conduit of impurity is the size of the drill-hole of a builder's drill, which in *Kelim* 17:12 is said to be equal to the size of a Neronian tetradrachma or a circular disk of about 25mm diameter. A window made for use to bring vessels to or from the building must be at least one handbreadth square; for people it must let a person crawl through. Since five successive windows of minimal size do not let light in, they are not made for light and do not transmit impurity. Then it is stated that a window which does not transmit impurity is an Egyptian window which cannot represent a right of possession (J. Benvenisti in *Śede Yehoshua.*)

(fol. 13d) **משנה יב:** אֵין עוֹשִׂין חָלָל תַּחַת רְשׁוּת הָרַבִּים בּוֹרוֹת שִׁיחִין וּמְעָרוֹת. רַבִּי אֱלִיעֶזֶר מַתִּיר כְּדֵי שֶׁתְּהֵא עֲגָלָה מְהַלֶּכֶת וּטְעוּנָה אֲבָנִים. אֵין מוֹצִיאִין זִיזִין וּכְצוֹצְטְרָאוֹת לִרְשׁוּת הָרַבִּים אֶלָּא אִם רָצָה כּוֹנֵס לְתוֹךְ שֶׁלּוֹ וּמוֹצִיא. לָקַח חָצֵר וּבָהּ זִיזִין וּכְצוֹצְטְרָאוֹת הֲרֵי זוֹ בְחֶזְקָתָהּ.

**Mishnah 12**: One makes no hollow under the public domain, cisterns, ditches, and caves. Rebbi Eliezer permits if a cart filled with stones can pass over it[155]. One does not build protrusions and balconies[156] above the public domain but if he wishes he builds inside his own property and adds them[157]. If somebody bought a courtyard and there are protrusions and balconies, that remains a right of possession[158].

155 Even for private use. A person who owns two parcels separated by a road may connect them by a tunnel on condition that he build a bridge strong enough to carry all expected traffic (*Bikkurim* 1:1, Note 20).

156 Greek ἐξώστρα, Latin *exostra* "gallery, lobby, balcony". The Babylonian spelling is גזוזטרא. Mishnah Ahilut 14:1 defines a זיז as

protrusion without a railing, גיזרא as one with a railing.

157 If the balconies do not extend over his property line, he may build on his property anything he wishes.

158 The buyer may assume that originally the property extended into what is now public domain and the balconies were built legally; he does not have to investigate their legality.

(14b line 33) **הלכה יב:** אֵין עוֹשִׂין חָלָל כול׳. נָפְלוּ וּמְבַקֵּשׁ לִבְנוֹתָן. רִבִּי יוֹחָנָן אֲמַר. וִיתֵּר. רֵישׁ לָקִישׁ אָמַר. לֹא וִיתֵּר. מַתְנִיתָא מְסַייְעָה לְדֵין וּמַתְנִיתָא מְסַייְעָה לְדֵין. מַתְנִיתָא מְסַייְעָה לְרִבִּי יוֹחָנָן. מִי שֶׁהָיְתָה דֶרֶךְ הָרַבִּים עוֹבֶרֶת בְּתוֹךְ שָׂדֵהוּ וּנְטָלָהּ וְנָתַן לָהֶן מִן הַצַּד. מַה שֶּׁנָּתַן נָתַן וְשֶׁלּוֹ לֹא הִגִּיעוֹ. מַתְנִיתָא מְסַייְעָה לְרֵישׁ לָקִישׁ. לָקַח חָצֵר וּבָהּ זִיזִין וּכְצוֹצְטְרָאוֹת וְנָפְלוּ בּוֹנֶה אוֹתָן בְּחֶזְקָתָן.

**Halakhah 12**: "One makes no hollow," etc. If they collapsed and he wants to rebuild[159]. Rebbi Johanan said, he gave up his rights[160]. Rebbi Simeon ben Laqish said, he did not give up his rights. A Mishnah supports one, a *baraita* supports the other. A Mishnah supports Rebbi Johanan[161]: "If a public road went through somebody's field and he took it and gave them on the side[162]. What he gave, he gave, but his own did not come to him." A *baraita* supports Rebbi Simeon ben Laqish[163]: "If somebody bought a courtyard and there are protrusions and balconies, if they collapsed he rebuilds them based on his right of possession."

159 This refers to the second part of the Mishnah. A person built a balcony above the public domain, i. e., he built inside his property and gave over the ground under the balcony to public use.

160 Since the strip which he surrendered is now in public use, if the balcony collapses the wall now borders the public domain; the Mishnah prohibits him from rebuilding. The Babli 60b agrees with the characterization of the opinions of R. Johanan and R. Simeon ben Laqish.

161 Mishnah 6:7.

162 He ploughed the road under and made a new road on the side of his field. The public has not lost its right of way through his field.

163 Tosephta 2:17.

## המוכר את הבית פרק רביעי

(fol. 14b) **משנה א**: הַמּוֹכֵר אֶת הַבַּיִת לֹא מָכַר אֶת הַיָּצִיעַ וְאַף עַל פִּי שֶׁהִיא פְתוּחָה לְתוֹכוֹ וְלֹא אֶת הַחֶדֶר שֶׁלְּפָנִים מִמֶּנּוּ וְלֹא אֶת הַגָּג בִּזְמַן שֶׁיֵּשׁ לוֹ מַעֲקֶה גָּבוֹהַּ עֲשָׂרָה טְפָחִים. רִבִּי יְהוּדָה אוֹמֵר אִם יֵשׁ לוֹ צוּרַת פֶּתַח אַף עַל פִּי שֶׁאֵינוֹ גָּבוֹהַּ עֲשָׂרָה טְפָחִים אֵינוֹ מָכוּר.

**Mishnah 1**: One who sells a house[1] did not sell the shed[2] even if it opened into it, nor the room which is in its interior[3], nor the roof if it has a railing ten handbreadths high[4]. Rebbi Jehudah says, if its entry point is shaped like a door it is not sold even if its railing is not ten handbreadths high.

1 "House" here means "apartment, ground floor apartment", cf. *Bava meṣia'* 10:1, Note 1, *Nedarim* 7:4, Note 47. This and the next three Chapters spell out the standard conditions of a contract. Any intended deviation from these has to be written into the sales contract.

2 A building ancillary to the main building (*1K.* 6:5,6,10). According to Maimonides it is a paved space surrounding the building.

3 A storage room in the central court.

4 Then it is accessible to be used (*Deut.* 22:8). It may be accessed from outside the house by a ladder.

(14c line 20) **הלכה א**: הַמּוֹכֵר אֶת הַבַּיִת כול'. רִבִּי נָחוּם בְּשֵׁם רִבִּי חִייָה בַּר בָּא. וְהוּא שֶׁיְּהֵא בָהּ אַרְבַּע עַל אַרְבַּע עַל רוּם עֲשָׂרָה. וּבִלְבַד בִּמְקוּרָה וּבִמְגוּפָף. אָמַר לוֹן רִבִּי זֵירָא. כָּל־הָדֵין פֵּירוּשָׁא הַפְרֵשׁ לְכוֹן רִבִּי חִייָה בַּר בָּא.

**Halakhah 1:** "One who sells a house," etc. Rebbi Nahum in the name of Rebbi Hiyya bar Abba: Only if it[5] is four by four [cubits] and ten [handbreadths] high, and only if it is roofed and waterproofed[6]. Rebbi Ze'ira told them, did Rebbi Hiyya bar Abba explain all this to you[7]?

5  A shed not covering at least 16 square cubits is not considered an independent building; it would be included in a contract to sell the adjacent apartment.

In measurements, feminine numbers refer to cubits, masculine to handbreadths.

6  So it can be used year-round.

7  In the Babli, 61a, Mar Zutra only stipulates the first of R. Hiyya bar Abba's four conditions.

(14c line 23) וְלֹא אֶת הַגַּג בִּזְמַן שֶׁיֵּשׁ לוֹ מַעֲקֶה גָּבוֹהַּ עֲשָׂרָה טְפָחִים. סוֹף דָּבָר מַעֲקֶה. הָיוּ אֲחוֹרֵי בָתִּים מַקִּיפִין אוֹתוֹ הָיוּ שָׁם עַמּוּדִים וְכָלוֹנְסִיּוֹת עַל גַּבֵּיהֶן. נִישְׁמְעִינָהּ מֵהָדָא. רִבִּי יְהוּדָה אוֹמֵר אִם יֵשׁ לוֹ צוּרַת פֶּתַח אַף עַל פִּי שֶׁאֵינוֹ גָּבוֹהַּ עֲשָׂרָה טְפָחִים אֵינוֹ מָכוּר. אָמְרִין. וְהוּא שֶׁיֵּשׁ שָׁם מַעֲקֶה גָּבוֹהַּ עֲשָׂרָה טְפָחִים.

"Nor the roof if it has a railing ten handbreadths high." Is a railing the last word? If it was surrounded by back walls of houses, if there were pillars and wooden superstructures[8] on top of them[9]? Let us hear from the following: "Rebbi Jehudah says, if its entry point is shaped like a door it is not sold even if its railing is not ten handbreadths high." They said, only if it has a railing ten handbreadths high[10].

8  Possibly Latin *columnas*, acc. pl. of *columna*, "projecting object, column, pillar, post" (Krauss).

9  If the railing is unnecessary because it is already provided automatically by the surrounding buildings.

10  Since the anonymous majority rejects R. Jehudah's rule it follows that for them a usable roof is sold with the house below if and only if it is accessible from the house by a door.

## HALAKHAH 2

**משנה ב**: וְלֹא אֶת הַבּוֹר וְלֹא אֶת הַדּוּת אַף עַל פִּי שֶׁכָּתַב לוֹ עוּמְקָהּ וְרוּמָהּ וְצָרִיךְ לִיקַּח לוֹ דֶּרֶךְ דִּבְרֵי רִבִּי עֲקִיבָה וַחֲכָמִים אוֹמְרִים אֵינוֹ צָרִיךְ לִיקַּח לוֹ דֶּרֶךְ. וּמוֹדֶה רִבִּי עֲקִיבָה בִּזְמַן שֶׁאָמַר לוֹ חוּץ מֵאִילּוּ שֶׁאֵינוֹ צָרִיךְ לִיקַּח לוֹ דֶּרֶךְ. מְכָרָן לְאַחֵר רִבִּי עֲקִיבָה אוֹמֵר אֵינוֹ צָרִיךְ לִיקַּח לוֹ דֶּרֶךְ וַחֲכָמִים אוֹמְרִים צָרִיךְ לִיקַּח לוֹ דֶּרֶךְ. (fol. 14b)

**Mishnah 2**: Neither the cistern nor the cellar[11] even though he wrote over to him "its bottom and height," and he has to buy himself access[12], the words of Rebbi Aqiba, but the Sages say that he does not have to buy himself access[13]. Rebbi Aqiba agrees that if he said "except these"[14], he does not have to buy himself access. If he sold them[15] to another person, Rebbi Aqiba said, he does not have to buy access[16], but the Sages say, he has to buy access[17].

11  This is a continuation of Mishnah 1. A sale contract for a house which does not mention either the cistern or the cellar, a masonry cavity used for storing wine or grain, does not include these items.

12  If the seller wants to use cistern or cellar, he has to buy access from the buyer, the new owner of the surrounding area.

13  They hold that nobody wants to make a contract which will hurt himself.

14  If cistern and/or cellar are mentioned as excluded in the sales contract.

15  A person sold cistern or cellar to a third party while retaining ownership of his house and courtyard. This part of the Mishnah is quoted in *Ketubot* 13:7, Notes 112-115.

16  In this situation, he adopts the reasoning of the Sages in the preceding case.

17  They hold that (particularly in an inflationary environment) a person may buy real estate purely as an investment without intention of using it personally. Therefore, nothing is sold which is not spelled out in the contract.

(14c line 28) **הלכה ב:** וְלֹא אֶת הַבּוֹר כּוּל'. לְאֵי זֶה דָבָר כָּתַב עוּמְקָא וְרוּמָא. שֶׁאִם רָצָה לְהַשְׁפִּיל יַשְׁפִּיל לְהַגְבִּיהַּ יַגְבִּיהַּ. רַבָּה בַּר רַב הוּנָא בְּשֵׁם רַב. הֲלָכָה כְּרִבִּי עֲקִיבָה דִּידָן דְּהוּא רַבָּנָן דְּרִבִּי חִייָה. רִבִּי זְעִירָא רַב יִרְמִיָה בְּשֵׁם רַב. הֲלָכָה כְּרִבִּי עֲקִיבָה דְּרִבִּי חִייָה דְּהוּא רַבָּנָן דְּבַבְלָאֵי.

**Halakhah 2:** "Neither the cistern," etc. Then why did he write "its bottom and height"? That if he wants to dig down, he may dig down and if he wants to increase its height, he may increase its height[18]. Rav Abba bar Rav Huna in the name of Rav: Practice follows Rebbi Aqiba in our version which is following the rabbis in Rebbi Ḥiyya's version. Rebbi Ze'ira, Rav Jeremiah in the name of Rav: Practice follows Rebbi Aqiba in Rebbi Ḥiyya's version which is following the rabbis in the Babylonians' version[19].

18   Tosephta 3:1, Babli 63b. It is necessary to convey the rights to the ground and the airspace separately. Compare Greek contracts which mention κάτω, ἄνω "downwards, upwards" cf. A. Gulak, *Das Urkundenwesen im Talmud im Lichte der griechisch-aegyptischen Papyri und des griechischen und römischen Rechts*, Jerusalem 1935 (Hebrew edition 1994 by Ranon Katzoff).

19   The same statements by Rav Huna and Rav Jeremiah are in the Babli, 64b/65a, which notes that there are opposite traditions about the possible requirement of providing separate contracts for access. The problem of access is not mentioned in the Tosephta, so it is not clear which version our Mishnah represents.

E formulates: "R. Ze'ura in the name of Rav: Rebbi Aqiba and Rebbi Ḥiyya parallel the Babylonian rabbis."

(14c line 32) תַּמָּן אָמְרִין. אַדְמוֹן וְרִבִּי עֲקִיבָה. אָמַר רִבִּי לָא. בִּסְתָמָם חֲלוּקִין. מָה נָן קַייָמִין. אִם דָּבָר בָּרִיא שֶׁיֵּשׁ לוֹ דֶּרֶךְ כָּל־עַמָּא מוֹדוּ שֶׁאֵין צָרִיךְ לִיקַּח לוֹ דֶּרֶךְ. אִם דָּבָר בָּרִיא שֶׁאֵין לוֹ דֶּרֶךְ כָּל־עַמָּא מוֹדוּ שֶׁהוּא צָרִיךְ לִיקַּח לוֹ דֶּרֶךְ.

אֶלָּא נָן קַייָמִין בִּסְתָם. רִבִּי עֲקִיבָה אוֹמֵר. אֵינוֹ צָרִיךְ לִיקַּח דֶּרֶךְ. וַחֲכָמִים אוֹמְרִין. צָרִיךְ לִיקַּח לוֹ דֶּרֶךְ.

[20]There, they said: Admon and Rebbi Aqiba. Rebbi La said, they disagree when nothing was specified. Where do we hold? If it is obvious that access was included, everybody agrees that he does not have to pay for access. If it is obvious that access was not included, everybody agrees that he has to pay for access. But we must hold that nothing was specified. Then Rebbi Aqiba said, he does not have to buy access, but the rabbis say, he does have to buy access.

20 This is a shortened version of a paragraph in *Ketubot* 13:7, Notes 111-116. The Mishnah there refers to the case when the access path to a field disappeared in the surrounding property of a single owner while this field's owner was on a prolonged absence overseas; Admon holds that the owner may choose for himself a short path through the other's domain while the Sages hold that he has to buy access or fly through the air.

**משנה ג:** הַמּוֹכֵר אֶת הַבַּיִת מָכַר אֶת הַדֶּלֶת אֲבָל לֹא אֶת הַמַּפְתֵּחַ. (fol. 14b) מָכַר אֶת הַמַּכְתֶּשֶׁת הַקְּבוּעָה אֲבָל לֹא הַמִּיטַּלְטֶלֶת. מָכַר אֶת הָאִיצְטְרוֹבִּיל אֲבָל לֹא אֶת הַקֶּלֶת. מָכַר הַתַּנּוּר מָכַר הַכִּירַיִם. בִּזְמַן שֶׁאָמַר לוֹ הוּא וְכָל־מַה שֶׁבְּתוֹכוֹ הֲרֵי כוּלָּן מְכוּרִין.

**Mishnah 3**: He who sold a house sold the door[21] but not the key. He sold a built-in mortar but not a movable one. He sold the pine cone but not the enclosure[22]. He sold the oven and the cooking stove[23]. But if he said to him, "it and all it contains," all is sold.

21 The door, while movable, is permanently connected to the building. But the key is removable. Anything built-in is sold, anything movable is not sold.

22 These two terms, referring to the grain mill, are explained in Chapter 2, Notes 17,18.

23 This is the reading of the Yerushalmi, Maimonides's autograph, and the Mishnah mss. in the Maimonides tradition. In the Babli and the Mishnah mss. of the Babylonian tradition: "Neither the oven nor the cooking stove." As explained in Halakhah 2:1, a (movable) oven or stove may be used inside a house only if it sits on a masonry basis. Therefore it is clear that the bases for oven or stove are sold; oven and stove themselves are not sold. Both versions lead to the same result.

(14c line 37) **הלכה ג:** הַמּוֹכֵר אֶת הַבַּיִת כול'. כֵּינֵי מַתְנִיתָא. מָכַר אֶת הַמַּכְתֶּשֶׁת הַחֲקוּקָה אֲבָל לֹא אֶת הַקְּבוּעָה.

**Halakhah 3**: "He who sold a house," etc. So is the Mishnah: He sold the hewn mortar but not the affixed one[24].

24 The same text is in the Babli, 65b. There, the commentary ascribed to R. Gershom gives the correct interpretation. A mortar hewn into rock is clearly part of the house and cannot be removed. Any mortar brought from the outside, even if it was permanently affixed to the house, can be removed and therefore is not part of the building which was sold.

(fol. 14b) **משנה ד:** הַמּוֹכֵר אֶת הֶחָצֵר מָכַר בָּתִּים בּוֹרוֹת שִׁיחִין וּמְעָרוֹת אֲבָל לֹא אֶת הַמִּטַּלְטְלִין. בִּזְמַן שֶׁאָמַר לוֹ הִיא וְכָל־מַה שֶׁבְּתוֹכָהּ הֲרֵי כוּלָן מְכוּרִין. בֵּין כָּךְ וּבֵין כָּךְ לֹא מָכַר לֹא אֶת הַמֶּרְחָץ וְלֹא אֶת בֵּית הַבַּד שֶׁבְּתוֹכָהּ. רַבִּי לְעֶזֶר אוֹמֵר הַמּוֹכֵר אֶת הֶחָצֵר לֹא מָכַר אֶלָּא אֲוִירָהּ שֶׁל חָצֵר.

**Mishnah 4**: He who sells a courtyard[25] sold houses, cisterns, ditches, and caves but nothing movable. But if he said to him, "it and all it contains," all is sold. In neither case did he sell the bath house or the olive press standing in it[26]. Rebbi Eliezer says, he who sells a courtyard only sold its airspace[27].

25 If a person be able to sell a courtyard, clearly he is the sole proprietor. In common speech, if one refers to "a courtyard" one understands the compound, all the houses accessible from the courtyard.

26 Since very few courtyards contain either a bathhouse or an olive press, the person acquiring the courtyard will not think of these unless they are mentioned in the contract.

27 This means, the area exposed to the sky, nothing built-up, since only the open area is called "courtyard" in exact speech. M. Gil [(1977) 46 חרביץ] reads the sentence as: "He who sells a compound only sells its door."

(14c line 38) **הלכה ד:** הַמּוֹכֵר אֶת הֶחָצֵר כול'. רִבִּי יִצְחָק שָׁאַל. עַל דַּעְתּוֹן דְּרַבָּנָן. מָכַר לוֹ חָצֵר סְתָם מָכַר בָּתִּים בּוֹרוֹת שִׁיחִין וּמְעָרוֹת אֲבָל לֹא הַמִּטַּלְטְלִין. אוֹ מָכַר לוֹ אֲפִילוּ הַמִּטַּלְטְלִין. רִבִּי יִצְחָק שָׁאַל. עַל דַּעְתֵּיה דְּרִבִּי לְעֶזֶר. מָכַר לוֹ חָצֵר סְתָם לֹא מָכַר אֶלָּא אֲוֵיר הֶחָצֵר. בִּזְמַן שֶׁאָמַר לוֹ. הִיא וְכָל־מַה שֶׁבְּתוֹכָהּ. מָכַר בָּתִּים בּוֹרוֹת שִׁיחִין וּמְעָרוֹת אֲבָל לֹא הַמִּיטַּלְטְלִין. אוֹ אֲפִילוּ הַמִּטַּלְטְלִין. אָמַר רִבִּי יוֹחָנָן. זֶנָהּ אַיְיתִיתֵיהּ מִדְּבֵית לֵוִי. הָיוּ שָׁם (חֲצֵירוֹת) [חֲנוּיוֹת] פְּתוּחוֹת לִפְנִים מְכוּרוֹת. פְּתוּחוֹת לַחוּץ אֵינָן מְכוּרוֹת. לִפְנִים וְלַחוּץ אֵילוּ וְאֵילוּ מְכוּרוֹת.

**Halakhah 4**: "He who sells a courtyard," etc. Rebbi Isaac asked: According to the rabbis, he who sells a courtyard without specifications sold houses, cisterns, ditches, and caves but nothing movable. Or maybe he also sold movables[28]? Rebbi Isaac asked: According to Rebbi Eliezer, he who sells a courtyard without specifications only sold the airspace. But if he said, "it and all it contains," he sold houses, cisterns, ditches, and caves but nothing movable. Or maybe he also sold movables?

Rebbi Johanan said, the following I brought from the House of Levi[29]: "If there were (courtyards)[30] [stores][31] open to the inside[32], they are sold; to the outside, they are not sold; to the inside and the outside, they are all sold."

28  He asks how the Mishnah should be understood. Is it to be understood the way it was translated, or does it mean that if he indicated that he was selling the courtyard together with the buildings bordering on it, then by implication he excluded movables, but if he mentioned only the courtyard, everything, including movables, was included? The same question may be asked about the formulation of R. Eliezer's statement.

29  Tosephta 3:1, Babli 67a.

30  Reading of L.

31  Reading of E, the Constantinople edition, the Tosephta, and the Babli; required by the context.

32  Accessible to buyers only from the courtyard.

(fol. 14b) **משנה ה:** הַמּוֹכֵר אֶת בֵּית הַבַּד מָכַר אֶת הַיָּם וְאֶת הַמֶּמָּל וְאֶת הַבְּתוּלוֹת אֲבָל לֹא מָכַר אֶת הַכִּירִים וְלֹא אֶת הַגַּלְגַּל וְלֹא אֶת הַקּוֹרָה. בִּזְמַן שֶׁאָמַר לוֹ הוּא וְכָל־מַה שֶּׁבְּתוֹכוֹ הֲרֵי כוּלָּן מְכוּרִין. רִבִּי לְעָזֶר אוֹמֵר הַמּוֹכֵר אֶת בֵּית הַבַּד מָכַר אֶת הַקּוֹרָה.

**Mishnah 5**: He who sells an olive-press building sold the lower stone of the olive mill[33], the upper stone[34], and the scaffolding for the beam of the press, but he sold neither the planks,[35] nor the wheel, nor the beam. But if he said to him, "it and all it contains," all is sold. Rebbi Eliezer said, he who sells an olive-press building sold the beam[36].

33  It is called "sea" similar to the "sea" constructed by Solomon in his Temple (*1K*. 7:44), shaped like a bowl to collect the oil which will drip from

the olives.

34 The technical terms in the Mishnah are translated following Maimonides's Mishnah Commentary.

35 Maimonides reads הכידין, the Babli העכירין. The planks cover the olives and are pressed down by the beam moved by the wheel.

36 Since without a beam there is no olive press as stated in the Halakhah (and the Babli, 67b).

(14c line 46) **הלכה ה:** הַמּוֹכֵר אֶת הַבַּד כול׳. כָּל־עַצְמוֹ אִם אֵין לוֹ קוֹרָה אֵינוֹ קָרוּי בֵּית הַבַּד. וְתֵימַר אָכֵן. וּמָאן תַּנִּיתָהּ. רִבִּי לְעָזָר. דְּתַנֵּי בְשֵׁם רִבִּי לְעָזָר. הַמּוֹכֵר אֶת בֵּית הַבַּד מָכַר אֶת הַיְקָבִין וְאֶת הָאֲסוּרִין וְאֶת הַמַּפְרִיכוֹת וְאֶת הָרֵיחַיִם הַתַּחְתּוֹנָה אֲבָל לֹא אֶת הָעֶלְיוֹנָה וְלֹא אֶת הַשַּׂקִּין וְלֹא אֶת הַמַּרְצוּפִין שֶׁבְּתוֹכוֹ. בִּזְמַן שֶׁאָמַר לוֹ. הוּא וְכָל־מַה שֶׁבְּתוֹכוֹ. בֵּין כָּךְ וּבֵין כָּךְ לֹא מָכַר הַיָּצוּעִין וְהַשָּׁבוֹין וְהַחֲרוּתִין שֶׁבְּתוֹכוֹ.

**Halakhah 5**: "He who sells an olive-press," etc. In fact, if it does not have a beam, it is not called an olive press[36]. You would say, who stated this? Rebbi Eliezer, since it was stated in the name of Rebbi Eliezer: [37]"He who sells an olive-press building sold the vats, the basket weaves[38], and the breakstones[39], and the lower millstone but not the upper one[40], nor the sacks nor the bags[41] it contains. But if he said to him, 'it and all it contains, ...'[42] In neither case did he sell the paved space surrounding the building[2], or the [ditches][43], or the [cellars][43]."

37 Tosephta 3:2, Babli 67b; anonymous in both sources.

38 Explanation of Rashbam. These are mats strung around the olive press to hold the olives together during the crushing process.

39 According to the Babli, 67b, מפרכת is synonymous with ממל.

40 Built-in mills are sold, movable ones not.

41 Greek μάρσιππος, ὁ, "bag, pouch", Latin *marsupium, marsuppium, -ii*.

42 One has to add: all is sold.

43 One has to read שיחין for שבוין and החדותין for החרורין, cf. Mishnah 1 (S. Lieberman).

**משנה ו**: הַמּוֹכֵר אֶת הַמֶּרְחָץ לֹא מָכַר אֶת הַנְּסָרִין וְאֶת הַסַּפְסָלִים (fol. 14b) וְאֶת הַבּוֹלָנִיּוֹת. בִּזְמַן שֶׁאָמַר לוֹ הוּא וְכָל־מַה שֶׁבְּתוֹכָהּ הֲרֵי כּוּלָּן מְכוּרִין. בֵּין כָּךְ וּבֵין כָּךְ לֹא מָכַר לֹא אֶת הַמְּגוּרוֹת שֶׁל מַיִם וְלֹא אֶת אוֹצָרוֹת שֶׁל עֵצִים.

**Mishnah 6**: He who sells a bathhouse sold neither the planks[44] nor the stools[45], nor the bath utensils[46]. But if he said to him, "it and all it contains," all is sold. In neither case did he sell the storage ponds of water or the stores of wood[47].

44  According to Rashbam, the planks to walk on in the wet heated sauna. According to Maimonides, planks to deposit one's clothes.
45  Latin *subsellium*, to sit on in the sauna.
46  Latin *balnearia, -orum*, "utensils, implements for bathing".
47  To heat the thermal bath.

(14c line 53) **הלכה ו**: הַמּוֹכֵר אֶת הַמֶּרְחָץ כול׳. תַּנֵּי. הַמּוֹכֵר אֶת הַמֶּרְחָץ מָכַר בָּתִּים הַפְּנִימִין וְהַחִיצוֹנִים וּבְסִלְקֵי וְקָמִין וּבֵית הָאוֹרְיָרִין. אֲבָל לֹא הַמִּגְדָּלִין וְלֹא הַיּוֹרָה. רִבִּי שִׁמְעוֹן בֶּן אֶלְעָזָר אוֹמֵר. מְקוֹם הַבַּלָּן מָכוּר וּמְקוֹם הָאוֹרְיָיר אֵינוֹ מָכוּר. בִּזְמַן שֶׁאָמַר לוֹ הִיא וְכָל־מַה שֶׁבְּתוֹכָהּ. אַף עַל פִּי שֶׁאָמַר לוֹ. הִיא וְכָל־מַה שֶׁבְּתוֹכָהּ. בֵּין כָּךְ וּבֵין כָּךְ לֹא מָכַר לֹא אֶת הַמְּגוּרוֹת שֶׁל מַיִם שֶׁמִּשְׁתַּמֵּשׁ בָּהֶן בֵּין בִּימוֹת הַחַמָּה בֵּין בִּימוֹת הַגְּשָׁמִים. וְלֹא בֵית הַכְּנָסָה שֶׁלָּעֵצִים. אָמַר לוֹ. הִיא וּמְשַׁמְּשֶׁיהָ אֲנִי מוֹכֵר לָךְ. הֲרֵי כּוּלָּן מְכוּרִין.

**Halakhah 6**: "He who sells a bathhouse," etc. It was stated[48]: "He who sells a bathhouse sold the inner and the outer rooms[49], the basilica[50], the heating chamber, and the storekeeper's[51] chamber, but not the chests nor the boiler[52]. Rebbi Simeon ben Eleazar said, the place of the bath attendant[53] is sold; the place of the storekeeper is not sold. But if he said to him, 'it and all it contains'? Even if he said to him, 'it and all it contains'[54]. In neither case did he sell the water ponds which he uses both in summer and in winter or the room in which wood is stored. But if he said to him, 'it and all its appurtenances,' all these are sold."

48  Tosephta 3:3; cf. Babli 67b.

49  In the inner rooms, people are naked; in the outer rooms they are dressed.

50  A large room supported by pillars.

51  Latin *horrearius* "superintendent of the storehouse, magazine" (E. G.).

In the Tosephta: האולייריו *olearii* "the oil sellers", cf. *Berakhot* 2:1, Note 94. In the Babli בית הוילאות "room of curtains". All commentators read the Tosephta into the Yerushalmi.

52  E adds: רִבִּי שִׁמְעוֹן בֶּן אֶלְעָזָר אוֹמֵר מָכַר אֶת הַיּוֹרָה. " Rebbi Simeon ben Eleazar said, he sold the boiler."

53  Latin *balneator* "bathkeeper", who collects the fee and hands out the bath towels.

54  In this case, the required formula is different. In the Tosephta, the wording is: But if he said to him, 'it and all it contains', *all is sold.* Even if he said to him, 'it and all it contains' he did not sell the water ponds . . .

(fol. 14b) **משנה ז:** הַמּוֹכֵר אֶת הָעִיר מָכַר בָּתִּים בּוֹרוֹת שִׁיחִין וּמְעָרוֹת מֶרְחֲצָאוֹת וְשׁוֹבָכוֹת בֵּית הַבַּדִּין וּבֵית הַשְּׁלָחִין אֲבָל לֹא אֶת הַמִּטַּלְטְלִין. וּבִזְמַן שֶׁאָמַר לוֹ הִיא וְכָל־מַה שֶּׁבְּתוֹכָהּ אֲפִילוּ הָיוּ בָהּ בְּהֵמָה וַעֲבָדִים הֲרֵי כוּלָּן מְכוּרִין. רַבָּן שִׁמְעוֹן בֶּן גַּמְלִיאֵל אוֹמֵר. הַמּוֹכֵר אֶת הָעִיר מָכַר אֶת הַסַּנְטָר.

**Mishnah 7**: He who sells a village sold houses, cisterns, ditches and caverns, bath houses and dovecots, the oil press and irrigated lots but not movables. But if he said to him, it and all that is in it, even if there were animals and slaves there, all of them are sold. Rabban Simeon ben Gamliel says, he who sells a village sold the steward.

(14c line 60) **הלכה ז:** הַמּוֹכֵר אֶת הָעִיר כול'. תַּנֵּי. הַמּוֹכֵר אֶת הָעִיר. רַבָּן שִׁמְעוֹן בֶּן גַּמְלִיאֵל אוֹמֵר. הַמּוֹכֵר הָעִיר מָכַר אֶת הַסַּנְטָר אֲבָל לֹא הָאִיקוֹמְנֹס. בִּזְמַן שֶׁאָמַר לוֹ הִיא וְכָל־מַה שֶׁבְּתוֹכָהּ. אַף עַל פִּי שֶׁאָמַר לוֹ. הִיא וְכָל־מַה שֶׁבְּתוֹכָהּ. בֵּין כָּךְ וּבֵין כָּךְ לֹא מָכַר לֹא אֶת הַשּׁוּרָה וּבְנוֹתֶיהָ וְהַטְּרָשִׁים הַמּוּקְצִין מִמֶּנָּה וְהַבִּיבָּרִין שֶׁל חַיָּה וְשֶׁל אוֹפוֹת וְשֶׁלְּדָגִים. שׁוּרָה בְזַיִיהּ. בְּנוֹתֶיהָ כּוּפְרָנָיָה. חוֹלֶק בַּיָּם וּבַנָּהָר. אִית תַּנָּיֵי תַנֵּי. מְכוּרִין. וְאִית תַּנָּיֵי תַנֵּי. אֵינָן מְכוּרִין. אָמַר רַב חִסְדָּא. מָאן דָּמַר. מְכוּרִין. אֶת שֶׁהֵן בִּתְחוּמָהּ. וּמָאן דָּמַר. אֵינָן מְכוּרִין. אֶת שֶׁאֵינָן בִּתְחוּמָהּ.

**Halakhah 7:** "He who sells a village," etc. It was stated[55]: "He who sells a village. Rabban Simeon ben Gamliel says, he who sells a village sold the steward but did not sell the administrator[56]. But if he said to him, 'it and all it contains'? Even if he said to him, 'it and all it contains'[54]. In neither case did he sell *širah* and its dependencies, and hard rocks hewn from it[57], and preserves [58] of wild animals, birds, and fish." *Širah* means outlying houses[59], dependencies are hamlets. Its part in ocean or river[60], there are Tannaïm who state, it is sold, and there are Tannaïm who state, it is not sold. Rav Ḥisda said, he who says, it is sold, as long as it is within its domain[61]; he who says, it is not sold, if it is not within its domain.

55   Tosephta 3:5; Babli 68b.

56   A slave trained in bookkeeping is too valuable to be sold as part of a package; cf. *Bava meṣia'* 9:1, Note 11. (In E: האונקומוס).

57   Some commentators read with Babli and Tosephta: וְהֶחֳרָשִׁים הַמּוּקְצִין מִמֶּנָּה "forests separated from it."

58   Latin *vivarium*.

59   The LXX translate *Jos.* 15:28: וּבְאֵר שֶׁבַע וּבְזִיּוֹתֶיהָ as καὶ Βηρσαβεε καὶ αἱ κῶμαι αὐτῶν καὶ αἱ ἐπαύλεις αὐτῶν "and Beer Sheba and its walls and its isolated houses." If וּבְזִיּוֹתֶיהָ is taken as an Aramaism, no emendation of the consonantal text is needed.

60   Ocean beach or fishing rights in the river.

61   In the formulation of the Babli, whether doors open to beach or river or do not.

**משנה ח:** (fol. 14b) הַמּוֹכֵר אֶת הַשָּׂדֶה מָכַר אֶת הָאֲבָנִים שֶׁהֵן לְצָרְכָּהּ וְאֶת הַקָּנִים שֶׁבַּכֶּרֶם שֶׁהֵם לְצָרְכּוֹ וְאֶת הַתְּבוּאָה שֶׁהִיא מְחוּבֶּרֶת לַקַּרְקַע וְאֶת מְחִיצַת הַקָּנִים שֶׁהִיא פְחוּתָה מִבֵּית רוֹבַע וְאֶת הַשּׁוֹמֵירָה שֶׁאֵינָהּ עֲשׂוּיָה בַטִּיט וְאֶת הֶחָרוּב שֶׁאֵינוֹ מוּרְכָּב וְאֶת בְּתוּלַת הַשִּׁיקְמָה.

**Mishnah 8**: He who sells a field sold the stones which are needed for it[62], and the posts in a vineyard which are needed for it[63], and grain standing on the ground, and a reed fence taking up less than a *bet rova'*, and a watchman's hut not made with mortar, and a carob tree not yet grafted, and a virgin sycamore tree[64].

**משנה ט:** אֲבָל לֹא מָכַר לֹא אֶת הָאֲבָנִים שֶׁאֵינָן לְצָרְכָּהּ וְאֶת הַקָּנִים שֶׁבַּכֶּרֶם שֶׁאֵינָן לְצָרְכּוֹ וְאֶת הַתְּבוּאָה שֶׁהִיא תְלוּשָׁה מִן הַקַּרְקַע. בִּזְמַן שֶׁאָמַר לוֹ הוּא וְכָל־מַה שֶּׁבְּתוֹכָהּ הֲרֵי כוּלָּן מְכוּרִין. בֵּין כָּךְ וּבֵין כָּךְ לֹא מָכַר אֶת מְחִיצַת הַקָּנִים שֶׁהִיא בֵית רוֹבַע וְאֶת הַשּׁוֹמֵירָה שֶׁהִיא עֲשׂוּיָה בַטִּיט וְאֶת הֶחָרוּב הַמּוּרְכָּב וְאֶת סַדָּן הַשִּׁיקְמָה.

**Mishnah 9**: But he sold neither the stones which are not needed for it, nor the posts in a vineyard which are not needed for it, nor grain harvested from the ground. But if he said to him, "it and all it contains," all is sold. In no case did he sell either a reed fence taking up more than a *bet rova'*[65], or a watchman's hut made with mortar[66], or a grafted carob tree, or an anvil sycamore tree[64].

**משנה י:** (fol. 14c) לֹא אֶת הַבּוֹר וְלֹא אֶת הַגַּת וְלֹא אֶת הַשּׁוֹבָךְ בֵּין חֲרֵיבִין בֵּין שְׁלֵימִין. וְצָרִיךְ לִיקַּח לוֹ דֶּרֶךְ דִּבְרֵי רַבִּי עֲקִיבָה וַחֲכָמִים אוֹמְרִים אֵינוֹ צָרִיךְ לִיקַּח לוֹ דֶּרֶךְ. וּמוֹדֶה רַבִּי עֲקִיבָה בִּזְמַן שֶׁאָמַר לוֹ חוּץ מֵאִילוּ אֵינוֹ צָרִיךְ לִיקַּח לוֹ דֶּרֶךְ. מִכְרָן לְאַחֵר רַבִּי עֲקִיבָה אוֹמֵר אֵינוֹ צָרִיךְ לִיקַּח לוֹ דֶּרֶךְ וַחֲכָמִים אוֹמְרִים צָרִיךְ לִיקַּח לוֹ דֶּרֶךְ.

**Mishnah 10**: Neither the cistern, nor the wine press, nor a dovecote[67] whether deserted or intact; and he has to buy himself access[12], the words of Rebbi Aqiba; but the Sages say that he does not not have to buy himself access[13]. Rebbi Aqiba agrees that if he said "except these"[14], he does not not have to buy himself access. If he sold them[15] to another person, Rebbi Aqiba said, he does not have to buy access[16], but the Sages say, he does have to buy access[17].

משנה יא: בַּמֶּה דְבָרִים אֲמוּרִים בְּמוֹכֵר אֲבָל בְּנוֹתֵן מַתָּנָה נוֹתֵן אֶת כּוּלָן. הָאַחִים שֶׁחָלְקוּ זָכוּ בַשָּׂדֶה זָכָה בְכוּלָן. הַמַּחֲזִיק בְּנִיכְסֵי הַגֵּר הֶחֱזִיק בַּשָּׂדֶה הֶחֱזִיק בְּכוּלָן. הַמַּקְדִּישׁ אֶת הַשָּׂדֶה הִקְדִּישׁ אֶת כּוּלָן. רַבִּי שִׁמְעוֹן אוֹמֵר הַמַּקְדִּישׁ אֶת הַשָּׂדֶה לֹא הִקְדִּישׁ אֶלָּא הֶחָרוּב הַמּוּרְכָּב וְאֶת סַדָּן הַשִּׁקְמָה.

**Mishnah 11**: When has this been said? For the seller. But one who gives a gift, gives everything[68]. Brothers who divided [an inheritance]: if one acquired a field he acquired everything[69]. Somebody taking possession of a proselyte's property: if he took possession of a field, he took possession of everything[70]. If somebody dedicated a field to the Temple, he dedicated everything; Rebbi Simeon says that he who dedicated a field to the Temple only dedicated a grafted carob tree and an anvil sycamore tree[64,71].

62   For fencing.
63   To support the vines.
64   The last two are young trees whose roots have not yet spread; therefore they are not included if their place was not sold. But an older carob tree grafted for better yield and a sycamore already cut once and now held for the production of logs (an "anvil sycamore") have large systems of roots spreading wide; they become part of the field.
65   114+ square cubits; the reeds themselves become a cash crop.
66   Which is valuable as dwelling by itself.

67  All of these are not intrinsically connected with a field.
68  A gift is supposed to be given in a magnanimous spirit.
69  Family relations are helped by clean divisions of property.
70  Since the proselyte died without relatives who could have inherited from him, the person who takes possession of his estate has no competitors with whom to share.
71  But nothing not included in the definition of "a field".

(14c line 68) **הלכה ח:** הַמּוֹכֵר אֶת הַשָּׂדֶה כול׳. **הלאכה ט:** אֲבָל לֹא מָכַר כול׳. **הלכה י:** לֹא אֶת הַבּוֹר כול׳. **הלכה יא:** הַמַּקְדִּישׁ אֶת הַשָּׂדֶה כול׳. דְּבֵית רִבִּי יַנַּאי אָמְרִין. בִּמְחַלְּקִין לִגְפָנִים. רִבִּי חִייָה רוּבָה שָׁאַל. הָיוּ שָׁם חֲלָיוֹת מְחוּלָקוֹת לִבְרוֹת. רִבִּי יִצְחָק בַּר טְבְלַיי שָׁאַל. הָיוּ שָׁם טַבְלִיוֹת שֶׁל שַׁיִישׁ מְחוּלָקוֹת לִכְתָלִין. רִבִּי יוּדָן בְּרִבִּי יִשְׁמָעֵאל שָׁאַל. הָיוּ שָׁם מַלְבְּנִין מְחוּלָקוֹת לַחַלּוֹנוֹת.

**Halakhah 8**: "He who sells a field," etc. **Halakhah 9**: "But he sold neither," etc. **Halakhah 10**: "Neither the cistern," etc. **Halakhah 11**: "If somebody dedicated a field to the Temple," etc. In the House of Rebbi Yannai they said, poles for vines[72]. The Elder Rebbi Ḥiyya asked, if there were split rings to select?[73] Rebbi Isaac bar Tebelai asked, if there were marble plates[74] for walls[75]? Rebbi Yudan ben Rebbi Ismael asked: If there were split rods to frame windows[76]?

72  This explains what is meant by "posts in a vineyard" in Mishnah 8; the same explanation is given in the Babli, 69a, where Rashbam explains that these poles in French are called *palis*.
73  This sentence is unintelligible. The thrust of the other two questions is very clear. If walls were covered with marble plates or windows framed with wood frames, the covering and the frames would be sold with the house. But what is the status of material prepared for installation which was not yet installed at the time of the sale? R. Ḥiyya seems to ask a similar question relative to agricultural property. חוליה

means "ring", from the root חלל, חול "to describe a circle", but it is not clear that חליה is the same as חוליה. The translation in the text follows R. Eliahu Fulda, not to leave the sentence untranslated. He reads חליות מחולקות as "half circles" formed by pliable twigs, such as willow branches, with both ends planted on the ground to support branches of fruit trees heavy with fruit. He also derives the *hapax* ברות from ברר "to select". [Starting with the Constantinople edition (1622), all printed editions read לכרות "to cut off", which replaces an unknown word by one well-known but devoid of sense in the context.] But one could as well read ברות as Arabic بَرَة "hunter's hut" and refer the question to the watchman's hut and ask about the status of such a hut built with split rings formed of any material. One also could read חַלָיוֹת

"מְחוּלָקוֹת לְבָרוֹת" "chopped herbs (خَل) for healing", whether these have the status of cut grain. Moïse Schwab translates: "S'il y a des morceaux de joncs divisées pour séparer les vignes, sont-ils tous considérés comme nécessaires"; it is difficult to read this into the text.

74    Greek τάβλα, Latin *tabula*.

75    In the Babli, 69a, a similar question is asked about stones prepared to be used to make a fence around an agricultural property but not yet displayed; it is determined that their status in a sale depends on a difference of opinion between R. Meïr and the anonymous majority.

76    In the Babli, 69a, the question is asked by R. Ze'ira about finished wood frames for windows (slits in the wall without glass) which are not structural but purely ornamental; the question is not answered.

(14c line 74) רִבִּי חִיָּיה בְּשֵׁם רִבִּי יוֹחָנָן. יֵשׁ שָׁם עֲרוּגָה שֶׁהִיא שִׁשָּׁה עַל שִׁשָּׁה וְיֵשׁ לָהּ שֵׁם בִּפְנֵי עַצְמָהּ אֵינָהּ מְכוּרָה. אָמַר רִבִּי יוֹחָנָן. הַקּוֹנֶה סַדָּן שִׁקְמָה בְּתוֹךְ שֶׁלַּחֲבֵירוֹ מַחֲלוֹקֶת רִבִּי יִשְׁמָעֵאל בֶּרְבִּי יוֹסֵי וְרַבָּנִין. רִבִּי יִשְׁמָעֵאל בֵּירְבִּי יוֹסֵי אוֹמֵר. קָנָה קַרְקַע. וְרַבָּנִין אָמְרִין. לֹא קָנָה. רִבִּי חִיָּיה בַּר וָא שָׁאַל. מָכַר לוֹ כָּל־הָאִילָן וְשִׁיֵּיר לוֹ סַדָּן שִׁקְמָה. עַל דַּעְתֵּיהּ דְּרִבִּי יִשְׁמָעֵאל בֵּירְבִּי יוֹסֵי. קָנָה קַרְקַע. עַל דַּעְתִּין דְּרַבָּנִין. לֹא קָנָה קַרְקַע. רִבִּי יִצְחָק בַּר טְבְלַיי שָׁאַל. מָכַר לוֹ כָּל־הָאִילָן וְזַיִת שֶׁבַּמָּקוֹם פְּלוֹנִי כָּל זֵיתִים שֶׁיֵּשׁ שָׁם מְכוּרִין. רִבִּי יוּדָן בֵּירְבִּי יִשְׁמָעֵאל שָׁאַל. הַקּוֹנֶה ג כִּיתֵּי קָנִים קָנָה אֶרֶז גָּדוֹל שֶׁבְּאֶרֶץ יִשְׂרָאֵל.

Rebbi Hiyya in the name of Rebbi Johanan: A vegetable bed which is six by six [handbreadths][76] and has its own name[77] is not sold[78]. Rebbi Johanan said: There is disagreement between Rebbi Ismael ben Rebbi Yose and the rabbis about one who bought an anvil sycamore[64] on another's property. Rebbi Ismael ben Rebbi Yose says, he acquired the land. The rabbis say, he did not acquire[79]. Rebbi Hiyya bar Abba asked: If somebody sold all trees but reserved for himself an anvil sycamore. In the opinion of Rebbi Ismael ben Rebbi Yose, he acquired the land[80]. In the opinion of the rabbis, he did not acquire the land[81]. Rebbi Isaac bar Tebelai asked: If somebody sold all trees and an olive tree at place X, are all olive trees at that place sold[82]? Rebbi Yudan ben Rebbi Ismael asked: If somebody bought three groups of reeds, did he buy the greatest cedar in the Land of Israel[83]?

76  The minimum size of a vegetable bed to be considered a unit of its own (Mishnah *Šabbat* 9:2, *Kilaim* 3:1).

77  For example, the name of the spice which usually is grown there such as "the bed of fenugreek".

78  Unless it is specifically mentioned in a sales contract of agricultural property.

79  As mentioned in Note 64, the anvil sycamore spreads its root widely. If the roots of the tree were restricted to the earth on which it stands, it could not live.

In practical terms, if the owner of the tree is the owner of the land, he may plant a new tree on its spot if the original tree dies; if he is not the owner of the land, he cannot plant a replacement. In view of Mishnah 5:5, there really should be no problem about a single tree.

80  He did not acquire it but never gave up his ownership.

81  He gave up ownership.

82  If an unspecified tree was sold and the seller had more than one tree at place X, the buyer might lay claim to any one of them. The treatment of the case is in dispute between R. Meïr and R. Yose, cf. *Qiddušin* 3:10.

83  If he bought reeds that cover more than a *bet rova'*, did he acquire only the reeds or everything that grows among them?

(14d line 7) בַּמֶּה דְבָרִים אֲמוּרִים. בְּמוֹכֵר. אֲבָל לֹא בְנוֹתֵן מַתָּנָה נוֹתֵן אֶת כּוּלָם. מַה בֵין מוֹכֵר וּמַה בֵין נוֹתֵן מַתָּנָה. רִבִּי בָּא בַר טְבַלַיי בְּשֵׁם רַב. שֶׁכֵּן דֶּרֶךְ הַנּוֹתֵן מַתָּנָה לִהְיוֹת נוֹתֵן בְּעַיִן יָפָה. רִבִּי שְׁמוּאֵל בַּר נַחְמָן בְּשֵׁם רִבִּי יוֹנָתָן. שֶׁכֵּן דֶּרֶךְ הַלְּקוּחוֹתִי לִהְיוֹת מְדַקְדְּקִין. וּמַה בֵינֵיהוֹן. הֶקְדֵּשׁ. מָאן דָּמַר. שֶׁכֵּן דֶּרֶךְ הַנּוֹתֵן מַתָּנָה לִהְיוֹת נוֹתֵן בְּעַיִן יָפָה. אַף הַמַּקְדִּישׁ בְּעַיִן יָפָה מַקְדִּישׁ. וּמָאן דָּמַר. שֶׁכֵּן דֶּרֶךְ הַלְּקוּחוֹתִי לִהְיוֹת מְדַקְדְּקִין. מַה אָמַר בְּמַקְדִּישׁ. נִישְׁמְעִינָהּ מֵהֲדָא. הָאַחִין שֶׁחָלְקוּ יֵשׁ לָהֶן דֶּרֶךְ זֶה עַל גַּבֵּי זֶה. וְאִית דְּבָעֵי מֵימַר. כֵּן אָמַר רִבִּי לְעָזָר. הָאַחִין שֶׁחָלְקוּ זָכוּ בַּשָּׂדֶה זָכוּ בְכוּלָן. הַמַּחֲזִיק בְּנִיכְסֵי הַגֵּר קָנָה. הֶחֱזִיק בַּשָּׂדֶה הֶחֱזִיק בְּכוּלָן. הַמַּקְדִּישׁ אֶת הַשָּׂדֶה הִקְדִּישׁ אֶת כּוּלָן. רִבִּי שִׁמְעוֹן אוֹמֵר. הַמַּקְדִּישׁ אֶת הַשָּׂדֶה לֹא הִקְדִּישׁ הֶחָרוּב הַמּוּרְכָּב וְשִׁיקְמָה הַיְשָׁנָה. מִפְּנֵי שֶׁיּוֹנְקִין מִשֶּׁל הֶקְדֵּשׁ. מִפְּנֵי שֶׁשִּׁיֵּיר לוֹ דֶרֶךְ. אִם לֹא שִׁיֵּיר לוֹ דֶרֶךְ אַף הֵן אֵין יוֹנְקִין מִשֶּׁל הֶקְדֵּשׁ.

"When has this been said? For the seller. But one who gives a gift gives everything." What is the difference between a seller and the giver of a gift? Rebbi Abba bar Ṭebelai in the name of Rav: Because the giver of a gift usually is magnanimous[84]. Rebbi Samuel ben Rav Naḥman in the name of Rebbi Joḥanan: Because buyers care about minutiae[85]. What is the difference between these opinions? A dedication to the Temple. He who says, because the giver of a gift usually is magnanimous, also the person vowing to the Temple usually is magnanimous. But he who says, because buyers care about minutiae, what does he say about a dedication to the Temple? Let us hear from the following[86]: "Brothers who divided [an inheritance], if one acquired a field he acquired everything. Somebody taking possession of the property of a convert aquired it; if he took possession of a field, he took possession of everything. If somebody dedicated a field to the Temple, he dedicated everything. Rebbi Simeon says that he who dedicated a field to the Temple, only dedicated a grafted carob tree and an old sycamore tree." Because they nurse from Temple property[87]. Because he reserved access to himself? If he had not reserved access for himself, would they not feed from Temple property[88]?

84  In the Babli, 71a, this is the conclusion reached after discussion.

85  Since the buyer gives the money, he can be specific and insist to spell out in the contract what he wants, but the recipient of a gift has to accept what he is given. Therefore, a sales contract has to be interpreted exactly but in the case of a gift it is up to the court to guess the donor's intention.

86  E here has an additional text: נִישְׁמְעִינָהּ מֵהָדָא. הָאַחִין שֶׁחָלְקוּ זָכוּ בַשָּׂדֶה זָכוּ בְכוּלָן. רִבִּי לֶעְזָר שְׁאִיל. עַל כָּל־הַפֶּרֶק הוּשְׁבָה אוֹ עַל הָרִאשׁוֹנָה הוּשְׁבָה. "Let us hear from the following: 'Brothers who divided [an inheritance], if they acquired a field they acquired everything.' Rebbi Eleazar asked: Does this refer to the entire Chapter or only to the first mention?"

87  Babli 72b. He holds that a gift to the Temple has to be interpreted narrowly, like a sale. The exeption are trees with widespread roots which must be included, even against the giver's wish, because of the severity of the sin of larceny from Temple property which would be committed if the donor profited from growth of the tree by the nutrients which its roots absorb from Temple property.

88  The brother whose inheritance is accessible only through another brother's property has the right of passage automatically, without specifically insisting on it at the time of the distribution, just as the anvil sycamore is part of Temple property even if the donor to the Temple does not specify it. Since the majority disagree with R. Simeon, they must hold that the donor to the Temple also is magnanimous.

## המוכר את הספינה פרק חמישי

(fol. 14d) **משנה א**: הַמּוֹכֵר אֶת הַסְּפִינָה מָכַר אֶת הַתּוֹרֶן וְאֶת הַנֵּס וְאֶת הַהוֹגִין וְאֶת כָּל־הַמַּנְהִיגִין אוֹתָהּ אֲבָל לֹא מָכַר לֹא אֶת הָעֲבָדִים וְלֹא אֶת הַמַּרְצוּפִין וְלֹא אֶת הָאֲנְתֵיקֵי. בִּזְמַן שֶׁאָמַר לוֹ הִיא וְכָל־שֶׁבְּתוֹכָהּ הֲרֵי כוּלָּן מְכוּרִין.

**Mishnah 1**: He who sells a ship sold the mast, and the sail, and the anchors, and all steering gear, but he neither sold the slaves, nor the storage bags[1], nor the load[2]. If he said, "it and all that is in it," all is sold.

**משנה ב**: מָכַר אֶת הַקָּרוֹן לֹא מָכַר אֶת הַפְּרָדוֹת. מָכַר אֶת הַפְּרָדוֹת לֹא מָכַר אֶת הַקָּרוֹן. מָכַר אֶת הַצֶּמֶד לֹא מָכַר אֶת הַבָּקָר. מָכַר אֶת הַבָּקָר לֹא מָכַר אֶת הַצֶּמֶד. רִבִּי יְהוּדָה אוֹמֵר הַדָּמִים מוֹדִיעִין. כֵּיצַד אָמַר לוֹ מְכוֹר לִי אֶת צִמְדְּךָ בְּמָאתַיִם זוּז הַדָּבָר יָדוּעַ שֶׁאֵין הַצֶּמֶד בְּמָאתַיִם זוּז. וַחֲכָמִים אוֹמְרִים אֵין הַדָּמִים רְאָיָה.

**Mishnah 2**: He who sold a truck[3] did not sell the mules; he who sold the mules did not sell the truck. He who sold the yoke did not sell the cattle[4]; he who sold the cattle did not sell the yoke. Rebbi Jehudah says, the price is an indicator. How is that? If he said to him, sell me your yoke and harness for 200 denars[5], it is obvious that yoke and harness are not worth 200 denars. But the Sages say, the price is no indicator.

**משנה ג**: הַמּוֹכֵר אֶת הַחֲמוֹר לֹא מָכַר אֶת כֵּלָיו. נָחוּם הַמָּדִי אוֹמֵר מָכַר אֶת כֵּלָיו. רִבִּי יְהוּדָה אוֹמֵר פְּעָמִים מְכוּרִין וּפְעָמִים אֵינָן מְכוּרִין. כֵּיצַד. הָיָה חֲמוֹר לְפָנָיו וְכֵלָיו עָלָיו וְאָמַר לוֹ מְכוֹר לִי חֲמוֹרְךָ זוֹ הֲרֵי כֵלָיו מְכוּרִין חֲמוֹרְךָ הַהוּא אֵין כֵּלָיו מְכוּרִין.

**Mishnah 3**: He who sells a donkey did not sell its gear[6]. Nahum the Mede says, he sold the gear. Rebbi Jehudah says, sometimes it is sold, sometimes it is not sold. How is this? If a donkey was standing there with his gear on it and he said, sell me *this* donkey, his gear is sold; your donkey, for this one the gear is not sold.

**משנה ד**: הַמּוֹכֵר אֶת הַחֲמוֹר מָכַר אֶת הַסְּיָח. מָכַר אֶת הַפָּרָה לֹא מָכַר אֶת בְּנָהּ. מָכַר אַשְׁפּוֹת מָכַר זִבְלָהּ. מָכַר בּוֹר מָכַר מֵימָיו. מָכַר כַּוֶּרֶת מָכַר דְּבוֹרִים. מָכַר שׁוֹבָךְ מָכַר יוֹנִים. הַלּוֹקֵחַ פֵּירוֹת שׁוֹבָךְ מַפְרִיחַ בְּרֵיכָה הָרִאשׁוֹנָה כַּוֶּרֶת נוֹטֵל ג נְחִילִים וּמְסָרֵס דְּבַשׁ וּמַנִּיחַ שְׁתֵּי חַלּוֹת. זֵיתִם לָקוֹץ מַנִּיחַ שְׁתֵּי גְרוֹפִיּוֹת.

**Mishnah 4**: He who sells a donkey sold the foal[7]; he who sold a cow did not sell its young[8]. He who sold a dungheap sold the manure; he who sold a cistern sold its water. He who sold a beehive sold the bees; he who sold the dovecote sold the pigeons. He who bought the yield of a dovecote leaves the first brood to fledge, of a beehive takes three swarms and then intermittently[9], honeycombs leaves two honeycombs[10], olive trees to cut down leaves two handbreadths[11].

1  Cf. Chapter 4, Note 41. Containers in which the load is stored.

2  Greek ἐνθήκη.

3  Greek κάρρος, κάρρον, Latin *carrus, carrum* "two-wheeled cart".

4  For ploughing.

5  In his time a sum whose possession disqualified one from receiving public assistance; Mishnah *Peah* 8:8.

6  The gear needed to fasten the animal.

7  As long as the foal is dependent on its mother it cannot be separated from her.

8  Since a calf can be slaughtered, it represents an independent value.

9  In order to preserve the population he takes only the second and all the odd-numbered swarms.

10  For the bees to survive the winter.

11 Interpretation of Maimonides. One might translate "two twigs" but it is difficult to see how the tree could be cut down and two twigs be left standing. But on a trunk extending two handbreadths above the ground a new olive tree can be grafted.

(15a line 7) **הלכה א:** הַמּוֹכֵר אֶת הַסְּפִינָה כול׳. תַּנֵּי. הַמּוֹכֵר אֶת הַסְּפִינָה מָכַר אֶת הָאַסְכָּלָה וּבוֹר הַמַּיִם שֶׁבְּתוֹכוֹ אֲבָל לֹא מָכַר הַיְצוּעִין וְהָעוֹבִין וְהָאִיסְקוּפָה וְהַבּוּצִית. סוּמְכוֹס אוֹמֵר. מָכַר דּוּגִית.

**Halakhah 1:** "He who sells a ship." etc. It was stated[12]: He who sells a ship sold the ladder[13] and the water tank in it but did not sell the sleeping gear, nor the mats, nor the barge[14] nor the rowboat[15]. Symmachos says, he sold the fishing boat.

12 Tosephta 4:1, Babli 73a.
13 Latin *scalae, -arum, f.*; to enter the ship.
14 Greek σκάφος "ship; hull of a ship".
15 A small boat used to reach the shore where there was no secure harbor. According to Rava in the Babli (*l. c.*), rowboat and fishing boat are one and the same, except that בוצית is Babylonian and דוגית Palestinian usage..

(15a line 9) תְּנָאִים שֶׁהִתְנָה יְהוֹשֻׁעַ. רַבִּי לֵוִי בֶּן בֵּירַיי בְּשֵׁם רַבִּי יְהוֹשֻׁעַ בֶּן לֵוִי. אַרְבָּעָה. מְלַקְּטִין עֲשָׂבִים מִכָּל־מָקוֹם חוּץ מִשָּׂדֶה תִּילְתָּן שֶׁאֲסוּרִין מִשּׁוּם גֵּזֶל. תַּמָּן תַּנִּינָן. וְכֵן תִּלְתָּן שֶׁהֶעֱלַת מִינֵי עֲשָׂבִים אֵין מְחַיְּיבִין אוֹתוֹ לְנַכֵּשׁ. כֵּינִי מַתְנִיתָא. אֵין מְחַיְּיבִין אוֹתוֹ לַעֲקוֹר. בְּתַנָּאֵי יְהוֹשֻׁעַ אַתְּ מַר. מְלַקְּטִין עֲשָׂבִים מִכָּל־מָקוֹם חוּץ מִשָּׂדֶה תִּילְתָּן שֶׁאֲסוּרִין מִשּׁוּם גֵּזֶל. הָדָא אֲמָרָה. שֶׁאֵינוֹ רוֹצֶה בָהֶן. אָמַר. תַּמָּן בְּשֶׁזְּרָעוֹ לְעָמִיר. בְּרַם הָכָא שֶׁזְּרָעוֹ לְזֶרַע. מַה הִתְנָה יְהוֹשֻׁעַ לְעוֹבְרֵי עֲבֵירָה. רַבִּי שְׁמוּאֵל בַּר נַחְמָן בְּשֵׁם רַבִּי יוֹנָתָן. שֶׁהוּא רוֹצֶה בָהֶן כְּאִילּוּ עֲקוּרִין וּמוּנָחִין לְפָנָיו. נָמַר בִּשְׂדֵה כֶרֶם. דָּמַר רִבִּי יַנַּאי. כָּל־הַסְּפִיחִין אֲסוּרִין חוּץ מִן הָעוֹלִים בִּשְׂדֵה בוּר וּבִשְׂדֵה נִיר בִּשְׂדֵה כֶרֶם וּבִשְׂדֵה זָרַע. בִּשְׂדֵה בוּר.

דְּלָא מַשְׁגַּח עָלֶיהָ. בְּשָׂדֶה נִיר. דּוּ בְעֵי מְתַקְּנָה חַקְלֵיהּ. בְּשָׂדֶה כֶרֶם. שֶׁלֹּא לֶאֱסוֹר אֶת כַּרְמוֹ. בְּשָׂדֶה זֶרַע. שֶׁאֵינוֹ רוֹצֶה בָהֶן. וְאִם תֹּאמַר רוֹצֶה בָהֶן כְּאִילוּ עֲקוּרִין וּמוּנָחִין לְפָנָיו.

[16]The conditions which Joshua imposed. Rebbi Levi ben Birai in the name of Rebbi Joshua ben Levi: four. One may collect grasses[17] everywhere except from a field of fenugreek where it is forbidden because of robbery[18]. There[19], we have stated: "Or fenugreek where grasses appeared, one does not require him to weed.[20]" So is the Mishnah: One does not require him to uproot. As one of Joshua's conditions you say, one may collect grasses everywhere except from a field of fenugreek where it is forbidden because of robbery. This implies that he does not want them. He said, there if he sowed it to make sheaves, but here when he sowed it for seeds[21]. Did Joshua made conditions for the benefit of sinners[22]? Rebbi Samuel bar Naḥman in the name of Rebbi Jonathan: He would like it if they were uprooted and lying before him[23]. And he mentions a vineyard field, as Rebbi Yannai[24] said: all spontaneous growth[25] is forbidden except for what appears on a fallow field, or a field ready to be ploughed under, a vineyard or a field grown for seeds[26]. A fallow field, for he does not care. A field ready to be ploughed under, for he wants to improve his field[27]. A vineyard, not to forbid his vineyard[28]. A field grown for seeds, for he does not want it; and if you say he does, he would like it if they were uprooted and lying before him.

16  This is a shortened reformulation of Halakhah *Kilaim* 2:5, Notes 73-89. The conditions of land use attributed to Joshua are discussed in the Babli in *Bava qamma* 80b-82a.

Since the distribution of land by Joshua was irrelevant for the Second commonwealth, a reference to "conditions of Joshua" is simply one to common law. In Tosephta *Bava qamma* Chapter 8,

Joshua is not mentioned.

17  As animal feed.

18  Fenugreek stems are very thin and valuable; it is impossible to tear out weeds without also damaging some stems, which inflicts a loss on the owner of the field. If the owner harvests his field, he might use the weeds to tie bundles of fenugreek for retail sale.

19  Mishnah *Kilaim* 2:5.

20  To avoid two different kinds growing on the field, which would be sinful.

21  If the fenugreek seeds are sold not as spice but as seeds, they are not sold on the stalk and, therefore, nothing is needed to bind the stalks; the weeds are unwanted in every respect and leaving them is not trespassing the prohibition of *kilaim*.

22  Since he forbade taking weeds from fenugreek even if they caused *kilaim*.

23  No farmer likes weeds in his field. The removal of weeds from fenugreek is impossible as explained in Note 18.

24  In *Kilaim*: R. Zeriqan in the name of the House of R. Yannai.

25  In a Sabbaticall year; *Lev.* 25:5,11.

26  The last category is not mentioned in *Kilaim*.

27  The ploughed-under aftergrowth will act as fertilizer.

28  Since produce growing in a vineyard will condemn the entire vineyard (cf. Introduction to Tractate *Kilaim*.)

(15a line 22) תַּמָּן תַּנִּינָן. הַמּוֹצֵא מֵת בַּתְּחִילָה מוּשְׁכָּב כְּדַרְכּוֹ נוֹטְלוֹ וְאֶת תְּבוּסָתוֹ. אָמַר רַב חִסְדָּא. זֹאת אוֹמֶרֶת. מֵת מִצְוָה מוּתָּר לְפַנּוֹתוֹ. דְּתַנִּינָן נוֹטְלוֹ וְאֶת תְּבוּסָתוֹ. וְכַמָּה. רִבִּי שְׁמוּאֵל בְּשֵׁם רִבִּי יוֹנָתָן. עַד ג׳ אֶצְבָּעוֹת עַד מָקוֹם שֶׁהַמּוֹחַל יוֹרֵד. אָמַר רִבִּי זְעִירָא. לֹא מִסְתַּבְּרָה דְלֹא. מֵת מִצְוָה אָסוּר לְפַנּוֹתוֹ. שֶׁאִם אוֹמֵר אַתְּ. מוּתָּר לְפַנּוֹתוֹ. אֵילוּ הוֹאִיל וּמְאַבְּדִין כָּל־הַשָּׂדֶה לֹא כָּל־שֶׁכֵּן שֶׁמּוּתָּר לְפַנּוֹתוֹ. מִמַּה דִפְשִׁיטָא לְתַנָּא. מֵת מִצְוָה אָסוּר לְפַנּוֹתוֹ. לְפוּם כֵּן צְרִיךְ מַתְנִיתָא. אָמַר רַב חִסְדָּא. אַתְיָיא כְּמַאן דָּמַר. מֵת מִצְוָה מוּתָּר לְפַנּוֹתוֹ. אֲנִי אוֹמֵר. בִּשְׁבִילֵי הָרְשׁוּת נִקְבַּר. וְחָשׁ לוֹמַר שֶׁמָּא מֵת מִצְוָה הָיָה וְאֵין מֵיתֵי מִצְוָה מְצוּיִין.

[29]There, we have stated[30]: "If somebody find a corpse in original position, lying as usual[31], he takes him and his surroundings." Rav Ḥisda said, this implies that it is permitted to remove a corpse of obligation, since we have stated: "he takes him[32] and his surroundings." And how much? Rebbi Samuel[33] in the name of Rebbi Jonathan: Up to three finger-breadths, the place where fluid penetrates. Rebbi Zeʿira says, this is not reasonable; it is forbidden to remove a corpse of obligation. If you would say, it is permitted to remove him, since you are going to ruin the whole field[34], would it be permitted to remove him? Since it is obvious for the Tanna that it is forbidden to remove a corpse of obligation, therefore, one needs the Mishnah[35]. Rav Ḥisda said, it follows him who said, it is permitted to remove a corpse of obligation; I am saying that he was buried on a permitted path[36]. But whould one not have to worry that maybe he *was* a corpse of obligation? Corpses of obligation are infrequent[37].

29 A parallel but quite different treatment of this subject is in *Nazir* 9:3, Notes 119-134. The Babli (*Bava qamma* 81a) notes that one of Joshua's stipulations was that a "corpse of obligation", an unattended corpse found far from any organized settlement, must be buried on the spot it was found.

30 Mishnah *Nazir* 9:3.

31 With his limbs stretched out, not in a compressed position which would characterize the corpse as Gentile.

32 An unqualified statement.

33 He is R. Samuel ben Rav Naḥman.

34 By digging a rather deep hole in the middle of somebody else's field.

35 Since the Mishnah tells one to remove the corpse, it must be done with minimal disturbance of the field, which cannot refer to a corpse of obligation.

36 A "permitted path", also mentioned in the next condition imposed by Joshua, is a path through a

grain field between harvest and the early rains, when the field is empty and traditionally everybody has permission to walk through the field. R. Ḥisda now holds that the Mishnah does not prove anything about a corpse of obligation; it could have been that a person was buried there during the time of permission with the intention of removing it later to a cemetary, but that something then intervened; the people knowing about the corpse died, and the provisional grave was forgotten.

37   Practically they never happen; the Mishnah certainly is not formulated for them.

(15a line 32) וּמוֹטְלִין[38] בִּשְׁבִילֵי הָרְשׁוּת. מִשֶּׁתֵּיעָקֵר הַתְּבוּאָה עַד שֶׁתֵּרֵד רְבִיעָה שְׁנִיָּה. וְלוֹקְחִין נְטִיעוֹת מִכָּל־מָקוֹם חוּץ מִשֶּׁלְזַיִת וּמִשֶּׁלְגֶּפֶן. בְּזַיִת מִן הֶחָדָשׁ שֶׁבְּחָדָשׁ וּמִן הַיָּשָׁן שֶׁבְּיָשָׁן. אֲבָל אִם הָיָה עָשׂוּי כְּמִין טרגול אֲפִילוּ מִן הֶחָדָשׁ שֶׁבְּחָדָשׁ אָסוּר.

One walks on permitted paths[36] from the moment the harvest is cleared up to the second rainfall[39], and one may take shoots to plant from everywhere[40] except from olive trees and vines. From olives trees from the very young and the very old[41], but if it was like a *trgwl*[42] even from the very young it is forbidden.

38   Reading מְטַיְּלִין "one takes a walk".

39   When the ploughing season starts (Babli *Ta'anit* 6b).

40   To start new trees.

41   Which do not bear olives. Cutting a twig of such a tree does not cause a loss to the tree's owner.

42   One might read פְּרַגּוֹל "whip", Latin *flagellum*, for טרגול (Krauss). Possibly טרגול is forbidden as looking like something used at the Athenian festival of the *Thargelia*, at which first fruits and humans were sacrificed (E. G.)?

(15a line 35) רִבִּי תַנְחוּם דִּכְפַר גּוּן בְּשֵׁם רִבִּי לָעֱזָר בֵּירִבִּי יוֹסֵי. אַרְבָּעָה מְלַקְּטִין עֲשָׂבִין מִכָּל־מָקוֹם וּבִלְבַד שֶׁלֹּא יְשָׁרֵשׁוּ. וּפוֹנִים לַאֲחוֹרֵי הַגָּדֵר. רִבִּי לָעֱזָר בֵּירִבִּי יוֹסֵי בְּשֵׁם רִבִּי תַנְחוּם. עַד מָקוֹם שֶׁמִּתְעַטֵּשׁ וְאֵין קוֹלוֹ נִשְׁמַע. וְרוֹאִין בַּחוֹרְשִׁין. אֲפִילוּ שֵׁבֶט יְהוּדָה בְשֵׁבֶט נַפְתָּלִי. וְנוֹתְנִין לְנַפְתָּלִי מְלֹא חֶבֶל לִדְרוֹמוֹ שֶׁל יָם. שֶׁנֶּאֱמַר יָם וְדָרוֹם יְרָשָׁה. דִּבְרֵי רִבִּי יוֹסֵי הַגָּלִילִי. רִבִּי עֲקִיבָה אוֹמֵר. יָם זֶה יָם שֶׁל סַמְכוֹ. וְדָרוֹם זֶה יָם שֶׁל טְבֶרְיָה. וּמִסְתַּלְּקִין לְצַדְדִין. רַב יְהוּדָה בְשֵׁם רַב. אֲפִילוּ שָׂדֶה מְלֵיאָה כַרְכּוֹם. מַה. נוֹתֵן דָּמִים אוֹ לֹא. מִן מַה דָּמַר רַב יְהוּדָה. אֲפִילוּ מְלֵיאָה כּוּרְכּוֹם. הָדָא אֲמָרָה. נוֹתֵן דָּמִים. אָמַר רִבִּי לָא. מִכֵּיוָן דָּמַר רַב יְהוּדָה. אֲפִילוּ לְשָׂדֶה מְלֵיאָה כּוּרְכּוֹם. הָדָא אֲמָרָה. אֵין נוֹתֵן דָּמִים. וְאֵינוּ יָכוֹל לְרַחוֹק אֶת עַצְמוֹ יוֹתֵר מִדַּאי. נִישְׁמְעִינָהּ מֵהָדָא. מַעֲשֶׂה בְּרַבָּן גַּמְלִיאֵל וְרִבִּי יְהוֹשֻׁעַ שֶׁהָיוּ מְהַלְּכִין בַּדֶּרֶךְ [וְהָיוּ מִסְתַּלְּקִין מִפְּנֵי יְתֵידוֹת הַדְּרָכִים] וְרָאוּ אֶת יְהוּדָה בֶן פַּפּוֹס שֶׁהָיָה מִשְׁתַּקֵּעַ וּבָא כְנֶגְדָּן. אָמַר רַבָּן גַּמְלִיאֵל לְרִבִּי יְהוֹשֻׁעַ. מִי זֶה שֶׁמַּרְאֶה עַצְמוֹ בְּאֶצְבַּע. אָמַר לוֹ יְהוּדָה בֶן פַּפּוֹס הוּא שֶׁכָּל־מַעֲשָׂיו לְשׁוּם שָׁמַיִם.

[42]Rebbi Tanḥum from Kefar Gun[43] in the name of Rebbi Eleazar ben Rebbi Yose: Four. One collects grasses from everywhere on condition that one not uproot. And one relieves himself behind a wall.[44] Rebbi Eleazar ben Rebbi Yose in the name of Rebbi Tanḥum[45]: Up to a place where he lets wind and is not heard[46]. And one grazes in forests, even the tribe of Jehudah in the tribe of Naftali, and one gives Naftali an entire region South of the lake, as it is said, "lake and South of it he inherits,[47]" the words of Rebbi Yose the Galilean. Rebbi Aqiba says, "lake" is Lake Samokhonites[48], "and South" is Lake Tiberias. [49]And one may step to one side. Rav Jehudah in the name of Rav: Even into a field full of saffron. How? Does one have to pay or not? Since Rav Jehudah said, even into a field full of saffron, that means, one pays[50]. Rebbi La said, since Rav

Jehudah said, even into a field full of saffron, that means, one does not pay[51]. But one cannot deviate more than necessary. Let us hear from the following: [49]Rabban Gamliel and Rebbi Joshua were on the road [and stepped aside because of obstacles on the road][52] when they saw Jehudah ben Pappos, who was sinking, coming towards them. Rabban Gamliël said to Rebbi Joshua: Who is this one who makes an exhibition of himself? He answered: This is Jehudah ben Pappos, all whose deeds are done for Heaven's sake.

42  This is an alternative version of the conditions imposed by Joshua; cf. Note 16.

43  He is R. Tanḥum bar Ḥiyya from Kefar Agin (Umm Jumia S. of Lake Genezareth), a third generation Amora.

44  In an agricultural area, even if the field is sown up to the wall; Babli *Bava qamma* 81a.

45  The names here have to be switched; the last generation Tanna Eleazar ben R. Yose cannot speak in the name of the third generation Amora R. Tanḥum.

46  From the road.

47  *Deut.* 33:23; cf. Tosephta *Bava qamma* 8:18, *Sifry Deut.* 355, Babli *Bava qamma* 81b. Since the territory of Naftali was the North-East corner of the Land of Israel, Joshua could not have understood the verse to mean: "West and South he inherited." The location of Naftali therefore is validly discussed among the rules attributed to Joshua.

48  Lake Huleh.

49  To avoid obstacles on the road, mainly in the rainy season on an unimproved road: *Berakhot* 2:9, Notes 347-353.

50  Reading of L. E: "one does *not* pay." The next sentence shows that the reading of L is correct. The argument here is that saffron is so valuable that any stepping into the field causes considerable damage to the farmer; it is unconscionable that he should not be indemnified.

51  If it is a right in common law, it cannot be disputed or subjected to payment. He holds that a very valuable crop should never be planted adjacent to a public road without leaving an ample shoulder at the side of the road.

52  From E, supported by the text in *Berakhot*.

(15a line 49) רִבִּי שְׁמוּאֵל בְּשֵׁם רִבִּי יוֹנָתָן. הָרוֹצֶה לִבְנוֹת עִיר כַּתְּחִילָּה נוֹתְנִין לוֹ אַרְבָּעָה דְּרָכִים לְד' רוּחוֹת הָעוֹלָם. רִבִּי חֲנִינָה בָּעֵי קוֹמֵי רִבִּי מָנָא. מָה. מֵאַרְבַּע אַמּוֹת עַד שְׁמוֹנֶה אוֹ מִשְּׁמוֹנֶה עַד שֵׁשׁ עֶשְׂרֵה. אָמַר לוֹ. מִשְּׁמוֹנֶה עַד שֵׁשׁ עֶשְׂרֵה. כְּדֵי שֶׁיְּהֵא קָרוֹן הוֹלֵךְ וְקָרוֹן בָּא.

Rebbi Samuel in the name of Rebbi Jonathan: If one wants to build a new village, one gives him[53] four roads to the four directions of the compass. Rebbi Ḥanina asked before Rebbi Mana, how? From four cubits to eight[54] or from eight to sixteen[55]? He told him, from eight to sixteen so that one truck may leave and the other come.

| | |
|---|---|
| 53 The district administration is required to build roads to connect the village to the existing network of roads. | 54 A private road (Mishnah 6:7). 55 A highway. A road 16 cubits wide is the definition of "public domain" (Mishnah 6:7). |

(fol. 14d) **משנה ה:** הַקּוֹנֶה שְׁנֵי אִילָנוֹת בְּתוֹךְ שֶׁל חֲבֵירוֹ הֲרֵי זֶה לֹא קָנָה קַרְקַע. רִבִּי מֵאִיר אוֹמֵר קָנָה קַרְקַע. הִגְדִּילוּ לֹא יָשֻׁפָּה. וְהָעוֹלֶה מִן הַגֶּזַע שֶׁלּוֹ וּמִן הַשָּׁרָשִׁים שֶׁל בַּעַל הַקַּרְקַע וְאִם מֵתוּ אֵין לוֹ קַרְקַע.

**Mishnah 5**: He who buys two trees on another's property did not acquire the land[56]; Rebbi Meïr says, he acquired the land. If they grew, he need not cut them[57]. What grows from the stem is his, from the roots[58] is the owner's of the ground. If they died, he has no land[59].

**משנה ו:** קָנָה שְׁלֹשָׁה קָנָה קַרְקַע. הִגְדִּילוּ יְשַׁפֶּה. הָעוֹלֶה מִן הַשָּׁרָשִׁים שֶׁלּוֹ וְאִם מֵתוּ יֶשׁ לוֹ קַרְקַע.

**Mishnah 6**: If he bought three, he bought the land. If they grew, he has to cut them[60]. What grows from the roots is his. If they died, he has the land.

56   On which the trees stand.

57   Anything that grows from the tree, neither new shoots nor expanding crowns which extend beyond the range they had at the time of sale.

58   A new tree coming out of the earth.

59   Cf. Chapter 4, Note 79.

60   Anything which will grow into the original owner's land is no different from trees growing in one orchard and overhanging another owner's property (Halakhah 2:14).

(15a line 54) **הלכה ה:** הַקּוֹנֶה שְׁנֵי אִילָנוֹת בְּתוֹךְ שֶׁלַּחֲבֵירוֹ כול׳. (דִּבְרֵי) [דְּבֵית] רִבִּי יַנַּאי אֲמְרֵי. הָרוֹאֶה אֶת הַצֵּל זֶהוּ שׁוֹרֶשׁ. הָרוֹאֶה אֶת הַחַמָּה זֶהוּ גֶּזַע. רִבִּי חָמָא בַּר עוּקְבָה בְּשֵׁם רִבִּי יוֹסֵי. הָעוֹלֶה מִשָּׁרָשָׁיו וּמִגִּזְעוֹ זֶהוּ שׁוֹרֶשׁ. מִגִּזְעוֹ וְלֹא מִשָּׁרָשָׁיו זֶהוּ אִילָן. אָמַר רִבִּי יוֹחָנָן. הַקּוֹנֶה שְׁלֹשָׁה אִילָנוֹת קָנָה קַרְקַע שֶׁבֵּינֵיהֶן וְתַחְתֵּיהֶן וְחוּצָה לָהֶן כִּמְלוֹא אוּרָה וְסַלּוֹ. אָמַר רִבִּי לָעְזָר וְדֶרֶךְ אֵין לוֹ וּמְלוֹא אוּרָה וְסַלּוֹ יֵשׁ לוֹ חוּצָה לוֹ.

**Halakhah 5**: "He who buys two trees on another's property," etc. (The words)[61] [In the House of][62] Rebbi Yannai they said, what sees the shadow is root, what sees the sun is stem[63]. Rebbi Hama bar Uqba in the name of Rebbi Yose: What grows from its roots and its stem is root, from its stem but not its roots is tree[64].

Rebbi Johanan said[65], he who buys three trees buys the land in between them, under them, and outside of them the width of the harvester and his bag[66]. Rebbi Eleazar said, while he has no access[67], he has the width of the harvester and his bag outside of them.

61   Reading of L.
62   Reading of E.
63   Babli 82a, in the name of R. Johanan. The question is, what is meant by "growth from the roots"? The entire tree grows from the roots. On

the other hand, unless lifted by man, most roots will feed just one stem. Where does one draw the line between stem and roots at the bottom of the stem?

64   Anything grown as a branch is the buyer's; anything else is the landlord's.

65   Babli 82a. It is understood that this only applies to trees which qualify for an orchard; i. e. that the distance between two trees be no larger than $\sqrt{250} = 15.81$ cubits (cf. *Ševi'it* 1:2, Note 18).

66   Four cubits around each tree (Chapter 2, Note 101; *Ševi'it* 1:2 Note 19)

67   Unless the trees are directly accessible from the road, buying the trees does not buy access. (But the person who only buys two trees rents the land and has free access as a renter; Babli 82b.)

(fol. 14d) **משנה ז:** הַמּוֹכֵר אֶת הָרֹאשׁ בִּבְהֵמָה גַּסָּה לֹא מָכַר אֶת הָרַגְלַיִם מָכַר אֶת הָרַגְלַיִם לֹא מָכַר אֶת הָרֹאשׁ. מָכַר אֶת הַקָּנֶה לֹא מָכַר אֶת הַכָּבֵד מָכַר אֶת הַכָּבֵד לֹא מָכַר אֶת הַקָּנֶה. אֲבָל בְּדַקָּה מָכַר אֶת הָרֹאשׁ מָכַר אֶת הָרַגְלַיִם מָכַר אֶת הָרַגְלַיִם לֹא מָכַר אֶת הָרֹאשׁ. מָכַר אֶת הַקָּנֶה מָכַר אֶת הַכָּבֵד מָכַר אֶת הַכָּבֵד לֹא מָכַר אֶת הַקָּנֶה.

**Mishnah 7:** He who sells the head of a large animal[68] did not sell the feet; if he sold the feet he did not sell the head. If he sold the windpipe[69] he did not sell the liver; if he sold the liver he did not sell the windpipe. But for a small animal[70], if he sold the head he sold the feet[71]; if he sold the feet he did not sell the head[72]. If he sold the windpipe he sold the liver; if he sold the liver he did not sell the windpipe.

68   Cattle.

69   With the lungs attached. {The use of קָנֶה "stick" for "reed, windpipe" might be induced by Latin *canalis animae* "windpipe" (Pliny) (E. G.)}

70   Sheep or goats.

71 Since the feet do not fetch much, it was customary to give them as a bonus to the buyer of the head. The upper part of the right leg had to be given to the Cohen in any case (*Deut.* 18:3).

72 The cheaper item is a gratuity for the more expensive one but not vice-versa.

(15a line 60) **הלכה ז**: הַמּוֹכֵר אֶת הָרֹאשׁ בִּבְהֵמָה גַסָּה כול'. רִבִּי יִצְחָק שָׁאַל. מָכַר חֲצִי הָרֹאשׁ מָכַר חֲצִי רַגְלַיִם. מָכַר חֲצִי קָנֶה מָכַר חֲצִי כָבֵד. [מָכַר חֲצִי הַכָּבֵד] מָכַר חֲצִי קָנֶה. נִישְׁמְעִינָהּ מֵהָדָא. מָכַר לוֹ יָד כְּמוֹת שֶׁהִיא רֹאשׁ כְּמוֹת שֶׁהוּא בְּנֵי מֵעַיִם כְּמוֹת שֶׁהֵן. נוֹתְנָן לַכֹּהֵן וְאֵינוֹ מְנַכֶּה לוֹ מִן הַדָּמִים. לְקָחָן בְּמִשְׁקָל נוֹתְנָן לַכֹּהֵן וּמְנַכֶּה לוֹ מִן הַדָּמִים.

**Halakhah 7**: "He who sells the head of a large animal," etc. Rebbi Isaac asked: If he sold half of the head, did he sell half of the legs? If he sold half of the windpipe, did he sell half of the liver? [If he sold half of the liver,]73 did he sell half of the windpipe? Let us hear from the following73: "If he sold him the entire foot, the entire head, the entire intestines, he gives to the Cohen and does not deduct from the price74. If he bought by weight, he gives to the Cohen and deducts from the price.75"

73 Reading of E, missing in L, required by the context.

74 Tosephta *Hulin* 9:8-9; Babli *Hulin* 132a.

75 If parts of the animal were separately sold by the piece, not by weight, the price is a lump sum for what is usable for the buyer. Therefore, if some of the obligatory gifts to the Cohen (the jaw, the upper leg, and the first stomach) were parts of the animal sold, the price was never intended to cover these gifts; nothing can be deducted.

76 If the meat is sold by weight, the parts given to the Cohen cannot be weighed. Therefore, the answer to R. Isaac's question is that it all depends; if the sale was by the piece, the additions are included, if by weight, they are excluded.

**משנה ח:** אַרְבַּע מִדּוֹת בַּמּוֹכְרִים. מָכַר לוֹ חִטִּים יָפוֹת וְנִמְצְאוּ רָעוֹת (fol. 14d) הַלּוֹקֵחַ יָכוֹל לַחֲזוֹר בּוֹ. רָעוֹת וְנִמְצְאוּ יָפוֹת הַמּוֹכֵר יָכוֹל לַחֲזוֹר בּוֹ. רָעוֹת וְנִמְצְאוּ רָעוֹת יָפוֹת וְנִמְצְאוּ יָפוֹת אֵין אֶחָד מֵהֶן יָכוֹל לַחֲזוֹר בּוֹ. שְׁחַמְתִּית וְנִמְצֵאת לְבָנָה לְבָנָה וְנִמְצֵאת שְׁחַמְתִּית עֵצִים שֶׁלְזַיִת וְנִמְצְאוּ שֶׁלְשִׁיקְמָה שֶׁלְשִׁיקְמָה וְנִמְצְאוּ שֶׁלְזַיִת יַיִן וְנִמְצָא חוֹמֶץ חוֹמֶץ וְנִמְצָא יַיִן שְׁנֵיהֶן יְכוֹלִין לַחֲזוֹר בָּהֶן.

**Mishnah 8**: Four situations for sellers. If one contracted to sell high quality wheat and it turned out to be low quality, the buyer may annul the contract. Low quality and it turned out to be high quality, the seller may annul the contract. Low quality and it turned out to be low quality, high quality and it turned out to be high quality, neither of them may annul the contract[77]. Brown grain and it turned out to be white grain, white grain and it turned out to be brown grain[78], olive wood and it turned out to be sycamore wood, sycamore wood and it turned out to be olive wood[79], wine and it turned out to be vinegar, vinegar and it turned out to be wine, either of them may annul the contract.

**משנה ט**: הַמּוֹכֵר פֵּירוֹת לַחֲבֵירוֹ מָשַׁךְ וְלֹא מָדַד קָנָה מָדַד וְלֹא מָשַׁךְ לֹא קָנָה. אִם הָיָה פִּיקֵחַ שׂוֹכֵר אֶת מְקוֹמָן. הַלּוֹקֵחַ פִּשְׁתָּן מֵחֲבֵירוֹ הֲרֵי זֶה לֹא קָנָה עַד שֶׁיְּטַלְטְלֶנּוּ מִמָּקוֹם לְמָקוֹם וְאִם הָיָה בִּמְחוּבָּר לַקַּרְקַע וְתָלַשׁ כָּל־שֶׁהוּא קָנָה.

**Mishnah 9**: If somebody sold produce to another and this one moved it without measuring, he took possession[80]. If he was measuring without moving, he did not take possession. If he is intelligent, he rents its place[81]. If somebody buys flax from another he he did not take possession until he moved it from place to place;[82] but if it still was standing on the ground and he plucked anything, he took possession.

**משנה י**: הַמּוֹכֵר יַיִן וְשֶׁמֶן לַחֲבֵירוֹ וְהוּקְרוּ אוֹ שֶׁהוּזְלוּ אִם עַד שֶׁלֹא נִתְמַלֵאת הַמִּידָה לַמּוֹכֵר מִשֶׁנִתְמַלֵאת הַמִּידָה לַלּוֹקֵחַ. וְאִם הָיָה סַרְסוּר בֵּינֵיהֶן נִשְׁבְּרָה הֶחָבִית נִשְׁבְּרָה לַסִּרְסוּר. חַיָב לְהַטִיף לוֹ שָׁלֹשׁ טִיפִין. הִרְכִּינָה וּמִיצַת הֲרֵי זֶה שֶׁל מוֹכֵר. וְהַחֶנְוָנִי אֵינוֹ חַיָב לְהַטִיף לוֹ שָׁלֹשׁ טִיפִין. רבִּי יְהוּדָה אוֹמֵר לֵילֵי שַׁבָּת עִם חֲשֵׁיכָה פָּטוּר.

**Mishnah 10**: If somebody sold wine or oil to another[83] and it rose or fell in price, if it was before the measure was filled it is for the seller, after the measure was filled for the buyer. If a broker was involved[84] and the amphora broke, it broke for the broker. He[85] is obligated to let it drip three drops. If he tilted and emptied it, [the remainder] is for the seller. The grocer does not have to let it drip three drops[86]. Rebbi Jehudah says, Friday evenings close to sundown he is not liable[87].

77  If the seller is unable to fill the contract as written, the party which would be disadvantaged can annul the contract without penalty or censure.

78  White grain is better quality than brown; the former is human food, the latter animal feed. If the delivery does not satisfy the buter's needs, he need not accept delivery.

79  Olive wood is more valuable than sycamore wood, but olive wood is for furniture and sycamore wood for building.

80  Moving merchandise after taking title always gives possession, Mishnah *Qiddušin* 1:5; *Bava meṣia'* 4:2.

81  If he is worried whether the seller may annul the sale, since real estate always conveys possession of what was acquired by its owner, Mishnah *Qiddušin* 1:5.

82  If he starts moving it, i. e., lifting it.

83  And the contract specified that it was sold at the market price on delivery.

84  Who transports the amphora from the seller to the buyer. A standard contract implies delivery f.o.b.

85  If less than an entire barrel is sold, the seller has to empty the measuring vessel into the buyer's vessel and after the flow has stopped has to wait until three single drops drip into

the buyer's vessel. The fluid which then still clings to the seller's vessel remains his property.

86 If he has many clients and the time spent in waiting for the three drops would seriously interfere with his business. (Mishnah *Yom Tov* 3:8 reports that a grocer who was a holy man never emptied measuring cups into his client's vessel but gave them his measuring vessel so they could pour themselves and take all the time to empty the vessel to the last drop.)

87 The retail grocer is required to wait until three drops drip exept for Fridays late in the afternoon when everybody is trying to get home quickly for the Sabbath.

(15a line 65) **הלכה ח:** אַרְבַּע מִדּוֹת בַּמּוֹכְרִים כול'. וְהֵיכִי. אִם בְּשֶׁהָיְתָה הַמִּידָה לַמּוֹכֵר חֲזָקָה לַמּוֹכֵר. אִם הָיְתָה לַלּוֹקֵחַ חֲזָקָה לַלּוֹקֵחַ. רַבִּי יְהוּדָה בְּשֵׁם שְׁמוּאֵל רַבִּי לָא בְּשֵׁם רַבִּי יְהוּדָה בְּרִיבִּי. כֵּינִי מַתְנִיתָא. בְּשֶׁהָיְתָה הַמִּידָה לְאָדָם אַחֵר. תַּנֵּי. רַבִּי יוּדָה אוֹמֵר. וּלֵילֵי שַׁבָּת עִם חֲשֵׁיכָה פָּטוּר מִפְּנֵי שֶׁהוּא רְשׁוּת. וַחֲכָמִים אוֹמְרִים. בֵּין כָּךְ וּבֵין כָּךְ חַיָּיב. מַאי טַעֲמָא אָמַר רַבִּי יוּדָן. אִם שָׂכִיר הוּא בָּא בִּשְׂכָרוֹ.

**Halakhah 8**: "Four situations for sellers.," etc. How is this? If the measuring vessel belonged to the seller, he has the property rights, if to the buyer, he has the property rights[88]. Rav[89] Jehudah in the name of Samuel, Rebbi La[90] in the name of the Great Rebbi Jehudah, so is the Mishnah: If the measuring vessel belonged to a third person.

It was stated: Rebbi Jehudah says, Friday evenings close to sundown he is not liable since he has permission, but the Sages say, in any case he is liable[91]. What is the reason for what Rebbi Jehudah said? "If he is hired, it is paid for by his wages.[92]"

88 This refers to Mishnah 10. Why should it make any difference when the measuring vessel was full? As long as the fluid is in the seller's vessel it is not delivered.

89 This has to be read here.

90 In the Babli, 97a, he identifies the third person as the broker. The passage is missing in E.

91 This *baraita* contradicts the Mishnah which frees the retail grocer from the obligation to wait for three drops.

92 *Ex.* 22:14. The quote has nothing to do with the preceding *baraita* but refers to the sentence in the Mishnah which holds the broker responsible for the delivery; in Tosephta 5:2 this is R. Jehudah's opinion. The verse quoted states that if a hired animal dies, the fee paid for it represents indemnification. The fee paid to the broker is indemnification for the risk which he assumes. Pseudo-Jonathan translates the verse: "If he works for a fee, his loss is covered by his fee."

(fol. 14d) **משנה יא:** הַשּׁוֹלֵחַ אֶת בְּנוֹ אֵצֶל חֶנְוָונִי וּמָדַד לוֹ בְּאִיסָר שֶׁמֶן וְנָתַן לוֹ אֶת הָאִיסָר שָׁבַר אֶת הַצְּלוֹחִית וְאִיבֵּד אֶת הָאִיסָר הַחֶנְוָונִי חַיָּיב. רִבִּי יְהוּדָה פּוֹטֵר שֶׁעַל מְנָת כֵּן שִׁילְחוֹ. וּמוֹדִים חֲכָמִים לְרִבִּי יְהוּדָה בִּזְמָן שֶׁהַצְּלוֹחִית בְּיַד הַתִּינוֹק וּמָדַד הַחֶנְוָונִי לְתוֹכָהּ הַחֶנְוָונִי פָּטוּר.

**Mishnah 11**: Somebody sent his son to a grocer who measured him oil for an *assarius* and he gave him the *assarius*; if he[93] broke the flask and lost the *assarius*[94], the grocer is liable. Rebbi Jehudah holds him not liable since for that he sent him[95]. The Sages agree with Rebbi Jehudah that if the flask was in the child's hand and the grocer measured into the flask, the grocer is not liable[96].

**משנה יב:** הַסִּיטוֹן מְקַנֵּחַ מִידּוֹתָיו אַחַת לִשְׁלֹשִׁים יוֹם וּבַעַל הַבַּיִת לִשְׁנֵים עָשָׂר חֹדֶשׁ. רַבָּן שִׁמְעוֹן בֶּן גַּמְלִיאֵל אוֹמֵר חִילּוּף הַדְּבָרִים. הַחֶנְוָונִי מְקַנֵּחַ מִידּוֹתָיו פַּעֲמַיִם בַּשַּׁבָּת וּמְמַחֶה מִשְׁקְלוֹתָיו פַּעַם אַחַת בַּשַּׁבָּת וּמְקַנֵּחַ מֹאזְנַיִם עַל כָּל־מִשְׁקָל וּמִשְׁקָל.

**Mishnah 12**: The wolesaler cleans his measuring vessels once every thirty days, the householder every twelve months. Rabban Simeon ben Gamliel says, it is the other way around[97]. The retail grocer cleans his measuring vessels twice a week, wipes his weights clean once a week, and cleans his scales after each weighing.

**משנה יג**: אָמַר רַבָּן שִׁמְעוֹן בֶּן גַּמְלִיאֵל בַּמֶּה דְבָרִים אֲמוּרִים. בַּלַּח אֲבָל בַּיָּבֵשׁ אֵינוֹ צָרִיךְ. וְחַיָּיב לְהַכְרִיעַ לוֹ טֶפַח. הָיָה שׁוֹקֵל לוֹ עַיִן בְּעַיִן נוֹתֵן לוֹ גֵּירוּמִים אֶחָד לַעֲשָׂרָה בַּלַּח וְאֶחָד לְעֶשְׂרִים בַּיָּבֵשׁ.

**Mishnah 13**: Rabban Simeon ben Gamliel said, when has this been said? For fluids, but for dry matter it is not necessary; he has to let [the scales] bend down a handbreadth[98]. If he weighed strictly by eyesight[99] he has to give him surplus, one tenth for fluids and one twentieth for dry products[100].

93    The child. The majority hold that if a child is sent to the grocer, the sender only intends to give the grocer a message that he should deliver the goods to the sender's house, not give them to the child.

94    It is difficult to see where the coin comes in. Rashbam reports that his grandfather Rashi changed the text of the Mishnah to the effect that the child was sent with a *dupondius*, to get oil for an *assarius* and an *assarius* in change. But the ms. evidence and Maimonides's text do not support the emendation.

95    In the Tosephta, 5:2, R. Jehudah explains that anybody sending money and a breakable vessel by a child expects the money to be lost and the vessel broken.

96    If he never took the vessel into his hand, he never became responsible.

97    He holds that the wholesaler uses his measuring vessels all the time; nothing will stick and, since each vessel is always used for the same commodity, no customer is disadvantaged. But the householder who only sells sporadically must clean his vessels lest some leftover fluid clot and diminish the volume.

98    The scales holding the

merchandise have to be visibly lower than the weights.

99   The lever of the balance being exactly parallel to the ground.

100   Which method is chosen will depend on local usage.

(15a line 71) **הלכה יא:** הַשׁוֹלֵחַ אֶת בְּנוֹ אֵצֶל חֶנְוָנִי כול'. אָמַר רִבִּי בָּא בַּר מָמָל. בָּעֲשִׂירוֹת חַיָּיב לְהַכְרִיעַ לוֹ טֶפַח. כְּתִיב מֹאזְנֵי צֶדֶק אַבְנֵי צֶדֶק. מִיכָּן אָמְרוּ חֲכָמִים. כָּל־מִצְוָה שֶׁמַּתַּן שְׂכָרָהּ בְּצִידָהּ אֵין בֵּית דִּין מוּזְהָרִין עָלֶיהָ. יִהְיֶה לָךְ. מְנֵה לָךְ אנגרמוס עַל כָּךְ. וְתֵימַר הָכֵין. אָמַר רִבִּי בּוּן בַּר חִייָה. כֵּינִי מַתְנִיתָא. כָּל־מִצְוָה שֶׁמַּתַּן שְׂכָרָהּ בְּצִידָהּ אֵין בֵּית דִּין נֶעֱנָשִׁין עָלֶיהָ. רַב מַנְיֵיהּ רֵישׁ גָּלוּתָא אנגרמוס וַהֲוָה מָחֵי עַל מְכִילָתָא וְלָא עַל שִׁיעוּרַיָּא. חֲבָשֵׁיהּ רֵישׁ גָּלוּתָא. עָאַל רַב קַרְנָא גַּבֵּיהּ. אָמַר לֵיהּ. אנגרמוס שֶׁאָמְרוּ לַמִּידוֹת וְלֹא לַשִּׁיעוּרִין. אָמַר לֵיהּ. וְהָא תַנִּית. אנגרמוס לַמִּידוֹת וְלַשִּׁיעוּרִין. אָמַר לֵיהּ. פּוּק אֱמוֹר לוֹן. אנגרמוס שֶׁאָמְרוּ לַמִּידוֹת וְלֹא לַשִּׁיעוּרִין. נְפַק וְאָמַר לוֹן. בַּר נָשׁ דְּתַנָּא כְּבָשָׁה דָא הִינוּ[110] חֲבָשִׁין לֵיהּ.

**Halakhah 11:** "Somebody sent his son to a grocer," etc. Rebbi Abba bar Mamal said, for the tenths he has to let bend down a handbreadth[101].

It is written[102]: "Fair scales, fair weights." From here[103] the Sages said that any commandment whose reward is noted, the court is not warned about. "You shall have,[104]" appoint market overseers[105] over this[106]. Rebbi Abun bar Ḥiyya said, so is the *baraita*: Any commandment whose reward is noted the court is not punished about.

Rav was appointed market overseer by the Head of the Diaspora[107]; he intervened about measuring vessels but not prices[108]. The Head of the Diaspora jailed him. Rav Qarna went to see him and said, the market overseer about whom they spoke was for measures but not prices. He answered, but you had stated: the market overseer is for both measures and prices[109]. He said to him, go out and tell them, the market overseer is for measures but not prices. He went out and said to them, a person who teaches hidden things they send to jail!

101 In the Babli, 88b, R. Abba bar Mamal explains that the bending down of the scales should correspond to $1/10$ of a pound for every 10 pounds, or 1%.

102 Lev. 19:36.

103 It is not from here but from Deut. 25:15: "A full and fair weightstone you shall have, a full and fair *ephah* you shall have, that your days be prolonged on the land which the Eternal, your God, gives to you."

104 Deut. 25:15; in Lev. 19:36 the plural is used, יִהְיֶה לָכֶם. It is a generally accepted talmudic principle of interpretation that a commandment formulated in the plural is addressed to every individual. In Lev. 19:36, the verse ends: I am the Eternal, your God, I Who took you out from the land of Egypt, on which *Sifra Qedošim Pereq* 8(10) notes: "On condition that you accept the obligation of fair measures, for every person who accepts the obligation of fair measures confirms the Exodus, and everyone who violates the obligation of fair measures negates the Exodus." But commandments in the singular are considered as commandments in the collective, addressed to the community.

105 Greek ἀγορανόμος. In *Demay* 2:1 (23c l. 26, Note 22) the transliteration is אגורנימוס.

106 Babli 89a, *Sifry Deut.* 294. This inference clearly contradicts the prior statement that oversight over measures is not a public duty.

107 Over Jewish markets in Babylonia.

108 In the Roman Empire, price control was introduced by Diocletian. But Rav was trained in Galilee under the Severans, almost a century before Diocletian. In *Demay* also, control of prices is described as an anomaly.

109 In the Babli, 89a, it is reported that Qarna taught this against the explicit instructions of Samuel; and that in consequence a horn grew on his forehead for which he was called Qarna.

110 The *editio princeps* mistakenly reads דתנא כבשה דאהינו "who stated about preserved palm shoots".

(fol. 15a) **משנה יד:** מָקוֹם שֶׁנָּהֲגוּ לָמוֹד בְּדַקָּה לֹא יָמוֹד בְּגַסָּה. בְּגַסָּה לֹא יָמוֹד בְּדַקָּה. לְמָחוֹק לֹא יִגְדּוֹשׁ. לִגְדּוֹשׁ לֹא יִמְחוֹק.

**Mishnah 14**: At a place where one is used to small measures he should not use large ones, to large measures he should not use small ones, to level one must not heap, to heap one must not level.

(15b line 6) **הלכה יד:** מָקוֹם שֶׁנָּהֲגוּ לָמוֹד בְּדַקָּה לֹא יָמוֹד בְּגַסָּה. בְּגַסָּה לֹא יָמוֹד בְּדַקָּה. לְמָחוֹק לֹא יִגְדּוֹשׁ. לִגְדּוֹשׁ לֹא יִמְחוֹק.

**Halakhah 14**: At a place where one is used to small measures he should not use large ones, to large measures he should not use small ones, to level one must not heap, to heap one must not level.

המוכר פירות פרק ששי

(fol. 15b) **משנה א**: הַמּוֹכֵר פֵּירוֹת לַחֲבֵירוֹ וְלֹא צִימֵּיחוּ וַאֲפִילוּ זֶרַע פִּשְׁתָּן אֵינוֹ חַיָּיב בְּאַחֲרָיוּתָן. רַבָּן שִׁמְעוֹן בֶּן גַּמְלִיאֵל אוֹמֵר זֵרְעוֹנֵי גִינָה שֶׁאֵינָן נֶאֱכָלִין חַיָּיב בְּאַחֲרָיוּתָן. הַמּוֹכֵר פֵּירוֹת לַחֲבֵירוֹ הֲרֵי זֶה מְקַבֵּל עָלָיו רוֹבַע טִינוֹפֶת לַסְּעָה. תְּאֵינִים מְקַבֵּל עָלָיו עֶשֶׂר מְתוּלָעוֹת לַמֵּאָה. מַרְתֵּף שֶׁל יַיִן מְקַבֵּל עָלָיו עֶשֶׂר קוֹסְסוֹת לַמֵּאָה. קַנְקַנִּים בַּשָּׁרוֹן מְקַבֵּל עָלָיו עֶשֶׂר פִּיטַסָאוֹת לַמֵּאָה.

**Mishnah 1**: If somebody sells grain to another and it did not sprout, or even flax seed, he is not responsible for it[1]. Rabban Simeon ben Gamliel said, for garden seeds which are not edible he is responsible[2]. If somebody sells produce[3] to another he has to accept a quarter [*qab*] of chaff per *se'ah*; for figs he has to accept ten worm-bitten ones per hundred; with a wine cellar he has to accept ten sour ones per hundred; with vessels in the Sharon[4] he has to accept ten *pitassaot*[4*] per hundred.

**משנה ב**: הַמּוֹכֵר יַיִן לַחֲבֵירוֹ וְהֶחֱמִיץ אֵינוֹ חַיָּיב בַּאֲחֲרָיוּתוֹ וְאִם יָדוּעַ שֶׁיֵּינוֹ מַחֲמִיץ הֲרֵי זֶה מֶקַח טָעוּת. אִם אָמַר לוֹ יַיִן מְבוּשָּׂם אֲנִי מוֹכֵר לָךְ חַיָּיב לְהַעֲמִיד לוֹ עַד הָעֲצֶרֶת. יָשָׁן מִשֶּׁל אֶשְׁתְּקַד. מְיוּשָּׁן מִשֶּׁל שָׁלֹשׁ שָׁנִים.

**Mishnah 2**: If somebody sells wine to another and it turned into vinegar, he is not responsible for it. But if it was known that his wine turns into vinegar, it is a buy in error[5]. If he told him, I am selling you spice wine, it has to keep until Pentecost[6]. "Old" is from the year before, "aged" from three years[7].

1 Since he may say that he sold it as food.

2 The prior argument does not apply.

3 Wholesale.

4 Local product. *Sharon* does not necessarily refer to the Palestinian plain, Latin *sarannus* may mean "Tyrian" or "Karthaginean".

4* In several Tosephtot (*Kelim Bava qamma* 4:16, *Ahilut* 10:3,15:11) פיטס means πίθος, "wine barrel, large vessel." This is the equivalent of Hebrew קַנְקַן; it is not relevant for the Mishnah.

Rabbenu Hananel explains the word פיטסאות here as a noun, קנקנים דשחלי "junk barrels". Since the Yerushalmi does not explain the Mishnah, one must have recourse to the Babylonian sources. Tosephta 6:4 supports Rabbenu Hananel's explanation of פיטסאות as "junk": "If somebody buys amphoras and they turn out to be פיטסות and broke, the seller has to return the price of the amphoras but not the value of the wine." The Babli, 97b, is somewhat ambiguous: תאנא פיטסות נאות ומגופרות "It was stated: *pitassot* half-baked and sulphured." It is not clear whether פיטסות is a noun or an adjective. An addition in the Munich ms. of the Babli, referred to by Rashbam, explains that instead of being fired in a kiln, the inner walls of the clay vessel were lined with sulphur, which then was lit, burned off, and gave the impression of a finished vessel while it was only superficially baked.

The three sources of Tosephta 6:3 have different texts:

Vienna ms.: קנקנים מקבל עליו עשר נאות פיטסות מגופרות למאה

Erfurt ms.: למאה קנקנים מקבל עליו עשר פוטסות נאות מגופרות

Editio princeps: קנקנים מקבל עליו עשר נאות פינוסות פוניסות מגופרות למאה

If the ms. before the Venice printer was none too clear, it was easy to misread ט as נו; therefore the *editio princeps* may count as confirmation of the Vienna text which clearly defines פיטסות as an adjective: "Barrels, he has to accept ten half-baked, *pytswt*, sulphured per hundred." S. Lieberman (*Tosefta kiFshutah Bava batra* p. 396) explains פיטסאות as Greek πισσωταί "pitched". Since Tosephta *Abodah zarah* 8:1 uses standard Hebrew זפות for "pitched", there is no reason why a Greek word should be used here. A clay vessel used for storage of fluids must be waterproofed; good vessels also are pitched. Therefore, פיטס is a word of unknown etymology, an adjective which denotes inferior quality which upon close inspection could have been detected. {But also cf. Greek ἐπιτάσσω "put upon, enjoin;

place beside, order"; ἐπίταξις "injunction, assessment". An *imposition* of 10% amphoras of lesser quality? (E. G.)]

5   The seller would have had to warn the buyer that the wine was only for immediate use; if he failed to do so, the buyer might return the merchandise for a full refund.

6   The wine has to keep from the harvest in the fall to the next Pentecost.

7   These are common trade terms.

(15b line 59) **הלכה א:** הַמּוֹכֵר פֵּירוֹת לַחֲבֵירוֹ כול׳. תַּנֵּי. הַמּוֹכֵר פֵּירוֹת לַחֲבֵירוֹ וְלֹא צִימֵחוּ אֲפִילוּ זֶרַע פִּשְׁתָּן אֵינוֹ חַיָּיב בְּאַחֲרָיוּתוֹ. וְאִם הִתְנָה עִמּוֹ מִתְּחִילַת הַזֶּרַע חַיָּיב בְּאַחֲרָיוּתוֹ. מָהוּ נוֹתֵן לוֹ. דְּמֵי זַרְעוֹ. וְיֵשׁ אוֹמְרִים. נוֹתֵן לוֹ דְּמֵי יְצִיאוֹתָיו.

**Halakhah 1**: "If somebody sells grain to another," etc. It was stated[8]: "If somebody sells grain to another and it did not sprout, even flax seed, he is not responsible for it. But if he made it conditional from the start as seeds[9], he is liable. What does he pay him? The value of the seeds. Some say, he gives him his expenses[10]."

8   Tosephta *Bava meṣia'* 9:16.

9   If the grain was sold as seed grain, rather than food.

10   All expenses to prepare the field for sowing; Babli *Bava batra* 93b.

(15b line 62) הָכָא מְקַבֵּל עָלָיו. בְּרַם תַּמָּן יְמָעֵט. הָכָא וּבִלְבַד טְנוּפָה. בְּרַם תַּמָּן מִין. הָכָא וּבִלְבַד כְּדֶרֶךְ מַגְּעוֹ. בְּרַם תַּמָּן וּבִלְבַד כְּדֶרֶךְ מַשּׂוֹאוֹ. הָכָא רִבִּי שִׁמְעוֹן מוֹדֶה. בְּרַם תַּמָּן רִבִּי שִׁמְעוֹן אוֹמֵר. שְׁנֵי מִינִין הֵן וְאֵין מִצְטָרְפִין.

Here, he has to accept it, but there[11] it should be diminished. Here only chaff, but there another kind. Here only the way he touched it, but there only the way he carried it[12]. Here Rebbi Simeon agrees, but there, Rebbi Simeon says they are two kinds and do not count together[13].

11  Mishnah *Kilaim* 2:1. While in commercial transactions $1/24$ of contamination is permitted and only more than $1/24$ is cause for rejection, for seed grain a contamination with $1/24$ of another kind of seeds must be rejected and only less than $1/24$ is acceptable.

12  This refers to the discussion in *Kilaim* 2:1, Notes 20-24, that the contamination with other seeds occurs during transport of the harvest to storage. But the chaff found in grain comes from the winnowing process, when the grain is touched during threshing.

13  In commercial transactions, anything which is not of the kind contracted for is a contamination; they all add together up to the statutory limit of $1/24$. But in matters of illicit mixing of seeds, R. Simeon counts each kind as a separate contamination.

(15b line 65) רִבִּי חִייָה בַּר בָּא שָׁאַל. סְאָה חִיטִּין שֶׁנָּפְלָה לְתוֹךְ מֵאָה שֶׁלִּשְׂעוֹרִין. כֹּהֵן וְיִשְׂרָאֵל מָהוּ שֶׁיְּחַלְּקוּ אֶת הַשֶּׁבַח. רִבִּי יִצְחָק בַּר טְבֶלַיי שָׁאַל. סְאָה תְּרוּמָה שֶׁנָּפְלָה לְתוֹךְ מֵאָה שֶׁלְּחוּלִּין. מוֹכֵר וְלוֹקֵחַ מָהוּ שֶׁיְּחַלְּקוּ אֶת הַשְּׁאָר. אָמַר רִבִּי בּוּן בַּר חִייָה. נִישְׁמְעִינָהּ מֵהָדָא. הַבּוֹרֵר צְרוֹרוֹת מִתּוֹךְ כֵּירָיו שֶׁלַּחֲבֵירוֹ חַייָב לִשְׁפּוֹת לוֹ. רִבִּי בּוּן בַּר כַּהֲנָא אָמַר. בְּאוֹמֵר. צְבוֹר וְאֶקְנֶה. אֲבָל אִם הָיוּ צְבוּרִין מִשָּׁעָה רִאשׁוֹנָה לֹא בְדָא.

Rebbi Hiyya bar Abba asked: One *se'ah* of wheat which fell into one hundred of barley, do the Cohen and the Israel split the increase in value? Rebbi Isaac bar Tebelai asked: One *se'ah* of heave which fell into one hundred of profane grain, do the seller and the buyer split the remainder[14]? Rebbi Abun bar Hiyya said, let us hear from the following[15]: He who takes out impurities from his neighbor's heap has to give him good grain in their stead.

Rebbi Abun bar Cahana said, if he said, collect and acquire[16]. But if it was collected from the start, this does not apply[17].

14  It seems that in the first question, one has to read "seller and buyer" and in the second "Cohen and Israel". The first question is about a sale of grain. If some of the more valuable wheat fell into a large

quantity of barley, the value of the barley is increased. Who benefits from that increase? It naturally is balanced by the loss incurred by the owner of the wheat which now is contaminated with barley.

The second question is about heave, which is forbidden to everybody except a Cohen in a state of purity. If one part of heave falls into more than 100 parts of profane grain, everything becomes profane but 1 part of the profane mixture has to be separated and given to a Cohen (Mishnah *Terumot* 4:8). But if there were only 100 parts it is *dema'* and the entire mixture must be sold to a Cohen to be eaten in purity. Here then it is a question of repartition of the loss.

15  Babli 93b/94a, *Kilaim* 2:1, Note 14. Since the farmer could have sold the contaminated grain, the person who cleaned it caused him monetary loss. As a fine, the person responsible is not permitted to put the contaminants back. As application to the questions asked, the person responsible for the mess-up is responsible for its financial consequences.

16  This refers to the statement in the Mishnah that the buyer of figs has to accept ten percent worm-infested ones.

17  For stored figs, the acceptable amount of bad ones is much smaller.

(15b line 71) תַּנֵּי. מֵאָה חָבִיּוֹת אֲנִי מוֹכֵר לָךְ. חַיָּיב לְהַעֲמִיד לוֹ יַיִן יָפֶה כְּרוֹב הַיַּיִן הַנִּמְכָּר בְּאוֹתוֹ מָקוֹם. מֵאָה חָבִיּוֹת יַיִן אֲנִי מוֹכֵר לָךְ. חַיָּיב לְהַעֲמִיד לוֹ יַיִן יָפֶה כְּרוֹב הַיַּיִן הַנִּמְכָּר בְּאוֹתוֹ חָנוּת. מֵאָה חָבִיּוֹת אֵילוּ אֲנִי מוֹכֵר לָךְ. אֲפִילּוּ חוֹמֶץ הִגִּיעוּ. רִבִּי חִיָּיא בַּר וָה. בְּשֶׁהָיוּ הַקַּנְקַנִּים לְלוֹקֵחַ יָכִיל מֵימַר לֵיהּ. לִשְׁתִּיָּיה מָכַרְתִּיו לָךְ.

It was stated[18]: "100 amphoras[19] I am selling to you, he has to deliver wine in the quality which is customarily sold at this place. 100 amphoras of wine I am selling to you, he has to deliver wine in the quality which is customarily sold at this store[20]. These 100 amphoras I am selling to you, even if they were vinegar they are delivered." Rebbi Ḥiyya bar Abba: If the vessels belonged to the buyer, he may tell him: I sold to you for [immediate] consumption[21].

18  Tosephta 6:8-9. A slightly different text in the Babli, 95a.

19  If these were wine amphoras.

20  The Babli holds that if wine was mentioned explicitly, best quality wine must be delivered.

21  It seems that the correct version is the expanded text of E:

רִבִּי חִייָה בַּר וָוה. בְּשֶׁהָיוּ הַקַּנְקַנִּים שֶׁל מוֹכֵר. אֲבָל אִם הָיוּ קַנְקַנִּים שֶׁל לוֹקֵחַ יָכִיל מֵימַר לֵיהּ. קַנְקַנֶּיךָ הֶחֱמִיצוּ הַיַּיִן. וְרִבִּי יוֹסֵי בֶּן חֲנִינָה אוֹמֵר. אֲפִילוּ קַנְקַנִּים שֶׁל מוֹכֵר יָכִיל מֵימַר לֵיהּ. לִשְׁתִּייָה מָכַרְתִּיו לָךְ.

Rebbi Ḥiyya bar Abba: If the vessels belonged to the *seller*. But if *the vessels belonged to the* buyer, he may tell him: *Your vessels turned the wine into vinegar. But Rebbi Yose ben Ḥanina said, even if the vessels belonged to the seller, he may tell him:* I sold to you for [immediate] consumption.

They hold that if the wine turned into vinegar in the buyer's possession, the seller cannot be held responsible unless he guaranteed a certain quality.

(15b line 75) בָּדַק חָבִית לִהְיוֹת מַפְרִישׁ עָלֶיהָ וְהוֹלֵךְ. עַד שְׁלֹשָׁה יָמִים וַדַּאי. מִיכָּן וְהֵילָךְ סָפֵק. רִבִּי סִימוֹן בְּשֵׁם רִבִּי יְהוֹשֻׁעַ בֶּן לֵוִי. שְׁלֹשָׁה יָמִים הָרִאשׁוֹנִים וַדַּאי יַיִן. הָאַחֲרוֹנִים חוֹמֶץ. אֶמְצָעִיִּים סָפֵק. אָמַר רִבִּי אַבָּהוּ. אֲנִי שְׁמַעְתִּיהָ מִמֶּנּוּ. מַה מְּעַבַּד וָמַר רִבִּי יוֹחָנָן. עַד שְׁלֹשָׁה יָמִים וַדַּאי. מִיכָּן וְהֵילָךְ סָפֵק. רִבִּי לָא בְשֵׁם רִבִּי לְעָזָר רִבִּי יָסָא בְּשֵׁם רַבָּנִין דְּעָלִין וְשָׁמְעִין מִבֵּי מִדְרָשָׁא דְּבַר עִיטִייָן בְּמַחַט כְּהָדָא דְּרִבִּי יְהוֹשֻׁעַ בֶּן לֵוִי בְּחָבִית. אִיבֵּד מַחַט שׁוּפָה וּבָא וּמְצָאָהּ חֲלוּדָה. רִבִּי סִימוֹן בְּשֵׁם רִבִּי יְהוֹשֻׁעַ בֶּן לֵוִי. שְׁלֹשָׁה יָמִים הָרִאשׁוֹנִים וַדַּאי טְמֵאָה. אַחֲרוֹנִים טְהוֹרָה. אֶמְצָעִיִּים סָפֵק. אָמַר רִבִּי אַבָּהוּ. אוּף שְׁמַעְתִּיהָ מִמֶּנּוּ. מַה מִיעַבַּד וָמַר רִבִּי יוֹחָנָן. עַד שְׁלֹשָׁה יָמִים וַדַּאי. מִיכָּן וְהֵילָךְ סָפֵק. רִבִּי חִייָה בַּר וָוה שָׁאַל. בָּא בְסוֹף (שָׁבוּעַ) [אַרְבָּעִים] וּמְצָאוֹ חֹמֶץ בָּרוּר [מִיַּד נַעֲשָׂה חָמֵץ בָּרוּר] אוֹ מִכָּן וּלְהַבָּא. רִבִּי יִצְחָק שָׁאַל. עָבַר הַפֶּרֶק בְּסוֹף אַרְבָּעִים יוֹם. כּוֹחוֹ שֶׁלְּפֶרֶק בִּיטֵּל כֹּחַ אַרְבָּעִים יוֹם אוֹ כֹּחַ אַרְבָּעִים יוֹם בִּיטֵּל כּוֹחוֹ שֶׁלְּפֶרֶק.

רִבִּי קְרִיסְפָּא שָׁאַל. בְּכָל־שָׁנָה בּוֹדֵק אוֹ אַחַת לְג שָׁנִים. נִישְׁמְעִינָהּ מֵהָדָא. הַמּוֹכֵר יַיִן לַשָּׁנָה חַיָּיב בְּאַחֲרָיוּתוֹ עַד הֶחָג. אָמַר רִבִּי יוּדָן. תִּיפְתָּר כְּגוֹן אִילֵּין גְּלִילָאֵי דְּלָא קָטְפִין כַּרְמֵיהוֹן אֶלָּא בָּתַר חַגָּא. וְלֵית שְׁמַע מִינָהּ כְּלוּם. וַיֵּידַע

אָמְרָה דָא. יָשָׁן מִשֶּׁלְאֶשְׁתְּקַד. מְיוּשָׁן שֶׁלּגׁ שָׁנִים. נֵימַר מִשּׁוּם הָדָא מַטְמוּעִיתָא. מַה חָבִית אַחַת הוּא בוֹדֵק כּוּלְהוֹן תְּלוּיוֹת בָּהּ. כָּל־אַחַת וְאַחַת הוּא בוֹדֵק וְאֵין מַחֲמִיצוֹת. אָמַר רִבִּי שַׁמַּי. אִית בְּנֵי נַשׁ מַקְשִׁין עַל גַּרְבָּא מִלְעֵיל וְיָדְעִין מָה אִית בֵּיהּ מִלְּנָיו.

[22]If one checked an amphora to continuously give heave from it[23]. Up to three days it is certain, after that in doubt.[24] Rebbi Simon in the name of Rebbi Joshua ben Levi: The first three days it certainly is wine, the last vinegar[25], the middle ones are in doubt. Rebbi Abbahu said, I heard this from him. What does and says Rebbi Johanan? For three days it is certain, after that in doubt. Rebbi La in the name of Rebbi Eleazar, Rebbi Yasa in the name of the rabbis, who come and hear from the House of Study of Bar Iṭyan, similar to the statement of Rebbi Joshua ben Levi about an amphora. If he lost a smooth needle and then found it rusty[26]. Rebbi Simon in the name of Rebbi Joshua ben Levi: The first three days it certainly is impure[27], the last pure, the middle ones are in doubt. Rebbi Abbahu said, I also heard that from him. What does and says Rebbi Johanan? The first three days it is certain, after that in doubt. Rebbi Hiyya bar Abba asked: If he came at the end of (a week)[28] [40 days][29] and found it clearly to be vinegar, [did it clearly become vinegar immediately][30] or only from that moment in the future[31]? Rebbi Isaac asked: If the crucial time passed at the end of forty days, did the importance of the crucial time invalidate that of forty days or did the importance of forty days invalidate that of the crucial time[32]?

[33]Rebbi Crispus asked: Does he check every year or only once every three years[34]? Let us hear from the following: If somebody sells wine for a year, he has to warrant it until after Tabernacles. Rebbi Yudan said, explain it for those Galileans who only harvest after Tabernacles and you cannot deduce anything. That is what was said, "old from the preceding

year, aged three years", should we say because of the tasting³⁵? ³⁶May one check one amphora on which all others depend [or] does he have to check every single one whether they would not turn into vinegar? Rebbi Shammai said, there are people who knock on the barrel at the top and know what is inside¹⁸⁵.

22  This is a reformulation of a paragraph in *Giṭṭin* 3:8, explained there in Notes 166-177 (Babli *Bava batra* 96a). The formulation here gives the impression of Notes which a lecturer made for himself to outline the argument to be presented in class.

23  At the beginning of the wine making season the vintner sets aside an amphora to give heave for all the wine he is going to produce. It is forbidden to give vinegar as heave for wine. Therefore, the amphora should periodically be inspected to make sure it still contains wine. In Mishnah *Giṭṭin* 3:8, R. Jehudah specifies three dates when wine might turn into vinegar because of damaging meteorological phenomena; Halakhah 3:8 also states that in the first 40 days of winemaking no vinegar is created.

24  This is R. Joḥanan's opinion. If the barrel was first checked and it contained wine, then rechecked and contained vinegar, any heave given during the first three days after checking is legitimate, the remainder questionable (but not unacceptable).

25  Heave for any wine produced then must be given anew.

26  A broken vessel or tool cannot be impure; a rusty needle is not touched by the laws of impurity.

27  Not actually impure but subject to the laws of impurity.

28  Reading of L.

29  Reading of E. The reading of E is more probable but both are possibly correct.

30  Reading of E, required by the context.

31  This question can be asked only for R. Joḥanan since R. Joshua ben Levi asserts retroactivity for three days.

32  If a meteorologically dangerous day occurred during the first 40 days of wine making, does one have to worry or not?

33  This is a truncated copy of a paragraph in *Giṭṭin* 3:8, Notes 178-185.

34  Following R. Jehudah, after meteorologically dangerous days.

35  The correct spelling is in *Giṭṭin* 3:8.

| 36 | There is a rather large lacuna here, compared to the text in *Giṭṭin*, | which leaves the text here with a logical lacuna; cf. Note 22. |

(fol. 15b) **משנה ג:** הַמּוֹכֵר מָקוֹם לַחֲבֵירוֹ לִבְנוֹת לוֹ בַיִת וְכֵן הַמְקַבֵּל מֵחֲבֵירוֹ לִבְנוֹת לוֹ בֵית חַתְנוּת לִבְנוֹ בֵּית אַלְמְנוּת לְבִתּוֹ בּוֹנֶה אַרְבַּע אַמּוֹת עַל שֵׁשׁ דִּבְרֵי רִבִּי עֲקִיבָה. רִבִּי יִשְׁמָעֵאל אוֹמֵר רֶפֶת בָּקָר הִיא זוֹ. הָרוֹצֶה לַעֲשׂוֹת רֶפֶת בָּקָר בּוֹנֶה אַרְבַּע אַמּוֹת עַל שֵׁשׁ בַּיִת קָטָן שֵׁשׁ עַל שְׁמוֹנֶה גָּדוֹל שְׁמוֹנֶה עַל עֶשֶׂר טְרַקְלִין עֶשֶׂר עַל עָשָׂר. רוּמוֹ כַּחֲצִי אָרְכּוֹ וְכַחֲצִי רָחְבּוֹ וּרְאָיָיה לַדָּבָר הֵיכָל וּכְתָלָיו. רִבָּן שִׁמְעוֹן בֶּן גַּמְלִיאֵל אוֹמֵר כְּבִנְיַין הֵיכָל.

**Mishnah 3**: If somebody sells a plot to another to build a house[37], or he contracts to build him a wedding building for his son[38], a widow's seat for his daughter, builds four by six cubits, the words of Rebbi Aqiba. Rebbi Ismael says, this is a cowshed[39]. If one wants to build a cowshed, he builds four by six cubits, a small room six by eight, a large one eight by ten, a dining hall[40] ten by ten, and its height equal to half its length and width[41]; the reason is the Temple and its walls. Rabban Simeon ben Gamliel said, a building like the Temple[42]?

| 37 A standard room, in the absence of specifications. | 40 Latin *triclinium*, a dining room for three couches. |
| 38 For his son to live in after his marriage when he still is dependent on his father. | 41 Height = (length + width)/2. |
| 39 No human should be forced to live in such a small space. | 42 It is presumptuous to try to imitate the architecture of the Temple for profane use. |

(15c line 20) **הלכה ג:** הַמּוֹכֵר מָקוֹם לַחֲבֵירוֹ כול׳. תַּנֵּא. קַנְטָר חַיָּיב לְהַעֲמִיד לוֹ שְׁתֵּים עֶשְׂרֵה עַל שְׁתֵּים עֶשְׂרֵה.

**Halakhah 3**: "If somebody sells a plot to another," etc. It was stated[43]: "For a large house[44] he must provide him with twelve by twelve [cubits]."

| | | |
|---|---|---|
| 43 | Tosephta 6:24; Babli 98b. | bridge"; root تنطر "to abandon Bedouin |
| 44 | Arabic نَطْرَة "large building, | way of life". |

(15c line 21) רַב הַמְנוּנָא סַפְרָא שָׁאַל לְרִבִּי חֲנִינָה. כָּתוּב אֶחָד אוֹמֵר קוֹמָתוֹ שְׁלֹשִׁים אַמָּה וְכָתוּב אַחֵר אוֹמֵר קוֹמָתוֹ עֶשְׂרִים אַמָּה. וְלָא הֲוָה דִשְׁמָעָהּ וְלָא אָמְרִין לֵיהּ כְּלוּם. שָׁאַל לְרִבִּי יִרְמְיָה. אֲמַר לֵיהּ. מִן הַקַּרְקַע וּלְמַעֲלָן שְׁלֹשִׁים אַמָּה. מִן הַדְּבִיר וּלְמַעֲלָן עֶשְׂרִים אַמָּה. אֲמַר רִבִּי אַבָּהוּ. מִפְכְּלֵיהּ דְּבִיר. דְּבִיר הָיָה עוֹמֵד מִן הַקַּרְקַע וְעַד הַקּוֹרוֹת. דִּכְתִיב וְסָפוּן בָּאֶרֶז מִן הַקַּרְקַע וְעַד הַקּוֹרוֹת. אֶלָּא מִן הַקַּרְקַע וּלְמַעֲלָן שְׁלֹשִׁים אַמָּה מִן הַכְּרוּב וּלְמַעֲלָן עֶשְׂרִים אַמָּה. אֲמַר רִבִּי תַנְחוּמָא. מְסוֹרֶת אֲגָדָה הִיא שֶׁאֵין מְקוֹם דְּבִיר עוֹלֶה מִן הַמִּנְיָין. אֲמַר רִבִּי לֵוִי. וְלֹא מְקוֹם אָרוֹן עוֹלֶה מִן הַמִּנְיָין. אֲמַר רִבִּי לֵוִי וְתַנֵּי כֵן בְּשֵׁם רִבִּי יוּדָה בֵּירִבִּי אִלְעָאי. אָרוֹן עוֹמֵד בָּאֶמְצָע וְחוֹלֵק הַבַּיִת עֶשֶׂר אַמּוֹת לְכָל־רוּחַ.

Rav Hamnuna the scribe asked Rebbi Ḥanina: One verse says, "its height thirty cubits,[45]" and another verse says, "its height twenty cubits.[46]" He had never heard this and they could not answer him anything. He asked Rebbi Jeremiah, who told him, from the ground up thirty cubits, from the inner room up twenty cubits. Rebbi Abbahu said, destroy the inner room[47]! The inner room was standing from the ground to the beams, as it is written, "covered with cedar from the ground to the beams.[48]" But from the ground up thirty cubits, from the Cherub up twenty cubits. Rebbi Tanḥuma said, it is an aggadic tradition that the space in the inner room not be counted. Rebbi Levi said, the space occupied by the Ark is not counted[49]. Rebbi Levi said, and it was stated in the name of Rebbi Jehudah ben Rebbi Illai, the Ark stands in the middle and divides the room, ten cubits in every direction of the compass.

45   *1K*. 6:2.
46   *1K*. 6:20.
47   The explanation given by R. Jeremiah is impossible; the inner room (the Holiest of Holies) was level with the Temple hall.
48   There is no such verse. A close verse is *1K*. 7:7, "covered with cedar from ground to ground," but it refers to Solomon's court, not the Temple. Possibly the reference is to *1K*. 6:16: "He built twenty cubits from the side of the Temple cedar siding from the ground to the walls," meaning that walls were constructed differently above and below twenty cubits' height.
49   What he wants to say is that the bodies of the Cherubim were not counted since v. 24 states that each wing of the Cherubim was 5 cubits, and v. 27 that the total span from one extreme wingtip to the other was 20 cubits, leaving no room for the bodies of the Cherubim.

משנה ד: מִי שֶׁיֵּשׁ לוֹ בוֹר לִפְנִים מִבֵּיתוֹ שֶׁל חֲבֵירוֹ נִכְנָס בְּשָׁעָה שֶׁדֶּרֶךְ (fol. 15b) בְּנֵי אָדָם נִכְנָסִין וְיוֹצֵא בְּשָׁעָה שֶׁדֶּרֶךְ בְּנֵי אָדָם יוֹצְאִין. וְאֵינוֹ מַכְנִיס בְּהֶמְתּוֹ וּמַשְׁקָה מִבּוֹרוֹ אֶלָּא מְמַלֵּא וּמַשְׁקָה מִבַּחוּץ זֶה עוֹשֶׂה לוֹ פּוֹתַחַת וְזֶה עוֹשֶׂה לוֹ פּוֹתַחַת.

**Mishnah 4**: If somebody has a cistern inside another's house, he may enter at times when people usually enter[50] and must leave when people usually leave. He cannot bring his animal and let it drink from his cistern but draws water and lets it drink outside. Each of them makes a lock for himself[51].

משנה ה: מִי שֶׁיֵּשׁ לוֹ גִינָה לִפְנִים מִגִּינָתוֹ שֶׁל חֲבֵירוֹ נִכְנָס בְּשָׁעָה שֶׁדֶּרֶךְ בְּנֵי אָדָם נִכְנָסִין וְיוֹצֵא בְּשָׁעָה שֶׁדֶּרֶךְ בְּנֵי אָדָם יוֹצְאִין. וְאֵינוֹ מַכְנִיס לְתוֹכָהּ תַּגָּרִים וְלֹא יִכָּנֵס לְתוֹךְ שָׂדֶה אַחֶרֶת וְהַחִיצוֹן זוֹרֵעַ אֶת הַדֶּרֶךְ.

**Mishnah 5**: If somebody has a vegetable garden inside another's vegetable garden, he may enter at times when people usually enter and must leave when people usually leave. He cannot bring traders inside[52] and cannot use it to go to another field; the outside owner may sow on the path[53].

**משנה ו**: נְתָנוּ לוֹ דֶּרֶךְ מִן הַצַּד מִדַּעַת שְׁנֵיהֶן נִכְנָס בְּשָׁעָה שֶׁהוּא רוֹצֶה וְיוֹצֵא בְּשָׁעָה שֶׁהוּא רוֹצֶה מַכְנִיס לְתוֹכָהּ תַּגָּרִים וְלֹא יִכָּנֵס לְתוֹךְ שָׂדֶה אַחֶרֶת. וְזֶה וָזֶה אֵינָן רַשָׁאִין לְזוֹרְעָהּ.

**Mishnah 6**: If he was allowed a path on the side by common accord, he may enter any time he wishes and leave any time he wishes; he can bring traders inside but cannot use it to go to another field; neither owner may sow on it.

50   Regular office hours only.
51   The cistern's owner makes a lock so the owner of the house cannot draw water from his cistern. The owner of the house puts a lock on the cistern so its owner cannot draw water without his knowledge.
52   To sell them his vegetables.
53   Since the owner of the inside plot may have a right of passage but has no property rights.

(15c line 31) **הלכה ד**: מִי שֶׁיֵּשׁ לוֹ בוֹר כול׳. תַּנֵּי. הַחִיצוֹן אֵין זוֹרֵעַ אֶת הַדֶּרֶךְ. דּוּ אֲמַר לֵיהּ. מְעַלֵּל אֲנָא שְׁרַע. הַפְּנִימִי אֵין זוֹרֵעַ אֶת הַדֶּרֶךְ. דּוּ אֲמַר לֵיהּ. אַתְּ חַיָּיס עַל דִּידָךְ וְדַיֵּישׁ עַל דִּידִי.

**Halakhah 4** "If somebody has a cistern," etc. It was stated[54]: The outer one cannot sow on the path for the other can tell him, I would walk on slippery ground[55]. The inner one cannot sow on the path for the other can tell him, you would take care of yours and step on mine[56].

54   This refers to the end of Mishnah 6.
55   I would have to tiptoe around your plants which is impossible for a person carrying agricultural tools.
56   To avoid stepping on your plants you will step on mine.

**משנה ז:** מִי שֶׁהָיְתָה דֶרֶךְ הָרַבִּים עוֹבֶרֶת בְּתוֹךְ שָׂדֵהוּ נְטָלָהּ וְנָתַן לָהֶן (fol. 15b) מִן הַצַּד. מַה שֶּׁנָּתַן נָתַן וְשֶׁלּוֹ לֹא הִגִּיעוֹ. דֶּרֶךְ הַיָּחִיד אַרְבַּע אַמּוֹת דֶּרֶךְ הָרַבִּים שֵׁשׁ עֶשְׂרֵה אַמָּה דֶּרֶךְ הַמֶּלֶךְ אֵין לָהּ שִׁיעוּר דֶּרֶךְ הַקֶּבֶר אֵין לָהּ שִׁיעוּר. הַמַּעֲמָד דַּיָּינֵי צִיפּוֹרִי אָמְרוּ בֵּית אַרְבַּעַת קַבִּין.

**Mishnah 7:** If a public way was passing through somebody's field, he took it away and gave them [a road] to the side of his property, what he gave, he gave, but what he wanted for himself he did not get[57]. A private way is four cubits wide[58], a public way sixteen cubits[59]; a king's highway[60] has no limit; the way to the cemetary has no limit[61]. The place for funeral orations, the judges of Sepphoris say an area of four *qab*[62].

**משנה ח:** הַמּוֹכֵר מָקוֹם לַחֲבֵירוֹ לַעֲשׂוֹת לוֹ קֶבֶר. וְכֵן הַמְקַבֵּל מֵחֲבֵירוֹ לַעֲשׂוֹת לוֹ קֶבֶר עוֹשֶׂה תוֹכָהּ שֶׁל מְעָרָה אַרְבַּע אַמּוֹת עַל שֵׁשׁ וּפוֹתֵחַ לְתוֹכָהּ שְׁמוֹנָה כּוּכִין שְׁלֹשָׁה מִיכָּן וּשְׁלֹשָׁה מִיכָּן וּשְׁנַיִם כְּנֶגְדָּן. וְהַכּוּכִין אָרְכָּן אַרְבַּע אַמּוֹת וְרוּמָן שִׁבְעָה וְרָחְבָּן שִׁשָּׁה. רִבִּי שִׁמְעוֹן אוֹמֵר עוֹשֶׂה תוֹכָהּ שֶׁל מְעָרָה שֵׁשׁ עַל שְׁמוֹנָה וּפוֹתֵחַ לְתוֹכָהּ שְׁלֹשָׁה עָשָׂר כּוּךְ. אַרְבָּעָה מִיכָּן וְאַרְבָּעָה מִיכָּן וּשְׁלֹשָׁה כְּנֶגְדָּן וְאֶחָד מִימִין הַפֶּתַח וְאֶחָד מִן הַשְּׂמֹאל. וְעוֹשֶׂה חָצֵר עַל פֶּתַח הַמְּעָרָה שֵׁשׁ עַל שֵׁשׁ כִּמְלוֹא הַמִּיטָה וְקוֹבְרֶיהָ. וּפוֹתֵחַ לְתוֹכָהּ שְׁתֵּי מְעָרוֹת אַחַת מִיכָּן וְאַחַת מִיכָּן. רִבִּי שִׁמְעוֹן אוֹמֵר אַרְבַּע לְאַרְבַּע רוּחוֹתֶיהָ. רַבָּן שִׁמְעוֹן בֶּן גַּמְלִיאֵל אוֹמֵר הַכֹּל לְפִי הַסֶּלַע.

**Mishnah 8:** If somebody sells a plot to another to build a grave[63], or he contracts to build him a grave makes the cavity of the cavern four cubits by six[64] and opens into it eight sepulchral chambers, three on each side and two at the back wall. The chambers are four cubits long, seven [handbreadths] high and six [handbreadths] wide[65]. Rebbi Simeon says, he makes the cavity of the cavern six by eight [cubits] and opens into it thirteen sepulcral chambers, four on each side, three at the back wall, one to the right of the entrance and one to its left[66]. In front of the cavern he excavates a courtyard of six by six [cubits] for the bier and its carriers.

He opens into it two caverns, one at each side. Rebbi Simeon says four, each to each direction of the compass[67]. Rabban Simeon ben Gamliel says, all depends on the rock[68].

57   An unpaved public way passing between two fields cannot be changed.

58   In all cases where there is a right of access, the access road has to be a minimum of four cubits.

59   Not only for civil law but also for the rules of the Sabbath.

60   A paved road, government built.

61   A funeral procession may overflow into adjacent areas.

62   Two thirds of a *bet se'ah* of 2500 square cubits or $1666^2/_3$ square cubits.

63   A rock cemetery.

64   4 cubits wide by 6 deep.

65   Since each chamber is one cubit wide, the chambers are spaced one cubit apart and the extreme ones half a cubit from the corner.

66   This is explained in the Halakhah.

67   His courtyard could not be excavated in front of the rock; it would have to be in the middle of a rock, accessible by ladders. No such construction was ever excavated.

68   The number of caves, of funeral chambers, their dimensions and spacing.

(15c line 31) **הלכה ז:** מִי שֶׁהָיְתָה דֶּרֶךְ הָרַבִּים כול' עַד סוֹף הַמִּשְׁנָה. רִבִּי חִייָה בַּר יוֹסֵף אָמַר. עוֹשֶׂה אוֹתָן כְּמוֹ נַגְרִין. אָמַר לֵיהּ רִבִּי יוֹחָנָן. וַהֲלֹא הַכְּלָבִים אֵינָן נִקְבָּרִין כֵּן. כֵּיצַד עוֹשֶׂה. בּוֹנֶה מִלְּפָנִים כְּבַחוּץ. וְאֵין הָעוֹבְרוֹת נוֹגְעוֹת בּוֹ. אֵינוֹ עָבַר. בָּנֵי חָדָא מִלְעֵיל וְחָדָא מִלְרַע.

**Halakhah 7:** "If a public way was passing through somebody's," etc., to the end of the Mishnah. Rebbi Ḥiyya bar Joseph said, he makes them like keyholes[69]. Rebbi Joḥanan told him, but dogs are not buried in that way! What does he do? He builds inside as if outside[70]. Do the crossings not interfere with one another[71,72]? They do not cross; he builds one higher and one lower[73].

69 He explains what R. Simeon means when he requires an extra chamber each right and left of the door. Would they not also be on the side walls? He proposes to build the two additional chambers vertically and to bury the dead standing up. In the Babli, 101a, this opinion is attributed to R. Yose ben R. Ḥanina; there also it is rejected by R. Joḥanan.

70 In the corners between the back wall and the sides, opposite the entrance, in a 45° angle to both walls meeting at the corner.

71 This refers to another problem with R. Simeon's plan. If four burial caves are dug from one center platform, by necessity the four cubits long burial chambers close to the entrance of each cave will intersect with the one dug for the cave at a right angle to it; the entire plan cannot be executed.

72 E reads עבד, עובדות for עבר, עוברות. This may be a scribal error.

73 The burial caverns have to be at least four cubits high so that the chambers in different caverns can be dug at different levels lest they intersect; or the caverns themselves have to be dug at different levels.

## האומר לחבירו פרק שביעי

(fol. 15c) **משנה א:** הָאוֹמֵר לַחֲבֵירוֹ בֵּית כּוֹר עָפָר אֲנִי מוֹכֵר לָךְ הָיוּ שָׁם נְקָעִים עֲמוּקִים עֲשָׂרָה טְפָחִים אוֹ סְלָעִים גְּבוֹהִים עֲשָׂרָה טְפָחִים אֵינָן נִמְדָּדִין עִמָּהּ פָּחוּת מִיכָּן נִמְדָּדִין עִמָּהּ. וְאִם אָמַר לוֹ כְּבֵית כּוֹר עָפָר הָיוּ שָׁם נְקָעִים עֲמוּקִים יוֹתֵר מֵעֲשָׂרָה טְפָחִים אוֹ סְלָעִים גְּבוֹהִים יוֹתֵר מֵעֲשָׂרָה טְפָחִים הֲרֵי אֵילּוּ נִמְדָּדִין עִמָּהּ.

**Mishnah 1:** If somebody says to another: I am selling you a *bet kor*[1] of dust[2], if there were depressions ten handbreadths deep or rocks ten handbreadths high[3], they are not measured with it[4]; less than that they are measured with it. But if he said, about a *bet kor* of dust, if there were depressions deeper than ten handbreadths or rocks higher than ten handbreadths, they are measured with it.

1  30 *bet se'ah* or 75'000 square cubits.
2  Agricultural land.
3  They cannot be cultivated with the rest.
4  To measure the exact size of the area delivered.

(15c line 68) **הלכה א:** הָאוֹמֵר לַחֲבֵירוֹ בֵּית כּוֹר עָפָר אֲנִי מוֹכֵר לָךְ כּוֹל׳. רִבִּי יָסָא בְשֵׁם רִבִּי יוֹחָנָן. וּבִלְבַד בִּמְעוּטֵי שָׂדֶהוּ בְּמוּבְלָעִים בָּהּ. וּבְסֶלַע שֶׁשִּׁילְּחוֹ בֵּית רוֹבַע אֵין נִמְדָּד עִמָּהּ. שֶׁבְּאֶמְצָע נִמְדָּד. שֶׁבַּצַּד אֵין נִמְדָּד. אֵי זֶהוּ צַד וְאֵי זֶהוּ אֶמְצָע. דְּבֵית רִבִּי יַנַּאי אָמְרֵי. כָּל־שֶׁמַּחֲרֵישָׁה סוֹבַבְתּוּ זֶהוּ אֶמְצָע. אֵין הַמַּחֲרֵישָׁה סוֹבַבְתּוּ זֶהוּ הַצַּד. אָתָא רִבִּי יוֹסֵי בְשֵׁם רִבִּי יוֹחָנָן. הָיָה רוּבָּהּ מִצַּד אֶחָד שֶׁאִם תְּפַזְּרֶנָּה וְיֵשׁ לָהּ מִיעוּט נִמְדָּד עִמָּהּ. רְחָבִין כַּמָּה. רִבִּי חַגַּי אָמַר. עַד אַרְבַּע אַמּוֹת. רִבִּי יוֹסֵי בֵּירִבִּי בּוּן אָמַר. עַד י׳ טְפָחִים. הָיָה שָׁם נֶקַע אֶחָד

עָמוֹק י טְפָחִים וְאֵין בּוֹ ד' מָהוּ. נִישְׁמְעִינָהּ מֵהָדָא. דָּמַר רִבִּי יָסָא בְּשֵׁם רִבִּי יוֹחָנָן. וּבִלְבַד בְּמִיעוּט הַשָּׂדֶה וּבְמוּבְלָעִין בָּהּ. וּבְסֶלַע שֶׁשִּׁילְחוֹ בֵּית רוֹבַע אֵין נִמְדָּד עִמָּהּ. הָיָה חָלוּק נִמְדָּד עִמָּהּ. הָדָא אָמְרָה. הָיָה רוּבָּהּ מִצַּד אֶחָד שֶׁאִם תְּפַזְּרֶנָּה וְיֵשׁ בָּהּ מִיעוּט אֵין נִמְדָּד עִמָּהּ. הָיָה שָׁם נֶקַע אֶחָד אָרוֹךְ וְהוּא מִסְתַּלֵּק לְבֵית רוֹבַע. רִבִּי חִייָה בַּר וָוא שָׁאַל. הָיָה עָשׂוּי כְּמִין מַקְלוֹת נִמְדָּד עִמָּהּ אִי לֹא. רִבִּי יוּדָן בַּר יִשְׁמָעֵאל שָׁאַל. הָיָה עָשׂוּי כְּמִין טַבְלִיּוֹת שֶׁל שַׁיִישׁ נִמְדָּד עִמָּהּ אִי לֹא. רִבִּי יִצְחָק בַּר טְבְלַיי שָׁאַל. הָיָה עָשׂוּי כְּמִין קַתֶּדְרִיּוֹת מִמְּקוֹם דּוֹפְנוֹ הוּא מוֹדֵד אוֹ מִמְּקוֹם שִׁיפּוּעוֹ מוֹדֵד. רַב הוּנָא בְּשֵׁם רַב [רִבִּי] חִייָה בְּשֵׁם רִבִּי יוֹחָנָן. וְהוּא שֶׁיְּהֵא שָׁם בֵּית ד' כּוֹר עָפָר.

**Halakhah 1**: "If somebody says to another: I am selling you a *bet kor* of dust," etc. Rebbi Yasa said in the name of Rebbi Johanan: Only if it[5] is the smaller part of his field and enclosed in it[6]. And a rock with a total surface area of a *bet rova'* is not measured with it[7]. If it is in the middle, it is measured, at the side it is not measured. What is a side and what is in the middle? In the House of Rebbi Yannai they said, any place surrounded by a ploughed area is in the middle; any place not surrounded by a ploughed area[8] is to the side.

Rebbi Yose came in the name of Rebbi Johanan: If it was a majority on one side, but if you spread it, it becomes a smaller part, and it is measured with it[9].

How wide[10]? Rebbi Haggai said, up to four cubits. Rebbi Yose ben Rebbi Abun said, up to ten handbreadths[11]. If there was a depression ten handbreadths deep but less than four[12] wide, what is the rule? Let us hear from the following, what Rebbi Yasa said in the name of Rebbi Johanan: "Only if it is the smaller part of his field and enclosed in it. And a rock with a total surface area of a *bet rova'* is not measured with it. If it was split, it is measured with it." This means that if the greater part of it was on one side, but if you spread it, it becomes the smaller part and is not measured with it[13].

If there was a long depression which added up to a *bet rova'*?[14] Rebbi Hiyya bar Abba asked: If it was shaped like sticks, is it measured with it or not? Rebbi Yudan bar Ismael asked: If it was like marble plates, is it measured with it or not?[15] Rebbi Isaac bar Tebelai asked: If it was formed like chairs, does he measure from the place of its wall or does he measure from its declivity[16]? Rav Huna in the name of Rav, [Rebbi] Hiyya in the name of Rebbi Johanan: Only if the total agricultural area was four *bet kor*[17].

5    The depressions or rocky areas.

6    The total of the area that is difficult or impossible to cultivate must be less than 50% of the total area and cannot be directly accessible from the boundary of the field.

7    No single bad area may be more than $1/24$ of a *bet se'ah* or $104 1/6$ square cubits. The Babli, 103a, restricts the total area of bad spots in a *bet kor* to 4 *batte rova'*.

8    "In the middle" means at least four cubits removed from the boundary line of the property. Four cubits is the customary space needed for the plough and the cattle which draw it.

9    This is the reading of L. Since later the opposite conclusion is reached by an argument, the readings of L are consistent with one another. The reading of E is: "is *not* measured." Then at the end the reading will be "is measured". This is the reading of *Šiṭṭah Mequbeṣet Bava batra* 102b, which always quotes from mss.

The question is whether the sale is legitimate if an entire area of the field is not usable for agriculture because of many unusable spots when each in isolation would be insignificant.

10    The Mishnah, while specifying depth or height of an unacceptable obstacle, fails to indicate length or width.

11    *Šiṭṭah Mequbeṣet* reads: R. Yannai says, 10 handbreadths, R. Yose bar Abun says, up to 4 cubits.

12    The mss., using letters as numerals, fail to indicate whether one refers to handbreadths or cubits. The printer of the *editio princeps*, spelling out the numeral as a word, by choosing the masculine form is referring to *handbreadths*. But *Šiṭṭah Mequbeṣet* (following Rashba and Ritba) quotes the question as about "4 by 4" and this in both Talmudim always refers to 4 by 4 *cubits* which characterizes the

minimum size of a piece of land for which separate title can be acquired. Then it is possible to read the question as referring to depressions less than 10 handbreadths deep but more than 16 square cubits wide, which as a separate area may be rejected by the buyer as a separate field.

13 *Šiṭṭah Mequbeṣet* reads: "is measured with it." This is the logical consequence of the quote that the rocks be measured with the field if the total area of the rocky surface was more than a *bet rova'* but no single piece of rock was of that size.

14 The question already was answered in the Mishnah, *viz.*, that this cannot be part of the area sold.

15 It is not clear what these questions mean.

16 The Mishnah does not specify how the area of depression has to be measured, whether from the upper rim or only on the bottom.

17 The remedy of the Mishnah, that the seller has to give the buyer additional land to make up for the bad spots, only works if there be enough adjacent agricultural land at the seller's disposal. If the buyer would have to accept a replacement plot separate from the main field, the sale would be annulled.

**משנה ב:** בֵּית כּוֹר עָפָר אֲנִי מוֹכֵר לָךְ מִדָּה בַחֶבֶל. פָּחַת כָּל־שֶׁהוּא יְנַכֶּה. הוֹתִיר כָּל־שֶׁהוּא יַחֲזִיר. אִם אָמַר הֵן חָסֵר הֵן יָתֵר אֲפִילוּ פָּחַת רוֹבַע לַסְּאָה אוֹ הוֹתִיר רוֹבַע לַסְּאָה הִגִּיעוֹ. יוֹתֵר מִכֵּן יַעֲשֶׂה חֶשְׁבּוֹן. (fol. 15c)

**Mishnah 2:** "I am selling you a *bet kor*[1] of dust measured by the surveyor's measuring tape," if a little bit be missing, he deducts, if it be a little more, he has to refund[18]. If he said "more or less," even if it was deficient by a quarter [*qab*] per *se'ah* or redundant by a quarter [*qab*] per *se'ah*, he received it[19]. For more than that one makes a computation[20].

18 The buyer pays exactly for the square cubits he received in land based on the fixed purchase price per *bet kor*.

19 A sale "more or less" allows a margin of ±4.1667%.

20. The sale price is proportional to the agreed price for 75'000 square cubits.

(15d line 10) **הלכה ב:** בֵּית כּוֹר עָפָר אֲנִי מוֹכֵר לָךְ כּוֹל'. הָכָא אַתְּ מַר. הִגִּיעוֹ. וְהָכָא אַתְּ מַר. לֹא אֶת הָרוֹבַע בִּלְבַד מַחֲזִיר לוֹ אֶלָּא כָּל־הַמּוֹתָר. אָמְרֵי. מִכֵּיוָן שֶׁאַתְּ מוֹצִיאוֹ לִפְחוֹת מֵחֶבֶל מַחֲזִירוֹ אַתְּ לְמִידָּה בַחֶבֶל.

**Halakhah 2**: "I am selling you a *bet kor* of dust," etc. Here, you say that "he has received it." But there, you say that "not only the quarter [*qab*] he has to return but all the excess"[21]? They said, since you exclude him from the rule of "less[22] than measured by the surveyor's measuring tape" you return him to the rules of "by the surveyor's measuring tape."

21  In Mishnah 2 it is stated that if the deviation of the delivered real estate from the contracted amount be less than $1/24$, the contract was validly satisfied. But in Mishnah 3 it is stated that if the difference was more than $1/24$, the entire excess beyond the contracted amount must be restituted, not only the excess beyond 104.167% over the contracted amount.

22  Short for "more or less than ..".

(fol. 15c) **משנה ג:** וּמַהוּ מַחֲזִיר לוֹ מָעוֹת וְאִם רָצָה מַחֲזִיר לוֹ קַרְקַע. וְלָמָּה אָמְרוּ מַחֲזִיר לוֹ מָעוֹת לְיַיפּוֹת כּוֹחוֹ שֶׁל מוֹכֵר שֶׁאִם שִׁיֵּיר בַּשָּׂדֶה בֵּית תִּשְׁעַת קַבִּין וּבַגִּינָּה בֵּית חֲצִי קַב. וּכְדִבְרֵי רִבִּי עֲקִיבָה בֵּית רוֹבַע. מַחֲזִיר לוֹ אֶת הַקַּרְקַע וְלֹא אֶת הָרוֹבַע בִּלְבַד הוּא מַחֲזִיר לוֹ אֶלָּא כָּל־הַמּוֹתָר.

**Mishnah 3**: What does he return[23]? Money. But if he[24] agreed, he returns land to him. Then why did they say, he returns money to him? To empower the seller[25], for if this one[24] retained for himself a space for nine *qab*[26], or in a vegetable garden the space for half a *qab* (or following Rebbi Aqiba a *bet rova'*) he returns land to him. Not only the quarter [*qab*] he has to return but all the excess.

**משנה ד:** מִדָּה בַחֶבֶל אֲנִי מוֹכֵר לָךְ הֵן חָסֵר הֵן יָתֵר בִּיטֵּל הֵן חָסֵר הֵן יָתֵר מִדָּה בַחֶבֶל. הֵן חָסֵר הֵן יָתֵר מִדָּה בַחֶבֶל בִּיטֵּל מִדָּה בַחֶבֶל הֵן חָסֵר הֵן יָתֵר

דִּבְרֵי בֶן נַנָּס. בְּסִימָנָיו וּבִמְצָרָיו פָּחוֹת מִשְּׁתוּת הִגִּיעוֹ עַד שְׁתוּת יְנַכֶּה.

**Mishnah 4**: "Measured by the surveyor's measuring tape, more or less;[27]" "more or less" invalidated "measured by the surveyor's measuring tape". "More or less, measured by the surveyor's measuring tape;" "measured by the surveyor's measuring tape" invalidated "more or less", the words of Ben Nannas. "By its description and its boundary strips,"[28] less than one sixth he received it, up to a sixth he shall deduct.

23  The buyer who received more than $25/24$ of the area agreed to for the stated purchase price.

24  The seller.

25  To protect the seller; to avoid his becoming the owner of a parcel too small for agricultural use which practically would be worthless.

26  If the seller retained at least 3750 square cubits of land for extensive agriculture or $208^1/_3$ square cubits of land for intensive agriculture, the seller automatically has a legal claim to receive the excess amount in land, rather than money.

27  The seller made two contradictory statements, viz., that the amount delivered will be exactly as stipulated, but it might not exactly be the amount stipulated. Ben Nannas holds that the last statement always is the operative one. The Babli in 105a and the Yerushalmi in *Bava meṣia'* 8:10 (Note 48) decide that practice does not follow Ben Nannas.

28  In addition to stating the surface area to be sold, the seller gave a topographical description of the field. If the latter disagrees with the former, less than a $16^2/_3\%$ error does not change the contract. An error of exactly $16^2/_3\%$ requires a monetary adjustment; a larger error invalidates the entire transaction.

(15d line 13) **הלכה ג:** וּמָהוּ מַחֲזִיר לוֹ. מָעוֹת כול'. תַּנֵּי רִבִּי חִיָּיה. הַמּוֹכֵר עֶבֶד לַחֲבֵירוֹ וְנִמְצָא גַּנָּב אוֹ קוּבְיָסְטוֹס הִגִּיעוֹ. נִמְצָא לִיסְטֵיס אוֹ מוּכְתָּב לַמַּלְכוּת לֹא הִגִּיעוֹ.

**Halakhah 3**: "What does he return? Money," etc. [29]Rebbi Ḥiyya stated: If somebody sell a slave to another and he turns out to be a thief or a gambler[30], he received him. But if he was a robber[31] or proscribed by the Government[32], he did not receive him.

29 Tosephta 4:7; Babli 92b, *Ketubot* 60b, *Qiddušin* 11a.
30 Greek κυβευτής "dicer, gambler."
31 Greek λῃστής. In contrast to the thief, a robber is armed and subject to capital punishment. He already is considered as dead; the sale of a dead slave is invalid.
32 A warrant is out for his arrest. The sale is invalid.

(fol. 15c) **משנה ה:** הָאוֹמֵר לַחֲבֵירוֹ חֲצִי שָׂדֶה אֲנִי מוֹכֵר לָךְ מְשַׁמְּנִין בֵּינֵיהֶן וְנוֹטֵל חֲצִי שָׂדֵהוּ. חֶצְיָהּ בַּדָּרוֹם אֲנִי מוֹכֵר לָךְ מְשַׁמְּנִין בֵּינֵיהֶן וְנוֹטֵל חֶצְיָהּ בַּדָּרוֹם. וְהוּא מְקַבֵּל עָלָיו מְקוֹם הַגָּדֵר חָרִיץ וּבֶן חָרִיץ. וְכַמָּה הוּא חָרִיץ. שִׁשָּׁה טְפָחִים. וּבֶן חָרִיץ שְׁלֹשָׁה.

**Mishnah 5**: If somebody say to another: I am selling you half a field, they estimate in common[33] and he takes half of his field. Its Southern part I am selling to you, they estimate in common and he takes the Southern half. He has to accept the place of the wall[34], the trench[35] or the small trench. How much is a trench? Six handbreadths[36]. And the small trench, three.

33 They together appoint the appraiser who will determine what exactly constitutes half a field in value.
34 If it is necessary to fence in the property, the owner of the fenced-in property also has to provide for the wall and the trench separating the wall from the field.
36 Width.

(15d line 16) **הלכה ה:** הָאוֹמֵר לַחֲבֵירוֹ. חֲצִי שָׂדֶה אֲנִי מוֹכֵר לָךְ כול'. רִבִּי הוּנָא אָמַר. הַשְׁתוּת עַצְמוֹ מְנָכֶה.

**Halakhah 5**: "If somebody say to another: I am selling you half a field," etc. [37]Rebbi Huna said, the sixth itself he shall deduct.

[37] This should be in Halakhah 3; it refers to the end of Mishnah 4, Note 28. In the Babli, 106a, *Rav* Huna declares that an error of one sixth follows the rules of errors less than one sixth; i. e., he holds that monetary adjustment is needed for any deviation from the area stated in the contract. It is not evident that *Rebbi* Huna here is a scribal error for *Rav* Huna even though *Rav* Huna is quoted reasonably frequently in *Neziqin* but *Rebbi* Huna is only mentioned three times, and this in *Bava meṣia'*.

(15d line 17) תַּנֵּי. הָאוֹמֵר לַחֲבֵירוֹ חֲצִי שָׂדֶה אֲנִי מוֹכֵר לָךְ וּפְלוֹנִי מַקִּיפָךְ וּפְלוֹנִי מַקִּיפָךְ וַחֲצִי פְלוֹנִי מַקִּיפָךְ. רַב הוּנָא וְרַב יְהוּדָה וְרִבִּי יִרְמְיָה. חַד אָמַר. נוֹתֵן לוֹ כְּמִין פַּנְדּוּר. וְחַד אָמַר. נוֹתֵן לוֹ כְּמִין מַטְלֵית. וְחַד אָמַר. נוֹתֵן לוֹ כְּמִין פְּסִיקְיָא.

It was stated: If somebody says to another: I am selling you half a field, and X and Y and half of Z surround you. Rav Huna, and Rav Jehudah, and Rebbi Jeremiah[38]. One said, he gives him [an area shaped] like a *pandur*[39]. And one said, he gives him something like a strip of cloth. And one said, he gives him something like patches[40].

[38] The Babylonian who in the Babli usually is called Rav Jeremiah.

[39] Greek πανδοῦρα "three-stringed lute."

[40] It is not clear which shape of a field is meant. In the Babli, 62a/b, the question is about a Gamma-shaped field or one given in separate pieces. If one assumes the original field to be rectangular, the indication of $2^1/_2$ boundary strips would indicate a surface composed of two rectangles forming a Γ. A "field in the form of patches" probably is a field of irregular shape, or even composed of disjoint triangles, discussed in *Kilaim* as "ox head" (*Kilaim* 1:9, Note 202; 2:7 Note 101). For this, one has to assume that one of the sides is not contiguous with the other two.

## יש נוחלין פרק שמיני

(fol. 15d) **משנה א**: יֵשׁ נוֹחֲלִין וּמַנְחִילִין. נוֹחֲלִין וְלֹא מַנְחִילִין. מַנְחִילִין וְלֹא נוֹחֲלִין. לֹא נוֹחֲלִין וְלֹא מַנְחִילִין. אִילּוּ נוֹחֲלִין וּמַנְחִילִין הָאָב אֶת הַבָּנִים וְהַבָּנִים אֶת הָאָב וְהָאַחִין מִן הָאָב נוֹחֲלִין וּמַנְחִילִין. הָאִישׁ אֶת אִמּוֹ וְהָאִישׁ אֶת אִשְׁתּוֹ וּבְנֵי אֲחָיוֹת נוֹחֲלִין וְלֹא מַנְחִילִין. הָאִשָּׁה אֶת בְּנָהּ וְהָאִשָּׁה אֶת בַּעֲלָהּ וַאֲחֵי הָאֵם מַנְחִילִין וְלֹא נוֹחֲלִין. וְהָאַחִים מִן הָאֵם לֹא נוֹחֲלִין וְלֹא מַנְחִילִין.

**Mishnah 1**: Some inherit and bequeath; inherit but do not bequeath, bequeath but do not inherit, neither inherit nor bequeath[1]. The following inherit and bequeath: The father from the sons, and the sons from the father, and the paternal brothers inherit and bequeath[2]. A man from his mother, a man from his wife, and the sons of sisters inherit but do not bequeath[3]. A woman to her son, a woman to her husband, and the mother's brothers bequeath but do not inherit[3]. But the maternal brothers neither inherit nor bequeath[4].

**משנה ב**: סֵדֶר נְחָלוֹת כָּךְ הוּא אִישׁ כִּי יָמוּת וּבֵן אֵין לוֹ וְהַעֲבַרְתֶּם אֶת נַחֲלָתוֹ לְבִתּוֹ. הַבֵּן קוֹדֵם לַבַּת וְכָל־יוֹצְאֵי יְרֵיכוֹ שֶׁל בֵּן קוֹדֵם לַבַּת. הַבַּת קוֹדֶמֶת לָאַחִין יוֹצְאֵי יְרֵיכָהּ שֶׁל בַּת קוֹדְמִין לָאַחִין. הָאַחִין קוֹדְמִין לַאֲחֵי הָאָב כָּל־יוֹצְאֵי יְרֵיכָן שֶׁל אַחִים קוֹדְמִין לַאֲחֵי הָאָב. זֶה הַכְּלָל כָּל־הַקּוֹדֵם בַּנַּחֲלָה יוֹצְאֵי יְרֵיכוֹ קוֹדְמִין. וְהָאָב קוֹדֵם לְכָל יוֹצְאֵי יְרֵיכוֹ.

**Mishnah 2**: The order of inheritances is the following: "If a man die without a son, you shall transfer his estate to his daughter[5]." The son precedes the daughter and all the son's descendants come before the daughter[6]. The daughter precedes the brothers and all the daughter's descendants precede the brothers. The brothers precede the father's brothers and all their descendants precede the father's brothers. This is the principle: For every one preceding in inheritance, his descendants precede[7]. But the father precedes all his descendants[8].

1   Among relatives.

2   The father inherits from his childless son. The sons inherit from their father. The brothers inherit from their childless brother after the father's death.

3   A son inherits from his widowed or divorced mother. A husband inherits from his wife. The sons of sisters inherit from an uncle who died without children or brothers. But women do not inherit except daughters of a man who died without sons.

4   Maternal halfbrothers are not considered relatives for the law of inheritance since *Num.* 26:55 restricts inheritance to "the paternal tribe."

5   *Num.* 27:8. Biblical law of inheritance is derived mainly from *Num.* 27:8-11.

6   If at the death of the father a daughter is alive and also a predeceased son's daughter, the granddaughter will inherit but not the daughter. On the other hand, the daughter has a claim on the estate for support or dowry, cf. Mishnah 11, *Ketubot* 13:3.

7   Only agnates inherit; all claims to inheritance are valid *per stirpes*.

8   But not his grandchildren. If a son dies during his father's lifetime, the father inherits only if the son left no descendants. Since the brothers only could inherit as their father's descendants, they cannot inherit if the father is alive.

(15d line 75) **הלכה א:** יֵשׁ נוֹחֲלִין וּמַנְחִילִין כּוֹל׳. כְּתִיב אִישׁ כִּי יָמוּת וּבֵן אֵין לוֹ וְהַעֲבַרְתֶּם אֶת נַחֲלָתוֹ לְבִתּוֹ. תַּנֵּי רִבִּי יִשְׁמָעֵאל. שִׁינָה הַכָּתוּב נַחֲלָה זֹאת מִכָּל נְחָלוֹת שֶׁבַּתּוֹרָה. שֶׁבְּכוּלָּן כָּתוּב וּנְתַתֶּם וְכָאן כָּתוּב וְהַעֲבַרְתֶּם. עִיבּוּר הַדִּין הוּא שֶׁתְּהֵא הַבַּת יוֹרֶשֶׁת. חַכְמֵי גוֹיִם אוֹמְרִים. בֵּן וּבַת שָׁוִין כְּאַחַת. דְּאִינּוּן דָּרְשֵׁי. וּבֵן אֵין לוֹ. הָא אִם יֵשׁ לוֹ שְׁנֵיהֶן שָׁוִין. הֲתִיבוֹן. וְהָכְתִיב. וְאִם אֵין לוֹ בַת. הָא אִם יֵשׁ לוֹ שְׁנֵיהֶן שָׁוִין. וְאַתּוּן מוֹדִין דְּלֵיתֵי בַּר אוּף הָכָא לֵיתֵי בַּר. הַצַּדּוּקִין אוֹמְרִים. בַּת הַבֵּן וְהַבַּת שְׁנֵיהֶן שָׁוִין. דְּאִינּוּן דָּרְשֵׁי. מַה בַּת בְּנוֹ[9]

הַבָּאָה מִכֹּחַ בְּנֵי יוֹרַשְׁתָּנִי. בִּתִּי הַבָּאָה מִכּוֹחִי אֵינוֹ דִין שֶׁתִּירָשֵׁינִי. אָמְרוּ לָהֶן. לֹא. אִם אֲמַרְתֶּם בְּבַת הַבֵּן שֶׁאֵינָהּ בָּאָה אֶלָּא מִכֹּחַ הָאַחִים תֹּאמְרוּ בַּבַּת שֶׁאֵינָהּ בָּאָה אֶלָּא מִכֹּחַ הַזָּקֵן. תַּלְמוּד לוֹמַר. וְכָל־בַּת יוֹרֶשֶׁת נַחֲלָה מִמַּטּוֹת וגו'. וְכִי הֵיאַךְ אֶיפְשָׁר לַבַּת לִירֵשׁ שְׁנֵי מַטּוֹת. אֶלָּא תִּיפָּתֵר אָבִיהָ מִשֵּׁבֶט זֶה וְאִמָּהּ מִשֵּׁבֶט אַחֵר.

**Halakhah 1**: "Some inherit and bequeath," etc. It is written: "If a man die without a son, you shall transfer his estate to his daughter[5]." Rebbi Ismael stated: The verse distinguished this inheritance from all other inheritances mentioned in the Torah, since for all of them it is written "you shall give,[10]" but here is written: "you shall transfer." It is an extension of the law[11] that the daughter shall inherit. The Gentile Sages say, son and daughter are equal[12], for they explain "if he have no son;" therefore, if he has one both are equal. One objected, is it not written "if he have no daughter;[13]" therefore, if he has one are both equal[14]? And you agree, if there is no child[15], here also, if there is no son[16]. The Sadducees say, the son's daughter and the daughter are equal[17], for they explain: Since my son's daughter who comes by force of her father does inherit from me, would it not be logical that my daughter who comes by force of myself should inherit from me? One told them, no. If you mention the son's daughter who only inherits by the power of the brothers, what could you say about the daughter who only inherits by the power of the old man[18]?

The verse says, "any daughter who is an heiress of the tribes[19]." How is it possible for a daughter to inherit from two tribes? But explain it if her father was from one tribe and her mother from another[20].

9   Read בְּנֵי.

10  The inheritance of the agnates,

verses *Num.* 27:9-11.

11  He reads the *hiph'il* "to transfer"

in the meaning of *pi'el* "to be pregnant", to express an exception to the usual rules. As stated at the end of the paragraph, the inheritance of the daughter implies a transfer of the property to her sons, who belong to her husband's family, not her father's.

12  This is the rule in Roman and Egyptian native law while in Egyptian Greek law the daughter inherited only if her dowry had not been paid (cf. R. Taubenschlag, *The Law of Greco-Roman Egypt in the Light of the Papyri*, New York 1944, §11.)

13  *Num.* 27:10.

14  Would a daughter have to share her inheritance with the agnate uncles?

15  A man's brothers only inherit in the absence of *stirpes*.

16  A daughter only inherits in the absence of sons.

17  Babli 116b.

18  The deceased son's daughter inherits her father's share in her grandfather's estate; her claim is the same as that of any of her uncles. But a daughter who has brothers has no claim whatsoever on her father's estate; she only has a lien on the estate for her dowry if at her father's death she was not yet married. The principles of the claims of a son's daughter and a daughter are different. *Sifry Num.* 134.

19  *Num.* 36:8. The verse really reads: Any daughter, heiress of property, of the tribes of the Children of Israel, . . . But the word מִמַּטּוֹת carries a (minor) dividing accent which may justify the truncation in the quote.

20  The same text in *Ta'aniot* 4:11, 69c l. 37 and the Babli 111a.

(16a line 11) עַד כְּדוֹן בֵּן אֶת הָאָב. הָאָב אֶת הַבֵּן. מָה אִם הַבֵּן שֶׁאֵינוֹ בָא אֶלָּא מִכֹּחַ הָאָב הֲרֵי הוּא יוֹרְשׁוֹ. הָאָב שֶׁאֵין הַבֵּן בָּא אֶלָּא מִכּוֹחוֹ אֵינוֹ דִין שֶׁיּוֹרְשׁוֹ. אָמַר קְרָא קָרוֹב. קָרוֹב קוֹדֵם.

So far the son [inherits from] the father. The father from the son? Since the son only inherits by the father's power, is it not logical that the father on whom the son depends inherit from him? The verse says, "close[21]"; the closer relative has precedence[22].

21  *Num.* 27:11.

22  The argument presented would imply that the father has precedence over his grandchildren. Therefore, the argument *de minore ad majus* has to be rejected and the rules all must be

found in the verse. It is asserted that a person's closest relatives are his children. The verse then also justifies the rule of the Mishnah that the heir is the agnate connected to the bequeather by a minimum of ascents in the genealogical tree.

(16a line 14) עַד כְּדוֹן בַּת. בֵּן. מָה אִם הַבַּת שֶׁהוֹרַעְתָּה כּוֹחָהּ בְּנִיכְסֵי הָאָב יִיפִּיתָה כּוֹחָהּ בְּנִיכְסֵי הָאֵם. בֵּן שֶׁיִּיפְּתָה כּוֹחוֹ בְּנִיכְסֵי הָאָב אֵינוֹ דִין שֶׁנְּיַיפֶּה כּוֹחוֹ בְּנִיכְסֵי הָאֵם. נִמְצֵאת הַבַּת לְמֵידָה מִן הַכָּתוּב וְהַבֵּן מִקַּל וַחוֹמֶר. בֵּן קוֹדֵם לַבַּת. רִבִּי שׁמְעוֹן בֶּן לָעֲזָר אוֹמֵר מִשּׁוּם רִבִּי זְכַרְיָה בֶּן הַקַּצָּב. כָּךְ הָיָה רִבִּי שִׁמְעוֹן בֶּן יְהוּדָה אוֹמֵר מִשּׁוּם רִבִּי שׁמְעוֹן. אֶחָד הַבֵּן וְאֶחָד הַבַּת שָׁוִין בַּמַּטֶּה הָאֵם. רִבִּי מַלּוּךְ בְּשֵׁם רִבִּי יְהוֹשֻׁעַ בֶּן לֵוִי. הֲלָכָה כְּרִבִּי זְכַרְיָה. רִבִּי יַנַּאי קַפּוֹדְקָיָיא הֲוָה לֵיהּ עוֹבְדָא וַהֲוּוֹ דַיְינִין רַב הוּנָא וְרִבִּי יְהוּדָה בֶּן פָּזִי וְרַב אֲחָא. אֲמַר לוֹן רַב אֲחָא. אַחֵינוּ שֶׁבְּחוּצָה לָאָרֶץ הַדְּיוֹטוֹת הֵן וְהֵן טוֹעִין אַה הַהֲלָכָה. וְעוֹד דְּאִינּוּן סָמְכוֹן עַל הָדָא דְרִבִּי מַלּוּךְ בְּשֵׁם רִבִּי יְהוֹשֻׁעַ בֶּן לֵוִי. וְלֵי תוּ כֵן. רִבִּי סִימוֹן בְּשֵׁם רִבִּי יְהוֹשֻׁעַ בֶּן לֵוִי. אֵין הֲלָכָה כְּרִבִּי זְכַרְיָה. רִבִּי בָּא בְּרֵיהּ דְּרִבִּי חִייָה בְּשֵׁם רִבִּי יוֹחָנָן. אֵין הֲלָכָה כְּרִבִּי זְכַרְיָה בֶּן הַקַּצָּב. רִבִּי לֶעְזָר אָבוֹי דְּרִבִּי יִצְחָק בַּר נַחְמָן בְּשֵׁם רִבִּי הוֹשַׁעְיָה . אֵין הֲלָכָה כְּרִבִּי זְכַרְיָה. רִבִּי יַנַּאי וְרִבִּי יוֹחָנָן הֲווֹן יָתְבִין. אָעַל רִבִּי יוּדָן נְשִׂייָא וְשָׁאַל. וְכָל־בַּת יוֹרֶשֶׁת נַחֲלָה מִמַּטּוֹת. מַהוּ. אָמַר לֵיהּ. מַקִּישׁ מַטֶּה הָאָב לְמַטֶּה הָאֵם. מַה מַּטֶּה הָאָב אֵין לַבַּת בִּמְקוֹם הַבֵּן אַף מַטֶּה הָאֵם אֵין לַבַּת בִּמְקוֹם בֵּן. אוֹ חִילּוּף. מַה מַּטֶּה הָאֵם יֵשׁ לַבַּת בִּמְקוֹם בֵּן אַף מַטֶּה הָאָב יֵשׁ לַבַּת בִּמְקוֹם בֵּן. אָמַר לֵיהּ רִבִּי יוֹחָנָן. אִיתָא מִן תַּמָּן לֵית אַהֵן גּוּבְרָא בָּעֵי מִישְׁמַע מִילָּה דְּאוֹרַייָא.

So far a daughter[23]. A son? Since the daughter, whose power is diminished regarding the father's property, has her power increased regarding the mother's property, should the son's power not be increased regarding the mother's property, since his power is increased regarding the father's property? It turns out that for the daughter one infers from the verse and for the son from an argument *de minore ad majus*. Does the son precede the daughter? Rebbi Simeon ben Eleazar said in the name of

Rebbi Zachariah the butcher's son: So did Rebbi Simeon ben Jehudah say in the name of Rebbi Simeon: Both son and daughter are equal for the mother's tribe[24]. Rebbi Mallukh in the name of Rebbi Joshua ben Levi: Practice follows Rebbi Zachariah. Rebbi Yannai the Kappadokian had a case; the judges were Rav Huna[25], Rebbi Jehudah ben Pazi, and Rebbi Aha. Rebbi Aha told them: Our brothers outside the Land are unqualified and err in practice; in particular they rely on Rebbi Mallukh in the name of Rebbi Joshua ben Levi, but it is not so. Rebbi Simon in the name of Rebbi Joshua ben Levi: Practice does not follow Rebbi Zachariah. Rebbi Abba the son of Rebbi Hiyya in the name of Rebbi Johanan: Practice does not follow Rebbi Zachariah. Rebbi Eleazar the father of Rebbi Isaac bar Nahman[26] in the name of Rebbi Hoshaiah: Practice does not follow Rebbi Zachariah. [24]Rebbi Yannai and Rebbi Johanan were sitting when Rebbi Yudan the Prince came and asked concerning: "Any daughter who is an heiress of the tribes," what is the rule? He[27] said to him, it binds the father's tribe together with the mother's tribe. Since from the father's tribe there is nothing for the daughter when there is a son, so also from the mother's tribe there is nothing for the daughter when there is a son. Or is it the other way around? Since from the mother's tribe there is something for the daughter when there is a son, so also from the father's tribe is there something for the daughter when there is a son[28]? Rebbi Johanan said to him[29], let us leave; that man does not want to listen to words of instruction.

23  In all paragraphs dealing with the laws of inheritance, *Num.* 27:6-11, 36:8-9, *Deut.* 21:15-17, only the father is mentioned. One might infer that these laws do not apply to the mother's estate. Since *Num.* 36:8 mentions the daughter as heiress, one infers that the daughter inherits from her mother

(*Sifry Num.* 134).

24    Babli 111a; Tosephta 7:10.

25    One has to read *Rebbi* Huna; the second generation Babylonian Rav Huna could not sit in a court together with two Galilean fourth generation judges, even though in the Babli, 111a, *Rav* Huna is reported to have erroneously followed R. Zachariah.

26    From here it seems that "bar Naḥman" was his family name.

27    R. Yannai. the senior authority.

28    This is R. Yudan the Prince's objection.

29    Probably one should read, parallel to the Babli: He said to R. Joḥanan; since the student R. Joḥanan could not tell his teacher R. Yannai to insult the patriarch to his face.

(16a line 33) וְהָאִישׁ אֶת אִמּוֹ וְהָאִישׁ אֶת אִשְׁתּוֹ. לֹא הוּא הָאִישׁ אֶת אִמּוֹ הוּא הָאִישׁ אֶת אִשְׁתּוֹ. רִבִּי יִצְחָק בָּעֵי מֵימַר פנסטא וְלָא אַשְׁכָּח. וָמַר הָדָא הִילְכְתָא תִינְיָיתָא.

"A man from his mother, a man from his wife." Is "a man from his mother" not the same as "a man from his wife"[30]? Rebbi Isaac: he wanted to enumerate all cases[31] and did not find them, so he formulated the rule twofold.

30    Neither rule has a direct scriptural root. The inheritance of a man from his mother was earlier derived from a biblical expression (Note 20). The inheritance of a man from his wife is not implied by this. In the Babli 111b and *Sifry Num.* 134 the husband's inheritance is inferred from *Jos.* 24:33; one explains that the "property of Phineas in the Mountains of Ephraim" must have come to him as inheritance from his wife since as a priest he would have been barred from receiving property outside of Levitic cities.

31    The word פנסטא in L's text defies explanation. E's reading פנטסה is read by S. Lieberman as πάντοσε "in all ways, in any way". The Mishnah often is formulated with redundancies, if the enumeration of all cases helps memorization.

In the Yerushalmi, the husband's right to his deceased wife's estate possibly remains a matter of common law [Halakhah 6, followed by Maimonides (*Neḥalot* 1:8, *Iššut* 12:3); rejected in the Babli as minority opinion (*Ketubot* 83b)]. Cf. M. A.

Friedman, *Jewish Marriage in Palestine*, Tel-Aviv and New York 1980, p. 391 ff.

(16a line 35) בֵּן. אֵין לִי אֶלָּא בֵן. בֶּן בַּת מְנַיִין. תַּלְמוּד לוֹמַר בֵּן. מִכָּל־מָקוֹם. בַּת. אֵין לִי אֶלָּא בַת. בֶּן בַּת בַּת בֶּן בַּת בַּת בֶּן בֶּן מְנַיִין. תַּלְמוּד לוֹמַר בַּת. מִכָּל־מָקוֹם. אָחִים. אֵין לִי אֶלָּא אַחִים. בְּנֵי אַחִים בְּנוֹת אַחִים בְּנֵי בְנוֹת אַחִים מְנַיִין. תַּלְמוּד לוֹמַר לִשְׁאֵרוֹ הַקָּרוֹב. מִכָּל־מָקוֹם.

[32]"Son." Not only a son, from where a daughter's son? The verse says, "a son[33]", from anywhere.

"Daughter." Not only a daughter, from where a daughter's son, a son's daughter, daughter's daughter, a son's son? The verse says, "a daughter", from anywhere.

"Brothers." Not only brothers, from where brothers' sons, brothers' daughters, brothers' sons' daughters? The verse says, "his flesh's relatives", from anywhere[34].

32  Cf. Babli 115a. The argument is intended to show a biblical source for the claim that the rules of inheritance are to be interpreted *per stirpes*.

33  No definite article is used in the paragraph, to allow maximum freedom of interpretation.

34  As long as an agnate exists, no matter how many generations one would have to go back, he becomes the heir. Only the male ancestors are considered since *Num.* 26:55 requires that inheritance be governed by "the names of the *fathers'* tribes."

(fol. 15d) **משנה ג:** בְּנוֹת צְלָפְחָד נָטְלוּ שְׁלֹשָׁה חֲלָקִים בַּנַּחֲלָה חֵלֶק אֲבִיהֶן שֶׁהָיָה עִם יוֹצְאֵי מִצְרַיִם וְחֶלְקוֹ עִם אֶחָיו בְּנִכְסֵי חֵפֶר וְשֶׁהָיָה בְּכוֹר נוֹטֵל שְׁנֵי חֲלָקִים.

**Mishnah 3**: Zelophehad's daughters[35] took three parts[36] in inheritance: Their father's who was of those who left Egypt, his part among his brothers in the estate of Hepher[37], and because he was firstborn he was taking two parts[38].

35 He had five daughters but no sons, *Num.* 27:1-7.
36 Cities with the names of the daughters dominate the entire Southern part of Cisjordan Manasseh. The problem to be discussed is how to compute the distribution of land by Joshua according to *Num.* 26:52-56 which prescribes first that the land be distributed to "those", i. e., those mentioned in the second desert census, *Num.* 26:5-51, but computed "by the names of their fathers' tribes" which means the names of those who left Egypt.
37 Who was supposed to have been alive at the time of the Exodus.
38 Mishnah 4.

(16a line 39) **הלכה ג:** בְּנוֹת צְלָפְחָד אָמְרוּ לִפְנֵי מֹשֶׁה רַבֵּינוּ. בְּנוֹת צְלָפְחָד כּוּל׳. אִם אָנוּ בְּנוֹת צְלָפְחָד נִירַשׁ אֶת אָבִינוּ. אִם אֵין בְּנוֹת צְלָפְחָד תִּתְיַבֵּם אִמֵּינוּ. מִיַּד וַיַּקְרֵב מֹשֶׁה אֶת מִשְׁפָּטָן לִפְנֵי י׳. אָמַר לוֹ הַקָּדוֹשׁ בָּרוּךְ הוּא. כֵּן בְּנוֹת צְלָפְחָד דּוֹבְרוֹת. תֵּן לָהֶן אֲחוּזַּת נַחֲלָה. תֵּן לָהֶן בַּקַּרְקָעוֹת. תֵּן לָהֶן בְּמִטַּלְטְלִין. תֵּן לָהֶן חֵלֶק אֲבִיהֶן בְּתוֹךְ אֲחֵי אֲבִיהֶן.

**Halakhah 3**: "Zelophehad's daughters," etc. [39]Zelophehad's daughters said before our teacher Moses: If we are Zelophehad's daughters, we should inherit from our father. If we are not Zelophehad's daughters, let our mother enter levirate marriage[40]. Immediately, "[41]he brought their suit before the Eternal." The Holy One, praise to Him, told him, "[42]Zelophehad's daughters speak correctly. Give them possession of inheritance," give them real estate, give them movables, give them their father's part among their father's brothers.

39 Babli 119b; Tanḥuma *Pineḥas* 6, 9, Tanḥuma Buber *Pineḥas* 8, 9, *Num. rabba Pineḥas* 11.
40 If daughters cannot inherit then the widow of a man who dies without sons should be treated like the widow of a childless man, *Deut.* 25:5-9. Since the latter conclusion obviously is

| impossible, so is the hypothesis from | 41 | *Num.* 27:5. |
| which it follows. | 42 | *Num.* 27:7-8. |

(16a line 43) רִבִּי יֹאשִׁיָּה אָמַר. לְיוֹצְאֵי מִצְרַיִם נִתְחַלְּקָה הָאָרֶץ. דִּכְתִיב לִשְׁמוֹת מַטּוֹת אֲבוֹתָיו. וְאִם כֵּן מַה תַּלְמוּד לוֹמַר לָאֵלֶּה. אֶלָּא מִפְּנֵי הַנָּשִׁים וּמִפְּנֵי הַקְּטַנִּים. רִבִּי יוֹחָנָן אָמַר. לְבָאֵי הָאָרֶץ נִתְחַלְּקָה הָאָרֶץ. שֶׁנֶּאֱמַר לָאֵלֶּה תֵּחָלֵק. אִם כֵּן מַה תַּלְמוּד לוֹמַר לִשְׁמוֹת מַטּוֹת אֲבוֹתָיו. מְשׁוּנָּה נַחֲלָה זוֹ מִכָּל־נְחָלוֹת שֶׁבָּעוֹלָם. שֶׁכָּל־נְחָלוֹת חַיִּים יוֹרְשִׁין מֵתִים וְכָא מֵתִים יוֹרְשִׁין חַיִּים. תַּנֵּי. רִבִּי הְהוֹשֻׁעַ בֶּן קָרְחָה אוֹמֵר. לְיוֹצְאֵי מִצְרַיִם וּלְעוֹמְדִים בָּעַרְבוֹת מוֹאָב נִתְחַלְּקָה הָאָרֶץ. כֵּיצַד. מִי שֶׁהָיָה מִיּוֹצְאֵי מִצְרַיִם וּמֵעוֹמְדִים בָּעַרְבוֹת מוֹאָב נָטַל שְׁנֵי חֲלָקִים. מִיּוֹצְאֵי מִצְרַיִם וְלֹא מֵעוֹמְדִים בָּעַרְבוֹת מוֹאָב מֵעוֹמְדִים בָּעַרְבוֹת מוֹאָב וְלֹא מִיּוֹצְאֵי מִצְרַיִם נָטַל חֵלֶק אֶחָד. בְּנוֹת צְלָפְחָד נָטְלוּ חֲמִשָּׁה חֲלָקִים. חֶלְקָן עִם יוֹצְאֵי מִצְרַיִם. וְחֶלְקָן עִם הָעוֹמְדִים בָּעַרְבוֹת מוֹאָב. וְשֶׁהָיָה בְּכוֹר נָטְלוּ שְׁנֵי חֲלָקִים. וְחֵלֶק אֲבִיהֶן בְּתוֹךְ אֲחֵי אֲבִיהֶן. אָמַר רִבִּי יוֹסֵי. מַתְנִיתָא לֹא אֲמָרָה כֵן. אֶלָּא נָתוֹן תִּתֵּן לָהֶן אֲחֻזַּת נַחֲלָה בְּתוֹךְ אֲחֵי אֲבִיהֶן. הָדָא הִיא דִכְתִיב וַיִּפְּלוּ חַבְלֵי מְנַשֶּׁה עֲשָׂרָה.

[43]Rebbi Joshiah said, the Land was distributed to those who left Egypt, as it is written: "By the names of the fathers' tribes they shall inherit.[44]" Then why does the verse say: "To those[45]"? Only because of women[46] and because of children[47].

Rebbi Johanan[48] said, the Land was distributed to those who entered the Land[49], as it was said, "to those it shall be distributed[45]." Then why does the verse say: "By the names of the fathers' tribes"? This inheritance was different from all other inheritances in the world. For in all other inheritances in the world the living inherit from the dead but here the dead from the living[50].

It was stated[51]: Rebbi Joshua ben Qorha said, the Land was distributed to those who left Egypt and to those who stood in the plains of Moab.

How is that? If one was both of those who left Egypt and those who stood in the plains of Moab, he took two parts[52]. Of those who left Egypt but not of those who stood in the plains of Moab, or of those who stood in the plains of Moab but not of those who left Egypt, he took one part. The daughters of Zelophehad took five parts: their part with those who left Egypt[54] and their part with those who stood in the plains of Moab. And because he[55] was a firstborn they took two parts. And their father's part among his brothers. Rebbi Yose said, the Mishnah says otherwise[56]. But "giving you shall give them inheritance among their father's brothers.[42]" That is what is written: "Ten measures fell to Manasseh[57]".

43 Babli 117a; a different version *Tanḥuma Pineḥas* 5 = *Num. rabba* 21(9).

44 *Num.* 26:55, referring to the census *Num.* 1.

45 *Num.* 26:53. The verse asserts that the distribution of land has to be based on the census of *Num.* 26.

46 The daughters of Zelophehad.

47 As will be explained later, Notes 63 ff.

48 One has to read with E and the Babli "Jonathan" as contemporary of R. Joshiah.

49 Each of the persons counted in the second census became a candidate for a piece of land similar in value to that of any other.

50 While the number of lots was determined by the second census, the final allotment was made through the first census as explained by Rebbi in the section after the next.

51 117a/b (R. Simeon ben Eleazar), slightly differently Tosephta 7:8 (R. Eliezer ben Jacob).

52 In the Tosephta: It was *given* to those who left Egypt and *distributed* to those who stood in the plains of Moab.

53 This applies only to Caleb and Joshua.

54 The decree that those who left Egypt could not enter the Land applied neither to women nor to Levites.

55 Zelophehad. Even though the rule that the firstborn takes a double portion does not apply to expected acquisitions of the estate, here it is considered already acquired because of God's promise in Egypt (*Ex.* 6:8).

56 They only received three parts. The Mishnah can only be interpreted

following R. Joshiah.

57  Jos. 17:5. It is explained in Jos. 17:2 that Gilead and Bashan were given to the seven male clans of Manasseh, and the Cisjordan territory to the five female clans. If together this made ten districts, it follows that the five females in the plains of Moab, while representing only one person of the Exodus, received $3/10$ of the entire territory of Manasseh.

(16a line 57) יְהוֹשֻׁעַ וְכָלֵב נָטְלוּ שְׁלֹשָׁה חֲלָקִים. חֶלְקָן עִם יוֹצְאֵי מִצְרַיִם. וְחֶלְקָן עִם הָעוֹמְדִים בְּעַרְבוֹת מוֹאָב. וְנָטְלוּ חֵלֶק מְרַגְּלִים. הָדָא הוּא דִכְתִיב. וִיהוֹשֻׁעַ בִּן נוּן וְכָלֵב בֶּן יְפֻנֶּה חָיוּ מִן הָאֲנָשִׁים וגו'. אֲבָל חֵלֶק מִתְלוֹנְנִים וַעֲדַת קֹרַח נָפַל לָאֶמְצַע. וּבְנֵיהֶם בִּזְכוּת אֲבִי אֲבִיהֶן וְאִמּוֹתֵיהֶן. הָדָא הִיא דִכְתִיב וּבְנֵי קֹרַח לֹא מֵתוּ.

Joshua and Caleb took three parts: Their part with those who left Egypt and their part with those who stood in the plains of Moab[53]; in addition they took the parts of the spies[58]. This is what is written: "Joshua bin Nun and Caleb ben Yephuneh lived off the men, etc.[59]" But the part of the complainers[60] and Korah's gang became common property; their sons [inherited] from their paternal and maternal grandfathers. That is what is written: "Korah's sons did not die.[61]"

58  Babli 117b.
59  Num. 14:38.
60  Num. 11:1 ff.

61  Num. 26:11. They were Levites not involved in the distribution of land.

(16a line 61) רְבִּי מוֹשְׁלוֹ מָשָׁל לְמַה הַדָּבָר דּוֹמֶה. לִשְׁנֵי אַחִים שׁוּתָּפִין שֶׁיָּצְאוּ מִמִּצְרַיִם. לָזֶה תִּשְׁעָה בָנִים וְלָזֶה בֵּן אֶחָד וְיָרְשׁוּ בֵּית עֲשֶׂרֶת כּוֹרִין. כָּל־אֶחָד וְאֶחָד נוֹטֵל לְתָךְ. הֶחֱזִירוּם לַאֲבוֹתֵיהֶן וְחִלְּקוּם. נִמְצָא בֶּן זֶה נוֹטֵל מֶחֱצָה וּבְנֵי זֶה נוֹטְלִין מֶחֱצָה.

Rebbi explained it by a parable; to what can this be compared? To two brothers, co-owners who left Egypt. One had nine sons, the other a single son. They inherited ten *bet kor*. Each of them takes a *letekh*[62]. They return it to their fathers and then split. It turns out that the single son takes half and the sons of the other take half[63].

62 Half a *bet kor*.

63 In the Babli, 117a, Rebbi is credited with the explanation by the parable credited here to R. Dositheos ben Jehudah.

The text here is inconsistent in several places. If together they took ten *bet kor*, each of them took a *bet kor* rather than a *letekh*, half a *bet kor*. If the fathers were above the age of twenty at the Exodus, there is no reason why the sons of one should be co-owners with the son of the other. If they were below age twenty at the Exodus, they should have survived and the entire question could not be raised. Therefore, one has to assume that the grandfather was alive at the time of the Exodus and the entire allotment was returned to the *grandfather*, from whom each son inherited the claim to half the estate which was then split for the ten grandsons.

(16a line 65) רִבִּי דּוֹסְתַּי בֶּן יְהוּדָה מוֹשְׁלוֹ מָשָׁל לְמָה הַדָּבָר דּוֹמֶה. לִשְׁנֵי אַחִים כֹּהֲנִים שׁוּתָּפִין שֶׁהָיוּ עוֹמְדִין עַל הַגּוֹרֶן. לָזֶה ט׳ בָּנִם וְלָזֶה בֵן אֶחָד וְנָטְלוּ (בֵּית) י׳ קַבִּין. הֶחֱזִירוּם לַאֲבוֹתֵיהֶן וְחִלְקוּם. נִמְצָא בֶּן זֶה נוֹטֵל מֶחֱצָה וּבְנֵי זֶה מֶחֱצָה.

Rebbi Dositheos ben Jehudah[64] explained it by a parable; to what can this be compared? To two brothers, Cohanim and co-owners[65] who stood by a threshing floor[66]; one had nine sons and the other had one. They took (the area of)[67] ten *qab*. They returned it to their father and split[68]. It turns out that the son of one takes half and the sons of the other take half.

64 A contemporary of Rebbi.

65 Both are still living at their father's house.

66 To ask for heave.

67 This has to be deleted since one refers here to volumes, not areas.

68 One has to assume that after they collected the heave, the grandfather and the fathers died, since otherwise the grandfather, on whose

property the entire family was living, would have received everything for distribution among his dependants.

Parables, situated in never-never land, cannot be subjected to stringent logical analysis.

(16a line 68) רִבִּי יוֹחָנָן מָתִיב. וְהֵבֵאתִי אֶתְכֶם אֶל אֶרֶץ אֲבוֹתֵיכֶם וגו'. אִם מַתָּנָה לָמָּה יְרוּשָׁה. וְאִם יְרוּשָׁה לָמָּה מַתָּנָה. אֶלָּא מֵאַחַר שֶׁנְּתָנָהּ לָהֶן לְשׁוּם מַתָּנָה חָזַר וּנְתָנָהּ לָהֶן לְשׁוּם יְרוּשָׁה. אָמַר רִבִּי הוֹשַׁעְיָה. כָּל־מָקוֹם שֶׁנֶּאֱמַר מוֹרָשָׁה לְשׁוֹן דִּיהָא. הֲתִיבוֹן. וְהָכְתִיב מוֹרָשָׁה קְהִילַת יַעֲקֹב. אָמַר. לֵית דִּיהָא סוֹגִין מִינֵּיהּ. מָן דּוּ לָעֵי הוּא מַשְׁכַּח כּוּלָּהּ.

Rebbi Johanan objected: "I shall bring you to your forefathers' land, etc.[69]" If it was a gift, why an inheritance? And if an inheritance, why a gift? But after he gave it to them as a gift, he turned around and gave it as inheritance[70,71].

Rebbi Hoshaia said, anywhere one mentions מוֹרָשָׁה it means weariness[72]. They objected, is it not written, "an inheritance (מוֹרָשָׁה) of the congregation of Jacob[73]"? He said, there is no weariness greater than this. He who studies forgets everything[74].

69  A misquote of *Ex.* 6:8. The verse ends: "I shall *give* it to you as an *inheritance*, I, the Eternal." *Giving* implies a voluntary act, a *gift*, whereas *inheritance* is automatic by law.

70  The rights of the people of the Exodus were established as *gift*; then those of the generation of the conquest already were an *inheritance* (Babli 117b).

71  E here has a parallel version:

רִבִּי יִצְחָק בַּר מַרְיוֹן בְּשֵׁם רִבִּי יוֹחָנָן. כָּתוּב וְטַפְּכֶם אֲשֶׁר אֲמַרְתֶּם לָבַז יִהְיֶה וּבְנֵיכֶם אֲשֶׁר לֹא יָדְעוּ הַיּוֹם טוֹב וָרַע הֵמָּה יָבֹאוּ שָׁמָּה וְלָהֶם אֶתְּנֶנָּה וְהֵם יְרָשׁוּהָ. אִם מַתָּנָה לָמָּה יְרוּשָׁה. וְאִם יְרוּשָׁה לָמָּה מַתָּנָה. אֶלָּא מֵאַחַר שֶׁנְּתָנָהּ לָהֶן בִּלְשׁוֹן מַתָּנָה חָזַר וּנְתָנָהּ לָהֶן בִּלְשׁוֹן יְרוּשָׁה.

Rebbi Isaac bar Marion in the name of Rebbi Johanan: It is written (*Deut.* 1:39): "Your little ones, of whom you said, they will be taken as prey, and your children who today do not know good or bad, they will come there, to them I shall *give* it, and they will *inherit* it." If it was a gift, why an inheritance? And if an inheritance, why a gift? But after he gave it to them *in the language of* a gift, he turned around and gave it *in the language of* inheritance."

72 It is unclear from which root he derives the word since the only candidate besides *yrš* "to inherit" would be *rwš* "to be poor."

73 *Deut.* 33:4: "Moses commended to us Torah, an inheritance ... " This verse should not have a negative connotation.

74 This is explained in *Eccl. rabba* on 1:13: "For his own benefit a person studies Torah and forgets it, for if a person could study Torah and not forget it, he would study it for two or three years and then never think of it again" and miss all rewards for the study of Torah.

(fol. 15d) **משנה ד:** אֶחָד הַבֵּן וְאֶחָד הַבַּת בַּנַּחֲלָה אֶלָּא שֶׁהַבֵּן נוֹטֵל פִּי שְׁנַיִם בְּנִכְסֵי הָאָב וְאֵינוֹ נוֹטֵל פִּי שְׁנַיִם בְּנִכְסֵי הָאֵם. וְהַבָּנוֹת נִיזּוֹנוֹת מִנִּכְסֵי הָאָב וְאֵינָן נִיזּוֹנוֹת מִנִּכְסֵי הָאֵם.

**Mishnah 4**: Both son and daughter[75] are equal for the rules of inheritance, except that the son take a double portion of the father's property[76] but no double portion of the mother's property. And the daughters can claim sustenance from the father's property[77] but not from the mother's property.

75 If there are no sons, the rules of inheritance apply to daughters as if they were sons.

76 *Deut.* 21:17. The entire paragraph only deals with father and son; since the mother is neither required nor empowered to recognize a child as hers, it cannot refer to the mother's inheritance.

It probably is correct to read פִּי שְׁנַיִם as "double portion" rather than "two thirds" which would read פִּים (*1S.* 13:21); cf. *Sifry Deut.* #217. The double portion of male first-borns is also found in the Egyptian native law both in Ptolemaic and in Roman times and the Syro-Roman law book.

77 After the father's death; cf. Mishnah 9:1, *Ketubot* 4:8.

(16a line 74) **הלכה ד:** אֶחָד הַבֵּן וְאֶחָד הַבַּת בַּנַּחֲלָה כול'. כָּתוּב בְּכָל־אֲשֶׁר יִמָּצֵא לוֹ וגו'. כֵּיצַד יוֹרֵשׁ בָּרָאוּי כְּבַמּוּחְזָק. כֵּיצַד. מֵת אָבִיו בְּחַיֵּי אֲבִי אָבִיו נוֹטֵל פִּי שְׁנַיִם מִנִּכְסֵי אָבִיו וְאֵין נוֹטֵל פִּי שְׁנַיִם מִנִּכְסֵי אֲבִי אָבִיו. וְאִם הָיָה אָבִיו בְּכוֹר כְּשֵׁם שֶׁנָּטַל מִנִּכְסֵי אָבִיו כָּךְ נוֹטֵל בְּנִכְסֵי אֲבִי אָבִיו. רִישׁ לָקִישׁ בְּשֵׁם אַבָּא בַּר דְּלָיָיה. נֶאֱמַר מִשְׁפָּט לְעִנְיַין כְּפֵילָה וְנֶאֱמַר מִשְׁפָּט לְעִנְיַין פְּשׁוּטָה. מַה לְעִנְיַין פְּשׁוּטָה אַתְּ רוֹאֶה אֶת הַבֵּן כִּילוּ קַיָּים לִיטּוֹל פְּשִׁיטוּת אָבִיו. אַף לְעִנְיַין כְּפֵילָה אַתָּה רוֹאֶה אֶת הַבֵּן כִּילוּ קַיָּים לִיטּוֹל כְּפֵילַת אָבִיו.

**Halakhah 4**: "Both son and daughter are equal for the rules of inheritance," etc. It is written[76,78]: "Of anything which will be found with him," etc. How could he inherit the expectancy like existing property? [79]How? If his father died during his father's father's lifetime, he takes a double portion of his father's estate but not a double portion of his grandfather's estate. But if his father was a firstborn, just as he takes from his father's estate so he takes from his grandfather's estate[80].

Rebbi Simeon ben Laqish in the name of Abba [Cohen][81] bar Delaiah: It was said "a rule of law[76]" in the matter of a double portion just as it was said "a rule of law[82]" in the matter of a single portion. Since for a single portion one considers the son as if he were alive to take his father's single portion[7] so for a double portion one considers the son as if he were alive to take his father's double portion[83].

78  The verse makes it clear that only property actually *at hand* in the estate at the moment of the father's death is subject to the double portion privilege of the firstborn son, but not *expected* income (*Sifry Deut*. 217).

79  Tosephta 7:7, *Bekhorot* 6:18.

80  If the grandfather dies after the father, the grandson can take a double portion of the former's estate only if he is the only son of a firstborn son. If his father had been a firstborn but has brothers, the rule of Mishnah 1 implies that their father's estate inherits a double portion in the grandfather's estate. Since this is future income, all brothers inherit equally. Cf. Babli *Bekhorot* 52b.

81 Reading of E; this is the name usually quoted.
82 *Num.* 27:11.
83 The rule of Mishnah 2 applies to double portions as well as single ones.

(fol. 15d) **משנה ה:** הָאוֹמֵר אִישׁ פְּלוֹנִי בְּנִי בְּכוֹר לֹא יִטּוֹל פִּי שְׁנַיִם אִישׁ פְּלוֹנִי בְּנִי לֹא יִירַשׁ עִם אֶחָיו לֹא אָמַר כְּלוּם שֶׁהִתְנָה עַל מַה שֶׁכָּתוּב בַּתּוֹרָה. הַמְחַלֵּק נְכָסָיו לְבָנָיו עַל פִּיו רִבָּה לְאֶחָד וּמִיעֵט לְאֶחָד וְהִשְׁוָה לָהֶן אֶת הַבְּכוֹר דְּבָרָיו קַיָּימִין. וְאִם אָמַר מִשּׁוּם יְרוּשָׁה לֹא אָמַר כְּלוּם. כָּתַב בֵּין בַּתְּחִילָה בֵּין בָּאֶמְצַע בֵּין בַּסּוֹף מִשּׁוּם מַתָּנָה דְּבָרָיו קַיָּימִין.

**Mishnah 5**: One who says, "my firstborn X shall not take a double portion," [or] "my son Y shall not inherit together with his brothers," did not say anything since he stipulated against what is written in the Torah[84]. One who distributes his property orally[85], if he increased for one, or diminished for another, or made the firstborn equal to the others, his words are upheld; except if, however, he formulated it in terms of inheritance[86], he did not say anything. But if he wrote in terms of gift, whether at the start, or in the middle, or at the end, his words are upheld[87].

84 Mishnah *Bava meṣia'* 7:14. The rules based on *Num.* 27:6-11 are prescriptive, rather than eventual rules in the intestate case.
85 If he makes the oral declaration of the will of a critically ill person.
86 If he wrote the entire will in terms of inheritance, the will is void.
87 In a document one has to follow the formal rules. If he used the language of gift but also mentioned inheritance, the will is valid as explained by R. Hoshaia in the Halakhah.

(16b line 5) **הלכה ה:** הָאוֹמֵר אִישׁ פְּלוֹנִי בְּנִי בְּכוֹר כול׳. רִבִּי לָא הִשְׁוָה אֶת הַבְּכוֹרָה לְאַחִין. אֲמַר לוֹן רִבִּי חַגַּיי. וְלָאו קְרָיָיא הִיא לֹא יוּכַל לְבַכֵּר. אֲמַר

רִבִּי לְעֶזֶר. הָעֲבוֹדָה שֶׁיָכוֹל אֶלָּא שֶׁאֵינוֹ רַשָּׁאי. אִי כֵן יָכִיל מִשֵּׁם מַתָּנָה.

**Halakhah 5:** "One who says, "my firstborn X shall not take a double portion,"' etc. Rebbi La made the right of the firstborn equal to that of the brothers[88]. Rebbi Ḥaggai said to them: Is that not a verse, "he shall not be able to declare as firstborn."[89] [90]Rebbi Eliezer said, by the Temple Service! He is able, but he is not permitted[91]. Except that he is able designating it as a gift[87].

88 He approved a will which gave the firstborn only what the other brothers received.

89 He thought that Rebbi La acted in error.

90 *Midrash Tannaïm* (*Midrash Haggadol Deut.* 21:16); *Sifry Deut.* 216.

91 What is missing here (compared to the other sources) is the statement that any action to deprive the firstborn of his inheritance be invalid. In general we hold that if a certain action is biblically forbidden, if it is done anyway it is valid in law since, if it were invalid, it could not be punishable. But an action by the father to deprive his firstborn of his double portion is not punishable; therefore, it is invalid.

(16b line 8) כָּתַב בֵּין בַּתְּחִילָּה בֵּין בָּאֶמְצַע בֵּין בַּסּוֹף מִשֵּׁם מַתָּנָה דְּבָרָיו קַיָּימִין. אָמַר רִבִּי הוֹשַׁעְיָה. יִנָּתֵן לְאִישׁ פְּלוֹנִי יְרוּשָׁה שֶׁהוֹרַשְׁתִּיו. יִירַשׁ פְּלוֹנִי מַתָּנָה שֶׁהוֹרַשְׁתִּיו. יִירַשׁ פְּלוֹנִי יְרוּשָׁה שֶׁנְּתַתִּי לוֹ. כִּתְבוּ וּתְנוּ שָׂדֶה פְּלוֹנִית לִפְלוֹנִי. רִבִּי לָעְזָר וְרִבִּי שִׁמְעוֹן בֶּן יָקִים אַעֲלוֹן עוֹבְדָּא קוֹמֵי רִבִּי יוֹחָנָן. אֲמַר לוֹן. אִם לְזִכְרוֹן דְּבָרִים כִּתְבוּ וּתְנוּ. אִם לְזַכּוּתוֹ בִּכְתָב כָּל־עַמָּא מוֹדוּ שֶׁאֵין אָדָם מְזַכֶּה בִּכְתָב לְאַחַר מִיתָה.

"But if he wrote in terms of gift, whether at the start, or the middle, or the end, his words are upheld." Rebbi Hoshaia said: "There *shall be given* to Mr. X the inheritance I want him to inherit." "X should inherit *the gift* I want him to inherit." "X shall inherit the inheritance which I *gave to him*."[92]

[93]"Write and give field X to person Y." Rebbi Eleazar and Rebbi Simeon ben Yaqim brought a case before Rebbi Joḥanan[94]. He told them, if it is documentation, then write and deliver. If it is to transfer property, everybody agrees that nobody can transfer property after his death[95].

92   These are examples of acceptable formulations in a will essentially formulated in the language of inheritance but with mention of *giving* or *gift* either before, or in between, or after mentioning inheritance. Cf. Babli 129a; Tosephta 7:17.

93   The paragraph is a reformulation of one in *Qiddušin* 1:5, Notes 495-499.

94   An oral death-bed will which is valid as if written during the bequeather's lifetime.

95   If the testator had said, I am giving it to him, you go and deliver the document, it is valid. If it were not a death-bed will, it would need an act of transfer, but the act of transfer is understood from the order given by the dying person. But if it is clear from the language of the testator that transfer of property should be effected by the delivery of the deed and he died in the meantime, delivery is impossible since a person's power over his property ends with his death because the biblical laws of inheritance are prescriptive (Babli 135b).

(16b line 14) שְׁמוּאֵל שָׁאַל לְרַב הוּנָא. מַתָּנָה שֶׁכָּתַב בִּלְשׁוֹן מֶכֶר מָהוּ. אָמַר לֵיהּ. אַרְכְּבֵיהּ אַתְּרֵי רִיכְשֵׁי בַּרְקֵי. אָמַר רִבִּי חִזְקִיָה. לָא אָמְרֵי אֶלָּא מַיְיתוּ תְּרֵין סוּסְוָן חִיוָורִין וּמַרְכִּיבִין עַל תְּרֵיהוֹן וְדֵין אָזְלָא בְּדָא וְדֵין אָזְלָא בְּדָא וּמִשְׁתַּכַּח לָא צָיַיד כְּלוּם.

[96]Samuel asked Rav Huna[97]: if one wrote a gift in the language of a sale[98]? He answered, he made it ride on two racing horses; Rebbi Ḥizqiah said, they only said that one brings two white horses and makes it ride on both. One goes in one direction and the other in another; it turns out that he caught nothing[99].

96   A reformulation of a paragraph in *Qiddušin* 1:5, Notes 490-492. Cf. Babli 152a.

97   To inquire about Rav's opinion after the latter's death.

98   A will formulated not as a true gift, as required by the Mishnah, but as a fictitious sale.

99   For Rav, the will is valid; for Samuel it is invalid since gifts and sales follow different rules.

(fol. 15d) **משנה ו:** הָאוֹמֵר אִישׁ פְּלוֹנִי יִירָשֵׁנִי בְּמָקוֹם שֶׁיֵּשׁ בַּת בְּתִּי תִּירָשֵׁינִי בְּמָקוֹם שֶׁיֵּשׁ בֵּן לֹא אָמַר כְּלוּם שֶׁהִתְנָה עַל מַה שֶּׁכָּתוּב בַּתּוֹרָה. רַבִּי יוֹחָנָן בֶּן בְּרוֹקָה אוֹמֵר אִם אָמַר עַל מִי שֶׁהוּא רָאוּי לִירוּשָׁה דְּבָרָיו קַיָּימִין וְעַל מִי שֶׁאֵינוֹ רָאוּי לִירוּשָׁה אֵין דְּבָרָיו קַיָּימִין.

**Mishnah 6:** One who says, Mr. X shall inherit from me while he has a daughter[100], or, my daughter shall inherit from me while he has a son, did not say anything since he stipulated against what is written in the Torah[84]. Rebbi Joḥanan ben Beroqah said, if he said that about anybody who can be his heir, his words stand; about anybody who cannot be his heir, his words do not stand[101].

100   But no son.   Tosephta 7:18.

101   As explained in the Halakhah;

(16b line 17) **הלכה ו:** הָאוֹמֵר אִישׁ פְּלוֹנִי יִירָשֵׁנִי כול'. אָמַר רִבִּי יוֹחָנָן. לֹא אָמַר רִבִּי יוֹחָנָן בֶּן בְּרוֹקָה אֶלָּא עַל בֵּן בֵּין הַבָּנִים וְעַל בַּת בֵּין הַבָּנוֹת. בַּת בֵּין הָאַחִין אַח בֵּין הַבָּנוֹת לֹא. אָמַר רִבִּי יוֹחָנָן. הֲלָכָה כְּרִבִּי יוֹחָנָן בֶּן בְּרוֹקָה. רִבִּי שָׁאַל לְרִבִּי נָתָן. בַּר בָּא אָמַר. אָכֵין שְׁאֵילָה. מַאי טַעֲמָא דְּרִבִּי יוֹחָנָן בֶּן בְּרוֹקָה. רִבִּי זְעִירָא אָמַר. הָכֵן שְׁאֵלָה. מָה רָאוּ לוֹמַר הֲלָכָה כְּרִבִּי יוֹחָנָן בֶּן בְּרוֹקָה. אָמַר לֵיהּ. וְאַתְּ לֹא שָׁנִיתָהּ לָנוּ כֵּן. אִינּוּן יְרָתוֹן. כֵּינֵי מַתְנִיתָא. אִינּוּן יִטְלוּן. אָמַר [רִבִּי] לָא. וַאֲפִילוּ כְּמָאן דְּאָמַר יְרָתוּן. כֹּחַ בֵּית דִּין מְיוּפֶּה. כַּמָּה

דְּתֵימַר תַּמָּן. אֵין אָדָם מְזַכֶּה בִּלְשׁוֹן מַתָּנָה. וְהָכָא מְזַכָּה. וְדִכְוָותָהּ. אֵין אָדָם מְזַכֶּה בִּלְשׁוֹן יְרוּשָׁה. וְהָכָא מְזַכֶּה.

**Halakhah 6**: "One who says, Mr. X shall inherit from me," etc. [102]Rebbi Johanan said, Rebbi Johanan ben Beroqa said only this about a son among sons or a daughter among daughters, but not a daughter among brothers[103] or a brother among daughters.

Rebbi Johanan said, practice follows Rebbi Johanan ben Beroqa. Rebbi asked Rebbi Nathan[104]; bar Abba[105] said, so was the question: What is Rebbi Johanan ben Beroqa's reason? Rebbi Ze'ira said, so was the question: What did they see to say that practice follows Rebbi Johanan ben Beroqa? He told him, did you not teach us so[106]: "they shall inherit"? So is the Mishnah: "they shall take."[107] [Rebbi][108] La said, even following him who said "inherit", is not the power of the court strengthened[109]? As you say, nobody can transfer property using the language of gift; here he may do it[110]. Similarly, nobody can transfer property using the language of inheritance; here he may do it[111].

102 Both following paragraphs are reformulations of a text in *Ketubot* 4:12, Notes 239-248. The statement of R. Johanan paraphrases Tosephta 7:18. It is clear that the Tosephta was unknown to the editors, if any, of this Yerushalmi. The Yerushalmi mentions neither the restriction of the Babli (130a) by R. Johanan ben Beroqa touching the privilege of the firstborn nor the extension of the Tosephta which includes grandchildren.

103 The daughter among the father's brothers is also mentioned in *Ketubot*, but naturally the father's brothers do not inherit if there be a daughter as stated in the same sentence. The two clauses "daughter among brothers," "brother among daughters" mean the same.

104 In *Ketubot*: Nathan the Babylonian.

105 In *Ketubot*: Rebbi Abba.

106 Mishnah *Ketubot* 4:12 states that in a polygamous family the sons of one wife inherit her *ketubah* in addition to their part in the father's estate. This shows that while the formulation of the

biblical law of inheritance presupposes equal parts for every son, there are situations where by common law inheritances are distributed unevenly.

107 Since the distribution of the deceased mother's *ketubah* is an obligation which the father accepted at his marriage, it is not an *inheritance* from the father (Babli 131a; *Ketubot* 52b, 55a).

108 Reading of E. In *Ketubot* R. Ze'ira.

109 The inheritance of the sons in a polygamous family is not a private contract but common law interpreted as an ordinance of the Court which promulgated the rules of *ketubah*.

110 Property can be transferred by a gift document but not by words unless accompanied by an act of acquisition. The rule is waived for a death-bed will.

111 Again, if the language of inheritance is used exclusively, the will is valid only as a death-bed will. Otherwise the terminology of giving must be used.

(16b line 25) תַּמָּן תַּנִּינָן. רַבָּן שִׁמְעוֹן בֶּן גַּמְלִיאֵל אוֹמֵר. אִם מֵתָה יִירָשֶׁנָּה. שֶׁהִתְנָה עַל מַה שֶּׁכָּתוּב בַּתּוֹרָה. רַב יִרְמְיָה בְּשֵׁם רַב. מִפְּנֵי שֶׁהִיתְנָה עַל הַכָּתוּב בַּתּוֹרָה. וְהַמַּתְנֶה עַל הַכָּתוּב בַּתּוֹרָה תְּנָייוֹ בָּטֵל. בִּתְנַאי שֶׁאֵינוּ שֶׁלְּמָמוֹן. וְכָא בִּתְנַאי מָמוֹן נָן קַיָּימִין. מַה טַעְמָא דְרַב. בַּסּוֹף הוּא זָכָה. אָמַר רִבִּי יוֹחָנָן. הֲלָכָה כְרִבִּי יוֹחָנָן בֶּן בְּרוֹקָה. דָּמַר רִבִּי יוֹחָנָן. מָכְרָה וְנָתְנָה בְּדִין הוּא לִהְיוֹת קַיָּים. וְלָמָּה אָמְרוּ מִכְרָהּ בָּטֵל. שֶׁלֹּא תְהֵא מַבְרַחַת נְכָסֶיהָ מִבַּעְלָהּ וְאוֹמֶרֶת שֶׁלִּי הֵן. רִבִּי יוּסְטִינֵי הֲוָה לֵיהּ עוֹבְדָא קוֹמֵי רַבָּנָן וְחִייְבוּנֵיהּ. קָם קוֹמֵי רֵישׁ לָקִישׁ. אָמַר. זִיל חוֹת לְנִיכְסָךְ. רִבִּי יִרְמְיָה בְּעָא קוֹמֵי רִבִּי זֵירָא. אָמַר רַב. בַּסּוֹף הוּא זָכָה בָּהֶן. אָמַר רִבִּי יוֹחָנָן. הֲלָכָה כְרִבִּי יוֹחָנָן בֶּן בְּרוֹקָה. אָמַר רֵישׁ לָקִישׁ. אֵיזִיל חוֹת לְנִיכְסָךְ. מָאן אִינּוּן רַבָּנָן. רַבָּנִין דְּרִבִּי יוּסְטִינֵי.

[112]There, we have stated[113]: "Rabban Simeon ben Gamliel said, if she dies, he should inherit from her since he made a condition contradicting what is written in the Torah." Rav Jeremiah in the name of Rav: "Since he made a condition contradicting what is written in the Torah and anybody's condition contradicting what is written in the Torah is invalid'"?

Conditions other than for money matters. But here we are dealing with a money matter![114] What is Rav's reason? Because in the end he acquired it[115]. Rebbi Joḥanan said, practice follows Rebbi Joḥanan ben Beroqa[116], for Rebbi Joḥanan said, if she sold or gave away[117], the rule should be that it is valid. Then why did they say that her sale is invalid? Lest she smuggle away her properties from her husband and say, they are mine. Rebbi Justinus had a case before the rabbis and they obligated him[118]. He came before Rebbi Simeon ben Laqish who told him, enter your properties[119]. Rebbi Jeremiah asked before Rebbi Ze'ira: Did not Rav say, because in the end he acquired it. Did not Rebbi Joḥanan say, practice follows Rebbi Joḥanan ben Beroqa? Did not Rebbi Simeon ben Laqish say, go and enter your properties? Who are these rabbis[120]? The rabbis of Rebbi Justinus[121].

112 A reformulation of texts in *Ketubot* 9:1, Notes 44-57.

113 Mishnah *Ketubot* 9:1. If a couple write a prenuptial agreement reserving the wife's property to her and her heirs, it is unconditionally valid for the rabbis but Rabban Simeon ben Gamliel denies the validity of the inheritance clause.

114 He agrees with Rabban Simeon that the inheritance clause is invalid but questions his reasoning since this is a money matter where stipulations are permitted which deviate from biblical rules; Babli *Qiddušin* 19b.

115 In the Babli, *Ketubot* 84a, it is stated explicitly that for Rav the husband's right to his wife's estate is rabbinic. Therefore his acquisition of the estate is a court decree. (In the Yerushalmi, *Ketubot* 8:5 Note 44, this is ascribed to R. Simeon ben Laqish.)

116 One is tempted to read instead: R. Joḥanan said, practice follows Rabban Simeon ben Gamliel, since the reason given in the next sentence has nothing to do with R. Joḥanan ben Beroqa's statement. This is the approach taken by all classical commentaries but it is impossible today since the text here and later is confirmed by E.

As explained in Note 109, R. Joḥanan holds that the rule of R,

Johanan ben Beroqa is common law modifying biblical rules. Therefore, he also must hold that an acceptance of Rabban Simeon ben Gamliel's rule cannot be based on the latter's reason. His explanation essentially is identical with that ascribed to Rav in the preceding sentence.

117  Her paraphernalia property, to which the husband has no property rights during her lifetime.

118  He and his wife lived under a regimen of separation of properties. When she died, the local court told him to surrender his wife's properties to her family.

119  He decided following Rabban Simeon ben Gamliel as rabbinic ordinance.

120  The greatest authorities of the first two Amoraic generations follow Rabban Simeon ben Gamliel. Which court could decide against him?

121  Courts of first instance sometimes do err.

(16b line 36) וְיָרַשׁ אוֹתָהּ. יָכוֹל כְּשֵׁם שֶׁהוּא יוֹרְשָׁהּ כָּךְ הִיא יוֹרְשָׁתוֹ. תַּלְמוּד לוֹמַר אוֹתָהּ. הוּא יוֹרְשָׁהּ. הִיא אֵינָהּ יוֹרְשָׁתוֹ. אָמַר רִבִּי יוֹחָנָן. דִּבְרֵי חֲכָמִים. אָבִיהָ יוֹרְשָׁהּ אֲחֵיהָ יוֹרְשִׁם אוֹתָהּ. הָתִיב רִבִּי בָּא בַּר מָמָל. אִם אוֹמֵר אַתְּ שֶׁאֵין יוֹרֶשֶׁת אִשָּׁה דְּבַר תּוֹרָה מֵעַתָּה יִירַשׁ אֶה אֲרוּסָתוֹ. כְּמָה דְתֵימַר תַּמָּן. הַקְּרוֹבָה. לֹא גְרוּשָׁה. וְדִכְוָותָהּ. הַקְּרוֹבָה. לֹא אֲרוּסָה. הָתִיב רַב הַמְנוּנָא. אִם אוֹמֵר אַתְּ שֶׁאֵין אִשָּׁה יוֹרֶשֶׁת דְּבַר תּוֹרָה מֵעַתָּה יִירַשׁ הַבַּעַל בָּרָאוּי כִּבְמוּחְזָק. אָמַר רִבִּי יוֹסֵי. כָּךְ שָׁנָה רִבִּי. אֵין הַבַּעַל נוֹטֵל בָּרָאוּי כִּבְמוּחְזָק. אָמַר רִבִּי יוֹסֵי בֵּירִבִּי בּוּן. הֲרֵי בְכוֹר הֲרֵי יְרוּשָׁתוֹ תּוֹרָה וְאֵינוֹ יוֹרֵשׁ בָּרָאוּי כִּבְמוּחְזָק.

"And he shall inherit from her[122]." I could think that just as he inherits from her, she should inherit from him[123]. The verse says, "from her." He inherits from her, she does not inherit from him[124]. Rebbi Joḥanan said, the words of the Sages are that her father inherits from her, her brothers inherit from her[125].

Rebbi Abba bar Mamal objected: If you say that the inheritance status of a woman is not from the Torah, should he not inherit from his preliminarily wedded wife[126]? As you say there, "the one close to him,[127]" not the preliminarily wedded one, so also here, "the one close to him," not the preliminarily wedded one.

Rav Hamnuna objected: If you say that a woman does not inherit by the word of the Torah, should not the husband inherit the expectancy like existing property[128]? Rebbi Yose said, so did Rebbi teach: The husband does not take the expectancy like that which is at hand[129]. Rebbi Yose ben Rebbi Abun said, there is the first-born whose inheritance is from the Torah but he does not take the expectancy like that which is at hand[79,130].

122  *Num.* 26:11: "If his father had no brothers, transfer his estate to his relative who is closest to him of his family; *he shall inherit (from) her.*" In the verse, the feminine *her* refers to the estate. The identification of *her* with the wife is R. Aqiba's (*Sifry Num.* 134). In *Lev.* 18, the *masculine* word שְׁאֵר "relative" is used exclusively for *female* relatives.

123  Babli 111b.

124  He explains the emphasis, "he shall inherit *her*" when the same could have been expressed by the shorter, וְיָרָשָׁהּ. The additional word used for *her* implies *not him*.

125  They reject R. Aqiba's derivation. *Her* in the verse refers to the estate; by biblical law her clan should be her heirs. The inheritance of the husband is purely rabbinical.

126  There really is no basis for this question since it is generally accepted that preliminary marriage be only relevant for criminal law whereas definitive marriage activates all financial aspects of a marriage (cf. Introduction to Tractate *Qiddušin*.) The question is rather whether there be a biblical basis for the common law practice that the husband's claim on the wife's property only starts with definitive marriage, when the couple starts living together.

127  Probably one should read הַקָּרוֹב both times for הַקְּרוֹבָה. In *Lev.* 21:2 the expression שְׁאֵרוֹ הַקָּרֹב אֵלָיו "the relative close to him" is explained as "his wife who is close to him," i. e., his definitively wedded wife, since all other closely related relatives are enumerated in vv. 2-3. The mention of closeness excludes the preliminarily wedded one since intimacy with her is forbidden to him [*Sifra Emor* (4)].

128  If the heiress wife dies before her father, his estate will go to her childen. Since in general common law

gives her inheritance to her husband, why not in this case also?

129 This is a statement of fact: Moneys due to the wife after her death go to her children, rather than her surviving husband. Babli 125b.

130 There is biblical precedent to exclude future income from present distribution.

(16b line 45) אָמַר רִבִּי יִצְחָק וִילֵּין דְּכָתְבִין. אִין מִיתַת דְּלָא בְנִין כָּל־דְּלָהּ יַחֲזוֹר לְאָבִיהָ. תְּנַאי מָמוֹן הוּא וּתְנָאוֹ קַייָם.

Rebbbi Isaac said: About those who write, if she should die without children, all that was hers shall revert to her father. This is a stipulation about money; the stipulation is valid[131].

131 This is repeated from *Ketubot* 9:1, Note 87.

(16b line 46) וּשְׂגוּב הוֹלִיד אֶת יָאִיר וגו'. וְכִי מְנַיִין הָיוּ לְיָאִיר עָרִים בְּהַר הַגִּלְעָד. אֶלָּא שֶׁנָּשָׂא אִשָּׁה מִבְּנוֹת מְנַשֶּׁה וָמֵתָה וִירָשָׁהּ. אִם אוֹמֵר אַתְּ שֶׁאֵין יוֹרֶשֶׁת אִשָּׁה דְּבַר תּוֹרָה גֵימַר וַיְהִי לִשְׂגוּב אֶלָּא וַיְהִי לוֹ לְיָאִיר. דְּכְוָותָהּ. וְאֶלְעָזָר בֶּן אַהֲרֹן מֵת. וְכִי מְנַיִין הָיוּ לוֹ לְפִינְחָס בְּהַר אֶפְרָיִם. אֶלָּא שֶׁנָּשָׂא אִשָּׁה מִבְּנוֹת אֶפְרַיִם וִירָשָׁהּ. אִם אוֹמֵר אַתְּ שֶׁאֵין יְרוּשַׁת אִשָּׁה דְּבַר תּוֹרָה. גֵימַר. וַיְהִי לְאֶלְעָזָר אֶלָּא וַיְהִי לְפִינְחָס.

[132]"Segub fathered Jair,[133]" etc. From where did Jair have cities on Mount Gilead? But he married a woman from the daughters of Manasse who died and he inherited from her. If you would say that the inheritance from a wife was not a word of the Torah it should not say that "Jair had" but that "Segub had.[134]" Similarly, "Eleazar ben Aaron died.[135]" From where did Phineas have property on the Mountain of Ephraim? But he married a woman from the daughters of Ephraim and inherited from her. If you would say that the inheritance from a wife was not a word of the Torah it should say that "Eleazar had" not that "Phineas had.[136]"

132 This paragraph is R. Ismael's argument to show that the husband's inheriting his deceased wife's properties, if not explicit in the Torah, at least was established practice already in the time of Joshua (*Sifry Num.* 134.) A different explanation of the verses quoted here is given in the Babli, 113a.

133 *1Chr.* 2:22. The verse states that Jair, a Calebite, had 23 villages in the land of Gilead (Manasseh).

134 In v. 21 it is reported that Jair's grandfather Hezron married a Gileadite wife. If the property came through her, the verse should have attributed ownership to her son Segub, rather than her grandson Jair.

135 *Jos.* 24:33, "they buried him on his son Phineas's hill which had been given to him on the Mountain of Ephraim."

136 As Rashi *ad. loc.* intimates, one cannot say that the tribe of Ephraim gave Phineas property among themselves since the Torah explicitly excluded priests from receiving any land outside the Levitic cities (*Deut.* 18:1). Therefore, ownership of property outside such cities must be by inheritance from a non-priestly wife. The tribal affiliation of Eleazar's father-in-law Puṭiel (*Ex.* 6:25) is not known.

**משנה ז:** הַכּוֹתֵב נְכָסָיו לַאֲחֵרִים וְהִנִּיחַ אֶת בָּנָיו מַה שֶּׁעָשָׂה עָשׂוּי אֲבָל אֵין רוּחַ חֲכָמִים נוֹחָה מִמֶּנּוּ. רַבָּן שִׁמְעוֹן בֶּן גַּמְלִיאֵל אוֹמֵר אִם לֹא הָיוּ בָנָיו נוֹהֲגִים כַּשּׁוּרָה זָכוּר לַטּוֹב. (fol. 15d)

**Mishnah 7:** If one writes his properties over to others[137] while neglecting his children, what he did is done[138] but the Sages do not approve of him. Rabban Simeon ben Gamliel says, if his children did not behave properly, let him be well remembered.

137 As a gift "from today, effective after my death".

138 If writing the document was accompanied by an act of acquisition on behalf of the beneficiary, it becomes irrevocable.

(16b line 52) **הלכה ז:** הַכּוֹתֵב נְכָסָיו לַאֲחֵרִים כול'. אָמַר רִבִּי בָּא בַּר מָמָל. הַכּוֹתֵב נְכָסָיו לַאֲחֵרִים וְהִנִּיחַ אֶת בָּנָיו. עָלָיו הוּא אוֹמֵר וַתְּהִי עֲווֹנוֹתָם עַל עַצְמוֹתָם. כְּהָדָא חַד בַּר נָשׁ אַפְקַד נִיכְסוֹי גַּבֵּי רִבִּי בָּא בַּר מָמָל. אֲמַר לֵיהּ. אִין הַוְיָין בָּנוֹי דַהֲנָיָיה הַב לוֹן פַּלְגָּא וְסַב פַּלְגָּא. אַתּוֹן בָּנוֹי וְנַסְבוּן פַּלְגָּא. בָּתַר יוֹמִין אַתּוֹן בְּעָיָין מֵיעוֹר עִימֵּיהּ. אֲמַר לוֹן. לָא אֲמַר אֲבוּכוֹן אֶלָּא אִי הַוְיָין בָּנוֹי דַהֲנָיָיה הַב לוֹן פַּלְגָּא וְסַב פַּלְגָּא. כְּדוֹן אַתּוֹן קַקוֹ פַּדְיפָטִי. הֲבוּ לִי מַה דִּיהֲבִית לְכוֹן.

**Halakhah 7**: "If one writes his properties over to others," etc. Rebbi Abba bar Mamal said, about one who writes his properties over to others while neglecting his children, the verse says: "their sins were on their bones[139]." As the following: A person deposited his properties with Rebbi Abba bar Mamal and told him, if my sons will be useful give them half and keep half. His sons came and took half. Later they came to appeal[140] against him. He told them, your father said only: If my sons will be useful give them half and keep half. Now you are badly educated[141], return to me what I gave to you.

139  Ez. 32:27. It is a sin which will cling to his bones even in the grave. In the Babli, 133b, Samuel told his student Rav Jehudah in his law practice never to help anybody to deprive a son of his inheritance.

140  The root of מיעור is ערר "to launch an appeal."

141  Greek κακο-παιδευτοί. E reads קקפריגמיניין which Lieberman explains as κακοτραγμόνες "unworthy, useless".

(fol. 15d) **משנה ח:** הָאוֹמֵר זֶה בְנִי נֶאֱמָן זֶה אָחִי נֶאֱמָן וְיִטּוֹל עִמּוֹ בְחֶלְקוֹ. מֵת יַחְזְרוּ נְכָסִים לִמְקוֹמָן. נָפְלוּ לוֹ נְכָסִים מִמָּקוֹם אַחֵר יִירְשׁוּ אֶחָיו עִמּוֹ. מִי שֶׁמֵּת וְנִמְצָא דְיָיתִיקֵי קְשׁוּרָה עַל יְרֵיכוֹ הֲרֵי זוֹ אֵינָהּ כְּלוּם. זִיכָּה בָהּ לְאַחֵר בֵּין מִן הַיּוֹרְשִׁין בֵּין מִן שֶׁאֵין מִן הַיּוֹרְשִׁין דְּבָרָיו קַיָּימִין.

**Mishnah 8**: He who says, this is my son, is to be believed[142]. This is my brother, he is not to be believed[143] but he shall split his part with him[144]; if he dies the properties shall return to their origin[145]. If he received property from another source, his brother shall inherit with him[146]. If somebody died and a will[147] was found tied to his hip, this is nothing[148]. If in it he transferred property to another[149], whether of the heirs or not of the heirs, his words are confirmed[150].

142 *Deut.* 21:17 is interpreted to mean that the father has the right to recognize a son without submitting a proof; his statement has to be accepted by the court. There is no difference whether the son was born from a licit or an illicit union; as long as the mother was Jewish the son frees the childless wife from levirate marriage and is entitled to a full share in the inheritance (Mishnah *Yebamot* 2:6).

143 If he presents an otherwise unknown person as his paternal half-brother, he is required to provide proof since the half-brother would 1º reduce his other brothers' share in their father's estate and 2º require levirate marriage in case the deceased had no other brothers and died childless. Since he acts to the detriment of others, he cannot be believed without solid proof.

144 Since a person can take an obligation on himself, by recognizing the stranger as his half-brother he acknowledged the latter as a co-heir. Since he cannot diminish the share of his other brothers, he must share his own inheritance with the stranger.

145 His heirs are not his own children but the sons of the man who recognized him as half-brother. Their father's unsubstantiated recognition of the stranger cannot impair his son's rights.

146 If the stranger accepted the status of paternal half-brother and then died without issue, the half-brother inherits.

147 Cf. *Bava meṣiaʿ* 1:7, Note 90.

148 Since a person can give away property only when he is alive, a will is valid only if either it was a public document (a death-bed will) or contains a note that an act of transfer of property was executed during the testator's lifetime. Without such a remark, the will is invalid

149 E. g., that it was signed by witnesses on behalf of the beneficiaries.

150 Once part of a will is valid, the entire will is valid.

## 681

(16b line 58) **הלכה ח:** הָאוֹמֵר. זֶה בְנִי. נֶאֱמָן כול'. אִם הָיוּ מוּחְזָקִין בּוֹ שֶׁהוּא בְנוֹ וּבִשְׁעַת מִיתָתוֹ אָמַר. אֵינוֹ בְנִי. וְשֶׁאֵינוֹ בְנוֹ אָמַר. בְּנִי. נֶאֱמָן. הָיָה עוֹמֵד בְּצַד הַמּוֹכֵס וְאָמַר. בְּנִי הוּא. וְחָזַר וְאָמַר. עַבְדִּי הוּא. נֶאֱמָן. עַבְדִּי הוּא. וְחָזַר וְאָמַר. בְּנִי הוּא. אֵינוֹ נֶאֱמָן. אִית תַּנָּיֵי תַנֵּי. נֶאֱמָן. אָמַר רִבִּי מָנָא. כְּגוֹן אִילֵּין נַפָּתָאֵי דִמְשַׁעְבְּדִין בִּבְנֵיהוֹן יָתִיר.

**Halakhah 8**: "He who says, this is my son, is to be believed," etc. [151]If it was the general belief that he was his son, but at the moment of his death he said, he is not my son, or about one not his son he said, he is my son, he is believed[152]. If he stood near the toll collector and said, he is my son[153] and then changed and said, he is my slave, he is believed. He is my slave, and then said, he is my son, he cannot be believed[154]. Some Tannaïm state, he is to be believed[155]. Rebbi Mana said, for example those Nabateans who particularly use their sons as slaves[156].

151 A materially different text in Tosephta 7:3, *Qiddušin* 4:7 Notes 182-194, Babli 127b as Amoraic statement.

152 Since *Deut.* 21:17 requires the father to recognize his son "on the day he distributes his estate", any statement he makes on his death bed in matters of recognizing sons must be believed without requiring proof.

153 To pay only the low rate applicable to persons, not the high rate payable for slaves as merchandise.

154 Since he acted to his own detriment.

155 Tosephta 7:3. If he always declares him a slave for toll collectors but never in other situations, he is believed but not otherwise.

156 They may switch between *slave* and *son* without inconsistency.

(16b line 63) הָאוֹמֵר. יִינָּתְנוּ נְכָסַיי לִפְלוֹנִי. וְהוּא כֹהֵן וְהָיוּ שָׁם עֲבָדִים. אַף עַל פִּי שֶׁאָמַר. אִי אֶיפְשִׁי בָהֶן. יֹאכְלוּ עֲבָדָיו בַּתְּרוּמָה. רַבָּן שִׁמְעוֹן בֶּן גַּמְלִיאֵל אוֹמֵר. מִכֵּיוָן שֶׁאָמַר. אִי אֶיפְשִׁי בָהֶן. זָכוּ בָהֶן הַיּוֹרְשִׁין. אָמַר רִבִּי לָא. בִּסְתָם חֲלוּקִין. מָה נָן קַיְימִין. אִם דָּבָר בָּרִיא שֶׁרוֹצֶה בָהֶן כָּל־עַמָּא מוֹדוֹ שֶׁיֹּאכְלוּ עֲבָדָיו בַּתְּרוּמָה. וְאִם דָּבָר בָּרִיא שֶׁאֵינוֹ רוֹצֶה בָהֶן כָּל־עַמָּא מוֹדוֹ שֶׁזָּכוּ בָהֶן

הַיּוֹרְשִׁין. אֶלָּא כִּי נָן קַייָמִין בִּסְתָם. וְרַבָּנִין סָבְרִין. מִשָּׁעָה רִאשׁוֹנָה הָיָה רוֹצֶה בָהֶן וְעַכְשָׁיו חָזַר בּוֹ. רַבָּן שִׁמְעוֹן בֶּן גַּמְלִיאֵל אוֹמֵר. מִכֵּיוָן שָׁאָמַר. אִי אֶיפְשִׁי. זָכוּ בָהֶן הַיּוֹרְשִׁין.

[157]"If somebody said that all his property should be given to X, a Cohen, and [the estate] contained slaves, even if [the Cohen] said 'I cannot have them' they eat heave. Rabban Simeon ben Gamliel said, since he said 'I cannot have them', the heirs acquired them." Rebbi La said, they disagree if he did not specify. How do we hold? If it is clear that he wants them, everybody agrees that his slaves may eat heave. If it is clear that he does not want them, everybody agrees that the heirs acquired them. But we deal with the case that he did not specify, where the rabbis think that at the start he wanted them and then he changed his mind. Rabban Simeon ben Gamliel said, since he said 'it is impossible for me', the heirs acquired them.

157  A reformulation of a paragraph in *Giṭṭin* 1:6, explained there in Notes 166-173 (Tosephta 8:1, Babli 138a, *Ḥulin* 39b, *Keritut* 24b).

(16b line 70) תַּנֵּי. רִבִּי שִׁמְעוֹן בֶּן גַּמְלִיאֵל אוֹמֵר. דִּייָתֵיקֵי מְבַטֶּלֶת דִּייָתֵיקֵי אֵין מַתָּנָה מְבַטֶּלֶת מַתָּנָה. רִבִּי אַבָּא בַּר חָנָה. רִבִּי יוֹחָנָן וְרֵישׁ לָקִישׁ תְּרֵיהוֹן אָמְרִין. כָּל־שֶׁאִילּוּ יַבְרִיא וְיַחֲזוֹר בְּדִייָתֵיקֵתוֹ חוֹזֵר אַף בְּמַתָּנָתוֹ. כְּהָהִיא אַחְתֵיהּ דְּרִבִּי חוֹנָיָיא כְּתָבַת נִיכְסָהּ לְרִבִּי חוֹנָיָיא. צָרְכַת וְזָבְנַת לְבַעֲלָהּ. מִן דְּדִמְכַת אֲתָא בָעֵי מֵיעוּר עִימֵּיהּ. אָמַר לֵיהּ. וְלָמָּה לָא תְבַעְתִּינוּן בְּחַיֶּיהָ. אָמַר לֵיהּ. לָא בְעִית מֵעִיקְתַּהּ. אַף עַל פִּי כֵן אַפֵּיק רִבִּי אַמִּי.

It was stated[158]: "Rebbi Simeon ben Gamiel says: A will invalidates a will, a gift does not invalidate a gift." Rebbi Abba bar Ḥana: Rebbi Joḥanan and Rebbi Simeon ben Laqish both are saying that in any case where he can invalidate his will if he recuperates, he also can repeal his gift[159]. As the following: Rebbi Onias's sister[160] wrote her property over to Rebbi Onias. She needed money and sold it to her husband. After she died, he[161] came to protest against him. He asked him, why did you not claim it[162] during her lifetime? He answered, I did not want to cause her pain. Nevertheless, Rebbi Immi removed it[163].

158 Tosephta 8:10, Babli 152b, *Peah* 3:9 (17d l. 66) Note 175.

159 The gift of a sick person, even if accompanied by an act of acquisition, follows the rules of death-bed wills, rather than that of gifts among healthy persons.

160 Who obviously lived under a regime of separation of properties.

161 R. Onias came to protest against his brother-in-law's taking his sister's properties as his own.

162 If the gift was irrevocable, the sale was impossible and R. Onias should have intervened immediately.

163 The reader may choose his own interpretation of this sentence. R. Eliahu Fulda explains that the gift was irrevocable among healthy people, that R. Onias became the proprietor of the real estate but had to refund the sale price to his brother-in-law. *Pene Moshe* explains that the gift was a death-bed gift which became meaningless when the woman recovered; therefore R. Immi confirmed the husband in his possessions and took away the gift document from R. Onias. In either case would R. Immi have followed the instructions of his teacher R. Johanan.

**משנה ט**: הַכּוֹתֵב נְכָסָיו לְבָנָיו צָרִיךְ שֶׁיִּכְתּוֹב מֵהַיּוֹם וּלְאַחַר מִיתָה (fol. 15d) דִּבְרֵי רִבִּי יְהוּדָה. רִבִּי יוֹסִי אוֹמֵר אֵינוֹ צָרִיךְ. הַכּוֹתֵב נְכָסָיו לִבְנוֹ אַחַר מוֹתוֹ הָאָב אֵינוֹ יָכוֹל לִמְכּוֹר מִפְּנֵי שֶׁהֵן כְּתוּבִין לַבֵּן וְהַבֵּן אֵינוֹ יָכוֹל לִמְכּוֹר מִפְּנֵי שֶׁהֵן בִּרְשׁוּת הָאָב. מָכַר הָאָב מְכוּרִין עַד שֶׁיָּמוּת מָכַר הַבֵּן אֵין לַלּוֹקֵחַ בָּהֶן כְּלוּם עַד שֶׁיָּמוּת הָאָב. הָאָב תּוֹלֵשׁ וּמַאֲכִיל לְכָל־מִי שֶׁיִּרְצֶה וּמַה שֶׁהִנִּיחַ תָּלוּשׁ הֲרֵי הוּא שֶׁל יוֹרְשִׁין.

**Mishnah 9**: One who writes his properties over to his sons must write: "from today and after my death[164]," the words of Rebbi Jehudah. Rebbi

Yose said, it is unnecessary[165]. If one writes his properties over to his son for the time after his death, the father cannot sell them because they are written over to the son; the son cannot sell because they are in the father's possession. If the father sold, they are sold until he dies. If the son sold, the buyer has no claim until the father dies. The father harvests and feeds anybody he pleases; what becomes part of his estate belongs to the heirs[166].

164 "Today" for the transfer of title to the property, "after my death" for the transfer of usufruct.

165 Without an explicit disclaimer, a deed is always deemed to be valid from the day it was written; *Gittin* 7:3 Note 67.

166 As movables, it is part of the estate, not only of the son inheriting the particular real estate.

(16b line 76) **הלכה ט:** הַכּוֹתֵב נְכָסָיו לְבָנָיו כול'. רִבִּי שִׁמְעוֹן בֶּן יָקִים אָעִיל עוֹבְדָא קוֹמֵי רִבִּי יוֹחָנָן. מֵהַיּוֹם לְאַחַר מִיתָתוֹ מַתָּנָתוֹ מַתָּנָה. מֵהַיּוֹם וּלְאַחַר מִיתָה אֵינוֹ גֵט. חַבְרַיָּיא אָמְרִין. כֵּן אָמַר לֵיהּ. אֵינָהּ הִיא אִיסְרַטָה. אָמַר רִבִּי יוֹסֵי בֵּירִבִּי בּוּן. כֵּן אָמַר לֵיהּ. אֵינָהּ בַּגִּיטִּין וְאֵינָהּ בַּמַּתָּנָה. אָמַר רִבִּי לָא. בְּמַתָּנָה אִם כָּתַב מֵהַיּוֹם מַתָּנָה בְרוּרָה הִיא. לְאִי זֶה דָבָר כָּתַב בָּהּ לְאַחַר מִיתָה. לְשַׁיֵּיר בָּהּ אֲכִילַת פֵּירוֹת. אֲבָל בְּגִיטִּין אִם כָּתַב בָּהּ מֵהַיּוֹם כָּרוּת הוּא. לְאִי זֶה דָבָר כָּתַב בָּהּ לְאַחַר מִיתָה. לְשַׁיֵּיר לוֹ גוּפָהּ. אָמַר רִבִּי בּוֹן בַּר כַּהֲנָא קוֹמֵי רִבִּי לָא. לְשַׁיֵּיר לָהּ מַעֲשֵׂה יָדֶיהָ. אָמַר לֵיהּ. לֹא מָצִינוּ אִשָּׁה נְשׂוּאָה לָזֶה וּמַעֲשֵׂה יָדֶיהָ לָזֶה. רִבִּי זֵירָא מְקַיֵּים לֵיהּ וְצָוַוח לֵיהּ. בְּנַיָּיהּ דְּאוֹרְיָיתָא.

**Halakhah 9**: "One who writes his properties over to his sons," etc. Rebbi Simeon ben Yaqim brought a case before Rebbi Johanan. "From today after his death," his gift is a gift. "From today and after death" it is no bill of divorce. [167]The colleagues say, so he told him: this is no condition. Rebbi Yose ben Rebbi Abun[168] said, so he told him: It applies neither to bills of divorce nor to gifts. Rebbi La said, for a gift; since he said "from today", the gift is clear. Why did he write "after death"? To reserve the yield to himself. But in bills of divorce, since he wrote "from today" in the bill, it would be a separation. Why did he write "after death"? To reserve her body to himself. Rebbi Abun bar Cahana said before Rebbi La, not to reserve her earnings for himself? He answered, we do not find a woman married to one man and her earnings belonging to another. Rebbi Ze'ira confirmed him[169] and called him "son of the Torah."

167 A slight reformulation of a paragraph in *Gittin* 7:3, explained there in Notes 67-75.

168 In *Gittin*: R. Ze'ira. For reasons of chronology, this is the more convincing reading.

169 Probably one should read with the text in *Gittin*: מְקַלֵּס לֵיהּ "he acclaimed him".

(16c line 9) הָאוֹמֵר. טַבִּי עַבְדִּי עָשִׂיתִי בֶּן חוֹרִין. עֲשִׂיתִיו בֶּן חוֹרִין. עוֹשֶׂה אֲנִי אוֹתוֹ בֶּן חוֹרִין. הֲרֵי הוּא בֶן חוֹרִין. הֲרֵי זֶה בֶן חוֹרִין. הֲרֵי זֶה זָכָה. רִבִּי חִיָיה בְּשֵׁם רִבִּי יוֹחָנָן. וּבִלְבַד בִּשְׁטָר. יֵעָשֶׂה בֶן חוֹרִין. רִבִּי אוֹמֵר. זָכָה. וַחֲכָמִים אוֹמְרִים. לֹא זָכָה.

[170]"If somebody says, I freed my slave Ṭabi, I freed him, I shall free him, he is free, this one is free; then he acquired." Rebbi Ḥiyya in the name of Rebbi Joḥanan: But only by a document. "He should be freed, Rebbi says, he acquired, but the Sages say, he did not acquire."

170 A slight reformulation of a text in *Gittin* 1:6, explained there in Notes 157-162. Tosephta 9:14.

(16c line 13) הָאוֹמֵר. שָׂדֶה פְלוֹנִית נָתַתִּי לִפְלוֹנִי. נְתוּנָה לוֹ. תְּהֵא שֶׁלוֹ. יִנְחַל פְּלוֹנִי בִנְכָסַיי. יַחֲזִק פְּלוֹנִי בִנְכָסַיי. לֹא אָמַר כְּלוּם. תִּינָתֵן לוֹ מַתָּנָה. רִבִּי אוֹמֵר. זָכָה. וַחֲכָמִים אוֹמְרִים. לֹא זָכָה. וְכוֹפִין אֶת הַיּוֹרְשִׁים לְקַיֵּים דִּבְרֵי

הַמֵּת. תַּנֵּי. רִבִּי שִׁמְעוֹן בֶּן גַּמְלִיאֵל אוֹמֵר. אַף הַכּוֹתֵב דִּיאֶתֵימוֹן בְּלַעַז הֲרֵי זוֹ כְמַתָּנָה. רִבִּי חָנִין בְּשֵׁם רִבִּי יְהוֹשֻׁעַ בֶּן לֵוִי. חִיזַּרְתִּי עַל כָּל־בַּעֲלֵי לְשׁוֹנוֹת לֵידַע מָהוּ דִּיאֶתֵימוֹן וְלֹא אָמַר לִי אָדָם דָּבָר.

If someone said, field X I gave to Y, it is given to him, it should be his, Y should inherit my property, Y should take possession of my property, he did not say anything[171]. It should be given to him as a gift, Rebbi says, he acquired[172], but the Sages say, he did not acquire; but one forces the heirs to fulfill the deceased's words.[173] It was stated[174]: Rebbi Simeon ben Gamliel says, also if one writes διέθεμεν[175] in Greek it is a gift. Rebbi Ḥanin in the name of Rebbi Joshua ben Levi: I turned to all linguists to know what is διέθεμεν and nobody told me anything[176].

171 Title to property cannot be transferred by simple declaration; cf. Mishnah *Qiddušin* 1:5. The Tosephta disagrees, 9:12. The Tosephta text is explained away by the Babli, *Giṭṭin* 40b.
172 If this was a death-bed declaration.
173 Babli *Giṭṭin* 14b,15a,40a; *Ketubot* 70a.
174 Tosephta 9:14.
175 "I disposed by will", from Greek "to dispose" (H. M. Pineles). A. Gulak, *Tarbiz* 1 fasc. 4 (1931) 144-146 has noted that the expression τάδε διεθέμην is used in Egyptian Greek deeds; also cf. R. Taubenschlag, *The Law of Greco-Roman Egypt in the Light of the Papyri*, New York 1944, p. 143. Since the expression is a legal Greek term, its use characterizes a valid deed even though the corresponding use of the past in Hebrew was declared invalid as statement of a deed. (S. Lieberman, *Tosefta kiFshutah Bava batra* p. 441, wants to infer that Rabban Simeon ben Gamliel validates also the Hebrew נָתַתִּי; this seems unjustified.)
176 They were not acquainted with Greek legalese.

(16c line 19) הָאוֹמֵר. יִינָּתְנוּ נְכָסַיי לִפְלוֹנִי. מֵת פְּלוֹנִי לִפְלוֹנִי. מֵת פְּלוֹנִי לִפְלוֹנִי. הָרִאשׁוֹן רִאשׁוֹן קוֹדֵם. מֵת הַשֵּׁינִי בְּחַיֵּי רִאשׁוֹן הָרִאשׁוֹן אוֹכֵל פֵּירוֹת.

וְאִם מֵת יַחֲזִיר לְיוֹרְשֵׁי הַנּוֹתֵן. מֵת הַשְּׁלִישִׁי בְחַיֵּי הַשֵּׁנִי הָרִאשׁוֹן אוֹכֵל פֵּירוֹת. וְאִם מֵת יַחֲזִיר לְיוֹרְשֵׁי הַנּוֹתֵן. מֵת הַשֵּׁנִי וְהַשְּׁלִישִׁי בְחַיֵּי רִאשׁוֹן הָרִאשׁוֹן אוֹכֵל פֵּירוֹת וְקוֹנֶה קַרְקַע. דִּבְרֵי רִבִּי. רַבָּן שִׁמְעוֹן בֶּן גַּמְלִיאֵל אוֹמֵר. אֵין לוֹ אֶלָּא אֲכִילַת פֵּירוֹת בִּלְבַד. חִזְקִיָּה אָמַר. הֲלָכָה כְּרִבִּי. אָמַר רִבִּי יַנַּאי. מוֹדֶה רִבִּי שֶׁאֵינוֹ נוֹתְנָהּ בְּמַתְּנַת שְׁכִיב מְרַע. רִבִּי יוֹחָנָן אָמַר. וְלֹא בְמַתְּנַת בָּרִיא. כְּהָדָא הַהִיא אִיתָּא כְּתָבַת נִיכְסָהּ לְחַד בַּר נָשׁ. צְרָכַת וְזִבְנַת לְבַעֲלָהּ. רִבִּי חִיָּיה בַּר מַדָיָיא אַעֵיל עוֹבְדָא קוֹמֵי רִבִּי יוֹסִי. לֹא כֵן אָמַר רִבִּי יַנַּאי. מוֹדֶה רִבִּי שֶׁאֵינוֹ נוֹתְנָהּ בְּמַתְּנַת שְׁכִיב מְרַע. אָמַר לֵיהּ רִבִּי יוֹחָנָן. וְלֹא כְמַתְּנַת בָּרִיא הוּא. הָדָא אִיתָּא מִכֵּיוָן דְּבַעֲלָהּ זָקוּק מְסַפְּקָא לֵיהּ מְזוֹנֵי. וְלֹא כְמַתְּנַת שְׁכִיב מְרַע הוּא. עַד כְּדוֹן זָקוּן מְסַפְּקָא פִּיתָּא וְקִיטְנֵי. דִּילְמָא בְּיֵי דְּלְמָא תִּרְנוֹגְלִין. מִמַּה דְּתַנֵּי. הָרִאשׁוֹן אוֹכֵל פֵּירוֹת וְקוֹנֶה קַרְקַע. מוֹכֶרֶת אֲפִילוּ לוֹכָל דְּבָרִים מְעוּלִּין. אָמַר רִבִּי יַעֲקֹב בַּר אָחָא. תַּנֵּי תַמָּן. קְבוּרָהּ בִּמְזוֹנוֹת. לֹא הָיָה לָהּ קְבוּרָה. מִן מַה דְּתַנֵּי. הָרִאשׁוֹן אוֹכֵל פֵּירוֹת וְקוֹנֶה קַרְקַע. הָדָא אָמְרָה. מוֹכֵר קַרְקַע וְלוֹקֵחַ קְבוּרָה.

[177] One who said, my property should be given to X, if X died to Y, if Y died to Z. The one who was mentioned earlier receives the property earlier. If the second died during the first's lifetime, the first one has the usufruct; when he dies the property reverts to heirs of the bequeather[178]. If the third died during the second's lifetime, the first[179] one has the usufruct; when he dies the property reverts to heirs of the bequeather. If both the second and the third die during the first's lifetime, the first has the usufruct and acquired the real estate[180], the words of Rebbi. Rabban Simeon ben Gamliel said, he only has the usufruct[181]. Ḥizqiah said, practice follows Rebbi. Rebbi Yannai said, Rebbi agrees that he cannot dispose of it by a death-bed will[182]. Rebbi Joḥanan said, not even as a gift from a healthy person[183]. As in the following: A woman wrote her properties over to a certain man[184]. She needed money and sold it to her husband. Rebbi Ḥiyya bar Madia[185] brought the case before Rebbi Yose.

Did not Rebbi Yannai say, Rebbi agrees that he cannot dispose of it by a death-bed will? Rebbi Johanan[186] said to him, is that not the gift of a healthy person? Since the husband of this woman is obligated to provide for her food, is that not like a death-bed will? So far, he is obligated to provide for her bread and legumes. Maybe eggs? Maybe chicken? Since it was stated that the first has the usufruct and acquired[180] the real estate, that means that she may sell the property even in order to eat delicacies. Rebbi Aha bar Jacob said, it was stated there[187] that her burial is part of her upkeep. If she did not have a burial site, since it was stated that the first has the usufruct and acquired[180] the real estate, it means that he may sell the real estate and acquire a burial site.

177  This is a reformulation of a paragraph in *Ketubot* 9:1, Notes 66-85. The text is partially problematic.

178  Since Z has to receive the property from Y's estate, if Y never got the property Z cannot get it. Babli 136b.

179  One has to read: The second.

180  The expression "my property should be given to X" is the language of a bequest. The bequest was conditional. If the condition becomes moot, the bequest becomes unconditional. In *Ketubot*, Rebbi is reported to permit the first holder to *sell* the real estate and use the proceeds for himself; then the second and third will receive nothing since the real estate for which the condition was formulated is no longer operative. Naturally, he may sell only if prior to the sale he had acquired the property. So here one should understand *acquired* as *acquired in order to sell*.

181  Babli 137a.

182  This is intelligible only in the *Ketubot* version. Since a death-bed will becomes valid only at the moment of death, the lien formulated by the bequeather already became active; the property is Y's before X's death-bed will is activated.

183  He holds that the property was given to X for his use; therefore he may sell it for profit but is barred from giving it away.

184  In her will. From the following it is clear that in this case, there was no separation of properties. During the woman's lifetime, her husband has the

| | |
|---|---|
| usufruct of her properties. Therefore, she can neither sell them nor give them away. | 186 One has to read: R. Yose; the story is dated three generations after R. Johanan and contradicts the latter's statement above. |
| 185 It is not clear whether his name was *bar Madia* or *bar Maria*. | 187 Mishnah *Ketubot* 4:6. |

(16c line 36) אָמַר רִבִּי יוֹסֵי. וְאִילֵּין דִּכְתָבִין. אִין סָנָת אִין סָנוּת. תְּנָאי מָמוֹן הוּא וְקִייָמְנוּהָ רַבָּנָן.

Rebbi Yose said: About those who write, "if she hates, if she is hated". This is a stipulation about money; the rabbis upheld it[188].

| | |
|---|---|
| 188 A prenuptial agreement about eventual divorce settlements disre- | garding rabbinic rules in the matter is valid. Cf. Note 131. |

(fol. 15d) **משנה י:** הִנִּיחַ בָּנִים גְּדוֹלִים וּקְטַנִּים אֵין הַגְּדוֹלִים מִתְפַּרְנְסִין עַל הַקְּטַנִּים וְלֹא הַקְּטַנִּים נִיזּוֹנִין עַל הַגְּדוֹלִים אֶלָּא חוֹלְקִין בְּשָׁוֶה. נָשְׂאוּ גְּדוֹלִים יִשְׂאוּ קְטַנִּים. וְאִם אָמְרוּ הַקְּטַנִּים הֲרֵי אָנוּ נוֹשְׂאִין כְּדֶרֶךְ שֶׁנְּשָׂאתֶם אַתֶּם אֵין שׁוֹמְעִין לָהֶן אֶלָּא מַה שֶׁנָּתַן לָהֶם אֲבִיהֶם נָתַן.

**Mishnah 10**: If he left[189] adult and underage sons, the adult ones cannot be provided for[190] at the expense of the underaged, nor the underaged fed at the expense of the adults, but they split evenly[191]. If the adult ones wed[192], the underaged may wed. But if the underaged said, we want to have weddings just as you had[193], one does not listen to them, because what their father gave them, he gave.

**משנה יא:** הִנִּיחַ בָּנוֹת גְּדוֹלוֹת וּקְטַנּוֹת אֵין הַגְּדוֹלוֹת מִתְפַּרְנְסוֹת עַל הַקְּטַנּוֹת וְלֹא הַקְּטַנּוֹת נִיזּוֹנוֹת עַל הַגְּדוֹלוֹת אֶלָּא חוֹלְקוֹת בְּשָׁוֶה. נִישְׂאוּ גְּדוֹלוֹת יִשְׂאוּ

הַקְּטַנּוֹת. וְאִם אָמְרוּ הַקְּטַנּוֹת הֲרֵי אָנוּ נוֹשָׂאִים כְּדֶרֶךְ שֶׁנְּשָׂאתֶם אַתֶּם אֵין שׁוֹמְעִין לָהֶן. זֶה חוֹמֶר בַּבָּנוֹת מִבַּבָּנִים שֶׁהַבָּנוֹת נִיזּוֹנוֹת עַל הַבָּנִים וְאֵינָן נִיזּוֹנוֹת עַל הַבָּנוֹת.

**Mishnah 11**: If he left adult and underage daughters[194], the adult ones cannot be provided for at the expense of the underaged, nor the underaged fed at the expense of the adults, but they split evenly. If the adult ones wed, the underaged may wed. But if the underaged said, we want to have weddings just as you had, one does not listen to them. It is a restriction about daughters which does not exist for sons, that daughters will be fed at the expense of sons[195] but not at the expense of daughters.

189 A father who died intestate.

190 With business suits and tools at the expense of the undistributed estate.

191 As long as the estate is not distributed, none of the brothers may receive more than any other.

192 If a brother marries after the father's death and the wedding expenses are borne by the estate, any other yet unmarried brother has a claim on the estate equal to the expenses of the one who was the first to marry.

193 During the father's lifetime.

194 If no sons survive the father.

195 In any marriage, the daughters have a lien on the estate to be supported by the estate until married, Mishnah *Ketubot* 4:13. Sons may not inherit until the claims of the daughters are satisfied. But in the absence of sons, daughters of all ages have identical claims on the estate.

(16c line 34) **הלכה י:** הִנִּיחַ בָּנִים גְּדוֹלִים וּקְטַנִּים כול׳. רִבִּי יִרְמְיָה בָּעֵי קוֹמֵי רִבִּי זֵירָא. נָסְבִין רַבְרְבַיָּיא מְאָה גַרְבִּין וְאִינּוּן טָבִין עֶשְׂרִים דֵּינָרִין. נָסְבִין זְעִירַיָּיא מְאָה גַרְבִּין דִּינּוּן טָבִין עֲשָׂרָה דֵינָרִין. אֲמַר לֵיהּ. כְּמָה דִּנְסַבִּין אִילֵּין יִסְבּוֹן אִילֵּין.

**Halakhah 10**: "If he left adult and underage sons" etc. Rebbi Jeremiah asked before Rebbi Ze'ira: Could the older ones take 100 barrels, each worth twenty denars, and the younger ones take 100 barrels, each worth ten denars[196]? He told him, what these take, those should be taking.

196 What is the meaning of the "even split" of the estate required by the Mishnah? Is it by quantity or price. The answer is that everything is computed by money's worth.

## מי שמת פרק תשיעי

**משנה א:** מִי שֶׁמֵּת וְהִנִּיחַ בָּנִים וּבָנוֹת בִּזְמַן שֶׁהַנְּכָסִים מְרוּבִּין הַבָּנִים יִירְשׁוּ וְהַבָּנוֹת יִיזּוֹנוּ. הַנְּכָסִים מְמוּעָטִין הַבָּנוֹת יִיזּוֹנוּ וְהַבָּנִים יִשְׁאֲלוּ עַל הַפְּתָחִים. אַדְמוֹן אוֹמֵר בִּשְׁבִיל שֶׁאֲנִי זָכָר הִפְסַדְתִּי. אָמַר רַבָּן גַּמְלִיאֵל רוֹאֶה אֲנִי אֶת דִּבְרֵי אַדְמוֹן. (fol. 16c)

**Mishnah 1:** [1]If somebody die and is survived by sons and daughters. If the estate is large, the sons inherit and the daughters will be sustained. If the estate is small, the daughters shall be sustained and the sons shall go begging. Admon said, because I am a male, shall I lose? Rabban Simeon ben Gamliel said, I am convinced by Admon's statement.

1   Mishnah *Ketubot* 13:1, explained there in Notes 50-52.

**הלכה א:** מִי שֶׁמֵּת וְהִנִּיחַ בָּנִים וּבָנוֹת כול'. כֵּינִי מַתְנִיתָא. הַבָּנוֹת יִיזּוֹנוּ וְהַבָּנִים (יִשְׁאֲלוּ) [יִסְחֲרוּ] עַל הַפְּתָחִים. (16d line 24)

**Mishnah 1:** "If somebody die and is survived by sons and daughters," etc. So is the Mishnah: "the daughters shall be sustained and the sons shall go (begging) [peddling][2].

2   The text in parenthesis is from L, the one in brackets from E. Since the L text is identical with the Mishnah, it is clear that the critical remark "so is the Mishnah" refers to the E text or a similar reading as reported in *Ketubot* (13:4, Notes 74-76). In contrast to the *Ketubot* text, here the alternate reading is endorsed.

According to the Mishnah and the L text, the sons are sent begging irrespective of their age. According to the revised version, small children covered by the decree of Usha (*Ketubot* 4:8,

Notes 187-193), who cannot earn money, must be supported with the daughters.

(16d line 25) רַב יִרְמְיָה בְּשֵׁם רַב. וְהוּא שֶׁיְּהֵא שָׁם לָאֵילוּ [וּלְאֵילוּ] מְזוֹנוֹת שְׁנֵים עָשָׂר חוֹדֶשׁ. שְׁמוּאֵל אָמַר. זוֹ דִּבְרֵי רַבָּן גַּמְלִיאֵל בְּרִבִּי. אֲבָל דִּבְרֵי חֲכָמִים. עַד שֶׁיִּבָּגְרוּ אוֹ עַד שֶׁיִּנָּשְׂאוּ. וְאִית בָּהּ לְקוּלָּא וְאִית בָּהּ לְחוּמְרָא. פְּעָמִים שֶׁסְּמוּכִין לְבֶגֶר וּפְעָמִים שֶׁרְחוֹקוֹת מִן הַבֶּגֶר. בְּעוֹן קוֹמֵי רִבִּי חִייָה בַּר וָוה. אֵיךְ שְׁמַעְתָּנָהּ מֵרִבִּי יוֹחָנָן. אָמַר לוֹן. אֲנָא לָא שְׁמָעִית מִינֵּיהּ הָדָא מִילְתָא אֶלָּא מַה דְּנָתָן בַּר הוֹשַׁעְיָה בְּעָא קוֹמֵי רִבִּי יוֹחָנָן. הָיָה שָׁם לָאֵילוּ וְלָאֵילוּ מָזוֹן י"ב חוֹדֶשׁ וְנִתְמָעֲטוּ נְכָסִין. אָמַר לֵיהּ. הוֹאִיל וְהִתְחִילוּ בְּהֶיתֵּר הִתְחִילוּ.

[3]Rav Jeremiah in the name of Rav: That there should be twelve months of sustenance for all of them. Samuel said, this is the opinion of Rabban Gamliel ben Rebbi, but the words of the Sages are, until they reach adulthood or are married. That is both a leniency and a restriction. Sometimes they are close to adulthood, sometimes far from adulthood. They asked before Rebbi Hiyya bar Abba, what did you hear from Rebbi Johanan? He said to them, I did not hear anything from him concerning this matter except what Nathan bar Hoshaia asked before Rebbi Johanan: what if there was sustenance for twelve months but the estate diminished in value? He answered him, since they started with permission, they started.

3   This is a reformulation of a paragraph in *Ketubot* 13:3, Notes 53-58.

(16d line 33) רִבִּי חֲנִינָה וְרִבִּי מָנָא. חַד אָמַר. וְהוּא שֶׁיְּהֵא שָׁם בְּסוֹף מָזוֹן י"ב חוֹדֶשׁ. וְחָרָנָה אָמַר. אֲפִילוּ מִתְּחִילָּה. לֹא הָיָה שָׁם לָאֵילוּ וְלָאֵילוּ מָזוֹן י"ב חוֹדֶשׁ וְהוֹתִירוּ יֵשׁ שָׁם מָזוֹן לָאֵילוּ וְלָאֵילוּ י"ב חוֹדֶשׁ. אָמַר רִבִּי אִמִּי בַּבְלַיָּיא. נִישְׁמְעִינָהּ מֵהָדָא. אִם עָמְדוּ יְתוֹמִין וּמָכְרוּ שֶׁלָּהֶן מָכְרוּ. כָּל־שֶׁכֵּן אִם הוֹתִירוּ יַחֲלִקוּ. הָיָה שָׁם לָאֵילוּ וְלָאֵילוּ מָזוֹן י"ב חוֹדֶשׁ וְאַלְמָנָה לָזוּן. מַהוּ שֶׁיֹּאמְרוּ בָנִים

לַבָּנוֹת. כְּלוּם אֵין לָכֶם אֶלָּא מָזוֹן י'ב חוֹדֶשׁ. אָמַר רִבִּי אַבְדּוּמִי. נִשְׁמִינָהּ מֵהָדָא. אִם אָמְרוּ הַיְתוֹמִים. הֲרֵי אָנוּ מַעֲלִין נִיכְסֵי אָבִינוּ יוֹתֵר דֵּינָר. אֵין שׁוֹמְעִין לָהֶן. רַב חִסְדָּא בָּעֵי. הָיָה שָׁם לָאֵילוּ וְלָאֵילוּ מָזוֹן י'ב חוֹדֶשׁ וְאַלְמָנָה לָזוּן. מַהוּ שֶׁיֹּאמְרוּ בָנִים לַבָּנוֹת. אֵין לָכֶם אֶלָּא מָזוֹן י'ב חוֹדֶשׁ. וָדָא דְּתֵימַר. וְהוּא שֶׁיְּהֵא שָׁם לָאֵילוּ וְלָאֵילוּ מָזוֹן י'ב חוֹדֶשׁ. חוּץ מִכְּתוּבַת אִשָּׁה מִמְּזוֹנוֹת אַלְמָנָה חוּץ מִפַּרְנָסַת בָּנוֹת חוּץ מִמִּלְוָה בִשְׁטָר חוּץ מִמִּלְוָה בָעֵדִים חוּץ מִקְּבוּרָתָהּ. אַלְמָנָה וּבָנוֹת שְׁתַּיִם שָׁווֹת אַלְמָנָה וּבָנִים שְׁנֵיהֶן שָׁוִין. אֵין אַלְמָנָה דּוֹחָה לְבָנוֹת וְלֹא בָנוֹת דּוֹחוֹת לָאַלְמָנָה. פְּעָמִים שֶׁאַלְמָנָה דּוֹחָה לְבָנוֹת עַל יְדֵי בָנִים. כְּשֵׁם שֶׁהָאַלְמָנָה דּוֹחָה לְבָנוֹת עַל יְדֵי בָנִים כָּךְ תִּדָּחֶה אַלְמָנָה לַבָּנִים. אָמַר. רְאוּיָה הִיא לִתְבּוֹעַ וּלְאַבֵּד מְזוֹנוֹתֶיהָ.

[4]Rebbi Ḥanina and Rebbi Mana. One said, only if at the end there be sustenance for twelve months. But the other said, even from the start[5]. If there was not sustenance for all of them for twelve months but they increased it so that now there is sustenance for all of them for twelve months[6]? Rebbi Immi the Babylonian said, let us hear from the following: If the heirs sold, they sold from their own property[7]. So much more, if they increased it, they should be able to divide it[8].

If there was sustenance for all of them for twelve months and a widow to support, may the sons say to the daughters: you have sustenance only for twelve months?[9] Rebbi Eudaimon said, let us hear from the following: [10]"If the orphans said, we accept the properties of our father for the value of an extra denar, one does not listen to them."

Rav Ḥisda asked[11]: if there was sustenance for all of them for twelve months and a widow to support, may the sons say to the daughters: you have sustenance only for twelve months?[9] But this means, only if there was sustenance for all of them for twelve months, except for *ketubah* of the wife, except for the sustenance of the widow, except for the dowries of the daughters, except for loans by document, except for loans by witnesses, except for her burial[12]. The widow and the daughters are of equal rank[13]. The widow and the sons are of equal rank. The widow does not push the daughters aside and the daughters do not push the widow aside. Sometimes the widow pushes the daughters out by means of the sons. Just as the widow pushes out the daughters by means of the sons, should the widow not push out the sons[14]? She might claim her *ketubah* and lose her right to sustenance[15].

4   Compare *Ketubot* 13:3, Notes 59-71.

5   The question which is answered here is only stated in *Ketubot*: What is the definition of a large estate? In the first opinion the estate is large if after 12 months there still is left enough money to sustain the entire family, sons and daughters, for 12 months. In the other opinion it is enough that there be sufficient funds for the first 12 months.

6   The sons could not be supported during the first 12 months. May they be supported now that the estate is large according to the first definition?

7   Cf. *Ketubot* 13:3, Note 63: If the male heirs sold real estate from a small estate, their sale is valid since they are the heirs in biblical law; the rights of the daughters are purely contractual. While the widow can take the real estate away from the buyer for her *ketubah* as prior mortgage holder, the daughters cannot since their claim was created only at their father's death, when the sons already were legal owners of the property.

8   The court-appointed guardian will have to include the sons for sustenance.

9   This question is difficult to understand since, as mentioned later, the widow's claim is paramount and the value of the estate is computed only after all claims of the widow are satisfied. Therefore, the mention of the widow here has to be deleted. In *Ketubot*, the question is: If there was more than enough to sustain only the daughters but not enough for both daughters and sons, according to the second definition of a large estate may the sons distribute among themselves the monies exceeding the daughters' claims for 12 months?

10   A truncated version of Mishnah 10:2. The Mishnah prohibits sons to manipulate the valuation of an estate in order to gain an advantage over their half-brothers. It is implied here that

they cannot manipulate the estate to the detriment of their sisters.

11  In *Ketubot*, Rav Ḥisda asked the first question, Note 6.

12  The value of an estate can only be determined after all actual and contractual liabilities were deducted.

13  In the Babli, 140b and *Ketubot* 43a, the widow's position is privileged. If there is not enough money to sustain both widow and daughters, the daughters are sent begging.

14  It seems that in the last two sentences, the places of "sons" and "daughters" should be switched. The question is whether the widow's sustenance is privileged over the daughters' claims to sustenance.

15  Her claim to sustenance is conditional; it cannot override the claim of the daughters which is absolute. The Babli disagrees.

(16d line 51) כְּהָדָא אַרְמַלְתֵּיהּ דְּרִבִּי שׁוּבְתַי הֲוָת מְבַזְבְּזָה בְּנִיכְסַיָּא. אָתוֹן בָּנוֹי קָרְבוֹן לְרִבִּי לְעָזָר. אָמַר לוֹן. וּמָה נִיעֲבִיד לְכוֹן וְאִינּוּן עַמָּא שַׁטְיָיא. מִי נַחְתּוֹן אָמְרוֹן אָמְרוּ לַכְּתוֹבָה מָה נַעֲבִיד. אָמַר לוֹן. אִיתְחַמּוֹן זַבְנוֹן מִן נִיכְסֵי וְאַתְיָיא וְתָבְעָה פְּרָנָא וְלֵית לָהּ מְזוֹנִין. בָּתָר יוֹמִין אָתַת וּקְרֵיבַת לְרִבִּי לְעָזָר. אָמְרָה לֵיהּ. יָבוֹא עָלַי אִם אָמַרְתִּי לָהֶן דָּבָר. וּמָה נַעֲבִיד וּמַכַּת פְּרוּשִׁין נָגְעוּ בָהּ.

[16]As the following: Rebbi Sabbatai's widow was wasting the estate. His sons came before Rebbi Eleazar. He said to them, what can one do for you; they are stupid. When they left, they said, let us ask the scribe what to do. He told them: Behave as if you would sell of the real estate and she will demand her *ketubah* and will no longer have support. After some time she came before Rebbi Eleazar. He said, It should come over me if I had told them anything. What can one do, this one was hit by predatory people.

16  A slight reformulation of the paragraph in *Soṭah* 3:4, Notes 143-148. The paragraph is inserted to show that the widow may be manipulated to forgo her claim of sustenance.

(16d line 57) רַב חֲנַנְאֵל בְּשֵׁם [רַב] רִבִּי זְעִירָא בְּשֵׁם אַבָּא בַּר יִרְמְיָה. שְׁנֵי דְבָרִים אָמַר חָנָן הֲלָכָה כְמוֹתוֹ. שִׁבְעָה דְבָרִים אָמַר אַדְמוֹן וְאֵין הֲלָכָה כְמוֹתוֹ. רִבִּי בָּא בַּר זַבְדָּא בְּשֵׁם רִבִּי יִצְחָק בֶּן חֲקוּלָה. כָּל־מָקוֹם שֶׁשָּׁנִינוּ אָמַר רַבָּן גַּמְלִיאֵל. רוֹאֶה אֲנִי אֶת דִּבְרֵי אַדְמוֹן הֲלָכָה כְאַדְמוֹן.

[17]Rav Ḥananel in the name of [Rav][18]; Rebbi Ze'ira in the name of Abba bar Jeremiah: Practice follows Ḥanan in his two statements; practice does not follow Admon in his seven statements. Rebbi Abba bar Zavda in the name of Rebbi Isaac bar Ḥaqula: In every case in which Rabban Simeon ben Gamliel said, I am convinced by Admon's statement, practice follows Admon.

17 An almost complete copy of paragraphs in *Ketubot* 13:1 (Notes 36,37), 13:4 (Note 77); Babli *Ketubot* 109a.

18 Missing in L, inserted from E; required by the parallel texts and reasons of chronology.

(16d line 61) שְׁמוּאֵל אָמַר. זָכִין לָעֲבָרִים. רִבִּי לָעְזָר אָמַר. אֵין זָכִין לָעוֹבָרִין. מַתְנִיתָא פְלִיגָא עַל רִבִּי לָעְזָר. גֵּר שֶׁמֵּת וּבִיזְבְּזוּ יִשְׂרָאֵל אֶת נְכָסָיו וְנוֹדַע שֶׁיֵּשׁ לוֹ בֵן אוֹ שֶׁהָיְתָה אִשְׁתּוֹ מְעוּבֶּרֶת כּוּלָּן חַיָּיבִין לְהַחֲזִיר. הֶחֱזִירוּ וְאַחַר כָּךְ מֵת הַבֵּן אוֹ שֶׁהִפִּילָה אִשְׁתּוֹ. הַמַּחֲזִיק בָּאַחֲרוֹנָה זָכָה. בָּרִאשׁוֹנָה זָכָה אִי לֹא. פָּתַר לָהּ מִשּׁוּם יֵיאוּשׁ וַאֲפִילוּ כִשְׁמוּאֵל לֵית הוּא פְלִיגָא. אוֹ אֲפִילוּ בָאַחֲרוֹנָה לֹא יִזְכֶּה. עוֹד הוּא מִשּׁוּם יֵיאוּשׁ.

[19]Samuel said, one can transfer benefits to the fetus; Rebbi Eleazar said, one cannot transfer benefits to the fetus. A *baraita* disagrees with Rebbi Eleazar. "If a proselyte died[20] and Jews plundered his estate, then it became known that he had a son[21] or that his wife was pregnant, everybody is required to return [what he took][22]. If they returned everything and then the son died or his wife had a miscarriage, the last one in possession acquires it.[23]" Did the first group acquire or not?

Explain it, because of hopelessness[24] and it does not even disagree with Samuel. Or should the last one not have acquired it[25]? Still it is because of hopelessness.

19 Cf. *Yebamot* 4:1, Notes 24-40; Babli *Bava batra* 141b/142a.

20 He died without Jewish children; his estate became ownerless with his death. His Jewish wife, who is not an heir, may take everything she can lay her hands on. (Halakhah 3:1, Notes 19,23; *Gittin* 4:4 Note 106).

21 A Jewish heir.

22 The unborn baby is an heir by biblical decree, *Num.* 27:8.

23 This *baraita* seems to follow Samuel. The unborn child acquired the inheritance; if he dies, the estate newly becomes ownerless and the last person to hold it acquires. Rebbi Eleazar should require that everything be returned to the first taker.

24 When the court decreed that the proselyte had a legal heir and the first takers returned the property, they gave up hope of owning it and with it any claim of ownership. Cf. *Bava meṣia'* 2:1 Note 6.

25 Since he got it under a false assumption.

(fol. 16c) **משנה ב:** הִנִּיחַ בָּנִים וּבָנוֹת וְטוּמְטוּם בִּזְמַן שֶׁהַנְּכָסִים מְרוּבִּין הַזְּכָרִים דּוֹחִין אוֹתוֹ אֵצֶל הַנְּקֵיבוֹת. נְכָסִים מְמוּעָטִין הַנְּקֵיבוֹת דּוֹחוֹת אוֹתוֹ אֵצֶל הַזְּכָרִים. הָאוֹמֵר אִם יָלְדָה אִשְׁתִּי זָכָר יִטּוֹל מָנֶה יָלְדָה זָכָר נוֹטֵל מָנֶה. וְאִם נְקֵיבָה מָאתַיִם יָלְדָה נְקֵיבָה נוֹטֶלֶת מָאתַיִם. אִם זָכָר מָנֶה וְאִם נְקֵיבָה מָאתַיִם וְיָלְדָה זָכָר וּנְקֵיבָה הַזָּכָר נוֹטֵל מָנֶה וְהַנְּקֵיבָה מָאתַיִם.

**Mishnah 2**: If he is survived by sons, daughters, and a sexless child[26], if the estate is large the males push him to the females; if the estate is small the females push him to the males[27]. If somebody says, in case my wife gives birth to a male, he shall take a mina; if she gave birth to a male he takes a mina. But if a female 200, if she gave birth to a female she takes 200. If a male a mina, if a female 200, if she gave birth to a male and a female, the male takes a mina and the female 200[28].

**משנה ג:** יָלְדָה טוּמְטוּם אֵינוֹ נוֹטֵל. אִם אָמַר כָּל־מַה שֶׁתֵּלֵד אִשְׁתִּי יִטּוֹל הֲרֵי זֶה יִטּוֹל וְאִם אֵין שָׁם יוֹרֵשׁ אֶלָּא הוּא יוֹרֵשׁ אֶת הַכֹּל.

**Mishnah 3**: If she gave birth to a sexless child, he does not take anything. If he said, any that my wife shall give birth to shall take, and if there is no heir but him, he inherits everything[29].

26  A child having neither male nor female sex characteristics (neither penis nor vagina).

27  Since the sexless is a claimant in an inheritance case, the burden of proof would be on him to show that he belongs to the advantaged class.

28  All these examples are only a preface to the statement that the sexless child has no claim on payments promised a child of a certain sex. Females need a larger trust fund at birth to pay for a future dowry.

29  In the absence of siblings the sexless inherits, whether he really is a male or a female.

(16d line 67) **הלכה ב:** הִנִּיחַ בָּנִים וּבָנוֹת כול'. תַּנֵּי. הָאוֹמֵר. הַמְבַשְּׂרֵינִי אִם יָלְדָה אִשְׁתִּי זָכָר יִטּוֹל מָאתַיִם. יָלְדָה זָכָר נוֹטֵל מָאתַיִם. אִם נְקֵיבָה מָנֶה. יָלְדָה נְקֵיבָה נוֹטֵל מָנֶה. זָכָר וּנְקֵיבָה אֵין לוֹ אֶלָּא מָנֶה. אָמַר רִבִּי מָנָא. בִּיטְּלָה צָרַת הַבַּת שִׂמְחַת זָכָר.

**Halakhah 2**: "If he is survived by sons, daughters,,," etc. It was stated: "If somebody says, he who brings me the news that my wife gave birth to a male shall take 200": if his wife gave birth to a male he takes 200. If she gave birth to a female he shall take a mina": if his wife gave birth to a female he takes a mina. If it was a male and a female, he only takes a mina[30]." Rebbi Mana said, the pain about the daughter invalidates the joy about the son.

30  Tosephta 9:5.

(fol. 16c) **משנה ד:** הִנִּיחַ בָּנִים גְּדוֹלִים וּקְטַנִּים הִשְׁבִּיחוּ הַגְּדוֹלִים אֶת הַנְּכָסִים הִשְׁבִּיחוּ לָאֶמְצַע. אִם אָמְרוּ רְאוּ מַה שֶׁהִנִּיחַ לָנוּ אַבָּא הֲרֵי אָנוּ עוֹשִׂין וְאוֹכְלִים הִשְׁבִּיחוּ לְעַצְמָן.

**Mishnah 4**: If he is survived by adult and underage children and the adult ones improved the property[31], the improvement goes to the estate. But if they said[32], make an inventory of what our father left[33] and we are going to work and profit from it, they improved it for themselves.

31  Before the estate was distributed.
32  Before the court.
33  To determine the underage brothers' share under the court's supervision.

(16d line 71) **הלכה ד:** הִנִּיחַ בָּנִים גְּדוֹלִים וּקְטַנִּים כול׳. אָמַר רִבִּי לָא. אִם אָמְרוּ בְּבֵית דִּין. דְּבֵי רִבִּי יַנַּאי אָמְרֵי. אֲפִילוּ עִירְנָיָה. רַב אָמַר. אֲפִילוּ סַל אֲפִילוּ קוֹרְדוֹם. תַּנֵּי רִבִּי חִיָּיה. אֲפִילוּ מַחַט אֲפִילוּ מוּקָף צָמִיד פָּתִיל.

**Halakhah 4**: "If he is survived by adult and underage children," etc. Rebbi La said, "if they said" in court. In the House of Rebbi Yannai they said, even a jug.[34] Rav said, even a basket, even an axe. Rebbi Ḥiyya stated: Even a needle, even a thread to tie down.

34  Latin *hirnea*, also *irnea, -ae*, "jug, pitcher" (E. G.).

(16d line 73) אָמַר רִבִּי חֲנִינָה. הַמַּשִׂיא אֶת בְּנוֹ בְּבַיִת זָכָה בַּבַּיִת. תַּנֵּי רִבִּי הוֹשַׁעְיָה. בַּבַּיִת וְלֹא בַּמִּטַּלְטְלִין. רִבִּי לָא חִילֵּק אֶת הַטְּרִיקְלִין בֵּינוֹ לְבֵין בְּנוֹ. רִבִּי חַגַּיי בְּעָא רִבִּי יוֹסֵי. חֲיָתָה חוּפָּתוֹ בַּקִּיטוֹן וְעָשָׂה לוֹ הֶסֵב בַּטְּרִיקְלִין מָהוּ. אָמַר לֵיהּ. לֵית חָמֵי לֵיהּ מַפְקָה.

[35]Rebbi Ḥanina said, if somebody definitively married off his son in a house, the latter acquired it[36]. Rebbi Hoshaia stated, the house but not the movables[37]. Rebbi La divided the dining hall[38] between himself and his son[39]. Rebbi Ḥaggai asked Rebbi Yose: If the ceremony was in the

bedroom⁴⁰ but the wedding party was in the dining room, what is the rule? He told him, one does not see him leaving⁴¹.

35  Cf. *Ketubot* 5:1 (Notes 23-26), 12:2 Note 41; Babli 144a.

36  This is qualified in *Ketubot* to apply only to a first marriage and in the Babli to the first marriage of the oldest son to a virgin, it being the first marriage of any of his children.

37  In *Ketubot* 5:1, R. Hoshaia is reported as saying "the movables but not the house".

38  Latin *triclinium*.

39  The newlyweds could use half the *triclinium* as their permanent abode.

40  Greek κοιτών, -ῶνος, m.

41  After the wedding the groom is expected to stay in the wedding chamber with his wife; he is not needed for the festivities and acquired only the bedroom.

(16d line 77) רִבִּי יְהוֹשֻׁעַ בֶּן לֵוִי אָמַר. חוֹלְקִין לַקְּטַנִּים מִפְּנֵי הַגְּדוֹלִים. אֶלָּא עָמְדוּ קְטַנִּים וּמָצְאוּ דְבָר יָתֵר וּמִיחוּ. רִבִּי אַבָּהוּ אוֹמֵר. נִשְׁבָּעִין לָהֶן. אָמַר רִבִּי מָנָא. כָּל־הַמּוֹצִיא מֵחֲבֵירוֹ עָלָיו הָרְאָייָה חוּץ מִזוֹ. רִבִּי חִייָה רוֹבָה אָמַר. סְתָם אַחִין שׁוּתָּפִין עַד שְׁלֹשָׁה דוֹרוֹת. אָמַר רִבִּי [ ] בַּר בּוּן. אַף רַב הַמְנוּנָא הוֹרֵי כֵן.

Rebbi Joshua ben Levi said: One divides for the underaged because of the adults⁴². But if the underaged found something additional and protested⁴³? Rebbi Abbahu said, they⁴⁴ have to swear for them. Rebbi Mana said, everywhere the burden of proof is on the claimant except in this case. The Great Rebbi Ḥiyya⁴⁵ says, without contract brothers are co-owners up to three generations⁴⁶. Rebbi [Yose]⁴⁷ bar Abun said, also Rav Hamnuna did instruct in this sense.

42  If the adults want to divide the estate in order to work for themselves, the court is obligated to separate the underaged's property and to transfer it to a guardian.

43  The underaged claim that the adults understated the value of the estate and that their portion should be greater.

44  The adults have to swear in court even though in general a claimant cannot make a defendant

swear unless he produce proof by at least one witness.

45 *Sefer Ha'ittur* I 42b reads: R. Ḥiyya bar Abba. In *Gen. rabba* 53(2), R. Abba. Our text is confirmed by Ravad *Temim De'im* §58.

46 Without any party objecting, an estate may stay undivided for up to three generations. After that it would need a contract of association.

47 Missing in the mss. but understood if any "bar Abun" is mentioned last in any paragraph.

(17a line 4) אָמַר רִבִּי אִימִי. בֵּן שֶׁנִּרְאָה חָלוּק בְּחַיֵּי אָבִיו מַה שֶׁסִּיגֵּל סִיגֵּל לְעַצְמוֹ. כְּהָדָא חַד בַּר נָשׁ אִיתְעֲבֵד סַפָּר. בָּעָא אֲחוֹי מִיפְלַג עִימֵּיהּ. אֲתָא עוֹבָדָא קוֹמֵי רִבִּי אִמִּי. אָמַר. כָּךְ אָנוּ אוֹמְרִים. אָדָם שֶׁמָּצָא מְצִיאָה אֶחָיו חוֹלְקִין עִמּוֹ. חַד בַּר נָשׁ נְפַק לִשְׁלִיחוּתָא. בָּעָא אֲחוֹי מִיפְלַג עִימֵּיהּ. אֲתָא עוֹבָדָא קוֹמֵי רִבִּי אִמִּי. אָמַר. כָּךְ אָנוּ אוֹמְרִים. אָדָם שֶׁיָּצָא לַלֵּיסְטַיָּא אֶחָיו חוֹלְקִין עִמּוֹ. רִבִּי הוֹרִיָינָה אֲחוֹי דְרִבִּי שְׁמוּאֵל בַּר סוֹסַרְטַיי בָּעָא אֲחוֹי מִיפְלַג עִימֵּיהּ. אָמַר לוֹ. אַלֶכְסַנְדְרִי אֲחוֹי. יְדַע אַתְּ דִּשְׁבַק אָבוּנָן אֲלָפִים.

Rebbi Immi said, if a son was seen separated during his father's lifetime, what he accumulated, he accumulated for himself[48]. As the following: A person learned to be a barber[49]. His brother wanted to share with him. The case came before Rebbi Immi who said, do we say that if a person found something, his brothers share with him[50]? A person became an agent. His brother wanted to share with him. The case came before Rebbi Immi who said, do we say that if a person went into robbery[51], his brothers share with him? A brother of Rebbi Horiana, brother of Rebbi Samuel ben Sosartai, wanted to share with him. He told him, brother Alexander, do you not know that our father left us thousands[52]?

48 The rules of the Mishnah only apply to sons living in their father's household, not those who are known to earn their money independently.

49 It is possible to read סָפֵר "scribe".

50 Even if a person still lives with his extended family, money made through his personal skill is not

| | |
|---|---|
| 51 Greek λῃστεία. | 52 He may claim only his share in the inheritance but nothing else. |

common property.

**משנה ה:** וְכֵן הָאִשָּׁה שֶׁהִשְׁבִּיחָה אֶת הַנְּכָסִים הִשְׁבִּיחָה לָאֶמְצַע. אִם אָמְרָה רְאוּ מַה שֶּׁהִנִּיחַ לִי בַעֲלִי הֲרֵי אֲנִי עוֹשָׂה וְאוֹכֶלֶת הִשְׁבִּיחָה לְעַצְמָהּ. (fol. 16c)

**Mishnah 5**: Similarly, a woman[53] who improved the property improved for the estate[54]. But if she said[32]: see what my husband left for me, I shall work it and eat from it[55]; then she improved it for herself.

| | |
|---|---|
| 53 A widow. | 55 She takes the property as her *ketubah* settlement. |
| 54 She acts as a guardian for the children as well as for herself. | |

**הלכה ה:** וְכֵן הָאִשָּׁה כול'. אָמַר רִבִּי לָא. אָמְרָה בְּבֵית דִּין. (17a line 12)

**Halakhah 5**: "Similarly, a woman," etc. Rebbi La said, "if she said" in court.

**משנה ו:** הָאַחִין הַשּׁוּתָּפִין שֶׁנָּפַל אֶחָד מֵהֶן לְאוּמָנוּת נָפַל לָאֶמְצַע. חָלָה וְנִתְרַפָּה נִתְרַפָּה מִשֶּׁל עַצְמוֹ. הָאַחִין שֶׁעָשׂוּ מִקְצָתָן שׁוּשְׁבִינוּת בְּחַיֵּי הָאָב חָזְרָה הַשּׁוּשְׁבִינוּת הַחֲזָרָה לָאֶמְצַע שֶׁהַשּׁוּשְׁבִינוּת נִגְבֵּית בְּבֵית דִּין. אֲבָל שִׁילַח לוֹ חֲבֵירוֹ כַּדֵּי יַיִן וְכַדֵּי שֶׁמֶן אֵינָן נִגְבִּין מִפְּנֵי שֶׁהִיא גְמִילוּת חֲסָדִים. (fol. 16c)

**Mishnah 6**: If one of co-owning brothers was requisitioned[56], he was requisitioned from the estate[57]. If he fell sick and was healed, the medical costs are his own. If some of the brothers together sent a wedding gift[58] during their father's lifetime, if a corresponding gift was returned[59], it returned to them in common since wedding gifts[58] can be sued for in court. But if somebody's friend sent him pitchers of wine or oil[60] they cannot be sued for since they represent deeds of charity.

56  He was ordered by the government to fulfill certain duties at his own expense.

57  If he was living off an undistributed estate, the estate had to bear the cost of government service.

58  Of money or valuables.

59  By the recipient on his wedding day.

60  Gifts of food are genuine gifts, not subject to a law of reciprocity.

(17a line 12) **הלכה ו:** הָאַחִין הַשּׁוּתָפִין כול'. תַּנֵּי. הָאַחִין הַשּׁוּתָפִין שֶׁנָּפַל אֶחָד מֵהֶן לָאוּמָנוּת הַמֶּלֶךְ. בִּזְמַן שֶׁבָּאִין מִכֹּחַ הָאָרִיס נוֹטְלִין מִכֹּחַ הָאָרִיס. מִכֹּחַ בַּעַל הַבַּיִת נוֹטְלִין מִכֹּחַ בַּעַל הַבַּיִת. כְּהָדָא דְרַב נַחְמָן בַּר שְׁמוּאֵל בַּר נַחְמָן נִתְפַּשׂ לַבּוּלֵי. אֲתָא עוֹבְדָא קוֹמֵי רִבִּי אִמִּי. אָמַר. אִין אִית בְּנִיכְסוֹי דְנַחְמָן שֶׁנִּתְפַּשׂ לוֹ יִנָּתֵן מִנְּכָסָיו. וְאִם לָאו יִינָּתֵן לוֹ מִן הָאֶמְצַע.

**Halakhah 6:** "If one of co-owning brothers," etc. It was stated[61]: If one of co-owning brothers was requisitioned for government service. If this was because of the sharecroppper[62], he takes because of the sharecropper[62]. If because of the head of household, he takes as head of household. As the following: Rav Naḥman bar Samuel bar Naḥman was appointed to the city council[63]. The case came before Rebbi Immi. He said, if Naḥman who was caught has enough property, it should be given from his property; otherwise it should be given to him from the common estate.

61  Cf. Tosephta 10:5.

62  This makes no sense. The correct reading is given in *Šiṭṭah mequbbeṣet ad* 144b in the name of Ravad and Rashba *Novellae ad* 144b: brothers. Since only rich and well-known people were ordered to pay for the city services, if the estate was renowned for its riches, the estate had to pay for the cost of services. If it was because of the personal renown of the person appointed, he had to bear

63 Greek βουλή, responsible not only for city services but also for the collection of taxes.

(17a line 18) חָלָה וְנִתְרַפָּה נִתְרַפָּה מִן הָאֶמְצַע. תַּנֵּי. רַבָּן שִׁמְעוֹן בֶּן גַּמְלִיאֵל אוֹמֵר. כָּל־מַכָּה שֶׁיֵּשׁ לָהּ קִיצָה מִתְרַפָּא מִכְּתוּבָּתָהּ. וְשֶׁאֵין לָהּ קִיצָה מִתְרַפָּא מִן הַנְּכָסִים. כְּהָדָא קְרִיבָתֵיהּ דְּרִבִּי שִׁמְעוֹן בַּר וָוא הֲוַת חֲשָׁשָׁה עֵיינָהּ. אֲתַת גַּבֵּי רִבִּי יוֹחָנָן. אֲמַר לָהּ. קְצִיץ הוּא אָהֵין אַסְיָיךְ. אִין קְצִיץ מִן פְּרִנֵךְ. אִין לָא קְצִיץ בַּעֲלִיךְ יְהִיב לִיךְ. וְלֹא כֵן תַּנִּינָן. אַל תַּעַשׂ עַצְמָךְ כְּעוֹרְכֵי הַדַּיָּינִין. וְאָמַר רִבִּי חַגַּיי בְּשֵׁם רִבִּי יְהוֹשֻׁעַ בֶּן לֵוִי. אָסוּר לְגַלּוֹת לְיָחִיד דִּינוֹ. אָמְרֵי. יָדַע הֲוָה רִבִּי יוֹחָנָן דְּהִיא אִיתָּא כְשֵׁירָה בְּגִין כֵּן גְּלֵי לָהּ. בַּעֲלָהּ בָּעֵי הֵן דְּקָצַץ וְהִיא בְּעָיָיהּ הֵן דְּלָא קְצַץ. לְמָאן שָׁמְעִין. לֹא לְבַעֲלָהּ. אָמַר רִבִּי מַתַּנְיָיה. הָדָא דְתֵימַר בְּהַהוּא דְּלֵית דִּינֵיהּ עִמֵּיהּ. בְּרַם בָּהוּא דְּאִית דִּינֵיהּ עִמֵּיהּ אָמַר לֵיהּ מִילְּתָא.

If she fell sick and was healed, the medical costs are on the estate[64]. It was stated: [65]"Rabban Simeon ben Gamliel says, for any hurt which has a fixed medical fee, she is healed from her *ketubah*; if it does not have a fixed medical fee, she is healed from the estate." As the following: The eye of a female relative of Rebbi Simeon bar Abba hurt. She came to Rebbi Joḥanan. He asked her: Did your doctor mention a fixed fee? If [the fee] is fixed, from your *ketubah*, if it is not fixed, your husband will give it to you[66]. But did we not state: "Do not turn yourself into a pleader[67]", and did not Rebbi Ḥaggai say in the name of Rebbi Joshua ben Levi, it is forbidden to disclose a judgment to a party? They said, Rebbi Joḥanan knew her to be an honest woman; therefore, he disclosed it to her. If her husband wants a treatment at a fixed rate, but she wants one without fixed rate, does one not listen to her husband? Rebbi Mattaniah said, only if the case not be before him. But if the case be before him, he has to tell it as it is[68].

64  It seems that this is a *baraita* which disagrees with the Mishnah.

65  Tosephta *Ketubot* 4:5, Babli *Ketubot* 52b. A shortened version of the paragraph is in *Ketubot* 4:11, Notes 231-236. It is commented on by Ran (*Ketubot* 4, *ad* Alfasi #249), and Rosh (*Ketubot* 4, #23).

66  Ran proves that Maimonides read this to mean: "From your husband's estate it will be given to you." He holds that the placement of the extended story in *Bava batra* indicates that it refers to an estate, not a living husband who bears unlimited responsibility for his wife's health.

67  Mishnah *Abot* 1:8. It is unethical for a judge to dispense legal advice.

68  If the case is before him, he can disclose the judgment. He is only prohibited to talk to one party separately before and during the trial.

(fol. 16c) **משנה ז:** הַשׁוֹלֵחַ סִבְלוֹנוֹת לְבֵית חָמִיו שִׁילַח שָׁם מֵאָה מָנֶה וְאָכַל שָׁם סְעוּדַת חָתָן אֲפִילוּ בְּדֵינָר אֵינָן נִגְבִּין. לֹא אָכַל שָׁם סְעוּדַת חָתָן הֲרֵי אֵילוּ נִגְבִּין. שִׁילַח סִבְלוֹנוֹת מְרוּבִּין שֶׁיָּבוֹאוּ עִמָּהּ לְבֵית בַּעֲלָהּ הֲרֵי אֵילוּ נִגְבִּין. סִבְלוֹנוֹת מְמוּעָטִין כְּדֵי שֶׁתִּשְׁתַּמֵּשׁ בָּהֶן וְהִיא בְּבֵית אָבִיהָ אֵינָן נִגְבִּין.

**Mishnah 7**: If somebody sent bridal gifts[69] to his father-in-law's house, if he sent there for 100 minas and ate there a marriage meal for at least a denar's worth, they cannot be collected[70]. If he did not eat there a marriage meal, they can be collected. If he sent large bridal gifts which she is expected to bring with her to her husband's house[71], they can be collected[72]. Small bridal gifts which she is supposed to use in her father's house[73] cannot be collected.

69  Gifts to his preliminarily married wife.

70  If for some reason there will be a divorce before the definitive marriage, he cannot sue in court to get the gifts back.

71  Clothing and jewellery.

72  Even if he ate at his in-law's house. The first part of the Mishnah deals with average gifts which cannot be characterized as either large or small.

73  Perfume and cosmetics.

(17a line 28) **הלכה ז:** הַשּׁוֹלֵחַ סִבְלוֹנוֹת לְבֵית חָמִיו כול׳. חַד בַּר נַשׁ שִׁילַח לַאֲרוּסָתוֹ סִבְלוֹנוֹת מְרוּבִּין. אָמְרוּ לֵיהּ קְרִיבוֹי. לֹא תִטְעוֹם תַּמָּן כְּלוּם. אֲזַל וְלָא שְׁמַע לוֹן וְכָל. וְנָפַל בֵּיתָא וּזְכוֹן בְּכוּלָּהּ.

חַד בַּר נַשׁ שִׁילַח לַאֲרוּסָתוֹ עֶשְׂרִים וְאַרְבַּע קָרָיוֹת מִינֵי חַרְת בֵּין פֶּסַח לַעֲצֶרֶת. וְלֹא אִיתְקַשִּׁי לְרַבָּנָן אֶלָּא מִנָּן אַיְיתֵי זֶרַע דְּכִיתָּן וְזֵיתִין.

רִבִּי פְּרִירָא אוֹקִיר לְרִבִּי יְהוּדָה נְשִׂייָא תְּרֵין פּוּגְלִין בֵּין רֵישׁ שַׁתָּא לְצוֹמָא וַהֲוָה פְּקֵי שְׁמִיטְּתָא וַהֲוָה בוֹן טְעוּנָא דְגַמְלָא. אֲמַר לֵי רִבִּי. לֵית אִינּוּן אֲסִירִין. לָאוּ סְפִיחִין אִינּוּן. אֲמַר לֵיהּ בְּפָקֵי שְׁמִיטְתָא אִיזְדַּרְעוּן. בְּאוֹתָהּ שָׁעָה הִתִּיר רִבִּי לִיקַּח יָרָק בְּמוֹצָאֵי שְׁבִיעִית מִיַּד.

**Halakhah 7**: " If somebody sent bridal gifts to his father-in-law's house," etc. A person sent to his preliminarily wedded wife large bridal gifts. His relatives told him not to taste anything there. He went, did not listen to them, and ate. The house collapsed; they kept everything.

A person sent to his preliminarily wedded wife 24 gourds filled with various kinds of agricultural produce[74] between Passover and Pentecost. It was only a problem for the rabbis: from where did he bring flax and olive seeds[75]?

[76]Rebbi Perira brought before Rebbi Jehudah the Prince two radishes between New Year's Day and the Fast. It was the year after a Sabbatical, and they were a camel's load. He said to him, rabbi, are they not forbidden? Are they no aftergrowth? He said to him, they were sown after the end of the Sabbatical year. At that moment did Rebbi permit to buy vegetables immediately after the end of the Sabbatical year.

---

74   The commentaries and editors read מיני חדח "new kinds". It is difficult to emend, only to end up with an uncommon expression. It seems preferable to read the word as حَرْث חרח "cultivated field".

75   Which are not found early in spring.

76   This is a slight reformulation of a paragraph in *Peah* 7:4, Notes 78, 81. The paragraph also is quoted in *Ševi'it* 6:4, Note 133.

**משנה ח:** שְׁכִיב מְרַע שֶׁכָּתַב כָּל־נְכָסָיו לַאֲחֵרִים שִׁיֵּיר קַרְקַע כָּל־שֶׁהוּא מַתָּנָתוֹ קַיֶּימֶת. לֹא שִׁיֵּיר קַרְקַע כָּל־שֶׁהוּא אֵין מַתָּנָתוֹ קַיֶּימֶת. לֹא כָתַב בָּהּ שְׁכִיב מְרַע הוּא אוֹמֵר שְׁכִיב מְרַע הָיִיתִי וְהֵן אוֹמְרִים בָּרִיא הָיָה צָרִיךְ לְהָבִיא רְאָיָיה שֶׁשְּׁכִיב מְרַע הָיָה דִּבְרֵי רִבִּי מֵאִיר. וַחֲכָמִים אוֹמְרִים הַמּוֹצִיא מֵחֲבֵירוֹ עָלָיו הָרְאָיָיה. (fol. 16c)

**Mishnah 8**: If a bedridden person distributed all his properties to others but reserved any real estate[77] his gift is permanent; if he did not reserve any real estate his gift is not permanent[78]. If [in the document] it was not written "bedridden"; he says, I was bedridden, but they are saying, he was healthy, he must prove that he was bedridden, the words of Rebbi Meïr[79]. But the Sages say, the burden of proof is on the claimants[80].

77  Since he reserves property for himself, it is a sign that he hopes to recover. The gift document written on his orders is not a death-bed will. But if in the document itself it is described as a last will and testament, it is revocable at all times.

78  A death-bed will (which may be written as a gift document and does not have to follow the formal rules of a will) is revocable if the patient recovers.

79  He holds that the actual situation before the court may serve as *prima facie* evidence that so was the prior state. If the bequeather is healthy now, proof is required that he was not healthy when the gift document was written.

An alternative interpretation would be that he holds that a duly executed and witnessed document is always valid unless proven invalid. The technical term for this position is: "the holder of a document is advantaged."

80  As long as the gift described in the document was not executed, the recipient is a claimant and the document is subject to the giver's interpretation unless the claimant can prove otherwise. The technical term for this position is: "the holder of a document is disadvantaged."

(17a line 37) **הלכה ח:** שְׁכִיב מְרַע שֶׁכָּתַב כָּל־נְכָסָיו לַאֲחֵרִים כול'. רַב יִרְמְיָה בְּשֵׁם רַב. שִׁייֵר מִטַלְטְלִין לֹא עָשָׂה כְּלוּם. אֶלָּא הִנִּיחַ לוֹ מָעוֹת וְלָקַח קַרְקַע כְּמִי שֶׁשִּׁייֵר לוֹ קַרְקָע. וְדָא דְתֵימַר. לֹא שִׁייֵר קַרְקַע כָּל־שֶׁהוּא אֵין מַתָּנָתוֹ מַתָּנָה. בְּאוֹתוֹ שֶׁלֹּא הִבְרִיא. אֲבָל אִם הִבְרִיא הָדָא הִיא דָמַר רִבִּי יוֹחָנָן בְּשֵׁם רִבִּי יַנַּאי. עָשׂוּ דִּבְרֵי שְׁכִיב מְרַע כִּבְרִיא שֶׁכָּתַב וְנָתַן. וְהוּא שֶׁמֵּת מֵאוֹתוֹ הַחוֹלִי. מְסוּכָּן שֶׁחִילֵּק נְכָסָיו בֵּין בַּחוֹל בֵּין בַּשַׁבָּת מַה שֶׁעָשָׂה עָשׂוּי. וְאִם הוּא בָּרִיא עַד שֶׁיִּכְתּוֹב בַּכֶּסֶף בַּשְּׁטָר וּבַחֲזָקָה.

**Halakhah 8**: "If a bedridden person distributed all his properties to others," etc. Rav Jeremiah in the name of Rav: If he reserved any movables, he did not do anything[81]. But if he reserved money and bought real estate it is as if he reserved real estate. And what you say that if he did not reserve any real estate his gift is not a gift, if he did (not)[82] recuperate. But if he did [not][82] recuperate, that is the case about which Rebbi Johanan said in the name of Rebbi Yannai, they treated words of a bedridden person like those of a healthy person who wrote and delivered[83]; but only if he died from that sickness. If a critically ill person distributed his property[84], whether on a weekday or on the Sabbath[85], what he did is valid. But if he was healthy [it is valid] only if he wrote "by money, or contract, or possession.[86]"

81  The Babli disagrees, 150a, if the amount reserved is more than minimal.
82  Clearly, the cases where the patient recovers and has occasion to revoke his will, or when he dies, are switched in the text.

83  *Ketubot* 11:1 Note 23; *Giṭṭin* 1:6, Note 201; Babli *Giṭṭin* 13a,15a; *Bava batra* 151a,175a.
84  By oral instruction.
85  When acquisition is forbidden.
86  Mishnah *Qiddušin* 1:5.

(17a line 44) אָמַר רִבִּי יוֹחָנָן. נִיטְמָא בְסָפֵק בְּקִעָה בֵּין בִּימוֹת הַחַמָּה בֵּין בִּימוֹת הַגְּשָׁמִים. מַחֲלוֹקֶת רִבִּי מֵאִיר וַחֲכָמִים. בָּא לִשְׁאַל בִּימוֹת הַחַמָּה נִשְׁאֲלִין לוֹ

בִּימוֹת הַחַמָּה. בִּימוֹת הַגְּשָׁמִים נִשְׁאָלִין לוֹ בִּימוֹת הַגְּשָׁמִים. אָמַר רִבִּי יוֹחָנָן. וּבִלְבַד יָמִים הַסְּמוּכִים לַגְּשָׁמִים.

Rebbi Johanan said: Somebody became possibly impure[87] in an agricultural area whether in summer or in winter; this refersn to the dispute between Rebbi Meïr and the Sages[88]. If he comes to ask in summer, one answers him according to the rules of summer; in the winter, one answers him according to the rules of winter. Rebbi Johanan said, only days close to the rainy season[89].

87 Mishnah *Tahorot* 6:6 declares that a doubt which arises about impurity in a private domain is treated as if the case were about certain impurity whereas in a public domain the same case is treated as one of purity. Mishnah 6:7 then notes that an agricultural area is treated like a private domain during the rainy season (the entire time between ploughing at the time of the first rains through harvest in early summer) but as a public domain after the harvest is completed and the fields are cleared.

88 Since R. Meïr holds that individual cases have to be decided according to the situation actually before the court (Note 79), for him the problem is not the state of the area when the question arose but when it is asked of the rabbinic authority.

89 Even R. Meïr will not decide according to the situation when the question was asked if there was a long interval between the creation of the problem and its resolution.

(17a line 48) רִבִּי יַנַּאי בְּשֵׁם רִבִּי. יַד הַשְּׁטָרוֹת לַתַּחְתּוֹנָה. אָמַר לֵיהּ רִבִּי יוֹחָנָן. וְלָאו מַתְנִיתָא הִיא. לֹא כָתַב לָהּ שְׁכִיב מְרַע וְהוּא אוֹמֵר שְׁכִיב מְרַע וְכוּל׳. וַהֲוָה רִבִּי יַנַּאי מְקַלֵּס לֵיהּ. הַזָּלִים זָהָב מִכִּיס. בְּנֵי אַל יָלִיזוּ מֵעֵינֶיךָ וגו׳. חַד טְלִי זְבִין נִיכְסוֹי. אֲתָא עוֹבְדָא קוֹמֵי רִבִּי חִייָה בַּר יוֹסֵף וְרִבִּי יוֹחָנָן. רִבִּי חִייָה בַּר יוֹסֵף אָמַר. חֲזָקָה עַל בֶּן דַּעַת חָתְמוּ. רִבִּי יוֹחָנָן אָמַר. מִכֵּיוָן שֶׁקִּיבֵּל עָלָיו לַעֲקוֹר נְכָסִין מִמִּשְׁפָּחָה עָלָיו לְהָבִיא הָרְאָייָה. אוֹמֵר רִבִּי יוֹחָנָן. יַד הַשְּׁטָרוֹת לָעֶלְיוֹנָה. רִבִּי יָסָא בְּעָא קוֹמֵי רִבִּי יוֹחָנָן. מַה בְּרִבִּי. דְּרִבִּי אָמַר. יַד בַּעַל הַשְּׁטָר לַתַּחְתּוֹנָה. אָמַר לֵיהּ. דִּבְרֵי הַכֹּל הִיא יַד הַשְּׁטָרוֹת לָעֶלְיוֹנָה. וְהֵיךְ אַתּוּן

אָמְרִין. אֲתָא עוֹבְדָא קוֹמֵי רִבִּי חִייָה בַּר יוֹסֵף וְאָמַר. חֲזָקָה עַל בֶּן דַּעַת חֲתָמוּ.
וְתִי⁹⁰ אָמְרַת. מִכֵּיוָן שֶׁקִּיבֵּל עָלָיו לַעֲקוֹר נְכָסִים מִמִּשְׁפָּחָה לְמִשְׁפָּחָה עָלָיו
לְהָבִיא רְאָיָיה. אָמַר לֵיהּ. אֲנָא לָא אֲמָרִית הָדָא מִילְתָא. אָמַר רִבִּי זֵירָא
קוֹמֵי רִבִּי יָסָא. אֲפִילוּ בָּעֵי רִבִּי יוֹחָנָן מִיכְפּוֹר. וְלָא כֵן אָמַר רִבִּי יוֹחָנָן בְּשֵׁם
רִבִּי. יַד בַּעַל הַשְּׁטָר לַתַּחְתּוֹנָה. אָמַר לֵיהּ רִבִּי יוֹחָנָן. וְלָאו מַתְנִיתָא הִיא. אֶלָּא
חֲכָמִים שֶׁהֵן כְּרִבִּי.

Rebbi Yannai in the name of Rebbi: The holder of documents is disadvantaged[80,91]. Rebbi Joḥanan said to him, is that not the Mishnah: "If [in the document] it was not written 'bedridden' but he says, I was bedridden," etc.[92] Rebbi Yannai praised him "those who pour out gold from the wallet[93]," "my son, they should not be removed from your eyes,[94]" etc.[95]

A young man was selling his properties[96]. The case[97] came before Rebbi Ḥiyya bar Joseph and Rebbi Joḥanan. Rebbi Ḥiyya bar Joseph said, the presumption is that they[98] signed for a mentally capable person[99]. Rebbi Joḥanan said, since he undertook to uproot the properties from the family, he has to bring proof[100].

Rebbi Joḥanan said, the holder of documents is advantaged[79]. Rebbi Yasa asked before Rebbi Joḥanan, how about Rebbi, since Rebbi said, the holder of documents is disadvantaged? He told him, everybody agrees that the holder of documents is advantaged. But how could you say that a case came before Rebbi Ḥiyya bar Joseph who said, the presumption is that they signed for a mentally capable person. And you said, since he undertook to uproot the properties from the family to another family, he has to bring proof! He told him, I never said this[101]. Rebbi Ze'ira said before Rebbi Yasa, even if Rebbi Joḥanan wants to deny it, did not Rebbi Yannai say in the name of Rebbi: The holder of documents is disadvantaged. Rebbi Joḥanan said to him, is that not the Mishnah? This is the opinion of the Sages[91] who follow Rebbi[102].

90 Vocalization of the ms.

91 In the Babli, 154b, the version is: The holder of a document of indebtedness or gift has to get judicial confirmation of its validity.

92 The position of the anonymous majority in the Mishnah.

93 *Is.* 46:6.

94 *Prov.* 3:21.

95 Similar texts are in *Kilaim* 8:1 Note 17, *Yebamot* 1:1 Notes 96-103, *Soṭah* 2:6 Note 177, *Qiddušin* 3:5 Note 166.

96 Real estate. Mishnah *Giṭṭin* 5:8 permits underage children to buy and sell movables as soon as they are able to handle money. The inference is that for real estate transactions one has to be an adult. The Babli, 156a, restricts the right to sell inherited real estate to people who have reached the age of 20. It is clear from the case discussed here that this is a purely Babylonian restriction.

97 The family objected to his selling inherited real estate. They disputed the validity of the deed on the grounds that the seller was underage.

98 The witnesses.

99 He agrees that the seller of real estate not only has to be an adult (13+ years for a male, 12+ years for a female) but also must understand the consequences of what he is doing.

100 That he was an adult understanding what he was doing.

101 He now holds that the person attacking the validity of a duly witnessed document, not the defendant, must prove his case. In the Babli (*Ketubot* 18b) this opinion is credited to R. Simeon ben Laqish, confirmed in his name by the Yerushalmi *Ševi'it* 10:5 Note 96 and *Giṭṭin* 4:2 Note 46, in R. La's name *Ketubot* 2:3 Note 61.

102 But R. Joḥanan himself decides practice to follow R. Meïr.

(17a line 62) רַב יִרְמְיָה בְשֵׁם רַב. הֲלָכָה כְרִבִּי מֵאִיר. שְׁמוּאֵל אָמַר. חִילוּפִין הִיא מַתְנִיתָא. מָהוּ חִילוּפִין הִיא מַתְנִיתָא. חַבְרַיָיא רַבְרְבַיָיא אָמְרֵי. עֵדִים. חַבְרַיָיא זְעִירַיָיא אָמְרֵי. אֵין עֵדִים. כְּלוּם פְּלִיגֵי אֶלָּא עַל הָעֵדִים. אָמַר רִבִּי אָחָא. כֵּיוָן שֶׁאָמַרְתִּי לָכֶם לִכְתּוּב שְׁכִיב מְרַע וְלֹא כְּתַבְתֶּם שְׁקָרִים אַתֶּם.

Rav Jeremiah in the name of Rav: Practice follows Rebbi Meïr[103]. Samuel said, the Mishnah is inverted[104]. In what is the Mishnah inverted? The senior colleagues said, "witnesses."[105] The junior colleagues said, no "witnesses": did they only disagree about witnesses[106]? Rebbi Aḥa said, since I told you to write "bedridden" and you did not write it, you are liers[107].

103  Since Rav and R. Joḥanan decide in the same sense, this is the established practice in the Yerushalmi. This opinion is not mentioned in the Babli.

104  The opinion ascribed to R. Meïr in this Mishnah is rejected by him in another.

105  In Mishnah *Ketubot* 2:3, an anonymous Mishnah which therefore is held to represent R. Meïr's opinion, witnesses may agree that they signed a deed but that nevertheless the deed is invalid since they acted under duress. Therefore, R. Meïr in the Mishnah here should not object to an investigation of the witnesses on a document of questionable validity.

106  There is no discrepancy between the two Mishnaiot since the question here is about the claim of the donor, not about the witnesses.

107  Even if the disagreement is about witnesses, it has nothing to do with the Mishnah in *Ketubot*. Since people who write down oral dispositions of a sick person are required to state in the document that it is a death-bed will, the donor claims that the document is invalid because it did not follow his instructions and, therefore, the genuine signatures on the document convict the signatories of lying.

(fol. 16c) **משנה ט:** הַמְחַלֵּק נְכָסָיו עַל פִּיו רִבִּי אֱלִיעֶזֶר אוֹמֵר אֶחָד וְאֶחָד מְסוּכָּן נְכָסִים שֶׁיֵּשׁ לָהֶן אַחֲרָיוּת נִקְנִין בַּכֶּסֶף וּבַשְּׁטָר וּבַחֲזָקָה וְשֶׁאֵין לָהֶן אַחֲרָיוּת אֵינָן נִקְנִין אֶלָּא בִּמְשִׁיכָה. אָמְרוּ לוֹ מַעֲשֶׂה בְּאִימָּן שֶׁל בְּנֵי רוֹכֵל שֶׁהָיְיתָה חוֹלָה וְאָמְרָה תְּנוּ כְּבִינָתִי לְבִתִּי וְהִיא בִּשְׁנֵים עָשָׂר מָנֶה וָמֵתָה וְקִייְמוּ חֲכָמִים אֶת דְּבָרֶיהָ. אָמַר לָהֶן בְּנֵי רוֹכֵל תִּקְבְּרֶן אִימָּם.

**Mishnah 9**: If somebody distributes his property orally, Rebbi Eliezer says that whether he is healthy or critical, guaranteed properties can be acquired by money, or contract, or possession. Not guaranteed properties can only be acquired by drawing close[108]. They said to him, it happened that the mother of the Bene Rokhel was sick and said, give my bonnet to my daughter, it is worth twelve minas. She died and the Sages confirmed her words. He answered them, the Bene Rokhel should have been buried by their mother[109].

108 He holds that oral dispositions must in every case fully comply with the rules laid down in *Qiddušin* 1:5.

109 They were of ill repute; the ruling of the Sages was a form of punishment.

(17a line 66) **הלכה ט:** הַמְחַלֵּק נְכָסָיו עַל פִּיו כול'. עַד כְּדוֹן בְּשֶׁהָיוּ קַרְקָעוֹת וּמִטַּלְטְלִין בְּמָקוֹם אֶחָד. הָיוּ קַרְקָעוֹת בְּמָקוֹם אֶחָד וּמִטַּלְטְלִין בְּמָקוֹם אַחֵר. אָמַר רִבִּי בּוּן. נִשְׁמְעִינָהּ מֵהָדָא. אָמַר לָהֶן רִבִּי אֱלִיעֶזֶר. מַעֲשֶׂה בְּמָרוֹנִי שֶׁהָיָה בִּירוּשָׁלֵם וְהָיוּ לוֹ מִטַּלְטְלִין הַרְבֵּה וּמְבַקֵּשׁ לְחַלְּקָן. אָמְרוּ לוֹ. אֵין לָךְ תַּקָּנָה אֶלָּא אִם כֵּן קָנִיתָ קַרְקַע. מֶה עָשָׂה. הָלַךְ וְקָנָה סֶלַע אֶחָד סָמוּךְ לִירוּשָׁלֵם. אָמַר. חֶצְיָיהּ צְפוֹנִי אֲנִי נוֹתֵן לִפְלוֹנִי וְעִמּוֹ מֵאָה צֹאן וּמֵאָה חָבִיּוֹת שֶׁל יַיִן. מֶחֶצְיָיהּ דְּרוֹמִי אֲנִי נוֹתֵן לִפְלוֹנִי עִם מֵאָה חָבִיּוֹת שֶׁל שֶׁמֶן. וּבָא מַעֲשֶׂה לִפְנֵי חֲכָמִים וְקִייְמוּ אֶת דְּבָרָיו. אָמַר רִבִּי חֲנַנְיָה קוֹמֵי רִבִּי מָנָא. וְלֹא שְׁכִיב מְרַע הוּא. לְפִי שֶׁבְּכָל־מָקוֹם אֵין אָדָם מְזַכֶּה אֶלָּא בִּכְתָב. וְכָא אֲפִילוּ בִדְבָרִים. לְפִי שֶׁבְּכָל־מָקוֹם אֵין אָדָם מְזַכֶּה עַד שֶׁיִּהְיוּ קַרְקָעוֹת וּמִטַּלְטְלִין בְּמָקוֹם אֶחָד. וְכָא אֲפִילוּ קַרְקָעוֹת בְּמָקוֹם אֶחָד וּמִטַּלְטְלִין בְּמָקוֹם אַחֵר. אָמַר לֵיהּ. וְלֹא רִבִּי אֱלִיעֶזֶר הִיא. שַׁנְיָיא הִיא. שְׁכִיב מְרַע דְּרִבִּי לִיעֶזֶר כִּבְרִיא דְּרַבָּנָן. אָמַר לֵיהּ. שְׁכִיב מְרַע דְּרִבִּי אֱלִיעֶזֶר כִּבְרִיא דְּרַבָּנָן.

[110]So far if real estate and movables were at the same place. If real estate was at one place and movables elsewhere? Rebbi Abin bar Ḥiyya said, let us hear from the following: Rebbi Eliezer said to them, it happened that a man from Meron was dwelling in Jerusalem who was rich in movables. He wanted to distribute them, to give them as gifts. They said to him, you cannot do that except if you acquire real estate. What

did he do? He went and bought a rock near Jerusalem and said: The Northern part I give to X with a hundred sheep and a hundred amphoras of wine, the Southern part I give to Y with a hundred amphoras of oil. The matter came before the Sages, who upheld his words.

Rebbi Hananiah said before Rebbi Mana: But was he not bedridden? For in general a person might give property rights only in writing, and here even orally. In general, a person might give only if real estate and movables are at the same place; here, however, the real estate was at one place and the movables elsewhere. He said to him: But is there a difference for Rebbi Eliezer? Would the sick person for Rebbi Eliezer be like the healthy person for the rabbis? He said to him: The sick person for Rebbi Eliezer is like the healthy person for the rabbis.

110   This paragraph and the next are a slight reformulation of a paragraph from *Peah* 3:8 (Notes 134-147), also quoted in *Qiddušin* 1:5, Note 500. A similar quote is in the Babli, 156b.

(17b line 4) תַּמָּן תַּנִּינָן. רִבִּי עֲקִיבָה אוֹמֵר. קַרְקַע כָּל־שֶׁהוּא. אָמַר רִבִּי מַתַּנְיָה. תִּיפְתָּר מָקוֹם שִׁיבּוֹלֶת אַחַת וּמַרְגָּלִית טְמוּנָה בּוֹ.

There, we have stated: "Rebbi Aqiba says, any real estate..." Rebbi Mattaniah said, explain it if it had space for one stalk but a pearl was hidden in it[111].

111   This is simply a note to look up the text in *Peah*:
"'Any real estate is subject to *peah* and first fruits, the words of Rebbi Aqiba.' What is the use of *any* real estate? Rebbi Mattaniah said, explain it if it had space for one stalk but a pearl was hidden in it."

(17b line 5) אָמַר רִבִּי יוֹסֵי בֵּירִבִּי בּוּן. עוּלָא הָיָה רוֹצֶה לְקַלְּלָן שֶׁהֵן זוֹרְעִין כּוּרְכְּמִין בַּכֶּרֶם.

Rebbi Yose ben Rebbi Abun said, he looked for a pretext to curse them since they were sowing saffron in a vineyard[112].

112 This is forbidden as a case of *kilaim*. The Babli, 156b, clearly knows of the Yerushalmi explanation since after stating Samuel's explanation that R. Eliezer wanted to curse them because they kept thistles in their vineyard, it asks: We understand that growing saffron is forbidden, but what is wrong with thistles?

**משנה י**: וַחֲכָמִים אוֹמְרִים בַּשַּׁבָּת דְּבָרָיו קַיָּימִין מִפְּנֵי שֶׁאֵינוֹ יָכוֹל לִכְתּוֹב אֲבָל לֹא בַחוֹל. רִבִּי יְהוֹשֻׁעַ אוֹמֵר בַּשַּׁבָּת אָמְרוּ קַל וָחוֹמֶר בַּחוֹל. (fol. 16d)

**Mishnah 10**: But the Sages say, on the Sabbath, his words are confirmed[113] since he cannot write, but not on weekdays. Rebbi Joshua says, they said that for the Sabbath, so much more for weekdays[114].

**משנה יא**: כַּיּוֹצֵא בּוֹ זָכִין לַקָּטָן וְאֵין זָכִין לַגָּדוֹל. רִבִּי יְהוֹשֻׁעַ אוֹמֵר לַקָּטָן אָמְרוּ קַל וָחוֹמֶר לַגָּדוֹל.

**Mishnah 11**: Similarly, one may acquire for an underage person[115] but not for an adult. Rebbi Joshua says, they said that for an underage person, so much more for an adult[116].

113 Even though on the Sabbath one is not permitted to change ownership actively or passively.

114 He accepts oral wills in all cases, provided that the statement was made before two unrelated witnesses in good standing and able to confirm the distribution in court.

115 He has no "hand" in the legal sense. A third person may accept gifts on his behalf and thereby effectuate the transfer of ownership.

116 Since it is a generally accepted principle that "one may act for the benefit of a person in his absence and without his knowledge, but not to his detriment."

(17b line 7) **הלכה י:** וַחֲכָמִים אוֹמְרִים בַּשַּׁבָּת דְּבָרָיו קַיָּימִין כוּל׳. אִית תַּנָּיֵי תַּנֵּי וּמַחֲלִיף. רִבִּי יְהוֹשֻׁעַ בֶּן לֵוִי אָמַר. כֵּינִי מַתְנִיתָא. אִם בַּשַּׁבָּת אָמְרוּ קַל וַחוֹמֶר בַּחוֹל. אִית תַּנָּיֵי תַּנֵּי וּמַחֲלִיף. רִבִּי יְהוֹשֻׁעַ בֶּן לֵוִי אָמַר. כֵּינִי מַתְנִיתָא. אִם בַּקָּטָן אָמְרוּ קַל וַחוֹמֶר לַגָּדוֹל.

**Halakhah 10**: "But the Sages say, on the Sabbath, his words are confirmed," etc. Some Tannaïm state it inversely[117]. Rebbi Joshua ben Levi said, so is the Mishnah: if they said that for the Sabbath, so much more for weekdays.

Some Tannaïm state it inversely[117]. Rebbi Joshua ben Levi said, so is the Mishnah: if they said that for an underage person, so much more for an adult.

117  In Tosephta 10:12 and Babli 156b, R. Meïr is reported in R. Eliezer's name to hold that one may orally dispose of one's property on a weekday but not on the Sabbath, and that one may acquire for an adult without his knowledge but not for an underage person. The text of the Mishnah there is attributed to R. Jehudah. In either case, it is presumed that a third person be available to formally accept the distribution for the beneficiaries. R. Joshua ben Levi confirms the text of the Mishnah, rejecting the Tosephta.

(fol. 16d) **משנה יב:** נָפַל הַבַּיִת עָלָיו וְעַל אָבִיו עָלָיו וְעַל יוֹרְשָׁיו עָלָיו וְעַל מוֹרִישָׁיו וְהָיְתָה עָלָיו כְּתוּבַּת אִשָּׁה וּבַעֲלֵי חוֹב יוֹרְשֵׁי הָאָב אוֹמְרִים הַבֵּן מֵת רִאשׁוֹן וְאַחַר כָּךְ מֵת הָאָב. וּבַעֲלֵי הַחוֹב אוֹמְרִים הָאָב מֵת רִאשׁוֹן וְאַחַר כָּךְ מֵת הַבֵּן. בֵּית שַׁמַּאי אוֹמְרִים יַחֲלוֹקוּ וּבֵית הִלֵּל אוֹמְרִים נְכָסִים בְּחֶזְקָתָן.

**Mishnah 12**: If the house collapsed on him[118] and his father, or on him and his heirs, or on him and one from whom he inherits, and a woman's *ketubah* and documents of indebtedness were on him. The father's heirs say that the son died first and then the father[119]; the holders of the debt say that the father died first and then the son[120]. The House of Shammai say that they shall split; the House of Hillel say the properties are in the possession of their holders[121].

**משנה יג**: נָפַל הַבַּיִת עָלָיו וְעַל אִשְׁתּוֹ הָאָב יוֹרְשֵׁי הָאִשָּׁה אוֹמְרִים הָאִשָּׁה מֵתָה רִאשׁוֹנָה וְאַחַר כָּךְ מֵת הַבַּעַל. יוֹרְשֵׁי הָאִשָּׁה אוֹמְרִים הָאִישׁ מֵת רִאשׁוֹנָה וְאַחַר כָּךְ מֵתָה הָאִשָּׁה. בֵּית שַׁמַּאי אוֹמְרִים יַחֲלוֹקוּ וּבֵית הִלֵּל אוֹמְרִים נְכָסִים בְּחֶזְקָתָן. כְּתוּבָּה בְּחֶזְקַת יוֹרְשֵׁי הַבַּעַל. וּנְכָסִים הַנִּכְנָסִין וְהַיּוֹצְאִין עִמָּהּ בְּחֶזְקַת יוֹרְשֵׁי הָאָב.

**Mishnah 13.** If the house collapsed on him and his wife[122]; the father's heirs say that the wife died first and then the husband[123]. The wife's heirs say that the man died first and then the wife[124]. The House of Shammai say that they shall split; the House of Hillel say the properties are in the possession of their holders, the *ketubah*[125] is in the hands of the husband's heirs; properties that enter and leave with her[126] are in the hands of her father's heirs.

**משנה יג**: נָפַל הַבַּיִת עָלָיו וְעַל אִמּוֹ אֵילוּ וְאֵילוּ מוֹדִין שֶׁיַּחֲלוֹקוּ. אָמַר רִבִּי עֲקִיבָה מוֹדֶה אֲנִי בָּזֶה שֶׁהַנְּכָסִים בְּחֶזְקָתָן. אָמַר לוֹ בֶּן עַזַּאי עַל הַחֲלוּקִין אָנוּ מִצְטַעֲרִין אֶלָּא שֶׁבָּאתָ לַחֲלוֹק עָלֵינוּ אֶת הַשָּׁוִין.

**Mishnah 13**: If the house collapsed on him and his mother[127], all agree that they shall split[128]. Rebbi Aqiba said, here I am agreeing that the properties are in the possession of their holders[129]. Ben Azzai said to him, we are sorry for their diagreements and you want to make a disagreement where they agree.

118  And he died without children.

119  The son did not inherit anything; the father's estate inherits from the son. The son's creditors can be satisfied only from his estate; they have no claim to the father's estate.

120  The son inherited from the father; the father's estate is available to satisfy the son's creditors.

121  The father's heirs have acquired

the father's estate at the latter's death. The son's creditors are claimants who have to bear the burden of proof.

122  And they have no children which would be the automatic heirs.

123  The husband inherited from his wife; all his estate now is the property of his agnates.

124  She has a claim on her *ketubah* which is inherited by her family.

125  Including the dowry which was given to the husband as his property to which the wife only has a claim at the dissolution of the marriage.

126  Paraphernalia property which never became the husband's; cf. Mishnah *Yebamot* 7:1.

127  When she was a widow or divorcee, he was her only son and he leaves no children. Her husband's heirs claim that the mother died first, the son inherited from her, and his agnates inherit everything. The mother's agnates claim that the son died first; he did not inherit anything; her inheritance belongs to her paternal family.

128  The mother's estate.

129  Her ex-husband's family has no claim to her estate.

(17b line 11) **הלכה יב:** נָפַל הַבַּיִת עָלָיו וְעַל אָבִיו כול'. אָמַר רִבִּי שְׁמוּאֵל בַּר רַב יִצְחָק. זֹאת אוֹמֶרֶת שֶׁבֶּן עַזַּאי חָבֵר וְתַלְמִיד לְרִבִּי עֲקִיבָה.

**Halakhah 12**: "If the house collapsed on him and his father," etc. Rebbi Samuel ben Rav Isaac said, this implies that Ben Azzai was a colleague and student of Rebbi Aqiba[130].

130  It is known that Ben Azzai was R. Aqiba's student. But had he not reached the status of a colleague, he could not have publicly criticized him.

## גט פשוט פרק עשירי

(fol. 17b) **משנה א:** גֵּט פָּשׁוּט עֵדָיו מִתּוֹכוֹ וּמְקוּשָׁר עֵדָיו מֵאֲחוֹרָיו. פָּשׁוּט שֶׁכָּתְבוּ עֵדָיו מֵאֲחוֹרָיו וּמְקוּשָׁר שֶׁכָּתְבוּ עֵדָיו מִתּוֹכוֹ שְׁנֵיהֶן פְּסוּלִין. רִבִּי חֲנַנְיָה בֶּן גַּמְלִיאֵל אוֹמֵר מְקוּשָׁר שֶׁכָּתְבוּ עֵדָיו מִתּוֹכוֹ כָּשֵׁר מִפְּנֵי שֶׁהוּא יָכוֹל לַעֲשׂוֹתוֹ פָשׁוּט. רַבָּן שִׁמְעוֹן בֶּן גַּמְלִיאֵל אוֹמֵר הַכֹּל כְּמִנְהַג הַמְּדִינָה.

**Mishnah 1**: The witnesses to an simple document[1] sign inside, to a knotted[2] one on its back. A simple document whose witnesses signed on its back[3] and a knotted one whose witnesses signed on its interior both are invalid. Rebbi Ḥananiah ben Gamliel says, a knotted one whose witnesses signed inside[4] is valid since one can turn it into a simple one. Rabban Simeon ben Gamliel says, everything follows local custom.

1 A normal document whose witnesses sign below the text.

2 A knotted document is signed on the verso, between the folds. According to Rashbam (Commentary to *Bava batra* 10:1), the document was written with wide spaces between the lines, then was folded and sewn so that the document text was hidden and a witness signed the fold on the back. The number of witnesses must equal the number of folds. But the text below indicates that the text was written before it was folded and sealed. A valid document must be folded at least three times.

The basic use for "knotted" documents was for real estate transactions, probably to hide the financial data from public knowledge. Such a document was certainly impossible in Egypt, where all real estate transactions had to be filed with the State registrar. Its validity in rabbinic tradition is given a biblical basis. It seems from the discussion in Babli *Bava batra* 10 that the use of "knotted" documents among Jews was mainly a Palestinian peculiarity (such documents have been found in the

Judean desert.) In fact, it was a typically Greek form of document (cf. S. Lieberman, יוונית ויוונות בארץ ישראל Jerusalem 1962, p. 20 ff.)

3  In order to eliminate fraud, witnesses on an open document must start to sign below the text, leaving exactly one line free.

4  Following the rules of open documents.

(17c line 4) **הלכה א:** גֵּט פָּשׁוּט עֵדָיו מִתּוֹכוֹ כוּל'. וּמְנַיִּין לְגֵט הַמְקוּשָׁר. אָמַר רִבִּי אִימִּי. וָאֶקַּח אֶת סֵפֶר הַמִּקְנָה. וְאֶת הֶחָתוּם. זֶה הַמְקוּשָׁר. וְאֶת הַגָּלוּי. זֶה הַפָּשׁוּט שֶׁבַּמְקוּשָׁר. וְאֶת הַמִּצְוָה וְאֶת הַחוּקִּים. שֶׁבֵּין זֶה לָזֶה. אֶלָּא שֶׁזֶּה בִּשְׁנַיִם וְזֶה בִּשְׁלֹשָׁה. זֶה מִתּוֹכוֹ וְזֶה מֵאֲחוֹרָיו.

וְרַבָּנָן דְּקַיְסָרִין אָמְרִין. וָאֶקַּח אֶת סֵפֶר הַמִּקְנָה. זֶה הַפָּשׁוּט. וְאֶת הֶחָתוּם. זֶה הַמְקוּשָׁר. וְאֶת הַגָּלוּי. זֶה הַפָּשׁוּט שֶׁבַּמְקוּשָׁר. וְאֶת הַמִּצְוָה וְאֶת הַחוּקִּים. שֶׁבֵּין זֶה לָזֶה. אֶלָּא שֶׁזֶּה בִּשְׁנַיִם וְזֶה בִּשְׁלֹשָׁה. זֶה מִתּוֹכוֹ וְזֶה מֵאֲחוֹרָיו.

רִבִּי אִידִי בְּשֵׁם רִבִּי יִרְמְיָה. הִלְכַת מְקוּשָׁר כָּךְ הוּא. כּוֹתֵב שֵׁם הַמַּלְוֶה וְשֵׁם הַלּוֹוֶה וְשֵׁם הָעֵדִים וּזְמָן. וּמְקַשְּׁרוֹ וְחוֹזֵר וְכוֹתֵב כֵּן מִלְמַטָּה. חָשׁ לוֹמַר שֶׁמָּא סִיֵּיף. אָמַר רַב הוּנָא. לְעוֹלָם אֵין הָעֵדִים חוֹתְמִין מִלְמַטָּן עַד שֶׁיִּקְרְאוּ בוֹ מִלְמַעְלָן. אֲנִי פְּלוֹנִי בֶּן פְּלוֹנִי מְקוּבָּל עָלַי כָּל־הַכָּתוּב לְמַעְלָן.

**Halakhah 1**: "The witnesses to an open document are inside," etc. [5]From where that a document can be knotted? Rebbi Immi said: "I took the sale document and the sealed[6]", that is the knotted [document]. "And the open," that is the simple, part of the knotted[7]. "And the orders and the rules"; orders and rules differ between these, for one is with two [witnesses], the other with three[8]; one in it, the other on its back[9].

But the rabbis of Caesarea say, "I took the sale document", that is the simple one. "And the sealed", that is the knotted [document]. "And the open," that is the simple, part of the knotted. "And the orders and the rules"; orders and rules differ between these, for one is with two [witnesses], the other with three; one in it, the other on its back.

Rebbi Idi in the name of Rebbi Jeremiah. The practice for a knotted one is the following. One writes the lender's name, and the borrower's name, the witnesses' names, and the time. Then one knots it and repeats the text below[10]. But should one not be afraid that maybe he falsifies[11]? Rav Huna said, witnesses never sign below unless they first read in the text above: "I X son of Y accept everything written above."

5   A similar text is in *Gittin* 8:12, Notes 107-112.

6   *Jer.* 32:11: "I took the document of acquisition, the sealed one, the orders and rules, and the public one." The verse clearly states that a sealed document is the main object, accompanied by a public document. The same argument is stated in the Babli, 160b.

7   The text of the document, whose formulation is identical whether sealed or public.

8   A public document needs two witnesses, a sealed (knotted) one at least three.

9   A simple document is signed by the witnesses on the recto of the sheet, starting exactly one line after the end of the text. A knotted document is signed on the verso, between the folds.

10   In fact, one folds the document and writes the main text a second time on the outside, followed by the witnesses' signatures, and ties the document. The document is valid only if the texts inside and outside coincide and the names of the witnesses are confirmed by the inside text.

11   How can the witnesses be sure that the writer of the document will not falsify the document after they affixed their signatures? For a simple document there is no problem since anything following the signatures has to be disregarded. For a sealed document with signatures at a right angle there is no problem since any text not covered by the signatures at the back has to be disregarded. But if the signatures are affixed while the document is being written, where are the guarantees?

(17c line 15) רִבִּי בָּא בְשֵׁם רַב יִרְמְיָה. צְרִיכִין הָעֵדִים לִהְיוֹת רְחוֹקִים מִן הַכְּתָב מָקוֹם שְׁתֵּי שִׁיטִין. רִבִּי אִידִי בְשֵׁם רַב יִרְמְיָה. מְקוּשָּׁר שֶׁכְּתָבוּ עֵדָיו לְאָרְכּוֹ.

פָּשׁוּט שֶׁכָּתְבוּ עֵדָיו לְרָחְבּוֹ. אָהֵין מִלְּגָיו וְאָהֵין מִלְּבַר. אֵיכִי עֲבִיד. אָמַר רִבִּי מָנָא. כֵּיצַד הָעֵדִים חוֹתְמִין בַּגֵּט הַמְקוּשָּׁר. אָמַר רַב חוּנָא. בֵּין קֶשֶׁר לַקֶּשֶׁר. אָמַר רִבִּי אִידִי. וּבִלְבַד שֶׁלֹּא יְהֵא בֵין עֵדִים לַשְּׁטָר מְקוֹם ב' שִׁיטִין.

שִׁמְעוֹן בַּר וָוא בְשֵׁם רִבִּי יוֹחָנָן. חָלָק מְקוֹם שְׁנֵי שִׁיטִין לְעִנְיָין אֶחָד אֲפִילוּ כָל־שֶׁהוּא. אָמַר רִבִּי שְׁמוּאֵל בַּר רַב יִצְחָק. מַתְנִיתָא אָמְרָה כֵן. עַד אֶחָד עִבְרִי וְעֵד אֶחָד יְוָנִי. וְעִבְרִי גַבֵּי יְוָנִי לֹא בְעֵינוֹ [12] אֶחָד הוּא. כַּמָּה יְהוּ הָעֵדִים רְחוֹקִים מִן הַכְּתָב. כְּדֵי שֶׁיְּהוּ מַקְרִין עִמּוֹ. דִּבְרֵי רִבִּי. רִבִּי שִׁמְעוֹן בֶּן אֶלְעָזָר אוֹמֵר. מְלֹא שִׁיטָה. רִבִּי דּוֹסְתַּאי בֶּן יְהוּדָה אוֹמֵר. מְלֹא חֲתִימַת יְדֵי הָעֵדִים. רַב יִרְמְיָה בְשֵׁם רַב אָמַר. מְשַׁעֲרִין אוֹתוֹ עַד כְּדֵי כְּדֵי לַךְ וָלָךְ. בְּאֵי זֶה כְּתַב מְשַׁעֲרִין אוֹתוֹ. רִבִּי יָסָא בְשֵׁם רִבִּי שׁוּבְתַּאי. מְלֹא חֲתִימַת יַד הָעֵדִים. חִזְקִיָּה אָמַר. וּבִלְבַד לְקוּלָא. שֶׁאִם הָיָה חוֹתָם יְדֵי הָעֵדִים דַּק וְהַכְּתָב גַּס הוֹלְכִין אַחַר הַגַּס. חוֹתָם יְדֵי הָעֵדִים גַּס וְהַכְּתָב דַּק הוֹלְכִין אַחַר הַדַּק. אָמַר רִבִּי יִצְחָק אֵין הֲנָה כְּגוֹן יוֹסֵי בֶּן יַנַּאי מְשַׁעֲרִין כְּדֵי מֶלֶךְ בֶּן מֶלֶךְ.

Rebbi Abba in the name of Rav Jeremiah: The signatures of the witnesses must be two blank lines away from the text[13]. Rebbi Idi in the name of Rav Jeremiah: On a knotted document the witnesses sign lengthwise[14]; on a simple document the witnesses sign across[15]. The first one on the outside, the latter one on the inside. Rebbi Mana said, [ ][16]. How do the witnesses sign on a knotted document? Rav Huna said, between two knots[17]. Rebbi Idi said, but between witnesses' signatures and the document there may not be space for two lines[18].

[19]Simeon bar Abba in the name of Rebbi Joḥanan: An empty space of two lines in a text about one subject in any case [invalidates][20]. Rebbi Samuel bar Rav Isaac said: The Mishnah says so[21]: "One Hebrew- and one Greek-writing witness . . ." Is not Hebrew combined with Greek one item? [22]"How far from the text should the witnesses sign? That they can be read with it[23], the words of Rebbi. Rebbi Simeon ben Eleazar says, one full line. Rebbi Dositheos ben Jehudah says, the width of the witnesses'

handwriting." Rav Jeremiah said in the name of Rav: One estimates לך ולך [24]. Rebbi Yasa in the name of Rebbi Sabbatai: the width of the witnesses' handwriting.

Ḥizqiah said, only for leniency[25]. If the witnesses' handwriting was small and the text large, one follows the large. If the witnesses' handwriting was large and the text small, one follows the small[26]. Rebbi Isaac says: If his name was, e. g., **Yose ben Yannai** one estimates as if it were **Melekh ben Melekh**[27].

12  Read בְּעִנְיָן.

13  The following discussion shows that one must read: "The signatures of the witnesses *may not* be two empty lines away from the text.

All talmudic sources require that on a simple document there be *exactly* one line between the concluding formula of a document and the witnesses' signatures. This is Hellenistic practice, cf. Taubenschlag (*loc. cit. Bava meṣia'* 1, Note 84) p. 36.

14  He follows up on his earlier statement that the names of the witnesses must be mentioned in the text of the document. Then the document is folded after completion and the witnesses sign lengthwise on the outside.

15  Below the text, as explained later in the following.

16  R. Mana's statement is missing. It is found in *Giṭṭin* 9:8 (Note 108): "R. Mana said, if he started at the end of the second line and ended at the fourth line, it is valid." If the first witness starts to sign towards the end of the second line after the text and the second witness then finishes on the fourth line, the document is valid since exactly one line is empty after the final clause; the document cannot be falsified by additions.

17  Since before opening the document one must verify that it has the required number of signatures, it must be folded in such a way that the signatures can be read when it is still tied.

18  Cf. Note 13.

19  This essentially is a text from *Giṭṭin* 9:8, Notes 105-115.

20  Since text may be inserted in the document after the witnesses signed.

21  Mishnah *Giṭṭin* 9:8, explained there Note 102.

22  Tosephta *Giṭṭin* 7:11-12.

| | |
|---|---|
| 23  The signatures can be read with a text if the first signature be exactly one line away from the text. | 26  For practical purposes, the scribe prepares lines on parchment or papyrus before writing the document; his lines determine everything. |
| 24  The line must accomodate letters extending both above and below the usual writing space; Babli 163a. | 27  This is a repetition of the argument of Note 23; in *Gittin* it is the answer to a question by R. Jeremiah. The statement is that יוסי נ' ינאי will get as much space above and below as מלך בן מלך. |
| 25  The larger of the handwritings of the scribe and the first witness is the measure of the width of "one line" in the Tosephta; Babli 162b. | |

(17c line 31) רִבִּי אִידִי בְּשֵׁם רִבִּי יִרְמִיָה. צָרִיךְ לְהַרְחִיק מִן הַמַּחַק מָקוֹם שְׁתֵּי שִׁיטִין. אָמַר רִבִּי יִצְחָק. אֲפִילוּ פָּשׁוּט. רַב אָמַר. מַחַק אוֹ תְלוּת שֶׁבְּכִתְבָה הַזֶּה זֶהוּ קִיּוּמוֹ. רַב אָמַר. זֶהוּ קִיּוּמוֹ. רִבִּי אַבָּהוּ בְּשֵׁם רִבִּי יִצְחָק בֶּן חֲקוּלָא. כָּל־מַה שֶּׁאַתְּ יָכוֹל לִתְלוֹת בְּמַחַק תְּלֵה. מַהוּ כָּל־מַה שֶּׁאַתְּ יָכוֹל לִתְלוֹת בְּמַחַק תְּלֵה. רִבִּי יָסָא קוֹצֵייָרָה חַתְנֵיהּ דְּרִבִּי יוֹסֵה בְּשֵׁם רִבִּי יוֹסֵה. סִמְפּוֹן כָּתוּב מִלְעֵיל וְסִימְפוֹן מְחִיק מִלְרָע. אֲנִי אוֹמֵר. גָּמְרוּ לַעֲשׂוֹתָן קִידוּשִׁין גְּמוּרִין. בְּגִין דְּלָא מֵיצָר בֵּינֵיהּ גֵּט מָחֲקֵיהּ. וְרַבָּנָן חָשְׁשִׁין דְּלָא מֵיצָר בֵּינֵיהּ גֵּט.

שְׁטָר נְפַק רִבִּי חוּנָה לְרִבִּי שַׁמִּי. אוֹגְדּוֹלֵי מְחִיק קוֹנְטָא לָא מְחִיק. אָמַר רִבִּי חוּנָה לְרִבִּי שַׁמִּי. פּוּק חֲמֵי עַד הַהֵן אָהֵן קוֹנְטָא מְשַׁמֵּשׁ. נְפַק וָמַר. עִם טְרַייָא קוֹנְטָא. מִי נְפַק אֲמַר. הָדָא מִתְגְּרָה תְּלַת אַפְסַדְתְּ עֲשָׂר.

Rebbi Idi in the name of Rebbi Jeremiah: One has to expand two lines from an erasure[28]. Rebbi Isaac said, even for a simple document[29]. Rav said, an erasure or an insertion must be confirmed in writing[30]. Rav said, "this is its confirmation"[31]. Rebbi Abbahu in the name of Rebbi Isaac ben Ḥaqula: Any erasure has to be given a maximal interpretation. What means, any erasure has to be given a maximal interpretation? Rebbi Yasa the fuller, son-in-law to Rebbi Yose, in the name of Rebbi Yose: "Contract"[32] is written on top, "contract" erased below. I am saying, they decided to make it an unconditional preliminary marriage. They erased it in order not to make an insertion in the document³³, because the rabbis are suspicious of insertions in documents³⁴.

Rebbi Huna³⁵ handed a document to Rebbi Shammai. Ὀγδοή- was on an erasure, -κοντα was not on an erasure. Rebbi Huna told Rebbi Shammai, find out what is the minimum with which -κοντα is used³⁶. He went out and said, τριάκοντα. After they left, he said, this one wanted to gain 30 and lost 20³⁷.

28   After an erasure, the text has to continue for at least another two lines.

29   Even for a simple document, the text has to continue for two lines since the last line simply contains the formula stating the validity of the preceding text, which cannot serve as a confirmation.

30   Both an erasure and an insertion by writing between lines must be referred to in the continuing text.

31   Rav prescribes the formula: "this is confirmation of [erasure/insertion] x". The same is required in the Babli, 161b, in the name of R. Johanan.

32   Cf. *Gittin* 7:6, Notes 133-139. The name of "contract", τὸ σύμφωνον, is given to the contract stating a conditional preliminary marriage. If the groom satisfies the condition within a certain time frame, the preliminary marriage is valid from the moment of signing the contract. If he fails to satisfy the condition in the pre-established time frame, the woman is not preliminarily married and may marry any other man.

33   Since they already had formulated all the financial terms of the marriage, they preferred to erase the mention of *symphon* in the final summary, which automatically made the *symphon* clause unenforceable, instead of inserting between the lines a note annulling the *symphon* clause.

34   The insertion would have required another lengthening of the document by a text confirming the insertion.

35   As a born Babylonian, he knew no Greek.

36   Since the amount of the debt stated in the document, ὀγδοήκοντα (80) was partially written on an erasure and the number was not confirmed later in the text, one had to assume that the document was falsified after it had been witnessed. But since κοντα was clearly readable as original text, the document was good to collect

τριάκοντα (30), the smallest multiple of 10 whose name is formed with -κοντα.

37 Rebbi Huna had the impression that the original document was for πεντήκοντα (50); instead of an intended gain of 30 the forgery resulted in a loss of 20 (H. M. Pineles). One has to read 'חלח (i. e., תלחין) instead of תלח, and 'עשר (i. e. עשרין) instead of עשר.

(17c line 42) חשיב[38] רִבִּי לְקַיֵּים דִּבְרֵי רִבִּי חֲנַנְיָה בֶּן גַּמְלִיאֵל. גוּפוֹ שֶׁלְּגֵט מוֹכִיחַ עָלָיו אִם פָּשׁוּט הוּא אִם אֵינוֹ פָשׁוּט. מָהוּ גוּפוֹ שֶׁלְּגֵט. אָמַר רִבִּי בָא. מִדָּמַר רַב הוּנָא. לְעוֹלָם אֵין הָעֵדִים חוֹתְמִין מִלְּמַטָּה עַד שֶׁיִּקְרְאוּ בוֹ מִלְּמַעְלָן. אֲנִי פְלוֹנִי בֶּן פְלוֹנִי מְקוּבָּל אֲנִי עָלַי כָּל־מַה שֶׁכָּתוּב לְמַעְלָן. וְהָתַנֵּי. טוֹפֶס שְׁטָרוֹת כֵּן הוּא. אָמַר רִבִּי מָנִי. טוֹפֶס שְׁטָרוֹת מְקוּשָּׁרוֹת כֵּן הוּא. אָמַר רִבִּי אָבִין. וַאֲפִילוּ תֵימַר. הוּא פָשׁוּט הוּא מְקוּשָּׁר. בְּפָשׁוּט מְעַכֵּב בִּמְקוּשָּׁר אֵינוֹ מְעַכֵּב. רִבִּי יוּדָה אוֹמֵר. בְּמוֹסִיף עַל הַהֲלָכָה. פָּשׁוּט בִּשְׁנַיִם מְקוּשָּׁר בִּשְׁלֹשָׁה. וְהֵן עוֹשִׂין אוֹתוֹ בִּשְׁלֹשָׁה. פָּשׁוּט מִתּוֹכוֹ מְקוּשָּׁר מֵאֲחוֹרָיו. וְהֵן עוֹשִׂין אוֹתוֹ מִתּוֹכוֹ וּמֵאֲחוֹרָיו.

"Rebbi answered to confirm the words of Rebbi Hananiah ben Gamliel: The main text of the document proves whether it is simple or not simple.[39]" What is the main text of a document? Rebbi Abba said, as Rav Huna said: witnesses never sign below unless they first read before them: "I X son of Y accept everything written above." And did we not state: this is the formula for documents of indebtedness[40]? Rebbi Mani said, this is the formula for knotted documents of indebtedness[41]. Rebbi Abbin said, even if you say, it is the same for simple and knotted, for a simple document it is indispensable, for a knotted one it is not indispensable[42]. Rebbi Jehudah[43] says, if one adds to the practice[44]. A simple document has two [winesses], a knotted one three, but they do it with three. A simple document inside, a knotted one on its back, but they do it inside and on its back.

38  One has to read הָשִׁיב.

39  In Tosephta 11:1 and Babli 164 a/b, Rebbi is reported to *disprove* R. Ḥananiah ben Gamliel's statement since the regnal year dating conventions for both kinds of documents are different. Also in the statement here, *confirm* somehow means *disprove*.

The Babli's argument would not apply to the Roman Empire under the Principate when years were still characterized by the names of the Consuls.

40  Of all kinds.

41  But it only has to appear on the second (outer) text.

42  Since the witnesses have to be enumerated by name in the inner text.

43  He is R. Yudan.

44  While the rules for simple and knotted documents are different, it is easy to write a document in compliance with both sets of rules. Therefore, R. Ḥananiah's statement can be confirmed (at least in most cases.) In contrast to the Babli, this presupposes that the same naming conventions apply to both kinds of contracts.

**משנה ב:** גֵּט פָּשׁוּט עֵדָיו שְׁנַיִם וּמְקוּשָּׁר עֵדָיו שְׁלֹשָׁה. פָּשׁוּט שֶׁכָּתַב בּוֹ (fol. 17b) עֵד אֶחָד וּמְקוּשָּׁר שֶׁכָּתוּב בּוֹ שְׁנַיִם שְׁנֵיהֶן פְּסוּלִין. כָּתוּב בּוֹ זוּזִין מְאָה דִּי הִימוּ סִלְעִין עֶשְׂרִין אֵין לוֹ אֶלָּא עֶשְׂרִים. זוּזִין מְאָה דִּי הִימוּ סִלְעִין תְּלָתִין אֵין לוֹ אֶלָּא מְנָה. כְּסַף זוּזִין דִּי אִינוּן וְנִמְחַק אֵין פָּחוֹת מִשְּׁנַיִם. כְּסַף סִלְעִין דִּי אִינוּן וְנִמְחַקוּ אֵין פָּחוֹת מִשְּׁנַיִם. דַּרְכּוֹנוֹת דִּי אִינוּן וְנִמְחַק אֵין פָּחוֹת מִשְּׁנַיִם.

**Mishnah 2:** A simple document has two witnesses and a knotted one three. A simple [document] in which one [witness] signed or a knotted one where two signed are both invalid. If there is written in it "100 *zuz* which are 20 tetradrachmas," he only has 20[45]. "100 *zuz* which are 30 tetradrachmas," he only has a *mina*[46]. "Silver *zuzim* which are" and the rest is erased, is for no less than two[47]. "Silver tetradrachmas which are" and the rest is erased, is for no less than two. "*Dareikos*[48] which are" and the rest is erased, is for no less than two.

45 If a document contains two different amounts, the smaller one is operative. Since 100 *zuz* (denars) equal 25 tetradrachmas, the contract only calls for payment of 20 tetradrachmas.
46 100 drachmas (denars).
47 Any indefinite plural has to be interpreted as 2, the smallest integer >1.
48 A Persian gold coin. The Yerushalmi in *Šeqalim* 2:3 identifies the Δαρεικός with the Roman gold denar.

(17c line 51) **הלכה ב:** גֵּט פָּשׁוּט עֵדָיו שְׁנַיִם כול׳. תַּנֵּי. זוּזִין דִּינוּן וְנִמְחֲקוּ. חֲמִשָּׁה. וַהֲלָה אוֹמֵר. אֵינוֹ אֶלָּא שְׁנַיִם. תַּמָּן אֱמְרִי. בֶּן עַזַּאי וְרִבִּי עֲקִיבָה. חַד אָמַר. נוֹתֵן שְׁנַיִם וְנִשְׁבַּע עַל הַשְּׁאָר. וְחַד אָמַר. כֵּיוָן שֶׁאִילּוּ לֹא הוֹדָה לוֹ כָּל־עִיקָּר לֹא הָיָה לוֹ אֶלָּא שְׁנַיִם אֵינוֹ נִשְׁבַּע אֶלָּא עַל מַה שֶּׁהוֹדָה.

**Halakhah 2:** "A simple document has two witnesses," etc. It was stated: "*Zuzin* which are" and the rest was erased[49]. Five[50], but the other says, they were only two. There[51], they say, Ben Azzai and Rebbi Aqiba. One of them said, he pays two and swears about the remainder[52]. But the other said, since if this one had not agreed to anything, the other could only have collected two, he should only have to swear on what he conceded[53].

49 A document where it is clear that the amount is written in the plural; therefore the IOU is worth at least two. The amount is illegible.
50 The amount claimed by the creditor.
51 In Babylonia.
52 Following the principle that in the absence of proof the debtor has to swear that he does not owe more than he admitted. The debtor has to swear only if either the creditor can prove that the debtor owes him something or the debtor admits to part of the creditor's claim (cf. *Bava meṣia'* 1:1, Note 9).
53 Since the Mishnah grants the creditor the right to collect two *zuzim*, the debtor did not confess to owing anything for which the creditor does not have documentary proof. Therefore, he should not have to swear. From the Babli, *Bava meṣia'* 4b, it seems that in its tradition this latter opinion is R. Aqiba's.

**משנה ג:** כָּתוּב בּוֹ מִלְמַעְלָה מָנֶה וּמִלְמַטָּה מָאתַיִם מִלְמַעְלָה מָאתַיִם (fol. 17b) וּמִלְמַטָּה מָנֶה הַכֹּל הוֹלֵךְ אַחַר הַתַּחְתּוֹן. אִם כֵּן לָמָּה כּוֹתְבִין הָעֶלְיוֹן. שֶׁאִם תִּימָּחֵק אוֹת אַחַת מִן הַתַּחְתּוֹן יִלְמַד מִן הָעֶלְיוֹן.

**Mishnah 3:** If at the start[54] there was written a *mina* but at the end[55] 200, or at the start 200 and at the end a *mina*, everything goes according to the end. If this is so, why does one write at the start? That if at the end a letter should become illegible, one may recoup it from the start.

54  The text of the document which states that it is an IOU for the amount of *x*.

55  The debtor's declaration that he owes *x* to the creditor, cf. Halakhah 1, after Note 11.

**הלכה ג:** כָּתוּב בּוֹ מִלְמַעְלָה מָנֶה כול׳. תַּנֵּי. לְעוֹלָם הַתַּחְתּוֹן יִלְמַד (17c line 55) מִן הָעֶלְיוֹן בִּמְקוּשָּׁר בְּאוֹת אַחַת אוֹ[56] בִּשְׁתֵּי אוֹתוֹת. בֵּין חָנָן לַחֲנָנִי בֵּין עָנָן לַעֲנָנִי בְּאוֹת אַחַת מְקַיְּימִין אוֹתוֹ. בִּשְׁתֵּי אוֹתוֹת אֵין מְקַיְּימִין אוֹתוֹ. רִבִּי יִצְחָק שָׁאַל. מִמַּעַל כָּתוּב חָנָן וּמִלְּמַטָּן נָנִי. מַהוּ לְלַמֵּד הַתַּחְתּוֹן מֵעֶלְיוֹן חָנָן וְעֶלְיוֹן מִתַּחְתּוֹן נָנִי.

**Halakhah 3:** "If at the start there was written a *mina*," etc. It was stated[57]: Always in a knotted document the bottom[58] should be instructed by the top for one letter (or) [but not][56] for two letters. One confirms between Ḥanan and Ḥanani, or Anan and Anani, a difference of one letter; of two letters one does not confirm[59]. Rebbi Isaac asked: At the top it was written Ḥanan, at the bottom Nani. May the top learn from the bottom for Ḥanan and the bottom from the top for Nani[60]?

56  The following text shows that one has to read אבל לא "but not" instead of או "or".

57  A similar *baraita* is in the Babli, 166b; that *baraita*, however, is formulated for *all* documents.

58  For a knotted document, the bottom would be the outer text, the top referring to the inner text.

59  For the Yerushalmi, there re

mains the possibility that for a simple document even a greater discrepancy could be acceptable.

60  The full name was Ḥanani, which was shortened in two ways to current forms of endearment.

(fol. 17b) **משנה ד:** כּוֹתְבִין גֵּט לָאִישׁ אַף עַל פִּי שֶׁאֵין אִשְׁתּוֹ עִמּוֹ וְהַשּׁוֹבָר לָאִשָּׁה אַף עַל פִּי שֶׁאֵין בַּעֲלָהּ עִמָּהּ וּבִלְבַד שֶׁיְּהֵא מַכִּירָהּ וְהַבַּעַל נוֹתֵן אֶת הַשָּׂכָר.

**Mishnah 4**: One writes[61] a bill of divorce for a man even though his wife not be present[62], and a receipt[63] for the wife even though he husband not be present[64] on condition that he know her[65]. The husband pays the fee[66].

61  "Writing" here means "writing and signing by witnesses."

62  Since by biblical standards a divorce does not need the wife's consent.

63  In which she absolves her ex-husband from all future payments due her on account of her *ketubah*.

64  Since the receipt is of advantage to the husband and "one may let a person acquire something without his knowledge."

65  The scribe and the witnesses must know the people involved, lest a woman write a receipt and hand it to another man, whose wife's name is the same as hers, who then may divorce his wife and claim that he does not owe her anything.

66  The scribe's fee for bill of divorce and receipt. In Babylonia they let the woman pay for the bill of divorce (Babli 168a).

(17c line 60) **הלכה ד:** כּוֹתְבִין גֵּט לָאִישׁ כול׳. אָמַר רִבִּי בָּא. צָרִיךְ שֶׁיְּהֵא מַכִּיר לִשְׁנֵיהֶן. אָמַר רִבִּי לָא. צָרִיךְ שֶׁיְּהֵא מַכִּיר לָאִישׁ בְּגִיטּוֹ וּלְאִשָּׁה בְּשׁוֹבְרָהּ. מַתְנִיתָא פְּלִיגָא עַל רִבִּי בָּא. הִתְקִין רַבָּן גַּמְלִיאֵל הַזָּקֵן שֶׁיִּכְתּוֹב. אִישׁ פְּלוֹנִי וְכָל־שֵׁם שֶׁיֵּשׁ לוֹ. אִשָּׁה פְּלוֹנִית וְכָל־שֵׁם שֶׁיֵּשׁ לָהּ. מִפְּנֵי תִיקּוּן הָעוֹלָם. וַאֲפִילוּ כְּרִבִּי [ ] לֵית הִיא פְּלִיגָא. בָּרִאשׁוֹנָה הָיָה מְשַׁנֶּה שְׁמוֹ וּשְׁמָהּ שֵׁם עִירוֹ וְשֵׁם עִירָהּ.

**Halakhah 4**: "One writes a bill of divorce for a man," etc. [67]Rebbi Abba said: He has to know both of them. Rebbi La said, he has to know the husband for his bill of divorce and the woman for her receipt. A Mishnah disagrees with Rebbi Abba: "Rabban Gamliel the Elder instituted that one should write Mr. X and all his names, Mrs. Y and all her names, for the public good." But even with Rebbi [La][68] it does not disagree: "In earlier times, his name and her name and the names of his and her towns could change."

67  This is a shortened version of a paragraph in *Gittin* 4:2, explained there in Notes 39-51.

68  Name missing in the text; supplied from the parallel in *Gittin*, required by the context.

(fol. 17b) **משנה ה:** כּוֹתְבִין שְׁטָר לַלּוֶה אַף עַל פִּי שֶׁאֵין הַמַּלְוֶה עִמּוֹ וְאֵין כּוֹתְבִין לַמַּלְוֶה עַד שֶׁיְהֵא הַלּוֶה עִמּוֹ. וְהַלּוֶה נוֹתֵן אֶת הַשָּׂכָר.

**Mishnah 5**: One writes[61] a document of indebtedness for the borrower even though the creditor not be present, but one does not write a document of indebtedness for the creditor if the borrower not be present[69]. The borrower pays the fee.

69  One may write and sign a document for an absentee beneficiary but not to the detriment of an absentee.

(17c line 65) **הלכה ה:** כּוֹתְבִין שְׁטָר לַלּוֶה כול'. תַּנֵּי. עִיצּוּמִים. רִבִּי אַבָּהוּ גָּבֵי רִבִּי אָחָא גָּבֵי רִבִּי אִמִּי גָּבֵי. רִבִּי יוֹנָה וְרִבִּי יוֹסֵי לֹא גָּבֵי. אָמַר רִבִּי מָנָא. אַף עַל גַּב דְּלֵית רִבִּי יוֹסֵי גָּבֵי עִיצּוּמִין מוֹדֶה בָּהוּ דִיהַב בְּרֵיהּ גּוֹ אוּמְנוּתָא וְעַצְמוֹן בֵּינֵיהוֹן דְּהוּא גָּבֵי.

**Halakhah 5**: "One writes a document of indebtedness," etc. It was stated, forfeits[70]. Rebbi Abbahu collected, Rebbi Aḥa collected, Rebbi Immi collected[71]. Rebbi Jonah and Rebbi Yose did not collect. [72]Rebbi Mana said, even though Rebbi Yose did not collect forfeits, he agrees if one gave his son to artisans and they mutually agreed to forfeits, he collects.

70 Whether a private contract containing forfeits automatically is enforceable in court or is to be considered an *asmakhta* contract (cf. *Giṭṭin* 5:9, Note 213) is a subject of controversy already of Tannaïm; Tosephta *Bava meṣia'* 1:16.

71 In the third generation of Amoraïm, forfeits were considered enforceable, following Egyptian and Greek practices. By the fifth generation, practice had changed and forfeits were considered *asmakhta*, following Roman law; cf. *Sefer Ha'iṭṭur* vol. 1, 49b, Note 42; Taubenschlag (Note 13) pp. 205 ff..

72 Cf. *Giṭṭin* 5:9, Notes 213-214.

**משנה ו**: כּוֹתְבִין שְׁטָר לַמּוֹכֵר אַף עַל פִּי שֶׁאֵין הַלּוֹקֵחַ עִמּוֹ וְאֵין כּוֹתְבִין לַלּוֹקֵחַ עַד שֶׁיְּהֵא הַמּוֹכֵר עִמּוֹ. וְהַלּוֹקֵחַ נוֹתֵן אֶת הַשָּׂכָר. (fol. 17b)

**Mishnah 6**: One writes[61] a sale contract[73] for the seller even though the buyer not be present, but one does not write a sale contract for the buyer if the seller not be present. The buyer pays the fee.

**משנה ז**: אֵין כּוֹתְבִין שְׁטָרֵי אֵירוּסִין וְנִישּׂוּאִין אֶלָּא מִדַּעַת שְׁנֵיהֶן. וְהֶחָתָן נוֹתֵן אֶת הַשָּׂכָר. אֵין כּוֹתְבִין שְׁטָרֵי אֲרִיסוּת וְקַבְּלָנוּת אֶלָּא מִדַּעַת שְׁנֵיהֶן. וְהַמְקַבֵּל נוֹתֵן אֶת הַשָּׂכָר. אֵין כּוֹתְבִין שְׁטָרֵי בֵירוּרִין וְכָל־מַעֲשֵׂה בֵית דִּין אֶלָּא מִדַּעַת שְׁנֵיהֶן וּשְׁנֵיהֶן נוֹתְנִין אֶת הַשָּׂכָר. רַבָּן שִׁמְעוֹן בֶּן גַּמְלִיאֵל אוֹמֵר לִשְׁנֵיהֶן כּוֹתְבִין שְׁנַיִם לָזֶה בְּעַצְמוֹ וְלָזֶה בְּעַצְמוֹ.

**Mishnah 7**: Documents of preliminary and definitive marriage one only writes[61] on the orders of both parties; the groom pays the fee. Documents of share-cropping and leases[74] one only writes[61] on the orders of both parties; the tenant pays the fee. Documents of arbitration[75] and court decisions one only writes[61] on the orders of both parties; both of them pay the fee. Rabban Simeon ben Gamliel says, one writes[61] them in duplicate, one for each party.

73 A contract for the sale of real estate which transfers title. The buyer has no power to transfer the title.

74 Agricultural leases for a fixed rental fee.

75 Contracts appointing a court of arbitration in a monetary dispute.

(17c line 69) **הלכה ו:** כּוֹתְבִין שְׁטָר לַמּוֹכֵר כּוּל׳. אָמַר רִבִּי עוּקְבָה. תַּנָּה בִּכְתוּבוֹת דְּבֵי לֵוִי. הָאוֹמֵר. אָבַד שְׁטָרִי. בֵּית דִּין עוֹשִׂין לוֹ קִיּוּם. תַּנֵּי. רַבָּן שִׁמְעוֹן בֶּן גַּמְלִיאֵל אוֹמֵר. אֲפִילוּ בִשְׁטָרֵי בֵירוּרִין בֵּית דִּין עוֹשִׂין לוֹ קִיּוּם.

**Halakhah 6**: "One writes a sale contract for the seller," etc. Rebbi Uqba said, it was stated in *Ketubot*[76] of the school of Levi: If one said, my document was lost, the court writes him a confirmation[77]. It was stated: Rabban Simeon ben Gamliel said, even for documents of arbitration one writes him a confirmation.

76 The *baraita* collection of the school of Levi about *Ketubot*.

77 This is really a commentary on Mishnah 9. Not only if part of a document became illegible can the holder go to court, present witnesses to the court who testify as to the exact wording that was lost, and get a court declaration certifying the text as belonging to the document, but even a lost document can be replaced by a court-issued confirmation if verified by witnesses and agreed to by the other party. The statement is inserted here as preliminary to the next statement about documents of arbitration mentioned in Mishnah 7.

(fol. 17b) **משנה ח:** מִי שֶׁפָּרַע מִקְצָת חוֹבוֹ וְהִשְׁלִישׁ אֶת שְׁטָרוֹ וְאָמַר לוֹ אִם לֹא נָתַתִּי לוֹ מִכָּן וְעַד יוֹם פְּלוֹנִי תֵּן לוֹ שְׁטָרוֹ הִגִּיעַ הַזְּמַן וְלֹא נָתַן רַבִּי יוֹסֵי אוֹמֵר יִתֵּן. רַבִּי יְהוּדָה אוֹמֵר לֹא יִתֵּן.

**Mishnah 8**: If somebody paid off part of his debt, deposited his bond with a third party,[78] and told him, if I have not paid him by date x, return the bond to him. If the time has passed while he did not pay, Rebbi Yose says, he shall return it; Rebbi Jehudah says, he shall not return it[79].

**משנה ט:** מִי שֶׁנִּמְחַק שְׁטָר חוֹבוֹ מַעֲמִיד עָלָיו עֵדִים וּבָא לִפְנֵי בֵית דִּין וְהֵן עוֹשִׁין לוֹ קִיּוּם אִישׁ פְּלוֹנִי בֶּן אִישׁ פְּלוֹנִי נִמְחַק שְׁטָרוֹ בְּיוֹם פְּלוֹנִי וּפְלוֹנִי וּפְלוֹנִי עֵידָיו.

**Mishnah 9**: If somebody's bond became illegible, he presents witnesses about it to the court and they confirm for him: The bond of Mr. X, son of Mr. Y, dated from day Z became illegible; U and V were his witnesses.

**משנה י:** מִי שֶׁפָּרַע מִקְצָת חוֹבוֹ רַבִּי יְהוּדָה אוֹמֵר יַחֲלִיף. וְרַבִּי יוֹסֵי אוֹמֵר יִכְתּוֹב שׁוֹבֵר. אָמַר רַבִּי יְהוּדָה נִמְצָא זֶה צָרִיךְ לִהְיוֹת שׁוֹמֵר שׁוֹבְרוֹ מִן הָעַכְבָּרִים. אָמַר לוֹ רַבִּי יוֹסֵה וְכֵן יָפָה לוֹ וְאַל יֵרַע כּוֹחוֹ שֶׁל זֶה.

**Mishnah 10**: If somebody paid off part of his debt, Rebbi Jehudah said, he shall exchange [his bond], but Rebbi Yose said, he shall write a receipt. Said Rebbi Jehudah, but then this one must guard his receipt from the rats! Rebbi Yose answered him, that comes to him rightly[80], not to impair the other one's rights[81].

**משנה יא:** שְׁנֵי אַחִין אֶחָד עָנִי וְאֶחָד עָשִׁיר וְהִנִּיחַ לָהֶן אֲבִיהֶן מֶרְחָץ וּבֵית הַבַּד. עֲשָׂאָן לְשָׂכָר לַשָּׂכָר לָאֶמְצַע עֲשָׂאָן לְעַצְמוֹ הֲרֵי הֶעָשִׁיר אוֹמֵר לָעָנִי קַח לָךְ עֲבָדִים וְיִרְחֲצוּ בַּמֶּרְחָץ. קַח לָךְ זֵיתִים וּבוֹא וַעֲשֵׂה בְּבֵית הַבַּד.

**Mishnah 11**: Two brothers, one poor and one rich, to whom their father left a bath house and an olive press. If they were built to be rented out, the rental fees are common property. If he built them for his own use, the rich one tells the poor, buy yourself slaves and have them bathe in the bathhouse, buy yourself olives and process them in the olive press[82].

78  The text of the bond cannot be changed; that would be falsifying it. The partial payment cannot be noted on the bond since everything written after the signature of the witnesses must be disregarded. It would be possible to write a separate receipt, cf. Mishnah 10. The alternative is to hand the bond to a third party as trustee with the instruction to deliver the document to the debtor upon payment of the remainder of the debt.

79  R. Yose considers the condition as valid; R Jehudah treats it as *asmakhta* (Note 70).

80  It gives the debtor an additional incentive to pay off his debt as quickly as possible.

81  Since a replacement document would have to be dated from the day it was written, the creditor might lose his privileged status if the debtor took on additional debt after the original bond was written. The original first mortgage would now be the second, and the second the first. This is an unacceptable outcome.

82  The poor one cannot force the sale of family heirlooms.

(17c line 72) **הלכה ח:** מִי שֶׁפָּרַע מִקְצָת חוֹבוֹ כול׳. רַב אָמַר. עוֹשִׂין לוֹ קִיּוּם בֵּית דִּין. תַּנֵּי רִבִּי חִייָה. אֵין עוֹשִׂין לוֹ קִיּוּם בֵּית דִּין. אָמַר רִבִּי יִרְמְיָה. אִילּוּ אָמַר רַב מַתְנַיָּיה לָא הֲוָה מֵימַר הָדָא מִילְתָא.

**Halakhah 8**: "If somebody paid off part of his debt," etc. [83]Rav said, the court writes him a confirmation. Rebbi Ḥiyya stated: the court does not write a confirmation. Rebbi Jeremiah[84] said, if Rav had heard this *baraita*, he would not have said what he did[85].

83  This refers to Mishnah 9.

84  He is Rav Jeremiah, Babylonian of the first generation.

85  The Babli confirms that Mishnah 9 never was accepted in Babylonian practice but that a completely new document had to be executed in which the debtor confirmed the original date of the creditor's foreclosure rights.

(fol. 17b) **משנה יב:** שְׁנַיִם שֶׁהָיוּ בְעִיר אַחַת שֵׁם אֶחָד יוֹסֵה בֶן שִׁמְעוֹן וְשֵׁם אֶחָד יוֹסֵה בֶן שִׁמְעוֹן אֵינָן יְכוֹלִין לְהוֹצִיא שְׁטָר חוֹב זֶה עַל זֶה וְלֹא אַחֵר יָכוֹל לְהוֹצִיא עֲלֵיהֶן שְׁטָר חוֹב. נִמְצָא לְאֶחָד בֵּין שְׁטָרוֹתָיו שְׁטָרוֹ שֶׁל יוֹסֵה בֶן שִׁמְעוֹן פָּרוּעַ שְׁטָרוֹת שְׁנֵיהֶן פְּרוּעִין. כֵּיצַד יַעֲשׂוּ. יְשַׁלֵּשׁוּ וְאִם הָיוּ מְשׁוּלָּשִׁין יִכְתְּבוּ סִימָן וְאִם הָיוּ בְסִימָנִין יִכְתְּבוּ כֹהֵן.

**Mishnah 12**: If two people lived in the same town, both called Yose ben Simeon, they cannot write a bond one on the other or a third party on one of them[86]. If somebody found between his bonds a bond of Yose ben Simeon which was paid off, the bonds of both of them are paid off. What can they do? They write three generations. If their names were identical for three generations, they should write a characteristic mark[87]. If they had identical charateristic marks, they should write "Cohen"[88].

86  Since such a document could be used against an innocent third party, it cannot be used at all.

87  A bodily characteristic like tall, red-faced, etc.

88  If one of them was a Cohen but not the other. This shows that in Mishnaic times it was not common practice to write Cohen or Levi in documents.

(17c line 75) **הלכה יב:** שְׁנַיִם שֶׁהָיוּ בְעִיר אַחַת כול׳. וְאֵין יְכוֹלִין לְהוֹצִיא שְׁטָר חוֹב זֶה עַל זֶה. כְּגוֹן דָּמְרִין כֵּן. אֲנִי פְלוֹנִי בֶּן פְּלוֹנִי לֹוֶה מִמְּךָ פְּלוֹנִי וּפְלוֹנִי עָרֵב.

רַב אָמַר. צָרִיךְ לְהַזְכִּיר זְמַן רִאשׁוֹן בַּשֵּׁינִי. וּשְׁמוּאֵל אָמַר. אֵין צָרִיךְ לְהַזְכִּיר זְמַן רִאשׁוֹן בַּשֵּׁינִי. תַּנֵּי רִבִּי חִייָה. אֵין צָרִיךְ לְהַזְכִּיר זְמַן רִאשׁוֹן בַּשֵּׁינִי. רִבִּי יוֹחָנָן בָּעֵי. אִם צָרִיךְ לְהַזְכִּיר זְמַן רִאשׁוֹן בַּשֵּׁינִי. עַל הָדָא אָמַר רִבִּי יוֹסֵי. וְכֵן יָפֶה לוֹ וְאַל יֵרַע כֹּחַ זֶה.

**Halakhah 12**: "If two people lived in the same town," etc. "They cannot write a bond one on the other." [89]As one formulates, "I, X ben Y, am taking a loan from you, Z, and U is guarantor."

[90]Rav said, one has to mention the earlier date in the second document[91]. But Samuel said, one does not have to mention the earlier date in the second document[92]. Rebbi Ḥiyya stated, one does not have to mention the earlier date in the second document. Rebbi Joḥanan asked, if one had to mention the earlier date in the second document, would Rebbi Yose have said, "that comes to him rightly, not to impair the other one's rights"[93]?

89  This does not belong here but to Halakhah 16, Note 128.

90  This refers to Mishnah 10 according to R. Jehudah who requires that a new document be written.

91  This is also Rav's opinion in the Babli, 170b.

92  Samuel's opinion is not mentioned in the Babli.

93  In Rav's version, the problem which R. Yose had with R. Jehudah's statement (Note 81) could not arise.

(fol. 17b) **משנה יג:** הָאוֹמֵר לִבְנוֹ שְׁטָר בֵּין שְׁטָרוֹתַיי פָּרוּעַ וְאֵין יָדוּעַ אֵי זֶהוּ שְׁטָרוֹת כּוּלָם פְּרוּעִין. נִמְצָא לְאֶחָד שָׁם שָׁנַיִם הַגָּדוֹל פָּרוּעַ וְהַקָּטָן אֵינוֹ פָּרוּעַ.

**Mishnah 13**: If somebody said to his son, a bond among my bonds is paid, but it is not known which one it is, all his bonds are paid[94]. If one finds there two [bonds] given by the same [debtor], the larger one is paid, the smaller one is not paid[95].

94  If any debtor mentioned in one of these bonds claims that he has paid off his bond, the heir has to accept his word.

95  If the father had used the singular, not more than one bond per debtor became questionable.

(17d line 4) **הלכה יג:** הָאוֹמֵר לִבְנוֹ כול'. תַּנֵּי. לֹא דוֹמָה אֵימַת שְׁטָר גָּדוֹל לְאֵימַת שְׁטָר קָטָן.

**Halakhah 13**: "If somebody said to his son," etc. It was stated: The worry caused by a large bond is not comparable to the worry caused by a small bond⁹⁶.

96  Everybody will try to pay off his large debt before small debts. Therefore it is almost certain that if a large or a small debt were paid off, the large one was paid.

(fol. 17b) **משנה יד:** הַמַּלְוֶה אֶת חֲבֵירוֹ עַל יְדֵי עָרֵב לֹא יִפָּרַע מִן הֶעָרֵב. אִם אָמַר עַל מְנָת שֶׁאֶפָּרַע מִמִּי שֶׁאֶרְצֶה יִפָּרַע מִן הֶעָרֵב. רַבָּן שִׁמְעוֹן בֶּן גַּמְלִיאֵל אָמַר אִם יֵשׁ נְכָסִים לַלּוֶֹה בֵּין כָּךְ וּבֵין כָּךְ לֹא יִיפָּרַע מִן הֶעָרֵב.

**Mishnah 14**: Somebody who gives a loan to another person with a guarantor may not request payment from the guarantor⁹⁷. If he said, on condition that I may request payment from whom I choose, he may ask payment from the guarantor. Rabban Simeon ben Gamliel said, if the debtor has real estate then in no case may he request payment from the guarantor⁹⁸.

97  The guarantor may be asked to pay only if the debtor was asked first and is unable or unwilling to pay. (In all three forms of law practices in Roman Egypt, the creditor always had the choice of first suing the surety.)

98  In his opinion, the creditor must first foreclose on the real estate before going to the guarantor.

(17d line 6) **הלכה יד:** הַמַּלְוֶה אֶת חֲבֵירוֹ עַל יְדֵי עָרֵב כול׳. רִבִּי אַבָּהוּ בְשֵׁם רִבִּי יוֹחָנָן. בְּשֶׁיֵּשׁ נְכָסִים לַלּוֶֹה. אֲבָל אֵין נְכָסִים לַלּוֶֹה יִפָּרַע מִן הֶעָרֵב. וְאִם אָמַר. עַל מְנָת שֶׁאֶפָּרַע מִמִּי שֶׁאֶרְצֶה. יִפָּרַע מִן הֶעָרֵב וַאֲפִילוּ יֵשׁ נְכָסִים לַלּוֶֹה. תַּמָּן מָרִין. בְּכָל־מָקוֹם הֲלָכָה כְרַבָּן שִׁמְעוֹן בֶּן גַּמְלִיאֵל חוּץ מֵעָרֵב וְצַיָּידָן וּרְאָייָה אַחֲרוֹנָה. אָמְרִין. וּבִלְבַד בְּמִשְׁנָתֵינוּ. רִבִּי אִמִּי בַּר קַרְחָה בְשֵׁם רַב.

וְלָמָּה אָמְרוּ. בְּכָל־מָקוֹם הֲלָכָה כְּרַבָּן שִׁמְעוֹן בֶּן גַּמְלִיאֵל. שֶׁהֲלָכוֹת קְצוּבוֹת הָיָה אוֹמֵר מִפִּי בֵית דִּינוֹ.

**Halakhah 14**: "Somebody who gives a loan to another person with a guarantor," etc. Rebbi Abbahu in the name of Rebbi Johanan: If the debtor has real estate. But if the debtor has no real estate, he may request payment from the guarantor. If he said, on condition that I may request payment from whom I choose, he may request payment from the guarantor[99].

There[100], they instruct that practice everywhere follows Rabban Simeon ben Gamliel except for the guarantor[101], Sidon[102], and the last proof[103]. They say, only in the Mishnah[104]. Rebbi Immi bar Qorḥa in the name of Rav: Why did they say, practice everywhere follows Rabban Simeon ben Gamliel? For he pronounced specific practices decided by his court[105].

99 The Babli, 173b, disagrees, also in the name of Rebbi Joḥanan, requiring the creditor under any circumstances first to foreclose the debtor's real estate, except if the debt had been assumed by another person.

100 In Babylonia (Babli 174a in the name of R. Joḥanan.)

101 The Mishnah here, *Bava batra* 10:14.

102 Mishnah *Giṭṭin* 5:5.

103 Mishnah *Sanhedrin* 3:13 (in most Mishnah editions, the *last* statement of Rabban Simeon in Mishnah 3:8 dealing with the right of the parties to submit proof to the court out of order.)

104 But not in the *baraitot*. The Babli agrees, *loc. cit.*

105 His pronouncements have the status of precedents decided by the Supreme Court.

(fol. 17b) **משנה טו**: כְּיוֹצֵא בוֹ הָיָה רַבָּן שִׁמְעוֹן בֶּן גַּמְלִיאֵל אוֹמֵר אַף הָעָרֵב לָאִשָּׁה בִּכְתוּבָּתָהּ וְהָיָה בַעְלָהּ מְגָרְשָׁהּ יַדִּירֶנּוּ הֲנָיָיה שֶׁמָּא יַעֲשׂוּ קָנוֹנְיָיא עַל נְכָסִים שֶׁל זֶה וְיַחֲזִיר אֶת אִשְׁתּוֹ.

**Mishnah 15**: Similarly did Rabban Simeon ben Gamliel say that if a person was guarantor for a woman's *ketubah* and her husband divorced her, the latter has to make a vow[106] not to have any usufruct from her so they could not plan a partnership[107] against that person's property and then he[108] would take back his wife.

106 The guarantor does not have to pay unless the husband publicly made the required vow. A public vow cannot be annulled.

107 Greek κοινωνία, in the Talmudim always used in the sense of "partnership in crime".

108 The husband. By his vow he is permanently barred from remarrying his divorcee.

(17d line 12) **הלכה טו:** כְּיוֹצֵא בוֹ הָיָה רַבָּן שִׁמְעוֹן בֶּן גַּמְלִיאֵל כּוּל׳. חָמוֹי דִּבְרַתֵּיהּ דְּרִבִּי חַגַּיי הֲוָה עֲרָבָא בִּפוֹרְנָהּ דִּבְרַתֵּיהּ דְּרִבִּי חַגַּיי וַהֲוָה מְבַזְבְּזָה בְּנִכְסַיָּיא. אֲתָא עוֹבְדָא קוֹמֵי רִבִּי אָחָא. אָמַר. צָרִיךְ לְהַדִּיר הֲנָיָיה. אָמַר רִבִּי יוֹסֵי. אֵין צָרִיךְ לְהַדִּיר הֲנָיָיה. אָמְרִין חֲבֵרַיָּיא קוֹמֵי רִבִּי יוֹסֵי. וּמָה אִילּוּ וְיַחְזוֹר וְיִסְבִּינָהּ לֵית מָרֵי חוֹבָה אָתֵי וּטְרִיף. אָמַר. דְּלָא יַחְזוֹר. וְיַעֲבְדִינוֹן מִטַּלְטְלִין אוֹ פָּרַאפְרְנוֹן וְלָא מַשְׁכַּח מָרֵי חוֹבָה מַה מִתְפַּס. וּנְפַק עוֹבְדָא כְּרִבִּי אָחָא.

**Halakhah 15**: "Similarly did Rabban Simeon ben Gamliel say," etc. The father-in-law of Rebbi Ḥaggai's daughter was guarantor for Rebbi Ḥaggai's daughter's *ketubah*. She turned out to be a spendthrift[109]. The case came before Rebbi Aḥa, who said that he would have to make a vow not to have usufruct. Rebbi Yose said, he does not have to make a vow not to have usufruct. The colleagues said before Rebbi Yose, but if he would take her back, the creditor would come and seize it[110]. He said, he would not take her back. But it could be transformed into movables[111] or paraphernalia[112] which the creditors could not seize. The case was decided following Rebbi Aḥa[113].

109  And therefore her husband divorced her. From the later argument it seems that he had to cover his wife's debts.

110  They argue that R. Yose should agree with R. Aḥa since otherwise he could pay his debts with his father's money by remarrying his wife after payment of the *ketubah* and then let her property be foreclosed by his creditors.

111  Which in general cannot be forclosed.

112  Which never become the husband's property and cannot be attached by his creditors (*Yebamot* 7:1 Note 1).

113  Which establishes practice.

(fol. 17b) **משנה יו:** הַמַּלְוֶה אֶת חֲבֵירוֹ בִּשְׁטָר גּוֹבֶה מִנְּכָסִים מְשׁוּעְבָּדִים. עַל יְדֵי עֵדִים גּוֹבֶה מִנְּכָסִים בְּנֵי חוֹרִין. הוֹצִיא עָלָיו כְּתָב יָדוֹ שֶׁהוּא חַייָב לוֹ גּוֹבֶה מִנְּכָסִים בְּנֵי חוֹרִין. עָרֵב הַיּוֹצֵא לְאַחַר חִיתּוּם הָעֵדִים גּוֹבֶה מִנְּכָסִים בְּנֵי חוֹרִין. מַעֲשֶׂה בָא לִפְנֵי רִבִּי יִשְׁמָעֵאל וְאָמַר גּוֹבֶה מִנְּכָסִים בְּנֵי חוֹרִין.

**Mishnah 16**: Somebody who lent to another by a document collects from encumbered property[114], by witnesses collects from free property[115]. If he presents a note in his own handwriting that he owes him[116], he collects from free property. From a guarantor who endorsed after the signature of the witnesses[117], one collects from free property. This case came before Rebbi Ismael who said, he collects from free property.

114  Unless otherwise noted in the contract, a secured loan is a mortgage on any real estate in the possession of the debtor at the moment the bond was executed. A sale by the debtor does not remove the creditor's lien. The creditor may foreclose from the buyer if no other property be left in the debtor's hand; the buyer is then left to try to get his money back from the debtor.

115  Since an oral loan before witnesses is a private transaction, it cannot be detected by a prospective buyer. Such a loan can only be used to forclose the debtor's unencumbered property. These are called "free properties".

116 An IOU can be collected in court but in the absence of witnesses' signatures only from the debtor's actual property.

117 If the guarantor endorsed the bond by a note below the witnesses' signatures that he would guarantee payment, he executed an IOU, not a witnessed document.

(17d line 19) **הלכה יו:** הַמַּלְוֶה אֶת חֲבֵירוֹ בִּשְׁטָר כול'. רַב הוּנָא אָמַר. הַקְדָּמָה פְּסוּלָה וְהַשְּׁטָר כָּשֵׁר. וְהָתַנִּינָן. פְּרוֹזְבּוֹל הַמּוּקְדָּם כָּשֵׁר וְהַמְאוּחָר פָּסוּל. הָדָא דַתְּ מַר. דְּרַב הוּנָא רִבִּי לֶעְזָר וְרִבִּי שִׁמְעוֹן בֶּן יָקִים. הָדָא דְרַב הוּנָא רִבִּי לֶעְזָר. אָמַר. אַף עַל פִּי שֶׁאֵין עָלָיו עֵדִים אֶלָא שֶׁנְּתָנוֹ לָהּ בִּפְנֵי עֵדִים כָּשֵׁר וְגוֹבָה מִנְּכָסִים מְשׁוּעְבָּדִין. שֶׁאֵין הָעֵדִים חוֹתְמִין עַל הַגֵּט אֶלָא מִפְּנֵי תִיקּוּן הָעוֹלָם. וְהֵיכִי. אִם בְּאוֹתָן שֶׁהִכְחִישׁוּ עֵדוּתָן. הִכְחִישׁ עֵדוּתָן כְּמִי שֶׁאֵינָהּ וְהַשְּׁטָר כָּשֵׁר. אִם בְּאוֹתָן שֶׁלֹּא הִכְחִישׁוּ עֵדוּתָן. אָמְרַת. הָא אָמַר רֵישׁ לָקִישׁ. עָשׂוּ הָעֵדִים הַחֲתוּמִין עַל הַשְּׁטָר כְּמִי שֶׁנֶּחְקְרָה עֵדוּתָן בְּבֵית דִּין. מַאי כְדוֹן. בְּאֵינוּן דֶאָמְרִין כֵּן. אֲנִי פְּלוֹנִי בֶּן פְּלוֹנִי לָוִיתִי מִפְּלוֹנִי וּפְלוֹנִי עָרֵב.

רַב אָמַר. צָרִיךְ לְהַזְכִּיר זְמַנּוֹ שֶׁלְּרִאשׁוֹן בַּשֵּׁנִי. וּשְׁמוּאֵל אָמַר. אֵין צָרִיךְ לְהַזְכִּיר זְמַנּוֹ שֶׁלְּרִאשׁוֹן בַּשֵּׁנִי. רַב וּשְׁמוּאֵל. רַב כְּרִבִּי יוֹחָנָן וּשְׁמוּאֵל כְּרִבִּי שִׁמְעוֹן בֶּן לָקִישׁ.

**Halakhah 16**: "Somebody who lent to another by a document," etc. Rav Huna said, predating is invalid but the document is valid[118]. But did we not state: "A predated *prozbol*[118*] is valid, postdated it is invalid"?[119] That means, Rav Huna, Rebbi Eleazar, and Rebbi Simeon ben Yaqim[120]. Rav Huna, quoted here. [121]"Rebbi Eleazar[122] said, it[123] is valid even if there are no signatures of witnesses on it if only he delivered it in the presence of witnesses; and she can use it to collect from encumbered property. For the witnesses sign on the bill of divorce only for the public good." How? If about those who denied their testimony[124], the denied testimony is as if nonexistent, and the document should be valid? If about those who did not deny their testimony, did not Rebbi Simeon ben Laqish say[125], that they considered witnesses who signed a document as if their testimony had been cross-examined in court[126]? What about it: As one formulates, "I, X ben Y, am taking a loan from you, Z, and U is guarantor."[127]

[128]Rav said, one has to mention the earlier date in the second document. But Samuel said, one does not have to mention the earlier date in the second document. Rav and Samuel, Rav parallels Rebbi Joḥanan[129] and Samuel parallels Rebbi Simeon ben Laqish[130].

118   A predated document can be made whole by testimony about the exact time it was signed. Then it can serve as basis for foreclosure procedures based on the oral testimony.

118*  Ševi'it 10:3, Note 80.

119   Mishnah Ševi'it 10:5. The question is not asked about this sentence, but about the following one: Predated documents of indebtedness are invalid, postdated they are valid. In the Halakhah there (Notes 98-99), R. Joḥanan holds that a predated bond is totally invalid; R. Simeon ben Laqish holds that it only counts from the time of signing, parallel to Rav Huna's opinion here. As explained in Note 114 (Ševi'it 10:1 Note 2), a bond creates a mortgage lien on behalf of the creditor which is not removed by sale of the property. A predated document may create a false lien; this makes it invalid.

120   Probably one should read instead "R. Simeon ben Laqish", R. Simeon ben Yaqim's teacher.

121   Mishnah Giṭṭin 9:5 (Notes 69-71).

122   R. Eleazar ben Shamua', the Tanna.

123   A bill of divorce.

124   If the witnesses claim that their signatures were forged, there is no document. Rav Huna cannot declare it valid.

125   Ševi'it 10:5 Note 96, Ketubot 2:3 Note 56, Giṭṭin 4:2 Note 46; Babli Ketubot 18b, Giṭṭin 3a.

126   A witness, once he has testified in court, may not change his story (Bikkurim 3:5 Note 72, Babli Sanhedrin 44b). Therefore the witnesses are not admitted to claim that they did not know the bond was predated.

127   A bond signed by the debtor witout any witnesses.

128   This is from Halakhah 12 (Mishnah 10, Notes 90-92).

129 Rav holds with R. Johanan (Note 119) that a predated bond is absolutely invalid. Therefore, a replacement for a bond which partially became invalid must be executed by a court which is empowered to make the copy retroactively valid to the time of the original as determined by testimony.

130 Samuel holds with R. Simeon ben Laqish that a predated bond is valid from the time of signing. Therefore, the replacement can be executed by the witnesses but cannot be made valid from a time before the actual signing of the replacement.

(fol. 17b) **משנה יז:** אָמַר לוֹ בֶּן נַנָּס אֵינוֹ גוֹבָה לֹא מִנְּכָסִים מְשׁוּעְבָּדִים וְלֹא מִנְּכָסִים בְּנֵי חוֹרִין. אָמַר לוֹ לָמָּה. אָמַר לוֹ הֲרֵי הַחוֹנֵק אֶת אֶחָד בַּשּׁוּק וְאָמַר לוֹ הַנַּח וַאֲנִי נוֹתֵן לָךְ פָּטוּר שֶׁלֹּא עַל אֱמוּנָתוֹ הִלְוָוהוּ. וְאֵי זֶהוּ עָרֵב שֶׁהוּא חַיָּיב לוֹ אָמַר לוֹ הַלְוֵוהוּ וַאֲנִי נוֹתֵן לָךְ חַיָּיב שֶׁכֵּן עַל אֱמוּנָתוֹ הִלְוָוהוּ. אָמַר רִבִּי יִשְׁמָעֵאל הָרוֹצֶה שֶׁיִּתְחַכֵּם יַעֲסוֹק בְּדִינֵי מָמוֹנוֹת שֶׁאֵין לָךְ מִקְצוֹעַ בַּתּוֹרָה גָּדוֹל מֵהֶן שֶׁהֵן כְּמַעְיָין הַנּוֹבֵעַ וְכָל־הָרוֹצֶה שֶׁיַּעֲסוֹק בְּדִינֵי מָמוֹנוֹת יְשַׁמֵּשׁ אֶת שִׁמְעוֹן בֶּן נַנָּס.

**Mishnah 17**: Ben Nannas said to him[131], he collects neither from encumbered nor from free property. He asked, why? He answered, if one would strangle another in the market place[132] and a third person would say, let him go, I shall pay you, he is not liable since the loan was not made on his faith[133]. Who is the guarantor who is liable? If he told him, "lend to him and I shall pay you," he is liable because the loan was extended on his faith.

Rebbi Ismael said, anybody who wants to train to become wise should study the laws of money matters since nothing greater is there in the Torah; they are like a flowing source, and anybody wanting to study the laws of money matters should serve Simeon ben Nannas.

131 This is a direct continuation of Mishnah 16; in the independent Mishnah mss. they form one Mishnah together.

132 A creditor tries to force the debtor to pay his debt by using physical force.

133 The use of "faith" for "credit worthiness" goes back to Latin *fides*.

(17d line 31) **הלכה יז:** אָמַר לוֹ בֶּן נַנָּס כול׳. רִבִּי יָסָא בְשֵׁם רִבִּי יוֹחָנָן אָמַר. אַף עַל פִּי שֶׁקִּילְסוֹ רִבִּי יִשְׁמָעֵאל אֶת בֶּן נַנָּס עַל מִדְרָשׁוֹ קִילְסוֹ. אֲבָל אֵינָהּ כְּבֶן נַנָּס. שִׁמְעוֹן בַּר וָוה בְשֵׁם רִבִּי יוֹחָנָן. אַף בְּחָנוּק הֲלָכָה כְּרִבִּי [יִשְׁמָעֵאל].¹³⁴ אָמַר רִבִּי יוֹסֵי. וְאַתְּ שְׁמַע מִינָהּ. בַּר נַשׁ דַּהֲוָה צַיְיד לְחַבְרֵיהּ בְּשׁוּקָא. אֲתָא חַד וָמַר. שְׁבָקֵיהּ וָנָא יָהֵב. מִן אָהֵן גָּבֵיי וּמִן אָהֵן לָא גָבֵיי.

**Halakhah 17**: "Ben Nannas said to him," etc. Rebbi Yasa in the name of Rebbi Johanan: Even though Rebbi Ismael praised Ben Nannas, he praised him only for his argument. But [practice] does not follow Ben Nannas¹³⁵. Simeon bar Abba in the name of Rebbi Johanan: Also in the case of the strangled person practice follows Rebbi Ismael¹³⁶. Rebbi Yose said, one infers from here that a person who caught another in the market place, when a third person came and said, let him go and I shall give, collects from the one but does not collect from the other.

134 Added from the Constantinople edition 1749, missing in ms. and *editio princeps*.

135 Babli 176a.

136 The Babli, *loc. cit.*, holds that in such a case a simple statement does not make the third person a guarantor; any guaranty given after the signing of the bond needs an act of acquisition by the creditor. It seems that R. Yose in the following sentence states the same; even for R. Ismael the intervening person does not become a guarantor by simple speech.

# Indices

## Index of Biblical Quotations

| | | | | | |
|---|---|---|---|---|---|
| Gen. 4:22 | 531 | 21:33 | 11,29,145,146,148 | | |
| 6:5 | 358 | 21:34 | 11,72,73,145 | Lev. 2:6 | 147 |
| 6:13 | 358 | 21:35 | 11,13,15,20,40,94, | 5:11 | 84,181 |
| 9:5 | 216 | | 110 | 5:14-16 | 189 |
| 18:20 | 358 | 21:36 | 11,13,21,60,131, | 5:21 | 32,223,239 |
| 20:7 | 218 | | 156 | 5:23 | 26,223,229 |
| 20:17 | 219 | 21:37 | 178,179,183,193, | 5:24 | 371 |
| | | | 329,331 | 7:18 | 84 |
| Ex. 3:1 | 197 | 22:3 | 26,241,330,331 | 7:20 | 84 |
| 3:2 | 167 | 22:4 | 11,13,16,34,166, | 7:23 | 84 |
| 6:8 | 662,665 | | 488 | 11:28 | 198 |
| 13:13 | 179 | 22:5 | 12,22,168,170 | 11:35 | 198 |
| 19:13 | 152 | 22:6 | 14,174,181,329, | 15:4 | 21 |
| 21:1 | 38,112 | | 331,449 | 15:25 | 61 |
| 21:3 | 178,179 | 22:7 | 346 | 19:1 | 25 |
| 21:8 | 178 | 22:8 | 180,241.273,331, | 19:3 | 323 |
| 21:12 | 133 | | 332,347 | 19:5 | 92 |
| 21:15 | 98,210 | 22:12 | 24 | 19:13 | 483 |
| 21:18 | 123 | 22:13 | 25,181 | 19:14 | 417,483 |
| 21:19 | 14,151,200 | 22:14 | 455,457,624 | 19:24 | 371 |
| 21:22 | 123,142,143,210 | 22:15 | 455 | 19:36 | 360,627 |
| 21:24 | 22 | 22:20 | 377 | 21:2 | 678 |
| 21:25 | 22,203 | 22:24 | 417 | 21:17 | 125 |
| 21:26 | 98,144,210,211 | 22:25 | 489 | 22:14 | 371 |
| 21:27 | 98,144,210,211 | 23:1 | 188,272 | 23:3 | 85 |
| 21:28 | 11,15,45,108,116, | 23:4 | 322 | 23:28 | 85 |
| | 118,120,123,129 | 23:5 | 153,322,325 | 23:29 | 84 |
| 21:29 | 11,45,114,118,121, | 23:12 | 153 | 24:18 | 23,24 |
| | 125,128 | 34:19 | 179 | 24:20 | 203 |
| 21:30 | 11,45,118,121,127 | 34:20 | 179 | 25:14 | 362,374 |
| 21:31 | 11,15,118,124 | 34:21 | 192 | 25:45 | 374 |
| 21:32 | 11,118,121,124 | 35:33 | 100 | 25:29 | 387 |

| | | | | | |
|---|---|---|---|---|---|
| Lev. 25:30 | 387 | 18:8 | 248 | | |
| 25:35 | 382,403 | 19:15 | 185 | Is. 5:5 | 13 |
| 25:36 | 379,381,403,417 | 19:19 | 184,203,574 | 32:20 | 13 |
| 25:37 | 417 | 19:21 | 203 | 46:6 | 712 |
| 25:47 | 403 | 21:18 | 82 | 57:19 | 167 |
| 25:55 | 425 | 22:1 | 153 | | |
| 26:39 | 286 | 21:15 | 657 | Jer. 20:19 | 167 |
| 27:1-8 | 237 | 21:17 | 555,666,680,681 | 32:11 | 722 |
| 27:19 | 371 | 22:1 | 322 | | |
| 27:31 | 371,373 | 22:3 | 299,309 | Ez. 32:27 | 679 |
| | | 22:4 | 322,324 | | |
| Num. 5:1 | 21 | 22:9 | 559 | Hos. 3:2 | 147 |
| 5:8 | 245,248 | 23:19 | 203 | Hab. 2:11 | 508 |
| 5:10 | 246 | 23:25 | 442,445,446 | 3:6 | 111 |
| 8:3 | 21 | 22:26 | 443 | | |
| 11:1 | 663 | 24:6 | 491 | Ps. 15:6 | 418 |
| 12:14 | 64 | 24:10-11 | 488,489 | 36:7 | 314 |
| 14:38 | 663 | 24:15 | 483 | 104:19-23 | 440 |
| 15:20 | 371 | 24:17 | 491 | 122:3 | 198 |
| 18:26 | 371 | 24:20 | 203 | | |
| 18:19 | 450 | 24:22 | 203 | Prov. 2:20 | 437 |
| 26:11 | 663,676 | 25:4 | 153,443 | 3:21 | 712 |
| 26:52 | 660 | 25:5 | 660 | 10:15 | 517 |
| 26:53 | 662 | 25:11 | 207,209 | 22:7 | 362 |
| 26:55 | 653,659,662 | 25:12 | 203 | 24:11 | 419 |
| 27:1 | 660 | 25:15 | 627 | | |
| 27:5 | 661 | 26:2 | 547 | Job 6:14 | 199 |
| 27:6 | 668 | 33:2 | 111 | 19:18 | 531 |
| 27:7 | 661 | 33:4 | 666 | 27:17 | 252 |
| 27:8 | 653,657,660 | 33:23 | 616 | 31:15 | 212 |
| 27:9 | 654 | | | 33:27 | 220 |
| 27:10 | 655 | Jos. 15:28 | 600 | 33:28 | 220 |
| 27:11 | 655,668 | 17:2 | 663 | 42:8 | 219 |
| 27:11 | 125 | 17:5 | 663 | | |
| 36:8 | 655,657 | 24:33 | 658.678 | 1Chr. 2:22 | 678 |
| | | | | 22:14 | 282 |
| Deut. 1:39 | 665 | 1K. 5:3 | 439 | 24:7-18 | 248 |
| 4:15 | 216 | 7:7 | 639 | | |
| 13:18 | 220 | | | | |
| 18:1 | 678 | 2K. 8:6 | 562 | Mat. 20:2 | 446 |
| 18:3 | 620 | | | | |

# Index of Talmudical Quotations

## Babylonian Talmud

| | | | | | |
|---|---|---|---|---|---|
| Berakhot 52b | 667 | 12b | 212 | 19b | 18,44,47,50 |
| | | 13a | 709 | 20a | 52,53,55 |
| Šabbat 7b | 454 | 14b | 686 | 21a | 55 |
| 63a | 199 | 40b | 686 | 22a | 58 |
| 91a | 83 | 42b | 211,212 | 23b | 60 |
| 106a | 99 | 48b | 488 | 24a | 60,62 |
| 151b | 220 | 76a | 453 | 26b | 22,103 |
| | | 84a | 453 | 27b | 217 |
| Eruvin 80a | 522 | | | 28a | 68,209 |
| 81b | 361 | Qiddušin 11a | 650 | 28b | 73 |
| | | 19b | 452,674 | 29b | 72,75 |
| Peasaḥim 13a | 338 | 20b | 403 | 30a | 77,78 |
| 22b | 129 | 24b | 144 | 30b | 80,381 |
| 113b | 91 | 26a | 361 | 31a | 88 |
| | | 28a | 361 | 31b | 68,88 |
| Yoma 52b | 91 | 42b | 347 | 32a | 91 |
| 87b | 220 | 52b | 32 | 32b | 92 |
| | | 65b | 277 | 33a | 92 |
| Roš Haššanah 26a | 147 | | | 34a | 96 |
| | | Soṭah 13a | 147 | 34b | 99 |
| Yom Ṭov 12b | 99 | 49b | 91 | 37a | 61,110 |
| | | | | 38a | 111,113 |
| Megillah 27b | 387 | Bava qamma 2b | 13,15 | 39a | 115 |
| | | 4a | 65 | 40a | 116 |
| Mo'ed qaṭan 25a | 327,328 | 4b | 14 | 41a | 108 |
| | | 9b | 27 | 41b | 120 |
| Yevamot 16b | 99 | 10a | 29 | 42b | 123,125 |
| | | 10b | 22,89 | 43a | 144 |
| Ketubot 18b | 712,744 | 11a | 24,25 | 43b | 124 |
| 31a | 83 | 12b | 32 | 44a | 45 |
| 33b | 104 | 13a | 32 | 44b | 116,128 |
| 43a | 696 | 14a | 34 | 45a | 116 |
| 52b | 658,706 | 14b | 38 | 46a | 126,137 |
| 60b | 650 | 15a | 38 | 46b | 136 |
| 70a | 686 | 15b | 38,40 | 48a | 140 |
| 83b | 658 | 16a | 41 | 48b | 141 |
| 84a | 674 | 17b | 16,50 | 49a | 142 |
| | | 18a | 46,48 | 50a | 78,147 |
| Giṭṭin 3a | 744 | 18b | 45 | 51a | 29,554 |
| 12a | 212 | 19a | 48 | 51a | 149 |

| | | | | | | | |
|---|---|---|---|---|---|---|---|
| Bava qamma 52a | 150 | 113b | 310 | 60b | 381 | | |
| 53a | 72 | 114b | 258 | 61b | 380 | | |
| 53b | 22 | 115a | 254 | 62b | 384,412 | | |
| 55a | 154 | 116a | 262 | 63a | 386,387,388 | | |
| 55b | 155,156,158 | 116b | 433 | 65a | 351 | | |
| 57b | 161 | 118a | 264 | 67a | 424 | | |
| 58a | 161,162 | 119b | 270 | 69a | 390,396,397,398 | | |
| 58b | 163 | | | 69b | 400 | | |
| 59a | 163 | Bava meṣi'a 3a | 273,274 | 70a | 412 | | |
| 59b | 163 | 4b | 729 | 71a | 418 | | |
| 60a | 166,168,169 | 5b | 274 | 71b | 404,405,406 | | |
| 61b | 173 | 7a | 275 | 72a | 381,405 | | |
| 62a | 174 | 12b | 285,291 | 72b | 393,410 | | |
| 62b | 180 | 13a | 289 | 74a | 410 | | |
| 65a | 226 | 17a | 293 | 75a | 406,416 | | |
| 65b | 228 | 20b | 297 | 75b | 418 | | |
| 72b | 188 | 22b | 300 | 76b | 422 | | |
| 73a | 188 | 24a | 302 | 77a | 426 | | |
| 76a | 190 | 25a | 303 | 78a | 427 | | |
| 76b | 192 | 25b | 306,307 | 78b | 428 | | |
| 78b | 194 | 26b | 309 | 79a | 429 | | |
| 80a | 196 | 28b | 315,317 | 80b | 431 | | |
| 80b | 611 | 29b | 317,320 | 83a | 437,440 | | |
| 81a | 504,613,616 | 30a | 320 | 83b | 440 | | |
| 81b | 616 | 32a | 323,325 | 87b | 442 | | |
| 82b | 258 | 32b | 325 | 89a | 443 | | |
| 83a | 191 | 33a | 324,327 | 91a | 403 | | |
| 83b | 174 | 34a | 331 | 93a | 446,447,450 | | |
| 84a | 203 | 37a | 331 | 94a | 453 | | |
| 84b | 204 | 38b | 338 | 95b | 456 | | |
| 85b | 202 | 40a | 340 | 97a | 25 | | |
| 93b | 224 | 43b | 347 | 100a | 462 | | |
| 94b | 252 | 44a | 347,351 | 101a | 226,464 | | |
| 96b | 228 | 44b | 351 | 101b | 465 | | |
| 97a | 230 | 47a/b | 361 | 102a | 466 | | |
| 98a | 232 | 46b | 348,361 | 102b | 467 | | |
| 100b | 234 | 48b | 359,360 | 103b | 473 | | |
| 102b | 236 | 49a | 360 | 105b | 477 | | |
| 103a | 413 | 49b | 359 | 106b | 482 | | |
| 109a | 247 | 52a | 369 | 108a | 240,523 | | |
| 111a | 250 | 52b | 372 | 111a | 483 | | |
| 111b | 253 | 53b | 373 | 111b | 486 | | |
| 112a | 256 | 58a | 32 | 113b | 488 | | |
| 113a | 253 | 58b | 375 | 115a | 491 | | |

# INDEX OF TALMUDICAL QUOTATIONS

| | | | | | | |
|---|---|---|---|---|---|---|
| Bava meṣi'a 116a | 492 | 63a | 387 | 141b | 698 |
| 116b | 497 | 63b | 592 | 144a | 701 |
| 117a | 498 | 64b | 592 | 150a | 709 |
| 117b | 236 | 65b | 594 | 151a | 709 |
| 118a | 79,501 | 67a | 596 | 152a | 671 |
| 118b | 504,505 | 67b | 597,599 | 152b | 683 |
| 119a | 457,506 | 68b | 600 | 154b | 712 |
| | | 69a | 604 | 156a | 712 |
| Bava batra 2b | 509 | 71a | 607 | 156b | 716,717 |
| 3a | 508 | 72b | 607 | 163a | 725 |
| 4a | 511 | 73a | 610 | 164a/b | 728 |
| 4b | 513 | 82a | 618,619 | 166b | 730 |
| 6a | 514 | 83b | 367 | 170a | 275 |
| 11a | 523 | 86a | 82 | 170b | 738 |
| 11b | 519 | 88b | 627 | 173b | 740 |
| 12b | 522 | 89a | 627 | 174a | 740 |
| 13b | 524 | 92a | 126 | 175a | 243,709 |
| 19a | 527 | 92b | 650 | 175b | 253 |
| 19b | 527 | 93b | 631,633 | 176a | 253,746 |
| 20b | 531,532,533 | 94b | 381 | | |
| 21b | 534 | 95a | 634 | Sanhedrin 27a | 166 |
| 22b | 537 | 96a | 636 | 32b | 88 |
| 23b | 539 | 97a | 624 | 62b | 98 |
| 25a | 542 | 97b | 630 | 78a | 125 |
| 25b | 545 | 98b | 637 | 112a | 32 |
| 28a | 552 | 102b | 646 | | |
| 36a | 555 | 106a | 651 | Ševuot 38b | 181 |
| 36b | 560 | 111a | 655,658 | | |
| 38a | 561 | 111b | 658,676 | Avodah zarah 2b | 111 |
| 38b | 562 | 113a | 678 | | |
| 39a | 563 | 115a | 659 | Zevaḥim 114a | 32 |
| 39b | 564 | 116b | 655 | | |
| 42b | 570 | 117a | 662,664 | Ḥulin 39b | 682 |
| 45b | 571 | 117b | 663,665 | 83a | 361 |
| 46a | 572 | 119b | 60 | 132a | 620 |
| 47a | 571,572 | 123b | 32 | | |
| 51a | 242 | 127b | 681 | Bekhorot 11a | 181 |
| 51b | 242 | 129a | 670 | 13b | 360 |
| 52b | 556 | 130a | 672 | 53b | 32 |
| 53a | 573 | 131a | 673 | 55a | 563 |
| 57b | 520 | 133b | 679 | | |
| 58b | 579 | 137a | 688 | Keritut 24a | 130 |
| 60b | 588 | 138a | 682 | 24b | 682 |
| 61a | 590 | 140b | 696 | | |

| Me'ilah 18a | 21 | | 386,387,388 | | |
|---|---|---|---|---|---|
| | | Temurah 8a | 32 | Niddah 68a | 61 |
| Arakhin 31a | | | | | |

## Jerusalem Talmud

| | | | | | |
|---|---|---|---|---|---|
| Berakhot 2:4 | 14 | | | | |
| 2:9 | 616 | Terumot 1:1 | 404 | Yoma 8:9 | 220 |
| 3:1 | 318 | 3:1 | 506 | | |
| 3:5 | 338 | 6:1 | 183 | Šeqalim 7:3 | 463 |
| | | 7:1 | 58,82,98,172,183, | | |
| Peah 3:8 | 715 | | 215 | Ta'aniot 4:11 | 655 |
| 3:9 | 681 | 7:5 | 254 | | |
| 4:2 | 281,282 | 8:10 | 221 | Yevamot 1:1 | 712 |
| 4:6 | 285 | | | 4:1 | 698 |
| 7:4 | 707 | Ma'serot 1:1 | 191 | 6:4 | 414 |
| 8:7 | 517 | 2:7 | 442,443 | 12:1 | 5645 |
| | | 4:1 | 191 | 15:9 | 337 |
| Demay 2:1 | 627 | | | 15:10 | 336,337 |
| 6:1 | 404,476 | Ma'aser šeni 2:7 | 369,372 | | |
| 6:3 | 387,558 | 4:1 | 352 | Ketubot 2:1 | 135,273 |
| 6:12 | 236 | 4:3 | 373 | 2:3 | 712,744 |
| | | | | 2:11 | 184,258 |
| Kilaim 1:6 | 300 | Orlah 3:1 | 129,198 | 3:1 | 58,82,172 |
| 1:8 | 480 | | | 3:10 | 127 |
| 2:1 | 632,633 | Bikkurim 1:1 | 546,587 | 4:8 | 217,666 |
| 2:5 | 611 | | | 4:9 | 290 |
| 6:2 | 506 | Šabbat 1:1 | 83,84 | 4:11 | 706 |
| 8:1 | 188,712 | 2:2 | 99 | 4:12 | 672 |
| 8:6 | 154 | 3 | 579 | 5:1 | 701 |
| | | 4 | 378 | 5:5 | 29,104,212,188, |
| Ševi'it 1:2 | 545 | 7 | 15 | | 362 |
| 4:5 | 480 | 11:2 | 502 | 6:1 | 285,286 |
| 4:7 | 463 | | | 6:2 | 287 |
| 4:10 | 216 | Eruvin 7:1 | 361,521, | 8:5 | 674 |
| 5:8 | 126 | | 580 | 9:1 | 674,677,686 |
| 6:4 | 707 | 7:11 | 347 | 9:5 | 334 |
| 7:4 | 198 | 10:12 | 99 | 10:4 | 106,107 |
| 8:1 | 347,361 | | | 11:1 | 709 |
| 9:2 | 561 | Pesaḥim 2:1 | 129,198 | 13:2 | 264 |
| 10:3 | 744 | 2:2 | 381 | 13:3 | 653,693,695,697 |
| 10:5 | 712,744 | 5:3 | 197 | 13:7 | 76,591,593 |
| 10:9 | 360 | 6:1 | 99 | | |

# INDEX OF TALMUDICAL QUOTATIONS

| | | | | | | |
|---|---|---|---|---|---|---|
| Soṭah 2:6 | 332,712 | 8:3 | 281,282 | 2:6 | 383 |
| 3:4 | 696 | 8:7 | 253 | 3:5 | 712 |
| 7:1 | 188 | 8:12 | 722 | 3:10 | 605 |
| 9:17 | 91 | 9:8 | 726 | 4:2 | 555,559 |
| | | | | 4:7 | 681 |
| Nedarim 3:4-5 | 369 | Nazir 7:1 | 76,258, | | |
| 4:2 | 264 | | 318 | Sanhedrin 6:2 | 130 |
| 5:1 | 93,520,577 | 7:3 | 548 | 9:3 | 123 |
| | | 8:1 188"9:3 | 613 | 10:8 | 130 |
| Giṭṭin 1:1 | 275 | 9:5 | 123 | | |
| 1:6 | 682,685,709 | | | Makkot 1:8 | 188 |
| 3:8 | 253,636 | Qiddušin 1:2 | 227,452 | 2:4 | 92 |
| 4:2 | 712,732,744 | 1:3 | 144,145 | | |
| 4:4 | 381,698 | 1:4 | 26,160,334,553, | Ševuot 6 | 265 |
| 4:6 | 434 | | 554,557 | 7:2 | 176 |
| 5:1 | 488 | 1:5 | 81,82,556,715,670, | 8:1 | 181 |
| 5:4 | 117 | | 671,686 | | |
| 5:5 | 226 | 1:6 | 31,348,352,354, | Avodah zarah 1:6 | 197 |
| 6:1 | 360 | | 356 | | |
| 7:3 | 685 | 2:1 | 359,427 | Horaiot 3:7 | 326 |
| 7:6 | 726 | | | | |

## Mishnah

| | | | | | |
|---|---|---|---|---|---|
| Peah 6:9 | 173 | 5:6 | 286 | Ševuot 7:1 | 174 |
| 8:8 | 609 | 7:9 | 354 | 7:4 | 272 |
| Demay 1:2 | 371 | 7:11 | 534 | 7:9 | 297 |
| 7:9 | 494 | 10:4 | 105 | Avot 1:8 | 706 |
| Kilaim 3:1 | 605 | 13:1 | 692 | | |
| Terumot 6:1 | 371 | Nedarim 1:1 | 242 | Bekhorot 2:4 | 402 |
| Ma'aser šeni 5:5 | 371 | Giṭṭin 7:8 | 454 | 4:1 | 396 |
| Bikkurim 1:1 | 150 | 8:2 | 282 | Keritut 3:4 | 84 |
| 2:1 | 371 | Qiddušin 1:1 | 371 | Arakhin 6:5 | 237 |
| | | 1:2 | 284 | Tamid 3:6 | 328 |
| Šabbat 4:1 | 527 | 1:5 | 622,709 | | |
| 9:2 | 605 | 1:6 | 350 | Ahilut 13:1 | 586 |
| Yom Ṭov 3:8 | 623 | 3:11 | 278 | 14:1 | 587 |
| | | 5:5 | 81 | Ṭahorot 6:6 | 710 |
| Yevamot 2:6 | 680 | . | | Parah 1:3 | 246 |
| Ketubot 2:2 | 567 | Sanhedrin 3:13 | 74p | Yadayim 4:7 | 213 |

## Tosephta

| | | | | | | | |
|---|---|---|---|---|---|---|---|
| Peah 2:2 | 282 | 6:22 | 171 | 2:17 | 315 | | |
| 4:9 | 517 | 6:23 | 171,188 | 2:20 | 317 | | |
| Demay 6:4 | 478 | 6:24 | 174 | 2:21-22 | 320 | | |
| | | 6:27 | 93 | 2:24 | 324 | | |
| Ketubot 4:5 | 667 | 6:28 | 175 | 2:30 | 327 | | |
| 5:1 | 104 | 7:18 | 194 | 3:11 | 357 | | |
| 10:4 | 106 | 7:21 | 32 | 3:14 | 360 | | |
| Soṭah 15:5 | 91 | 8:18 | 616 | 3:17-19 | 369 | | |
| Giṭṭin 5:7 | 453 | 9:1 | 14,201 | 3:24 | 375 | | |
| 5:12 | 452,453 | 9:3 | 205 | 4:2 | 386 | | |
| 7:11 | 724 | 9:4 | 206 | 4:4 | 387 | | |
| Qiddušin 3:8 | 452 | 9:29 | 219 | 4:8 | 393 | | |
| | | 9:30 | 220 | 4:16 | 413 | | |
| Bava qamma 1:1 | 27 | 9:31 | 222 | 4:17 | 393 | | |
| 1:2 | 38 | 9:32 | 221 | 4:18 | 392 | | |
| 1:3 | 38 | 10:2 | 224 | 4:20 | 236 | | |
| 1:4 | 41 | 10:3 | 227 | 4:21 | 393 | | |
| 1:6 | 16 | 10:5-7 | 226 | 4:22 | 392,393,474 | | |
| 1:9 | 34 | 10:8 | 232 | 4:23 | 412 | | |
| 2:1 | 50,91 | 10:16-17 | 247 | 5:3 | 384 | | |
| 2:5 | 79,96,501 | 10:18 | 250 | 5:5 | 396,397,398 | | |
| 2:6 | 78 | 10:20 | 254 | 5:6 | 390 | | |
| 2:8 | 88 | 10:21 | 256 | 5:7 | 396 | | |
| 2:9 | 88,89 | 10:28 | 261 | 5:8 | 398 | | |
| 2:11 | 91 | 10:29 | 261 | 5:9 | 399 | | |
| 3:3 | 94,96,104,208 | 10:33 | 342 | 5:11-12 | 398 | | |
| 3:6 | 135 | 11:1 | 292 | 5:13 | 400,401 | | |
| 4:2 | 112 | 11:14 | 268 | 5:15 | 406 | | |
| 4:5 | 45 | | | 5:16 | 404 | | |
| 4:6 | 128 | Bava meṣi'a 1:1 | 275 | 5:17 | 405 | | |
| 5:4 | 116 | 1:2 | 275 | 5:19 | 407 | | |
| 5:7 | 131,156 | 1:4 | 283 | 5:20 | 406 | | |
| 5:9 | 140 | 1:5 | 288 | 5:21 | 405 | | |
| 5:10 | 140 | 1:15 | 275 | 5:25 | 252 | | |
| 6:1 | 72 | 1:16 | 733 | 5:26 | 252 | | |
| 6:4 | 78 | 2:1 | 301,302 | 6:17-18 | 418 | | |
| 6:8 | 29 | 2:2 | 258,308,463 | 7:1 | 422 | | |
| 6:9 | 29 | 2:5 | 300 | 7:7 | 428 | | |
| 6:12 | 30 | 2:8 | 301 | 7:10 | 431 | | |
| 6:14 | 22,73 | 2:11 | 307 | 7:13 | 433 | | |
| 6:20 | 160 | 2:12 | 307 | 7:14 | 433 | | |
| 6:21 | 163 | 2:13 | 307 | 8:7 | 443 | | |

| Bava meṣia' 8:25 | 433 | 1:4 | 527,532,533,534 | 7:8 | 662 |
| --- | --- | --- | --- | --- | --- |
| 8:27 | 465 | 1:5 | 537 | 7:10 | 658 |
| 9:14 | 471 | 1:8 | 542 | 7:17 | 670 |
| 9:32 | 481 | 1:12 | 545 | 7:18 | 671,672 |
| 10:2 | 483 | 2:4 | 566 | 8:1 | 682 |
| 10:3 | 483 | 2:6 | 571 | 8:10 | 683 |
| 10:5 | 485 | 2:9 | 188 | 9:5 | 699 |
| 10:8 | 489 | 2:13 | 579 | 9:12 | 686 |
| 10:10 | 491 | 2:14 | 578 | 9:14 | 685,686 |
| 10:11 | 492 | 2:15 | 584 | 9:16 | 631 |
| 11:4 | 495,499 | 2:17 | 588 | 10:5 | 704 |
| 11:5 | 505 | 3:1 | 592,596 | 10:12 | 717 |
| 11:6 | 505 | 3:2 | 597 | 11:1 | 728 |
| 11:7 | 79,157,501 | 3:3 | 599 | | |
| 11:8 | 504 | 3:5 | 600 | Ševuot 3:1-3 | 158 |
| 11:12 | 523 | 4:1 | 610 | Horaiot 2:5,6 | 326,327 |
| 11:15 | 519 | 4:7 | 650 | | |
| 11:17 | 516 | 5:2 | 624,625 | Hulin 9:8 | 620 |
| 11:18 | 522 | 6:4 | 630 | Bekhorot 6:18 | 667 |
| 11:20 | 523 | 6:8-9 | 634 | 7:3 | 563 |
| 11:21 | 523 | 6:24 | 638 | Arakhin 3:8 | 212 |
| | | 7:3 | 681 | 3:9 | 137 |
| Bava batra 1:3 | 528 | 7:7 | 667 | | |

## Midrašim

| | | | | | |
| --- | --- | --- | --- | --- | --- |
| Gen. rabba | 314,331, 358,702 | Midrash Ps. | 418 | Sifra | 21,32,85,125,201, 203,286,360,627,676 |
| Ex. rabba | 490 | Mekhilta dR. Ismael | 15,22,24,29,58,62,73,94, 96,99,112,120,129,131, 132,144,150,151,169,179 204,205,211,286,322,324 325,377,456,490 | Sifry Num.. | 21,247, 655,658,676,678 |
| Lev. rabba | 111,314 | | | Sifry Deut. | 92,111, 112,203,209,309,320,322, 325,442,446,483,485,488, 490,616,627,666,669 |
| Num. rabba | 660,662 | | | | |
| Deut. rabba | 111,310 | | | | |
| Eccl. rabba | 197,268, 666 | | | | |
| Tanḥuma | 111,490,549,660, 662 | Mekhilta dR. Simeon ben Ioḥai | 15,22,24,120,125, 129,142,150,163,169,179, 193,194,286,322,325,347, 377,456,490 | Onqelos | 197,322 |
| Tanḥuma Buber | 111,660 | | | Pseudo-Jonathan | 111,322, 492,624 |
| Midrash Tannaïm | 111,113, 114,115,120,123,325,669 | Derekh Ereṣ | 88 | | |

## Rabbinic Literature

| | | | | | |
|---|---|---|---|---|---|
| Alfasi | 174,176,287,295, | | 276,305,306,353,395, | | 597,598,603,625, 720 |
| | 322,383,444 | | 431,444,447,496,501, | Rashi | 50,215,295,302, |
| Arukh | 215,353,421 | | 523,589,594,597,598, | | 322,395,421,424,496, |
| Azulai, H.Y.D. | 347,353 | | 610,625,658,706 | | 523,625,678 |
| Caro, Y. | 236,362 | Meïri | 563 | Ravad | 21,353,702,704 |
| De Lonzano, M. | 311,343, | Mordokhai | 362 | Ritba | 646 |
| | 353 | Musaphia, B. | 301,347 | Rosh (Ašer b. Ieḥiel) | |
| Fulda, E. | 14,36,212,275,283, | Nahmanides | 103,174 | | 174,201,469,531,706 |
| | 352,378,394,477,604, | Nimmuqe Yosef | 322 | Saadya Gaon | 268 |
| | 683 | Or Zarua | 144,393, | Šakh (Cohen, S.) | 265 |
| Gershom, Rabbenu | | | 469,555 | Sefer ha'Iṭṭur | 296,297, |
| | 541,594 | Pardo, D. | 424 | | 362,507,535,563,702 |
| Hananel (Raḥ) | 217,295 | Pene Moshe | 265,279, | Šem-Tov Gabbai | 353 |
| Hizquni | 240 | | 378,424,580,683 | Simeon b. Ṣemaḥ Duran | |
| Ibn Ezra, A. | 166,240 | Ran | 383,706 | | 70 |
| Isserles, M. | 276 | Rashba | 18,132,144,174, | Šiṭṭa Mequbeṣet | 646,704 |
| Kaftor wapperaḥ | 360,437 | | 194,258,584,646,704 | Tosaphot | 144 |
| Maggid Mishneh | 276 | Rashbam | | Yalqut Šim'onī | 144,247 |
| Maimonides | 201,216, | | | | |

## Index of Greek, Latin, and Hebrew Words

| | | | | | |
|---|---|---|---|---|---|
| ἀγγαρεῖα | 426 | ἐξώστρα | 587 | οἰκονόμος | 460 |
| ἀγορανόμος | 627 | ἐπίταξις | 631 | πανδοκεῖον | 308 |
| βάρβαρος | 310 | ἐπιτάσσω | 631 | πανδοῦρα | 267,651 |
| βασιλική | 428 | ζημία | 517 | πάντοσε | 658 |
| βουλή | 705 | κάθισμα | 143 | παράφορον | 344 |
| βωμός | 505 | κακο-παιδευτοί | 679 | πάρδαλις | 40,451 |
| γαϊδάρια | 398 | κακοτραγμόνες | 679 | πλαστός | 418 |
| γλωσσοκομεῖον | 294 | κάρρος, κάρρον | 609 | πλατεῖα | 302 |
| δεράνιον, δεράιον | | κλυστήριον | 342 | πορεῖοφόροι | 420 |
| | 311 | κοινωνία | 291 | πόρευμα | 420 |
| διαθήκη | 292 | κοιτών | 701 | πρᾶξις | 314 |
| δίαιτα | 524 | κυβευτής | 650 | πρατήριον | 356 |
| διέθεμεν | 686 | λῃστής | 257,650 | πυριατήρ | 58 |
| δισάκκιον | 338 | λιμήν | 424 | σκάφος | 610 |
| δόμος | 505 | μάρσυππος | 597 | στρατιώτης | 311 |
| ἐμπορία | 301 | μέταξα | 359 | στρόβιλος | 528 |
| ἐνθήκη | 609 | ξενία | 523 | σύμφωνον | 295,726 |
| ἐξέδρα | 523 | ξέστης | 414 | τάβλα | 604 |

| | | | | | |
|---|---|---|---|---|---|
| ταώς | 154 | horrearius | 599 | בית | 493 |
| τόμος | 201 | involucrum | 353 | בעי | 11 |
| τραπεζίτης | 356 | marsupium | 597 | ברות | 604 |
| τριάκοντα | 736 | missicius, missitius | | דעקין | 260 |
| ὕαινα ὄψις | 40 | | 263 | האוררין | 598 |
| φασιανός | 154 | pardalis | 451 | זז | 216 |
| φέρετρον | 420 | platea | 302 | חלף | 50 |
| χάραξ | 370 | prunus persica | 501 | חררה | 56 |
| χρυσάργυρος | 70 | saltuarius | 407 | חרת | 707 |
| | | sarannus | 630 | כייל | 471 |
| amictorium | 302 | scalae | 610 | מדבר | 197 |
| balnearia | 598 | semita | 302 | נחשול | 433 |
| balneator | 599 | stibadium | 532 | נמר | 40 |
| carrus, carrum | 609 | subsellium | 598 | סלע | 216 |
| columna | 590 | tabula | 604 | סנוקרט | 217 |
| compendiarium iter | | tomus | 201 | סרד | 378 |
| | 428 | triclinium | 637,701 | עני | 282 |
| exostra | 587 | vivarium | 600 | פיטסות | 630 |
| foris | 58 | xenoparochus | 70 | קרט | 352 |
| forum | 58 | | | תוקע | 215 |
| funda | 344 | איסטרכין | 268 | | |
| hirnea | 700 | בזיה | 600 | حفش | 294 |

## Author Index

| | | | | | |
|---|---|---|---|---|---|
| Abramson, S. | 352 | Josephus Flavius | 440 | Rappoport, S.I.L. | 3,4 |
| Ben Jehudah, E. | 541 | Klein, S. | 563 | Rosenthal, E. S. | 5,58 |
| Corpus iuris | 547 | Kohut, A. | 378 | Schechter, S. | 8 |
| Dessau, A. | 70 | Levy, J. | 378 | Schreiber, A. | 563 |
| Epstein, J.N. | 4,67,217, | Lewy, I. | 3,36,120 | Schwab, M. | 604 |
| | 388 | Lieberman, S. | 3,4,75, | Sheftel, H. Y. | 352 |
| Frankel, Z. | 3,8 | 116,242,261,290,301,307, | | Sperber, D. | 348,349, |
| Freimann, A. H. | 53,75 | 331,343,344,390,394,396, | | | 352 |
| Friedman, M. A. | 659 | 398,404,407,414,424,428, | | Sussman, J. | 8,9 |
| Gil, M. | 595 | 471,541,571,585,597,630, | | Taubenschlag, R. | 291,295, |
| Ginzberg, L. | 3,9,549 | 658,686,721 | | | 556,655,686,724 |
| Guggenheimer, E. | 230 | Lifshitz, B. | 388 | Torczyner, H. | 541 |
| Guggenheimer, H. | | Loew, I. | 50 | Wewers, G. A. | 8,9 |
| | 9,61,64, 230 | Melamed, E.Z. | 9 | Zuckermandel, M. | |
| Gulak, A. | 9 | Neusner, J. | 4 | | 1,563 |
| Halevi, J. I. | 8,592,686 | Pineles, S. | 14,686 | | |
| Jastrow. M. | 378,563 | | | | |

## Subject Index

| | | | |
|---|---|---|---|
| Abandoned property | 257 | Bond, Babylonian practice | 736 |
| Accidents, follow-on | 75 | partial payment | 735 |
| Acquisition | 556 | Book scrolls | 524 |
| by change | 224,228 | Boyfriend's rights | 144 |
| by domain | 281 | Bribe | 70 |
| by money | 348,363 | Bridal gifts | 706 |
| by moving | 622 | Broker trading for own account | 393 |
| by oath | 231 | Broker's risk | 624 |
| by proxy | 279 | Building standards | 637 |
| by unborn | 698 | Burden of proof | 137,354 |
| claim to | 347 | Burial caves | 643 |
| in barter | 347,353 | Bystander, passive | 166 |
| of animal | 195 | | |
| of ownership | 278 | *chrysargyros* tax | 8,70 |
| Activity, detrimental | 531 | Camel's load | 431 |
| Agent, Gentile's | 404 | Caracalla | 9 |
| Agricultural land | 710 | Censure, judicial | 357 |
| marginal | 646 | Change of control | 160 |
| sale of | 650,651 | Changing testimony | 277,744 |
| Agriculture, extensive | 511 | Cheating | 364 |
| intensive | 511 | Cherubim | 639 |
| minimal plots | 518,605,649 | Child in store | 625 |
| repairs | 523 | Child, fatherless | 142 |
| Alexander legend | 313 | Circumventing interest | 384 |
| Anastasius I | 4 | Circus animals | 39 |
| Animal dung | 46 | Cisjordan Manasseh | 660 |
| Animal leases | 429,430,431 | Claims, certain or probable | 265 |
| Animal, deaf-mute | 152 | of Gentiles | 34 |
| Animals, unattended | 12 | subordinated | 102 |
| Apartment, rental | 496 | Co-owner's veto power | 534 |
| Arab traders | 409 | Coin, as merchandise | 349 |
| Area measures | 163 | as token | 349 |
| Argument *de minore ad majus* | 64 | defective | 368,372 |
| Arson | 58,169,173 | false | 370 |
| *Asmakhta* | 733 | invalidated | 230 |
| Assertion of claim | 461 | Commandments, in plural | 627 |
| | | in singular | 627 |
| Banker | 406 | Common law | 611,658 |
| Banker's deposits | 407 | Compaint, righteous | 392 |
| Bankruptcy problems | 271 | Conditions, of Joshua | 76,258,611,616 |
| Bees, swarming | 257 | Condominium | 495,499,506,508 |
| Bill of divorce | 292 | building | 513 ff. |

## SUBJECT INDEX

| | |
|---|---|
| cistern | 519 |
| dissolution | 509 |
| reserved space | 518 |
| Confession, partial | 273 |
| Conspiracy | 291 |
| Constantine | 8 |
| Contamination | 632,633 |
| Contract termination | 398,421,422 |
| Contract, agricultural | 470 |
| long term | 481 |
| self-contradictory | 649 |
| Contracting, for animal care | 397 |
| Corpse of obligation | 613 |
| Corral | 304 |
| Court officer's immunity | 209 |
| Court power | 567 |
| Court, competent | 38 |
| Courtyard | 595 |
| Crime for hire | 220 |
| Crime, prosecutable | 192,210 |
| Criminal intent | 188 |
| Crop rotation | 479 |
| | |
| Daily wages | 446 |
| Damage, by animals | 11 |
| by borrower | 25 |
| by bull | 11 |
| by devourer | 11 |
| by fire | 11,27,168 |
| by foot | 14 |
| by humans | 14,66,94 |
| by goring | 20 |
| by pit | 11,16 |
| by tail | 46 |
| by thief | 25,26 |
| by tooth | 14 |
| derivative | 15 |
| fundamental | 15 |
| indirect | 48 |
| in public domain | 52,53 |
| invisible | 227 |
| Damages, for minors | 124 |
| for slaves | 124 |
| Danger in private domain | 78 |

| | |
|---|---|
| Danger, categories of | 39 |
| Daughters' rights | 690,692 |
| Death-bed gift | 708 |
| Death-bed will | 670,672,708 |
| Deaths, simultaneous | 719 |
| Debts, profane | 32 |
| towards Heaven | 32 |
| Dedication and redemption | 191 |
| Deed, split | 684 |
| Deferred sale | 408,410 |
| Discount | 384 |
| Doctor's oath | 729 |
| Document, authorization | 734 |
| inconsistent | 729 |
| knotted | 720 |
| lost or illegible | 734,745 |
| power of | 711 |
| predated | 291,744,745 |
| signatures | 724 |
| simple | 722 |
| Dung in public domain | 80 |
| | |
| Egyptian fractions | 272 |
| Elijah, prophet | 306,335 |
| Employment contract | 425 |
| *Eruv* | 521 |
| Escurial ms. | 1 |
| Estate, debts of | 718 |
| distribution | 701 |
| evaluation of | 691 |
| large | 695 |
| undistributed | 702 |
| Evil eye | 581 |
| | |
| Fair wages | 420 |
| Fake theft | 259 |
| Farmhand's food | 446 |
| Father's honor, limit | 322,323 |
| Felon, barred from oath | 272 |
| Fenugreek | 612 |
| Fifths, multiple | 240 |
| Finder's obligations | 319,322 |
| Finds, archeological | 307 |
| in store | 308 |

| | | | |
|---|---|---|---|
| of dependents | 283,285 | by sexless | 699 |
| Fines | 37,38 | Egyptian law | 655 |
| in criminal cases | 82,98,182,186,188 | from mother | 677 |
| | | interethnic | 556 |
| Firstborn, double portion of | 666,667,669 | Greco-Egyptian law | 655 |
| | | Sadducee reading | 655 |
| Flux | 61 | Insult | 98 |
| Foreclosure | 740 | Interest, definition | 351,379 |
| Forfaits | 733 | dust of | 380 |
| Forgiveness | 218 | in court | 381 |
| Free offering | 32 | rabbinic | 380,385 |
| Futures contracts | 408 | Investment gain | 413 |
| | | Investment, legitimate | 400 |
| Gang murder | 125 | Investor's risk | 389 |
| Gift, of stolen goods | 254 | IOU | 743 |
| to Temple | 607 | | |
| Gifts, to Cohen | 620 | Joshua's distribution | 661 |
| Giving spree | 101 | Journeyman, in suit | 484 |
| Grain, sorts | 622 | payday | 482 |
| Guarantor | 739 | Justinian | 4 |
| protection of | 741 | | |
| Guardians, temporary | 131 | *Karmelit* | 16 |
| | | Keeper's oath | 332 |
| Handbreadth | 21 | Keeper, four categories | 449 |
| *Ḥazaqah* | 29.551,552,569,576,578 | paid | 24 |
| limitations | 569 | Keeper, unpaid | 132,324,449 |
| of artisans | 571 | *Kefar Othnay* | 454 |
| of partners | 570 | *Ketubah* | 292 |
| of real estate | 188,262 | *Kutaḥ* cheese | 338 |
| Heave, of wine | 636 | | |
| Hebrew slavery | 210 | Ladder, Egyptian | 578 |
| Hedging, prohibition | 408 | short | 579 |
| Heir's title | 568 | Tyrian | 578 |
| Highway, standards | 617,642 | Law, unapplicable to Gentiles | 112 |
| Husband's right of succession | 126 | Lease, yearly | 467 |
| | | Leavened matter on Passover | 338 |
| Impurity, doubtful | 710 | Lessee | 333 |
| by sitting | 579 | Liability, agents | 394 |
| of beds | 21 | consignee's | 395 |
| of the dead | 586 | created | 166 |
| of textiles | 21 | for fire | 170,174 |
| Inheritance, biblical | 653 ff. | of artisan | 232,233 |
| by court rule | 673,674 | of incompetents | 115,165,213 |
| by husband | 676,678 | of married women | 213 |

| | | | |
|---|---|---|---|
| transfer of | 29 | Ownership | 553 |
| Liquids, change of | 167 | delayed | 295 |
| Loan, antichretic | 434,435 | of sacrifice | 374 |
| of seed grain | 408 | transfer of | 236 |
| Loan, oral | 742 | transferred by agreement | 331 |
| undocumented | 253 | | |
| Loans of merchandise | 351 | Payment, for torts | 488 |
| Local law | 4 | Payments, for disability | 207,208 |
| Lock, composite | 328 | for injuries | 200,206 |
| Loss ratio | 340 | *Peah* | 282 |
| Lump sum indemnity in lieu of accounting | 393 | People of Sodom | 522 |
| | | Perjurer, disqualification | 575 |
| | | Perjury, punishment | 184,203,594 |
| Manslaughter | 120,123 | Permitted path | 613 |
| Marriage, incestuous | 144 | Perpetual rent | 400,401 |
| Measure, honest | 622,623 | *Peruṭah* standard | 371 |
| *Mem* partitive | 373 | Pit, covered | 148 |
| *Mezuzah* | 464 | for vessels | 77 |
| *Mil* | 171 | Possession | 553 |
| *Mina* (Greek) | 273 | undisturbed | 561,562 |
| Minimum | 61 | Poverty line | 609 |
| *Modius* | 234 | Preliminary marriage, conditional | 726 |
| Money in doubt | 134,272 | Prenuptial agreement | 674 |
| Moral obligations | 158 | Price control | 627 |
| Mortgage *omnium bonorum* | 288,742 | *Prima facie* evidence | 293 |
| | | Privacy, rights of | 580,583,584 |
| *n* parts | 73 | Proof of identity | 731,737 |
| Negligence | 18 | Property, unencumbered | 289 |
| Notice, public | 315 | Proselyte's estate | 245,247 |
| Notorious | 44,45,60 | Proselyte's wife | 698 |
| | | Proselyte, childless | 555,556 |
| Oath | 174 | Protest | 562,565 |
| affirmatory | 276 | *Prozbol* | 744 |
| judicial | 273 | Public domain, fair use | 503 |
| Objects, deposited | 305 | tunnelling under | 587 |
| not returnable | 298 | balcony over | 588 |
| Obstacle, dangerous | 29 | Public road, use of | 44 |
| Olive press | 500 | Publicans | 251 |
| Orchard, minimal | 473 | Purification offering | 84 |
| Orchard, standard | 619 | | |
| *Orlah* | 447 | Real estate, title to | 557,559 |
| Overcharging | 364 | Rebellious son | 82 |
| Overseas trade | 414 | Recognition, of brother | 680 |
| Ownerless | 299 | of son | 666,680 |

| | | | |
|---|---|---|---|
| Redmption, right of | 387 | *Stadion*, itinerant | 325 |
| Rental fee | 384,476,479 | Standard field | 160 |
| paid in kind | 478 | Stipulation, imposible | 452,453 |
| Rental, of animal | 457 | monetary | 453 |
| Reparation offering | 84 | Suffering, payment for | 14 |
| Requisition | 702,704 | Sycamore | 480 |
| Resident taxpayer | 517 | | |
| Responsibility, strict | 16,22 | Taxes, other people's | 264 |
| Restitution | 38 | Temple acquisition | 31 |
| by robber | 26,223 | Tenant farmer | 399,476 |
| double | 178 | Tenant in perpetuity | 572 |
| Right of access | 607,640 | Tent impurity | 547 |
| Robber, repentant | 336 | Term, for payment | 487,501 |
| Robbing a proselyte | 245,247 | Testimony, invalid | 188 |
| Roman arches | 514 | *Tevel* | 494 |
| Roman pound | 176 | *Thargelia* | 614 |
| | | Theology, systematic | 6 |
| Sadducees | 521,522 | Thinking work | 100 |
| Sale "more or less" | 647 | Time limits | 317 |
| Sale contracts | 589 ff. | Time of claim | 347 |
| Sale does not break lease | 469 | Title, to property | 686 |
| Sale, completion of | 349 | Torts | 31 |
| *Sancta*, most holy | 32 | Town projects | 516 |
| simple | 32 | Trade, future | 352 |
| Sapor I | 535 | Trades, classification | 356 |
| Second divorce | 282 | Transfer, direct | 363 |
| Seed grain | 631 | Transport | 82,83 |
| *Sela'* | 216 | Trees, cutting down | 463 |
| Separation of properties | 675 | Replanting | 464 |
| Septuagint | 600 | Trigger event | 48 |
| Sequential bequests | 688 | Trustee's responsibilities | 342 |
| Sexless | 699 | Trustee, unfaithful | 180,181 |
| Shame, payment for | 14 | | |
| Sharon | 630 | Underage heirs | 256 |
| Shepherds | 267 | Underaged, legal transactions of | 712 |
| Short sale | 382,408 | Upper floor | 361 |
| Shoulder, of road | 616 | Usage supersedes practice | 459 |
| Signing for absentee | 732 | | |
| Sins, against fellow man | 433 | Valley | 36 |
| multiple | 489 | Veterans receiving land | 263 |
| Slave, freed for injury | 210,212 | Volume measures | 340 |
| law | 227 | Vow | 32 |
| potentially Jewish | 210 | Wedding chamber | 701 |
| Sojourner | 401 | Weight, honest | 627 |

# SUBJECT INDEX

| | | | |
|---|---|---|---|
| Welfare cut-off | 216 | Witnesses, under duress | 713 |
| Weregilt | 45 | Worker's right to strike | 424 |
| Wholesale measurement | 625 | Working day | 438 |
| Will, oral | 714 | | |
| Wills | 292,668,670,678,680 | Zephyrium | 247 |
| Window | 604 | Zoning, agricultural | 543,545 |
|   Egyptian | 578 |   regulations | 525 ff. |
|   Tyrian | 578 | Zuz | 216 |

www.ingramcontent.com/pod-product-compliance
Lightning Source LLC
Chambersburg PA
CBHW031841220426

**43663CB00006B/458**